MEXICO

a travel survival kit

John Noble
Dan Spitzer
Scott Wayne

Mexico – a travel survival kit
  3rd edition

Published by
  Lonely Planet Publications
  Head Office: PO Box 617, Hawthorn, Victoria 3122, Australia
  US Office: PO Box 2001A, Berkeley, CA 94702, USA

Printed by
  Singapore National Printers Ltd

Photographs by
  Chris Bold (CB)
  David Hiser – Photographers Aspen (DH)
  James Lyon (JL)
  John Noble (JN)
  Dan Spitzer (DS)
  Scott Wayne (SW)
  Tony Wheeler (TW)
  Front cover: Quetzal Dancer (DH)
  Back cover: The Palace, Palenque (TW)

First Published
  1982

This Edition
  February 1989

Although the author and publisher have tried to make the information as accurate as possible, they accept no responsibility for any loss, injury or inconvenience sustained by any person using this book.

National Library of Australia Cataloguing in Publication Data

Wayne, Scott.
  Mexico, a travel survival kit.

  3rd ed.
  Includes index.
  ISBN 0 86442 047 1.

  1. Mexico – Description and travel – 1981– – Guide-books. I. Spitzer, Dan. II. Noble, John. III. Richmond, Doug. Mexico, a travel survival kit. IV. Title. V. Title: Mexico, a travel survival kit.

917.2'04834

Scott Wayne

Scott Wayne was born in Philadelphia, Pennsylvania, but grew up in Newport Beach, California. He has travelled extensively and written much about Mexico, Europe, the Middle East and Africa. He graduated from Georgetown University's School of Foreign Service and did graduate studies at the Royal Institute of International Affairs in London and the University of Southern California. He travelled to Egypt and the Sudan to research and write his first travel survival kit. He then ventured into Mexico to write *Baja California – a travel survival kit* and co-write this book. He is now writing *Adventuring in North Africa*. When Scott isn't travelling, he lives in Venice, California.

Dan Spitzer

Dan Spitzer received a BA from the University of Michigan, undertook graduate studies at Berkeley and earned a PhD in Latin American Studies from the University of Michigan. After teaching Caribbean studies, political theory and political economy at a small college in Vermont, Dan began a career as a journalist and author. He has written articles for many publications and several books, including *Wanderlust*, *Asia Overland*, and *Fielding's All-Asia Budget Guide*. After a stint of writing and producing radio news programmes in San Francisco, he went to the College of Marin. He then went to Mexico to research and co-write this book. Dan lives in Berkeley, California.

John Noble

John Noble was born in 1951 and comes from Clitheroe, Lancashire, England. After a Cambridge University degree in English literature and philosophy, he pursued a career as a journalist, interspersed with trips to Europe, Mexico, Guatemala and North America. In 1982 wanderlust finally got the better of him and since then he has spent most of his time travelling in Latin America, Asia

and Australia, earning a living as a freelance writer and editor. His first project for Lonely Planet was an update of *Sri Lanka – a travel survival kit* in 1986. Other publications for which he has written or edited include the *Observer*, the *Guardian* and the *Times* (London), *South* magazine, *Far Eastern Economic Review* and the *Jakarta Post*.

Acknowledgements

All three of us would like to thank the many helpful tourist offices around Mexico and the Mexican Government Tourism office in Los Angeles for their help while we were researching this book. Lastly, this wouldn't be a book without the tremendous editorship and patience of Elizabeth Kim, LP USA.

Scott would like to thank friends and fellow travellers who helped him before, during and after his travels through Mexico: Jonathan Burton (USA), Ravi Prasad (Australia) who hitch-hiked through Baja, Steffen Layer (West Germany) who bicycled from San Francisco to Cabo San Lucas, Molly Frink (USA), Steve Rigney (USA), Jay Valentine and Dusen Mills of the Baja High Wind Center, USA, Robert Wheeler (USA) for his help on Sonora and letter about working in Mexico, and last, but not least, Shirley Cotten for her love and superhuman patience and understanding. Also, of course, a dog bone of thanks to Roxie, the wonder dog, who faithfully accompanied Scott through Baja and part of Mexico until her howls of homesickness got her a return ticket on Aeroméxico.

John would like to thank everyone who helped him on his slice of this book – especially Dallas (NZ), Susan Forsyth, Armando García Salas, Miguel Guerrero, Terry Hennessy, Sarah Noble, Bill Paul, John and María Taylor, Yolo of Monterrey, and the guy in Tapachula who said he'd write about the train to Arriaga (you probably did but I was late getting to Veracruz to pick up my mail, and the post office had 'returned' it – write again!).

Dan would like to thank the many people who helped him on his part of the book. He extends special thanks to Ann Emerson for her love and encouragement.

Lonely Planet Credits

Editors	Elizabeth Kim
	Tony Wheeler
	Adrienne Ralph
	Michelle de Kretser
Cover design	Chris Lee-Ack
Maps	Chris Lee-Ack
	Valerie Tellini
Design	Margaret Jung
	Vicki Beale
Illustrations	Margaret Jung
Typesetting	Ann Jeffree
	Tricia Giles

Thanks also to James Lyon for proofing the maps; Tom Smallman for help with the corrections; Sue Mitra, Lindy Cameron, Debbie Lustig, Debbie Rossdale and Lyn McGaur for compiling the index. Thanks to Greg Herriman for doing the colourwraps.

A Warning & a Request

Things change – prices go up, schedules change, good places go bad and bad places go bankrupt – nothing stays the same. So if you find things better or worse, recently opened or long since closed, please write and tell us and help make the next edition better! All information is greatly appreciated and the best letters will receive a free copy of the next edition, or any other Lonely Planet book of your choice.

Extracts from the best letters are also included in the *Lonely Planet Update*. The *Update* helps us make useful information available to you as soon as possible – it's like reading an up-to-date noticeboard or postcards from a friend. Each edition contains hundreds of useful tips, and advice from the best possible source of information – other travellers. The *Lonely Planet Update* is published quarterly in paperback and is available from bookshops and by subscription. Turn to the back pages of this book for details.

Contents

Introduction

Mexico's extraordinary diversity goes back to pre-Hispanic times when several civilisations often occupied the country at the same time. It's also largely a result of the rugged geography. Cortés, asked to describe the map of Mexico, crumpled up a piece of paper and laid it on a table.

The mountains which isolate parts of the country make Mexico a much bigger country to travel through than it may appear on the map. Communications are much slower than in western countries, which helps preserve the separate identities of each region. To go for instance the 200 km from hot, coastal, music-loving Veracruz to the dry, quiet mountain fastnesses of Oaxaca is to travel to a different world.

As for the people of Mexico, at one extreme are the superficially westernised middle classes of the cities, at the other the 50-plus Indian peoples, each with their own language, scattered over the remotest parts of the country. Between the two are the mestizo (mixed blood) populations, each with a strong pride in its traditions.

Land of many faces, Mexico is a country where the more you learn, the more you realise how little you knew.

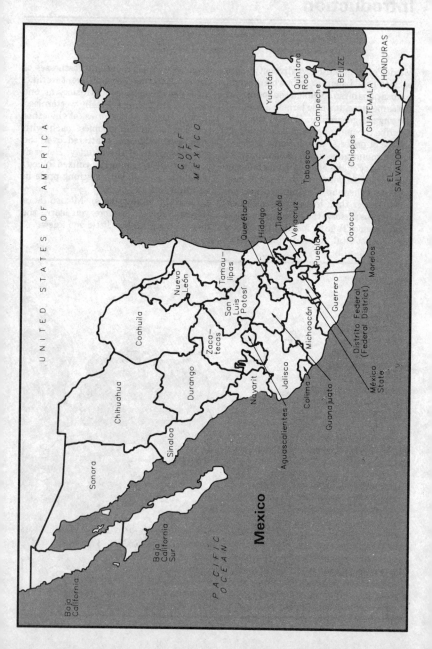

Facts about the Country

HISTORY
Pre-Hispanic Mexico
Pre-Hispanic Mexico was the site of some of the world's greatest civilisations. During the past two centuries, speculation has produced numerous theories concerning their origins. Ethnocentric theories traced them back to Europe; more recently, best-selling idiocies like *Chariots of the Gods* linked the civilisations to visitors from outer space. Carbon dating has unquestionably revealed that they developed strictly in the New World, though the origin of the people themselves has been traced to Asia.

Myan god

The First Mexicans Prior to 10,000 BC, nomadic peoples crossed a land bridge connecting Siberia to Alaska and began to populate the New World. When the Ice Age ended, the land bridge was flooded and became the Bering Strait. This ended migration from Asia, leaving cultures in the New World to evolve independently. By the end of the Ice Age, bands of nomadic hunters had roamed as far south as the tip of South America.

Archaic Period (5000-1500 BC) Carbon dating reveals that nomadic Indians hunted for survival in Mexico as far back as 4000 BC. It was during the Archaic Period that many of these hunters and gatherers began to turn to agriculture. Beans, tomatoes and particularly corn were cultivated, baskets were woven to carry in the crops, and turkeys and dogs were domesticated for food. Crude stone tools emerged and primitive pottery as well as elementary clay figurines symbolising fertility were produced. The first trade routes appeared, with sea peoples exchanging salt for highland tribes' obsidian used in tools and arrowheads.

Pre-Classic Period (1500 BC-300 AD) In the lowland jungles of Tabasco and Veracruz, the first great Mesoamerican civilisation evolved. The Olmecs, famous today for the legacy of their huge stone carvings of heads, were to deeply influence the religion, agronomy, art and agriculture of later peoples.

Olmec culture was at its height between 700 and 400 BC. It produced a written system of hieroglyphics and the first New World calendar of 365 days. The Olmecs' jaguar-god and the art inspired by it became widespread through Mesoamerica. Their huge, mysterious basalt-carved heads weighing up to 60 tons were sculpted with characteristic 'jaguar mouths' and Negroid features. How the heads were hewn with the lack of sophisticated tools and moved some 100 km from basalt quarries to the Olmecs' capital city of La Venta remains a puzzle to this day.

It is believed that Olmec civilisation

Olmec pendant of distorted figure

ultimately succumbed to waves of barbarian invaders. Meanwhile, throughout Mesoamerica, tribes became more settled as slash-and-burn agriculture provided sustenance. Irrigation ditches around the valleys and terracing in the highlands of what is now the region of Mexico City permitted settlements of considerable size to thrive. Religions and secret societies, some influenced by the Olmecs, made their first appearance.

Classic Period (300-900 AD) Sophisticated agrarian advancements, particularly in terracing and irrigation, permitted villages to grow into cities. It is thought that the evolution of a class system permitted an elite to develop the technological, theoretical and artistic works that gave the Mesoamerican civilisations of this period their greatness. The earliest of these cultures was centred in the Zapotecan city of Monte Albán, where there was strong Olmec input. Another major culture of the period was the Mayan, in what is now the Yucatán, northern Chiapas, Guatemala and northern Honduras; the city of Teotihuacán near Mexico City; and the Totonac centres on the Gulf coast of El Tajín and Zempoala.

The Mayan cities represent the quintessence of the great Mesoamerican civilisations. Their achievements are still visible architecturally in the extraordinary ruins of sites like Chichén Itzá and Uxmal in the Yucatán Peninsula as well as Palenque in Chiapas. Their intellectual accomplishments include the use of the zero in mathematical calculations and a calendar as complex as any in Europe, capable of predicting the movement of the stars and eclipses of the sun and moon. Although the Mayan cities in Guatemala and northern Honduras declined during this period, some of the great Yucatán Peninsula cities like Chichén Itzá reached their peak during the Post-Classic period.

Mexico's first major urban settlement evolved just outside the area that is now Mexico City. Encompassing about 30 square km, Teotihuacán numbered at its height more than 100,000 residents. Of the cities that existed about 500 AD, it is thought to be among the world's largest.

It took 10,000 Indians 20 years to construct the monumental Pyramids of the Sun and Moon at Teotihuacán, among the grandest structures built anywhere at that time. Teotihuacán, which means 'the place where men become gods', was a theocracy whose influence spread far and wide. Atop the pyramid, priests performed bloody human sacrifices and ruled the political destiny of the city. Teotihuacán was ultimately abandoned about 650 AD, perhaps after a series of barbarian invasions.

Even as Teotihuacán fell, the Zapotecan cities of Monte Albán and Mitla in Oaxaca were becoming more prominent. A 52-cycle calendar, a bar-and-dot mathematical system and exceptional architecture are highlights of these cities' impressive achievements. Today, you can see their hieroglyphs inscribed on stone stelae; the influences of the earlier Olmecs can be seen in Zapotecan sculptures.

On the Gulf coast, the Totonacs too built splendid settlements and produced fine sculptures. In El Tajín ball games were a major part of life, with at least seven ball courts constructed.

Post-Classic Period (900-1540 AD) Wave after wave of invasions by nomadic tribes from the north into the valley of Mexico led to some interesting fusions. After conquering the region, each tribe assimilated the parts of their predecessors' culture which they considered of value. Although all these tribes were termed *Chichimeca*, or 'barbarians', and none really approached the Classic civilisations, they were hardly primitive and created vibrant cultures. Hieroglyphs and paintings show that wars and migration were prevalent, one dominant tribe succeeding another.

The Toltecs, who, some archaeologists claim, destroyed Teotihuacán, reached their peak between 950 and 1150. They were an extremely warlike people and human sacrifice was a regular practice. The Toltecs also propagated the myth of Quetzalcóatl or the plumed serpent. According to legend, Quetzalcóatl was a fair-haired, bearded god who fled into exile, promising he would one day return from the east. The blond, bearded Cortés later reaped the benefits of this widely believed legend in his conquest of Mexico.

When the last of the northern invaders, the Aztecs, entered the valley of Mexico toward the end of the 12th century, they found it divided into several city states; none were dominant. The Aztecs initially appeared to wield little power but when a religious leader spied an eagle seated atop a cactus devouring a rattlesnake, he took this as a sign to build the city of Tenochtitlán on a lake which today is covered by Mexico City.

The Aztecs constructed remarkable causeways to link their insular capital with the mainland. They also built 'floating gardens' of reed islands which grew food for the city while safeguarding farmers from attacks. As their numbers and strength grew, the Aztecs forged an alliance in 1429 with the powerful states of Tlacopan and Texcoco. The Aztecs viciously suppressed and taxed conquered tribes. In little less than a century, they came to dominate much of central and southern Mexico.

Elsewhere in Mexico during this period, the Mixtecs conquered the Zapotecan cities of Monte Albán and Mitla. They thereby dominated Oaxaca, bringing brilliant techniques of pottery and smithing. The Mixtecs were eventually conquered by the Aztecs just prior to the arrival of the Spanish; the Aztecs eventually vanquished the Gulf coast settlements as well.

Although the Maya were never completely dominated by northern barbarians, their great civilisation ultimately declined. There are a number of theories for this, including rebellion from within against the ruling priestly class, natural disaster or a combination of these factors coupled with the intrusion of barbarians from the north. We do know that by the time Cortés reached Tenochtitlán, there was little left that approached the heights of the Mayan civilisations of the Classic and early Post-Classic periods.

Characteristics of Mesoamerican Civilisations
Mexico had roughly 10,000 cities in the pre-Hispanic epoch, yet few were more than 500 km north of where Mexico City lies today because the aridity was not conducive to agrarian settlement. While highland civilisations like those of Teotihuacán generally had sizeable

centralised states, lowland tribes like the Maya had several centres of power.

Although some of the civilisations wrote hieroglyphs on deerskin or bark paper, the Spanish clergy destroyed these writings while attempting to purge the 'heathen' Indians of their past. Archaeologists have attempted to reconstruct their way of life through stelae hieroglyphs, pottery drawings, and interpretations of bones and plants.

Trade & Tools Commerce in the pre-Hispanic era helps account for shared features like religious beliefs, calendars and astronomical calculations, hieroglyphs and diet. The extraordinary architecture and intricate artwork were accomplished without metal tools. Pack or draft animals were not used either, which might explain why the wheel, found on some Mayan toys, was not utilised more seriously.

Diet Diet was similar in most of the major Mexican civilisations. Based on corn and beans, it was supplemented by tomatoes, chiles and squash. Turkey, fish, deer and dog were also consumed. Food was sweetened by honey rather than sugar. The Spaniards found the Indians smoking a plant then unknown in Europe, tobacco.

Mathematics The Mayan mathematical and calendar systems reflect their intellectual advancement. They developed the concept of zero, unknown even to the Roman Empire. Similar to the decimal system, their positional system of numbers was based on 20 instead of 10.

Calendar The Mayan calendar is more accurate than the Gregorian calendar we use today. All major Mexican civilisations used a dating system which assisted them in planning for agriculture and religious ceremonies. This dating system has been traced back to as early as 1200 BC.

Without sophisticated technology, Mesoamerican calendars were able to compute the length of the solar year, the lunar month and the Venus year. Their calculations enabled them to pinpoint eclipses with uncanny accuracy; their lunar cycle was a mere seven minutes off today's sophisticated technological calculations, and their Venus cycle errs by only two hours for periods covering 500 years.

Astronomical observations played such a pivotal role in Mesoamerican life that astronomy and religion were linked, and the sun and moon worshipped. Most Mesoamerican cities were constructed in strict accordance with celestial movements. One remarkable example of this is Chichén Itzá. During equinoxes, the setting of the sun illuminates the serpent railing on El Castillo, making the snake undulate!

Religion Religion was tied to the movement of the stars. The Indians believed that they could determine the will of the gods by studying the heavens from exactingly aligned observatories. Activities were undertaken in accordance with celestial movements. Ceremonies were held during eclipses and the rising of Venus to prevent catastrophes. The passage of the sun was studied to determine when to begin planting.

Rituals were performed to appease the gods so that droughts could be averted, earthquakes avoided and floods prevented. Gods of the sun, moon, rain, fire, wind and earth predominated. Four worlds were thought to have existed prior to earth. The Indians believed that each had been destroyed: the first eaten by jaguars; the second levelled by hurricanes; the third obliterated by volcanic eruptions; the fourth inundated by floods.

The present world was also perceived to be constantly endangered and the Indians took steps to avert catastrophe through ceremony and sacrifice. Their priests deemed certain days appropriate for fasting and declared when acts of self-mutilation were necessary to appease the deities. Human sacrifice was considered absolutely vital - particularly by the Aztec, who believed that without it the sun would be extinguished and all life would perish.

Sports The recreation most favoured by Mesoamerican peoples was hip-ball. Using a hard rubber ball on stone courts, players tried to stop the ball from hitting the ground, keeping it airborne by batting it with any part of their body other than their hands, head or feet. A wooden bat may have been used. In some regions, a team was victorious if one of its players hit the ball through stone rings a little larger than the ball itself.

The ball game was taken quite seriously and often used to settle disputes between tribes. On occasion, it is thought that the captain of the losing team was punished by the forfeiture of his life.

One archaeological theory links ball games with astrology. Some ball courts were constructed in the path of the setting sun and it is thought that the batted ball either symbolised *el sol* or was seen as a ceremonial means to facilitate the sun's movement across the sky.

Aztec human sacrifice

The Spanish Conquest

Ancient Mexican civilisation, a tradition nearly 3000 years old, was shattered in two short years from 1519 to 1521. A tiny group of invaders destroyed the Aztec empire, brought a new religion and reduced the native people, including their all-powerful overlords, to second-class citizens and slaves. So alien to each other were the newcomers and the Indians that each doubted that the other was human. The period was marked by violence: the Aztecs sacrificed thousands of people to keep the sun rising, and the Spanish killed thousands in the interests of their own survival.

From this traumatic meeting arose modern Mexico. Most Mexicans are descendants of both cultures. While Cuauhtémoc, the last Aztec emperor, is now an official hero, Cortés, the leader of the Spanish conquerors, is a villain, and the Indians who helped him are seen as traitors. Nevertheless, Spanish is the national language, Catholicism is the national religion and Spanish influence is obvious and pervasive.

The Spanish had been in the Caribbean since Christopher Columbus arrived in 1492, with their main bases on Santo Domingo (now Haiti and the Dominican Republic) and Cuba. Realising that they had not reached the East Indies, they began looking for a passage through the land mass to their west but were distracted by tales of gold, silver and a rich empire. Trading, slaving and exploring expeditions from Cuba were led by Francisco Hernández de Córdoba in 1517 and Juan de Grijalva in 1518 but didn't penetrate inland from Mexico's Gulf coast, where they were driven back by hostile natives.

In 1518 the governor of Cuba, Diego Velázquez, asked Hernán Cortés to lead a new expedition westward. As Cortés gathered ships and men, Velázquez became uneasy about the costs and Cortés' loyalty, and cancelled the expedition. Cortés ignored him and set sail on 15 February 1519 with 11 ships, 550 men and 16 horses.

Cortés' cunning and Machiavellian tactics are legendary, but it's less widely known that the Aztecs played military politics too. The story of the confrontation between the two sides is one of the most bizarre in history. A first-hand, detailed account may be found in the *True History of the Conquest of New Spain* by one of Cortés' soldiers, Bernal Díaz del Castillo.

Landing first at Cozumel off the Yucatán, the Spaniards were joined by Jerónimo de Aguilar, a Spaniard who had been shipwrecked there several years earlier. Moving west along the coast to Tabasco, they defeated some hostile Indians and Cortés delivered the first of many lectures to Indians on the importance of Christianity and the greatness of King Carlos V of Spain. The Indians gave him 20 maidens, among them 'La Malinche' who became an interpreter, aide and lover to Cortés.

The expedition next put in near the present city of Veracruz, where the local Totonac Indians were friendly. Meanwhile, in the Aztec capital of Tenochtitlán tales of 'towers floating on water' – the Spanish ships – bearing fair-skinned beings had been carried to Moctezuma II, the Aztec god-emperor. Lightning struck a temple, a comet sailed through the night skies, a bird 'with a mirror in its head' was brought to Moctezuma, who saw warriors in it, and according to the Aztec calendar the next year, 1519, marked legendary god-king Quetzalcóatl's return from the east to claim his throne. Cortés and Moctezuma began their battle of wits, in which key elements were the Aztecs' fear that Cortés might be Quetzalcóatl, and Cortés' skilful use of this weakness. Moctezuma discouraged Cortés from travelling to Tenochtitlán.

The Spanish were well received at the nearby Totonac towns of Zempoala and Quiahuiztlán, which resented Aztec domination. Cortés told their chiefs to imprison five Aztec tribute collectors who were in the area, promising to protect the locals. He then secretly freed two of the Aztecs, told them he was their friend and sent them to Moctezuma with a request for a meeting. The Totonacs, finding that the two had escaped, decided they now had nothing to lose by rebelling against the Aztecs. Cortés had thus gained his first allies, while keeping the Aztecs guessing.

Cortés set up a settlement called Villa Rica de la Vera Cruz in the name of the King of Spain, and appointed town officials who duly elected him their leader. This gave him a semblance of legality with which to counter the hostility of Diego Velázquez, and he sent a ship to Spain to gain royal support for his actions. Still facing doubts and hostility among his own men (some of whom were Velázquez supporters), Cortés apparently scuttled his remaining ships to remove any ideas of retreat. Then, leaving about 150 men at Villa Rica, the Spaniards and Zempoalan carriers set off inland for Tenochtitlán.

On the way Cortés convinced the Tlaxcalan Indians that he was their friend, and they became his most valuable allies. Moctezuma finally invited Cortés to meet him, denying responsibility for an ambush at Cholula. The Spanish and 6000 Indian allies crossed the pass between the volcanoes Popocatépetl and Iztaccíhuatl on the edge of the Valley of Mexico, where in the distance they saw for the first time the Aztecs' lake-island capital – a city bigger than any in Spain.

Entering Tenochtitlán on 8 November 1519 along one of the causeways which joined it to the lake-shore, Cortés was met by Moctezuma, who was carried by nobles in a litter with a canopy of feathers and gold. Only his kinsmen were allowed to look into his face, and when he descended from the litter cloaks were placed on the earth. Cortés tried to hang a glass-bead necklace round Moctezuma's neck but was prevented because it was considered an indignity to the god-emperor. They exchanged courtesies and the Spaniards were lodged – as befitted gods – in the former palace of Axayácatl, Moctezuma's father.

Though attended to with considerable luxury, the Spanish were trapped; one wrong move and the Aztecs could easily have retaliated. The Spaniards' advantages in this situation were the fear they inspired among the natives and the still-prevalent belief that they could be gods. Some of the Aztec leaders nevertheless advised Moctezuma to attack the Spaniards. The emperor's hesitation eventually made the decision for him.

To guarantee their own safety, the Spaniards took Moctezuma hostage. Cortés went to the emperor with a small armed band, saying he could no longer trust him because Spaniards had been attacked by Indians on the coast. According to Díaz, the two men spent half an hour arguing before Cortés said, 'Either we take you prisoner or you die by the sword'. Moctezuma seemed to believe the imprisonment was his gods' doing, and kept his people from rebelling by telling them that he went willingly. The Spanish allowed him to live in his accustomed luxury and to continue running his empire.

Gradually, however, hostile voices rose in the city, aggravated by the Spaniards' destruction of some of the Aztec idols. Then, after the Spanish had been in Tenochtitlán about six months, Moctezuma told Cortés that another fleet had arrived on the Veracruz coast. This was led by Pánfilo de Narváez, sent by Diego Velázquez to arrest Cortés. Now it was Moctezuma's turn to play off enemy factions against each other, and he sent gifts to Narváez. Gonzalo de Sandoval, head of Cortés' garrison at Villa Rica, refused to submit to Narváez but the newcomers made friends with the leaders of Zempoala and installed themselves there.

Cortés left 140 Spaniards under Alvarado in Tenochtitlán and sped to the coast with the others. They routed Narváez' much bigger force one night in May 1520 and most of the defeated men joined Cortés.

In their absence the long-feared confrontation took place in Tenochtitlán. Apparently fearing an attack, the Spanish under Alvarado had struck first and killed about 200 Aztec nobles trapped in a square during a festival. Cortés and his enlarged force returned to the Aztec capital and were allowed to rejoin their comrades – only then to come under the fiercest attack they had yet encountered. Trapped in Axayácatl's palace, Cortés persuaded Moctezuma to try to pacify his people. The emperor went onto the roof to address the crowds but was unable to calm them and, wounded by missiles, he died soon afterwards.

The Spanish had no choice but to flee. They built a portable bridge to help them cross the gaps in the causeways and tried to sneak out one night. They were spotted and several hundred Spaniards and thousands of their Indian allies were killed. In some places the dead and dying formed the bridges between causeways. Alvarado reputedly escaped only by pole-vaulting with his spear across the last gap.

To their relief the survivors were welcomed at Tlaxcala, whose leaders had been impressed by the Spaniards' valour. They prepared for another campaign by building boats in sections which could be carried across the mountains for a waterborne assault on Tenochtitlán. When the 900 Spaniards re-entered the Valley of Mexico, they were accompanied by 100,000 native allies. For the first time, the odds were in their favour.

Moctezuma had been replaced by his nephew, Cuitláhuac, who then died of smallpox, a new disease brought to Mexico by one of Narváez's soldiers. He was succeeded by another nephew, the 18-year-old Cuauhtémoc. The attack started in May 1521 and the Spaniards' boats soon bested the Aztecs' canoes. But the besieged Aztecs didn't give in easily and Cortés resorted to razing Tenochtitlán to the ground bit by bit, to give his horses and cannon the advantage of open ground. Slowly the defenders were worn down and on 13 August 1521 the last resistance ended. Cuauhtémoc escaped in a canoe but was captured. He asked Cortés to kill him, but was denied.

Spanish Rule

Establishing their headquarters at Coyoacán on the southern shore of the lake, the Spanish organised the rebuilding of Tenochtitlán. In an unsuccessful bid to discover the whereabouts of the fabled treasure hoards, they reputedly tortured Cuauhtémoc and other Aztec nobles by burning the soles of their feet.

To satisfy his soldiers, who were disgruntled at the lack of material reward for their efforts, Cortés began giving them Indian towns as *encomiendas*. Under this system the Spaniards were entitled to Indian tribute and labour and in return were supposed to look after 'their' Indians' welfare and convert them to Christianity. In reality *encomiendas* were often little more than slave encampments. The rest of the 16th century saw a long, mainly successful struggle by the Spanish crown to bring them under royal control since the crown was uneasy about letting the conquistadors and their descendants have such power.

Several exploratory expeditions were sent out by Cortés to other parts of Mexico even before the fall of Tenochtitlán, and by 1524 virtually all of the Aztec empire, plus some outlying regions such as Colima, the Huasteca and the Tehuantepec area, were under at least loose Spanish control. Some native peoples accepted Spanish rule, others resisted fiercely and met with equal violence. Pedro de Alvarado set off in 1523 to conquer Guatemala and El Salvador, eventually being appointed their governor by Carlos V.

The ambitious Spaniards' internal squabbles proved as much of a handicap to Cortés as any native enemies. Another conquistador, Cristóbal de Olid, was sent to take Honduras but betrayed Cortés and agreed to fight in Diego Velázquez's name instead. Cortés sent a force to Honduras to punish him and then decided to follow it himself in 1524 with a bigger expedition. After an extremely arduous march – during which Cuauhtémoc, taken along as a hostage, was hanged for trying to stir up an Indian revolt – Cortés found that Olid had been killed by the first expedition.

Away from Mexico for 19 months, Cortés was presumed dead. Rivals took *encomiendas* from the conquistadors and sent letters to Spain accusing Cortés of cheating the crown. Cortés restored the situation in Mexico on his return but Carlos V, keen to keep the new colony in crown hands, appointed officials to take over its government. Cortés went to Spain in 1528 with an entourage of Mexican nobility and animals, and managed to persuade the King that he was indeed loyal. He was granted 22 towns of his own choosing as *encomiendas* and given the title Marqués del Valle de Oaxaca, but not restored as governor. Slowly squeezed out of positions of power in the colony, he returned to Spain in 1540, briefly joined a foray to Algeria, and died near Seville in 1547. Despite his black image in Mexico today and his undeniable cunning, ruthlessness and opportunism, he appears to have resorted to violence only when his men's survival was at stake. He was also loyal to his King, a pious Christian of a crude but not then rare variety, and undoubtedly one of history's most brilliant explorer-conquerors, whatever the morality of his exploits.

In 1527 the King set up Mexico's first *audiencia*, nominally a high court but with government functions. Its leader, Nuño de Guzman, was a supporter of Diego Velázquez and one of the worst of Mexican history's long list of corrupt, violent men. Guzman again deprived Cortés' supporters of *encomiendas* and made an enemy of Mexico City's first bishop, Juan de Zumárraga, who was shocked by the maltreatment of the Indians. He then set off on a bloody conquest of western Mexico, from Michoacán up to Sonora. Eventually Guzman was recalled to Spain.

The second *audiencia* (1530-35) brought some order to the colony. The King then appointed Antonio de Mendoza as Mexico's first viceroy – his personal representative who governed Mexico, though legal matters remained in the hands of the *audiencia*. Mendoza, who ruled for 15 years, gave the colony the stability it badly needed, limited the worst exploitation of the Indians, encouraged the spread of Christianity and ensured steady revenue to the Spanish crown.

The crown claimed one-fifth of any bounty from the colony, including Indian treasure and gems or precious metals. Taxes and, later, the selling of government jobs provided further cash for the crown. From the beginning the Mexican economy was run for the benefit of Spain; all imports, for instance, had to come from the mother country.

The Yucatán was subdued in the 1540s by two men both called Francisco de Montejo (relatives of a conquistador of the same name who had failed in the same task in 1527). This meant that all of 'civilised' Mexico was in Spanish hands, despite several bloodily quashed rebellions of which the most serious was the Mixtón war in the west (1540-41). That left the huge 'Chichimec frontier' – roughly, the area north of a line between modern Tampico and Guadalajara, inhabited by the fierce semi-nomads known to the Aztecs as Chichimecs ('barbarians' or 'Descendants of Dogs').

The discovery of big silver deposits in Zacatecas in the mid-1540s, soon followed by further major finds at Guanajuato, San Luis Potosí and Pachuca, spurred Spanish attempts to pacify the Chichimec area but they did not do so until the 1590s. Northerly outposts like Monterrey remained threatened until the 18th century. Other Spanish expeditions in the 1540s unsuccessfully scoured the Pacific coast in search of mineral riches and penetrated as far north as Kansas.

Despite the efforts of Bishop Zumárraga and Viceroy Mendoza, the position of the natives deteriorated fast, not only because of harsh treatment at the hands of the colonists but also because of a series of plagues, many of them new diseases brought by the Spanish. The Indian population of New Spain, as the colony was called, was decimated from 20 million at the time of conquest to two million in

1580. It reached its low point of one million in the mid-17th century. On the Baja peninsula, the Indian population was almost completely wiped out. This disaster was probably accelerated by *congregaciones* set up in the 1550s; Indians were forced to abandon their villages and settle in a few places where they could more easily be controlled. Earlier, there had even been debates as to whether the Indians were capable of reason and could be considered human. (The Pope decided in their favour in 1537.)

The Indians' only real allies were some of the Christian monks who started arriving in New Spain to convert them in 1523. Many were compassionate and brave men; the Franciscans and Dominicans distinguished themselves by protecting the Indians from the colonists' worst excesses. One Dominican monk, Bartolomé de Las Casas, persuaded the King to enact new laws in 1542 and 1543 to protect the Indians. When this nearly caused a rebellion among the *encomienda* holders the laws were not put into practice.

The monks' missionary work also helped extend Spanish control over Mexico. By 1560 they had built over 100 monasteries (some fortified) and carried out millions of conversions. These monastic orders were distinct from the 'secular' clergy under bishops, a division which later gave rise to serious rivalry.

Under the second viceroy, Luis de Velasco, Indian slavery was abolished in the 1550s (to be partly replaced by black slavery). Forced labour on *encomiendas* was also stopped, but since the population of workers was plummeting, a new system of about 45 days' forced labour a year – the *cautequil* – for all Indians was introduced. This too was widely abused by the Spanish until abolished about half a century later. Indians who worked for wages were often induced to take loans which they could not pay off, thus becoming debt *peones* – workers whose debts to their bosses could be passed on to their sons, which reduced families to virtual slavery again. Harsh labour in mines and mills, on plantations and as porters killed many of them. While Indians were in numerous cases allowed to retain their traditional lands, they were often cheated out of it as the colonial centuries wore on. Ownership disputes between peasants and big landowners still provoke serious conflict today.

By 1575 there were 60,000 Spanish in New Spain. While as a group they were the elite, not all were powerful or rich; a few apparently resorted to begging. There were also 20,000 black slaves in the colony. Inter-marriage among the different groups produced today's mestizo.

The administrative system of New Spain was an often-changing hotch-potch of sub-divisions with varied powers. The viceroy was the King's representative, but the *audiencia*, also royal-appointed, was the highest legal body. *Alcaldes mayores, corregidores* and *gobernadores* were royal officials in charge of provincial areas, subject to higher authorities in Mexico City. *Cabildos* or *ayuntamientos* were 'town councils', theoretically independent of the royal officials but in practice influenced by them. *Cabildos* of Indian towns were usually composed of Indian leaders. All these lesser posts often gave holders licence to exploit the local people. Positions were often sold to the highest bidder. Royal officials were paid so little that they added to their salaries by a variety of dubious means, commencing a Mexican tradition which still thrives and is now known as *la mordida* (literally 'the bite').

The boundaries of the area governed from Mexico City also changed repeatedly. For example, the western region conquered by Nuño de Guzman around 1530 was for a time administered separately under the name Nueva Galicia, as later were Durango and Chihuahua (as Nueva Vizcaya). Guatemala was separated from Mexico in 1530, and from 1530 to 1544 highland Chiapas, on the Mexico-Guatemala border, went back and forth three times between control from Mexico City and the Guatemalan capital. By 1700 the viceroy in Mexico City was responsible for all territory from Panama to northern Mexico, plus some Caribbean islands and even the Philippines – but there were separate *audiencias* for Central America, the Caribbean and the Philippines!

From the 16th to the 18th centuries, a sort of political-economic 'apartheid' system was in effect in Mexico. One's place in society was determined by skin colour and birthplace. Although they were a minuscule part of Mexico's population, *peninsular* Spaniards or *gachupines* were at the top of the socio-economic ladder and were automatically considered nobility in Mexico however humble their status in Spain. Their white, Spanish background made them the richest, most powerful people in Mexico.

Next on the ladder were *criollos*, whites born in Mexico who differed from Spaniards only in birthplace. By the 18th century some criollos had managed to acquire fortunes in ranching, mining, agriculture and commerce; not surprisingly, they also sought political power commensurate with their wealth.

In the first half of the 18th century, the Spanish Kings Philip V and Ferdinand VI assented to appointing eight criollos to the 12-member *audiencia* of Mexico. They hoped that the appointments would bring greater cooperation with and increased tax revenues from a growing Mexican population of criollos and non-whites. Spain desperately needed the additional revenue.

After almost half a century of stagnation under the feeble-minded King Charles II (1665-1700), Philip V, a grandson of Louis XIV of France, assumed the throne. Almost immediately he was faced with the War of the Spanish Succession, which saw him and a succeeding dynasty of Bourbons established in Spain. Because the war almost completely ruined Spain, Philip looked to the colonies, particularly prosperous Mexico, for rejuvenation. Philip instituted several successful reforms, especially in the Manila-to-Acapulco trade route and in Mexico's silver mines. The most significant economic resurgence in Spain and Mexico, however, came about when Charles III (1759-88) became king.

Charles sought not only policy reforms, but also a complete revamping of the political-economic structures of both Spain and Mexico. He believed this was necessary because Mexico was increasingly threatened by British and French encroachments on its northern flank. In 1764 he sent two permanent regiments of Spanish troops to Mexico in a show of force. A year later he sent José de Gálvez, a royal inspector, to devise a more efficient economic and political structure. Several important changes were made. Criollo representation in the *audiencia* was reduced. The colony was reorganised into 12 *intendencias* under a single general in Mexico City who reported directly to Charles. Free trade was established so that all Spanish colonies could trade with Mexico, and a tax hike was imposed on local merchants. Royal monopolies were established in Mexico on gunpowder and tobacco. The Jesuits, two-thirds of whom were criollos, were expelled from Mexico because they were regarded as too influential in Mexican society.

Expulsion of the Jesuits was only the beginning of an attack on church organisations. From bequests of money, property and personal belongings, the Catholic Church in Mexico had amassed a fortune large enough to allow it to lend money to local entrepreneurs. To the Spaniards this represented a loss of control. In 1804 the 'Amortisation and Consolidation Law' was passed, which called for the immediate transfer of all church funds to the royal coffers. Most of the church property holdings had to be sold to meet royal demands. The result was economic chaos and the creation of conditions ripe for rebellion. The catalyst came in 1808 when Napoleon Bonaparte invaded Spain and crown control over Mexico suddenly rested solely with loyalists in Mexico.

Independence From Spain

By 1810, although demonstrations had begun to whittle away Spanish control over Mexico, a revolt did not gather momentum until Miguel Hidalgo y Costilla, a parish priest in the town of Dolores (now named Dolores Hidalgo in his honour), began actively planning a rebellion for 8 December 1810. News of his plans leaked to the government before that date, so Hidalgo decided to act immediately. On 15 September 1810 (now celebrated as Mexico's Independence Day), he summoned his supporters to the church and issued the *Grito de Dolores*, a call to rebel against the Spanish. Translated, the gist of the *Grito* is:

My children, a new dispensation comes to us this day. Are you ready to receive it? Will you be free? Will you make the effort to recover from the hated Spaniards the lands stolen from your forefathers three hundred years ago? We must act at once .... Long live our Lady of Guadalupe! Death to bad government! ... Mexicans! Long live Mexico! ....

An angry mob formed, marched on Guanajuato and, over the next month and a half, also captured Zacatecas, San Luis Potosí and Valladolid. They scored a few minor victories as they tried to take Mexico City, but were forced northward where Spanish troops captured them and executed the rebel leaders, including Hidalgo.

Struggle for independence

As you will soon notice while travelling around Mexico, Hidalgo is revered as one of Mexico's greatest leaders. Few cities and towns in Mexico don't have at least a street named after him; and there's a state named Hidalgo. The same can be said about Hidalgo's successor, José María Morelos y Pavón.

After Hidalgo's execution, Morelos, who was also a parish priest, assumed the leadership of the rebel forces. He led them back to Mexico City where they besieged the city for several months. Meanwhile, Morelos convened a congress of representatives at the town of Chilpancingo in the state of Guerrero. They agreed on a set of guiding principles including the abolition of slavery, elimination of royal monopolies, universal male suffrage and, most importantly, popular sovereignty. Morelos, however, was captured in 1815 and his forces were dispersed into several bands of guerrillas, the most successful of which was led by Vicente Guerrero.

Hidalgo's flag

1821-1867 Sporadic fighting continued until 1821 when Viceroy Agustín de Iturbide defected and conspired with the rebels to declare independence from the Spanish Crown. By September 1821 a compromise called the Plan de Iguala had been worked out between various factions in Mexico. The plan established 'three guarantees': religious dominance of the Catholic Church, a constitutional monarchy, and equality of rights for criollos and peninsular Spaniards. The plan was accepted by both loyalists and rebels.

With great pomp and circumstance Iturbide entered Mexico City and signed the Treaty of Córdoba with Captain General Juan O'Donojú. The treaty recognised Mexico's independence from Spain. Iturbide's army cronies staged a rally of soldiers calling for Iturbide as the new leader of Mexico. Under the terms of the Plan de Iguala, he assumed control as Emperor Agustín I and had a personal palace built in Mexico City.

Emperor Agustín's reign lasted only two years before he was booted from power and a 'United States of Mexico' was formed by a junta consisting of Nicolás Bravo, Guadalupe Victoria and Pedro Celestino Negrete. They drew up a constitution in 1824 that established Mexico as a federal republic of 19 states and four territories. Victoria became Mexico's first president. Over the next seven years, though, Victoria was overthrown by Bravo who, in turn, later lost an election to a centralist candidate. Guerrero staged a coup d'état and in 1829 had General Antonio López de Santa Anna lead the final expulsion of Spanish troops from Mexico. Santa Anna turned around in 1831 and had Guerrero executed.

Santa Anna was voted in as president in 1833. His tenure marked the beginning of a 22-year period of severe political instability in which the presidency changed hands 36 times; 11 of these terms went to Santa Anna. His main contributions to Mexico were manifestations of his megalomaniac personality. Statues and busts of himself appeared throughout the country, and the Gran Teatro de Santa Anna in Mexico City was erected in his honour. Most memorably, he had his amputated, mummified leg (which he lost in an 1838 battle with the French) disinterred in 1842 and paraded through the streets of Mexico City with a full military guard in attendance. His sanctified leg was then presented to the people of

Mexico to be placed atop a specially erected pillar.

Santa Anna is also remembered for his attempts to keep Texas a part of Mexico (see under 'The North-East Border' in the 'North-East Mexico' chapter). After a war with the United States, the Mexican government signed the Treaty of Guadalupe Hidalgo on 2 February 1848 which ceded Texas, California and New Mexico territories to the US. Crippled by the war and a weakened economy, Santa Anna's government decided to raise much-needed capital by ceding – for a price – more land to the US. In 1853 the US government negotiated what is known as the 'Gadsden Purchase' and bought the Mesilla Valley (today Arizona and southern New Mexico) from Mexico for US$10 million. This loss precipitated the Revolution of Ayutla, the ousting of Santa Anna from power in 1855 and a violent three-year civil war starting in 1858.

The civil war resulted in the temporary formation of two capitals – Mexico City for the conservatives and Veracruz for the liberals. By 1855 Santa Anna was finally out of power and a provisional government was formed to implement the Plan of Ayala drawn up the year before by Benito Juárez, a Zapotec Indian turned politician and lawyer, and a group of liberals. Several reform laws were passed including the 'Iglesias Law' which diminished financial gains made by churches since the passage of the 1804 Amortisation and Consolidation Law. The reform laws and a new constitution precipitated the War of the Reform (1858-1861) between conservatives and liberals.

Under the leadership of Juárez, the liberals won the war and came to power in 1861. Juárez was elected president in March. When he entered office, the country was in shambles – roads, public buildings, fields of crops and bridges were all in ruins – and heavily in debt to England, France and Spain. All three countries agreed to temporarily occupy Mexico to collect their debts, but France decided to go even further and colonise Mexico. The first significant resistance to the French was in 1862 when the French army was defeated at Puebla by General Ignacio Zaragoza on 5 May. A year later, the French took Puebla and went on to capture Mexico City. In 1864 Emperor Napoleon III of France sent Austrian Archduke Ferdinand Maximilian of Hapsburg to Mexico City to rule as emperor of Mexico. Juárez and his government were forced by the French army to withdraw from power.

Maximilian and his wife Carlota entered Mexico City on 12 June 1864 and moved into Chapultepec Castle. His reign was short-lived; under pressure from the US government, Napoleon III began to withdraw Maximilian's main base of power – the French troops occupying Mexico – 1½ years after his rule began. By early 1867 most of the French troops had left and Maximilian was forced to surrender to Benito Juárez in May 1867. He was executed by a firing squad on 19 June 1867.

1867-1876 Juárez was again elected president and immediately set an agenda emphasising economic and educational reform. The education system was completely revamped and, for the first time, made mandatory. A railway line was built between Mexico City and Veracruz. A rural police force was organised to secure the transportation of cargo through Mexico. When Juárez was re-elected after a run-off election, however, José de la Cruz Porfirio Díaz, one of his opponents, rebelled in November 1871. Díaz won by default – Juárez had a heart attack in July 1872 – and pushed Sebastián Lerdo de Tejada into the presidency. Four years later, Díaz sent Lerdo into exile and grabbed control of Mexico.

The Porfiriato Porfirio Díaz spent his first four-year term in office implementing various economic reforms and clamping

Cartoon of Porfirio Díaz

down on smuggling and banditry. He left office in 1880 and was followed by Manuel González, who continued Díaz's modernisation programme for four more years. Díaz then returned to power in 1884 with a modernisation philosophy based on Positivistic writings of Auguste Comte and the slogan 'order and progress'.

Order and progress became the catch-words of Mexican society as Díaz followed the economic advice of technocrats led by José Ives Limantour. Buildings and public-works projects were constructed throughout Mexico, particularly in Mexico City where a 48-km canal and 10-km tunnel were built to solve the city's age-old drainage problems. Telephone and telegraph lines were strung and underwater cables were laid. In the 1890s railroad tracks were extended to a total of 3200 km from a mere 640 km in 1876. By 1911, more than 20,000 km of track criss-crossed Mexico. Mexico began to experience a

modicum of stability and prosperity that attracted foreign investors. Mining and oil exploration were opened up to greater foreign investment. In Baja California, for example, a French-owned copper-mining company was established in Santa Rosalía and British investment was encouraged in Ensenada and the San Quintín area.

To maintain this economic progress, however, required a great deal of order, sometimes forced. According to Díaz, order and progress could not be maintained with political opposition, free elections and a free press. He eliminated these potential threats, made Mexico's rich richer and kept the poor under control with a repressive army and rural police force – all of which was contrary to Mexico's 1857 constitution.

In the early 1900s, a liberal opposition formed, but was forced into exile in the USA. The most important group of exiles included Antonio Villareal, Librado Rivera, Juan Sarábia and the Flores Magón brothers, all of whom issued an independence proclamation from St Louis, Missouri in 1906 and began an opposition publication, *La Redención*. Their actions precipitated strikes throughout Mexico and, by late 1910, a revolution.

The Mexican Revolution
In 1910, Francisco Madero, a liberal from a wealthy family in the state of Coahuila, campaigned for the presidency and probably would have won if Díaz hadn't imprisoned him. Madero was released and immediately began reorganising an anti-Díaz opposition. After he drafted the revolutionary Plan of San Luis Potosí in November 1910 the revolution spread quickly across the country and prompted Díaz to suspend all civil liberties and to allow the use of force against the opposition. By May, however, revolutionaries under the leadership of Francisco 'Pancho' Villa (born Doroteo Arango) and uncertain political leadership of Madero took Ciudad Juárez and caused Díaz to resign

later that month. Madero was elected president in November.

Madero was unable to create a stable government and contain the various factions fighting for power throughout the country. Emiliano Zapata, a peasant leader from Morelos, withdrew support from Madero because of Madero's reluctance to immediately restore hacienda land to the peasants. Madero sent federal troops to Morelos to disband Zapata's rebel forces, but matters were only made worse because the Zapatista movement was born.

In November 1911 Zapata promulgated the Plan of Ayala calling for the restoration of all land to the peasants. Zapatista forces won battles against federal troops in Morelos, Guerrero, México, Tlaxcala, Puebla and Mexico City. Pascual Orozco became the titular head of the rebellion. At about the same time, General Bernardo Reyes rebelled in the north and formed the short-lived Reyista movement, but he was quickly defeated by federalist troops.

In January 1912 Emiliano Vásquez Gómez, a former opposition candidate, organised yet another movement – the Vasquistas – and took Ciudad Juárez. Pascual Orozco broke away from Zapata two months later and led a march of Orozquistas on Mexico City, but he was defeated by Victoriano Huerta and his federal troops. In October 1912, Félix Díaz, nephew of Porfirio, organised a conservative, counter-revolutionary army in Veracruz – the Felicistas – and unsuccessfully tried to march out of the city. Félix was imprisoned in the Mexico City penitentiary where he met Bernardo Reyes. Together, they plotted yet another revolt.

Reyes and Díaz were sprung from prison in February 1913 by General Manuel Mondragón and several artillery regiments. The fighting quickly spread to the streets of Mexico City as Díaz (Reyes died in the first street battle) and the soldiers took control of the Ciudadela, a major army arsenal in the city. From 9 February to 18 February – a period now called the *decena trágica* or 10 tragic days – the city was besieged by artillery fire. Thousands of civilians and soldiers were killed and many buildings were destroyed. The fighting ended only after the US ambassador to Mexico, Henry Wilson, negotiated for Madero's General Huerta to support the rebels in deposing Madero's government. As Madero and his vice president José María Pino Suárez were executed by the rebels, Huerta stepped into the ensuing power vacuum to take control of the government.

Wanted poster of Pancho Villa

Huerta did nothing for Mexico except foment greater opposition and strife. In March 1913, three revolutionary factions united against Huerta under the Plan of Guadalupe: Francisco 'Pancho' Villa in Chihuahua, Venustiano Carranza in Coahuila and Álvaro Obregón in Sonora.

Zapata and his forces were also fighting against the government. Terror reigned in the countryside as Huerta's troops fought unsuccessfully on three fronts and, for reprisals, pillaged and plundered many villages. Huerta was forced to resign on 8 July 1914.

Carranza called all the revolutionary leaders to a conference in the hope that a new government could be formed. Instead, another civil war erupted and each faction formed its own government. Carranza eventually emerged as the victor and formed a government that was recognised by the USA. A constitutional convention was held in 1916 and the Constitution of 1917 resulted. Carranza was sworn into office on 1 May 1917.

Unfortunately for Carranza, the revolution continued, especially in Morelos where the Zapatistas demanded more social reforms. However, he was able to eliminate the Zapatista threat by having Jesús M Guajardo, a colonel in the federal army, feign defection to the Zapatistas. Guajardo called a meeting with Zapata on 10 April 1919 at a hacienda in Chinameca. As Zapata entered the building, Guajardo's men shot him point-blank. Carranza's problems, however, were not over yet. The following year, opposition leaders Adolfo de la Huerta and Álvaro Obregón raised an army, chased Carranza out of office and had him assassinated.

From Recovery to WW II

The 1920s ushered in some peace and prosperity as political stability was regained and the economy rebuilt. Álvaro Obregón served as president from 1920 to 1924 and, through his Minister of Education José Vasconcelos, stimulated a significant trend in Mexican art. Art was regarded as an important part of a new, all-encompassing educational structure. In keeping with this attitude, Vasconcelos commissioned Mexico's top artists – Diego Rivera, David Alfaro Siqueiros and José Clemente Orozco – to do murals on the walls of several public buildings. The murals were intentionally painted with dramatic colours and scenes to convey a clear sense of Mexico's past and present and the ideals of the Revolution. Today, these and other murals painted in subsequent years are on display throughout Mexico City.

Plutarco Elías Calles followed Obregón in 1924 and a period of political stability and economic prosperity ensued. Calles expanded the education system by 2000 schools. He implemented many agricultural reforms, the most significant of which was the distribution of more than three million hectares of land. Relations with the US improved with the appointment of Dwight Morrow as US ambassador to Mexico.

However, Calles' administration was not without problems. Like some of his predecessors, he implemented measures against the power of the Catholic Church in Mexico. These included the closure of all monasteries and convents, deportation of all foreign priests and nuns, and the prohibition of religious processions. The bloody Cristero Rebellion resulted and lasted until 1929.

At the end of his term in 1928, Calles called for the return of Obregón to office, this time for the newly expanded presidential term of six years. Obregón won re-election, but was assassinated not long after. On Calles' recommendation, Emilio Portes Gil was then elected for a two-year interim term while Calles reorganised his political supporters to found the National Revolutionary Party (El Partido Nacional Revolucionario or PNR), Mexico's first well-organised political party and the beginning of a long list of official acronyms.

Although some reforms had been implemented since the Revolution, in 1934 Mexico was still ripe for a social revolution. As governor of the state of Michoacán, Lázaro Cárdenas recognised this and won the presidency with the support of the PNR.

During his six-year term, Cárdenas

proved to be a true president of the people. He instituted an extensive land reform system by redistributing almost 20 million hectares, mostly through the establishment of *ejidos* for Mexican peasants. (An *ejido* is land owned collectively and used by a peasant community or an individual.) He encouraged better church-state relations and reorganised the labour movement into the Confederation of Mexican Workers (La Confederación de Trabajadores Mexicano or CTM).

Other changes implemented by Cárdenas included expropriation of foreign oil company operations in Mexico; formation of the Mexican Petroleum Company (Petróleos Mexicanos or Pemex; and reorganisation of the PNR into the Party of the Mexican Revolution (Partido de la Revolución Mexicana or PRM), a coalition party of representatives from four sectors of Mexican society – agrarian, military, labour and the people-at-large.

Cárdenas' reforms and changes were at the expense of increased foreign investment and general growth in the economy. After the expropriation of foreign oil company operations in 1938, investors stayed away from Mexico, thus depriving it of much needed foreign capital. Combined with the tremendous cost of implementing various social programmes, this made the Mexican economy sluggish, but only temporarily; Cárdenas had laid the foundation for future development. He recognised a need, however, for a more conservative approach to governing Mexico, so in 1940 he recommended a conservative candidate, Ávila Camacho. Camacho's easy win established a political tradition: whoever a Mexican president recommends as his successor during his last year in office receives the PRM's candidacy and is elected president of the Republic.

WW II was the key event during Camacho's presidency. As a supporter of the Allied war effort, he sent Mexican troops to help the Allies in the Pacific, and supplied raw materials and labour to the USA. At home, the war proved a boost to Mexico's economy because many manufactured goods could no longer be imported from the industrialised countries, but had to be produced in Mexico. At the same time, Mexico was able to increase its exports.

The Post-WW II Era

As the Mexican economy expanded, so did the PRM because new groups had to be represented. The party was again renamed, this time the Institutional Revolutionary Party (El Partido Revolucionario Institucional or PRI). In 1946 the post-war boom ushered in Miguel Alemán Valdés as president.

Alemán continued the industrialisation and development of Mexico by building the National Autonomous University of Mexico (Universidad Nacional Autónoma de México or UNAM), hydroelectric stations and irrigation projects, and by expanding Mexico's road system fourfold. In addition, Pemex drilling operations and refineries grew dramatically and, with the rapid rise of other industries, spawned some of Mexico's worst corruption.

Alemán's successor, Adolfo Ruíz Cortines, was elected in 1952 and immediately set out to eliminate much of the graft and corruption that had plagued his predecessor's administration. Cortines also began to tackle a problem that Mexico didn't have to cope with before – explosive population growth. In two decades the population had doubled and many people began migrating to urban areas to search for work.

Confronting the problems of the poor became one of the priorities of Cortines' successor, López Mateos. His main objective became the revival of the Mexican Revolution in the countryside. He pursued this goal through various social reforms such as redistribution of 12 million more hectares of land, nationalisation of foreign utility concessions, implementation of social-welfare programmes for the poor, and public-health campaigns to combat tuberculosis, malaria and polio. Almost every village was given assistance in the construction of schools and provided with teachers and textbooks. His programmes were helped by strong economic growth, particularly in tourism and export sectors.

The changes, however, were not being implemented fast enough for the Mexican people. Between 1959 and 1962, there were numerous strikes, riots and demonstrations against the government, most of which involved labour issues. The formation of a National Commission for the Implementation of Profit Sharing quelled much of the labour unrest because organised labour was apportioned five to 10% of each company's profits.

1960s to 1980s

President Gustavo Díaz Ordaz (1964-1970) came to power on a platform that emphasised business more than social programmes. One of his first actions was to fire the new liberal-minded president of the PRI, Carlos Madrazo. His reputation, already soured by his pre-presidency nullification of Baja California's elections, was worsened by this action against liberals. Groups of university students in Mexico City were the first to express their outrage with the Ordaz administration.

Protest demonstrations began at the National University in the spring of 1966, but were quelled by federal troops. Their discontent came to a head as Mexico City prepared for the 1968 summer Olympics, the first ever held in a Third World country. While the last coats of paint were being applied to new hotels, a subway system and athletic facilities, the students organised massive demonstrations in the zócalo in Mexico City; more than half a million rallied on 27 August. A few weeks later on 2 October the Olympics had already begun and another rally was organised nearby at the Plaza de las Tres Culturas. The government, fearing that this would disrupt the games, encircled the protesters with riot police who were armed with tear gas, clubs and guns. Even today, no one is certain how many people died in the ensuing melee, but estimates have been put at 300 to 400.

When President Luis Echeverría Álvarez came to power in 1970, Mexico was a political and economic mess. He sought a strategy by which Mexico could continue to expand economically and wealth could be redistributed more equitably. His first target of reform was the agricultural sector where technical assistance and government investment were desperately needed to forestall a complete collapse. He instituted new government credit projects and expanded rural health clinics, the social security system and family planning. More government control was acquired over the telephone company and the tobacco industry. Echeverría also granted land to peasants occupying the Yaqui Valley in protest at government policies.

Despite Echeverría's progressive actions, though, civil unrest in Mexico was increasing – political kidnappings, bank robberies, an insurrection in Guerrero, all of which were partially fuelled by the corruption rife among government officials. Some of the corruption was spawned by the economic boom that resulted when oil prices sky-rocketed after an Arab oil boycott.

Fortunately for Echeverría, the most infamous case of corruption occurred during the subsequent administration of José López Portillo. Mexico City's chief of police Arturo Durazo somehow parlayed his weekly US$65 salary into a fortune that allowed him to buy race race horses, build palatial residences in Mexico City and Zihuatenejo and funnel more than US$600 million into Swiss bank accounts. Much of the money has not yet been recovered.

López Portillo's administration, however, was blessed with rapidly rising oil revenues, which could be applied to both industrial and agricultural investments. Suddenly, Mexico was seen as a safe investment; international banks and lending institutions lent Mexico billions of dollars until, just as suddenly, a glut of oil on the world market sent prices plunging. To stem a flight of capital from the country and assuage inflation, López Portillo nationalised all private banks and instituted currency controls. The peso was horribly over-valued, so López Portillo loosened the controls, let it float on 17 February 1982 and watched, probably in horror, as the value of the peso plunged and the worst economic recession since the Depression began. Later that year he passed on the legacy to his successor, Miguel de la Madrid.

1982 to the Present

De la Madrid's term of office lasted until 1988, but he was largely unsuccessful in coping with the problems of his predecessors. The population has grown at Malthusian rates, meaning that it has increased faster than its means of subsistence and unless it's checked by moral restraint or disaster, widespread poverty and degradation will result. Mexico's population growth is not being 'checked' by anything – since 1970 the number of people has increased from about 47 million to 80 million. This increase has dramatically outpaced economic growth, particularly in the agricultural sector, and increased migration to big cities.

The result is a vicious cycle. An average of more than 2000 people migrate to Mexico City every day, which means that fewer people are working in agriculture. Resulting food shortages and an increased need to import food mean that hard currency, which should be spent on capital-intensive, infrastructural projects, has to be applied to the short-term goal of feeding people and subsidising certain foodstuffs and essentials like gasoline and electricity.

De la Madrid's government believed that if it were up to free-market forces to determine prices, then everything would cost more and greater numbers of people

would be impoverished. Consequently, Mexico has found it increasingly difficult to make even the interest payments on its US$80 billion debt. Housing shortages are resulting, especially in Mexico City, and squalid, unhealthy slums are sprouting up that indirectly strain the health care and social service systems.

Madrid's economic policies were not helped by an earthquake on 19 September 1985. The earthquake registered eight on the Richter scale, caused more than US$4 billion in damage to hundreds of buildings in Mexico City, dislocated thousands of people and killed at least 8000. One side-effect of the earthquake was the discovery of tortured bodies in the ruined head-quarters of the Distrito Federal attorney-general in Mexico city. The national attorney-general was forced to admit that torture went on, and a new law banning it was passed later the same year amid scepticism about its effectiveness.

Not surprisingly, in this climate of economic chaos people began to question the country's political system. Since the 1930s and '40s a single party had dominated Mexican politics – first the PNR, then the PRM and now the PRI. Although dissenting parties had existed since the beginning of the PNR, they never really managed more than a token influence on Mexican politics. The 1980s, however, saw an increase in organised political dissent, even within the PRI.

Northern Mexico, where comparisons with the affluent USA are all too easy to make, saw growing support for the right-wing opposition party PAN – and frustration with election fraud – as the national economy declined in the 1980s. Big protest marches resulted in Monterrey. At Piedras Negras in December 1984, when the PAN claimed 16 victories in 38 seats at local elections but was awarded only a few, the city hall was set on fire. The same year angry PAN supporters in Escobedo, Coahuila, kidnapped the mayor, stripped him naked and left him tied to a post.

Outside the official political groupings, peasant and Indian unrest, which dates back to at least the Spanish conquest, has continued going strong – along with equally traditional violent reprisals. These days the unrest is provoked mainly by exploitative caciques who control local business and politics, by big landowners taking over peasant land, or by the failure of the authorities to hand over land to its rightfully recognised peasant owners.

Small armed guerrilla movements still occasionally spring up – such as those in the 1970s led by Genaro Vázquez Rojas and Lucio Cabañas Barrientos in Guerrero and by Francisco Medrano in Oaxaca – but these were put down with a ruthlessness which helped to further alienate the local people.

Since the official national peasant organisation, the Confederación Nacional Campesino (CNC), is controlled by the government party PRI, the peasants' only hope for real progress in land disputes is to form independent campaigning groups. Numbers of these come and go in many parts of Mexico, often accompanied by violent repression. The Coordinadora Nacional Plan de Ayala is an association of several such groups in southern states, united under the name of Emiliano Zapata's 1911 land reform programme. Another national body is the Independent Union of Agricultural Workers and Peasants (CIOAC), which is affiliated with PSUM, the Unified Socialist Party of Mexico. Locally based groups include the Triqui Unification and Struggle Movement (MULT) and the Isthmus Worker Peasant Student Coalition (COCEI), both in Oaxaca; the Emiliano Zapata Peasant Organisation (OCEZ) in Chiapas; and the Independent Peasant Union (UCI) in Puebla.

The army was sent into Oaxaca city in 1976 after riots over land. In 1980 the town of Juchitán in Oaxaca state managed to elect a COCEI mayor. Three years later he was removed from office by the state government after violence between COCEI and PRI supporters but he and his supporters refused to leave the town hall until, following new elections in which all COCEI candidates were defeated, the army forced them out.

In 1984 and 1985 the international human rights body Amnesty International sent teams to investigate reports of killings, disappearances and torture of peasants in land disputes in Oaxaca and Chiapas. The quarrels arose mainly from local elections, peasant occupations of disputed lands, and arguments over boundaries between Indian communities. Amnesty International stated, 'In some cases such disputes have apparently led to deliberate killings of members of peasant organisations in circumstances suggesting that municipal authorities or members of the security forces were involved . . . . '

Peasant organisations reported the killing of 37 Triqui Indians between 1976 and 1981, 22 COCEI members or supporters between 1974 and 1984, more than 20 Tzotzil Indian leaders in Chiapas since the mid-1960s, and 12 peasants in Huizitlán de Serdán, Puebla, in 1984. Amnesty also documented the killing of 12 supporters of CNPA-affiliated groups in Hidalgo since 1983. The victims tended to be supporters of groups opposed to the CNC, landowners, commercial interests, or municipal or state authorities.

Amnesty added: 'The available evidence suggests that when members of opposition peasant organisations are killed by armed civilians, those responsible have rarely been brought to justice . . . (it was) frequently alleged that internal divisions within communities were fostered and exploited by landowners closely associated with the municipal authorities . . . (there were) clear differences in the success rate of police investigations according to the political affiliation of the victim . . . . '

Another tactic open to the peasants is to make highly public protests. Amnesty International named Jorge Enrique Hernández, a Chiapas peasant, one of its 'Prisoners of the Month' in January 1987, after he had taken part in a demonstration on the Pan-American Highway demanding a maize subsidy. The protest dispersed peacefully when police and soldiers arrived, and the Chiapas state government apparently agreed to receive a delegation from the protesters, but the delegation members were then arrested. Hernández, one its members, was charged with terrorism.

Other protests included hunger strikes in April 1987 by Chiapas peasants in Mexico City zócalo (demanding release of political prisoners and punishment for murderers of peasants) and by three women in San Luis Potosí zócalo (demanding to be shown 24 prisoners who had disappeared).

In a few places the church gives the peasants some support, but clergy who speak out are usually branded leftists. Samuel Ruíz García, the bishop of San Cristóbal in Chiapas, is called the Obispo Rojo (Red Bishop) for this reason.

Discontent on all sides finally mounted to the point where it at last made an impact on even the *official* results of the 1988 presidential election. Cuauhtémoc Cárdenas, son of the charismatic 1930s president Lázaro Cárdenas, walked out of the PRI to lead the new centre-left National Democratic Front (FDN) into the election. One of his close aides was murdered on the election eve but despite discouragement, many people believe Cárdenas received more votes than anyone else. Officially he was awarded 31% of the vote, while the PRI candidate Carlos Salinas de Gortari (a former member of de la Madrid's cabinet) received 50.36% – the lowest of any PRI presidential candidate in history. The PAN candidate Manual Clouthier won 17%.

Cardénas claimed he had been cheated of victory by fraudulent counting, etc, and a wave of anti-government protests followed, but it didn't look as if the PRI was even remotely willing to loosen its hold on power. Nevertheless the size of the vote officially awarded to the opposition proved that the PRI was finally being forced to admit to at least some of its unpopularity.

A Brief Who's Who of Mexico

Gerónimo de Aguilar Spanish priest shipwrecked on the Yucatán Peninsula seven years before Cortés arrived. He had learned the Mayan language and proved an invaluable ally to Cortés.

Ahuizotl Aztec emperor from 1486 to 1502, who expanded the empire.

Captain Ignacio Allende One of the instigators of the independence struggle in 1810.

Pedro de Alvarado One of the leading conquistadors, conqueror of Guatemala and El Salvador.

Axayácatl Aztec emperor from 1469 to 1481.

Luis Echeverría Álvarez President of Mexico from 1970 to 1976, he increased government technical assistance for agriculture and expanded rural social services. His administration, however, was blighted by violent civil unrest and the beginnings of severe corruption. He definitely isn't revered as one of Mexico's great leaders.

Carlota Maximilian's wife.

Plutarco Elias Calles Mexican Revolution leader and then president of Mexico from 1924 to 1928. He started to unite regional political elites into a national party while president, creating a modicum of stability in the country. In 1929 Calles' national party became the National Revolutionary Party, the precursor to the PRI, Mexico's dominant party today.

Lázaro Cárdenas Considered a true president of the people, Cárdenas carried out major land reforms, established a system of *ejidos*, expropriated foreign oil company operations, and reorganised the PNR into the PRM (Party of the Mexican Revolution) in the late 1930s and early '40s.

Venustiano Carranza Succeeded the intensely disliked Huerta in 1914, but since he did not implement land reforms, he wasn't able to end the Revolution. One of his most memorable actions was the ambush and execution of rebel leader Emiliano Zapata. He was overthrown by the alliance formed by Álvaro Obregón and Huerta and assassinated while fleeing the country.

Bernal Díaz del Castillo Captain (some say lieutenant) in the army of Cortés and author of the *True History of the Conquest of New Spain*, an eyewitness account of the Spanish conquest of Mexico.

Hernán Cortés Spanish conquistador, sometimes known as Hernando or Fernando, who invaded Mexico and conquered the Aztecs. Much maligned today in Mexico, Cortés was the chief person responsible for introducing Hispanic civilisation into Mexico.

Martín Cortés Name of two sons of Hernán Cortés.

Miguel Hidalgo y Costilla Parish priest of Dolores who sparked the independence struggle in 1810 with his famous *Grito* or call for independence. He led an unsuccessful attempt to take Mexico City. Mexican cities and towns usually have at least a street or plaza named after him.

Cuauhtémoc Successor to Moctezuma and Cuitláhuac and last Aztec emperor. Defeated and later executed by Cortés.

Cuitláhuac Aztec emperor who briefly succeeded Moctezuma Xocoyotzin in 1520 before dying in the same year.

Porfirio Díaz Was elected president in 1876 and re-elected on numerous occasions on a slogan of 'order and progress'. He gradually moved further and further to the right, effectively becoming a dictator. He pursued many public-works projects and encouraged foreign investment; this was, however, at the expense of certain freedoms. His policies precipitated the 1910 Revolution and forced his abdication in 1911.

Ricardo Flóres Magón One of the brothers who were leading opponents of Porfirio Díaz.

Juan de Grijalva Leader of early Spanish expedition to Mexican Gulf Coast in 1518.

Vincente Guerrero A leader in the later stages of the fight for independence from Spain. Later a liberal president but deposed and executed by the conservative Anastasio Bustamente in 1829.

General Victoriano Huerta Huerta's first major accomplishment was quashing rebel leader Orozco's attack on Mexico City in March 1912. The following year he stepped into a power vacuum and became one of Mexico's most disliked and ineffective leaders. He was forced to resign in 1914.

Agustín de Iturbide Iturbide was viceroy of Mexico in 1821 until he conspired with rebels to declare independence from Spain. He deftly negotiated a settlement that led to his instalment as Emperor Agustín I of Mexico, but his reign lasted only two years.

Benito Juárez A Zapotec Indian turned politician and lawyer who led a group of liberals in deposing Santa Anna, then passed laws against the church that precipitated the three-year War of the Reform. Elected president in 1861, he served until forced to flee because of the French takeover by Napoleon III and Emperor Maximilian. After Napoleon III removed his soldiers from Mexico, Juárez was again able to assume the presidency which he held until his death in 1871.

La Malinche Cortés' Indian mistress and interpreter, she is considered to have had a major influence on Cortés' strategy in subduing the Aztecs.

Bartolomé de Las Casas Bishop of Chiapas who campaigned for Indian rights in the 16th century.

José López Portillo President from 1976 to 1982, López Portillo's administration was blessed with high oil revenues but cursed with a corrupt police chief, a plunge in the price of oil and a mammoth external debt because of poor financial management. He left Mexico with a recession that the country is still reeling from today.

Francisco I Madero A liberal politician, Madero led the first major opposition to Díaz and succeeded in forcing him to abdicate. He proved unable to quell the factional fighting throughout Mexico and only made matters worse. His term ended in 1913 in front of a firing squad.

Ferdinand Maximilian Austrian archduke sent by Napoleon III of France to rule as emperor of Mexico. His rule was short-lived (1864-1867) and he was forced to surrender to Benito Juárez. Maximilian was executed by firing squad in 1867.

Antonio de Mendoza First Spanish viceroy of Mexico (1535-50).

Moctezuma Ilhuicamina Aztec emperor 1440-1468.

Moctezuma Xocoyotzin Aztec emperor at the time of the Spanish invasion in 1519.

Francisco de Montejo Conquistador who failed to conquer the Yucatán in 1527 and later became governor of Honduras. His son and nephew, both also called Francisco de Montejo, pacified the Yucatán in the 1540s.

Pánfilo de Narváez Leader of 1520 expedition sent to Veracruz dy Diego Valázquez to try to arrest Cortés.

Álvaro Obregón Obregón led a faction against Madero from Sonora, but he wasn't elected president of Mexico until after the Revolution in 1920. His major accomplishment was a restructuring of Mexico's education system that included stimulating a new trend in Mexican art – murals.

José Clemente Orozco One of the three great 20th century muralists, with Rivera and Siqueiros.

Diego Rivera Founder of a Mexican tradition of mural painting linking art and politics. Some of his best work was done on the walls of the National Palace in Mexico City.

Carlos Salinas de Gortari Elected president in 1988 with 50.36% of the official vote count – the lowest of any PRI candidate in history.

Gonzalo de Sandoval One of the leading conquistadors.

General Antonio López de Santa Anna A thorn in the side of newly independent Mexico for 30-odd years, Santa Anna unseated Iturbide, the head of Mexico's first independent government, in 1823. During the first 30 years of Mexico's independence there were 50 governments, 11 of them headed by Santa Anna. He was a lead player in Mexico's squabbles with the USA, and when Texans cry 'Remember the Alamo' they're recalling Santa Anna's massacre of the American defenders of the Alamo mission.

David Alfaro Siqueiros One of the three great 20th century muralists, with Rivera and Orozco.

Leon Trotsky A Bolshevik organiser and leader of the Russian Revolution, Trotsky sought refuge in Mexico City in 1937, but was murdered by ice-pick-wielding Stalinists in 1940. He had been attempting to organise opposition to the dictatorial bureaucracy of Stalin.

Diego Velázquez Spanish governor of Cuba who originally commissioned Hernán Cortés' 1519 expedition to Mexico.

Guadalupe Victoria Republican president following the removal of Inturbide in 1823.

Francisco 'Pancho' Villa An infamous, charismatic revolutionary leader whose destructive forays into the USA and throughout Mexico have become legendary. US troops pursued him into Mexico, but were unable to find him. Pancho has been written about extensively in the book *Insurgent Mexico* by John Reed (Penguin Books, New York 1983).

Emiliano Zapata A peasant rebel leader from the state of Morelos who organised one of Mexico's first land-reform fights with the Plan of Ayala in 1911. After winning numerous battles throughout Mexico, he was ambushed and executed in 1919 on President Carranza's orders.

GEOGRAPHY

Covering almost two million square km, Mexico is shaped like a wide-handled scythe that narrows towards the south/south-east at the Isthmus of Tehuantepec and then curves north-eastward into the Yucatán Peninsula. It's bordered by the

Sea of Cortés (also known as the Gulf of California) on the north-west, and by the Pacific Ocean along the Baja California coast and the western and south-western mainland coasts. The Sea of Cortés also separates Baja from mainland Mexico. For the purposes of this book, 'mainland Mexico' refers to that part of Mexico separate from the Baja California peninsula. Mexico's east coast is bordered by the Gulf of Mexico and curves south-east and then east from Veracruz and north-eastward to Campeche and the Yucatán Peninsula. This curved part of the Gulf is called the Bahía de Campeche (Bay of Campeche). Heading east along the Yucatán and then south, the peninsula is bordered by the Caribbean.

The rest of Mexico is demarcated by a 3326-km-long northern border with the USA and, along the south and south-east, a 251-km border with Belize and an 871-km border with Guatemala.

Apart from Baja California, northern and central Mexico –as far south as Mexico City - is roughly striped from north to south with two mountain ranges, two sets of coastal plains and two broad plateaus.

On the west coast, a relatively dry coastal plain stretches south from Mexicali almost to Tepic. Several rivers cut through the plain and empty into the Sea of Cortés and the Pacific Ocean, including the Río Colorado, Río Sonora, Río Yaqui, Río Fuerte and, just north of Tepic, the Río Grande de Santiago. The rivers flow out of the Sierra Madre Occidental mountain range, an extension of the Sierra Nevada range in the USA. The mountains are rugged and have made this area almost completely impassable. There are only two surface transportation routes from the coast through the mountains to the great plateaus - the Copper Canyon train from Los Mochis to Chihuahua and the harrowing highway from Mazatlán to Durango.

The plateaus are divided into northern and central parts and range in altitude from about 1000 metres in the north to around 2000 metres near San Luis Potosí, 1500 metres around Guadalajara and 2300 metres in Mexico City. The Sonoran Desert occupies a large part of the northern plateau and extends northward into the southern fringes of Arizona and California. The central plateau is mostly a series of rolling hills and broad valleys, all of which includes some of the best farming and ranching land and the two largest cities (Mexico City and Guadalajara) in the country. Not surprisingly, more than half the population lives on this plateau.

Both plateaus are bounded to the east by the Sierra Madre Oriental mountain range, which is an extension of the Rocky Mountains in the USA. This range runs as far south as the northern part of the state of Puebla and includes peaks as high as 3700 metres.

On the east side of the Sierra Madre Oriental is the Gulf Coastal Plain, an extension of a similar coastal plain in Texas. In the north-eastern corner of Mexico the plain begins as a wide area, semi-marshy near the coast, and gradually narrows as it nears Veracruz, a major port.

The Central Plateau, Sierra Madre Oriental range and Gulf Coastal Plain reach as far as the Cordillera Neo-Volcánica mountain range, just south of Mexico City. This range runs east-west and includes Mexico's highest peaks – Pico de Orizaba (5639 metres), Popocatépetl (5452 metres) and Iztaccíhuatl (5286 metres) - as well as the smaller extinct volcanoes of Parícutin (2700 metres) and Nevado de Colima (4330 metres).

To the west, the Pacific Coastal Lowlands become a narrow coastal plain as the Sierra Madre Occidental mountains become the Sierra Madre del Sur just south of Cabo Corrientes (west of Guadalajara). The Sierra Madre del Sur extends south all the way to the 250-km-wide Isthmus of Tehuantepec, the narrowest part of Mexico. As the range approaches the Isthmus, a lower range

North

South

East

West

Glyphes for the world directions

past the Highlands is a lush tropical rainforest area called El Petén. The jungle melts into a region of tropical savanna on the Yucatán Peninsula and, at the tip of the Peninsula, a very arid desert-like region. North of El Petén the jungle and isthmus open onto the marshy Tabasco Plain.

The last major geographic feature of Mexico is the Baja California peninsula, which has long been isolated from most of the rest of Mexico. It is a peninsula of mountains, deserts, plains and beaches stretching from a border with the USA between latitudes 32° and 33° to Cabo San Lucas 1300 km to the south, making it the world's longest peninsula. Its width ranges from 48 to 234 km. The peninsula is separated from mainland Mexico by the Colorado River at the north-eastern corner of the peninsula and by the Sea of Cortés (Gulf of California). Baja is a geographic microcosm of mainland Mexico, with a mountainous region down its middle, and narrow coastal plains cut by a few (usually dry) rivers and streams. As with mainland Mexico, its mountains are an extension of North American ranges, in this case the Sierra Nevada range in California.

CLIMATE

The two most important factors in determining climatic conditions in Mexico are elevation and parallels of latitude. Although the Tropic of Cancer, which cuts across Mexico just north of Mazatlán, roughly determines the northern edge of the tropics, it's not safe to assume that the climate from here southward will be hot and humid. It's hot and humid along the coastal plains of both coasts south of the Tropic of Cancer; however, inland at higher elevations such as in Guadalajara or Mexico City, the climate is much more dry and temperate with mountain peaks that are often capped with snow.

The hot, wet season is May to October, with June to September the hottest and wettest months of all. Low-lying coastal

called the Oaxacan Highlands branches northward from Oaxaca.

From the isthmus a narrow stretch of lowlands runs along the Pacific coast south to Guatemala. The lowlands are demarcated to the north-east by the Sierra Madre de Chiapas (also called the Sierra de Soconusco), beyond which is the Río Grijalva basin and then the Chiapas Highlands. Travelling farther north-east areas get more rain and higher temperatures than elevated inland ones. In the east, rainfall is particularly high on the eastern slopes of the Sierra Madre Oriental and on the northern side of the Isthmus of Tehuantepec. The Altiplano Central is one of the driest parts of the country. December to February are generally the coolest months and north winds can make inland northern Mexico chilly, with temperatures (°C) often in single figures.

In general, the climate varies according to the landscape. The following chart adapted from *Estadística Anuario de Mexico*, a Mexican government publication, should be useful in planning your travels through Mexico. Figures indicated are in °C and mm.

		Jan	Feb	Mar	Apr	May	June	July	Aug	Sept	Oct	Nov	Dec
Tijuana	temp	14	15	15	16	19	20	23	23	22	19	17	14
	rain	40	60	50	10	–	–	–	–	–	10	30	30
Mexicali	temp	12	15	17	20	24	30	33	32	23	23	16	12
	rain	10	10	10	10	–	–	–	20	20	20	10	20
La Paz	temp	16	16	18	21	23	27	28	29	28	25	20	17
	rain	10	–	–	–	–	–	10	30	60	10	10	10
Cabo San Lucas	temp	19	19	20	21	23	26	28	29	28	27	22	20
	rain	–	10	–	–	–	–	10	10	60	30	40	10
Acapulco	temp	26	26	26	27	29	29	29	29	28	28	27	26
	rain	10	–	–	–	300	440	220	250	360	170	30	10
Cancún	temp	26	25	26	28	28	29	29	29	29	28	27	26
	rain	100	60	40	40	120	180	110	150	230	220	100	110
Ciudad Juárez	temp	6	9	12	18	21	26	27	26	22	17	10	6
	rain	–	10	10	10	20	10	30	30	30	30	10	10
Colima	temp	22	22	24	25	26	26	26	26	25	26	25	23
	rain	10	10	–	–	10	140	200	180	200	80	20	30
Chihuahua	temp	10	11	15	18	24	26	25	24	22	18	13	10
	rain	–	–	10	10	10	30	80	90	90	40	10	20
Guadalajara	temp	15	16	18	21	22	22	21	20	20	18	16	15
	rain	20	–	–	–	20	190	250	200	180	50	20	0
Guanajuato	temp	14	16	18	20	22	20	19	19	18	17	16	15
	rain	10	10	–	–	30	140	180	140	150	50	20	20
Hermosillo	temp	16	17	20	23	26	31	32	31	31	26	21	16
	rain	–	20	10	–	–	–	70	80	60	40	–	–
Ixtapa/Zihuatenejo	temp	24	24	28	30	31	30	28	27	27	27	26	26
	rain	20	–	–	10	30	180	250	230	180	80	–	–
Manzanillo	temp	24	24	24	25	26	27	29	29	27	27	26	25
	rain	20	10	–	–	–	100	140	190	390	130	20	50

		Jan	Feb	Mar	Apr	May	June	July	Aug	Sept	Oct	Nov	Dec
Mazatlán	temp	20	20	20	21	24	26	27	27	27	26	24	21
	rain	10	10	–	–	–	30	170	240	270	60	10	40
Mexico City	temp	12	13	16	17	18	17	16	16	16	15	13	12
	rain	10	10	10	10	–	110	120	100	120	30	20	10
Monterrey	temp	15	17	20	24	26	27	27	28	26	22	17	14
	rain	20	20	20	30	40	80	70	60	210	110	30	20
Morelia	temp	14	16	18	20	21	20	18	18	18	17	16	15
	rain	10	10	10	10	40	130	170	160	160	60	20	10
Oaxaca	temp	17	19	21	22	23	22	21	21	21	20	18	18
	rain	–	–	10	30	60	120	90	100	170	40	10	10
Pátzcuaro	temp	14	13	16	18	20	20	17	17	17	16	15	13
	rain	20	10	10	10	40	200	250	240	220	80	30	20
Puebla	temp	12	16	17	18	19	18	17	17	17	16	15	13
	rain	10	10	10	10	70	160	140	150	190	60	20	10
Puerto Vallarta	temp	22	21	24	24	26	29	28	30	29	30	28	26
	rain	20	10	10	10	10	230	350	330	330	140	10	10
San Cristóbal	temp	12	13	14	16	16	16	16	16	16	15	13	13
	rain	10	–	10	40	130	260	140	160	250	150	20	20
San Luis Potosí	temp	13	15	17	21	21	21	20	20	20	18	17	14
	rain	10	10	10	10	30	70	60	40	90	20	10	20
Tampico	temp	18	20	22	25	27	28	28	28	27	26	22	20
	rain	50	20	10	10	50	200	150	150	340	180	60	40
Taxco	temp	19	21	22	24	25	22	21	21	21	21	20	20
	rain	–	10	10	20	80	270	300	350	330	90	10	–
Tlaxcala	temp	13	14	16	17	18	17	16	16	16	16	15	14
	rain	10	–	10	20	70	120	130	150	140	50	10	10
Uruapan	temp	16	17	20	21	22	22	21	21	21	20	18	16
	rain	20	20	10	10	30	280	350	330	410	180	40	30
Veracruz	temp	21	22	23	25	26	27	27	27	27	26	24	22
	rain	20	20	10	20	50	270	350	300	350	150	90	20

PEOPLE

The Mexican character is complex to say the least – try reading Octavio Paz's *The Labyrinth of Solitude* for an assessment of it – but two general features of Mexican society which quickly become obvious are strong nationalism and greater stereotyping according to sex than in other western countries.

Machismo is an exaggerated masculinity aimed at impressing other males rather than women. Its manifestations range from aggressive driving and the carrying of weapons to heavy drinking. Women, in

Old Chenalho woman

turn, exaggerate their femininity and don't question male authority. This behaviour is often no more than a front, and at its extreme applies only to a minority. Nevertheless, feminism has a long way to go and not many women hold responsible jobs. The only recent female politician of any renown was Rosa Luz Alegría, President López Portillo's tourism minister and mistress.

The macho image probably has its roots in Mexico's violent past, and seems to hinge on a curious network of family relationships: as several writers have pointed out, it's fairly common for Mexican husbands to have mistresses. In response, wives lavish affection on their sons, who end up idolising their mothers and, unable to find similar perfection in a wife, take a mistress .... The strong mother-son bond also means that it's

crucial for a Mexican wife to get along with her mother-in-law. And while the virtue of daughters and sisters has to be protected at all costs, other women are often seen as 'fair game' by Mexican men. This applies particularly to foreign women without male companions. Before AIDS, few middle-class Mexico City males passed their teens without a trip to Acapulco to see how many of those reputedly sex-hungry gringo women they could pick up.

Despite tensions – or perhaps to hide them – family loyalty is very strong. One gringo who has lived in Mexico for several years commented that Mexicans never really reveal their true selves outside the family: 'However well you think you know someone, you eventually realise that everything they say or do is an act of one kind or another – but that doesn't stop them being friendly, loyal or charming'. If you have any friends or contacts who live in the country, don't waste the opportunity. An invitation to a Mexican home is an honour for an outsider; as a guest you'll be treated royally and will enter a part of real Mexico which surprisingly few outsiders are admitted to.

Nationalism stems from Mexico's 11-year war for independence from Spain in the early 19th century and subsequent struggles against Spanish, American and French invaders on Mexican soil. Foreign economic domination – by the British and Americans around the turn of this century and more recently by the Americans again – has also been impossible to throw off. But while Mexicans present a fiercely patriotic front to foreigners, they're well aware that their country, like any other, has its shortcomings. Politicians, police and officials are universally despised for their corruption, and inefficiency in public organisations is accepted as the rule, not the exception. As one Mexican passenger at the Dallas airport confided when our Continental flight to Mexico City was delayed four hours: 'We're not in Mexico, we're not travelling on a Mexican airline, but we are going to Mexico, so we are late'.

Machismo and nationalism were gruesomely combined in one incident when John Noble was hitch-hiking with an American companion near San Blas in Nayarit:

Our driver was tearing with calm insanity along an empty country road when we rounded a bend and saw a flock of turkeys daydreaming in our path, not far enough ahead for comfort. I braced myself for a violent swerve or a screeching halt ... but no, the driver hit the accelerator even harder and thud, thud, thud went the turkeys as we drove straight through the middle of them. Not believing this had really happened, I looked back. Several mangled birds and a few drifting feathers forced the reality upon me. I peered sideways at the driver. His eyes had a hard, satisfied gleam: he'd shown these gringos that nothing, not even a flock of turkeys, stops a real *hombre* when he's behind the wheel.

More often, Mexicans are friendly, humorous and willing to help. Language difficulties can obscure this fact; some people are shy or will ignore you because they haven't encountered foreigners before and don't imagine a conversation is possible – just a few words of Spanish will often bring you smiles and warmth, not to mention lots of questions. Then someone who speaks a few words of English will pluck up the courage to try them out.

Some Indian peoples adopt a cool attitude to visitors; they have learned to mistrust outsiders after 4½ centuries of exploitation by Spanish and mestizos. They don't like being gaped at by crowds of tourists and are sensitive about cameras, particularly in churches and at religious festivals.

If you have a white skin in Mexico, you'll be assumed to be a citizen of the USA and may provoke any reaction from curiosity or wonder to fear or, occasionally, hostility. The classic Mexican attitude to the US is a combination of the envy and resentment that a poor neighbour feels for a rich one. While the US is still seen by some as the land where everything you touch turns to dollars (or at least cars, cassette players and Disneyland T-shirts), enough Mexicans have worked as wetback labourers for it to be known that the US doesn't share its wealth too willingly. The *norteamericanos* have also committed the sin of sending their soldiers into Mexican territory three times.

Towards individual Americans any hostility usually evaporates as soon as you show that you're human too. And while the word 'gringo' isn't exactly a compliment – you may hear it in an annoying undertone after you've walked past someone – it can also be used with a brusque friendliness. (On a street in Acayucan, Veracruz, John heard the call, 'Gringo!' and looked round to see a truckload of smiling, waving boys who wanted to greet him.)

If you're not an American, and say so, you may well be seen (in rural areas particularly) as a freak of nature who'll get the benefit of the doubt. John writes:

Reactions to the revelation that I was *inglés* have included 'How many days in the bus to England?' (from a trainee teacher in Chiapas); 'England ... that is Germany? Or France?' (a Oaxaca restaurant-owner); 'What part of England is Britain in?' (a Mexico City telephone operator); and, from a fisherman on the Chiapas coast, 'Is England that way (pointing out to sea) or that way (inland)?' to which I pointed inland (the more accurate of the two choices) and he replied, 'Ah, in the sierra'. The three things most commonly associated with England these days are Las Malvinas, football hooligans and Margaret Thatcher ('Why don't you have a man – strong – for prime minister?'). A New Zealander with whom I travelled for a few days usually evoked blank incomprehension with the words *Nueva Zelandia*, nor did the addition of *cerca de Australia* help much. But then what use do most Mexicans have for any knowledge about our countries?

As for the Mexican attitude toward time – the fabled *mañana* syndrome – it's no more casual than in any other non-western country and has probably become legendary simply from comparison with the US. Sometimes one gets the feeling that Mexicans adopt a deliberately relaxed attitude to prevent any underlying tensions from breaking out. But it's certainly true, especially outside the big cities, that the urgency or promptness westerners are used to is lacking – which many will think is all to the good. If something's really worth doing, it gets done. If not, it can wait .... Most buses still leave on time and shops open at more or less regular hours.

POPULATION

Mexico can be roughly divided into two population groups – mestizos and Indians. Mestizos, the overwhelming majority of Mexico's populace, are people of mixed blood. The term dates back to 16th-century colonial society in Mexico when whites – born in either Mexico or Spain – sought to distinguish themselves from people of mixed blood born of white and Indian parents. Today, 'mestizo' and 'Mexican' are practically synonymous, although Indians are distinguished as a separate ethnic group.

Indians *Indígenas*, as they are formally and perhaps more respectfully known, are those descendants of Mexico's pre-Hispanic peoples who have retained their distinct cultures, languages and identity – usually at the cost of isolation, oppression and poverty. Despite various attempts by the government to strengthen or obliterate the Indians' differences from the rest of society in the name of progress, they remain in general second-class citizens, often occupying the worst land and exploited by mestizos. Their main wealth is traditional and spiritual; the Indian way of life is synonymous with communal custom and ritual closely bound up with nature.

Many Indian groups have lost their distinct identity in the 4½ centuries since the Spanish conquest, and the gradual modernisation of Mexican life continues this process in some cases. Researchers have listed at least 139 vanished Indian languages; about 50 Indian peoples remain. An Indian in Mexico is hard to define, and estimates of the Indian population range from four to 10 million. Basically it comes down to those who speak an Indian language and regard themselves as Indian. Official figures usually count only those who list themselves in censuses as speakers of Indian tongues. The following estimates of Indian numbers and the states they live in are derived from mainly the 1970 and 1980 censuses; in some cases they may be too low.

Amuzgo	20,000	(17,500 Guer, 2500 Oax)
Chatino	20,000	(Oax)
Chichimec	1500	(Guan)
Chinantec	70,000	(Oax)
Chocho	2000	(Oax)
Chol	95,000	(78,000 Chis, 17,000 Tab)
Chontal de Oaxaca	8000	
Chontal de Tabasco	30,000	
Chuj	800	(Chis)
Cochimí	150	(BCN)
Cora	12,000	(Nay)
Cucapá	200	(BCN)

Cuicatec	15,000	(Oax)
Guarijío	3000	(Son & Chih)
Huastec	105,000	(53,000 SLP, 50,000 Ver, 2000 Tam)
Huave	10,000	(Oax)
Huichol	50,000	(41,000 Jal, 9000 Nay)
Ixcatec	250	(Oax)
Jalaltec	1000	(Chis)
Kikapoo	500	(Coah)
Kiliwa	200	(BCN)
Kumiai	100	(BCN)
Lacandón	300	(Chis)
Mame	4000	(Chis)
Matlatzinca	2000	(Mex)
Maya	653,000	(500,000 Yuc, 82,000 QR, 71,000 Cam)
Mayo	58,000	(37,000 Son, 21,000 Sin)
Mazahua	185,000	(181,000 Mex, 4000 Mich)
Mazatec	118,000	(110,000 Oax, 6000 Ver, 2000 Pueb)
Mixe	75,000	(Oax)
Mixtec	290,000	(213,000 Oax, 66,000 Guer, 11,000 Pueb)
Motozintlec	4000	(Chis)
Nahua	1,335,000	(375,000 Pueb, 350,000 Ver, 180,000 Hid, 130,000 Guer, 130,000 SLP, 85,000 DF, 27,000 Tlax, 24,500 Mor, 23,000 Mex, 4500 Oax, 3000 Jal, 3000 Mich)
Ocuiltec	5000	(Mex)
Opata	500	(Son)
Otomí	300,000	(125,000 Hid, 104,000 Mex, 21,000 Guan, 21,000 Quer, 19,000 Ver, 7000 Pueb, 1500 Tlax, 600 Mich, 600 Mor)
Pai-pai	300	(BCN)
Pame	5000	(SLP)
Pápago	200	(Son)
Pima	500	(350 Chih, 150 Son)
Popoloca	9000	(7000 Pueb, 2000 Oax)
Popoluca	25,000	(Ver)
Seri	500	(Son)
Tarahumara	58,000	(57,000 Chih, 1000 Dur)
Tarasco/Purépecha	100,000	(Mich)
Tepehua	8000	(6500 Ver, 1500 Hid)
Tepehuano	17,000	(13,500 Dur, 2500 Chih, 1000 Nay)
Tlapanec	55,000	(Guer)
Tojolabal	25,000	(Chis)
Totonac	192,000	(125,000 Ver, 67,000 Pueb)
Trique	9000	(Oax)
Tzeltal	220,000	(mostly Chis)
Tzotzil	135,000	(Chis)
Yaqui	20,000	(Son)
Zapotec	350,000	(mostly Oax)
Zoque	27,000	(Chis)

BCN – Baja California Norte; Cam – Campeche; Chih – Chihuahua; Chis – Chiapas; Coah – Coahuila; DF – Distrito Federal; Dur – Durango; Guan – Guanajuato; Guer – Guerrero; Hid – Hidalgo; Jal – Jalisco; Mex – State of México; Mich – Michoacán; Mor – Morelos; Nay – Nayarit; Oax – Oaxaca; Pueb – Puebla; QR – Quintana Roo; Quer – Querétaro; Sin – Sinaloa; SLP – San Luis Potosí; Son – Sonora; Tab – Tabasco; Tam –Tamaulipas; Tlax – Tlaxcala; Ver – Veracruz; Yuc – Yucatán

CULTURE

Traditional Dress

One of the most intriguing aspects of Mexican Indian life is the colourful, usually hand-made traditional clothing. This comes in infinite and exotic variety, often differing dramatically from village to village. Under the onslaught of modernity, such clothing is less common in everyday use than a few decades ago, but in some areas - notably around San Cristóbal in Chiapas - it's actually becoming more popular as Indian pride reasserts itself and the commercial potential of handicrafts is developed. In general, Indian women have kept to traditional dress longer than men.

Some styles still in common use go back to pre-Spanish times. Among these (all worn by women) are the *huipil*, a long, sleeveless tunic; the *quechquémitl*, a shoulder cape; and the *enredo*, a wrap-around skirt. Blouses are post-conquest introductions. Indian men's garments owe more to Spanish influence; nudity was discouraged by the church, so shirts, hats and *calzones* (long baggy shorts) were introduced.

What's most eye-catching about these costumes is their colourful embroidery - often entire garments are covered in a multicoloured web of stylised animal, human, plant and mythical shapes which can take months to complete. Each garment identifies the group and village from which its wearer comes. *Fajas* (waist sashes) are also important in this respect.

The designs often have multiple religious or magical meanings. In some cases the exact significance has been forgotten, but among the Huicholes of Jalisco, for instance, *fajas* are identified with snakes (fertility symbols) and serve as appeals for rain; the embroidered design of the white *totó* flower which grows in the rainy season is a request for maize. To the Indian weavers of Chiapas, descendants of the Mayas, diamond shapes represent the universe (the ancient Mayas believed the earth was a cube), while wearing a garment with saint figures on it is a form of prayer.

Materials and techniques are changing but the pre-Hispanic back-strap loom is still widely used. The warp (long) threads are stretched between two horizontal bars, one of which is fixed to a post or tree, while the other is attached to a strap which goes round the weaver's lower back. The weft (cross) threads are then woven in.

Yarn is hand-spun in many villages. Some Otomí women in Hidalgo make cloaks from maguey cactus fibres. Palm hats are common. Vegetable dyes are not yet totally out of use, and natural indigo is employed in several areas. Red dye from cochineal insects and purple dye from sea snails are used by some Mixtecs in Oaxaca. Modern luminescent dyes go down very well not only with Indians but with other Mexicans, who are happily addicted to bright colours.

The variety of techniques, materials, styles and designs is bewildering. Read Chloë Sayer's *Mexican Costume* (British Museum Publications, London), one of the most fascinating books written in recent years on any aspect of Mexico. (For more on clothing and other handicrafts, see 'Things to Buy' in the 'Facts for the Visitor' chapter.)

Music & Dance

In Mexico you're likely to hear live music at any time on streets, plazas or even buses. The musicians are playing for their living and range from marimba teams (with big wooden 'xylophones') and mariachi bands (violinists, trumpeters, guitarists and a singer, all dressed in 'cowboy' costume) to ragged lone buskers with out-of-tune guitars and hoarse voices. Marimbas are particularly popular in the south-east and on the Gulf coast.

Mexico has a thriving popular music business - old folk songs are in demand alongside rock and even punk music, while styles imported from elsewhere in the Americas include tango, bossanova, salsa and Andean pan-pipe music. The name of one band going the rounds in Oaxaca was 'Mike y Su Tropical Salvaje Show' (Mike & His Wild Tropical Show). Classical music is not neglected; there are several venues in Mexico City and other cities where you can hear recitals.

Music is an important part of the many colourful festivals on the Mexican calendar. The festivals also feature traditional dances. They're mainly performed to honour Christian saints, but in many cases they have pre-Hispanic roots and retain traces of ancient ritual. There are hundreds of traditional dances: some are popular in many parts of the country, others can be seen only in a single town or village. Nearly all of them feature special costumes, often including masks. One of the most spectacular is the *voladores*, performed by Totonac and Nahua Indians in the states of Veracruz and Puebla. Four men 'fly' (with ropes attached to one leg) from the top of a 20-metre-high pole in re-enactment of an old fertility rite. Among the most superb of all dance costumes are those of the Zapotec feather dance in Oaxaca and the Nahua quetzal dance in Puebla, which feature enormous feathered headdresses or shields.

Some dances tell stories of clear Spanish or colonial origin. Moros y Cristianos is a fairly widespread one which re-enacts the victory of Christians over Moors in medieval Spain, while the spring carnival at Huejotzingo, Puebla, sees a mock battle between Mexicans and French. At carnival time in Zaachila, Oaxaca, whip-wielding 'devils' are defeated by 'priests' with crosses and buckets of water. Near San Miguel de Allende in May, the festival of Las Yuntas sees 'Indians' confront 'Federales'.

Other dances – like the *voladores* – have even older roots. In a tradition which goes back to before the Spanish conquest, groups of dancers from several states meet at a spot outside San Miguel de Allende in late September, then wend their way to the town wearing bells, feather headdresses, scarlet cloaks and masks, carrying flower offerings and in some cases playing lutes made of armadillo-shell. The Huastec dance Zacamson from San Luis Potosí state mimics animal movements to the music of harp and fiddles. It has more than 75 parts, danced at different times of day and night.

Sometimes the meaning of the dances has become confused over time; in one Holy Week dance in Pinotepa Nacional, Oaxaca, white-painted youths called *Judíos* (Jews) recite old Mixtec incantations while firing arrows into the air. The Mardi Gras dance of Los Tejorones in the nearby villages of Pinotepa de Don Luis and San Juan Colorado has four episodes – a tiger or snake hunt, a wedding, a baptism and a cockfight.

Some dances are these days performed outside the religious context as simple spectacles. The *voladores*, for instance, can regularly be seen at El Tajín, Zempoala and Papantla. The Ballet Folklórico in Mexico City brings together traditional dances from all over the country. Veracruz state also has its own Ballet Folklórico, and folklore festivals like the Guelaguetza in Oaxaca and the Atlixcáyotl in Atlixco, Puebla, also gather performers from wide areas.

Sports

Bullfighting To gringo eyes, bullfighting hardly seems to be sport or, for that matter, entertainment. Mexicans, however, see it as both and more. It's a traditional spectacle, more a ritualistic dance than a fight, that originated in Spain and readily lends itself to a variety of symbolic interpretations, mostly related to *machismo*. Symbolism aside, the importance of the bullfight to Mexican society is underscored by the oft-heard saying that Mexicans arrive on time for only two events – funerals and bullfights.

The *corrida de toros* or bullfight begins promptly on Sundays at 4 pm in the winter and 5 pm in the summer with the presentation of the matador and his assistants. Everyone leaves the ring except for the matador and his 'cape men', before the first of six bulls is released from its pen. The cape men try to tire the bull by working him around the ring.

After a few minutes, a trumpet sounds to mark the beginning of the first of three parts *(tercios)* of each 'fight'. Two men on thickly padded horses enter the ring with long lances called *picadores* and trot around until they are close enough to the bull to stick their lances into its shoulder muscles. Their main objective is to weaken the bull just enough to make him manageable, but not enough to kill him.

The second *tercio* begins after the *picadores* leave the ring. Men with *banderillas*, one-metre-long stilettos, then enter the ring on foot. Their objective is to jam three pairs of banderillas into the bull's shoulders without impaling themselves on the bull's horns.

With that done, the third *tercio* – the part everyone has been waiting for – begins. The matador has exactly 16 minutes to kill the bull by first tiring him with fancy cape-work. When he feels the time is right, the matador trades his large cape for a smaller one (the *muleta*) and takes up a sword. He baits the bull towards him and gives it what he hopes will be the death blow, the final *estocada* or lunge from the sword. If the matador succeeds, and he usually does, you can expect a quick and bloody end.

The bull collapses and an assistant dashes into the ring to slice its jugular and chop off an ear or two and sometimes the tail for the matador.

Soccer *(fútbol)* is probably the country's second favourite sport; Mexico hosted the World Cup finals in 1970 and 1986. Neither time did the home team get beyond the quarter-finals – a fair reflection on local standards. If Mexico produces a really good player, chances are he'll go to Spain or Italy to improve his game and earn more. There's a decent national professional league and several impressive stadiums but crowds at games are small – perhaps because games are shown on TV. América (of Mexico City) and Guadalajara are among the top clubs.

Baseball *(béisbol)* is also popular, and there's a national professional league. Mexican stars often move to the States, and ageing Americans sometimes stretch out their careers south of the border.

Charreada is the rodeo, held particularly in the northern half of the country, both during fiestas and in regular venues often called *charros*.

Lucha Libre is free-style wrestling, a down-to-earth spectacle.

Horse Racing is held at several *hipódromos* around the country. It's popular in towns on the US border and at the Hipódromo de las Américas in Mexico City.

Jai Alai ('high-a-lie') is the Basque game *pelota*, brought to Mexico by the Spanish. It's a bit like squash with a hard ball on a very long court, played with curved baskets attached to the arm instead of a racket – and it can be fast and exciting. You can see it played by semi-professionals in Mexico City and Tijuana, among other places.

Tennis & Golf are popular among those who can afford them. Many upper-range hotels have tennis courts.

Outdoor Activities Mexicans aren't, in general, great lovers of nature or the wilderness experience – not surprising since there are large tracts of inhospitable country, and a great deal of what's left is inhabited or cultivated. There are a few popular day trails; the one up Popocatépetl can get pretty busy. There's also a small rock-climbing fraternity (see the 'Puebla & Tlaxcala' chapter). For many middle-

Jai Alai

class Mexicans, the countryside is either a place where peasants work or, if it's picturesque, somewhere to go in your car, have a family picnic, look at the view and probably leave some litter.

Fishing and shooting may be bigger news than hiking and camping, but that doesn't keep intrepid gringos from trekking off into what Mexicans consider absurdly rough country. The trails in Copper Canyon are a breeze for the Tarahumara Indians, but a challenge that's increasingly popular among gringo backpackers. *Mexico's Volcanoes* and *Backpacking in Mexico & Central America* are two useful guides (see 'Books' in the 'Facts for the Visitor' chapter). Nor is cycling a common pastime. Campsites are usually also trailer parks though tent camping there is possible. In some places it's possible to hire horses for the day.

Sport fishing is especially popular off the Pacific and Sea of Cortés coasts of mainland Mexico and the Baja peninsula. Check the *Angler's Guide to Baja California* by Tom Miller (Baja Trail Publications).

Water sports are popular in the main coast resorts. Most of the resorts and surrounding towns have shops that will rent equipment such as snorkels, masks and fins, and arrange boat excursions. Elsewhere, you're on your own.

Surfing is popular on the Pacific coast of Mexico. A few of the best surf spots include Punta Mesquite and Santa Rosalillita in Baja, and Bahía de Metanche near San Blas where they boast the world's longest wave. Ixtapa and Puerto Escondido are also considered good.

ARCHITECTURE

One of the Spaniards' first preoccupations upon their arrival in Mexico was to replace 'pagan' temples with Christian churches, often in the same location. A classic case is the Great Pyramid of Cholula, the biggest in the Americas, which is now surmounted by a small colonial church. Religious buildings remained among the most important of all the fine buildings erected in Mexico during the 300 years of Spanish rule. Many of the mansions and plazas which today contribute so much to the beauty of Mexico were also built then. Most of them are in basically Spanish styles but often with unique local variations.

Gothic & Renaissance styles and influences dominated the 16th and early 17th-century architecture of Mexico. The gothic style of the European Middle Ages is typified by soaring buttresses, pointed arches, clusters of round columns and ribbed vaults (ceilings). The renaissance style saw a return to Greek and Roman ideals of harmonious proportion; classical shapes like the square and the circle predominated, along with classical motifs; also featured were columns or 'orders', which, from the simplest to the most elaborate, were called Tuscan, Doric, Ionic, Corinthian and Composite.

The usual renaissance style in Mexico was called plateresque – from the Spanish for silversmith, *platero*, because plateresque often resembled the elaborate ornamentation that went into silverwork. Plateresque is commonly a style of decoration for the façades of buildings, particularly church doorways, which have round arches bordered by classical columns and often a variety of stone sculpture. A later version of the renaissance style was called 'pure' or herreresque after the Spanish architect Juan de Herrera. This was more austere and less decorative than plateresque.

Gothic and renaissance influences are combined in numerous 16th-century Mexican buildings – including many of the fortified monasteries that were built as Spanish monks carried their missionary work to all corners of the country. Monasteries usually had a large church, a cloister where the monks lived and worked, a big atrium (churchyard) sometimes with small *posa* chapels in the corners where processions would pause, and often a *capilla abierta* (open chapel) from which in the early days the priests could address large crowds of Indians gathered in the atrium.

Capillas abiertas – many of which have a simple beauty – are rare outside Mexico. Besides their practical functions before the monastery church was completed, they were probably a subtle attempt to simulate the feeling of pre-Hispanic religious ceremonies, at which the people would gather in plazas while priests carried out their tasks on pyramids or platforms.

Notable monasteries include Actopan, Acolmán and Huejotzingo (all in central Mexico); and Yanhuitlán, Coixtlahuaca and Teposcolula in Oaxaca state. The Casa de Montejo in Mérida has a fine plateresque façade. Mérida cathedral shows a mixture of plateresque and pure renaissance, while Mexico City and Puebla cathedrals mingle purist renaissance and the later baroque style. The interior of Guadalajara Cathedral is a bit of an anomaly, built later but more gothic in style.

The influence of the Arabs who had occupied much of Spain until fairly recently was also carried across the Atlantic to Mexico. Examples of this style, which is known as *mudéjar*, can be seen in beautifully carved wooden ceilings and in the *alfíz*, a rectangle framing a round arch (such as on the plateresque side door of San Francisco church in Puebla). The Capilla Real in Cholula is one of the strangest Arabic-influenced buildings in Mexico: its 49 domes almost resemble a mosque.

Baroque, which first came to Mexico in the early 17th century, was in turn a reaction against the strictness of renaissance styles. It used classical influences but combined them with other elements and aimed at creating dramatic effect rather than classical proportion. Curving shapes and lines, use of colour, contrasts of light and dark, and a decorativeness that became increasingly elaborate were among its hallmarks. Painting and sculpture were integrated with architecture for further elaborate effect – most notably in ornate, often enormous altarpieces. The classical 'orders' were used but often the 'wrong' way round, with the lighter or more elaborate columns placed below the heavier, simpler ones.

Mexican baroque went through several phases and, between 1730 and 1780, took on what some people consider a distinct style in itself – churrigueresque. Named after a Barcelona carver and architect, José Benito de Churriguera, the style was characterised by riotous surface ornamentation of which the hallmark is the *estípite* – a pilaster (vertical pillar projecting only partially from the wall) in the form of a very narrow upside-down pyramid. The estípite helped give churrigueresque its frequent dramatic 'top-heavy' effect.

Early, more restrained baroque buildings include the churches of Santiago Tlatelolco in Mexico City, San Felipe Neri in Oaxaca and San Francisco in San Luis Potosí. Later baroque structures are the churches of San Cristóbal in Puebla and La Soledad in Oaxaca, and the Zacatecas cathedral façade. Outstanding churrigueresque works include the façade of the Sagrario Metropolitano and the La Merced monastery patio in Mexico City; the churches of San Martín in Tepotzotlán, of San Francisco, La Compañía and La Valenciana in Guanajuato and of Santa Prisca y San Sebastián in Taxco; the Ocotlán sanctuary at Tlaxcala; and the interiors of Santa Rosa and Santa Clara churches in Querétaro.

Mexican Indian artisanry came into its own in the baroque era with a profusion of detailed sculpture in stone and polychrome stucco. Among its most exuberant examples are the Capilla del Rosario in Santo Domingo church, Puebla, and the village church of Tonantzintla, near Puebla. Arabic influence continued with the popularity of coloured tiles – *azulejos* – on the outside of buildings, particularly in and around the city of Puebla. The House of Tiles in Mexico City and Acatepec church near Puebla are notable tiled buildings, though in these cases the designs aren't particularly Arabic.

Neoclassic was another return to Greek and Roman ideals. In Mexico it lasted from about 1780 to 1830. Outstanding examples are the Escuela de Minería in Mexico City, El Carmen church in Celaya, the Alhóndiga de Granaditas in Guanajuato and the 2nd storey of the Mexico City cathedral towers.

19th & 20th Centuries Early independent Mexico mainly saw revivals of earlier styles and imitation of contemporary European fashions. There were gothic and colonial revivals and towards the end of the century many buildings copied French or Italian styles – none of them very original. Bellas Artes in Mexico City is one of the best.

After the Revolution of 1910-21 there was an attempt to return to pre-Hispanic roots in the search for a national identity – a trend generally known as Toltecism – and many public buildings exhibit the 'heaviness' of, say, Aztec or Toltec monuments. This movement culminated in the famous Mexico City university campus, built in the early 1950s, where many buildings are covered with colourful murals. Since then major buildings in Mexico have been more responsive to international trends and there have been a few dramatic innovations, perhaps the most spectacular being the Faro del Comercio in Monterrey – a tall, thin block of orange concrete which emits green laser beams across the city at night.

RELIGION

The Spanish missionaries of the 16th and 17th centuries succeeded less in converting the indigenous people than in grafting Catholicism onto the pre-Hispanic religions. Often old gods were simply given saints' names and old festivals and rituals continued to be celebrated, little changed, on whichever saint's day was nearest to the traditional date. Acceptance of the new religion was greatly helped by the dark-skinned Virgin Mary who appeared in a vision in 1531 to an Indian called Juan Diego, on a hill near Mexico City where Tonantzin, the mother of the Aztec gods, had long been worshipped. Today the 'Virgin of Guadalupe' is virtually the national patron saint.

The picture has changed little since those early Spanish days, despite some decline in traditional practices as the modern world makes inroads into Indian life. While nearly all Indians are Christian, their Christianity is fused with more ancient beliefs. Indeed, among some of the remoter peoples it's only a sideshow.

Triqui witch doctors in Oaxaca, for instance, reputedly carry out magical cures in churches after services, and for the Day of the Dead Triquis pour a broth made from sacrificed oxen over the church floor to feed the dead.

The Huicholes of Jalisco, who never really accepted Christianity, have two Christs but neither is a major deity. Much more important is Nakawé, the fertility goddess. The hallucinogenic plant peyote is a crucial source of wisdom in the Huichol world. Elsewhere, especially among the Tarahumara in the Copper Canyon, drunkenness is an almost sacred element at festival times. Even among the more orthodox Indians it's not uncommon for saints' festivals in spring, or the pre-Lent carnival, to be accompanied by remnants of fertility rites. The famous Totonac *voladores* dance of Veracruz is one such ritual, though it's losing much of its sacredness today through being performed as a spectacle for tourists. The Guelaguetza dance festival, which draws thousands of visitors to Oaxaca every summer, has its roots in pre-Hispanic maize god rituals which Christian priests replaced with masquerades.

In the traditional Indian world almost everything has a spiritual (some would say superstitious) dimension – trees, rivers, plants, wind, rain, sun, animals and hills have their own gods or spirits, and travellers have seen offerings of Coca-Cola bottles at festivals in Chamula, Chiapas. Sometimes whole hierarchies of 'pagan' gods co-exist side by side with the Christian Trinity and saints.

Witchcraft and magic survive. As with the deities, beliefs are complicated and differ from one group to the next, but illness is widely seen as a 'loss of soul' caused by the sufferer's wrongdoing or by the influence of someone with magical powers. A soul can be 'regained' if the appropriate ritual is performed by a witch doctor *(brujo)* and sometimes these ceremonies involve the use of hallucinogenic mushrooms. Another common belief is in the *tono* or *tona* – a person's animal 'double' in the spirit world whose welfare closely parallels that of the person's.

Catholicism

More than 90% of the population professes Catholicism. This is remarkably high considering the rocky history that the Catholic Church has had in Mexico, particularly in the last two centuries.

The Catholic Church was present in Mexico from the very first days of the Spanish conquest. It remained the second most important institution after the crown and its royal colonial representatives (the viceroy, etc), and was really the only unifying force in Mexican society until independence. Almost everyone – Indians, mestizos and whites – belonged to the church because, spirituality aside, it was the principal provider of social services and education in Mexico.

The Jesuits were the foremost providers and administrators, having established several missions and settlements throughout Mexico by the late 18th century. In the eyes of the French-influenced Bourbon administration in Spain they were mistakenly seen as one of the causes of Mexico's economic demise over the previous century and a half, so they were expelled in 1767. This marked the beginning of stormy church-state relations.

In the 19th and 20th centuries (up to 1940) colonial Mexico and then independent Mexico passed numerous measures restricting the power and influence of the Catholic Church. The bottom line was money and property, both of which the church was amassing faster than the generals and political bosses. The 1917 Constitution includes several anti-clerical provisions: marriage is a civil, not a religious, contract; clergy can't speak out about government policies and decisions; religious groups can't own property; and all church buildings must first be authorised and approved by the government. Most of these provisions are still in the Constitution, but they are almost never enforced.

Today, the church remains the unifying force that it was when Mexico was a Spanish colony. Since 1531, its most binding symbol has been the dark-skinned Virgin of Guadalupe. According to legend, a Christian Indian named Juan Diego saw the Virgin Mary three times in December 1531. The third time, the Virgin commanded Diego to pick up some roses and go to the Bishop to request that a church be built in her honour. In the Bishop's office Diego unfolded his cloak to present him with the roses and both saw an image of the Virgin imprinted on it. The image was deemed a miracle and a church was built on the spot.

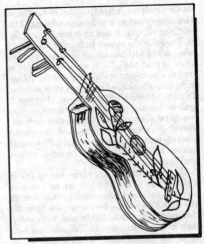

The appearance of a dark-skinned Virgin has been regarded as a link between the Catholic and non-Catholic Indian worlds. More importantly, since Mexico is now a predominantly mestizo society, the Virgin has come to symbolise a coming-of-age for the country. Evidence of this abounds in Mexico; the name of the Virgin of Guadalupe is invoked in religious ceremonies, political speeches and literature.

Protestantism

With only 4% of the population professing Protestantism, it has not been significant in Mexico. Several denominations, however, are represented: the Methodist Church, Jehovah's Witnesses, Seventh-Day Adventist Church, Seventh-Day Baptist Church, Church of Jesus Christ of Latter-Day Saints (Mormons) and National Presbyterian Church.

Judaism

Jews make up one tenth of 1% of Mexico's population. Most of them live in the state of Mexico and Mexico City, where there are several synagogues.

FESTIVALS & HOLIDAYS

The abundance of fiestas in the Mexican calendar has been explained by some writers, notably Octavio Paz, as an attempt to escape from the horrors of everyday existence – not only poverty but also a kind of blackness in the soul which perhaps stems from the country's violent past and its roots in the joining of two antagonistic groups, the Indians and the Spanish. Be that as it may, Mexican fiestas are full-blooded, highly colourful affairs which often go on for several days.

Festivals may be held for harvests of local products like grapes, apples, lemons, even radishes. There are festivals of the arts, local dance and music. Even trade and business fairs add a bit of a festival atmosphere to a town. Most Mexican festivals are religious at heart and often serve as an excuse for general merrymaking. Parades, special costumes, dancing, lots of music and plenty of drinking are all part of the scene. Some are celebrated nationwide – for example Carnival, Easter, Independence Day, the Day of the Dead, the Day of the Virgin of Guadalupe and Christmas. Others are very local, such as celebrations for a village's patron saint. But even near-universal events like the pre-Lent Carnival have their unique local variations, comprehensible only to the participants (if anyone!). John writes:

At Carnival time in San Cristóbal de Las Casas, two of us rented a car to look round some of the outlying villages. It was an extraordinary day. In Chamula the square in front of the church was packed with thousands of people who had come in from the hills. It was a market day as well as a fiesta, but in odd corners of the village, men in multicoloured costumes were gathered in tight, slowly-revolving groups, chanting to guitar accompaniment. Occasionally they would be plied with small cups of an obviously potent beverage as they worked themselves towards some kind of sacred 'high'. The church too was full of chanting amid the incense fumes and flowers.

On to Mitontic, where there was no one in sight except a few children whose curiosity about us couldn't quite overcome their fear. In the church we found a few women sitting on the floor making garlands. All the men, apparently, were away at Chamula. At Chenalhó, our next stop, the people seemed exhausted; in the square quiet groups of women were still hoping to sell some leftovers from the morning market, while men were draped here and there in advanced inebriation, most of them well past being able to move, let alone get home. Carnival was clearly several days old here already. Two of the less paralytic men gave us a slurp from their bottle – the contents were fiery and not unlike brandy. Liveliest person in the village was the priest – a Frenchman with a St Bernard dog who had been here donkey's years. He invited us into his house for rum and a chat in bits of three languages about the amazingly convoluted local church politics.

As we lurched along the deeply rutted 'road' to our final destination, San Andrés Larrainzar, the weather closed in and it started to drizzle. Every couple of km now we were passing bands of wandering minstrels, all strumming what seemed the same tune on guitars as they ambled solemnly from one hamlet to another, dressed in flowing red and black robes, pointed 'wizard' hats that streamed with rainbow-coloured ribbons, and – despite the weather – sunglasses. They too were clearly not teetotallers. In San Andrés the main activity came from what appeared to be a group of village elders, who were having grave difficulty lining up in the correct order for their entry into the church. Down a couple of side streets more bands of minstrels walked in circles. Another group went round and round the village square.

Heading back to San Cristóbal, we picked up an ageing couple whose Spanish was worse than ours. The woman seemed sober but the man was responsible for trying to communicate with us. He was well the worse for wear and had a bleeding gash on one leg. We stopped at what we gathered was the track leading to their home but by then he seemed to want to leave his wife behind to continue with us to Chamula. We hailed another man standing by the roadside to do some interpreting. No one seemed to understand anyone else but eventually the couple struggled out of our vehicle and we drove back to San Cristóbal, little wiser about what Carnival meant in the highlands of Chiapas.

Following is a list of some of the main holidays, celebrations and events, along with dates (some change each year and are therefore approximations). Banks, post offices and government offices are closed on most of these days or weeks.

1 January
   New Year's Day
5 February
   Constitution Day
24 February
   Flag Day
Late February-early March
   Carnaval (Carnival) – Held the week or so before Ash Wednesday, usually in February. Celebrated all over the country but most grandly in Veracruz and Mazatlán, with huge parades, music, food, fireworks and other events.
19 March
   Día del Señor San José – The Festival of St Joseph, patron saint of San José del Cabo in Baja California, is celebrated with street dances, horse races, cock fights, food fairs and fireworks.
21 March
   Birthday of President Benito Juárez
April
   Palm Sunday & Good Friday – Celebrated throughout Mexico on variable dates in March and April.
April
   Semana Santa (Holy Week) – Easter Week is one of the biggest holiday periods in Mexico. Transport and accommodation are heavily booked at this time. Around 60,000 people a day pass through Mexico City's northern bus terminal, and the two national

airlines carry the same number of travellers. Virtually the entire population of the Distrito Federal makes at least one trip out of the city. Some parts of the country become so overrun that gasoline has to be rationed.

1 May
Labour Day

5 May
Cinco de Mayo – Anniversary of Mexico's victory over the French Army in Puebla in 1862. Celebrated grandly in Puebla.

10 May
Día de la Madre (Mother's Day)

1 June
Navy Day

1st Sunday in July
Tecate en Marcha (Tecate in Progress); also known as *La Romería (the Pilgrimage)* – Celebrated in Tecate with colourful parades and rodeos.

Last two Mondays in July
Guelaguetza Festival – Regional dance performances in Oaxaca city.

August
La Pamplonada (Running of the Bulls) – Celebrated in Tecate and meant to resemble the running of the bulls in Pamplona, Spain.

15-16 September
Día de la Independencia – Commemoration of Mexico's independence from Spain in 1821. The biggest celebrations take place in Mexico City beginning with a recitation of Hidalgo's *Grito* or cry for independence followed by fireworks, horse races, folk dances from all over Mexico and mariachi bands.

September
Día de San Miguel – This saint's day held on one of the last Fridays in September brings big celebrations in San Miguel de Allende, Guanajuato.

September
Atlixcáyotl – Dance and music festival held the last weekend in September at Atlixco, Puebla. Performers come from a wide area.

3 October
International Seafood Fair – Held at Riviera del Pacífico in Ensenada.

12 October
Día de la Raza (Columbus Day) – Commemoration of Columbus' discovery of the New World.

1-2 November
All Saints/All Souls Day – 2 November is also called Day of the Dead. Festivities take place throughout Mexico with especially colourful celebrations on the island of Janitzio in Lake Pátzcuaro. In many places the celebrations recall ancestor-worship, as families build altars in their homes in honour of their dead and spend the day in the graveyards – which often have quite a festive atmosphere. It's widely believed that the spirits of the dead return on this day. Breads and sweets made to resemble human skeletons are sold in almost every market and bakery; papier-mâché skeletons and skulls appear everywhere.

November
The Baja 1000 off-road race – Early in the month a race takes place through most of the peninsula. This was the world's first off-road race. Mexican government tourist officials were uncertain whether the race would be held every year.

20 November
Anniversary of the Revolution of 1910

12 December
Día de Nuestra Señora de Guadalupe (Festival of Our Lady of Guadalupe) – Our Lady of Guadalupe is the patron saint of Mexico. Supposedly she made her miraculous appearance to a peasant on this day in 1531 in present-day Mexico City, 10 years after Cortés' conquest of Mexico. The biggest celebrations take place at the Basilica de Guadalupe in Mexico City.

25 December
Christmas Day – This marks the end of a week of *posadas*, parades of costumed children re-enacting the journey of Mary and Joseph to Bethlehem. The children also

Shrine

break piñatas (papier-mâché animals) full of candy. *Posadas* are held throughout Mexico. Christmas is celebrated with a service in almost every church in the country.

There isn't a village, town or city in Mexico that doesn't have at least one patron saint who is venerated first in the church and then in the streets. Some claim that the tradition is a throw-back to pre-Hispanic days when local gods and goddesses were fêted with the same vigour. The following is a month-by-month list of saint's days.

January

2	San Macario
6	Los Santos Reyes
13	San Gumersindo
15	San Mauro
16	San Marcelo
17	San Antonio Abao
19	San Mario
24	Nuestra Señora de la Paz
30	Santa Martino
31	Santa Virginia

February

1	San Ignacio
3	San Blas
5	San Felipe de Jesús
10	San Guillermo
11	Nuestra Señora de Lourdes
13	San Benigno
14	San Valentín
16	San Onesimo
23	Santa Marta
28	San Hilario

March

2	San Federico
6	Santa Felicitas
8	San Juan de Dios
14	Santa Matilda
17	San Patricio
19	San José
22	San Octaviano
28	Santa Dorotea
31	San Benjamín

April

2	Santa Ofelia
3	San Ricardo
5	Santa Emilia
8	San Alberto
12	San Julio
18	San Perfecto
21	San Anselmo
23	San Jorge
25	San Marcos

May

1	Santa Berta
8	San Bonifacio
10	San Antonio
15	San Isidoro
20	San Bernardino
25	Corpus Christi
26	San Felipe Neri
27	Santa Carolina
30	San Fernando

June

3	Santa Clotilde
7	San Roberto
9	San Feliciano
15	San Modesto
17	San Gregorio
21	San Luis Gonzaga
24	San Juan Bautista
26	San Antelmo
29	San Pedro y San Pablo
30	Santa Luciana

July

1	San Aaron
2	San Martiniano
7	San Fermín
8	Santa Isabel
11	San Abundio
19	Santa Rufina
24	Santa Christina
27	San Celestino
28	San Victor
31	San Ignacio de Loyola

August

1	Santa Esperanza
6	San Justo
9	San Roman
10	San Lorenzo
12	Santa Clara
20	San Bernardo
25	San Luis Rey
27	San Armando
28	San Agustín
31	San Ramón

September

1 Nuestra Señora de los Remedios
4 Santa Rosalía
8 San Sergio
19 San Genaro
21 San Mateo
25 Santa Aurelia
27 San Cosme
29 San Miguel
30 San Jerónimo

October

3 San Gerardo
4 San Francisco de Asís
5 San Placido
13 San Eduardo
15 Santa Teresa de Jesús
17 Santa Margarita
18 San Lucas
24 San Rafael
27 San Florencio
30 San Claudio

November

4 San Carlos
6 San Leonardo
7 San Ernesto
8 San Victoriano
11 San Martín
13 San Diego
17 San Gregorio
23 San Clemente
25 Santa Catalina
30 San Andrés

December

1 Santa Natalia
4 Santa Barbara
7 San Ambrosio
13 Santa Lucía
15 San Arturo
17 San Lázaro
18 San Ausencio
20 San Filogonio
27 San Juan

LANGUAGE

Spanish is the predominant language of Mexico. Mexican Spanish is unlike Castilian Spanish, the literary and official language of Spain, in two respects: the Castilian lisp has more or less disappeared and several Indian words have crept in.

Travellers in the towns, cities and larger villages can almost always find someone who speaks at least some English. All the same it is still useful and courteous to know at least a few words and phrases of Spanish. Mexicans will generally respond more positively if you attempt to speak to them in their own language.

Spanish Alphabet *ch, ll* and *ñ* are letters of the Spanish alphabet and come after c, l and n respectively in alphabetical lists like dictionaries or phone books.

Pronunciation Spanish has five vowels, *a, e, i, o* and *u*. They are pronounced something like the highlighted sections of the following English words: father, end, India, or and pull.

Most of the consonants in Spanish are pronounced in much the same way as their English counterparts, but there are a few exceptions:

c is pronounced like 's' in 'sit' when before *e* or *i*; elsewhere it is like 'k'
g is pronounced like English 'h' (with more friction) before *e* or *i*; before *a* or *o* it is like the 'g' in 'go'
gu is pronounced like the 'g' in 'go', but the *u* is not pronounced
h is not pronounced at all
j is pronounced like English 'h', only with a lot more friction
ll is similar to English 'y'
ñ is like the 'ny' in 'canyon'
qu is the same as English 'k' (the *u* is not pronounced)
r is a very short rolled r, whereas *rr* is a longer rolled 'r'
x is like *j* when it comes after *e* or *i*, otherwise it is like English 'x' as in 'taxi'
z is the same as English s; under no circumstances should *s* or *z* be pronounced like English *z* – this sound does not exist in Spanish.

There are a few other minor pronunciation

problems, but the longer you spend in Mexico, the easier they will become.

Accents & Stress Knowing which part of a word to stress in Spanish is a big aid to being understood. The rule is: if the word has an accent, put the stress on the syllable containing the accent; if not, stress the last syllable unless the word ends in a vowel or 'n' or 's', in which cases stress the second-last syllable. Examples:

zócalo	ZO-ca-lo
kilómetro	ki-LOM-et-ro
mazatlán	maz-at-LAN
méxico	ME-xi-co
cortés	cor-TES
favor	fa-VOR
catedral	cat-e-DRAL
monterrey	mon-te-RREY
comer	com-ER
estoy	es-TOY
acapulco	ac-a-PUL-co
naranja	na-RAN-ja
estados unidos	es-TA-dos u-NI-dos
casa	CA-sa
joven	JO-ven

More than 50 Indian languages are spoken in Mexico by over four million people, of whom about 20 to 25% don't speak Spanish.

Following is a list of some helpful words and phrases. Words pertaining to food and restaurants are covered in the 'Food' section of the 'Facts for the Visitor' chapter.

Entering Mexico

tourist card	*tarjeta de turista*
visa	*visado*
passport	*pasaporte*
identification	*identificación*
birth certificate	*certificado de nacimiento*
driver's licence	*licencia de manejar*
car owner's title	*título de propiedad*
car registration	*registración*
customs	*aduana*

immigration	*inmigración*
the border (frontier)	*la frontera*

Greetings & Civilities

hello/hi
hola
good morning/good day
buenos días
good afternoon
buenas tardes
good evening/good night
buenas noches
goodbye
adiós
Pleased to meet you.
mucho gusto
How are you? (to one person)
como está usted?
How are you? (to a group)
como están ustedes?
I am fine.
estoy bien

General Expressions

yes	*sí*
no	*no*
please	*por favor*
thank you	*gracias*
you're welcome	*de nada*
excuse me	*perdóneme*
good/okay	*bueno*
bad	*malo*
better	*mejor*
best	*el mejor*
more	*más*
less	*menos*
very little	*poco* or *poquito*

How much?
cuánto?
How much does it cost?
cuánto cuesta? or *cuánto se cobra?*
I want ....
yo quiero ....
I do not want ....
no quiero ....
Give me ....
déme ....
What do you want?
que quiere usted?

Do you have ....?	*tiene usted ....?*
Is/are there ....?	*hay ....?*

I	*yo*
you (familiar)	*tu*
you (formal)	*usted*
you (plural)	*ustedes*
he/him	*el*
she/her	*ella*
we/us	*nosotros*
they/them (masculine)	*ellos*
they/them (feminine)	*ellas*

my wife	*mi esposa*
my husband	*mi esposo*
my sister	*mi hermana*
my brother	*mi hermano*
sir/mr	*señor*
madam/mrs	*señora*
miss	*señorita*

I am .... (condition or place)	*estoy*
tired	*cansado*
sick/ill	*enfermo*

I am .... (state)	*soy*
a student	*estudiante*
a worker	*trabajador*

Nationalities

American (m)	*americano*
American (f)	*americana*
Australian (m)	*australiano*
Australian (f)	*australiana*
British (m)	*británico*
British (f)	*británica*
Canadian	*canadiense*
French (m)	*francés*
French (f)	*francesa*
German (m)	*alemán*
German (f)	*alemána*

Languages

I speak	*yo hablo ....*

I do not speak	*no hablo ....*
Do you speak ....?	*usted habla ....*
Spanish	*español*
English	*inglés*
German	*alemán*
French	*francés*

I understand.	*entiendo*
I do not understand.	*no entiendo*
Do you understand?	*entiende usted?*
Please speak slowly.	*por favor hable despacio*

Getting Around

Where is ....?	*dónde está........?*
the bus station	*la estación del autobús*
the train station	*la estación del ferrocarril*
the post office	*el correo*
the telephone office	*la caseta de teléfono*
the airport	*el aeropuerto*

street	*calle*
boulevard	*bulevar*
avenue	*avenida*
road	*camino*
highway	*carretera*
corner (of)	*esquina (de)*
corner (or) bend	*vuelta*
block	*cuadra*
to the left	*a la izquierda*
to the right	*a la derecha*
on the right side	*al lado derecho*
on the left side	*al lado izquierdo*
left (hand side)	*(mano) izquierda*
right (hand side)	*(mano) derecha*
straight ahead	*adelante*
straight on	*todo recto* or *derecho*
this way	*por aquí*
that way	*por allí*
north	*norte*
south	*sur*
east	*este*

east (in an address)	*oriente*
	(abbreviated *ote*)
west	*oeste*
west (in an address)	*poniente*
	(abbreviated *pte*)

How far is ....?
   á que distancia está ....?
How long? (how much time?)
   cuanto tiempo?

Accommodation

hotel	*hotel*
guest house	*casa de huéspedes*
inn	*posada*
room	*cuarto*
single room	*cuarto solo* or
	cuarto sencillo
double room	*cuarto para dos* or
	cuarto doble
double bed	*cama de*
	matrimonio
with twin beds	*con camas gemelas*
with bath	*con baño*
shower	*ducha*
hot water	*agua caliente*
air-conditioning	*aire acondicionado*
blanket	*manta*
towel	*toalla*
soap	*jabón*
toilet paper	*papel higiénico*
the bill	*la cuenta*

What is the price?
   cuál es el precio?
Does that include taxes?
   están incluídos los impuestos?
Does that include service?
   está incluído el servicio?

Using the Telephone

telephone office	*caseta de teléfono*
telephone booth	*cabina de teléfono*
local call	*una llamada local*
long-distance call	*una llamada de*
	larga distancia
person to person	*persona a persona*
collect call	*por cobrar*
busy	*ocupado*

Money

money	*dinero*
travellers' cheques	*cheques de viajero*
bank	*banco*
exchange bureau	*casa de cambio*

I want to change some money.
   quiero cambiar dinero
What is the exchange rate?
   cuál es el cambio?
Is there a commission?
   hay comisión?

Driving in Mexico

gasoline/petrol	*gasolina*
unleaded	*sin plomo*
leaded	*con plomo*
fill the tank	*llene el tanque*
full	*lleno*
tyre	*llanta*
spare tyre	*llanta de repuesto*
puncture	*agujero*
flat tyre	*llanta desinflada*

How much is gasoline per litre?
   cuánto cuesta el litro de gasolina?
My car has broken down.
   se me ha descompuesto el carro
I need a tow truck.
   necesito un remolque
Is there a garage near here?
   hay garage cerca?

Time

now/in a few minutes	*horita, ahorita*
tomorrow (but in practice 'maybe' or 'sometime')	*mañana*
What time is it?	*que hora es?*

Numbers

0	*cero*
1	*un, uno* (masculine)
	or *una* (feminine)
2	*dos*
3	*tres*
4	*cuatro*
5	*cinco*
6	*seis*

7	siete
8	ocho
9	nueve
10	diez
11	once
12	doce
13	trece
14	catorce
15	quince
16	diez y seis
17	diez y siete
18	diez y ocho
19	diez y nueve
20	veinte
21	veinte y uno
22	veinte y dos
30	treinta
40	cuarenta
50	cincuenta
60	sesenta
70	setenta
80	ochenta
90	noventa
100	cien
101	ciento (y) uno
200	doscientos
1000	mil
2000	dos mil
3000	tres mil

WILDLIFE

Mexico has an impressive list of wild animals, from the fabled jaguar to the volcano rabbit *(romerolaqus diazi)* which only exists around Popocatépetl and Iztaccíhuatl volcanoes. There is also much splendid bird life, from the abundant coastal species and the hawks, eagles and buzzards which roam the mountain areas to magnificent tropical creatures such as the multicoloured red macaw and a few quetzal birds said to inhabit the Mexico-Guatemala border area. Unfortunately much of this wildlife is disappearing because of hunters and the destruction of the forests. Conservation laws, where they exist at all, are widely disregarded. In Chiapas one friendly hotel manager said he could arrange a jaguar shoot for John. While presented as a 'privilege', nothing could have been further from John's wishes.

Nor is Mexico geared up for visitors who merely want to observe animals in the wild, rather than shoot them. The best places to see wildlife are zoos, and probably the best zoo in the country is at Tuxtla Gutiérrez in Chiapas, where animals are kept in fairly spacious enclosures in an extensive forest area. All the species in the zoo are native to the state of Chiapas. Here you'll see jaguar, tapir, ocelot, puma and lynx, as well as vicious-looking snakes (including boa constrictors) and spiders that will put paid to any dreams you might have of unaccompanied jungle safaris.

If you're interested in the wildlife – particularly the birds – of the Gulf and Yucatán coasts, get hold of Donald Schueler's *Adventuring Along the Gulf of Mexico* (Sierra Club Books, San Francisco, 1986).

Baja California is home to a variety of animal life, some of which is unique: grey whales which migrate every year to Scammon's Lagoon near Guerrero Negro to mate and nurse their young, rattlesnakes without rattles, a black jack rabbit, a bat that catches and eats fish, and over 800 species of fish in the Sea of Cortés.

Facts for the Visitor

ENTERING MEXICO
Tourist Cards

Regardless of age, anyone who plans to travel farther south than Maneadero or Mexicali in Baja California, or beyond any of Mexico's other border crossings, will need a tourist card. This also applies to those entering the country by air.

Tourist cards are available from several automobile travel clubs in the USA and Canada, Mexican government tourist offices, Mexican consulates and embassies, Mexican immigration authorities at border crossings, airlines flying to and from North America and Mexico, and some travel agencies. The card must be validated by Mexican immigration authorities at the port of entry. This is most easily done at the border crossings.

Going from west to east there are 24 official border crossings. Along the California border there are border crossings

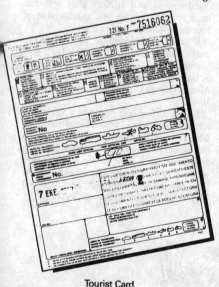

Tourist Card

at Tijuana, Otay Mesa, Tecate, Mexicali and Algodones. The Tijuana and Mexicali crossings are open 24 hours every day. The Otay Mesa crossing is open only from 6 am to 10 pm. Tecate and Algodones are open daily from 7 am to 8 pm. Along the Arizona border the crossings are San Luis Río Colorado, Sonoita, Sasabe, Nogales, Naco and Agua Prieta; Nogales and Agua Prieta are open 24 hours daily. Along the New Mexico border the crossings are Palomas and, right at the south-west corner of Texas, Ciudad Juárez. Along the Texas border the crossings are Guadalupe Bravos, Praxedis Guerrero, Ojinaga, Ciudad Acuña, Piedras Negras, Nuevo Laredo, Ciudad Alemán, Camargo, Reynosa, Nuevo Progreso and Matamoros. The crossings at Ciudad Juárez, Nuevo Laredo and Matamoros are open 24 hours a day.

To obtain a validated tourist card from the *migración* (immigration) offices at border crossings you will need several items, depending on your nationality:

Native-born Americans need a photo identification such as a driver's licence or state-issued identification card plus proof of American citizenship (a passport, birth certificate or notarised affidavit of citizenship). An American passport satisfies both requirements. Although a driver's licence that includes your photograph is usually sufficient identification, a US passport is highly recommended. If you bring a birth certificate it must clearly show official certification from a government agency in the USA.

Naturalised Americans need a photo identification (as above) and proof of American citizenship (an American passport or a certificate of naturalisation from the US Immigration & Naturalisation Service). Again, a US passport is highly recommended.

Citizens of Canada and Great Britain

need to show a current passport or birth certificate.

Citizens of Australia, New Zealand, France and West Germany must obtain visas stamped directly in their passports as well as tourist cards. No photographs are required and the visas and tourist cards are issued free.

Double-check these requirements at any of the places that distribute tourist cards. According to Mexican tourist offices and consulates, citizens of countries other than the USA or Canada must apply in advance for a tourist card. In practice, however, it seems that they can obtain a tourist card in the USA or at the border and have it validated at the border.

Two types of cards are issued: a multiple-entry card which allows unlimited entries for a period of 180 days (two photographs are required); and a single-entry card which is valid for 90 days. Three photographs are occasionally requested for issuance of the 180-day tourist card. The photograph requirement, however, seems to be more stringent if you apply for a tourist card outside of North America.

Do not overstay the time limit or you might be subject to a fine. Chances are slim, however, that you will be asked to show your tourist card if you drive, walk or take a bus across the border. The most likely places you will be asked for your card are the airports in Tijuana, Mexicali, Ciudad Juárez, Nuevo Laredo and Brownsville as you arrive from some other point in Mexico. Even then, you can probably bluff your way out of having to present it by showing the official a big messy bag full of papers and saying that 'it must be in there somewhere'.

Do not lose your card. If you do, prepare yourself for what could be a frustrating tour of Mexican bureaucracy as you try to obtain a replacement from Mexican immigration authorities.

You do not need a tourist card for visits of less than 72 hours to the border towns and cities and to the places between Tijuana and Maneadero (just south of Ensenada), but proof of citizenship may be needed when returning to the USA. A driver's licence or identity card issued by your local Department of Motor Vehicles is sufficient to prove US citizenship.

Citizens of other countries must have their passports and appropriate US visas if planning to return to the USA. Be certain of the entry and re-entry status of your US visa before departing for Mexico.

Embassies & Consulates

Australia
Embassy of Mexico, 14 Perth Avenue, Canberra ACT 2600 (tel (062) 677-520)

Canada
Embassy of Mexico, 130 Aldrich St, Ottawa KIP 5J4 (tel (613) 233-8988)

France
Embassy of Mexico, 9 rue de Longchamps, 75116 Paris (tel 727-4144)

West Germany
Embassy of Mexico, Rathausgasse 30, Bonn 5300, Bonn 1 (tel 221-63-12-26)

Great Britain
Embassy of Mexico, 8 Halkin St, London SW1 (tel (01) 253-6393)

For the USA: apart from the embassy in Washington DC there are consular offices in many other cities, particularly in the border states:

Arizona
515 10th St, Douglas, Arizona 85607 (tel (602) 364-2275)
135 Terrace Avenue, Nogales, Arizona 85621 (tel (602) 287-2521)
5755 North 19th Avenue, Phoenix, Arizona 85015 (tel (602) 242-7398)

California
Imperial Avenue at 7th St, Calexico, California 92231 (tel (714) 357-3863)
2839 Mariposa St, Fresno, California 93721 (tel (209) 233-3065)
125 Paseo de la Plaza, Los Angeles, California 90012 (tel (213) 624-3261)
2100 Capitol Avenue, Sacramento, California 95816 (tel (916) 446-4696)
588 West 6th St, San Bernardino, California 92401 (tel (714) 888-2500)

225 Broadway St, San Diego, California 92101 (tel (619) 231-8414)

870 Market St, Suite 528, San Francisco, California 94102 (tel (415) 392-5554)

12 South First St, San Jose, California 95113 (tel (408) 294-3414)

Colorado

1670 Broadway, Denver, Colorado 80202 (tel (303) 832-2621)

Florida

1444 Biscayne Boulevard, Miami, Florida 33132 (tel (305) 371-5444)

Georgia

410 South Omni International Building, Atlanta, Georgia 30303-2776 (tel (404) 688-3258)

Illinois

540 North LaSalle St, Chicago, Illinois 60606 (tel (312) 670-0240)

Louisiana

1140 New International Trade Mart Building, 2 Canal St, New Orleans, Louisiana 70130 (tel (504) 522-3596)

Massachusetts

1 Post Office Square, Boston, Massachusetts 02109 (tel (617) 426-4942)

Missouri

823 Walnut St, Kansas City, Missouri 64106 (tel (816) 421-5956)

1015 Locust St, St Louis, Missouri 63101 (tel (314) 436-3233)

New Mexico

Western Bank Building, 505 Marquette NW, Albuquerque, New Mexico 87102 (tel (505) 247-2139)

New York

8 East 41st St, New York, New York 10017 (tel (212) 689-0456)

Pennsylvania

575 Bourse Building, Philadelphia, Pennsylvania 19106 (tel (215) 922-4262)

Texas

716 Brazos St, Austin, Texas 78701 (tel (512) 478-2866)

940 East Washington St, PO Box 1711, Brownsville, Texas 78520 (tel (512) 542-4431)

160 Guaranty Bank Plaza Building, Corpus Christi, Texas 78475 (tel (512) 882-3375)

4229 North Central Expressway, Dallas, Texas 75205-4593 (tel (214) 522-9740)

1010 South Main St, Del Rio, Texas 78840 (tel (512) 775-2352)

140 Adams St, Eagle Pass, Texas 78852 (tel (512) 773-9255)

910 East San Antonio St, PO Box 812, El Paso, Texas 79901 (tel (915) 533-3644)

2502 Fannin St, Houston, Texas 77002 (tel (713) 654-8880)

1612 Farragut St, Laredo, Texas 78040 (tel (512) 723-6360)

1220 Broadway Avenue, Lubbock, Texas 79401 (tel (806) 765-8816)

1418 Beech St, McAllen, Texas 78501 (tel (512) 686-0243)

127 Navarro St, San Antonio, Texas 78205 (tel (512) 227-9145)

Washington

1402 Third Avenue, Seattle, Washington 98101 (tel (206) 682-3634)

Washington DC

Consular Section, 1019 19th St NW, Washington, DC 20036 (tel (202) 293-1710)

CUSTOMS

Almost anything can be brought into Mexico from North America or elsewhere. Motor vehicles that are being transported or driven south of the mainland border towns or north from Guatemala or Belize must have automobile permits (see below). Firearms are prohibited except during hunting season when you must also have the proper hunting and firearms permits. If you are bringing foreign-manufactured items such as cameras, radios and televisions into Mexico from the USA, it is a good idea to first register them with US customs before crossing the border. If you have the original receipts for these items, then registration is unnecessary. Though we have never heard of anyone being checked upon return to the USA, it's best to be prepared.

Each US resident returning from Baja or other parts of Mexico to the USA may bring in duty-free items that do not exceed a total retail value of US$400. These items must be for personal use only and not for resale. The exemption applies to each 30-day period you are out of the country. This limit is rarely ever invoked because, according to US customs, 'Mexico is a developing country'. More than 2700 items, including handicrafts, are exempt from this US$400 limit. If the limit is applied at all, it is towards clothing manufactured in Mexico. However, limits on the importation of liquor are stricter. Adult US residents (21 years or older) may bring only one litre of hard liquor into the USA per person.

INSURANCE
Automobile
Mexican law only recognises Mexican automobile insurance. Accordingly, non-Mexican insurance is not considered valid anywhere in Mexico. Insurance is not required by law, but is highly recommended because all parties involved in an automobile accident are considered guilty until proven innocent. Everyone involved must show proof to the police of their means to pay all injuries and damages, or else wait in jail until the case goes to court. Insurance keeps you from going to jail.

There are many companies represented in the USA border towns just before you cross the border into Mexico. Some insurance offices are open 24 hours a day. Some even have 'drive-thru' windows so that you don't have to get out of your car to buy a policy.

All rates are government controlled and thus fairly standard on both sides of the border. Policies can be arranged through several representatives in the USA. Most of the major American and Canadian insurance companies and automobile clubs (which usually require membership) can help you arrange coverage. If you intend to spend more than a few days in Mexico, contact representatives who offer group coverage. Their rates are usually discounted by as much as 20 to 30% of the cost of standard policies.

Following is a list of a few USA-based organisations which offer Mexican insurance policies:

International Gateway Insurance Brokers, 3450 Bonita Road, Suite 103, Chula Vista, California 92010-3209 (tel (619) 422-3057 or toll-free from California (800) 423-2646).

Mexico West Travel Club, Inc, 2424 Newport Boulevard, Suite 91, Costa Mesa, California 92627 (tel (714) 662-7616). In addition to insurance, they publish an informative newsletter, offer discounts on books about Mexico and entitle members to discounts at certain trailer parks, restaurants and hotels in Baja.

MacAfee & Edwards Mexican Insurance Specialists, 2500 Wilshire Boulevard, Suite 1018, Los Angeles, California 90057 (tel (213) 388-9674). They offer insurance policies for automobiles, aeroplanes and boats. Maps and tourist cards are also available.

Mexico Services, 12601 Venice Boulevard, Los Angeles, California 90066 (tel (213) 398-5797). The owner/manager, Raoul Martinez, is extremely helpful with travel plans for Mexico. He arranges insurance policies for automobiles, aeroplanes and boats, and can arrange permits, licences or documents for autos, fishing, hunting, firearms and pets. He also runs a reservation service for hotels throughout Mexico.

Sample premiums of a year-long full coverage policy range from US$155 to US$278 for a vehicle valued from US$1000 to US$29,999. Sample daily premiums for a vehicle valued at US$5000 are US$5.60. After 30 days of coverage the daily premium drops. The more days covered, the lower the daily premium.

Travel & Medical
Get some before you go! You may never need it, but if you do you'll be glad you got it. If you plan to spend an extended period of time in the country then you should have medical insurance. The many different travel insurance policies cover medical costs for illness or injury, the cost of getting home for medical treatment, life insurance and baggage insurance. Some protect you against cancellation penalties on advance-purchase tickets should you have to change travel plans due to illness. Any travel agent should be able to recommend a policy, but check the fine print, especially regarding baggage

insurance. Many American insurance companies will extend their coverage to travel in Mexico; Blue Cross is one such company.

Legal

If you are the type of person who looks for trouble, you might also consider obtaining legal or juridical insurance. This insurance secures you against damage caused to 'federal' property such as street signs, and injury to a person whom you may have hit with your vehicle or your fist. Basically, it allows the insurance adjuster to get you out of jail without having to post a bond.

LICENCES & PERMITS
Automobiles

Auto permits are required only for travel to mainland Mexico, not for travel in Baja California. An automobile permit also serves as the bearer's tourist card. If you plan to take the ferry from Baja to the mainland, you must get the permit stamped at the *migración* (immigration) office just after you cross the border. If you are travelling from La Paz or Cabo San Lucas, then the permit must be stamped and approved at the Registro Federal de Vehículos in either Tijuana or La Paz (See the 'La Paz' section). Recently, the officials at the Tijuana office (on the right side of the border post just after you cross) seemed keen on insisting that all final approvals must be obtained in La Paz. The permits are valid for periods ranging from 90 to 180 days.

To obtain an auto permit, if you are a US or Canadian citizen then you must show proof of citizenship such as a passport or birth certificate. You must also show the original current registration or a notarised bill of sale for each vehicle including motorcycles and boats. You must obtain permits for additional vehicles. If the vehicle belongs to or is registered in the name of a company, then a notarised affidavit of authorisation is required along with the original current registration.

You must have a permit for each vehicle that you bring into Mexico. For example, if you have a motorcycle attached to your car, you must also have a permit for the motorcycle, but there is a catch: one person cannot have more than one permit even if that person owns both vehicles. Consequently, another person travelling with you must obtain the second permit. As with all rules of this sort, though, they are not written in stone. Changes, exceptions and neglect of the rule are not unheard of, especially if the official who might enforce the rule is somehow induced to do otherwise.

Another rule for drivers intending to travel to the mainland: you cannot leave Mexico without your vehicle even if it breaks down, unless you obtain permission from either the Registro Federal de Vehículos (Federal Registry of Vehicles) in Mexico City or a *hacienda* (treasury department) office in another city or town. This rule exists because the Mexican government is trying to prevent the illegal import of vehicles for resale in Mexico and forestall threats to its fledgeling auto industry.

Hunting

A slew of forms and permits is needed to bring hunting guns into Mexico. For the latest information about the necessary permits and hunting season dates, contact a Mexican consulate or one of the following organisations:

Mexair Insurance, (tel (213) 398-5797), 12601 Venice Boulevard, Los Angeles, California 90066

Romero's Mexico Service, (tel (714) 548-8931), 1600 West Coast Highway, Newport Beach, California 92663

The Mexican Hunting Association, Inc, (tel (213) 421-1619), 3302 Josie Avenue, Long Beach, California 90808

The Wildlife Advisory Services, (tel (213) 385-9311), PO Box 76132, Los Angeles, California 90075

Fishing & Boating

If you are 16 years or older and plan to do any fishing on your own from the beach or offshore anywhere in Mexico, you will need a fishing licence. Applications can be obtained from the Mexico Department of Fisheries (tel (619) 233-6956), 1010 2nd Avenue, Suite 1605, San Diego, California 92101. One of the hunting or insurance organisations mentioned earlier should be able to tell you the latest fees, daily bag limits and prohibited species. These are all subject to seasonal changes.

If you want to bring fish back to California, then first check with the California Fish & Game Department (tel (619) 237-7311), 1350 Front St, San Diego, California, 92101 for information about declaration forms, permits and limits. For other states or provinces, check with the local Department of Fish & Game.

Mexican boat permit applications can also be obtained from the Mexico Department of Fisheries. Romero's Mexico Service mentioned earlier runs a very helpful yacht documentation service which can assist you with the numerous forms required for sailing to Baja and other parts of Mexico.

Pets

Mexican consular officials claim that you must have a special US$15 visa and an International Health Certificate for your pet if you wish to bring it into Mexico. More than once, Scott's 36-kg half pit bull/half labrador dragged him right past Mexican customs officials at the Tijuana border crossing without Scott showing any documents. Perhaps they don't ask for documents from the owners of dogs with big sharp teeth.

On the other hand, US customs officials do ask to see your pet's rabies certificate before allowing you and your pet back into the USA. It is also a good idea to carry the International Health Certificate. This can be obtained from any veterinarian.

LEGAL MATTERS

The Mexican judicial system is based on the Napoleonic Code system, which presumes that a person is guilty until proven innocent. There is no trial by jury. Consequently, if you encounter troubles such as a car accident (and the police arrive on the scene), everyone involved is considered guilty and liable until proven otherwise. If you do not have car insurance, then you will be held in jail until it has been established who was at fault in the accident.

If you should encounter legal troubles with public officials or local business-people anywhere in Mexico, contact La Procuraduría de Protección al Turista (The Attorney General for the Protection of the Tourist). English-speaking aides are on the staff at each attorney general's office. There are offices in Tijuana (tel 85-21-38, 24-hour national hotline) and Ensenada (tel 76-36-86) in Baja California and the state capital of every state in the rest of Mexico. There's another 24-hour national hotline in Mexico City (tel 250-01-51, 250-04-93, 250-05-89, 250-01-23); ask the operator for emergency assistance.

Traffic Fines

In downtown Tijuana, various traffic violations will cost you approximately the following amounts if you decide to settle the fine on the street:

*minor equipment violation such as a faulty tail-light: US$2

*driving the wrong way on a one-way street: US$2.50

*drunk driving: US$32 plus a night in jail

*going through a stop sign or stoplight or driving without a licence: US$5

*speeding or having alcohol on your breath: US$10

Fines are probably lower in Mexico City.

MONEY

Mexican pesos (MEX$) are the main

currency in Mexico, although US dollars (US$) are used throughout Baja California and in most Mexican border towns. US dollars will not be accepted, though, in some small towns and villages, even in Baja. The symbol '$' is used for both currencies. Occasionally, restaurants, hotels, gasoline stations and other establishments which often deal with North Americans will put *Dlls* or *mn* after prices to indicate whether they are in dollars or *moneda nacional* (national money).

Mexican coins come in denominations of one, five, 10, 50, 100 and 500 pesos and 20 and 50 centavos (one peso = 100 centavos). Bills are in denominations of 50, 100, 500, 1000, 2000, 5000, 10,000, 20,000 and up.

Money exchange is at free-market floating rates, thus subject to change. Exchange rates for pesos have changed dramatically. Since 1980 the value of the peso has gone from MEX$22 = US$1 to more than MEX$1300 = US$1 in 1987 and MEX$2200 = US$1 in late 1987. The rate continues to change almost every day because of severe inflation and continual devaluation of the peso.

Money can be exchanged at banks, hotels and *casas de cambio* (exchange houses). Banks and casas de cambio offer basically the same rates of exchange. At both places, rates for cash are usually lower than rates for travellers' cheques because, according to one bank official, cash costs more to transport.

Banks never charge commissions on any exchange transactions. Instead, they may change only a certain minimum amount of foreign currency. For example, the bank in the Baja town of Mulegé will not change any amount less than US$100.

Some casas de cambio may charge a commission. This occurs mostly with the casas de cambio in the border towns on the USA side; the casas de cambio of San Ysidro (across the border from Tijuana) are notorious. Big signs in front of practically every San Ysidro casa de cambio advertise 'no commission'. Careful! What they really mean is that no commission is charged on the exchange of pesos into dollars, not vice versa. You do not realise that they have charged you as much as a 7% commission on travellers' cheques until you sit down to count your money. Always ask before you change money.

Hotels offer the worst exchange rates. You are charged a commission on top of receiving an exchange rate considerably lower than those offered by banks and casas de cambio.

COSTS

It cannot be emphasised enough that because of dramatic changes in the MEX$/US$ exchange rate, *prices are approximate*. All prices listed in this book are in US$, but they must be considered estimates. Peso prices were converted to

US$ at various rates current during research.

Costs of food and accommodation vary most dramatically as you move from Baja and coastal resorts popular with gringos to the less-visited and thus more inexpensive inland towns and cities. It is easy to eat for as little as US$2 per day if you buy food from fruit and vegetable markets or corner food stalls. Accommodation is generally a different matter. Except for Youth Hostels, most cheap hotel rooms and casas de huéspedes (guest houses) will start at about US$3 (for a flea-bag sort of place). In Baja, however, it is hard to find a double room for less than US$10.

Camping is the cheapest and sometimes the easiest way to go. You can camp for free on almost any beach in Mexico. Most official campgrounds are trailer parks designed for motor homes. Full hook-ups – electrical outlets, water faucet, sewerage outlet – are normally available. Clean bathrooms with hot showers are sometimes available. Prices for two people and a vehicle average about US$5 to US$8 per night. Tent camping is less and usually subject to negotiation. Aside from camping, at the cheapest end of the scale you can rent a hammock on a beach like Zipolite in Oaxaca for US$0.75 a night and eat a seafood meal there for US$1 to US$1.50 – so that you can exist on US$5 a day or less if you don't travel anywhere. Buying food and drinks in markets and shops helps keep costs down too.

A single budget traveller staying in bottom-end or lower middle-range accommodation and eating two meals a day in restaurants will be paying somewhere around US$7 a day for those basics. Add in the costs of travel (very roughly, US$1 per hour on long-distance buses), the odd beer, film, clothes, city buses, snacks, soft drinks, toothpaste, souvenirs, etc, and you're getting to US$10 or US$12 a day. Of course the more moving around you do the more it all costs. On the other hand, if there are two or more of you sharing accommodation,

costs per person come down considerably. Double rooms are often little dearer than singles, and triples or quadruples only a little more expensive than doubles.

Even when you're economising to the utmost, you'll probably still want to splash out now and then on a more luxurious hotel, a slap-up meal or a costly handicraft item – so save enough for that.

Student Discounts

Discounts for foreign students are virtually unknown in Mexico. A few places offer small discounts on already minuscule admission fees to students under 26 who hold a card from either the Servicio Educativo de Turismo de los Estudiantes y la Juventud de México (SETEJ) or Consejo Nacional de Recursos para la Atención de la Juventud (CREA). These cards also entitle you to Youth Hostel membership. CREA cards can be obtained at most Youth Hostels in Mexico.

Both CREA and SETEJ occasionally conduct group tours of Baja and other parts of Mexico. For more information, write to the Asociación Mexicana de Albergues de la Juventud, AC, Avenida Francisco 1 Madero No 6, Despachos 314 y 315, Mexico 1, DF.

Shops & Markets

Most shops have fixed prices but it's probably worthwhile to ask for a discount if you're buying several things in, say, a handicrafts shop.

In markets bargaining is the order of the day and foreigners tend to be regarded as walking silver-mines who will pay absurd prices. It's often said that you should aim to pay half what the seller first asks for, but you'll be doing well if you achieve that very often. Using even a few words of Spanish gives you an advantage – they somehow indicate that you're a bit wiser to Mexico than regular tourists. Don't ever offer a price you're not prepared to pay. For food and other everyday items, the difference between what you're initially asked for and the regular price isn't as high as for craft or souvenir goods.

Shops are good places to get an idea of a reasonable price for something if you're thinking of looking for it in markets later. Also, watch the locals to see what they're paying before you make an offer.

Credit Cards

The Visa card is widely used in Mexico in hotels, shops, airlines, etc. Bancomer is the local Visa representative bank and you can usually get cash advances without too much fuss in its many branches. Be prepared for interest rates higher than rates in the USA.

La Mordida

Another cost occasionally levied is called the *mordida* (bite) or bribe. The most common 'bite' is requested by traffic cops when motorists commit certain infractions such as driving the wrong way on a one-way street or not stopping for a stop sign. *Mordidas* may also be requested by immigration/border officials, ferry officials and other bureaucratic officials.

WORKING IN MEXICO

Aside from many opportunities for teaching English in Mexico, there isn't much else, unless you are sent to Mexico by a foreign company. Mexico City is obviously the best place to pick up English-teaching work; Guadalajara is also good. It should also be possible in Monterrey, Puebla and other sizeable cities as well as places where there are 'gringo' communities, for example San Miguel de Allende and Oaxaca.

The following letters are from two Americans who have worked in Mexico as teachers of English. Their experiences are fairly typical.

It should be relatively easy for native speakers of English to find positions teaching in language schools/cultural institutes, private and even public school systems, or by offering personal tutoring. More than anything else, it is a matter of timing. Obviously, positions are more likely to become available with the beginning of the new term. Language schools tend to offer short courses, so that opportunities come up more often, and any commitment is for a shorter time. The remuneration, however, tends to be less than that paid at the *preparatoria* (high school) and university levels. The pay scales are going to be low, regardless, but travellers can at least cover their expenses if able to work enough hours and willing to live somewhat frugally (by our standards). Of course, teaching offers rewards aside from the financial ones, particularly for travellers who really want to meet the people of their host country and gain insights into their language and culture, while sharing those of their own.

By law, a foreigner working in Mexico must have a permit to do so, but there are ways around this. A school will often pay a foreign teacher in the form of a scholarship or *beca*, and thus circumvent the law. If someone wants to teach for an indefinite period of time, then the school's administration will work to procure the appropriate papers. The basic credentials for teaching English, or any subject in English, of course depend on the particular institution. Being a native speaker is enough for most language classes. Holding a degree of any kind might afford you the opportunity to teach a variety of subjects in a bilingual school. A person with a BA in History could end up teaching a course in chemistry, assuming he or she would be comfortable in doing so. I was told that I should apply for a position at the university level teaching philosophy in Spanish, even though I hold a degree in English Literature and Agriculture and my Spanish is spotty. By the way, it is usually not necessary to speak Spanish to hold teaching positions in English. Generally, administrators prefer that you don't, in order to force the class to communicate with you only in English. I will say that it is helpful to know a little of their street language, however, for the sake of maintaining discipline. If a quick-witted little boy jumps up in front of the class and addresses you, it is nice to know if you should compliment him or wash his mouth out with soap.

Tutoring can potentially be the most lucrative form of teaching, and allow you the most freedom in structuring your class and schedule. You are paid in effect under the table, so you shouldn't need a work permit. The main problem is that it will take a while to establish your clientele, since your method of advertising will probably be word-of-mouth.

The best way to look for a teaching position, assuming you have not made any connections in advance, would be to go through the yellow pages (of almost every major city and town in Mexico) and contact the various institutions and schools that offer bilingual programmes or classes in English. I have found that the school directors are very helpful and encouraging. Even if they do not have any openings, they will often refer you to other schools that might. If there are any universities in your area, it would be advisable to arrange an appointment with the director of the language department.

– Robert Wheeler

There are lots of opportunities for teaching English in Mexico, though the pay isn't much and you need to wear conservative clothing.

I looked through the *Mexico City News* (English newspaper) and got a job with a school downtown that paid considerably less than some of the bigger chain schools. The problem with the chain schools is that they require a two-year commitment.

I worked three hours per night, one two-hour class and a one-hour class. I worked five hours on Saturdays, but had a friend in to help me teach. While I earned about US$1.60 per hour, teachers at chain schools were earning US$6 to US$7 per hour. Quite a difference, but in a country where the minimum wage is US$4 per day, I could get by on my wage fairly well.

The only place I came across that didn't care about how long you taught with them was called Quick Learning. They hire foreigners as 'consultants' and do not ask for a number or work papers. Another place to try is Harmon Hall, a big chain who advertise in subway stations (in Mexico City).

Some schools may require you to have a number, like a Social Security number – it's referred to as a Registro Federal de Contribuyentes and you can 'borrow' one (with permission of course!) from a native Mexican.

In the larger chain schools, the speaking of Spanish is not permitted in class. Where I worked, the students demanded that I explain things to them in Spanish.

– Andrea Spignesi

STUDY PROGRAMMES

There are Spanish-language schools in many cities – some private, some attached to the universities. Course length can range from a week to a year. Often you can enrol in a course on the spot, though some places prefer you to make the arrangements before you come to Mexico. You may be offered accommodation with a local family as part of the deal – and living with Spanish-speakers will help your Spanish as much as any formal tuition. UNAM in Mexico City is one university which offers such courses. The Universidad Veracruzana in Jalapa does summer courses, as does the university in Saltillo. Guadalajara also has a Spanish-language school.

Cuernavaca has several private Spanish-language schools, most of which offer courses ranging from a few days to a few months. One of its most prominent schools is Cuauhnahuac – Instituto Colectivo de Lengua y Cultura (tel 12-36-73, 12-16-98) at Avenida Morelos Sur 1414, Colonia Chipitlán, 62070 Cuernavaca. Their mailing address is APDO 5-26, 62501 Cuernavaca. They provide all levels of intensive training, with classes limited to four students. The Instituto Teopanzolco (tel 17-30-40, 13-64-64, 13-66-20) at Calle Teopanzolco 102-BIS, Colonia Vista Hermosa, Cuernavaca 62290 offers a similar series of programmes plus a unique programme specially designed for deaf or hearing-impaired students from English-speaking countries. Their mailing address is: APDO Postal 103-A, Cuernavaca, Morelos, Mexico 62280. In the USA contact John Diaz (tel (408) 732-0807), 410 Escobar St, Fremont, California 94539. Another popular school is the Concepto Experiencia Educativa Bilingue (tel 12-23-44) at J H Preciado 306 (mailing address: APDO 1801, Cuernavaca, Morelos 62000) with three-student intensive Spanish classes. As at the other two schools, you may opt for a week-long course and participate in culturally-oriented classes and programmes. See the 'Cuernavaca' section for further information.

Private Spanish lessons are easy to fix

up in most places. If you're in southern Mexico, consider moving on to Antigua in Guatemala for a Spanish course. Antigua is a small, beautiful colonial city with several Spanish-language schools where foreigners take short language courses at ridiculously cheap prices. One traveller reported getting a month's course, with five or six hours' instruction a day, plus accommodation and meals with a local family, for just US$180 all in!

There are also a few colleges where foreigners can study Mexico and Latin America in depth – often with credit for college courses at home. Apart from Mexico's regular universities, these include the Universidad de las Américas at Cholula near Puebla, and the Academía Hispano Americana in San Miguel de Allende. Also in San Miguel, the Instituto Allende is popular with foreigners for art, craft and language courses. In Oaxaca, the Instituto Cultural Oaxaca runs courses in the Spanish, Zapotec and Mixtec languages and in weaving, ceramics and regional dance.

Many Mexican towns have Casas de la Cultura, which are adult education centres offering part-time, usually cheap courses, both practical and theoretical, in a wide variety of arts and crafts. Foreigners are often welcome to join these. In San Miguel de Allende the function of the Casa de la Cultura is performed by Bellas Artes.

For information about other Spanish-language programmes in Mexico, in the USA contact The National Registration Center for Study Abroad (tel toll-free (800) 558-9988), 823 North Second St, Milwaukee, Wisconsin 53203. In Canada contact Ms Doreen Desmarais, 341 Main St, Ottawa, Ontario K1V 8Y6.

The Council on International Educational Exchange (tel (212) 661-1414), 205 East 42nd St, New York, New York 10017, lists a wide variety of programmes in various states in the USA. Contact them for more information.

The Smithsonian Institution occasionally organises expeditions and study tours to Mexico. Write to National Associates, Capital Gallery 455, Smithsonian Institution, Washington, DC 20560; or call (202) 287-3362 for tour brochures, (202) 357-1350 for seminar brochures.

Society Expeditions Cruises (tel (206) 285-9400 or toll-free (800) 426-7794), 3131 Elliott Avenue, Suite 700, Seattle, Washington 98121, conducts a 24-day annual cruise from San Diego that stops at several points in Baja before continuing down the Pacific coast of Mexico and Central America to the Panama Canal and then into the Caribbean. A highly qualified lecture team of anthropologists, biologists, historians others lead discussion sessions and guides nature excursions. Rates range from US$12,700 for the deluxe 'Owner's Suite' to US$3150 for a partial cruise in the most inexpensive rooms.

TOURIST INFORMATION

Mexican government tourist offices are a fair source of information. The offices outside Mexico do not know much about Baja California, but they do have the latest information on the most visited areas and on official tourist matters such as tourist card requirements. They can also issue tourist cards and automobile permits. If they cannot issue what you need or answer your query, then they can usually direct you to someone who can. Following is a list of their offices:

USA

10100 Santa Monica Boulevard, Suite 2204, Los Angeles, California 90067 (tel (213) 203-8151)

Two Illinois Center, 233 North Michigan Avenue, Suite 1413, Chicago, Illinois 60601 (tel (312) 565-2785)

405 Park Avenue, Suite 1002, New York, New York 10022 (tel (212) 755-7261)

2707 North Loop West, Suite 450, Houston, Texas 77008 (tel (713) 880-5153)

Canada
    1 Place Ville Marie, Suite 2409, Montreal,
    Quebec H3B 3M9, (tel (514) 871-1052)
    181 University Avenue, Suite 1112, Toronto,
    Ontario M5H 3M7 (tel (416) 364-2455)
Great Britain
    7 Cork St, London W1X 1PB (tel (441)
    734-1058)
France
    34 Avenue George V, 75008 Paris (tel (331)
    720-6907)
Italy
    Via Barberini No 3, 00187 Rome (tel (396)
    474-2986)
Spain
    Calle de Velázquez No 126, Madrid 28006
    (tel (341) 261-1827)
West Germany
    Wiesenhuettenplatz 26, D600 Frankfurt
    Am Main 1 (tel 49-69-25-3413)

Tourist information can also be obtained
from any of three types of tourist offices in
Mexico: federal, state and local offices.

The *Baja Times* and *Ensenada News &
Views* are English-language publications
distributed free at hotels, restaurants,
souvenir shops and tourist offices throughout Baja California. Both provide the
most recent information available about
events, restaurants and tourist-related
news in Northern Baja.

Other sources of current information
about travel in Mexico include the
newsletter published by the Mexico West
Travel Club (2424 Newport Boulevard,
Suite 91, Costa Mesa, California 92627)
and *Los Cabos News*, a newsletter
focusing on Southern Baja published by
the travel club *Vagabundos del Mar* (PO
Box 824, Isleton, California 95641).

GENERAL INFORMATION
Post
Almost every city and town in Mexico has
an Oficina de Correos (post office) where
you can buy postage and send or receive
mail.

Letters or postcards sent by air mail to
North and Central America cost about
15c, to Europe 20c and to Australasia
US$.030. Service is relatively dependable,

but not predictable. If you are sending something by air mail, be sure to clearly mark it with the words 'Por Avión'. An air mail letter sent from Cabo San Lucas at the tip of the Baja peninsula to Los Angeles may take anywhere from four to 14 days. Mail to Europe can take anywhere from one to three weeks.

Receiving mail in Mexico can be tricky. You can send or receive letters and packages care of a post office if they're addressed as follows:

Jane SMITH (last name should be capitalised)
a/c Lista de Correos
Cabo San Lucas, Baja California Sur
00000 (postal code if possible) MEXICO

When the letter arrives at the post office, the name of the addressee is placed on an alphabetical list which is updated daily. If you can, check the list yourself because the letter might be listed under your first name instead of your last.

To claim your mail, present your passport or other identification; there's no charge. The snag is that many post offices only hold 'Lista' mail for 10 days before returning it to the sender. If you think you're going to pick mail up more than 10 days after it has arrived, have it sent to you at Poste Restante, Correo Central, Town/City, State, Mexico. Poste restante usually holds mail for up to a month but no list of what has been received is posted. Again, there's no charge for collection.

If you can arrange a private address to send mail to, do so. There's less chance of your mail getting put aside, lost or returned to the sender if you're late in picking it up.

American Express If you have an American Express card or American Express travellers' cheques, you can have mail sent to you c/o the American Express offices in Mexico, which will hold it for you. You must show your card or a travellers' cheque when you collect the mail. Their office in the zona rosa (principal deluxe shopping area) of Mexico City, at Hamburgo 75, was put out of action by the 1985 earthquake but mail addressed there is redirected to the new office nearby at the corner of Reforma and Havre. Call American Express before you leave home to find out the latest mailing addresses.

Telephone

Dialling telephone numbers in Mexico is often a confusing chore. The most perplexing part is trying to figure out how many digits to dial. The number of digits in a telephone number varies according to distance even within a city. For example, to place a call from certain points in Tijuana a five-digit number may suffice, whereas from other points to the same places you must dial six or seven digits. Outside the cities this can become even more confusing. Ask locals for help or go to a *caseta de teléfono*, a telephone office which is usually part of a shop or other office. It is indicated by a telephone-shaped sign.

Local calls are inexpensive and easy to place from casetas and call-boxes. Sometimes hotels don't charge you for them. If you aren't placing the call from a caseta, be sure you have the small-denomination coins accepted by public call-boxes. Sometimes call-boxes don't work; other times they work and refuse to take any money.

International and domestic long-distance calls are exorbitantly taxed and sometimes difficult to place. If you don't have a private or hotel line you have to find a Lada caseta *(larga distancia)* or long-distance office, of which there are usually several around the centres of larger towns and at least one in most other towns. These casetas are often in shops; an operator will connect your number and you speak from a booth. Price examples: A three-minute call to the USA costs US$12, to Australia US$55 and to West Germany US$65; an eight-minute call from San Luis Potosí to Monterrey costs US$10.25.

Collect calls *(llamadas por cobrar)* sometimes go through without a hitch; on the other hand you may wait a long time to get through to the operator, or a hotel or Lada caseta will either refuse to place a collect call or charge a supplement for doing so.

Telegrams

Most towns have a *telégrafos* office where you can send domestic and international telegrams – a simple but not always very quick means of communication (one from Mexico City to Melbourne, Australia, took five days). From Mexico City, a telegram to the USA costs US$4.25 for the first 15 words, then 15c for each extra word, and you don't have to pay for the address you send it to. To Britain or Australia you pay US$4 for the first seven words, then US$0.50 for each extra word, and you have to pay for the address.

Telex

If you have a telex number to send to, this can be a good alternative to both phone and telegram. Most towns have public telex facilities where you can both send and receive telexes (ask in the post office or telégrafos office for the location). Telexes are usually cheaper than international phone calls and don't involve hassling with international operators or busy lines. They're more expensive than telegrams but get there quicker.

Electricity

Electrical current, plugs and sockets in Mexico are the same as in the USA and Canada: 110 volts, 60 cycles and flat, two-pronged plugs.

Time

Baja California is divided into two time zones. Northern Baja California is on Pacific Standard Time. Southern Baja is on Mountain Standard Time, which is one hour ahead of PST. During the summer, PST is moved ahead one hour for Pacific Daylight Time and thus becomes the same as MST. Northern Baja California is always on the same time as the state of California. PST is eight hours behind Greenwich Mean Time, MST is seven hours behind.

Business Hours

Banks are open from 9 am to 1.30 pm, Monday to Friday. Businesses are generally open from 9 am to 2 pm and 4 to 7 pm, Monday to Friday. Siesta or break time is between 2 and 4 pm, Monday to Friday. Outside Mexico City, many shops and offices close for siesta from roughly 1 to 4 pm, then stay open until 7 or 8 pm.

Measurements & Weights

Mexico uses the metric system. Following are conversion charts:

km	miles
1	.62
3	1.86
4	2.49
9	5.59
10	6.21
15	9.32
50	31.07
90	55.92
100	62.14

litres	gallons
3.8	1
7.6	2
11.4	3
15.1	4
18.9	5
37.9	10
56.8	15
75.7	20
94.6	25
132.5	35
189.3	50

One km = 1000 metres
One metre = 39.37 inches
One kg (kilogram) = 2.20 pounds

Archaeological Sites

Most of Mexico's archaeological sites are open daily (some close on Monday) and admission fees are low. Even when excavations are going on you can usually still visit the sites. If you want special access – for instance to the frescoes at Cholula, which are closed to the general public – contact INAH, the Instituto Nacional de Antropología e Historia. Its head office is at Córdoba 45 in Colonia Roma, Mexico City. INAH also has regional offices including one in Puebla (tel 32-01-78) at 18 Pte 103.

One site which should soon appear on more itineraries is the important early Olmec site at San Lorenzo in southern Veracruz. There are plans to make the site, currently undeveloped, more interesting to visitors. For information contact INAH or the museum in Jalapa (tel 5-49-52, 5-07-08).

Churches

Most Mexican churches are in frequent use, so be careful not to disturb services when you visit them. Many – particularly those that contain valuable works of art – are locked when not in use.

MEDIA

Newspapers & Magazines

English-language *Atención San Miguel* is a weekly paper in English published in San Miguel de Allende. Mexico City has the *Mexico City News* and various small tourist-oriented papers; the *News* is distributed throughout Mexico. Almost every other city or region that attracts English-speaking tourists and retirees in droves – Lake Chapala, Guadalajara, Baja California, Puerto Vallarta, for example – has an English-language newspaper or newsletter.

Mexican Mexico has a thriving local press as well as national newspapers. Even small cities often have two or three newspapers of their own.

For those interested in a non-establishment view of events, *La Jornada* is a good national daily with a mainly left-wing viewpoint which covers a lot of stories that other papers don't. *Proceso* is a weekly news magazine with a similar approach. Both cover international and cultural events as well as domestic news. Another interesting opposition magazine is the weekly *Quehacer Político*. The south-eastern state of Chiapas has its own excellent independent magazine, *Perfil del Sureste*, which comes out every two months and covers many issues that the authorities would prefer to keep quiet. *Fem* is a national feminist magazine.

Ovaciones is a national paper with a whole section devoted entirely to Mexican and international sport. North American baseball and football scores and European soccer results can often be found in *Excelsior* and *El Universal*.

México Desconocido is an interesting travel magazine in Spanish devoted to little-known destinations in Mexico.

Television

There's much less freedom of expression on TV than in the printed media. Watching TV – which you can do in many hotel rooms – isn't a bad way of picking up some Spanish, but the quality of programmes leaves a lot to be desired. Unfortunately there are a lot of ageing American movies dubbed into Spanish.

HEALTH

Vaccinations

Vaccinations are not required for travel anywhere in Mexico, including Baja California. If you plan to spend more than a week in the country, it is a good idea to be up to date on at least your tetanus shot. A gamma globulin shot is also recommended for protection against infectious hepatitis.

The advice given to travellers going to Mexico from the London Hospital for Tropical Diseases was to be vaccinated against typhoid and polio, and to take 200 mg of Proguanil daily and 300 mg of Chloroquine weekly for protection against malaria. The malaria doses should start two weeks before you arrive in

Mexico and continue six weeks after you leave. Malaria-carrying mosquitoes are more common in coastal areas, particularly in the southern half of the country, than in the highlands. They're most active around dusk and dawn and are attracted to dark colours and repelled by white – so be bright at night in mosquito-ridden areas! You can buy mosquito repellent in Mexican pharmacies if they are persistent.

You only need a yellow fever certificate to enter Mexico if you have recently been to a country where yellow fever is present.

Medical Kit

It is always a good idea to travel with a small first-aid kit. Some of the items that should be included are: Band-Aids, a sterilised gauze bandage, elastoplast, cotton wool, a thermometer, tweezers, scissors, antibiotic cream or ointment, an antiseptic agent (Dettol or Betadine), burn cream (Caladryl is good for sunburn, minor burns and itchy bites), insect repellent and multi-vitamins.

Don't forget a full supply of any medication you're already taking; the prescription might be difficult to match in Mexico.

Recommended traveller's medications include diarrhoea tablets such as Lomotil or Imodium, and Tylenol or Motrin for pain and fever.

Food & Water

One of the biggest fears about travelling in Mexico is health problems resulting from the food and water. Most of these problems relate to upset stomachs and diarrhoea which can be avoided or at least minimised by taking a few precautions.

Cooked food is generally safe to eat as long as you don't punish your stomach by immediately consuming large portions. Take it easy. If you are prone to indigestion, you may want to eat your first truly Mexican meal in one of the many restaurants which mainly caters to North Americans. You don't have to avoid the local restaurants, taco stands and street-corner fish-cocktail and fruit carts; just introduce yourself to them gradually. Eating a clove of garlic every day for a week prior to your trip has also been highly recommended by many travellers as a way to stave off stomach problems.

Avoid uncooked or unpasteurised dairy products such as raw milk and homemade cheeses. Dairy products bought at a supermarket are usually *pasteurizado*, but in a restaurant you can't be sure. Milkshakes *(licuados con leche)* made at a juice stand are usually safe because the government requires the stands to use pasteurised milk and purified water.

Avoid most raw fruits and vegetables unless you can wash or peel them yourself. Don't eat already-peeled fruit or anything that's been lying around where insects can get at it. This obviously applies to food stalls, but salads in restaurants are also risky. Of course if you are *too* careful you may miss out on some of Mexico's best food and drink; use your own judgement, and you'll develop a sense of how fresh something is. Buying your own fruit in markets and shops is one way of ensuring freshness.

Meat, chicken and most types of seafood are all safe as long as they have been thoroughly cooked. Raw oysters can also be safely eaten, but be sure they haven't spoiled from sitting in the sun too long.

Everyone has heard the infamous warning about Mexico: Don't drink the water. Well, it's true. In some areas the water is potable, but bacterial differences will still make you sick. Locals can drink this water because they are used to it. In other areas, however, even the locals won't touch the water. Generally, it is best not to use the water for drinking, ice cubes, brushing your teeth, or washing fruit and vegetables.

Purified water *(agua purificada)* and ice are available throughout Mexico from supermarkets, small grocery stores (*ultramarinos*) and liquor stores (*licorerías* or *vinos y licores*).

If you plan to travel off the main roads and into the middle of nowhere, a water-purification system is recommended if you cannot take enough bottled water with you. This system should consist of one or more of the following:

Iodine (*yodo*) sold in pharmacies; add about seven drops per litre of water.
Water-purification drops or pills called *gotas* or *pastillas para purificar agua*; sold in pharmacies and supermarkets.
Water-purification tablets called *hidroclonazone*; usually sold in supermarkets.
Water boiled for at least 30 minutes.
A portable water filter. Compact units are available from major camping supply stores in the USA such as Recreational Equipment, Inc (REI) (tel (206) 431-5804), PO Box C-88126, Seattle, Washington 98188; and Mountain Equipment Inc (MEI) (tel (800) 344-7422), 1636 South Second St, Fresno, California 93702.

Contaminated food and water can cause dysentery, giardia, hepatitis A and, in extremely rare instances, typhoid and polio.

Ailments

Diarrhoea Almost every traveller going to Mexico fears and loathes the moment when diarrhoea, more commonly known as Montezuma's Revenge or *la turista*, will strike his or her innards. There is usually nothing you can do to prevent the onslaught; it is simply your system trying to adjust to a different environment and can happen anywhere. In fact, Mexicans claim that it happens to them when they visit the USA. There is no 'cure', but certain regimens will eventually eliminate or suppress it.

The regimen is fairly basic: drink plenty of fluids, though not milk, coffee, strong tea, soft drinks, cocoa or anything alcoholic. Avoid consuming anything other than fruit juices, especially apple juice, apples, yoghurt and perhaps a little dried toast if you are very hungry, for at least one or two days.

If you are travelling, it may be difficult to follow this regimen and you might have to resort to one of the following diarrhoea suppressants: Lomotil (*paregórico*), codeine phosphate tablets, Entero-Vioformo, a liquid derivative of opium prescribed by a doctor, or a medicine with pectin (like Kaopectate). Lomotil is convenient because the pills are tiny, although it is currently subject to some medical debate. These suppressants are not cures for diarrhoea, nor should they be considered substitutes for the regimen mentioned. If you are still ailing after using a suppressant and following the regimen, then you might have dysentery and should see a doctor.

Dysentery There are two types of dysentery, both of which are characterised by diarrhoea containing blood and/or mucus. Bacillary dysentery, the most common variety, is short, sharp and nasty but rarely persistent. It hits suddenly and lays you out with fever, nausea, cramps and diarrhoea but, as it's caused by bacteria, responds well to antibiotics. Amoebic dysentery is caused by amoebic parasites and is more dangerous. It builds up slowly, cannot be starved out and if untreated will get worse and can permanently damage your intestines. Do not have anyone other than a doctor diagnose your symptoms and administer treatment.

Hepatitis This is a viral liver disease. There are two types – infectious hepatitis (Type A) and serum hepatitis (Type B). Type A, the most common, can be caught by eating food, drinking water or using cutlery or crockery contaminated by an infected person. Type B can only be contracted by having sexual relations with an infected person or by using the same syringe. Symptoms appear 15 to 50 days after infection (generally around 25 days) and consist of fever, loss of appetite, nausea, depression, lack of energy and pains around the base of the rib cage. Skin turns yellow, the whites of the eyes yellow to orange, and urine deep orange or brown. Do *not* take antibiotics. There is no cure for hepatitis except complete rest and good food. The worst is over in about 10 days, but rest is still important. A gamma globulin injection provides protection against Type A for three to six months but its effectiveness is still debatable. If you follow the food and water precautions mentioned, it is extremely unlikely you will contract hepatitis.

Rabies If you are bitten, scratched or even licked by a rabid animal and do not start treatment within a few days, you may die. Rabies affects the central nervous system and is certainly an unpleasant way to go. Typical signs of a rabid animal are: mad or uncontrolled behaviour, inability to eat, biting at anything, frothing at the mouth. If you are bitten by an animal, react as if it has rabies – there are no second chances. Get to a doctor and begin the course of injections that will prevent the disease from developing.

If you plan to spend a lot of time around animals, consider getting a rabies vaccine. In the USA, call your county public health office to find out where you can obtain it. In Great Britain, the British Airways Medical Service in London can provide the vaccine if given advance notice.

Tetanus This is a killer disease but it can easily be prevented by immunisation. It is contracted by cuts and breaks in the skin caused by rusty or dirty objects, animal bites or contaminated wounds. Even if you have been vaccinated, wash the wound thoroughly.

Taking the Heat

Protect yourself against the sun's heat in Mexico. For example, in the desert regions of Baja it is difficult to gauge how quickly you are losing body water because the humidity can be low. Headaches, dizziness and nausea are signs that you have lost too much water and might have heat exhaustion. To prevent this, take a bit of extra salt with your food, drink plenty of fluids and wear a hat and sunglasses. The salt helps prevent dehydration. Incidentally, the caffeine in coffee, tea and certain soft drinks contributes to dehydration. Sunscreen will prevent the sun from frying your skin. Lastly, the sunshine on the beach and in the water is deceptive and will burn you quickly, so wear a T-shirt while snorkelling or swimming.

Hospitals & Clinics

Almost every town and city in Mexico now has either a hospital or medical clinic and Red Cross (Cruz Roja) emergency facilities, all of which are indicated by road signs which show a red cross. Hospitals are generally reliable and inexpensive for typical ailments (diarrhoea, dysentery) and minor surgery (stitches, sprains). Clinics are often too understaffed and overburdened with local problems to be of much help, but they are linked by a government radio network to emergency services.

If you have a serious medical problem which requires immediate treatment at more sophisticated facilities, Air-Evac International (tel (619) 278-3822, (619) 571-8944 or toll-free in California (800) 247-8326, telex 182822 AIREVAC CHUL), a San Diego-based organisation, can arrange to have you flown to the USA at any time of the day or night.

John got a first-hand look at the Mexican health system while travelling through the country. He writes:

My only experience of Mexican medicine took place once in San Cristóbal de Las Casas. How typical it was I don't know, but it certainly displayed the charming side of Mexico as well as its Third World limitations.

A friend and I who had both eaten at the same restaurant woke next morning with headaches so appalling that we couldn't face the daylight even with our eyes closed. He had acute diarrhoea, I was constipated. Things got worse as the day progressed; a doctor was called and said we should go into the local hospital. We got there in a taxi and were given a clean two-bed room all to ourselves.

After a few tests, the doctor told us next day that we both had typhoid and paratyphoid. I was given some pink medicine which turned constipation into the worst diarrhoea I've ever known, and we lay there feeling pretty weak for eight days while our bowels returned to something like normal. A North American and an Englishman living in the town got to hear about us and paid regular visits to see how we were doing. One of them arranged plain meals from a local restaurant for us.

The hospital treated us as honoured guests and, when the time came for us to leave, the doctor asked only for minimal charges as he knew we were on tight budgets. We spent a further week convalescing in San Cristóbal and then headed on. It was a few more weeks before I recovered my full strength but there were no lasting ill-effects. When I was checked by a doctor on my return to England, he said there was no evidence of my having had typhoid or paratyphoid and that my weakness was probably the result of the 'medicine' rather than anything else.

The only lesson I can draw from the experience is that you should see a doctor back home as soon as possible if you've had serious health problems. If an illness persists in Mexico, head for a doctor or hospital that has been recommended by someone whose judgement you are sure you can trust, such as an embassy or consulate, or perhaps a resident expatriate or perhaps a luxury hotel. It's also well worth taking out health insurance before you go to Mexico – in case the doctors are less understanding than they were in San Cristóbal!

Pharmacies Mexican chemists' shops are usually well stocked with a wide range of drugs and medicines. Many which require a prescription in Western countries are available over the counter.

DANGERS & ANNOYANCES
Mexico has some reputation as a violent country thanks mainly to Pancho Villa, foreign movies and *machismo*. However, there's really little to fear on the score of physical safety unless you get deeply involved in a quarrel. More at risk are your possessions, particularly those you carry around with you. Reports of theft from rooms are scarce but pick-pockets are all too common, especially on transport and in cities, especially Mexico City.

Crowded buses, bus stops, metro trains and metro stations are among the thieves' favourite haunts. They often work in small teams: one may grab your bag or camera, and while you're holding on to it for dear life another will pick your pocket. Or one may 'drop' a coin in a crowded bus and as he 'looks for it', a pocket will be picked in the jostling. Thieves also often carry razor blades with which they slit pockets, bags or straps.

The best precautions are to wear a money belt beneath your clothes and carry as little as possible. Most hotels will lock things up for you and there are *guarderías* (left-luggage offices) in many bus stations.

On long-distance buses or trains keep your baggage with you if you can. If you let it disappear into a bus baggage compartment the chance of not seeing it again increases – or it may emerge considerably the worse for wear. (John's came out covered in wet chicken shit at Tuxtla Gutiérrez.) Parked vehicles are also a prime target for thieves.

There's little point in going to the police after a robbery unless your loss is insured, in which case you'll need a statement from the police to present to your insurance company. You'll probably have to communicate with them in Spanish, so if your own is poor take a more fluent speaker with you to the police station. Say you want to *poner una acta de un robo* (make a record of a robbery). This should make it clear that you merely want a piece of paper and aren't going to ask the police to do anything inconvenient like look for the thieves or recover your goods. With luck you should get the required piece of paper without too much trouble.

Women Travelling Alone
In general, Mexicans aren't great believers

in the equality of the sexes (what would you expect from the home of *machismo*?), and women alone have to expect numerous attempts to chat them up. It's commonly believed that foreign women in Mexico without male companions are easy game for Mexican men. Before AIDS, few middle-class Mexico City males got through their teens without a trip to Acapulco to see who they could pick up.

This can get tiresome at times; the best discouragement is a cool but polite initial response and a consistent firm 'No'.

FILM & PHOTOGRAPHY

According to customs laws in Mexico you are allowed to bring in no more than one camera and 12 rolls of film. I have never heard of this ever being enforced. Camera stores, pharmacies and hotels are the most common outlets for buying film. Be suspicious of film that is being sold at prices lower than what you might pay in North America – it is often outdated. You may not know this by glancing at the date on the back of the film carton because sometimes it's obscured by a sticker bearing the new lower price. Look under the sticker before you buy the film. Most types of film are available. Colour print film is plentiful. Slide (transparency) film is occasionally more difficult to find, especially in smaller locales in Baja. Film prices in Mexico are usually about US$1 or US$2 higher than prices in North America.

Mexico is a photographer's paradise, especially for shots of magnificent landscapes and coastline; a wide-angle lens is useful. It helps to have a polarising filter to cut down glare from reflections of sunlight on the ocean.

For in-depth information and tips on all aspects of travel photography, including hints for Mexico, get a copy of *Travel Photography Pocket Mate* by Jason Rubinsteen (Travel/Photography Press, PO Box 4486, Inglewood, California 90309, USA). It costs US$11 including postage (California residents must add US$0.65 for sales tax).

ACCOMMODATION

Accommodation in Mexico ranges from luxury resort hotels, tourist vacation hotels, budget hotels and motels to *casas de huéspedes* (guest houses) and *albergues para jóvenes* (Youth Hostels).

Hotels & Motels

The luxury resort hotels are mainly found along the coasts, although there are deluxe hotels in most major inland cities such as Mexico City and Guadalajara. They are all expensive, with double-room rates starting at about US$80 per night and going as high as US$250. A few resemble mini-palaces (the Hotel Palmilla and Hotel Cabo San Lucas) and are worth visiting just to look around.

Most of the tourist vacation hotels are affiliated with hotel chains based in the USA and Mexico. The USA-based chains represented in Mexico include Quality Inns, Comfort Inns, Travelodge and Holiday Inn. Their rates in Baja tend to be lower than rates for comparable accommodation in the USA – anywhere from US$35 to US$60 for a double room.

Principal Mexican chains include the La Pinta, El Presidente and Castel hotels. La Pinta and El Presidente are actually the same chain. Rates for double rooms at all three are about US$50 per night. Standards at these hotels are on a par with those at USA-based chains.

By American standards, most of the other hotels and motels in Mexico can be considered in the budget range. Double-room rates normally start at about US$10. Hotels and motels with rates less than this are usually dives or flophouses. However, standards vary from hotel to hotel; room rates and outside appearance are not always true indicators of the quality of accommodation. Ask to see a room, sniff around and sit on a bed to see how much it sags.

Casas de Huéspedes

The next cheapest option is the casa de huéspedes, or a home converted into simple guest lodgings. A double can cost anywhere from US$2 to US$10 with or without meals.

Youth Hostels

The *albergues para jóven* or Youth Hostels are usually run by the Consejo Nacional de Recursos para la Atención de la Juventud (CREA), which is associated with the International Youth Hostel Association (IYHA). IYHA cards can be used or you can obtain a CREA card at the hostel. The charge is US$2 to US$3 per night for members and non-members.

Camping

You can camp for free on most beaches. Wherever facilities are available for campers, though, expect to pay from US$1 to US$10 per night. Most equipped campgrounds are trailer parks designed for motor homes. If you plan to camp much, I highly recommend *Camping in Mexico* by Carl Franz (John Muir Publications, Santa Fe, New Mexico) as a resource for what to bring, how and where to camp, outdoor cooking and other camping topics.

In the north-east, Veracruz, Oaxaca and Chiapas campgrounds are none too common, though there are one or two in or near most major travellers' destinations. They're usually privately owned trailer parks with electrical, water and often sewerage hook-ups, where you can pitch a tent too. Prices vary but the average is US$4 for two people.

Cabañas & Hammocks

These are the two cheapest forms of accommodation, usually found in low-key beach spots. Cabañas are palm huts, sometimes with a dirt floor and nothing inside but a bed, other times more solidly built with electric light, mosquito nets, fans, even a cooker. Prices range from US$1.50 up to US$10 for the most luxurious.

You can rent a hammock and a place to hang it for less than US$1 in some beach places – usually under a palm roof outside a small casa de huéspedes or a fishing family's hut. If you bring your own hammock the cost may be even less. It's easy enough to buy hammocks in Mexico; Mérida in Yucatán and Mitla in Oaxaca are two places specialising in them.

FOOD

You can find almost any type of food and restaurant in Mexico – everything from succulent steaks in a family-run restaurant to Mexicanised Chinese food in a pagoda and abalone burritos at a roadside stand.

Mexicans eat three meals a day: breakfast *(el desayuno)*, lunch *(la comida)* and dinner *(la cena)*. Each includes one or more of three national staples:

Tortillas are thin round patties of pressed corn or wheat flour dough cooked on griddles. Flour (harina) tortillas are prevalent mostly in Northern Mexico and Baja. Corn (maíz) tortillas are found throughout Mexico. Both can be wrapped around or served under any type of food.

Frijoles are beans eaten boiled, fried, refried, in soups, on tortillas or with eggs.

Chiles come in many varieties and are consumed in hundreds of ways. Some types such as the *habanero* and *serrano* are always hot while others such as the *poblano* vary in spiciness according to when they were picked. If you are unsure about your tolerance for hot chiles, ask if the chile is *picante* (spicy hot) or *muy picante* (very spicy hot).

Breakfast is coffee or juice *(jugo)*, a sweet roll *(el bolillo* or *pan dulce)* or toast *(pan tostado)* and eggs, which are served in a variety of ways:

huevos revueltos scrambled eggs; *con chorizo* chor-ree-so) is with sausage; *con frijoles* is with beans *huevos revueltos estilo mexicano* eggs scrambled Mexican-style with tomatoes, onions, chiles and garlic

huevos estrellados or *huevos fritos* fried eggs

huevos rancheros rancho-style eggs fried, smothered with spicy tomato sauce and placed on a tortilla

When you ask for eggs, never ask the waiter *'tiene huevos?'* ('Do you have eggs?') because *huevos* also translates as a crude word for testicles. Instead, ask him *'hay huevos?'* ('Are there eggs?').

Lunch, the biggest meal of the day, is served at about 2 pm. Dinner *(la cena)* is a lighter version of lunch served at about 7.30 pm. In restaurants which do not cater primarily to tourists, lunch and dinner menus – if available – might change every day, every week or not at all. Meals might be ordered a la carte or on a fixed-price basis. A fixed-price *comida corrida* (the bargain or daily special meal) is sometimes offered for as little as US$1. Most fixed-price meals include soup, a main dish, one or two side dishes and dessert. Dishes for lunch or dinner can include the following:

burrito – any combination of beans, cheese, meat, chicken or seafood seasoned with salsa or chile and wrapped in a flour tortilla

chilaquiles – scrambled eggs with chiles and bits of tortillas

chiles rellenos – *poblano* chiles stuffed with cheese, meat or other foods, dipped in egg whites, fried and baked in sauce

enchilada – ingredients similar to those used in tacos and burritos wrapped in a flour tortilla, dipped in sauce and then baked or fried

machaca – cured, dried and shredded beef or pork mixed with eggs, onions, cilantro and chiles

quesadilla – flour tortilla topped or filled with cheese and occasionally other ingredients and then heated

taco – a soft or crisp corn tortilla wrapped or folded around the same filling in a burrito

tamale – steamed corn dough stuffed with meat, beans, chiles or nothing at all, wrapped in corn husks

tostada – flat, crisp tortilla topped with meat or cheese, tomatoes, beans and lettuce

Soups

la sopa – soup

sopa de arroz – rice soup more rice than soup; commonly served with lunch

sopa de pollo – chicken's feet in a thin chicken broth

el pozole – hominy soup with meat and vegetables

el menudo – popular soup made with the spiced entrails of various four-legged beasts

gazpacho – chilled vegetable soup spiced with hot chiles

Seafood

Many people come to Baja just for the seafood; the variety can't be beat. In restaurants you often have to specify what type of fish *(pescado)* you want.

Fish

All of the following types of seafood are available in seafood restaurants most of the year. Clams, oysters, shrimp and prawns are also often available as *coctels* (cocktails) from sidewalk stands. There are stands in almost every town and city in Baja.

pez – fish which is alive in the water

pescado – fish after it has been caught

pescado al mojo de ajo – fish fried in butter and garlic

ceviche – raw seafood marinated in lime and mixed with onions, chiles, garlic and tomatoes

filete de pescado – fish filet

dorado – dolphin

lenguado – flounder or sole

sierra – mackerel

huachinango or *pargo* – red snapper

la cabrilla – sea bass
trucha de mar – sea trout
tiburón – shark
pez espada – swordfish
atún – tuna
jurel – yellowtail

Shellfish

mariscos – shellfish
abulón – abalone
almejas – clams
jaiba – small crab
cangrejo – large crab
ostiones – oysters
langosta – lobster
camarones – shrimp
camarones gigantes – prawns
tortuga or *caguama* – turtle

Meat & Fowl

carne – meat
carne asada – tough but tasty grilled meat
carne al carbón – charcoal-grilled meat
biftec – any cut of meat, fish or fowl
biftec de res – beefsteak
el asado – roast
barbacoa – literally barbecued, but a different process: the biftec is covered and placed under hot coals
la birria – barbecued on a spit
milanesa – breaded
milanesa de res – breaded beefsteak
el hígado – liver
puerco – pork
carnitas – deep-fried pork
chorizo – pork sausage
chicharrones – deep-fried pork rinds
costillas de puerco – pork ribs or chops
chuletas de puerco (not often used) – pork chops
jamón – ham
patas de puerco – pig's feet
tocino – bacon or salted pork
el borrego – sheep
el cordero – lamb
la cabra – goat
el conejo – rabbit
pollo – chicken

pollo asado – grilled chicken
pollo frito – fried chicken
pollo con arroz – chicken with rice
el pavo or *el guajolote* – turkey
el pato – duck
la codorniz or *la chaquaca* – quail

Fruit

las frutas – fruits
el coco – coconut; can often be bought from roadside stands in Southern Baja
el dátil – date
las fresas – strawberries, but also used to refer to any berries
la guayaba – guava
el higo – fig
el limón – lime or lemon
el mango – mango
el melón – melon
la naranja – orange
la piña – pineapple
la papaya – papaya
el plátano – banana
la toronja – grapefruit
la uva – grape

Vegetables

Vegetables are rarely served as separate dishes, but are often mixed into salads, soups and sauces.

verdura or *legumbres* – vegetables
las aceitunas – olives
la calabaza – squash or pumpkin
la cebolla – onion
los championes – mushrooms
los chícharos – peas
los ejotes – green beans
elotes – corn on the cob; commonly served from steaming bins on street carts
la jícama – a popular root vegetable which resembles a potato and an apple; eat with a sprinkling of lime, chile and salt
la lechuga – lettuce
la papa – potato
las papitas fritas – potato chips
el tomate – tomato
la zanahoria – carrot

Desserts

la postre – dessert
helado – ice cream
paleta – flavoured ice on a stick
nieve – Mexican equivalent of the American 'snow cone' – flavoured ice with the consistency of ice cream
flan – custard; extremely popular throughout Mexico
el pan de dulce – sweet rolls
el bolillo or *el birote* – French-style rolls, sometimes sweet
el pastel – cake

Other Foods

sel – salt
pimienta negra – black pepper
azúcar – sugar
leche – milk
crema – cream
queso – cheese
mantequilla – butter
mole – a nationally popular sauce made from more than 30 ingredients including unsweetened chocolate, chiles and many spices; often served over chicken or turkey
guacamole – mashed avocados mixed with onions, chile sauce, lemons, tomatoes and other ingredients
salsa – sauce made with chiles, onions, tomato, lemon or lime juice and spices

At the Table

el menú – menu
la cuenta – bill
la propina – the tip, 10 to 15% of the bill
el plato – plate
el tenedor – fork
el cuchillo – knife
la cuchara – spoon
la servilleta – napkin
la tasa – cup
el vaso or *la copa* – glass

DRINKS

Tea & Coffee

Té and *café* are available throughout Baja, but they are not as popular as in the USA. *Té de manzanillo* (camomile tea) is more common in restaurants than standard *té negro* (black tea). Regular *café* is either instant or ground and almost always served heavily sweetened unless you specify otherwise. In restaurants, coffee or tea rarely arrive before your meal unless you ask for them; otherwise either is served with your meal. Types of coffee you can order:

nescafé – instant coffee; practically an institution in Mexico
café sin azúcar – coffee without sugar. This keeps the waiter from adding heaps of sugar to your cup, but it doesn't mean your coffee won't taste sweet; sugar is often added to and processed with the beans.
café negro or *café americano* – black coffee with nothing added except sugar, unless made with sugar-coated coffee beans
café con leche – coffee with hot milk
café con crema – coffee with cream, served separately

Fruit Drinks

Fresh fruit and vegetable juices (*jugos*), shakes (*licuados*) and flavoured waters (*aguas frescas*) are popular drinks in Mexico. Almost every town has a stand serving one or more of these. All of the fruits and a few of the squeezable vegetables mentioned are used either individually (as in *jugos* or *aguas frescas*) or in some combination (as in *licuados*).

A basic licuado is a blend of fruit or juice with water and sugar. Other items can be added or substituted: raw egg, milk, ice, flavourings such as vanilla or nutmeg. The delicious combinations are practically limitless.

Aguas frescas are made by mixing fruit juice or a syrup made from mashed grains or seeds with sugar and water. You will usually see them in big glass jars on the counters of juice stands. Try the *agua fresca de arroz* (literally 'rice water'); it has a sweet nutty taste certain to please your taste buds.

Soft Drinks (refrescos)

Almost every type of soft drink that can be bought in the USA can also be bought in Mexico. If you are a soft-drink fan, try some of the Mexican refrescos. Apple-flavoured sidral and manzanita are two of the better soft drinks. Other types such as fresa (strawberry), limón (lime) and cereza (cherry) tend to be too sweet.

Alcoholic Beverages

Mexico, particularly the border towns, is a shopper's paradise when it comes to buying inexpensive liquors and liqueurs made in Mexico: Bacardi rum, brandy ('Pedro Domecq' is produced in Baja), Controy (Cointreau – orange liqueur), Kahlua (coffee liqueur popular with North Americans) and Oso Negro vodka.

USA customs allows only one litre of liquor per person (over 21 years of age) into the USA.

Mezcal, Tequila & Pulque Mezcal, tequila and pulque are all made from the sap of the maguey plant, which resembles a porcupine with long, wide, slightly curved spikes.

Mezcal can be made from several species of maguey, but tequila is made from the agave tequilana which grows only in and around the mainland town of Tequila. The spikes of the maguey are stripped away to expose the plant's core or piña. The piña is chopped, roasted, shredded and then pressed to remove the juice. Sugar is added to the juice and, after the resulting mixture ferments for four days, it is put through two distillation processes.

After distillation the mezcal and tequila are aged in wooden casks for periods ranging from four months to seven years. The final product is a golden liquid which is at its most potent as tequila. The longer the ageing, the higher the price.

The traditional steps in drinking mezcal or tequila are:
1) lick the back of your hand and sprinkle salt on it
2) lick the salt
3) suck on a lime
4) down the mezcal or tequila in one gulp
5) lick more salt

When the bottle is empty, you are supposed to eat the worm (preferably fried) traditionally added to each bottle before it's filled.

For foreigners not used to the potency of straight tequila, it is more popular as part of a mixed drink called a Margarita. There are more than 100 types of Margaritas, but most of them are made with tequila (always), lime juice, orange liqueur and a salt-rimmed glass. One type of Margarita calls for 1½ ounces of tequila, ¾ ounce of orange liqueur such as Cointreau and ¾ ounce of fresh lime juice. Fresh fruit such as strawberries and peaches can be added. Other variations include Triple Sec or a Baja-produced liqueur called Damiana.

If you are shopping for a bottle of tequila, look for the letters DGN which mean Dirección General de Normas or Bureau of Standards. This government certification signifies that the tequila is real and not phoney stuff made with magueys other than the agave tequilana.

Pulque is a mildly alcoholic drink derived directly from the sap of the maguey. The foamy, milky drink spoils quickly and thus cannot be bottled and easily shipped throughout Mexico. Most pulque is produced in the region around Mexico City and served in pulquerías. In Mexico City there are several excellent pulquerías in Plaza de Garibaldi.

Beer (cerveza) Baja's claim to fame in Mexico's thriving beer industry used to be Tecate lager beer produced exclusively at the Tecate brewery. However, it was bought by Mexico's second largest brewery conglomerate, Cervecería Cuauhtémoc.

Beer label

The Tecate brewery now produces other brands such as Carta Blanca in addition to its namesake beer.

Breweries were first established in Mexico by German immigrants in the late 19th century. European techniques and technology have been continuously used and are probably a major factor in making Mexican beer extremely popular throughout Mexico and North America today.

Mexico's breweries now produce more than 25 brands of beers. Besides Tecate, popular beers are Corona, Carta Blanca, Dos Equis and Sol Especial.

Which is the best? The answer depends, of course, on your tastes. If you ask five people, you will get five different answers. Everyone does agree on one point though – most Mexican beers are generally smooth and tasty. The current taste-testing rage is to drink Tecate or Corona from a salt-rimmed glass with a slice of lemon or lime.

In restaurants and bars unaccustomed to tourists, beer is usually served at room temperature. If you want a cold beer, ask for *una cerveza fría*.

Our official Mexican beer evaluation:

Chihuahua – a dog of a beer that's really too light

Hussong – overly carbonated beer without the bite of the cantina in Ensenada

Superior – lives up to its name

Pacifico Clara – not so clean in taste

Negro Modelo – rich and savoury; a dark, full-bodied beer in squat little bottles. Don't be deceived by the small size – it's big in taste.

Noche Buena – one of the better things to come out of Orizaba

Bohemia – bottled in Monterrey, Bohemia is not a true Bohemian; it's somewhat malty but without a distinctive taste. Although flat-tasting, it's smooth.

Sol – brewed in Orizaba. Extremely light and not particularly flavourful; it's the Miller High Life of Mexico.

Wine Wine is not as popular in Mexico as beer and tequila. Nevertheless, there are three big wineries in Mexico, all of them in Baja: Industrias Vinicolas Domecq, Formex-Ybarra and Bodegas de Santo Tomás. All three are in and around Ensenada.

Domecq is renowned in Mexico for its Los Reyes table wines. Formex has more than 800 acres of vineyards in the Valle de Guadalupe and is known for its Terrasola table wine. Bodegas hopes to eventually produce wines which can compete with California's. It is run by the Tchelistcheffs, a California-based vintner family. They have planted several varieties of grapes from California and have recently begun producing Pinot Noir, Chardonnay and Cabernet wines which are worth a try.

BOOKS

Although you can find books in English in most major centres, the choice is not extensive, apart from in Mexico City. The Mexican-produced titles mentioned – such as the guides to pre-Hispanic sites – are widely available in Mexico, but with other books it is wise to find what you want before arriving in the country.

The Mexican Book Service, 204 Worthington Drive, Exton, Pennsylvania 19341, USA, maintains a comprehensive list of 215 books covering all aspects of Mexico including travel, pre-Hispanic history, mythology and economics. Most of the books mentioned can be obtained from this service.

Guides & Maps

Michael D Coe's books *The Maya* and *Mexico* (see 'History' books section) have detailed information on all the important ancient sites and are handy enough to take along with you.

The large hardback *The Complete Visitor's Guide to Mesoamerican Ruins* by Joyce Kelly (University of Oklahoma Press, 1982) gives good directions on how to reach some of the remoter sites.

Baja California – a travel survival kit by Scott Wayne (Lonely Planet Publications, 1988) is one of the best guides available on Baja California. In typical Lonely Planet fashion, it is packed with useful tips and information about Mexico's last frontier.

Adventuring Along the Gulf of Mexico by Donald G Schueler (Sierra Club Books, San Francisco, 1986) is an interesting guide to the whole Gulf coast from Florida to the Yucatán, concentrating on wildlife, the environment and opportunities to get away from other people.

Mexico's Volcanoes by R J Secor (The Mountaineers, Seattle, 1981) is a thorough guide to routes up the seven main peaks of Mexico's central volcanic belt. It contains much practical information on how to reach the mountains, what to take and safety precautions.

Backpacking in Mexico & Central America by Hilary Bradt & Rob Rachowiecki (Bradt Enterprises, Cambridge, Massachusetts, and Chalfont St Peter, Bucks, England, 1982) covers only a few hikes in Mexico but has some useful general information plus details of hikes in all the other Central American countries.

The Baja Book III by Tom Miller & Elmar Baxter (Baja Trail Publications, Huntington Beach, California, 1987) is a mile-by-mile guide to Baja which uses a series of aerial photographs taken by the USA's National Aeronautic & Space Agency (NASA) satellites.

Angler's Guide to Baja California by Tom Miller (Baja Trail Publications) is one of the best guides to all aspects of fishing in Baja. It is packed with information on how to identify various species of fish and on where, when and how to fish. Maps, drawings and charts are included.

Camping in Mexico and *The People's Guide to Mexico* by Carl Franz (John Muir Publications, Santa Fe, New Mexico) are excellent guides to the practical aspects of travelling in Mexico. The People's Guide, long an essential for anyone planning an extended trip, has been something of a modern classic, apart from having originated the phrase, 'Wherever you go ... that's where you are'. It doesn't attempt to give hotel-restaurant-transport-sightseeing specifics but instead provides an all-around general introduction to Mexico with information on everything from how to get around to what and where to eat.

In Spanish, the Guía Aurea series of fold-out guides to some cities and states provides good maps, information and illustrations on off-beat places as well as major destinations. You can get them in some Fonart shops.

Those who love old guidebooks should try to find a copy of *Terry's Guide to Mexico*, which was produced from 1922 to 1947. It's highly detailed, though hopelessly out of date of course – but look at those wonderful old multi-coloured fold-out maps. A copy of the 1935 edition at the Lonely Planet office reveals that the 1934 Mexican Customs regulations didn't have much to say about how many cigarettes or bottles of wine you could bring in with you, but did list exhaustively what clothes a female visitor was permitted to import duty-free:

Eighteen pieces of each kind of underwear, 12 night dresses or six pyjamas, 24 pairs of stockings, 24 handkerchiefs, six collars, two aprons, one pair of bath slippers, one bathing cap, one bathrobe, one bathing suit, one pair of slippers, 12 pairs of shoes, one pair of riding boots, one pair of rubber shoes, six house robes, one automobile robe, three overcoats or wraps, one mackintosh, three sweaters, four mufflers, six pairs of gloves, six belts, 12 street-dresses, two evening dresses, three sports gowns, one parasol, one umbrella and 10 hats.

Insight Guides - Mexico from Apa Productions (Singapore 1983) is another in this excellent series of lavishly illustrated guidebooks. There are plenty of photographs to fire the imagination for a Mexico visit.

Those with a passionate interest in pre-Hispanic sights should look for *A Guide to Ancient Mexican Ruins* and *A Guide to Ancient Maya Ruins*, both by C Bruce Hunter (University of Oklahoma Press, 1974 & 1977). Small, locally produced guides to most of the sites are usually available, in English and in other languages, at each site. The *Official Guide* series to each site are probably the most authoritative, but others, such as the extensive Richard Bloomgarten *Easy Guide* series, are also interesting.

One of the best overall maps of Mexico is published by Bartholomew in its World Travel Map series at a scale of 1:3 million - which means that it folds out to about 1.2 by 0.8 metres. It shows altitudes, rivers, cities and towns, roads, railways and state boundaries clearly and accurately. You can also get a good 1:3.5 million 'Tourist Road Map' of the country, which includes good street plans of some cities, free from many tourist offices. For motorists, the best road atlas is generally reckoned to be the *Pemex Atlas de Carreteras*, available from some Pemex petrol stations.

Travel & Description

Barbarous Mexico by John Kenneth Turner (University of Texas Press, 1969) is a superb account by a US journalist of travels in Mexico early this century, written to tell North Americans the truth about the barbarity of the Porfirio Díaz regime - a job in which it succeeds admirably and very readably. When translated into Spanish in 1955, the book was entitled *Problemas Agrícolas e Industriales de México* (Agricultural & Industrial Problems of Mexico) - no doubt a less offensive title for a Mexican audience.

Other interesting books by foreigners who have lived in or travelled in Mexico are *Life in Mexico* by Frances Calderón de La Barca, the Scottish wife of Spain's ambassador to Mexico in the turbulent 1840s (reissued by Dent, London in 1970); *Viva Mexico!* by Charles Macomb Flandrau (Eland paperback) which tells of life on a coffee plantation at the turn of this century; *Thomas Gage's Travels in the New World* (University of Oklahoma Press, 1969), by a 17th-century English Puritan; and *A Visit to Don Otavio* by Sybil Bedford (Eland paperback).

Time-Life Books' well-illustrated American Wilderness series includes an interesting volume on *The Sierra Madre*.

Incidents of Travel in Central America, Chiapas & Yucatán and *Incidents of Travel in Yucatán* by John L Stephens are fascinating accounts of adventure, discovery and archaeology by the enthusiastic 19th-century amateur archaeologist. Both are available in Dover paperback editions.

Graham Greene's *The Lawless Roads* was originally published in 1939 and entertainingly traces his wanderings through Mexico at a particularly troubling time when violent clashes were taking place between state and church.

Aldous Huxley travelled through Mexico too; *Beyond the Mexique Bay*, first published in 1934, has interesting observations on the Mayans. It's also worth reading if you're going to be staying long in Oaxaca.

Writers haven't stopped finding Mexico a worthwhile place to travel in and write about. *So Far from God (A Journey to Central America)* by Patrick Marnham (Viking, New York, 1985 and now in a Penguin paperback) was the winner of the 1985 Thomas Cook Travel Book Award.

It's an insightful and often amusing account of a leisurely meander from Texas down to Mexico City and on through Oaxaca and San Cristóbal de las Casas into Central America. Paul Theroux rides the rails through Mexico on *The Old Patagonian Express*.

The Children of Sánchez by Oscar Lewis (Random House) is a brilliantly readable look at the Mexican family. The anthropologist Lewis compiled his data through taped oral histories and it's essential reading if you want to understand the pivotal importance of the family in Mexican society. *Five Families* (Basic Books) is by the same author.

Literature

Mexico's best-known novelist is Carlos Fuentes, who has achieved major international recognition. His most highly regarded novel is *Where the Air is Clear* (Farrar Straus & Giroux, New York, 1971), written in the 1950s. Like *The Death of Artemio Cruz* (Panther), another of his best-known works, it's an attack on the failure of the Mexican Revolution. Fuentes' *Aura*, a short tale of a young scholar who falls in love with the niece of an old widow whose husband's memoirs he is editing, is a magical book with one of the most stunning endings of any novel in any language. It's available in a parallel-text (Spanish and English) paperback published by Farrar, Straus & Giroux. Fuentes was Mexico's ambassador to France briefly in the mid-1970s, but resigned in protest at the appointment of former president Díaz Ordaz as ambassador to Spain. His other novels include *Terra Nostra*, *Distant Relations*, *A Change of Skin* and *The Old Gringo*, which poses a solution to the mysterious disappearance in Mexico of American writer Ambrose Bierce during the Revolution.

The only other Mexican novelist widely known outside the country is Jorge Ibargüengoitia, who was killed in the Madrid air disaster of 1983. His *The Dead Girls* and *Two Crimes*, both published in paperback by Chatto & Windus, London, are black comic thrillers, the first based on the real murders of six prostitutes in a provincial Mexican brothel, the second the story of a radical on the run from the security forces.

The Labyrinth of Solitude, The Other Mexico: Critique of the Pyramid (Grove Press, New York, 1972) is a passionate, insightful book by Octavio Paz. It was written after the 1968 Tlatelolco massacre and assesses the lingering influence of the savage Aztec world view in modern Mexico. Paz's *Alternating Currents* is a less known but still brilliant collection of essays combining literary criticism, philosophy and political and social insight. Like Fuentes, Paz combined his literary career with diplomacy; he resigned as ambassador to India in protest against the Tlatelolco massacre.

D H Lawrence's *The Plumed Serpent* asks the big questions about life, death and relationships in a Mexican setting. Heavy going even for Lawrence fans, it was first published in 1926 and is available in Penguin paperbacks. Lawrence wrote at least part of *The Plumed Serpent* in Oaxaca in 1924. His frail health didn't stand up to the country very well: he got malaria, dysentery and tuberculosis. *Lawrence in Oaxaca* by Ross Parmenter is a recently published account of the time he spent in the state. *Mornings in Mexico* (also in Penguin paperback) is a collection of short stories by Lawrence set in both New Mexico and Mexico.

Recently made into a widely acclaimed film with the same name, *Under the Volcano* by Malcolm Lowry (Lippincott 1965; also in Penguin paperback) follows a British diplomat who drinks himself to death. Sounds simple, but it delves deeply into the Mexican psyche at a time (1938) of deep conflict.

Carlos Castaneda's *Don Juan* series of novels (Penguin), which reached serious cult status in the 1970s, tells of an American's experiences with a peyote guru somewhere in northern Mexico.

Those who want to delve into the curious inspiration Mexico has offered to writers in English could seek out *Infernal Paradise: Mexico & the Modern English Novel* by Ronald G Walker.

History

General *Sons of the Shaking Earth* by Eric Wolf (University of Chicago Press, 1959) is a wonderfully readable introduction to Mexican history. Other good general introductions to the country's history include *A Short History of Mexico* by J Patrick McHenry (Doubleday).

There are various worthwhile books to look for on the pre-Hispanic period, on the Spanish conquest and its aftermath, and on recent events in Mexico. Starting at the beginning of the Mexican story there's Nigel Davies' *The Ancient Kingdoms of Mexico* (Alan Lane, London, 1982; also available in Pelican paperback). This is a succinct but scholarly study of four of Mexico's ancient civilisations: the Olmecs, the builders of Teotihuacán, the Toltecs and the Aztecs. Diagrams, illustrations, plans and maps complement the text.

Atlas of Ancient America by Michael Coe, Dean Snow & Elizabeth Benson (Facts on File, New York and Oxford, 1986) covers North, South and the rest of Central America as well as Mexico. It's too big to carry in a backpack but is a fascinating, superbly illustrated, up-to-date book. The whole course of ancient Mexico is charted and there are maps showing the areas controlled by the different Maya cities and the expansion of the Teotihuacán, Toltec and Aztec empires.

The Daily Life of the Aztecs by Jacques Soustelle (New York, 1962) is something of a classic on its subject. *Burning Water* by Laurette Séjourné (Shambhala, Berkeley, 1976) is an interesting book on Aztec myths, religion and thought.

The multi-volume *Handbook of Middle American Indians* (University of Texas Press, Austin, 1964-1976) edited by Robert Wauchope is an encyclopaedic work which covers both the pre-Hispanic and more recent stages of Indian history and culture in great detail.

The Works of Hubert Bancroft by Hubert Bancroft (A L Bancroft & Company, 1884) is an immense multi-volume history of Central America, Mexico and California by one of the most pre-eminent American historians. This is probably the most comprehensive study ever written on these areas and includes extremely informative sections about Baja California. Unfortunately, the collection is available only at a few libraries, mainly in universities, but it is definitely worth tracking down.

The Course of Mexican History by Michael C Meyer & William L Sherman (Oxford University Press, 1986) is one of the best general histories of Mexico.

Spanish Conquest *The Conquest of New Spain* by Bernal Díaz del Castillo (Penguin paperback, abridged version) is an eyewitness account of the Spanish arrival. Díaz was one of Cortés' soldiers or lieutenants. *Cortés & Moctezuma* (Avon Books, 1954 & 1978) is a fast-moving story of the Spanish conquest.

There's a very readable account of the Spanish conquest, based on Bernal Díaz's writings, in the small paperback Panorama series widely available in Mexico. It's called *The Conquest of Mexico* and is by Fernando Orozco L.

Soldiers, Indians & Silver by Philip W Powell is an interesting history of the bloody and little-known Chichimec War fought by the Spanish for control of northern Mexico in the 16th century.

Mexico Today *Mexico in Crisis* by Judith Adler Hellman (Holmes & Meier, New York and London, 1983) is a well-researched leftist attack on the failure of Mexico's recent governments to provide any real remedies for the country's poverty.

Worth looking for at bookstalls, if you can understand some Spanish, are the satirical cartoon books by Rius, with titles like *Su Majestad el PRI* (His Majesty PRI) and *La Deuda y Como No Pagarla* (The Debt & How Not to Pay it).

For disturbing documentation of recent political violence against Mexico's poor, dig out *Mexico – Human Rights in Rural Areas*, a short report published by Amnesty International in London in 1986.

Distant Neighbors by Alan Riding (originally published by Knopf, New York in 1984 but now available in paperback) is subtitled 'A Portrait of the Mexicans'. This is probably the best guide to understanding modern Mexico and its ongoing love-hate relationship with the United States. The book delves into the Mexican political system, economy, people, mixed blessing of oil, headlong growth of Mexico City and more. It's easily readable.

Indians There are libraries full of anthropologists' writings on modern Mexican Indians but few works in English which give an overall picture. The best introduction we've come across is *Of Gods & Men* by Anna Benson Gyles & Chloë Sayer (BBC, London, 1980), which traces the path of several Indian peoples from pre-Hispanic to modern times. Otherwise, there's the *Handbook of Middle American Indians* (University of Texas Press, Austin), a multi-volume encyclopaedic work edited by Robert Wauchope. In Spanish, there's *Grupos Indígenas de México* by Lillian Scheffler in the Panorama paperback series which is quite widely available in Mexico. With luck this will soon be translated into English like many other books in the series. There's also the two-volume *Grupos Etnicos de México* published by INI, the Instituto Nacional Indigenista.

A Treasury of Mexican Folkways by Frances Toor (Bonanza Books/Crown Publishers, New York, 1985) was written in the 1940s but still has much interesting detail on mainly Indian customs, ceremon-

ies, beliefs and ways of life. *Mexico South* by Miguel Covarrubias (Alfred A Knopf, New York, 1946), an account of life and customs of the Zapotecs on the Isthmus of Tehuantepec, is also fascinating but much of what it describes has sadly disappeared. Covarrubias was an artist who also wrote one of the best books on Bali in Indonesia.

Culture, Art & Architecture

Books on Mexico's great 20th-century artists include Diego Rivera's autobiography *My Art, My Life* (Citadel Press, New York), *The Fabulous Life of Diego Rivera* by B D Wolfe (Stein & Day, New York) and *The Mexican Muralists* by Alma M Reed (Crown, New York).

Mexico's post-1521 architectural heritage isn't nearly so well documented as the pre-Hispanic, scene but *Art & Time in Mexico* by Elizabeth Wilder Weismann & Judith Hancock Sandoval (Harper & Row) is a good, fairly handy, recent book on colonial architecture, with many photos. *A Guide to Mexican Art* by Justino Fernández (University of Chicago Press, 1969) covers architecture as well as art fairly thoroughly.

One of the most fascinating of all recent books on Mexico – but unfortunately too big for a backpack – is Chloë Sayer's *Mexican Costume* (British Museum Publications, 1985). This book is the fruit of immense research but very readable and not too long. It traces the designs, materials and techniques of the country's highly colourful and varied costumes from pre-Hispanic times to the present, and includes many photos and a great wealth of other intriguing detail about Mexican life past and present. The same author has also written *Crafts of Mexico* (Aldus Books). Another good book in English is *Mexican Folk Crafts* by Carlos Espejel (Editorial Blume, Barcelona, 1978).

Michael D Coe has two interesting books available as Thames & Hudson paperbacks. *The Maya* (1984) traces the history, art and culture of the Maya while *Mexico* (also 1984) concentrates on the other pre-Hispanic civilisations of Mexico. These two books give a handy and well-illustrated overall view of the great cultures of Mexico. Charles Gallenkamp's *Maya* is also widely acclaimed.

The Blood of Kings (Dynasty & Ritual in Maya Art) by Linda Schele & Mary Ellen Miller (George Braziller, New York 1986) is a heavily illustrated guide to the art and culture of the Maya period with particular emphasis on sacrifices, bloodletting, torture of captives, the ball game and other macabre aspects of Mayan culture. The illustrated analyses of Mayan art are fascinating.

Other Subjects

Publisher Minutiae Mexicana produces a range of pocket-size guides to various aspects of Mexico including *A Bird Watcher's Guide to Mexico*, *A Guide to Mexican Mammals & Reptiles*, *A Guide to Mexican Archaeology*, *A Guide to Mexican Ceramics*, *A Guide to Architecture in Ancient Mexico* and even *A Guide to Tequila, Mezcal & Pulque*. They're useful, compact introductions to specific topics and are widely available in Mexico.

Another interesting Mexican-produced paperback series with many titles in English is Panorama. These include *History of Mexico*, *The Conquest of Mexico*, *The Mexican Revolution*, *Truth & Legend on Pancho Villa*, *Pre-Hispanic Gods of Mexico*, *Codices of Mexico*, *Mural Painting of Mexico* and *Indian Costumes of Mexico*.

THINGS TO BUY

Most *artesanías* (handicrafts) originated in objects made for everyday use or for specific occasions such as festivals. Today many objects are made simply to sell as 'folk art' – some purely decorative, others with a useful function – but that doesn't necessarily reduce their quality. Although traditional materials, particularly textiles,

are rarer than they used to be, some craftspeople have used the opportunity to develop their artistic talents to high levels.

The places where crafts are made aren't always the best places to buy them. There's wide trade in artesanías and you'll often find a better selection in shops and markets in towns and cities than in the original villages. Nor do prices necessarily get much higher in the bigger centres. Oaxaca city, for instance, is the major clearing-house for handicrafts from all over the state of Oaxaca, and the number of stores selling them helps keep prices competitive. On the other hand, goods from Oaxaca become more expensive when they're transported to Mexico City or elsewhere.

You can get a good overview of the best that's available and an idea of prices by looking round some of the city stores devoted to these products. Buying in these places also saves the time and effort of seeking out the sometimes remote towns and villages where items are made. The government-run Fonart shops in several cities usually have good ranges of

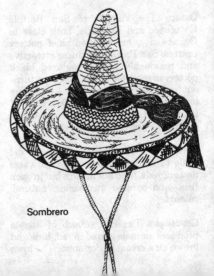

Sombrero

high-quality stock at decent prices. In Mexico City and San Miguel de Allende the shops have a wide range of crafts from all over Mexico. The Bazar Sábado (Saturday Bazaar) at San Ángel in Mexico City always has some of the best of Mexican folk art. Sanborn's House of Tiles is another shop in the capital with a good range. There are several craft stores in Oaxaca and other cities too. San Cristóbal de Las Casas is the centre for crafts from all over Chiapas.

The local markets in Oaxaca, Toluca, Cuetzalán (Puebla), Ocotlán and Tlacolula (near Oaxaca) are among those with good ranges of crafts.

Pottery

This comes in a huge variety of local forms. There are basically two types – unglazed earthenware and sturdier, Spanish-influenced, often highly decorated, glazed ware. You can pick up attractive items for a couple of dollars or less in many places.

Talavera This is a glazed, colourfully painted pottery from Puebla. Its many forms include plates, cups and tiles.

Oaxaca The villages of San Bartolo Coyotepec and Atzompa, both close to Oaxaca city, are the two chief pottery centres. San Bartolo produces attractive and reasonably priced unglazed black pottery in multiple forms. Atzompa turns out 'embroidered' clay pieces – including interesting pagan-looking 'earth mother' figures and Last Supper scenes – as well as distinctive green-glazed ware.

Chiapas The village of Amatenango del Valle turns out earthenware jugs, vases and animals, fired not in kilns but in open fires, and painted in pleasing 'natural' colours.

Guadalajara The city suburb of Tonalá produces animals glazed in red, blue and brown on a cream background. The town of Patamba, Michoacán makes green-glazed pineapple-shaped pots and jars.

Tzintzuntzan Tarascan pottery decorated with simple swan, fish and fishing designs is produced in Tzintzuntzan in Michoacán.

Trees of Life One of Mexico's most intriguing and distinctive pottery forms is the tree of life. The lavishly worked, candelabra-like forms are often colourfully painted, usually with a religious, mythological or contemporary theme. The works of Heron Martínez of Acatlán in Puebla are reckoned to be the best. There are also several craftspeople in Izucar de Matamoros, Puebla. Metepec in the state of Mexico is another tree of life centre, also known for its clay suns.

Textiles

These provide the greatest variety of all. For a start there are the colourful hand-woven and embroidered Indian costumes, which come in a number of basic shapes and as many designs as there are weavers. The states of Oaxaca, Chiapas and Puebla are three of the most interesting from this point of view, with truly bewildering variety. Some of the finest huipiles are made in Mérida in Yucatán. Cheaper are the colourful waist sashes *(fajas)*.

Teotitlán del Valle in Oaxaca turns out an enormous number and variety of excellently designed blankets and rugs. A *sarape* is a type of blanket which can also be worn poncho-style: among the best are those of Jocotepec near Guadalajara and Pátzcuaro in Michoacán.

Santa María del Río near San Luis Potosí and Tenancingo in the state of Mexico produce some of the best wool or cotton shawls known as *rebozos*.

The Huichol Indians of Jalisco make colourful and interesting 'yarn paintings' with designs clearly influenced by peyote, which is central to Huichol culture.

Attractive table cloths and wall hangings, embroidered with multitudes of colourful animals and plants, are produced in several places in central and southern Mexico. Tenango de Doria (Hidalgo), San Pablito (Puebla) and San Mateo del Mar (Oaxaca) are three villages where they are made, but they can be found in many towns and cities.

Other Woven Goods

Many goods are woven all over the country from palm, straw, reeds or sisal (rope made from the henequén cactus). Mérida is a centre for sisal mats, hammocks, bags and hats. The state of Oaxaca also turns out many palm mats and baskets, as well as useful string bags *(bolsas)*. Ocotlán and Oaxaca markets are good places to find them. The Tarascan Indians of Tzintzuntzan in Michoacán produce mats and figurines from reeds.

Silver, Gold & Copper

Taxco is Mexico's main silversmith centre; San Miguel de Allende and Oaxaca also have good jewellery. Guanajuato is a centre for gold jewellery, sometimes decorated with turquoise. Santa Clara del Cobre in Michoacán, a copper-mining centre since 1553, has over 50 workshops producing well-worked bowls, candlesticks, lamps and hand-hammered plates. A cheap and quite attractive product found widely is tin, beaten and painted into a multitude of designs – the sort of thing that would hang well on a Christmas tree.

Woodwork

Ceremonial masks are widely used and you can buy them in cities like Oaxaca, San Cristóbal de Las Casas and Mexico City. San Miguel de Allende and Cuernavaca are centres for wooden furniture. Probably the finest guitars are made in Paracho. Some villages around Oaxaca city are now producing attractive, colourfully painted wooden animals and birds. *Amate* paintings (done on tree bark) are widely available and make pleasing, affordable souvenirs.

Lacquerware

This attractive craft involves the decoration of wood – boxes, trays, etc – or gourds with layers of colourful and protective lacquer paint. Several towns specialise in it and the best work is from Olinalá in Guerrero and Uruapan in Michoacán.

WHAT TO BRING

Clothing for travellers in much of Mexico resembles clothing in California – cool and casual. Men can wear jeans or shorts, tennis shoes or sandals and T-shirts, although more conservative wear is in order when visiting churches. Women can wear almost the same type of clothes as men anywhere except those places which are off the beaten track and unaccustomed to tourists. In general, it is better for women to dress somewhat conservatively when in town – no shorts, tank tops, etc. Sweaters and light jackets are often necessary in winter, but only occasionally in summer. A light rain-jacket, preferably a loose-fitting poncho, is also useful. Consult the climate chart for an idea of temperatures and rainfall.

Toiletries such as shampoo, shaving cream, razors, soap and toothpaste are readily available throughout Mexico in all but the smallest villages. You should bring your own contact lens solution, tampons, contraceptives and deodorant.

Other recommended items are sunglasses, flashlight, hat, disposable lighter, pocket knife, two to three metres of cord, diving or snorkelling equipment, fishing equipment, sunscreen, small sewing kit, money belt or pouch, small Spanish-English dictionary and lip balm.

Getting There

FROM THE USA
Air

There are direct scheduled flights from the USA to several cities in Mexico, including Baja California. The principal airlines flying to Mexico include: Aeroméxico, Mexicana de Aviación (Mexicana), Pacific Southwest Airlines (PSA, Baja only), Sun Pacific Airlines (Baja only), Continental, American Airlines and Delta. Each offers different routings, fares and package deals.

Aeroméxico non-stop flights link Atlanta with Cancún, Cozumel and Mexico City; Houston with Cancún, Guadalajara, Mérida, Mexico City and Monterrey; Los Angeles with Guadalajara, La Paz, Los Cabos, Monterrey and Tijuana; Miami with Mérida and Mexico City; New York with Cancún and Mexico City; Tucson with Guaymas and Hermosillo. Mexicana non-stop flights go between Baltimore/Washington and Cancún; Chicago and Acapulco, Cancún, Cozumel, Mexico City, Monterrey and Puerto Vallarta; Dallas/Fort Worth and Acapulco, Cancún, Cozumel, Guadalajara, Monterrey and Puerto Vallarta; Denver and Los Cabos, Mazatlán and Puerto Vallarta; Philadelphia and Cancún and Mexico City; Los Angeles and Guadalajara, Mazatlán, Mexico City and Puerto Vallarta; Miami and Cancún and Cozumel; San Antonio and Monterrey, Puerto Vallarta and Mexico City; San Francisco and Guadalajara, Mazatlán and Puerto Vallarta; Seattle and Tacoma with Mazatlán and Puerto Vallarta.

Continental has direct flights between Houston and Acapulco, Cancún, Cozumel, Guadalajara, Mexico City, Monterrey and Puerto Vallarta. Some of these services also enable you to start or end your journey in St Paul in Minneapolis, Denver, Salt Lake City, Detroit, New York or Colorado Springs without changing planes. Continental also offers tickets which allow you to fly into one destination in Mexico and out of another. The cities covered are Mexico City, Cancún, Cozumel, Monterrey and Acapulco.

The Singapore Airlines and Continental's joint round-the-world ticket, which covers many destinations in Europe, the Middle East, Asia, Australasia and North America, also allows you (for the normal Continental Houston to Mexico return fare) to make a side-trip into Mexico (any of about six places) and back to Houston, without this being counted as backtracking.

If you want to travel overland down through northern Mexico, there are flights to most US cities on the Mexican border.

Aeroméxico ticket

Continental, for instance, serves Laredo, McAllen (Texas) and San Diego. Transtar links Brownsville (Texas) with several cities in the south-eastern USA.

The major North American addresses and telephone numbers for Aeroméxico and Mexicana are:

Aeroméxico (tel toll free (800) 237-6639)
  912 Dallas St, Houston, Texas (tel (713) 691-3091)
  1005 West Beverly Boulevard, Montebello (Los Angeles), California (tel (213) 646-0335)
  2055 Peel St, Montreal, Quebec, Canada (tel (514) 288-0000)
  444 Madison Avenue, New York, New York (tel (212) 391-2900)
  246 Broadway Avenue, San Diego, California (tel (619) 238-1319)
  360 Post St, Suite 506, San Francisco, California (tel (415) 982-1424)
  85 Richmond St West, Suite 103, Toronto, Ontario, Canada (tel (416) 363-9017)
  209-1111 West Georgia St, Vancouver, British Columbia, Canada (tel (604) 685-4433)
Mexicana (tel toll free (800) 531-7921)
  55 East Monroe, Chicago, Illinois (tel (312) 346-8414)
  1808 Main St, Dallas, Texas (tel (214) 651-8303)
  5757 Century Boulevard, Suite 600, Los Angeles, California (tel (213) 553-2902)
  500 Fifth Avenue, Suite 1715, New York, New York (tel (212) 687-0388)
  400 Post St, San Francisco, California (tel (415) 982-1424)
  203 Columbia Center Building, Seattle, Washington (tel (206) 441-5480)
  60 Bloor St West, Suite 1206, Toronto, Ontario, Canada (tel (416) 961-2080)
  Oceanic Plaza, 1066 West Hastings St, Suite 650, Vancouver, British Columbia (tel (604) 682-8364)

Fare Information When you book flights on Aeroméxico and Mexicana, check into special fares and combined air fare/hotel packages. Fares are generally US$20 to US$30 lower on flights that arrive and depart Monday to Thursday. Accommodation at resort-style hotels throughout

Mexico is often much more inexpensive if arranged through an airline or travel agency. A few sample packages are described in the 'Tours' section.

Flight Information For flight information to a certain city in Mexico, see the 'Getting There' section for that city. You can safely assume that flights are scheduled for frequent departures for almost every major city in Mexico. The 'Overseas Airline Guide' devotes many pages of microscopic print to flights from the USA to Mexican cities. Your travel agent should have a copy, or you can consult it in the library. Many flights to Mexico, especially from cities in the western USA, are routed through Los Angeles.

Warning At the time of publication Aeroméxico was undergoing a change of management and as a result may not be operating for any or all domestic and international services.

Overland

Mexico can be entered by land from the USA at 24 points: San Ysidro (Tijuana), Otay Mesa, Tecate, Calexico (Mexicali) and Algodones, San Luis Río Colorado, Sonoita, Sasabe, Nogales, Naco, Agua Prieta, Palomas, Ciudad Juárez, Guadalupe Bravos, Praxedis Guerrero, Ojinaga, Ciudad Acuña, Piedras Negras, Nuevo Laredo, Ciudad Alemán, Camargo, Reynosa, Nuevo Progreso and Matamoros.

Bus & Trolley Greyhound is the major bus company operating buses to the border cities from American cities. If you plan to travel extensively by bus in the USA, you might consider purchasing an Ameripass or International Ameripass. The Ameripass costs US$189 for seven days of travel, US$249 for 15 days and US$349 for 30 days. The International Ameripass is a better deal if you qualify. It is available to foreign students, research scholars and lecturers (with their families) who have been in the USA for less than a year. It costs US$99 for seven days, US$150 for 15 days and US$225 for 30 days. Additional days can be added to each pass for US$12 per day.

The Ameripass is sold at every Greyhound terminal. The International Ameripass can be bought only at Greyhound terminals in New York City, Miami, Los Angeles and San Francisco after completing an affidavit and presenting your passport to Greyhound officials.

The Greyhound bus network provides several services daily from within the US to all the main towns on the US side of the border. There are a few Mexican buses to destinations deep inside Mexico from the towns on the US side of the border, but these usually cost significantly more than buses from the towns on the Mexican side. To save money it's better to walk or take a local bus across the border and then get a long-distance bus from the Mexican side. See the sections on the border towns for more detail.

Rail There are seven Amtrak passenger trains daily to and from Los Angeles and San Diego. From San Diego's Santa Fe Amtrak depot you can take a trolley car directly to the border at San Ysidro. Following is schedule information:

departs Los Angeles	arrives San Diego
8.00 am	10.45 am
10.45 am	1.35 pm
12.45 pm	3.30 pm
2.45 pm	5.25 pm
4.45 pm	7.30 pm
6.40 pm	9.15 pm
8.45 pm	11.30 pm

departs San Diego	arrives Los Angeles
6.45 am	9.30 am
8.00 am	10.00 am
9.45 am	12.30 pm
12.45 pm	3.30 pm
2.45 pm	5.30 pm
4.45 pm	7.30 pm
7.45 pm	10.25 pm

From Monday to Thursday one-way/round-trip fares are US$20/27.50. On Friday, Saturday and Sunday the round-trip fare is US$41, one-way fare US$20.50. For the latest fare and schedule information call Amtrak toll free on (800) 872-7245.

Car Millions of people drive their own vehicles across the border into Mexico every year. If you do not plan to travel farther south than the border town of Ensenada in Baja, and are not staying more than 72 hours, then you will not need a tourist card or visa. If you are going to mainland Mexico either by ferry from Baja or overland across the border to the east of Mexicali, then you will need a car permit/tourist card (if you are the driver) or a tourist card.

Mexican automobile insurance is highly recommended for any visit by car to Mexico because the policies of other countries are invalid in Mexico.

For more information about car permits and insurance coverage as well as tourist cards, see the 'Facts for the Visitor' chapter.

Sea

Cruise ships, private yachts and a 'shuttle' boat between San Diego and Ensenada are the only ways to travel by sea to Mexico from California.

The cruise ship *Tropicale* of Carnival Cruise Lines (tel (800) 327-9501) sails every Sunday from Pier No 93A at the Port of San Pedro near Los Angeles. The cruise lasts for a week and visits Cabo San Lucas, Puerto Vallarta and Mazatlán. Prices vary from US$775 to US$1045 per person.

Exploration Cruise Line (tel (800) 426-0600, (206) 625-9600) sails the 158-passenger MS *Northstar* from San Diego to Cabo San Lucas and several mainland ports between October and April for prices ranging from US$1585 to US$1885.

Society Expeditions (tel (800) 426-7794) runs luxurious cruises from San Diego to Cabo San Lucas, several mainland ports, the Panama Canal and various Caribbean destinations only in September for prices ranging from US$3100 to US$12,000.

The Ensenada Express (tel (800) 422-5008), PO Box 81823, San Diego, California 92138-1823, sails a 100-foot (30½-metre) 'luxury' vessel from San Diego to Ensenada every day at 9 am, returning at 9 pm. At US$79 round trip it is a very popular way to travel to Baja. Advance reservations are essential.

If you know something about boats and sailing, you might try talking your way into a crew position on one of the many boats sailing from California's harbours to Mexico. The marinas at Dana Point, Newport Beach, Belmont Shores and Marina del Rey are good places to begin your enquiries.

Tours

General and special-interest tours are an increasingly popular way to explore Mexico. Whale-watching expeditions in Baja, cycling, kayak and wind-surfing trips in the Sea of Cortés, beach-camping and fishing trips are only a few of the many types of tours available. Following are a few of the tour operators which offer these trips:

Baja High Wind Center is a wind-surfing centre based in the San Francisco area that relocates each winter and early spring (November to early April) to the Rancho Buena Vista Hotel in Los Barriles (south of La Paz). Courses are held weekly with world-class instructors and prototypes of the latest wind-surfing equipment direct from the manufacturers. They offer various all-inclusive packages. Contact them at PO Box 1374, Sausalito, California 94966 (tel (415) 332-0110, toll free in California (800) 323-1991, or toll free in the rest of the USA (800) 222-5697).

Pacific Adventures (tel (714) 684-1227), PO Box 5041, Riverside, California 92517 offers trips oriented to horseback riding, kayaking, scuba diving and sailing.

Baja Frontier Tours (tel (619) 262-2003), 4365 New Jersey Avenue, San Diego, California 92116 specialise in back-country mule trips and whale-watching journeys in Baja.

Green Tortoise Alternative Travel (tel (213) 392-1990, (805) 569-1884, (408) 462-6437, (415) 821-0803, (503) 937-3603, (503) 225-0310, (206) 324-7433, (604) 732-5153, (212) 431-3348, (617) 265-8533 or toll free for all other areas (800) 227-4766), PO Box 24459, San Francisco, California 94124 is a national organisation which offers funky bus trips through Baja and all the way to the Yucatán for two or three weeks of beach camping and wind-surfing. The trips are usually offered only in November and December.

Mayan Adventure Tours (tel (206) 523-5309), PO Box 15204, Wedgwood Station, Seattle, Washington 98115-15204 offers unique tours of obscure Mayan sites which are not easily accessible. Small groups of nine to 12 travel in private vehicles and stay in local hotels. Among the trips are Chichén Itzá during the equinox, the Yucatán coast to coast, the indigenous crafts centres of Oaxaca and Guatemala, and hidden beaches of the Yucatán.

Package holidays to Mexico are available from just about every Western country. Many of them are of the 'nine nights in Acapulco plus a couple in Taxco' variety but others are more varied and worth considering if you want to pack a lot of Mexico into a little time. Mexican government tourist offices around the world can give you armfuls of brochures about these trips. A few examples follow (food is not always included in the price):

Expeditions Inc (tel (817) 861-9298), PO Box 13594, Arlington, Texas 76094-0594, can take you to about 16 archaeological or colonial destinations in two weeks (send for prices).

Sun Pacific Airlines offers two nights and three days at the Hotel Castel in San Felipe for US$259, including round-trip air fare from Long Beach, California.

Mexicana and Aeroméxico offer various air fare/hotel packages through companies such as Firstours (tel (800) 423-3118), 8134 Van Nuys Boulevard, Suite 200, Panorama City, California 94102.

Quality Air Tours, Inc (tel (800) 752-8687), 6048 South Clementine, Anaheim 92802 arrange packages of three nights and four days in La Paz at the Hotel El Presidente or Hotel Los Arcos for US$234 (including air fare).

Reforma Mex (tel (213) 283-1300), 36 West Bay State St, Alhambra, California 91801, are one of the few agencies that arranges packages for Loreto – three nights and four days at the Hotel El Presidente for US$210 including air fare and other extras.

Travel agents at most USA agencies can arrange package deals with a variety of operators: Simplex Tours, American Leisure, Petrabax, Guerra Tours and A-Avanti. All of them offer similar deals with rates that vary greatly depending on the season.

A Simplex Los Angeles-to-Mazatlán tour for eight days and seven nights costs US$519 (winter/high rate) and includes round-trip air fare, in-flight meals and beverage service, airport-hotel transfers, accommodation, dinner at the Lazy Crab Restaurant, bay cruise, two-for-one meals at Casa Maria, the services of a Simplex host/hostess, 15% tax and flight insurance.

Another special deal called 'The Golden Pass' with a Los Angeles-based company, Mexico Travel Advisors, costs US$499 per person and covers hotel rooms for 30 consecutive nights including two meals daily. This has to be used in Mexico City, Taxco and Tehuacán. Only your first night must be booked in advance. Contact USA travel agents for further details, since it usually must be booked through an agent.

FROM THE UK & EUROPE
Air
At the time of writing, only the Spanish airline Iberia was flying direct between Europe (Madrid) and Mexico City. You can get flights (often at discount rates) with numerous other airlines such as Air France, KLM, Continental, United, American, Eastern, Aeroméxico and British Caledonian, but they all involve a stop and sometimes a change of plane on the way – usually in the USA. Some airlines such as Continental also offer fares to other destinations in Mexico like Cancún, Cozumel, Acapulco and Monterrey. For Guadalajara and Oaxaca you usually need to make an internal connection in Mexico – but for Mérida it's probably easier to fly to Miami (Virgin has some of the cheapest flights from London) and then on by Mexicana or Aeroméxico. The total London/Mérida return cost by this route starts from US$750. Most nationalities, by the way, are advised to have a US visa even if they're only changing planes there.

If you want to stop over in the USA on the way to Mexico, there are many options: several airlines including Continental, American, United and Aeroméxico serve Europe, the US and Mexico; or you can simply get a ticket to the US and buy another ticket to Mexico or the border from there. You may have to show 'sufficient funds' to enter the USA if you haven't already got an onward ticket.

The commonest types of ticket from Europe to Mexico are one-ways, fixed-date returns, open returns, circle trips and ticketed surface sectors. Most of them are available at discount rates from cheap ticket agencies in Europe's bargain flight centres like London, Amsterdam, Paris and Frankfurt.

Fixed-date returns (sometimes called excursion fares) require you to decide dates of travel when you buy the ticket. Open tickets allow you to choose your dates later; they're usually valid for 180 days or a year and are a bit more expensive than fixed-date returns. Circle trips and surface sectors are useful if you want to travel from one part of Mexico to another or between Mexico and elsewhere in the

Americas, without backtracking. On both you usually depart from and return to the same city in Europe: circle trips give you flights between your different destinations in Mexico or Latin America en route, while with surface sectors you make your own way between your entry and exit points in Latin America. Some bargain fares (notably with KLM) are only open to students, teachers or people under 26. Fares can also vary considerably between high and low seasons.

London For cheap tickets, pick up a copy of *Time Out, LAM* or any of the other magazines which advertise discount (bucket shop) flights, and check out a few of the advertisers. Agents which offer good-value fares to Mexico include Journey Latin America (tel (01) 747-3108) at 16 Devonshire Road, Chiswick, London W4 2HD (this company also has an information service for its customers and runs some small-group tours to Mexico); STA Travel (tel (01) 581-1022) at 74 Old Brompton Road, London W1 and 117 Euston Road, London NW1; and London Student Travel (tel (01) 730-3402) at 52 Grosvenor Gardens, London SW1.

Fares quoted by Journey Latin America at the time of writing are: London/Mexico City one-way (student, teacher or under 26) US\$375; London/Mexico City or Cancún or Cozumel or Monterrey or Acapulco one-way (anyone) US\$400, fixed-date return (up to 180 days) US\$710; London/Mexico City 180-day open return (student, teacher or under 26) US\$750; London/Mexico City one-year open return US\$775; six-month return from London with a surface sector available between any two of Mexico City, Cancún, Cozumel, Monterrey or Acapulco US\$710; London/Bogotá/Mexico City/London one-year circle trip US\$1160; London/Mexico City/Lima/London six-month circle trip (students or under 26) US\$1450; London/Santiago/Mexico City/London open-jaw US\$925.

An unusual and potentially interesting

route to Mexico is via Paris and Havana with the Cuban airline Cubana. Journey Latin America quotes around US\$650 one-way, US\$1050 return for this.

Elsewhere in Europe Discount tickets are available at prices similar to London's in several European cities. Amsterdam, Paris and Frankfurt are among the main cheap flight centres. Air France, KLM, Iberia and the Colombian airline Avianca are some of the airlines whose tickets are handled by discount agents. KLM, Air France and Iberia all offer surface sector fares between Europe and numerous places in Latin America (Iberia's are particularly good value), and Avianca has some interesting round-trip options.

The following agencies in various cities might be worth contacting for information on discounted flights:

London
    STA Travel, 74 Old Brompton Road, London SW7 (tel (01) 581-1022)
Amsterdam
    NBBS Reiswinkels, Dam No 17, Amsterdam (tel 020 237686)
Brussels
    ACOTRA, 38 rue de la Montagne, Brussels (tel 5134480)

Tours
Journey Latin America (tel (01) 747-3108), 16 Devonshire Road, Chiswick, London W4 2HD, runs a few small-group tours using local transport in Mexico. One two-week trip costing around US\$1600 from London takes in Mexico City, Teotihuacán, Oaxaca and nearby sites, San Cristóbal de Las Casas, Palenque, Mérida and some Maya sites in the Yucatán.

Explore Worldwide does a 24-night small-group trip with 'expert leaders', which includes Mexico City, Oaxaca, San Cristóbal de Las Casas, Palenque, Tikal, Belize City, Ambergris Cay, Mérida, Uxmal, Chichén Itzá, Sayil and Labna. The company has offices in Aldershot, England (tel (025) 231 9448); Sydney, Australia (tel (02) 290 3222); Remuera, Auckland, New Zealand (tel 545-118); Edmonton, Canada (tel (403) 439-9118); Oakland, California (tel (415)

654 1879); and Hong Kong (tel 5-225181). From London the trip costs about US$2100.

The Travel Business of Dulwich (tel (01) 299 0214) at 94 Dulwich Village, London SE 21 offers a tour covering Mexico City, the Copper Canyon railway trip and a week at a coastal resort for around US$2100.

Swan Hellenic offers a 20-day Mayan art treasures tour from London with 1st-class hotels and guest lecturers for US$3500.

Mancunia Travel of Manchester, England (tel (061) 228 2842) and Mississauga, Ontario (tel (416) 823-3640), specialises in religious destinations. Once a year this company runs a two-week trip (US$1600 from England) which takes you to the Basilica of Guadalupe in Mexico City plus Teotihuacán, Tula, Taxco and Acapulco.

FROM AUSTRALASIA

There are no direct flights from Australia to Mexico. The cheapest way of getting there is via the USA – often Los Angeles. Discount returns from Sydney to Los Angeles cost from US$850. Cheap flights from the USA to Mexico are hard to find in Australia. Regular Los Angeles/Mexico City fares are US$220 one-way, US$350 return – but you may be able to pick up cheaper tickets if you are stopping a day or two in Los Angeles. There are also numerous flights between North American cities and several other destinations in Mexico.

If you want to combine Mexico with South America, the cheapest return tickets from Sydney to Lima or Rio de Janeiro are about US$1920. Santiago and Buenos Aires are a little cheaper at about US$1860. If you want to fly into South America and out of the USA, or vice-versa, the best option is to get a return ticket to South America on an airline such as United, which flies to South America via the USA, and simply don't use one of the legs you have paid for. Fortunately, at the time of writing, United's fares for this route were much the same as those of airlines which go directly to South

America – discount returns via the States from Sydney to Buenos Aires, Lima, Santiago or Rio de Janeiro were all available at around US$1980 .

Round-the-world tickets with a Mexico option are sometimes available in Australia. STA Travel, with 40 offices around the country, is one of the most popular discount travel agents in Australia. It also has sales offices or agents all over the world.

FROM CANADA

Japan Airline's one-month excursion return fare between Vancouver and Mexico City is good value at US$340. Aeroméxico has non-stop flights between Acapulco and Montreal and Toronto.

FROM CENTRAL & SOUTH AMERICA & THE CARIBBEAN

Aeroméxico flies between Mexico City and Panama City, Caracas and Bogotá. Mexicana links Mexico City with Guatemala City, San Juan (Puerto Rico), Havana and San José (Costa Rica); it also has flights between San Juan and Cancún, and Havana and Mérida. Avianca, the Colombian airline, also links Mexico with South America. Cubana flies between Havana and Mexico City.

Ferries sail at least once a week between Guaymas and Santa Rosalía; Topolobampo (near Los Mochis), Mazatlán, Puerto Vallarta and La Paz; and Puerto Vallarta and Cabo San Lucas. Fares are ridiculously cheap for seats, cabins, automobiles, motorcycles and anything else you may want to transport. For specific fare and schedule information, see the sections on 'Santa Rosalía', 'La Paz' and 'Cabo San Lucas'.

Guatemala

Bus Buses run frequently from main points in Guatemala such as Guatemala City, Huehuetenango and Quezaltenango to the main border points of La Mesilla (near Ciudad Cuauhtémoc, Chiapas) and Talismán (near Tapachula, Chiapas).

The borders are usually open 24 hours but you may have to pay a few extra charges on the Guatemalan side if you want to go through the border before 9 am, after 6 pm or between noon and 2 pm. At night you'll probably also have to wait longer for onward transport into Mexico. (See the 'Chiapas' chapter for more detail on these border points.)

Boat The Flores/El Naranjo/La Palma/Tenosique river route from Guatemala to Mexico is a seven-hour bus ride from outside the San Juan Hotel in Santa Elena near Flores, Guatemala, to El Naranjo on the San Pedro River, upstream from El Progreso (still in Guatemala). There's one 'bad' hotel in El Naranjo. From El Naranjo the boat takes four to five hours to La Palma in Mexico and costs 25 quetzals. It goes most days (Saturday and Sunday are the least reliable) and leaves before 9 am. Guatemalan border control is at El Naranjo; Mexican border control is at the first settlement along the river after you cross the border. From La Palma it's about 1½ hours to Tenosique, Chiapas, by bus (US$0.50). There's usually a departure at about 4 pm. The traveller who told me this said the border formalities went smoothly. Before setting off, travellers should check the military situation on this border, which is sometimes affected by the guerrilla war in Guatemala.

LEAVING MEXICO
Buying Air Tickets
You can get information and make reservations on Mexicana flights at any time of day or night by calling 660-44-44 in Mexico City. Aeroméxico provides the same service at 553-48-88 or 553-15-77 in Mexico City from 6 am to midnight every day.

One-way tickets from Mexico City to London cost around US$320 with airlines like United, American and Continental. Fares to most other western European capitals are similar.

The simple fact of crossing the international border between Mexico and the USA tends to add a lot to the price of an air ticket, even if the extra distance travelled is small. With Mexicana or Aeroméxico for instance, Mexico City/San Diego is US$230 while Mexico City/Tijuana is US$135. It's therefore possible to save significantly by flying to a Mexican border town, making your own way across the border and picking up other transport once back in the USA.

Airport Tax
There's a US$10 departure tax (payable in pesos if you like) for all international departures. You pay it at your plane's last stop in Mexico.

To the USA
There are a few buses from places inside Mexico to towns on the US side of the border – but these cost considerably more than buses to the towns on the Mexican side, so it often pays just to go to, say, Matamoros, then make your own way over the international bridge to Brownsville in Texas.

To Guatemala
Most nationalities need visas to enter Guatemala, and while travellers have reported that these can be obtained at the border (even for citizens of the UK, with which Guatemala has been in a state of tension over the Belize issue), the situation is changeable. If you're unsure, the Guatemalan embassy in Mexico City is the best place to get a visa and find out if any other formalities are needed. There are also Guatemalan consulates in some southern Mexican cities, but these won't always issue visas or be open more than a few hours a week.

The two main border points are at Talisman near Tapachula and La Mesilla near Ciudad Cuauhtémoc, both in Chiapas. Mexican buses and local transport run pretty often to these borders, and frequent buses will take you on into Guatemala from the other side. Expect a few miscellaneous 'charges' on your way through Guatemalan customs or immigration – especially if you want to go through outside the 'regular working hours' of 9 am to noon and 2 to 6 pm.

Another possible route is by boat along the San Pedro River from La Palma in Tabasco to El Naranjo in Guatemala.

Be aware that a guerrilla war has been going on in northern Guatemala for years.

Getting Around

For journeys in Mexico by any means of transport at the peak travel periods of Semana Santa (the week before Easter) and Christmas/New Year it's wise to book as far ahead as possible.

AIR
Mexicana & Aeroméxico

These two Mexican airlines between them serve 50 cities and towns in Mexico as well as many others abroad. Flights are fairly frequent and though domestic fares rise daily as the peso slides, they're still good value. Mexico City to Oaxaca, for instance, costs US$44, Mexico City to San Luis Potosí US$30. Thus San Luis Potosí to Oaxaca, which requires making a connection at Mexico City, costs only US$55 – not bad for a journey that would otherwise involve about 14 hours on buses plus a trip across Mexico City from one bus terminal to another.

The only drawback is that both airlines are by-words for unreliability: delays are almost the norm.

Attempting to get from San Luis Potosí to Oaxaca in one day, we booked an 8 am departure from San Luis for the 45-minute flight to Mexico City, and an 11 am flight from Mexico City to Oaxaca. But the plane that was taking us out of San Luis didn't turn up until 10.20 and we didn't leave until 10.40. We asked for the Oaxaca flight to be held, without success. We landed at Mexico City at 11.25 to find that the Oaxaca flight had also left late, but not quite late enough. We arranged seats on another flight to Oaxaca that evening, Mexicana gave us a voucher for as much as we could consume in meals at the airport restaurant, and we filled the rest of the time with a quick taxi-and-bus trip to Teotihuacán.
- John Noble

Mexicana and Aeroméxico have ticket offices in every place they fly to and some other places too. You can get information and make reservations 24 hours a day on any Mexicana flight by calling Mexico City 660-44-44. Aeroméxico provides the same service at 553-48-88, 553-15-77 (also Mexico City) from 6 am to midnight every day.

Other Domestic Airlines
Aerocalifornia This airline which flies between Guadalajara, Los Mochis, Hermosillo and Tijuana doesn't serve Mexico City but has an office there at Reforma 332 (tel 514-66-78, 207-13-92). Aerocalifornia is commonly used by travellers headed to the Copper Canyon because Los Mochis is the train terminus for the Copper Canyon train to Chihuahua.

Aerovías Oaxaqueñas This tiny airline is one of the minor delights of travel in Mexico. It has just a couple of ageing 28-seat DC-3s which trundle once or twice most days between Oaxaca city and Puerto Escondido and Salina Cruz on the Oaxaca coast. Flights last half an hour and cost US$25 one way. The trips from Oaxaca city are spectacular as the twin-prop craft rumble over the mountains and down to the coastal plain. Take-off and landing are infinitely smoother than on any Mexicana or Aeroméxico jet. Leaving Puerto Escondido for Oaxaca, the plane makes a big loop out over the Pacific to gain height for the mountain crossing. It's an interesting alternative to the seven-hour bus haul between Oaxaca and the coast. Not surprisingly, seats are often booked up a week or more ahead. Aerovías Oaxaqueñas has offices in Oaxaca, Puerto Escondido and Salina Cruz and at Despacho 514, Balderas 32 (tel 510-01-62) in Mexico City.

Chartering Planes
You can charter planes at many Mexican airports but the only reason most travellers do so is to get to remote

archaeological sites like Bonampak and Yaxchilán in the Chiapas jungle. Four-seater aircraft to Bonampak and Yaxchilán may be chartered from Palenque, San Cristóbal de Las Casas or Tenosique in Tabasco. See the 'Chiapas' chapter for details.

John met an American in Puerto Escondido who said he'd not only chartered a plane to get there from Oaxaca but had piloted it over the mountains. He also said he was tripping on LSD at the time.

BUS

Buses are frequent, cheap and go almost everywhere. Not surprisingly, they're the most usual form of public transport. Local buses in towns are described under 'Local Transport' in this chapter. Long-distance buses vary enormously from comfortable, non-stop, air-conditioned 1st-class services to ancient, decaying, suspensionless ex-city buses that grind out their dying years on dirt tracks to remote settlements. Fortunately Mexico has not yet caught the compulsory high-volume video disease which afflicts bus travellers in many other parts of the world.

Most cities and towns now have a single bus station where all long-distance buses arrive and depart. This is called the Central Camionera, Central de Autobuses, Central de Camiones or simply El Central, and is usually a long way from the centre of town. This reduces heavy traffic downtown but is a lot less convenient for bus users, though frequent city buses often link bus station and town centre. Note the crucial difference between the Central (bus station) and the Centro (town centre). Sometimes there are separate Centrales for 1st and 2nd-class buses, and sometimes the different bus companies have their own terminals scattered around town – potentially confusing but at least these are usually close to the town centre.

Most bus lines have schedules posted in their bus station ticket offices, but these are by no means comprehensive, so always ask. There may well be more services than are listed – and even if your destination isn't listed, it may be en route to one that is. If for instance you're in Tampico and want to go to Tuxpan, to which there are few services listed but which is on the road to Poza Rica, ask if the Poza Rica buses (of which there are many) will stop at Tuxpan on the way.

On long journeys it helps to work out on which side the sun will be, and sit on the other side. It's also a good idea to get a seat where you can control the opening and shutting of the window – Mexicans often have odd ideas about what's too warm or too cool! And keep your luggage with you; if you let it go into the baggage compartment, the chances of not seeing it again increase, or it may come out covered in oil or chicken-shit.

There are various bus types and classes:

Primera (1a) clase 1st class, usually with air-conditioning, a comfortable numbered seat for each passenger, and a locked toilet to which the driver may or may not have a key. They make infrequent stops and serve all sizeable towns. You can usually book 1st-class tickets several days, even weeks, in advance, which is useful at busy times like Semana Santa and Christmas/New Year. Some offices of the ADO line even have computer terminals showing seating plans which enable you to choose your seat. Several different companies often operate on the same route, and fares – roughly US$1.30 per 100 km – differ insignificantly. Examples: Monterrey to Mexico City, 960 km, 12 hours, US$11.50; Mexico City to Oaxaca, 500 km, nine hours, US$6.75; Oaxaca to San Cristóbal de Las Casas, 620 km, 12 hours, US$7.75; Veracruz to Jalapa, 100 km, 2½ hours, US$1.50. Among the best 1st-class lines are ADO (east Mexico and Mexico City), Cristóbal Colón (the south-east and Mexico City) and Transportes del Norte (the north-east and Mexico City). In southern Oaxaca, '1st class' usually means what would elsewhere be called 2nd class.

Segunda (2a) clase 2nd class, older, tattier, less comfortable, more prone to break down than 1st class – and considerably slower because they'll stop anywhere for someone to get on or off. No apparent limit on capacity, which means that if you board mid-route you may have to stand. Often no tickets – you just pay the conductor, so beware of rip-offs. Fares are about 10% less than 1st class. The long-distance services of the 2nd-class line AU in the east and south-east can be almost as quick and comfortable as 1st-class buses; at the other extreme Flecha Amarilla (north-central Mexico) and Transportes Tuxtla Gutiérrez (south-east) are among the slowest, least comfortable and most unreliable, which is a pity because both of them dominate in areas where 1st-class buses are rare. In southern Oaxaca, '2nd class' means 3rd class.

Tercera (3a) clase 3rd class consists of old city buses with low seat-backs and poor suspension. In some areas these serve outlying villages.

Directo 'Non-stop' (1st class) between departure point and destination – which sometimes means a few stops anyway.

Semi-directo A few more stops than directo.

Ordinario Stops wherever passengers want to get on or off. 1st-class buses are never ordinario.

Express Ultra-directo.

Locales Buses which start their journeys from the town in which you start yours. They leave on time and have more seats available than they will at mid-route.

De paso Bus which started its journey somewhere else. Often late, and you may have to wait until it arrives before any tickets are sold.

RAIL

Advance reservations are necessary for all special accommodation such as sleepers and 1st-class reserved seats. Regular 1st and 2nd-class coach seats do not require reservations. Some intermediate stations have no sleeping-car space assigned for sale (San Miguel de Allende for example).

Stopovers are allowed at any point en route within the limit of the 1st-class ticket and upon request to ticket agents at

time of purchase, with payment of a 15% surcharge; sleeping arrangements must be made in these cases from point to point.

Sleeping Cars

Sections Lower and upper berths which during the day are converted into seats facing each other and at night are surrounded by heavy curtains.

Bedrooms One upper and one lower berth, washing facilities and sitting space in daytime in a private room.

Roomettes One lower berth and washing facilities in a private room.

Two adults and one child under five years of age are allowed to sleep in one lower berth. Up to four adults and one child are allowed in a section for the same price of sleeping accommodation.

Occupancy of sleepers in Mexico requires the following minimum number of adult 1st-class railroad tickets: bedroom – two, single roomette – one, lower berth – one, upper berth – one.

A through sleeper is operated between Mexico City and Nogales, Sonora, as well as between Mexico City and Mexicali, Baja California, on National Railways of Mexico train Nos 5-6, Pacific Railroad train Nos 1-2 and Sonora-Baja California Railway train Nos 3-4.

Cancellations should be made at least 24 hours before trains depart; otherwise no refund will be granted.

Dining-car service is available on National Railway train Nos 5-6 and 71-72, and on Pacific train Nos 1-2.

Fares

First-class railroad tickets entitle the ticket-holder to buy sleeping-car accommodation or to travel in 1st-class reserved-seat coaches where operated. These reserved seats have to be requested at the time of purchase.

First-class coach tickets entitle the ticket

Train Facilities

Train No	2nd class coach	1st class coach	1st class resrvd	lower berth	upper berth	roomettes	bdrm	dining car
252			•					•
71/72						•	•	•
1/2	•	•	•					
139/140	•	•						
111–114	•	•	•					
113/112	•	•						
51/52	•	•						
53/54	•	•	•					
102/101	•	•				•	•	
222/221	•	•						
49/50	•	•						
29/30	•	•						
27/28	•	•	•	•	•	•	•	
7/8	•	•	•	•	•	•	•	
55/56	•	•						
57/58	•	•						
5/6	•	•	•	•	•			
11/12	•	•						

Pacific Railroad

Train No	2nd class coach	1st class coach	1st class resrvd	lower berth	upper berth	roomettes	bdrm	dining car
1/2	•	•						
3/4	•	•						

Sonora-Baja California Railway

Train No	2nd class coach	1st class coach	1st class resrvd	lower berth	upper berth	roomettes	bdrm	dining car
1/2	•	•	•			•	•	•
3/4	•	•						

Chihuahua-Pacific Railway

Train No	2nd class coach	1st class coach	1st class resrvd	lower berth	upper berth	roomettes	bdrm	dining car
21/22	•							

holder to transportation in regular 1st-class coaches.

Second-class tickets entitle the ticket holder to transportation in 2nd-class coaches only.

Children Children aged between five and 12 years of age are charged one-half the adult fare plus a small fee for insurance when accompanied by a ticketed adult. One child under five years of age not occupying a separate seat may travel free with each ticketed adult.

For information concerning rail service and rates from Guatemala onward, contact International Railways, Avenida 10 & Calle 18, Zona 1, Guatemala City, Guatemala.

Baggage & Pets

Baggage weighing up to 50 kg can be checked in the baggage car on each full-fare 1st-class ticket. On a half-fare ticket you can check 25 kg.

Pets may be transported in baggage cars upon presentation of a veterinarian's certificate of rabies vaccination. They cannot travel in passenger cars.

Reservation Requests

Reservation requests must be presented in advance, in writing, stating exact dates of travel, number of passengers, accommodation desired and age of children, if any. They should be addressed to the representative at the border gateway where entry is planned, or to the railroad officer handling your starting point.

Following are the station officials to whom you should address your requests:

Mr Javier Sánchez Méndez, Chief Passenger Traffic Department, National Railways of Mexico, Buenavista Grand Central Station, 063858 Mexico DF (tel 547-89-72). For trips from Mexico City to any point in Mexico including railroad stations over the Pacific Railroad and Sonora-Baja California Railway. Also from: Monterrey, Veracruz, Chihuahua, Uruapan and Guadalajara to Mexico City.

Mrs Guadalupe Contreras de López, Commercial Agent, National Railways of Mexico, Passenger Station, Nuevo Laredo, Tamaulipas (tel 2-80-97); or PO Box 595, Laredo, Texas 78042, USA. For trips starting at Nuevo Laredo, Tamaulipas (opposite Laredo, Texas).

Mr A Barraza Silva, Commercial Agent, National Railways of Mexico, Ciudad Juárez, Chihuahua (tel 2-25-57); or PO Box 2200, El Paso, Texas 79951, USA. For trips originating at Ciudad Juárez.

Mr Francisco Hernández, Ticket Agent, Pacific Railroad, Calle Internacional No 10, Nogales, Sonora (tel 2-00-24). For trips from Nogales, Sonora to Sufragio, Culiacán, Mazatlán, Tepic, Guadalajara and Mexico City.

Mr Antonio Velarde Zatarain, General Passenger Agent, Pacific Railroad, Calle Tolsá 336, Guadalajara, Jalisco (tel 26-31-02). For trips from Guadalajara to Tepic, Mazatlán, Culiacán, Sufragio, Nogales and Mexicali.

Traffic Superintendent, Sonora-Baja California Railway, PO Box 182, Mexicali, Baja California (tel 7-23-86, 7-21-01); or PO Box 231, Calexico, California 92231, USA (tel (706) 567-2386). For trips from Mexicali to Sufragio, Culiacán, Mazatlán, Tepic, Guadalajara and Mexico City.

Mr Alfonso Avitia, General Freight & Passenger Agent, Chihuahua-Pacific Railway, PO Box 46, Chihuahua, Chihuahua (tel 2-22-84, 2-38-67). For trips on the Chihuahua Pacific Railway: Chihuahua, La Junta, Creel, San Rafael, Sufragio, Los Mochis.

Payment After one of these agents confirms your reservations, payment must be made in pesos in the form of a bank draft, cashier's check or certified check payable to National Railways of Mexico.

In 1987 a new deluxe train called *El Tapatío* was inaugurated for the Guadalajara to Mexico City route, complete with sleeping cars, dining cars and a bar car.

The principal train routes (including routes in the opposite directions) are:

Nogales to Benjamín Hill – stops en route at Magdalena and Santa Ana.
Mexicali to Benjamín Hill – stops en route at Coahuila, Puerto Peñasco and Caborca.
Benjamín Hill to Guadalajara – stops en route at Hermosillo, Empalme (Guaymas), Ciudad Obregón, Navajoa, Sufragio (junction with Los Mochis-Chihuahua/Copper Canyon train), Guamuchil, Culiacán, Quila, Mazatlán, Rosario, Escuinapa, Acaponeta, Tepic and Compostela.
Los Mochis to Chihuahua – stops en route at Sufragio, El Fuerte, Temoris, San Rafael, Divisadero, Creel, La Junta and Cuauhtémoc.
Ciudad Juárez to Mexico City – major stops en route include Chihuahua, Torréon, Zacatecas, Aguascalientes and Querétaro.
Nuevo Laredo to Mexico City – major stops en route at Monterrey, San Luis Potosí and Querétaro.
Mexico City to Uruapan – stops include Morelia and Pátzcuaro.

Mexico City to Veracruz
Mexico City to Mérida

For more information about these and various secondary routes, see the 'Getting There & Away' sections within each regional or state chapter. For the latest fare and schedule information, write to the station officials listed above.

FERRY
A fleet of ferries operates between Baja California and mainland Mexico, but in 1987 and 1988 the fleet was overloaded and becoming increasingly unreliable. The routes are: Guaymas/Santa Rosalía (daily), La Paz/Mazatlán (daily), La Paz/Topolobampo (four times weekly) and Cabo San Lucas/Puerto Vallarta (twice weekly). Refer to the 'Getting There & Away' sections under these cities for schedule and fare information.

CAR
Driving a car in Mexico is not as easy as in North America, but it is often easier and more convenient than the bus and sometimes the only way to get to some of the most beautiful places and isolated towns and villages. Wherever you drive in Mexico, whether it be in the cities and towns, on the highways or in the countryside, you must have a driver's licence, Mexican automobile insurance, an open mind about road conditions and lots of patience.

Driver's Licence & Car Permit
To drive in Mexico you must have a valid US, Canadian or International Driver's Licence (IDL). The US and Canadian licences are widely recognised in Mexico, but the IDL is not. In fact, if a policeman asks to see your licence and you show him the IDL, you will probably have to explain it to him.

A car permit is required only if you are driving south of Mexicali or Ensenada in Baja or planning to drive in mainland Mexico. The car permit also serves as a tourist card for the driver. Both can usually be validated at the checkpoint in Maneadero just south of Ensenada or at any border post. For more information about car permits and tourist cards, see the 'Facts for the Visitor' chapter.

Gasoline
All gasoline in Mexico is sold by government-controlled Pemex (Petróleos Mexicanos or Mexican Petroleum) stations at prices a few cents lower than American prices. Almost every town, village and major road junction has a Pemex station. Extra or unleaded gas is dispensed from silver pumps; Nova or regular gas is dispensed from blue pumps. Extra is sometimes difficult to find on the smaller highways and roads.

Road Conditions
In towns and cities you must be especially wary of stop *(alto)* signs, speed bump *(topes)* signs and potholes. These often appear when you least expect them.

Wide one-way streets in, for example, Tijuana are renowned for stop signs

Road signs

placed on one street corner or the other, but not on both. Consequently, if you are driving in the far left lane and a stop sign appears on the right corner, chances are you won't see the sign until you are already in the intersection. Sometimes *alto* signs aren't on the corners, but on the streets in bold painted letters just before intersections. If, though, you are looking for stop signs on the corners, chances are you won't see the painted letters. Catch-22! Drive slowly through town and you probably won't miss too many stop signs.

Speed-bump signs, speed bumps and potholes are also sometimes easy to miss. You'll know that you didn't see the signs if your car suddenly jolts and your head hits the roof. This can happen often if you don't develop an eye for distinguishing asphalt bumps from the asphalt road. Potholes can be equally difficult to notice, especially if they resemble mud puddles. These unobtrusive little puddles have been known to swallow and slash tires and crack a few axles. Again, drive slowly through town.

Highway driving is smoother, but still not without its problems and challenges. Some highways are toll roads and thus maintained in better condition than non-toll roads and highways. If you must go off the road and on to the highway shoulder, slow down and ease your car off the pavement. Be careful, though: the shoulder begins a few cm below the ledge-like pavement and then slopes steeply downward. Driving off the ledge too quickly will rattle your car as well as your nerves.

Help!

Whatever car problems you may have on the highways, Mexican government teams called *Ángeles Verdes* (Green Angels) are prepared to assist you. The Green Angels are bilingual mechanics in bright green trucks who patrol each major stretch of highway in Mexico at least twice daily searching for motorists in trouble. They can make minor repairs, replace small parts, provide gasoline and oil, arrange towing and other assistance by short wave and citizen band radio if necessary. Service is free, but parts, gasoline and oil are provided at cost. If you are near a telephone when your car has problems, you can contact them through their national 24-hour emergency hot-line number: 5-250-01-23.

Most serious mechanical car problems can be fixed efficiently and inexpensively by mechanics in towns and cities as long as the parts are available. On the other hand, don't expect miracles if your car's problems are linked to its state-of-the-art computerised systems. Volkswagens (without fuel-injection engines) are the easiest cars to have repaired in Mexico.

Off-Road Driving

Beyond the paved highways and streets, much of Mexico, especially Baja, is criss-crossed by hundreds of miles of rough dirt roads and paths. A few can be traversed in an ordinary passenger car, but for most you should have a four-wheel drive with high ground clearance. Wherever you go in the back-country, your trip is bound to be an adventure. You must be well prepared and travel only in a vehicle which is in excellent condition.

Renting a Car

Renting a car is possible in most of Mexico's cities. Hertz, Avis, Budget and National car-rental agencies are well represented across the country, and there are several local agencies. Their daily rates vary from about US$19.10 to US$37.45 depending on the agency, when and how long you rent the car, the amount of insurance you want, the number of km you plan to drive, whether you make your reservations in the USA or in Mexico, where you return the car, etc. Since rates and special deals change almost daily, call each agency toll free in the USA: Hertz, (800) 654-3131; National, (800)

328-4567; Budget, (800) 527-0700; and Avis, (800) 331-2112.

Small private car-rental agencies operate in many cities. Their rates tend to be slightly lower, but as with the USA-based companies they change frequently so shop around. Prices vary widely from town to town – they're notoriously high in Oaxaca – and local agencies tend to be a bit cheaper than the big names. If you can find a reasonable deal, and two or three people to share the costs with, car hire can be economical. It's certainly useful if you want to visit several different places in a short time, or to go off the beaten track where public transport is slow or scarce.

You usually pay a fixed rate, plus insurance, per day, and an extra fee for each km you drive. For one day and 200 km in a Volkswagen Sedan – usually the cheapest car available – this works out to US$30 to US$35. On top of that you pay for your own petrol, and a hefty deposit (frequently more than your probable final bill) is usually demanded. In some towns like San Miguel de Allende, Oaxaca and San Cristóbal de Las Casas, the supply of rental cars isn't equal to demand and you often have to book a week or more ahead. You should be ready to produce a driver's licence and some other ID – though they may not be required – and ensure that the price you're quoted includes all taxes, etc. You should also get a signed rental agreement, and read its small print.

HITCHING

Hitch-hiking is relatively easy in Mexico as long as you stick to the highways and main roads, have a sign and don't look scruffy. Don't be surprised if you're asked to pay the driver.

LOCAL TRANSPORT

Taxi

Taxis are common in towns and cities and are often surprisingly economical – useful if you have a lot of baggage, or need to get from A to B quickly, or are worried about theft on public transport. In Mexico City they're usually yellow Volkswagen Beetles. Some taxis, especially in Mexico City, have meters – but the meter fare usually has to be converted in line with a chart which should be displayed in the vehicle. If a taxi has a meter, ask the driver if it's working *('Funciona el taxímetro?')* and if it's not, establish the price before getting in. For a 10-minute journey, US$0.75 is a fair price.

Taxis may be outwardly indistinguish-able from colectivos or peseros (see below).

Combi, Colectivo & Pesero

These light green or white minibuses or minivans have functions halfway between those of a taxi and a bus. They run along set routes – sometimes displayed on the windscreen – and will pick you up or drop

you on any corner along that route. Go to the curb and wave your hand when you see one. As the driver approaches, he may indicate how many places are free by holding up the appropriate number of fingers. Tell the driver where you want to go and pay at the end of the trip. The fare depends on how far you go; they're cheaper than taxis, quicker and less crowded than buses. In Mexico City most peseros are lime-green minibuses.

Local Bus

Generally known as *camiones*, local buses are the cheapest way of getting around cities and to nearby villages. They run everywhere, are dirt cheap (within a city the fare is rarely more than 20c) and as often as not are noisy, dirty and crowded. In cities they halt only at specific points *(paradas)*, which may or may not be marked. Mexico City buses are notorious haunts of thieves and pick-pockets, so be careful.

Bicycle

Cycling is an increasingly popular way for foreigners to tour Mexico. Intrepid cyclists have begun taking tours of isolated areas such as the Vizcaíno peninsula in Baja California (offered each winter by The Touring Exchange, PO Box 265, Port Townsend, Washington 98368, USA). Thrill-seeking masochistic cyclists are also riding the entire length of the peninsula, sometimes alone. In 1986 a 19-year-old German named Steffen Layer was one such cyclist.

Steffen started his journey in San Francisco, crossed the border at Tijuana and eventually rode all the way to Cabo San Lucas. This was his first ever overnight bicycle journey. His bicycle was loaded with a tent, sleeping bag, tools, spare tyre tubes and tyres, food, several jugs of water, a first-aid kit and many other supplies. He often camped in the desert; rattlesnakes and scorpions were occasionally a problem. Boredom was a bigger problem, especially on long roads through

the desert. After three weeks of pedalling through Baja he made it to Cabo San Lucas.

This is not a trip for every cyclist. You must be in top physical shape and have excellent equipment which you can repair on your own, sometimes in the middle of nowhere. Bicycle shops are found only in the big cities and are too small to help you with complicated parts and repairs.

Cycling on the highways and roads in mainland Mexico is not recommended because drivers can become maniacs behind the wheels of fast-moving vehicles. True to the character of *machismo*, vehicles becomes extensions of themselves, so they've got to look tough. Consequently – cyclists beware!

Finding Your Way in Cities

The person-in-the-street in Mexico is no more likely than anyone else in the world to know the name of the street, let alone the way to the one you're looking for. However, Mexicans have an excuse, since thanks to different governments' varying ideas about who the nation's heroes were, any Mexican street is likely to have at least two names – both of them hard to remember, like Calle Maximilian Avila Camacho or Boulevard Niños Héroes Ferrocarrileros, and both destined to evaporate 50 metres further on. There the street may take on yet another identity such as Avenida Doctor Alfonso Ibarguengoitia, before metamorphosing into Calzada Diagonal Sur Xicoténcatl as it leaves the downtown area and continues out of the city altogether as Carretera Periférico Aguascalientes-Coatzacoálcos.

On the other hand some cities whose streets are on right-angle grid plans dispense with real names and just call their streets 1 Norte, 2 Norte, 1 Oriente, 2 Oriente (1 North, 2 North, 1 East, 2 East) and so on. Simple though this sounds, in practice it can be confusing, for in many cities the system of allocating these names defies human understanding (see the sections on Puebla and Orizaba.

When asking directions, it's better to ask for a specific place, such as the Hotel Central, the Museo Regional or the Correos, rather than the street it's on. To achieve any degree of certainty, ask three people and take the average.

Mexico City

Population of Mexico City: 9,500,000
Population of Greater Metropolitan Area: 18,000,000

Mexico City is a place to both love and loathe. It has everything you would expect in a city that's the world's largest metropolitan area (2018 square km or 779 square miles) and second largest city (after Shanghai, but this claim is disputed). Like mysterious ingredients added to a bubbling cauldron, the best and worst of the country have been combined in the high, flat valley where what is now considered Mexico City continually grows upward and outward. The result is a bustling cosmopolitan megalopolis of music and noise, brown air and green parks, colonial palaces, world-renowned museums, sprawling slums and much, much more.

History

As early as 10,000 BC, humans and animals were attracted to the shores of what was eventually called Lake Texcoco. Until 7500 BC when the lake began drying up, it was a hunting haven for early humans in the Valley of Mexico because many animals, including mammoths and bison, used it as a watering place. Although the lake didn't completely dry up, the change brought fewer animals and prompted people to begin farming and establishing small permanent settlements along the shores. The farms expanded, food production increased and the settlements grew as more sophisticated farming techniques such as the *chinampas* or floating gardens (versions of which are still seen in Xochimilco near Mexico City) were used.

Although a loose federation of farming villages evolved around Lake Texcoco by approximately 200 BC, their influence in the region palled compared to Teotihuacán

or 'Place of the Gods', a rapidly developing city-complex of immense pyramids and temples to the north-east. Teotihuacán fell in 650 AD, leaving a power vacuum that was not to be filled until the Toltecs, a nomadic Chichimec tribe from north of the Valley of Mexico, founded Tula 81 km (50 miles) north-west of present-day Mexico City.

By the 12th century the Tula empire had also collapsed, leaving yet another vacuum in the Valley of Mexico or, as the Indians called it then, the Valley of Anáhuac, which means 'near the water'. The Lake Texcoco villages had by this time evolved into small city-states, all of which were vying for control of the valley. It was another Chichimec tribe invading from the north, though, that eventually won the power struggle.

These latest arrivals were called Mexica ('meh-SHEE-kah') or Aztecs. At first they settled on the hill of Chapultepec, but other valley inhabitants strongly objected to certain Aztec practices such as wife-stealing, human sacrifice and interference in the volatile relations between the various city-states. By the early 14th century King Coxcox, the leader of Culhuacán, had pushed the Aztecs on to poor land, but he offered to resettle them on better land if they helped him in a battle against Xochimilco. The Aztecs won the battle and sent King Coxcox 8000 human ears as gruesome proof of their victory.

The King granted the Aztecs land and even complied with their request to make his daughter an Aztec queen and goddess, though he didn't know what this was to entail. As described in *The Course of Mexican History* by Michael Meyer and William Sherman,

... the princess was sacrificed and flayed. When her father attended the banquet in his honour, he was horrified to find that the entertainment included a dancer dressed in the skin of his daughter. Having finally had enough of the Aztecs, Coxcox raised an army which scattered the barbarians . . . .

Between 1325 and 1345 – historians disagree over the exact year – the Aztecs came to believe that Huitzilopochtli, one of their gods, had sent them a signal by causing an eagle, which was eating a snake, to land on a *tenuch* or cactus on an island in Lake Texcoco. They interpreted this to mean that the island should become Tenochtitlán or the 'Place for the High Priest of Tenuch'.

Tenochtitlán became a sophisticated city-state, which over the next century and a half was the centre of an empire that extended throughout central and southern Mexico. From 1450 to 1455, though, the empire was beset with terrible floods and famines caused by what the Aztec priests thought were angry gods. To appease the gods, daily rituals of human sacrifice were institutionalised to assure a steady supply of human hearts. The priests had problems in procuring enough victims, so they formed a pact with the neighbouring city-state of Tlaxcala. They agreed to wage *xochiyaoyotl* or 'flowery wars', with rules that specified limited battles for the express purpose of taking live prisoners who would then be sacrificed to the gods.

In 1487 these sacrificial rituals were performed at a frenzied pace to dedicate a new temple to the blood-thirsty god Huitzilopochtli. Meyer and Sherman write in *The Course of Mexican History*:

In a ceremony lasting four days sacrificial victims taken during campaigns were formed in four columns, each stretching three miles. At least twenty thousand human hearts were torn out to please the god . . . . In the frenzy of this ghastly pageant, the priests were finally overcome by exhaustion . . . .

Aside from appeasing the gods, these rituals also probably served to intimidate the Aztecs' potential rivals. The resulting peace and prosperity allowed them to build an immense city of canals, streets, causeways, botanical gardens, ponds, zoos, pyramids and temples. At the centre was a double pyramid dedicated to Huitzilopochtli, which today is the great plaza known as the zócalo. By the early 16th century the population was estimated at 100,000. This was the city the Spanish saw when they arrived in 1519.

The Fall of Tenochtitlán In 1519 the Spanish explorer Hernán Cortés set sail from Cuba for Mexico. At Tenochtitlán the Aztec emperor Moctezuma II discouraged a meeting with Cortés but eventually invited him to stay. After a series of events leading to an attack by the Spanish and a counter-attack by the Aztecs, Cortés retreated to Tlaxcala and plotted the destruction of Tenochtitlán. On 10 May 1521 Cortés, his soldiers and Indian allies began their attack. The battles raged until Tenochtitlán fell on 13 August 1521. What had not already been destroyed by the fighting was ordered levelled by Cortés. Bricks and stones from the rubble were used to build the capital of New Spain – Mexico City.

The Rise of Mexico City At first, Cortés ruled over the city as governor and captain general and directed its reconstruction, but by 1524 he was replaced with royal officials sent by King Charles V of Spain because of his past insubordination. In 1527 Spanish judges who had served in *audiencias* – omnipotent groups with broad legislative, executive and judicial functions – replaced the officials in Mexico City. Reconstruction of the city was somewhat stymied by the judges because most of their efforts seemed directed at destroying what Cortés had created. By 1528 King Charles realised that what he really needed in New Spain was a 'vice-king' or viceroy who would supplant the past influence of Cortés.

The first viceroy, Antonio de Mendoza,

did not arrive until 1535, but once he was installed in power, Mexico City developed quickly as the capital of New Spain. By 1550, the last year of Mendoza's rule, Mexico City was the beautiful, thriving capital of a viceroyalty that extended as far south as Panama. Streets were carefully laid out and baroque-style buildings constructed according to Spanish designs with local materials such as tezontle, a light red, porous volcanic rock that the Aztecs had used to build their temples. Hospitals, schools, churches, palaces, cathedrals, parks, a university and even an insane asylum were built.

From 1550 until struggles for independence from Spain began in 1821, 60 viceroys ruled over New Spain from Mexico City. During the 16th and 17th centuries the economy began to flourish under the centralised political control of the viceroys, but not without problems. In 1624 a rift developed between the viceroy and the archbishop because of political and religious rivalries. The archbishop excommunicated the viceroy who in turn banished the archbishop, thus precipitating violent protests in Mexico City from the many supporters of the prelate. Many people died and several government buildings were damaged or destroyed in the ensuing riot. Similarly violent riots occurred again in 1692 due, in part, to severe food shortages caused by crop failures. The viceregal palace (now the National Palace) and several other government buildings were destroyed. Throughout this period and even up to the late 19th century, Mexico City was also threatened by severe floods caused by the partial destruction in the 1520s of the Aztecs' drainage canals. Lake Texcoco often overflowed into the city, damaging streets and buildings necessitating the relocation of thousands of people.

Surprisingly, despite the frequent inundation of the city construction was continual in the 17th and 18th centuries. Architectural forms and styles remained the most outward sign of continuous cultural and political links to Spain. This was most evident in the dramatic and riotous decorations of church façades, particularly those of the Church of Santo Domingo, the Sagrario chapel and the Templo de la Santísima, near the zócalo of Mexico City. This extremely decorative style was considered ultra-baroque and named 'churrigueresque' after its originator, Spanish architect José Churriguera. It was perhaps reflective of excessive Spanish control over the politics, economy and society of what, by the 18th century, had become a uniquely Mexican society.

Independence from Spain By the early 1800s, demonstrations and revolts began to whittle away Spanish control over New Spain. Since Mexico City was the seat of Spanish power in the colony, control over the city became the principal objective of the independence movement. On 30 October 1811, parish priest Miguel Hidalgo y Costilla, whose *Grito* or cry for independence is considered one of the main catalysts of the independence struggle, led an unsuccessful march on Mexico City with 80,000 peasant-soldiers. Two years later, parish priest José María Morelos y Pavón attempted to encircle Mexico City with rebels, but the Spaniards broke through his defences.

Sporadic fighting continued until 1821, when Viceroy Agustín de Iturbide defected and conspired with the rebels to declare independence from the Spanish crown. By September 1821 a compromise called the Plan de Iguala had been worked out between various factions in New Spain and Iturbide entered Mexico City to assume control as Emperor Agustín I. Two years later he was booted from power and a 'United States of Mexico' was formed by a three-man junta. A decade later, General Antonio López de Santa Anna was voted in as president. His tenure marked the beginning of a 22-year period of severe political instability in which the presidency changed hands 36 times, 11 times to Santa Anna.

Meanwhile, Mexico City and the rest of the country were falling apart as battles with Texas evolved into border disputes and, by 1846, war with the USA. The loss of land to the US precipitated the Revolution of Ayutla, the ousting of Santa Anna from power in 1855 and a violent three-year civil war starting in 1858. Two capitals were established – Mexico City for the conservatives and Veracruz for the liberals. By 1860 liberals led by Benito Juárez had taken control of Mexico City and in early 1861 installed Juárez in power; he was officially elected in March 1861.

When Juárez entered office, the country was in shambles and heavily in debt to England, France and Spain. All three countries temporarily occupied Mexico to collect their debts, but France went further and sent Austrian archduke Ferdinand Maximilian of Hapsburg to Mexico City in 1864 to rule as emperor of Mexico, forcing Juárez and his government to withdraw from power. By early 1867, however, most of the French troops had left Mexico and Maximilian surrendered to Juárez. He was executed on 19 June 1867.

By this time Mexico City was a booming city of 200,000 that was quickly being transformed into an urban monster of both great beauty and extreme ugliness. On the one hand, various social problems such as prostitution, crime and begging had increased dramatically. Flooding and a lack of adequate drainage created pools of stagnant water alongside fetid open sewers in the streets. Until the 1870s, various Mexican governments seemed unable to deal with Mexico City's problems and instead offered escapes to affluent suburbs such as Tacubaya and lush green parks like the gas-lit Alameda Park.

The Reign of Díaz Porfirio Díaz came to power in 1876 and ushered in an unprecedented building boom in Mexico City. He solved the city's drainage problem by commissioning the British company S Pearson & Son, Ltd to construct a 48-km canal and 10-km tunnel in and around Mexico City. Paseo de la Reforma was redesigned after the Champs Élysées of Paris. Buildings and other boulevards were built with plans adapted from those used by architect Baron Haussman in many parts of Paris. Statues and huge monuments such as the Niños Héroes monument were erected. Most of the city had electricity, street-cars and cabs were plentiful, and several new hotels and hospitals had been completed by the time Díaz gave one of his last orders – the construction of yet another monument, a column topped with a gold angel in honour of Mexico's independence.

Díaz's lavish concern for monuments and modernisation had been concentrated in Mexico City at the expense of the rest of the country. Not surprisingly, his actions precipitated a revolution, a civil war and his overthrow by Francisco Madero in May 1911.

Revolution Madero was unable to create a stable government and contain the various factions fighting for power throughout the country. By February 1913 the fighting had spread to the streets of Mexico City as two rebel leaders and their soldiers took control of the Ciudadela, a major army arsenal in the city. From 9 February to 18 February – a period now called the *decena trágica* or 10 tragic days – the city was pounded by artillery fire. Thousands of civilians and soldiers were killed and many buildings were destroyed. The fighting ended only after US Ambassador to Mexico Henry Wilson negotiated for a general under Madero, Huerta, to support the rebels in deposing Madero's government. As Madero and his vice president José María Pino Suárez were executed by the rebels, Huerta stepped into the ensuing power vacuum to take control of the government.

For the next seven years Mexico City

was unable to fully recuperate because war and civil strife raged throughout the country. The 1920s ushered in a modicum of peace and prosperity as political stability was regained and the economy rebuilt. Álvaro Obregón served as president from 1920 to 1924 and, through his Minister of Education José Vasconcelos, stimulated a significant trend in Mexican art.

Recovery Vasconcelos commissioned Mexico's top artists – Diego Rivera, David Alfaro Siqueiros and José Clemente Orozco – to paint murals on the walls of several public buildings. The murals were intentionally painted with dramatic colours and scenes to convey a clear sense of Mexico's past and present, especially during the world Depression. Today, these and other murals painted in subsequent years are on display throughout Mexico City.

The growth and reconstruction of Mexico City were temporarily stymied by the Depression, but by 1940 a drive to industrialise was attracting more people – 1,726,858 by 1940 – and money to the city. In the 1940s and '50s factories and skyscrapers rose almost as quickly as Mexico City's population, which was growing at an average annual rate of 7%.

1960s to the Present Despite the continuation of this rapid economic growth into the 1960s, political and social reform lagged far behind. The government of President Gustavo Díaz Ordaz (1964-1970) made an already bad situation worse by yielding to PRI pressure in firing the new liberal-minded president of the PRI, Carlos Madrazo, and nullifying elections in Baja California when opposition candidates won office. Groups of university students in Mexico City were the first to express their outrage at the system.

Protest demonstrations began at the National University in the spring of 1966, but were quelled by federal troops. The discontent came to a head as Mexico City prepared for the 1968 summer Olympics. More than half a million students rallied in Mexico City's zócalo on 27 August. A few weeks later on 2 October the Olympics had already begun, and at the Plaza de las Tres Culturas protesters were encircled by riot police. To this day, no one is certain how many people died in the ensuing melee, but estimates have been put at 300 to 400.

Mexico City in the 1970s continued to expand and spread into the surrounding Federal District. In the mid-1970s rises in world oil prices spawned an economic boom in the city that also brought political corruption.

Petroleum was regarded as the panacea of Mexico's economic ills, but when the price dropped there was an economic recession and in the early 1980s people migrated in droves from the countryside hoping to find work in Mexico City. With less attention being paid to the agricultural sector, the government had to begin importing food. This occurred as the population of metropolitan Mexico City began increasing at an annual rate of 700,000, or 2000 people daily. This means that Mexico City's population increases annually by more than the population of San Francisco or Boston.

People have continued to flow into Mexico City at about the same rate despite the earthquake on 19 September 1985 which registered eight on the Richter Scale, caused more than US$4 billion in damage to hundreds of buildings in Mexico City, displaced thousands of people and killed at least 8000. Earthquake-damaged buildings, some on the verge of collapse, are still visible throughout the city.

In 1986 the population of Mexico City and surrounding areas was estimated at 18 million, with a daily increase of 3000, making it one of the world's most densely populated metropolitan areas. The United Nations estimates that by the year 2000 the population will be at least 37 million.

The effects of overcrowding have been predictable. Crime has risen to the point where a robbery is committed every five minutes and a murder every 90 minutes. The one million-plus vehicles on the streets daily create grid-locked traffic that, with the presence of heavy industry in metropolitan Mexico City, produces some of the worst smog in the world.

Mexico City is the centre of Mexico's industry, retail businesses, banking, transportation and communications. There are more than 450 industrial plants – about half the country's industries – in the metropolitan area. Tourism is also a big industry: more than one million tourists visit annually. As much as 70% of the country's banking transactions occur here. The city has five television stations, 20 daily newspapers, whose circulation in Mexico City accounts for more than half of the country's total, and 30 radio stations.

With so much commerce concentrated here, it is hardly surprising that hundreds of thousands of people continue to migrate and settle in the metropolitan area. Because of this concentration of power the citizens of Mexico City have been given a slightly derogatory nickname – *chilangos* – by the rest of the country. As a group, *chilangos* are traditionally unpopular in the rest of the country, no doubt because of jealousy and resentment.

Geography & Orientation

Like the spreading tentacles of a mammoth, growing octopus, Mexico City's 350 *colonias* or neighbourhoods and suburbs have spread across the ancient lake beds of the Valley of Mexico to form a densely populated city, federal district and state. At an altitude of 2309 metres (7525 feet) above sea level, the valley is hemmed in by mountain ranges: the Sierra Nevada volcanoes of Iztacíhuatl 5286 metres (17,340 feet) and Popocatépetl 5452 metres (17,887 feet) to the east, the Sierra de las Cruces to the west, the Sierra de Pachuca to the north, and the Serranía del Ajusco to the south. Because of Mexico City's expansion, the city's borders are hard to map.

For the purposes of this book, starting from the ancient and traditional city centre called the zócalo or Plaza de la Constitución, Mexico City stretches south to the suburbs of Tlalpan and the 'floating gardens' of Xochimilco, north to Tlalnepantlá and Tenayuca, east to the International Airport, and west to the Plaza El Toreo and Hipódromo Las Américas. The main area of interest in central Mexico City for travellers and tourists is concentrated around the zócalo, then west to an area called the Alameda and south-west to the zona rosa and the Bosque de Chapultepec.

You could also easily spend days wandering around the many interesting places in the south of the city. The old Spanish-built villages of San Angel and Coyoacán, now well within the city, have markets, plazas, parks, cafés, restaurants, shops and some fascinating galleries and museums – including the former homes of Trotsky and Diego Rivera. Further south, the modern splendour of the University City and the ancient site of Cuicuilco stand in a lava field called El Pedregal.

Getting around central Mexico City is relatively easy because ever since the Aztecs founded their city of Tenochtitlán (in the area now called the zócalo) in the 14th century, streets have been arranged in a grid-like pattern to run north-south or east-west.

Street names and numbers, however, can be confusing because both change as the street goes from one *colonia* or neighbourhood to the next. Also, maps and residents vary in their classification of streets. For example, Mexico City's streets are known as *calles* ('streets' in Spanish), *calzadas* (avenues or highways), *avenidas* (avenues), *ejes* (axes), *paseos* (boulevards) or, more often than not, as just a name. Fortunately the street names within a colonia do have some organisation. For example, many of the streets near the zócalo are named after Latin American countries while streets near the zona rosa are named after European cities.

In the central area, Avenida Lázaro Cárdenas and 34-km Avenida Insurgentes run north-south roughly marking the east-west boundaries of the city's central *colonias*. Names change and numbers revert to zero as the streets go west from the zócalo and cross Lázaro Cárdenas. For example, Francisco Madero becomes Avenida Benito Juárez and Tacuba becomes Hidalgo as they go west across Lázaro Cárdenas. This area from around the zócalo to Lázaro Cárdenas is packed with historical sites and, for the sake of organisation, will be referred to as 'the zócalo'.

Going west from Lázaro Cárdenas is an area dominated by the Alameda Park and the Plaza de la República that will be referred to as 'the Alameda'. It is roughly bounded on the east by Avenida Insurgentes and on the north by Mina. For this book, only the area south-east of Paseo de la Reforma and due south of Alameda Park will be considered part of the Alameda area. Although this latter area was particularly hard-hit by the earthquake, there are still many good budget hotels concentrated here as well as just north of Alameda Park and near the Plaza de la República.

From the north-west corner of Alameda Park, the Paseo de la Reforma – the widest street in Mexico City – passes south-west through one of the city's most affluent business and tourism districts – the zona rosa or pink zone – and into the Bosque de Chapultepec (referred to here as Chapultepec Park). There are several luxury and tourist-class hotels and restaurants on Paseo de la Reforma and nearby side streets. The most deluxe and thus most expensive establishments are in the heart of the zona rosa, which is mostly south-east of Paseo de la Reforma, west of Avenida Insurgentes and north of Avenida Chapultepec. This area will be referred to as Chapultepec Park and the zona rosa.

South of the zona rosa lie Mexico City's poshest suburbs: Tacubaya, San Ángel, Coyoacán, Lomas de Chapultepec (Chapultepec Hills), Ciudad Universitaria, the Bosque del Pedregal and Tlalpan.

North of the zócalo and the Alameda is a historic area called Tlatelolco where the Plaza de las Tres Culturas and the Basilicas of Guadalupe are located.

To the east of the zócalo is the Benito Juárez International Airport, easily accessible by taxi or metro. See the Getting There & Away section later in this chapter for more information.

Smog The severity of air pollution in Mexico City is due to a climatic phenomenon called thermal inversion, whereby the layer of smog traps the air below it and further reduces the amount of oxygen. This can usually happen several times a year in Mexico City. When it happened a couple of times in London in the 1950s, some people died; most of them were already suffering from severe asthma, bronchitis or other breathing problems. On an average day, breathing the air in Mexico City is, for a non-smoker, equivalent to smoking two packs of cigarettes.

Theft
Mexico City's buses and metro are notorious stomping grounds for pickpockets and thieves, particularly when they're crowded – and unsuspecting foreigners are among the most common victims. Any tightly packed crowd is a risk since you may not notice a hand dipping into your pocket in the crush.

Thieves often work in groups of two or three. One of them may drop something and cause a crush or melee looking for it, while a colleague picks a pocket or two in the process. At other times, one of them will try to pull your bag from your hand, and while you're struggling to keep hold of it a second person will pick your pocket. Yet another trick is to push and shove so that people lose balance and ease their

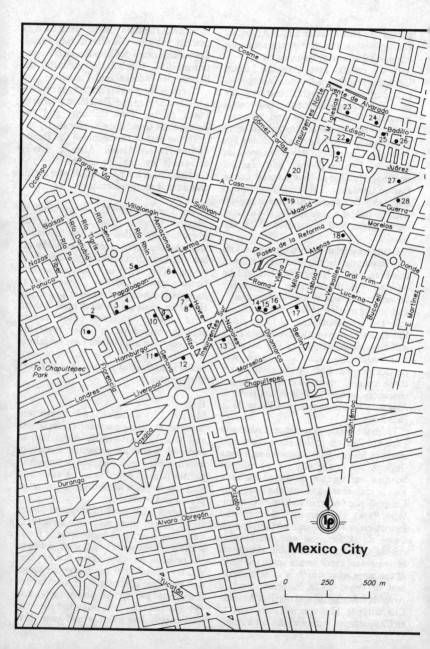

Mexico City

0   250   500 m

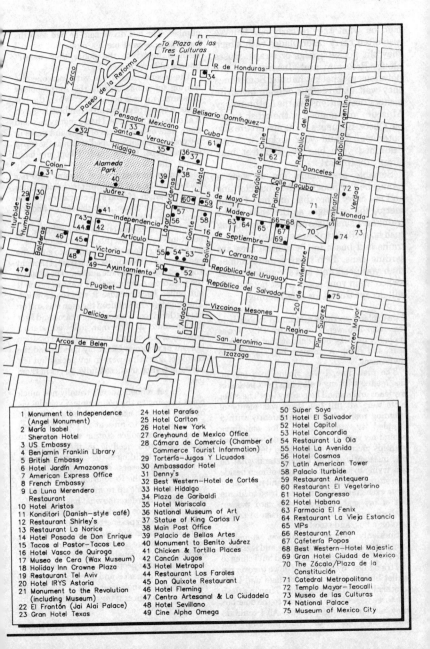

1 Monument to Independence
  (Angel Monument)
2 María Isabel
  Sheraton Hotel
3 US Embassy
4 Benjamin Franklin Library
5 British Embassy
6 Hotel Jardín Amazonas
7 American Express Office
8 French Embassy
9 La Luna Merendero
  Restaurant
10 Hotel Aristos
11 Konditori (Danish-style café)
12 Restaurant Shirley's
13 Restaurant La Norice
14 Hotel Posada de Don Enrique
15 Tacos al Pastor—Tacos Leo
16 Hotel Vasco de Quiroga
17 Museo de Cera (Wax Museum)
18 Holiday Inn Crowne Plaza
19 Restaurant Tel Aviv
20 Hotel IRYS Astoria
21 Monument to the Revolution
  (including Museum)
22 El Frontón (Jai Alai Palace)
23 Gran Hotel Texas

24 Hotel Paraíso
25 Hotel Carlton
26 Hotel New York
27 Greyhound de Mexico Office
28 Cámara de Comercio (Chamber of
  Commerce Tourist Information)
29 Tortería—Jugos Y Licuados
30 Ambassador Hotel
31 Denny's
32 Best Western—Hotel de Cortés
33 Hotel Hidalgo
34 Plaza de Garibaldi
35 Hotel Mariscala
36 National Museum of Art
37 Statue of King Carlos IV
38 Main Post Office
39 Palacio de Bellas Artes
40 Monument to Benito Juárez
41 Chicken & Tortilla Places
42 Cancún Jugos
43 Hotel Metropol
44 Restaurant Los Faroles
45 Don Quixote Restaurant
46 Hotel Fleming
47 Centro Artesanal & La Ciudadela
48 Hotel Sevillano
49 Cine Alpha Omega

50 Super Soya
51 Hotel El Salvador
52 Hotel Capitol
53 Hotel Concordia
54 Restaurant La Ola
55 Hotel La Avenida
56 Hotel Cosmos
57 Latin American Tower
58 Palacio Iturbide
59 Restaurant Antequera
60 Restaurant El Vegetarino
61 Hotel Congresso
62 Hotel Habana
63 Farmacia El Fenix
64 Restaurant La Vieja Estancia
65 VIPs
66 Restaurant Zenon
67 Cafetería Popos
68 Best Western—Hotel Majestic
69 Gran Hotel Ciudad de Mexico
70 The Zócalo/Plaza de la
  Constitución
71 Catedral Metropolitana
72 Templo Mayor—Teocalli
73 Museo de las Culturas
74 National Palace
75 Museum of Mexico City

hold on what they're carrying. Thieves also often carry razor blades with which they slit pockets, bags or straps. Buses along Reforma and Insurgentes are notorious pickpocket haunts. Sometimes they wait at bus stops outside favourite visitors' destinations like the Anthropology Museum and pounce in the crush to get on. Check-in queues at the airport are also notorious. While your ticket is being examined your bag by your feet may simply disappear!

Sensible precautions are to wear a money belt or pouch *under* your clothing and not carry more than one bag. On the metro, the carriages at the ends of the trains are usually less crowded, but during rush hours (6.30 to 9 am and 4 to 7 pm) all trains and buses in the central area are sardine cans. Don't carry more money than you need and leave your valuables locked up in your hotel. Most hotel desks will accept things for safe-keeping.

I was subject to three attempted robberies in less than two weeks in Mexico City. I was probably unlucky but it shows that the risk is real and that a money belt is a wise investment.

The first time, I was sitting in a bus on Insurgentes with my wallet in a front pocket of my jeans and a small bag on my lap. The other seats were all full but there was plenty of standing room. A youth, apparently with a crippled leg, started looking for something behind my seat. I looked too and found a card with his picture on it, which he then showed me, insistently. I didn't understand what he was trying to say until a couple of men beside him started motioning me to stand up – one of them even grabbed my arm and tried to lift me out of my seat. I guessed the card was an authorisation for a disabled person to take a seat on a bus, and stood up.

Suddenly I was off-balance, somehow trapped by the three men's arms and legs. One tried to pull my bag from my hand but I clung to it. I tried to get my other hand down to cover my wallet but my arm was being held and I felt another hand lift the wallet out. Then in a flash the three were off the bus. I ran to the door but they had already disappeared. All I could do was make a note of the time, place and bus number. The bus driver said he had seen the incident and gave me his name but when I made a report to the police they weren't interested in witnesses.

The second time, I was with someone else waiting for a bus outside the Anthropology Museum as it was going dark. When the bus came, a crowd of people all scrambled to get on it at once. By this time, I had a money belt and there were only a couple of thousand pesos in my pocket. A man 'dropped' a coin at the top of the bus steps. In the crush, I kept my hand round the banknotes in my pocket. My companion spotted a hand dipping into her pocket but elbowed the culprit in the ribs. Once out of the crush, I found a 15-cm razor slit down the side of my pocket, but the cash – and my hand – were intact.

Episode three was on the metro, during the build-up to the afternoon rush-hour. As I walked along the station platform to enter the end carriage of the approaching train, I thought I noticed a man follow me and stand near me on the platform. A train came, I went to get on it but pulled back because it was too crowded. The train left and I noticed the man was still on the platform too. A second train came and I got straight onto it. The man followed, started pushing and shoving, and managed to position himself next to me. I kept my hand round the couple of notes that were in my pocket but felt his hand trying, unsuccessfully, to get in there too.

If you get robbed, there's usually not much point in going to the police unless your loss is insured, in which case you'll need a statement from the police to present to your insurance company. One police station which seems to understand this need is in the Delegación Cuauhtémoc building at the corner of Avenida Central and Héroes Ferrocarrileros, a few blocks north of the Revolution Monument. If your Spanish isn't up to much, take someone with you who can describe what has happened – some of the police speak some English, that's all. Also take your passport and tourist card. Go in the side door on Aldama and say you want to *poner una acta de un robo* (make a record of a robbery). You'll probably have to wait a while with all the other people who have been robbed but a bit of patience and a couple of polite inquiries as to when your turn is coming up should see an officer typing out your report in an hour or two.

– John Noble

Information

Tourist Office Information about events, exhibitions, hotels, restaurants, transportation and museums in and around Mexico City is provided by English-speaking staff at any of several tourist offices, or over the telephone through a special computerised tourist information service.

The Secretaria de Turismo (tel 250-01-51), the Ministry of Tourism's representative at Avenida Presidente Mazaryk 172, is a federal-level office that stocks information about tourism throughout Mexico. Although they have some brochures and maps of Mexico City and surrounding areas and will assist you with hotel reservations, they did not seem as helpful as the district tourism office. They're two or three blocks north of Chapultepec Park and are open Monday to Friday, 8 am to 8 pm.

The district office is officially known as Dirección de Turismo, Departamento del Distrito Federal (tel 528-94-69) and is at Amberes 54 on Londres in the zona rosa. The English-speaking staff are helpful and can provide brochures and maps, but be sure to visit the adjacent lobby/waiting room where several shelves of detailed brochures are available. Hours are 9 am to 9 pm daily.

The district office also maintains a special telephone line called Infotur (tel 525-93-80) that can link you to English-speaking operators who will run a computerised information search for any tourist or travel-related queries you may have about Mexico City. This free service is available daily from 9 am to 9 pm.

There are branch offices at Mexico City's four inter-city bus terminals, the Buenavista train station and the Benito Juárez International Airport. Hours are 8 am to 4 pm, daily.

The Mexico City Chamber of Commerce (La Cámara de Comercio de la Ciudad de México) at Paseo de la Reforma 42, between Juárez and Morelos, has a friendly and helpful tourist information office (tel 592-26-77, ext 226) which gives out copies of *Codex*, its excellent English-language colour-printed publication. Each issue is devoted to a different aspect of Mexico City's artistic and cultural heritage (from pre-Hispanic to modern times) and where and how to see it today. The office is open 9 am to 2 pm and 3 to 5.30 or 6 pm Monday to Friday.

If you're approached by the law on Reforma, you needn't be alarmed. Several English-speaking policemen are posted there to help tourists and if they see you looking lost they'll be quick to offer help.

Other Tourist Services Tourist-card extensions should be requested at least two weeks in advance of expiration by visiting the Secretaria de Turismo or calling the Dirección General de Protección al Turista (24-hour tel 250-01-51, 250-05-89) for specific instructions about the extension process. If your card is lost or expired, contact your consulate and they will advise you about the necessary paperwork.

The numbers for the Dirección General de Protección al Turista can also be called for other reasons, such as legal problems, complaints and emergencies.

If you need information about or assistance with car-related problems within Mexico City, call the Ángeles de Plata or Silver Angels (tel 250-82-21), the city version of the Ángeles Verdes (Green Angels) who serve the highways.

Money Mexico City is full of banks; the majority of the country's banking is conducted here. For the traveller that means you should have no problem finding a bank open Monday to Friday, 9 am to 1.30 pm. However, some banks may only exchange foreign currency or travellers' cheques for Mexican pesos in the morning or after 12 noon. Since the banks are government-controlled, they all offer the same exchange rates.

Casas de cambio can be found at the international airport and concentrated in the zona rosa area of Mexico City. Except for the airport and American Express exchange counters, casas de cambio are open longer hours and usually don't offer exchange rates competitive with bank rates, especially for travellers' cheques. American Express is probably the best place in Mexico City to exchange American Express travellers' cheques. The airport casa de cambio claims to be open 24 hours daily, though it seemed to open only when a big international flight arrived.

Casas de Cambio de Moneda Genova is one chain with several branches in central Mexico City which will change travellers' cheques. Its Reforma 284 branch is supposedly open every day until 6 pm, and the Reforma 80 and Amberes 69 branches are open Monday to Saturday until 5.30 pm. Other branches are at Reforma 408 and Amberes 11.

If you need to have money wired to you from outside Mexico, do not go through a Mexican bank; instead have it wired through the American Express office, the Barclays Bank representative's office (Paseo de la Reforma 390-1203, 06695; tel 525-18-70) or the main Mexico City telegram and telex offices: Telegramas Internacionales, Balderas 14-18, tel 519-59-20; Central de Telégrafos, Museo Nacional del Arte building, Tacuba 8 east of Lázaro Cárdenas. All three offices are near the Alameda and the zona rosa. The latter two offices are open for *giros internacionales* (international money-wire transfers) Monday to Friday 9 am to 1 pm and 2.30 to 6.30 pm, Saturday 9 am to 1 pm, Sunday 9 to 11 am.

Other (legal) ways to get money include cash advances on credit cards such as the Visa, Mastercard and American Express Gold cards and cashing personal cheques if you have an American Express card.

Post The central post office of Mexico City is on Avenida Lázaro Cárdenas at Tacuba across from the Palacio de Bellas Artes and Alameda Park. The stamp windows are marked with signs reading *estampillas* and the poste restante or general delivery window is marked *Lista de Correos*. Hours for all services are 8 am to 12 midnight Monday to Saturday, and 8 am to 4 pm on Sunday.

Other post office branches are at the corner of Varsovia and Londres in the zona rosa and at Mariscal and Arriaga, north of the Monumento de la Revolución.

American Express The main American Express Office (tel 533-03-80) has financial services, a travel bureau and a mail pick-up desk. They moved in 1986 from earthquake-damaged quarters on Hamburgo to new offices at Paseo de la Reforma 234 around the corner from the French Embassy on Le Havre.

The staff speaks English and is helpful with mail enquiries and American Express card and cheque problems. If you have lost your travellers' cheques, they will replace them as quickly as possible. Before issuing new cheques, if you don't have your cheque receipts they will have to send a telex to the place where you purchased them. A 24-hour 'lost cheque' hotline staffed by English-speaking operators can be called collect from anywhere in Mexico at (905) 598-79-66, extension 2367 or 2368.

Client mail is usually processed and filed as it is received. The travel bureau and mail pick-up desk are open Monday to Friday from 9 am to 6 pm. The cashier (for money-exchange and other financial matters) is open from 9 am to 5 pm. Both are open on Saturday from 9 am to 1 pm.

Other branches of American Express are at Avenida Patriotismo 635 (tel 598-79-66), hours Monday to Friday 9 am to 6 pm and Saturday 9 am to 1 pm; and Centro Comercial Perisur Periférico Sur 4090 (tel 652-27-88, 652-27-99), hours Tuesday to Saturday 10 am to 8 pm.

Telegrams You can send domestic and international telegrams from the Central de Telégrafos on the east side of the Museo Nacional del Arte at Tacuba 8, just east of Lázaro Cárdenas. It's open until 11 pm. A telegram to the USA costs US$4.25 for the first 15 words, then 15c for each extra word, and you don't have to pay for the address you send it to. To Britain or Australia you pay US$4 for the first seven words, then US$0.50 for each extra word, and you have to pay for the address. You can also send telegrams from a private phone: dial 518-08-80 for international ones, 519-59-20 for domestic.

Telephone Calls Offices for long-distance calls are known as *casetas de larga distancia* and, unless you're staying at a hotel with a patient reception desk staff, you must go to one of these offices to make a long-distance domestic or international call. Domestic calls are much easier and cheaper to make than international calls because they are not subject to the same exorbitant taxes, and because domestic line operators are more readily available.

To make a direct international call, the operator at the hotel reception desk or the caseta must first connect with an international line operator, which can take anywhere from 30 seconds to an hour or more even from Mexico City. If you are calling the USA direct, be prepared to spend US$4 per minute; for Europe and Australasia, the rate skyrockets to US$15 to US$20 per minute. International calls placed from your hotel can cost even more because they are subject to the hotel's service charges in addition to the usually hefty government taxes.

International collect calls are known as *una llamada por cobrar* and can often be made from any pay telephone in Mexico City by dialling 09 to get an English-speaking international operator.

Local calls to anywhere within Mexico City can be made free from any pay telephone.

Casetas for toll calls outside of Mexico City, including international calls, are located throughout Mexico City and are indicated by a telephone-shaped sign. Following is a list of casetas and hours of operation:

Airport
   Sala E, 6.30 am to 9.30 pm daily; Sala A, 7 am to 11 pm daily
Buena Vista Train Station
   8 am to 9 pm Monday to Friday, 9 am to 2 pm Saturday and Sunday
Central Bus Station *(Central Camionera del Norte)*
   Room No 4, 7 am to 10 pm daily
Insurgentes District
   Jalapa 12, 10 am to 6 pm Monday to Saturday, closed Sunday.
Gift Market *(Mercado de la Merced)*
   Local 1, 8.30 am to 7 pm Monday to Saturday, 9 am to 1 pm Sunday
Raza District
   Seris 18, 9 am to 8 pm Monday to Friday, 9 am to 2 pm Saturday
Tarqueña District
   Cerro Caporo 94, Local 2, 8 am to 8 pm Monday to Saturday, 9 am to 4 pm Sunday
Tlatelolco District
   Guerrero 395, 10 am to 3 pm and 4 to 8 pm Monday to Saturday

Other casetas are listed in the Mexico City phone book.

Bookstores American Bookstore, Madero 25, has many English-language books and current magazines and newspapers (usually only two or three days late). Hours are 9 am to 6 pm daily except Sunday. There's another branch in the San Ángel suburb of Mexico City at Avenida Revolución 1570, open the same hours.

Librería Británica, Madero 30A in the Hotel Ritz building, specialises in, as its name suggests, English-language books and magazines. Evidently book prices have not been rising as quickly as the value of the peso has been dropping because prices here are much lower than in the USA. Some books seem to have had the same price they had when first put on the shelf. For example, a copy of *The Course of Mexican History* by Michael Meyer and William Sherman cost US$8 while in the USA the same edition cost US$20. Hours are 8 am to 5 pm daily except Sunday. There's another branch at Avenida Universidad and México, next to the Coyoacán metro stop in the Coyoacán suburb of Mexico City.

Most Sanborn's department store branches have a book and newsstand section with a fairly good selection of English-language books, magazines and newspapers (sometimes only a day or two old). The Casa de Azulejos or 'House of Tiles' at Madero and Correo a block east of Avenida Lázaro Cárdenas is home to a main branch of Sanborn's. Librería Misrachi on Juárez 4 at the corner of Avenida Lázaro Cárdenas is a good source of English-language books about Mexico and Mexico City and maps for all parts of Mexico.

Libraries Benjamin Franklin Library (tel 211-00-42) is the library of the United States Information Agency, which is part of the US State Department. A wide range of books about the USA, Mexico and other parts of Latin America is available, as well as current English-language periodicals. It is open to the public, but only residents of Mexico City can check out books. It used to be on Londres near the zona rosa, but earthquake damage prompted a move to the 7th floor of a building at Reforma 295, between Danubio and Sena. It's open 9 am to 6 pm, Monday to Friday.

The Canadian Embassy Library (tel 254-32-88) has a wide selection of Canadian books and periodicals in English and French. It is at Schiller 529 in the Polanco area, just north of Chapultepec Park. Hours are Monday to Friday, 9 am to 5 pm.

Newspapers & Magazines The most popular and oldest English-language newspaper in the city is the *Mexico City News*, which until early 1987 was also one of the most controversial.

Under the editorship of Pete Hamill, a well-known American journalist and novelist, the paper began covering political events, such as a student strike, much more frankly and openly than Mexico's Spanish-language publications. Hamill was not at all bashful or intimidated by Mexico's political establishment and described events as they actually were, rather than as the establishment said they were. However, when Romulo O'Farrill, the owner of the *Mexico City News* and *Novedades* (a popular Spanish-language magazine), told Hamill not to run interviews with student strike leaders, Hamill and 18 of his staff resigned because of what they considered censorship.

Despite the paper's return to Mexican editorship for visitors to Mexico City it is still one of the best sources of information in English about concerts, art exhibitions, plays, movies and English-as-a-second-language teaching positions. It can be bought for 25c from most newsstands, the bookstores listed and Sanborn's department stores.

Less reliable, but still packed with useful information, is the *Mexico City Daily Bulletin*, a 20-page paper distributed free in the lobbies of most major hotels. The snippets of news included in the paper tend to be quite sensationalist; some recent headlines: 'Boy Charged with Attack on Elderly Lady', 'Rebels Attacked . . .', 'Mysterious Stranger Visits Poe's Grave', 'German Kidnap Linked to Arab's Arrest' – all on the same page. It does, however, offer a fair review of restaurants, cultural events and places of interest around Mexico City every day except Monday.

Also available for free in some hotel lobbies is the monthly English/Spanish magazine *Ciudad de Mexico Guide*, more like a directory of restaurants, hotels, nightclubs, museums and other places of interest for tourists than a descriptive guide.

One of the best all-round publications for information about cultural events, sporting events, restaurants, TV programmes and movies in and around Mexico City is the weekly Spanish-language magazine *El Tiempo Libre* ('Free Time'). Even if you don't know Spanish, you should be able to recognise some cognates. It can be bought at most newsstands and bookstores for 25c.

Some major English-language newspapers and magazines from North America and Europe are sold at a few hotels, newsstands and bookstores in Mexico City and the suburbs.

French publications such as *L'Expres, Le Point, Paris Match* and *Le Nouvel Observateur* are carried by the Servicio Expreso Mexicano (tel 533-68-33, 525-27-00, 528-67-78) at Florencia 57 in the zona rosa.

Maps The *Guía Roji Ciudad de México* is a good street atlas of the city, with an index. It costs US$2.25 and is available in bookshops and some street stalls. The Mexico and Central America map published by the American Automobile Association (available only to members in the USA) includes an excellent map of central Mexico City.

Airlines Most of the world's major airlines operate in and out of Mexico City, maintain offices here or, at the very least, have representatives in the city. They include:

Aeroméxico
    More than 20 ticket offices in Mexico City, including one at Paseo de la Reforma 445 (tel 553-15-77, 553-48-88 for reservations 6 am to 12 midnight daily; 762-40-22 for arrivals and departures)
Air France
    Paseo de la Reforma 404, 15th floor for administrative offices; Paseo de la Reforma 287 for ticket offices (tel 566-00-66 reservations; 511-38-83 ticket information)
American Airlines
    Paseo de la Reforma 300 (tel 571-32-19 information)

Continental Airlines
    Paseo de la Reforma 325, corner of Río Danube (tel 203-11-48 reservations; 571-36-61 arrivals and departures; 525-37-10 ticket information)
Eastern Airlines
    Paseo de la Reforma 30, 1st floor (tel 592-60-11 information)
Icelandair
    Calle Durango 193-302 (tel 511-84-61 information)
Mexicana
    More than 19 ticket offices in Mexico City (tel 660-44-44 reservations, open 24 hours; 571-88-88 arrivals and departures, open 24 hours)
Pan Am
    Edificio Plaza Comerex, Boulevard M Avila Camacho 1-702 (tel 520-16-99 ticket information; 571-32-79 flight information)
Republic Airlines
    Paseo de la Reforma 300, 20th floor (tel 207-05-15 reservations)
United Airlines
    Calle Leibnitz 100 (tel 531-83-44, 531-45-28, 545-90-25 and 545-51-47 reservations and ticket information)

Embassies & Consulates

Australia
    Paseo de la Reforma 195, 6th floor (tel 566-30-55); open 9 am to 5 pm Monday to Friday
Canada
    Schiller 529, Polanco, 11580, Mexico DF (tel 254-32-88, 254-38-07 for emergencies); open 9 am to 5 pm Monday to Friday
Costa Rica
    Paseo de la Reforma 133, 2nd floor, ZP 06 (tel 535-98-30)
Cuba
    Avenida Presidente Masaryk 554, ZP 5 (tel 540-01-84)
France
    Havre 15 between Hamburgo and Paseo de la Reforma (tel 511-08-47)
Nicaragua
    Calle Nuevo León 144, Mezz CP 06170 (tel 553-97-91)
Panama
    Campo Eliseos 111-1, ZP 5 (tel 250-40-45)
UK
    Río Lerma 71 at Cuauhtémoc (tel 511-48-80); open 9 am to 5 pm Monday to Friday

USA
    Paseo de la Reforma 305 (tel 211-00-42, or
    553-33-33 Saturday for emergencies); open
    9 am to 5.30 pm Monday to Friday, closed
    on Mexican and American holidays

Laundromat There's a decent laundromat
in the Revolution Monument area –
Lavandería Automática on Edison half a
block west of Arriaga. It's open daily from
9.30 am to 8 pm. For three kg of clothes,
the wash costs US$0.60, 10 minutes'
drying is US$0.50. They'll do it for you for
another US$0.50.

Festivals

Every major festival and fiesta described
in the Facts about the Country Chapter is
celebrated in or around Mexico City.
Some of these, as well as special
celebrations that take place only in
Mexico City, include:

Cinco de Mayo On El Peñon Hill near the
International, Airport, a mock battle
between 'French' and Mexican 'soldiers'
is conducted in the afternoon to commemorate the Battle of Puebla on 5 May 1862.
On that day, Brigadier General Porfirio
Díaz led the Second Brigade of the
Mexican Army to victory against an
invading French army led by General
Charles Latrille. It was a temporary
victory, though, because about a year
later the French army besieged Puebla
with two months of mortar and artillery
attacks before marching on Mexico City
and taking control of the country.

Independence Day On 15 September
hundreds of thousands of people gather in
front of the National Palace in the zócalo
to hear a reading of Hidalgo's *Grito* or call
for independence, listen to music and
throw lots of confetti.

Virgin of Guadalupe At the Basilicas de
Guadalupe north of central Mexico City,
12 December caps a week of colourful

festivities venerating and celebrating the
dark-skinned Virgin who mysteriously
appeared before an Indian convert to
Christianity in 1531.

Around the Zócalo

The historic and traditional centre of
Mexico City is the Plaza de la Constitución,
more commonly known as the zócalo.
Until the early 19th century, the plaza
was known variously as the Plaza de
Armas and the Plaza Real (Royal Plaza),
but it was more a maze of market stalls
and narrow passageways than an open
plaza. The market, called the Mercado
del Parián, existed for most of the 16th
and 17th centuries until it had to be torn
down because the many stalls had
overcrowded the plaza. In 1812 the plaza
was renamed Plaza de la Constitución to
commemorate a liberal constitution
drawn up by the local assembly in protest of
Napoleon's invasion of Spain. The word
zócalo, which means plinth or stone base,
was adopted in 1843 when a tall monument
commissioned by then-President Santa
Anna was constructed only as far as the
base. Today, the central plaza of almost
every Mexican city, town and village is
known as the zócalo.

The plaza was first paved in the 1520s
by Cortés with stones from the ruins of
what had been the grandest and most
important set of temples and palaces of
the Aztec empire. With each side
measuring exactly 240 metres (792 feet), it
has remained one of the world's largest
city plazas. To get a true sense of its
immensity, visit the open-air terrace
restaurant that overlooks the plaza from
the 7th floor of the Hotel Majestic, at the
corner of Francisco Madero and República
del Brasil.

Every year on the night of 15 September,
hundreds of thousands of people gather in
this and almost every other zócalo in
Mexico to celebrate Mexico's Independence
Day. Here in Mexico City it is commemorated with a reading of Hidalgo's *Grito* or
call for independence, performances by

mariachi bands and other music groups and lots of confetti.

El Palacio Nacional Home to the offices of the president of Mexico, the Federal Treasury, the National Archives, a museum in honour of President Benito Juárez (1855-72) and the dramatic murals of Diego Rivera, the National Palace fills the entire east side of the zócalo. The present structure was built in the late 17th and early 18th centuries over the ruins of two previous palaces.

The first palace on this spot was built of tezontle (a light reddish volcanic stone) by Moctezuma Xocoyótzin (Moctezuma II) in the early 16th century before Cortés and his Spanish conquistadors arrived. Cortés destroyed the palace in 1521 and rebuilt it with a large enclosed courtyard so that he could entertain visitors with Mexico's (or New Spain's, as it was then known) first recorded bullfights. The palace remained with Cortés' family until the King of Spain bought it in 1562 to house the viceroy rulers of New Spain. It was destroyed during riots in 1692, rebuilt again using tezontle and continued serving as a residence for the viceroys until Mexican independence in the 1820s. The government of the Republic of Mexico moved in and still occupies the south-east wing.

Facing the palace, you will see three gates: the first one on your right is the guarded entrance for the president of Mexico and his officials; the centre gate is the entrance to a courtyard surrounded by Diego Rivera's colourful depictions of Mexico's history and people; and the third entrance leads to a courtyard where the seldom-visited *El Recinto de Homenaje a Benito Juárez* (the place of homage to Benito Juárez) is located.

Diego Rivera's bright, colourful murals are the prime attraction of the palace. In general, they summarise the history of Mexican civilisation from the arrival of Quetzalcóatl – the plumed serpent god believed to be personified first in Cortés –

to Mexico's 1910 Revolution. Detailed guides to the murals are available at the foot of the stairs just inside the entrance gate. The murals are open for public viewing from 9 am to 3 pm and 6 to 9 pm daily. Admission is free.

If you have time, enter the northernmost gate and visit *El Recinto Homenaje a Benito Juárez* on the 2nd floor. Benito Juárez was an Indian who led Mexico's reform movement in the 1850s and the fight against the French in the 1860s. He ordered Emperor Maximilian's execution in 1867 and then assumed the presidency of Mexico which he held until his death in this wing of the National Palace in 1872. The room where he died and his library have been preserved along with a mask of his face and several personal effects. The rooms are open Tuesday to Friday from 10 am to 6 pm and on Saturday and Sunday from 10 am to 3 pm. Admission is free.

Every year on 15 September at 11 pm the president of Mexico addresses more than a million people from the National Palace and recites the *Grito de Dolores* (Cry of Dolores), Mexico's most famous speech, from a balcony. The *Grito*, a call to rebel against the Spaniards, was first proclaimed in 1810 by Miguel Hidalgo y Costilla in the town of Dolores (now named Dolores Hidalgo in his honour). Translated, the gist of the *Grito* is:

My children, a new dispensation comes to us this day. Are you ready to receive it? Will you be free? Will you make the effort to recover from the hated Spaniards the lands stolen from your forefathers 300 years ago? We must act at once . . . Long live our Lady of Guadalupe! Death to bad government! . . . Mexicans! Long live Mexico! . . .

El Templo Mayor – Teocalli Until 1978 the precise location of the Aztecs' principal temple of the *teocalli* or sacred city was unknown because most of the Aztec capital of Tenochtitlán had been destroyed by Spanish conquistadors in the 1520s. However, in February 1978, workers unearthed an intriguing eight-tonne stone as they were digging a hole just north of the National Palace. The stone, a replica of which is displayed here (the original is in the Anthropology Museum), was decorated with the figures and symbols of a violent Aztec legend and prompted more archaeological excavation.

One version of the stone's story, as anthropologists have interpreted it, shows Coatlicue, the goddess of death and earth, becoming pregnant while sweeping the temple. In her moon goddess daughter Coyolxauqui's opinion, she should have stuck to her sweeping and stayed away from the gods' bedrooms. Coyolxauqui whined to her 400 brothers and conspired to kill Coatlicue, but they couldn't agree on how to kill her. Meanwhile, Coatlicue gave birth to a healthy full-grown man named Huitzilopochtl who heard about the conspiracy and immediately sought to prevent it. He cut up his siblings and threw the pieces into the heavens to become stars and planets.

More excavation showed that this was the site of the Aztecs' principal temple. A raised walkway around the site gives you some idea of the temple's layout and multiple layers of construction. The temple pyramid that once stood here was enlarged at least five times. For a better idea of the layout of the entire city of Tenochtitlán, retrace your steps to the zócalo and stop at the pool of water between it and the excavation site. A brass model of the city is displayed in the pool. Or visit the Museo de la Ciudad de México, described below, to see a scale model of Tenochtitlán. Another option is to telephone 542-17-17 for an English-speaking guide who knows the history and legends of the *teocalli*. The site (on the left side of the National Palace) is open Tuesday to Sunday from 9 am to 5 pm. Admission is free.

La Catedral Metropolitana The Metropolitan Cathedral at the north end of the zócalo was one of the first buildings constructed by the Spanish in the 1520s. With a three-naved basilica design of vaults on semi-circular arches rather than pointed Gothic arches and an apse that faced east to Jerusalem where Christ's tomb is, it was constructed to resemble cathedrals in the Spanish cities of Toledo and Granada. The first cathedral here was not finished until 1548, but it was later superseded by a larger cathedral, parts of which were expanded, redesigned or torn down.

The tall twin doors that face Calle República de Guatemala were added in the early 17th century and are a good example of neoclassical renaissance-style portals with pilasters that resemble columns. The cathedral's other grand portals were constructed later in the 17th century with markedly different elements – baroque designs that include three levels of exterior columns and marble panels with bas-reliefs.

The cathedral's exterior was not completed until 1813 when architect and sculptor Manuel Tolsa added statues of faith, hope and charity atop the clock tower and a great central cupola or dome to create a sense of unity and balance.

Inside, the cathedral includes 14 heavily decorated chapels, a central nave, two processional or side naves and two chapel naves. The eye-catching Chapel of the Holy Angels is an exquisite example of baroque sculpture and painting with its huge main altarpiece that is all one sculpture and three smaller altarpieces decorated by the 17th-century painter Juan Correa. Paintings by Correa also grace the walls of the sacristy with depictions of Jesus' arrival in Jerusalem, the coronation of the Virgin and St Michael's slaying of the dragon.

Most of the rest of the artwork in the cathedral was, unfortunately, damaged or completely destroyed in a 1967 fire. Ongoing restoration efforts have repaired most of the works, notably the intricately carved wooden choir stalls of late 17th-century artist Juan de Rojas and the huge gilded Altar of Pardon.

Restoration work is continually necessary, particularly since the building's immense weight is causing it to gradually sink into the marshy subsoil. Work had begun to correct a noticeable tilt in the building, when the September 1985 earthquake struck and exacerbated the sinking.

El Sagrario Connected to the cathedral is its 18th-century parish church El Sagrario (The Sacred). It was originally built to house the archives and sacred vestments and vessels of the archbishop. The church's southern and eastern façades are prime examples of the ultra-decorative architectural style fostered by Spanish architect José Churriguera.

Inside, the church was laid out in a square so that it resembles a Greek cross and fits neatly next to the rectangular cathedral.

Monte Nacional de Piedad Founded in 1775 by the Count of Regla, Mexico's national flea market is worth a visit to see what

must be one of the world's largest 'department stores' for second-hand goods. It is housed in a large, dark building across from the west side of the cathedral and is open daily except Sunday. Though erratic, hours are generally normal business ones.

Iglesia de Santo Domingo Built in 1527, the original Church of Santo Domingo was one of Mexico's first Dominican churches and convents. However, the present building, still on the original site near the zócalo at the intersection of Calles República del Brasil, República de Venezuela and República de Colombia, only dates back as far as 1736. It is a beautiful example of baroque architecture decorated on its eastern side with the statues of Saint Domingo and Saint Francis. Below the statues, the arms of both saints are symbolically entwined as if to convey a unity of purpose in their lives. The front or southern façade is equally beautiful with its statues and 12 columns

El Sagrario

around the main entrance. Between the columns are statues of Saint Francis and Saint Augustine and in the centre at the top is a bas-relief of the Assumption of the Virgin Mary.

Museo Nacional de las Culturas The National Museum of Cultures has a collection of exhibits showing the art, dress and handicrafts of several cultures. The 2nd-floor rooms each highlight a different culture or set of cultures: for example, there's an Asian room with displays from India and China. The ground-floor rooms include a small temporary exhibit hall, a library with magazines from several countries and a paleontological exhibit.

The museum is at Calle Moneda 13 near the north-east corner of the National Palace, in a building constructed in 1567 to house the Casa de Moneda or Treasury. Hours are Tuesday to Saturday 9.30 am to 6 pm, and Sunday 9.30 am to 4 pm. Admission is 10c.

Templo de la Santísima The Church of the Holy Sacrament, a magnificent example of churrigueresque architectural style, is two blocks east of the National Museum of Cultures on Calle Moneda at Calle de la Santísima. The profusion of ornamental sculptures on the front façade is the main reason to visit this church, most of which was designed and carved by sculptor and architect Lorenzo Rodríguez between 1755 and 1783. The most important features of the façade include the ghostly busts of the 12 apostles and the sculpted depiction of Christ with his head in God's lap.

Suprema Corte de Justicia Mexico's Supreme Court, at the corner of Pino Suárez and Corregidora, would not be a visitor attraction were it not for the five immense murals on the walls of the 2nd-floor foyer and near the entrance to the library. As you enter the courthouse, the steps to the 2nd floor and the four murals

painted by José Clemente Orozco will be directly in front of you. The mural on the east wall is a bright tribute to workers' rights while on the opposite wall the pride and national conscience of Mexico are depicted in the form of a great tiger atop the country's mineral wealth. The other two murals are called *La Justicia* and show 'Justice' sleeping while a man is transformed into a destructive fire-bolt. The fifth mural is by American artist G Biddle. Admission is free.

Museo de la Ciudad de México The Museum of Mexico City at Pino Suárez 30, three blocks south of the south-east corner of the zócalo, is often skipped by travellers, but it should not be missed for an overview of the geological, demographic and political history of Mexico City.

The museum is housed in a baroque mansion built in 1528 as a residence for one of Cortés' cousins and then rebuilt in 1781 for the counts of Santiago de Calimaya. A stone sculpture of a feathered serpent embedded in the building's cornerstone at Pino Suárez and República d'El Salvador shows that the mansion was partly constructed from Aztec ruins. On the ground floor, models chronicle the volcanic eruptions that created the valley now occupied by Mexico City. Displays show that humans began settling the valley in 8000 BC and gradually built the magnificent temples and pyramids of Teotihuacán. By the 14th century AD, the Aztec Indians had settled in the area of present-day Mexico City to build Tenochtitlán. An impressive small-scale model sits in Room 6. In the next room, a huge mural by Mexican painter Francisco Moreno Capdevila depicts the fiery conquest of Tenochtitlán by Cortés in 1521. The rise of New Spain is presented in Room 8 with displays of construction plans for various 15th-century buildings, several of which still stand. A chart of ethnic equations shows the peoples and cultures that evolved in New Spain:

Top: Mexico City (Dept. of Tourism)
Bottom: Guanajuato (DS)

Top: Plaza Mayor, Mérida (TW)
Left: Colonial Doorway, Mexico City (JL)
Right: Museo Regional de Oaxaca (TW)

Spanish + Indian	=	Mestizo
Mestizo + Spanish	=	Castizo
Castizo + Spanish	=	Spanish
Spanish + Black	=	Mulatto
Morisco + Spanish	=	Chino

Room 9 is devoted to immense topographical models.

Exhibits on the 1st floor cover Mexico City's contemporary history from the 18th century to the present.

A 2nd-floor room once served as the studio of Joaquin Clausell, a Mexican Impressionist painter, who used the studio's walls as a floor-to-ceiling canvas.

Concerts, plays and special art exhibits are often presented in the inner courtyard of the museum building. A sound & light show depicting the history of Tenochtitlán (in Spanish) is shown daily at 11 am in the museum's ground-floor conference room.

Museum hours are Tuesday to Sunday, 9.30 am to 7.30 pm.

Around the Alameda

The Alameda, one of Mexico's first public parks, dates back to 1593 when Viceroy Luis de Velasco decided the growing city needed a pleasant area of pathways, fountains and trees. Before then, the area was used to burn or hang heretics. The Alameda became a strolling-ground for the wealthy. By the late 19th century, bandstands offered free concerts, hydrogen gas lamps were installed and the poor mingled with the rich. Today, the park is a popular and easily accessible refuge from the maddening crowds and traffic of Mexico City. It's a great place to have a small picnic, people-watch or just relax. Just over Mora from the north-west corner of the Alameda there are usually several games of open-air chess going on, with crowds gathered round to watch.

Monument to Benito Juárez
On the south side of the park on Avenida Juárez is yet another tribute to Benito Juárez, a semicircular marble monument with columns. Almost every city, town and village in

Mexico has at least a street named after him because his leadership marked a break with the power struggles and political turmoil of the first half of the 19th century.

Museo Nacional de Artes Industrias
The Museum of Industrial Arts at Avenida Benito Juárez 44, across from the Benito Juárez monument in Alameda Park, displays and sells (at fixed prices) handicrafts from all over Mexico. Items include hide-covered drums, hand-blown glassware, intricately woven baskets and shawls. Hours are Tuesday to Friday, 10 am to 2 pm. It might also be open the same hours on Saturday and Monday.

Palacio de Bellas Artes
Dominating the east end of the Alameda is the Palace of Fine Arts, an impressive example of the excesses of President Porfirio Díaz, who ruled Mexico from 1877 to 1880 and again from 1884 to 1911. Construction began in 1904 under Italian architect Adam Boari and was supposed to be completed by 1910, in time for the grandiose centennial celebrations planned by Díaz. However, before the interior was finished, the heavy marble shell of the building began to sink into the spongy subsoil. Construction was subsequently interrupted for several years by the Revolution and civil war and not completed until 1934. Architect Federico Mariscal changed and completed the interior so that it would reflect the popular art deco styles of the 1920s and '30s - that explains the prevalence of bright natural lighting, sharp geometric forms and columns.

The Palace serves a dual function as home to one of Mexico's finest and most dramatic collections of murals and home to the world-renowned Ballet Folklorico. This is also the place to come for tickets to most of Mexico City's major cultural events, including those held here.

Murals by David Alfaro Siqueiros, José Clemente Orozco and Diego Rivera dominate immense wall space on the 3rd level of the Palace. As social activist and artist, Siqueiros used murals to express his outrage at social injustices and support for class struggle. Displayed here are *Cain en los Estados Unidos*, expressing his indignation at racism against blacks in the USA; and *Nacimiento del fascismo*, his graphic interpretation of the birth of fascism and dictatorships in the world.

Rivera also used murals as a form of dramatic political expression. On the western wall is one of his most famous murals, *Man at the Crossing of the Ways*, which first appeared at the Rockefeller Center in New York as *Man in Control of his Universe*. The Rockefeller family commissioned the piece in the 1930s but had it destroyed because of its rebellious, anti-capitalist themes. Rivera reproduced it here with the same themes of struggle against a class system and dehumanising

Palacio de Bellas Artes

industrialisation that he expressed in his original, but probably more wildly.

Another highlight of the Palace is a beautiful glass curtain hanging in the main theatre that colourfully depicts the Valley of Mexico. Based on the work of Mexican painter Gerardo Murillo ('Dr Atl'), Tiffany Studios of New York (creators of Tiffany lamps) assembled the curtain from almost a million pieces of coloured glass. On Sunday mornings and just before performances, the curtain is illuminated for public viewing.

The Ballet Folklorico is a superb performance of Mexican dances and music that should not be missed. Shows are on Wednesday at 9 pm and Sunday at 9.30 am and 9 pm. Ticket prices are US$5.25 for 1st-floor seats, US$4.25 2nd floor and US$2.25 3rd floor. Buy your ticket as early as possible at the Bellas Artes ticket office or through a local travel agency (though with added commissions).

Tickets can be bought for various cultural events (including the Ballet Folklorico) from the ticket windows in the main lobby Monday to Saturday 11.30 am to 3 pm and 4 to 9 pm, and Sunday 10.30 am to 1 pm and 4 to 7 pm. This schedule has been known to change without notice, so you may want to call 529-05-09, 529-93-20 or 529-78-05.

Museo Nacional de Arte The National Museum of Art is housed in an early 1900s building of eclectic architectural styles, which originally served as the Department of Communications and the National General Archives. Outside, a distinctive bronze statue of Spanish King Carlos IV de Borbón stands in front of the museum's main entrance at Calle Tacuba 8, half a block east of the north side of the Palacio de Bellas Artes. The statue, called *El Caballito* or 'little knight', was sculpted by Don Manuel Tolsa in the late 18th century and had to be hidden at the University of Mexico between 1824 and 1852 because of anti-Spanish sentiment. Inside, before you see any of the museum's collections, the most striking feature is the grand and polished Italian marble staircase. The central staircase with its beautifully baroque lampposts was the work of Italian architect Silvio Contri and, along with the brilliant blue and gold ceilings of Florentine artists, was first completed in Europe and then shipped to Mexico.

The museum's collections represent every style and school of Mexican art. First-floor collections include a fascinating series of paintings by Mexican artist José Velasco depicting late 19th and early 20th-century life in Mexico City and the countryside. One of his landscapes shows that Mexico City was still surrounded by lakes even in the late 19th century. Second-floor collections include 17th-century religious paintings by Antonio Rodríguez, Juan Correa and José de Ibarra; 18th and 19th-century sculptures; portraits by Antonio Poblano; sketches and prints of skeletal figures sweeping streets; and anonymous paintings with social and political themes. Hours are 10 am to 6 pm, Tuesday to Sunday. Admission is 5c or free with a student card.

Plaza de Garibaldi Plaza de Garibaldi, a 10-minute walk up Avenida Lázaro Cárdenas north of the Alameda, is the place to hear what must be the world's biggest congregation of mariachi bands, drink at a cantina with tough-looking Mexican 'machos' and get your purse snatched or pocket picked.

The mariachi bands gather here every evening to serenade whoever invites them to their table; the going rate is US$3 to US$4 per song. If you get to the plaza any time between 10 pm and 3 am – the prime playing hours – you will be amazed by the cacophony caused by several bands playing simultaneously.

Around the plaza are several cantinas and *pulquerías* (places specialising in pulque, the fermented juice of the maguey plant) where you can hobnob with Mexican machos or, as is common here but not in the rest of Mexico, Mexican families (minus their children). By custom rather than law, women are not normally permitted in drinking establishments in Mexico. One of the better pulquerías is the Pulquería Hermana Hortensia near the corner of Calle República de Honduras and Calle Amargura. The Guadalajara de Noche is often recommended for a taste of cantina life.

After you've numbed your senses with drink, try your heart at the shock boxes. A group of people form a line by linking hands, and the two end persons each grab the metal tubes attached to each shock box. The owner of the boxes then begins generating electrical current by turning a crank, gradually increasing it until someone breaks the link or has a heart attack. Nice business!

Because the plaza can become crowded, you must guard your valuables, particularly wallets and purses. Pickpockets and purse-snatchers abound here. If you can, don't carry a purse or a wallet; wear a money belt or pouch under your clothing and keep only a small amount of cash in a more accessible pocket.

La Casa de los Azulejos At Avenida Francisco Madero and Calle Correo about a block east of the Alameda is the 'House of Blue Tiles', a late 16th-century building adorned with intricately designed blue tiles. Although Moorish in style with a combination of Spanish and North African geometric designs, the tiles were actually produced in China and shipped to Mexico on the Manila *naos* (typical Spanish sailing vessels used from the late 16th to the early 19th centuries). Some of the tiles were also produced in Puebla. Since the tiles were considered a symbol of wealth and status, the house was thought suitable for a personal palace for the Counts of the Valley of Orizaba.

Today, the blue tiles, a high-ceilinged inner courtyard surrounded by columns, and a Moorish fountain are the principal signs of its palatial past. A branch of Sanborn's, a nationwide department-store chain, now occupies the building. The courtyard functions as a restaurant and coffee-shop between 7.30 am and 10 pm.

Palacio Iturbide One block east of the 'House of Blue Tiles' at Avenida Francisco Madero 17 is the Palace of Iturbide or, as he was better known, Emperor Agustín I. He ruled Mexico during its stormy, first year of independence from late 1821 to early 1823 and resided at this house with his family. The house was built in the 18th century with churrigueresque designs by architect Francisco Guerrero Torres for the Counts of San Mateo de Valparaiso and the Marquises of Jarral de Berrio. Iturbide transformed it into a mini-palace and, after his self-exile in 1823, it became a hotel. Today, the Banco Nacional de México (National Bank of Mexico) has restored the building for use as administrative offices and an art gallery. The ground-floor gallery has different exhibits every three months and is open from 9 am to 6 pm. Admission is free.

La Torre Latinoamericana With 42 floors, the Latin American Tower is the tallest building in Mexico City (and supposedly one of the tallest in Latin America). Impossible to miss, it's at the intersection of Lázaro Cárdenas and Avenida Francisco Madero, the latter street being a continuation of Avenida Benito Juárez. From 11 am to 12 midnight daily you can take an elevator to the observation deck on the 42nd floor. Buy a ticket (US$1) from the kiosk in the ground-floor lobby or go for free to the bar and restaurant on the 41st floor where you can have a slightly overpriced drink or meal.

The view is fantastic, especially after a day of rain or strong winds has temporarily cleared away Mexico City's yellowish-brown blanket of smog. Even on smoggy days, though, the snow-capped peaks of the Popocatépetl and Ixtacchíhuatl volcanoes can be seen on the eastern horizon poking through the dirty air. Most of the other mountains surrounding the Valley of Mexico are visible; like a wall, they cause an inversion layer of thick smog to form ominously over the city.

Have a look at the Acuario (Aquarium) on the 37th floor. This was hardly something I expected to see 37 floors above ground – aquarium tanks full of a variety of sea life from the Atlantic and Pacific oceans. According to a sign at the entrance, it's the 'highest' aquarium in the world. As you tour the tanks, even stranger is the soundtrack from an American-made cowboy movie coming from overhead speakers.

Hotel del Prado This used to stand near the south-western corner of the Alameda but was destroyed by the 1985 earthquake. Fortunately, its most famous attraction – the Diego Rivera mural *Dream on a Sunday Afternoon in Alameda Park* – was not seriously damaged. It was transferred to a temporary home at the Secretaria de Comunicación.

The mural, painted in 1947-48, is a brilliant and colourful depiction of Mexican history from the Spanish conquest to the 1910 Revolution.

Centro Cultural José Martí At the north-western corner of the Alameda is a small building that serves as a cultural centre dedicated to Cuban poet and leader of the anti-Spanish independence movement José Martí (1853-1895). The only interesting sight here is a huge, multicoloured mural spread across three inside walls that depicts foreign, predominantly American, intervention in Mexico, Cuba, Nicaragua, Guatemala and the Dominican Republic. According to an adjoining chart, foreigners invaded Mexico 270 times. The rest of the centre is used for special cultural events such as baroque or folkloric music performances, poetry readings and art exhibits. The centre's programme of events is always in the magazine *Tiempo Libre* (available at newsstands). The mural can be seen Monday to Friday from 10 am to 3 pm and 5.30 to 9 pm, and on weekends from 9 am to 2 pm. Admission is free.

Pinacoteca Virreynal de San Diego The Pinacoteca, at Dr Mora 7 across from the north-west corner of the Alameda Park, is a former church and Dominican monastery that is now home to a collection of 17th and 18th-century baroque and religious motif paintings. A mural by contemporary painter Federico Cantú is also displayed. Hours are 10 am to 5 pm, Tuesday to Sunday; at the time of writing it was temporarily closed for remodelling.

La Ciudadela y Centro Artesanal A little more than one km south of the south-western corner of the Alameda, the 'Citadel' and 'Artisans' Centre' are sometimes referred to as the same place even though both are separated by two small streets and Plaza de la Reforma. The Citadel, which can't be visited today, has an important place in Mexico's Revolution because it was from here in February 1913 that Díaz supporters waged bloody street battles that resulted in the ouster and eventual execution of President Francisco Madero.

The Artisans' Centre is where you should buy arts and crafts from throughout Mexico.

La Lotería Nacional Mexico's lottery is a national passion, making a visit to the 1930s art deco-style lottery building at the junction of Paseo de la Reforma and Avenida Juárez an interesting spectacle. Any Monday, Wednesday or Friday at exactly 8 pm, the lottery numbers are ceremoniously selected from two cages of numbered wooden balls on the stage of a small auditorium. The ceremony is televised live throughout Mexico and the results are listed like important news on the front pages of some of Mexico's largest newspapers.

Museo de San Carlos The Museum of San Carlos, at the corner of Calle Ramos Arizpe and Puente de Alvarado a block and a half east of the 'Revolución' metro station, is housed in a beautiful late 18th-century two-storey building with columns encircling an interior courtyard. In 1785 the building was dedicated as the Art Academy of San Carlos, one of the first schools of art in Mexico. During the late 19th century, Diego Rivera and José Clemente Orozco were two of the school's most prominent students. The school was gradually converted into a museum.

The ground floor is reserved for temporary exhibits that change every three to six months. One exhibit was an extensive collection of documents, sculptures, paintings and memorabilia chronicling the history of the Mexico City lottery.

Upstairs is the museum's permanent collection of paintings. Several periods are represented: 15th-century religious paintings with thick gilded frames, 17th-century paintings from the Spanish and Dutch schools, Flemish portraits and several rococo and neoclassical works. One example of a 15th-century painting – the *Retablo de la Encanración* – covers an entire wall. Paintings by the 17th-century Spanish baroque painter Francisco de Zurbarán have an uncanny life-like quality, particularly his life-size portrait of San Juan de Dios with a wide-open eye that seems to follow you around the room. Paintings by Goya and the French caricaturist Honoré Daumier are also displayed. Hours are 10 am to 3 pm and 4 to 7 pm. Admission is free.

Monumento a la Revolución A few blocks west and within sight of the Alameda is the Plaza de la República and the huge 'Monument to the Revolution'. The monument was built in the early 1900s by Porfirio Díaz and was supposed to be a meeting-chamber for senators and deputies, but construction was interrupted by the Revolution. Instead, the remains of two Revolution-era presidents – Venustiano Carranza and Francisco Madero – were interred in the wide pillars of the structure and, in the 1930s, it was dedicated as a monument to the 1910 Revolution.

Museo Nacional de la Revolución The National Museum of the Revolution, one of Mexico City's newest museums, is located beneath the base of the Monument to the Revolution in the Plaza de la República. This subterranean museum is devoted to exhibits about life during the 1910 Revolution. A life-size model of a typical bank, the front pages of several newspapers, tools and equipment from various industries, old photographs and a silent movie about the 1910 Centenary celebration are all among the exhibits. The museum is open from 10 am to 7 pm Tuesday to Friday and 9 am to 5 pm on Saturday and Sunday. Admission is free.

El Frontón México – Jai Alai Across from the Monument to the Revolution in a plain, office-like building is Mexico City's Jai Alai Palace. Jai alai, a fast-moving game that originated in the Basque region of Spain, is played with two teams of two players each in a long, walled-in court. Players wear small wicker baskets on their arms, which are used to catch and throw a hard, goatskin-covered rubber ball. Spectators are allowed to bet on each match. Games are played all year every Tuesday, Thursday, Saturday and Sunday from 6.30 pm. Admission is 25c.

Edificio Pasquel at Boulevard Insurgentes 86 is an ordinary office building hardly worth visiting were it not for the unusual display in the lobby. A stuffed menagerie that includes a lion, antelope, water buffalo and two large bears greet you at the entrance.

Zona Rosa Area

The zona rosa area on the south-west side of central Mexico City is comprised mostly of Paseo de la Reforma from its junction with Insurgentes at the statue of Cuauhtémoc to the entrance of Chapultepec Park, as well as those streets on either side of the Paseo named after foreign rivers (on the north-west side) and cities (on the south-west side). The costly (by Mexican standards) pink zone offers glittering hotels, chic nightspots and good restaurants.

Museo de Cera de la Ciudad de Mexico Housed in a stately old zona rosa home, the Wax Museum of Mexico City has an eclectic collection of wax works representing everything from great historical events to freakish fantasies. Figures include Mexican leaders Juárez and Hidalgo, Emperor Maximilian and Empress Carlota in full regal dress, Ayatollah Khomeini, a dapper-looking young Ronald Reagan, Prince Charles and Lady Diana, R2D2 from *Star Wars* and the Creature from the Black Lagoon. The museum is on Londres between Berlin and Bruselas. It is open Monday to Friday 11 am to 7 pm, and Saturday and Sunday 10 am to 7 pm. Admission is US$1.

Bosque de Chapultepec According to popular legend, Chapultepec Park first gained prominence when one of the last kings of the Toltecs and Chichimecs escaped from Tula to the woods of Chapultepec, establishing the area as a convenient place of refuge. Later, the hill for which the park was named (Chapultepec means 'Hill of the Grasshoppers' in the Indian language of Nahuatl) served as a refuge for the Mexica tribe and then as a fortress for Moctezuma I (1440-1469) before becoming a summer vacation residence for Aztec nobles. In the 16th century, Netzahualcóyotl, the King of nearby Texcoco, gave his official sanction to a plan to make the area a park. It has remained Mexico City's largest and attracts hundreds of thousands of visitors daily. The park covers more than four square km (1000 acres) and has lakes, a zoo, botanical gardens, a sculpture garden and museums.

There are several ways of getting to and from the park. Bus Nos 76 and 55 – the 'Zócalo - Km 13' buses – run frequently between it and the zócalo. The bus stop is conveniently located a short distance from the front of the National Anthropology Museum. The metro is also a convenient way of getting to the park. Line 1, the 'Observatorio - Zaragoza' metro - stops at the eastern end of the park near the Museum of Modern Art and the Niños Héroes monument.

El Museo de Arte Moderno The Museum of Modern Art (tel 553-63-13) is one of several museums in Chapultepec Park. It is located near the park entrance and the intersection of Paseo de la Reforma and Calzada Mahatma Gandhi. The smaller round building holds temporary international exhibits, the other houses the permanent collection including works by Mexico's most famous artists: Siqueiros, José Luis Cuevas, Diego Rivera, Velasco and Juan O'Gorman. Hours are Tuesday to Sunday 10 am to 6 pm. Admission is 5c.

Castillo de Chapultepec This overlooks Mexico City from atop Chapultepec Hill. Although Cortés built a fortress here, it was abandoned after his death and fell into ruin. Part of the present castle was built in 1785 as a residence for the viceroy leaders of New Spain until it was again briefly abandoned after independence. Some changes were made in 1843 when the then-vacant residence was converted into a military college, which on 13 September 1847 became the final battle-ground of the Mexican-American War.

When Emperor Ferdinand Maximilian and Empress Carlota arrived in 1864, they moved out of the National Palace in the zócalo and reconverted the castle, with the help of painter Santiago Rebull and architect Vicente Manero, into a royal residence. After their fall from power the castle remained a residence for Mexico's presidents until 1940, when Mexican president Lázaro Cárdenas established a museum here.

Today, the castle houses the Museo Nacional de Historia (The National History Museum), with two floors of exhibits chronicling the rise and fall of New Spain, the establishment of an independent Mexico, the dictatorship of Porfirio Díaz and the Mexican Revolution. In La Lucha de Independencia (The Struggle for Independence) Hall, a magnificent mural by Diego Rivera covers the walls from floor to ceiling and stretches completely around the room.

To get to the castle from Paseo de la Reforma, walk into the park towards the six immense pillars that comprise the Monumento a los Niños Héroes (Monument to the Boy Heroes). The monument was erected at the base of Chapultepec Hill in honour of six army cadets who fought until death rather than surrender the castle to an invading American army on 13 September 1847. Every year on this date, a ceremony is held at the monument to commemorate their act. To the right of the monument, follow the road that curves up towards the castle. You can either take a 10-minute hike up to the Museo del Caracol and Chapultepec Castle or wait for the free shuttle bus. The bus stops in front of the elevator entrance at the foot of the hill road. At the time of writing, the castle elevator was not working. Hours are Wednesday to Monday, 9 am to 5 pm. Admission is less than 5c.

Museo del Caracol Shaped like a snail (caracol), the museum honours 'la lucha del pueblo Mexicano por su libertad', or 'the struggle of the Mexican people for their liberty'. The first of 12 halls also functions as the Gallery of History where temporary exhibits present highlights of Mexican history. Most of the museum is a series of displays and dioramas covering social and political life in Mexico from Spanish colonial days, the divisions of New Spain in the 18th century, Miguel Hidalgo y Costilla's leadership in the struggle for independence, and Francisco Madero's rule in the early 1900s. Your Spanish doesn't have to be excellent to understand the exhibits because most, especially the dioramas, are self-explanatory. The tour ends in a round room that contains only one item – the 1917 Constitution of Mexico. Overall, the museum offers a good summary of Mexican history from the late 18th to the early 19th centuries. It is in Chapultepec Park near the top of Chapultepec Hill, on the south side of Chapultepec Castle. Hours are 9 am to 5 pm, Tuesday to Sunday. Admission is free.

Parque Zoológico de Chapultepec The Zoological Park of Chapultepec dates back to when King Netzahualcóyotl first created Chapultepec Park in the early 16th century and set aside part of it for what was probably the first zoo in the Americas. After Cortés conquered Tenochtitlán in the 1520s he added a bird sanctuary. Today one of the highlights is panda bears, a gift from the People's Republic of China. The zoo is on the west side of Lake Chapultepec and the south side of Paseo de la Reforma across from the National Museum of Anthropology. Once inside, walk or take the zoo tram tour. Hours are 10 am to 4.30 pm.

Jardín Botánico Near the zoo are the Botanical Gardens, a collection of plants and trees from all over Mexico and several other countries. It's open from 9 am to 5 pm and admission is free.

Museo Nacional de Antropología If you have time to visit only one sight in Mexico City, make it the National Museum of Anthropology in Chapultepec Park. It has been deservedly hailed as one of the greatest museums of its kind in the world. The museum is open 9 am to 7 pm

Tuesday to Saturday, and 10 am to 6 pm on Sunday. The restaurant is open daily between 9 am and 7 pm. Admission is free on Sunday and 25c the rest of the week.

From the moment you walk through its doors into the entrance hall, your eyes widen with awe at the architectural splendour of the building, which was designed and built by Mexican architect Pedro Vásquez and his team of fellow architects in the early 1960s at a cost of more than US$20 million. Through the high glass windows of the entrance hall, you can see a long, rectangular courtyard flanked on three sides by the museum's two-storey exhibit halls – a total of four km of hallways. An immense stone pillar, which resembles a giant mushroom, rises from the centre to cover half the courtyard. A pond fills most of the uncovered half.

In the entrance hall is a bookstore with many books in English and Spanish about archaeology and anthropology in Mexico. There's a section for temporary exhibits and an orientation theatre where a 20-minute film presents the history of 'Man in Mesoamerica' (Mesoamerica is Mexico and Central America as far south as Panama). Although the film is in Spanish, most of it is pictorial and can offer a fairly comprehensible introduction to the museum. Daily showtimes are 11 am, 12 noon, 1 pm, 2 pm, 3.30 pm and 4.30 pm, except on Friday when the film is also shown at 5, 6 and 7 pm. Admission is a few token pesos.

Directly above the bookstore is the National Library of Anthropology with research materials covering every archaeological site and major anthropological study in Mexico. Access to the materials is available only to new students and research scholars who have obtained prior permission. There's also the National School of Anthropology where Mexico's future anthropologists and archaeologists study and conduct research.

The museum itself is divided by floor into two subject areas. The ground-floor rooms cover Mexico's prehistoric days and later history with an emphasis on archaeological artefacts. The 2nd-floor rooms cover the diverse ethnography of Mexico with a mind-boggling array of displays from all over the country. Do not attempt to cover the entire museum in a day or even in two days. Instead, visit those rooms with exhibits you are most interested in or, better yet, visit rooms with exhibits representing regions of Mexico that you plan to visit or have visited. Here's a brief guide to the regions and archaeological sites covered:

Rooms 1-4, 13 Introductory/orientation rooms covering 'Introduction to Anthropology', 'Mesoamerican Civilisations', 'Origins of Man in Mexico' and 'Introduction to Ethnography'
Room 3 Origins Room – Santa Isabel Ixtapan and the Valley of Mexico
Room 4 Pre-Classic Civilisations Room – Michoacán, Cuicuilco and Tlatilco
Room 5 Teotihuacán Room – Near Mexico City
Room 6 Toltec Room – Tula, Xochicalco, Campeche, Chichén Itzá and Tenayuca
Room 7 Mexica Room – Tenochtitlán (Mexico City/Templo Mayor)
Room 8 Oaxaca Room
Room 9 Gulf of Mexico – Gulf coast including Tajin and Cempoala, Veracruz
Room 10 Mayan Room – Yucatán Peninsula including Palenque, Yaxchilán, Bonampak and Copan
Room 11 Northern Mexico Room
Room 12 Western Mexico – Michoacán and area from Mazatlán to Acapulco
Room 14 Cora-Huichol Indian Room – Jalisco
Room 15 Purpecha Indian Room – Michoacán
Room 16 Otomí Indian Room – Querétaro and Toluca
Room 17 Sierra de Puebla Room – Puebla region
Room 18 Oaxaca Room
Room 19 Totonac and Huastec Room – Gulf of Mexico
Room 20 Mayan Room – mostly Chiapas, but also parts of Tabasco and the state of Yucatán
Room 21 Northern Mexico – Tarahumara and Yaqui Indians
Room 22 Nahua Room – Central Mexico including San Luis Potosí, Veracruz, Hidalgo

Room by room, here are some of the highlights:

Room 1 has exhibits explaining human evolution and the development of different races. Tools and artefacts from peoples as diverse as the Eskimos and Egyptians are presented as proof of the similarity of cultural development throughout the world. A few exhibits explain archaeologists' methods. Overall, these exhibits are a useful introduction to the rest of the museum.

Room 2 is the Mesoamerican Room with displays covering civilisations and societies in an area that includes present-day Mexico and Central America as far south as Panama. Murals, paintings and models of pyramids, including a scale model of Teotihuacán, are used to show the development of Aztec, Mayan and other civilisations.

Room 3 or the Origins Room offers a survey of human settlement of Mexico. One exhibit features a model of an excavation pit and hunting implements found in an important archaeological dig at Santa Isabel Ixtapan. The implements found at this site and others in the Valley of Mexico suggest that humans settled and hunted here as early as 12,000 years ago.

Room 4 is the Pre-Classical Room, highlighting the transition from a nomadic life of hunting to a more settled life of farming in Mexico about 1000 BC. This transition can be seen in the types of pottery and models of religious structures exhibited in the room – from the simple to the more decorative and symbolic.

Room 5 is the Teotihuacán Room, one of the premier rooms of the museum because Teotihuacán was one of the first major civilisations of Mexico. A topographic scale model and immense photo mural show the capital's past and present splendour. The room's highlight is an actual-sized model of the Temple of Quetzalcóatl.

Room 6 or the Toltec Room contains artefacts representing the Toltecs, the predominant race of people in Mexico from 900 to 1200 AD. Several of the items displayed are from Tula, once the Toltec capital, and include the many small clay figurines made from moulds (probably the first mass-produced art objects of Mesoamerica). The Toltecs were also known for their ball and court game, parts of which are on display and have led some to believe that this was the origin of modern-day basketball. The object of the game was to get a small rubber ball through a stone ring mounted high up on walls on either side of a court-like area.

Room 7 is the Mexica Room, with exhibits and relics from the Mexica or, as it came to be known, the Aztec civilisation. This room is packed with important Aztec relics, including the Aztec stone calendar showing different animal symbols for each day. There's also a scale model of the Tlatelolco market, which according to Cortés was visited daily by more than 60,000 people. In addition you'll see statues of almost every known Aztec god and goddess.

Room 8 or the Oaxaca Room covers Zapotec (the valley people) and Mixtec (the hill people) culture and civilisation. Artefacts from some of Mexico's most important and impressive archaeological sites, particularly Monte Albán, Mitla and Yagul, are displayed. Among the artefacts are Monte Albán pottery and gold burial jewellery.

Room 9 is the Gulf of Mexico Room with exhibits of the diverse civilisations and cultures that existed along the eastern Gulf shore of Mexico. Roughly, they can be divided into three groups from south to north: the Huastecs (present-day Veracruz city area), Totonacs (Villa Rica area) and Olmecs. As with almost every other room in the museum, this one is packed with statuettes, stelae and pieces of pottery.

Room 10 is the Mayan Room with many artefacts from the ancient Mayan sites of Palenque and Bonampak, among others. A short film in Spanish (but somewhat comprehensible to non-Spanish speakers) about the Mayan calendar is shown in a small theatre. Their calendar is considered astronomically more accurate than our Gregorian calendar. Also noteworthy are the tomb of Palenque with its beautiful jade death mask, and the Mayan Cross (dated 642 BC) dedicated to corn.

Rooms 11 & 12 are the North Mexico and West Mexico rooms covering northern Mexico and the south-western USA, and Acapulco to Mazatlán respectively. As evidenced by the displays in these rooms, the peoples in these regions never developed empires or sophisticated architectural and artistic styles similar to those of various Indian groups farther south.

Huastec female

2nd Floor

Room 13 is the Introduction to Ethnography Room. Various examples of daily life, rituals and ceremonies, craftwork and food preparation are presented.

Room 14 contains exhibits that elaborate on certain aspects of people and culture in Mexico. A photographic montage is used to show the different 'faces' of Mexicans. A model of a typical Mexican home is, in a sense, a study of social organisation and family structure. The meaning and ritualistic use of peyote are explained with photographs of ceremonies and displays of implements. Exhibits on the Cora and Huichol Indians are also presented.

Room 15 is devoted to the Purpecha Indians of Michoacán. Implements used in their daily lives for fishing, farming and forestry are displayed. There is also a model of a 'Tarascan' wood cabin with carved cedar pillars and a small front porch (quite unlike most homes in Mexico). Next to the cabin are colourful samples of earthenware pots and dishes.

Room 16 highlights the beautiful basketwork, weaving and leatherwork of the Otomiano Indians of the Toluca Valley. Photographs, diagrams and charts show how they produce the materials necessary for weaving and basket making.

Room 17 is called the Sierra de Puebla Room. The Sierra de Puebla is a mountainous region around the city of Puebla, which is home to four ethnic groups: the Totonacs, Nahua, Otomí and Tepehua. Displays in this room highlight each of these groups with information, photographs and charts describing their dances, social organisation, religion and customs.

Room 18 has a fascinating presentation of Oaxacan Indian herbal medical remedies still used today by many Indians. In addition to herbs, certain roots, leaves, spices and vegetables are also used. For example, one type of tomato is claimed to be helpful in improving circulation and curing varicose veins.

In the same room, an impressive mural shows life in a supposedly typical Oaxacan Indian village and the types of clothing and jewellery worn by Indians such as the Mixtecs, Chinantecos, Cuicatecos and Mazatecos.

Room 19 covers the descendants of Totonac and Huastec Indians in the Gulf of Mexico region. Items on display include native costumes, musical instruments and artwork. Diagrams and photographs explain the famous *voladores*.

Room 20 contains displays about the people of Chiapas, mostly Mayan descendants, who live near Guatemala.

Room 21 covers the Yaqui and Tarahumara Indians of north-western Mexico. Many of the Tarahumaras still live in caves in the Copper Canyon west of Chihuahua.

Room 22 is the Nahua Room with somewhat absurd contemporary exhibits covering the Nahua Indians of central Mexico, the predominant Indian group in the country. For example, a small wooden shack with a big television set and Indian mannequins in work clothes is called a typical Nahua Indian home in the suburbs of Mexico City! Frankly, it is difficult to distinguish this 'Indian' home from thousands of others that have sprung up in the suburbs.

Museo Tamayo de Arte Contemporáneo Internacional

The Tamayo Museum of Contemporary International Art, a modern, multi-level concrete and glass building, opened in 1981 to house the art collection donated by the renowned Mexican painter Rufino Tamayo and his wife Olga to the people of Mexico. Part of the collection is devoted to 20th-century art, including paintings by Andy Warhol and Picasso. Other works include a mammoth rope wall-hanging that resembles a squirming mass of red, black and brown worms and snakes, and a model of a Rolls-Royce made from twigs and branches. The museum is just off Paseo de la Reforma to the east of and on the same side of the street as the National Museum of Anthropology and is open Tuesday to Sunday from 10 am to 6 pm. Admission is less than 10c.

Museo Sala de Arte Público David Alfaro Siqueiros Less than a month before his death in January 1974, David Alfaro Siqueiros, one of Mexico's greatest painters and muralists, donated his house and studio at Calle Tres Picos 29 to the government for use as a museum. Siqueiros' private papers and photographs, along with some of his lithographs, murals and drawings, are on display. Call 531-33-94 to arrange a free guided tour (the only way to visit) Monday to Friday 10 am to 2 pm and 5 to 7 pm, and Saturday 10 am to 2 pm.

Places to Stay – bottom end

Mexico City is full of inexpensive hotels where you can get a good, clean, centrally located room for US$5 to US$10, sometimes even less. Many of these hotels are concentrated in the areas immediately north, south and west of the Alameda. To the west, the area within a two to three-block radius of the Monument to the Revolution offers a fair selection of inexpensive hotels.

West of the Alameda The *Hotel Oxford* (tel 566-05-00), on the quiet Plaza Buenavista at Ignacio Mariscal 67 near the corner of Ramos Alcazar, has clean, carpeted, well-furnished rooms with private bath, plenty of hot water, TV and phone for US$4.50 single, US$5.75 double. Some of the rooms need a new coat of paint and those on the upper floor are brighter.

The extremely popular *Hotel Carlton* at Ignacio Mariscal 32 across Plaza Buenavista from the Oxford is a favourite among budget travellers. Get here early if you want a room; it fills up quickly. Rooms are clean, carpeted and equipped with radios and TVs. The hotel restaurant serves basic meals for US$1. Room rates are US$4.50/5 singles/doubles.

The *Gran Hotel Texas* (tel 546-46-26) is yet another popular travellers' hotel. Rooms are clean, bright and airy but stark. Carpeting – though worn and brown – a telephone, TV and a carafe of mineral water in each room help. Singles/doubles are US$7.25/8.75.

Half a block from the Monument to the Revolution at Gómez Farías 20 is the *Hotel Arizona* (tel 546-28-55). Fairly decent carpeted rooms with telephones and showers, including some with views of the city, are US$7.50 singles, US$8.50 doubles, US$9.50 triples.

Less than a block from the Arizona at Avenida Insurgentes Centro 96 is the plain, almost drab, but clean *Hotel IRYS Astoria*. Some of the rooms on each floor are rented out as office space. Singles/doubles are US$4.75/5.

Within sight of the Plaza de la República and the Monument to the Revolution at Paris 9 is the modern and relatively inexpensive *Hotel Regente* (tel 566-89-33). Clean, comfortable rooms with telephones and large windows, which offer great views of the city, are US$8.50/11 singles/doubles. The hotel restaurant serves a very filling comida corrida for about US$3.75 that includes a daiquiri, Russian salad, a main dish (such as steak, burritos or tacos) and a dessert. Parking is available for restaurant and hotel patrons.

The *Hotel Frimont* (tel 546-25-80) at Jesús Terán 35 is an inexpensive hotel with clean, comfortable rooms, all with private bathrooms. It is often recommended by budget travellers because the rooms are a particularly good deal for the price: US$5 single, US$6 double, US$7 triple.

The *Hotel New York* (tel 566-97-00) at Edison 45 is an excellent bargain with colour TVs, telephones, cushioned chairs and a long counter that doubles as a desk and a dresser in every room. There's even in-house laundry service and room service from the adjoining restaurant. Some of the staff speak English and will help you however they can. Free parking is available in a locked garage next door. Singles/doubles are US$6 to US$8.

Also on Edison at No 106 is the *Hotel Edison* (tel 566-09-33) half a block west of Arriaga. It has parking spaces and clean singles/doubles for US$6.75/7.75 set around a pleasant courtyard. Its only drawback is that it doesn't have many rooms and is sometimes full.

The *Palace Hotel* (tel 566-24-00) at Ignacio Ramírez 7, a block south of the Monument to the Revolution, has good clean rooms with faint pretensions to luxury but little character for US$9.50 single, US$10.75 double.

There are several cheap hotels around the Plaza San Fernando at the junction of Guerrero and Orozco y Berra, ¾ km northeast of the Monument to the Revolution. One traveller recommended the *Hotel San Fernando* where big, light rooms with private bath go for US$3/4.

South of the Alameda The *Hotel Fleming* (tel 510-45-30) at Revillagigedo 35 is in the heart of downtown Mexico City, only a five-minute walk south of the Alameda. At rates of US$7.50/8 for singles/doubles with one or two beds, this place is a bargain. Rooms are clean and include TVs, carafes of drinking water and large tiled bathrooms; some rooms on the higher floors offer great views of the downtown area. Downstairs, the hotel coffee shop offers a filling comida corrida of four dishes, dessert and coffee or tea for US$1.75.

The *Hotel Metropol* (tel 510-86-60) on the west side of Luis Moya between Independencia and Artículo 123 has comfortable, airy rooms with wall-to-wall carpeting, TVs and a water purifier/filter attached to each bathroom sink faucet. None of the rooms offers a great view, but the hotel's central location (only two blocks from the Juárez metro station and the Alameda) is compensation. Singles/doubles are US$9.25/10.25.

From the outside, the *Hotel Conde* (tel 585-23-88) at Calle Pescaditos 15 looks more like a new but dull office building than a hotel. Its antiseptic lobby and frosted glass windows at the reception desk heighten this effect. The rooms, however, are far from stark with fluorescent bedspreads and wall-to-wall carpeting.

Each room has a telephone, TV, carafe of drinking water, shower and bidet. Parking is available on the hotel grounds. Rates are US$5.50 for one or two people.

The *Hotel Sevillano* (tel 512-67-15), on the south side of Calle Victoria between Revillagigedo and Luis Moya, is an older hotel with rooms around a quiet courtyard. Drinking water, bidets and hot showers are available in each room. Rates are US$2.75/4.25 singles/doubles.

The *Hotel La Avenida* (tel 518-10-07) at Lázaro Cárdenas 38 is hard to beat. Don't be fooled by the dark, gloomy lobby. Clean, carpeted rooms with new, tiled bathrooms, filtered water, soap and towels are US$5.25 single, US$6.25 double, US$7.50 for twin beds. Rooms overlooking Lázaro Cárdenas have great views, but the traffic below can be noisy.

The *Hotel Cosmos* (tel 521-98-89) at Lázaro Cárdenas 12 is near the Hotel La Avenida and has clean basic rooms that vary in price from floor to floor. The cheapest and simplest rooms are on the top floor (the 5th) and cost US$2.50. Other rooms cost more because they are carpeted and include TVs, radios and telephones – US$4.75 for a single and US$6.75 for a double. Soft drinks, coffee and hot chocolate are sold in the lobby.

Although the owners of the *Hotel Roble* (tel 522-78-30) at Uruguay 100 seem to have a fetish for orange walls, it is one of the best low-budget deals in Mexico City. Bright, cheery rooms with new wall-to-wall carpeting, framed museum prints on the walls and carafes of purified water are US$5.25 single, US$6.50 double, US$7.25 triple. Some rooms have TVs. Restaurant Mapple, next to the ground-floor reception area, serves a comida corrida for US$1.75 and various other dishes such as spaghetti, soup and sirloin steak starting at US$2.

Small, quiet rooms with carpeting, TVs and filtered water from hallway jugs are available at the *Hotel El Salvador*, República del Salvador 16 half a block east of Avenida Lázaro Cárdenas. Singles/

doubles are US$6.75/8.50 including a 15% tax.

Another good place to stay is the *Hotel Concordia* (tel 510-41-00) at Uruguay 13, also half a block east of Avenida Lázaro Cárdenas, where clean singles/doubles with hot water and telephones are US$4.75/5.25 and US$6.25. A cafeteria attached to the hotel serves sandwiches and tortas in the morning and afternoon.

One of the most inexpensive places to stay is the *Hotel Capitol* (tel 518-17-50) at Uruguay 12 across from the Concordia. The rooms smell like old dusty books, but are otherwise clean. Aside from low rates of US$2.50/3.25 for singles/doubles, its chief attribute is that the rooms surround a large, bright and airy courtyard where you can relax with a cup of muddy coffee from the coffee machine next to the reception desk.

North of the Alameda The grey, monolithic *Hotel Hidalgo* (tel 521-87-71) sits at Calle Santa Veracruz 37, a small back street hidden north of the Alameda. Everything is relatively new. The rooms are carpeted and almost antiseptically clean; all have telephones, TVs and carafes of purified water. A restaurant is attached to the hotel. Room rates are reasonable: US$7.25/9.75 singles/doubles.

If you don't mind rooms with green drapes and views of electrical power lines, then the *Hotel Mariscala* (tel 585-42-88) at Santa Veracruz 12 is a good deal. The rooms are big, clean and carpeted. Most have telephones, TVs and small desks. A restaurant downstairs serves a comida corrida for US$1.50. Room rates are US$6 single, US$8.50 double, US$9.75 triple.

Some travellers have recommended the *Hotel Cuba* (tel 518-13-80) at República de Cuba 69 as a decent, inexpensive place to stay, even though there is hot water only in the mornings and the street can be noisy. Rates are US$3 single, US$3.25 double, US$4 triple.

For a clean, basic, nondescript place to stay, try the *Hotel Florida* (tel 585-32-33)

at Belisario Domínguez 57. Carpeted rooms with TVs and bathrooms that include bidets are US$4.25 for one or two people in a double bed and US$6.25 for two people in twin beds.

If you can get past the pseudo-medieval fortress-style wallpaper in the lobby of the *Hotel Antillas* (tel 526-56-74), then you will find decent rooms with carpeting, bright red bedspreads, carafes of purified water and hot showers for US$6.50 to US$9.50. And who can forget the in-house entertainment – piped-in muzak. A restaurant attached to the hotel serves a comida corrida for about US$1.75. They are at Belisario Domínguez 34.

The *Hotel Congresso* (tel 510-44-46) at Allende 18 has dark rooms with carpeting, drinking water and, in a few, TVs. Free parking is available. Rates are US$3.75 single, US$4.25 double, US$4.75 triple.

Zócalo Area If you want an inexpensive hotel room near the zócalo, the *Hotel Moneda* at Calle Moneda 8 just across from the Museum of Cultures is one of the better places to stay for the price. The rooms are simple and somewhat noisy, but basically comfortable. Singles are US$3.25, doubles US$4.25, triples US$4.75.

Zona Rosa Area The *Hotel Posada de Don Enrique* (tel 566-84-03) at Dinamarca 42 is proof that you can find an excellent and inexpensive place to stay near the zona rosa. Clean rooms with telephones and hot showers large enough for a grizzly bear are US$6/7.25 singles/doubles.

One of the cheapest places to stay in Mexico City – the *Casa SETEJ* (Youth Hostel) – is also near the zona rosa. The hostel (tel 286-91-53) is at Cozumel 57 between Colima and Durango with five beds in each of its 12 single-sex rooms. A SETEJ card is required, but is sold here for US$0.50. Bed and breakfast cost US$2.50.

There is another Youth Hostel – the *CREA Hostel* (tel 573-77-40) – in Mexico

City, but its Villa Olimpica location is too far from central Mexico City.

Northern Bus Terminal Area *Hotel Brasilia* (tel 587-85-77) at Avenida de los Cien Metros 4823, 2½ blocks to the left as you exit the bus station, has comfortable, modern, air-conditioned singles/doubles for US$10.50/11.50.

Places to Stay – middle
West of the Alameda The *Ambassador Hotel* (tel 518-01-10), Humboldt 38, is a sparkling clean and comfortable place to stay. Bevelled windows and muzak in the lobby create a slightly surreal atmosphere. The rooms are less impressionistic with padded vinyl headboards, plain tables and chairs, telephones and colour TVs. A covered and guarded parking structure across the street is available for guests with cars. The Restaurant del Valle attached to the hotel serves a fair comida corrida for US$4. Singles/doubles with bathrooms are US$20.50/21.75.

Also near the Alameda at Jesús Terán 12 is the *Hotel Jena* (tel 566-02-77), a new, gleaming building with some of the best-priced rooms in the middle range. Rooms are ultra-clean with telephones, carpeting, piped-in music, TV and 'sanitised' toilets. Purified water is available from special hallway taps. Singles/doubles are US$14.50/17; suites are US$24.

South of the Alameda The *Hotel Bamer* (tel 521-90-60) at Juárez 52 is a tourist-class hotel in a spectacular central location overlooking the Alameda. In the lobby and reception area, the polished floor, white statues, huge globe and Mexican businessmen shuffling in and out give you the impression that the rooms are expensive. Actually, for what you get – large, comfortable rooms with fantastic views of the Alameda – the rates are reasonable. Singles are US$21, doubles US$22, triples US$25, an excellent bargain if this is in your budget. A restaurant on the 15th floor serves a

comida corrida of salad, two typical Mexican dishes and dessert for US$2.75.

North of the Alameda At Avenida Hidalgo 85, the north-west corner of the Alameda, is the colonial-style Best Western *Hotel de Cortés* (tel 518-21-81), which from the outside looks plain and unappealing. However, just past the reception desk is a quiet stone courtyard with thick, sinewy plants and pink arches, which doubles as a relaxing café and restaurant. The rooms are spotless and comfortable with radios, telephone and small windows that look out on the courtyard. Even if you don't plan to stay here, it's a pleasant refuge from the noise and chaos on the streets and a chance to enjoy an 'inn' that dates back to 1780. Rates average US$36/38 singles/doubles.

Zócalo Area Another colonial-style Best Western-run establishment is the *Hotel Majestic* (tel 521-86-00) at Avenida Madero 73 with many rooms overlooking the zócalo. Avoid the rooms near Madero (too noisy) and the rooms facing the inner glass-floored courtyard (unless you don't mind people looking in at you). It's a bit unnerving to walk across the glass floor because it also serves as the lobby ceiling. Considering the great location and relatively high level of standards here, the room rates are surprisingly low (by average American standards): US$32/34 for singles/doubles. Even if you don't stay here, be sure to visit the rooftop café/restaurant for a great view of the zócalo and, sometimes, the snow-capped peaks of the volcanoes of Popocatépetl and Ixtacchíhuatl.

Also near the zócalo and run by Best Western is the *Gran Hotel Ciudad de México* (tel 510-40-40) at Avenida 16 de Septiembre 82. With old cage-like elevators, a crystal chandelier in the foyer and brass lamps in the lobby, it has a palatial turn-of-the-century aura. Rooms are pleasant and, as with other Best Western hotels, the rates are reasonable for what you get: singles US$35, rooms with double bed US$40, with queen-sized bed US$50.

Zona Rosa Area For large, sparkling rooms with kitchenettes near the zona rosa, try the *Hotel Jardín Amazonas* (tel 533-59-50) at Río Amazonas 73. With a swimming pool, parking garage and smiling staff, it resembles a fancy American-style motel without parking. A restaurant is attached to the hotel. Rates average US$14.50/US$18 for one or two people.

A personal favourite in this price range is the beautiful colonial-style *Hotel Vasco de Quiroga* (tel 546-26-14) at Londres 15 near the principal thoroughfares of the zona rosa. At first it doesn't seem like a hotel because the reception lobby and adjoining sitting room resemble a luxurious living room. Dark wood and 19th-century prints of Mexico grace the walls of the lobby and hallways. Bookcases and a baby grand piano make the sitting-room a pleasant refuge after touring the city. The rooms are equally impressive and romantic, with antique furniture and terraces in most rooms, wall-to-wall carpeting, TVs, telephones and newly tiled bathrooms with shower/bathtub combinations. Singles/doubles are US$20.50/21. A restaurant/bar is downstairs just off the lobby.

Places to Stay - top end

Mexico City has several deluxe and 1st-class hotels with room rates starting at US$40. Most of these are located in or around the zona rosa and the Chapultepec Park area. A few major international hotel chains are represented here: the *María Isabel-Sheraton, Hotel Geneve Calinda Quality Inn, Camino Real (Westin Hotels), Hotel Galería Plaza (Westin Hotels)* and *Holiday Inn Crowne Plaza*. There are also several national (chains and independents) hotels in this category: *El Presidente Chapultepec, Hotel Aristos, Hotel Century Zona Rosa* and *Hotel Krystal Zona Rosa*. These hotels are renowned more for their modern architecture, plushly comfortable surroundings and excellent but pricey restaurants than for any historical or distinctly Mexican character.

For full descriptions of these and other hotels in the same category, most travel agents in the USA should be able to help you. Mexican government tourist offices and foreign representatives of the hotel chains can also be helpful.

Places to Eat

Near the Zócalo For a simple, inexpensive meal near the zócalo, try the *Cafetería Popos*, two doors down from the Hotel Majestic. A breakfast of scrambled eggs, bacon or ham, potatoes or beans and free refills of coffee costs US$1. They also serve tacos for 25c each and small sandwiches *(tortas)* for US$0.30 to US$0.50.

If you are hungry before or after visiting the National Museum of Cultures on Moneda, stop across the street at the *Café Moneda* for a chicken comida corrida. A quarter-chicken plate costs US$1.75, a half-chicken US$3.

For good, cheap tacos and enchiladas try the row of *taquerías* on Uruguay between Bolívar and Avenida Lázaro Cárdenas. Although these stands may not look like the cleanest places in the world, your innards are generally safe if you eat tacos made right in front of you.

Since 1939 the *Restaurant Zenon* at Palma (pedestrian mall) and Avenida Madero has been serving excellent Mexican food at reasonable prices. Various a la carte dishes are US$1.75. A three-taco combination plate is US$1.50.

Between the Zócalo & the Alameda *Sanborn's* Casa de los Azulejos (House of Tiles) branch on Madero, half a block east of Lázaro Cárdenas, is worth a visit to see this superb 16th-century Puebla-tile-bedecked building which used to be the home of the condes (counts) of Orizaba. The main restaurant is in an old courtyard (now covered) with a Moorish fountain and odd murals of mythical landscapes and creatures, to which have been discreetly added, in one corner, two owls which are the Sanborn's symbol. The food is the usual Sanborn's mixture of Mexican and North American; a big bacon & eggs breakfast costs US$4. There's also a cheaper counter area. Both eating areas are open from 7.30 am to 10 pm. While you're here you could check the Orozco mural on the stairs and the crafts store upstairs.

Restaurant El Vegetarino at Filomeno Mata 13 between Madero and 5 de Mayo specialises in – you guessed it – vegetarian food. Their specials (US$2) change daily, according to the availability of certain vegetables. Tomato-based dishes almost always seem to be offered here. Spaghetti with tomato and mushroom sauce costs US$2.25.

Restaurant Antequera, across Filomeno Mata from Restaurant El Vegetarino, specialises in chile relleno. It is sometimes included as part of their comida corrida, which costs US$1. Their various dishes and specials are displayed in the window.

Café La Blanca at Cinco de Mayo 40 near the zócalo always seems crowded with foreigners and Mexicans. It's a great place to chat, eat inexpensively (jumbo shrimp US$1 and various sandwiches US$0.65), relax and people-watch with a cup of coffee.

Restaurant La Vieja Estancia is a small, elegant place with white table cloths and a fair selection of red and white wines. A filling breakfast of eggs, beans, tortillas, coffee and juice costs US$1 to US$1.25; a 'New York' steak costs US$4. It is on Madero just to the east of Motolinia.

Near the Alameda & the Monument to the Revolution *Restaurant Montemar*, across from the Jai Alai Palace on Ramos Arizpe, serves a very filling and inexpensive comida corrida that includes fruit salad, soup, *paella* (chicken, seafood, rice and vegetable stew), tasteless *quesadillas* (tortillas with melted cheese), rice pudding and coffee for US$2.

Pepe's Pizza y Pollo is a pizza-and-chicken joint across from the Hidalgo metro station. As you come out of the station, look for the big, bright red neon 'Pizza y Pollo' sign over the doorway; it is at Puente de Alvarado 5. Several types of pizza, including one with a jalapeño pepper topping, are served at prices ranging from US$1.60 to US$2.10. Unless your tolerance for extremely hot peppers is high, don't try any topping with jalapeño peppers. Conveniently, they also serve ice cream.

A favourite restaurant for inexpensive meals which seems to attract many Mexican businessmen is the Italian-style *Cafetería y Restaurant Trevi* named after Rome's famous Trevi fountain. Breakfast is a good deal here: US$1 for juice, eggs, ham and coffee, and US$0.75 for juice, hotcakes, and coffee or milk. For lunch and dinner they serve various Italian dishes as part of a six-course comida corrida – excellent value at US$1.25. The Trevi faces the western end of the Alameda at Colón 1 and Dr Mora.

For a good, clean, Mexicanised coffee-shop, try the *Restaurant y Cafetería Covadouga* at Edison 57-B at the corner of Edison and Alcazar around the corner from the Hotel New York. They serve various Mexican dishes for US$1 to US$2 including a specialty of *milanesa con papas* (breaded potatoes).

For Jewish-Mexican food try the *Restaurant Tel Aviv* across from the Hotel Regente on Paris. A breakfast of steak, eggs, toast and coffee costs US$2. Other items on the menu include omelettes for less than US$1, blintzes (an East European pancake) and a corned beef-and-pastrami sandwich on rye with a side of coleslaw for US$1.25.

The *Café Rosales* at the corner of Rosales and Mariscal, a block north of the national lottery building on Reforma, is a popular and economical Chinese restaurant. One traveller wrote: 'The food is OK. The owner is Chinese. The decor is Chinese. And sometimes (if you ask) you can even hear Chinese music.'

Café La Habana at the corner of Bucarelli and Morelos, a couple of blocks beyond Reforma if coming from the Revolution Monument, is a coffee hangout for an interesting cross-section of Mexico City people, from journalists at the nearby newspaper offices to bohemian-looking characters out of the 1960s. It's a large, bare place that reputedly serves the best coffee in Mexico City. You can eat a tasty torta Habana (with bacon, chile, avocado, onion and tomato) for US$1, good enchiladas Suizas (US$1.25) or meat dishes (around US$3.25). The Habana is open until 11.30 pm daily.

The *Tortería – Jugos y Licuados* across Humboldt from the Ambassador Hotel serves a good selection of freshly squeezed juices, milk shakes (with bananas, strawberries or anything else you want) and small sandwiches.

A sidewalk stall on Emparan, a few metres from the corner of Edison, serves up seafood cocktails that rival any restaurant's. A steady stream of customers testifies to its cleanliness and there's a long list of choices at US$1 or US$2. The larger-sized cocktails are almost meals in themselves.

The *Restaurant El Puerto* at the corner of Iglesias and Ignacio Mariscal does a comida corrida of soup and bread, fish with lettuce and vegetables, and a refresco for US$1 from 11 am to 6 pm.

The restaurant of the Palace Hotel at Ignacio Ramírez 7, a block south of the Revolution Monument, does a good five-course dinner for US$2.50 (sample menu: avocado cocktail, potato soup, enfrijoladas, chicken and dessert). Grills and other specialities go up to US$4.25.

The *Restaurant La Taberna* at Arriaga 14, on the corner of Ignacio Mariscal, is nothing special – the chilaquiles are moderate though lots of good bread comes with them. Paella (US$2) is the speciality

and there are meat dishes up to US$2.75.

The *Hotel Carlton* restaurant on the corner of Ignacio Mariscal and Ramos Alcazar has antojitos and salads for US$1.25, meat dishes for US$1.50 to US$2.50.

The *Hotel New York* restaurant at Edison 45 can be better than it looks with a good selection of meat and poultry dishes offered at prices ranging from US$1 to US$5. They also serve various juices and coffees. The lunchtime comida corrida is popular with local business people.

South-East of the Alameda *Restaurant La Ola Uruguay* is a big, bustling place next to the Hotel Concordia where you can have a breakfast of eggs, tortillas, coffee and juice for US$1.25. They also serve a comida corrida at lunch for US$2.50.

Super Soya at Lázaro Cárdenas 50 is a health-food store with boxes of All-Bran and bottles of vitamins stacked strategically around the store like gun emplacements. Bright, glowing signs plastered on the walls advertise every imaginable type of fruit-juice combination and milk shake. They supposedly serve more than 150 types of muffins and pastries. Hours are Monday to Saturday 9 am to 9 pm and Sunday 10 am to 10 pm.

South of the Alameda *Don Quixote* at Luis Moya 55 between Artículo 123 and Victoria is a basic restaurant devoid of any hint of its romanticised literary namesake. It's the place to come for food that's not tasty, but definitely inexpensive and filling. Service is quick; in fact so quick the chicken wings in the house soup still have a few feathers. The travellers, women with operators' headsets, and dapper military cadets who frequent Don Quixote's don't seem to mind. The comida corrida menu changes daily, but the price hovers at just under US$1. A breakfast of orange juice, coffee, toast with jam and ranch-style eggs is US$0.50.

Restaurant Los Faroles at Luis Moya 41 between Artículo 123 and Independencia serves a good comida corrida of soup, grilled chicken and rice or spaghetti for US$1. At lunch it is full of local businesspeople, but you should be able to find a table.

Cancún Jugos is a popular health-food restaurant on Luis Moya between Independencia and Artículo 123. They offer more than 10 types of fruit-juice mixtures and concoctions, vegetable salads and various fruit salads.

Also on Luis Moya, from Independencia north one block to the Alameda, is a row of grilled chicken and taco stands where you can stuff yourself for less than US$1. Tortillas and salsa are usually served with the chicken.

Near the Zona Rosa If you're in the zona rosa and want a fast, inexpensive meal, head for *Barry Pollo* at Hamburgo and Florencia or *Antojería* at Hamburgo and Niza. Barry Pollo serves roast chicken *(pollo asado)*, cheese fondues and tacos for US$2.25 to US$2.75. Antojería is known for inexpensive chicken enchiladas, tacos, licuados and fruit juices; a meal averages US$1 to US$1.75.

Although *La Cucaracha* (the cockroach) isn't an appetising name for a restaurant, the French and Italian food served here is delicious. Their specialities include pizzas, pasta dishes and French fondues. With average prices of US$4.25 to US$5.25, it attracts fashionable young Mexicans. The restaurant is near Florencia at Hamburgo 177.

Copenhague is a pedestrian-only thoroughfare, renowned for its pleasant sidewalk cafés and restaurants where people-watching is as good as the food. Lunch and dinner prices here are considered high relative to those of most Mexican restaurants.

Mesón del Perro Andaluz (No 28) and *The Piccadilly Pub* (No 23) are two of the better-known restaurants on Copenhague. The Mesón serves a dish of duck in olive sauce that you'll never forget, as well as various reasonably priced lunch specials (US$4 to US$6). If the weather is pleasant, the outside tables are always crowded, especially in the evenings.

A typical English pub and restaurant in the heart of Mexico City seems unlikely, but somehow the *Piccadilly* has succeeded in transplanting a bit of Britain in Mexico. Such English dishes as Yorkshire pudding and roast beef-and-oyster pie are decent here. Prices range from US$4 to US$6 for lunch and higher for dinner.

Around the corner from Copenhague on Oslo is an inexpensive little diner called *La Luna Merendero* ('the lunch-room mirror'). A comida corrida of such mainstays of Mexican cuisine as beans, tacos, burritos and chicken costs US$0.50, but don't expect *haute cuisine*.

Slightly below street level on Londres between Napoles and Havre is a charming, inexpensive little restaurant with straw-back chairs called *La Norice*. They serve a good 'home-made' meal *(comida casera)* for US$0.75. Try their specially spiced *sopa de fideos* (noodle soup).

Tacos al Pastor – Tacos Leo at Plaza Washington (Londres and Dinamarca) is a good, clean place for a plateful of steaming tacos for under US$1.

Restaurant Bar La Estancia, next to the Hotel Jardín Amazonas on Río Amazonas near Paseo de la Reforma, is a pleasant place to munch on a salad and listen to a band in the evenings.

On the edge of the zona rosa at Reforma 292, nearly opposite the US Embassy, the *Restaurant Latino* does one of the best-value comidas corridas in the area for US$1.25.

For a more expensive meal, *La Trucha Vagabunda* (Vagabond Trout) on Londres between Niza and Genova is very hard to beat. Seafood, often cooked at the table, is the speciality; main-dish prices range from US$2.75 to US$7.75. *Huachinango a las brasas* (braised snapper) at US$4 and *trucha del río al pescador* (trout with shrimp) for US$2.75 are both delicious.

Service is with style: order crepes Suzette, sit back and watch the show!

Konditori at Genova 61 between Londres and Hamburgo is a popular Danish and Mexican joint effort, with a vase of flowers on every table and piped-in Viennese waltzes and Mozart concertos. You can choose to sit either inside with the piped-in classical music and tempting scents of freshly baked pastries, or outside under an awning on the sidewalk. Breakfast is their speciality; various egg dishes with coffee or tea, orange juice, bread or pastries cost US$1.90 to US$2.75. A pot of coffee is US$0.75. Their weekend breakfast buffet is a special treat – a large spread of pastries, cereals, eggs made to your liking, juices and many other foods.

Fantasía Tropical on the corner of Niza and Insurgentes does vegetarian salad or a large plate of fruit salad for US$1, yoghurt and fruit for US$0.75, tortas and sandwiches around US$0.50, plus juices and licuados. *Makai* on Genova between Londres and Liverpool is similar and slightly dearer.

Best Tacos in Mexico City At night, the large corner taco stand *El Tizóncito*, which means 'the little charcoal chip', is bustling with hungry customers in designer suits and white-coated waiters bearing stacks of steaming tacos. Catch a waiter and order three or four *tacos al carbón, tacos al pollo* (chicken tacos) or whatever other types of tacos they happen to be selling that day. Condiments like guacamole, salsa and tomatoes are available at most tables. Save the small square of greasy paper that comes with each taco because this is the only way the cashier can tell how many you have eaten. Its two locations – at Tamaulipas and Campeche (the original stand) and Campeche and Cholula – are near each other, but outside of central Mexico City. They are ¾ km (½ mile) east of the Juanacatlán metro station (line 1). From the station, follow Michoacán east until

Campeche and then head south-east seven or eight blocks to the taco stands. It's worth the trek!

Mexican-American Food For desperate devotees of American hamburgers, there are now two *McDonald's* in Mexico City. Or you can resort to one of the 11 Mexico City branches of *Denny's* or other American-style coffee-shops such as *Shirley's* and *VIPs*.

For tourists and travellers these coffee-shops are convenient and predictable because the food is standard American fare – club sandwiches, bacon & eggs, pancakes, steak with potatoes, etc. For Mexicans, however, going to a coffee-shop where prices are higher than in most other restaurants amounts to going out for a special meal.

In central Mexico City, there are *Denny's* restaurants at Mariano Escobedo 402, Juárez and Humboldt, Paseo de la Reforma 509, and Londres and Amberes.

At *Shirley's*, Londres 102 and Paseo de la Reforma 108, breakfast averages US$1 to US$2, and entrees for lunch and dinner are US$3 to US$4. Two specialities are the 'Yankee pot roast' and the 'Smokey Ridge Kentucky ham steak'. If you are truly hungry, the all-you-can-eat buffets are a good deal. During the week the buffet costs US$3.50, on weekends except Sunday mornings US$4, and Sunday mornings US$3.25. You can count on prompt, smiling service here.

VIPS is as ubiquitous and American as Shirley's. Breakfast is their speciality. A continental breakfast of toast or pastry, coffee and juice is US$1.15. A fuller Mexican breakfast of eggs, toast or pastry, sausage, ham or bacon, beans, tortillas and salsa is US$4 and will leave you stuffed. If you want only scrambled eggs with mushrooms, that costs US$1.75. There are 50 branches in Mexico City, including the ones at Niza 2 in the zona rosa and on Madero between República de Chile and Palma (between the zócalo and the Alameda).

Entertainment

Two publications in Spanish give very complete listings of Mexico City's huge variety of entertainment and cultural events. *Tiempo Libre* (Free Time) is a weekly magazine available from bookstalls for 25c. *En Eventos Culturales . . . México te da a Escoger* ('In cultural events . . . Mexico City gives you choice') is monthly, and free from tourist offices. The *Mexico City News* is also a good source of information.

Movies These are a common and inexpensive diversion in Mexico City. American movies are usually dubbed, but a few theatres do show movies with the original soundtrack and Spanish sub-titles. Look in the *Mexico City News* and *Tiempo Libre* for the latest listings. Some of the theatres include the *Tele-Cine Arcadia* at Balderas 39 near the Juárez metro station, the *Cine – Alfa Omega* at Luis Moya 64 between Victoria and Ayuntamiento, *Cine Ciudadela* at Balderas 108 near La Ciudadela, *Cine Diana* at Paseo de la Reforma 423 between Mississippi and Río Nilo, and *Cine Paris*, also on Reforma at No 92 near Lisboa. Average ticket price is US$0.50.

Nightlife Mexico City has many nightclubs where you can listen to music or dance the night away. Some have a cover charge and a minimum drink requirement and can average US$5 to US$10.

For a night of salsa, reggae and Cuban-style tropicale music, try *Catacumbas* at Dolores 16 half a block south of the south-east corner of the Alameda. *La Azteca* in the *Torre de America Latina* is another good nightspot for Latin American music.

For a New York-style discotheque with lots of high-tech lighting and a penetrating sound system, there is *Studio 54* in San Angel. Admission costs US$4.25.

Closer to central Mexico City is the *Florencia* discotheque on Hamburg in the zona rosa. Everything from rock, reggae and salsa to tropicale music emanates from this club.

The *Carrousel Restaurant-Bar* on the corner of Hamburgo and Niza in the zona rosa has live jazz every night. Although there's no cover charge and beer is only US$1, there's no room for dancing and you often have to queue up to get in. Jazz is featured in the *Salon Luz* restaurant-bar on Genova between Londres and Liverpool.

For brassy Cuban-Puerto Rican salsa rhythms, the *Tropicoso* on the corner of Reforma and Niza in the zona rosa is probably Mexico City's most popular venue among Mexicans and visitors alike. It's open 9 am to 4 pm Monday to Saturday. Cover charge is US$1.50 and you have to pay at least US$10 for a half-bottle of alcohol. You can observe proceedings from outside through the big upstairs window before deciding whether to part with your money. There is also a disco and a rumba-tango-paso doble spot in the same building.

Salsa fans can check out *Marciano's* on Bucarelli between Morelos and Atenas, a half km south-west of the Alameda Central. Formerly called El Africa, it used to be a very lively place with irresistible music, dim lighting, a few prostitutes and a lot of people having a good time, where you could buy a bottle of rum between a few people and wiggle the night away. Now it's a bit smarter and has a new name but still purveys the same kind of music.

One traveller reported being taken to a 'superb' student/young people's musical hangout called *Contigo* where drinks were cheap and people from the audience could get up and jam with the informal group of musicians. Unfortunately he didn't know where it was, but he reckoned a lot of locals would.

Four km south of Reforma at the corner of Insurgentes and Filadelfia, the popular disco of the *Hotel de México* has a superb view (it's at the top of a 50-storey building). The music is mainstream and the entry charge of US$5 entitles you to drink as much as you like of beer or cocktails.

Mariachi music abounds at Garibaldi Plaza where several smartly attired mariachi bands vie for attention and tourist dollars.

Sport Soccer is popular on TV but crowds at most games are small. Mexico isn't a first-rank soccer nation despite hosting the World Cup finals twice. The city has several major league clubs and games in a number of stadiums most weekends. The biggest match of the year is usually América (a Mexico City club) against Guadalajara.

The main bull ring is in the Ciudad de los Deportes, off Insurgentes. Sunday is the main bullfight day with fights starting at precisely 4 pm.

Horse races are held Tuesday (winter only), Thursday, Saturday and Sunday all year (except for a few weeks in September and October) at the *Hipodromo de las Américas* north-west of central Mexico City. Most days the races start at 2.15 pm. To get there, take any pesero or combi minivan marked 'Hipodromo' and going south-west or north-west on Paseo de la Reforma. Admission is free except for the small tax that's paid when you purchase a programme. Obviously, the expectation is that you will bet on the races, which can be done at the windows.

Jai Alai This old Basque game (pronounced 'high-a-lie'), introduced to Mexico by the Spanish, is a fast, skilful and elegant sporting spectacle when played by experts, and some of the best can be seen every night except Monday or Friday at the Frontón México on the north side of the Plaza de la República (the plaza with the Monument to the Revolution).

Jai alai is rather like squash played on a very long court, and even more like the English game of racquets. Instead of a racquet the players – two or four – attach a long curved basket to one arm and use it to catch the hard ball and thump it straight back against the end wall of the court. The ball must not bounce twice before being played, must land between an upper and a lower line on the end wall, and must not go off the open side of the court. Only the server or serving pair can score a point. If they lose a rally, the opposition takes the next serve. Most games end when one player or pair reaches 30 points.

Players at the Frontón México are usually semi-professionals earning US$10 to US$15 a night. Some of the best ones leave Mexico City for Tijuana, where pay is higher. The attraction for the spectators is not just the game but the chance to bet on it. The betting system is complicated but is partly explained in the nightly programme. Bookmakers call out changing odds as each game goes on: if a player or pair is way behind and the game is approaching its end, the odds on them will be very long. Admission at the Frontón México is US$1 and play lasts from 6 pm to 12 midnight (you can come and go any time). There's a restaurant and bar, and you can take drinks in to watch the play. It's also possible to see amateurs at play in the mornings by using the back entrance.

Things to Buy

Mercado de Artesanías Also known as La Ciudadel, the market near the army barracks and the metro stations Balderas and Juárez is a souvenir-hunter's paradise of curio shops. Handicrafts from all over Mexico are sold here at prices that are fair even before you begin bargaining. You'll find life-size brass storks, brightly dyed sarapes, multicoloured ceramic parrots, paintings on leather or felt, silver jewellery, guitars, plaster-of-paris statuettes, ceramic slices of watermelon and baskets of every shape and size – some large enough to hide in. Before you buy anything, though, you may want to first visit a Fonart shop to get an idea of prices, selection and quality.

Fonart Fondo Nacional para el Fomento de las Artesanías (National Fund for the

Promotion of Arts & Crafts) is a government-run organisation with shops throughout Mexico that sell handicrafts such as glassware, hand-woven wall-hangings, baskets, ceramic animals and many other items from all over the country. No bargaining is allowed because the government sets the prices, which are still reasonable. The Exposición Nacional de Arte Popular at Juárez 89 and the National Museum of Popular Arts at Juárez 44 are both run by Fonart. There's another shop in the zona rosa at Londres 136. Hours are 10 am to 7 pm, Monday to Saturday.

Sanborn's House of Tiles When looking for handicrafts, it's useful to check out some of the bigger stores first. These give a good idea of what's available and of prices at the middle and upper ends of the spectrum. Sanborn's on Madero, half a block east of Lázaro Cárdenas in downtown Mexico City, is one such store.

La Lagunilla Sunday bazaar is a sprawling flea-market of over 1500 stalls selling antiques, old books (some in English), stamps, pottery, watches, guitars, leather,

clothes, blankets, hats and much more. It spreads out from the corner of Comonfort and Rayón, just east of the intersection of Reforma and Lázaro Cárdenas and about a km north-east of the Alameda Central.

The market has had many homes and survived several attempts to close it, going back to 1792 when its ancestral *vendedores ambulantes* (walking vendors) were ordered out of the zócalo. In the 1930s it settled down on República de Paraguay until in 1957 the city authorities made one last effort to kill it off. The plan backfired and La Lagunilla now has official recognition and a permanent building.

Guerrero is the nearest metro station and bus 'La Villa' along Reforma takes you within a couple of blocks.

La Merced Even larger than La Lagunilla market is the Merced market, a sprawling collection of buildings about two km south-east of the zócalo. Markets for produce, clothing, household goods and almost anything else you may want are housed in separate buildings. Although you can find deals here on baskets and some leather goods, it's not as good as the Mercado de Artesanías.

The Merced metro station (line 1) is near the market.

Getting There & Away
Air – Overseas
Many international airlines fly into Mexico City from North America, Latin America, Europe and Asia, including KLM, Iberia, Air France, Continental, Pan Am, AeroPeru, Lineas Aereas Paraguayas, Delta, Lasca, American Airlines, Taca International Airlines, Transportes Aereos Nacionales, Air Panama International, Avianca, Varig, Lufthansa and Empresa Ecuatoriana de Aviación.

From the USA There are many daily flights or at least connecting flights to Mexico City from almost every major American city including:

Atlanta One direct flight daily on Aeroméxico and several daily connecting flights through Miami International Airport and a few other international airports.

Boston No direct flights, but several daily connections are available on Continental, American Airlines, Eastern, Delta and United Airlines through Philadelphia, Dallas, New York (JFK airport) and Chicago (O'Hare airport).

Chicago Direct daily flights on Mexicana and American Airlines (via Dallas/Fort Worth) and many connecting flights through other USA cities.

Cleveland No direct flights, but several daily connections are available on Delta, Continental, American Airlines and United Airlines through Atlanta, Dallas/Fort Worth and Chicago (O'Hare).

Dallas Several direct daily flights on American Airlines and Mexicana.

Detroit No direct flights, but several daily connections are available on Delta, Continental, American Airlines, Pan Am, Northwest Orient, Braniff via Dallas/Fort Worth, New York (JFK airport) and Kansas City.

Houston More than one direct daily flight on Aeroméxico, Air France and Continental.

Kansas City Usually at least one direct daily flight on Braniff.

Las Vegas Connecting flights through either Los Angeles or Kansas City.

Los Angeles Many direct daily flights on Mexicana, Aeroméxico (usually with stops first in other Mexican cities), Delta and Lasca.

Miami Several direct daily flights on American Airlines and Pan Am.

New Orleans Connecting flights available on American Airlines, Delta, Continental and Aeroméxico through Dallas/Fort Worth and Atlanta.

New York Several direct daily flights on Aeroméxico, Braniff, Continental and Pan Am, and a multitude of connection possibilities.

Philadelphia Direct daily flights on Aeroméxico and American Airlines.

Phoenix Daily connections on United Airlines, Aeroméxico, Delta and Braniff via Los Angeles or Tucson.

Portland Daily connections via Los Angeles or Seattle on Delta or United Airlines.

San Antonio More than one direct daily flight.

St Louis One direct daily flight on Continental.

San Francisco All connections through Los Angeles.

Seattle At least one direct daily flight on Mexicana (usually stopping first in other Mexican cities).

Washington, DC – Dulles International Direct daily flights on Mexicana.

From Canada Direct flights from Canada to Mexico City are not as frequent as flights from the USA. The second-best option is to connect with a direct daily flight departing from a USA city.

Montreal Direct flights four times weekly on either Iberia (Spanish airlines) or Aeroméxico.

Toronto One direct flight every Friday on Aeroméxico.

Vancouver One direct flight twice weekly on Japan Airlines.

From Latin America
Buenos Aires, Argentina Daily connections via Guayaquil (Ecuador), Miami (circuitous route), Rio de Janeiro and Lima (Peru).

Belize City, Belize Connecting flights via Tegucigalpa (Honduras) or El Salvador on Taca International Airlines and Transportes Aereos Nacionales (TAN).

La Paz, Bolivia Connecting flights via Panama City or Lima on Air Panama International and AeroPeru.

Rio de Janeiro, Brazil Daily connections on

Avianca, Pan Am, Aeroméxico and Varig via Bogotá, Lima and Miami.

Santiago, Chile One weekly direct flight on Avianca.

Bogotá, Colombia Direct flights on Avianca and Varig four times weekly.

San José, Costa Rica Direct daily flights on Lasca and Mexicana.

Quito, Ecuador Direct daily flights on Empresa Ecuatoriana de Aviación.

El Salvador Direct daily flights on Transportes Aéreos Nacionales.

Guatemala City, Guatemala Direct daily flights on Mexicana and three times weekly on Aviateca.

Tegucigalpa, Honduras Direct daily flights on Taca International Airlines and Transportes Aéreos Nacionales.

Managua, Nicaragua Direct flights four times weekly on Aerolineas Nicaraguenses (Aeronica).

Lima, Peru Direct flights three times weekly on Aerolineas Argentina and three times on AeroPeru. Also flights on Aeroméxico and Pan Am.

Montevideo, Uruguay One direct flight weekly on Avianca.

Caracas, Venezuela Direct daily flights on Avensa.

From Europe Direct or connecting flights to Mexico City are possible from several European cities, for example:

Amsterdam Direct flights are available almost every day on KLM Royal Dutch Airlines. Several daily connecting flights through other European cities can be arranged.

Brussels No direct flights, but connecting flights can be arranged through Frankfurt, Paris, New York, London, Amsterdam or Madrid.

Frankfurt Direct daily flights on Lufthansa and many connections are possible.

London Direct daily flights through Gatwick Airport on Continental Airlines and many connections through other European cities.

Madrid Direct daily flights on Iberia and four times weekly on Aeroméxico. Several connections available through Miami, San Juan in Puerto Rico, New York, London and Amsterdam.

Moscow Direct flights twice weekly on Aeroflot.

Paris Direct daily flights from Charles de Gaulle and Orly airports and many possible connections.

From Australia & New Zealand No direct flights; the most direct connections are via Los Angeles and San Francisco.

From Japan Direct flights twice weekly from Tokyo on Japan Airlines and many connecting flights through Los Angeles, San Francisco and Dallas-Fort Worth.

Air - Domestic Flights
Aeroméxico and Mexicana have several daily flights between Mexico City and almost every major city and town in Mexico including:

Acapulco Several direct daily flights on Mexicana and Aeroméxico.

Cancún Several direct daily flights on Mexicana and Aeroméxico.

Chihuahua Two flights daily on Aeroméxico and one flight four times weekly on Mexicana.

Ciudad Juárez Several daily flights on Aeroméxico – both direct and with intermediate stops.

Cozumel Several daily flights on Aeroméxico and Mexicana - both direct and with intermediate stops.

Durango Two flights on Aeroméxico - one daily and the other three times weekly.

Guadalajara Many direct daily flights on Aeroméxico and Mexicana.

Hermosillo Several direct daily flights on Aeroméxico and Mexicana.

La Paz Daily flights on Aeroméxico and Mexicana – direct and with stops.

Manzanillo Flights on Aeroméxico and Mexicana every day except Saturday and Sunday.

Mazatlán Several daily flights on Aeroméxico and Mexicana, most with stops.

Mérida Several direct daily flights on Aeroméxico and Mexicana.

Monterrey Several direct daily flights on Aeroméxico and Mexicana.

Nuevo Laredo Two flights on Mexicana – one daily and the other four times weekly.

Oaxaca Several direct daily flights on Aeroméxico and Mexicana.

Puerto Vallarta Several daily flights on Aeroméxico and Mexicana, a few with intermediate stops.

Tijuana Many daily flights on Aeroméxico and Mexicana, almost all with intermediate stops.

Villahermosa At least two direct daily flights on Aeroméxico and Mexicana.

Ixtapa, Zihuatenejo Several direct daily flights on Aeroméxico and Mexicana.

Bus

Buses arrive at and depart from four main terminals 24 hours a day in Mexico City. It is possible to arrive at one of these terminals any time of the day or night and not have to wait long for a bus to almost any town or city in Mexico.

The following guide should help you figure out which terminal you will arrive at or depart from:

Sur	Poniente	Oriente	Norte
Acapulco	Toluca	Acayucan	Aguascalientes
Chilpancingo	–	Amecameca	Chapala
Cuernavaca	–	Cancún	Chihuahua
Iguala	–	Campeche	Colima
Ixtapa	–	Chetumal	Durango
Taxco	–	Córdoba	Guadalajara
Zihuatenejo	–	Cozumel	Guanajuato
Cuautla	–	Fortín de las Flores	Guaymas
Oaxtepec	–	Ixta-Popo volcanoes	Hermosillo
Tepoztlán	–	Jalapa	Los Mochis
–	–	Mérida	Manzanillo
–	–	Oaxaca	Monterrey
–	–	Orizaba	Morelia
–	–	Palenque	Pachuca
–	–	Puebla	Pátzcuaro
–	–	San Cristóbal de las Casas	Puerto Vallarta
–	–	Tehuacán	Querétaro
–	–	Tuxpan	Saltillo
–	–	Tuxtla Gutiérrez	San Juan
–	–	Veracruz	San Miguel de Allende
–	–	Villahermosa	Teotihuacán
–	–	Zempoala	Torreón
–	–	–	Tula
–	–	–	Zacatecas

Terminal de Autobuses del Norte (tel 587-15-52) is the terminal for buses to and from anywhere in northern Mexico, as far south as Pachuca, Papantla and Tuxpan in the east, Guadalajara and Morelia in the west. There are even some buses to Manzanillo. It's at Avenida de los Cien Metros 4907, a half km north off Insurgentes Norte and five km north of the zócalo, the Alameda Central and the Monument to the Revolution. Trolleybus 'Eje Central' and bus No 17-B, 'Central Camionera del Norte-Villa Olimpica', stop in front of the terminal, the former going down Lázaro Cárdenas and the latter down Insurgentes to downtown Mexico City and points farther south.

The terminal is an enormous place with its own post office (open 8 am to 7 pm Monday to Friday, 9 am to 1 pm Saturday, 9 am to 12 noon Sunday), telégrafos office (Monday to Friday 9 am to 8 pm, Saturday 9 am to 12 noon) and bank. As you enter, 1st-class bus lines are generally to the right, 2nd-class to the far right and the left (no political comment intended). There's a left-luggage office at the far right end.

The Terminal Autobuses Norte metro station is just outside the terminal. For city buses and taxis to/from the terminal, see Getting Around. Some of the principal companies and their routings include:

Omnibus de México (tel 567-76-98, 567-67-56, 567-72-87) runs 1st-class buses to more or less everywhere north or north-west of Mexico City including Guadalajara, but not the west coast or the border west of Reynosa. It has 16 buses daily to San Luis Potosí (US$5.25) and three to Ciudad Valles (US$5.75).

Transportes del Norte (1st class, tel 587-55-11, 587-54-00) goes to Nuevo Laredo (US$14.50) 10 times daily (nine of them after 3 pm), Monterrey (US$11.50) about 15 times, Saltillo (US$10.50) six times, San Luis Potosí (US$5.25) 23 times, Querétaro (US$2.75) 11 times, Matamoros (US$13) four times, Reynosa (US$13) twice, Ciudad Valles (US$5.75) once, Tampico (US$7.50) direct at 10 pm, Matehuala

(US$7.50) and Ciudad Victoria. It also sells Greyhound tickets for the USA and Canada.

ADO (1st class, tel 567-15-77, 567-53-22) goes to Papantla (US$3.75) at 1, 8 and 11.30 pm, Poza Rica (US$3.75) 20 times daily, Tuxpan (US$4.25) 17 times, Tampico (US$7.50) 10 times, Pachuca (US$1.25) every 20 minutes, Huejutla, Tantoyuca and Tecolutla.

Tres Estrellas de Oro (1st class, tel 567-71-31, 567-72-74) has expresses to Tijuana (US$36.50) and Mexicali (US$34.25) six times daily. It also has eight buses daily to Los Mochis (US$19.75); many to Guadalajara; several to Morelia; 11 to San Luis Potosí (US$5.25); direct buses to Monterrey (US$11.50) at 7.30 and 10 pm; a few a day to Matamoros (US$13), Brownsville Texas (US$21), Reynosa (US$13) and Nuevo Laredo (US$14.50); and one bus to Mazatlán (US$14.50) at 10 pm.

Transportes del Pacífico (1st class, tel 587-58-21, 587-52-21) has buses to Mexicali (US$34.25), Tijuana (US$36.50), Guadalajara, Mazatlán, Tepic, Hermosillo and Nogales (US$29.25) at 7.30 and 11.30 pm.

Transportes Chihuahuaenses (1st class, tel 587-52-66, 587-53-99) goes to Chihuahua (US$18) and Ciudad Juárez (US$22.50) 13 times daily each, San Luis Potosí (US$5.50) 10 times, Fresnillo, Zacatecas, Querétaro and Guadalajara.

Anáhuac (tel 587-53-01, 587-52-12, 587-52-09) has 1st-class buses to Querétaro (US$2.75) four times daily, San Luis Potosí (US$5.25) 10 times, Matehuala (US$7.50) nine times, Saltillo (US$10.50) seven times, Monterrey (US$11.50) six times, Piedras Negras (US$15.75) at 10 am and 9.30 pm, Ciudad Acuña (US$16.50) at 3 pm.

Approximate 1st-class journey times: Tijuana 24 to 27 hours, Ciudad Juárez 26 hours, Nuevo Laredo 16 hours, Monterrey 12 hours, Saltillo 11 hours, San Luis Potosí 5½ hours, Matehuala seven hours, Ciudad Valles 10 hours, Ciudad Victoria 13 hours, Reynosa 16 hours, Matamoros 18 hours, Tampico 9 to 11 hours, Guadalajara seven hours, Pachuca 1½ hours.

Anáhuac has 2nd-class buses to the same destinations as its 1st-class services at about the same frequency for 10% less.

Estrella Blanca (2nd class, tel 587-53-44, 587-53-66, 587-52-55) goes to Guadalajara (US$7) 23 times daily, Puerto Vallarta (US$11.50) twice, Mazatlán three times, Zacatecas (US$7.25) and Fresnillo 16 times each, Torreón (US$11.50) 10 times, Durango (US$10.25) eight times, Poza Rica (US$3.25) 19 times direct with a toilet on board (!), San Luis Potosí (US$4.75) 21 times direct, Monterrey 14 times, Nuevo Laredo (US$13) eight times direct, Matamoros (US$11.75) and Reynosa (US$12) four times each, Ciudad Juárez (US$20.50) six times, Aguascalientes, Guanajuato, Chihuahua, Tuxpan, Tampico and Ciudad Victoria.

Flecha Amarilla (2nd class, tel 567-78-87) goes to Guadalajara (US$7) 41 times daily via Atotonilco, Manzanillo (US$9.25) three times and León four times. Buses also run with varying frequency to Toluca, Uruapan, Lagos de Moreno, Morelia, Aguascalientes, Querétaro, Guanajuato, San Luis Potosí, San Miguel de Allende, and most other places in between.

Herradura de Plata (2nd class) goes to Querétaro (US$2.50), San Miguel de Allende (US$3.25) and Dolores Hidalgo (US$3.50) every hour, and to Morelia direct every hour from 6 am to 4 pm.

Flecha Roja (2nd class, tel 567-08-97, no 'Flecha Roja' sign above its ticket office) goes to Pachuca (US$1) direct every 10 minutes, to Ciudad Valles (US$5.25) about 15 times daily, also to Ixmiquilpan and Tamazunchale.

Mexico-Tuxpan-Tampico (2nd class) goes direct to Pachuca (US$1) every 15 minutes.

Transportes Norte de Sonora (2nd class, tel 587-55-66, 587-56-33) serves the north-west.

Autobuses San Juan Teotihuacán (at the far left end) go to the Teotihuacán pyramids (US$0.65, one-hour journey) every 20 minutes from 6 am to 6 pm.

Autotransportes Valle del Mezquital (also at the far left end) has frequent buses to Tula (US$1.25). The 'Refinería' route is the quicker and more comfortable of the two options.

Terminal Autobuses Pasajeros del Oriente
The Terminal Autobuses Pasajeros del Oriente (TAPO for short) is the departure and arrival point for buses serving east and south-east Mexico, including Puebla, central and southern Veracruz, Oaxaca, Chiapas, the Guatemalan border and the Yucatán.

For Papantla, Tuxpan and Tampico you have to depart from the northern terminal.

TAPO is on Calzada Ignacio Zaragoza between Avenida Eduardo Molina and Avenida Oceanía, about two km east of the zócalo. The San Lázaro metro station (line 1) is right next door. Bus No 20 ('Hipodromo-Pantitlán') runs from Donceles in downtown Mexico City, along Hidalgo and then Alvarado to the terminal. For other transportation to/from TAPO, see Getting Around. There's a tourist office in the terminal – often closed but helpful when open.

ADO (1st class, tel 522-29-33, 522-61-53, 522-94-00) goes to Puebla (US$1.75) direct every 15 minutes from 5 am to 10 pm, to Acayucan (US$8.50) 10 times, Campeche (US$16.75) six times daily, Cancún (US$22.75) four times, Catemaco (US$7.50) three times, Coatzacoalcos (US$9.25) 18 times, Córdoba (US$4.25) 26 times, Fortín de las Flores (US$4) five times, Jalapa (US$4) 23 times, Mérida (US$19) six times, Oaxaca (US$6.75) 30 times, Orizaba (US$4) 29 times, Palenque (US$13) at 4 and 6 pm, San Andrés Tuxtla (US$7.25) 13 times, Santiago Tuxtla (US$7.25) three times, Tehuacán (US$3.25) six times, Tlaxcala (US$1.50) five times, Veracruz (US$5.50) 30 times, Villahermosa (US$11.25) 19 times and Zempoala (US$5) three times. Some of these services are direct or semi-direct, some stop along the way.

Cristóbal Colón (tel 542-72-63) has 1st and 2nd-class services. Among the 1st-class ones are Amecameca (US$0.75) every hour, Chiapa de Corzo (US$13.25) once a day at 6.15 pm, Comitán (US$15.25) at 2.15 and 11 pm, Cuautla (US$1.25) hourly, Juchitán (US$10.25) three times daily, Puebla (US$1.75) six times, Salina Cruz (US$10.75) three times, San Cristóbal de Las Casas (US$14.25) at 2.15, 6.15 and 11 pm, Talismán on the Guatemalan border (US$15, with connections on to Guatemala City available for US$6.75) four times daily, Tapachula (US$14.75) eight times, Tehuantepec (US$10.50) three times, Tlaxcala (US$1.50) a few times, Tonalá in Chiapas (US$12) three times, Tuxtla Gutiérrez (US$13) at 7.30 and 9.30 pm.

Approximate 1st-class journey times: Amecameca 1½ hours, Acayucan 11 hours, Córdoba four hours, Jalapa 4½ hours, Juchitán 14 hours, Mérida 24 hours, Oaxaca nine hours, Palenque 16 hours, Puebla two hours, San Andrés Tuxtla nine hours, San Cristóbal de Las Casas 21 hours, Tapachula 21 hours, Tehuantepec 14 hours, Tlaxcala two hours, Tuxtla Gutiérrez 19 hours, Veracruz 6½ hours, Villahermosa 14 hours.

Cristóbal Colón 2nd-class services include buses to Arriaga in Chiapas (US$10.50), Juchitán (US$9.25), Tapachula (US$13.25) and Tehuantepec (US$9.50).

AU (2nd class) goes to Puebla (US$1.50) direct every 15 minutes from 5 am to 10 pm, Puebla via Cholula (US$1.50) every 30 minutes from 5 am to 7 pm, Acayucan (US$7.50) seven times, Arriaga (US$10.50) four times daily, Catemaco (US$6.75) twice, Coatzacoalcos (US$8.50) seven times, Córdoba (US$3.75) 25 times, Jalapa (US$3.75) 14 times, Juchitán (US$9) six times, Orizaba (US$3.50) 25 times, Salina Cruz (US$9.50) twice, San Andrés Tuxtla (US$6.50) twice, Santiago Tuxtla (US$7) twice, Tehuacán (US$2.75) 12 times, Tehuantepec (US$9.25) twice, Tuxtepec (US$5.50) six times, Veracruz (US$5) 12 times, Villahermosa (US$10.25) three times.

Other 2nd-class lines operating from Tapo: Estrella Roja (tel 571-6157, 522-3687) runs buses to Puebla (US$1.50) direct every 15 minutes from 6 am to 9 pm, to Huejotzingo (US$1.25) and Cholula (US$1.50) every 15 minutes from 5 am to 10 pm. Mexico-Texcoco runs buses to Tlaxcala 11 times daily, Puebla six times, Cuetzalán at 7.20 pm, Jalapa and Veracruz. Lineas Unidas Mexico-Oaxaca runs buses to Oaxaca (US$6) hourly from 5 to 7.45 am and direct every 15 minutes from 8 to 11 pm, to Putla (US$6) three times daily.

Terminal de Autobuses de Poniente (tel 271-04-81, 271-05-78) is a relatively small terminal whose buses primarily service the Mexico City-to-Toluca route. The terminal is at Río Tacubaya 102 near the line 1 metro station 'Observatorio'. Bus No 76 ('Zócalo-Km 13') runs from the terminal to Paseo de la Reforma, Avenida Juárez, Avenida Madero and the zócalo. It also handles a few of the slower buses to Guadalajara and Morelia. Flecha Roja has buses to Toluca (US$0.75) every two minutes from 5 am to 11 pm. Turismos Mexico-Toluca (tel 271-14-33) runs buses to Toluca (US$0.75) every 10 minutes.

Terminal Central de Autobuses del Sur (tel 689-05-00) serves several destinations from Mexico City to Acapulco and Zihuatenejo on the west coast. The terminal is next to the Tasqueña metro station (line 2) at Tasqueña 1320. Trolleybus 'Eje Central' runs from the terminal to Avenida Lázaro Cárdenas downtown and then all the way to the northern terminal. Taxis and peseros are plentiful and inexpensive. A hotel kiosk at the station entrance is open from 10 am to 5 pm Monday to Friday for making reservations in Acapulco.

Estrella de Oro (1st-class express, tel 549-85-20, ext 184) has buses to Cuernavaca (US$0.80, 1½ hours) 15 times, Taxco (US$2.25, three to 3½ hours) six times daily, Acapulco (US$6, 7½ hours) 20 times, Zihuatenejo (US$9.50) three times and Ixtapa (US$9.60, 12 hours) three times. Unlike the other companies in the terminal, Estrella de Oro has ticket windows with their own lines and computer terminals for check-in – very efficient service.

Autos Pullman de Morelos (1st class, tel 672-38-90) serves Cuernavaca (US$0.80) with buses every 10 minutes from 5.30 am to 9 pm and every half-hour from 10 pm to midnight. Buses to Las Grutas de Cacahuamilca (US$1.50) leave every two hours from 6.50 am to 2.50 pm and make several stops along the way.

Estrella Roja (1st class) has buses to Oaxtepec (US$1, one hour 20 minutes) and Cuautla (US$1.05, one hour 40 minutes) more than 20 times daily from 7 am to 9 pm. At 10 p.m there's

a bus to Zihuatenejo via Altamirano (US$3).
Buses to Taxco (US$1.60) leave daily at 7, 9 and
11 am, and at 12.30, 1.30, 2.30, 4.30 and 6.30
pm.

Flecha Roja Lineas Unidas del Sur has direct
buses every 15 minutes to Cuernavaca
(US$0.55) from 6 am to 9.30 pm and frequent
departures to Acapulco, Ixtapa, Taxco and
Iguala.

Omnibus Cristóbal Colón (1st class) has buses
to Tepoztlán (US$0.80, 1¼ hours) every hour
from 6.45 am to 9 pm and to Cuautla (US$1)
every half-hour from 6 am to 11 pm.

Greyhound Bus Booking Office The USA-
based Greyhound bus company has a
ticket office at Paseo de la Reforma 27 (tel
591-03-38). Although they serve only as
far south as the Mexican border towns and
cities, tickets can be bought here for most
USA destinations. In addition, tickets for
most inter-city Mexican bus lines are also
sold here.

Rail
All trains in and out of Mexico City arrive
at and depart from the city's equivalent of
Grand Central Station – Estación Buenavista, a wide, cavernous building at
Insurgentes Norte and Mosqueta about
1½ km or a 20-minute walk from the
Monument to the Revolution (a budget-
hotel area). If you don't feel like walking
between the station and central Mexico
City, you can take any bus or pesero/
colectivo going north along Insurgentes.
Private taxis from in front of the station
are another option, but be sure to set the
fare in advance or check that the meter
actually works.

Inside the station, if you have any
questions, skip the information kiosk in
the main hall and head straight for the
well-marked 'International Passengers
Office', open daily from 7.30 am to 3 pm
(sometimes longer if necessary). Guadalupe
Olvera, the office manager, speaks fluent
English – she lived in the USA for a few
years – and can help you with information

and reservations. You can call her too at
547-89-71. Ticket and reservation information in English can be obtained by calling
547-65-93.

Ticket offices *(taquillas)* are open 6 am
to 9.30 pm daily. Tickets for sleeping
accommodation and 1st-class reserved
seats must first be reserved at the *mudolo
de asignaciones* on the main concourse
and then purchased at a taquilla.

The station has a left-luggage office and
a slow, over-priced restaurant (scrambled
eggs, bacon and bolillos US$1.50) upstairs.

According to the International Passengers
Office, reservations for train trips originating or ending in Mexico City should be
made at least 30 days in advance if you
plan to travel during holiday periods and
you want a space in a sleeper car. For trips
originating in Mexico City, write to
Señora Guadalupe Olvera or Señor Javier
Sánchez Méndez, c/o Passenger Traffic
Department, National Railways of Mexico,
Buena Vista Grand Central Station
06358, Mexico DF.

Your reservation request should include
all itinerary details and the type of seat or
space you want. For a full explanation of
what's available and where to write for
reservations from cities other than
Mexico City, see the Getting There
chapter.

The official in charge of the station will
reply with a preliminary confirmation
and a request for a bank draft, cashier's
cheque or certified cheque in pesos for the
amount of the ticket desired. Cancellations
or changes are accepted up to 24 hours
before departure.

In theory, this is how the system is
supposed to work; in practice, reservations
don't always seem to be necessary. If you
are on a very definite itinerary and require
a reserved 1st-class seat or sleeper
compartment, then we recommend that
you make reservations 30 days in
advance. On the other hand, if your
itinerary is more flexible, then you can
probably afford to wait and see if there are
any cancellations.

Supposedly, you can also make reservations at the office of the Chihuahua-Pacific Railroad (Ferrocarriles del Chihuahua-Pacífico) near the Buenavista station for the Copper Canyon trip between Los Mochis and Chihuahua or vice versa. It's on the 6th floor of the white earthquake-damaged office building across from the station; you can't miss it because it's the tallest white building in the immediate area.

Following are the daily schedules of trains to and from Mexico City, but be forewarned that according to the International Passengers Office at Buenavista station, these schedules are subject to change without notice:

Mexico City-Mérida

(35½ hours)
Train 49

departs	Mexico City	6.30 pm
	Córdoba	1.15 am
	Tierra Blanca	3.35 am
	Medias Aguas	7.50 am
	Empalme FUS	10.20 am
	Teapa	5.09 pm
	Palenque	7.45 pm
	Campeche	2.40 am
arrives	Mérida	6.00 am

Train 50

departs	Mérida	10.00 am
	Campeche	1.05 am
	Palenque	8.37 am
	Teapa	11.07 am
	Empalme	3.20 pm
	Medias Aguas	6.30 pm
	Tierra Blanca	11.02 pm
	Córdoba	1.35 am
arrives	Mexico City	9.15 am

According to the Passenger Office, no sleeper cars are available on either train, only 1st and 2nd-class coach seats.

Mexico City to Puebla and Oaxaca

(14 hours, 32 minutes)
Train 113/114

departs	Mexico City	5.32 pm
	Puebla	10.55 pm
arrives	Oaxaca	8.05 am

Train 114/113

departs	Oaxaca	6.20 pm
	Puebla	3.30 pm
arrives	Mexico City	8.52 am

2nd-class coach, 1st-class coach and 1st-class reserved seats are available.

Mexico City to Morelia-Pátzcuaro-Uruapan

(14 hours, 10 minutes)

		Train 29	Train 27
departs	Mexico City	6.55 am	9.29 pm
	Toluca	9.35 am	11.46 pm
	Morelia	5.12 pm	6.08 am
	Pátzcuaro	6.46 pm	7.36 am
arrives	Uruapan	9.05 pm	10.07 am

		Train 28	Train 30
departs	Uruapan	7.15 pm	6.35 am
	Pátzcuaro	9.25 pm	8.45 am
	Morelia	10.57 pm	10.22 am
	Toluca	5.27 am	6.00 pm
arrives	Mexico City	7.50 am	8.50 pm

2nd-class coach, 1st-class coach and 1st-class reserved seats, berths, roomettes and bedrooms are available on train Nos 27 and 28. Only 2nd-class coach, 1st-class coach and 1st-class reserved seats are available on train Nos 29 and 30.

Mexico City-Ciudad Juárez

(35½ hours)
Train 7

departs	Mexico City	7.50 pm
	Tula	9.28 pm
	Querétaro	12.53 am
	Irapuato	2.50 am
	Silao	3.52 am
	Aguascalientes	7.40 am
	Zacatecas	10.33 am
	Chihuahua	1.47 am
arrives	Ciudad Juárez	7.20 am

Train 8

departs	Ciudad Juárez	6.25 pm
	Chihuahua	11.25 pm
	Zacatecas	3.41 am
	Aguascalientes	6.10 pm
	Silao	10.35 pm
	Irapuato	11.00 pm
	Querétaro	1.30 am
arrives	Mexico City	6.15 am

All seating and accommodation arrangements are available on both trains.

Mexico City-Querétaro Express A new express train called *El Constitucionalista* was inaugurated in 1987 for service between Mexico City and Querétaro. The trip takes two hours and 57 minutes and includes breakfast on the first run and dinner on the second. It departs Mexico City at 7 am and Querétaro at 6 pm. Only 1st-class reserved seats are available.

Mexico City-Monterrey-Nuevo Laredo
(23 hours, 20 minutes)

		Train 71	Train 1
departs	Mexico City	6.00 pm	8.00 am
	Querétaro	–	12.56 pm
	San Miguel de Allende	–	2.35 pm
	San Luis Potosí	12.46 am	5.08 pm
	Saltillo	6.34 am	11.53 pm
	Monterrey	9.00 am	2.20 am
arrives	Nuevo Laredo	–	7.20 am

		Train 2	Train 72
departs	Nuevo Laredo	6.55 pm	–
	Monterrey	11.30 pm	6.00 pm
	Saltillo	2.35 am	8.10 pm
	San Luis Potosí	10.05 am	1.50 am
	San Miguel de Allende	1.09 pm	–
	Querétaro	2.42 pm	–
arrives	Mexico City	7.20 pm	8.46 am

Roomettes, bedrooms and dining cars are available on train Nos 71 and 72. Only 2nd-class coach, 1st-class coach and 1st-class reserved seats are available on train Nos 1 and 2.

Mexico City-Guadalajara
(13¼ hours)
Guadalajara is the transfer point for Pacific Railways, which runs north to San Blas (junction with the Chihuahua and Pacific 'Copper Canyon' train), Benjamín Hill (junction with Sonora and Baja California Railways to Mexicali) and Nogales.

		Train 11	Train 5
departs	Mexico City	6.05 pm	8.30 pm
	Querétaro	11.30 pm	1.34 am
	Irapuato	1.58 am	3.33 am
arrives	Guadalajara	7.20 am	8.10 am

		Train 6	Train 12
departs	Guadalajara	8.55 pm	7.30 pm
	Irapuato	1.17 am	11.12 am
	Querétaro	3.35 am	2.43 am
arrives	Mexico City	8.08 am	7.40 am

Train Nos 5 and 6 have only sleeper cars and a dining car. Train Nos 11 and 12 have 2nd-class coach, 1st-class coach and 1st-class reserved seats only.

Mexico City-Fortín-Veracruz
(11 hours, 26 minutes)

		Train 51	Train 53
departs	Mexico City	7.34 am	9.32 am
	Fortín	4.00 pm	4.24 am
	Córdoba	4.12 pm	4.35 am
arrives	Veracruz	7.00 pm	7.00 am

		Train 54	Train 52
departs	Veracruz	9.30 pm	8.00 am
	Córdoba	11.41 pm	10.25 am
	Fortín	12.03 am	10.50 am
arrives	Mexico City	7.37 am	7.12 pm

Coach seats only on train Nos 51 and 52; coach seats, 1st-class reserved seats, roomettes and bedrooms on train Nos 53 and 54.

One-Way Fares from Mexico City As with the schedules, fares are also subject to change without notice. All of the following are approximate US$ amounts:

From Mexico City to:	2nd cl coach	1st cl coach	1st cl rsrved	lower berth	upper berth	single roomette	bedroom
Aguascalientes	$ 2.25	$ 3.75	$ 3.75	$ 4.75	$ 3.75	$ 6.50	$ 9.25
Benjamín Hill	$ 8.00	$14.00	$17.25	-	-	$22.00	$31.50
Campeche	$ 5.25	$ 9.25					
Ciudad Juárez	$ 7.00	$12.50	$15.25	$13.25	$10.50	$18.50	$26.50
Chihuahua	$ 5.75	$10.25	$12.50	$11.25	$ 9.00	$15.50	$22.25
Córdoba	$ 1.25	$ 2.25	$ 2.50	$ 2.75	$ 2.25	$ 3.75	$ 5.50
Empalme FUS	$ 2.50	$ 4.75	-	-	-		
Guadalajara	$ 2.25	$ 4.00	$ 4.75	$ 4.75	$ 3.75	$ 6.75	$ 9.50
Irapuato	$ 1.25	$ 2.25	$ 2.75	$ 2.75	$ 3.00	$ 2.25	$ 4.00
Mazatlán	$ 4.25	$ 7.50	$ 9.25	-	-	$13.25	$18.75
Mexicali	$10.00	$17.50	$21.50	-	-	$28.00	$40.00
Mérida	$ 5.75	$10.25	-	-	-	-	-
Monterrey	$ 3.50	$ 6.25	$ 7.75	-	-	$ 9.75	$14.00
Morelia	$ 1.50	$ 2.50	$ 3.00	$ 3.00	$ 2.50	$ 4.25	$ 6.00
Nuevo Laredo	$ 4.50	$ 8.00	$10.00	-	-	-	-
Nogales	$ 8.50	$15.00	$18.25	-	-	$ 2.50	$ 3.50
Oaxaca	$ 2.00	$ 3.75	$ 4.50	-	-	-	-
Palenque	$ 3.75	$ 6.50					
Pátzcuaro	$ 1.50	$ 2.75	$ 3.50	$ 3.50	$ 2.75	$ 5.00	$ 7.00
Puebla	$ 0.75	$ 1.50	$ 1.75	-	-	-	-
Querétaro	$ 1.00	$ 1.50	$ 2.00	$ 2.50	$ 2.00	$ 3.50	$ 5.00
Saltillo	$ 3.25	$ 5.50	$ 7.00	$ 6.25	$ 5.00	$ 7.00	$12.50
San Luis Potosí	$ 2.00	$ 3.25	$ 4.00	-	-	$ 5.00	$ 7.00
San Miguel de Allende	$ 1.25	$ 2.00	$ 2.50				
Teapa	$ 3.50	$ 6.00	-	-	-		
Tepic	$ 3.25	$ 5.50	$ 6.75	-	-	$10.25	$14.50
Toluca	$ 0.25	$ 0.50	-	-	-	-	-
Tula	$ 0.45	$ 0.50	$ 0.75				
Uruapan	$ 2.00	$ 3.25	$ 4.00	$ 4.10	$ 3.25	$ 5.75	$ 8.10
Veracruz	$ 1.50	$ 2.75	$ 3.50	$ 3.50	$ 2.75	$ 5.00	$ 7.00
Zacatecas	$ 2.50	$ 4.50	$ 5.50	$ 5.50	$ 4.25	$ 7.50	$10.75

Getting Around

Airport Terminal Information Domestic and international arrivals and departures are in five clearly marked sections (*salas*) of the one and only terminal: Sala A – domestic arrivals, Sala B – domestic departures and ticket counters for national airlines, Sala C – European airlines ticket counters, Sala D – North American airlines ticket counters, and Sala E – all international arrivals.

Money-exchange counters that offer some of the best rates in Mexico City are across from the gates in each arrival section and are supposedly open 24 hours. A post office and telegram/telex centre are set up near the domestic departures sections.

If you need them, there are guarded left-luggage lockers in Sala A. They cost US$0.60 for 24 hours.

Banks of public telephones are located throughout the terminal. Local calls are free.

Car-rental kiosks can be found at the international arrivals section (Sala E). If no one is present, check the kiosk for a telephone number to call.

A tourist information booth in Sala A offers a map and leaflets about Mexico City from 8 am to 9 pm.

Airport Transport Unless you are renting a car, the only two ways to go the 6½ km between the zócalo and the airport are metro and taxi. Buses and minibuses run near the airport, but the extra walking you'd have to do is inconvenient, especially if you have baggage.

Officially, you're not supposed to travel on the metro with anything larger than a shoulder bag. However, this rule isn't always enforced before 7 am and after 9 pm, the only times when the metro is not too crowded. The airport metro station is 200 metres up the sidewalk from Domestic Departures, Section A. If you are coming from the terminal and you can see a parking structure on your right, then you are headed in the right direction.

If you're going to the airport by metro, don't make the mistake of believing that the Aeropuerto metro stop serves the airport; you'll find yourself a km or two away. Termina Aerea is the stop you want; follow the 'Salida – Avenida Aeropuerto Municipal' signs as you leave the station.

Taxis from the airport are relatively inexpensive because fares are government-controlled. Just outside the international arrivals section is a taxi ticket window where you pay for your fare in advance. The ticket-seller will ask the name of your hotel and then determine your fare according to a zone chart. You can expect to pay US$3 to US$4 to go to a hotel in the downtown Plaza de la República area. The ticket is valid with any of the cabbies hovering around the terminal. Tips aren't expected, but are appreciated.

The easiest way to get to the airport from downtown is to call Transporte Terrestre (tel 571-93-44) between 8 am and 9 pm. If you're going to the airport from east of Mexico City, ADO buses from Puebla will drop you at Boulevard Aeropuerto in the capital, from where you can get a taxi or pesero to the airport – much quicker than going in to the bus terminal and then out to the airport. Keep your luggage with you and tell the driver in advance.

Bus Getting around by bus is the most popular (and sometimes most crowded) mode of transportation in Mexico City. According to Mexican government studies, over 15 million people use Mexico City's 6000 buses daily; this is less than a third of the buses actually needed. Routes are most crowded during the morning and late afternoon/early evening rush hours when people are commuting to and from work. During other hours, those routes of interest to the traveller are not too crowded. Whenever travelling in Mexico City by bus, however, beware of pickpockets and thieves. Hang on to your bags and be sure your money and passport are well hidden beneath your clothing, not in your pockets. Some pick-pockets are so deft that you may not know that your pocket has been picked or cut open until after you're off the bus.

As long as you don't ride during rush hours and are careful with your valuables, buses are a good, inexpensive (2c per ride, paid as you enter) way to get around.

Here are a few major routes and route maps:

No 17 Various No 17 buses cover different lengths of Insurgentes. Southbound, 'Rectoría', 'Villa Olimpica' and 'Fovisste' all go past Buenavista railway station and close to the Revolution Monument, cross Reforma at the edge of the zona rosa, then continue to Insurgentes metro station, San Ángel and the university. Northbound 'Indios Verdes' follows the same route in reverse, and passes close to the Guadalupe Basilica before terminating at Indios Verdes in the north of the city, while 'Central Camionera Norte' turns off before the Guadalupe Basilica to go to the northern long-distance bus terminal. 'M Insurgentes', in either direction, only goes as far as Insurgentes metro station.

No 20 'Pantitlán-Metro Colegio Militar' runs from Pantitlán near the Terminal de Autobuses de Pasajeros de Oriente (TAPO, eastern destinations) and the Alameda (along Avenida Hidalgo), and continues along Puente de Alvarado (near the Monument to the Revolution).

No 22 'Metro Pantitlán-Metro Cuatro Caminos' passes the Buenavista railway station on Mosqueta and continues east to pass the intersection of Norte 17 and Boulevard Puerto Aereo (south-east corner of the airport runways, still a bit less than a km from the terminal). You can change to any northbound bus on Boulevard Puerto Aereo if you don't feel like walking.

No 24 'Santa Martha-Metro Cuatro Caminos' passes along Puente de Alvarado near the Monument to the Revolution, Avenida Hidalgo near the Alameda and near the Terminal de Autobuses de Pasajeros de Oriente (TAPO).

No 26 'Sta Cruz Meyehualco-Hipodromo' runs from Pino Suárez metro station (not origin or end point) along 20 de Noviembre, República de Uruguay and Victoria to the Hipodromo.

No 55 'La Villa-Auditorio Nacional' runs from La Villa metro station (line 6, near the Basilica de Guadalupe), Plaza de Tlatelolco (nearby), along Paseo de la Reforma to the National Anthropology Museum and the Auditorio.

No 76 'Zócalo-Km 15.5' runs from the zócalo to the Alameda, Paseo de la Reforma, the National Anthropology Museum and El Auditorio. From El Auditorio, the 'Por Palmas' bus proceeds along Paseo de las Palmas and joins Paseo de la Reforma later. The 'Por Reforma' bus stays on Reforma to the end of the route.

To/From Long-Distance Bus Stations The eastern bus terminal, TAPO, is next door to San Lázaro metro station. For city buses from TAPO, follow the signs to Calle Eduardo Molina and when you hit the street the bus stop is 50 metres to the right. Bus No 16 'Alameda' goes to the Alameda Central; bus No 24 links TAPO with the Alameda Central and the Revolution Monument area, passing Hidalgo and Revolución metro stations on the street Puente de Alvarado.

The northern bus terminal has the Terminal Autobuses Norte metro station right outside it. For city buses to downtown, cross under the road through the metro subway. Bus No 27 goes to Tlatelolco metro station and Bellas Artes metro station near the Alameda Central. Bus No 17 goes down Insurgentes, passing near the Revolution Monument, crossing Reforma at the edge of the zona rosa, and continuing on to Insurgentes metro station. Bus No 17 'Rectoría' follows the same route and continues to San Ángel and the university in the south of the city. Heading out to the northern bus station from downtown, take a 17 'Central Camionera Norte' bus going north on Insurgentes.

Metro The seven lines of Mexico City's

metro system offer the cheapest (2c per ride including transfers), quickest and most crowded way to get around Mexico City.

Over five million people ride the metro on an average day. The station platforms become dangerously packed with passengers, especially during the morning and evening rush hours, and it's not unusual to see police officers with billy clubs shoving people into each car. When it gets crowded enough to require the police officers, separate cars are made available to women and children.

With such crowded conditions, it is not surprising that large bags aren't allowed and pick-pocketing is rife on the metro. However, if you're careful with your belongings, especially your money, you should have no problem.

The metro is easy to use: buy a ticket (boleto) or a packet of tickets (more convenient) at the booth as you enter the station and follow the signs to the metro line that's going in the direction you want to go. First consult the metro map in this chapter to figure out the station, metro line and direction you want. Information desks give out maps of the system at La Raza, Hidalgo, Insurgentes, Pino Suárez and other stations. The metro operates from 6 am to 12 midnight.

The stations are generally clean and well-organised. On display at the Pino Suárez station is a small Aztec pyramid unearthed during construction of the station.

Combi, Pesero & Colectivo Route 2 is the most common route for travellers because it goes between the zócalo and Chapultepec Park along Juárez and Paseo de la Reforma. Peseros 'Indios Verdes' (northbound) and 'San Ángel' (southbound) run up and down most of the length of Insurgentes. From Insurgentes metro station, the fare is 20c to San Ángel (8½ km), 15c to the corner of Edison near the Revolution Monument (three km).

Taxi Most Mexico City taxis are yellow Volkswagen Beetles. They usually have meters but what the meter shows is not what you pay: you have to refer to a conversion chart which should be posted inside the cab. Ask if the meter is working – 'Funciona el contador?' – before you get in, or you'll be at the driver's mercy when it comes to paying. Drivers often demand higher fares at night in any case.

Sample fares: zona rosa to Buenavista railway station US$0.75; Tasqueña metro station to San Ángel (15 minutes in moderate traffic) US$1.50; Monument to the Revolution to airport US$1.50; Monument to the Revolution to northern or eastern bus terminals US$0.80.

To the Revolution Monument area from the airport under the official taxi ticket system, the fare is US$3; from the northern or eastern bus terminals it's US$1.25. But picking up your own cab as it cruises past or drops off other passengers should cost US$1.50 to US$2 from the airport, US$0.75 to US$1 from the eastern or northern bus terminals.

Car Touring Mexico City by car is strongly discouraged, unless you are familiar with the streets and have a healthy reserve of stamina and patience and reflexes quick enough to weave through frequent traffic jams. See the Orientation section at the beginning of this chapter for information about the principal routes in and out of Mexico City.

Renting a car is easy in Mexico City. Several local and international car-rental chains have offices in downtown Mexico City and at the airport. Rental rates for a Volkswagen sedan are comparable to, if not higher than, American rates – an average of US$39 daily or US$227 weekly including unlimited km, collision damage waiver and a 15% value added tax. Allotting for gasoline might boost the daily cost by US$5 or US$10.

Budget Rent-a-Car has offices at Atenas 40 (tel 566-88-15, 566-79-23) behind the Holiday Inn Crowne Plaza and

Hamburgo 71 (tel 533-04-50) in the zona rosa. Nearby at Paseo de la Reforma 100-B, half a block from the Crowne Plaza, is ANSA Rent-a-Car (tel 592-88-24, 703-00-81). Dollar Rent-a-Car has an office in the lobby of the María Isabel Sheraton (tel 211-00-01, ext 3336). National Car Rental (tel 211-00-92, ext 320) maintains an office in Hotel Krystal.

MEXICO CITY SUBURBS
North
Tlatelolco - Plaza de las Tres Culturas About two km north of the Palacio de Bellas Artes and the Alameda up Avenida Lázaro Cárdenas is the Plaza de las Tres Culturas. It was given this name because three cultures and periods of Mexican history are represented on the plaza by the ruins of the Aztec pyramid of Tlatelolco, the 17th-century Spanish colonial church of Santiago and the modern Foreign Affairs building (which suffered severe damage in the 1985 earthquake and may be torn down).

Until 1473 when it was annexed to the Aztec capital of Tenochtitlán, Tlatelolco was the seat of an independent dynasty and home to the largest market in the Valley of Mexico. Spaniard Bernal Díaz del Castillo saw the market when he arrived in 1520 and later described it in great detail in his book *The True History of the Conquest of New Spain* (Farrar, Strauss & Giroux, New York, 1966).

The Pyramid (Temple) of Tlatelolco was the most prominent feature of the area until the Spanish conquest. Today, you can see the ruins of this and other temples from a causeway erected over them.

The Spanish recognised the religious significance of the temples, so after reducing much of this area to rubble, they built first a church, then a Franciscan monastery and finally, in 1609, the Church of Santiago that stands today. Santiago was the patron saint of Spain, who supposedly enabled the Spanish to conquer the Aztecs. Inside, the principal item of interest on display is the baptismal font of Juan Diego (see under Las Basilicas de Nuestra Señora de Guadalupe).

The plaza was the scene of the student rally on 2 October 1968 to protest government policies. At the time of writing the modern side of the plaza was in ruins and ready to collapse from earthquake damage.

The easiest way to get to Plaza de las Tres Culturas is to take the metro (line 3) to the Tlatelolco station, go out the Manuel González exit and turn right. Walk up to Lázaro Cárdenas and turn right and you will see the plaza just ahead of you.

Las Basilicas de Nuestra Señora de Guadalupe The Churches of Our Lady of Guadalupe are on the small hill of Tepeyac near the north-eastern end of Avenida Insurgentes Norte just before it leaves what is generally considered central Mexico City. The obviously older of the two churches dates back to 1533 and was built after a dark-skinned Virgin of Guadalupe who supposedly appeared on the hill before Juan Diego, a recent Indian convert to Christianity. Diego approached Brother Zumárraga, a prominent figure in the introduction of Catholicism to Mexico, with the idea of building a church on the hill to venerate the Virgin. Zumárraga didn't take Diego seriously until an image of the Virgin miraculously appeared on Diego's cloak. The church was built and the enshrined cloak became an object of pilgrimage which probably contributed significantly to an increase in conversions of Indians to Christianity.

The older basilica became too small and old to accommodate the millions of pilgrims who crawl in penitence across the plaza every year to see the cloak, so it was moved to the newer basilica, completed in 1976 by the same architect who designed the National Museum of Anthropology (Pedro Ramírez Vázquez).

To get to the basilicas, take a 'Basilica'

pesero or combi minivan north on Avenida Insurgentes Norte and get off at Avenida Montevideo. Walk ¾ km east on Montevideo. Alternatively, take metro line 3 to the Basilica station, exit on Avenida Montiel and walk ¾ km east/north-east on Montiel straight to the basilicas. Another option, which might be the most crowded, is to take bus No 27 ('Reculsorío Cd – Jardín') north on Avenida Insurgentes Norte.

One of the most colourful times to visit the basilicas is the week preceding 12 December, the Day of the Virgin of Guadalupe, when crowds of pilgrims fill the plaza and celebrate with brightly costumed groups of dancers, artists and musicians from throughout Mexico. A special Virgin-shaped corn cake called *la gordita de la Virgen*, which is eaten only during this week, is available from vendors in the plaza.

South

Insurgentes Sur South of its junction with Reforma at the Cuauhtémoc monument, this major thoroughfare ('in-soor-HEN-tez') – the longest avenue in Mexico City – is dotted with up-market shops and restaurants for much of the way to San Ángel 8½ km away. There are several places of interest en route.

Southbound along Insurgentes, buses '17 Rectoría' and '17 Ciudad Universitaria (CU)' go to San Ángel and then the University City. Buses '17 Fovisste', '17 Villa Olimpica' and '17 Tlalpan' go even further and will take you to Cuicuilco. Pesero or combi minivan 'San Ángel' goes to the junction with La Paz in San Ángel, which is a major pesero terminal, with the tree-shaded Parque de la Bombilla a landmark for it on the east side of Insurgentes. Pesero 'Huipulco' from Insurgentes and La Paz goes on down Insurgentes to the University City and Cuicuilco.

Returning north, buses '17 Indios Verdes' and '17 Central Camionera Norte' go straight up Insurgentes to Reforma and far beyond; bus '17 M Insurgentes' goes only to Insurgentes metro station. Pesero San Ángel goes north from Cuicuilco and the University City to the corner of Insurgentes and La Paz in San Ángel. Pesero 'Indios Verdes' goes north from there up Insurgentes to Reforma and beyond.

Siqueiros Poliforum & Hotel de México The bizarre Poliforum Cultural Siqueiros (tel 536-45-20), designed by muralist David Alfaro Siqueiros, is the site of one of his last and biggest murals and a centre for other arts. Opened in 1971, it stands on the corner of Insurgentes and Filadelfia, 4½ km south of Reforma.

The 12-sided exterior of the building is covered with murals by young artists on wide-ranging subjects like the atom as the triumph of peace over destruction, the drama unleashed by love during the Spanish conquest, and Moses breaking the Tablets of the Law. The wall backing Insurgentes shows five leaders of the Mexican artistic resurgence of the late 19th and 20th centuries: Diego Rivera, José Clemente Orozco, the cartoonist and print-maker José Guadalupe Posada, the engraver Leopoldo Méndez, and Dr Atl (Gerardo Murillo). Some of them bear a curious resemblance to Stalin, Trotsky and Marx, with whom Siqueiros' life was deeply entangled. The poliforum is open daily from 10 am to 7 pm, but closes from 3 to 4 pm Monday to Friday.

Inside, the ground floor houses contemporary art exhibitions while downstairs are some crafts stores and the 'youth forum' with a circular stage. Entry to these parts is free.

The most important part of the building is upstairs (admission 25c). Here the walls and ceiling of an auditorium are covered with an enormous Siqueiros mural called *The March of Humanity on Earth and Towards the Cosmos*. Grand in scale and concept – it took six years and a team of 50 to finish it – the work combines Mexican and universal themes. The

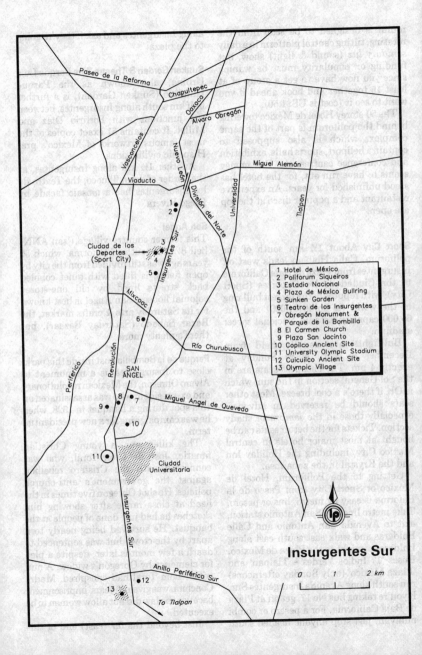

1 Hotel de México
2 Poliforum Siqueiros
3 Estadio Nacional
4 Plaza de México Bullring
5 Sunken Garden
6 Teatro de los Insurgentes
7 Obregón Monument & Parque de la Bombilla
8 El Carmen Church
9 Plaza San Jacinto
10 Copilco Ancient Site
11 University Olympic Stadium
12 Cuicuilco Ancient Site
13 Olympic Village

Insurgentes Sur

0   1   2 km

To Tlalpan

mural is designed to be seen from the rotating, tilting central platform in a daily *sonido y luz* (sound & light) show, but funding or popularity must be waning since you now have to get a group of at least 15 together and book ahead if you want to see it (cost is US$1.50).

The 50-storey Hotel de México towering behind the poliforum is part of the same complex, which is also supposed to contain a heliport, sports halls, exhibition and conference centres, etc. But money seems to have run out, for the hotel has stood unfinished for years. An expensive restaurant and a popular disco at the top are open.

Sport City About 1½ km south of the poliforum, Calle Holbein leads west off Insurgentes from Plaza de Baja California to the Ciudad de los Deportes (Sport City), with reputedly the largest bull ring in the world (it holds 64,000) and the 65,000-capacity Estadio Nacional soccer stadium.

Bullfights are usually held from December to April every Sunday at exactly 4 pm. The cheapest seats are in the Sol General section in the sun, which is OK if there's a cool breeze. Most other seats should be reserved in advance, especially those in the *sombra* or shady section. Tickets for the better seats can be bought at most major hotels in central Mexico City, including the Holiday Inn and the Krystal in the zona rosa.

Getting to the Poliforum, Hotel de México or Sport City from Paseo de la Reforma is easy by metro, bus or pesero. Take metro line 7 to San Antonio station, exit to Avenida San Antonio and Calle Balderas and walk east/south-east along Balderas straight to the Plaza de México. Buses '17 Indios Verdes – Tlalpan' and 'Plaza México' (only Sunday afternoons) run south along Avenida Insurgentes Sur. If you're taking bus No 17, get off at Plaza de Baja California. For a pesero or combi minivan, just stop anyone headed south along Insurgentes and ask if they're going to the plaza.

Sunken Garden & Theatre The Parque Luis Urbina, also known as the Parque Hundido (Sunken Garden), is a further half km south along Insurgentes, between the junctions with Porfirio Díaz and Millet. It contains 51 exact copies of the most famous artworks of Mexico's pre-Hispanic civilisations.

Another 1½ km along Insurgentes, at the corner of Juan Tinoco, the Teatro de los Insurgentes has a mosaic façade by Diego Rivera.

San Ángel

This former country village ('san ANN-hell 8½ km south of Reforma, which 50 years ago was still divided from the city by open fields, is filled with quiet cobbled back streets lined by old one-storey colonial houses. San Ángel is best known for its Saturday arts & crafts market, the Bazar Sábado (Saturday Bazaar), but there's plenty more.

Parque de la Bombilla Just inside this park, close to Insurgentes, is a monument to Álvaro Obregón, the Mexican revolutionary and ex-president who was assassinated on this spot during a banquet in 1928, when he was campaigning for a new presidential term.

The killer was a young Christian fanatic, José de León Toral, who was connected with the Cristero rebellion against the government's anti-church policies. He shot Obregón five times in the head at close range after showing him sketches he had just done of people at the banquet. He survived being nearly torn apart by the crowd but was sentenced to death a few months later, despite a plea for clemency by Obregón's widow. A nun with whom Toral had conspired, Madre Conchita, was given 20 years' imprisonment because the law did not allow women to be executed.

Just beyond the far (east) end of this

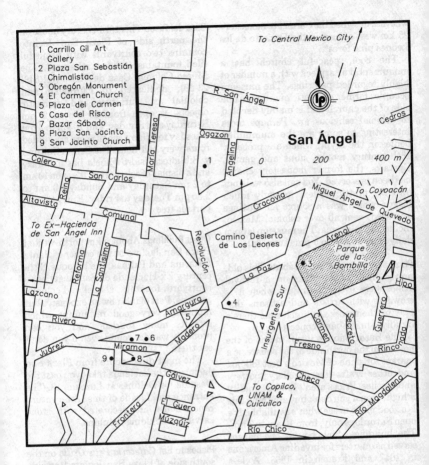

1 Carrillo Gil Art Gallery
2 Plaza San Sebastián Chimalistac
3 Obregón Monument
4 El Carmen Church
5 Plaza del Carmen
6 Casa del Risco
7 Bazar Sábado
8 Plaza San Jacinto
9 San Jacinto Church

San Ángel

0   200   400 m

To Central Mexico City

To Coyoacán

Parque de la Bombilla

To Ex-Hacienda de San Ángel Inn

To Copilco, UNAM & Cuicuilco

pleasant park is the Plaza San Sebastián Chimalistac, surrounded by old colonial houses and a little church with a 16th-century open chapel.

Carrillo Gil Gallery At Revolución 1608, two blocks north of La Paz past a very picturesque streetside flower market, is one of Mexico City's best art galleries, the Museo de Arte Carrillo Gil (tel 548-74-67). It offers temporary and permanent exhibitions of Mexican and foreign artists of the first rank. In the permanent collection are many works by Rivera, Siqueiros, Orozco (including some of his grotesque, satirical early drawings and watercolours), Picasso, Villon, Nishisawa and Paalen. Hours are Tuesday to Sunday from 10.30 am to 7 pm (free).

El Carmen The tile-domed church and museum (tel 548-28-38) of El Carmen are a few metres south along Revolución from La Paz. This ex-monastery was built between 1615 and 1617. The architect was Andrés de San Miguel, a Carmelite monk who also designed the Carmelite monastery 25 km west of here in the Desierto de los Leones pine forest.

The cool, peaceful church has a monumental altarpiece with a number of highly regarded paintings. The museum occupies former monastic quarters to one side of the church and is mainly devoted to colonial religious art. Perhaps more interesting to some are the mummified bodies in the crypt, which are probably 18th-century monks, nuns and gentry. Upstairs, the former monastery chapel has been preserved. You can also walk out into the pretty garden, formerly much bigger, which was a source for cuttings and seeds sent all over colonial Mexico, including California. The museum is open daily from 10 am to 5 pm (entry 5c).

Plaza San Jacinto & Bazar Sábado This old, pretty little plaza takes on a festival atmosphere every Saturday, when it is crowded with artists and artisans displaying their work. At lunch time there's usually a brass-band concert.

The Bazar Sábado itself, in one of the houses on the north side of the square, is a market for some of Mexico's best folk art and other crafts like jewellery, pottery and textiles. Prices aren't low but quality is high; even if you don't buy anything this is a good place to see what's available. It's open Saturdays only, from 10 am to 7 pm. The building which houses the bazaar served as quarters for invading Americans in 1847 and French in 1863. A less expensive crafts market is also held outside, at the north-west corner of the plaza.

The 16th-century church of San Jacinto, off the west side of the plaza, was originally part of a Dominican monastery and has a peaceful garden where you can take refuge from the crowded market areas. You enter it by walking up Juárez, beside the open-air crafts market. Continuing up this street brings you into an area of old colonial villas, side by side with a few expensive modern houses.

Casa del Risco This 18th-century house on the north side of Plaza San Jacinto contains two courtyards with beautiful tiled fountains and two museums. The Museo Colonial Casa del Risco (tel 548-23-29), dedicated to European and colonial art, furniture and domestic objects, is open from 10 am to 2 pm Saturday and Sunday, and 10 am to 3 pm Tuesday to Friday, when there are guided tours every half-hour. The Centro Cultural y Biblioteca Isidro Fabela has a library and a display of colonial art. It's open 10 am to 2 pm Saturday and Sunday, 10 am to 2.30 pm Tuesday to Friday. Entry to both parts is free.

Other Buildings About a km north-west of Plaza San Jacinto at the corner of Santa Catarina and Palmas, the baroque 18th-century Ex-Hacienda de San Ángel has a courtyard, fountain, chapel and colonial gardens. Part of it is now an expensive but reputedly very good restaurant which attracts many tourists, and you can probably wander round even if you don't eat there.

The most direct route from Plaza San Jacinto to the hacienda takes you past the Casa de los Delfines at Lazcano 18. The entrance and façade of this 18th-century ranch house are decorated with stone carvings, including dolphins.

Places to Eat *Cafetería Pepe Grillo* on the south side of Plaza San Jacinto (the side opposite the Bazar Sábado) is a cool, quiet place which serves delicious cakes for US$0.50, antojitos for US$1.50 to US$2, and a five-course comida corrida for US$2.25. There are tables both inside and outside on the sidewalk, and friendly young waiters. A couple of restaurants on the north side of the plaza – including one inside the Bazar Sábado – are more expensive. Probably the cheapest place on the plaza is *Ninfa's* on the north-east corner, where you can get tortas for US$0.50 and a basic comida corrida for US$1. There are a couple of similar places on Madero, going down towards Revolución.

The *Ex-Hacienda de San Ángel Inn* (tel 548-67-46), a km north-west of the plaza at the corner of Santa Catarina and Palmas, is expensive but has a good culinary reputation, and the 18th-century surroundings are lovely.

Getting There & Away See Insurgentes Sur, above, for peseros and buses along Insurgentes to and from the corner of La Paz in San Ángel. Quevedo metro station is ¾ km east of this junction.

For the Plaza San Jacinto, which is the heart of San Ángel and site of the Bazar Sábado, walk west along La Paz from Insurgentes, passing a Fonart shop, until it meets another busy road, Revolución, after 250 metres. The small plaza across Revolución is the Plaza del Carmen. Madero, the street going up its left (south) side, leads straight to Plaza San Jacinto.

To reach Coyoacán, two km east of San Ángel, one way is to take a 'Río Guadalupe – Ruta 116A – General Anaya' bus from the corner of Camino Desierto de los Leones and Revolución or Insurgentes. From Coyoacán to San Ángel, pick up a 'Gen Anaya/San Ángel' bus at the corner of Allende and Malintzin. Taxis between San Ángel and Coyoacán cost US$1.

Copilco
A km south of La Paz along Insurgentes, then 500 metres east along Avenida Copilco and Calle Victoria, is the site of one of the earliest villages in the Valley of Mexico. Copilco probably already existed in 1200 BC when the Olmec civilisation of the Gulf coast was emerging, and remained inhabited until 400 BC. It was at least partly contemporary with the bigger, Olmec-influenced village of Tlatilco further north, and both were near the shore of the great lake that filled much of the valley at that time. It's thought that Copilco was a trade and religious centre for a large agricultural area and may have been ruled by priests.

The village was buried by an eruption of the volcano Xitle around 100 BC to 100 AD, but archaeologists have found several tombs containing skeletons, pottery, stone implements and clay figurines beneath three metres of lava. Some of these are displayed in a museum which is open from 10 am to 5 pm except Monday. The nearest metro station is Quevedo, a km north-east.

University City
Breeding-ground of Mexico's most vocal political dissent and the nation's modern architectural showpiece, the main campus of the Universidad Nacional Autónoma de México (UNAM, the National Autonomous University of Mexico) is beside Insurgentes 11 km south of Reforma. It stands on the vast dried-up lava field of El Pedregal, the site of some of Mexico's most avant-garde modern homes.

The university was originally founded in the 1550s but was suppressed from 1833 to 1910. Most of the present Ciudad Universitaria's main buildings were built between 1950 and 1953 by a team of 150 young architects and technicians headed by José García Villagrán, Mario Pani and Enrique del Moral. It's a grandiose monument both to national pride, with its buildings covered in optimistic murals linking Mexican and global themes, and to an idealistic education system in which almost anyone, often regardless of qualifications, is entitled to free or cheap university tuition.

UNAM is the biggest university in Latin America, with 340,000 students and 25,000 teachers, but even so has to turn away tens of thousands of applicants a year. Other current problems include a drop-out rate approaching 70%, a falling budget in the recent national economic crisis, declining academic standards (partly because teachers have to take other jobs to make ends meet) and a lack of the technological courses which the country needs. In 1987, proposals by university authorities to raise academic entry standards and fees during the economic crisis brought the whole place to a standstill in an 18-day strike while demonstrations of 100,000 or more filed through downtown Mexico City. The reforms were suspended.

Left-wing politics are the norm on this and most other Mexican campuses but they have had little influence on wider national events since the 1968 Tlatelolco massacre, when 300 to 400 people at an open-air meeting were shot dead by soldiers as a student-initiated protest movement gathered momentum on the eve of the Mexico Olympics.

Stadium The University Olympic Stadium, across Insurgentes from the campus, is designed to resemble a volcano cone and holds 80,000 people. The Diego Rivera mosaic over its main entrance was originally intended to be the first of a series. You can peep inside the stadium when it's closed by going to Gate 38 at the south end.

Library As you enter the campus from Insurgentes, it's easy to spot the Central Library, Mexico's most photographed modern building. Ten floors high, the almost windowless structure is covered on every side with mosaics by Juan O'Gorman.

The south wall, with two prominent circles towards the top, covers colonial times. The theme of the north wall is Aztec culture. The east wall shows the creation of modern Mexico. The mosaic on the west wall is harder to interpret but may be dedicated to Latin American culture as a whole.

La Rectoría According to one architecture critic, this administration building south-west of the library achieves 'a harmonic equilibrium of horizontal and vertical masses'. Whether or not that's so, there's a spectacular 3D mosaic by Siqueiros on its south wall, which shows students urged on by the people.

Museum With your back to the Siqueiros

Central Library, University City

Port of Siqueiros Mural and Central Library

mural, the building in front and a bit to the left contains the university science & arts museum, open Monday to Friday 10 am to 3.30 pm and 4.30 to 7 pm (free). The archaeological section includes some pieces from Veracruz.

More Murals Two more interesting mosaics lie just past the far (east) end of the wide grassy Jardín Central, which is reached by steps down from the Rectoría. The science auditorium, fronting the east side of the garden, has on its north end a mural by José Chávez Morado showing the conquest of energy. Humanity progresses from the shadow of the primitive jaguar-god to the use of fire and then the atom, before emerging into an ethereal, apparently female, future. The east side of the same building shows the progression from primitive agriculture to modern science.

A little further east, on the west wall of the medical school, a mosaic in Italian stone by Francisco Eppens interprets the theme of life and death in Mexican terms.

The central mask has a Spanish profile on the left, an Indian one on the right, together making up a mestizo face in the middle. A maize cob and symbols of Aztec and Mayan gods represent the forces of life and death.

Espacio Escultórico Still within the Ciudad Universitaria, but a km south of the main buildings, past the Sala Netzahualcóyotl concert hall and close to Insurgentes, is a work by Mathias Goeritz which no one can explain but most people agree is striking. It consists of concrete shapes about a round platform, set on the bare lava bed.

Getting There & Away See Insurgentes Sur, above, for buses and peseros along Insurgentes. Insurgentes passes between the university stadium on its west side and the campus on the east; the bus stop is only a few metres from both. The nearest metro station, Copilco, is a km east of the most interesting university buildings.

Cuicuilco

About three km beyond the university is the early archaeological site of Cuicuilco, set in the Parque Ecológico Cuicuilco just left off Insurgentes immediately after the big intersection with the Periférico Sur. You can recognise the spot by what's best described as a big round green thing with a hole in the middle, on the opposite (west) side of Insurgentes.

The site's open Tuesday to Saturday 10 am to 5 pm, Sundays and holidays 10 am to 4 pm. Entry to the museum (tel 533-22-63) costs 25c except on Sundays and holidays when it's free.

History Cuicuilco was near the lake that filled much of the Valley of Mexico and was probably the biggest settlement in the valley from approximately 600 to 200 BC. It was still occupied when it was buried by the eruption of Xitle volcano, to the south, some time between 100 BC and 100 AD.

The valley at that time was something of a backwater, far from the centres of Mexican civilisation on the Gulf coast, but Cuicuilco is estimated to have had a population of 20,000 and traces of a street lay-out have been found. The whole site covered an area 4½ km from north to south and one km from east to west. Its pyramid shows that Cuicuilco must have been, as well as a residential settlement, a ceremonial centre of a probably priest-dominated society, organised enough to build large monumental structures. Earlier temples in the Valley of Mexico were thatch-roof affairs on low earth mounds. The next important centre to arise in central Mexico was the splendour of Teotihuacán.

Pyramid The most important excavated structure is the round, tiered pyramid 118 metres across and now 23 metres high which you can see as you approach from Insurgentes. The 10-metre lava layer which buried the lower levels has been removed to show the stone facing of the mound, whose interior is of sand and rubble. The stone facing itself was probably originally plastered with stucco. Ramps on the west and east sides lead to the top of the pyramid, where the remains of an altar are protected by a modern roof. Beneath this altar are the remains of two earlier ones, built over when the whole pyramid was enlarged, which happened at least twice.

Museum Just south of the main pyramid, the museum contains information on Cuicuilco's inhabitants and the development of the valley in ancient times, objects found at the site and a painting of the eruption which destroyed it. There's an image of the fire-and-volcano god, Xuihtecuhtli, with a brazier on his back, who was – not surprisingly – Cuicuilco's most important deity.

Other Structures Several other mounds, four of them restored, can be seen on the far side of Insurgentes, where some of them were incorporated into the landscaping of the Olympic Village built to accommodate athletes for the 1968 Olympics. The village is now local housing.

Coyoacán

About eight km south of downtown Mexico City, Coyoacán ('Place of Coyotes' in Nahua) was Cortés' base after the fall of Tenochtitlán and for four centuries remained a small town outside Mexico City until the urban sprawl surrounded it 40 years ago. It still has its own identity, with its own café-ringed plazas and a student-artist atmosphere which stems from its closeness to the university and from having been home to people such as Trotsky, Diego Rivera and Frida Kahlo. Their interesting former homes are preserved for the public to visit. Other places to visit in the area are Churubusco monastery – site of a heroic Mexican stand against US invaders – and the Anahuacalli, a building designed by Rivera, which contains his pre-Hispanic art collection and some of his own work.

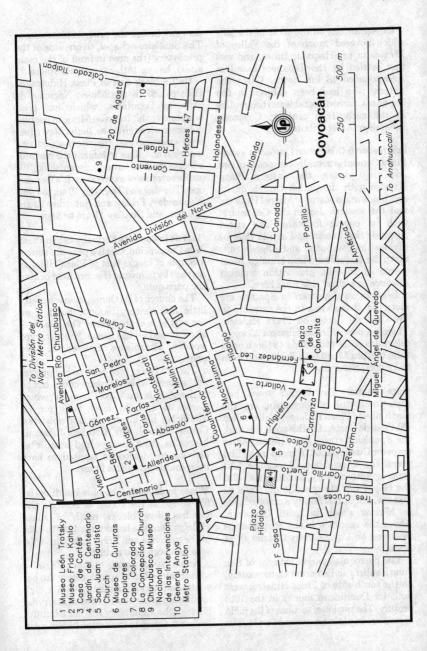

1 Museo León Trotsky
2 Museo Frida Kahlo
3 Casa de Cortés
4 Jardín del Centenario
5 San Juan Bautista Church
6 Museo de Culturas Populares
7 Casa Colorada
8 La Concepción Church
9 Churubusco Museo Nacional de las Intervenciones
10 General Anaya Metro Station

Coyoacán

To Anahuacalli

0   250   500 m

To División del Norte Metro Station

Coyoacán was on the shore of the lake which covered much of the Valley of Mexico in pre-Hispanic times, and was first settled by the Tepanecs based in Azcapotzalco 18 km north. When the Aztecs, who had been subject to the Tepanecs, turned the tables on their rulers in the early 15th century, Coyoacán became an Aztec tributary.

Information & Orientation Coyoacán's wide Plaza Central is actually composed of two adjoining plazas, the eastern Plaza Hidalgo with the parish church on its south side and a statue of Miguel Hidalgo, and the western Jardín del Centenario with its coyote fountain. The street Aguayo (also known as Carrillo Puerto) divides the two parts, and Allende runs down the east side of Plaza Hidalgo. Most points of interest are within walking distance or a short ride from here.

Leaflets on Coyoacán in Spanish are given out at the kiosk in the entrance to the Casa de Cortés on Plaza Hidalgo. There's a post office at Higuera 23 and a telégrafos office at Allende 45 (both open 9 am to 8 pm Monday to Friday and 9 am to 12 noon Saturday).

Plaza Central The former town hall (*ayuntamiento*) of Coyoacán, on the north side of Plaza Hidalgo, is also called the Casa de Cortés. On this spot, it is said, the Spanish tortured the defeated Aztec emperor Cuauhtémoc to try to make him reveal the whereabouts of treasure. The existing 18th-century building was also the HQ of the Marquesado del Valle de Oaxaca, the Cortés family's private lands in Mexico which included Coyoacán. Above the entrance is the coat of arms bestowed on Coyoacán by Charles IV of Spain.

The parroquia (parish church) of San Juan Bautista and adjacent ex-monastery, on the south side of Plaza Hidalgo, were built for Dominican monks in the 16th century. The two lower sections of the main façade are in plain renaissance style. The

doorway beside the tower is plateresque. The Santísima chapel, to one side of the presbytery (the area in front of the main altar), has an 18th-century altarpiece.

Half a block east of Plaza Hidalgo, at Hidalgo 289, is the Museo Nacional de Culturas Populares, which has good temporary exhibitions on Mexican popular culture such as circuses, *lucha libre* (free-style wrestling) and *nacimientos* (nativity models), and likes to lament the harmful effect of modern 'entertainments' like TV on these forms of expression. It's free and open Tuesday and Thursday 10 am to 4 pm, Wednesday, Friday and Saturday 10 am to 8 pm, and Sunday 11 am to 5 pm.

Plaza de la Conchita Formally called Plaza de la Concepción, this is a peaceful square a couple of blocks east of Plaza Hidalgo, reached by following Higuera from behind the parroquia.

The church of La Concepción is a pretty little 18th-century baroque building on the east side of the plaza. The interior – often closed – has some finely carved wooden altarpieces covered in gold paint.

The red house (not open to the public) at the corner where Higuera comes out on to the plaza is the 'Casa Colorada', which Cortés is said to have built for La Malinche, his interpreter and mistress. Cortés' Spanish wife, Catalina Juárez de Marcaida, who disappeared soon after arriving in Mexico, is reputed to have been murdered in this house.

Museo Frida Kahlo The blue building (tel 554-59-99) at the corner of Allende and Londres, five blocks north of Plaza Hidalgo, was the home from 1929 to 1954 of Diego Rivera and Frida Kahlo, his wife, who was born here in 1910.

Kahlo spent most of her life in a wheelchair after a spinal injury in her youth and became an artist with a high reputation in her own right after marrying Rivera, who apparently was not a faithful husband. Given to the nation by Rivera in

1955 in memory of his wife after her death, the house and garden are a very interesting three-in-one gallery/museum. Their fine collection of pre-Hispanic objects and Mexican folk art, as well as works by Kahlo, Rivera, Marcel Duchamp, José Clemente Orozco, Paul Klee and others, give glimpses of the artist-revolutionary couple's life style.

The paintings, carvings and sculptures by Kahlo express the anguish and hopes of her existence: one called *Marxism Will Give Health to the Sick* shows her casting away her own crutches. Trotsky lived only a few streets away, and Rivera and Kahlo were part of a high-powered but far from harmonious, leftist, artistic-intellectual circle. Stalin appears as the hero of some of Kahlo's paintings, done after Rivera and Trotsky had fallen out.

Regional costumes (used by Kahlo), ex-voto paintings done to give thanks for miracles, colourful and grotesque papier-mâché Easter week procession figures, lacquerwork and ceramics are included in the folk art collection.

The house is open daily except Monday from 10 am to 2 pm and 3 to 6 pm (free). Free guided tours are given at 11 am on Saturday and Sunday.

Museo León Trotsky Having come in second to Stalin in the power struggle in the Soviet Union in 1927, Trotsky was exiled and eventually found refuge in Mexico under President Lázaro Cárdenas in 1937, thanks to the support of Diego Rivera. Trotsky and Natalia, his wife, lived in Coyoacán at Viena 45, on the corner of Morelos, two blocks north and three east of the Museo Frida Kahlo.

The house has been left pretty much as it was on the day in 1940 when Trotsky was killed here and it's a fascinating monument to a revolutionary's life, with secrecy and danger ever-present. High walls and watchtowers surround the house and small garden, and you have to ring the bell to get in. Hours are Tuesday to Friday 10 am to 2 pm and 3 to 5.30 pm; Saturdays,

Sundays and holidays 10.30 am to 4 pm. Free guided tours in Spanish or English are compulsory.

The garden contains Trotsky's and Natalia's ashes. The watchtowers were put up, the outside walls heightened and the windows made smaller after the first attempt on their lives here on 24 May 1940. A group of attackers, which probably included the artist David Alfaro Siqueiros, pumped bullets into the house but the couple survived by hiding under their bedroom furniture. The bullet holes remain. Several interesting old photos in the house include one of Trotsky, Natalia, Rivera, Frida Kahlo and the surrealist painter André Breton in Chapultepec Park in 1938.

The most interesting room is Trotsky's study, where he died. The assassin was Ramón Mercader, a Spanish Stalinist agent who managed to become the lover of Trotsky's secretary and gradually gained the confidence of the household, making frequent visits over two or three months. On 20 August 1940 he went to Trotsky, who was sitting at his desk in his study, and asked him to look at a document. Standing beside him, he then pulled an ice-axe from under his coat and smashed it into the back of Trotsky's skull. Trotsky died next day; Mercader was arrested and spent 20 years in prison. Trotsky's desk has been left exactly as it was at the time of his death: books and magazines lying on it include *Should Socialists Support the War? Wall Street's War – Not Ours, Statistical Abstract for the UK, British India, Statesman's Yearbook 1939, If Germany Attacks* and *British Trade Unionism Today.*

Churubusco A km east of Trotsky's house stands the 17th-century ex-monastery of Churubusco, scene of one of Mexico's heroic military defeats and now partly given over to an interesting museum on foreign imperialism in Mexico. The occasion of the heroism was the US invasion in 1847. The Americans had taken Veracruz with high loss of Mexican life and were advancing on the capital. On 20 August, Mexicans who had fortified the old monastery resisted a bigger and better-armed American force until they ran out of ammunition and were only finally beaten in hand-to-hand fighting. General Pedro Anaya, asked by US General Twiggs to surrender his ammunition, is said to have answered: 'If there was any, you wouldn't be here'. During the Reform War the monastery served again as military quarters and later as a hospital for contagious diseases.

Some of the peaceful old monastery gardens are also open. Cannons and memorials outside the monastery recall the events of 1847. Inside, the Museo Nacional de las Intervenciones (National Interventions Museum) is open from 9 am to 8 pm Monday to Friday, 10 am to 5 pm Saturday and Sunday (entry 20c, free on Saturdays, Sundays and holidays).

It's a big museum, and the interesting displays include references to present-day US 'interventions' (eg Libya 1986) and the US military presence in the Caribbean, an American map of the Mexico City area showing operations in 1847 (note how far outside the city Churubusco was at the time), material on the Texas war, the French occupation in the 1860s (with a death mask of Emperor Maximilian), foreign economic dominance in the late 19th and early 20th centuries, and the plot by US Ambassador Lane Wilson to bring down the Madero government in 1913. Numerous interesting old photos include one of US troops in Veracruz in 1914.

The monastery is on Calle 20 de Agosto, two blocks east of Avenida División del Norte along Catita and 1½ km from central Coyoacán. General Anaya metro station is half a km south-east, and most peseros between there and Coyoacán pass Churubusco on the way. Bus and pesero 59 'metro División del Norte – metro Tasqueña', south along Avenida División del Norte from División del Norte metro station, also pass within a couple of blocks

of Churubusco. Get out at the junction with Xicoténcatl and Catita.

Anahuacalli Not strictly in Coyoacán, but near enough to be included in the same visit, is this museum (tel 677-29-84) designed by Diego Rivera to house his own excellent collection of pre-Hispanic objects – mostly pottery and stone figures of humans, animals or gods. The name means House of Anáhuac (Anáhuac is a name for the Valley of Mexico).

An inscription over the door reads: 'To return to the people the artistic inheritance I was able to redeem from their ancestors'. The building is a fortress-like edifice of dark volcanic stone incorporating many pre-Hispanic stylistic features of pre-classic, western Mexico, Aztec, Veracruz, Zapotec, Mixtec, Toltec and Teotihuacán cultures.

The museum also houses Rivera's studio and some of his own works. The most interesting are studies for major murals like *La Paz* (Peace) and *El Hombre en el Cruce de los Caminos* (Mankind at the Crossroads) done for the Rockefeller Center, New York, in 1933 but now in the Bellas Artes in Mexico City. Another huge sketch shows Mao Zedong offering the dove of peace to Uncle Sam, John Bull and France. If the atmosphere's clear, there's a great view over the city from the roof.

The Anahuacalli is open daily except Monday from 10 am to 2 pm and 3 to 6 pm. Entry is free. One of the easiest ways to get there directly from central Mexico City is to take the metro to Tasqueña, then the Tren Ligero (a kind of cross between the metro and a real train) from Tasqueña metro station to Xotepingo (2c), the fourth stop. Xotepingo station is beside an intersection where a sign points to 'museo'. Take the direction indicated, continuing three blocks to traffic lights at Avenida División del Norte, then continue ahead for five blocks as the road (Calle Museo) curves left and uphill. The grey, fortress-like Anahuacalli is unmistakable on the right. Alternatively, take the metro to División del Norte station, then a bus/pesero No 59 south along Avenida División del Norte for six km to the corner of Calle Museo (check that it's going far enough – some 59s turn off before reaching Calle Museo). To get to and from Coyoacán or Churubusco, take bus/pesero No 59 along Avenida División del Norte.

Aztec Stadium This 100,000-seat soccer stadium, scene of World Cup triumphs by Brazil in 1970 and Argentina in 1986, is five km south of Coyoacán. Games are played here frequently in the Mexican season. The metro to Tasqueña, then the Tren Ligero to Estadio Azteca is probably the quickest way of getting there from downtown Mexico City.

Places to Eat There are several places on or near Coyoacán's Plaza Central. *El Parnaso* on the Jardín del Centenario at the corner of Carrillo Puerto is an arty hangout with a good bookshop in the back. A sandwich will cost you US$1.50. About 50 metres away on the Tres Cruces corner of the Jardín del Centenario, *Jugos y Frutos Coyoacán* (tel 554-62-12) is cheaper, with tortas around US$0.50, also fruit juices and coffee.

On Avenida Sosa, leading west from the Jardín del Centenario, *Café Los Geranios* at No 19 is cool, popular and a touch elegant with a good but not huge avocado salad at US$2, patés or cheese plates for US$1.75 to US$2.75, fish soup US$2, *conejo a la Española* (Spanish-style rabbit) US$3.50, *huachinango a la Veracruzana* (Veracruz-style snapper) US$3.75, pasta, other salads and eggs. A bit further along Sosa, the *Restaurant Villa de Sosa* at No 38 does salads for US$1.50 to US$2, chicken or meat dishes for US$3.75 to US$4.75, soups around US$1.

La Boricua at the corner of Tres Cruces and Sosa does a comida corrida for US$1. There are several more restaurants of varying price levels on Allende and Hidalgo.

Getting There & Away There are several ways of getting to Coyoacán from downtown Mexico City. One of the best is to take the metro to General Anaya two km east of Coyoacán, then a 'Santo Domingo/Coyoacán' pesero to Allende in Coyoacán, or a 'Gen Anaya/San Ángel' bus to the corner of Allende and Malintzin. The latter goes on to San Ángel after Coyoacán. Another route is the metro to División del Norte, then a bus or pesero (such as No 59 'metro Div del Norte – metro Tasqueña') three km south along Avenida División del Norte to the corner of Hidalgo, then a one-km walk west along Hidalgo. Viveros, 1½ km west of central Coyoacán on Avenida Universidad, is actually the nearest metro stop of all.

From Camino Desierto de los Leones in San Ángel, bus 'Río Guadalupe – Ruta 116A – General Anaya' takes you close to central Coyoacán. A taxi between Coyoacán and San Ángel costs US$1.

Leaving Coyoacán, a 'M Gen Anaya' pesero, colectivo or bus from the corner of Xicoténcatl and Allende or Aguayo will take you to General Anaya metro station.

Xochimilco

Pronounced 'zo-chee-meel-ko', Xochimilco – a Nahuatl Indian word which means 'place where flowers grow'– is a suburb of 'floating gardens' 24 km south-east of central Mexico City. In the 13th century, the Chinampaneca Indians who settled here built rafts on the lake to grow food and flowers. The rafts eventually became rooted to the lake bottom and were named *chinampas*. Because of their proliferation the lake was transformed into more than 80 km of canals.

Today, more than 3000 boats, including *trajineras* or colourfully decorated flat-bottom boats, cruise the canals with loads of tourists, mariachi bands, 'official' photographers, taco bars and big steaming pots of corn-on-the-cob. On the weekends the town and waterways are jammed with people trying to arrange a boat, cruising the canals or fast-talking you into buying something. The hawkers are bothersome because they hound you even when you're on the canals. Many of them disappear during the week, so that's a much quieter time to visit, but then you have to pretend that you don't see the mounds of weekend rubbish floating on the water.

Getting There & Away The easiest and fastest way to get there via public transportation is to take metro line 2 to Taxqueña station and then any 'Xochimilco' bus running south along Calzada Tlalpan in front of the metro station. You could also catch a 'La Villa-Xochimilco' bus southbound on Pino Suárez (Nos 33 & 31, at Correo Mayor) near the zócalo, but that takes much longer. Get off at the end of the line in central Xochimilco and look for the 'Los Embarcaderos' signs.

A visit to Xochimilco can be combined with a short visit to one of the other previously mentioned southern Mexico City suburbs – Coyoacán, San Ángel, Copilco and Ciudad Universitaria. If you are coming from downtown and want to visit these areas first, then follow the directions above for getting there and to the General Anaya metro station. From this station, which is the last one before Taxqueña station, you can then hop on a southbound bus to Xochimilco.

Near Mexico City – North & West

To the north and west of Mexico City, easily accessible by public transport, is a wealth of sights worth seeing. Those interested in antiquities should not miss the pre-Hispanic sites of Teotihuacán's spectacular pyramids and the towering statues of Tula. Ruins buffs will enjoy less-visited Tenayuca and Santa Cecilia Acatitlán.

Colonial Mexico is represented in the architecture of Pachuca and the baroque San Francisco Javier Church of Tepotzotlán, also famous for its museum of the vice-regal period.

Also worth a visit is what some call Mexico's largest market, held Friday at the town of Toluca, capital of the state of Mexico.

Most of these places – including Teotihuacán, Tepotzotlán, Toluca and Tula – can be visited in day trips from Mexico City, but unless you have your own vehicle it's hard to fit more than one

or two into a single day. Toluca and, to the north, Pachuca can be used as bases for more in-depth exploration.

North of Mexico City

TENAYUCA & SANTA CECILIA ACATITLÁN
Just beyond the federal district's northwestern border lie two archaeological sites that pre-date the Aztec capital of Tenochtitlán. Last ruled by a son of Moctezuma who was converted to Christianity, Tenayuca has a pyramid which is a dead ringer for the Templo Mayor in Mexico City's zócalo, though smaller. You will see striking serpent sculptures on three sides of the pyramid – imagine what they looked like when they were painted bright red, yellow and green. Archaeological excavation has revealed that this pyramid covers temples built as

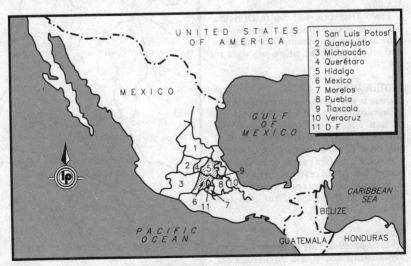

```
                    UNITED  STATES
                       OF  AMERICA          ┌─────────────────────┐
                                            │  1  San Luis Potosí  │
                                            │  2  Guanajuato       │
                                            │  3  Michoacán        │
                                            │  4  Querétaro        │
        MEXICO                              │  5  Hidalgo          │
                                            │  6  Mexico           │
                                            │  7  Morelos          │
                                   GULF     │  8  Puebla           │
                                    OF      │  9  Tlaxcala         │
                                  MEXICO    │ 10  Veracruz         │
                                            │ 11  D F             │
                                            └─────────────────────┘
                      1
                    2  4  5        9
         3            8 10
                                                  CARIBBEAN
        6  11    7                                    SEA

                                              BELIZE
         PACIFIC
         OCEAN
                              GUATEMALA    HONDURAS
```

far back as the 11th-century reign of the Toltecs at Tula. Some archaeologists believe that the architecture of Tenayuca significantly influenced Aztec designers.

Beyond Tenayuca is Santa Cecilia Acatitlán, whose 16th-century church was built with the stones of an Indian temple. The small Aztec pyramid behind the church is particularly interesting, as it is the sole Aztec temple which is completely intact. As an Aztec settlement, Acatitlán was ruled from Tenayuca. For a good view of the surrounding area, climb to the top of the pyramid. Also at Acatitlán, a small museum has been fashioned from a lovely old hacienda. It contains some interesting Aztec sculptures and a replica of an Aztec sacrificial skull rack as well as colonial artefacts.

Getting There & Away

To reach Tenayuca, take the brown-and-yellow 'Reclusorio-Cd. Jardín' city bus No 27 northbound. Ask to be let off at Avenida Aqueducto Tenayuca and walk one km west on that avenue to the pyramid. A small museum on the north-eastern side of the pyramid is open during the day.

From Tenayuca, you can reach Santa Cecilia Acatitlán by taking the yellow or blue bus from the pyramid's eastern side and telling the driver where you want to get off.

TEOTIHUACÁN

If there is any 'must see' attraction in the vicinity of Mexico City, it is the pyramids of San Juan Teotihuacán. Before the coming of the Spaniards Teotihuacán was the New World's greatest city, with a quarter of a million people occupying 150 square km. At its centre were two of the most imposing temples you will see in Mexico, the Pyramids of the Sun and Moon.

History

Historic parallels may be drawn between Teotihuacán and Rome. Archaeological

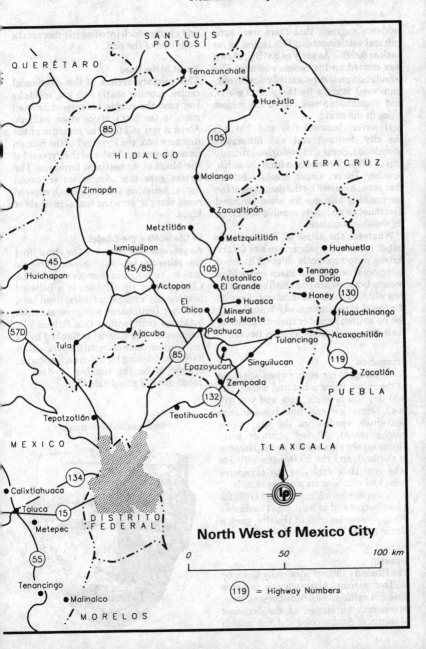

SAN LUIS
POTOSÍ

QUERÉTARO

Tamazunchale

85

Huejutla

105

HIDALGO

VERACRUZ

Molango

Zimapán

Zacualtipán

Metztitlán

Metzquititlán

Ixmiquilpan

Huehuetla

45

45/85

105

Tenango
de Doria

Huichapan

Actopan

Atotonilco
El Grande

Honey

130

El Chico

Huasca

Mineral
del Monte

Huauchinango

57D

Ajacuba

Pachuca

Acaxochitlán

Tula

Tulancingo

119

85

Singuilucan

Zacatlán

Epazoyucan

Zempoala

PUEBLA

132

Tepotzotlán

Teotihuacán

MEXICO

TLAXCALA

Calixtlahuaca

134

Toluca

15

Metepec

DISTRITO
FEDERAL

North West of Mexico City

55

0   50   100 km

Tenancingo

Malinalco

119 = Highway Numbers

MORELOS

evidence suggests that there were agricultural settlements in this region as far back as 600 BC. As early as 200 BC, a town was erected on the ceremonial site. The population grew substantially until it outnumbered Rome's by the year 600 AD, and Teotihuacán was one of the largest cities in the world.

However, between 600 and 700 AD the city declined and was ultimately abandoned. Some archaeologists attribute this to barbarian invasion from the north, possibly Toltec. Other scholars believe that erosion caused by the denuding of the surrounding hillsides for wood rendered Teotihuacán no longer capable of feeding its sizeable populace.

Whatever the cause of Teotihuacán's fall, it remained a pilgrimage site for the Aztecs, who reverently dubbed its great ceremonial centre 'The Place where Men become Gods'. When you visit Teotihuacán, you will find the name most apt. Despite the fact that the Indians who built the city left no written record of their civilisation, their impressive stone legacies live on.

Information

Some things to remember when you come to the ruins: Bring a hat and water. The mid-day sun is brutal here and you will need protection and liquid sustenance (soft-drink vendors on the site charge mucho pesos). During summer early afternoon showers are the norm. Because of the heat and the 2300-metre altitude take your time exploring the expansive ruins and climbing its steep pyramids.

Unless you are willing to spend US$2 for a hamburger and at least US$4 to dine at the expensive eateries at the site, pack a picnic lunch.

Museum

The Unidad Cultural is a worthy first stop at Teotihuacán. Although the museum does not exhibit the art discovered here, which may be viewed at the National Museum of Anthropology, it has models and charts which intelligently discuss the evolution of the city.

Street of the Dead

This primary avenue of the ceremonial centre, running nearly four km, will take you past the rubble of unreconstructed ruins to the city's major stone edifices. Along it you will find the museum at the southern end, the Pyramid of the Sun on its north-eastern flank and the Pyramid of the Moon at its northern terminus. The Aztecs gave this avenue its erroneous name, believing that the earth-covered ruins along it were the burial mounds of kings.

La Ciudadela – the Citadel

As you cross the Street of the Dead from the museum you will see an immense sunken rectangular complex called La Ciudadela, or the Citadel. It is believed that the city's religious leaders lived here, and that Teotihuacán was governed from buildings built within this fortress-like compound. The Citadel is flanked by 12 buildings on three sides with a pyramid on its fourth, totalling 13, which archaeologists believe to be the number of days in Teotihuacán's ritual calendar.

Teotihuacán stone mask

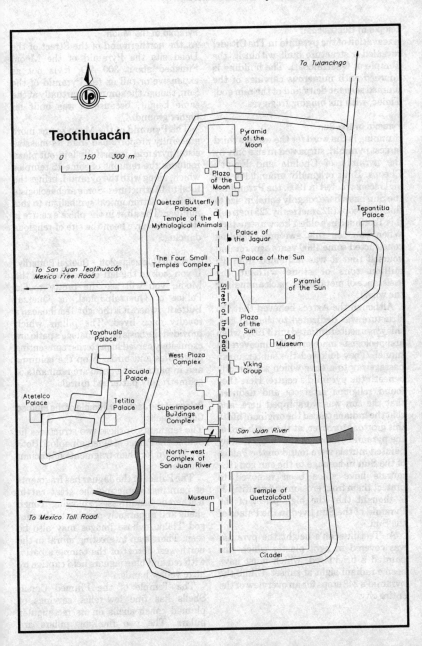

Teotihuacán

0   150   300 m

To Tulancingo

Pyramid of the Moon

Plaza of the Moon

Quetzal Butterfly Palace

Temple of the Mythological Animals

Tepantitla Palace

Palace of the Jaguar

Palace of the Sun

The Four Small Temples Complex

Pyramid of the Sun

To San Juan Teotihuacán Mexico Free Road

Street of the Dead

Plaza of the Sun

Yayahuala Palace

Old Museum

West Plaza Complex

Zacuala Palace

Viking Group

Atetelco Palace

Tetitla Palace

Superimposed Buildings Complex

San Juan River

North-west Complex of San Juan River

To Mexico Toll Road

Museum

Temple of Quetzalcóatl

Citadel

Temple of Quetzalcóatl

Excavation of the pyramid in The Citadel revealed a structure built within it, the Temple of Quetzalcóatl. The building is adorned with numerous carvings of the plumed serpent deity and of the rain god, Tlaloc, with his bulging frog-eyes.

Pyramid of the Sun

Stunning is the word for the world's third largest pyramid, surpassed in size only by the pyramid of Cholula and Egypt's Cheops. Built originally around 100 AD and reconstructed in 1908, the Pyramid of the Sun has a base roughly equal in size to that of Cheops (222 metres by 225 metres). It is Teotihuacán's oldest known structure. When you see this awesome building constructed some 1900 years ago, remind yourself that it was fashioned from 3½ million tons of stone without the assistance of metal tools, pack animals or the wheel!

Although the Aztecs believed that the structure was dedicated to the sun god, this was unsubstantiated until 1971, when archaeologists inadvertently uncovered a tunnel. They followed the subterranean passageway to a cave which sat directly beneath the pyramid's centre. Here they found religious artefacts and deduced that the sun was worshipped here, and that the Indians traced the origins of life to this grotto. Moreover, at the north end of the pyramid's Plaza of the Sun, ornately painted murals were found on the Palace of the Sun in homage to the sun god (the murals have since been removed to protect them from erosion and graffiti). It is thought that the high priest of the Pyramid of the Sun lived in the Palace of the Sun.

At Teotihuacán's height the pyramid was covered in light plaster which was painted a bright red, which must have been a radiant sight at sunset. Climb the pyramid's 248 steps for an overview of the entire city.

Pyramid of the Moon

At the northern end of the Street of the Dead sits the Pyramid of the Moon. Finished about 300 AD, it is not as expansive or tall as the Pyramid of the Sun, though the summit is virtually at the same height, because it was built on higher ground.

The Pyramid of the Moon seems more gracefully proportioned than its massive sister pyramid. Its artfully laid-out plaza includes the remains of some 12 temples which, along with the pyramid, brings the total to 13 structures. Some archaeologists attribute astronomical symbolism to this number. The altar in the plaza's centre is thought to have been the site of religious dancing.

Palace of Quetzalpaplotl – Quetzal Butterfly

If you look to the left of the Plaza of the Moon, you will see the pretty roofed Palace of Quetzalpaplotl, or Quetzal Butterfly, where it is thought Teotihuacán's royalty once lived. The pillars which provided the basis for the palace's patio are exquisitely carved in patterns representing butterflies and birds. Atop the columns and in parts of the patio are remnants of geometrically patterned murals.

Palace of the Jaguar & Temple of the Plumed Conch Shells

The remnants of these two structures lie behind the Palace of Quetzalpaplotl. Both are known for their fragments of ancient murals.

The Palace of the Jaguar has fragments of paintings depicting the great cat in feathered headdresses, blowing conch shells and apparently praying to the rain god Tlaloc, whose images may also be seen. There's an interesting mural in the north-west corner of the temple's patio, with red and blue jaguars held captive by huge yellow hands.

The Temple of the Plumed Conch Shells has fine low-relief carvings of plumed conch shells on its rectangular pillars. The two flanking pillars are carved with flowers. At the temple's base is a colourful green-and-blue mural of birds with water streaming from their beaks.

Tepantitla

For more well-preserved frescoes, sitting next to Parking Lot 2 across from the Pyramid of the Sun are some of the former apartment buildings of priests. These retain a portion of the famous mural *Paradise of Tlaloc*. The mural is fully reproduced at the National Museum of Anthropology, but you can still make out human figures playing in and around a lake set at the base of a mountain.

There is also a representation of a sacrificial figure, blood spurting from his chest along with a ribbon of a river's blue waters. This illustrates the Indians' use of ritual sacrifice to appease the gods, thereby keeping the life forces of nature flowing. Another mural provides evidence that a ball game was played at Teotihuacán, using a kind of bat. Although a ball court has yet to be excavated here, some archaeologists hypothesise that the Street of the Dead served as the field.

Sound & Light Show

Every night but Monday during the dry season, from October to May, there is a sound & light show at Teotihuacán beginning at 7 pm. Admission is US$2. Bring warm clothing, as it is cold and windy at night. Blankets and sarapes are available for rent at the entrance.

Getting There & Away

The ruins are open daily from 8 am to 5 pm, admission US$0.30. Get here as early as possible to avoid the tourist crush. Buses run virtually every half-hour between 5 am and 10 pm, departing from the Terminal Central de Autobuses del Norte. Tickets are sold at the northern end of the terminal; the one-hour ride costs US$0.65.

TEPOTZOTLÁN

Forty-three km north of Mexico City, in a

pleasant little town surrounded by mountains, sits the most splendid example of churrigueresque architecture in Mexico, the Church of San Francisco Javier, as well as the Museo del Virreynato with a fine collection of colonial artefacts.

In the late 16th century the Jesuits carried on missionary work in Tepotzotlán. They were so beloved that one of their converts, the Indian nobleman Don Martín Maldonado, donated land and houses to the priests when he heard they were thinking of leaving the village. On that land in 1582 the Jesuits established the first school in Mexico exclusively for Indian children.

In 1670 ground was broken on the donated land for the Church of San Francisco Javier, which was finished 12 years later. Over the years, the church was embellished in a lavish, downright ostentatious manner. The façade is a phantasmagoric array of baroque designs, the interior the quintessential example of Mexican churrigueresque style. One gilded altar gives way artfully to another, each carved with mirrors accentuating the dazzle. There is even an appropriately placed mirror reflecting the dome.

In 1964, the National Institute of Anthropology & History restored the church and the adjacent older (1584) monastery, transforming the complex into the Museo del Virreynato, or National Museum of the Viceroyal Period. The institute restored the monastery's gardens, chapels and dining hall to their original appearance and placed within its rooms some of the great art of the colonial period. Among the antiques are silver chalices, pictures constructed with inlaid wood, folk art and some of the finest examples of religious paintings and statues from the vice-regal epoch.

The museum complex's hours are 11 am to 6 pm, Tuesday to Sunday, closed Monday. The admission charge is US$0.30 on weekdays and 15c on Sunday. There are free guided tours of the museum on Saturdays at 11.30 am and 1 pm.

Classical music concerts are frequently presented on the premises. From 16 to 23 December Christmas plays are performed in a courtyard of the monastery. It is necessary to book tickets for this popular event considerably in advance from Mexico City tourist agencies.

Places to Eat
If you are hungry while in Tepotzotlán, try the comida corrida at the *Virreyes Restaurant*.

Getting There & Away
There are a couple of ways to reach Tepotzotlán by public transport from Mexico City. Ride line 2 of the metro to Tacuba station and take a 20c white or blue bus, both with yellow stripes, to Tepotzotlán. Or catch the Tula-bound Valle de Mezquital bus from the Central de Autobuses del Norte terminal (US$0.60) and get off at the first toll booth. Either take a local bus to the church from here or walk two km west on Insurgentes.

TULA
The capital of central Mexico's second great civilisation, the Toltec, stood 65 km north of what is now Mexico City, on the edge of the Valley of Mexico. Less spectacular than Teotihuacán, Tula is still a very interesting site, best known for its fearsome 4½-metre-high Atlante statues of warriors. It has good views over hilly countryside north towards the altiplano central. There's nothing exciting about the dusty modern town of Tula de Allende, but it offers adequate accommodation and you can travel on to Pachuca, San Juan del Río or Querétaro without going back to Mexico City.

History
The history of Tula and the Toltecs is enlivened and confused by legends that grew up about them, some of which were written down by the Aztecs after the Spanish conquest. Many later peoples in pre-Hispanic Mexico revered the Toltec era (950 to 1150 AD) as a golden age, and some rulers, including Aztec emperors and even Mayan leaders as far away as Chiapas, claimed to be descended from the Toltecs.

Topiltzin After the decline of Teotihuacán in the 6th or 7th century AD, there was a power vacuum in central Mexico. Among the nomadic Chichimec tribes from the north who moved into the Valley of Mexico in this period was a group led by Mixcoatl (Cloud Serpent) who probably settled at a place called Colhuacán by about 900. Mixcoatl's son Topiltzin, born in 935 or 947, reputedly had fair skin, long hair and a black beard and studied at the religious centre of Xochicalco. He transferred his people's capital first to Tulancingo in eastern Hidalgo and then, probably in 968, to Tula (originally called Tollan, 'Place of Reeds'). These Toltecs ('Artificers') were joined by the Nonoalca, a group possibly brought in from Puebla and the Gulf coast to help build Tula.

The events of Topiltzin's life are mostly legend, partly supported by history. He became identified with Quetzalcóatl, the feathered serpent god who had already been worshipped at Teotihuacán and Xochicalco. Topiltzin was probably a priest-king dedicated to the peaceful, non-human-sacrificing worship of Quetzalcóatl. His enemies at Tula seem to have been followers of the less likeable Tezcatlipoca (Smoking Mirror), the god of warriors, witchcraft, life and death. The story goes that Tezcatlipoca appeared in various guises to provoke Topiltzin-Quetzalcóatl: as a naked chile-seller he aroused the lust of Topiltzin's daughter and ended up marrying her, and as an old man he persuaded the sober Topiltzin to get drunk. Eventually the humiliated leader burnt or buried his treasures and left for the Gulf coast.

There are at least two stories of what he did when he got there. One is that he put on his turquoise mask and quetzal feather headdress, set himself on fire and became

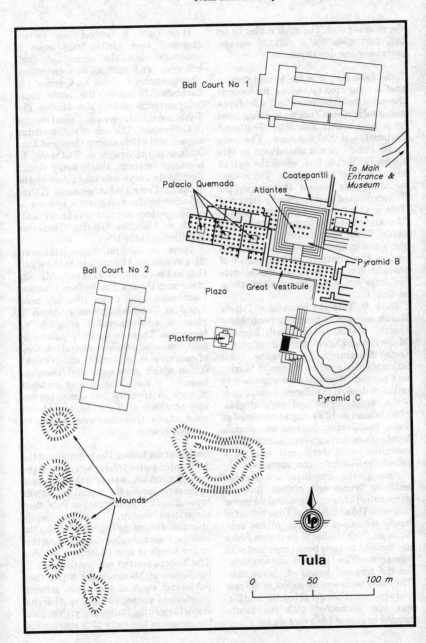

Ball Court No 1

To Main
Entrance &
Museum

Coatepantli

Palacio Quemada

Atlantes

Ball Court No 2

Pyramid B

Great Vestibule

Plaza

Platform

Pyramid C

Mounds

Tula

0   50   100 m

the morning star. The other is that he set sail eastwards on a raft of snakes, promising one day to return.

Toltec Expansion It is the second version that is supported by history, for towards the end of the 10th century the Puuc Mayan culture of northern Yucatán was conquered by a man called Kukulcán (Feathered Serpent) and his followers. The only major Puuc site not abandoned at this time was Chichén Itzá, where the style of many of the buildings is Toltec-like. Archaeologists suggest that wandering Toltecs created an even grander version of Tula in this outpost, gathering the local Mayas in one centre to control them more easily. Toltec control over a good part of the Yucatán lasted about 200 years. (To add to the mystery, another school of thought has it that the Toltec-style buildings at Chichén Itzá pre-date those at Tula.)

Back in Tula the home-base Toltecs built a militaristic kingdom, dominating central Mexico where Calixtlahuaca, Malinalco and Xochicalco were all part of their domain, and extending their influence over much of the rest of Mexico and beyond. Warriors were organised in orders dedicated to different animal-gods – the coyote, jaguar and eagle knights. Mass human sacrifice may have started at Tula. Fortification became widespread. Sombre stone carvings – almost exclusively concerned with death and warriors – reflect the Toltecs' preoccupations.

Among the carvings are strange reclining figures with pitiless, mocking gazes called chac-mools, found wherever there was Toltec influence. Their helmeted heads are raised and look to one side, while on their stomachs lie dishes which are thought to have been connected with human sacrifice, perhaps as receptacles for the torn-out hearts of the victims. They may represent an aspect of the rain god who, as the bringer of fertility and life, was also connected with the deaths needed to ensure life's continuity.

How tight a control the Toltecs exercised over further-flung areas is uncertain, but the spread of their influence and culture was enormous. They probably founded La Quemada in Zacatecas to guard the trade route bringing turquoise from New Mexico. The Toltec hand is also seen at Casas Grandes in Chihuahua. The cult of the feathered serpent still exists among Hopi and Zuni Indians in the American Southwest. In northern Veracruz, the Huastec site of Castillo de Teayo was taken over by the Toltecs. There's also probable Toltec influence in old temple mounds, ceremonial plazas, pottery and artefacts found as far north as Alabama, Georgia, Tennessee and Illinois in the US.

There are several Toltec-influenced sites in western Mexico, and to the south they had some hold over the early Mixtecs of northern Oaxaca. Pottery from Chiapas, Guatemala, even Costa Rica has been found at Tula, which was evidently a place of some splendour alongside its harshness. Legends speak of palaces of gold, turquoise, jade and quetzal feathers, of enormous cobs of maize and coloured cotton which grew naturally. There is, however, a surprising lack of evidence of work in anything but stone, pottery and obsidian at Tula. Quite possibly most of its treasures were looted by Chichimecs.

Decline of the Toltecs The beginning of the fairly rapid end of Toltec glory came in the mid-12th century, when the ruler Huémac apparently moved the capital to Chapultepec after factional fighting at Tula, then committed suicide. Tula was finally abandoned about the beginning of the 13th century, seemingly after violent destruction at the hands of new Chichimec raiders. The Toltecs started new settlements in the Valley of Mexico, from which they influenced some of the newly arriving Chichimecs who were setting up other city states there in the 13th century. (Not until the Aztecs in the early 15th century did any one of these groups emerge as the undisputed power in the valley.) Other Toltecs went further afield, taking over Cholula for a few decades from 1292. Some went as far as the Gulf coast, Guatemala, even Nicaragua – where the Nahuatl-speaking Pipil Indians of today are probably their descendants.

Strangely enough, although archaeologists had been poking around the ruins at Tula since at least 1888, it was only in the 1930s or 1940s that it was identified as the site of the Toltec capital.

The modern town of Tula de Allende has seen industrial development in recent decades. A large oil refinery and cement works stand on the outskirts.

Information & Orientation

To leave the Autotransportes Valle del Mezquital bus station you walk through a small courtyard with a few food stalls and you emerge in a corner of the town's main plaza. Juárez is the street leaving the plaza to the right. It comes out on Valle after 100 metres. The street with the Tollan Restaurant on it, stretching across the far side of the plaza when you emerge from the bus station, is Quetzalcóatl. To reach the market, walk left along Quetzalcóatl. You can change money at the bank on Juárez.

The archaeological site is three km from the main plaza. A taxi costs US$0.60. By foot from the main plaza, it's quickest to walk to the right along Quetzalcóatl. At the end of Quetzalcóatl cross the footbridge over the river and turn right along the far bank. The path becomes a road and at the street sign 'Oriente 14' another road comes down from the left. If you double back up this road, you can nip through a gap in the site's boundary fence on the right and save a long walk round to the official entrance.

If you prefer the official entrance, don't double back at the Oriente 14 sign but follow the road you're on as it curves left, then uphill past La Palapa restaurant. You come out on a busier road which you

follow to the left until you reach the site entrance road.

An alternative is to get off your bus by the railway tracks as the bus turns right into central Tula along Ocampo. Signs here to 'Parque Nacional Tula' will lead you to the site. While this route is better for motorists, it's no quicker on foot than the routes described above.

The Site

Tula ruins are open daily except Monday from 9.30 am to 4.30 pm. Entry is 25c (free on Sundays and holidays). The restored area stands on a small hilltop. Dating from 950 to 1150 AD, these are the remains of the main ceremonial centre of a town of 30,000 to 40,000 people, covering nearly 13 square km and stretching to the far side of the modern town. The Mexico City-Querétaro railway circles the site on a viaduct. There's a restaurant at the entrance. If you want a miniature Atlante or chac-mool, numerous stalls selling them line the path from the entrance to the main structures.

Museum The museum at the site entrance has some informative displays on the history and life style of the Toltec inhabitants and shows the large scale of the old settlement. The collection includes a chac-mool, a jaguar statue, stelae and other finds from the site.

Ball Court 1 This is the first structure you reach from the main entrance. It's I-shaped, 37 metres long, and a copy of an earlier one at Xochicalco.

Coatepantli Pyramid B, topped with the famous 'Atlante' statues, stands to the south of Ball Court 1. As you approach it you first reach a wall a few metres from the pyramid's north side, which is called the Coatepantli (serpent wall). Forty metres long and 2¼ metres high, the wall is carved with rows of geometric patterns and a row of snakes devouring human skeletons. Traces remain of the bright colours with which this and most other structures at Tula were originally painted.

Pyramid B Also known as the temple of Quetzalcóatl or of Tlahuizcalpantecuhtli (the morning star), this is the most interesting building at Tula and is climbed by a flight of steps on the south side. The row of four basalt Atlantes which faces you at the top, and the row of pillars behind, supported the wood-beamed roofs of the two rooms of a temple which originally stood here. Two round stone columns, representing feathered

Tula Atlantes

serpents with their heads on the ground and their tails in the air, stood at the top of the stairway to form part of the entrance to the temple. Parts of these, carved with feather patterns, remain.

The left-hand Atlante is a replica of the original, which is in the Mexico City Anthropology Museum. Part of the right-hand one was missing and has been reproduced. All were originally carved in four sections. These warriors symbolise Quetzalcóatl in his guise as the morning star. Their headdresses are vertical feathers set in what may be bands of stars; the breastplates are in the shapes of butterflies. Short skirts cover most of the front of the thighs but leave the buttocks bare and are held in place behind by discs representing the sun. Their right hands hold spear-throwers called *atlatls*; in their left hands are spears or arrows and incense bags. Their sandals have serpent motifs.

The rectangular columns behind the Atlante statues depict crocodile heads (symbolising the earth), warriors and symbols of the warrior orders, weapons and the head of Quetzalcóatl. In this rear part of the temple was an altar resting on smaller Atlantes.

On the east wall of the pyramid, protected by scaffolding, are some of the carvings which once surrounded all four sides. These show the symbols of the Toltec warrior orders: jaguars, coyotes, eagles eating hearts and what may be a human head in the mouth of Quetzalcóatl or Tlahuizcalpantecuhtli.

A colonnaded hall known as the Great Vestibule extends along the front of the pyramid, facing the open plaza. You'll see the remains of a stone bench decorated with carved warriors, which originally ran the length of the hall, possibly for the use of priests and nobles observing ceremonies in the plaza.

Palacio Quemada This 'burnt palace' immediately west of Pyramid B is a series of halls and courtyards with more low benches and relief carvings, one of which

Top: La Venta, Villahermosa (TW)
Left: Temple of Quetzalcóatl, Teotihuacán (TW)
Right: Atlante, Tula, Hidalgo (JN)

shows a procession of nobles. These areas were probably used for meetings or ceremonies, and the walls painted with frescoes.

Plaza At the centre of the plaza in front of Pyramid B is a small altar or ceremonial platform with a low stairway on each side. This plaza would have been the scene of religious and military displays of many kinds. Pyramid C, the biggest structure at Tula, is on the east side of the plaza; it has not been excavated. To the west is Ball Court 2, the largest in central Mexico at over 100 metres long, with a chac-mool at each end.

El Corral This curious circular structure stands on a dirt track, 1½ km north of the main centre of the site. The two rectangular wings were probably added later. Temples once topped the structure, and the circular part may have been dedicated to the wind god Ehécatl. Between El Corral and the main ceremonial centre are the remains of some residential areas. Tula houses tended to be in small groups of three to five, each with a central shrine. The dead were generally buried under the house floors.

Places to Stay
Hotel Rodríguez at Zaragoza 20 (no sign) has basic but reasonably clean singles/doubles with communal bathrooms for US$2/3.25. From the main plaza, walk left along Quetzalcóatl, then turn right along Zaragoza just before the church. The hotel is towards the far end on the right.

Auto Hotel Cuellar at Cinco de Mayo 23 has parking space, a restaurant and smallish singles/doubles with private baths for US$3.25/4.25 (extra for TV). From the main plaza, go left along Quetzalcóatl, right on Zaragoza, then left on Cinco de Mayo at the end of Zaragoza.

Motel Lisbeth (tel 2-00-45) at Ocampo 42 is the best place in town but poor value at US$9.50/12.50. Rooms have private baths and TV and there's parking space and a restaurant. From the bus station, go out of the vehicle entrance on to Ocampo and walk to the right for 300 metres.

Places to Eat
The *Tollan Restaurant* on Quetzalcóatl facing the main plaza is a bakery too and a decent, not too expensive place at which to stop between the bus station and the ruins. Enchiladas, quesadillas, etc cost US$1 to US$1.50, meat dishes US$1.25 to US$2.50.

Restaurant-Grill La Palapa, not far from the ruins, does a four-course lunch for US$2. To get there from the ruins' main entrance, go down the driveway, turn right along the main road, then take the first fork to the right.

Cafetería El Cisne, on the corner of Juárez and Valle 100 metres from the main plaza, does mainly Western-type snacks and light meals. Fried chicken at US$1 is the most expensive item. Also on the menu are burgers and ice cream.

There's a restaurant at the entrance to the ruins.

Getting There & Away
Bus Tula's main bus station is just off the main square. Autotransportes Valle del Mezquital (2nd class) has buses every 20 minutes from Mexico City northern bus station to Tula (US$1.25). There are two routes; the 'Refinería' is shorter and uses better roads. The trip takes 1¼ hours. The same company runs buses between Tula and Pachuca (US$1.25) every 15 minutes.

Flecha Amarilla has three buses a day to San Juan del Río, Querétaro and León. These depart from an office at Cinco de Mayo 41 at the corner of Zaragoza.

Rail There are trains from Mexico City to Tula at 8 am and 6 pm, but the station is no nearer the ruins than the bus station is. The train trip supposedly takes 1½ hours and costs US$0.50 in 1st class. A return train to Mexico City leaves Tula at 6 pm.

Hidalgo State

PACHUCA

The capital of the state of Hidalgo, 90 km from Mexico City, is faintly reminiscent of Andalusia in Spain. It's set 2426 metres high, where the altiplano central meets the Sierra Madre Oriental, with whitewashed or brightly painted houses climbing the dry hillsides around the centre. The pleasant, calm town has some interesting history and some colonial buildings, but lacks any outstanding attractions. Pachuca is a good example of a relatively prosperous, fairly large (140,000 people), ordinary Mexican town, which could serve as an offbeat retreat from Mexico City or a base for exploring deeper into Hidalgo.

History

The Spanish settlement of Pachuca dates from the first half of the 16th century. Silver was found in the area by the Spanish as early as 1534, though the Aztecs may have worked the mines in the last few decades before the Spanish arrival. It was in Pachuca that the 'patio' process of separating silver from ore by amalgamating it with mercury was invented by Bartolomé de Medina. The Pachuca tank, used in the cyanide process for silver, was also developed here.

The mines of Real del Monte founded in 1739, nine km north-east, still produce significant amounts of silver, but in recent decades other mining-related industries have been replacing silver as the backbone of the local economy – among them smelting and ore-reduction plants.

Orientation

Pachuca's centre is the Plaza de la Independencia, with its high clock tower – the *reloj monumental* – in the middle. Places to stay and eat are nearly all within a few blocks of the plaza. Matamoros is the street running along its east side. From the south-west corner, Allende runs south to meet Matamoros after 300 metres.

A short street leading off the plaza midway along its west side (near the Hotel Grenfell) meets Guerrero, another important street, after 100 metres. If you go left along Guerrero you come to the modern Plaza Juárez. You would also reach Plaza Juárez by going south along Matamoros for about four blocks from Plaza de la Independencia. Plaza Constitución is another downtown square, a couple of blocks north-east of the Plaza de la Independencia.

The bus station is some way south-west of the centre, not far off the road to Mexico City. Green-and-white colectivo taxis (10c) or regular taxis (US$0.30) wait outside the bus station to take you to the Plaza de la Independencia.

Pachuca is making an effort to beautify itself. A couple of streets east of the Plaza de la Independencia have been pedestrianised and several small modern plazas have been added to the older ones. Murals stressing Hidalgo's Otomí Indian heritage are appearing and a particularly good one depicting animals and plants in local style covers a roadside wall just south of the fountain where Matamoros meets Arista.

Pachuca's various 'palacios' can be confusing: in addition to the new Palacio de Gobierno, there's also the former Palacio de Gobierno, a French-chateau-like building on Plaza General Pedro María Anaya three blocks east of the Plaza de la Independencia, and the Palacio Municipal on Plaza Constitución.

Information

Tourist Office There are two tourist offices. One, federally run, is near the plaza de toros (bull ring) on the road from Mexico City as it enters Pachuca. The state tourism office (tel 3-05-10 – closed Saturday afternoons and Sundays) is on the 2nd floor of the new Palacio de Gobierno on Plaza Juárez.

Money There are banks on the Plaza de la Independencia.

Post The post office is at the corner of Juárez and Iglesias.

Centro Cultural de Hidalgo

Pachuca's only real 'sight' is well worth the effort if you're already in town, but hardly worth travelling from Mexico City for unless you have a special interest. Next to the 17th-century church of La Asunción on Arista at Jardín Colón, the ex-monastery of San Francisco has been turned into the Centro Cultural de Hidalgo which contains Mexico's national photography museum, a regional museum, theatres, a cinema and an exhibition gallery. Admission is free (unless you're attending a performance) and the centre is open from 10 am to 2 pm and 4 to 7 pm Tuesday to Saturday, 11 am to 5 pm on Sunday.

To reach the Centro Cultural, go south down Matamoros from the Plaza de la Independencia until you reach a crossroads with a fountain after three blocks. Turn left here on to Arista and you come to the Jardín Colón at the junction with Hidalgo, after about two blocks – altogether about ¾ km from the centre.

Museo Nacional de la Fotografía combines early film technology – such as a reconstructed daguerrotype studio and an array of antique cameras – with selections from the 1.5 million photos in the archive of INAH, the national anthropology and history institute. These provide fascinating glimpses into Mexico's past (since 1873) and present, capturing both the big names and the ordinary people. The collection is particularly strong on the early 20th century revolutionary period: you'll see folk heroes Emiliano Zapata and Pancho Villa, as well as the pomp and circumstance of dictator Porfirio Díaz.

Museo Regional de Hidalgo This has exhibits on Indian dress, life styles and crafts, and as informative displays on the state's archaeology and history. On display are mammoth teeth, beautiful early obsidian tools, a stone jaguar from Tula, and relics of the Aztec and colonial periods.

La Asunción This church is often locked, but if you get in you can look for the mummified body of Santa Columba (who died in Europe in 273 AD) on one of the side altars, the Capilla Secreta (Secret Chapel) in the rear of the church and the eight-sided sacristy covered with oil paintings.

Reloj Monumental

The clock tower in the middle of the Plaza de la Independencia was built in 1904 in the French style popular at the time. Four marble sculptures, one on each side, represent Independence, Liberty, the Constitution and Reform.

Colonial Buildings

These include the Casa Colorada, now a school a short way north along Hidalgo from the Centro Cultural, and the Cajas Reales (Royal Treasuries) behind the north side of the Plaza Constitución.

Foro Cultural Efrén Rebolledo

Located at Bravo 8, 1½ blocks west of the Plaza de la Independencia, the historical research centre and science & arts college often has exhibitions of various kinds. There was a Punch and Judy show on when we visited it!

Places to Stay

Hotel Grenfell (tel 2-02-77) at Plaza de la Independencia 16 occupies an imposing building on the west side of the main plaza but is much less impressive inside. Clean, sizeable, bare rooms with private bath around a large but wasted courtyard give the place an institutional feel. Rooms with one bed are US$2.75, with two beds US$3.50. *Hotel Juárez* (tel 2-12-95) on the southern side of the same plaza is dark, with cubicle-like rooms. It's cheap (singles/doubles with private bath are US$1.75/2.25) but says it's 'full' when it doesn't look it.

The *Hotel Noriega* (tel 2-50-00, 2-50-01) at Matamoros 305, two blocks south of the Plaza de la Independencia, is the best bet in town, an excellent-value colonial-style place with a good restaurant. There's a covered courtyard, a fine staircase, wide rambling corridors, and lots of plants. Rooms are pleasant with TV, phone and private bath. Singles cost US$4.25 or US$4.75, doubles US$5.50 or US$6. For garage space, you pay an extra US$0.50.

Hotel de los Baños (tel 3-07-00, 3-07-01), at Matamoros 205 a block nearer the Plaza de la Independencia, is more expensive and less appealing, but still OK. Rooms have ageing decor and no fans but are clean and quite big. Some have TV. Singles/doubles are US$5.50/7.

Hotel Emily (tel 2-65-17, 2-65-18), also on the south side of Plaza de la Independencia, is Pachuca's newest place but is characterless and has few advantages over the cheaper Noriega. Rooms have balconies (some looking onto the plaza, others on to walls a few feet away), TV and pine panelling but are box-like. Singles are US$5.50, doubles US$6 with one bed, US$6.25 with two beds. There are also suites from US$7.25 to US$9.75.

Hotel Plaza Eldorado (tel 2-52-85, 2-53-25) at Guerrero 721 has 92 pleasant and sizeable rooms at US$4.75 for one single or double bed, US$8 for two beds. To reach it from Plaza de la Independencia, take the short street leading off the middle of the west side of the plaza (near the Hotel Grenfell), and turn left along Guerrero at the first corner.

Places to Eat

The renowned place for local specialities like *barbacoa* (baked lamb) and *gusanos de maguey* (maguey worms) is the village of Pachuquilla, nine km east of Pachuca on Highway 130.

For more familiar fare, *Pizza 2000* on Bravo half a block from Plaza de la Independencia has only four tables but prepares good pizzas before your eyes. An *ordén* (two pieces) costs US$0.40. Four to eight pieces make a meal, depending on your appetite. Bravo is the street leading west from the north-west corner of the plaza. There's another pizzeria on the street going north from the same corner.

The *Restaurant Noriega* in the Hotel Noriega at Matamoros 305 has a touch of elegance (including prints of old London on the walls), but prices are reasonable. It's especially popular for Sunday lunch, for which you pay US$2.75. Also popular is *Chip's Restaurant*, attached to the Hotel Emily on the Plaza del Independencia, which is more of a cappuccino, antojito and ice cream bar.

The large *Restaurant La Blanca* (tel 2-18-96), also on the plaza at the corner of Matamoros and Valle a few metres from the clock tower, serves fairly ordinary Mexican food. The five-course comida corrida is US$1.50. There are several other restaurants on Matamoros including the *Ostionería El Puerto de Acapulco*, which provides seafood and a would-be seaside atmosphere. One pair of travellers recommended the *Casino Español*, upstairs at Matamoros 207, where the comida corrida is US$2.

Restaurant Ciro's is an unimaginative modernish place on the north side of the plaza (go down a few steps from street level to enter). The usual aves and carnes are in the US$1.75 to US$3 range. There are also antojitos (enchiladas Suizas are tasty at US$1.50), eggs and unremarkable ice cream.

Things to Buy

The Casa de las Artesanías (tel 3-04-12, 3-09-65), by the Glorieta Independencia roundabout on Avenida Juárez (the Mexico City road) two km south-west of the Plaza de la Independencia, displays and sells crafts from the state of Hidalgo.

Pachuca has at least three markets. The main one is on Plaza Constitución.

There are also the Juárez market, a couple of blocks north of the Plaza de la Independencia's north-west corner, and the Barreteros market on Guerrero.

Getting There & Away
Road Pachuca is the meeting point of several main roads. Highway 85, the Pan-American, goes south-west to Mexico City (90 km) and north through the Sierra Madre to Ixmiquilpan (79 km), Tamazunchale (280 km) and Ciudad Valles (395 km). Highway 45, west from Ixmiquilpan to San Juan del Río, is surfaced but rough.

Two beautiful but twisting and sometimes poorly surfaced roads go north and east from Pachuca through the Sierra Madre to the Gulf coast plain. Highway 105, particularly tortuous, goes north to Atotonilco El Grande (35 km) and Huejutla (215 km), and is the most direct – but probably not the quickest – route to Tampico (380 km). Highway 130 goes east to Tulancingo (46 km) and on through Huauchinango to Poza Rica (200 km). All roads through the Sierra Madre are subject to fog. You can also get to Tula, Teotihuacán and Tlaxcala by paved roads.

Bus Pachuca's bus station (Central Camionera) is along a few maze-like streets not far east of the Mexico City road in the south-west of town. Fortunately green-and-white colectivo taxis (10c) run between the Plaza de la Independencia and the bus station door. A taxi all to yourself will cost US$0.30.

Buses, mostly 2nd class, go anywhere you want to go. ADO (1st class, tel 3-35-63) runs every 15 or 20 minutes to Mexico City (US$1.25), to Huejutla (US$3) twice daily, Poza Rica (US$2.50) and Tampico (US$6.25) once each.

Autobuses México-Tuxpan-Tampico (tel 3-32-58) has 1st and 2nd-class buses (prices given are 1st class – subtract 10% for 2nd class). Buses run several times daily to Mexico City (US$1), Huejutla (US$3) and Querétaro (US$2.75) via Actopan (US$0.50), Ixmiquilpan (US$1) and San Juan del Río (US$2.25). They run a few times daily to Reynosa (US$10), Matamoros (US$10), Tamazunchale (US$3.25), Tampico (US$6.25), Tuxpan (US$3), Huauchinango (US$1.25), Poza Rica (US$2.50), Ciudad Victoria, Ciudad Mante, Ciudad Valles, San Juan de los Lagos, Lagos de Moreno, León, Irapuato, Salamanca and Celaya.

Estrella Blanca (2nd class, tel 3-37-47) goes to most of the same places, including Querétaro (US$2.50), every two hours up to 6.30 pm. Flecha Roja (2nd class, tel 3-33-43) concentrates on Mexico City (US$1) every five minutes, Ciudad Valles (US$4.25) every 40 minutes, Actopan (US$0.50) and Ixmiquilpan (US$1) every 20 minutes. Autotransportes Valle del Mezquital (2nd class) runs buses to Tula (US$1.25) every 15 minutes up to 8 pm, also to numerous other local towns and villages. AMTH (2nd class) serves Texcoco, Tlaxcala, Puebla and Mexico City. Transportes de Hidalgo (2nd class) will take you 45 km south-east to Ciudad Sahagún, from where you could get another bus 30 km west to Teotihuacán.

Travelling times: Mexico City (1st class) 1½ hours, Actopan (2nd class) 45 minutes, Ixmiquilpan (2nd class) 1½ hours, San Juan del Río (2nd class) four hours, Huejutla about six hours, Ciudad Valles about nine hours, Poza Rica about five hours.

AROUND HIDALGO
Though well off the beaten tourist track, Hidalgo has some spectacular country and a number of other interesting destinations, many of them within an hour or two of Pachuca. If you're based in Mexico City for a while, or just want to go somewhere different, some of them would make worthwhile trips. You're unlikely to see any Westerners and should be prepared for a bit of back-country travel. Unless you have your own car most of these places require at least one night

outside Mexico City. See Getting There & Away under Pachuca for information on buses around Hidalgo.

The state has a bizarre shape and borders Querétaro on the west, San Luis Potosí on the north, Veracruz and Puebla to the east, Tlaxcala and México to the south. It also has a dramatic geography, as dry rolling country in the south gives way to the forested Sierra Madre Oriental in the north and east. Several deep canyons cut through the countryside. Hidalgo's population of 1.8 million includes over 300,000 Indians – mostly Otomíes and Nahuas but also a few Tepehuas. Many of them are located in the remote east and north-east of the state. There are also Otomí concentrations in the west, centred on Ixmiquilpan, Actopan and Zimapán. About 125,000 of Mexico's 300,000 Otomíes live in Hidalgo – more than in any other state. They are also scattered around México, Guanajuato, Querétaro and Veracruz states. Traditional women's dress is a quechquémitl on top of an embroidered cloth blouse.

History

The Otomí people, who may already have been in Hidalgo before and during the period of Toltec supremacy from 950 to 1150 AD, became the main inhabitants after the fall of Tula, the Toltec capital. In the second half of the 15th century the south and north of the state fell under Aztec dominance. The statelets of Metztitlán in the centre and Tutotepec in the east managed to remain independent, however, and initially welcomed the Spanish, who found early allies among the Otomíes. But things quickly went sour: Cortés himself led an expedition to put down a rebellion in Tutotepec in 1523 and the Otomíes, despite helping the Spanish pacify some Chichimecs to the north, found themselves faring no better than most other Indians.

Silver and other mineral deposits made Hidalgo important to the Spanish from the early 16th century. Among its monuments are many monasteries built during the early and mid-16th century as Augustinian monks set about converting the local people. The state of Hidalgo came into existence in 1869 and was named after Miguel Hidalgo y Costilla, the Mexican independence hero.

Today its economy is still predominantly agricultural and it is one of Mexico's poorer states, though efforts are being made to bring new industries to the south, around towns like Pachuca, Tula and Tulancingo. Hidalgo produces 31% of Mexico's barley, 11% of its alfalfa, 7% of its coffee and 6% of its silver; it has 9% of its six million sheep.

West of Pachuca

Pan-American Highway 85 runs north-west through dry, alternately rugged and rolling country to Actopan, Ixmiquilpan and Zimapán (all with large Otomí Indian populations), then turns north-east through the Sierra Madre to Tamazunchale and Ciudad Valles in the state of San Luis Potosí. Eight km after Ixmiquilpan, Highway 45 branches west through Huichapan to meet the Querétaro-Mexico City road just south of San Juan del Río, which is 175 km from Pachuca.

Ajacuba Ten km north-west of Pachuca, the road to Tula (85 km from Pachuca) branches west. After 38 km it reaches the small town of Ajacuba, where three hot springs have been diverted into swimming pools. One of them, Balneario La Carreta, is also equipped with a hotel (tel Mexico City 515-12-26) and restaurant. Another, Balneario Ajacuba, has 44°C radioactive waters containing sulphates and chlorides (said to be good for rheumatism, arthritis and stomach and skin problems!) and 1600 square metres of pools.

Actopan Located 37 km from Pachuca along Highway 85 (45 minutes by bus), Actopan has Hidalgo's finest Augustinian fortress-monastery (founded 1548), typical of such buildings put up in the early decades after the Spanish conquest and still in an excellent state of preservation.

The monastery church has a lovely plateresque façade with Corinthian columns, and its single tower shows mudéjar (Moorish) influence. The nave has gothic vaulting.

The cloister, where the monks lived and worked, is to the right of the church. Mexico's best 16th-century frescoes are in its Sala De Profundis (where hermits are depicted), and on its stairs (saints, leading Augustinians and one mural showing Father Martín de Acevedo, one of the leading early monks at Actopan, with two important Indians, Don Juan Inica Actopa and Don Pedro Ixcuincuitlapilco). There's a religious art museum here too. The refectory (dining hall) has a finely decorated ceiling.

To the left of the church a large, vaulted open chapel is also decorated with frescoes. At the top of the arch is carved the Augustinian shield.

Actopan's Wednesday market goes back at least 400 years. Places to stay include the *Hotel Del Convento* at Plaza Juárez 15 and the *Hotel Rirra* at Lerdo de Tejada 50.

Ixmiquilpan This town of 25,000 people is 75 km from Pachuca in the arid Mezquital Valley, a long-time Otomí enclave. It's 1½ hours by bus from Pachuca and has a busy Monday market which is probably the best place of all to look for Otomí crafts such as miniature musical instruments made of juniper wood with pearl or shell inlay, numerous objects made of reed, colourful drawstring bags and embroidered textiles. You may if you're lucky come across a dark blue cotton quechquémitl coloured by the ikat tie-dyeing technique. Until recent decades these were widely used by the Otomíes of the Mezquital Valley.

The Otomíes of the Mezquital Valley are also noted for making Mexico's finest *ayates*, cloths woven from ixtle, the fibre of the maguey cactus. The process they

follow has changed little since it was described in the 16th century by Fray Bernardino de Sahagún, the greatest early Spanish chronicler of Indian ways. It involves baking the leaves, soaking them in water, beating and scraping them, soaking the resulting fibres with soap or dough, then drying, combing and spinning them. The Otomíes also use maguey for many other purposes including food, drink, soap, house-building and needles.

There's a Casa de Artesanías (tel 3-03-13) displaying and selling local crafts on Felipe Ángeles.

Ixmiquilpan's Augustinian monastery was built under the direction of Andrés de Mata, the monk who also designed Actopan. Its church has a plateresque façade and a huge gothic vault. The cloister corridors and rooms have old frescoes by Indian artists showing combats between Indians and mythical pre-Hispanic figures, as well as religious scenes.

Places to stay include the *Hotel Saisa* (tel 3-01-12) at Insurgentes 99, *Hotel Diana* (tel 3-07-58) at Insurgentes 103, *Hotel Jardín* (tel 3-03-08) and *Hotel Palacio* (tel 3-01-08) both on Plaza Juárez, and the more expensive *Hotel Club Alcantara* (tel 3-04-90) with a swimming pool at Peña Juárez 8.

From Cardonal, a village 17 km north of Ixmiquilpan by paved road, a rough dirt road leads 22 km east into the Barranca de Tolantongo. This is a 10-km-long ravine, 800 metres deep in parts, formed by the thermal Río Blanco which emerges from a cave surrounded by waterfalls at the head of the ravine. While most of the ravine is semi-desert, with tall and ancient cacti, the area round the cave is semi-tropical! The road goes right down to the bottom of the ravine – don't try it in wet weather.

Tasquillo This site 16 km beyond Ixmiquilpan just off Highway 85 is the location of the Balneario Tzindejeh, a 35°C hot spring with alkaline waters, a hotel and restaurant.

Zimapán Located 40 km north-west of Ixmiquilpan a few km west of Highway 85, this is an old mining town at the foot of the Sierra Madre. There are a couple of hotels. Some long-distance buses make a detour here off the highway. The road north through the Sierra Madre passes some pine forests.

Pachuca to Huejutla

Highway 105 winds north into the picturesque Sierra Madre Oriental towards Huejutla, 215 km away. Buses should go from Pachuca to all the places mentioned here:

El Chico Nine km from Pachuca, a road heads off north-west from Highway 105 into El Chico National Park, an area of evergreen forest and impressive rock formations sometimes used by climbers. The *Albergue Miguel Hidalgo*, in the park 10 km from the turn-off, is an alpine hostel where you can get a bed on Friday or Saturday nights for a little over US$1. There's a restaurant a couple of km before it. Beyond the hostel, the road winds on to Mineral del Chico, an old mining village 29 km from Pachuca.

Mineral del Monte Formerly called Real del Monte, this small mining town 12 km from Pachuca claims to have been the scene of the first strike in the Americas (1776) and still produces silver from at least four mines. The local people eat *pastes*, a type of meat pie introduced by English miners in the last century. Turn right off Highway 105 about 10 km from Pachuca.

Huasca, San Miguel Regla & San Juan Hueyapan A turn-off to the right, 25 km from Pachuca, leads nine km to the pretty little village of Huasca, from where roads lead three km to San Miguel Regla and five km to San Juan Hueyapan, both of which have old haciendas turned into hotel-restaurants. The one in San Miguel Regla (tel Huasca 2) is more luxurious and

expensive. A dirt road leads eight km north from Huasca to Santa María Regla, where a 50-metre-deep ravine is fringed by bizarre 'basalt prisms', thin hexagonal fingers of rock. This is a popular Mexican weekend outing. There's an old hacienda in the bottom of the ravine.

Atotonilco el Grande This small town 35 km from Pachuca has the remains of one of several Augustinian monasteries built in Hidalgo in the 16th century; a few frescoes can still be seen. The monastery church façade is in renaissance style. Market day is Thursday. After Atotonilco the road descends 800 metres into the fertile valley of the Río Tulancingo, which contrasts strongly with the dry landscape higher up.

Metztitlán This village in the Río Tulancingo valley has a better-preserved monastery. It's reached by a 23-km paved road up the valley. The turn-off from Highway 105 is to the left soon after crossing the Río Tulancingo, 65 km from Pachuca. Metztitlán was the centre of an Otomí state which the Aztecs couldn't conquer. The monastery stands in the highest part of the village. It has a big atrium (yard) with posa chapels. The façade is plateresque/pure renaissance. The church has six gilded baroque altarpieces. The cloister has been restored.

Metzquititlán About 78 km from Pachuca, this town has a 16th-century church with a fine Indian-influenced plateresque façade. Two km east by dirt road, the little church of Santa María Xoxoteco has Indian frescoes depicting the world's transformation from paganism to Christianity. Eighteen km beyond Metzquititlán, the village of Tlahuelompa is famed for its copperwork and has produced bells for many of Mexico's churches. Beyond Metzquititlán, Highway 105 climbs on to a dry plateau then enters the forested Sierra Madre.

Zacualtipán Located 100 km from Pachuca,

Zacualtipán also has a 16th-century Augustinian monastery with a plateresque façade showing Indian influence.

Molango This town 137 km from Pachuca has one of the most interesting monasteries. From the tree-shaded atrium there is a good view of the surrounding valley. Its bells are hung in an *espadaña*, a wall separated from the church. The plateresque façade has a gothic-style rose window. Some of the cloister has been restored. If you want to stay in Molango try the *Hotel Plaza* (tel 58) at Plaza de la República 27.

Huejutla ('way-HOOT-la') This town of 40,000 is very close to the Veracruz border and 215 km from Pachuca. Here you have descended to the semi-tropical lowlands which stretch to the Gulf coast. The big Sunday market in the town square brings many Nahua Indians from outlying villages. The villagers of Chililico and Jaltocan are known for their glazed pottery and embroidered costumes respectively. Palm furniture, reed baskets and huarache sandals are other things you'll see here. Huejutla has another 16th-century Augustinian monastery, whose atrium forms part of the square. For accommodation try the *Hotel Posada Huejutla* (tel 6-03-00) at Morelos 32 or the *Hotel Fayad* (tel 6-00-40) on the corner of Hidalgo and Morelos.

East of Pachuca
Highway 130 runs east to Tulancingo, 46 km away. Beyond Tulancingo the road leaves Hidalgo and crosses a part of the Sierra Madre Oriental known as the Sierra Norte de Puebla before descending to Poza Rica on the Gulf coast plains. See under Sierra Norte de Puebla in the Puebla & Tlaxcala chapter for more on this route.

Zempoala Reached by a different road south-east from Pachuca, Zempoala is 28 km from the state capital. It has a 16th-century church. Nearby is the one km-long arched aqueduct known as Los Arcos del Padre Tembleque. Designed by an untrained 16th-century monk called Francisco de Tembleque, it took 17 years to build and was originally intended to carry water 44 km from the Cerro del Tecajete to Otumba. It crosses a valley and its highest arch is 35 metres high.

Pachuquilla Nine km from Pachuca along Highway 130, Pachuquilla is known for its restaurants specialising in local delicacies such as *gusanos de maguey* and *escamoles*, worms and insect eggs from the maguey plant. Barbacoa (baked lamb) is another Hidalgo favourite.

Epazoyucan Nine km beyond Pachuquilla by Highway 130, then three km south, Epazoyucan has a fine 16th-century Augustinian fortress-monastery. Its church has a plateresque façade. The cloister contains four colourful renaissance frescoes with Indian influence, which are considered some of the most important produced in 16th-century Mexico. There is a large atrium with posa chapels.

Singuilucan Located 36 km east of Pachuca along Highway 130, then 12 km south-west by Highway 132, Singuilucan has a 16th-century monastery with a chapel containing a gilt baroque altarpiece, eight large 17th-century oil paintings on religious subjects, and a roof decorated with plant and flower motifs. In the 18th-century village church is a crucifixion image known as the Señor de Singuilucan, which according to legend detached itself from its cross, sweating profusely, during a procession in 1651. Highway 132 continues south-west to Teotihuacán.

Tulancingo Hidalgo's second biggest town (70,000 people) lies 46 km east of Pachuca along Highway 130, at an altitude of 2222 metres. It was probably the Toltec capital briefly before Tula. There's a Toltec pyramid at the foot of a cliff at Huapalcalco, three km north. Tulancingo is the centre of a vegetable-growing area and has a sizeable textile industry. Market day is Thursday. If you need to stay, try the *Hotel Colonial* (tel 3-02-87) at the corner of Avenida Juárez and Zaragoza. There's also the *Hotel La Joya* (tel 3-32-97) out on the Pachuca road.

People interested in Indian textiles might like to make an expedition to the remote villages of Tenango de Doria and Huehuetla, 40 or 50 rugged km north of Tulancingo (the dirt roads are sometimes impassable). In Tenango the Otomíes embroider cotton with multitudes of animal, human, plant and imaginary figures to make attractive tablecloths or wall-hangings. In Huehuetla, one of the few communities of the tiny Tepehua Indian group embroider colourful floral and geometric patterns on their quechquémitls and enredos. For more on the Tepehua, see the Veracruz chapter.

Pahuatlán & San Pablito These are two very traditional villages actually in Puebla state but approached from a turn-off to the north from Highway 130, about 12 km east of Tulancingo. A spectacular dirt road winds downhill for most of the 30 km to Pahuatlán, which has a Nahua population and a lively Sunday market.

San Pablito, 10 km beyond Pahuatlán, is an Otomí village with a rich and still flourishing textile tradition. Colourfully embroidered blouses and quechquémitls abound here: the women also cover large factory-woven cotton cloths with animal, plant and human motifs to make attractive tablecloths or wall-hangings. At least until recently, San Pablito was still making *amate* (tree-bark paper) by the pre-Hispanic method of boiling bark until it's soft, laying it in strips as a mesh, then beating it with a stone hammer. *Amate* is sometimes used for ritual purposes.

Acaxochitlán Highway 130 continues east into a Nahua Indian area. Acaxochitlán is 23 km east of Tulancingo. The market day

is Sunday; local specialities are fruit wine and preserved fruit. Indian women here often wear very richly embroidered blouses. The road then skirts the large El Tejocotal Reservoir before entering the state of Puebla. Just over the state boundary, Highway 119 branches south to Zacatlán, Apizaco and Tlaxcala.

West of Mexico City

DESIERTO DE LOS LEONES
One fairly short trip out of Mexico City recommended by travellers is to this 2000-hectare national park 30 km west. Its name means Desert of the Lions but in fact it's a pine forest 800 metres higher than the city. There are walking trails (one said to be 30 km long), a campsite, comedores, and a 17th-century Carmelite ex-monastery with pleasant gardens. Free concerts are often held in the monastery on Sunday. Park fauna includes deer and armadillos.

It was at Las Cruces, within the park area, that the 1810 revolutionaries led by Miguel Hidalgo defeated the Spanish loyalists but decided not to go on and attack Mexico City, which was at their mercy – thus, it is claimed, prolonging the independence war by 10 years. The road to Desierto de Los Leones heads west from Insurgentes just north of San Ángel. It's called Camino al Desierto.

TOLUCA
Population: 200,000
Toluca, at 2680 metres the highest of Mexico's capital cities, is surrounded by towering peaks. The extinct volcano Nevado de Toluca, at 4583 metres, sits like a crown jewel above the town. If it were not for the Friday market there would be little reason to visit the town, which is a centre of heavy industry. As to whether you decide to visit what is billed as Mexico's largest market, if you are going to any other major Indian market

town in Mexico, skip Toluca – it's a madhouse.

Before you enter the market, stop at the Casa de Artesanías just east of the market on the main street, Paseo Tollocan. Here you will see goods made in the region and get a sense of what they should cost (prices are fixed here). Then enter the market and ignore the horde of vendors who will try to hustle you. Bargain hard; you'll have plenty of stalls from which to choose. Crafts from nearby Indian villages include rebozos from Tenancingo, table cloths from Almoloya, pottery from Metepec and sarapes from Tianguistengo.

To unwind from the madness of the market, walk a block east of the zócalo and to the Cosmic Glass Botanical Gardens. Light reaches these pleasant gardens through unique stained-glass murals. Also visit the Museo de Arte Popular at the eastern entrance to the city on Highway 15. The quality of the goods here is higher than you will find in the market, illustrating the decline of crafts in this region.

Getting There & Away
Buses leave Mexico City's Terminal Poniente near the Observatorio metro station for Toluca every 20 minutes. The journey takes about an hour and costs US$0.80.

Puebla & Tlaxcala

East of Mexico City lies the state of Puebla, extending 300 km from Poza Rica in the north to the borders of Oaxaca and Guerrero in the south. Tucked into its centre is Tlaxcala, Mexico's smallest state. This is a very diverse region offering fine colonial towns and cities (notably Puebla and Tlaxcala, after which the states are named), the largest ancient pyramid in the Americas (Cholula), some of Mexico's finest frescoes (Cacaxtla), plus some beautiful mountain country and, in parts, a strong Indian presence.

Some of these places can be visited in a day from Mexico City, others require an overnight stop and several reward a much longer stay. Conveniently, they are nearly all on the way from Mexico City to somewhere else: Puebla city is en route to both Veracruz and Oaxaca, while parts of northern Puebla aren't far from Jalapa or El Tajín.

Among the greatest of the area's attractions are the volcanoes Popocatépetl and Iztaccíhuatl, which stand about halfway between Mexico and Puebla cities. You can reach the 3950-metre saddle between these two mountains by bus and taxi in a day trip from the capital.

On the opposite (eastern) border of Puebla state, 150 km away, stands the highest mountain in Mexico, the 5700-metre Pico de Orizaba. Roughly halfway between these great peaks is another, lower volcano, La Malinche, surrounded by plains with the cities of Puebla and Tlaxcala to its west. To the north, in what's called the Sierra Norte de Puebla, Puebla state runs up into the remote southern end of the Sierra Madre Oriental mountains (where there's a high Indian population), then descends to the fringe of the semi-tropical Gulf coast plain in the far north-east. The far south of the state is also mountainous, but dry.

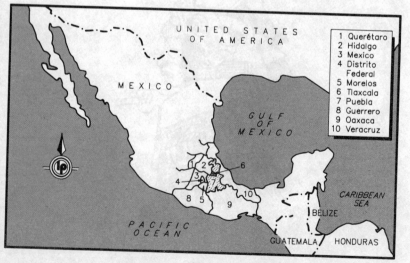

History

Archaeologists have managed to trace in some detail the beginnings of agriculture in the high, dry Tehuacán Valley in south-east Puebla. A variety of sites including caves and rock shelters show that probably before 7000 BC a few small groups lived in the valley, moving from place to place at different times of year, eating plant foods and hunting animals such as horses (which later became extinct in Mexico), jack rabbits and antelope. By 7000 to 5000 BC they were planting avocados, chiles, cotton and squashes, and around 5000 BC the first tiny forms of domestic maize were cultivated. Later, stone metates were made for grinding these crops, and around 3400 to 2300 BC, when the people were still semi-nomadic, the first stone bowls and jars appeared. Pottery, the sign of a truly settled existence, occurred about 2000 BC.

It wasn't until after 400 BC that the Puebla-Tlaxcala region arrived on the map of pre-Hispanic civilisations. By this time the Tezoquipan culture in what's now the state of Tlaxcala had progressed beyond the stage of a few scattered farming settlements to develop a number of villages and small towns with ceremonial centres where there were streets, plazas, platforms, sculpture and the ball game. Terraces and irrigation were also features of this culture, which lasted until 100 AD before Tlaxcala returned to a more scattered agricultural way of life.

Contemporary with the Tezoquipan culture was the more important rise of Cholula, in the Puebla Valley just south of Tlaxcala. During the supremacy of Teotihuacán 100 km to its north-west (0 to 600 AD), Cholula became one of the most important cities in central Mexico and was heavily influenced by its powerful nearby neighbour.

The Puebla Valley, located on routes from central Mexico to the Gulf coast and Oaxaca, has long been a cultural crossroads: among the artistic influences at Cholula was that of El Tajín. One of the groups of people who arrived in the area around the time of the decline of Teotihuacán were the Olmeca-Xicallanca, thought to have been a Mayan people from the Tabasco-Campeche border area, no relation to the earlier Olmecs. Sooner or later they took control of the Puebla Valley and southern Tlaxcala, and Cacaxtla was probably their capital.

The area saw many other comings and goings of peoples from different parts of Mexico. Northern Puebla became part of the Veracruz-centred Totonac domain, and then, along with the Cholula area after the end of the Olmeca-Xicallanca period some time between 800 and 1100, received waves of usually aggressive Chichimec newcomers from the north and west. The scattering of the Toltecs from their capital of Tula in the 12th and 13th centuries also contributed to the mix of peoples in Puebla and Tlaxcala.

From this confusion a variety of small states emerged in the last few centuries before the Spanish conquest. Cholula regained its importance and by the early 16th century was a city of an estimated 100,000 people. In Tlaxcala arose a number of small kingdoms (señoríos), at least some of which came to be loosely linked in the so-called republic of Tlaxcala. The most important seems to have been Tizatlán, on the outskirts of modern Tlaxcala town. Others were Tepeticpac, Ocotelulco and Quiahuixtlán. Another piece in the jigsaw was Huejotzingo, 20 km north-west of Cholula, which controlled Cholula briefly in the 14th century. Speakers of Nahua, the language also spoken by the Aztecs, moved into northern Puebla around the same time. Like the Aztecs, they were probably ultimately of Chichimec origin.

The Aztec empire which spread out from the nearby Valley of Mexico in the 15th century brought most of Puebla, including Cholula, under its sway but the Tlaxcalans managed to remain independent – partly thanks to the curious Flower Wars, in

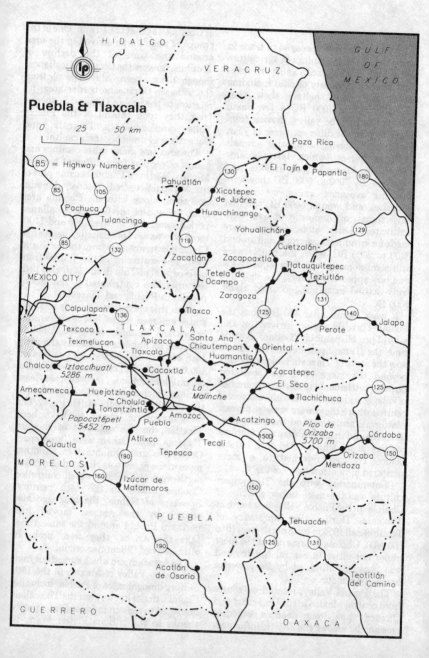

which actual fighting was limited and the main purpose was to take prisoners for sacrifice. In Aztec symbolism, flowers represented human blood.

When the Spanish turned up in 1519 the Tlaxcalans fought them fiercely but were persuaded to make an alliance with them against the Aztecs. Henceforth they became Cortés' staunchest allies – with the exception of one chief, Xicoténcatl the Younger, who tried at least twice to rouse the Tlaxcalans against the Spanish, and was hanged for his pains during the final campaign against the Aztec capital in 1521. In line with modern Mexico's official rejection of its Spanish past, Xicoténcatl is now a bit of a national hero.

Cholula met a different fate at Spanish hands. On arrival there after his initial success with the Tlaxcalans, Cortés got wind of an Aztec-inspired plot to ambush him and his men. The result was the Cholula massacre, in which up to 6000 locals were killed and Cortés' reputation of invincibility was heightened.

After the conquest the Tlaxcalans were rewarded with privileges and used by the Spanish to help pacify Chichimec areas to the north. They were among the early settlers in San Miguel de Allende, San Luis Potosí and Saltillo. In 1527 Tlaxcala town became the seat of the first bishopric in New Spain. A disastrous plague in the 1540s, however, decimated the whole area's population and neither Tlaxcala nor Cholula ever played an important role in Mexican history again. But Tlaxcalan loyalty to the Spanish remained and in the independence struggle of the early 19th century they were on the losing side. The mainly Nahua Indian people of mountainous northern Puebla, however, lost many of their lands to Spanish overlords and after repeated rebellions joined enthusiastically in the independence movement.

The city of Puebla, founded for Spanish settlers in the 1530s, became the most important in the area and for a long time was Mexico's second biggest, a key strategic point in the many wars which engulfed the country in the 19th century. Today it's still the fourth biggest city in the country, a major industrial centre with over a million people.

This one city apart, the states of Puebla and Tlaxcala are primarily rural. Maize, barley, sugar cane, cattle and maguey cactus (for pulque) are among the main products, with coffee, fruit and flowers also grown in humid parts of northern Puebla. Tlaxcala has Mexico's only female state governor, Beatríz Paredes Rangel of the PRI, who was chosen for a six-year term in 1986 at the age of 33.

People

Puebla is predominantly rural but still the fifth most populous state in Mexico, with some four million people. Tlaxcala has another 700,000. Puebla's population includes nearly 500,000 Indians – among them the biggest number of Mexico's most numerous Indian people, the Nahuas, of whom nearly 400,000 are scattered around the state. In the north there are also 60,000 Totonacs, 7000 Otomies and a few Tepehua; in the southeast, near the Oaxaca border, there are some 12,000 Mixtecs, 7000 Popolocas and a few Mazatecs.

The strong Indian presence gives Puebla in particular a rich handicrafts output; fine hand-woven and embroidered textiles with a multitude of unique designs, pottery and carved onyx are among the best things to look out for. Most of these are made in outlying villages and towns but often sold in Puebla city. These days many Indians reserve their fine traditional costumes for fiestas and other special occasions.

POPOCATÉPETL & IZTACCÍHUATL

The snow-capped peaks of Mexico's two most famous mountains ('po-po-ka-TEH-pettle' and 'iss-ta-SEE-wattle') used to be visible almost daily from Mexico City, 65 km away. Nowadays, thanks to the city's smog, you usually

IZTACCÍHUATL

La Cabeza
▲ 5100 m

El Pecho
▲ 5286 m

5000 m

Los Pies
▲ 4700 m

La Joya
Car Park

TV
Transmitter

**Popocatépetl &
Iztaccíhuatl**

0   1   2 km

Paso
de Cortés
(3650 m)

Cortés
Monument

To Cholula

To
Amecameca

Tlamacas
(3950 m)

Las
Cruces
(4480 m)

Querétano (4460 m)

Ventorrillo 5000 m

Teopixcalco
(4930 m)

5452 m

Crater
Rim

5000 m

4500 m

POPOCATÉPETL

4000 m

have to go closer to get a decent look, but
it's well worth the trouble. In clear
weather the mountains and the views
from them are superb.

There are usually better views of these
two giants from the Puebla side. The
Mexico City to Puebla road also often
affords a good view – Iztaccíhuatl (5286
metres) is the nearer to the road,
Popocatépetl (5452 metres) the more
cone-shaped peak. Much better, a road
(and public transport) go up to Tlamacas,
3950 metres high on the saddle between
the two mountains. Here, on the edge of a
pine forest, there's a lodge with dormitory
beds and a restaurant, making this a very
popular weekend outing for people from
Mexico City.

You can walk from Tlamacas to the top
of Popo and back in a strenuous day if you
have the right equipment. The heights of
Izta, however, are mainly for climbers.
There are plenty of other good walks and
strolls on and around the mountains.

The peaks are Mexico's second and
third highest and their names are Aztec.
Popocatépetl means Smoking Mountain,
Iztaccíhuatl White Woman. The legend is
that Popo was a warrior, in love with Izta,
the emperor's daughter. She died of grief
while he was away at war. On his return,
he built the two mountains, laid her body
on one and stood holding her funeral torch
on the other. Plumes of steam still
sometimes rise from Popo's crater and,
with a touch of imagination, Izta does look
a bit like a woman lying on her back.
Different sections of Izta are named after
parts of her body. As you approach from
Mexico City you can make out four peaks
from left to right known as La Cabeza
(head), El Pecho (breast), Las Rodillas
(knees) and Los Pies (feet). Between head
and breast is El Cuello (neck); between
breast and knees is La Barriga (belly).

History

The mountains were first thrown up about
10 million years ago and their present
shape dates from 2.5 million years ago.

Both are classified as dormant, but while Iztaccíhuatl is now craterless, Popocatépetl sometimes belches steam. The Spanish conquistadors recorded eruptions on Popo, and as recently as 1921 a small new cone formed on the floor of the crater.

Both mountains were worshipped by the Aztecs, and high on the Ventorrillo of Popocatépetl (the rugged lower peak on the Tlamacas side) is a small enclosure dating from 900 AD, reckoned to be the work of Toltecs. It's therefore possible that pre-Hispanic Mexicans were the first conquerors of Popo.

Better chronicled are the amazement and antics with which the Spanish conquistadors reacted to the mountain. On reaching Cholula in October 1519 Cortés, curious about a mountain that emitted clouds of smoke, sent a party of 10 Spaniards and some Indians up Popo. The mountain was erupting at the time. Cortés wrote to the King of Spain that the party hadn't quite reached the top because of the snow, flying ashes, wind and cold. Because the party's leader, Diego de Ordaz, became an enemy of Cortés at some point after the ascent, some people credit the story of another conquistador, Bernal Díaz del Castillo, which said that Ordaz and two others did make it to the summit.

From Cholula the conquistadors pressed on towards Tenochtitlán by way of the pass between the two volcanoes, now called the Paso de Cortés. Here they saw in the distance for the first time the lake cities at the heart of the great empire which they were to conquer. A statue of Cortés on the Paso is one of only two in the country – he's not too popular among Mexicans!

After the fall of Tenochtitlán in 1521 the Spanish ran short of ammunition, and five conquistadors were sent back to Popo to get sulphur from the crater for making gunpowder. Again it was erupting. The expedition managed to dodge the flying hot rocks and four reached the top, one having retired exhausted. Standing on the rumbling crater rim, they could see molten lava below when the smoke cleared. Undaunted, two men were lowered into the crater by rope 13 times between them, each time coming up with a bag of sulphur. They were reportedly received as heroes by Indians waiting at the foot of the mountain. Their exploits were equalled on a daily basis nearly four centuries later by the workforce of a sulphur-mining company around the turn of this century.

The first documented ascent of Iztaccíhuatl was by a Swiss, James de Salis, in 1889 – though some say a German called Sonneschmidt had managed it over 100 years earlier.

Tlamacas

At the head of the road (3950 metres) and the base of the black, towering, cone of Popo is the Tlamacas hut – an excellent, modern, 98-bed establishment which charges US$0.75 per person for a dormitory bed and locker (bring your own padlock). It also has a bar and a restaurant open to non-residents. You can rent ice axes and crampons (US$3 each) as well as snow-glare sunglasses here and get helpful advice about the mountains. There are great views of Popo and Izta. At weekends the Tlamacas car park can be packed with a few hundred vehicles. Winds can produce a distinct chill even in sunshine.

Walks

For some, a ramble through the pine forests around Tlamacas or a stroll towards Popo is enough at this altitude. Another possibility is to walk the four km between Paso de Cortés and Tlamacas; there are several short cuts between the bends in the road which climbs/descends 300 metres between the two points. Longer but flat is the eight km from Paso de Cortés to La Joya car park on the flank of Izta – take drinks (at least) with you. From La Joya there are trails across the west flank of Izta to the Chalchoapan hut beneath the 'neck', and back down to Amecameca (six hours). To experience Popo itself without going all the way to the top, you can walk to Las Cruces at 4480 metres, three hours up from Tlamacas (see Ascents). It's ill-advised to leave anything in a vehicle anywhere – the lockers at Tlamacas hut are probably the only safe refuge for belongings you don't want to carry.

Ascents

This section is for hikers who want to go higher than Tlamacas. For more information on rock-climbing routes, see Books, below. Register at the Tlamacas hut or with the Mountain Rescue people (Socorro Alpino) at Tlamacas before embarking on any ascent more demanding than the walk to Las Cruces – for your own safety. It's advisable to have experience in at least mountain-snow hiking before embarking on Popo, and it's not wise to go alone. Izta is even more formidable. Take great care – people have died on these mountains.

Altitude Anyone, even the most experienced climbers, can be affected by altitude problems – which can kill, so don't play around if you think you or one of your party has symptoms. Descend and seek medical help. Fitness helps you avoid these problems, and acclimatisation is another key; if you've already spent a few days around Mexico City (2240 metres) that will help. A day at Tlamacas before trying a long ascent is also a good idea. There are three main types of altitude problem: severe mountain sickness, pulmonary oedema and cerebral oedema. All are usually caused by ascending too fast above 3000 to 3500 metres.

The symptoms of severe mountain sickness include short breath, headaches, sleeplessness, coughing, urine retention, dizziness, nausea and vomiting. It's usually relieved by resting and descending. Severe mountain sickness is different from acclimatisation problems, which cause some of the same symptoms in milder form (you may experience them even in Mexico City).

Pulmonary oedema comes on fast and can cause coma or death. Fluid collects in the lungs; symptoms include breathlessness even when not moving, coughing (sometimes with blood or foam), gurgling in the chest and weakness. Descend and take oxygen if available.

Cerebral oedema is caused by fluid collecting in the brain. It is rarer and can also cause coma or death. It usually occurs above 4000 metres. Symptoms include severe headache, staggering, confusion and hallucinations.

Conditions & Seasons It can be windy and well below freezing on the upper slopes of either mountain at any time of year and is nearly always below freezing near the summits at night. Ice and snow are permanent; the average snow line is 4200 metres but it's higher in the hot dry months of October and November. The very best months for ascents are December and January, when there's a reasonable amount of snow for cramponing. In October and November more hard walking up scree is needed. February and March are sometimes prone to storms and poor visibility. The rainy season, April to September, is the least suitable: this is the time of most snow but it's often soft. At this time there can be thunderstorms, clouds, white-outs, even occasional avalanches. Crevasses (grietas) are a possibility on Popo at any time of year.

Equipment Unless you're just walking to Las Cruces, take ice axes and crampons, since you'll be going up steep, icy or snowy slopes. You can rent them at Tlamacas hut (US$3 each). You should also have at least the following: decent boots; clothing for temperatures below freezing and, at some times of year, for rain; protection for your head against sun and cold; first-aid gear; food and water (though you can melt snow once you reach the snow line); sunglasses (also available at Tlamacas hut) and sunblock for glare; and a very warm sleeping bag if you're thinking of spending the night in a hut or tent.

Huts on Popo Above Tlamacas, there are three huts known as *refugios* – one on the summit and two on the rock-climbers' routes. These are just shelters with no equipment or facilities. They hold eight people each and at weekends and holidays can be full, so take a tent if you're planning a night on the mountain at a busy time.

Books There are at least two books in English which give fuller information on Popo, Izta and other hikes and climbs in Mexico. R J Secor's *Mexico's Volcanoes* (The Mountaineers, Seattle, 1981) is an excellent guide to seven mountains and covers hikes and many rock-climbing routes on Popo and Izta. *Backpacking in Mexico & Central America* (Bradt Enterprises, Cambridge, Massachusetts and Chalfont St Peter, Bucks, 1982) by Hilary Bradt and Rob Rachowiecki is for hikers. It includes routes on Popo, Izta and elsewhere in Mexico as well as lots of useful general information.

Groups & Guides You may well, particularly at Tlamacas, be invited to join a group of Mexican climbers or hikers. In Mexico City you can try contacting the Club de Exploraciones de México (tel 578-57-30) for information on climbing the mountains. The club apparently holds frequent meetings and presentations and runs some trips which are open to non-members. Another possibility is the Mountain Rescue Club at Lázaro Cárdenas 80, No 305, in central Mexico City. They reportedly rent equipment.

Coordinadores de Guías de Montaña (tel 584-46-95, 584-89-97) at Tlaxcala 47 in Colonia Roma, Mexico City provide qualified guides for Popo, Izta, Pico de Orizaba and Nevado de Toluca. For a 1½-day trip from Mexico City to the top of Popo or Izta and back they charge US$120

(equipment and food extra). You can also find guides at Tlamacas – but for the Las Cruces route it's not really necessary because the trail is well-worn and sometimes busy.

Las Cruces Route This is the hiker's way to the top of Popocatépetl. From Tlamacas the total ascent is 1500 metres. It takes an average of eight hours to reach the summit, a bit less just to the crater rim, and two to four hours to come down, so a 4 am start is normal. You can walk the beginning of the route – to Las Cruces and back – as a few hours' stroll. From Tlamacas, take the clear trail going east (left) across the base of the volcano. Las Cruces, where there used to be a hut, is three km along this path and 550 metres higher than Tlamacas, at 4480 metres.

From Las Cruces to the crater rim at 5100 metres you head straight up the 30° slope – by far the hardest part but if you make it you will be rewarded by awesome views down into the crater. Its sides are sheer with a maximum depth of nearly 500 metres. On the floor are a small lake and a few minor cones. The crater is 2½ km round. If you turn right on reaching the crater and follow the rim round, you reach the hut on the 5452-metre summit after an hour.

Other Popo Route R J Secor, in his book *Mexico's Volcanoes*, mentions the trip to the Queretano hut on the Ventorrillo as a possibility for adventurous hikers. You fork right off the Las Cruces trail at 4100 metres, following the path to the north-east ridge of the Ventorrillo, which is the craggy formation visible between Tlamacas and the crater. From the ridge the path reaches the Queretano hut at 4460 metres, overlooking the canyon between the Ventorrillo and Popocatépetl's glaciers.

Iztaccíhuatl This is an even more serious proposition. Nearly all the routes to its peaks – the highest is El Pecho (the Breast) at 5286 metres – involve some rock-climbing, and a night on the mountain is usually necessary. There are three shelter-huts (one ruined) between 4500 and 4900 metres high on the way from La Joya car park to Las Rodillas (The Knees), which can be used during an ascent of El Pecho. On the average, it takes six hours from La Joya to the huts, another four to six hours from the huts to El Pecho and four to six hours to descend. There are a few other huts and many other routes on Izta, which is in many ways a more beautiful mountain than Popo. Before tackling any of them, find out as much as you can from Tlamacas and from other hikers/climbers. Secor's book is very useful.

Getting There

Amecameca From the Mexico City side, you first have to get to Amecameca, a town of 25,000 people some 60 km by road from the city. There are a few restaurants and one hotel, the *San Carlos*, here. Cristóbal Colón buses (1st class) leave Mexico City eastern bus station (TAPO) for Amecameca every hour from 6 am to 8 pm. The trip takes 1½ hours and costs US$0.75. The last bus back to Mexico City leaves Amecameca at 9 pm. A small hill called El Sacromonte just outside Amecameca is an important pilgrimage goal on Ash Wednesday. A church on the hill has a supposedly miraculous Christ image.

Two-and-a-half km south of Amecameca, among the trees just to the left off the Cuautla road, is the bizarre Popo-Park. In the 1940s and 1950s this was an exclusive country retreat for the rich of Mexico City, including the president. Houses in all manner of styles from pseudo-gothic to Spanish villas were built but many of them are now abandoned, overgrown and ruined. Cuernavaca has become more fashionable. The lovely little chapel, however, is still beautifully kept. Near Popo-Park, at Km 66.5 on the Amecameca-Cuautla road, the *Restaurant Español*

Popocatépetl does a good daily comida for US$2.50.

Amecameca to the Volcanoes From the bus station in Amecameca walk a couple of blocks to the zócalo, where taxis wait to take people 30 or so twisting km up the hill to Paso de Cortés or Tlamacas, both on the high saddle between the two peaks. These taxis charge US$3 to US$4 for the 45-minute journey. There may also be buses from Amecameca to Tlamacas – some certainly go to San Pedro, a few km up the hill. Particularly on weekends, it's easy enough to hitch a lift one way or the other. The road to Tlamacas branches east off the Amecameca-Cuautla road a km south of Amecameca.

Your last chance to get water (quality not guaranteed) if you're heading straight for Izta is at the entrance to the Izta-Popo National Park on the way up from Amecameca. At the Paso de Cortés (3650 metres), five km before Tlamacas, the road passes the Cortés monument on the left. Here two dirt roads branch off to the left. The left-hand one goes eight km to La Joya car park on the south-west side of Iztaccíhuatl, passing a TV transmitter on the way; the right-hand one heads east down to Cholula 45 km away and is reportedly passable (but might be tricky in wet weather). Quite a lot of cars go along the Izta road at weekends, and hitching a lift shouldn't be too hard.

PUEBLA

Probably no other Mexican city preserves the Spanish imprint as strongly as Puebla. There are over 70 churches and 1000 other colonial buildings in the downtown area alone – many of them embellished with the lovely hand-painted tiles for which the city is famous. Set in a broad valley at 2162 metres with the volcanoes Popocatépetl and Iztaccíhuatl rising to the west, Puebla is on the important road from Veracruz to Mexico City and has always played a big part in national affairs.

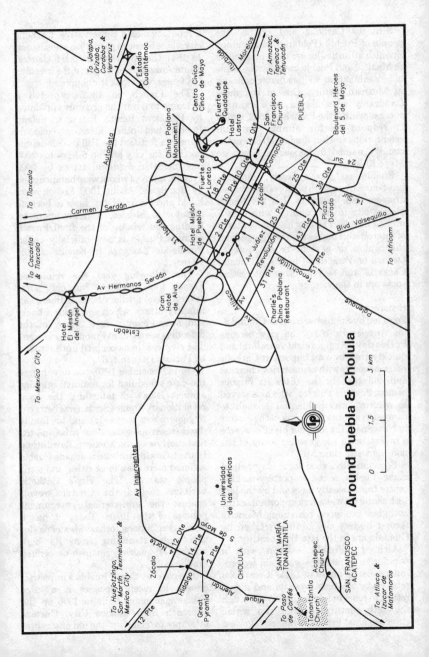

Around Puebla & Cholula

Strongly Catholic and criollo, the people of Puebla (Poblanos) maintained Spanish affinities longer than most cities in Mexico, and Puebla has been the scene of ignominious as well as heroic episodes in Mexican history. One of the more favourably remembered is a military success against the French in 1862, which is responsible for annual national celebrations and hundreds of streets in the country named in honour of Cinco de Mayo (5 May).

Puebla is also a lively, modern, prosperous place, with plenty of fashionable dressers and boutiques. It's the fourth biggest city in the country, with over a million people. The city has many places of interest and makes a good change from the capital or a stopover en route to Oaxaca or Veracruz. Cholula, Tlaxcala, Cacaxtla and several other interesting spots are in the vicinity.

History

Founded by Spanish settlers as Ciudad de los Ángeles in 1531, the city became Puebla de los Ángeles eight years later and quickly grew into an important Catholic religious centre with monasteries, churches and colleges. By the 1640s its famous bishop, Juan de Palafox, who also served as viceroy, was influential enough to campaign against the power of the Jesuits in New Spain (he lost, but his efforts were a milestone in the growing power of the non-monastic church).

Economically, good local clay helped make Puebla a major pottery-making centre from its early days and by the late 18th century it was a very important textile and glass producer, remaining Mexico's second biggest city until overtaken by Guadalajara in the late 19th century.

Although Puebla – then with a population of 50,000 – was held by pro-independence forces in 1811, it was soon retaken by Spanish loyalists and didn't return to rebel hands until 1821. Through the 19th century, despite two heroic stands against French invaders, it gained

a reputation as a conservative, Catholic city whose Mexican patriotism was suspect. In 1847 the city refused to let General Santa Anna defend it against the invading US forces, who took it unopposed.

The French, in 1862, expected a welcome too, but the generals appointed by President Benito Juárez to defend Puebla had other ideas. Ignacio de Zaragoza fortified the Hill of Guadalupe north of the city and on 5 May his 2000 men defeated a frontal attack by 6000 French, many of whom were handicapped by diarrhoea. About 1000 French were killed and Porfirio Díaz, later to become dictator of Mexico, won his spurs by leading the repulse of the final French assault. Puebla is now officially called Puebla de Zaragoza in honour of this victory.

The following year the reinforced French took Puebla – but only after several days' artillery bombardment, an infantry attack which was beaten back, and a two-month siege. Many of the defenders were sent to France as prisoners. The city was then occupied until retaken by Porfirio Díaz in 1867.

On 18 November 1910, two days before the date scheduled for national uprising against Díaz's dictatorship, the local revolutionary Aquiles Serdán was betrayed to government forces. He and his family died in the ensuing shoot-out, to become the first martyrs of the Mexican Revolution. In the following turbulent decade Puebla suffered more than most cities, and some people starved. The city's Catholic heritage fuelled the Cristero revolt against the anti-clerical government policies of the 1920s. Today it has a reputation among other Mexicans for snootiness, stemming from its high number of wealthy, Spanish-descended families.

The clearest sign of Puebla's industrial growth in recent decades is a huge Volkswagen plant built in 1970 on the approach from Mexico City. Current attempts to 'clean up' the old city centre have involved not only renovating buildings and closing some streets to traffic but also banning street sellers and relocating the market to several different sites on the edges of the city. This goes down well with the middle class but isn't popular among the poor, who also fear that they may be moved out of their *vecindades* – old apartment blocks in the city centre.

Recently the city has also become a major clearing house for *fayuca* – electrical goods smuggled in (often by politicians) from the USA. No one tries to hide the fact – there are even buses marked 'Fayuca' which will take you to the markets where the stuff is sold!

Architecture
Puebla developed a number of distinctive baroque styles which set its buildings apart from those of other Mexican cities. In the 17th century locally made tiles – some in Arabic designs – began to be used on church domes and with red brick on the façades of buildings, to fine effect. Then in the 18th century *alfeñique* became popular in the city. Named after a candy made from egg whites and sugar, alfeñique is an elaborate white stucco ornamentation. Throughout the colonial period the local grey stone was carved into a variety of forms to embellish many buildings. Also notable is the local Indian influence, seen most clearly in the proliferation of stucco ornamentation in churches like Tonantzintla and the Capilla del Rosario of Santo Domingo.

Pottery
Puebla became a pottery-making centre from its very early days, thanks to a combination of good local clay and the skills of its Spanish colonial inhabitants. Known as Talavera after a town in Spain, Puebla's colourful hand-painted glazed ceramics took many forms – plates, pots, cups, bowls, vases, fountains – and its designs showed Asian, Spanish-Arabic and Mexican Indian influence. The finest

of all is the white ware known as majolica. In colonial times Puebla pottery was not used by the rich, who preferred silver or Chinese porcelain. The potter's – or rather painter's – art also reached heights in the pretty tiles *(azulejos)* used to adorn buildings. Talavera is still made and sold in Puebla.

Orientation
The grid lay-out of Puebla's old central streets makes it an easy city to find your way round, though the street-naming system takes a bit of getting used to. The centre of town is the spacious, tree-shaded zócalo, with the cathedral occupying the block to its south. The majority of places to stay, eat and visit are within a few blocks of the zócalo.

A new Central de Autobuses is being built in the north of the city but at the time of writing work on it appeared to have stopped (money problems), so the old downtown stations may still be in use. Under this old arrangement each bus line has a different terminal – slightly confusing but convenient, since all of them are close to the city centre. From ADO walk 2½ blocks west along Camacho (to the right out of the entrance) to reach the zócalo; from AU go 5½ blocks south (left) along 4 Norte, then one block west (right) along Camacho.

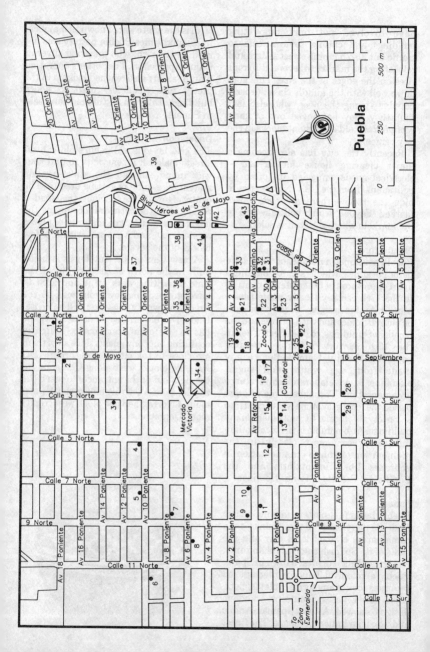

1	San José	22	Hotel del Portal &
2	Santa Mónica		Hostería de Los Angeles
3	Santa Rosa	23	Casa del que mató al animal
4	La Merced	24	Casa de Cultura
5	Transportes Puebla- Tonantzintla	25	Tourist Office
6	Autobuses Tlaxcala-Apizaco-	26	Bishop's Palace
	Huamantla	27	Post Office
7	Autobuses Puebla-Cholula	28	La Concordia
8	Autobuses Puebla-Tlaxcala-	29	Santa Inés
	Calpulalpan	30	Hotel Colonial
9	San Marcos	31	University
10	Benjamin Franklin Library	32	La Compañía
11	Palacio de Gobierno	33	Restaurant Nevados Hermilo
12	Estrella Roja	34	Santo Domingo
13	Fonda Santa Clara	35	Museo de la Revolución
14	Hotel Teresita	36	San Cristóbal Church
15	Museo Bello	37	A U
16	Hostal de Halconeros	38	Teatro Principal
17	Restaurant-Café El Vasco	39	San Francisco Church &
18	Foto-Aguirre Café		Craft Centre
19	Hotel Gilfer	40	Barrio del Artista
20	Hotel Palacio	41	Casa del Alfeñique
21	Casa de Los Muñecos	42	El Parián
		43	A D O

The crucial corner as far as street names go is the north-west corner of the zócalo. From here, 5 de Mayo goes north, 16 de Septiembre goes south, Reforma goes west and Camacho goes east. Other north-south streets are called Calles and given even numbers when they're east of this junction, odd ones when they're west of it. Thus Calle 2 is one block east, Calle 4 is two blocks east, etc, while Calle 3 is one block west, Calle 5 is two blocks west. (There is no Calle 1.) In addition, north-south streets are called Norte (Nte) when they're north of the crucial corner, Sur when they're south of it. An address on Calle 7 Sur is therefore three blocks west of the zócalo and somewhere south of Reforma. East-west streets are called Avenidas and have even numbers (2, 4, 6, etc) when they're north of the crucial corner, odd (3, 5, 7, etc) when south of it. West of the crucial corner, they're Poniente (Pte), east of it they're Oriente (Ote).

If you grasp this system it enables you to locate addresses precisely: 5 Pte 336 will be west (Poniente) of the crucial corner, on Avenida 5, the east-west street two blocks south. The number 336 shows that the building is in the block after Calle 3 Sur. Thus, from the north-west corner of the zócalo, you would go two blocks south, then 1½ blocks west. (On the other hand, you could just look at a map – or ask!)

The downtown street 5 de Mayo shouldn't be confused with Boulevard Héroes del 5 de Mayo, a ring-road that runs north-south a few blocks east of the zócalo.

The smart downtown shopping area is in the few blocks north of the zócalo. Beyond that to the north and west you soon enter dirtier, poorer streets.

An area of smart modern restaurants and shops – the zona esmeralda – stretches along Avenida Juárez, one to two km west of the zócalo.

Information

Tourist Office The helpful, English-speaking tourist office (tel 46-12-85, 46-09-28) is at Avenida 5 Ote 3, facing the cathedral yard. It's open 8 am to 8 pm Monday to Friday, 9 am to 2 pm Saturday and Sunday.

Money Banks include two on Reforma just west of the zócalo.

Post The post office is just round the corner on 16 de Septiembre, a couple of doors south of Avenida 5 Ote.

Books *Guía Turística de Puebla* by Enrique Cordero is an interesting and well-informed guide (in Spanish) to the city's sights, which you can pick up for US$1.50 in some of the museums. Most of Puebla's many museums are open daily except Monday from 10 am to 5 pm, but you usually can't enter after 4.30 pm.

Airlines Mexicana (tel 48-56-00) is at Calle 23 Sur 506 on the corner of Avenida Juárez. Aeroméxico (tel 32-00-13/4/5) is at Avenida Juárez 1514A.

Zócalo & South

Puebla's central plaza served as a marketplace where hangings, bullfights and theatre took place before it acquired its current garden-like appearance in 1854. The *portales* (arcades) surrounding it are all 16th century.

Casa del que Mató al Animal Now a newspaper office, the 'House of the Animal-Killer' at the corner of Avenida 3 Ote and Calle 2 Sur (just off the south-east corner of the zócalo) is worth a look for its interesting 16th-century carved doorway showing hunters and dogs in a style similar to that of 15th-century French tapestries. The building's name comes from the legend that a monstrous snake from the forests of La Malinche was terrorising the people of Puebla and had killed the child of a wealthy citizen.

A reward was offered to whoever would get rid of the monster. A young soldier who arrived in town heard of this and managed to cut off the creature's head.

Cathedral Occupying the block south of the zócalo, Puebla's massive cathedral is considered one of Mexico's finest for its harmonious proportions. The successful blend of severe herreresque renaissance style and early baroque was begun in 1550 but most of the building took place under the dynamic Bishop Juan de Palafox in the 1640s. Like Mexico City's cathedral, this one has a typically renaissance rectangular ground plan. The towers are the highest in the country at 69 metres; some of their bells date from the 17th century and are immortalised in the traditional rhyme *'Para mujeres y campanas, las Poblanas'* – 'For women and bells, Puebla's (are best)'.

The dome is covered with local glazed tiles. The main (west) façade built in the 1660s adhered to renaissance stylistic dictates, moving from simpler Doric columns on the lowest level through Ionic to ornate Corinthian columns on the 3rd level.

Inside is the domed main altar, an outstanding neoclassical work by Manuel Tolsá and José Manzo from 1800; the gilded wrought-iron screen and wooden mosaic seats in the choir (between the west door and main altar); some fine baroque altars and altarpieces; and the murals by Baltasar de Echave y Rioja in the sacristy.

Bishop's Palace This building at Avenida 5 Ote 1, facing the south side of the cathedral, is a classic example of Puebla architecture. It now contains government offices.

Casa de Cultura At Avenida 5 Ote 5, this is another fine colonial building. Today it's mainly devoted to local cultural activities. Upstairs is the Biblioteca Palafoxiana (Palafox Library), founded by the 17th-century bishop, which contains thousands of valuable old books including atlases and bibles from the 17th and 18th centuries and the 1493 Nuremberg Chronicle with more than 2000 engravings. The Casa de Cultura also has a cafeteria.

Callejón del Sapo This little street between Avenida 5 and 7 Ote, a few metres east of Calle 4 Sur, has a market selling antiques, old books and bric-a-brac. It's busiest on Sunday. Mariachis also hang around here.

Museo Bello This house at Avenida 3 Pte 302 is filled with the amazing fine-art collection of 19th-century industrialist José Luis Bello and his son Mariano. Ceramics, furniture, glass, clothes, watches, paintings, musical instruments, ivory and more come not only from Mexico but also Europe, China, Japan, Guatemala and the Philippines. Among the more curious and outstanding items are nuns' spiked metal flagellation chains; spurs from Amozoc; beautiful French, English, Japanese and Chinese porcelain; a 17th-century wooden Mexican organ; and a door made of glass columns, each with a different musical pitch. Admission is 10c. Guided tours are conducted in Spanish and English (guides ask for a tip).

East of the Zócalo
Casa de los Muñecos The exterior of 'house of the figures' on Calle 2 Nte, just off the north-east corner of the zócalo, is decorated with big tiles grotesquely depicting the city fathers who took the house's owner, Agustín de Ovando y Villavicencio, to court because his building was taller than theirs.

Academía de Bellas Artes Now the Instituto de Artes Plásticas, this fine colonial building at Camacho 406 holds some interesting local and visiting exhibitions.

La Compañía This Jesuit church at the corner of Camacho and Calle 4 Sur, also called Espíritu Santo, has a churrigueresque façade from 1767. It is said to contain the tomb of a 17th-century Asian princess who was captured, sold into slavery in Mexico and finally freed. She is supposed to have originated the colourful *china poblana* costume of shawl, frilled blouse and embroidered skirt, to which were often added gold and silver adornments – a kind of peasant chic which became fashionable in the 19th century. The real origins of the costume are probably a little less exotic – *china* also meant maid-servant and the style may have developed from Spanish peasant costumes.

University The 16th-century building next door to La Compañía on Calle 4 Sur, formerly a Jesuit college, is now part of Puebla University. It has pretty courtyards and on the left at the top of the stairs, the *paraninfo* (hall) has an elaborate marquetry rostrum. Further along the corridors, the Salón Melchor de Covarrubias has a typical Puebla 'sugar candy' ceiling of churrigueresque stucco.

El Parián This is a crafts market bounded by Calles 6 and 8 Nte and Avenidas 2 and 4 Ote. There are Talavera, onyx and trees of life here but they're not very high quality.

Casa del Alfeñique This house at the corner of Calle 6 Nte and Avenida 4 Ote is the most outstanding example of Puebla's 18th-century churrigueresque decorative style, alfeñique. Inside is the Museo del Estado (10c) with a variety of paraphernalia from the 18th and 19th centuries including china poblana costumes, carriages, maps, furniture and paintings.

Barrio del Artista Calle 8 Nte between Avenidas 4 and 6 Ote is occupied by artists' and sculptors' workshops and showrooms. The small plaza at its north end is a modern reconstruction in 17th-century style.

Teatro Principal This theatre on Calle 6 Nte between Avenidas 6 and 8 Ote dates from 1756 and is one of the oldest in the Americas. Destroyed by fire in 1902, it was rebuilt in the 1930s. You can look inside between 10 am and 5 pm when the theatre's not in use. In the late 19th century a local writer predicted that if Puebla ever had two theatres, one would burn down. This came true three times: the Teatro Principal went up in flames while the Teatro Guerrero was being built; the Guerrero followed suit in 1909 while the Variedades was under construction; and the Variedades burnt in 1922 after the Constantino had opened. The Constantino, not to be left out, went up in flames in 1930.

San Francisco One of Puebla's most attractive churches, with an 18th-century tower and brick-and-tile façade added to a mid-16th-century basic structure, stands just east of the ring-road on Avenida 14 Ote. The north doorway is a good example of the 16th-century plateresque style. The Franciscans were the first monks to come to Puebla and their monastery buildings stand beside the church. In a glass case in the north chapel is the body of San Sebastián de Aparicio, a Spaniard who came to Mexico in 1533 and planned out many of the country's roads before becoming a Franciscan monk. He died in Puebla and later was canonised; his shrine sees a constant stream of worshippers and his body is in a remarkable state of preservation. The chapel contains many paintings of his life, and his statue stands outside the church.

In one of the monastery buildings is the state-run Centro Artesanal, selling a good range of handicrafts from Puebla state (closed Monday).

San Cristóbal This church, at the corner of Avenida 6 Ote and Calle 4 Nte, has a lovely 17th-century baroque façade. Its towers, destroyed in the French bombardment of 1863, were rebuilt in the 1950s.

Museo de la Revolución This house at Avenida 6 Ote 206 was the scene of the first battle of the 1910 Revolution. Betrayed two days before the national uprising was due to start, the Serdán family (Aquiles, Máximo, Carmen and Natalia) plus 16 other men and one other woman fought 500 soldiers and police – many firing from the roof of nearby Santa Clara church – until only Aquiles, their leader, and Carmen were left alive. Aquiles had been hidden under the floorboards by the women and might have survived if the cold and damp hadn't provoked a cough which gave him away. The house now contains a bullet-shattered mirror and many other interesting Revolution memorabilia. Entry is 10c.

North of the Zócalo

Santo Domingo This church is 2½ blocks north of the zócalo on 5 de Mayo. Its chief glory is the Capilla del Rosario (Rosary Chapel) south of the main altar. Built between 1680 and 1720, the chapel is a sumptuous example of Mexican baroque – an amazing proliferation of gilded, coloured plaster and carved stone with angels, cherubim and plants leaping out all over the place. See if you can spot the heavenly orchestra. An equally elaborate altar in the centre of the chapel is dedicated to the Virgin Mary.

Mercado Victoria A little further up 5 de Mayo from Santo Domingo, then to the left, is what used to be Puebla's main market, an elegant 1912 construction where everything from vegetables and clothes to herbal medicines was sold. It has now been renovated and 'cleaned up' as part of the programme to make the city centre more respectable, and has lost some of its liveliness, but is still worth a visit. The ordinary markets of Puebla have been 'decentralised' to a variety of locations on the edges of the city with catchy names like 'Tianguis Popular 28 de Octubre No 2' and so on.

Santa Rosa This 17th-century nunnery on Calle 3 Nte between Avenidas 12 and 14 Pte now houses the excellent Museo de Artesanías del Estado de Puebla – an extensive collection of the many fine handicrafts produced in the state of Puebla. The only snag is the compulsory tours in Spanish led by apparently bored guides – find an excuse to wander round at your own pace. There's a great variety of Indian costumes, some fine pottery (including superb trees of life), onyx, glass, even *amate* (tree-bark paper). After all this you reach the kitchen, beautified with 20th-century tiles and full of old pottery and cooking implements. Entry is 5c.

Santa Monica Another nunnery-museum, with one of the city's most beautiful tiled courtyards, can be found at Avenida 18 Pte 101 near the corner of 5 de Mayo. According to Enrique Cordero, author of an authoritative guide to Puebla, the tale that Santa Monica functioned secretly during the anti-clerical movements of the 19th century is false. Today it houses mainly religious art, but you can wander freely round the well-preserved convent buildings and look into some of the former nuns' cells where, among other items, their self-flagellation weapons are laid out. Entry is 10c.

San José This church at the corner of Avenida 18 Ote and Calle 2 Nte is one of Puebla's best-looking religious buildings. It dates from 1590 and its Capilla del Sagrario, with a profusion of carved stone, is thought by some to be more splendid than the Capilla del Rosario in Santo Domingo.

Centro Cívico Cinco de Mayo

Behind this boring name lies a collection of interesting historic sites and museums in a hilltop park stretching one km east of Calle 2 Nte, two km from the zócalo. Take the bus marked 'Fuertes' from downtown to get there.

The hill in question was where a small Mexican force under Ignacio de Zaragoza defeated a bigger French army on 5 May 1862 in one of the few truly successful episodes of Mexican military history. A few roads criss-cross it now between the trees.

The Fuerte de Loreto at the west end of the park was one of the Mexican defence points on 5 May 1862. Today it holds the Museo de la Intervención, which chronicles the French invasion and occupation of Mexico (entry 5c).

East of this fort, beyond the large domed auditorium, are the Museo de Antropología e Historia, Museo de Historia Natural and Planetario, all built recently. The first traces the course of human history in the state of Puebla from pre-Hispanic times to the beginning of the 20th century. The planetarium (US$0.50) has shows at 4, 6 and 8.30 pm daily except Monday, plus an extra one on Saturday and Sunday at 3 pm.

At the eastern end of the park, beyond the Centro Cultural y Recreativo with a theatre, gallery and restaurant, is the Fuerte de Guadalupe, which played a part on 5 May 1862, when the chapel inside was ruined.

Africam

If Mexico isn't providing enough variety for you, try a bit of the rest of the world. Africam, Mexico's only safari park, has 3000 animals of 250 species on 30 hectares. It's 20 km south-east of Puebla off Road 708 to Tecali, and is open daily from 10 am to 5 pm. Entry is US$2. For information in Puebla contact the office (tel 35-87-13, 35-87-00) at Avenida 11 Ote 2405.

AU buses leave Puebla for Africam at 11 am, 1 pm and 2.30 pm, with an extra one at 3.15 pm on Saturday, Sunday and holidays. The last bus back to Puebla is at 5 pm. AU also runs a package from Mexico City to Africam. For US$7 you get bus rides from the TAPO terminal to Africam and back (changing in Puebla), plus admission to the park and a meal.

Places to Stay – bottom end

Puebla's budget hotels are unfortunately among Mexico's worst. Some of them bear a strong resemblance to prisons, with gloomy concrete walkways, clanging doors and spartan rooms. There are just two relatively pleasant places in this category. One, often full, is the *Hotel Teresita* (tel 41-70-72) at Avenida 3 Pte 309. Rooms are small and usually windowless but clean. Singles/doubles with bath (hot water limited) are US$2.75/3.25.

The *Hostal de Halconeros* (tel 42-74-56) at Reforma 141, half a block west of the zócalo, is the other of the better bets. Rooms are generally dingy, pillows lumpy and paint flaky but at least it's clean, the staff are friendly and there's a decent restaurant in the place. Singles/doubles with bath are US$3.50/4.25.

Hotel San Agustín (tel 41-50-89) at Avenida 3 Pte 531 is moderately clean and has a grassy courtyard but the rooms (US$3.25) smell damp. Slightly better is the *Hotel Embajadoras* (tel 41-26-37) on 5 de Mayo between Avenidas 6 and 8 Ote. Rooms are quite big but dark and the private bathrooms are extremely antiquated. Singles/doubles cost US$5.25/5.75.

The *Hotel Astomba* (tel 42-39-33) on Avenida 10 Pte between Calles 3 and 5 Nte has singles with common bath at US$1.50, with private bath at US$2.75, but it's poorly kept and prison-like. The *Hotel Victoria* (tel 41-89-92) at Avenida 3 Pte 306 next to the Museo Bello is similar. Rooms are US$4.25 single or double. The *Hotel Ritz* (tel 41-44-57) on Calle 2 Nte between Avenidas 2 and 4 Ote is smelly and run-down. Singles/doubles cost US$3.25/4.25.

Places to Stay – middle

Cheapest in this range is the *Hotel Palacio* (tel 42-40-30) next door to the Hotel Gilfer at Avenida 2 Ote 13. Rooms are clean but a bit poky and cost US$6.75/8.25 for singles/doubles.

Well worth the extra pesos is the *Hotel Colonial* (tel 46-47-09, 46-41-99) at the corner of Avenida 3 Ote and Calle 4 Sur, which is one of Puebla's pleasantest hotels. It's part of a former Jesuit monastery, about 400 years old. The elevator is not much newer. The rooms, mostly set round open-air courtyards, are spacious, bright and beautifully tiled, and have TVs. Singles/doubles are US$9.25/10.75. The hotel also has an old glass-domed dining room.

Another good bet is the *Hotel Del Portal* (tel 46-02-11) at the north-east (Camacho) corner of the zócalo. It has a spacious, bright lobby and rooms are pleasant and well-kept but smaller than the Colonial's. Some of them overlook the zócalo but are noisy. Singles/doubles are US$11.75/13.50.

The *Hotel Gilfer* (tel 42-89-90, 42-00-39) at Avenida 2 Ote 11 has light, clean rooms for US$9.50/11 but could be noisy and the staff are offhand. The *Hotel Royalty* (tel 42-02-02) at Portal Hidalgo 8 on the north side of zócalo has a touch of elegance but the rooms at US$12.50/14.50 are small.

The *Hotel Lastra* (tel 35-97-55) is at Calzada de los Fuertes 2633 two km north of the centre on a hill. Singles/doubles are US$11.75/14.50.

Places to Stay – top end

Most of Puebla's top hotels are away from the city centre. One that isn't is the *Hotel Posada San Pedro* (tel 46-50-77) at Avenida 2 Ote 202. It has a small, open-air swimming pool and two restaurants but the rooms, while pleasant, are none too big and could be noisy. Singles/doubles are US$16.75/18.75.

The best place in town is generally reckoned to be the 200-room *Hotel El Mesón del Angel* (tel 48-21-00) at Avenida Hermanos Serdán 807, six km from downtown, ½ km off the Mexico city autopista. Singles/doubles are US$24/28.75. There are two swimming pools, tennis courts, colour TVs, several restaurants and bars, etc.

Other top-end hotels are the 400-room *Gran Hotel de Alva* (tel 48-60-55) three km west of downtown near the corner of Avenida 6 Pte and Avenida Hermanos Serdán (singles/doubles US$24/28.75); and the *Hotel Misión de Puebla* (tel 48-96-00) at Avenida 5 Pte 2522, between Calles 25 and 27 Sur in the zona esmeralda (singles/doubles US$26.50/27.75).

Places to Eat

Puebla is home to many food specialities, invented in its monasteries and convents in colonial times. The most famous is *mole Polbano*, the spicy chocolate sauce served with turkey (*pavo* or *guajolote*) or chicken. Supposedly invented by Sister Andrea de la Asunción, a nun in the Santa Rosa convent, on the occasion of a visit by the Spanish viceroy to Puebla, it traditionally contains fresh chile, *chipotle* (smoked chile), pepper, peanuts, almonds, cinnamon, aniseed, tomato, onion, garlic and of course chocolate. It's imitated all over the country and you'll find it on almost every menu in Puebla.

Puebla is also known for its *dulces* (sweets or candies) and there's a nun story behind these too. A young 19th-century novice with a sense of humour is said to have mixed *camote*, a type of bulb, into a sweet being prepared for visiting empress Carlota. The result was surprisingly tasty and the camote de Santa Clara became a speciality. Several shops on Avenida 6 Ote, the street where Santa Clara convent stood, deal in a variety of exotic candies.

Another local speciality is *chiles en nogada*, said to have been created in 1821 to honour Agustín de Iturbide, the first ruler of independent Mexico. Its colours are red, green and white, after the national flag. Large chiles stuffed with meat and fruit are covered with a creamy nut sauce (sometimes containing cheese and brandy) and sprinkled with pome-granate seeds. Other Poblano foods include *semitas* (a kind of taco) and *chalupas* (a greasy type of tortilla with chicken and hot sauce).

A good place to try some of these is the *Fonda Santa Clara* (tel 42-26-59, closed Monday) at Avenida 3 Pte 307. Apart from mole Poblano, the menu includes chalupas, *molotes* (fried maize pancakes), *mixiotes* (lamb tamales wrapped in cactus leaves) and various seasonal dishes such as chiles en nogada (August and September) and *escamoles* and *gusanos de maguey* (April to June), which are maguey worms or their eggs prepared with avocados or hen eggs.

Of the restaurants on the zócalo, the *Hostería de los Angeles* on the north-east corner is pleasant and reasonably priced, good for breakfast (around US$1.50) and the comida corrida (US$2 three courses, US$2.50 four courses).

La Princesa, at Portal Agustín de Iturbide 101 on the west side of the zócalo, is a big, busy place which does a good six-course comida corrida for US$2. It's also popular for breakfast.

A door or two away, the *Restaurant-Café El Vasco* (tel 41-86-89) is a quieter place where couples and old friends meet for a chat – and it's worth a visit for a look at its bilingual menu alone. Sadly, the 'ostopussy into its own ink' which used to adorn the English-language side of the menu has become plain old octopus but you can still feast on filet sol overflow, shrimps at curry, viky soisse, pathé de foie grass, smoked pork shops, friend chicken 1/2, beef shop, veal chicken friend steak, lamb citops garlie sauce and red enapper with carlie sauce. Names apart, the fare's not bad and the portions sizeable – chicken and steaks are around US$2, seafood US$3.50, enchiladas Suizas US$1.25, avocado with tuna and sardines US$1.

The *Restaurant-Bar Royalty* (tel 42-47-40) at Portal Hidalgo 10 on the north side of the zócalo is a stylish place where the waiters wear jackets and bow ties, a

Hammond organ plays in the evening, and the octopus is 'into its tint'. The cheaper end of its menu includes spaghetti (US$1.50 to US$2). Meat and fish dishes range from US$2.25 to US$5.25 and turkey in mole Poblano is US$3.

Just off the zócalo on 5 de Mayo, the *Foto Aguirre Café* is a busy place which does a four-course comida corrida for US$1.75. The restaurant in the Hostal de Halconeros at Reforma 141 does breakfast for US$0.75, lunch for US$1.25 and dinner for US$1. There's a *Sanborn's* at Avenida 2 Ote No 6. The *Hotel Colonial* on the corner of Avenida 3 Ote and Calle 4 Sur also has a good restaurant. Try the Yucatán-style *huevos motuleña* (US$1.75) at breakfast – a meal in itself consisting of tortilla, frijoles, egg, tomato sauce and a large banana which, not surprisingly, is known as *platano macho*!

The *Restaurant Nevados Hermilo* (tel 41-79-63) at Calle 4 Nte and Avenida 2 Ote is famous among Poblanos for its tortas (US$0.75), enchiladas with mole Poblano (US$1.50) and *caldo Atlixqueño* (US$1.25), a chicken consommé with floating chile. You can get also get tasty little cocktails called *nevados* here – try the Marijuana (mint and vodka), Pinguino (cacao, rum and nut) or Popocatépetl (tequila and mint).

There's a vegetarian restaurant, *El Vegetariano*, at Avenida 3 Pte 525, open from 8 am to 9 pm, with a long menu and comida corrida for US$1.50. The cafeteria in the Casa de Cultura on Avenida 5 Ote sells yoghurt.

For a splash-out meal in the semi-Westernised surroundings that many Mexicans enjoy, go to *Charlie's China Poblana* (tel 46-31-59) at Juárez 1918 in the zona esmeralda. An excellent meal with wine from a Mexican and international menu costs around US$10 to US$12. The zona esmeralda has lots more swish restaurants – including German, Italian and Chinese.

Entertainment

The serious nightlife in the Puebla area is in fact at Cholula, a few km west, where there are several discos. As a consequence the Puebla-Cholula road is an accident blackspot late at night! The bar at Charlie's China Poblana restaurant at Juárez 1918 in the zona esmeralda has a reputation as a pick-up spot. The Hotel Mesón del Angel bar has a jazz group.

For cultural events – of which there are quite a few – check the noticeboards in the tourist office and the Casa de Cultura on Avenida 5 Ote and in the university building on Calle 4 Sur.

Things to Buy

Apart from Puebla's own glass and Talavera pottery, the city is also a good place to look for crafts and folk art from elsewhere in the state. Among the specialities are onyx from Tecali, black and red earthenware pottery from Acatlán de Osorio and Amozoc, trees of life from the same two places and Izucar de Matamoros, and Indian textiles from a number of towns and villages. A visit to the Museo de Artesanías del Estado de Puebla on Calle 3 Nte between Avenida 12 and 14 Pte will give you a good idea of the range.

The Creart shop just east of 16 de Septiembre, south of the zócalo, has a good selection. There's also a state crafts sales centre (closed Monday) in one of the monastery buildings attached to San Francisco church.

There are a few onyx and Talavera shops on Avenida 18 Pte near the corner of 5 de Mayo, more or less opposite the entrance to Santa Monica convent.

El Parián at Calle 6 Nte and Avenida 2 Ote is another crafts market. Trees of life, Talavera and onyx are among the items on sale but they're not very high quality.

There's a street market in antiques and old books in Callejón del Sapo between Avenidas 5 and 7 Ote, a few metres east of Calle 4 Sur. It's busiest on Sunday.

The three smart shopping areas are in

Top: Monte Albán Plaza (TW)
Bottom: View from the Pyramid of the Moon, Teotihuacán (TW)

the streets just north of the zócalo, along Avenida Juárez one to two km west of the zócalo, and in the Plaza Dorada, beside Boulevard Héroes del 5 de Mayo opposite its junctions with Avenidas 35 and 39 Ote.

Getting There & Away

Air Puebla has an airport, west of Cholula. There's talk of using it as a second airport for Mexico City but at present there are only flights to and from Guadalajara (by Mexicana, three days a week).

Road Puebla is 130 km from Mexico City by a good fast autopista, Highway 150-D. Good roads also lead to Tlaxcala (35 km north), Córdoba (170 km east), Veracruz (298 km east), Jalapa (190 km northeast), Atlixco (35 km south-west), Izucar de Matamoros (70 km south-west) and Tehuacán (115 km south-east). Oaxaca is 361 km away.

Bus Puebla's new Central de Autobuses, inconveniently placed on the northern edge of the city, may be in operation by the time you read this. Until then, each bus company has its own downtown terminal.

ADO (1st class, tel 42-22-61) is at Camacho 604, 2½ blocks east of the zócalo. Buses go to Mexico City (US$1.75) every 15 minutes from 5 am to 11 pm, and hourly through the night. If you're heading for Mexico City airport, these buses will let you get off at Boulevard Aeropuerto in the capital, from where you can get a taxi or pesero to the airport – much quicker than going in to the bus terminal and then out to the airport. Keep your luggage with you and tell the driver in advance.

On other ADO services, such as to Oaxaca or Jalapa, it's advisable to get your ticket in advance as the buses are often booked up. ADO has frequent buses to Tlaxcala (US$0.75); 20 daily to Tehuacán (US$1.50); 13 to Córdoba (US$2.50); 11 each to Orizaba (US$2.25) and Veracruz (US$3.75); nine to Villahermosa (US$9.75); eight to Jalapa (US$2.50); six to Oaxaca

(US$5); four each to Huajuapan (US$2.75) and San Andrés Tuxtla (US$5.75); three each to Campeche (US$15) and Mérida (US$17.50); two each to Tehuantepec (US$9), Salina Cruz (US$9.25), Juchitán (US$8.75), Tonalá, Tapachula (US$13), Acatlán (US$2), Cuetzalán (US$2.75) and Poza Rica (US$4.75); and one each to Zempoala (US$3.50), Santiago Tuxtla (US$5.50), San Cristóbal de Las Casas (US$9.25), Comitán (US$11.25) and Cancún (US$21).

Approximate 1st-class journey times: Mexico City two hours, Jalapa 2½ hours, Córdoba 2½ hours, Veracruz four hours, Tehuacán 2½ hours, Oaxaca seven hours.

Second-class bus prices are 10% less than those of ADO. The best 2nd-class buses are usually those of AU (tel 46-65-00, 46-66-50) at Calle 4 Nte 1004. It has a direct, reserved-seat service to Mexico City (US$1.50) every 15 minutes from 6 am to 10 pm. There are also 18 direct buses daily to Orizaba; 16 to Córdoba; 10 to Veracruz; eight (more at weekends) to Tehuacán; seven to Jalapa; six to Oaxaca; five each to Acayucan (US$6.25) and Coatzacoalcos; four each to San Andrés Tuxtla and Catemaco (US$5.25); two to Santiago Tuxtla; and one each to Villahermosa, Tuxtepec (US$4), Huajuapan, Juchitán, Salina Cruz and Arriaga (US$9.25).

Autobuses Puebla-Cholula (tel 41-43-09) at Avenida 8 Pte 713 goes to Cholula and Tonantzintla every few minutes. Transportes Puebla-Tonantzintla (tel 41-87-44) at Avenida 10 Pte 705 serves San Francisco Acatepec.

Autobuses México-Puebla Estrella Roja (tel 46-97-30, 41-76-71, 42-23-33) at Calle 5 Sur 105 has buses to Mexico City frequently and to Mexico City airport (US$4.75) at 4 and 6 am. It also serves Cholula and Huejotzingo.

Autobuses Puebla-Tlaxcala-Calpulalpan (tel 46-53-62) at Avenida 6 Pte 908 goes frequently to Tlaxcala.

Autobuses Tlaxcala-Apizaco-

Huamantla (tel 42-28-38) at Avenida 10 Pte 1107 goes to Nativitas (three km from Cacaxtla), Tlaxcala, Pachuca, Poza Rica and Mexico City.

Autobuses Unidos Flecha Roja del Sur, also called Frosur (tel 41-27-08), at Avenida 14 Pte 906 serves Izucar de Matamoros (US$0.75) and Atlixco (US$0.50).

Lineas Unidas del Sureste (tel 42-13-60) at Avenida 12 Ote 212 has buses to Tepeaca, two a day to Acatlán (US$0.50) and one daily to Huehuetlán.

Getting Around

Most hotels and places of interest in Puebla are within walking distance of the zócalo. Bus 'Fuertes' (10c) goes from downtown to the Loreto fort and nearby points of interest in the north of the city. Taxis charge US$0.75 for a two-km trip from downtown to the outskirts of town.

CHOLULA

Ten km west of Puebla stands the biggest ancient pyramid in the Americas, the Great Pyramid of Cholula, larger in volume than Egypt's Pyramid of Cheops at 425 metres square and 60 metres high. Now a town of 40,000 and overshadowed by Puebla, Cholula in pre-Hispanic times was one of the largest cities and religious centres in Mexico, inhabited for nearly 2000 years before the Spanish turned up. Archaeological interest apart, it's a pleasant, easygoing town, also known for its large number of churches – Cortés vowed to build one for each day of the year, or one on top of every pagan temple, depending on which legend you prefer. He didn't get very far: there are 38 or 39 now. More splendid are the village churches of Tonantzintla and Acatepec, a few km south of Cholula.

History

First occupied around 300 BC, Cholula grew steadily in stature during the Teotihuacán period (1 to 600 AD) when much of the major building took place.

The Great Pyramid was built over several times; one of the earlier structures was bigger than the Pyramid of the Sun at Teotihuacán. These superimpositions have made it difficult to unravel the early history of Cholula and there's considerable confusion about what happened here after the fall of Teotihuacán. Cholula was an important crossroads open to influences from many different directions. Apart from the clear Teotihuacán style of some of the earlier structures, there are, for instance, stelae in typical Classic Veracruz style.

Around 600 AD, Cholula fell under the sway of the Olmeca-Xicallanca who built nearby Cacaxtla. Then, some time between 900 and 1300, it was taken over by Toltecs and/or Chichimecs. There's a legend that Quetzalcóatl Topiltzin, the god-king of Tula, stayed here for several years after his flight from the Toltec capital in the 10th century. For part of the 14th century Cholula was controlled by nearby Huejotzingo and later came under Aztec dominance. There was also artistic influence from the Mixtecs to the south. The finest pottery in the land in the years before the Spanish conquest was the colourful glazed ware in the so-called Mixtec-Puebla style. When the Spanish arrived in 1519 Cholula had a population of 100,000, although the Great Pyramid was by that time overgrown.

Cortés, having made friends with the nearby Tlaxcalans, was asked by Moctezuma to travel on to Cholula before heading to Tenochtitlán. At first welcomed by the Cholula chiefs, the Spanish soon realised they had walked into a trap. Aztec warriors were waiting outside the city and two Cholulan chiefs confessed that Moctezuma had instructed them to attack the Spanish and take some of them as prisoners to Tenochtitlán. Apparently deciding that they had to strike first, the Spanish launched what is now known as the massacre of Cholula, in which up to 6000 Cholulans were killed before the city was looted by the Tlaxcalans.

1 Estrella Roja
2 Red Buses to Puebla
3 San Pedro Church
4 Café y Artes Los Portales
5 Hotel Calli Quetzalcóatl
6 Zócalo
7 Capilla Real
8 San Gabriel Monastery
9 Autobuses Puebla—Cholula
10 Hotel Reforma
11 Museum
12 Hotel Las Américas
13 Villa Arqueológica
14 San Andrés Church

Cholula

0   250   500 m

Despite a severe plague in the 1540s Cholula continued to exist but never regained its former importance, though it remained an important market centre until this century.

Orientation

As you approach Cholula from Puebla you can see the Great Pyramid, topped with a church, to your left. If you have a car, you can park beneath the north side of the pyramid. Buses will drop you near Cholula's spacious zócalo, 300 metres

north-west of the pyramid. The east side of the zócalo is mainly taken up by the ex-monastery of San Gabriel. The other side has an arcade, the Portal Guerrero, with a few restaurants and the Hotel Calli Quetzalcóatl.

Cholula's streets are on a grid plan and their naming system is similar to that in Puebla. Unfortunately, the whole numbering system is used twice, once in the north-west half of the town, once in the south-east. You could thus be walking east along 23 Ote and suddenly find yourself on 9 Pte. But unless you're actually proposing to live in Cholula – as some foreign students at the nearby University of the Americas do – the town is small enough to get around without the need to familiarise yourself with this bizarre arrangement.

Festivals

La Virgen de los Remedios Not surprisingly, the abundance of churches in the town gives rise to many festivals – one local says there are at least 10 a year in each church. Among the most important is the Festival de la Virgen de los Remedios and regional feria (first week of September), with daily traditional dances outside the church on top of the Great Pyramid. Local firework-makers are renowned for their spectacular shows.

Great Pyramid & Museum

The pyramid, probably originally dedicated to Quetzalcóatl, is now surmounted by one of the chapels built by the Spanish – a classic symbol of their conquest. Entrance to the archaeological zone, open from 10.30 am to 5 pm daily, costs 20c (free on Sundays and holidays). The main track to the top of the pyramid starts from the north-west corner, by the railway tracks. Just south of this corner (to the right if approaching from Cholula town centre) is a restored part of an impressive outer pyramid in Teotihuacán talud-tablero style.

The small museum, with an interesting model showing the different layers of the pyramid, is down some steps opposite the north side of the pyramid. Archaeologists have burrowed eight km of tunnels beneath the pyramid, and you can walk through some of these to see the earlier layers which have been exposed. The entrance is on the north side and you emerge on the east side. Guides who approach you at the tunnel entrance could be useful in explaining the significance of all the unlabelled structures in the bowels of the pyramid. Expect to pay them US$1.50.

Great Plaza

On the south side of the pyramid the Great Plaza, or Patio de los Altares, stands between exposed layers of other constructions. This plaza was the main approach to the pyramid. It is surrounded by platforms, diagonal stairways unique to Cholula and a number of carved stone monuments. Three large stone slabs on the east, north and west sides are carved in the Veracruz interlocking-scroll design. At the south of the plaza is an Aztec-style altar in a pit dating from shortly before the Spanish conquest. Human bones indicate that this was possibly a sacrificial site.

One of the buildings just west of the Great Plaza, unfortunately not open to the general public, contains a spectacular 50-metre-long mural, probably from the 3rd century AD, depicting a drinking ceremony whose life-size participants are mostly naked and in an advanced state of inebriation. If you want to see this mural, try applying to INAH at Avenida 18 Pte 103 in Puebla (tel 32-01-78).

San Gabriel Monastery

There are three churches in this complex taking up most of the east side of Cholula zócalo. On the left is the Capilla Real, dating from 1540, an Arabic-style construction unique in Mexico with 49 domes. In the middle is the 17th-century Tercer Orden church, and on the right the San Gabriel church, originally founded in 1530 on the site of a pre-Hispanic pyramid.

On the north side of the zócalo stands the parroquia (parish church) of San Pedro (1640).

Places to Stay

Cholula is a very easy day trip from Puebla but if you want to stay here there are a couple of uninviting bottom/middle-range places and two at the upper end. *Hotel Reforma* on Morelos, a block towards the pyramid from the zócalo, has doubles/triples with private bath for US$7.25 and smaller rooms with common bath for US$3.25. It's clean enough but overpriced. *Hotel Las Américas* (tel 47-09-91) at Avenida 14 Ote 6, 2½ blocks straight on beyond the pyramid from the town centre, has doubles for US$4.25, is clean and may be pleasant when its current renovations are finished.

Hotel Calli Quetzalcóatl (tel 47-15-55) on the zócalo at Portal Guerrero 11 has good modern rooms, a dining-room and bar, all around a courtyard with a fountain in the middle. Doubles cost US$10.50. Top place is the *Villa Arqueológica* (tel 47-19-66) a couple of fields south of the Great Pyramid, with tennis, a heated swimming pool, and singles/doubles at US$23/26.

The *Trailer Park Las Americas* (tel 47-01-34), on the north edge of Cholula at Avenida 30 Ote 602 near the corner of Calle 6 Nte, charges US$5 for two people with all hook-ups.

Places to Eat

There are several places to eat in the Portal Guerrero on the west side of the zócalo. At the north end the *Café y Artes Los Portales* is a friendly place where the amiable English-speaking manager, Roberto Malagón, acts as an unofficial tourist information source. There are art exhibitions here too, and live music on Friday nights. The comida corrida is US$1.75, tortas US$0.75, and there are also 10 breakfast menus (each named after a different barrio of Cholula), 15 types of coffee and yoghurt.

Next along the portales is the smarter *Tío Nico Restaurant*, with a Mexican and international menu. Then there's *Tacos Suez* (20 to 40c per taco), the Hotel Calli Quetzalcóatl with a restaurant, and *Pizzería La Parroquia*, where a three-course comida corrida costs US$1.

Half a block south of the zócalo on Alemán, *Pepe's Fish* also does a comida corrida. *La Casona*, a block south of the zócalo along Alemán, then half a block left

at Avenida 3 Ote 9, has tables in rooms around a pleasant courtyard and does a variety of local specialities at US$2.

You can get a comida corrida for US$1 in *Restaurant El Norteño* on Morelos half a block towards the pyramid from the zócalo.

Getting There & Away

Road From Cholula, Huejotzingo is 30 km north-west by Highway 150. Atlixco is 31 km south-west by Highway 190. Between Cholula and Tonantzintla, a road branches west to Paso de Cortés on the saddle between Popocatépetl and Ixtaccíhuatl. It's 40 km and unpaved most of the way, but passable in dry weather.

Bus Autobuses Puebla-Cholula run from Puebla to Cholula (15c) every few minutes from their terminal at Avenida 8 Pte 713 in Puebla. In Cholula their terminal (tel 47-00-17) is at Calle 3 Sur 502, 2½ blocks south of the zócalo portales.

Estrella Roja run from Cholula to Puebla, Huejotzingo and Mexico City and back again. In Puebla their terminal is at Calle 5 Sur 105, in Cholula it's at the corner of Avenida 6 Pte and Calle 3 Nte – that's one block west from the Café y Artes Los Portales on the corner of the zócalo, then one block north. From here buses run to Huejotzingo (20c) and Mexico City's TAPO terminal (US$1.50) every 20 minutes.

Red buses to Puebla (10c) also go every few minutes from the corner of Avenida 4 Pte and Calle 3 Nte in Cholula, one block west of the Café y Artes Los Portales.

To get to Tonantzintla or Acatepec from Cholula, take bus 'Chipilo' from outside the Estrella Roja station.

AROUND CHOLULA

Four and five km south of Cholula respectively are two quiet little villages whose small churches are among the loveliest examples of Puebla baroque architecture. Tonantzintla is outstanding even on a national scale. Fourteen km north-west of Cholula is the interesting town of Huejotzingo.

Tonantzintla & Acatepec

The baroque church of Santa María Tonantzintla (open 9 am to 1 pm and 3 to 5 pm) has a pretty but simple tiled façade. Inside is one of the most exuberantly decorated of all Mexican church interiors. Particularly on and beneath the dome, every available inch is covered with colourful stucco shapes of fruit, saints, devils, flowers, birds and more – a superb example of Indian craftsmanship applied to Christian themes. Blue, white and gold are among the most prominent colours. You could spend several hours working out what's what in this riot of sculpture. Tonantzintla holds a procession and traditional dances for the Festival of the Assumption on 15 August.

The church of San Francisco Acatepec, 1½ km south-east of Tonantzintla, dates from about 1730. Its ornately but attractively shaped churrigueresque façade shows an inspired use of blue, green and yellow Puebla tiles set in red brick. Some of the tiles are painted with animals and birds. The interior, partly damaged by fire in the 1930s, has some exuberant decoration but isn't as striking as Tonantzintla.

Getting There You can get to Tonantzintla and Acatepec from Cholula by bus 'Chipilo' from the Estrella Roja station at the corner of Avenida 6 Pte and Calle 3 Nte. Between the two villages you can wait for the next bus or walk; it's only 1½ km.

From Puebla, Autobuses Puebla-Cholula at Avenida 8 Pte 713 runs buses to Tonantzintla, and Transportes Puebla-Tonantzintla at Avenida 10 Pte 715 goes to Acatepec.

Huejotzingo

From Cholula, Highway 150 heads north-west to meet the road to Mexico City at San Martín Texmelucan. Huejotzingo ('way-hot-ZIN-go'), 14 km along Highway 150 from Cholula, was the capital of a small pre-Hispanic state that was friendly with the Tlaxcalans – and therefore the Spanish – at the time of the conquest.

Franciscan monks founded a fine monastery here in the 16th century. Mainly in the plateresque style, the monastery churchyard has four posa chapels – used as halts during processions – with Moorish-style alfizes, and the fortified church has gothic ribbing on its roof. The church nave contains an altarpiece with oils by Simón Pereyns, a Flemish painter who made his name and living in late 16th-century Mexico. The cloisters have some old frescoes and, upstairs, a small monastic museum.

Today Huejotzingo is a town of 25,000 people known for its cider and sarapes. Market days are Tuesday and Saturday. Carnival is celebrated actively here, particularly on Shrove Tuesday, when one of the masked dances re-enacts a battle between French and Mexicans. There's also an annual cider festival at the end of September. See under 'Puebla', 'Cholula' and 'Mexico City' (eastern bus terminal) for getting to Huejotzingo by bus.

TLAXCALA

About 120 km east of Mexico City and 30 km north of Puebla, this sleepy town of some 25,000 people is the capital of Mexico's second smallest state (after the Distrito Federal). It makes a pleasant, off-the-beaten-track trip out of the big city, with a number of places to visit in the town and round about.

Orientation

Tlaxcala's bus station (Central Camionera) is a km west of the town centre. A pesero downtown costs 10c. The most central place to disembark is at the corner of Independencia and Diego Muñoz, where two plazas meet. The squarer of these plazas, surrounded by colonial buildings with the tile and red-brick church of San José off one corner, is the zócalo,

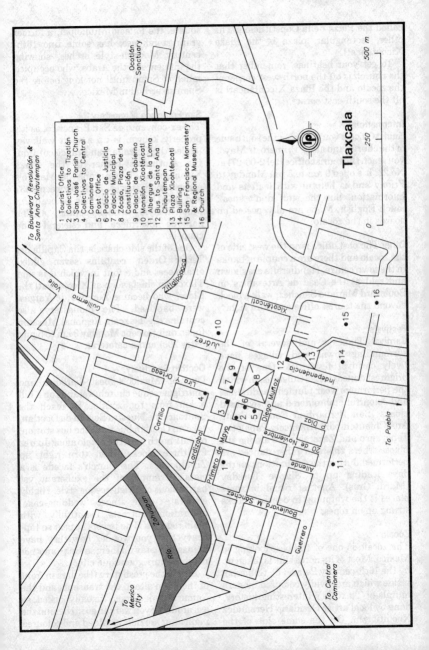

Tlaxcala

1 Tourist Office
2 Colectivos to Tizatlán
3 San José Parish Church
4 Colectivos to Central
   Camionera
5 Post Office
6 Palacio de Justicia
7 Palacio Municipal
8 Zócalo, Plaza de la
   Constitución
9 Palacio de Gobierno
10 Mansión Xicohténcatl
11 Albergue de la Loma
12 Bus to Santa Ana
    Chiautempan
13 Plaza Xicohténcatl
14 Bullring
15 San Francisco Monastery
    & Regional Museum
16 Church

called the Plaza de la Constitución. The other, rectangular, plaza is the Plaza Xicohténcatl.

To get your bearings, remember that the church is off the north-west corner of the zócalo and the Plaza Xicohténcatl is off the south-east corner.

Information

Tourist Office If you walk past the south side of the church and along Primero de Mayo, you reach the tourist office (tel 2-00-27) at No 22. It's open 9 am to 5 pm Monday to Friday and is helpful with leaflets and information, but the staff don't speak much English. Maps are also posted on boards in the zócalo.

Other The post office is on the west side of the zócalo and there are a couple of banks in the town centre. Handicrafts are shown and sold at the Casa de Artesanías on Boulevard Mariano Sánchez; walk a block beyond the tourist office and turn right.

Festivals

Carnival Tlaxcala and several of the surrounding towns and villages have lively carnival festivities. One of the brightest dances is Las Culebras, in which the performers wear plumed headdresses and colourful embroidered and sequined cloaks. San Bernardino Contla, Santa Ana Chiautempan, Amaxcac, Papalotla, Tepeyanco and Zacatelco are among the places where this and other dances are performed during the celebrations on the days leading up to Shrove Tuesday (Mardi Gras). Another ritual in some places is the whipping to death of cocks strung up on ropes.

Zócalo

The zócalo is one of the best-looking in Mexico. Most of its north side is taken up by the 16th-century Palacio de Gobierno, inside which are vividly coloured modern murals of Tlaxcala's interesting history, done by local artist Desiderio Hernández Xochitiotzin. On the same side of the

square, the Palacio Municipal, a former grain storehouse, has some fine 16th-century Moorish-style arches, showing the influence of the Arabs, who occupied much of Spain until not long before the Spanish arrival in Mexico.

San Francisco Monastery

The ex-convento de San Francisco, as it's properly known, is up a short walkway (called the Calzada San Francisco) from the south-east corner of the Plaza Xicohténcatl. It was one of Mexico's earliest monasteries, built between 1537 and 1540. Its church has a beautiful Moorish-style wooden ceiling, a fine baroque altarpiece and several side chapels.

One of the side chapels, the Capilla del Tercer Orden, contains seven gilded altarpieces and a font in which it is said Tlaxcalan chiefs such as Xicoténcatl the Elder, who became Lorenzo de Vargas, were baptised. The monastery also contains the Tlaxcala Regional Museum (open daily except Monday 9 am to 5 pm, entry 20c) and a cafeteria.

Ocotlán Sanctuary

One of Mexico's best baroque and churrigueresque churches stands on a hill a km from the zócalo. To reach the Santuario de Nuestra Señora de Ocotlán, take an Ocotlán bus from the bus station, or walk north from the zócalo along Juárez for three blocks, then turn right up Zitlalpopoca. The church's façade is a classic example of the exuberant yet harmonious churrigueresque style. Highly elaborate white stucco 'wedding-cake' decoration contrasts beautifully with plain red tiles. The towers appear so top-heavy that you wonder how they have managed to stay up there so long – another notable churrigueresque effect.

Inside, the presbytery (the area in front of the main altar), the transepts and the Camarín de la Virgen (usually locked, so ask around if you want to go in) behind the main altar are riots of gilded and coloured ornamentation. The 18th-century Indian Francisco Miguel spent 25 years on the decoration of the camarín and the altarpieces of the presbytery. Around the camarín walls are eight 18th-century oil paintings on the life of the Virgin Mary by Cristóbal de Villalpando. The camarín is the 'dressing room' for the image of the Virgin which stands on the church's main altar in memory of a 1541 apparition. Paintings in the church nave depict this miracle. The church is still a pilgrimage goal and on the third Monday in May the Virgin's image is taken round other churches in a procession.

Tizatlán

The scanty remains of Xicoténcatl's HQ stand on a small hill four km from the town centre. The position is impressive, with views of three volcanoes (Popocatépetl, Iztaccíhuatl and La Malinche) if the weather's clear. You can get there by taking a 'Tizatlán' colectivo (10c) from Tlaxcala bus station or from the corner of Primero de Mayo and 20 de Noviembre behind the parish church. Get off at the bottom of a lane on the left leading up to a church with a yellow dome.

All that's to be seen is the remains of a palace and two altars with some rather faded frescoes in Mixteca-Puebla style. They show gods such as Tezcatlipoca (Smoking Mirror), Tlahuizcalpantecuhtli (Morning Star) and Mictlantecuhtli (Underworld).

The church of San Estéban next to the ruins is 19th century but has a 16th-century Franciscan open chapel with some frescoes (showing angels playing medieval musical instruments) at the far end. There's also a small museum of religious art, a pre-Hispanic statue beside the church wall, and a statue of Xicoténcatl the Younger looking out towards La Malinche. The ruins, museum and open chapel are officially closed on Monday.

Places to Stay

Tlaxcala has a few options if you want to stay. On Juárez, the street leading north from the zócalo, the *Mansión Xicoténcatl* (tel 2-19-84, 2-19-89) at No 15 has biggish but slightly grubby rooms, a bit overpriced at US$5.75 single, US$6.75 double. The *Hotel Oriental* (tel 2-08-58) at Juárez 37 is cheaper: sizeable singles or doubles round a courtyard are US$3.25 with common bath, US$5.25 with private bath, but they're dingy.

The *Albergue de la Loma* (tel 2-04-24), on a small height overlooking the town at the corner of Guerrero and 20 de Noviembre, has singles/doubles for US$3.75/5.25. It's one block south and one west of the south-west corner of the zócalo.

More expensive are two places on the continuation of Juárez which leads out to Santa Ana Chiautempan. *Jeroc's Hotel* (tel 2-15-77) at Boulevard Revolución 4 has singles/doubles for US$10.75/12. *Challet's Hotel* (tel 2-03-30) at Boulevard Revolución 3 charges US$12.50 for both singles and doubles.

Places to Eat

There are several reasonably priced restaurants along Juárez close to the zócalo. One of them, *Cafetería Patti's* opposite the Hotel Oriental, does a comida corrida for US$1. *Marisquería El Cangrejo Hermitaño* at Juárez 12 specialises in seafood.

On the east side of the zócalo, *Fuente de Sodas Guimache* offers little except tortas (US$0.40). For snacks try the fondas on Calle Cuautla along the north side of Plaza Xicohténcatl, or *Carnes Ossie's* a little further down the same street. There are a few other restaurants on the same plaza.

A step up in class is *Mesón Taurino* at the corner of Independencia and Guerrero just beyond the south end of Plaza Xicohténcatl. Pasta or queso fundido costs US$1.75, fish or meat are mostly

US$2.50, a few other dishes go up to US$5.25.

Getting There & Away

Road From Mexico City, Highway 150D (the autopista to Puebla) takes you to within 25 km of Tlaxcala, after which you turn left. Puebla is 30 km south of Tlaxcala by a decent enough road. About 20 km north of Tlaxcala at Apizaco, Highway 136 heads west to Texcoco and east to Huamantla and eventually Jalapa, while Highway 119 goes north into the Sierra Madre to Zacatlán, eventually emerging at the Tulancingo-Poza Rica road.

Bus Tlaxcala's bus station (Central Camionera, tel 2-02-17) is a km west of the town centre. ADO buses (1st class) travel between Tlaxcala and Puebla every 15 or 30 minutes up to 7 pm. Fare is U$0.75 and the trip takes 45 minutes. Flecha Azul has slightly cheaper and slower, but also frequent, 2nd-class buses on the same route up to 10 pm.

From Mexico City, ADO leaves the eastern bus terminal (TAPO) five times a day for Tlaxcala (US$1.50, two hours). The last ADO bus returning to Mexico City is at 7 pm. Autobuses Tlaxcala-Apizaco-Huamantla have more frequent 2nd-class buses to/from Mexico City, while Autobuses Estrella de Oro serves local destinations plus Puebla and Cholula.

Getting Around

To get back to the bus station from downtown, you can catch a colectivo on the corner of Lardizal and Lira y Ortega, just to the right of the front of the parish church.

SANTA ANA CHIAUTEMPAN

This town of 25,000 people a few km east of Tlaxcala is a textile crafts centre, selling both its own products and those of villages elsewhere in the state. Sarapes, jorongos, blankets, jumpers and rugs are among the items you'll find. The designs aren't in general as attractive as in other parts of Mexico. Several central shops sell the goods, particularly on Ignacio Picazo Norte. There's also the Centro Comercial de Artesanías Plaza Abandames, on Bernardo Picazo. The town holds a Feria Nacional del Sarape in late June and early July.

The *Restaurant Artesanías*, inside the Plaza Abandames, will do you quesadillas or enchiladas for US$1 or meat dishes for US$1.75. *Hotel Aloha*, at Ignacio Picazo Sur 8, has basic rooms with private bath round a courtyard-garden for US$2.50 downstairs, US$4 upstairs.

You can get a bus to Santa Ana (10c) from the corner of Plaza Xicohténcatl nearest to the zócalo in Tlaxcala.

CACAXTLA

The archaeological site at Cacaxtla was first recorded in the 16th century by Diego Muñoz Camargo, but not until looters started emerging with pieces of a highly coloured mural in 1974 did archaeologists get round to digging there. What they found ranks among the most exciting post-war discoveries in Mexico – a fortified ceremonial and palace complex of the 8th and 9th centuries AD, embellished with some of the most vivid and best-preserved murals in the country.

History

Cacaxtla was the capital of a group of Olmeca-Xicallanca or Putún Mayas, a Campeche-based, Mayan-speaking, trading and seafaring people who reached their greatest importance after the downfall of classic Mayan civilisation from around 800 AD. They arrived in central Mexico possibly as early as 400 AD and may also have had a settlement at Teotihuacán.

After the decline of Cholula about 600 AD (which they may have helped bring about), the Olmeca-Xicallanca became the chief power in southern Tlaxcala and the Puebla valley. Cacaxtla was at its peak from 650 to 900 AD before being abandoned in 1000 or 1100, when the

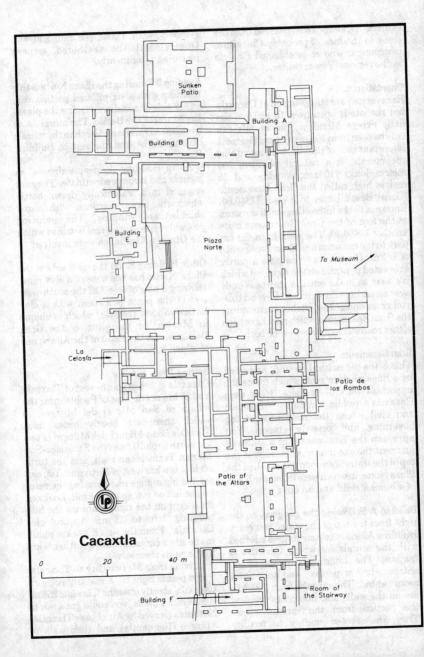

Sunken
Patio

Building A

Building B

Building
E

Plaza
Norte

To Museum

La
Celosía

Patio de
los Rombos

Patio of
the Altars

Cacaxtla

0   20   40 m

Room of
the Stairway

Building F

Olmeca-Xicallanca disappeared from the scene in the face of probably Chichimec newcomers, who re-established Cholula as the regional power centre.

Orientation

Excavations are still going on at Cacaxtla but the site is open from 10 am to 5 pm daily except Monday. The murals can only be seen from 10 am to 1 pm. The most important part of the site, which contains the murals, is a natural platform 200 metres long, 110 metres wide and 25 metres high called the Gran Basamento (Great Base). Entry to it costs US$0.50. Entrance to the interesting small museum at the foot of the Gran Basamento costs another US$0.40. The walk from the car park to the museum and Gran Basamento is ¾ km. On the way you pass a partly excavated pyramid on the right, on which it's easy to make out the staircase built over an earlier construction. Beyond this, you cross one of the ditches surrounding the Gran Basamento which may have been either roadways or defences, or both.

Gran Basamento

This is the big natural mound, protected by a huge modern roof, which forms the important part of Cacaxtla's public buildings – religious and civil – and the residences of the governing and priestly classes. You approach the Basamento up a stairway just past the site museum. In front at the top of the stairs is an open space called the Plaza Norte, in which were found the bones of a human child and an onyx vase.

Building A Following the gangway to the right from the top of the steps, you reach Building A, one of two structures adorned with the murals for which Cacaxtla is famous. The building consists of an entrance-hall or portico, and an interior room behind. The murals, from 750 AD, are on the walls and doorposts dividing the portico from the interior room. They are devoted mainly to fertility

symbols, with Tláloc the rain god and Quetzalcóatl the feathered serpent featuring prominently.

Building B Fronting the Plaza Norte is this building with a six-pillared portico and, either side of a stairway facing the plaza, the Mural of the Battle. The mural dates from 650 AD and is earlier than the murals of Building A and the rest of Building B.

As in Building A, people dressed as jaguars and birds predominate. They are engaged in a realistically drawn battle which the jaguar-warriors, with round shields, are winning. The painting probably represents a real battle in which the Olmeca-Xicallanca were involved.

Other Building E, on the west side of the Plaza Norte, has the base of a clay relief showing a pair of feet. Off the south-west end of the plaza is a room with a clay lattice-window (celosía) which is unique in Mexico. At the south of the Gran Basamento is the Patio of the Altars, one of which remains.

Getting There & Away

Cacaxtla is 20 km south-west of Tlaxcala and 35 km north-west of Puebla, near the village of San Miguel del Milagro, to which there are hourly buses from Tlaxcala. San Miguel del Milagro is two km north (uphill) from the Zacatelco-San Martín Texmelucan road, and the turn-off to it is a km west of Nativitas. You can see the big orange roof covering the ruins on the left as you go up the hill. Look out for a sign on the right a km up the hill, pointing left to 'Zona Arqueológica Cacaxtla'. From the sign it's ½ km uphill to the site's car park, then a further ¾ km to the ruins themselves.

Driving from Mexico City to Tlaxcala, a sign points right to 'Zona Arqueológica Cacaxtla' shortly after the 'Tlaxcala 25 km' sign. From Puebla, you could get a bus to Nativitas (served by Autobuses Tlaxcala-Apizaco-Huamantla) and then walk or pick up a San Miguel del Milagro bus there, or go to Tlaxcala first.

HUAMANTLA

This town of 25,000 people, 41 km from Tlaxcala, holds a colourful feria in August (usually early in the month), which includes bull-running through the town in the style of Pamplona in Spain, and the laying of 'carpets' of flowers and coloured sawdust in the streets. From Tlaxcala, you first go north to Apizaco, then east to Huamantla. Autobuses Tlaxcala-Apizaco-Huamantla is the bus company to use.

SOUTHERN PUEBLA

Markets, handicrafts and colonial buildings are the main attractions here. You can visit these places as day trips from Puebla, or en route to/from Oaxaca or Veracruz. For more information on buses, see Getting There & Away in the Puebla city section.

Puebla to Tehuacán

Highway 150 to Tehuacán in the southeast of the state parallels the Veracruz road, 150D, for the first 40 km or so east of Puebla city.

Tepeaca Forty km east of Puebla on Highway 150, Tepeaca has a big Friday market noted, among other things, for its metates (grinding stones) and petates (mats). In the zócalo stands a tower called El Rollo, built in the 16th century as a symbol of Spanish rule. There's also a Franciscan monastery. Tepeaca holds its regional feria in early October.

Tecali This village of 2000 people 11 km south-west of Tepeaca by a minor paved road, is a centre for the carving of onyx from the nearby quarries. Stalls and shops in the main plaza and on the roadside sell the stuff. A 16th-century Franciscan monastery once stood here, of which the ruins remain. You can also reach Tecali by the local Highway 708 from Puebla.

Tehuacán This town, 115 km from Puebla, is a sizeable place of 100,000 people, famed for its mineral waters sold in bottled form all over Mexico. Many buses to Oaxaca go through Tehuacán. It's a pleasant enough town, with a zócalo called the Parque Juárez a block east of the main street intersection where Independencia (running east-west) meets Reforma (north-south). But there's no particular reason to stop here unless you're keen to bathe in cold mineral water or interested in very early archaeology.

The development from nomadic hunting to settled agriculture in the Tehuacán Valley between 9000 and 4000 years ago was thoroughly researched by archaeologists led by Richard MacNeish in the 1960s, and now there's a museum in Tehuacán explaining their finds – including some ancient and very small cobs of maize which were among the first to be cultivated. The Museo del Valle de Tehuacán is in the Ex-Convento del Carmen, two blocks north and one west of the zócalo.

There are plenty of hotels and restaurants in town to choose from. At the cheaper end, the *Hotel Madrid* (tel 2-00-72) at 3 Sur 105 has singles/doubles for US$2.75/3.50. A little dearer is the *Hotel Posada de Tehuacán* (tel 2-04-91) at Reforma Nte 213, a block west of the zócalo and then 1½ blocks north. There's also the *Hotel Puerto de Veracruz* at 2 Ote 101; the *Hotel Casa Colorada* at 3 Nte 114; several casas de huéspedes, including *La Castellana* and *La Consentida* (tel 2-03-65), next door to each other at 3 Nte 103 and 101; *La Yucateca* at Reforma Nte 110 and *La Colonial* at Reforma Nte 100.

In the middle range, the *Hotel Iberia* (tel 2-11-22), just east of the zócalo on Independencia, is an old building with some rooms round a courtyard and singles/doubles for US$4.25/5.25. There's also the *Hotel Monte Carlo* (tel 2-07-00) at Reforma Nte 500.

At the top end there's the *Hotel México* (tel 2-00-19), a block west of the zócalo at

Independencia Pte 101, where singles/doubles are US$9.50/12. One traveller reported that this hotel had one of the best restaurants in town and changed travellers' cheques at the bank rate. There's also the modern *Bogh Suites Hotel* at the corner of Independencia and 1 Nte with similar prices.

Outside the town centre is the luxurious but slightly faded old *Hacienda Spa Peñafiel* (tel 2-01-90, 2-04-85), two km from the town centre just off the Orizaba road. It has a golf course, fine gardens and a mineral-water swimming pool. Singles/doubles cost US$15/20. The *Hotel El Riego* (tel 2-00-75) four km south-west of downtown in an old hacienda also has a large pool. There's also the new *Hotel Aldea del Bazar* on the Puebla road just outside town.

The Balneario San Lorenzo just off the Puebla road, five km from the zócalo, is a public mineral-water swimming pool.

Puebla to Huajuapan de León

Highway 190 heads south to Huajuapan, just over the state border in Oaxaca, 216 km from Puebla city.

Atlixco This town of 50,000 people, 31 km from Puebla and 1700 metres high is known for its avocados and near-perfect climate. It has a colonial and 19th-century town centre. The annual Atlixcáyotl festival on the last weekend in September is a chance to see many traditional costumes, dances and music from Puebla state and sometimes further afield. The performances are held in an open-air theatre on the Cerro de San Miguel, a hill near the town centre.

Izúcar de Matamoros This town, 67 km from Puebla, produces some pottery, including fine trees of life. Market day is Monday. There's a 16th-century Dominican monastery in the town.

Acatlán de Osorio This town, 154 km from Puebla, is a flower-growing centre also known for its black and red earthenware pottery. The workshop of Héron Martínez, creator of probably Mexico's finest trees of life, is here, though you could hardly find anything less easy to tuck into a backpack or more likely to break during travels. These elaborate pottery sculptures on a multitude of themes, resembling if anything candelabra, are in a way the modern successors of the superb Indian-style sculpted plasterwork in many of Mexico's colonial churches, such as at Tonantzintla near Puebla. You don't have to go to Acatlán for Martínez's work: you can find it in Puebla city, Oaxaca, even Mexico City.

SIERRA NORTE DE PUEBLA

This is the mountainous, remote northern part of Puebla state, which often rises over 2500 metres before falling towards the Gulf coast plain on the Veracruz border. Even though some of the land has been deforested, it's fertile and beautiful with high rainfall. There are pine forests at higher altitudes and luxuriant semi-tropical vegetation lower down. Low cloud often covers the hills.

The area has a high Indian population – mostly Nahua and Totonac but also some Otomíes and one small community of Tepehua in Pantepec in the far north of Puebla.

The Nahua are Mexico's most numerous Indian group: 1.4 million of them are scattered over at least 12 states. Traditional Nahua women's dress consists of a black wool enredo, waist sash, and embroidered blouse and quechquémitl. In Cuetzalán it's accompanied – these days on special occasions only – by the *maxtahual*, which refers to strips of fabric wound into the hair to raise it up to an almost hat-like appearance.

The Nahua are Christian but also believe in various supernatural beings such as *nahuales* (people who can change into fierce, harmful animals), *tonos* (people's animal 'doubles'), witches who can become blood-sucking birds and cause illness, and spirits of natural things like mountains and rivers. Nahua dances in this area include the *voladores*, made famous by their Totonac neighbours.

The Nahua language was spoken by the Aztecs and, like the Aztecs, the Nahua of Puebla are probably of ultimate northern Chichimec origin. Their ancestors are thought to have arrived in the Sierra Norte in the 14th century, probably after first settling in the Valley of Mexico and southern and central Puebla. For more on the Totonacs and Tepehua, see the Veracruz chapter. For the Otomíes, see under Hidalgo state.

The many handicrafts of the Sierra Norte – among them rebozos, quechquémitls, wood-carving, candles, gourds and baskets – are sold in markets at Cuetzalán, Zacapoaxtla, Tlatlauquitepec, Tetela de Ocampo, Huauchinango, Pahuatlán and other places, as well as in Puebla and Mexico cities.

Three decent routes lead into the Sierra Norte. From Puebla, one of them follows Highway 150D to Amozoc, then Highway 129 to Oriental where it meets Highway 125, which heads north-east to Teziutlán, with a turn-off to the north for Zacapoaxtla and Cuetzalán. (There are also good roads to Teziutlán from Nautla and Perote in Veracruz.) A second route is Highway 119 through Tlaxcala and Apizaco to Zacatlán. This road continues north to meet the third route, Highway 130, which crosses far northern Puebla from east to west en route from Poza Rica in Veracruz to Pachuca in Hidalgo.

Bus connections from surrounding cities such as Puebla, Tlaxcala, Jalapa, Poza Rica and Pachuca are regular but not very frequent and you will have to use more than one bus to get to many places. See under those cities for more information.

Cuetzalán

This is one of the most interesting towns in the Sierra Norte, famed for its Sunday market which brings in Nahua and Totonac Indians from miles around.

Flowers and textiles (embroidered blouses, quechquémitls and sashes) are just a few of the items bargained over.

Set 1200 metres high in a lush coffee-growing area, Cuetzalán is a colonial town dominated by a large church and is the setting of the Mexican XEW TV soap opera *El Padre Gallo*. For several days around 4 October it sees lively celebrations of the festival of San Francisco de Assisi, combined with a coffee fair. Another colourful festival in mid-July attracts traditional dance groups from all over the area. One of the dances performed is the Quetzales, in which the dancers wear huge circular headdresses of feathers, ribbons and reeds.

Places to Stay There are several places to stay in Cuetzalán, among them the *Posada Las Garzas* (tel 21) on the zócalo at the corner of Guadalupe Victoria and 2 Abril, the *Posada Jackelin* next door and the *Posada Cuetzalán* at Zaragoza 8. Singles/doubles in all these cost around US$4/5 but some rooms don't have private baths. There are also the *Hotel Rivello* at Guadalupe Victoria 3 and the *Hotel Marquéz* at Alvarado 11.

Getting There From Puebla, two ADO buses a day make the 4½-hour, 180-km, trip to Cuetzalán for US$2.75. Driving yourself, you turn north off Highway 125/129 just west of Zaragoza, from where it's a further 51 paved km.

Yohuallichán

Eight km from Cuetzalán by a poor dirt road, this is the only known pre-Hispanic site with a pyramid of niches similar to the one at El Tajín, which is 50 km north-east. It's in seven tiers, less impressive than its more famous cousin but interesting nonetheless, standing beside a large plaza 66 by 40 metres wide with more pyramids on the other sides. Some restoration has been done here to make it worth a visit. The structures retain traces of their original red paint. There is also a ball court.

Huehuetla

A remote 25 km north of Cuetzalán, Huehuetla holds colourful celebrations with dances and candlelit processions for the festivals of the Birth of the Virgin Mary (8 September) and the Virgin of Guadalupe (12 December).

Teziutlán

With 50,000 people, this is probably the biggest town in the Sierra Norte. It sits at an altitude of 2000 metres. There are several hotels on Hidalgo. Market days are Friday and Saturday. To the north-west is Hueyapán, a crafts centre noted in particular for its black wool rebozos adorned with multicoloured animals, birds and flowers. Hueyapán's main fiesta is for San Andrés (30 November).

Zacatlán

Market day is Sunday in this fruit-growing town on the Apizaco-Huauchinango road. About 20 km west is the valley of Piedras Encimadas, a collection of bizarre rock formations. One of Zacatlán's major festivals is San Isidro Labrador (15 May). There's also an apple festival in mid-August.

Huauchinango

This is the centre of a flower-growing area, and you'll also find fruit and embroidered textiles on sale in the busy Saturday market. The town is on Highway 130 roughly halfway between Poza Rica and Pachuca. The vegetation around here is semi-tropical. Huauchinango holds a week-long flower festival, including traditional dances, centred on the third Friday in Lent.

Pahuatlán

A traditional Nahua village, Pahuatlán has a sizeable Sunday market. It's 15 km north-west of Huauchinango but is approached from further west (see under

Hidalgo state). Beyond Pahuatlán is San Pablito, another traditional village, this time with an Otomí population.

OTHER VOLCANOES

Mexico's highest mountain, the 5700-metre Pico de Orizaba or Citlaltépetl, lies on the boundary of Puebla and Veracruz. Another volcano, La Malinche, stands on the border of Puebla and Tlaxcala states, 30 km south-east of Tlaxcala town and a similar distance north-east of Puebla city. Both mountains, as well as Popocatépetl and Iztaccíhuatl, can be seen from the Mexico City-Córdoba-Veracruz road. Both are dormant and neither appears to have erupted in recent centuries.

Pico de Orizaba

Named after the city to its south-east and also called by the Aztec name Citlaltépetl (Star Mountain), Mexico's highest peak is topped by a small crater and a permanent snow-cap. The only higher peaks in North America are Mt McKinley in Alaska and Mt Logan in Canada. A legend says that the god-king Quetzalcóatl, after fleeing in shame or defeat from the Toltec capital Tula where he had reigned, died near the Pico de Orizaba and that his body was burnt on top of the mountain. After four days of dense fog, he reappeared as a bright new morning star.

The approaches to the mountain are from the west side, reached as easily from Puebla or Jalapa as from Orizaba. The mountain is popular with climbers but is not for hikers – the most common route is up a steep, sometimes crevasse-ridden glacier.

Getting There The main approach is from the village of Tlachichuca, 23 km east of the Jalapa-Puebla road, Highway 140. The turn-off to Tlachichuca is signposted and is seven km north of El Seco and 33 km north of Acatzingo. First and 2nd-class buses from Jalapa and Puebla run past the turn-off; some will stop there for you. Local buses will then take you up to

Tlachichuca. From Orizaba, 2nd-class AU buses go to El Seco; then you need other buses north and east.

From Tlachichuca (2700 metres) a very rough dirt road (four-wheel drive is required) leads 23 km east to two huts which can accommodate 70 people at Piedra Grande (4230 metres) on the north flank of the mountain, which most climbers use as the base for their ascents. Señor José Amador Reyes (tel Tlachichuca 26), in the shop opposite the Pemex station in Tlachichuca, is one person who can fix you up with lodging in Tlachichuca and transport to Piedra Grande. He also has a representative in Mexico City, Señor Francisco Reyes Rodríguez (tel 595-12-03).

Conditions Señor Reyes warns that weather conditions can turn critical on the mountain and that training is needed before embarking on a climb. The Pico de Orizaba is a very serious proposition; you should be an experienced climber, fit and well equipped. To find out more – including other approaches and routes – see R J Secor's guide *Mexico's Volcanoes*, mentioned in the Popocatépetl & Iztaccíhuatl section, or contact one of the organisations also listed in that section. The Pico de Orizaba

has a seasonal pattern similar to those of Popocatépetl and Iztaccíhuatl.

The most popular route, by the north or Jamapa Glacier, is an ascent of six to nine hours from Piedra Grande.

La Malinche

Named after the Indian woman who became Hernán Cortés' interpreter and lover, this 4450-metre mountain has an easily identified profile. In contrast to the awesome Popo, Izta and Pico de Orizaba, La Malinche offers a relatively easy three or four-hour walk to its summit from the nearest road. It has snow only for a few months of the year.

The approach is by way of a microwave transmitting station and government resort, IMSS La Malintzin, on the north side of the mountain. Turn south from Highway 136 halfway along its 26-km stretch between Apizaco and Huamantla. From this turn-off there's 15 km of road (paved most of the way) past the radio station and IMSS. The road becomes impassable for vehicles at 3000 metres. Then it's 1000 metres of ascent by a marked path, through trees at first, onto the ridge which leads to the summit.

Morelos

The state of Morelos is close enough to Mexico City to be visited in a day trip from the Federal District, but still far away enough to offer a pleasant respite from Mexico City's overwhelming crowds, smog and traffic. Most people come to Morelos to visit Cuernavaca, the state's colourful capital city with lively plazas, beautiful colonial-style architecture and sidewalk cafés. Cuernavaca is also a retreat for Mexico's political bosses and the wealthy as well as for a growing community of American retirees. It hosts several of Mexico's largest and most internationally popular schools for studying Spanish as a second language.

The surrounding towns and countryside are also interesting. They include the pre-Columbian ruins of Teopanzolco and Tepozteco; Tepoztlán, a mystical town steeped in Aztec, Tlahuican and colonial history with the ex-Convento de Tepoztlán cathedral; and Cuautla, a bustling market town known for its scenic train excursion to Yecapixtla and nearby hot-spring resorts at Oaxtepec.

History

Morelos is named for José María Morelos y Pavón, one of Mexico's early leaders of the independence movement. As a mestizo priest, he was a follower of Miguel Hidalgo's 1810 rebellion and, after Hidalgo was executed in 1811, became leader of the independence movement. Although Chilpancingo in the neighbouring state of Guerrero became the site of his constitutional congress (the Congress of Chilpancingo, 1813), much of his support came from peasants in the area of the present state of Morelos. He was able to use this area as both a base and refuge until Spanish royalist forces caught and executed him in 1815. Morelos was in a sense following a long line of Spaniards and Aztecs who had considered this area,

especially Cuernavaca (now the capital of Morelos), either a holiday retreat or a refuge from political problems.

Before Cortés built a palace in Cuernavaca in 1531, the Tlahuicans and Aztecs established religious centres in Morelos with the construction of pyramids and temples in Tepoztlán. In the 18th century, José de la Borda, king of Mexico's silver mines, was attracted to Morelos by the pleasant climate and decided to establish a palatial residence and beautiful garden in Cuernavaca. In the 1860s the garden appealed to Emperor Maximilian and his wife Carlota so much that they decided to build a summer residence here. During the revolutionary years Morelos was a favourite stomping grounds for Emiliano Zapata and his rebellious Zapatistas.

Today, Morelos is still a popular refuge for international celebrities and *chilangos* (residents of Mexico City). Despite its small size it is a prominent agricultural centre, particularly for fruits, vegetables, corn, rice, sugar cane and wheat. The University of Morelos was established here in 1953.

Geography & Climate

Covering 4941 square km, the state is one of Mexico's smallest and most densely populated. Much of it lies on the mountainous and hilly southern slope of a major geographical region called the central Mexican plateau. Small valleys at different elevations throughout Morelos have given it a variety of micro-climates, which in turn makes the land suitable for a variety of fruits, vegetables and grains.

The main road from the north is Highway 95D, a six to eight-lane super-highway toll road *(cuota)* connecting Mexico City to Cuernavaca. After Cuernavaca it becomes a two to four-lane

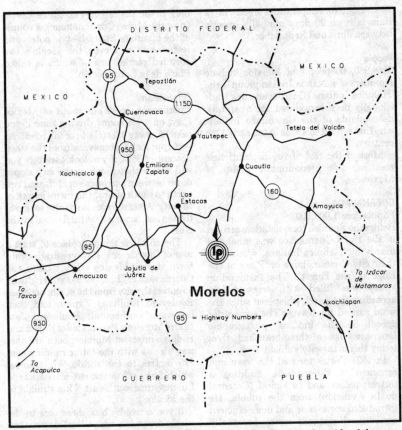

highway that remains a toll road for another 102 km and continues on to Acapulco. Highway 95 runs parallel to 95D until it crosses into the state of Guerrero and branches off south-west to Taxco.

The toll portion of 95D between Mexico City and Cuernavaca is one of Mexico's most scenic stretches of highway, as it climbs more than 3000 metres from the Valley of Mexico and into the refreshing pine forests of the Ajusco and Pelado mountains and the Tres Cumbres pass. As you leave the valley, look back for a breath-taking (not only because of the smog) view. On the other side of the pass you'll get a view of the Valley of Morelos and, to the north-east, the volcano of Popocatépetl.

The state's capital city, Cuernavaca, is in the north-central part of the state and can be seen as you descend Highway 95D to the Valley of Morelos (elevation 1500 metres).

The major rivers of the Río Amacuzac, the Río Balsas and their tributaries have, through the millennia, cut several small valleys across the state's mountain ranges.

In Cuernavaca temperatures average

20°C. High/low temperatures are 28°/13°C. Rain falls on 90 days annually, mostly between June and September.

People

The 980,000 people of Morelos include members of a Nahua Indian group – the Tlahuica Indians (Cuernavaca has traditionally been considered their capital), descendants of the Chichimec Indians who first settled this area in the early 13th century.

Most of the rest of the population is mestizo, the predominant group of Mexico.

CUERNAVACA

Population: 1,009,000

Before the Spanish conquistadors arrived in the 1520s Cuernavaca was inhabited mostly by Tlahuica Indians, who called their city Cuauhnáhuac or 'Place at the Edge of the Forest'. The surrounding valley was filled with trees which, according to legend, whispered when the wind rustled the leaves. The symbol for speech in the Indians' pictographic language was a three-branched tree; today this is the city's shield.

In 1521 Cortés torched the town and renamed it Cuernavaca, building a fortress-palace and cathedral (Catedral de la Asunción) from the rubble. He introduced sugar cane and more efficient agricultural methods which eventually transformed Cuernavaca into a major colonial agricultural centre.

Today Cuernavaca is overrun by visitors, particularly on the weekends. Hotel rooms are often hard to come by, elbow-to-elbow crowds flow through the zócalo and patrons at sidewalk cafés can't take a sip without an aggressive pedlar waving blankets, cheap paintings or doilies in their faces. During the week, the situation is not much better; the recent construction of an industrial complex just outside the city has helped create more traffic and smog.

Cuernavaca is worth visiting though, if only to see the famed Palacio de Cortés (now the Museo Cuauhnáhuac), a couple of the luxurious Spanish-style hotels and restaurants and even the zócalo's two crowded plazas, one of which is called Plaza de la Constitución.

Orientation

Cuernavaca is 84 km south of Mexico City, only 1½ hours' driving time if you take Highway 95D (*cuota* or toll road). As you approach Cuernavaca from the steep descent of 95D, if you look carefully you will notice that much of the city slopes down between *barrancas* or cliffs that run north to south almost the entire length of the city. After the zócalo the city seems to flatten out, though it is still flanked by the cliffs.

The zócalo is the best place to start a tour of Cuernavaca. If you're driving into town from Mexico City, take the Cuernavaca or Highway 95 exit. Highway 95 enters the city from the north, becomes Boulevard Emiliano Zapata and then one-way (southbound) Boulevard José María Morelos y Pavón. Calles Rayón and Hidalgo intersect Morelos; both are one-way streets with the latter running east 325 metres to the zócalo. Matamoros, which forks off to the left after Ricardo Linares, runs south-east ¾ km straight to the zócalo.

If you arrive by bus, directions to the zócalo depend on which bus line you took because each line has its own terminal. See the Getting There & Away section for more information.

Information

Tourist Office The tourist office is run by the state of Morelos at Morelos Sur 802 (tel 14-39-27, 14-39-20), south of the Jardín Borda. The staff are helpful and willing to provide heaps of information about hotels, language schools, archaeological sites and cultural activities in Morelos. Some English is spoken. Hours are 9 am to 8 pm Monday to Friday, 9 am to 6 pm on Saturday, and 9 am to 3 pm on Sunday.

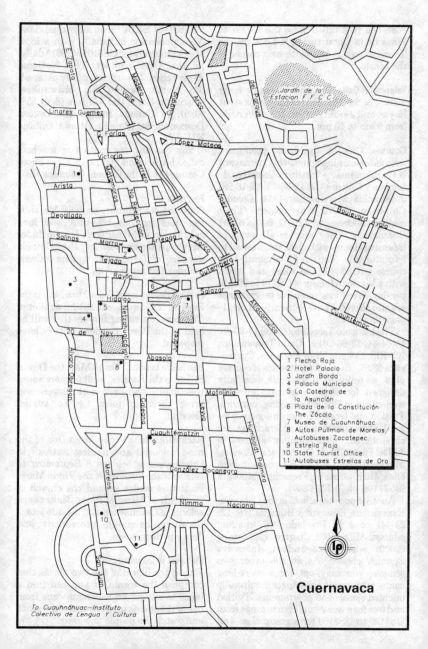

1 Flecha Roja
2 Hotel Palacio
3 Jardín Borda
4 Palacio Municipal
5 La Catedral de la Asunción
6 Plaza de la Constitución The Zócalo
7 Museo de Cuauhnáhuac
8 Autos Pullman de Morelos/ Autobuses Zacatepec
9 Estrella Roja
10 State Tourist Office
11 Autobuses Estrellas de Oro

To Cuauhnáhuac—Instituto Colectivo de Lengua Y Cultura

Cuernavaca

Post The post office is on the zócalo at Plaza de la Constitución 3. Look for the 'Correos' sign at the south-east corner of the zócalo.

Telephone Calls There's a caseta de larga distancia in the Farmacia Central at Rayón and Jardín Juárez. It's open daily from 9 am to 10 pm.

Courses One of the most prominent schools for learning Spanish in Cuernavaca is Cuauhnáhuac – Instituto Colectivo de Lengua y Cultura (tel 12-36-73, 12-16-98) at Avenida Morelos Sur 1414, Colonia Chipitlán, 62070 Cuernavaca. Their mailing address is APDO 5-26, 62501 Cuernavaca. They provide all levels of intensive classes with class size limited to four students. Tuition for a month-long course is US$440, and room and board with a Mexican family is US$10 to US$15 per day. Week-long intensive programmes are also offered. Write to them for their 21-page brochure.

The Instituto Teopanzolco (tel 17-30-40, 13-64-64, 13-66-20) at Calle Teopanzolco 102-BIS, Colonia Vista Hermosa, Cuernavaca 62290 offers a similar series of courses plus a unique programme specially designed for deaf or hearing-impaired students from English-speaking countries. Tuition and fees for a month-long course are US$450; week-long programmes are also offered. Their mailing address is APDO Postal 103-A, Cuernavaca, Morelos, Mexico 62280. In the USA contact John Diaz, 410 Escobar St, Fremont, California 94539 (tel (408) 732-0807).

Another popular school is the Concepto Experiencia Educativa Bilingue (tel 12-23-44) at J H Preciado 306 (mailing address: APDO 1801, Cuernavaca, Morelos 62000) with three-student, intensive Spanish classes. As at the other two schools, you may opt for a week-long course or more and participate in culturally oriented classes and programmes. Tuition and fees for a week-long course range from US$120 to US$160 for a group class and US$190 to US$270 for an individual class. Accommodation is usually with a local Mexican family for US$10 to US$15 daily. In the USA contact The National Registration Center for Study Abroad, 823 North Second St, Milwaukee, Wisconsin 53203 (tel toll free (800) 558-9988). In Canada contact Ms Doreen Desmarais, 341 Main St, Ottawa, Ontario K1V 8Y6.

You can also try contacting a school called Experiencia (tel 12-70-71) at Paseo Cozumel 16 in the Colonia Quintana Roo.

Festivals

Carnival Late February or early March is the time for this colourful week-long celebration of Mardi Gras that includes street performances by the Chinelo dancers of Tepoztlán, among others, parades and art exhibits.

Festival de las Flores From 2 to 8 May is the Festival of Flowers, a beautiful exhibit of Cuernavaca's spring flowers that will be held in the Borda Gardens, if they have reopened.

San Isidro Labrador On 15 May, the Day of St Isidro the Farmer, local farmers adorn their mules and oxen with flowers and bring them to town for an annual blessing.

Nacimiento de la Virgen María One of the most colourful and noisiest festivals in Cuernavaca is held on 8 September to celebrate the birthday of the Virgin Mary. Festivities centre around the church of Our Lady of Miracles in the Tlaltenango colonia of Cuernavaca and include lots of fireworks, candle-lit processions and dance performances.

Plaza de la Constitución

This is the bigger of the two plazas that comprise the zócalo. If you can find a place to sit, get an ice-cream cone from one of the stands in the centre of the plaza and watch the people flow past.

Palacio de Cortés – Museo de Cuauhnáhuac

The imposing medieval-style fortress stands at the eastern end of Plaza de la Constitución. Construction of this two-storey stone palace-fortress began between 1522 and 1532 over the ruins of a small pyramid. During the 1530s when Charles V finally bestowed a title of nobility upon him, Cortés resided here as Marquis del Valle de Oaxaca; he departed for Spain in 1540. The palace remained with Cortés' family for most of the next century, but by the 18th century it was being used as a prison and, during the days of Porfirio Díaz in the late 19th century, served as a government 'palace'.

Today, the palace serves as the Museum of Cuauhnáhuac with two floors of exhibits highlighting the history and cultures of Mexico. On the 1st floor, exhibits focus on several cultures prominent in pre-Hispanic times, including the Aztec, Mayan, Olmec, Xochilimilca, Chalcha and Tlahuica. On the 2nd floor, exhibits boldly and sporadically cover the range of events from the Spanish conquest to today. An attempt is made to show how

Olmec jadeite mask

the Tlahuica Indians have changed through the years, with the reproduction of a 'typical' Tlahuica dirt-floor hut furnished, of course, with a big TV set.

On the balcony of the 2nd floor is a fascinating Diego Rivera mural, one of the museum's most outstanding features. Commissioned by the US Ambassador to Mexico in the mid-1920s, Dwight Morrow, as a gift to the people of Cuernavaca, the mural stands as yet another stunning Rivera monument to Mexico's history from the conquest to the 1910 Revolution. The mural emphasises the horrors of oppression – Spaniards over Aztecs, Spaniards over Mexicans, Mexicans over Indians and the wealthy over the poor.

The museum is open 9.30 am to 7 pm, Tuesday to Sunday (closed Monday).

Palacio Municipal

For more wall paintings showing Mexico's history, visit the Palacio Municipal, also known as the Honourable Ayuntamiento de Cuernavaca or Honourable Town Council of Cuernavaca. It's near the Jardín Borda at the corner of Morelos and Callejón Borda. The paintings are displayed on the walls of the 1st and 2nd floors around a lovely inner courtyard. Some show life in pre-Hispanic Cuernavaca: Aztec tax collectors harass Tlahuican Indians and other Indians harvest cotton or weave cloth. The paintings can be seen for free from 9 am to 2 pm and 4 to 6 pm, Monday to Friday.

Jardín Borda

The gardens behind the Palacio Municipal and parallel to Morelos have not been well maintained and were supposed to be closed for renovation. If they have reopened, stop by to get some idea of what was once a favourite retreat for Mexico's aristocrats.

The gardens were laid out with pools and fountains by Manuel de la Borda in 1783 as an addition to the neighbouring stately residence built by his relative José de la Borda, the Taxco silver magnate.

Emperor Maximilian and Empress Carlota were big fans of the garden, but after they left not much was done to maintain them. When it's open, hours are daily 9 am to 6 pm.

La Catedral de la Asunción

The 16th-century cathedral stands at the corner of Hidalgo and Morelos across from the Palacio Municipal. Most of the church was finished by 1552, making it one of the oldest in Mexico. Over the main entrance is a skull and crossbones, symbol of the Franciscan order that once maintained a monastery here. Inside is a hodge-podge of architectural and artistic styles. Most of the building was constructed like a plain, sturdy fortress with high walls and towers, but the wall reliefs are good examples of churrigueresque style. Early 17th-century Japanese frescoes were accidentally discovered more than two decades ago, when the nave was renovated so that the priest could face the congregation when leading a sermon. The frescoes show the persecution of Christian missionaries in Sokori, Japan and are believed to have been painted by a Japanese convert to Christianity who settled in Cuernavaca. This church was renowned as a Franciscan centre for missionary activities that extended throughout the Orient.

La Casa del Olvido

The 'House of Forgetfulness' was one of Maximilian's favourite hideouts where he and 'La Bonita India' would meet. Maximilian 'forgot' to include a room for his wife.

Today, the house is the Museo de la Herbolaria, a museum of traditional herbal medicine. Many of the herbal remedies on display are still used and can be bought at any open-air market. According to the exhibits, the curative powers of the herbs cover everything from nervous disorders to birth pains. The museum is on Calle Galeana in the

Colonia Acapantzingo, 1½ km south-east of the zócalo.

Pyramid of Teopanzolco

This archaeological site which doubles as a park is at the end of Calle Río Balsas east of the railway station. The pyramid is actually two pyramids, one inside the other, once a typical Tlahuica Indian method of expanding pyramids. A wide stairway leads up the side of the more recent pyramid to an upper platform and the pit-like entrance to the descending stairway of the first pyramid. The first pyramid dates back more than 800 years and the outside pyramid was left unfinished when Cortés arrived in the 1520s. The grassy area is a good place for a picnic.

Places to Stay

Cuernavaca offers a good selection of hotels for all budgets, but don't bother trying to find a hotel room on the weekends or holidays. Don't despair, though, because you may find a bed and possibly a meal at the home of a Cuernavacan family. Many local families are accustomed to hosting (for a price) students from the city's language schools, and a few have opened their homes to travellers. Check with the tourist office for the latest list of families. The daily room and board rate averages US$10 to US$15.

Places to Stay – bottom end

The *Hotel Iberia* (tel 12-60-40) at Rayón 9, just north of the Jardín Juárez, has long been a favourite of travellers and foreign students. Rooms are clean, quiet and set around a courtyard full of tropical vegetation. Singles/doubles are US$5.50/7.50.

The *Hotel Palacio* (tel 12-05-53) at Morrow 204, next to the Bancomer offices, is another favourite, with clean, basic rooms that include great bathtubs and brass bedposts. Singles/doubles are US$6.50/7.50.

For an eclectic tropical atmosphere, try

the *Hostería/Hotel Peñalba* (tel 12-41-66) at Matamoros 22B, three blocks north of the zócalo. Rooms are clean and simple, quite adequate for a night or two, but you may want to stay longer just to savour the tropical jungle-like courtyard. A monkey swings from vine to vine while exotic birds squabble and a cat that's for sale meows from a cage near the reception desk. Singles/doubles are US$5/6.50; reservations are usually necessary for weekends.

A fair traveller's hang-out is the renovated *Hotel Colonial* (tel 12-00-99) at Aragón y León 104, three blocks north of the zócalo, between Morelos and Matamoros. Rooms are arranged around a pleasant courtyard, a great place to sit and chat. Singles/doubles are a bargain at US$4/5.

Places to Stay - top end

Hostería del Sol (tel 12-12-27, 12-44-04) is conveniently located near the zócalo and the Palacio de Cortés at Las Casas 107. From the outside it's a nondescript place with high white-washed walls, but inside it's a quiet, romantic gem with a small garden, pool and fountains. This colonial hide-away just around the corner from the chaos of the zócalo is perfect for a vacation. A spacious double is US$35.

The luxurious colonial-style *Posada Las Mañanitas* (tel 14-14-66) is at Ricardo Liñares 107. The rooms are next to an equally impressive restaurant and set amidst beautiful tropical gardens. Before the sun sets, peacocks wander around the grounds and between the tables before being herded into nearby cages. Although the room rates (US$55 to US$90) and meal prices make this a splurge for budget travellers, it is worth visiting just to view it.

Places to Eat

Las Mañanitas restaurant (tel 12-46-46), attached to the Posada Las Mañanitas, is one of Mexico's best and most famous restaurants. The menu features exotic food from around the world with an average meal costing US$8 to US$15, expensive by Mexican standards.

For simpler, more inexpensive fare try the restaurants and sidewalk cafés around the zócalo. The *Café Los Arcos* next to the post office on the zócalo is a popular hang-out for foreign students from the language schools. The comida corrida changes almost daily and is a good deal at US$3. A la carte options include steak, sandwiches and fried or grilled fish from US$0.75 to US$5.

On the other side of the zócalo at or near the corner of Rayón and Galeana are *El Portal* and *La Cueva*, both relatively inexpensive but often crowded restaurants/sidewalk cafés. Their four-course comidas are similar in price and content – US$2 for soup, a rice dish, beef or fish, dessert and coffee. Unfortunately, these restaurants are favourite targets for persistent hawkers trying to sell drawings, irritating little squeaky toys, hand-woven table cloths and a bevy of other items.

Nearby at Guerrero 104 is the popular and noisy *Café Vienna* which reputedly serves some of the best pastries, ice cream and cappuccinos in Cuernavaca. They also serve decent American-style club sandwiches for US$2.

For a quieter and tastier meal, try *Restaurant Palacio* in the Hotel Palacio at Morrow 204. A four-course comida of basic Mexican fare is US$4 to US$5. A very filling Spanish paella (US$3) and mole poblano (US$2.75) are two of their specialities and definitely worth trying.

Getting There & Away

Bus Four bus companies serve Cuernavaca from Mexico City's Terminal Central de Autobuses del Sur (tel 689-05-00). All of these companies operate frequent service to Mexico City. Here's a run-down of the lines and their terminals:

Autos Pullman de Morelos/Autobuses Zacatepec (1st class) - Corner of Abasolo and Netzahualcóyotl; a block east of Morelos and a long block south of Hidalgo, just less than ½ km south-west of the zócalo.

Autobuses Estrellas de Oro (1st class) – Las Palmas Circle and Morelos on the west side (of the circle), 1½ km south of the zócalo.

Estrella Roja (1st & 2nd class) – South-east corner of Galeana and Cuauhtémotzin; Galeana runs into Hidalgo and the zócalo 450 metres to the north while Cuauhtémotzin intersects Morelos two blocks west of the terminal.

Flecha Roja (2nd class) – Morelos 504, Arista and Morelos, just south of the Morelos-Matamoros fork described earlier in this section.

Autos Pullman de Morelos (tel 672-38-90) serves Cuernavaca (US$1.25) with buses every 10 minutes from 5.30 am to 9 pm and every half-hour from 10 pm to midnight. The first Cuernavaca stop is La Selva, but don't get off until the last stop (Centro).

To Taxco, Acapulco, Zihuatenejo and Ixtapa you can use Estrella de Oro, Estrella Roja and Flecha Roja (Acapulco and Taxco only).

To Tepoztlán, Onitochili, buses depart from the Mercado on López Mateos several times daily. Ask the tourist office for the latest schedule.

Service is offered to Las Grutas de Cacahuamilpa by Autos Pullman de México (every two hours) and by Flecha Roja.

Estrella Roja buses run several times daily to Cuautla and Oaxaca.

Rail It's possible to arrive in Cuernavaca by train, but this is so inconvenient it's not worth describing. The station is in the north-east part of the city on the road to Cuautla, 1½ km south-east of the junction with Boulevard Emiliano Zapata (Highway 95) and a bit less than a km north-east of the zócalo.

Getting Around

Although most of central Cuernavaca is within walking distance, numerous local buses and taxis are available for outlying destinations. Avenida Morelos is the principal thoroughfare for the buses before they veer towards the colonia or neighbourhood marked on their signs. The average bus fare is 5c. Taxis are subsidised by the Cuernavaca city government and thus allow you to go almost anywhere in the city for US$0.45.

CUAUTLA

Population: 140,000

First impressions of Cuautla ('KWAHT-la') are deceiving because it doesn't appear to live up to its reputation as a favourite resort for Mexico City's rich and powerful. Grandiose monuments and remnants of Mexico's pre-Hispanic and Spanish past are nowhere visible, nor are there any signs of 19th and early 20th-century Mexico. But there are many signs of today – Coca Cola, billboards, department stores, loud choking buses. Beneath these blights are the attractions that have lured visitors here for centuries.

Hot mineral springs *(los balnearios)* and a pleasant year-round climate have been the area's main attractions at least as far back as Moctezuma; he was reputedly an avid fan of soaking in the sun and sulphur springs. It is not surprising that Cuautla has also catered to Mexico's beleaguered political bosses and earned itself a place in the history books.

In 1811 it was more than hot springs, though, that attracted José María Morelos y Pavón, one of Mexico's first leaders in the independence struggle. Morelos' military strategy was to use Cuautla as a base from which his forces would encircle the royalist forces in Mexico City. However, before he could launch an attack, the royalist army under General Calleja besieged the city from 19 February 1812 to 2 May 1812 (both dates are now street names in Cuautla). Morelos and his army were forced to evacuate when their food gave out and many people died of starvation. A house

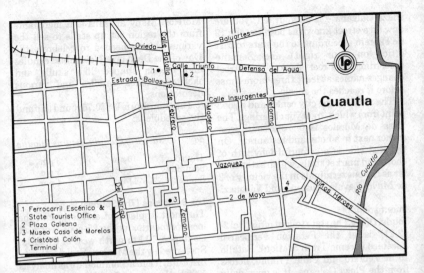

1 Ferrocarril Escénico &
  State Tourist Office
2 Plaza Galeana
3 Museo Casa de Morelos
4 Cristóbal Colón
  Terminal

in Cuautla's zócalo where Morelos lived during the siege is the only reminder of his presence.

A century later Cuautla was again significant in Mexico's history, this time as a key centre of support for the revolutionary army of Emiliano Zapata. In June 1916 the federal army of then-President Carranza attempted to wrest control of the state of Morelos from the Zapatistas, but their success was limited to the execution and deportation of thousands of peasants. Zapata remained in control and was able to rout the federalist forces from Cuautla.

An epidemic of Spanish influenza in 1918, however, killed thousands of his soldiers and opened the door to another federalist offensive which had the Zapatistas on the run. When a federalist colonel named Jesús Guajardo pretended to defect to Zapata's side, Zapata welcomed the additional support and agreed to have lunch with the colonel at a hacienda in Chinameca. He was shot dead as he rode through the gate. Today, every year on 10 April the agrarian reform minister lays a wreath at Zapata's statue

in Cuautla and makes a speech quoting his ideas about land reform.

Cuautla's altitude is 1291 metres. The average temperature is 22°C.

Orientation

Cuautla lies 42 km east of Cuernavaca and is the second largest city in the state of Morelos. The city extends from north to south approximately parallel to the Río de Cuautla, with the centre concentrated around the area where a tributary of the river branches off to the north-east and then north. Also parallel to the river are Cuautla's two principal avenues, commonly known as Reforma and Insurgentes, but known by an assortment of other names as they pass through the city. Both avenues merge in the northern part of the city just past the westbound *carretera federal* (federal highway) to Cuernavaca and south of the highway to Tepoztlán and Oaxtepec.

If you are heading south on Insurgentes and the Hotel de Cuautla is on your left, you are now actually on Batalla 19 de Febrero. If you continue south on this street and the city's first major plaza –

Plaza Galeana – is on your left, you are now on a street known as both Batalla 19 de Febrero (according to the state tourist office on your right) and Zemano (according to street signs). This street changes names at least three more times before it reaches the zócalo.

The zócalo is the city centre and a good point from which to get your bearings. The Casa de Morelos is on the south-west corner next to a hotel and restaurant. On the east side is a colourful labyrinth of shops and market stalls, which extends as far as the bus terminals in the vicinity of 2 de Mayo, Zavala, Costeño and Vázquez.

Information

Tourist Office The state tourist office (tel 2-52-21) is at the Estación Ferrocarril Escénico (Scenic Train Station), Batalla 19 de Febrero and Calle Triunfo, across from the Plaza Galeana. It is open daily from 9 am to 8 pm, but no English is spoken. Lots of brochures, information leaflets and a cryptic map are available.

Ferrocarril Escénico – Cuautla-Yecapixtla

The one-hour scenic train trip on an old steam locomotive from Cuautla to Yecapixtla is a pleasant way to visit the Mexican countryside. It departs three times weekly (see schedule below) from the old station at Batalla 19 de Febrero, one of Cuautla's principal thoroughfares.

Yecapixtla At the end of the line 17 km north-east of Cuautla, you arrive at Yecapixtla station 2½ km from the village. Take a taxi or bus from the station into the village to get a taste of what is probably a fairly typical Mexican village of 5000, but be back at the station in time for the return trip to Cuautla because there's no place to stay in Yecapixtla.

While in the village try one of its renowned specialities – *cecina* or beef jerky.

On 31 October this normally quiet farming village wakes up to celebrate the Feria del Gran Tianguis (Market Fair), one of the most spectacular markets in Morelos. Many artisans and merchants from the region set up stalls to sell the various objects needed to celebrate the Day of the Dead on 1 November: candies and breads shaped like skulls and skeletons, black candles and various decorations.

The train fare is US$0.75 round trip and the schedule is:

day	*departs Cuautla*	*returns Cuautla*
Thursday	10 am	3 pm
Saturday	1 pm	5 pm
Sunday	11 am	4 pm

Los Balnearios (The Springs)

The most resplendent and largest of the local *balnearios* is the 25-pool centre at Oaxtepec, 10 km north-west of Cuautla. Sponsored by the Mexican Social Security Institute, it can accommodate as many as 5000 bathers and often does on weekends and holidays. In addition to the pools, there's an aerial tram that takes bathers from pool to pool, resort-style hotels and a restaurant.

This area first began attracting visitors when Moctezuma established his private botanical gardens here. By 1604 the Hospital of Santa Cruz was established to take advantage of the waters; it operated for two centuries. Ruins of the hospital can still be seen.

Buses to Oaxtepec (15c) depart from the Cristóbal Colón terminal on 2 de Mayo every half hour from 8 am to 6 pm.

Closer to Cuautla are the popular sulphur pools of the Agua Hedionda or 'Stinking Water' centre. It is a 15-minute bus ride north-east of Cuautla's zócalo in the Colonia Agua Hedionda. Catch the 'Agua Hedionda' bus from in front of the Palacio Municipal on the zócalo for 5c. Centre hours are 7 am to 7 pm daily.

There are several other balnearios in the area, including El Almeal, El Colibri, Las Tazas and Taza de Calderón. Ask at the tourist office for more information.

Museo Casa de Morelos

The 'House of Morelos Museum' on the zócalo was one of Morelos' favourite retreats while he led Mexico's struggle for independence. It is now a museum with a few exhibits chronicling the role of Cuautla in Mexico's history. Old, yellowed photographs, newspaper clippings and a few paintings grace the peeling walls while outside in the centre courtyard a variety of tropical plants are dying. Admission is free; hours are Wednesday to Sunday 10 am to 5 pm.

Places to Stay – bottom end

The *Hotel El Oasis* (tel 2-01-01) at Galeana 21 or Guerrero 21 has clean rooms with cheap tiled floors and private bathrooms. It's an adequate place to stay for a night, but, compared to what you get in Mexico City for the same price, it isn't a great bargain. Singles are US$6, doubles US$7.50, triples US$9.

The *Hotel Colón* (tel 2-29-90) is down the street from the Oasis and right on the zócalo. Most rooms have jugs of drinking water, fans, TVs and piped-in music; some also offer good views of the zócalo. At rates of US$3.25 single, US$4.25 double, US$5 triple, this is a good deal.

The *Hotel España* (tel 2-21-86) at 2 de Mayo 22 has 29 rooms and could be an excellent place to stay if all the bathrooms had toilet seats. Otherwise the rooms are fine – clean, basically comfortable with hand-painted, Spanish-style tiles gracing the walls. Rates range from US$3.75 to US$6 for singles, US$4.75 to US$7.25 for doubles, US$6.50 to US$8.75 for triples and US$7.50 for four people.

The *Hotel Jardines de Cuautla* (tel 2-00-88, 2-51-35) across from the Omnibus de Cristóbal Colón bus terminal at Calle 2 de Mayo 94 is a cool, stark hotel with cold tile floors and a few plants in each room. Small balconies in some rooms don't overlook much, but they help. Singles are US$4.50, doubles US$6, triples US$8.

Camping This is possible at the *Santa Ines*

Trailer Park (tel 2-94-32), supposedly at Felipe Neri 2 (at the corner of Nicolás Bravo) only one km west of the Alameda in central Cuautla. In fact none of the three streets named Nicolás Bravo are anywhere near the one named Felipe Neri! If you do find the park, according to its flyer it has hot water, bathrooms, electricity and a swimming pool. Their mailing address is APDO 308, Cuautla, Morelos.

Places to Stay – top end

The *Hotel de Cuautla* (tel 2-72-33, 2-72-55, 2-72-77) at Batalla 19 de Febrero 114 is a spotless, modern hotel that welcomes you with a bright orange stucco lobby and clean, comfortable rooms. At US$23 single, US$25 double, US$27 triple, with air-conditioning and access to a swimming pool, it still seemed overpriced.

Places to Eat

The restaurant at the *Hotel Colón* does a good comida corrida for US$1. The restaurant's gaudy little wrought-iron tables don't give the place much in the way of atmosphere, though the tacos al carbon and beef burritos are tasty.

Also on the zócalo is the *Cafetería El Cid*, which serves a comida corrida for US$1 and has outdoor tables perfect for people-watching.

Getting There & Away

All of the bus lines are in an area near the market stalls at 2 de Mayo and Zavala and at Vázquez, Costeño and Mongoy. Mexico-Zacatepec and Cristóbal Colón lines offer 2nd-class service to Mexico City (US$1) every half-hour from 5.30 to 12.30 am from the 2 de Mayo terminal.

Omnibus de Cristóbal Colón also has 1st-class buses to Taxco daily every 15 to 30 minutes from 4.30 am to 9.30 pm. Second-class buses depart for Oaxaca at 7 am, 12.30 pm, 2 pm and 8 pm.

Autotransportes Estrella de Roja (tel 2-05-49, 2-08-55) is at the latter terminal and has 1st-class buses to Cuernavaca

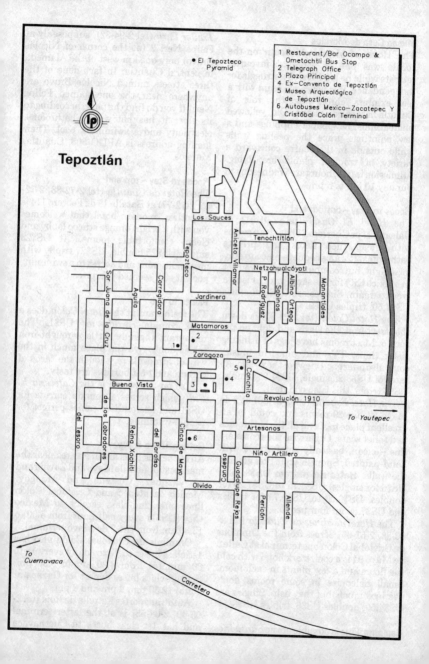

El Tepozteco
Pyramid

Tepoztlán

1 Restaurant/Bar Ocampo &
  Ometochtli Bus Stop
2 Telegraph Office
3 Plaza Principal
4 Ex-Convento de Tepoztlán
5 Museo Arqueológico
  de Tepoztlán
6 Autobuses Mexico-Zacatepec Y
  Cristóbal Colón Terminal

Los Sauces

Tenochtitlán

Aniceto Villamar

Netzahualcóyotl

Tepozteco

Corregidora

Aguila

Sor Juana de la Cruz

Jardinera

P Rodríguez

Sabinos

Albina Ortega

Manantiales

Matamoros

2

1

Zaragoza

5

La Conchita

Buena Vista

3

4

Revolución 1910

To Yautepec

de los Labradores

del Tesoro

Reina Xóchitl

del Paraíso

Cinco de Mayo

6

Artesanos

Niño Artillero

Osapusu

Guadalupe Rejas

Pericón

Allende

Olvido

To Cuernavaca

Carretera

every half-hour and Mexico City every 45 minutes.

Estrella de Roja buses depart from the same terminal and go to Cuernavaca (US$0.75) via Yautepec every day at 5, 5.30, 5.50 and 6.05 am and then approximately every 15 to 30 minutes until 8.30 pm; to Cuernavaca via La Pera at 6, 7, 9 and 11 am, and at 1 and 3 pm. Buses to Mexico City (US$1.50) via La Pera depart every half-hour from 4.30 am to 7.30 pm.

TEPOZTLÁN

Population: 24,109

Situated in a beautiful valley surrounded by high jagged cliffs 22½ km north-east of Cuernavaca, the town of Tepoztlán justifiably claims to be a magical place. A variety of sooth-sayers, astrologists and just ordinary folk frequent Tepoztlán in hopes of experiencing the legendary force that spawned the birth of Quetzalcóatl, the omnipotent serpent god of the Aztecs, more than 1200 years ago.

Tepoztlán is 1701 metres above sea level, with an average temperature of 19°C. The rainy season is May to September.

Orientation

The town is small enough for everything except the Pyramid of Tepozteco to be easily accessible by walking. As with many other Mexican cities, streets change names. For example, the carretera to Cuernavaca becomes Avenida Cinco de Mayo as it enters town and then Avenida Tepozteco as it passes the zócalo. At what precise point it changes names is unknown and can cause problems for a place like the Restaurant/Bar Ocampo, which uses both street names.

Information

The telegraph office is on Avenida Tepozteco across from the Restaurant/Bar Ocampo bus stop. The post office is on the Plaza Principal. The long-distance tele-phone office is also near the Plaza Principal at Avenida Revolución 24.

Festivals

Carnival Held in late February or early March, this features the colourful dances of the Huehuenches and Chinelos. The dancers' feather headdresses and beauti-fully embroidered costumes alone are worth seeing, apart from any performances.

Feria de Santa Catarina On 16 January various regional dances are performed during this festival, including the 'Apache' dance done to the strange, resonating music of instruments made from armadillo shells.

Fiesta del Brinco More dances are performed during the three-day Festival of the Hop which takes place during Holy Week. Decked out in bright costumes of feathers and silk, the dancers jump around like gymnasts trying to amuse the spectators.

Fiesta del Tepozteco On the night of 7 September this festival is celebrated on Tepozteco hill near the pyramid, with copious consumption of pulque in honour of the god Tepoztécatl.

Pyramid of Tepozteco

Tepoztécatl was the Aztec god of fertility, the harvest and pulque. The 10-metre-high Pyramid of Tepozteco was built three km above the valley to honour him and is accessible from a steep, narrow path that begins at the end of Avenida Tepozteco. The hike takes one hour and offers a spectacular view of Tepoztlán and the valley. Hours are 8 am to 4.30 pm. Admission is 10c.

Ex-Convento de Tepoztlán

The fortress-like ex-convent was built by Dominican priests between 1580 and 1588. On the arch of the church façade are Dominican seals interspersed with floral designs and various figures. The inside was being renovated at the time of writing, but was open to visitors. Look out of the window on the 2nd floor for a magnificent view of the Valley of Tepoztlán.

On a bulletin board just outside the church entrance is an interesting set of newspaper clippings and notices in Spanish about American intervention in Mexico and the impending effects of the new USA immigration law which forbids US employers from hiring undocumented workers or illegal aliens, a large number of whom are Mexican.

The church can be visited Tuesday to Sunday from 9 am to 5 pm.

Museo Arqueológico

The Archaeological Museum at Calle Pablo González 2 (behind the church) was being renovated at the time of writing. When it reopens, you should be able to see the collection of old Aztec, Olmec, Zapotecan and Mayan clay figures and pieces of pottery donated by Tepoztlán's benefactor Carlos Pellicer. Its hours were 10 am to 2 pm and 4 to 6 pm every day except Monday.

Places to Stay - bottom end

La Casa de Huéspedes 'Las Cabañas' at Avenida Cinco de Mayo 54 and El Mesón del Indio at Avenida Revolución 40 are the least expensive places in town. La Casa has 20 rooms, each with a bathroom and hot water; a double is US$2. El Mesón has only eight rooms, each with a bathroom but no hot water.

Camping This is possible near town, at the Campamento Comohmila or YMCA (tel 5-01-10) at Km 3.5 just off the Carretera Tepoztlán-Yautepec and near a recreation area, swimming pool and playing fields. Reservations are supposedly required, probably for weekends and holidays. Another campground, Campamento Meztitla (tel 5-00-68), which belongs to the Boy Scouts, is near the beginning of the Tepoztlán-Yautepec highway (see map).

Places to Stay - top end

The Posada del Tepozteco (tel 5-03-23), Calle del Paraíso 3, is a modern hillside resort hotel built to resemble an old Spanish mission. It sports a swimming pool, a restaurant/bar and badminton court. Room rates average US$20 for a double, but were due to increase soon.

The Hotel Tepoztlán (tel 5-05-22, 5-05-23, 5-05-04), Calle de las Industrias 6, is a resort-style hotel with 36 rooms and two suites, jacuzzis, a heated swimming pool, restaurant and bar. Rooms are spotlessly clean with showers and tiled sinks; some offer spectacular views of the surrounding hills and cliffs. Rates are US$16/18 single/double and US$38 to US$55 for suites.

Places to Eat

Inexpensive restaurants and food stalls are concentrated around the Plaza Principal. El Pan Nuestro on the Plaza Principal is a good place for yoghurt-based Mexican dishes and people-watching from miniature tables and stools fit for midgets. Hours are 10.30 am to 8.30 pm.

Restaurant Diana, Plaza Principal 7, is a fairly clean establishment on the Plaza Principal tucked back next to the food stalls of the market. They serve a variety of basic dishes, including carne asada (roast meat, usually beef, US$2.25), fried chicken (US$2.15) and something called a botana especial. Try their sangria (US$0.80).

The Restaurant/Bar Ocampo, Cinco de Mayo 6, has been recommended by travellers as a good place for a comida corrida.

Getting There & Away

The Ometochtli bus line has buses to and from Cuernavaca (2nd class, 25c, 45 minutes either direction) every 20 minutes from 6 am to 9 pm. Catch the bus in front of the Restaurant/Bar Ocampo on Cinco de Mayo/Avenida Tepozteco, slightly north-west of the Plaza Principal.

Autobuses Mexico-Zacatepec y Cristóbal

Colón, a bus line with a terminal on Avenida Cinco de Mayo south of the Plaza Principal, has several 2nd-class buses running daily between Tepoztlán, Mexico City and Yautepec. Buses to Mexico City (US$1.15) depart at 5.15, 6.30, 7 and 7.30 am, and every hour after that until 5.30 pm, with the last bus at 6.45 pm. Buses to Yautepec (US$0.75) depart at 7.55 am and every hour until 9.55 pm.

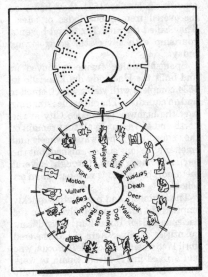

Stone calendar

XOCHICALCO

Atop a desolate plateau 15 km south-west of Cuernavaca is the ancient ceremonial centre of Xochicalco ('ko-CHEE-cal-koh'), one of the most important archaeological sites in central Mexico. In the Indian language Nahuatl, Xochicalco means 'Place of Flowers', which it probably was for Toltecs in the 7th century, but today it is a collection of white stone ruins representing the various cultures – Toltec, Olmec, Mayan, Zapotec, Mixtec and Aztec – that once ruled empires or parts of empires from here.

The most famous monument here is the Pyramid of the Plumed Serpent with its well-preserved bas-reliefs from which archaeologists have surmised that astronomer-priests met here at the beginning and end of a 52-year cycle of the Aztec calendar to 'correct' the calendar.

Unless you have your own transport, getting to Xochicalco can be difficult because only two Flecha Roja buses make the daily trip from Cuernavaca, and their schedules are unpredictable. The option is to take a bus to Miacatlán from the Autos Pullman de Morelos terminal in Cuernavaca and, after an hour, get off at the Crucero de Xochicalco. From there you have a one-hour, four-km hike uphill to the principal site.

The site is open Tuesday to Sunday from 9 am to 6 pm and admission is 20c.

Guerrero – Taxco to the Coast

The state of Guerrero, named after Independence War hero General Vicente Guerrero, is a mountainous and hilly area of 64,281 square km. Four mountain ranges dominate the state, the most important being the Sierra Madre del Sur, which parallels the Pacific Ocean from the Río Balsas border with Michoacán to the border with Oaxaca. The states of Puebla, Morelos and Mexico border Guerrero on its north/north-eastern side.

Guerrero's principal thoroughfare – Highway 95 – begins in Mexico City and ends in Acapulco. On the way it runs through Morelos, Taxco, Iguala and Chilpancingo before cutting through the Sierra Madre del Sur. On the western side of the Sierra Madre, be prepared for the highway's descent from the relatively cool, dry air of the mountains and central Mexican plain to the hot, humid climate of the coast.

Although much of the state's terrain is mountainous and lacks roads, the towns that are accessible are worth visiting. Taxco, a city renowned for its silver work and abundance of red-tiled colonial architecture, is often touted as one of Mexico's most beautiful cities. Tranquil Iguala is the historic site of Mexico's first proclamation of independence. Chilpancingo is worth a stop if only to see a fairly typical state capital and university city. Acapulco was one of Mexico's first ports and beach resorts and continues to be one of its biggest and most popular shipping centres and vacation destinations.

Acapulco sits on a narrow plain of tropical savanna and jungle that extends along most of the Guerrero coast and includes the tropical town of Zihuatenejo ('zee-whah-ten-NAY-ho') and its nearby mega-resort complex of Ixtapa ('ees-STOP-pah') – two more destinations worth visiting.

TAXCO
Population: 30,000

Before the Spanish arrived in 1529, Taxco was called Tetelcingo or 'Small Hill' by the Aztecs, who had dominated the region since 1440. The Spanish came searching for tin, which they found in small quantities, but by 1534 they had also discovered tremendous lodes of silver. They called the area Taxco and began a courtship with silver still going strong today.

Spanish mining engineers moved in and built the Hacienda del Chorrillo in 1534 complete with water wheel, smelter and an aqueduct. The old arches standing over the highway to Mexico City at the north end of Taxco are all that remain of the aqueduct. The water wheel and smelter have long since vanished, but the hacienda has gone through several metamorphoses and is now part of an art school.

The engineers and prospectors quickly emptied the first veins of silver from the hacienda and left Taxco. Further significant quantities of silver were not discovered until 1743 when Don José de la Borda, who had arrived in 1716 from Spain to work with his miner brother, accidentally uncovered one of the area's richest veins. According to a frequently related Taxco legend, Borda was walking with his horse where the Cathedral of Santa Prisca now stands when his horse stumbled, dislodged a stone and exposed the silver.

Borda went on to make a fortune and build mansions, gardens (such as the Jardín de Borda in Cuernavaca) and the Cathedral of Santa Prisca. His new-found wealth attracted many prospectors and the veins were again emptied.

With most of the silver gone, Taxco once more became a quiet town with a dwindling population and economy. In 1932 a North American professor named

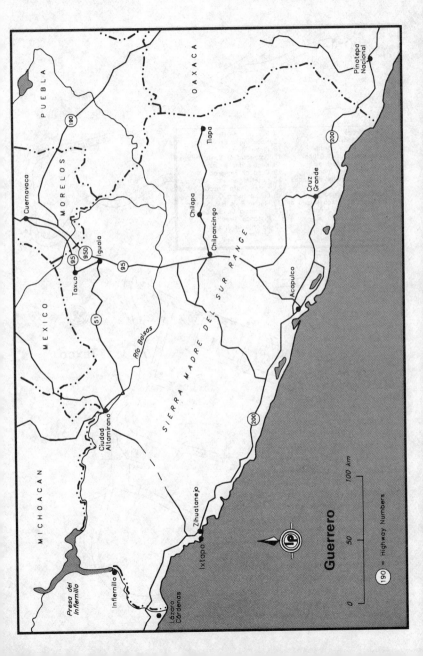

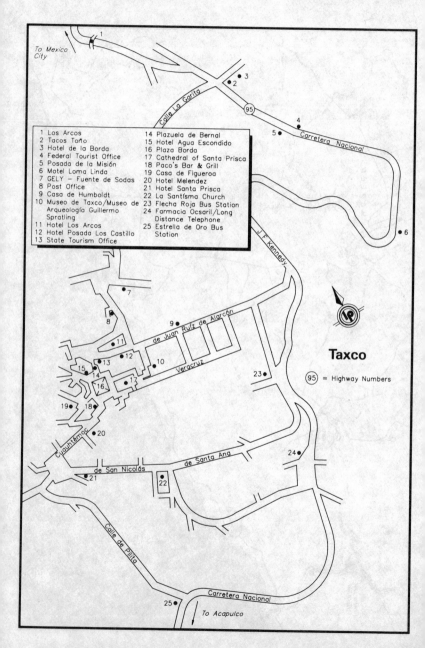

1 Los Arcos
2 Tacos Toño
3 Hotel de la Borda
4 Federal Tourist Office
5 Posada de la Misión
6 Motel Loma Linda
7 GELY – Fuente de Sodas
8 Post Office
9 Casa de Humboldt
10 Museo de Taxco/Museo de Arqueología Guillermo Spratling
11 Hotel Los Arcos
12 Hotel Posada Los Castillo
13 State Tourism Office
14 Plazuela de Bernal
15 Hotel Agua Escondido
16 Plaza Borda
17 Cathedral of Santa Prisca
18 Paco's Bar & Grill
19 Casa de Figueroa
20 Hotel Melendez
21 Hotel Santa Prisca
22 La Santísma Church
23 Flecha Roja Bus Station
24 Farmacia Ocsaril/Long Distance Telephone
25 Estrella de Oro Bus Station

Taxco

95 = Highway Numbers

William Spratling arrived and, at the suggestion of then-US Ambassador Dwight Morrow, set up a small silver workshop as a way to rejuvenate the town. The workshop became a factory and Spratling's apprentices began establishing their own shops. Today there are more than 300 silver shops in Taxco selling some of the finest silverwork in the world.

Taxco is also an attraction in itself. With its labyrinth of winding, cobblestone streets and passageways and a jumble of red-tiled buildings, the town conjures up romantic images of old Spain. Fortunately, local laws preserve Taxco's colonial-style architecture and heritage. The federal government has gone one step further and declared the entire city a national monument.

Orientation

At an altitude of 1660 metres, Taxco is a hilly town of steep, narrow streets and hidden plazas, located 185 km south-west of Mexico City along Highway 95. You may feel like a mouse in a maze when you try to find your way to the city centre, Plaza Borda.

As Highway 95 enters the city and winds through the hills around the perimeter of central Taxco, it becomes Avenida John F Kennedy. If you follow Avenida Kennedy from the north, Calle La Garita will be the first major street on your right, directly across from the Pemex station and the entrance to the Hotel Borda. La Garita winds through the city to the Plazuela de Bernal and the Plaza Borda or zócalo as it is also known. From the Plazuela de Bernal, the first major street on your left – Calle Juan Ruíz de Alarcón – leads down to Avenida Kennedy.

The next major street off Kennedy is Calle Santa Ana, which changes names to Calle San Nicolás as it climbs back towards central Taxco to end west of the zócalo at the Plazuela de San Juan. Farther along Kennedy, Calle de San Miguel also climbs back towards central Taxco to intersect with Calle Santa Ana/San Nicolás at La Santisima Church. The last major street along Kennedy that leads to Plazuela de San Juan is Calle Pilita, across from the Estrella de Oro bus station.

Information

Tourist Office The federal tourism office (tel 2-15-25), Avenida John F Kennedy 28-9, is staffed by a couple of sleepy bureaucrats who will, if nudged awake, provide some information about Taxco and the state of Guerrero.

The English-speaking staff at the Secretaria de Fomento Turístico del Gobierno del Guerrero – the state tourism office (tel 2-17-05), Plazuela de Bernal 2 – are much more helpful and eager to answer any questions about Taxco, particularly its hotels and restaurants. Hours are Monday to Friday 9 am to 3 pm and 5 to 7 pm, Saturday 9 am to 3 pm.

Post The post office is near the state tourism office at Juárez 6. Hours are Monday to Friday 8 am to 7 pm and Saturday 9 am to 1 pm.

Telephone Calls Casetas de larga distancia can be found in the Farmacia Oscaril on Avenida Kennedy not far from the Flecha Roja bus terminal (hours are 9 am to 8 pm) and the Farmacia de Cristo near the Plazuela de San Juan.

Festivals

Try to time your visit to Taxco during one of its several annual festivals, but be sure to make hotel reservations in advance because finding a room can be difficult.

Santa Prisca & Blessing of the Animals On 18 January mass is celebrated in the cathedral while people parade by the entrance with their pets and farm animals in tow for an annual blessing. Just outside the cathedral's gates game booths are set up and groups of dancers entertain the many pilgrims who come for the mass.

En El Atrio de la Parroquia de Ojeda or 'In the Front Court of the Parish Church of Ojeda' on 24 February includes colourful performances by various music and dance groups.

Palm Sunday Jesus Christ's triumphal entrance into Jerusalem on a donkey is re-enacted in the streets of Taxco.

Maundy Thursday On the Thursday before Easter, the institution of the Eucharist is commemorated with beautiful present-ations and street processions of hooded penitents. During this week, known as Semana Santa or Holy Week, visitors from around the world pour into the city to see the processions.

San Miguel Day Regional dance groups perform in the front court of the beautiful 18th-century chapel of Archangel San Miguel on 29 September.

Feria de la Plata (Silver Fair) On 1 December Mexico's best silversmiths, most of whom are from Mexico City, display their most prized works.

Las Posadas From 16 to 24 December nightly candle-lit processions pass through the streets of Taxco singing from door-to-door. The children are usually dressed up to resemble various Biblical characters. At the end of the processions, decorated piñatas stuffed with candy are hung from ropes in the streets and blindfolded children take turns trying to break them open while adults control the ropes.

Cathedral of Santa Prisca
Located on Plaza Borda, this is Taxco's second most popular attraction after the silver shops. Constructed by Spanish architect Diego Durán from 1748 to 1758 for Don José de la Borda and his son Manuel, a priest, the rosy-stoned church is a masterpiece of baroque architecture. The façade is a churrigueresque riot of elaborately sculpted figures and decor-

ations. Over the doorway, the bas-relief depicts Christ's baptism. Inside, the intricately sculpted altarpieces covered with gold leaf are equally fine examples of churrigueresque art. On both sides of the main altar and in the sacristy are paintings by Miguel Cabrera, including one showing Mary pregnant.

Casa de Humboldt
On Calle Juan Ruíz de Alarcón just down the street from the tourist office stands one of the oldest colonial homes in Taxco. This was the house of German explorer and naturalist Baron von Friedrich Heinrich Alexander Humboldt in 1803. The ground floor of the house is now used as a store and museum for Mexican handicrafts.

Museo de Taxco
Also known as the Museo de Arqueología Guillermo Spratling, the three-storey archaeological and history museum is located at Porfirio Delgado 1 directly behind the Cathedral of Santa Prisca.

Polychrome vessel

Pre-Hispanic art exhibits on the two upper floors include jade statuettes, Olmec crafts and ceramics mostly from William Spratling's collection. On the ground floor, exhibits cover the history of Taxco as a city and mining centre and Spratling's role in introducing silver shops to Taxco.

Joyería Elemad los Ballesteros
This jewellery store at Calle Celos Muñoz 4 carries only the highest-quality silverwork and could easily be mistaken for a small museum. If you want to see or buy some of the best silverwork in Mexico, this is the place to come.

Casa de Figueroa
The 26-room house at Guadalupe 2 was built in 1767 by the Count de la Cardena and had only two windows and one door. It acquired the name 'House of Tears' because it was built by workers who had neglected to pay their taxes.

Upon the count's death the house was briefly owned by one of his descendants, who left an infamous mark on the place by murdering his daughter's suitor in the family room. Before the Figueroa family bought the house in 1848, it served as a monastery and reformatory and was the site of several more murders.

Over time, the Figueroas divided the house in half, added windows and dug a labyrinth of tunnels underneath. One half was the family chapel complete with a statue of an opal-teared Virgin and a wooden chair that includes a carving of severed hands set on a purple cushion. Just past the chair is a small room which the family used to hide the women from sex-crazed revolutionaries who harassed them in the early 1900s. The tunnels were used for the same purpose and are believed to have led all the way to the Cathedral of Santa Prisca and further up into the hills of Taxco.

In the 1950s and '60s Richard Nixon, Bette Davis and General MacArthur stayed at the house at different times.

Hours are 9 am to 1 pm and 3 to 7 pm Monday to Saturday; admission is 15c.

Cable Car
At the northern end of Taxco near Los Arcos is an unexpected sight – a million-dollar, Swiss cable-car system that ascends to the luxurious Monte Taxco resort. The panoramic view of Taxco from the cable car and the resort is fantastic and, on a clear day, probably worth the US$0.90 one-way or US$1.80 round-trip fare. The cable car runs daily from 8 am to 5 pm. You can use the resort's facilities for a price: swimming pool and steam baths US$1.75, horseback riding in the mountains US$1.90 per hour and tennis US$2 per hour.

Places to Stay - bottom end
The *Casa de Huéspedes Arellano* (also known as the Casa de Huéspedes El Humil) (tel 2-02-15) offers 10 simple rooms in a central location tucked away in a back street across from the Mercado de Artesanías. The old woman who owns the house is often grumpy in the mornings, but she does keep the place clean and homey. Singles are US$2.25, doubles US$3.25, triples US$4.25.

The *Hotel Casa Grande* (tel 2-01-23) is right on Plazuela de San Juan and has clean, basic rooms arranged around an inner courtyard. Rooftop rooms are nicest because they open outwards. There is a cafeteria and cinema. Singles are US$3.75, doubles US$6, triples US$7.50.

Camping The *Motel Loma Linda* (tel 2-02-06), Avenida John F Kennedy 52, allows two or three vehicles to park overnight in a small lot next to the motel. Sunset views of the city from the lot are spectacular. Hook-ups for electricity and water are available for two vehicles. The shower and bathroom are next to the motel's reception desk. They charge US$3 per night. Tent camping is not impossible here.

Places to Stay – middle

Hotel Los Arcos (tel 2-18-36), Juan Ruíz de Alarcón 2, is near the zócalo and has 26 beam-ceilinged rooms around a cool courtyard and small fountain. Some rooms have antique roll-top desks and crank-style telephones. Potted plants appear in every hall. There's a small pool, piano bar, restaurant and wonderful rooftop terrace. Room rates are reasonable for what you get: US$8.50 single, US$11 double, US$13 triple. Rates are 15% lower from January to April.

Hotel Posada Los Castillo (tel 2-13-96, 2-34-71), across from Hotel Los Arcos at Juan Ruíz de Alarcón 7, has very clean rooms with tiled bathrooms and carved furniture. If possible, get a room overlooking the eclectic collection of statues in the lobby. Singles are US$7, doubles US$9, triples US$11.50.

The *Hotel Agua Escondido* (tel 2-07-26) is located at Guillermo Spratling 4 near Plaza Borda. Although the fluorescent-lit lobby has stark white walls that give this place an almost institutional atmosphere, the rooms are comfortable and airy. Singles and doubles are US$12.75 and triples are US$16.

Posada de la Misión (tel 2-00-63) is a converted old Spanish mission with cedarwood singles, doubles and triples at very reasonable rates of US$16.50, US$23.50 and US$31. Located at Avenida John F Kennedy 32, it also has a swimming pool, bar, disco and restaurant with a Juan O'Gorman mural.

The *Hotel Melendez* (tel 2-00-06), Cuauhtémoc 6, is an older place with slightly musty rooms, but it's in a good location between the Plazuela de San Juan and the zócalo. Singles are US$10, doubles US$15.80, triples US$20 including breakfast.

The colonial-style *Hotel Santa Prisca* (tel 2-00-80, 2-09-80), Cena Obscuras 1 (roughly south of the Cathedral of Santa Prisca), is one of the best deals in Taxco. Most of the rooms have antique dressers, huge bathtubs and terraces. Breakfast is served in the hotel dining-room for US$1.25 to US$2.50. Singles are US$12 to US$18 and doubles US$16 to US$25.

The *Motel Loma Linda* (tel 2-02-06), Avenida John F Kennedy 52, is a decent American-style motel with colonial decor. Its chief attribute is its location on the ledge of a beautiful chasm, a view often painted by visiting Americans. Singles and doubles are US$12 to US$18 depending on the view.

Places to Stay – top end

Hotel de la Borda (tel 2-00-25), Cerra de Pedegral 2 across from the junction of Kennedy and Calle La Garita, is a modern mission-style hotel with large, anti-septically clean singles for US$30, doubles US$32, triples US$33, some overlooking the swimming pool. A few rooms offer panoramic views of the city. Rooms on the ground floor are still comfortable, but views of the city are blocked by trees.

The *Hotel Monte Taxco* (tel 2-13-00) is a mountain-top resort overlooking Taxco from the northern end of town near Los Arcos. The air-conditioned rooms and suites are comfortable and range in price from US$40 to US$50, including access to the hotel's facilities.

Places to Eat

Restaurant Santa Fe, around the corner from Plazuela de San Juan at Hidalgo 2, is a good place for an inexpensive breakfast (under US$1). They also serve various seafood dishes including a shrimp in garlic sauce platter that will titillate your taste buds. Their spicy chicken dishes (US$1.50) aren't as tasty, but still a good deal for the price.

The restaurant at the *Hotel de la Borda* serves a full lunch of roast beef or turkey, tomato salad, green beans and dessert for US$5. It's worth eating here just for the panoramic view of the city.

Tacos Toño, just to the right of the main gate of the Hotel de la Borda, is a hole-in-the-wall taco stand that serves a variety of simple and typical but delectably spiced taco dishes. While you munch on a *pollo desmenuzado* (shredded chicken) taco (US$0.40) or a *cecina* (dried beef) taco (US$0.50), several cages of parakeets in front of the stand serenade you.

Restaurant Olimpico, Benito Juárez 89 (2nd floor), caters mostly to Mexican families even though they do have a menu in English. Their US$2.50 super meal includes a fruit cocktail, soup or salad, a choice of fish, chicken, baked pork or grilled veal cutlets and dessert – adequate compensation for the crude plastic chairs and folding tables.

Cafetería El Puerte, Benito Juárez 42, serves an inexpensive comida corrida of chicken soup, beans and veal cutlet tacos for US$1.25.

'GELY' – Fuente de Sodas/Antojitos Mexicanos, across from the ex-convent, is the Mexican version of an American soda fountain/diner with some outdoor seating. Specialities include *chalupas* (tortilla in special chile sauce, three for US$0.75), *pozole grande* (hominy and pig's-head stew, US$0.90) and *mole con arroz* (turkey with chile-chocolate sauce and rice). Malts, milk shakes and freshly squeezed juices are available from the soda fountain counter.

Restaurant Los Reyes, across from the post office, serves a full meal almost exactly the same as Restaurant Olimpico's for US$2.60, but the wooden tables, woven chairs and 2nd-floor location overlooking a small plaza make it a more pleasant place to dine.

The Hotel Los Arcos restaurant serves baked iguana and a cow's-head filet (speciality of the house) for US$3.25 per dish.

Señor Costilla's is a restaurant overlooking the zócalo that resembles the several gringo-style Carlos 'n' Charlie's that have sprouted up throughout Mexico. Loud American rock & roll music shakes the many old photographs and pictures on the walls. A lot of gringos come here to party and, even though the prices are high by Mexican standards, chicken with the usual assortment of tortillas and beans for US$2.50 or grilled fish (whatever they can catch in nearby lakes and haul up to Taxco) for US$4 aren't unreasonable.

Paco's Bar & Grill at Plaza Borda 12 serves a large meal of typical Mexican food for US$4. If you order à la carte, you could easily spend much less than this for an equally filling meal.

Arnold's (tel 2-12-72) at Plazuela de los Gallos serves Mexican and Continental food for US$2.75 and less. The collection of ceremonial masks on the walls almost earns it museum status.

Restaurant La Hacienda, next to the Hotel Agua Escondido, serves a delicious special Mexican meal of *sabrosa cecina con chorizo* (tasty dried beef with sausage), rice, beans, guacamole, fried pork rinds and cheese for US$3.75.

La Parrilla Taxqueña at Calle Benito Juárez in front of the Pemex station specialises in tacos al pastor.

Pizza Bel near the Posada de la Misión and *Pizza Bora Bora* near the Casa de Figueroa serve a good selection of pizzas. Right on the zócalo is the popular *Pizza Dama* – 10 types of pizza costing US$1 for a small one, US$2 for a medium and US$3 for a large. Don't ask for *caliente* unless your stomach and taste buds have been well initiated to hot peppers.

Entertainment

For good mariachi music and a great view from a terrace overlooking the zócalo, try *Bar Bertha* across from the Cathedral of Santa Prisca. William Spratling supposedly invented the Margarita here. The bar is often full of tourists.

Bar Paco, Plaza Borda 12, also overlooks the zócalo and is often crowded with tourists, but it is a great people-watching vantage point. Mariachi bands stroll from table to table in the afternoons.

Things to Buy

Silver is why many people come to Taxco. There are more than 300 shops specialising in silverwork; the selection of jewellery is mind-boggling. If you are careful and willing to bargain a bit, good deals can be obtained. Don't buy anything that doesn't have the Mexican government '.925' stamp and spread-eagle hallmark (sometimes only one symbol appears), which certify that the piece is 92.5% pure sterling silver. Anything else might be silver-plated tin or copper or *alpaca*, a cheap silver-like metal. Anyone who is discovered selling forged 925 pieces is sent to prison. The shops in and around the Plaza Borda tend to have higher prices than shops farther from the centre.

Getting There & Away
Bus Estrella de Oro (1st class) buses arrive and depart from a small station at Avenida John F Kennedy and Calle de Pilita. Direct buses to Mexico City (US$1.85) depart at 7 am, 12 noon and 6 pm. Other buses to Mexico City depart at 9 am, 4 pm and 8 pm, but stop first in Cuernavaca (US$1). Buses to Acapulco (US$3.30) via Iguala (US$0.40) and Chilpancingo (US$1.70) depart at 9 am, 3.30 pm and 6 pm. The 6 pm bus goes past Acapulco all the way to Zihuatenejo (US$6.15).

Flecha Roja (2nd class) buses arrive at and depart from a station at Becerra and Tango 1, just off Avenida Kennedy. Buses to Mexico City (US$1.80) depart at 5 am, 8 am and then every two hours until 8 pm. To Cuernavaca (US$0.95) they run every hour from 5.40 am to 7.50 pm; to Acapulco (US$3.25) they run at 5.30, 8.20, 9.20 and 11.10 am, and at 1.10 and 6.10 pm. To Las Grutas de Cacahuamilpa (US$0.60) and Toluca (US$2.65) buses run at 1.10, 2.20, 3.10 and 6.10 pm.

Getting Around
Aside from walking, combis and taxis are the most popular ways of getting around the steep winding streets of Taxco. The 'Los Arcos' combi departs from the zócalo (in front of the silver store La Platería Conchita) and the Plazuela de San Juan along the Avenida Kennedy to Los Arcos

or The Arches at the northern end of town. The 'Zócalo' combi goes in the opposite direction along approximately the same route. The 'La Vista' combi goes from the zócalo into the hills above to the Church of Guadalupe. The 'Huejojutla' and 'La Azul' combis run from the zócalo past The Arches to various small farming communities north of Taxco. The combis are often full when they are about halfway to or from the zócalo and can't pick up additional passengers. An average combi ride costs less than US$0.50.

Taxis are plentiful and an average ride costs US$0.75.

AROUND TAXCO
Las Grutas de Cacahuamilpa
The underground caverns of Cacahuamilpa are a beautiful, natural wonder of stalactites, stalagmites and twisted rock formations 31 km north-east of Taxco. Although you are required to tour the 20 *salones* or halls of the caverns with a guide, the two-km tour is worthwhile.

Tours leave every hour on the hour from 10 am to 5 pm from the touristy visitor's centre. Admission is US$1. To get here from Taxco, take a Flecha Roja bus to Toluca, get off at the crossroads and walk down the street to your right. Autos Pullman de Morelos buses depart daily from Mexico City's Terminal del Sur every two hours from 6.50 am to 2.50 pm. Flecha Roja buses depart daily from Cuernavaca every 20 minutes from 6 am to 9.30 pm and Autos Pullman de Morelos buses every hour from 8.20 am to 4.20 pm.

IGUALA
Population: 45,000
Iguala is an industrial city on Highway 95 about 36 km south of Taxco and 180 km south of Mexico City. The main reasons to visit it are for its past rather than its present.

On 24 February 1821, at the height of Mexico's struggle for independence from Spain, Colonel Agustín Iturbide and rebel leader Vicente Guerrero met here and

Iturbide's regimental flag

issued the historic Plan de Iguala, an unusual declaration of independence. The declaration was the result of Iturbide's defection from the Spanish and offer to make peace with Guerrero.

Iturbide and Guerrero recognised the need for conservative support in Mexico for a new government to succeed. They also wanted to appease liberal factions clamouring for an independent republic. Consequently, rather than berate Spain in the declaration, they stated that Spain was the most magnanimous of nations but, after 300 years as a colony, it was time for Mexico to become a nation in its own right. After some badgering, Spain agreed to the plan, Mexico's first flag was sewn and raised in Iguala and a provisional junta was installed in Mexico City as a prelude to an independent Congress.

When the Congress was formed, it immediately began chopping away at Iturbide's military support. Iturbide sensed that his hope of being ruler of Mexico was slipping away, so he engineered a demonstration of soldiers who demanded that he declare himself emperor. The ruse succeeded and, on 19 May 1822, Congress was intimidated into proclaiming him constitutional emperor of Mexico. So much for Mexico's break with Spain's imperial style of governance.

Iguala's only interesting sight is the block-like Stalinistic Monument to the Flag & the Young Heroes of the Revolution on the zócalo. Built in 1942, it features the sculpted figures of Mexico's independence heroes: Morelos, Guerrero and Hidalgo.

Tamarind trees planted around the zócalo in 1832 in honour of the Plan de Iguala established tamarind as the city's fruit. Try an *agua de tamarind* at any of the juice stands near the zócalo.

Every year from 17 February to 28 February, Iguala hosts the Flag Fair, colourful celebrations with a parade, rodeos, horse-racing and exhibits from local farms and businesses.

The *Iguana Loca* (Crazy Iguana) restaurant, south-east of downtown next to the Club de Leones (Lion's Club) on Highway 95, has been recommended by travellers as the place to go if you have always wondered about the taste of iguana.

CHILPANCINGO

Population: 62,000

Chilpancingo (elevation 1360 metres), capital of Guerrero, is a university city and agricultural centre on Highway 95, 129 km north of Acapulco and 138 km south of Taxco. As with Iguala, the main reasons to visit are for its past rather than its present.

Murals in the former City Hall showing the 1813 Congress of Chilpancingo are the only remaining signs of the city's important place in Mexico's history. In the spring of 1813, rebel leader José María Morelos y Pavón encircled Mexico City with his guerrilla army and then called for a congress to meet in Chilpancingo. The Congress issued a Declaration of Independence and began to lay down the principles of a new constitution. Their achievements, however, were short-lived because Spanish troops broke the circle around Mexico City and recaptured most of Guerrero, including Chilpancingo. Morelos was tried for treason and shot by a firing squad.

Places to Stay & Eat

If you have to spend the night in Chilpancingo, the *Hotel Parador del Marqués* (tel 2-67-73) at Km 255 on

Highway 95 just south of town has 29 rooms and a trailer park with full hook-ups. Rooms are clean, carpeted and cosy with telephones and modern bathrooms. The ground-floor rooms are better because they were recently renovated. There's a restaurant just off the lobby. Room rates are US$11 and a space in the trailer park is US$2.25 including access to hotel showers. Tent camping is possible in the trailer park.

ACAPULCO

Population: 500,000

Acapulco is the grand-daddy of Mexican resort cities and ports. Its name is derived from the ancient Nahuatl Indian words meaning 'where the reeds stood' or 'place of giant reeds', which was, perhaps, all that was here when Spanish sailors first discovered the Bay of Acapulco in 1512. Spanish settlement of the area, however, was postponed until 1530 when a port and ship-building facilities were established because of the bay's substantial natural harbour. Acapulco became the only port in Mexico authorised to receive the *naos* or trading galleons from the Philippines and China.

By the 17th century, trade with the Orient was flourishing and Dutch and English pirate ships abounded in the Pacific Ocean and along the coastlines of Mexico and Baja California. To ward off the pirates, the San Diego Fort was built atop a low hill overlooking the bay. The *naos* continued trading until the early 19th century when they were replaced by bigger and better sailing ships.

With independence, Mexico severed most of its trade links with Spain, and Acapulco declined as a port city. It became relatively isolated from the rest of the world and Mexico until a paved road was built in 1927 linking it with Mexico City. As Mexico City grew larger and *chilangos* (inhabitants of Mexico City) began flocking to the Pacific coast for vacations, Acapulco became a booming resort by the 1950s.

Today, Acapulco is a city of dual personalities. Along the bay and for two blocks inland, it's a place of beaches, hotels, motels, discos, restaurants with trilingual menus (many French Canadians come here) and designer shopping plazas. Beyond this is a city of auto parts stores, a polluted river, tacky billboards, crowded apartment buildings and long lines of fuming buses that choke passers-by.

Throughout the year you can expect average daytime temperatures of 27 to 33°C and night-time temperatures of 21 to 27°C. Afternoon showers are common from June to September, but rare the rest of the year.

Orientation

Acapulco sits on a narrow, coastal plain along the 11-km shore of the Bay of Acapulco. Reached by Highway 200 from the east and west and by Highway 95 from the north, it is 400 km south of Mexico City and 239 km south-east of Ixtapa/Zihuatenejo.

At the western end of the city, the Peninsula de las Playas (Peninsula of Beaches) juts south from downtown Acapulco. From Playa Caleta on the southern edge of the peninsula, Avenida López Mateos climbs west and then north to Playa La Angosta and La Quebrada before curling east back towards downtown.

Playa Caleta also marks the beginning of Avenida Costera Miguel Alemán (known simply as 'La Costera'), Acapulco's principal avenue. Most of Acapulco's major hotels, restaurants, discos and other points of interest are along or just off La Costera. From Playa Caleta, La Costera cuts north/north-west across the peninsula and then follows the bay shore past Playa Larga, Playa Manzanillo, the zócalo, the port facilities, the Fort of San Diego, Río de Mendoza, Río Camarón, Playa Hornos, Papagayo Park, Playa Hornitos and Playa Condesa before running south out of the city.

After passing the naval base, La Costera

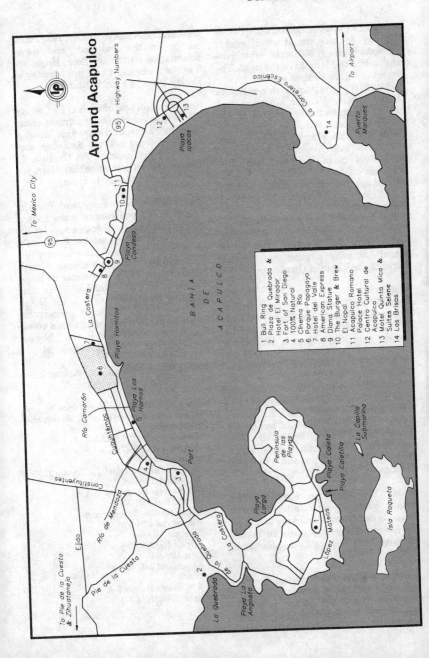

Around Acapulco

95 = Highway Numbers

To Pie de la Cuesta & Zihuatanejo

To Mexico City

To Airport

La Carretera Escénica

La Costera

BAHÍA DE ACAPULCO

Playa Icacos

Playa Condesa

Playa Hornitos

Playa Los Hornos

Río Camarón

Cuauhtémoc

Constituyentes

Río de Mendoza

Port

Elido

Pie de la Cuesta

La Quebrada

La Costera

Playa La Angosta

López Mateos

Playa Larga

Peninsula de las Playas

Playa Caleta

Playa Caletilla

La Capilla Submarina

Isla Roqueta

Puerto Marques

1 Bull Ring
2 Plaza de Quebrada &
   Hotel El Mirador
3 Fort of San Diego
4 100% Natural
5 Cinema Río
6 Parque Papagayo
7 Hotel del Valle
8 American Express
9 Diana Statue
10 The Burger & Brew
   El Nopal
11 Acapulco Romano
   Palace Hotel
12 Centro Cultural de
   Acapulco
13 Motel Quinta Mica &
   Suites Selene
14 Las Brisas

becomes La Carretera Escénica (the Scenic Highway) for nine km, at which point it intersects Highway 200 on the left and the road to Puerto Marqués on the right. The airport is 2½ km straight ahead.

Back in the city, from north/north-west of the zócalo, Vicente Guerrero and Escudero/Aquiles Serdán lead to Calzada Pie de la Cuesta, which, in turn, goes to Pie de la Cuesta, a lagoon and beach area 13 km to the west. Avenida Cuauhtémoc – Acapulco's main business district – branches off to the right from Aquiles Serdán and runs approximately parallel to La Costera until it turns inland north of Playa Condesa.

Just south of the Peninsula de las Playas is the popular Isla de la Roqueta and, nearby, the so-called 'underwater chapel', actually a submerged bronze statue of the Virgin of Guadalupe.

Information

Tourist Office There are two main tourist offices in Acapulco. The federal tourism office (Sectur), on the south side of La Costera near Playa Hornos, isn't worth visiting. The state tourism office (tel 4-10-14, 4-61-36) – La Secretaria de Turismo/Procuraduria del Turista – is more helpful, although the staff are occasionally lethargic. They are at La Costera 54 right across from the bright blue CICI watersports centre. The 'Ciné-Río' bus passes by here from the Ciné Río, which is just west of the Río Camaron on La Costera. Hours are 9 am to 2 pm and 4 to 8 pm, Monday to Saturday.

Money The American Express office usually offers a good rate of exchange. Casas de cambio and banks are plentiful, the latter usually only open for money exchange from 9 am to 1 pm, Monday to Friday.

American Express The American Express office (tel 4-15-20, 4-15-10), La Costera 709A near La Diana statue, is a full-service office – money matters including

travellers' cheques on the 1st floor, mail service on the 2nd floor and travel information on the 3rd floor. Hours are 9 am to 2 pm and 4 to 6 pm Monday to Friday, 9 am to 1 pm Saturday.

Post The main post office is at La Costera 125 next to Sanborn's department store. Hours for stamps are 8 am to 8 pm Monday to Friday, 9 am to 8 pm Saturday, and 9 am to 1 pm Sunday. For the lista de correos (general post office list), hours are 8 am to 8 pm Monday to Friday.

Telephone Calls There are several offices in Acapulco, but you cannot make collect calls from any of them because supposedly you can do that from most of Acapulco's pay phones. Your best option is to try the phones in the zócalo. For domestic long-distance calls, there are casetas de larga distancia at Calle Hidalgo 13 in the shopping passageway next to the Hotel Imperial, Calle D Morro around the corner from the American Express office (La Costera 709A), and in the lobby of Hotel Mary at Velásquez de León 24.

Airlines Seven international airlines have flights to and from Acapulco:

Aeroméxico (daily flights to and from Mexico City and various other cities in Mexico and North America)
    La Costera 286 (tel 5-23-85)
    Airport (tel 4-22-37)
American Airlines
    Condesa del Mar Hotel, La Costera 1260 (tel 4-12-44)
Braniff Airways de México, S A
    Airport (tel 4-29-30)
Canadian Airlines International
    Airport (tel 4-34-95)
Continental Airlines
    Airport (tel 4-33-08)
Eastern Airlines
    Airport (tel 4-63-63)
Mexicana
    V Nuñez de Balboa 3-A (tel 5-27-49, 5-14-14)

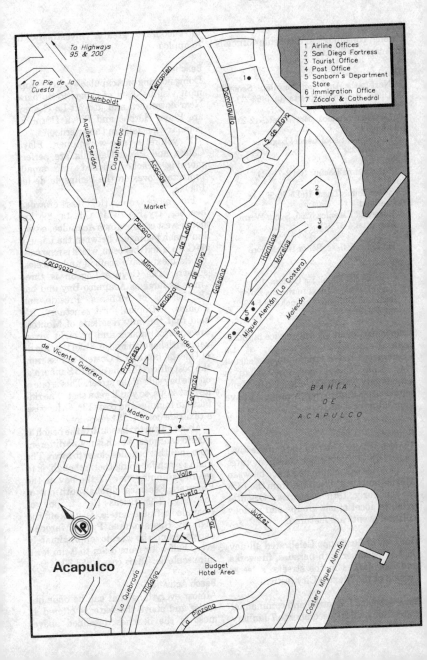

Acapulco

1 Airline Offices
2 San Diego Fortress
3 Tourist Office
4 Post Office
5 Sanborn's Department Store
6 Immigration Office
7 Zócalo & Cathedral

To Highways 95 & 200

To Pie de la Cuesta

Humboldt

Aquiles Serdán

Cuauhtémoc

Teocolpan

Domingullo

5 de Mayo

Acaxolos

Market

Parana

Mina

V de León

5 de Mayo

Zaragoza

Galeana

Mendoza

Hornitos

Morelos

Escudero

Miguel Alemán (La Costera)

de Vicente Guerrero

Progreso

Carranza

5 4
6

Malecón

Madero

7

BAHÍA DE ACAPULCO

Valle

Azuela

20

Juárez

La Quebrada

Hidalgo

La Pinzona

Budget Hotel Area

Costera Miguel Alemán

Consulates

Foreign consulates and consular officials in Acapulco include:

Canada
    Next to the American Consulate, Señora Diana Mclean de Huerta (tel 5-66-21)
France
    Lic Vidal Mendoza Bravo (tel 2-12-29)
Guatemala
    Laurel 150, Señor Leonel Lagunes (tel 5-73-23)
Italy
    Señor Jaime Bachur (tel 2-71-51)
Spain
    Señor Tomás Lagar (tel 5-70-99)
Switzerland
    Carretera Escénica 5255, Señor Werni Eisen (tel 4-87-94)
UK
    Hotel Las Brisas, Señor Derek Gore (tel 4-16-50)
USA
    Club del Sol Hotel, La Costera y Reyes Católicos (next to the Big Boy's Restaurant), Señor Urbanek (tel 5-66-21 ext 273, 3-19-69).

Laundromat There's a self-service laundromat, Commercial Mexicana, at La Costera and Todeo Arredondo, just east of the zócalo. Closer to Playa Caleta is Lavandería Caleta at Calle 2 No 8. Many hotels in Acapulco can arrange to have your laundry done.

Festivals

The Nao of China This arts and crafts festival from 7 to 30 November commemorates the galleons that conducted trade between Mexico and the Philippines from the 16th to the early 19th centuries. Oriental exhibits, local music groups and various cultural events are featured.

Our Lady of Guadalupe Celebrated all day on 12 December with parades, fireworks and folk dances in the streets; a lesser version of the Mexico City festival.

Expo-Acapulco Industrial and commercial exposition held 20 December to 7 January

to encourage greater investment in Acapulco.

Beaches

Doing nothing on Acapulco's beaches tops most visitors' lists of things to do here. Near downtown and just off La Costera are Playa Hornos and Playa Hornitos, popular especially in the afternoon.

If you're a sun-worshipper, Playa Caleta and Playa Caletilla are perfect morning beaches tucked into small, protected coves on the Peninsula de las Playas.

For more romantic, less crowded beaches, try Pie de la Cuesta, 8½ km north-west of downtown Acapulco, a two-km beach peninsula between the Laguna de Coyuca and the ocean, which is renowned for its inexpensive seafood and priceless sunsets. The Coyuca Lagoon is three times as large as Acapulco Bay and has the islands of Montosa, Presido and Pájaros, a tropical bird sanctuary. It's said that the only residents of Montosa are a mezcal-maker and his eight wives, each with her own house. Take the 'Pie de la Cuesta' bus on La Costera across from the post office (the one next to Sanborn's) on the bay side of the street. This is one of its first stops, so you'll get a seat. The ride takes 25 minutes and costs 13c. Otherwise, a taxi ride costs US$1 one way.

About 18 km to the south is the beach at Puerto Marqués, which is not so different from the other beaches closer to town. The main reason for going there, though, is to see the stunning view of the bay as the Carretera Escénica climbs south out of the city. Las Brisas Resort, one of Acapulco's finest hotels, is just off the highway. Buses marked 'Puerto Marqués' depart from the zócalo approximately every half-hour from 5 am to 9 pm for a minuscule 3c. Taxis cost US$3.30.

Beach Activities

Almost everything that can be done on, under and above the water is offered at most of the beaches described above.

Para-sailing – hanging from a parachute high above the water as a speedboat keeps you aloft – costs US$14 for a few minutes, but none of the hotels nor the tourist office recommend it as safe. Water-skiing costs US$10 and up per hour. Sailing is US$8.25 per hour. Small paddle boats can be rented for US$0.75 per hour. Water-skiing is particularly popular at Pie de la Cuesta, where there are several water-skiing clubs.

Scuba diving and snorkelling are possible off Isla Roqueta, just south of Playa Caleta and Playa Caletilla, where the highlight is a submerged bronze statue of the Virgin of Guadalupe dubbed La Capilla Submarina (the underwater chapel). If the water isn't murky you might also see some colourful fish and discarded beer bottles. 'The Brothers Arnold' – actually a father-son team – will gladly rent equipment and arrange a boat from their shop near the Fort of San Diego. Or you could take the Isla Roqueta boat (US$0.75) from Playa Caleta. The glass-bottom boat (US$1.60 round trip) will also show you the bronzed Guadalupe.

A variety of other boat tours and cruises are offered on the malecón across from the zócalo. Some are multi-level boats with blaring salsa music and open bars, while others are yachts offering quiet sunset cruises around the harbour. The *Yate Hawaiano* has daily departures at 11.30 am, 4.30 pm and 10.30 pm from a pier near the zócalo. The first two trips each last three hours and cost US$5.50, while the last one, which includes two variety shows and a beach party, is US$17.50 for three hours. If you are keen to take a cruise, every travel agent and almost every hotel can arrange one for you.

Tropical 'jungle' cruises in the Laguna de Coyuca at Pie de la Cuesta are also popular. Boats take you from a landing near Highway 200 across the lagoon to the place where Sylvester Stallone filmed *Rambo*. Prices for the boat trips are definitely subject to negotiation and are set by the boat rather than per person.

Divers of La Quebrada

Better than waddling your way around the bay is to watch the world-renowned cliff divers of La Quebrada jump with amazing finesse from heights of 25 to 45 metres into the shallow water beneath the Hotel El Mirador. Not surprisingly, the divers on the highest ledges pray at a small chapel before leaping over the edge. So did Elvis Presley in the film *Fun in Acapulco*. Views of the diving from the terraces of the Hotel El Mirador are good, but if you want decent photographs you should descend the stone stairway adjacent to the hotel before the crowds arrive. If you arrive more than 15 minutes in advance of the starting times – 1, 7.15, 8.15, 9.15 and 10 pm – you probably won't be asked for an admission fee at the hotel entrance (US$0.30 at 1 pm and US$2.65 later). To get here, either walk up Calle Quebrada from the zócalo (20 minutes) or take a taxi.

Bullfights

South-east of La Quebrada and north-west of Playas Caleta and Caletilla is Acapulco's Plaza de Toros or bull ring. Bullfights are held on Sundays at 5 pm; you can buy tickets at the ring starting at 4.30 pm. The 'Caleta' bus, which leaves from a point two blocks west of the zócalo, passes near the bull ring.

Parque Papagayo

Papagayo amusement park is across from Playas Hornos and Hornitos and is full of rides for both kids and adults. Take the *teleférico* or cable car from Playa Papagayo, between Playa Hornos and Playa Hornitos, to the top of a hill in the park for a spectacular view of the city (US$0.50). A chair lift (US$0.30) takes you to the top of another, smaller hill from which you can then take an alpine-style toboggan (US$0.30) to the bottom.

The gardens and lake around the amusement park are well-kept and offer a pleasant escape from city traffic and crowded beaches. Boats can be rented at the lake from 11 am to 3 pm and 4 to 7 pm daily. Park hours are 10 am to 6 pm daily; admission is free.

Bullfights and rodeos are hosted in the adjoining stadium according to an irregular schedule. Check with the park office at the entrance (tel 5-24-90) for the latest schedule. Hours are 6 am to 8 pm Monday to Friday, and 6 am to 9 pm Saturday and Sunday.

Fort of San Diego

Built in 1616 atop a hill just east of the zócalo, the Fort of San Diego was supposed to protect the *naos* or galleons that conducted trade between the Philippines and Mexico from marauding Dutch and English pirates. It must have done some good because this trade route lasted until the early 19th century. The fort had to be rebuilt after a 1776 earthquake, but apparently it was also strong enough to forestall independence leader Morelos' take-over of the city for four months. There's an interesting new museum in the fort. Hours are 10 am to 5 pm Monday to Wednesday and Friday to Sunday.

El Mercado de Curiosidades

Acapulco's main crafts market is east of the zócalo between Cuauhtémoc and Vicente de León and is a good place to get better deals on everything that you see in the hotel shops and on the beaches – sarapes, hammocks, silver jewellery, sandals, etc. Bargaining is definitely the rule here.

Centro Cultural de Acapulco

Museo Arqueológico/Instituto Guerrerense de la Cultura The Cultural Centre of Acapulco, the Archaeological Museum and the Cultural Institute of Guerrero are spread among several small buildings around a garden at La Costera 4834, very near to the CICI water-sports centre. Classes in dance, English-as-a-second language, guitar and music are often held here. The archaeological museum has exhibits of pre-Hispanic artefacts such as

funeral urns, exaggerated carvings of skulls, pottery and ancient Indian millstones and grinding implements. One of the buildings is also used as a gallery for temporary art exhibits. Hours are 9 am to 2 pm and 5 to 8 pm.

Places to Stay – bottom end

Most of Acapulco's budget hotels are concentrated around the cathedral and zócalo, but there are several closer to the beach just off La Costera.

The *Hotel Colimense* (tel 2-28-90), José María Iglesias 11, is near the zócalo and may be one of the best deals in Acapulco. A man and a monkey greet you at the reception desk. Rooms are clean, cool and arranged around a quiet courtyard. Rates are US\$2.75 per person for two and US\$3.15 for one.

The *Hotel California* (tel 2-28-93), La Paz 11, is clean and basic, a fair second choice to the Colimense. There are fans in every room. Rates are US\$3 for a double.

The *Hotel Sutter* (tel 2-02-09), Azueta 10 y La Paz, has rooms with bathrooms and fans, somewhat dirty, but tolerable for the price – singles/doubles US\$4.25/7.50. A group of Americans staying here seemed content with the place. It's advertised as *exclusivo* for families and travel agents, and you're urged to feel at home.

The *Hotel Arteaga* (tel 3-19-30), Azueta 8, is a bit old and worn out, but cheap – US\$2.65 for one and US\$5.25 for two. Window shutters give the place some character.

The *Hotel Mary* (tel 2-33-07), Velásquez de León 24, has dirty rooms with balconies, fans, private bathrooms and cell-like doors, but no window screens. There's a clean, shallow swimming pool. Singles/doubles are US\$3.15/US\$6.30.

The *Hotel Betty* (tel 3-50-94) is at Avenida Cuauhtémoc and Belisario Domínguez 4. Although the rooms and bathrooms seem clean, don't look under the beds at the mattresses and pretend that you didn't see the torn curtains. The fan in each room keeps you cool and calm for middle-of-the-night surprises.

The *Hotel Sevillano* (tel 3-83-58, 3-83-59, 3-83-05), Tadeo Arredondo 7, is a multi-storey hotel that seems to be popular with Mexican sarape merchants. Piles of sarapes lined the corridors of every floor and the courtyard below. Rates are US$4.75 for one person, US$5.80 for two, US$6.35 for twin beds and US$7.50 for three. There's an inexpensive cafeteria downstairs.

Avoid the *Hotel María Isabel* (tel 6-03-18) on Avenida Cuauhtémoc – at US$8 for one and US$16.75 for two, it's terribly over-priced. If you insist on staying here, get a room away from the street; otherwise the noisy traffic will keep you up all night. Purified water is available in the hallway.

The *Hotel del Valle* (tel 5-83-36, 5-83-88), Gómez Espinosa 8 y La Costera, is a small two-star hotel managed by a pleasant elderly couple. It's right across from the Papagayo Park and only one block from the beach. There's also a swimming pool. Rates vary according to whether rooms have fans or air-conditioning: US$5.25 to US$7.35 for one and US$9 to US$18 for two. It's hard to beat this for the price.

The *Hotel Jacqueline* (tel 6-93-18) is at Consalo Gómez 6 next to Papagayo Park and across from the beach. Its 10 rooms are arranged around a pleasant little garden. Rooms for one or two are US$10.50 with air-conditioning.

Several other hotels in downtown Acapulco near the zócalo that have been mentioned by travellers include the family-style *Casa de Huéspedes de Alicia* (tel 2-78-02) at Azueta 9 (with or without bathrooms for US$4 to US$5); *Hotel Acuario* (tel 2-17-84), Azueta 11 (US$5 to US$8); *Hotel Sacramento* (tel 2-08-21), Emiliano Carranza 4 (US$5 to US$13); the old mission-style *Hotel Misión* (tel 2-36-43), Felipe Valle 12 (US$10.50 to US$15.80); and the *Hotel Faro* (tel 2-13-

65, 2-13-66), Quebrada 83 across from the Hotel El Mirador (US$5 to US$12).

The most noteworthy of these hotels is the *Hotel Misión*, a beautiful place with rooms arranged around a cool courtyard. It's popular and fills up quickly, so be sure to make reservations. It's one of the best bargains in Acapulco.

Camping This is possible at two trailer parks on Pie de la Cuesta. The *Acapulco Trailer Park*, on the ocean side of the road, has 60 spaces and 15 bathrooms that are a bit on the dirty side probably because a sign at the bathroom entrances urges guests to clean up after themselves. There's a grocery store at the park entrance. Rates range from US$4 to US$7. The *Trailer Park Quinta Dora*, just across the road from the Acapulco Trailer Park, is cheaper, less crowded and cleaner, particularly the lagoon-side sites. Full hook-ups are available in both parks. Campers pay US$1 per person to use the facilities.

Places to Stay – middle
There are many hotels in this range with rooms starting at US$10. The following is just a sample.

The *Hotel Isabel* (tel 2-21-91), La Paz 16, has singles for US$13 and doubles for US$16.80 – greatly over-priced for what you get, which isn't much. They did say, however, that prices were supposed to go down and quality up soon. Let us know.

The *Motel Quinta Mica* (tel 4-01-21, 4-01-22), Cristóbal Colón 115 in front of the CICI water-sports centre, is modern and close to the beach. Most of the rooms have air-conditioning and kitchenettes with refrigerators. There's also a swimming pool on the premises. A room for one or two, which could probably accommodate two more, is US$31.60.

Suites Selene (tel 4-29-77), Cristóbal Colón 170, is similar to the Quinta Mica – a modern building near the beach. Full suites that include kitchens, dining-rooms, air-conditioning and two double beds are reasonably priced at US$28 for two. Some rooms have balconies.

The *Autotel Ritz* (tel 5-80-23) is on Avenida Wilfrido Massieu (no number), one block inland from La Costera. All rooms have carpeting and air-conditioning; rooms on the upper floors have great views of Acapulco. Singles/doubles are US$30/34.

The *Acapulco Romano Palace Hotel* (tel 4-77-30), La Costera 130, is a high-rise that caters mostly to Canadian tourists. For some reason, the hotels' designers insisted on decorating the place in ancient Roman motif, which accounts for the plaster-of-Paris columns in the lobby and cheap prints of Roman gladiators in the hallways. If you like this and don't feel like walking across the street to the beach, there are two pseudo-Roman swimming pools attached to the hotel. Its 430 rooms are air-conditioned and have balconies with great views of the bay. Singles/doubles range in price from US$30/37 to US$60/74 depending on the season; the latter rates apply in winter.

The *Hotel El Mirador* (tel 2-11-11), Calle La Quebrada 74, is the launching pad for Acapulco's famous cliff divers. The hotel is run by Mexico's 1st-class hotel chain, Hoteles El Presidente, but prices are kept at a moderate level. The structure has rooms staggered at different levels along the hill. Singles/doubles range in price from US$36/40 to US$72/80 (winter).

Places to Stay – top end

As with the middle-range hotels, rates are sometimes as much as 50% lower in the summer. However, even in the winter, good deals can often be obtained through any of the several air-fare/hotel packages offered by USA travel agents. Package deals are offered with 1st-class and deluxe hotels such as the Acapulco Plaza, the Exelaris Hyatt Regency, the Sheraton Acapulco and Las Brisas.

One of Acapulco's best hotels, *Las Brisas* (tel 4-16-50), is worth visiting just

to see it. In the USA it has topped lists of favourite honeymoon destinations. There are 300 private *casitas*, many with their own private swimming pools, set on a hillside of manicured gardens. The views of Acapulco Bay, particularly at night, seem too good to be true. Rates start at US$105 per night.

Places to Stay – Pie de la Cuesta

The *Casa de Huéspedes y Restaurant Rocio*, on your left as you enter the Pie de la Cuesta area, is owned by a local primary-school teacher. Prices are US$3.15 for one person and US$5.25 for two in simple but clean rooms which all have fans and screens on the windows. The restaurant is right on the beach, a perfect place for watching the sunset. Philippe, the manager, chef, nightly singer and guitarist as well as bartender, will make just about anything you want to eat or drink.

The next place down is *Bungalows Guillermo* with bungalows for two (US$16). Each bungalow has a complete kitchen and is separated from the beach by a brick wall. Fans are available when the temperature and humidity are high.

The *Quinta Karla Casa de Huéspedes y Restaurant* has several rooms set around a sandy court area with many palm trees. A dog named 'Doggo' insists on playing frisbee with every person who walks through the gate. The simple beach front place is run by a man named Rudolpho and his wife. According to their card, they offer 'a tranquil place on the Pacific with a magnificent beach and the world's most beautiful sunsets', which is a fairly accurate description.

La Cabañita has bungalows for US$2.10 per person. Most of the rooms have bathrooms, fans and painted concrete floors. There are also 'cabins' available for US$6.30 per day. The restaurant serves various specialities such as barbecued red snapper, octopus and shrimp.

The *Hotel Puesta del Sol* has plain but clean rooms and bungalows with kitchenettes, hot water and fans for US$16 to

US$26.30. The rooms face either the beach or the tennis courts and swimming pool. The hotel was once owned by Señor Silveti, one of Mexico's greatest bullfighters. The atmosphere is casual: if you want more food you just go into the kitchen. The bar is open until midnight.

Places to Eat

El Amigo, María Iglesias 13, is a hole-in-the-wall restaurant that serves decent home-cooked food to the Mexican pensioners who hang out here. Tacos and beans with salad costs less than US$1. *Restaurant Los Braseros*, La Costera 225, has an old wagon wheel in front that is supposed to attract gringos hungry for a 'western-style' steak. Their most expensive dish is something that resembles steak for US$3.15. Breakfast is a fair bargain at US$0.95. Open 24 hours.

Restaurant Sinbad's is an intriguing place tucked away on a side street around the corner from Los Braseros. They offer a tasty lunch of spaghetti, meatballs and tortillas for US$1.25.

Restaurant Hong Kong, La Costera 222, specialises in fair-priced meals of Mandarin-style food. Chop suey, fried rice, egg rolls, tea and a fortune cookie is US$2. Their highest priced meal is US$3.75.

The *Burger & Brew El Nopal*, next to the Acapulco Romano Palace Hotel, offers a fair breakfast deal for US$1.60 to US$2.50. It seems to be a refuge for homesick gringos: not a Mexican in sight except behind the counter.

100% Natural is the name of a chain of juice stands found throughout Acapulco. They serve a variety of creative mixtures of juices and other ingredients in huge glasses for US$0.85. Try their licuado with bananas, coconut slivers, chocolate, cinnamon and vanilla flavouring. It's a great place for a unique breakfast. One outlet is located in the shopping passageway next to the Hotel Imperial; another is across from the Radisson Hotel and next to Papagayo Park.

La Flor de Acapulco, Plaza Alvarez on the zócalo, is known more for its great people-watching location than its food. The food is fairly *típico*, with a few American dishes to satisfy the many Americans who frequent the place. Meals range in price from US$1.65 to US$3.70. A small steak costs US$2.

Mariscos Pipo, Almirante Breton 3 near Juárez, serves snails and octopus patties among other types of seafood for US$2.50 to US$3.50.

Also for seafood, try the restaurants at Playas Caleta, Caletilla and La Angosta. Most of them are in small bay-front shacks. Prices vary, so compare restaurants here.

The restaurants at Pie de la Cuesta, most of which are attached to hotels and casas de huéspedes, are renowned for their seafood. The *Ramiro Lago Club* has a piano bar, a green swimming pool and chicken and fish dinners by the lagoon. You will see its sign near the trailer parks. *Tres Marías II* supposedly has some of the best food in the area. *Steve's Hideaway*, at the southern end of the lagoon, is known for its steak and seafood specialities.

Other restaurants frequently recommended by travellers are the *Restaurant Rocio*, which is attached to the Casa de Huéspedes Rocio, the *Quinta Karla Casa de Huéspedes y Restaurant*, *La Cabañita* and the *Hotel Puesta del Sol Restaurant*.

Entertainment

Nightlife in Acapulco revolves around its many discos and nightclubs. *The Gallery*, Avenida de los Deportes 11 near the Holiday Inn, is a disco also known for its 11.30 pm and 1 am shows of female impersonators. *The Peacock* is a predominantly gay bar, and has some of the best music in Acapulco. *Fantasy* has a laser-light show, disco dancing and a 2 am fireworks show. *Baby O's*, at La Costera and Horacio Nelson, also has a laser-light show and is supposedly one of the best discos in Acapulco. *Magic*, across from Baby O's, is an exclusive place with a bouncer at the door who selects the clientele. *Le Dome* and *Jackie O's* are popular with gringos on the go. *Boccacio's* is another good disco often recommended by disco fans.

Getting There & Away

Air There are direct flights to Acapulco from many cities in Mexico and North America on Aeroméxico, Mexicana, American Airlines, Delta, Continental, Braniff, Canadian Airlines International and Eastern Airlines.

Direct international flights to Acapulco arrive from Atlanta, Georgia three times weekly; Chattanooga, Tennessee daily; Chicago, Illinois daily; Cincinnati, Ohio daily; Dallas, Texas daily; Houston, Texas daily; Indianapolis, Indiana daily; Jacksonville, Florida daily; Los Angeles, California four times weekly; Miami, Florida three times weekly; Montreal, Quebec once weekly; Nashville, Tennessee daily; New York, New York daily except Wednesday; Philadelphia, Pennsylvania daily except Tuesday and Wednesday; Savannah, Georgia daily; Toronto, Canada once weekly.

Bus Most inter-city buses in Acapulco are associated with either Tres Estrellas de Oro (1st class) or Flecha Roja (2nd class). The Tres Estrellas terminal is at Avenida Cuauhtémoc 158; the Flecha Roja terminal is nearby at Avenida Cuauhtémoc 97.

Flecha Roja has slightly lower fares and more frequent departures than the Tres Estrellas buses. Some of the major destinations and frequency of departure from Acapulco are: Cuernavaca five times daily (US$3.60), Mexico City every half-hour 24 hours daily (US$4.75), Zihuatanejo every half-hour (US$2.50), Puerto Escondido every hour (US$5.30) and Taxco three times (US$2.75).

Tres Estrellas has buses to Mexico City every hour (US$5), Zihuatanejo six times daily (US$2.70), Taxco twice daily (US$3.20) and Cuernavaca six times daily (US$4.15).

Getting from the bus stations to town is easiest by taxi (US$1.30 to the zócalo), but there are also public buses. Ask locals to point the way. You can also walk: from Tres Estrellas to town takes 30 minutes and from Flecha Roja to town 20 minutes.

Getting Around

Airport Transport Acapulco's airport is 22½ km south of downtown, beyond the junction for Puerto Marqués. Before you leave the terminal, buy a ticket from the Transportaciones de Pasajeros desks for transportation into town. You can go by bus (US$1.75), Volkswagen minibus/combi (US$2.50) or taxi (US$7 for two people). To return to the airport, call them at 5-23-32 or 5-25-91.

Local Transport The 'Cine Rio' bus runs along La Costera from La Cinema Río to the Naval Base at the southern end of Acapulco. The 'Pie de la Cuesta' bus leaves from La Costera opposite Sanborn's department store. Along the Costera there are buses which go to Puerto Marqués.

Taxis are plentiful in Acapulco and taxi drivers are happy to take gringos for a ride, especially for fares higher than the government-set rates. From the zócalo to Pie de la Cuesta or to Puerto Marqués, the fare should be US$3.30. From the zócalo to Playa Caleta, expect to pay US$1.30. Always ask the fare before the trip begins.

ZIHUATENEJO & IXTAPA

Population: 22,000 (Zihuatanejo only)

Less than 10 years ago, Zihuatanejo ('zee-wha-ten-NAY-ho') was a small fishing village, and nearby Ixtapa ('ees-STOP-pah') was a coconut plantation. Then, Fonatur, the Mexican government tourism development organisation that built Cancún, decided that the Pacific coast needed a Cancún-like resort to bring more tourist dollars into Mexico.

Using various market studies of

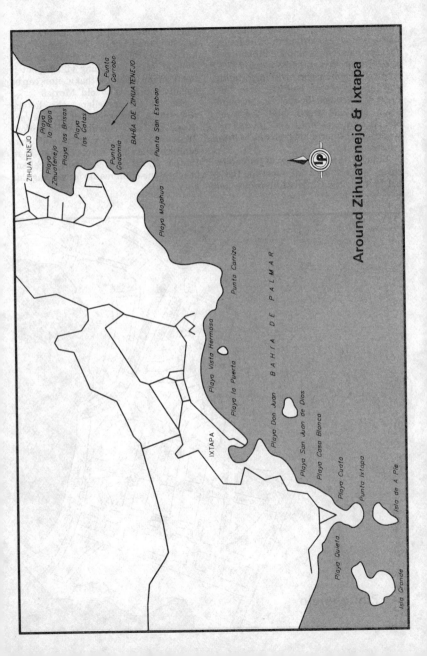

Around Zihuatenejo & Ixtapa

ZIHUATENEJO

Punta Garrobo
Playa la Ropa
Playa Zihuatenejo
Playa las Brisas
Playa las Gatas
Punta Gadomia
BAHÍA DE ZIHUATENEJO
Punta San Esteban

Playa Majahua

Punta Carrizo

Playa Vista Hermosa
Playa la Puerta

BAHÍA DE PALMAR

IXTAPA

Playa Don Juan
Playa San Juan de Dios
Playa Casa Blanca
Playa Cuata
Punta Ixtapa

Playa Quieta

Isla Grande
Isla de A Pie

American tourists, Fonatur economists chose Ixtapa, 210 km north of Acapulco, for their new resort complex. Proximity to the USA, an average temperature of 27°C, tropical vegetation and, most importantly, the quality of the beaches were their criteria. They bought the coconut plantation, laid out streets, built reservoirs, strung electrical lines and invited the world's best-known hotel chains to begin construction.

Today, Ixtapa is a string of impressive resort hotels spread out along the Bahía del Palmar; the Club Méditerranée and Playa Linda Ixtapa are farther west beyond Punta Ixtapa. Zihuatenejo, five km to the south, is supposed to be a 'typical' Mexican fishing village, but it has been spruced up so that visitors can be equally impressed by 'old' Mexico.

For budget travellers, the hotels, restaurants and shops of Ixtapa are expensive and should be avoided. Zihuatenejo, though touristy and over-commercialised, is much cheaper than Ixtapa. Both places have excellent beaches, the main reason for visiting this area.

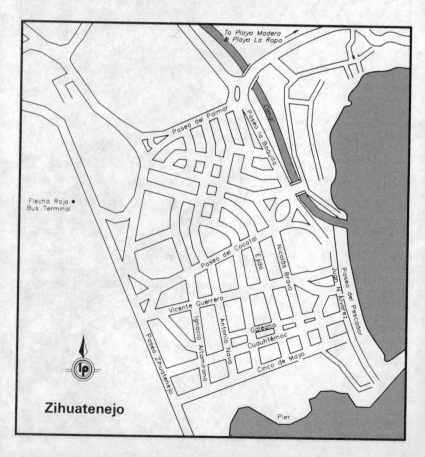

Zihuatenejo

Orientation

Ixtapa is spread out along the Bahía de Palmar, while most of Zihuatenejo is squeezed into a relatively compact area at the north end of the smaller Bahía de Zihuatenejo. Across the bay from downtown Zihuatenejo are Playa La Ropa and Playa Las Gatas, where you'll find Zihuatenejo's better beaches and hotels. Closer to town, and consequently less appealing, are Playa Madera and Playa Principal (also known as Playa Zihuatenejo).

It's difficult to get lost in Zihuatenejo because almost all of its downtown streets, most of which are cobblestoned, are laid out in a rectangular grid pattern bounded by 'Paseos' on each side. Along the waterfront is Paseo del Pescador, on the west is Cinco de Mayo, east is Paseo del Coctal (also known as Avenida Benito Juárez), and north is Paseo Zihuatenejo, the main street in and out of town.

Information

Tourist Office The state and federal governments maintain tourist offices in Zihuatenejo; there's also a federal office in Ixtapa in front of the Hotel El Presidente.

The state tourist office (tel 4-22-07), Paseo del Pescador 20 near the pier, has a few brochures and maps of the area. Hours are 9 am to 2 pm and 5 to 7 pm, Monday to Friday.

The federal tourist office (tel 4-38-35), Ascensio 5, is unlike others in Mexico because the staff seemed more knowledgeable about the area than the state office staff. Hours are 9 am to 6 pm daily including holidays.

Money Zihuatenejo has several banks and a casa de cambio where you can exchange money. Rates are somewhat better at the banks, but the lines are longer and hours shorter (only until 12 noon, Monday to Friday). Some souvenir shops in Zihuatenejo will also change money. If you change at a hotel, though, you'll usually get a lower rate and may be charged a commission.

Bancomer is at Paseo Ixtapa, in front of the Centro Comercial 'La Puerta'. Bánamex is at Cuauhtémoc 4 at Alvarez. Multibanco Comerex may be found at Ramírez and Vicente Guerrero. Banco Mexicano Somex is on Avenida Benito Juárez across from Hertz Rent-a-Car and next to the Central Market. A casa de cambio on Galeana between Bravo and Ascensio is open daily from 8 am to 10 pm.

Post The post office is across from Ruly's Burgers at Calle Catalina González 7 between Vicente Guerrero and Galeana. Hours are 8 am to 7 pm Monday to Friday, and 9 am to 1 pm Saturday.

Telephone Calls The caseta de larga distancia in the ice cream shop on Ascensio at Galeana is open 8 am to 8 pm daily.

Airlines Three airlines have offices in Zihuatenejo. Mexicana (tel 4-22-08) is at Vicente Guerrero and Nicolás Bravo. Aeroméxico has three offices – Cinco de Mayo 14 (tel 3-08-53), Juan Alvarez 34 (tel 4-20-18) and Centro Comercial 'La Puerta' (tel 3-08-53). Continental (tel 4-32-50) is at Vicente Guerrero and Nicolás Bravo.

Laundromat The Lavandería Darbet is around the corner from La Panadería Francesca, which is on Calle Catalina González.

Beaches

As in Acapulco, lazing on any of the idyllic beaches in and around Zihuatenejo and Ixtapa is the thing to do.

Starting from north of Punta Ixtapa across from Isla Ixtapa (or Isla Grande as it's also known) are Playa Cuatas, Playa Linda and Playa Quieta. The latter is claimed by the Club Méditerranée but is open to the public. Playa Cuatas is on the south side of Punta Ixtapa.

Isla Ixtapa, two km offshore from Playa Quieta, also has beautiful beaches and can be reached by boat from Playa Quieta (US$1 round trip) and the Zihuatenejo pier (US$3.30 round trip). The boat departs the pier daily at 11.30 am while the one from Playa Quieta departs every 15 minutes from 9 am to 5 pm.

Farther east towards hotel row in Ixtapa are the small, isolated beaches of Playa Casa Blanca, Playa San Juan de Dios and Playa Don Juan. These are probably some of the most beautiful but inaccessible beaches in the area.

Going farther east along the Bahía del Palmar, the marshy outlet of the Laguna de Ixtapa prevents a crossing from Don Juan to the area's longest and most popular beach, Playa del Palmar. To get there from the west, you have to follow the road inland and around the lagoon. Or swim. Ixtapa's major hotels are all along this beach, which theoretically is open to the public.

In Zihuatenejo skip the beach in town, Playa Principal (also known as Playa Zihuatenejo), and head farther east to Playa Madera and then south to Playa La Ropa and Playa Las Gatas. Playa Madera is worth visiting only if you don't want to walk more than 15 minutes to get to La Ropa and Las Gatas. To get to La Ropa from Playa Madera, follow the road along the canal until you see a sign that says either 'Entrada a la Playa Ropa' or 'Hotel Catalina Sotavento'. The path to La Ropa leads through the hotel down to the beach.

From Playa La Ropa you can hike to Las Gatas and join the crowds of tourists who arrive by boat. The boats depart every 10 minutes, 8 am to 5 pm, from the Zihuatenejo pier. Save your ticket because you'll need it for the return trip. The reef just offshore is a superb diving and snorkelling spot. Equipment can be rented at Las Gatas from either Oliverio's Scuba or Carlos Scuba, or in town at Casa del Mar. They also rent pedal-boats (US$0.75 per hour) and sailboards (US$7 to US$10) and arrange water-skiing (US$20 per boat).

Places to Stay

There are no budget hotels in Ixtapa, only in Zihuatenejo. However, even in Zihuatenejo hotel rates are not particularly great, especially considering what you would get for the same price in Acapulco or Puerto Vallarta. Also, during the high season from December to late February or early March, all hotels and casas de huéspedes in Zihuatenejo tend to be full.

Places to Stay – bottom end

If you arrive during the high season and want an economical place to stay, try the *CREA Youth Hostel* on Paseo Zihuatenejo, a 15-minute walk from the bus stations. They charge US$2.75 per night for a bed in a clean, single-sex dormitory.

The *Hotel Casa Bravo* (tel 4-25-28), Bravo 11, has a cool, inviting lobby with a hammock strung in front of the reception desk. The rooms are not as inviting, but they're clean and not bad for the price. Singles are US$10, doubles US$12, triples US$15. The *Casa de Huéspedes Miriam*, on Calle Antonio Nava between Cuauhtémoc and Cinco de Mayo, may seem like a good deal at first with its courtyard and fans in every room, but the rooms are shabby and overpriced. Singles/doubles are US$5/10.

Unfortunately, the rooms at the *Hotel Rubi* on Paseo Zihuatenejo are also disappointing, although its location alongside a hill overlooking the town gives you a great first impression. A steep stairway leads up to the hotel from the Paseo. The rooms are drab and steamy when it's humid, even though they have fans. Singles are US$4, doubles US$6, triples US$10.

The recently renovated *Hotel Imelda*, on Calle Catalina González, has small but airy rooms for US$10. A restaurant attached to the hotel serves fairly good economical meals.

The *Hotel Casa Aurora* (tel 4-30-46),

Bravo 27 between Galeana and Vicente Guerrero, is generally clean, but check more than one room. Rates are US$5 per person.

Camping This is possible at *Camping Playa Ropa*, near the Hotel Catalina Sotavento, for US$1 per person plus US$0.75 for a car. Showers and bathrooms are available next to the sites. You can also camp at the deluxe *Camping Playa Linda* at the north-western end of Ixtapa for US$1 per person for tents or hammocks. Tents can be rented here for US$4 and up.

Places to Stay - middle
Bungalows Allec (tel 4-20-02) is at the top of a hill leading into the Playa Madera hotel zone and built over a set of terraces leading down to the beach. All of the bungalows are clean and have full kitchens, bedrooms, a living room and verandas. The small units (US$20) are for two people, while the larger ones (US$40) are for four people. Playa Madera, which you can see from most of the bungalows, is only 30 seconds away. Its German managers claim that it is the only hotel with palm trees in front of it.

Also on Playa Madera is the *Hotel Posada Caracol* (tel 4-20-35) with air-conditioned rooms and access to the hotel's swimming pools, restaurants and night-club. Singles/doubles are US$28/30.

Places to Stay - top end
Except for the Villa del Sol beach club and hotel at Playa La Ropa in Zihuatenejo, all of the top-end hotels are in or around Ixtapa. These are the *Camino Real Ixtapa, Palmar Ixtapa, Club Méditerranée, Dorado Pacífico, El Presidente Ixtapa, Holiday Inn, Krystal Ixtapa, Playa Linda Ixtapa, Riviera del Sol* and *Sheraton Ixtapa*. If you want more information about them, including how to get the best rates, most travel agents in the USA should have brochures and package deals.

Places to Eat
La Panadería Francesca, Calle Catalina González 15, is a French-style Mexican bakery that sells reasonably priced (for Zihuatenejo) little pizzas and various French and Mexican pastries. A good place to stock up on picnic supplies.

La Madera Beach Club, in front of Bungalows Allec, serves moderately priced meals at US$2 to US$5. Seafood, especially the red snapper platter, is their speciality. Breakfast isn't really special, but it's cheap – US$2 for eggs, tortillas, beans, juice, coffee and whatever else the cook feels likes including.

The *Café Marina*, Paseo del Pescador near Cuauhtémoc, is owned and run by a transplanted California surfer-boy who serves everything from fruits and nuts with honey or yoghurt or both to chocolate cake and pizza. Prices range from US$1 to US$3.50.

Pollo Loco, on Bravo next to the Casa Bravo, serves some of the best chicken on the coast. It's a ramshackle place, open to the street, where the chicken is cooked over a grill of hot coals. A full meal of spicy chicken, tortillas and salad costs US$1.50.

Things to Buy
Prices of Mexican artwork and crafts tend to be higher here than in bigger resort cities such as Acapulco, Manzanillo and Puerto Vallarta. If you can't wait, then you'll have no problem finding a decent selection because it seems as though every other shop in Zihuatenejo sells souvenirs. For a survey of what's available, first visit the Casa de Artesanías de Zihuatenejo on Juárez.

Getting There & Away
Air Continental, Aeroméxico and Mexicana have regularly scheduled international and domestic (not Continental) flights between Ixtapa/Zihuatenejo and the following cities: Atlanta (two to three times per week), Chicago (twice), Dallas (four times), Guadalajara (daily), Houston (three to five times), Los Angeles (three to

five times), Manzanillo (four times), Mazatlán (three times), Mexico City (daily), Miami (twice), New York (two to five times), Puerto Vallarta (two to five times), San Francisco (three times) and Seattle (three times).

Flights to Ixtapa/Zihuatenejo from other cities in the world must be made through the above cities.

Bus Tres Estrellas de Oro (1st class), Paseo del Palmar 54, has buses departing north for Lázaro Cárdenas (US$1.30) and points in between at 6 am, 2.30 pm and 6.15 pm; Acapulco and points in between at 8 am, at noon, and at 6, 7, 8 and 9 pm (US$0.40 to Petatlan, US$0.90 to Papanoa and US$3 to Acapulco); Mexico City (US$8) six times daily and Cuernavaca (US$7).

Flecha Roja (2nd class), Paseo de Zihuatenejo, has buses to Lázaro Cárdenas (US$1.50) 26 times daily, Acapulco (US$3) every half-hour from 4 am to 8 pm and Mexico City (US$8) four times daily.

Getting Around
Airport Transport The Ixtapa/Zihuatenejo airport is 16 km south of Zihuatenejo, just off Highway 200. Taxis and minibuses are available for the trip between the airport and town. Rates are negotiable, but expect to pay anywhere from US$2 to US$5.

Local Transport The same taxis are available for trips between Zihuatenejo and Ixtapa (US$1 to US$2) and to Playa La Ropa from central Zihuatenejo (US$0.50 to US$1). The cheapest way to get to Ixtapa is to take the local bus that leaves from Juárez and Altamirano every 15 minutes from 6 am to 11 pm.

Oaxaca

This mountainous southern state ('wa-HA-ka') is famed above all for its Indians – nearly a million of them representing at least 17 different peoples. They make up a third of the state's population and a fifth of all Indians in Mexico. The Indian presence is felt throughout Oaxaca in their colourful costumes, delicate handicrafts, busy markets and exotic festivals, and in the groups of small wiry people on the buses or walking along the roads. Some Indian traditions are giving way under the pressure of modern ways but others remain strong.

Oaxaca is a rugged place and many visitors don't get beyond Oaxaca city or the Pacific coast, where Spanish and mestizo influence is stronger. Many of the most traditional Indians live in harsh country and may give a cool reception to outsiders, since they have been driven to these retreats by centuries of conflict with each other and with the Spanish and mestizos. Shy and self-contained, they have a healthy suspicion of strangers. Few paved roads reach these parts, which may be as far from Oaxaca city in culture and travelling time as Oaxaca is from Mexico City. Be prepared for the unexpected if you venture into these remote areas!

The heart of the state in every sense is Oaxaca city and the Central Valley in which it stands. This is the meeting point of the state's diverse cultures, a fascinating, lively place of colonial buildings, intriguing history and mixed population, which draws tens of thousands of visitors yearly. Not least of its attractions are the ruins of pre-Hispanic Indian towns like Monte Albán, Mitla and Yagul.

By contrast, the Oaxaca coast offers some of Mexico's most laid-back beach spots. In the rest of the state there's enough rugged (but quite heavily populated) country to offer a lifetime's exploring. In the east is Mexico's narrow 'waist', the low-lying Isthmus of Tehuantepec.

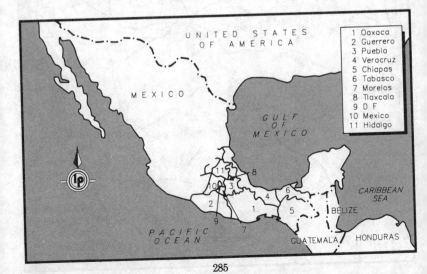

285

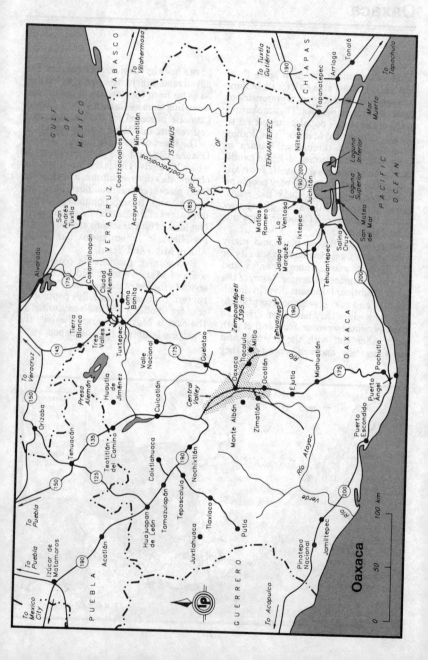

Place Names

One clear sign of the Indian influence in Oaxaca is the names of its towns and villages, most of which have Spanish-Christian and pronunciation-defying Indian components. (Test your tongue on Santa Cruz Xoxocotlán, San Lorenzo Cuaunecuiltitla, or San Miguel Ahuehuetitlán!)

Usually places are known by only one of these components and that's the practice we follow here, except where the full name is given to avoid confusion with similarly-named places nearby. This is sometimes necessary since Oaxaca's 570 municipalities include 56 Santa Marías, 55 Santiagos, 53 San Juans, etc.

Drugs

Oaxaca is one of Mexico's main marijuana-growing areas. Magic mushrooms, used by some Indians for ceremonial or medical purposes, are common. If you buy any, take extreme care who you buy them from.

History

Zapotecs & Mixtecs Oaxaca's pre-Hispanic civilisations, isolated behind hard-to-penetrate mountains, were left more or less undisturbed to reach heights rivalling those of central Mexico. The influence of the Olmecs, Mayas, Teotihuacán and probably Toltecs was felt here, and Oaxaca traded with other parts of Mexico, but until the Aztecs turned up in the 15th century the only enemies Oaxacans seem to have had were each other.

The Central Valley has always been the hub of life in Oaxaca. Evidence of human habitation goes back to around 8000 BC. By 1350-1000 BC, there was a village of about 100 houses at San José Mogote, 15 km north-west of Oaxaca city. In 500 BC building began at the great hilltop site of Monte Albán in the Central Valley. Some of its founders may have come from San José Mogote and may have had cultural connections with the Olmec to the north-east, whose civilisation was coming to an end. By the start of the Christian era the occupants of Monte Albán were probably Zapotec-speaking and the place remained the centre of Zapotec power until 700 or 800 AD.

The Zapotecs extended their control over the Central Valley and other parts of the state by conquest. Their culture peaked between 250 and 750 AD, by which time there were at least 200 other settlements or ceremonial centres in the Central Valley, plus extensive irrigation. Monte Albán became a true town, with perhaps 25,000 people – all proof of a highly organised and sophisticated society. As in all pre-Hispanic Mexican cultures, the priests were either highly influential or were themselves the rulers.

The most important Zapotec deities included Cocijo, the rain god, who is often shown with a forked tongue representing lightning; Pitao Cozobi, the maize god; Xipe Tótec, the god of spring and the flayed, who wears a human skin representing new vegetation (a classic example of the ancient Mexican belief that human death was necessary to keep nature going); the bat god, who usually has a headdress and shoulder ornaments representing wings; and the feathered serpent.

Xochiquetzal, Goddess of Beauty and Love

Monte Albán declined rapidly and by about 750 AD was largely deserted, as were many other Zapotec sites in the Central Valley. Places like Yagul, Zaachila and Mitla became the main centres, and many of them came under the growing influence of the Mixtecs from the north-west of the state. The Mixtecs first established dominance of their own area by the 11th century and then from about 1200 started to control much of the Central Valley – perhaps as a small but powerful aristocracy.

Mixtec and Zapotec cultures became entangled in the Central Valley; Oaxaca's second greatest archaeological site, Mitla, had both Zapotec and Mixtec phases. Famous for its 'palaces' covered with intricate stone mosaics, Mitla flourished in the few centuries preceding the Spanish conquest. Before the Spanish arrived Oaxaca also had to contend with Aztec imperialism. The Mixtecs and Zapotecs managed to keep the Aztecs out of the south and east of the state, but between the mid-15th century and 1521 the Central Valley and the north-west became tribute-payers, with textiles and cochineal dye among the items they had to send to the Aztecs. There were Aztec garrisons at Oaxaca and near Coixtlahuaca and Tlaxiaco.

Archaeologists divide the pre-Hispanic era of the Central Valley into six phases named after Monte Albán, its most important site.

Colonial Era Despite early help from the Chinantecs of northern Oaxaca in their capture of the Aztec capital Tenochtitlán, the Spanish received a very hostile reception in Oaxaca. Resistance by the Mixtecs, Zapotecs, Chinantecs and Mixes of the north-east brought at least four Spanish expeditions to the state between 1520 and 1526.

The city of Oaxaca was finally founded in 1529. Cortés donated large parts of the Central Valley to himself and was officially named Marqués del Valle de Oaxaca.

Much of the rest of the state was divided up under the infamous *encomienda* system, by which Spanish overlords were supposed to look after the welfare of the Indians in their charge but in many cases exploited them mercilessly.

Just as elsewhere in Mexico, the Indian population slumped disastrously in the first century of Spanish rule. A plague in the Mixteca killed about 75% of its population in 1591. The Central Valley, which had about 150,000 Indians in 1568, had only 40 to 50,000 70 years later. Some of the remoter Indian tribes such as the Mixes and Triquis were brought under a form of loose control only with the help of missionaries. Indian rebellions continued into at least the 18th century – one of the biggest was in the Tehuantepec area in 1660 – but rarely did the different Indian peoples unite to form a serious threat. There were conflicts between different Indian groups and villages as well as between Indians and Spanish – a pattern that goes back to pre-Hispanic days and continues today.

The struggle for Mexican independence was marked mainly by apathy on the part of the alienated Indians, but the mountainous north-west of the state and the remote south served as refuges for the independence leaders Guerrero and Bravo when the tide of war was against them. From the Mixteca in the north-west Guerrero launched his 1820 campaign, which eventually led to the final defeat of the Spanish.

19th Century Two of the great figures of turbulent 19th-century Mexico, Benito Juárez and Porfirio Díaz, were Oaxacans.

From 1848 to 1852 Juárez was a liberal state governor of Oaxaca, opening new village schools and cutting back the bureaucracy. He refused refuge in Oaxaca to General Santa Anna after the disaster of conquest by the United States. Then in 1853 the restored Santa Anna exiled him to New Orleans, where he found other Mexican liberals already installed. Juárez

Top: Playa de los Muertos, Puerto Vallarta (SW)
Left: La Quebrada Divers, Acapulco (TW)
Right: Acapulco (TW)

Top: Acapulco Fort (TW)
Bottom: Aripo Craft Shop, Oaxaca (TW)

returned to Mexico to assist in the Revolution of Ayutla, which deposed Santa Anna in 1855 and became justice minister in the new liberal government, as well as governor of Oaxaca after the defeat of a conservative revolt in the state. After a series of events he won national presidential elections in March 1861.

Promoted in the army by Juárez, Díaz played a decisive part as a commander in a defeat of the French at Puebla in 1862, and was appointed governor of Oaxaca by Juárez before being taken prisoner when the French captured the city in 1865. He escaped and retook Oaxaca the next year, going on to drive the French from Mexico City itself. He was already noted both as a cruel leader and a cruel enemy, which also became apparent during his later reign as Mexico's president.

Valle Nacional in northern Oaxaca was a notorious example of the depths to which rural Mexico sank under Díaz. The Chinantec Indians who lived there were apparently swindled out of their land in the early Díaz years by tobacco planters who set up virtual slave camps. According to the American writer J K Turner who visited them, almost the entire 15,000-strong plantation workforce was replaced annually because workers died of disease, starvation and beating. In theory they were labourers working to pay off debts to their bosses. Turner reported that workers were recruited from outside, mainly by the offer of a US$5 advance which they could never repay. Recruiting agents all over southern Mexico were supported by the local government authorities, who offered cheap transportation to Valle Nacional, made the now-feared *rurales* available for guarding the labourers and took a cut of the profits.

When Díaz was finally thrown out in the Mexican revolution of 1910-11, having fixed his own re-election in 1910, few were sorry. In contrast to Juárez's national hero status, monuments to Díaz in Mexico today are rare, though there are two streets named after him in Oaxaca city.

20th Century The revolutionary decade of 1910-20 saw Oaxaca dissolve into a chaos of opposing armed factions and shifting allegiances. The conservative supporters of Victoriano Huerta were strong early on, and liberals supporting Venustiano Carranza and the Constitutionalists were persecuted by the pro-Huerta state government in 1913, but there were also anti-Huerta uprisings.

That same year a group of *jefes serranos* (strongmen from the hills), among them Guillermo Meixueiro and José Luis Dávila, opposed to both Huerta and the Constitutionalists, managed to take control of the state government. They decided to dissociate Oaxaca from the national factions and declared self-government for the state the same year. Oaxaca city was taken by the Constitutionalists in 1916 but the jefes serranos carried on fighting from the hills. In 1920 they allied themselves with Álvaro Obregón to help depose the national Constitutionalist government. In return they were allowed to take control of Oaxaca, but were soon replaced as Obregón and Plutarco Calles consolidated their hold on the country.

Despite some land redistribution in the state after the Revolution – about 300 *ejidos* (communal land-holdings) were set up in the 1930s – land ownership remains a source of serious friction to this day.

Juárez & Díaz

The strangely intertwined careers of Benito Juárez and Porfirio Díaz were in complete contrast to each other – a real 'hero and villain' story.

Juárez was a Zapotec, born in 1806 in the village of Guelatao 60 km north of Oaxaca. Orphaned at three, he went to the city at 12, unable to speak Spanish, and worked in the home of a Franciscan lay brother who paid for his schooling. He started training for the priesthood but abandoned it to study law instead and graduated in 1831 – the year after Díaz, also soon to be orphaned, had been born in Oaxaca city into a horse trainer's family. According to one tale, Díaz showed an early tendency to violence by stuffing the nose of his brother Félix with gunpowder during a quarrel and setting it alight. Félix became known as 'Chato' (pugnose).

Juárez worked as a lawyer for poor villagers and became a member of the city council, then of the state government, then a delegate to the national congress in Mexico City. Díaz studied for the priesthood and the law too but was no great scholar and joined the national guard during the American invasion (1846-48).

After the Revolution of Ayutla, which established a liberal government in Mexico, Juárez became justice minister and promulgated a new national law, the Ley Juárez, which decreed that soldiers and priests charged with civil crimes would be tried in civil courts, not in their own special courts as previously. This was the first of the Reform Laws which sought to break the power of the church. Few of Juárez's liberal policies were aimed at really radical change which would improve the lot of the poor or of the Indians, but the Reform Laws were enough to provoke the Reform War of 1858 to 1861 – between liberals on one side and conservatives fighting for 'Religión y Fueros' (religion and rights) on the other.

In Oaxaca the conservative José María Cobos besieged government troops in the city's Santo Domingo church but was defeated by liberal forces led by Díaz. In Mexico City Juárez was arrested, the liberal president resigned, and a conservative named himself president. Juárez escaped to Querétaro to be declared rightful president by the liberals, later setting up his government in Veracruz and issuing more laws which, among other things, outlawed the monastic orders and nationalised all church property.

After early setbacks the liberals won the war, and Juárez won national presidential elections in March 1861. He had only been in office a few months when the French, supported by many conservatives and clergy, invaded Mexico. By mid-1863 Juárez was off into government-in-exile again, chased out of northern Mexico into the USA by the French. In 1866, with military support from the USA, he was back. The French troops supporting their puppet emperor in Mexico, Maximilian, were withdrawn and Juárez's troops defeated Maximilian and his small Mexican force at Querétaro in May 1867. Maximilian was tried and executed and Juárez won new presidential elections later in the year.

Juárez tried to pull Mexico's disastrous economy round by attracting foreign investment for transport and the mining industry. He also channelled more funds to the *rurales*, a police force he had set up to play a much-needed peace-keeping role in the countryside, and made primary education theoretically free and compulsory.

In 1871 Juárez ran for a fourth presidential term but this time faced opposition from younger members of the liberal party, including Díaz. Juárez won and Díaz rebelled, declaring himself opposed to continuous re-election of the same president. His campaign won little support and he was on the brink of defeat when Juárez died in 1872. Today the memory of Juárez is preserved by countless statues and by streets, schools and plazas named after him all over Mexico. His maxim *'El respeto al derecho ajeno es la paz'* ('Respect for the rights of others is peace') is widely known.

New elections followed and Díaz was defeated by Sebastián Lerdo de Tejada, who continued with moderate liberal policies similar to those of Juárez. But when Lerdo stood for re-election in 1876, Díaz rebelled again – this time successfully – under the banner of the Plan de Tuxtepec, which declared that presidents and state governors should not be re-elected.

The following year Díaz was the only candidate in the presidential election and for the next 33 years he ran Mexico. Though he stepped down from the presidency in 1881 in accordance with his own no re-election rule, and went back to Oaxaca as state governor, he remained the power behind the scenes.

Returning to the presidency in 1884, Díaz began the first of six successive terms known as the Porfiriato. Taking an extremely ruthless line against any opposition, he kept Mexico free of the civil wars which had plagued it for over 60 years – his dictatorship is also called La Paz Porfiriana (The Porfirian Peace) – and brought the country into the industrial age. The price of such development was not only foreign ownership of many of Mexico's resources, but also increasing corruption, and oppression of industrial and peasant workers.

Geography & Climate

At 94,000 square km, Oaxaca is Mexico's fifth biggest state, and was perfectly represented by Cortés' illustration of

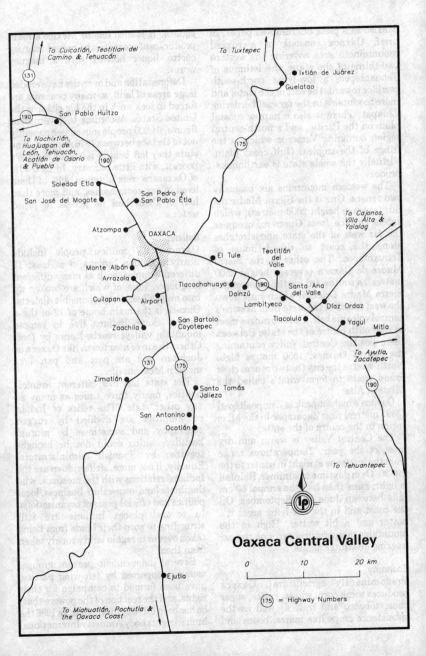

To Cuicatlán, Teotitlán del Camino & Tehuacán

To Tuxtepec

131

190

Ixtlán de Juárez

Guelatao

San Pablo Huitzo

To Nochixtlán, Huajuapan de León, Tehuacán, Acatlán de Osorio & Puebla

190

175

Soledad Etla

San Pedro y San Pablo Etla

San José del Mogote

To Cajones, Villa Alta & Yalalag

Atzompa

OAXACA

El Tule

Teotitlán del Valle

Monte Albán

Arrazola

Tlacochahuaya

Dainzú

Santa Ana del Valle

Cuilapan

Airport

Lambityeco

Díaz Ordaz

Zaachila

San Bartolo Coyotepec

Tlacolula

Yagul

Mitla

To Ayutla, Zacatepec

190

Zimatlán

131

175

Santo Tomás Jalieza

San Antonino

Ocotlán

To Tehuantepec

lp

Oaxaca Central Valley

0   10   20 km

175 = Highway Numbers

Ejutla

To Miahuatlán, Pochutla & the Oaxaca Coast

Mexico as a piece of crumpled paper. In brief, Oaxaca consists of a rugged mountainous area covering the western two-thirds of the state; the Isthmus of Tehuantepec, a low-lying north-south corridor towards the east of the state; and more mountains in the far east bordering Chiapas. There is also a narrow coastal plain on the Pacific, and a north-central region bordering Veracruz which is the fringe of the tropical Gulf coast plain. Virtually the whole state is earthquake-prone.

The western mountains are basically two ranges. One is the Sierra Madre del Sur (average height 2000 metres), which enters Oaxaca from Guerrero, occupies the far west of the state and stretches along the coast to the Isthmus of Tehuantepec. The other is the Sierra Madre de Oaxaca (average height 2500 metres), a southward continuation of the Sierra Madre Oriental which runs down the west centre of the state from Mexico's central volcanic belt. The two ranges meet in the south centre of the state. Between them lies the Central Valley containing the city of Oaxaca, 1550 metres high. North-west of the city the two ranges close round again to form what's called the Mixteca Alta.

Oaxaca's highest peak is Zempoaltépetl (3395 metres) near Zacatepec in the Mixe region in the centre of the state.

The Central Valley is warm and dry most of the year. Temperatures range from the low teens at night in winter to the low 30°Cs in daytime in summer. Rainfall is light; more than half the annual 60 cm falls between June and September. On the coast and in the low-lying areas it's hotter and a bit wetter. High in the mountains temperatures can sink to near freezing on winter nights.

Economy

Predominantly agricultural, Oaxaca produces some corn, wheat, coffee, sugar cane, tobacco and fruit as well as the subsistence crops like maize, beans and squash. It is also one of Mexico's main producers of *mezcal* – the potent maguey cactus liquor bottled with a maguey worm.

Deforestation and over-use have eroded large areas of land, so many peasants are forced to seek work in the big cities or the United States. According to government figures, 94,000 people moved permanently out of Oaxaca between 1976 and 1980. The state they left behind is one of Mexico's poorest, with little industry. In 1980 33% of Oaxacans were illiterate, 48% of them lived in one-room homes, and more than half of them had no access to piped water.

Indians

Oaxaca's 2.7 million people include nearly a million Indians of at least 17 different peoples, with as many different languages, some of which are broken up into mutually incomprehensible dialects. Oaxaca is the main home of 12 of these groups. Some Indians live in remote mountain valleys reached only by foot. Others live in or near towns like Oaxaca or Juchitán and are part and parcel of modern Mexican life.

The state has 570 different municipalities, nearly three times as many as any other state. The relics of Indian communities are divided by rugged geography and sometimes by mutual hostility, which could not be brought together by Spanish administrators. Equally, if not more, strife-ridden are the Indians' relations with the mestizos, who dominate land-ownership, business, local politics and official peasant organisations. In several places Indians are still struggling to stop their lands from being taken over or to regain land wrongly taken from them.

Several independent peasant groups, usually supported by left-wing parties, have been formed to campaign for their rights, and the reaction of the powers-that-be has been literally murderous. In 1986 the human rights body Amnesty International

Indian girl

published reports that 22 members or supporters of the Coalición Obrero-Campesino-Estudiantil del Istmo (Isthmus Worker-Peasant-Student Coalition, or COCEI), which draws its support mainly from Zapotec Indians, were killed between 1974 and 1984, and that 37 Triqui Indians were assassinated between 1976 and 1981. Amnesty International said the circumstances of at least some of these killings suggested the involvement of the security forces or municipal authorities, adding that the culprits were rarely brought to justice.

Indian land today is often the poorest and most eroded in the state, with a shortage of the irrigation, paved roads and credit that could make it more profitable.

Typically, Indians live in one-room houses made of local natural materials. They own land communally and share work – for instance on the building of a new home. Perhaps three-quarters of them speak Spanish as a foreign language.

Chatinos About 20,000 Chatinos live in the remote areas around Juquila and Sola de Vega north of Puerto Escondido. Their language is tonal – that is, the meaning of a word depends on the pitch. They eat mainly maize, beans, squash and chile that they grow themselves by the slash-and-burn method, but in lower-lying areas also grow coffee, cotton, sugar cane and fruit to sell. They have as little contact as possible with non-Chatinos, though for economic reasons they often have to leave their lands to pick coffee on nearby estates.

Men and women wear waist-sashes woven on backstrap looms, but otherwise modern dress is taking over. Chatinos are known for going on long journeys for trade or pilgrimage which may take them beyond Mexico's southern border.

Chinantecs The 70,000-strong Chinantecs live mostly in the hard-to-reach valleys and hills known as La Chinantla, which extend 30 or 40 km east and west of Valle Nacional in the north of the state. Part of the area is high and dry, part is low, subtropical and fertile. Many Chinantecs grow tobacco, chile, sugar cane, coffee and rice but the trade is usually controlled by outsiders. Thousands have been displaced from fertile lands near Ojitlán by the construction of the Cerro de Oro reservoir.

Chochos Just 2000 Chocho-speakers (also called Chochones or Chocholtecs) survive in Mixtec territory in the mountainous north-west, in and between Coixtlahuaca and Teposcolula. Their language is closely related to that of the Popolocas to their north. The Chochos and Popolocas may have come from Tula, the Toltec capital, in the 12th century. Later the area was conquered by the Mixtecs, then the Aztecs, then the Spanish. The Chochos' main economic activity is making hats of palm or synthetic material, which they sell to supplement their small agricultural output.

Chontales About 8000 Oaxaca Chontales (also known as Tequistlatecos and no relation to the Tabasco Chontales) live along the coast and in the mountains west of Salina Cruz. They are mainly concentrated in Astata, San Pedro Huamelula, Ecatepec and Tequisistlán. This remote area was not subdued by the Spanish until 1569, and the Chontales have a tradition of conflict with mestizos and neighbouring Zapotecs which continues today in land disputes. The women can wear huipiles after marriage or pregnancy. Maize and beans are their chief crops but they also grow maguey (for mezcal) and, on the coast, fruit and sugar cane. In the dry season (January-May) some Chontales work as low-paid labourers in factories and plantations on the Isthmus of Tehuantepec or in Chiapas.

Cuicatecs The 15,000 or so Cuicatecs inhabit a remote, very varied region of mountains and deep valleys, between 600 and 3300 metres high. The region lies east of Cuicatlán in northern Oaxaca, surrounded by Chinantec territory to the east, Mazatecs to the north and Mixtecs to the west. The Cuicatecs are thought to be descended from Toltecs who moved here in the 11th century.

Huaves The 10,000 Huaves live in four villages – San Mateo del Mar, Santa María del Mar, San Francisco del Mar and San Dionisio del Mar – around the saltwater Laguna Inferior at the south end of the Isthmus of Tehuantepec. Their main activity is fishing in the lagoons; they also practise some agriculture and produce sea salt. Huave weaving – mainly of cloth attractively embroidered with little animal designs – has revived recently because of its commercial potential. At the end of the dry season Huaves carry saints' images into the sea and pray for rain.

Ixcatecs By 1981 fewer than 200 Ixcatecs remained to make up about a fifth of the people in their only centre, the village of Ixcatlán in one of the driest and poorest parts of the Mixteca, 21 km north-east of Coixtlahuaca. In pre-Hispanic times Ixcatlán is thought to have ruled several other now-abandoned villages to the west, with a total Ixcatec-speaking population of about 10,000. Like the nearby Chochos, the Ixcatecs make palm hats.

Mazatecs The 100,000-plus Mazatecs of Oaxaca's far north are one of Mexico's most distinctive Indian groups. The huge Miguel Alemán reservoir lies in the middle of their territory, which includes a hot, wet, low-lying eastern zone in the Papaloapan valley (with the Mazatec centre of Ojitlán) and a temperate western mountain area around Huautla de Jiménez, San José Tenango and

Carrying a child

Mazatlán de Flores. About 22,000 Mazatecs were moved from their lands in the 1950s when the reservoir was created. The modern world is making inroads into Mazatec culture but they retain, more than many Indians, their traditional dress and their belief in a magical and ritual world.

Mixes Some 70,000 Mixes are spread over central Oaxaca from the mountains just east of Mitla and Yalalag to the low-lying Isthmus of Tehuantepec. This is very isolated country with few roads. The Mixes are among the least modernised and most self-contained of Oaxaca's Indians; more than half of them don't speak Spanish, and they don't allow outsiders to attend their ceremonies. Like other groups they have witch-doctors, who diagnose and cure illnesses, sometimes with the help of magic mushrooms.

Today the Mixes of lower-lying regions produce some cash crops, but those from the highlands often have to emigrate temporarily to add to their land's meagre produce. The Mixes are by no means united; two groups in particular, from the Zacatepec and Ayutla areas, have a tradition of bloody feuding.

Mixtecs Some 300,000 Mixtecs are spread around the mountainous borders of Oaxaca, Guerrero and Puebla. Of these, over two-thirds are in western Oaxaca. They are far removed from their pre-Hispanic glories, usually consigned to poor, shrinking, often eroded land where a minority mestizo population controls most business and politics. Many Mixtecs are forced to emigrate for work; some go to big farms in California, Sinaloa and Baja California Norte. In the two latter places they earn US$3 or US$4 a day, and much of it is sent back home to help feed their families.

The 'Mixteca' of Oaxaca consists of three adjoining zones: a high (1000-1700 metres), dry, eroded north-western zone around Huajuapan and stretching into Puebla, called the Mixteca Baja (Low); an even higher, rugged, badly eroded central zone of extreme climate which contains the towns of Tlaxiaco and Coixtlahuaca, called the Mixteca Alta (High); and a south-western zone stretching back up into the hills from the coast, called the Mixteca de la Costa (Coast), where Jamiltepec is one of the main Mixtec settlements. Highways cross the Alta and the Costa from east to west, but only one partly-paved road links them from north to south. There are also a few Mixtecs in the Central Valley.

Despite their large numbers, most of the Mixtecs live in isolated areas (their own villages or barrios) and maintain many traditional customs and beliefs. Mixtecs are known for the hats, *petates* (mats), baskets and toys that they weave from palm and sell to supplement the small income from their land.

Triquis The 10,000 or so Triquis of western Oaxaca have had some of the worst luck of all Mexican Indians. Even before the Spanish arrived, they were apparently driven off their lands first by the Zapotecs and then by the Mixtecs, until they settled in their present small area surrounded by Mixtecs between the towns of Tlaxiaco, Putla and Juxtlahuaca. Not surprisingly the Spanish found them rebellious and nearly impossible to convert to Christianity.

There are some fertile areas in the Triqui territory, which ranges between 800 and 3000 metres high, but in general it doesn't produce enough food to go round. Triquis are forced to leave home as migrant workers or rent their land to mestizo cattle-raisers and then work on it as paid labourers. There's a long history of bloody conflict between Triquis and mestizos or Mixtecs over land rights, particularly for timberland. The introduction of coffee as a cash crop around the town of San Juan Copala has only made things worse: Triquis dispute with each other about the ownership of their now more valuable land.

Zapotecs All visitors to Oaxaca come into contact with the Zapotecs, the state's most numerous and widespread Indian group. Some 350,000 live mainly in the Central Valley, the mountains to its north and south, along the coast around Pochutla and on the Isthmus of Tehuantepec. While some villages are remote, Zapotecs generally have had more contact with the outside world than other Oaxacan Indians and their status as second-class citizens in their own land is to a lesser degree. Quite a few are highly educated and speak good English.

In addition to agriculture Zapotecs are involved in the trade of their produce, including mezcal, but many of them still have to emigrate temporarily to find work. Crafts – notably textiles and pottery – produce extra income, particularly in the Central Valley where tourism provides a big market. Sandals, baskets and *petates* (mats) woven from palm or reed are widespread.

The Zapotec language has 16 or 17 dialects, some of which are incomprehensible to other dialect speakers. Each Zapotec village is its own close-knit world; marriages outside the village are rare and villages sometimes come into conflict with each other.

Others Oaxaca has minorities of at least five other Indian groups whose main populations lie beyond the state boundaries. There are about 2000 Amuzgos near the south-western border with Guerrero; about 5000 Nahuas and 2000 Popolocas in the far north of the state; and about 5000 Zoques and 2500 Tzeltals in the east.

Festivals

Oaxaca's Indian heritage makes it one of Mexico's liveliest states as far as fiestas are concerned. Almost every village holds several colourful events each year, among the most important being the one for the village's patron saint. Churches are usually the focus of these events but many of them also involve processions and costumed or masked dances whose origins are lost in the mists of time. As elsewhere in Mexico, the celebrations for Carnival (February or March, just before Lent), the Day of the Dead (2 November) and the day of the Virgin of Guadalupe (12 December) are also widely celebrated.

Prominent fiestas are mentioned in this chapter following the places where they happen. One other well-known site is Santiago Juxtlahuaca, 90 km south of Huajuapan de León by partly paved road; fireworks, parades and masked dances are held here on Carnival Sunday, Monday and Tuesday. Processions and dances take place here from 24 to 28 July, around the Day of Santiago Apóstol, and on 8 September.

OAXACA

Population: 150,000

The state's capital and only sizeable city is a Spanish-built place of narrow, straight streets liberally sprinkled with colonial buildings, among them many churches. It lies 1550 metres high in the heart of the Central Valley, meeting point of the valley's three arms – Tlacolula to the east, Zimatlán to the south, Etla to the north.

Oaxaca is a good-looking city but really no more spectacular than any another Mexican colonial town. What's special is its atmosphere – at once relaxed and energetic, isolated and cosmopolitan. On one hand the sun, dry mountain air, Indian presence, and many old buildings, plazas and cafés help slow the pace of life. On the other, the historical continuity of the Indian peoples' residence here, their artistic heritage and that of the Spanish, and the city's reputation as a meeting point of diverse cultures (Oaxacan, Mexican and international) all make it a place of deep interest to foreigners, some of whom end up returning year after year.

Head for the zócalo to get a taste of this atmosphere.

Not least of Oaxaca's attractions are the abundant Indian crafts for sale and the many other fascinating places within day-trip distance in the Central Valley, notably the Zapotec ruins at Monte Albán; other ruins at places like Mitla, Yagul and Cuilapan; the Indian markets and the craft-making centres.

Foreign and Mexican tourists are an important source of income to Oaxaca, but somehow it accommodates them with minimal impact on its way of life. The changes that have come to the city – for example the near-disappearance of *burros* (donkeys) as a form of transport – have more to do with the slow overall modernisation of Mexican life.

History

The Aztecs established first a garrison and then a settlement here to reinforce their hold over the tribute-paying local peoples in the second half of the 15th century. They called it Huaxyacac (Place of Gourds), from which the name Oaxaca is derived. The Spanish occupied the same part of the valley, calling their first settlement, in what's now the barrio of Jalatlaco about 1½ km north-east of the centre, Segura de la Frontera.

After several Indian uprisings were put down in the 1520s, a new town was laid out around the existing zócalo in 1529. It was called Antequera (after a part of Andalusia in Spain) until 1532, when its name was changed to Oaxaca. It quickly became the most important town in southern Mexico, an administrative centre, the seat of a bishopric and site of numerous churches and monasteries. The religious orders based here played a big part in pacifying the Indians of the region by conversion and by more humane behaviour than the other Spaniards. Early building was interrupted several times by earthquakes, one of which destroyed the cathedral in 1560, and by more Indian rebellions, but by 1620 Oaxaca had about 2000 inhabitants.

In the second half of the 18th century Oaxaca grew rich from exports of cochineal to Europe. An estimated 30,000 peasants in outlying areas of the state were involved in producing this red dye from tiny insects, but many of them were virtual slaves from their debts to the cochineal traders in the city, who had lent the peasants money and goods they couldn't hope to pay back. The banning of this practice by the Spanish crown in 1783 ended the city's cochineal boom but Oaxaca continued to thrive as a textile centre. By 1796 it was probably the third biggest city in New Spain, with about 20,000 people (including 600 clergy) and 800 cotton looms.

The elite of Oaxaca were opposed to the independence movement of the early 19th century. Two envoys from the insurgent leader Miguel Hidalgo were shot in the city in 1810. (The street Armenta y López is named after them. Others are named after Valerio Trujano and Manuel Mier y Terán, rebel leaders in the Mixteca.) José María Morelos took the city for the insurgents in 1812 but after he left for Acapulco the next year, the royalists took it back.

Several mostly conservative rebellions sprang up in the city and state over the following decades while Benito Juárez quietly climbed the ladder of local and then national power. A major earthquake in 1854 destroyed much of the city. In 1857, at the beginning of the Reform War, liberal forces were besieged in Santo Domingo monastery. Porfirio Díaz led the liberals who retook Oaxaca but was taken prisoner here in 1865 when the French occupied the city. Next year he escaped and led the forces which retook the city from the French.

Under the mainly peaceful national presidency of Díaz towards the end of the century Oaxaca began to grow again; in the 1890s it passed the 30,000 population mark and became the seat of an archbishopric. The railway arrived, and the Juárez market (initially called the

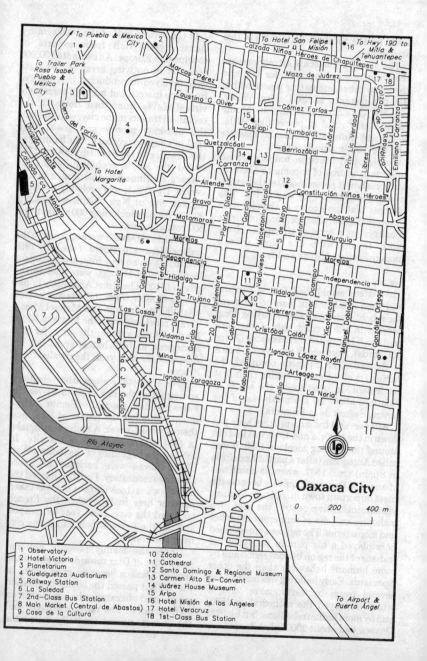

To Puebla & Mexico City
1
2
To Trailer Park Rosa Isabel, Puebla & Mexico City
3
Marcos Pérez
Faustino G Oliver
Cerro del Fortín
4
To Hotel San Felipe u Misión
16
Calzada Niños Héroes de Chapultepec
To Hwy 190 to Mitla & Tehuantepec
Maza de Juárez
17
18
Gómez Farías
Quetzalcóatl
15
Cosijopi
Humboldt
Carranza
13
Berriozábal
Juárez
Priv Lic Verdad
Libres
Emiliano Carranza
Calzada Niños Héroes
To Hotel Margarita
Allende
12
Constitución Niños Héroes
Bravo
García Vigil
Abasolo
Matamoros
Porfirio Díaz
Macedonio Alcalá
5 de Mayo
Reforma
Murguía
División Oriente
Calzada Fco Madero
División Oriente
5
Morelos
6
Morelos
Independencia
Valdivieso
Independencia
Victoria
Galeana
Hidalgo
11
Hidalgo
Ocampo
Mier Y Terán
Trujano
10
Melchor
Xicoténcatl
Manuel Doblado
González Ortega
7
Las Casas
Díaz Ordaz
20 de Noviembre
Cabrera
Guerrero
8
Aldama
J P García
Cristóbal Colón
Ignacio López Rayón
9
Mina
C Mabustamante
Arteaga
La J C J P García
Ignacio Zaragoza
Fiallo
La Noria

Río Atoyac

Oaxaca City

0   200   400 m

To Airport & Puerto Ángel

1 Observatory	10 Zócalo
2 Hotel Victoria	11 Cathedral
3 Planetarium	12 Santo Domingo & Regional Museum
4 Guelaguetza Auditorium	13 Carmen Alto Ex−Convent
5 Railway Station	14 Juárez House Museum
6 La Soledad	15 Aripo
7 2nd−Class Bus Station	16 Hotel Misión de los Ángeles
8 Main Market (Central de Abastos)	17 Hotel Veracruz
9 Casa de la Cultura	18 1st−Class Bus Station

Porfirio Díaz market) was built by an English company.

During the Revolution, as in the War of Independence, the Oaxaca establishment was conservative, but there were numerous rebel movements in the countryside. The *jefes serranos* (strongmen from the hills) who took control of the state in 1913 were driven out of the city by Constitutionalist forces in 1916, but returned in 1920 in the Obregón rebellion, which saw the national defeat of the Constitutionalists. The decade of turmoil cut the city's population from over 35,000 to under 28,000. An earthquake in 1931 left 70% of the city uninhabitable, and another one lasting three minutes in 1978 caused extensive damage.

Oaxacan Artists

Miguel Cabrera (1695-1768) Born here and went on to found Mexico's first Academy of Painting in 1753. His best canvases, on religious themes, are in churches elsewhere in the country; he also painted a famous portrait of Sor Juana Inés de la Cruz, a nun and one of Mexico's best love poets.

Rufino Tamayo A Zapotec born in the city in 1899, is sometimes regarded as the fourth great Mexican 20th-century muralist (with Rivera, Siqueiros and Orozco), but he has painted canvases too and his work is very different from the other muralists'. Less concerned with details of Mexican history, his work is more universal and may be either more abstract or intent on everyday scenes. Tamayo was orphaned, moved to Mexico City in 1911 and has lived much of his life outside the country, but he gave his collection of pre-Hispanic art to the people of Oaxaca and it now forms one of the city's most interesting museums.

Francisco Toledo Born in 1940 in Juchitán but moved to Oaxaca in 1969. As well as his paintings, his woodcarvings are well known and he has designed blankets woven in Teotitlán del Valle.

Orientation

Big maps of the city and state are posted in the 1st and 2nd-class bus stations and the zócalo. The centre of Oaxaca is the zócalo, a big, shady, traffic-free square surrounded by cafés and restaurants. Adjoining it to the north-west is another traffic-free plaza, the Alameda, with the cathedral fronting its east side. Streets in the central area are on a right-angled grid plan and usually change their names when they pass the north-east corner of the cathedral. Alcalá, which runs north from this corner, is mostly pedestrians-only and leads past some beautifully preserved old buildings to the famous church of Santo Domingo with the Oaxaca Regional Museum next door.

There are many hotels and restaurants of all varieties within a few blocks of the zócalo. The 1st-class bus station is north of the centre on Calzada Niños Héroes de Chapultepec, about a 20-minute walk from the zócalo. The 2nd-class bus station is slightly nearer the centre but west of it, near the main market.

Information

Tourist Office Oaxaca has two tourist offices. One is at the corner of García Vigil and Independencia (tel 6-38-10, 6-04-63) usually open from 9 am to 3 pm and 6 to 8 pm. The other, at the corner of 5 de Mayo and Morelos (tel 6-48-28), is officially open 9 am to 3 pm and 4 to 8 pm Monday to Friday, 10 am to 1 pm Saturday, closed Sunday. The staff usually have plenty of maps and leaflets but their knowledge of English is erratic, and how much they can tell you depends on who's on duty. The man with the withered arm in the 5 de Mayo office is particularly knowledgeable not only about the city but about the surrounding area too. The tourist offices can also usually tell you what festivals are on in the city and outlying villages.

Money Several banks change travellers' cheques and foreign cash. For some reason the queues in Banpais on García Vigil, half a block north of Independencia, are usually a lot shorter than in other central branches. Outside bank hours try the American Express representatives, Viajes

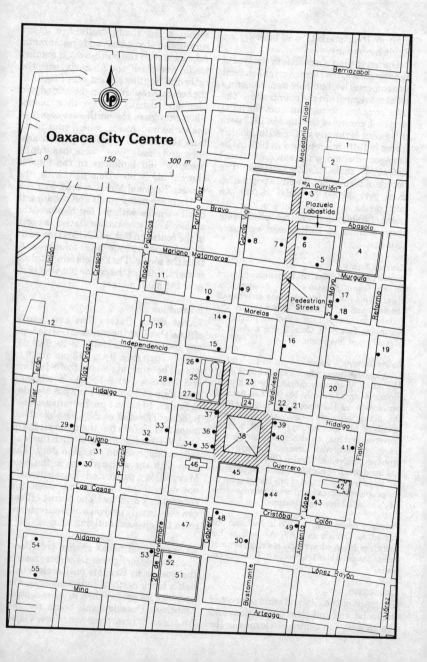

Oaxaca City Centre

0   150   300 m

Berriozabal

Macedonio Alcalá

1
2

A Gurrión
3
Plazuela
Labastida

Porfirio Díaz
Bravo

García Vig

Abasolo

Palacios

Mariano Matamoros

8   7   6   4

5

Murguía

Crespo

Tinoco

11

10   9

Morelos

5 de Mayo

Pedestrian
Streets

17
18

Reforma

Unión

12

14

13

Díaz Ordaz

Independencia

15

16

19

Mier Y Terán

León

26
25
27

28

23

24

Valdivieso

20

22 21

Hidalgo

Hidalgo

29

37
36
34 35

32   33

31
30

38

39
40

41

Fiallo

Trujano

P. García

46

45

Guerrero

Las Casas

44

42

43

Cabrera

48

Cristóbal

Colón

49

Armenta Y López

47

50

54

Aldama

53   52

20 de Noviembre

51

55

Mina

López Rayón

Bustamante

Arteaga

Juárez

1	Museo Regional	30	Hotel Vallarta
2	Santo Domingo	31	Restaurants Montebello & Flamingo
3	Pizzería Alfredo da Roma	32	Hotel Mesón del Rey
4	Hotel El Presidente	33	Hotel Francia
5	El Sol Y La Luna	34	Hotel Plaza
6	El Topil	35	Café El Jardín &
7	Biblioteca Circulante		Restaurant Asador Vasco
8	Hotel Calesa Real	36	Hotel Señorial
9	Cocijo	37	Mi Casita
10	Hotel Pomba	38	Zócalo
11	Museo Rufino Tamayo	39	Café del Portal
12	Jardín Socrates	40	El Zaguan
13	San Felipe Neri	41	Posada San Pablo
14	Restaurant Catedral	42	San Agustín
15	Tourist Office	43	Restaurant La Flor de Oaxaca
16	Yalalag	44	Hotel Ruíz
17	Hotel Principal	45	Palacio de Gobierno
18	Tourist Office	46	La Compañía
19	Hotel Reforma	47	Juárez Market
20	Teatro Macedonio Alcalá	48	Hotel Trebol
21	Hotel Antequera	49	Hotel Colón
22	El Mesón	50	Hotel Aurora
23	Cathedral	51	20 de Noviembre Market
24	Hotel Marqués del Valle	52	San Juan de Díos
25	Alameda	53	Hotel Rivera
26	Post Office	54	Hotel Del Valle
27	Hotel Monte Albán	55	Hotel Mesón del Ángel
28	Hotel Central		(Buses to Monte Albán)
29	Café Alex		

Micsa, at the corner of Hidalgo and Valdivieso by the zócalo (open for changing travellers' cheques until 8 pm Monday to Friday, 6 pm Saturday) or Casa de Cambio San Felipe in the Aerovías Oaxaqueños office at Armenta y López 209 (open mornings and 4 to 7 pm, Monday to Saturday). Rates in these last two places are usually lower than in the banks.

Books Many books have been written on different aspects of the city and state of Oaxaca but there doesn't yet seem to be a good general guide. Miguel Guerrero of El Topil restaurant is working on what looks like a very thorough and useful handbook to the city and area, called *Auster*. He plans to have it published in 1988, initially in Spanish only.

The Biblioteca Circulante de Oaxaca (Oaxaca Lending Library) at Alcalá 305 has quite a big collection of books and magazines in English and Spanish, many of them on Oaxaca and Mexico. It's open 10 am to 1 pm and 4 to 6 pm Monday to Friday, except holidays. For a year's membership fee of US$3 you can borrow books. The library has a copy of *Lawrence in Oaxaca* by Ross Parmenter, an account of D H Lawrence's time in the state, where he wrote and set part of his novel *The Plumed Serpent*.

Librería Universitaria at Guerrero 108 just off the zócalo has quite a few books on Oaxaca and Mexico, mostly in Spanish but a few in English. The regional and Rufino Tamayo museums and the Aripo craft shop at García Vigil 809 also have interesting books for sale.

Courses The Instituto Cultural Oaxaca (tel 5-34-04), open 9 am to 2 pm and 4 to 6 pm, is a private college offering courses in the Spanish, Zapotec and Mixtec languages and in weaving, ceramics and regional dance. A full-time Spanish course costs US$137 for two weeks, US$275 for four weeks. It's at Avenida Juárez 909 on the corner of the Pan-American Highway. Private Spanish lessons are easy to fix up in Oaxaca – just ask around.

Airlines Aeroméxico (tel 6-37-65, 6-10-66; at the airport 6-28-44) is at Hidalgo 513. Mexicana (tel 6-84-14, 6-73-52; at the airport 69229) is at the corner of Independencia and Fiallo. Aerovías Oaxaqueñas (tel 6-38-33, 6-38-24), which flies between Oaxaca, Puerto Escondido and Salina Cruz, is at Armenta y López 209. Its Mexico City office (tel 510-01-62) is at Despacho 514, Balderas 32. Several travel agents in Oaxaca also sell air tickets. If you're into hiring planes, you can arrange that at the airport.

Market Days Village markets in and around the valley take place on different days of the week: Tlacolula is Sunday, Miahuatlán and Ixtlán are Monday, Soledad Etla Tuesday, Zimatlán and San Pedro y San Pablo Etla Wednesday, Zaachila and Ejutla Thursday, Ocotlán Friday (see the Central Valley sections).

Other Most shops and businesses close between 1.30 and 4 pm and almost always on Sundays. The post office is on the Alameda, just off Independencia. The US Consulate (tel 6-06-54) is at Crespo 213, the Canadian Consulate (tel 6-46-88) is at Fortín 128. Other consulate telephone numbers: France 6-35-20, West Germany 6-56-00, Spain 5-00-31.

Festivals

Guelaguetza Oaxaca's best-known festival is the Guelaguetza (a Zapotec word meaning 'offering'), which takes place on the last two Mondays of July in a big amphitheatre on Cerro del Fortín hill, about 1½ km north-west of the zócalo. The celebrations have very ancient roots.

For several hours from about 10 am, troupes of richly costumed dancers from different parts of the state walk in procession to the stage, deposit offerings of local produce in front of it, do a traditional dance (these days to the accompaniment of recorded music), and then throw their offerings to the crowd. One of the best-known dances is the Zapotec feather dance (Danza de las Plumas) by men only, which represents the Spanish conquest of Mexico. All wear glorious feather headdresses; the dancer portraying Moctezuma wears one of red, green and white, the colours of the Mexican flag.

In pre-Hispanic times the Zapotecs, Mixtecs and Aztecs who occupied the valley held a festival in the same place at the same time of year, in honour of their maize gods (Pitao Cozobi to the Zapotecs, Centéotl and Xilómen to the Aztecs). Different traditions have it that food was given to the poor for eight days, with dancing on the eighth day, or that the nobles and priests held ceremonies each morning – reputedly sometimes with the sacrifice of virgin girls – while the people would gather on the hill in the evenings. Christian priests substituted masquerades of monsters, then giants before such pagan goings-on were abolished altogether in 1882, but people continued to make pilgrimages to the hill for the fiesta of the Virgen del Carmen on 15 or 16 July. Then in the 1930s the celebrations were revived in their present form. The amphitheatre was opened in 1974.

Blessing of Animals This takes place at La Merced church around 31 August.

La Virgen de la Soledad (Virgin of the Solitude) The day of the state's patron saint on 18 December sees processions and traditional dances at La Soledad church.

Fiesta de los Rábanos (Festival of the Radishes) Growers display their products and figures carved from radishes in the zócalo. You're supposed to eat *buñuelos* (a type of crepe) and throw your plate in the air afterwards. It takes place on 23 December.

Christmas Eve A week of festivities climaxes in a parade in which an image of the baby Jesus is carried round the zócalo and churches.

Zócalo

The zócalo is both the geographical and social heart of Oaxaca. Traffic-free and lined with cafés and restaurants, it's the perfect place to relax and watch the city go by. Here people will try to sell you everything from shoeshines or songs to blankets from Teotitlán del Valle. The adjacent Alameda, without the cafés, is also a popular gathering place for locals.

On the south side of the zócalo, the stairway of the neoclassical Palacio de Gobierno has a mural depicting Oaxacan history. Its centre panel is devoted mainly to the 19th-century reformers, notably Benito Juárez (with his wife) but also José María Morelos and Ricardo Flores Magón. Porfirio Díaz, who early in his career was one of Juárez's generals, appears below in blue. At bottom right, the death of Vicente Guerrero at nearby Cuilapan is shown. The left wall shows ancient Mitla while the right wall is dominated by women, notably Sor (Sister) Juana Inés de la Cruz, a 17th-century nun and famous love poet. Traditional activities of Indian women are shown, as well as the anti-clerical reforms of the 19th century.

The cathedral, begun in 1553 and finished (after several bouts with earthquakes) in the 18th century, stands on the north side of the zócalo, partly behind the Hotel Marqués del Valle. Its main façade on the Alameda has some fine baroque carving, while the interior includes later neoclassical remodelling.

Regional Museum

The Museo Regional de Oaxaca is housed in the beautiful two-storey green stone cloister of the ex-monastery attached to Santo Domingo church, five blocks up Alcalá from the zócalo. It's open 10 am to 6 pm Tuesday to Friday, 10 am to 5 pm Saturday and Sunday. Entry fee is 20c (free on Sundays and holidays). The museum's archaeological contents will probably prove more interesting if you visit it after seeing some of the sites in the Central Valley.

A special section of the museum is devoted to the Mixtec treasure from Tomb 7 at Monte Albán. In the mid-14th century the Mixtecs, extending their domain into the Central Valley, re-used an old Zapotec tomb from period IIIB at Monte Albán to bury one of their kings and his sacrificed servants. With the bodies they placed a hoard of beautifully worked silver, turquoise, coral, jade, amber, jet, rock crystal, pearls, jaguar and eagle bone, and above all gold. It was discovered in 1932 by Alfonso Caso.

Santo Domingo

The famous church of Santo Domingo is next door to the Regional Museum. Built between 1570 and the early 17th century (though additions and decorative work went on longer), it was originally part of one of the many monasteries of the Dominican monks in Oaxaca. The Dominicans were founded by Santo Domingo de Guzmán, a 13th-century Spanish monk who was at odds with the church establishment and started a new order with strict vows of poverty, chastity, obedience and intense study and teaching of the holy writ. In Mexico they won themselves a reputation for protecting the Indians from exploitation by other colonists. The finest artisans were reputedly brought from Puebla and elsewhere to help in Santo Domingo's construction. Along with other large buildings in this earthquake-prone region, it has immensely thick stone walls.

Santo Domingo is usually locked for a few hours in the early afternoon. At other times there are often services going on, so enter with care. The church's chief glory is its interior, where the amazing ornamentation in gilded and polychromed stucco is among the most lavish in Mexico. Just inside the main door, on the ceiling, is an elaborate family tree of Santo Domingo de Guzmán.

Museo Rufino Tamayo

The Mixtec treasure apart, this house on Morelos between Porfirio Díaz and Tinoco y Palacias has a more interesting and better displayed pre-Hispanic collection than the Regional Museum. The objects here were collected and donated to Oaxaca by the painter Rufino Tamayo. The museum is open on Sunday from 10 am to 3 pm, and every other day except Tuesday from 10 am to 2 pm and 4 to 7 pm. Admission is US$0.50.

Museo Casa de Juárez

The Juárez House Museum is where the 19th-century president and national hero Benito Juárez lived as a boy after he arrived in Oaxaca from the village of Guelatao, a Zapotec with only a few words of Spanish. Thanks to his elder sister who was already a servant in the city, Benito found work in 1818 in this house at García Vigil 609, between Carranza and Quetzalcóatl. The owner – Antonio Salanueva, a lay preacher and bookbinder – spotted the boy's potential and helped pay for an education he otherwise might not have received.

The house, round a central courtyard, shows how wealthy people lived in the first half of the 19th century. The bookbinding workshop is preserved, along with pictures and a death mask of Juárez,

some of his correspondence and other documents. It's open daily except Monday from 10 am to 2.30 pm and 3.30 to 7 pm. Entrance is 10c (free on Sundays and holidays).

Planetarium

The Nundenui Planetarium on Cerro del Fortín, a hill 1½ km north-west of the zócalo, does three or four shows daily except Monday, most of them after 5 pm. The nearby observatory is also often open.

Other Buildings

Oaxaca has many colonial churches, usually with lovely carved stone façades. San Agustín on Guerrero, 1½ blocks east of the zócalo, shows scenes from the saint's life. In the old market area are La Compañía (by the south-west corner of the zócalo) and the popular San Juan de Díos, dating from 1526 and the oldest church in Oaxaca, at the corner of Aldama and 20 de Noviembre. The large building opposite the Juárez House Museum is the ex-convent of Carmen Alto, now a school.

San Felipe Neri On the corner of Independencia and Tinoco y Palacios is this colonial church with some elaborate altars and a southern façade in a typically baroque mixture of styles. The emblem of the Oratorio religious movement founded by San Felipe Neri (a 16th-century Florentine) is visible on the façade's lowest level – it consists of the four-point Jesuit cap and a lily on a book, with the symbol of the Holy Spirit above. In this church Benito Juárez married Margarita Maza, daughter of the family for whom his sister had been a servant, in 1843.

La Soledad This is a 17th-century church with another rich baroque façade, three blocks west of San Felipe Neri along Independencia. The church's much-revered image of Oaxaca's patron saint, the Virgen de la Soledad (Solitude), is said to have miraculously appeared in a donkey-pack on this spot, which is why the church is where it is. Today the image is adorned with a two-kg gold crown, 600 diamonds and a huge pearl. Processions and dances take place here on the saint's day, 18 December. The adjoining convent buildings contain a religious museum, open 10 am to 2 pm Monday to Saturday and 12 noon to 2 pm on Sunday.

Teatro Macedonio Alcalá This theatre, at the corner of 5 de Mayo and Independencia, was completed in 1903. It's a fine example of the French style which became fashionable among the rich during the dictatorship of Oaxacan Porfirio Díaz, when foreign influences dominated many aspects of Mexican life. The entrance hall is in Louis XV style with a marble stairway. The five-tiered auditorium holds 1300, has more marble and a giant candelabrum. The theatre's usually open for evening performances.

Places to Stay

Compared with less-visited cities, accommodation in Oaxaca is a bit expensive for what you get, in all parts of the price spectrum. There are plenty of budget places but the atmospheric old buildings are reserved for the middle and top ranges.

Places to Stay – bottom end

There are hordes of cheap hotels within a few blocks of the zócalo, but nowhere outstanding. Some of them are quite small so you may have to look at a couple in busy periods. Among the best value in the range are the Hotels Reforma, Pomba and Aurora.

The *Hotel Reforma* (tel 6-71-44) is east of the zócalo at Reforma 102, half a block north of Independencia. They're friendly and most of the rooms are clean, big and light. There's a roof to sit on and singles/doubles with bath are US$4.50/6. Rooms on the street side can be noisy.

The *Hotel Pomba* (tel 6-26-73) at

Morelos 601 between García Vigil and Porfirio Díaz, north of the zócalo, is a rambling place with 50 varied rooms and nearly always some vacancies. It's spartan but basically clean with some open-air walkways. Rooms with bath are US$2.75/3.25.

South-east of the zócalo, the *Hotel Aurora* (tel 6-41-45) at Bustamante 212 between Colón and Rayón is the same price as the Pomba but the bathrooms are communal (and hot water irregular). The rooms, round a big, pleasant courtyard, are large, cool and tidy and the management is friendly.

Not far from the Aurora, the *Hotel Colón* (tel 6-47-26) at Colón 120 near the corner of Armenta y López has a pleasant courtyard with a fountain and plants. Rooms are clean with private bathrooms taking up one corner but the partitions between rooms don't always reach up to the ceiling. Rates are US$5.25/6.50. *Hotel Yagul* (tel 6-27-50), in the same area on the corner of Mina and Bustamante, has rooms for US$2.75/3.25. They have private baths but need a good clean.

On the pleasant Plazuela Labastida between Alcalá and 5 de Mayo four blocks north of the zócalo, the *Posada Margarita* is a small, friendly, family-run place with a view of the towers of Santo Domingo. Rooms have private bath but aren't huge and cost US$5.50 double. North-west of the zócalo the *Hotel Central* on 20 de Noviembre between Hidalgo and Independencia has clean, bright rooms with private bath for US$4.75/6.

South of the zócalo, the *Hotel Pasaje* on Mina between 20 de Noviembre and García is friendly and clean with doubles for US$5. Two travellers reported that the private bathrooms were immaculate and the parrot talked. Opposite the 20 de Noviembre market the *Hotel Chayo* at 20 de Noviembre 508 has clean enough but mostly small singles/doubles with bath for US$3.25/4.25. *Hotel Nacional* at 20 de Noviembre 512 is similar at US$4/5. *Hotel Rivera* (tel 6-38-04) at 20 de Noviembre

502 on the corner of Aldama is a step up, with echoing tiled corridors and big, clean rooms. One double bed costs US$5.50, two beds are US$7.75. In the same area *Hotel La Cabaña* (tel 6-59-18) at the corner of Mina and Cabrera is clean but very institutional and noisy with banging doors. Singles/doubles are US$3/3.50 with common bath, US$5/6.50 with private bath.

The rougher streets between the zócalo and the 2nd-class bus station are packed with hotels, many of them among the cheapest in town. Expect cockroaches in some of these places. Among the better places here is the *Hotel Del Valle* on Aldama between Díaz Ordaz and Mier y Terán, which has a pleasant lobby, parking space, a restaurant and tiled stairs – though the rooms are a bit dark. Singles/doubles are US$5/7.

The very cheapest places in this area include the *Hotel Lishiviusa* at Díaz Ordaz 404, half a block south of Las Casas, where damp, dirty doubles cost US$2. *Hotel Vallarta* (tel 6-49-67) at Díaz Ordaz 309 between Las Casas and Trujano is better – well kept, clean and bright, with rooms at US$4.50/5.50.

At Trujano 412 the *Hotel San José* is basic and dank with rooms (common bath) for US$2.25/3. *Hotel Del Pacífico* at Trujano 420 is bare but the rooms are bigger and brighter than at the San José and seem clean. Doubles are US$3 with common bath, US$3.25 with private bath. *Hotel Jiménez* on Mier y Terán half a block from Trujano is a step up from both these places. Rooms are bigger, brighter, have more furniture, and cost US$4.50/5.50.

Hotel Las Américas on Aldama between Díaz Ordaz and Mier y Terán has small but clean rooms with private bath for US$2.50/3.25, and a sign banning drunks and *mujeres a la vida galante* (prostitutes).

Camping *Trailer Park Oaxaca* (tel 5-27-96) is in the north of the city at the corner

of Violetas and Heroica Escuela Naval Militar. The rates are US$6.50 for a vehicle with all hook-ups, US$5 for a tent alone. To get there turn north off Calzada Niños Héroes de Chapultepec, five blocks east of the ADO bus station, and go seven blocks along Calzada Manuel Ruíz, which becomes Violetas.

Trailer Park Rosa Isabel (tel 6-07-70) is six km from the city centre on Highway 190 towards Puebla. Rates are US$4 for a vehicle with hook-ups, about US$1.75 for a tent.

Places to Stay – middle

Probably the best value hotel in Oaxaca is the *Hotel Principal* (tel 6-25-35) at 5 de Mayo 208, between Morelos and Murguía. It's very well kept, with large rooms opening on to a sunny, peaceful courtyard, and is popular with travellers. The rooms lack fans but are built to retain the cool of the night. Doubles/triples round the main courtyard are US$9/11. There are also a couple of singles/doubles on a less attractive rear courtyard for US$7.25/9. The Principal has fewer than 20 rooms and is sometimes full, so you may have to wait a day or two for a room – but it's worth it for a touch of old-fashioned elegance at what, for Oaxaca, is a decent price.

Also a good bet and equally popular is the *Hotel Plaza* (tel 6-22-00) at Trujano 112, half a block west of the zócalo. The entrance is via a flight of stairs. Like the Principal it's well kept with a pleasant atmosphere and rooms on two levels round a courtyard. Singles/doubles are US$7.75/10 and there are double suites for US$12. Continental breakfast is served in the courtyard.

Hotel Trebol, tucked away opposite the Juárez market a block south of the zócalo at the corner of Las Casas and Cabrera, has big, bright rooms for US$7.50/9.50. The new, clean rooms are well furnished.

The *Hotel Monte Albán* (tel 6-27-77), very centrally located opposite the cathedral at Alameda de León 1, is about

400 years old with a beautiful old pillared courtyard-dining-room (unfortunately covered to keep rain out). Rooms are on two floors around this and cost US$10.50/13.25. The ones at the front are bigger but the whole place is comfortable and has colonial atmosphere.

Another interestingly housed hotel is the *Posada San Pablo* (tel 6-49-14) two blocks east of the zócalo at Fiallo 102 between Hidalgo and Guerrero. The building is a converted part of an ex-convent. It's cool, clean and well kept and rooms are US$8.50/10.75. Some rooms have stove and fridge. The monthly rates are US$150/180.

The *Hotel Francia* (tel 6-48-11), at 20 de Noviembre 212 near the corner of Trujano, is where D H Lawrence stayed and isn't too bad value at US$7.75/10. It's a rambling place with a variety of rooms – some modern and quite big with balconies, some small and dark – on two floors around a pair of covered courtyards.

Hotel Mesón Del Rey (tel 6-00-33) at Trujano 212, 1½ blocks west of the zócalo, is pleasant, modernish, clean and well-kept, with its own restaurant and rooms for US$8.25/10. *Hotel Antequera* (tel 6-46-35, 6-40-20), at Hidalgo 807 half a block east of the zócalo, is very central and has a lovely wide stone staircase but the covered courtyard keeps in heat and cooking smells. Rooms, which have TV but could be cleaner, cost US$8.50/10.

Hotel Ruíz (tel 6-36-60) at 103 Bustamante, half a block south of the zócalo, is a 1930s-style building with a wide staircase taking up most of the lobby. Rooms cost US$8.25/10 and are big enough but the bathrooms could be cleaner. *Hotel Isabel* (tel 6-49-00), at Murguía 104 between Alcalá and 5 de Mayo, has rooms for US$6.50/8 but many of them are dark and need paint. Still, it has a pleasant-enough lobby and a glass lift, and you might be offered one of the better rooms.

Places to Stay - top end

The ultimate splurge for colonial atmosphere is the *Hotel El Presidente* (tel 6-06-11) at 5 de Mayo 300 between Murguía and Abasolo. The entire 16th-century convent of Santa Catalina was converted to create this hotel and the transformation was a success. The old chapel is a crafts showroom/banquet hall, one of the courtyards houses a swimming pool, and thick old stone walls – some still bearing original frescoes – keep the place cool. There are 91 rooms, ranging from singles at US$46 and doubles at US$53 to suites at US$59. Upstairs rooms tend to be brighter, while those on the road side or near the kitchens can be noisy. Some say the service should be better, but the setting can't be beat! You can also make reservations by calling Mexico City 395-03-33, Monterrey 44-65-85, Guadalajara 16-35-84, or (toll-free in the US) 800-472-2427.

The other top-of-the-top-end place is the 154-room *Hotel San Felipe Misión* (tel 5-01-00, 5-06-00) in the far north of the city on Calzada San Felipe. Singles/doubles, all with private balconies, are US$23/28.75, and facilities include a swimming pool, live music in the bar, a disco and two restaurants. A shuttle bus runs between the hotel and the city centre.

The 164-room *Hotel Misión de los Ángeles* (tel 5-15-00, 5-12-22), in the not-quite-so-far-north of the city at Calzada Porfirio Díaz 102, has singles/doubles at US$16.50/20.75, plus swimming and tennis. In the 63-room *Hotel Margarita* (tel 6-41-00, 6-40-85) at Calzada Madero 1254 (just off the main road to Puebla) singles/doubles are US$15.25/17. Also out of the centre and in the top bracket, with prices midway between the last two places, is the *Hotel Victoria* (tel 5-26-33) just off the Pan-American Highway on the hill of Cerro del Fortín, about 1½ km from the zócalo.

Back in the central area the *Hotel Calesa Real* (tel 6-55-44) at García Vigil

306, between Bravo and Matamoros, is pleasantly tiled, with a tiny swimming pool and singles/doubles for US$13/14.25. Right on the zócalo the *Hotel Señorial* (tel 6-06-11) at Portal de Flores 6 is much used by tour groups and has a swimming pool, restaurant, cafeteria, roof garden and TV in rooms. Singles/doubles are US$10.25/11, two-room suites are US$13.75/14.50. *Hotel Marqués del Valle* (tel 6-32-95, 6-33-77) on the north side of the zócalo at Portal de Clavería has singles/doubles for US$15.25/17. Some of the rooms have great views over the square.

Hotel Mesón del Ángel (tel 6-66-66) at Mina 518 near the corner of Mier y Terán is an unimaginative modern place with a swimming pool and singles/doubles for US$15.25/17.

Places to Eat

Oaxacan restaurant food has never won any prizes and it's said that nowhere in Mexico is there a greater quality gap between home and restaurant cooking. But in recent years standards have improved as the Oaxacans have become more used to catering to outsiders. Among local specialities is *mole Oaxaqueño* – a sauce made from chiles, bananas, chocolate, pepper and cinnamon, usually served over chicken or tamales.

Three places are at the top of the list for reasonably priced, tasty and sizeable meals. One is *Café Alex*, a clean, lively, hole-in-the-wall place with just seven tables, out on the corner of Trujano and Díaz Ordaz but well worth the walk for great-value breakfasts. For example, US$0.60 buys you orange juice, an onion-ham-potato omelette, frijoles refritos, bolillo and coffee. Also on the menu are yoghurt, fruit and honey. Later in the day you can get soup (US$0.35), spaghetti (US$0.40), chicken and chips a la Mexicana (US$0.65), or an order of enchiladas or tacos for US$0.70.

More upmarket is *Pizzeria Alfredo da Roma* (tel 6-50-58) at Alcalá 400 just down from Santo Domingo, where delicious and generous portions of spaghetti, ravioli or lasagne cost US$1.50, and pizzas come in four sizes and many combinations – eg Margarita US$1.25 to US$2.25, 7 Mari (Seven Seas) US$2.50 to US$4.50. There are good salads too, and you can rinse it all down with a glass of sangría (US$0.60 without alcohol, US$0.80 with) or wine (US$3.50 to US$6.50 for three-quarters of a litre).

Just off the zócalo on Hidalgo is *El Mesón*, a fast-service place which does a wide selection of tasty, mainly charcoal-grilled Mexican food at reasonable prices. You tick off your order on a printed list – which can be a problem if you don't understand what all the items are, but *alambres* (meat kebabs on tacos) and *tacos razas con crema* (bean tacos with cream) are both delicious.

Oaxaca's markets are the cheapest places in town to eat. The 20 de Noviembre market is almost entirely given over to *fondas* (small sit-down eating places) and it's especially good value for breakfast. This is also the place to try authentic local hot chocolate – not to everyone's taste but interesting.

The zócalo harbours a variety of busy restaurants but one thing they nearly all have in common is slow service. *El Zaguan* on the east side is an exception – a small, friendly place with just a few tables, great for a snack or lingering over a drink. Two tasty burritos cost US$0.50, fruit cocktail US$0.40.

Next door to El Zaguan, the *Refresquería Bum Bum* is good for fruit juices squeezed before your eyes, but on the other side of El Zaguan, the *Café y Restoran Guelatao* wins our Oaxaca Zócalo Award for Slow Service. The waitresses are apparently happy to let their customers die of thirst to save the trouble of taking an order. If you insist on going to the Guelatao (which a lot of people seem to, perhaps because of its US$0.75 four-course comida corrida) you can nip two doors away to the Bum Bum for drinks in between waiting for the menu to turn up, waiting for the waitress to come back for the order, waiting for the food to turn up, waiting for the waitress to appear so you can ask for the bill, waiting for the bill to turn up, and waiting for the change.

Elsewhere on the zócalo, the *Café del Portal* on the north-east corner is more expensive but the meals are quite good. They range from spaghetti napolitano in cream sauce (US$1.25) to pickled fish kebab *(brocheta de pescado adobada)* at US$3.50 and red snapper *(huachinango)* mornay at US$3.75. The top side of the zócalo is occupied by the *Restaurant Marquis*, whose location is better than its fare. Omelettes can be leathery but the guacamole (US$0.60) is good. Mexican dishes are US$1 to US$2.25.

On the south-west corner of the zócalo the *Café El Jardín* is always bustling and is the favourite place with locals. It's more of a drink and snack place than a restaurant but the seafood cocktails (US$1.25 to US$1.75) are good, the hearty *tasajó* (US$2.25) is a huge slab of beef with frijoles and *chilaquiles* (tortilla chips with chile sauce), and there are tacos and tortas too.

Above El Jardín, the *Restaurant Asador Vasco* (tel 6-97-19) is the zócalo's most expensive restaurant. The waitresses appear to be dressed German-style but the food is Spanish, Mexican and international and good enough for a bit of a splurge. If you want a table with a view, reserve earlier in the day. Main dishes are mostly in the US$3 to US$4 bracket – the *brochetas* (kebabs) are good. *Carne asada Oaxaqueña* (a slab of beefsteak with tortilla chips in a rather tame mole plus something unidentifiable but tasty) is average. You'll probably be serenaded by quite good musicians as you dine. *Mi Casita* (tel 6-92-56), upstairs on the north-west corner of the zócalo, is another more expensive place recommended by locals – it's usually open only at lunch time.

There are a number of restaurants in the streets north of the zócalo. For carefully prepared Oaxacan food try *El Topil* (the name is Zapotec for The Police) on Plazuela Labastida. Tasajó with guacamole is one speciality for US$2, and there's a range of soups, of which garbanzo (chick pea) is delicious, plus some good antojitos (enchiladas US$1.25 to US$2.25). *Tito's* (tel 6-73-79) at García Vigil 116 is popular with Mexicans and foreigners; they serve a comida corrida from 1.30 pm for US$1, also tasty hamburgers (US$0.75 to US$1.25), roast meats (US$1.25 to US$1.50), chiles rellenos with frijoles (US$1), chicken tacos with guacamole (three for US$1), tortas (US$0.35 to US$0.45) and good pozole.

Quicklys on Alcalá, half a block down from Morelos, just about lives up to its name. Like the decor (potted plants, white trelliswork, folksy Mexican bird murals) the food is a gringo-Mexican mix, sometimes a bit bland but the helpings are big. *Parrilladas* are meat, rice and vegetable plates (there are vegetarian varieties too). There's a *menú del día* (US$1.25) of soup, meat, vegetable, salad and pasta – also burgers, burritos and tortas. *Cafetería Frutimundo* on Valdivieso-Alcalá just north of the zócalo offers 'bionic salads' (six fruits, nuts, coconut, wheat germ, etc) for US$1.25, also yoghurt, licuados, burgers and *sincronizadas* (ham and cheese between two hot tortillas).

A block east of the zócalo, the clean *Restaurant La Flor de Oaxaca* (tel 6-55-22) at Armenta y López 311, between Colón and Guerrero, has lots of non-meat items on the menu. The food is Mexican, with main dishes around US$1.50. The comida corrida (US$1.50) is popular.

Some of the best-value comidas corridas are along Trujano, west of the zócalo. At the *Restaurant Montebello* (Trujano 305, between García and Díaz Ordaz) you pay US$0.90. *Restaurant Flamingo* at Trujano 301 is also popular for its four-course comida corrida (US$1). Travellers recommend a nameless restaurant on García between Mina and Aldama, where a four-course comida corrida of soup, rice, main course and desert costs just US$0.60.

At Trujano 118 (the zócalo end), *Tartamiel* is a French bakery with some delicious sweet pastries and tables to sit at. A couple of doors away you can get yoghurt, granola, fruit and cappuccino at *Chip's*.

A good-value vegetarian comida corrida can be found at the friendly *Restaurant Pisces* at Hidalgo 119, not far west of the zócalo, between 11 am and 4 pm Monday to Friday. It costs US$1.25 (salad, soup, tacos, cauliflower in tomato sauce, lemon water and herb tea). Ring the bell to enter. *El Arca de Emmanuel* (tel 5-64-12) at Calzada Niños Héroes de Chapultepec 1023, almost opposite the 1st-class bus station, is another vegetarian place.

Two more pizzerias are just west of the zócalo. *Pizza Rych's*, on Hidalgo a block west of the cathedral, does pizzas from US$1.50 to US$2.25 and spaghetti for US$1.25, and stays open until 11 pm. At *Gino's* (Independencia 503) pizza prices range from US$1.75 to US$5 and there is also a variety of queso fundidos.

Two middle to top-bracket places with high reputations and courtyard settings are the family-run *La Fontana* on Plazuela Labastida, where a meal from a wide-ranging menu costs around US$5, and *Dona Elpidia* (tel 6-42-92) at Cabrera 413, south of the zócalo, which serves only a Oaxacan comida corrida for about US$5. Dona Elpidia has no sign outside; La Fontana is closed Sunday.

For a breakfast splurge, the all-you-can-eat buffet in the *Hotel El Presidente* costs US$4.

Finally, there's a bunch of open-air *neverías* (sorbet and ice cream places) in the Jardín Socrates, also called Plaza de la Danza, on Independencia next to La Soledad church. The *Cali Fresco Fruti Bar* on 5 de Mayo between Independencia and Morelos does a great mixed-fruit drink called Conga for about 25c.

Entertainment

Oaxaca has a lively cultural and entertainment life thanks mainly to its Indian heritage, high student population and visitor interest. To start with there's live music – marimbas or a brass band – Sunday lunch times and almost every night in the zócalo.

High on the list must also come *El Sol y La Luna* on Murguía between Alcalá and 5 de Mayo. If you've ever dreamed about tropical rhythms, Latin American folk music or jazz under the stars on a balmy Mexican night, this is your place. The open courtyard of an old house is packed with tables where you can sit over a drink or two (beer US$0.50) and listen to good live bands from 7 pm until late every night except Sunday. There's an art gallery in a back room, and food too – spaghetti US$1.50, hamburgers US$2.25 – but it's not as good as the music or the setting. There's a cover charge of US$0.50 per person.

Another good live music spot is the downstairs bar of the *Restaurant Catedral* (tel 6-32-85) at García Vigil 105, on the corner of Morelos. It's open until 1 am most nights (closed Sunday) and the music and clientele are more Mexican than at El Sol y La Luna. At the time of writing there was also an excellent four-piece bossanova band in residence at the *Hotel San Felipe Misión*, which got even better when they let their hair down and played jazz. The *San Felipe Misión* and the *Misión de los Ángeles* hotels have popular but expensive discos. *Chaplin's* disco near the corner of Independencia and Porfirio Díaz is more relaxed, with students among its clientele.

For Oaxacan Indian and folk dances, try the nightly *danzas folkloricas* shows in the *Hotel Monte Albán* (US$1.50, starting at 8.30 pm). The *Hotel El Presidente* puts on similar shows.

The *Casa de la Cultura Oaxaqueña* (tel 6-24-83, 6-18-29), based in an ex-monastery east of the zócalo at González Ortega 403 between Colón and Rayón, runs an almost daily programme of exhibitions, concerts, dance, theatre, classes, etc, at different venues in the city.

You can pick up a programme at the tourist office or keep an eye on the noticeboard at the north side of the zócalo, which also has monthly lists of festivals in the state. *Centro Cultural Ricardo Flores Magón* at Alcalá 302 also has frequent events, as does the *Teatro Macedonio Alcalá* at the corner of 5 de Mayo and Independencia.

Craft, art and photo exhibitions, open-air or street theatre, dance, music, lectures and slide shows are likely to pop up anywhere at any time. One evening started with children dressed as animals and fairies parading through the zócalo; continued with folk-dancing in front of the cathedral; moved on to an open-air ballet of *Peter & the Wolf* in front of Santo Domingo; and was followed by marimbas back in the zócalo! All free.

Things to Buy

Oaxacans come to the city from all over the Central Valley and much further afield to buy and sell food, clothes, shoes, handicrafts, tools, motor parts, animals, sandals, mezcal, you name it. The city is also the best place to find what's now called 'folk art' – Indian-made handicrafts with such appeal for visitors and merchants that they are made in large numbers.

The distinction between 'genuine' items actually used by the people and items made for sale is blurred – but in any case, items made for sale may well be of higher quality, and why try to strip the Indians of their cultural heirlooms? The folk art business is even giving birth to some completely new forms. Techniques, however, are still often very traditional – the backstrap loom is used alongside the pedal loom, pottery is turned by hand.

Like any other business, folk art turns out good work and bad work, so look around before you buy. In general, the better (and more expensive) work in the city is to be found in just a few shops. You'll probably be pleasantly surprised by the prices, which are generally lower in Oaxaca than outside the state, and not necessarily higher in the city than in the villages where they are made.

Things to look out for include black pottery from the village of San Bartolo Coyotepec; blankets and sarapes from Teotitlán del Valle; huipiles and other Indian clothing from anywhere (those from Yalalag and the Triquis are among the prettiest); brightly painted wooden animals from San Martín Tilcajete, Arrazola Xoxo and Cuilapan; hand-woven belts from Santo Tomás Jalieza; knives, daggers and swords from Ejutla; embroidered blouses and dresses from San Antonino and Mitla; woven reed (including baskets) from Ocotlán; stamped and coloured tin from Oaxaca itself. For more on some of these places see the Central Valley section of this chapter.

A special mention must go to the pottery from the village of Atzompa, just north of Oaxaca, where by a unique method of 'embroidering' clay the villagers make intricate, very pagan-looking 'earth mothers' and other figures – including whole Last Supper scenes – in easily recognisable light brown clay. The earth mothers range from miniatures a few cm high which sell for less than US$1 to superb, highly detailed figures a metre or more high (which cost maybe US$30). From Atzompa also comes distinctive dark-green glazed pottery.

If you're in Oaxaca before the Day of the Dead at the beginning of November, you'll see lots of little model skeletons in the markets, doing everything from riding bicycles to getting married – Mexico's way of reminding itself that worldly happiness and success are temporary.

Markets Oaxaca's main market is in the west of town next to the 2nd-class bus station. Officially called the Central de Abastos (Supplies Centre), it's a big maze and has several permanent buildings. Saturday is the main market day, but the place is a hive of activity any day of the week.

Zapotec women are among the traders here and you can find almost anything if you look for it long enough. The care that goes into the displays of food, particularly vegetables (every bunch of chiles becomes a work of art) would put any Western shop-window to shame. Bargaining is expected so don't be shy! In addition to the everyday items that Oaxacans come here to buy and sell, you can find some special handicrafts - look out for huipiles and other textiles, black pottery from San Bartolo Coyotepec, green pottery from Atzompa, or reed baskets from Ocotlán. Quality is variable but you stand as good a chance of a bargain here as anywhere. You may also find medicinal herbs and numerous things whose identity you can only discover by asking. Innumerable eating stalls are scattered round the market.

Oaxaca's two central indoor markets still function daily too - nowadays with some specialisation. They're next door to each other, close to the zócalo. The Juárez market, bounded by the streets 20 de Noviembre, Las Casas, Cabrera and Aldama, concentrates on food - fruit, vegetables, meat, honey, 1001 varieties of chile, cheese and *quesillo* (tiny cheese balls). There are also flowers and, at the northern end (closest to the zócalo) and down the 20 de Noviembre side, some crafts - huipiles, other embroidered clothing, sarapes, blankets, knives, daggers, swords and pottery.

One block south of the Juárez market, the 20 de Noviembre market is devoted mainly to *fondas* (sit-down food stalls) but there are a few craft stalls along the west and south sides.

A small open-air textile crafts market functions every day in the Plazuela del Carmen Alto, six blocks north of the zócalo between Alcalá and García Vigil. Triqui women weave at backstrap looms here.

Other plazas - including the zócalo - are used as informal markets by wandering sellers. The zócalo cafés are favourite spots for sellers of Teotitlán del Valle blankets.

Shops The shops most used by ordinary Oaxacans are in the streets west of the zócalo, but those specialising in folk art are north of it. The quality stuff is to be found in about half a dozen shops. One of the farthest away, but well worth the effort, is Aripo at García Vigil 809 (corner of Cosijopi). This emporium-like place is run by the state government and has rooms devoted to different crafts –blankets, masks, clothing, pottery, woodwork, etc; much of it is among the best you'll find in Oaxaca. Weavers work at treadle looms in a back room and the shop is open Sunday morning until 1 pm as well as 9 am to 1.30 pm and 4 to 7.30 pm every other day.

Cocijo at García Vigil 212, between Matamoros and Morelos, is another place with a wide range of high-quality goods (notably trees of life, fine brown pottery from Acatlán in Puebla, and masks), and so is Yalalag at Alcalá 104, near the corner of Independencia.

Other good shops are Fonart at the corner of García Vigil and Bravo, Victors at Porfirio Díaz 111 (between Morelos and Independencia), and Casa Brena at Pino Suárez 58 on the Paseo Juárez park out towards the ADO bus station. Casa Brena produces its own gold-painted glazed earthenware. Artesanías Chimalli at García Vigil 513, El Cactus at Alcalá 401 (for blankets and sarapes) and Copil at

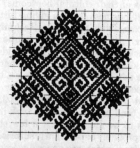

Alcalá 303 are also well worth a look. Nearly all these shops will pack stuff and mail it home for you if you want.

At Oro de Monte Albán on Gurrión, just off Alcalá, you can see goldsmiths at work – and pick up a pair of excellent imitation Mixtec treasure ear pendants or other gold items for up to US$400.

Getting There & Away

Air Mexicana has two to four flights daily to and from Mexico City. Aeroméxico has one daily direct flight to and from Mexico City, Acapulco, Tapachula and Villahermosa. Aerovías Oaxaqueñas runs 28-seater DC-3s to and from Puerto Escondido (US$25) twice daily and Salina Cruz (US$27) daily except Sunday. See Information for where to buy tickets.

Road Oaxaca is about 510 km from Mexico City and 410 km from Puebla. The exact distance depends on the route you take – the Pan-American Highway, Route 190, runs from Mexico City, by-passing Puebla, via Atlixco, Izucar de Matamoros and Huajuapan de León to Oaxaca, but buses often take an alternative route (Highways 150 and 125 via Tehuacán) from Puebla to Huajuapan. A third, more mountainous and poorer route (Highway 131) goes from Tehuacán through Teotitlán del Camino, meeting highway 190 again about 40 km before Oaxaca. All these roads traverse long, isolated, twisting mountain stretches as they enter northwest Oaxaca state.

East of Oaxaca, the Pan-American Highway continues to Tehuantepec (250 km away), Tuxtla Gutiérrez (540 km), San Cristóbal de Las Casas (620 km) and Ciudad Cuauhtémoc on the Guatemalan border (790 km). The coastal route to Guatemala branches off 138 km after Tehuantepec to reach the border just past Tapachula (660 km from Oaxaca).

To the south, Highway 175 is paved for its spectacular mountainous 238 km to Pochutla near the Pacific coast, where it meets Highway 200 running along the coast from Acapulco to Tehuantepec. Highway 131 to Puerto Escondido is paved less than half the way – the longer route via Pochutla is highly advisable. North of Oaxaca, Highway 175 winds through yet more mountains to Tuxtepec (215 km away), then continues to the Gulf coast near Alvarado (350 km).

Bus Oaxaca's 1st-class bus station is on Calzada Niños Héroes de Chapultepec, just east of Pino Suárez. ADO (tel 5-09-03, 5-17-03) runs to Mexico City (US$6.75) 28 times daily, Huajuapan (US$2.50) 14 times, Puebla (US$5) 12 times, Tehuacán (US$3.75) eight times, Córdoba (US$4.75) three times, Veracruz (US$6.50) and Orizaba (US$4.50) twice, Tuxtepec (US$3) once, also to Nochixtlán (US$1.50) and Tamazulapan (US$2). Huajuapan and Tamazulapan buses will usually drop you at Yanhuitlán and the turn-offs for Teposcolula and Coixtlahuaca if you want.

Cristóbal Colón (tel 5-12-14) goes to Tehuantepec (US$3.25) 11 times daily; Juchitán (US$3.50) nine times; Salina Cruz (US$3.50) seven times; Tuxtla Gutiérrez (US$6.50) three times; Villahermosa (US$8.50), Teposcolula (US$1.75) and Tlaxiaco (US$2.25) twice each; San Cristóbal de las Casas (US$7.75); Arriaga (US$5.25); Tonalá (US$5.50) and Tapachula (US$8) once each. You can usually book tickets from 5 pm the day before departure.

First-class journey times: Puebla about seven hours, Mexico City nine hours, Tehuantepec 4½ hours, Tuxtla Gutiérrez 10 hours, San Cristóbal de las Casas 12 hours, Tapachula 12 hours.

Cuenca del Papaloapan (tel 2-02-02), a 2nd-class line, also runs from the 1st-class station. Its buses go to Tuxtepec (US$3) six times daily, Loma Bonita (US$3.25) and Cosamaloapan (US$3.50) twice.

The 2nd-class bus station is a large building between Trujano and the main market, about 10 blocks west of the zócalo.

It's a maze of confusingly-named bus lines but is the departure point to most places in the Central Valley and south to Puerto Ángel and Puerto Escondido. There are also some slow, uncomfortable buses to more distant places like Puebla, Mexico City, Tehuantepec, Tuxtla Gutiérrez, Tuxtepec and Tapachula.

For the Pacific coast, Estrella del Valle/Oaxaca Pacífico (tel 6-54-29) is your only serious option. Its ticket office is between Gates 22 and 23. Its '1st class' buses are really 2nd class and its '2nd class' buses are town or village buses, with low seatbacks, pressed into long-distance service. At the last count there were '1st class' departures at 7.30 am, 9.30 pm and 9.45 pm to Puerto Escondido (US$3.75, seven hours or more), 10 and 11 pm to Pochutla (US$3, six hours or more), 10.30 pm to Puerto Ángel (US$3, 6½ hours or more), 8.30 pm to Pinotepa Nacional (US$4.50), 9 pm to Jamiltepec (US$4.50), 10.15 pm to Huatulco (US$3.50) and 5 am to Río Grande (US$4.25). The '2nd class' buses go to Ocotlán (US$0.35) every 15 minutes, Ejutla (US$0.65) and Miahuatlán (US$1.25) every 30 minutes, Pochutla (US$2.75) at 3 and 5 pm, and Puerto Escondido (US$3.50) at 6 am, 9 am and 12 noon. You can generally buy tickets the day before departure.

La Solteca at Gate 32 has low-seatback buses to Puerto Escondido (US$3) at 6 am and 9 pm and Pinotepa Nacional at 9 pm, but they take the half-unpaved cross-country route via Sola de Vega. La Solteca also runs to Zimatlán every half-hour.

Transportes Oaxaca-Istmo (tel 6-36-64) at Gate 9 goes to Tlacolula (US$0.30) and Mitla (US$0.50) every 20 minutes; also to Tuxtepec, Salina Cruz, Arriaga and Tuxtla Gutiérrez. Its service to Puerto Escondido goes via Salina Cruz, takes 13 hours, and costs US$5.75.

Valle del Norte (Gate 30) serves El Tule, Tlacochahuaya and Teotitlán del Valle. Autobuses de Oaxaca goes to Cuilapan and Zaachila every 20 minutes and costs 10c. Lineas Unidas Mexico-Oaxaca has nine buses a day to Mexico City (US$6) via Yanhuitlán (US$1.25), Acatlán (US$3) and Puebla (US$4.50).

Fletes y Pasajes (tel 6-22-70, 6-12-17) leaves for Arriaga five times daily, Tuxtepec twice, Tuxtla Gutiérrez (US$6) four times, Puebla (US$4.50) three times, Mexico City 12 times, Tehuantepec (US$2.75) and Juchitán once, also Salina Cruz. Servicios Unidos del Istmo goes to Tlacolula, Tehuantepec, Salina Cruz, Juchitán, Arriaga, Tonalá, Tapachula (US$7.25) and Coatzacoalcos.

Other buses, minibuses and colectivos run to villages near the city from a variety of points around the market.

Rail Oaxaca's railway station (tel 6-26-76, 6-48-44) is on Calzada Madero (the westward continuation of Independencia) about two km west of the zócalo. Like most Mexican trains, those from here are slow, not particularly reliable and cheap. There are night trains to and from Tehuacán, Puebla and Mexico City but they have no sleeping accommodation. A 1st-class reserved seat to Mexico City costs US$8.50, 1st-class unreserved US$3.75, 2nd class US$2.25. For Oaxaca, the train leaves Mexico City at 5.32 pm and Puebla at 10.35 pm, reaching Oaxaca at 8.05 am. The return train leaves Oaxaca at 6.20 pm, reaching Puebla at 3.30 am and Mexico City at 8.52 am. There's one other 2nd-class train each way between Oaxaca, Tehuacán and Puebla, taking over 11 hours.

Getting Around
Most points of interest in the city are within walking distance of each other. For transport around the Central Valley, see the sections on Getting There and your particular destination.

Airport Transport Oaxaca airport is a few km south of the city off the road to Ocotlán and Pochutla. Yellow colectivo taxis marked 'Transportes Terrestre' meet incoming flights at the airport. For US$1 per person they'll drop you anywhere in the city. They'll also pick you up from your hotel – book at the Transportaciones Aeropuerto office on Valdivieso just north of the zócalo. If it's a very early morning departure they may charge you US$1.50.

Car Rental Oaxaca is one of Mexico's most expensive cities for car hire, but even so you often have to book a week ahead for a vehicle, even at non-peak periods. For the smallest available car, a Volkswagen sedan, Avis (tel 6-50-30) at Alameda de León 1H, next to the Hotel Monte Albán, charges US$26 a day plus 15c per km, while Budget (tel 6-06-11), in the El Presidente Hotel at 5 de Mayo 300, charges US$25.25 a day plus 15c per km. You pay for your own petrol in both cases.

A better bet for price is Señor Guzmán, a freelance car-hire operator who can be contacted through the Estambres Paty shop on 5 de Mayo almost opposite the Hotel Principal. He can be bargained down to cheaper rates than either Avis or Budget and the Volkswagen Beetle he provided us with was in good condition. There's also Renta Automática (tel 5-03-30) at Manzanos 100 in Colonia Reforma, off the street Heroico Colegio Militar, which in turn is off Calzada Niños Héroes de Chapultepec four blocks east of the 1st-class bus station.

Tours Oaxaca's a compact city, and half the fun of trips to other places in the Central Valley is making your own way there, but if you're short of time there are several companies offering day-tours in and around the city. One with a good choice of itineraries is Viajes Chimali (tel 6-68-69, 6-11-33) at Alcalá 201.

MONTE ALBÁN

The ancient Zapotec capital ('MON-teh al-BAN' – 'White Mountain') stands on a long, artificially flattened hilltop 400 metres above the valley floor, nine km west of Oaxaca. Its distinctive outline can be clearly seen from the airport and from some places in the city if you know what you're looking for. Monte Albán's hilltop position, with views over the often dry, moonscape-like hills and valleys for many km around, makes it well worth visiting even if you're bored stiff by old stones.

History

The site was first occupied some time between 800 and 400 BC, probably by Zapotec-speakers from the very start. One theory about Monte Albán's origins is that when the peoples of the three arms of the Central Valley first became a single political unit, they agreed – or were forced – to create one centrally located governing and religious settlement.

Monte Albán I, the first phase, lasted until about 200 BC and saw the levelling of the hilltop, the building of temples and probably palaces, and the growth of a town of 10,000 or more people on the hillsides. From this period come the 'Danzante' carvings which are probably portraits of slain enemies and have, in many cases, Olmec-like down-turned mouths. These same carvings also bear date and possibly name inscriptions – the earliest known true writing in Mexico.

Monte Albán II (200 BC-250 AD) was a gradual development from phase I. The arrow-shaped Building J (the 'observatory') was constructed and lined with engraved slabs recording military victories. Some influences from the early Mayas are apparent in the pottery of the period. Buildings were typically constructed of huge stone blocks with steep walls.

Monte Albán III (250-750 AD) was when the place reached its peak. The slopes of the main and surrounding hills were terraced for dwellings and the population reached about 25,000 – a size not exceeded by Oaxaca until the late 19th century. There was extensive irrigation and at least 200 other settlements and ceremonial centres

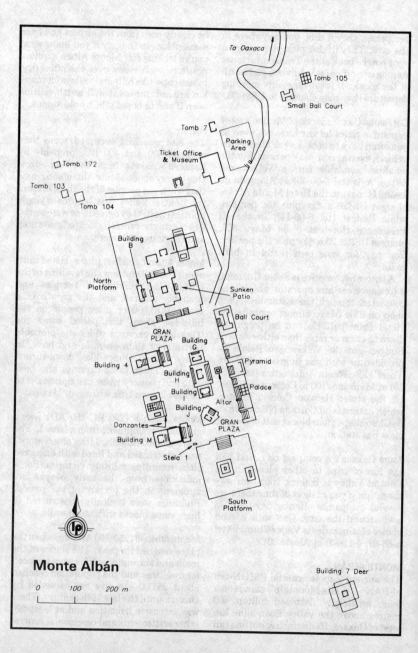

To Oaxaca

Tomb 105

Small Ball Court

Tomb 7

Parking Area

Ticket Office & Museum

Tomb 172

Tomb 103

Tomb 104

Building B

North Platform

Sunken Patio

Ball Court

GRAN PLAZA

Building G

Building 4

Building H

Pyramid

Building I

Palace

Building J

Altar

GRAN PLAZA

Danzantes

Building M

Stela 1

South Platform

Building 7 Deer

Monte Albán

0   100   200 m

in the Central Valley. Monte Albán was the centre of a highly organised, sophisticated, priest-dominated society.

Most of what we see today dates from this time. Several old buildings on the hilltop ceremonial centre were knocked down or built over, and new ones were put up in previously unused parts of the site, including the big ones covering unlevelled parts of the hilltop. Many of them were plastered with stucco and painted red. The use of talud-tablero architecture (alternating sloping and vertical sections giving a 'step' effect to buildings) in this period probably indicates influence from Teotihuacán, with which Monte Albán seems to have co-existed peacefully (there was a Oaxaca barrio at Teotihuacán). A ball court was built on the hilltop.

Nearly 170 underground tombs from Phase III have been found at Monte Albán – many of them elaborate and decorated with frescoes (Tomb 104 is the most exciting). Pottery urns depicting Zapotec gods were found in many of these. In the same period a little-understood script related to that of Monte Albán I and II was often engraved beside relief carvings of human figures – it usually seems to record yet more conquests.

The people of Monte Albán ate tortillas, corn dough, beans, squash, chile, avocado and other plants plus sometimes deer, rabbit and dog. In the dry season water was probably carried up to them from the valley.

Decline Around 700 or 800 AD Monte Albán was largely abandoned, for reasons unknown – perhaps because the effort of maintaining and supplying a growing town was beyond the resources of the rest of the Central Valley. Despite some minor construction work later, Monte Albán gradually fell into ruin and Zapotec life centred instead around several different places in the Central Valley.

When the Mixtecs arrived in the valley some time between 1100 and 1350 they re-used old tombs at Monte Albán to bury their own dignitaries. In Tomb 7 they left one of the greatest treasure hoards ever found in the Americas, which is now in Oaxaca's Regional Museum. Later the Spanish conquistadors were among a long line of people who excavated Monte Albán and other Central Valley sites, seeking not knowledge of the past but treasure.

The Mexican archaeologist Alfonso Caso led the most important archaeological digs at Monte Albán in the 1930s and 1940s. He discovered the Tomb 7 treasure, but much of the site is still to be explored.

Information

Entry to the site is 25c (free on Sundays) and it's open from 8 am to 5 pm daily. If you want to linger for sunset it wouldn't be too difficult to disappear for a few minutes while the site is being cleared at closing time, but you'd have to walk most of the way back to Oaxaca afterwards! There's a good little museum at the entrance containing stone carvings from the site and explanatory text in Spanish, plus a small cafeteria and a couple of shops. Take a flashlight (torch) so that you can look in the tombs – but ask at the entrance if the tombs are open, since they sometimes aren't and the main ones are a bit of a walk from the rest of the site.

Gran Plaza

The track up from the museum comes out at the north-east corner of the Gran Plaza, which is the main levelled area and was the centre of Monte Albán. It's about 300 metres long, 200 metres wide, and aligned roughly north-south. Most of the important structures are on and around this plaza and what's visible is nearly all from the main building period, Monte Albán III. Some of the buildings were temples, others were residential.

Ball Court As you go along the east side of the plaza, this deep, I-shaped court is the first structure. The stone terraces on the sides were probably part of the playing area, not stands for spectators. The round stone in the middle may have been used for bouncing the ball at the start of the game.

Pyramid This is halfway along the line of structures down the east side of the plaza. A tunnel runs from the south side of what was a small pillared temple on top to the buildings in the middle of the plaza. From the altar in front of this building came a well-known bat-god mask made of jade, probably from Phase II and now in the Mexico City Anthropology Museum.

Palace This structure, towards the south end of the east side, has a broad stairway. Under the inner patio that stood on top was found a cross-shaped tomb probably from the Monte Albán IV phase, constructed after the site had been largely abandoned.

South Platform This is the big mound with the wide staircase occupying the whole southern end of the plaza. It has been only partly excavated but is a good place for a panorama of the whole plaza. Two or three hundred metres to the south-east, off the Gran Plaza, is a big structure called Building 7 Deer, from an inscription on its entrance lintel. At the foot of the south platform's north-west corner stands Stela 1, which seems to show a jaguar wearing the mask of Cocijo, the rain god. More stelae originally stood at the other corners.

Building J The arrow-shaped 'observatory' stands in front of the main staircase of the south platform, at an angle of 45° to the other structures. Its positioning gives it significant alignments with a bright star called Capella, but it's not certain whether it was used for astronomical purposes. There's a tunnel inside the building at the end opposite the point. Figures and hieroglyphs carved on its walls probably record military conquests. Building J dates from Phase II. The

remains of a similar building, dating from 250 BC, have been found at Caballito Blanco in the east of the Central Valley near Yagul.

Building M This is the southernmost building on the west side of the plaza. The remains of four columns on top were part of a temple. There's also a cross-shaped tomb on top but, like other structures with tombs built into or on top of them at Monte Albán, Building M was not primarily a funerary construction. The front parts of Building M and of Building IV (at the north end of the same side of the plaza) were added in Phase III. This was apparently an attempt to conceal the plaza's lack of symmetry, since owing to the positioning of the great rock mounds on which they are built, the south and north platforms are not directly opposite each other.

Danzantes The next building along the west side is an amalgam of a Phase I building which contained the famous Danzante (Dancer) carvings, and a Phase III structure which was built over it. The Danzantes – some of which are seen around the lower part – do not actually represent dancers, but rather slain enemies. They generally have open mouths, closed eyes, and in some cases blood flows from where their genitals have been cut off. The hieroglyphs accompanying many of them represent dates and possibly names. Some of the Danzantes were later moved and used again elsewhere in the site.

Building IV This building at the north end of the west side of the plaza, is similar to Building M. An underground tunnel from its north side enables you to see the big stone block construction typical of Phase II. The main stairway and the front part of the building were added in Phase III. Stela 18 (originally five metres high) which stands close to the tunnel entrance is also from Phase II.

Buildings G, H & I These are one complex, lined up from north to south in the middle of the plaza. They cover a rocky rise which the builders could not remove when they flattened the plaza, and probably topped with altars.

North Platform This huge structure covers an area almost as big as the Gran Plaza. Chambers on either side of the main staircase contained tombs. Columns on the top once supported the roof of a hall, and further on is the sunken patio, with an altar in the middle. West of the sunken patio stand the remains of Building B, which was probably a late Mixtec addition. North of the north platform are many unexplored mounds.

Tombs

Nos 104 & 172 A marked path, branching left from the track back to the museum, leads to the 5th-century Tomb 104, which is beneath the remains of a patio with four pillars. There's a replica of this tomb in the Mexico City Anthropology Museum. Above its elaborate underground entrance stands an urn in the form of a person wearing a Cocijo mask. The heavy stone slab covered with hieroglyphs in the antechamber originally blocked the doorway between the antechamber and the tomb proper.

Inside, the tomb walls are covered with frescoes related in style to those at Teotihuacán. The figure on the left wall is probably Xipe Tótec, the flayed god and god of renewal; the figure on the right wall wearing a big snake and feather headdress is Pitao Cozobi, the Zapotec maize god. The tomb contained a male skeleton and several urns.

Tomb 172, lower down in the same mound that contains Tomb 104, retains skeletons and funeral offerings as they were found by excavators. These and several other tombs were built near or beneath other buildings which served as residences.

No 7 This partly restored tomb, just off the car park, dates from Phase III but in the 14th or 15th century it was re-used by Mixtecs to bury a dignitary along with two other bodies – probably sacrificed servants – and the great treasure hoard now in the Regional Museum in Oaxaca.

No 105 On a hill called Cerro del Plumaje on the far side of the access road is another tomb reproduced in the Mexico City Anthropology Museum. It's famous for its Teotihuacán-influenced murals, now somewhat decayed, which show four figures walking along each side. These and other figures may represent nine gods of death or night and their female consorts. A band of decoration round the top seems to show eyes (or stars) falling from divine jaws.

Getting There & Away

The only buses to Monte Albán are run by Autobuses Turísticos from the Hotel Mesón del Ángel on Mina, between Díaz and Mier y Terán, in Oaxaca. They depart for the 20-minute journey at 9.30 and 11.30 am and 1.30 and 3.30 pm daily, returning at 12 noon and 2, 4 and 5.30 pm. A return ticket is US$0.75 and you can come back by any of the buses. It's easy enough to hitch a lift up or down provided you don't leave too late. A taxi from Oaxaca costs about US$3.50 one way. As the road climbs towards Monte Albán, you can see mounds on other hilltops which demonstrate the great size of the ancient settlement.

CENTRAL VALLEY – EAST

Of the three arms of the Central Valley which radiate out from the city of Oaxaca, the Valley of Tlacolula to the east probably has most to offer. The ruins of Mitla are almost as well-known as Monte Albán, and Teotitlán del Valle is one of Mexico's most-visited craft-making villages, but there's much more. There are a couple of places to stay in Mitla if you want to base yourself at this end of the valley or venture into the Mixe country to the east.

Getting There & Away

All the places mentioned here are on or not far off the Oaxaca to Mitla road, and the Transportes Oaxaca-Istmo buses to Mitla, which leave every 20 minutes from Gate 9 of the 2nd-class bus station in Oaxaca, will drop you wherever you want. Tlacochahuaya and Teotitlán del Valle are also served direct – but not so frequently – by Autotransportes Valle del Norte from the same bus station.

El Tule

An *ahuehuete* tree (a type of cypress) in the churchyard here, 10 km along the Mitla road, is claimed to have the biggest girth of any tree in the world. It's certainly a wonderful monster, 42 metres round and 2000 or more years old. Unfortunately it's protected by a fence so you can't get too close. It stands right by the road, so you can get a glimpse from the bus if you're in a hurry.

Guelaguetzas are held here for Candelaria (Candlemas, early February) and the Festival of the Assumption (mid-August). The annual Feria del Árbol (Fair of the Tree) is on the second Monday in October.

Tlacochahuaya

About 18 km from Oaxaca, a turn-off to the right leads two km to this little-visited village ('tla-co-cha-WHY-ah'), whose church San Jerónimo is known for wonderfully decorative Zapotec folk paintings of flowers on its walls and ceiling. The church – originally part of a 16th-century Dominican monastery but redecorated several times since – is often locked but the caretaker lives in front of it, and if he's there he'll open it and explain things for you. There's some fine woodcarving in the church too, and some more formal canvases, also by Zapotec artists – altogether a fine showcase of Indian art.

Tlacochahuaya's main fiesta is for San Jerónimo during the week following 30 September.

Dainzú

Twenty-one km from Oaxaca, a track to the right leads a km across a hillside to this small but interesting set of ruins (open daily 8 am to 6 pm, entrance 15c). Dainzú ('Dine-ZOO') has remains from several different periods between 300 BC (or earlier) and 1000 AD. If it was occupied all that time, it outlasted Monte Albán.

To the left as you approach the site is Building A, a pyramid-like structure 50 metres long and eight metres high. This was built about 300 BC. Along its bottom wall (mostly to the right of the stairs) are a number of engravings from the same date or perhaps earlier, similar to the Danzantes at Monte Albán which date from before 200 BC. The difference is that the Dainzú carvings nearly all show ball players – with masks or protective headgear, collars, protective hand-gear and a ball in the right hand.

It's said by some experts that these figures, like the Monte Albán Danzantes, have 'Olmecoid' features – which might mean that the inhabitants of the Central Valley at that early stage were somehow related to the Olmecs, whose centre at La Venta in Tabasco to the north was probably not extinguished until 100 or more years after Monte Albán and Dainzú were founded. Like some of the Danzantes, the Dainzú carvings may well have been removed to their present positions some time after they were made – which would explain their disorderly arrangement.

The stairway running up the middle of Building A dates from about the 7th century AD. Behind the ball-players wall, steps descend to a tomb, converted from a stairway at the same time the central stairway was added.

On the hillside below Building A are more remains, some from about 300 BC. Among them, to the right if you look down from the main building, is a sunken tomb

Top: Puerto Escondido (JN)
Bottom: Oaxaca Market (JN)

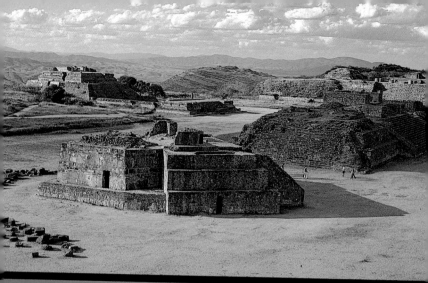

Top: Observatory, Monte Albán (JN)
Left: Iglesia Santo Domingo, Oaxaca (TW)
Right: Church of Coixtlahuaca, Oaxaca (JN)

with its entrance carved into the form of a crouching jaguar. Over on the left side is a ball court (half restored) from about 1000 AD. Between the ball court and the tomb is a big building with many rooms and a large patio.

At the top of the hill behind the main building are more carvings in natural rock similar to the ball-players, but it's a stiff climb and you'll probably need a guide to find them. There are many more unexplored structures at Dainzú.

Teotitlán del Valle
A few km beyond Dainzú, about 26 km from Oaxaca, a sign points left off the Mitla road to 'Entrada a T del Valle'. The actual turning is 500 metres or so later, and then it's about four km up a paved road to one of Mexico's most famous weaving villages. Blankets, rugs and sarapes wave at you from almost every other house as you enter the village, and signs point to the *mercado de artesanías* in the centre, where there are hundreds more on sale in an enormous variety of designs – from Zapotec gods and Mitla-style geometric patterns through birds and fish to good imitations of artists like Picasso, Miró and Escher. The weaving tradition here goes back to pre-Hispanic times and although it's now a big industry (you'd be extremely lucky to be offered anything coloured with Teotitlán's old dyes made from cochineal, sea snails, wood, moss or leaves) the quality is still very high in many cases. You can see people at work on treadle looms and sometimes spinning their own wool. Prices in Teotitlán are not necessarily lower than in Oaxaca, but there's certainly far more to choose from here. The very best works may well be hidden away in weavers' houses; if you show interest you will probably be asked in to see someone's techniques and merchandise.

Teotitlán celebrates the fiesta of the Virgen de la Natividad on 3 April with the Feather Dance.

The buses of Autotransportes Valle del Norte run all the way to Teotitlán from Oaxaca's 2nd-class bus station, and the last one returns from the village about 7 pm. It's not too hard to get a lift up from the main road, though.

Lambityeco
Another partly explored archaeological site lies next to the roadside 29 km from Oaxaca, on the right. Lambityeco was probably occupied from as early as 500 BC, but during the couple of centuries around the decline of Monte Albán (about 600-800 AD) it seems to have become a sizeable Zapotec place of about 3000 people. It may then have been abandoned and its people may have moved to Yagul a few km away – a more defensible site in what was probably a time of turmoil after the abandonment of Monte Albán.

The chief interest lies in two patios. The first, immediately left of the main pyramid beside the car park, is part of a building known as the Palace of the Caciques (leaders). On one side of the patio, either side of a small altar, are carved stone friezes. Each frieze shows a bearded man holding a bone (symbol of hereditary rights) and a woman with Zapotec hairstyle, accompanied by their name glyphs – actually birth dates. All three couples are thought to have occupied the building and ruled Lambityeco in the 7th century AD.

On the far side of this patio (going away from the road) is the second patio – in the 'Palace of the Priests' – which has two reconstructed sculpted heads of the rain god Cocijo, one of which is quite fearsome. A huge feather-like headdress spreads out above his stern face and in the middle forms itself into the face of a jaguar, which was also a hieroglyph.

Both patios are fenced off but the caretaker will let you in for a closer look if you show interest. Lambityeco is officially open from 10 am to 5.30 pm daily. Entrance costs 10c except on Sundays, when it's free. Buses from Oaxaca are US$0.30.

Lambityeco is usually classed as period Monte Albán IV – which doesn't necessarily mean that it post-dated the decline of Monte Albán, but rather that its artefacts are in a 'decadent' style that followed the end of the great Phase III at Monte Albán. Some pottery made here was even in an imitation-Mayan style.

Tlacolula

Four km beyond Lambityeco and 33 km from Oaxaca, this town of about 20,000 people holds one of the Central Valley's major markets every Sunday. The area around and behind the church becomes a packed throng of sellers and buyers, many of them Zapotecs. Teotitlán del Valle blankets are among the goods sold at food and clothing stalls. Like that of Ocotlán in the southern branch of the Central Valley, this market has even more of an Indian feel than Oaxaca's. It's busiest in the morning; traders start to pack up from early afternoon onwards. An extra-big market is held on the second Sunday in October. Buses from Oaxaca cost US$0.30.

Church Tlacolula's church was one of several founded in Oaxaca by Dominican monks. Inside, the domed chapel of Santo Cristo (probably 17th century) is a riot of golden ornamentation comparable with, but earlier than, the Rosary Chapel in Santo Domingo, Oaxaca city. Martyrs can be seen carrying their heads under their arms, and the decoration shows clear Indian influence. There's a lot of silver in this chapel too. The chapel gate and the pulpit are fine examples of colonial wrought-iron work.

Some books say the church was built in the 16th century. Its style, however, is baroque, which was used in the 17th and 18th centuries. The façade is basically similar to the one at San Felipe Neri church in Oaxaca – both are in three 'storeys' with a large central door, round arches, columns, niches and a window near the top.

Santa Ana del Valle & the Zapotec Sierra

A left turn off the main road at Tlacolula, towards Díaz Ordaz, brings you after about a km to a junction where, if you go left, you enter the village of Santa Ana. This is another village with a textile tradition going back before the Spanish (like Teotitlán it had to pay tribute to the Aztecs in the form of cloth). A museum (open daily from 10 am to 2 pm and 3 to 6 pm) has recently been set up here with some archaeological pieces, a photographic record of the village during the Mexican Revolution, and a display of Santa Ana's traditional textile methods, including local designs and the preparation of cactus and cochineal dyes.

Today the village produces mainly blankets, sarapes and bags made of wool on treadle looms. Natural dyes have not entirely disappeared and traditional designs – flowers, birds and geometric among them – are still in use.

Santa Ana has a richly decorated 17th-century church. Minibuses run frequently from Tlacolula to the village.

The road to Díaz Ordaz also leads to a remote mountain Zapotec region served only by dirt roads, of which San Ildefonso Villa Alta, about 60 km north of Santa Ana, is considered the heart. Yalalag, source of some of Oaxaca's loveliest huipiles, is in this region, reached by heading a few km east from Cajonos, about halfway to Villa Alta. According to one Oaxacan who has travelled widely in the state, buses leave Oaxaca for Villa Alta at 12 noon and take six or seven hours, and it's possible to find lodgings there.

Yagul

This site ranks after Monte Albán and Mitla as one of the most interesting and spectacular ruins in Oaxaca. It's reached by a 1½-km paved road to the left, 35 km from Oaxaca, and is set on a hill with good views around sunset. The site is open from 8 am to 6 pm daily (15c but free on Sundays and holidays). If you want to see

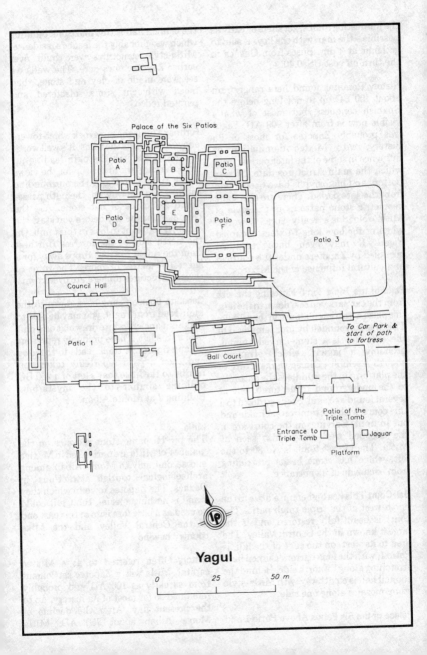

Palace of the Six Patios

Patio A

Patio B

Patio C

Patio D

Patio E

Patio F

Patio 3

Council Hall

Patio 1

To Car Park &
start of path
to fortress

Ball Court

Entrance to
Triple Tomb

Platform

Patio of the
Triple Tomb

Jaguar

Yagul

0   25   50 m

the interesting tombs, get there as early as possible – the man with the keys is said to go home at 3 pm. Buses from Oaxaca to the turn-off cost US$0.40.

History Remains found here range from about 400 BC up to not long before the Spanish conquest, but most of what's visible now is from after 900 AD. Yagul was probably Zapotec for most of its history, with Mixtec domination or influence in some of the later period, from which the main structures date. Mixtec pottery and hieroglyphs have been found from this late period. There are also some geometric stone patterns in the style of Mitla. No one's really sure, however, when or for how long Mixtecs occupied Yagul. It may even have remained occupied by Zapotecs under the political and cultural influence of the Mixtecs.

Patio of the Triple Tomb Entering the site from the car park you see, down to the left, this plaza with a low platform in the middle. This was surrounded by four temples. On the east side is a stone-carved animal, probably a jaguar, which strangely enough resembles Olmec works. Next to the platform in the middle is the entrance to the underground triple tomb, one of several found at Yagul. Steps go down to a tiny court, with one tomb on each side and one in front. Carvings in the court are in the 'stepped fret' design also seen at Mitla. The largest tomb is No 30 to the left, which has stone heads protruding from each side of its entrance.

Ball Court This lies higher up, a little to the north-west of the triple tomb patio. The court is beautifully restored and is the largest known in the Central Valley. The area to its west, on the edge of the hill, is Patio 1, with the long narrow 'council hall' stretching along its north side. Behind the council hall is a pathway with Mitla-style stone mosaics along one side.

Palace of the Six Patios Above Patio 1 and

the council hall is this maze of a building which was probably the leader's residence. Mitla-style structures were built over earlier Zapotec ones here. The walls we see were made of clay and stone, then faced with cut stone, plastered and painted red.

Fortress This is the huge rock which towers above and dwarfs the ruins. It's well worth the effort to climb the path leading up from the car park to the top for the views of the ruins below and the surrounding country. On the way up, the path passes Tomb 28, made of cut stone. Ask the caretaker for the key before you start the climb, if you want to look in this tomb. On the north side of the fortress (furthest from the ruins) the rock drops away for a sheer 100 metres or more. The ruins of several structures up here are overgrown.

Caballito Blanco Going back down to the main road from Yagul, you may be able to make out ancient white drawings on a cliff face to the left. These probably represent human figures. A track leads to the area and then a path reportedly takes you nearby to the little that's left of a 250 BC building similar to the mysterious Building J at Monte Albán.

Mitla

The pre-Hispanic stone mosaics on the 'palaces' of Mitla are unrivalled in Mexico and second only to Monte Albán among archaeological tourist attractions in Oaxaca. The Zapotec town in which they stand is nothing special, though it could be used as a base for visits to this east end of the Central Valley and the Mixe country beyond.

History Often referred to as a Mixtec capital, Mitla was a Zapotec settlement from as early as 100 AD and probably remained so for most of its history, up to the present day. After the decline of Monte Albán about 750 AD, Mitla

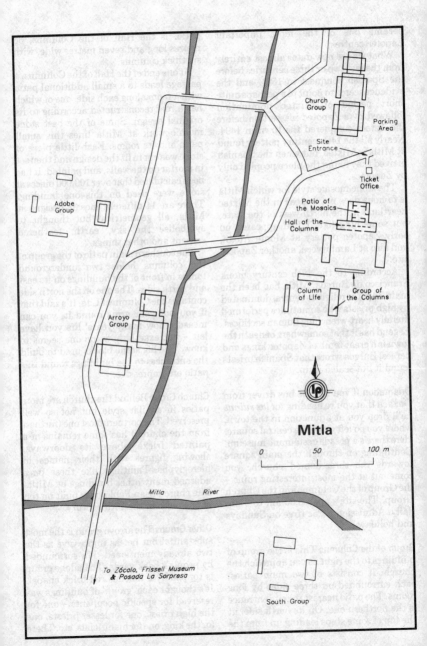

Church Group

Parking Area

Site Entrance

Ticket Office

Patio of the Mosaics

Hall of the Columns

Adobe Group

Column of Life

Group of the Columns

Arroyo Group

Mitla River

Mitla

0   50   100 m

To Zócalo, Frissell Museum & Posada La Sorpresa

South Group

became one of the most important Zapotec centres.

What we see now dates almost entirely from the last two or three centuries before the Spanish conquest in 1521, and the evidence seems to point to a perhaps quite short period of Mixtec domination followed by a Zapotec reassertion before the Aztecs conquered the town in 1494. Nearly all the 14th-century pottery found at Mitla is Mixtec, but when the Spanish arrived they found the place peopled only by Zapotecs.

The stone mosaic style for which Mitla is famous does not appear in the Mixtec heartland in the north-west of the state, but something like it had appeared on early Zapotec pottery at Monte Albán, and also at Lambityeco, another Zapotec site.

According to the 17th-century monk Francisco de Burgoa, Mitla had been the main Zapotec religious centre, dominated by high priests who sometimes performed literally heart-wrenching human sacrifices. Legend has it that somewhere beneath the town is a great tomb of Zapotec kings and heroes; Burgoa wrote that Spanish priests found it but sealed it up.

Orientation If you tell the bus driver from Oaxaca that you're heading for *las ruinas* he'll drop you at a junction in the town, where you go left up to the central square. Here there's a posada-restaurant-museum. Continuing on through the main square towards the three-domed church, you come out at the most interesting ruins – the Group of the Columns and the Church Group. The site's open 8.30 am to 6 pm daily. Admission is 25c (free on Sundays and holidays).

Group of the Columns This is the group of buildings to the right as you approach the church. It consists of two main patios, each surrounded on three sides by long rooms. The patio nearest the site entrance is the northern one. On its north side, at the top of some steps leading up from the

patio, is the Hall of the Columns, 38 metres long and seven metres wide, with six thick columns.

At one end of the Hall of the Columns, a passage leads to a small additional patio with a room along each side, one of which has a roof reconstructed according to its original design. Some of the best stone mosaic work at Mitla lines this small patio and its rooms. Each little piece of stone was cut to fit the design and then set in mortar on the walls, and painted. It has been calculated that over 100,000 pieces of stone were used on this one building. There are 14 different mosaic designs at Mitla, all geometrical but thought to symbolise the sky, earth, feathered serpent and other things.

The southern main patio of the group of the columns holds two underground tombs in front of the buildings on its east and north sides. The one on the north side contains the Column of Life. It's said that if you put your arms round it, you can measure how many years' life you have left – but exactly how, no one seems to know. The big stone blocks used to build the entrances to the buildings round this patio are impressive.

Church Group Behind the church are more patios in similar style but not so well preserved. The northernmost one (furthest from the church) has some remains of a painted frieze above its doorways, showing figures with their names in hieroglyphs. Paintings like these once adorned many other buildings at Mitla. The church (San Pablo) was built on top of one patio in the 16th century.

Other Groups The arroyo group is the most substantial but not as impressive as the two already mentioned. It's surrounded by people's back yards. The adobe group is topped by a hideous red brick chapel. It's thought each 'group' of buildings was reserved for specific occupants – one for the high priest, one for lesser priests, one for the king, one for his officials, etc. There are also the remains of forts outside the town, and tombs and other remains scattered over the countryside for many km around, which indicate that the population was large in ancient times.

Museum The Frissell Museum (open 9 am to 6 pm daily, free) in the Posada La Sorpresa building (see below) has a sizeable collection of archaeological material from Oaxaca – including several clay figures of the rain god Cocijo, some jade and painted pottery – but it's very poorly labelled.

Places to Stay & Eat *Posada La Sorpresa* off the town square has tables round a very pleasant courtyard where good breakfasts (US$1) and lunches (US$2) are served. There are also large, clean rooms of various sizes at the back. They have private bathrooms and cost US$2.50 to US$5 single, US$3 to US$6.25 double. Running water's a bit scarce though – a sign in the restaurant bathroom reads, 'Please put a water in the toilet with the tray', which means, 'Fill a bucket from the well to flush the toilet'!

Across the road from La Sorpresa the *Hotel y Restaurant Mitla* has singles/doubles with bath for US$2.50/3. There's also the *Hotel y Restaurant Zapoteca* on the road between the town square and the church.

Things to Buy The main streets of the town have several shops selling textiles – embroidered dresses and blouses, huipiles, wool and cotton rebozos, table cloths, blankets, ponchos, rugs with attractive geometric patterns, even hammocks. There's also a craft market strategically placed next to the entrance to the ruins, with the same sort of stuff, much of it made here in Mitla. Some of the striped rebozos are an original Mitla design.

Getting There & Away Oaxaca-Istmo buses (US$0.50) depart for Mitla every 20 minutes from the 2nd-class bus station in Oaxaca. The town is 42 km from Oaxaca; the last four km is up a side road to the left off Highway 190.

If you want to travel on to Tehuantepec from Mitla, you have to get back down to Highway 190 and hail a passing bus.

The Mixe Region
Mitla is the starting point for buses into the remote western Mixe country. The bus to Zacatepec 100 km away, where there is said to be accommodation, supposedly leaves at 12 noon and takes six hours, passing through San Pedro y San Pablo Ayutla (where there is also accommodation) about halfway. San Juan Cotzocón is about 10 km beyond Zacatepec.

CENTRAL VALLEY – SOUTH
Three roads head south from the city of Oaxaca. One goes to Cuilapan and Zaachila. The main one is Highway 175 to the Pacific coast, which goes through San Bartolo Coyotepec, Ocotlán, Ejutla and Miahuatlán. The third is Highway 131, which veers south-west off Highway 175 about 14 km from Oaxaca towards Zimatlán. Estrella del Valle/Oaxaca Pacífico buses go down Highway 175 every 15 or 30 minutes from Oaxaca 2nd-class bus station.

Arrazola
About 10 km out of Oaxaca on the Zaachila road, a sign points to this village five km down a side-road, known for the brightly painted wooden animal and human figures made here. Manuel Jiménez of Arrazola Xoxo is the best-known craftsperson. Colectivos direct to Arrazola go from the main market in Oaxaca.

Cuilapan
The people of Cuilapan ('kwi-LAP-an'), 12 km from Oaxaca, speak Spanish but are mostly Mixtecs – one of the few Mixtec enclaves in the predominantly Zapotec Central Valley today. Shortly before the

Spanish conquest Cuilapan was a large Mixtec town of over 10,000 people; Cortés included it in his private domain, the Marquesado del Valle de Oaxaca, but like the rest of the Marquesado it became the subject of legal wrangles between Cortés and other Spaniards over land rights.

Today Cuilapan is of interest mainly because of its big, beautiful and historic ruined monastery. Probably started in 1555, it was built for the Dominican monks who were responsible for Santo Domingo in Oaxaca and numerous other churches and monasteries in the state. The monastery is made of pale stone and seems almost to grow out of the land. Part of the church still functions, but is closed when not in use.

In 1831 the Mexican independence hero Vicente Guerrero was imprisoned and shot dead at the monastery by soldiers supporting the rebel conservative Anastasio Bustamante, who had just thrown the liberal Guerrero out of the presidency. Trying to flee the country, Guerrero booked passage on a ship out of Acapulco but its captain handed him over to the authorities for 50,000 pieces of gold. Guerrero was transported to Puerto Escondido, then to Cuilapan to die.

The first part of the monastery complex you reach from the entrance gate is the long, low *capilla abierta* (open chapel). To its right and beyond it is part of the original body of the main monastery church. The room off this, containing a font decorated with cherubim, is the baptistry. Continuing through a row of arches, you reach the entrance to the cloister on the left. The cloister has two storeys and is a rare example of pure renaissance architecture in Mexico. The rooms at the back on the ground floor have some 16th and 17th-century wall paintings. A painting of Guerrero hangs in the room where he was held. Through a nearby window you can see a monument to him, which stands on the spot where he was shot.

The closed part of the church is said to contain the Christian tombs of Juana Donají (daughter of Cocijo-eza, the last Zapotec king of Zaachila) and her Mixtec husband.

Getting There & Away Autobuses de Oaxaca runs from Oaxaca's 2nd-class bus station to Zaachila every 20 minutes, passing right by Cuilapan monastery. The fare to Cuilapan is 10c. The site is open from 10 am to 6 pm daily (admission 15c).

Zaachila

This village ('za-CHEE-la'), with a busy market on Thursdays, is part Mixtec and part Zapotec. It was a Zapotec capital from about 1400 to the Spanish conquest but was controlled for at least some of that period by the Mixtecs. The 15th-century Zapotec king Zaachila III allied with the Aztecs to try to drive the Mixtecs out. His son and successor Cocijo-eza – whose daughter, according to one account, was married to a Mixtec prince – tried to enlist Spanish help against the Mixtecs in the 1520s. Cocijo-eza was baptised a Christian with the name Juan Cortés and died in 1523, the last Zapotec king. Apparently some hostility between Zapotecs and Mixtecs survives in Zaachila today. The village is the scene of a masked mock-battle at Carnival time in which *diablos* (devils) use whips on *curas* (priests) who defend themselves with crosses and buckets of water. The *curas* win.

Tombs Up the road behind the church, then up a path to the right marked 'zona arqueológica', are some ancient mounds which contain at least two tombs that were used by the Mixtecs. In one of them was found a Mixtec treasure hoard comparable with that from Tomb 7 at Monte Albán. So strong was local opposition to any disturbance of these relics that the famous Mexican archaeologists Alfonso Caso and Ignacio Bernal were forced to flee when they tried to dig in the 1940s and 1950s respectively. Finally Roberto Gallegos excavated the tombs under armed guard in 1962 – all of which is clear proof of the continuity between pre-Hispanic and modern Indian cultures.

There doesn't appear to be any greater enthusiasm in the village today for outsiders to see the tombs: they're nominally open from 10.30 am to 5 pm daily (admission US$0.35, free on Sundays and holidays) but there's often no one around to open them up. Market day, Thursday, is probably the best day to try; Monday and Tuesday are apparently bad days. Ask in the Palacio Municipal on the zócalo if you can't find anyone to help you.

The tombs are underneath the sparse remains of a Mixtec patio in front of the site kiosk. The treasure found in Tomb 2 is now in the Mexico City Anthropology Museum. Much typical Mixtec polychrome pottery was found in both tombs. There are also six pre-Hispanic monoliths in the zócalo.

Getting There & Away Zaachila is six km beyond Cuilapan, 18 km from Oaxaca. There are frequent colectivo taxis (US$0.30) between Oaxaca and Zaachila zócalo. In Oaxaca they leave from a parking lot on Fiallo between La Noria and Xochitl – two blocks east from the south-east corner of the zócalo, then 4½ blocks south. Autobuses de Oaxaca from Oaxaca 2nd-class bus station also go to Zaachila (12c) every 20 minutes. From the Zaachila bus station, walk up the main street to the zócalo and church, then turn left for the tomb site.

San Bartolo Coyotepec

All that polished, black, amazingly light pottery you see in Oaxaca comes from San Bartolo Coyotepec ('san barr-TOL-o co-yo-te-PEC'), a small village about 12 km south of the city on Highway 175, past the airport. Look out for the roadside sign to Doña Rosa's Alfarería, which is to the east, up one of the village's few streets. Several houses in the village make and sell the 'blackware' but Rosa Valente Nieto Real was the woman who, a few decades

ago, invented the method of burnishing it with quartz stones for the distinctive shine. Doña Rosa died in 1979 but her family carries on the business and gives very skilful demonstrations.

The pieces are hand-moulded by an age-old technique in which two saucers play the part of a potter's wheel. The pottery is fired in pit kilns and goes black because of the iron oxide in the local clay and because smoke is trapped in the kiln.

The village saint's day, 24 August, is celebrated with dances, including the Feather Dance.

Buses heading for Ocotlán will drop you at San Bartolo (fare 15c).

Highway 131

This is the cross-country route to Puerto Escondido, which forks west from Highway 175 a couple of km south of San Bartolo Coyotepec. It's paved for the first 75 km to Sola de Vega, then dirt road for another 170 km to Puerto Escondido. Zimatlán, 13 km from the Highway 175 junction, has a Wednesday market. La Solteca runs 2nd-class buses from Oaxaca half-hourly to Zimatlán, less often to points beyond.

Santo Tomás Jalieza

This little Zapotec village ('santo to-MASS hal-i-EY-za'), just east of Highway 175, about 25 km south of Oaxaca, is famous for cotton textiles – in particular its woven waist sashes which are used by Mixtecs as well as Zapotecs and are even reportedly sought by Guatemalan Indians. They have pretty animal or plant designs and, for the technically minded, are warp-patterned and made with rigid heddles. The village holds a textiles market on Friday to coincide with market day in Ocotlán.

San Antonino

Textiles are also the attraction in this village just off the road shortly before Ocotlán, about 30 km from Oaxaca. The specialities here are blouses and dresses very finely embroidered with floral patterns in silk, cotton or wool. In the best pieces, crochet joins different embroidered sections. Such garments are for sale but local women only wear them for fiestas.

Ocotlán

The big, bustling Friday market at Ocotlán ('oc-ot-LAN') goes back to pre-Hispanic days. Local specialities include reed baskets, and there's other merchandise from far and wide – Mitla embroidery, palm hats from Huajuapan de León, Teotitlán del Valle sarapes, San Bartolo blackware, green Atzompa pottery. Among the local dishes you might find served up in the numerous fondas is *mole de pavo* (turkey in mole sauce). Like other village markets, this one starts to wind down in early afternoon. If you're interested in pottery, seek out the Aguilar sisters and Luis Valencia Mendoza, who are renowned as Ocotlán's finest clay-figure makers.

Buses from Oaxaca (2nd class) take about 45 minutes; fare is US$0.35.

Ejutla

Some 60 km from Oaxaca down Highway 175, this village ('e-HOOT-la') has a Thursday market and is known for its engraved knives, machetes and swords – and for its mezcal, reputedly the finest in Oaxaca. Second-class bus fare from Oaxaca is US$0.65.

Miahuatlán

Market day is Monday here, 100 km from Oaxaca and halfway to the coast. This is the biggest place between Oaxaca and Pochutla, and there are a couple of places to stay. Second-class bus fare from Oaxaca is US$1.25.

CENTRAL VALLEY – NORTH

Except for Guelatao, these places are on or close to Highway 190 (the Pan-American) as it heads north from Oaxaca city up towards the Mixteca in the north-west of the state. Most 2nd-class buses heading for Tamazulapan or Huajuapan de León from Oaxaca will drop you anywhere along this road. For places off the road, ask around the market and 2nd-class bus station in Oaxaca – or walk from the main road!

Atzompa

This village, six km north of the city and then three km west along a dirt road, is the source of two distinctive types of pottery. One, with a dark green glaze, is often in the form of goats or oxen. The other, invented by Teodora Blanca, is an ornate and fascinating light brown pottery in the form of 'earth mother' dolls and other figures. Plenty of both kinds can be found in Oaxaca itself. Some of the Central Valley's little-explored ancient mounds lie on a nearby hill.

San Pedro y San Pablo Etla

Ten km from Oaxaca, then three km east, this village has a Wednesday market and the remains of a 16th-century convent.

San José del Mogote

This tiny village is probably little bigger now than it was 3000 years ago. Excavations by the University of Michigan here have disproved the old notion that before the rise of Monte Albán, about 500 BC, the Central Valley was filled with a lake. San José already had a population of 500 around 1150 to 850 BC. Life was quite organised: houses were about six metres long with whitewashed walls and thatched roofs, and there was an industry of making mirrors from polished magnetite, a kind of iron ore. These were probably traded to the Olmecs. Some people were buried with jade and shell ornaments. The food of these early Oaxacans included domestic dogs and turkeys, wild rabbits and deer, maize, chile, squash and walnuts.

A stone-built mound probably dates from Monte Albán's beginnings. A carving of a dead captive found here may be a precursor of the Monte Albán Danzantes. There's also a small museum with a reconstructed wall that contains probably the oldest adobe in Mexico, and some reconstructed burials.

The turning to San José, which is eight km from the main road, is 15 km from Oaxaca. Turn off to the west (left), passing through Soledad Etla (which has a market on Tuesday) after four km.

San Pablo Huitzo

This town 28 km from Oaxaca, just off the main road, was the site of a large pre-conquest Zapotec centre which according to some archaeologists was nearly as big as Monte Albán. But the remains are little explored and the zona arqueológica offers little unless you're very dedicated. One restored tomb has carved stone animals on its outside. Pottery and Spanish records indicate that Huitzo ('WEET-soh') was taken over by Mixtecs at a late stage before the Spanish arrived. You can get to the site by going through the town, which is left of the highway. Huitzo also has a 16th-century church.

Guelatao

Not actually in the Central Valley but close enough (74 km) to Oaxaca city to be visited on a day trip, the small town of Guelatao is the birthplace of Benito Juárez and something of a monument to one of the few unquestioned heroes of Mexican history. There's a mausoleum with his remains, at least two statues of him, a small museum devoted to him (open Tuesday to Saturday, 9 am to 1 pm and 3 to 5 pm), and more memorabilia in the Palacio Municipal. All these are around the Plaza Cívica. Mexican presidents and visiting statesmen sometimes pay homage here. If you're interested in history and politics, Guelatao is well worth the trip – if not, the scenery en route isn't bad either. On Juárez's birthday, 21 March, national ceremonies are held here.

Ixtlán de Juárez, a km north of Guelatao on the same road, has the 16th-century church where baby Benito was baptised.

Getting There & Away Guelatao is on Highway 175, which winds up through the mountains north-east from Oaxaca city towards Tuxtepec. Highway 175 turns off Highway 190 about four km east of the city. Buses for Tuxtepec go through Guelatao, taking about 2½ hours.

MIXTECA ALTA

Most of this rugged, sometimes forbidding area lies over 2000 metres high. Located in the north-west of the state, it is crossed by nearly every traveller entering Oaxaca from Puebla or Mexico City, but few stop to explore it. The Mixteca Alta (High Mixteca) is a country of bare highlands and evergreen valleys where settlements tend to be small and scattered. However, it offers a chance to get well off the beaten track, and has three ruined 16th-century monasteries which are among colonial Mexico's great works of art.

You can visit the Mixteca Alta in a day or two-day trip from Oaxaca city or Huajuapan de León, or by a rough ride up from Pinotepa Nacional near the Pacific coast.

The far north-western borderlands of Oaxaca, around Huajuapan de León and Santiago Juxtlahuaca, are part of what's called the Mixteca Baja (Low Mixteca), which stretches across into Puebla state. The Mixteca Alta is the wide area of high country between the Mixteca Baja and the Oaxaca Central Valley. The Pan-American Highway, 190, runs across the Mixteca Alta on its 204-km stretch between Huajuapan and Oaxaca city, passing right by Yanhuitlán monastery. Another highway, 125, cuts south from the Pan-American through the towns of Teposcolula, Tlaxiaco and Putla to reach Oaxaca's southern coastal plain near Pinotepa Nacional. The southern half of Highway 125, beyond Putla, is not paved.

Fifteen or so daily 1st-class buses pass

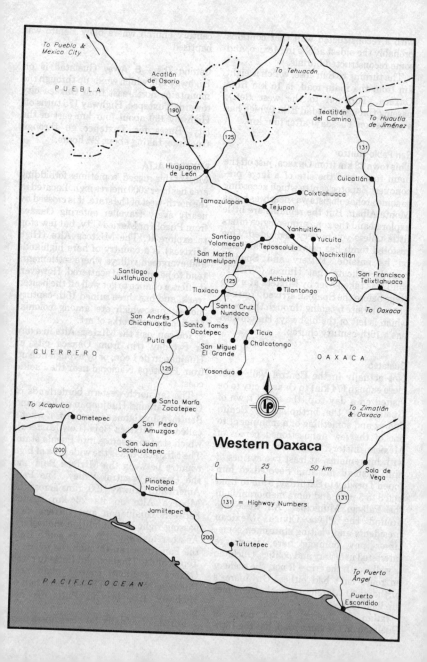

To Puebla & Mexico City

To Tehuacán

PUEBLA

Acatlán de Osorio

190

125

Teotitlán del Camino

To Huautla de Jiménez

131

Huajuapan de León

Cuicatlán

Coixtlahuaca

Tamazulapan

Tejupan

Yanhuitlán

Santiago Yolomecatl

Teposcolula

Yucuita

San Martín Huamelulpan

Nochixtlán

San Francisco Teotitláhuaca

Santiago Juxtlahuaca

190

Achiutla

Tlaxiaco

Tilantongo

125

Santa Cruz Nundaco

To Oaxaca

San Andrés Chicahuaxtla

Santo Tomás Ocotepec

Ticua

Putla

Chalcatongo

San Miguel El Grande

GUERRERO

Yosondua

OAXACA

125

Western Oaxaca

To Acapulco

Ometepec

Santa María Zacatepec

To Zimatlán & Oaxaca

0   25   50 km

San Pedro Amuzgos

San Juan Cacahuatepec

Sola de Vega

Pinotepa Nacional

131

200

Jamiltepec

131 = Highway Numbers

200

Tututepec

PACIFIC OCEAN

To Puerto Angel

Puerto Escondido

each way along Highway 190 between Oaxaca, Huajuapan, Tehuacán, Puebla and Mexico City and often stop at main points along the way like Nochixtlán, Yanhuitlán, Tamazulapan, Huajuapan and the turn-offs for Teposcolula, Tlaxiaco and Coixtlahuaca. There are a few 1st-class buses serving Teposcolula and Tlaxiaco directly from Oaxaca.

Frequent 2nd-class buses go almost everywhere and stop anywhere – including some which link the Mixteca Alta with the Pacific coast. You can certainly get to Tlaxiaco in one bus from Oaxaca, Huajuapan, Puebla or even Mexico City.

Huajuapan has quite a few hotels and there is accommodation in several of the smaller places too. There are petrol stations at Tamazulapan, Huajuapan, Teposcolula and Tlaxiaco.

History

The Mixteca, particularly the Alta, has been the heartland of the Mixtec people for at least 1000 years, possibly 4000. The Mixtecs of Tilantongo, south-west of Nochixtlán, started to make their presence felt about 700 or 800 AD when they brought most of the Mixteca Alta under their control. Tilantongo reached its peak in the 11th century under a king called Eight Deer, who started to spread Mixtec dominion over the Central Valley and the Tehuantepec area. The Mixtecs were influenced by the Toltecs of Tula at this stage, and Eight Deer appears to have gone to Tula to pay homage to the Toltec leaders.

The second known important Mixtec dynasty was that of Coixtlahuaca, which was probably the most pre-eminent of a collection of small Mixtec states. Not always friendly with each other, these states emerged by the 15th century and exerted a measure of control over the Zapotecs of the Central Valley. Coixtlahuaca flourished only briefly, for despite fierce resistance the Mixteca Alta – though not the southern Mixtec kingdom of Tututepec – was subjugated by the Aztecs in the mid-15th century.

Famed as workers of gold and precious stones, the Mixtecs also helped develop a fine type of painted pottery known as Mixteca-Puebla which, it is said, was the only type that the Aztec emperor Moctezuma would eat from. Little excavation or research has been done in the Mixteca itself and much of what we know of the pre-Hispanic Mixtecs comes from Central Valley sites.

After the Spanish conquest the Mixtecs suffered the usual Indian fate – servitude, epidemics which in some places cut the population by half, loss of lands, reduction to second-class status. During the Mexican Revolution many Mixtecs supported Emiliano Zapata and his radical land-reform goals. Today much of the Mixteca is badly eroded, owing to over-farming and deforestation, and local politics and business are controlled mainly by mestizos. The *juego de pelota Mixteca*, a game probably descended from the pre-Hispanic ball game, is sometimes still played.

Monasteries The grand mid-16th century monasteries at Yanhuitlán, Coixtlahuaca and Teposcolula were built, like most monasteries in Oaxaca, by the Indians for the Dominicans, a powerful order of monks who did much to protect their Indian converts from the worst colonial excesses.

In architectural style, these buildings are a successful fusion of medieval, plateresque, pure renaissance and Mexican Indian. The restrained carving of their stonework is in contrast to the over-profuse decoration of many Mexican churches. They also contain a number of important paintings. Their history is shrouded in uncertainty and subject to much learned – and sometimes heated – argument. It's thought that these three monasteries, which in architecture and setting are the most outstanding in the state, were all designed by the same hand.

Nochixtlán

This town, 100 km from Oaxaca on Highway 190, has a couple of very basic hostelries – the *Hotel Central* on the zócalo and the *Casa de Huéspedes Santillana* on the main road on the Puebla side of town. There's also the *Hotel Sarita* at Porfirio Díaz 50. *Restaurant Lucy* on the highway at the edge of town does decent and reasonably priced Mexican food. First-class bus fare from Oaxaca is US$1.50.

For the festival of San Isidro Labrador (15 May) local people dress up their animals and take them to be blessed. The town's 16th-century church is the focus of pilgrimages from surrounding villages for the Festival of the Assumption (15 August). The Mixtec ball game is sometimes played at festivals here.

Yucuita

Three km west of Nochixtlán, a road turns north off Highway 190 for six km to San Juan Yucuita ('yoo-KWEE-ta'). At the entrance to the village are some partly-restored remains of a settlement of about 3000 people from some time between 500 BC and 300 AD. Yucuita was one of several such villages in the Mixteca at that time and carried on some trade with Monte Albán. At the other end of the village is a small archaeological museum.

Yanhuitlán

The best-known and easiest-reached of the Mixteca monasteries is in this village ('yan-wit-LAN') on Highway 190, 120 km from Oaxaca and 77 km from Huajuapan. It towers above the village, designed not only to impress, but also to withstand earthquakes and serve as a defensive refuge (historians tell of an attack on Yanhuitlán from Teposcolula in the 1540s, during the building of the monastery).

The *Restaurant Lupita*, to the right as you face the monastery from the main

road, has some grubby rooms with private bath for US$2.75 (one double bed), US$4 (two beds). First-class bus fare from Oaxaca is US$1.50, 2nd class is US$1.25. The journey takes about two hours.

History Before the Spanish conquest, Yanhuitlán had been a sizeable Mixtec settlement which fiercely resisted the Aztec invasion. The monastery was built in the mid-16th century. In the 17th century the village was apparently devastated by an epidemic that may also have caused the abandonment of the monastery in the same century. In 1812, royalist forces holed up in the monastery managed to beat off an attack by 3000 pro-independence rebels. Allegedly, they afterwards shot 40 prisoners, including local Mixtec leaders. French and other troops are also reported to have used the place at different stages of Mexico's various wars – so it's quite surprising that so much remains there.

Cloister This has an interesting little museum of items from the monastery (open daily 10 am to 6 pm, admission 5c). A fresco of San Cristóbal on the stairs is one of the few survivors of the wall-paintings that once adorned the Oaxaca monasteries.

Church The monastery church, still in use, contains valuable works of art and is usually locked. Try asking in the Presidencia Municipal, on the zócalo behind the monastery, for the key – or persuade the museum caretaker to open the church. Its main exterior façade (altered after it was built) is a mixture of medieval fortress-like bulk and plateresque decoration.

If you can get inside the church, the nave has a gothic rib vault, and the fine roof supporting the choir is timber in mudéjar style. The early baroque *retable* (altarpiece) of gilded wood behind the main altar contains some of the few known paintings by the Spaniard Andrés de la Concha, an important figure in early colonial art in Mexico.

Coixtlahuaca

A 16th-century Dominican monastery which rivals Yanhuitlán in both architecture and setting may be seen in this small, remote town ('coyce-tla-WAC-a'), 22 km north-east of Highway 190 by a paved road. The turn-off, 50 km east of Huajuapan and 154 km north-west of Oaxaca city, is at Tejupan ('te-HOO-pan'), which has its own large 16th-century Dominican church. The bus ride from Oaxaca to Tejupan takes about 2½ hours.

As you approach Coixtlahuaca the monastery church stands out from several km away on the far side of the valley. The village was the centre of an important pre-Hispanic Mixtec kingdom. Its former wealth is shown by the tribute it had to send to the Aztecs who conquered it in the mid-15th century: gold, quetzal feathers, rubber, cacao, cotton shawls, huipiles, underskirts, cochineal and precious stones. There are some remains of the ancient settlement in the village, but the local people don't want them excavated.

Coixtlahuaca has a small restaurant and a couple of basic posadas where you can stay the night. There are only a few buses from Tejupan but taxis (US$2.25) are nearly always waiting there to take people to Coixtlahuaca. If you want to know more about Coixtlahuaca and the Mixteca, and can speak some Spanish, ask the friendly young director of the Casa de la Cultura on the main street, Alejandro Mendoza García. He'll let you use the library, and can probably help with other questions or problems too – such as getting into the church.

Open Chapel To one side of the monastery church stands its ruined open chapel, completed before the rest of the complex to enable the Dominicans to immediately minister to the Indians. The graceful building once had a ribbed vault, and has many stylistic similarities to the bigger open chapel at Teposcolula.

Church As at Yanhuitlán, the monastery church is usually locked because of the art treasures inside it. If the caretaker of the cloister museum can't help, someone should know where the priest is!

Like Yanhuitlán's church, this one is strongly built, with a simple rectangular ground plan. Its façades are if anything more beautiful. An unusual feature of the main façade is the large number of niches lining its sides. The interior of the church has a beautiful rib-vaulted roof with carved keystones. The former baptistry, on the right as you enter the church, has Solomonic twisted columns and decorations which were probably added in the 17th century.

Teposcolula

The small town of San Pedro y San Pablo Teposcolula lies on Highway 125, 13 km south of Highway 190. The junction of the two highways is 15 km west of Yanhuitlán, 62 km east of Huajuapan. The church and remains of the 16th-century Dominican monastery stand beside the zócalo, which borders the road through the town. The monastery's chief glory is an open chapel which reportedly inspired the Mexican art historian Manuel Toussaint to devote his life to rediscovering his country's colonial art heritage.

From the street to the right of the complex, a path leads into the church. The original 16th-century structure was probably destroyed by an earthquake. In the transept to the left of the main altar is a confessional chair elaborately carved from a single piece of wood. The nave has many *retables*, some with paintings by Andrés de la Concha and Simón Pereyns.

Leaving the church by the end door, you can see carved saints from the original church on the façade above you. To the left are the remains of the old monastery cloister, now a museum (open 10 am to 6 pm daily, admission 5c). A restored chapel to the right of the cloister entrance has beautiful pillars and a 17th-century *retable* of the Virgin of Santa Gertrudis. To the right as you leave the church end-door is the open chapel, constructed in pure renaissance style: it consists simply of three elegant open bays.

Getting There & Away Cristóbal Colón runs two 1st-class buses a day each way between Oaxaca and Teposcolula. Fare is US$1.75, journey time about 2½ hours. There are also four or five 2nd-class Fletes y Pasajes buses. Alternatively, you can get a bus along Highway 190 to the junction with Highway 125 and pick up local transport for the remaining 13 km south to Teposcolula. There are quite frequent 2nd-class buses from Huajuapan to Teposcolula, and even a few from Mexico City (run by Cristóbal Colón and Lineas Unidas México-Oaxaca from the eastern bus terminal, and Fletes y Pasajes).

San Martín Huamelulpan
Archaeology fanatics might want to detour one km east off Highway 125, 23 km south of Teposcolula, to this small village ('wam-eh-LOOL-pan'). In the Palacio Municipal is a small museum which includes an 'Olmecoid' statue of uncertain date but probably pre-300 BC. A 10-minute walk uphill from here are some remains of a Mixtec settlement dating from the centuries around 100 BC, when this was one of the Mixteca's most important places. The nearby church, built on a pre-Hispanic platform, has some pre-Hispanic carvings (including two human heads) set into its entrance arch and another (a jaguar) in one of its walls.

Tlaxiaco
This town ('tla-hi-AC-o') 43 km south of Teposcolula on Highway 125 is one of the biggest in the Mixteca, with about 25,000 people. Before the Mexican Revolution it was known as 'Paris Chiquita' (Little Paris), because of the quantities of fashionable French luxuries like clothes and wine which were imported here for a few rich land and mill-owning families. During the revolution the town was for three years (1916 to 1919) the headquarters of the 'independent' government of Oaxaca led by José Luis Dávila.

Today the only signs of Tlaxiaco's former elegance are some surprisingly grand portales round the zócalo and a few large houses with courtyards. Foreigners are a rarity and provoke a range of reactions from fear and apparent loathing to surprise and friendliness. There's a 16th-century Dominican monastery two blocks south of the zócalo but most of it now seems to be a court and prison. The monastery church, still in use, has gold-painted ribs on its gothic vault and a plateresque façade. There's a market area off the south-east corner of the zócalo which is worth looking in for Mixtec and possibly Triqui handicrafts.

Tlaxiaco's main fiesta takes place the week following the second Sunday in October.

Places to Stay & Eat It might be worth staying in Tlaxiaco if you want to try the rough road between here and the coast – or if you've just left it too late to get back to Oaxaca or Huajuapan! The *Hotel del Portal* on the zócalo has clean rooms with private bath round a pleasant courtyard and charges US$2.75 single, US$5.50 for two beds, US$6.75 for three beds. *Casa Habitación San Michell* on Independencia is the other of the town's better places, with rooms from US$3.75. There is also the *Hotel Colón* one block east of the zócalo at the corner of Colón and Hidalgo, and the *Hotel México* 1½ blocks south along Hidalgo from Colón.

Restaurant Superior on Hidalgo serves decent meals – noodle soup, bolillo, tomato-pineapple fried rice, meat, frijoles and an awesome chile sauce – but make sure you establish the price first (around US$2), or the owner will charge whatever he thinks he can get away with.

Getting There & Away Cristóbal Colón has two 1st-class buses daily each way between Oaxaca and Tlaxiaco (fare US$2.25, journey time about 3½ hours), plus other buses between Tlaxiaco, Huajuapan and Mexico City. Fletes y Pasajes (2nd class) has four services a day to and from Oaxaca, five to Huajuapan and Mexico City, and three south to Pinotepa Nacional. Flecha Roja runs once a day (5 am) to Huajuapan, Acatlán and Puebla from outside the Restaurant Superior. Lineas Unidas Mexico-Oaxaca runs three overnight 2nd-class buses from Mexico City (TAPO) to Tlaxiaco and Putla.

Tlaxiaco to Pinotepa Nacional

South-west of Tlaxiaco, Highway 125 winds into the Sierra Madre del Sur, passing through San Andrés Chicahuaxtla in Triqui Indian country. There may be a chance to pick up Triqui handicrafts here. The only sizeable place between Tlaxiaco and Pinotepa Nacional is Putla, 87 km from Tlaxiaco. South of Putla, the road is unpaved for the remaining 125 km to Pinotepa Nacional.

Santa María Zacatepec, 49 km south of Putla, has a population of Tacuate Indians often regarded as distinct from the surrounding Mixtecs. Their men are instantly recognisable by their white cotton shirts and trousers embroidered with hundreds of tiny, colourful animals, birds and insects. Their long tunics are rolled at the waist to form a bag. Tacuates gather for the Zacatepec feria in the first week of December, when the Moros y Cristianos (Moors and Christians) and other dances are performed. People of African descent from the nearby coast reputedly also attend this fiesta.

The Amuzgo Indians of San Pedro Amusgos, 73 km south of Putla, are known for their fine huipiles (sometimes for sale). There are dances and processions for the fiestas of San Pedro (end of June) and the Virgen del Rosario (first Sunday in October). Eleven km south of San Pedro Amusgos, San Juan Cacahuatepec cel-ebrates Carnival Sunday to Tuesday with a number of mask dances.

NORTHERN OAXACA

Tuxtepec

This town is the 'capital' of a low-lying area of northern Oaxaca which in culture and geography is equally akin to neighbouring Veracruz. Tuxtepec is on the Papaloapan River, 53 km from Cosamaloapan and 128 km from Alvarado on the Veracruz coast. Highway 175 winds south through the mountains to Oaxaca 210 km away. Tuxtepec is therefore on a possible coast-to-coast route and quite a transportation centre. It has several moderately priced hotels and is served by ADO and Cristóbal Colón (1st class) and AU (2nd class) buses from most places in Oaxaca and Veracruz, as well as several smaller lines. Roads also cut across the flat country from Ciudad Alemán, 12 km north, to Córdoba and Acayucan.

To the north you can reach the Miguel Alemán dam at Temascal, which holds back the waters of the huge Alemán reservoir. To the west are some Mazatec villages and to the south, around Valle Nacional – scene of infamous slave plantations in the Porfiriato period – is the territory of the Chinantecs.

Mazatecs and Chinantecs celebrate the festival of San Sebastián (20 January) together in Jalapa de Díaz, 56 km west of Tuxtepec. They wear traditional costumes and put on dances and a procession.

Huautla de Jiménez & La Cañada

Huautla de Jiménez ('WOWT-la de him-EYN-ez') is known for the use of hallucinogenic mushrooms in the Mazatec Indians' approach to spiritual problems – and for the availability of mushrooms to visitors (not necessarily with spiritual problems). Huautla is easiest approached from Tehuacán in Puebla. It's 67 km by dirt road up into the hills east from Teotitlán del Camino (also called Teotitlán de Flores Magón), which is 68 km south of Tehuacán by paved Highway 131. One

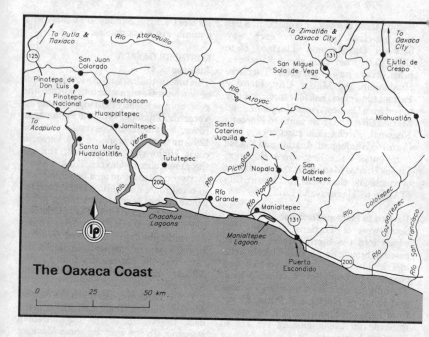

The Oaxaca Coast

traveller reported that there's accommodation in Huautla and that mushrooms are easy to pick up. Out of season, they are apparently preserved in honey.

One of Huautla's main fiestas is held on the third Friday in Lent, which usually falls in March. Village Mazatecs come to the town in colourful processions.

You can get to Teotitlán from Oaxaca by Highway 131 north from Highway 190, just west of San Pablo Huitzo. The road climbs through a rugged wooded area called La Cañada ('ca-NYA-dah', area called La Cañada ('ca-NYA-dah') to Cuicatlán, on the edge of the Cuicatec Indian area. Oaxaca to Teotitlán is 188 km.

The Oaxaca Coast

If you've had enough of stones and bones, or just fancy a spot of sea, sun and fun, the Pacific coast of Oaxaca is the answer. For some people, even Oaxaca city is only a stopover on the way to a laid-back beach stint at Puerto Escondido or Puerto Angel. Though new paved roads have brought this once-isolated coast closer to the rest of Mexico in the last decade, these two fishing-villages-cum-travellers'-rests are still much smaller and more relaxed than other Pacific resorts. But to their east, in keeping with the recent Mexican tradition of creating one new resort during every presidency, the beautiful bays of Huatulco are being developed into a complex which some claim/fear will put even Cancún in the shade.

From Oaxaca city, you can drive to the coast through the tortuous Sierra Madre del Sur, or fly to Puerto Escondido. You can also fly from Mexico City or reach the two Puertos by the coastal highway from the Isthmus of Tehuantepec or Acapulco.

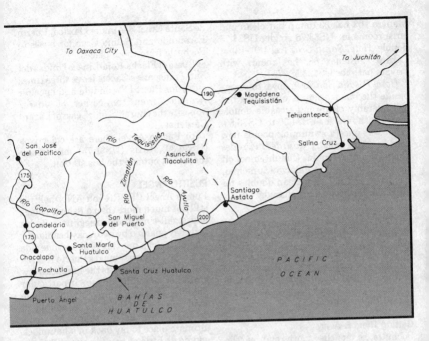

Getting There & Away

Buses travelling to and along the Oaxaca coast west of Salina Cruz are classed differently from most others in Mexico. There are no real 1st-class services; buses that go under the label '1st class' would be 2nd class anywhere else (though they might stop less often). 'Second-class' buses here are usually city or village buses, with low seatbacks and not much suspension.

POCHUTLA

For travellers this small town ('poh-CHOOT-la') is no more than a way station between Oaxaca city and Puerto Angel or Puerto Escondido. There's not usually any need to stay overnight in Pochutla, but people often have to wait for buses here. Pochutla also has the nearest bank to Puerto Angel and the nearest humane bank to Puerto Escondido. The town's patron saint's festival is 29 June.

Information & Orientation

Lázaro Cárdenas is the narrow, noisy main street running north-south. The bus station of Oaxaca Pacífico/Estrella del Valle is towards its south end. Streets running east off the middle section of Lázaro Cárdenas are, in south-north order, Juárez, Madero and Allende. Juárez and Madero both lead to the Plaza de la Constitución, where the church and Palacio Municipal stand.

Bancomer at the corner of Lázaro Cárdenas and Allende changes travellers' cheques and foreign cash between 9.30 am and 12 noon, Monday to Friday. The post office is on Progreso, behind the church.

Places to Stay

There are a few options if you do need to stay in Pochutla. *Hotel Izala* (tel 4-01-15) at Lázaro Cárdenas 59 is the best in town. Clean rooms with fans cost US$4.50 per person. *Hotel Pochutla* (tel 4-00-33) at

Madero 102 has 33 damp but clean and large rooms for US$3.75 single, US$4.75 double. *Hotel Santa Cruz* (tel 4-01-16) at Lázaro Cárdenas 88, has rooms with private bath for US$2.25/2.75.

Hotel Posada San José, down the track beside the bus station, is uninviting but has tolerably clean and sizeable double rooms with fans for US$4.50 to US$6.50. What was once a swimming pool is now used for drying laundry. *Casa de Huéspedes Tropical* on Avenida Cuauhtémoc off Progreso, behind the Palacio Municipal, has basic and not very clean doubles for US$2.75. Bathrooms are shared.

Places to Eat

Los Arcos on Lázaro Cárdenas opposite the corner of Madero is the busiest restaurant. *Restaurant Lupita*, on Lázaro Cárdenas 50 metres north of Allende, has pictures of psychedelic-phase Beatles on the wall. Their eggs with ham and onion (US$0.75) taste great.

Getting There & Away

Pochutla is at the south end of the mountainous Highway 175, 238 km from Oaxaca. A km south of the town is a crossroads where coastal Highway 200 runs west to Puerto Escondido (74 km) and Acapulco (474 km), east to Salina Cruz (185 km) and Tehuantepec (201 km); the road to Puerto Ángel (12 km) goes south.

Bus The Oaxaca Pacífico/Estrella del Valle bus station is towards the south end of the main street, Lázaro Cárdenas. At the last count the '1st class' services to Oaxaca (US$3, six hours or more) left at 5 and 10.30 am and at 1.30, 10.30 and 11 pm. The '2nd class' services (US$2.75) left at 7 and 9 am, at 12 noon, and at 3, 5 and 8.30 pm. Buses also depart from the same place every half-hour for Puerto Ángel (15c); hourly to Puerto Escondido (US$0.75, 1¼ hours), Santa Cruz Huatulco (US$0.50) and Salina Cruz (US$2.25, five hours); and four times daily to the Bahías

de Santa Cruz. See under Oaxaca, Puerto Escondido and Salina Cruz for buses to Pochutla from those places.

Buses of Flecha Roja/Lineas Unidas del Sur/Transportes Cacela leave three times a day for Puerto Escondido and once for Acapulco from the corner of Juárez opposite the church, a block east of Lázaro Cárdenas.

To Puerto Angel there are colectivos (US$0.30), taxis (US$1.75) and buses; these wait outside the bus station.

PUERTO ÁNGEL

Puerto Ángel ('PORR-toh ANN-hell') is still not much more than a fishing village and small-time port straggling round a little bay guarded by two rocky headlands. There's a clean but tiny beach on one side of the bay, but what makes Puerto Ángel a true travellers' haven is the beaches a few km either side of the village – in particular Zipolite. This long, empty stretch of pale sand has been fabled for a couple of decades now as southern Mexico's ultimate place to lay back in a hammock and do as little as you like, in as little as you like, for almost as little as you like.

Ten years ago access to Puerto Ángel was only by unpaved road over the Sierra Madre del Sur from Oaxaca. Now you can fly to Puerto Escondido, a couple of hours away by bus, and paved roads lead from Oaxaca, Salina Cruz and Acapulco. There's a bigger (but still limited) range of accommodation in Puerto Ángel now and a few more people are coming here – but it's still a sleepy place where a small naval base makes as little difference to the tenor of local life as do the visitors.

Like Puerto Escondido, Puerto Ángel gets pretty hot and any breath of wind can be a big bonus. May is usually the hottest month and most rain falls between June and September.

Information & Orientation

The paved road from Pochutla, 13 km north, emerges at the east end of the small Puerto Ángel Bay and what you can see

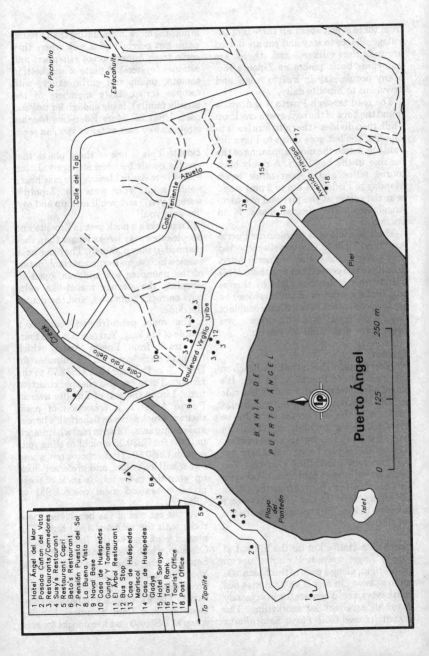

Puerto Ángel

1 Hotel Ángel del Mar
2 Posada Cañon del Vata
3 Restaurants/Comedores
4 Susy's Restaurant
5 Restaurant Capri
6 Beto's Restaurant
7 Pensión Puesta del Sol
8 La Buena Vista
9 Naval Base
10 Casa de Huéspedes Gundy Y Tomas
11 El Árbol Restaurant
12 Bus Stop
13 Casa de Huéspedes Mariscol
14 Casa de Huéspedes Gladys
15 Hotel Soraya
16 Taxi Rank
17 Tourist Office
18 Post Office

To Pochutla

To Estacahuite

Calle del Tajo

Calle Teniente Azueta

Avenida Principal

Boulevard Virgilio Uribe

Calle Palo Bello

Creek

BAHÍA DE PUERTO ÁNGEL

Pier

Playa del Panteón

Islet

To Zipolite

250 m

125

0

from there is just about all there is of the village. Places to stay and eat are dotted around the village, and there are numerous basic places at Zipolite too. Many people stay in Puerto Ángel and travel out to Zipolite daily.

The road through Puerto Ángel winds round the back of the bay, over a creek, up a hill, then divides – the right fork leads to Zipolite, the left goes down to Playa del Panteón, much the more appealing of the beaches in the bay itself. A rarely open tourist office and a post office (open Monday to Friday, 11 am to 2 pm) stand near the corner at the pier end of Puerto Ángel Bay. The nearest bank is in Pochutla.

Theft is a bit of a problem in Puerto Ángel and Zipolite. One traveller reported that going to the police in Puerto Ángel does help. His possessions and those of his friends were stolen one night by thieves who broke a window in their vehicle; he got the possessions back within a couple of days. Take equal care with drugs – you never know who might set you up.

Beaches

Playa del Panteón This is the little beach on the west side of Puerto Ángel Bay. It's clean, shallow and calm and at low tide you can swim out to a sandspit which joins the shore to the islet on the right. In the evenings diving pelicans and locals in boats fish the same waters close inshore. There are a couple of restaurants here and you can rent snorkelling gear too. You could probably get a fisherman to take you for a boat trip from here or from the pier on the other side of the bay – but they won't take you to Zipolite because the surf's too rough there.

Estacahuite Half a km up the hill out of Puerto Ángel towards Pochutla, a sign points right, along a path to this beach '500 metres' away. In fact it's 700 metres but worth every step. There are three tiny sandy bays, all excellent for snorkelling. The grandly named *Club Playa Estacahuita*

is nothing more intimidating than a round palm hut perched on a rock where they serve fresh *huachinango* (snapper) and *ostiones* (oysters). A plate of spaghetti in tomato, onion and garlic sauce, with *totopos* (crisp, tasty members of the tortilla family), is big enough for two and costs US$1.25. More Eden-like beaches stretch away east as far as you can see.

Zipolite This is one of those places that creates bonds between strangers. Later, somewhere else in Mexico, you may hear a voice ask, 'You were in Zipolite, weren't you?' and you'll look up and say, 'So were you!'

Time takes a back seat in Zipolite and people often stay weeks longer than they planned (*if* they planned). The place has a magic which stems from some combination of the pounding sea and sun, open-air sleeping, the strange rocket-like palm huts on rocky pinnacles, and (no doubt) the dope.

The wide, palm-fringed beach is a couple of km long. You reach it by a four-km track from Puerto Ángel, which frequent taxis cover in 10 minutes for US$1.75 to the near end, US$2.75 to the far end. There are also cheaper colectivo taxis. Lining the end of Zipolite nearest Puerto Ángel is a collection of palm shelters which serve as fisherfolk's homes and restaurants. You can rent a hammock in these for US$0.75 a night or sling your own for US$0.50. Try to choose one whose owner will look after, and preferably lock up, your things for you. In most of these places a seafood meal costs US$1 to US$1.50.

At the far end of the beach rise those rocks with the rocket-shaped huts. The nearest rock marks the *Restaurant Lo Cosmico*, which has a handful of cabañas. Some of the others are part of the *Shambhala Posada*, usually called the *Casa Gloria* after its North American owner. There's a variety of basic accommodation here from hammock-hanging space at US$0.50 and hammocks for rent at US$0.75, to hammocks in cabañas for US$1.50 to US$1.75. The sitting/eating area has a great view back along the beach, and vegetarian food is served (most items US$0.75 or less). A track, passable for vehicles, leads along behind the beach to Casa Gloria.

The sea at Zipolite can be quite rough so don't wander too far out, and keep away from the rocks at both ends. Particularly at the Casa Gloria end there can be strong undertow. Nudity is usually no problem – just occasionally, men in uniforms wander along asking people to cover up.

Beyond Zipolite A path that's hard to find, but fine once you're on it, leads from behind Casa Gloria to the first of two long, sandy beaches, about a km away. A few pelicans fishing from a rock are usually the only living creatures here. The second long, sandy beach is a different story. It's the site of the infamous Zipolite turtle slaughterhouse, where dogs sniff round giant turtles flapping on their backs in the sand. Unable to turn over, the turtles wait to die and be shipped out in trucks as meat. If you want to become vegetarian, pay a visit.

Places to Stay

Several excellent places in Puerto Angel – some run by young Mexican-European or Mexican-North American couples – provide a comfortable alternative to Zipolite's basic accommodation. Some of them have a bit of a water shortage; there's usually enough to wash yourself but not always your clothes.

Places to Stay – bottom end

The friendly *Casa de Huéspedes Gladys* is up the hill above the pier, past the Hotel Soraya. It has eight clean rooms with fans ranging from a small single for US$2.75 to doubles/triples with shared bath at US$5.50/6.50 and doubles with private bath for US$6.50. There are balconies and a roof with bay views.

The *Pensión Puesta del Sol* is up to the right as you climb the hill past the creek. Rooms have no fans or mosquito nets but are large and clean and cost US$3.75 for one or two people. Open-air hammocks are US$0.75. Bathrooms are shared and there are light eats - eggs, yoghurt, fruit.

Places to Stay – middle

The *Posada Cañon del Vata* isn't the cheapest place but it's so beautifully laid out that many are happy to pay the extra cost. There are just a few comfortable rooms (with fans and private bathrooms) scattered among trees and along walkways on a secluded hillside. A breezy sitting/hammock-swinging area tops one hillock, tiles are used decoratively and there are lots of English-language books to read. The dining area at the back has open sides and a palm roof and is hung with paintings. Singles/doubles cost US$8.25/9. Reach it by following the track down to Playa del Pantéon, then going on round to the right. The entrance is up a flight of steps on the right beside an empty building.

Casa de Huéspedes Gundy y Tomás, breezily placed up a track opposite the naval base, has eight rooms ranging from US$3.75 to US$5.50. All have either mosquito nets or mosquito screens on the windows. You can also rent an open-air hammock for US$1. The shared bathrooms are clean and there's enough water for washing clothes. Food is available (omelette, vegetable soup and yoghurt with fruit are all around US$0.75) and there are pleasant sitting areas.

In a similar vein but a bit more up-market is *La Buena Vista*, which has 10 big clean rooms with private bathrooms, mosquito screens and fans. There are lots of flowers around and they'll bring breakfast to your room! Singles are US$6.50 or US$7.25, doubles US$7.25 or US$8.25. If you want to wash clothes, ask to do it in the house. Turn right immediately after the creek, then take the first left to get there.

Hotel Soraya, on the hill above the pier, is one of Puerto Ángel's two true hotels. There are 32 clean rooms with private baths and communal balconies. Some have sea views. Singles/doubles are US$7.75/9.50 with fan, US$13.25 with air-conditioning. The hotel has its own restaurant.

Places to Stay – top end

The *Hotel Ángel del Mar*, on the hilltop above Playa del Panteón, has 33 bright, clean, fan-cooled rooms with their own balconies at US$20/24.50/29 for one/two/three people, plus nine suites. There's a restaurant, a small swimming pool, plenty of breeze and great views.

Places to Eat

The cheapest places are those lining the road between the pier and naval station, of which *El Árbol*, on the land side, is one of the best.

Also popular and reasonably priced for seafood is *Beto's*, up the hill past the creek. For a treat go to the rooftop *Restaurant Capri* on the right at the beginning of the track that descends to Playa del Panteón. It's deliciously cool in the evenings and the food's good and still well-priced. *Huachinango* (snapper) Veracruzana or in garlic sauce is US$1.75, oysters or beefsteak US$1.25, shrimp US$2.25 and guacamole US$0.50.

On Playa del Panteón, *Susy's* does big seafood cocktails for US$1.75 to US$2.75, fish dishes for US$1.50, seafood soup or octopus for US$1.75, and shrimp dishes for US$2.75.

Non-residents can also eat in the excellent restaurant at the *Posada Cañon del Vata*, where a three-course dinner (often vegetarian) with a fruit drink and home-baked bread is served at 7 pm for US$2.50 (book earlier in the day). At other times you can get things like yoghurt with granola and bananas or sandwiches (cheese, avocado, tomato and onion) for around US$0.75, enchiladas for US$1.

Getting There & Away

The bus stop in Puerto Ángel is in front of El Árbol restaurant, between the pier and naval base. There are buses to and from Pochutla (15c) every half-hour. Colectivos (US$0.30) and taxis (US$1.75) also cruise around most of the time to take people between the two places.

From Oaxaca there's one Estrella del Valle/Oaxaca Pacífico '1st class' bus daily to Puerto Ángel. It leaves Oaxaca at 10.30 pm, costs US$3 and takes about 7½ hours. There's also one a day going back to Oaxaca. However, there are 10 other buses a day run by the same company in each direction between Oaxaca and Pochutla, and it's easy enough to make a connection to or from Puerto Ángel in Pochutla. See under Oaxaca and Pochutla for details.

For Puerto Escondido, Salina Cruz and other places along the coast, you have to change buses in Pochutla.

HUATULCO

A series of picturesque sandy bays – the Bahías de Huatulco ('wa-TOOL-koh') – is strung along the coast for about five km each side of the village of Santa Cruz Huatulco 40 km east of Pochutla. According to tradition, the area was settled in pre-Hispanic times by Zapotec and Mixtec outcasts from elsewhere in Oaxaca. The English navigators Francis Drake and Thomas Cavendish landed at Santa Cruz Huatulco in 1578 and 1587, and some accounts say it was here, not at Acapulco, that the Mexican revolution hero Vicente Guerrero was betrayed to his enemies by an Italian for 50,000 pieces of gold.

Those events apart, Huatulco looked likely to remain in obscurity, known by just a few outsiders as a great place for a quiet bathe and fresh seafood – until one day in 1984, when the local people heard for the first time that a big tourist development was planned for their villages and bays. Quite how big they didn't discover until later, when in 1987 it was reported that by the beginning of the

21st century Huatulco was due to have 9000 hotel rooms, 800,000 visitors a year and a permanent population of 100,000. Thirteen hundred rooms and 146,000 visitors were planned for 1989.

The Mexican government has already pumped huge sums into the project, work has proceeded quickly, and stories are rife of presidential money and influence being involved too. One magazine reported that the ball started rolling after President José López Portillo took a boat trip along the coast in 1982 with his Minister of Tourism (and mistress) Rosa Luz Alegría.

An international airport, and a 554-room *Club Méditerranée* at Tangolunda Bay, were scheduled for completion in late 1987. The first hotel in operation was the relatively small *Benigenda* at Santa Cruz (rooms about US$30 a night). Also in the pipeline are an *El Presidente* hotel at Tangolunda and a 500-room *Sheraton*. A replica of the Oaxaca zócalo is said to be planned for one development.

Local people complain of official trickery over compensation for their lands, and of appearances (though not violence) by the military to frighten them into cooperation.

In west-east order, the Huatulco bays are Cacaluta, El Maguey, El Organo, Santa Cruz (with the village of Santa Cruz Huatulco), Chahue, Tangolunda and Conejos. Buses go from Pochutla to Santa Cruz Huatulco every hour (US$0.50), and there are four a day from Pochutla to the Bahías de Huatulco.

PUERTO ESCONDIDO

A haunt of surfers since long before paved roads came to this part of Oaxaca, Puerto Escondido ('PORR-toh ess-con-DEED-o', meaning Hidden Port) is as much a resort as a fishing village now, but remains small, relaxed and relatively cheap. Scattered across a hillside above the ocean, it has no big hotels, few paved streets and is still too remote to make a serious appearance on the package holiday map. There's talk of more hotel development along Zicatela Beach and in a purpose-built zone to the west of the town, now that Puerto Escondido has a new international-size airstrip, but at present it's still a world away from Acapulco, Puerto Vallarta and other Pacific resorts further north.

There are several beaches in and near the town, an interesting coastline to explore, a range of reasonable accommodation, some fine cafés and restaurants, and a dash of nightlife. It's a convivial place for travellers to get together, and Puerto Ángel, even more laid-back, is only 1½ hours east.

Puerto Escondido is truly tropical – hotter and more humid than the highlands of Oaxaca. Any breath of breeze can be at a premium and you're more likely to get one up the hill a bit, rather than down at sea-level. The rainy season is May to October, with July and August the wettest months.

Orientation

The town is set on a hillside which rises from a small, south-facing bay (the main beach). The Sierra Madre del Sur rises behind the town. Avenida Pérez Gasga is a partly traffic-free street which runs along behind the beach and loops up to the Carretera Costera, the Acapulco-Salina Cruz coastal highway which runs across the town, halfway up the hill. On Pérez Gasga you'll find the small clutch of restaurants, shops and hotels which constitutes Puerto Escondido's 'resort area'.

The bay curves round, at its east end, to Zicatela Beach, a long, empty stretch of sand good for surfing but dangerous for swimming. It is backed by a few groups of cabañas which are favourite hang-outs for budget travellers. Other beaches line a series of bays dotted along the coast to the west.

The bus stations and homes of most of the local people are in the streets uphill from the Carretera Costera.

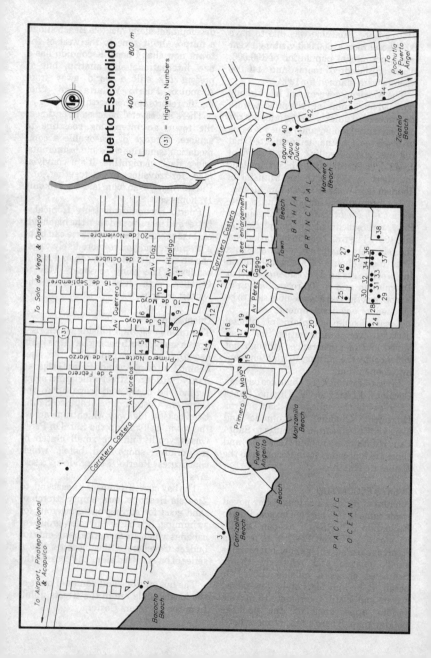

1	Hotel Rancho del Pescador
2	Castel Puerto Escondido
3	Trailer Park Carrizalillo
4	Hotel Palacio Azteca
5	Hotel Cruz del Ángel
6	Los Arcos Restaurant
7	Hotel Posada del Puerto
8	Oaxaca-Istmo Bus Station
9	Flecha Roja/Lineas Unidas del Sur Bus Station
10	Laundromat
11	Estrella del Valle/Oaxaca Pacifico Bus Station
12	El Picapiedra Disco
13	Post Office
14	Hotel El Crucero
15	Casa de Huéspedes Las Dos Costas
16	Hotel Paraíso Escondido
17	Mexicana
18	Hotel Nayar
19	Hotel Loren
20	Lighthouse
21	Hotel Ribera del Mar
22	Hotel Rocamar
23	Macumba Disco
24	Lucy's Restaurant
25	El Fogón Restaurant
26	Bancomer
27	Restaurant San Ángel
28	Restaurant Los Crotos
29	Pizza Parlor
30	Hotel Las Palmas
31	Tourist Office
32	Hotel Rincón del Pacifico
33	Aerovías Oaxaqueñas
34	Ostería Viandante
35	Il Cappuccino
36	Bananas
37	Palmas de Cortés
38	Neptuno
39	Restaurant Las Cabañas
40	Restaurant Liza
41	Villa Marinero
42	Hotel Santa Fe
43	Casas de Playa Acali
44	Bungalows Acuario

Information

Tourist Office There's a helpful tourist office (tel 2-01-75) on Pérez Gasga, between the hotels Las Palmas and Rincón del Pacífico. It's open mornings except Sunday, and evenings Monday to Friday.

Money Bancomer on Pérez Gasga is more or less the only blot on the Puerto Escondido landscape. It's the only bank in town which will change foreign money or travellers' cheques, and unfortunately this monopoly allows some of its staff to exact a sadistic punishment on foreigners for enjoying themselves. Long queues of visitors stand motionless while clerks endlessly check and recheck countless documents in between lengthy breaks for coffee, chats, etc.

When I complained to the bank clerk that he had allowed a Mexican woman to jump the queue, he disappeared for a few minutes, then came back to consult his manager. The manager called me over and told me the Mexican entry stamp in my passport had been altered, pointing to an indecipherable purple smudge. I pointed to the real date stamp, which clearly had not been altered and tallied with my tourist card. He then informed me that the signature on my travellers' cheque was different from the one on my passport and he therefore couldn't change the cheque.

I told him his bank was *basura*, left and hopped on a bus for Pochutla, where I changed my cheque in another branch of Bancomer, and was back in Puerto Escondido three hours later – a process not very much longer and a lot less aggravating than waiting for the Puerto Escondido branch to go through its 'paces'.

– John Noble

The only other answers to Bancomer in Puerto Escondido are an early start (it opens at 9 am) and infinite patience. Or change as much money as you feel safe carrying before you get to Puerto Escondido.

Post The post office is on Carretera Costera, just west of the junction with the west end of Pérez Gasga.

Airlines The Mexicana airline office (tel 2-04-14, 2-04-22) is at Pérez Gasga 302, up the hill a bit. Aerovías Oaxaqueñas (tel 2-

01-32) is on Pérez Gasga opposite Bancomer.

Other There's a laundromat, Lavandería Automática, on Avenida Hidalgo next to the sport centre. Il Cappuccino café on Pérez Gasga has a ride board. There are a few English-language books and magazines in a shop just up Pérez Gasga from the Hotel Nayar.

Beaches

Town Beach The main town beach is long enough to accommodate a few restaurants at its west end, a small fishing fleet in the middle, sun-worshippers at the east end, and occasional flights of pelicans which wing in inches above the waves. A few vendors wander up and down offering textiles and necklaces, but the beach is rarely other than relaxed. The water's pretty shallow and the swell fairly gentle, but don't get too close to the rocks at the east end.

Zicatela Beyond the rocky outcrop at the east end of the town beach, Zicatela is on the open ocean and is for strong-swimming surfers only. There are big waves – including the 'Mexican Pipeline' – and a dangerous undertow here. People have drowned.

Puerto Angelito This bay, about a km west of the town beach as the crow flies, has two small beaches separated by a few rocks which you can walk across. The smaller one's known as Manzanilla. This is a good place to come if you find the town beach too busy – though at weekends and holiday times Puerto Angelito can get just as busy. The sea floor slope's a bit steeper than at the town beach but it's very calm. Snorkelling's good here and you can rent equipment for US$2.75 an hour from in front of the small restaurant.

You can reach Puerto Angelito by *lancha* (motor launch) from the town beach. There's usually a boatman or two waiting somewhere in front of the Hotel Las Palmas – price US$0.50 per person.

By land, you have to go west along the Carretera Costera for a few hundred metres from the top of Pérez Gasga. A sign points left off the carretera down to Puerto Angelito. On the way down you fork left at the *Bienvenidos a PEPSI Puerto Angelito* sign – altogether a 30 to 40-minute walk from Pérez Gasga. A taxi from town to Puerto Angelito costs about US$1.

Carrizalillo This is a small cove a bit further west from Puerto Angelito – rockier but OK for swimming, with a little beach. Lanchas from the town beach will bring you here too. By land, Carrizalillo is reached by a path down from the Trailer Park Carrizalillo. From the town, follow the directions above for Puerto Angelito but fork right at the Pepsi sign to get to the trailer park. You can also reach Carrizalillo by cutting left through the trees as you ascend the track from Puerto Angelito, and then walking across to the trailer park.

Bacocho This is a long stretch of beach on the open ocean west of the Castel Puerto Escondido hotel. It has rough seas and a reputedly dangerous undertow.

Places to Stay

Puerto Escondido has a wide range of accommodation, but even at non-peak times of year the more popular hotels are often full. Try to make advance reservations if you're dead set on Las Palmas, Rincón del Pacífico, the Nayar, the Santa Fe or the Paraíso Escondido. Otherwise the best chance of getting a room in such places is to ask about 9 or 10 am, when they should know if there'll be any vacancies the same day.

Prices in the lower and middle ranges may rise at peak periods like Christmas, New Year, Semana Santa and July and August.

Places to Stay – bottom end

You have the choice of campgrounds and cabañas – cane walls, palm roof, dirt floor

– near the beach or the cheaper hotels up the hill.

Palmas de Cortés and *Neptuno* are set back from the town beach, among trees either side of the short lane that runs down beside Bananas café. *Palmas de Cortés* is a campground/trailer park charging US$1 per person and vehicle, with showers and electrical hook-up available, and fireplaces. *Neptuno* is a quite spacious but sociable place where a two-bed cabaña (no mosquito nets, a few mosquitoes) costs US$1.75 and you can camp (US$0.75 per person) or park a vehicle (US$1.25). Electricity is available. There's a big central fireplace, and the toilets and showers are clean. Noise from the disco over the road might be a disturbance if you're an early sleeper.

Further along the beach, just beyond the small lagoon, *Restaurant Las Cabañas* has similar two-bed cabañas crowded together in a quieter but more mosquito-ridden location for the same price as Neptuno – US$1.75. Toilets and showers are reasonably clean.

Still further along, behind the next beach (Zicatela) and past the more up-market Acali cabañas, you'll find a nameless place with Coca-Cola ads on the fence. The cabañas here are good value – US$10 for three people, with mosquito nets, fans, fridges and a place to cook. Just beyond, *Bungalows Acuario* has big, well-built wood-and-thatch cabañas for US$5.50 single, US$6.75 double.

The *Casa de Huéspedes Las Dos Costas* is at Pérez Gasga 302, on the left going up the hill. Large clean rooms with fan and private bath cost US$5 double, US$7.75 triple.

Up in the town, hotels are cheaper because they're uphill from the beach, but you also stand more chance of a breeze. *Hotel Posada del Puerto* (tel 2-02-64) at Hidalgo 104 is popular with Mexican families. There are about 15 basic two-bed rooms with fan and private bath round a courtyard. Cost is US$4.50 for two people, US$6.50 for four. *Hotel Cruz del Angel* (tel 2-01-22) at Díaz 202 has 16 clean rooms with fan and private bath for US$4 single, US$6 double, US$7.75 triple. The front rooms at the top have good views. *Hotel Palacio Azteca* (tel 2-02-46) at the corner of Díaz and Primera Norte has clean, quite big rooms with fan and small balcony for US$4.75 single, US$6 double, US$7 triple.

About 1½ km west of the town, the *Trailer Park Carrizalillo* is a big bare area with a fine clifftop position. Water and electrical hook-ups are included at US$4.50 for two people. Follow the 'Puerto Angelito' sign to the left off the Carretera Costera going out of town, then fork right at the Pepsi sign.

Places to Stay – middle

Best bets in this range are some of the hotels on Pérez Gasga or a couple of more up-market cabaña places on Zicatela Beach.

The *Hotel Rincón del Pacífico* (tel 2-00-56) is good value for its beachside position at Pérez Gasga 900, and for that reason is often full. There are 26 clean, sizeable glass-fronted rooms with fans round a shady courtyard, from which you walk onto the beach. Singles/doubles are US$7.75/9.75.

Another good choice, with the same prices and also sometimes full, is the *Hotel Nayar* (tel 2-01-13, 2-03-19), slightly up the hill at Pérez Gasga 407. There are 36 rooms with fans and small balconies; some rooms have sea views. The hotel also has airy sitting areas/ walkways and its own restaurant.

Next door to the Nayar, just down the hill, the box-like and smaller *Hotel Loren* (tel 2-00-57) has the same prices again and slightly bigger rooms than the Nayar, but less breeze and less space outside the rooms.

Hotel El Crucero (tel 2-02-25), near the top of Pérez Gasga at No 106, has 19 simple, clean, quite big rooms with fans and private bath for US$7.75 single, US$9.75 double, US$11.50 triple. The

Hotel Ribera del Mar is on the dirt track parallel to Pérez Gasga, halfway up the hill to the main road. It's a U-shaped building with trees in the middle. Rooms are clean and quite large, and have fans. Singles/doubles/triples are US$6.50/8.25/11. A few rooms have sea views.

About 300 metres along the track at the back of Zicatela Beach, *Casas de Playa Acali* has well-built wood cabañas with fridge, mosquito nets, comfortable beds and communal baths for US$9.75 single, US$11.50 double, US$15.50 quadruple. Further along the same beach, *Bungalows Acuario* has a few rooms with private bath for US$8.25 single, US$9 double, US$11.75 quadruple, as well as cheaper cabañas.

Back at the east end of the main beach, *Villa Marinero* has a few brick bungalows at US$9.50 for one double bed, US$18.25 for two beds. Nearby, *Restaurant Liza* has a few rooms in the back. They're clean but not very big and a bit airless. Singles/doubles are US$11/12.75.

Places to Stay – top end

There are three places in town, all with their merits, and a few more a km or two to the west. *Hotel Las Palmas* (tel 2-00-56) has a prime position on both the beach and the traffic-free part of Pérez Gasga. It has 20-odd fan-cooled rooms at US$11.75 single, US$13.50 double, which are often full. Rooms are a bit bigger than in the cheaper Rincón del Pacífico next door, the garden's a bit more artistic, and there's a little restaurant right on the beach.

At the east end of the main beach, beside the rocky outcrop, the *Hotel Santa Fe* (tel 2-01-70) has about 30 rooms artistically set around small terraces and a palm-fringed swimming pool. The stairways are tiled and there's an airy restaurant/bar overlooking the sea, as well as a small library of English-language books. Singles/doubles/triples (with fans but no air-conditioning) are US$21/24.25/27.50. The dirt track on which the hotel stands is officially Calle del Morro and its postal address is Apartado Postal 96, Puerto Escondido, Oaxaca.

Almost as charming is the *Hotel Paraíso Escondido* (tel 2-04-44) on Calle Unión, which shortcuts the loop in Pérez Gasga. This is a rambling, old-fashioned whitewash-and-blue-paint place on several levels with lots of tile, pottery and stone sculpture decoration. There's an attractive restaurant/bar/swimming pool area. The 20 spotless rooms are air-conditioned and some have stained-glass window panes. Some have better views than others and the price range is US$25 to US$30. You can make reservations by calling Mexico City 604-08-34 between 3 and 8 pm, or by writing to Apartado Postal 20-187, Mexico 20 DF.

Puerto Escondido's very top hotel, the *Castel Puerto Escondido* (tel 2-01-33, 2-03-46), is about two km out of the town on Boulevard Benito Juárez (turn left off the Carretera Costera going west). It has 100 air-conditioned three-bed rooms, a big palm-shaded garden with a swimming pool, three bars and a restaurant and is sited on a headland overlooking Bacocho beach. Singles/doubles/triples are US$25/31.25/37.50. You can make reservations in Mexico City through Casteles de México (tel 528-57-79, 528-86-13), at Álvaro Obregón 275-5, Mexico DF 06700.

Places to Eat

You can catch or buy your own fish and grill them over a cabana campfire, or maybe get a restaurant to cook them for you. A varied clutch of visitor-oriented restaurants has grown up on the beach and the traffic-free section of Pérez Gasga, and some of them are pretty good.

For seafood, the *Restaurant Los Crotos* towards the west end of the town beach is very good though not the cheapest. Most seafood dishes are in the US$1.75 to US$2.50 range. Try *pescado papillon* (fish – usually snapper – in shrimp, beer and capsicum sauce) with avocado salad and French fries, or *camarones gigantes al mojo de ajo* (truly giant shrimp in garlic sauce). Other items on the menu include seafood cocktails (US$2.25), fish soup (US$1.50), spaghetti (US$1.50 to US$1.75) and eggs (US$1).

Osteria Viandante is an excellent and very popular little Italian restaurant with quick service on the beach side of Pérez Gasga. Spaghetti dishes cost US$1 to US$1.50, salads US$1, one-person pizzas US$1.75 to US$2.25. The *pay de limón* (lemon pie) is tasty too, and the music is by The Grateful Dead, Hendrix, Dylan and Springsteen.

Next door, *Il Cappuccino* is a pleasant place for breakfasts, snacks and drinks. Not surprisingly, the coffee's great. Vegetarian omelette with rice, fruit, Russian salad and bolillo costs US$1.75. There's a ride board here.

More expensive but very popular in the evenings – when there's usually live music – is *Bananas*, a few more metres along Pérez Gasga. You can play chess or table tennis and read the papers. The food is quite expensive but includes yoghurt and granola (US$1.25, small helping), crepes (US$1.50 to US$1.75), carrot or beetroot juice (US$0.75), cappuccino (US$0.75), cakes and cocktails.

Also popular on Pérez Gasga are the *Restaurant San Angel*, opposite Il Cappuccino, where fish dishes are US$1.75 to US$2.25, shrimp US$2.75, spaghetti US$1 to US$1.75; and the cheaper *Lucy's* on the beach side (fish, oysters, seafood cocktails, eggs). *El Fogón* nearly opposite Lucy's does tacos, tortas, tostadas, queso fundido and breakfasts.

On the beach just east of Restaurant Los Crotos, *The Pizza Parlor* does brick-oven pizzas for US$1.25 to US$1.75, *picante* seafood cocktails including *caracol* (sea snail) for US$1.50, fish or beefsteak dishes (US$1.50 to US$1.75) and spaghetti (US$0.75 to US$1.25).

At the east end of the beach, *Liza's* is more expensive but the seafood comes in huge platefuls and is good. *Huachinango* (snapper) grilled with garlic, plus a large salad and French fries, will cost you

US$4.50. They sometimes have lobster (US$8.25 per lb). The *Hotel Santa Fe* restaurant is an elegant place, often with a live guitarist in the evenings and some tasty seafood and vegetarian offerings. Cheaper ones include spinach and Swiss cheese enchiladas (US$4); and yoghurt, granola, fruit and honey (US$1.75).

Up in the town, there are a few cheaper restaurants along Hidalgo around the bus stations. *Los Arcos* on Díaz near the corner of 5 de Mayo does fish dishes for US$2, seafood soup for US$2.50 and seafood cocktails for US$1.75. Unfortunately the cheapest meals of all have moved with the market to the far north-west edge of town, a considerable distance from anywhere else.

Entertainment

Many Puerto Escondido evenings start at the beachside happy hours in the *Hotel Las Palmas* (6 to 7 pm, two piña coladas US$1) or *Liza's* (5 to 8 pm, more expensive but the 'matador' mezcal cocktail is interesting!). Then there are usually musicians in *Bananas* and the *Hotel Santa Fe*, and if you're still lively later, a few discos throb into the night. The most popular at the last count were *Macumba* at the west end of the traffic-free part of Pérez Gasga, and *El Picapiedra* up on the Carretera Costera, just east of the top of Pérez Gasga.

Things to Buy

The purpose-built Juárez market is way out on the north-west edge of town where even the townspeople don't bother to go. You can buy fruit and a few other things from stalls that set up around the Posada del Puerto on Hidalgo. Jewellery and coral sellers set up on Pérez Gasga most evenings. There are some T-shirt and craft shops in the same street, and a few vendors sometimes wander along the town beach.

Getting There & Away

Air A spectacular, quick and reasonably

priced alternative to the bus is the usually twice-daily air service of Aerovías Oaxaqueñas between Oaxaca and Puerto Escondido. The ageing little DC-3s have just 28 seats but the ride's more comfortable than any Mexicana or Aeroméxico jet. Leaving Puerto Escondido, the planes make a big loop out over the ocean to gain height for the crossing of the Sierra Madre del Sur. One-way fare between Oaxaca and Puerto Escondido is US$24.75 and it's advisable to book as far ahead as possible. There may also be flights between Puerto Escondido and Salina Cruz. Aerovías Oaxaqueñas has offices in Puerto Escondido (tel 2-01-32) on Pérez Gasga opposite Bancomer, in Oaxaca (tel 6-38-33) at Armenta y López 209, and in Mexico City (tel 510-01-62) at Despacho 514, Balderas 32.

Mexicana has four direct flights a week each way between Mexico City and Puerto Escondido.

Road Puerto Escondido lies on the coastal highway (No 200) which is now paved all the way from Tepic to Tehuantepec. To the west, Acapulco is 400 km away, to the east Pochutla is 74 km, Salina Cruz 259 km and Tehuantepec about 275 km. From Pochutla, Highway 175 (paved) climbs and winds 238 km north through the Sierra Madre del Sur to Oaxaca. Highway 131 goes direct from Puerto Escondido to Oaxaca but it's not paved for the first 170 km from Puerto Escondido to Sola de Vega.

Bus Flecha Roja runs two '1st class' (really '2nd class') buses a day from Mexico City's southern bus terminal near Tasqueña metro to Puerto Escondido (US$11). The same company also has 16 daily buses from Acapulco to Puerto Escondido (US$6) – a seven or eight-hour trip.

From Oaxaca to Puerto Escondido, Estrella del Valle/Oaxaca Pacífico runs '1st class' buses at 7.30 am, 9.30 pm and 9.45 pm. The journey takes seven hours or more and the road is spectacular but very twisty. At busy times these buses are often full – you can book a day ahead at Oaxaca 2nd-class bus station. Fare is US$3.75. The same line also has '2nd class' buses which leave Oaxaca for Puerto Escondido at 6 am, 9 am and 12 noon and cost US$3.50. An alternative is to get one of the same line's buses to Pochutla, then one of the frequent services along the coast to Puerto Escondido.

The buses of La Solteca take the direct, mostly unpaved, route from Oaxaca to Puerto Escondido and are much slower and even less comfortable. They leave Oaxaca at 6 am and 9 pm and the fare is US$3. From Puerto Escondido to Oaxaca, Estrella del Valle/Oaxaca Pacífico's '1st class' buses leave at 9.30 am, 10 pm and 10.30 pm from their terminal on Hidalgo. The '2nd class' departures are at 7.30 am and 1 pm. Again it's advisable to book ahead if possible on these.

Estrella del Valle/Oaxaca Pacífico also has hourly services from Puerto Escondido along the coast to Pochutla (US$0.75, 1¼ hours in '1st class') and Salina Cruz (US$3, about 6½ hours in '1st class'), and a few buses west to Jamiltepec and Pinotepa Nacional.

Oaxaca-Istmo ('2nd class') covers the route to Pochutla and Salina Cruz five times a day. Fare to Salina Cruz is US$2.75 and the terminal in Puerto Escondido is also on Hidalgo. You can buy advance tickets at the restaurant diagonally across the junction from the terminal.

Flecha Roja/Lineas Unidas del Sur ('1st class'), also on Hidalgo, goes to Acapulco (US$6, seven to eight hours) 16 times a day, with one faster direct departure at 10.30 am. It also has two daily buses to Mexico City (US$11), four to Pochutla and three just to Pinotepa Nacional (US$2.50). For Puerto Ángel, take a bus to Pochutla and a bus, colectivo or taxi from there.

Getting Around

Airport Transport Puerto Escondido's new airport is a few km west of the town.

Colectivo taxis (US$1 per person) meet incoming flights and will drop you anywhere in town. You can book them to take you back to the airport at Pérez Gasga 601 (tel 2-01-14) on the right going up the hill.

Local Transport You can walk to Puerto Angelito or Carrizalillo beaches, but it's more fun to take a lancha from the town beach in front of the Hotel Las Palmas (US$0.50 to Puerto Angelito). Taxis cruise around and will take you to any local destination (US$1 to Puerto Angelito).

The lancha operators are often also willing to take people fishing or on trips along the coast – perhaps as far as Manialtepec Lagoon. Expect to pay about US$6 an hour. There are a couple of tour companies with offices on Pérez Gasga which run trips to places like Manialtepec and Chacahua and the Sunday markets in Jamiltepec and Pinotepa Nacional. See 'West of Puerto Escondido' for information on these places – you could go by public transport or hired car to some of them.

Car Rental Avis (tel 2-04-43) has offices at the airport and at the Hotel Rancho del Pescador, which is up a track to the right about a km west of the town along the Carretera Costera. A VW Sedan will cost you US$48 per day plus 15c for every km beyond 200 km.

WEST OF PUERTO ESCONDIDO

A number of places which might be worth exploring lie on and off Highway 200 as it heads towards Acapulco. The route passes through the area inhabited by Chatino Indians, which stretches north from Río Grande, into a mainly Mixtec region around Jamiltepec and Pinotepa Nacional where many people still hold to traditional costumes and customs. Buses of Estrella del Valle/Oaxaca Pacifico and Flecha Roja/Lineas Unidas del Sur cover the main road from Pochutla and Puerto Escondido to Pinotepa Nacional and on to Acapulco and even Mexico City. There

are also overnight buses from Oaxaca to Jamiltepec and Pinotepa Nacional (both US$4.50) by Estrella del Valle/Oaxaca-Pacifico.

Manialtepec

The jungle and the 12 km-long mangrove-surrounded lagoon here, 13 km from Puerto Escondido, are reputedly the haunt of types of raccoon *(mapache)* and badger *(tejón)*, herons *(garzas)*, pelicans, divers and several fish species. You can get here by road; then ask a local boatman to take you out on the lagoon. You may also be able to reach the lagoon by lancha from Puerto Escondido.

Chacahua

There are three more tropical lagoons – Chacahua, La Pastoría and Tianguisto – here, reached by a 28-km side-road to the left 57 km from Puerto Escondido. The forest roundabout and the lagoon islands contain black orchids, mahogany and cedar trees, deer and mapaches. Alligators and turtles are among the water life. You can probably rent a local lancha here too.

Tututepec

This village, 72 km along the highway from Puerto Escondido, then nine km north from the village of Santa Rosa, was probably the capital of the very little studied southern Mixtec kingdom which fought off the Aztec invasion in the 15th century. There are reportedly stone carvings including a jaguar and an atlante here. Saints' images are carried through the village in a torchlight procession for the Day of the Dead.

Jamiltepec

This mainly Mixtec town 105 km from Puerto Escondido has a Sunday market. Jamiltepec figures in D H Lawrence's *The Plumed Serpent*. An image of the Virgin of Guadalupe, discovered carved in a rock in 1978, has become an object of pilgrimage. Easter week sees candlelight processions every night in the town. The fiesta of the Virgen de los Remedios is celebrated with dances and parades in mid-September.

Santa María Huazolotitlán Eleven km west of Jamiltepec, then four km south, is this Mixtec village known for its crafts. Carnival and the Festival of the Assumption (mid-August) are celebrated with traditional dances.

Huaxpaltepec This village, about 15 km west of Jamiltepec, is an Indian gathering point for fairs and festivities on Carnival Sunday and the day of Jesús Nazareno (fourth Friday in Lent).

Mechoacan This village, a few km north of Huaxpaltepec, has a colourful procession and traditional dances for its patron, Santa Catarina, on 25 November.

Pinotepa Nacional

The biggest town between Puerto Escondido and Acapulco lies 135 km from Puerto Escondido. It has a high Mixtec population, a Sunday market and several places to stay, of which probably the best is the *Hotel Carmona* (tel 3-22-22) at Porfirio Díaz 123. There is also the *Hotel Rodríguez* at Juárez 402, the *Hotel Tropical* at Progreso 103, and *Bungalows Marlyn* outside town on the highway. About three Fletes y Pasajes buses a day take the half-unpaved Highway 125 north to Tlaxiaco, 212 km away, from where you could get other buses on to Oaxaca, Huajuapan de León, Puebla or even Mexico City. For places between Pinotepa Nacional and Tlaxiaco, see the Mixteca Alta section.

Semana Santa is the occasion of important celebrations here. In one strange ceremony, white-painted youths called *Judíos* (Jews) recite old Mixtec formulae and fire arrows into the air. On Good Friday a large cross is carried through part of the town. On Easter Day a local mestizo dance called the 'Chilenas' is performed.

Pinotepa de Don Luis This is one of the most traditional Mixtec villages, where until quite recently most women went topless in the home. It's about 15 km north-east of Pinotepa Nacional. Fiestas include San Sebastián's Day (20 January, a fair, dances and fireworks), Carnival Sunday (traditional dances, parades, fireworks), Easter Saturday (burning of Judas effigies) and the Assumption (mid-August, dances and horse races).

At least until recently, violet dye from *caracoles* (sea snails) was still being used by weavers here. Village men carry cotton thread to sections of the coast where caracoles are found on the rocks. When squeezed, the creatures give off a secretion which is rubbed on to the thread; they are then replaced unharmed. The dark red dye of the cochineal insect is also reportedly still in use – though that is apparently brought to the area from further north in the Mixteca.

San Juan Colorado This village, six km north of Pinotepa de Don Luis, is the scene of the Tejorones dance on Mardi Gras (Carnival Tuesday), in which four episodes – a tiger or snake hunt, wedding, baptism and cockfight – are enacted. Other dances are performed for the fiesta of San Andrés (late November-early December).

Isthmus of Tehuantepec

Eastern Oaxaca occupies the southern half of the 200 km-wide Isthmus of Tehuantepec ('teh-wan-teh-PECK'), which is Mexico's narrowest point and only coast-to-coast stretch of low-lying land. The mountains of Oaxaca climb to the west, those of Chiapas to the east. Roads from Chiapas, Oaxaca city, the Oaxaca coast and the north of the isthmus converge on the three isthmus towns of Tehuantepec, Salina Cruz and Juchitán.

This is hot, humid, unpretty country, and for most travellers it's little more than a place to change buses. Of the towns, Tehuantepec is the smallest (about 30,000 people) and most appealing but Salina Cruz and Juchitán – with about 50,000 people each and containing a sizeable share of Oaxaca's limited industry – are better stepping-off points for bus travel along the Oaxaca coast and into Chiapas respectively. East of Juchitán, around the aptly-named road junction of La Ventosa, strong winds sweep down from the north and frequently blow high vehicles off the road.

History

The mainly Zapotec people of the isthmus have a tradition of fierce independence. They managed to repulse the 15th-century Aztec invaders from the hilltop fortress of Guiengola near Jalapa del Marqués, and the isthmus never became part of the Aztec empire. Later some of the strongest resistance against the Spanish took place here – notably in 1524-27 (by an alliance of Zapotecs, Mixes, Zoques and Chontales) and in 1660 (when the mayor of Tehuantepec was stoned to death by rebels).

After the building of a railway across the isthmus at the turn of the century, linking the Atlantic and Caribbean with the Pacific, Salina Cruz became an important port. But hopes of major oil finds in the area were disappointed at that time, and the chaos of the Mexican Revolution and the creation of the Panama Canal further south soon ended its prosperity. In recent years, however, the area has received some spin-offs from the oil boom in Tabasco, Veracruz and Chiapas, and Salina Cruz is developing again as a pipeline terminal.

In 1980 Juchitán managed to elect a communist-supported mayor, Leopoldo de Gyves, who was a member of COCEI, an independent organisation campaigning for peasants whose land had been taken by big landowners. He was removed from office by the state government after violence between COCEI and PRI supporters three years later. He and his supporters refused to leave the town hall until the army forced them to do so, following new elections in which all COCEI candidates were defeated.

People

Another feature of the isthmus people is the strength of the women, who are not only physically well-built but also take a leading role in business and politics. They are much more open and confident than women in the rest of Mexico, and in no way live in the shadow of their menfolk.

The women of Juchitán and in particular Tehuantepec are also famous for their costumes. For everyday use younger women have now turned to Western dress, but older ones still wear embroidered huipiles and voluminous printed skirts. For fiestas, the women of Tehuantepec and Juchitán turn out in velvet or sateen huipiles and skirts embroidered with fantastically colourful silk flowers. The design goes back to manila shawls popular in 19th-century Mexico. They also deck themselves in the gold and silver jewellery which is a sign of wealth, and often wear bizarre headgear known as the *huipil grande*. According to tradition, this lace bonnet with sleeves hanging down behind has its origins in babies' christening robes. These costumes are worn not only in parades and processions but also in a local dance called the 'Zandunga'.

Isthmus fiestas are also noted for the curious *Tirada de Frutas* in which women climb on the roofs and throw fruit on the men below. Apart from those in Tehuantepec and Juchitán, fiestas where you might see this are in Santa María Petapa (a couple of days each side of the Festival of the Assumption, 15 August), Santo Domingo Petapa (Day of Santo Domingo, 4 August) and Ixtepec (late September, around the Festival of San Jerónimo). The Petapas are a few km south-west of Matías Romero on the road to Acayucan; Ixtepec is 16 km north of Juchitán.

Niltepec, 52 km east of Juchitán on the Pan-American Highway, has lively festivals for the days of Santo Cristo de Esquipulas (14 January, processions carrying Christian standards) and Santiago Apóstol (25 July, procession and local dances).

Miguel Covarrubias, the Mexican artist who wrote one of the best books on the folklore and customs of the island of Bali in Indonesia, did the same for the Isthmus of Tehuantepec with *Mexico South*, published in 1946. It's a fascinating read but sadly a lot of what he describes has now disappeared.

TEHUANTEPEC

This is a jolly, friendly town where there's often a fiesta going on in one of the barrios. A curious form of local transport is the *motocarro* – a kind of three-wheel buggy in which the driver sits on a front seat while the passenger stands behind him on a platform, holding a rail.

Information & Orientation

Every bus entering Tehuantepec goes through the zócalo and passes at least two of its three downtown hotels, so there's little difficulty getting your bearings. Facing the market (a dark but intriguing warren) on the zócalo, the main bus stations and one hotel are along Hidalgo, to the right, and the other two hotels are on Juárez and Romero, to the left. The post office is on the zócalo, at the corner of Hidalgo.

Festivals

Each Tehuantepec barrio has its own main fiesta, which continues for several days and includes parades, *Tiradas de Frutas*, lots of marimba music and a good time for all. Dates of fiestas are:

Lieza Barrio On and around Day of San Sebastián, 22 January.

Guichiveri & Atotonilco Barrios On and around Day of San Juan, 24 June.

Vishana Barrio On and around Day of San Pedro, 30 June.

Santa María, San Jacinto & Santa Cruz Barrios On and around the Feast of the Assumption (15 August).

Laborio Barrio Ten days up to the Festival of Birth of the Virgin Mary, 10 September.

San Jerónimo & Cerrito Barrios On and around Day of San Miguel (1 October).

Guiengola & Tequisistlán

The old Zapotec stronghold of Guiengola, where the Aztecs were repulsed in 1496, is reached by going 15 km along the Oaxaca road, then turning right along a track for six km, then walking up a 350-metre hill. You can see the remains of a big pyramid, a few smaller buildings, and a thick, high defensive wall.

The village of Magdalena Tequisistlán, just off the Oaxaca road 46 km from Tehuantepec, is home to Chontal Indians and known for its onyx carvings – ashtrays, chess boards, tables.

Places to Stay

Hotel Donají (tel 5-00-64) at Juárez 10, two blocks from the zócalo, has clean rooms on two upper floors, most of them round a central court with wide, open-air walkways. Singles and doubles with private bath (intermittent hot water) are US$3. The rooms in the middle are quietest; you get street noise on the two sides, cinema noise at the back.

Hotel Oasis (tel 5-00-08) at the corner of Romero and Ocampo, one block from the zócalo, has the same prices as the Donají and similar standards but slightly smaller rooms. *Hotel Istmo* at Hidalgo 31 (past the Cristóbal Colón station if coming from the zócalo) has a nice courtyard but the rooms (US$2) are shabby.

On the highway going east, *Hotel Calli*

(tel 5-00-85) two km out of town is the only top-end place. Rooms are air-conditioned and in the US$17 to US$22 range. There is a disco and swimming pool.

Places to Eat

Sometimes you can get iguana (said to taste like chicken) in the upstairs fondas of the market in the mornings, but armadillo (like pork) is now rare and considered a delicacy. A more approachable local food is the *totopo*, a light, crisp, tasty member of the tortilla family. It's also less harmful to endangered species.

Mariscos Rafa on the zócalo near the corner of Hidalgo does good fish dishes (around US$1.50) and seafood cocktails (US$0.75 to US$1.50) as well as lobster (US$4). Also on the zócalo at 22 de Marzo No 23, *Restaurant La Carreta* does good fish Veracruzana (in tomatoes, onions, garlic, olives and herbs) for US$1.50. *Restaurant Café Colonial* at Romero 66, two blocks from the zócalo, has main dishes for US$1.50 to US$2, antojitos for US$1 to US$1.50. In the evenings tables are set up around the zócalo for cheap open-air eating.

Getting There & Away

Road Highway 190 by-passes Tehuantepec to the north, with Juchitán 30 km away to the east, Oaxaca 242 km through the mountains to the north-west. Just west of Tehuantepec, the coastal highway (No 200 most of the way) branches south for Salina Cruz (16 km), Pochutla (201 km), Puerto Ángel (213 km), Puerto Escondido (275 km) and Acapulco (678 km).

Bus Travelling by bus into Chiapas or Veracruz, it's often quicker to get a local bus first to Juchitán (US$0.30), where there are more long-distance connections. For the coast road east to Pochutla and Puerto Escondido, there's only one unreliable bus daily from Tehuantepec – instead, get a local bus to Salina Cruz (20c) and then another bus on from there. Local buses to Salina Cruz and Juchitán frequently pass in front of the Restaurant Bar El Dorado on the corner of the zócalo where the crowd stands on the steps – if you want a seat, walk back up the street a bit to where the buses wait. The last bus to Salina Cruz is at about 9 pm.

Tehuantepec's 1st-class bus station, Cristóbal Colón, is on Hidalgo a block from the zócalo. There are eight buses a day each to Oaxaca (US$3.25) and Juchitán (US$0.35); seven to Salina Cruz (25c); six to Acayucan (US$2.75); five to Coatzacoalcos (US$3.50); three each to Tuxtla Gutiérrez (US$3.75) and Tuxtepec (US$4.50); two each to Mexico City (US$10.50), Córdoba (US$6.50), Villahermosa (US$5) and Veracruz (US$7.25); and one each to Puebla (US$9), San Andrés Tuxtla (US$5.25), San Cristóbal de Las Casas (US$4.50), Arriaga (US$2.25), Tonalá (US$2.50) and Tapachula (US$5.25). Approximate journey times: Oaxaca 4½ hours, Tuxtla Gutiérrez five hours, San Cristóbal de Las Casas seven hours, Mexico City 14 hours, Tapachula 6½ hours.

The 2nd-class bus station is a block further up Hidalgo from Cristóbal Colón, then a few metres right on Guerrero. There are 18 departures a day to Oaxaca, four to Tuxtla Gutiérrez, three to Tuxtepec and an unreliable one to Puerto Escondido at 6 pm (Salina Cruz is a much better departure point for Puerto Escondido). There are also a few 2nd-class buses run by Fletes y Pasajes to Veracruz and Mexico City from in front of the Hotel Donají.

SALINA CRUZ

Recent port development has given Salina Cruz a lively air of incipient brash prosperity, and its wide, breezy zócalo has a smattering of smartish restaurants and even boutiques. But for most travellers this is nothing more than a place to change buses on the way to or from Puerto Ángel or Puerto Escondido. Nearby Playa Ventosa used to be a bit of a paradise beach, but it's now dirty from pollution that's also killing off the caracoles.

Orientation

The road from Tehuantepec comes into Salina Cruz along Avenida Tampico, passing the zócalo which is a block away to the left. The market is a block behind the far left corner of the zócalo as you enter the zócalo from Avenida Tampico. From the Fletes y Pasajes bus station to the zócalo, walk left along Avenida Tampico for 2½ blocks, then one block to the right. From the Cristóbal Colón bus station, the zócalo is just a block away.

San Mateo del Mar

This is the biggest of the four Huave Indian villages around the large saltwater Laguna Superior and Laguna Inferior. The Huaves' main income comes from fishing and they are a distinct people from the Zapotecs, with their own language. Their traditions are slowly disappearing and they have a reputation for coolness towards outsiders, but a commercial revival of their textiles in the last decade might make them more welcoming to foreigners. They weave cotton rebozos, cloths, bags and huipiles with small animal motifs and apparently still use backstrap looms and some dyes derived from caracoles, mangrove and maize.

Buses from Salina Cruz to San Mateo del Mar leave roughly every two hours from the corner of Calle Mazatlán and Avenida Puerto Ángel, which is one block from the market and two blocks from the zócalo. The journey takes about two hours and the last bus coming back from San Mateo leaves about 3 pm.

Places to Stay

Hotel Rios at Avenida Tampico 405, 1½ blocks from the zócalo and two blocks along Tampico from the Fletes y Pasajes station in Salina Cruz, has doubles with private bath for US$4. The better *Hotel Jacarandas*, at the corner of Camacho and Miramar, about three blocks from the zócalo, has a pleasant leafy restaurant and doubles for US$8.50 with fan, US$10 with air-conditioning.

Getting There & Away

Air Salina Cruz has an airport, served by Aerovías Oaxaqueñas with daily flights to and from Oaxaca (except Sunday). One-way fare is US$27.

Road Salina Cruz is at the eastern end of coastal Highway 200. Tehuantepec is 16 km north; to the west Pochutla is 185 km, Puerto Ángel 197 km and Puerto Escondido 261 km.

Bus Salina Cruz is good for buses to Pochutla and Puerto Escondido but poor for buses into Chiapas. If you're heading for Chiapas, it's usually better to start with a local bus to Tehuantepec (20c) or preferably Juchitán (US$0.50), then pick up a long-distance bus from there. Local buses to these two places run along Avenida Tampico frequently. For Puerto Ángel, get a Fletes y Pasajes bus to Pochutla, then another bus or a colectivo or taxi from there.

Cristóbal Colón runs 1st and 2nd-class buses from the same station on the corner of 5 de Mayo and Coatzacoalcos, one block from the zócalo. The 1st-class ones go to Oaxaca (US$3.50, about five hours) and Acayucan (US$3, four hours) six times each daily; Tuxtepec (US$4.75) four times; Mexico City (US$10.75, 14 hours) three times; Córdoba (US$6.75), Villahermosa (US$5.75) and Veracruz (US$7.50) twice each; and Puebla (US$9.25), Tuxtla Gutiérrez (US$3.75, 5½ hours) and San Cristóbal de las Casas (US$4.75, 7½ hours) once each. Second-class buses serve Arriaga five times daily; Tonalá and Tapachula (US$5, seven hours) twice; Tuxtla Gutiérrez once; plus Oaxaca, Tuxtepec, Coatzacoalcos, Tehuantepec and Juchitán.

Fletes y Pasajes at Avenida Tampico 40 (turn left along Tampico if coming from the zócalo) has 2nd-class buses every hour from 4 am to 4 pm to Pochutla (US$2.25, five hours) and Puerto Escondido (US$3, 6½ hours), plus one more to Pochutla at 5 pm.

JUCHITÁN

Despite its political feat of being allowed to elect an opposition party mayor in 1980, there's little to detain the casual visitor in this scrappy, growing town ('hooch-i-TAN') unless perhaps you turn up during one of its festivals. These include the Fiestas of San Isidro Labrador (14-16 May), and Las Velas (The Candles, 18-19 May, 13-14 August and 3-5 September). The Casa de la Cultura (open Tuesday to Sunday, 9 am to 7 pm) apparently has an archaeological display and paintings by Diego Rivera and Salvador Dalí in a collection donated by the artist Francisco Toledo, who was born here in 1940.

Orientation

The long-distance bus stations are just off the highway so you don't need to go into town at all. Don't miss them if you're arriving on a local bus from Salina Cruz or Tehuantepec: the bus will turn right at a crossroads as it hits the edge of Juchitán, and the stations are on the right after about 100 metres. Cristóbal Colón's 1st and 2nd-class services operate from different ends of the same building; the 2nd-class buses of Fletes y Pasajes and Oaxaca-Istmo go from a parking lot to the left as you face Cristóbal Colón.

Places to Stay

Hotel Malla, entered through the Cristóbal Colón 1st-class ticket hall, has cool, quite clean rooms with private bathrooms. Singles/doubles are US$3.50/4.50. For more comfort, the *Hotel La Mansión* (tel 2-10-55) at Prolongación 16 de Septiembre No 11, two blocks into town from the bus stations, has singles/doubles for US$10/11 and its own restaurant.

Getting There & Away

Road West of Juchitán the Pan-American Highway (No 190) runs 30 km to Tehuantepec, then on to Oaxaca. To the east the same road crosses a long, flat isthmus stretch, then slowly climbs to Tuxtla Gutiérrez in Chiapas, 253 km from Juchitán, and San Cristóbal de Las Casas (334 km). Two important roads split off from the Pan-American before it reaches Tuxtla Gutiérrez. At the sometimes dangerously windy La Ventosa, just 15 km east of Juchitán, Highway 185 heads 177 km north across the isthmus to Acayucan. Just after San Pedro Tapanatepec, 106 km east of Juchitán, Highway 200 heads off south-east for Tonalá, Arriaga and Tapachula (near the Guatemalan border, 390 km from Juchitán).

Bus The long-distance bus stations are just off Highway 190, on Prolongación 16 de Septiembre. Cristóbal Colón 1st-class services go to Oaxaca (US$3.50), Acayucan (US$2.50) and Coatzacoalcos (US$3.25) five times each daily; Tuxtla Gutiérrez (US$3.50) and Tuxtepec (US$4) four times each; Mexico City (US$10.25) three times; Veracruz (US$7), Villahermosa (US$5.25) and Córdoba (US$6.25) twice each; San Cristóbal de las Casas (US$4.25), Tapachula (US$4.75) and Puebla (US$8.50) once each. Approximate journey times: Acayucan three hours, Oaxaca 5½ hours, Tuxtla Gutiérrez 4½ hours, San Cristóbal de las Casas 6½ hours, Tapachula six hours, Mexico City 14 hours, Veracruz eight hours, Villahermosa seven hours.

Cristóbal Colón 2nd-class services include four a day to Tapachula and three to Arriaga. Oaxaca-Istmo and Fletes y Pasajes go to Oaxaca (US$3.25) 16 times daily, Arriaga (US$1.75, three hours) 11 times and Tuxtla Gutiérrez (US$3) four times. They also go to Veracruz, Puebla and Mexico City.

Local buses to Tehuantepec (US$0.30) and Salina Cruz (US$0.50) can be picked up at the crossroads on the highway about 100 metres from the main bus stations.

Rail From Juchitán, there are two 2nd-class trains a day to Arriaga, Tonalá and Tapachula (theoretically 10 hours away); and one a day to Veracruz (13 hours).

Chiapas

Mexico's southernmost state is one of our favourites and its remoteness is part of the appeal. Chiapas has enormous variety and most of it is well off the beaten tourist path. Palenque, perhaps the most beautiful of all Mayan sites, and San Cristóbal de las Casas, a tranquil hill-country colonial town surrounded by very traditional Indian villages, are well known – but there's much more. Between Palenque and San Cristóbal are the Agua Azul waterfalls, some of Mexico's most beautiful. The surprisingly modern state capital, Tuxtla Gutiérrez, has probably the country's best zoo – devoted entirely to Chiapas' very varied fauna – and a good new museum.

Nearby is the 1000-metre-deep Sumidero Canyon, through which you can take an awesome boat ride. Near the border with Guatemala, with which Chiapas has always had much in common, is the lovely Montebello Lakes region. Other fine Mayan sites include Yaxchilán and Bonampak, both deep in the Lacandón jungle, one of Mexico's largest areas of tropical forest. Chiapas even has a few laid-back Pacific beach spots, among them Puerto Arista near Tonalá.

If you're heading for Guatemala, Chiapas is the gateway. If you're not, try to fit Chiapas into your plans anyway. Most travellers who stumble upon it by chance stay longer than they planned.

Roads Chiapas has just four major roads. Highway 200 runs along the coastal plain from the Guatemalan border near Tapachula to Tonalá and Arriaga before entering Oaxaca. Highway 190, the Pan-American, runs from Ciudad Cuauhtémoc, inland on the Guatemalan border, to Comitán, San Cristóbal de las Casas, Chiapa de Corzo and Tuxtla Gutiérrez, then heads on into Oaxaca where it meets Highway 200 before Juchitán.

The two other roads both head north off Highway 190. One, from 12 km south of San Cristóbal de las Casas, goes to Ocosingo and Palenque before meeting

the Villahermosa-Campeche road. It's now paved most of the way and where it isn't, the dirt surface is even. The other road is Highway 195, from just east of Chiapa de Corzo to Villahermosa.

Buses First-class buses are scarcer in Chiapas than in most other states. The only 1st-class line is Cristóbal Colón, and everywhere it pays to book seats a couple of days ahead if you can. The usual alternatives – apart from Cristóbal Colón itself, which also runs 2nd-class buses – are Transportes Tuxtla Gutiérrez and Fletes y Pasajes, both of which run some of the most battered, slow and crowded vehicles in Mexico.

History

For most of its long history Chiapas has been more intimately connected with Guatemala, culturally and politically, than with Mexico. Pre-Hispanic civilisations in the area spread across the modern international border, and for most of the colonial era Chiapas was governed from Guatemala.

Pre-Hispanic The human presence in Chiapas goes back to at least 6700-5000 BC, when the Santa Marta cave near Ocozocoautla in the west of the state was occupied by people who left behind pottery, dart points, metates and burials. Village life, based on both agriculture and fishing, has been traced back to the Barra and Ocós cultures on the Chiapas-Guatemala Pacific coast plain around 1600 and 1500 BC. Inland, village life at Chiapa de Corzo in central Chiapas dates from about 1500 BC. Later, both central and coastal Chiapas came under some influence – conquest, trade or missionary – from the Olmecs who flourished further north from about 1300 to 400 BC.

Izapa, in the south-western corner of Chiapas near Tapachula, was the centre of a culture which peaked around 200 BC to 200 AD and is thought to be a link between the Olmecs and the Mayas.

Polychrome Mayan statuette

During the Classic Mayan era (approximately 300-900 AD) coastal and central Chiapas were relative backwaters, affected more in the earlier centuries by the Kaminaljuyú civilisation centred near Guatemala City than by the Mayas. Kaminaljuyú itself was under strong influence from Teotihuacán in central Mexico. But the low-lying, jungly east and north-east of Chiapas gave rise to at least two important and splendid Mayan city states – Palenque and Yaxchilán, both of which flourished in the 7th and 8th centuries. Further west, Toniná and Chinkultic were also Mayan centres.

After the Classic Mayan collapse, the

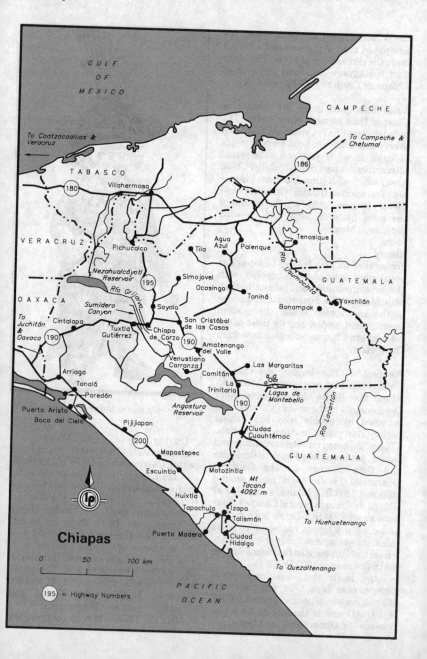

Chiapas

GULF OF MEXICO

To Coatzacoalcos & Veracruz

To Campeche & Chetumal

CAMPECHE

TABASCO

(186)

(180) Villahermosa

VERACRUZ

Pichucalco

Tila

Agua Azul

Palenque

Tenosique

Río Usumacinta

Nezahualcóyotl Reservoir

Río Grijalva

Simojovel

Ocosingo

Toniná

GUATEMALA

OAXACA

Sumidero Canyon

Soyalo

Bonampak

Yaxchilán

To Juchitán & Oaxaca

(190)

Cintalapa

Tuxtla Gutiérrez

Chiapa de Corzo

San Cristóbal de las Casas

(190)

Amatenango del Valle

Arriaga

Venustiano Carranza

Las Margaritas

Tonalá

Paredón

Comitán

Río Lacantún

Puerto Arista

Boca del Cielo

Angostura Reservoir

La Trinitaria

(190)

Lagos de Montebello

Pijijiapan

(200)

Ciudad Cuauhtémoc

GUATEMALA

Mapastepec

Escuintla

Motozintla

Mt Tacaná 4092 m

To Huehuetenango

Huixtla

Tapachula

Izapa

Talismán

To Quezaltenango

Puerto Madero

Ciudad Hidalgo

Chiapas

0   50   100 km

(195) = Highway Numbers

PACIFIC OCEAN

influence of the Toltecs, spreading out from central Mexico, was felt in coastal and central Chiapas around 1000-1200 AD. Lowland Chiapas took its turn to become a backwater, while highland Chiapas and Guatemala came to be divided among a number of often warring mini-empires, many with cultures descended from the Mayas but some also with rulers claiming Toltec ancestry.

Coastal Chiapas, a rich source of cacao from which chocolate is made, was conquered by the Aztecs at the end of the 15th century and became their empire's most distant province, under the name Xoconochco (from which the area's present name, Soconusco, is derived).

Spanish Era Soconusco was the first part of Chiapas to be subdued by the Spanish, lying as it did on Pedro de Alvarado's route to conquer Guatemala in 1524. The same year, after pleas from the Zoques for help against the tyranny of the Chiapa, Luis Marín was sent to take central Chiapas for the Spanish. It wasn't until Diego de Mazariegos led a second expedition in 1528 that central Chiapas came under effective Spanish control.

Accompanied by friendly Tlaxcalans and Aztecs, Mazariegos' forces first defeated the Chiapa, many of whom jumped to death in the Sumidero Canyon rather than be captured, and founded the town of Chiapa de los Indios (now Chiapa de Corzo). Shortly afterwards, in March 1528, the settlement was moved east to Villa Real de Chiapa (now San Cristóbal de las Casas) in the highlands, where the Indians were less hostile than before. Potentially more of a problem for Mazariegos was a rival Spanish force under Pedro de Puertocarrero, sent to Chiapas from Guatemala by Alvarado the previous year; they had already established the settlement of San Cristóbal de los Llanos near Comitán. The two leaders met amicably at Huixtán and Puertocarrero agreed to retire and send some of his men to join Mazariegos. Further outlying areas

of Chiapas were subdued in the 1530s and 1540s.

Soconusco and inland Chiapas – apart from the sparsely populated eastern jungle which the Spanish never occupied – were administered separately but both were controlled from Guatemala for most of the Spanish era, which in effect meant that they lacked outside supervision for long periods. There was little check on colonists' excesses against the Indians, and the local Spaniards developed an independent streak which persists today. Aside from being sold into slavery, forced to work on *encomiendas* and haciendas, and paying severe taxes, the Indians suffered from being moved out of their villages into small settlements where they could be easier controlled and evangelised, and from new diseases brought by the Spanish. One epidemic in 1544 killed about half the Indians of Chiapas, and the state's population slumped from 350,000 when the Spanish arrived to 95,000 in 1600 and as little as 76,000 in 1800. Numerous rebellions by the Indians were all brutally put down.

The only light in the Indians' darkness was the work of some Spanish church leaders, of whom the most illustrious was Bartolomé de las Casas (1474-1566), appointed the first bishop of Chiapas in 1545. Las Casas had come to the Spanish Caribbean as an ordinary colonist, but in 1510 he entered the Dominican monastic order and spent the rest of his life pressuring the Spanish crown for protection of Indian rights in the new colonies. His achievements, including partly observed laws reducing compulsory labour (1543) and banning Indian (but not black) slavery (1550), earned him the hostility of Spanish colonists but the lasting affection of the Indians (San Cristóbal de las Casas is named after him). He spent only six months in his diocese, being occupied with campaigns on a wider scope, but the missionary work of other Dominicans made them generally protective toward the Indians. Juan de Zapata y Sandoval, bishop from 1613 to 1621, was one of the Indians' strongest defenders.

19th & 20th Centuries The years following the end of Spanish rule over Mexico and Central America (including Guatemala) in 1821 were the most confused in Chiapas' history. In 1821 Chiapas' leaders declared their wish to join Mexico, were accepted, and sent deputies to the national congress. Then in 1823 Agustín Iturbide was deposed and the Mexican congress was dissolved. Chiapas set up its own junta, with representatives from each of its districts, to govern temporarily. The Central American states, annexed by Mexico in 1822, declared themselves independent as the United Provinces of Central America. To protect Mexico's interests, Mexican troops entered Chiapas from Guatemala and dissolved its junta. However, the *Chiapas Libre* (Free Chiapas) movement persuaded the troops to withdraw – apparently without bloodshed and with agreement from Mexico City – so that Chiapas could decide its own future.

Chiapas rejoined Mexico in 1824 after a referendum, organised by the restored junta, in which 96,829 Chiapanecos voted to rejoin Mexico against 60,400 in favour of joining Central America. (Quite how the votes were cast or counted is unclear!) Support for the Central American option had been stronger in Soconusco than elsewhere; only in 1882 did Guatemala (by then a separate country) officially recognise Mexico's dominion over Soconusco.

Ángel Albino Corzo, after whom Chiapa de Corzo is named, was a liberal state governor who organised the troops to quash the 1855 rising. In 1863 he survived an attempt to take control of Chiapas by pro-church conservatives supporting the French invasion of Mexico. The conservatives, led by Juan Ortega, captured San Cristóbal de las Casas but their campaign ended in defeat at Chiapa de Corzo.

Corzo also tried policies to benefit the highland Indians but his efforts made no more difference to their lot than freedom from Spain had. Their lands continued to be taken from them and the most symbolic event of the 19th century was the 1869-70 Chamula rebellion. Sparked by the arrest of a young Tzotzil girl who was at the centre of a religious cult, the rebellion aimed more at regaining Indian lands. This revolt spread over central Chiapas and narrowly failed to take San Cristóbal de las Casas.

San Cristóbal was capital of the state until 1892, when the title went to Tuxtla Gutiérrez. This was apparently because of hostility in San Cristóbal toward Mexico's dictator at the time, Porfirio Díaz, who encouraged the takeover of peasant land by big landowners. In the same era the Soconusco coffee plantations were notorious for the near-slavery of their Indian workers.

The question of which city was to be the state capital was not taken lightly. In 1911 there was a mini-war between the two rivals, with Tuxtla victorious and many Tzotzil Indians massacred.

Today the position of the peasants is still little improved. Just 1% of Chiapas' landowners – now including descendants of more recent German immigrants in the Soconusco as well as the older Spanish and mestizo families – hold nearly half the state and there are still clashes over land rights. Many Indians have to work for pitiful wages in poor conditions on coffee and cotton plantations. Samuel Ruíz García, the bishop of San Cristóbal, who follows in the worthy tradition of Bartolomé de las Casas with his support for Indian causes, is known by the establishment press as the *Obispo Rojo* (Red Bishop) for his pains.

The caciques, who control not only the land but also business, politics and the security forces, clamp down, often violently, against movements like OCEZ, the Organización Campesina Emiliano Zapata, which campaigns for the return of lands which have been awarded to the peasants by the courts but not handed over. In 1986

Amnesty International published reports that more than 20 Tzotzil leaders had been assassinated since the mid-1960s in the Venustiano Carranza and Villa de las Rosas areas.

Recently there have been rumblings in Soconusco, the richest part of Chiapas, in favour of its becoming a separate state, on the grounds that as long as it remains part of Chiapas it can't fulfil its economic potential.

Refugees Mexico was finally forced to take official notice of the decades of political violence in Central America when in 1981 Guatemalan Indians began fleeing to Chiapas to escape the Guatemalan army. The first arrivals were sent back at gunpoint but others replaced them and by the next year there were about 40,000 Guatemalan refugees in Chiapas in their own hastily built camps.

The Mexican government, afraid that the refugees would not only upset its relations with Guatemala but also stir up discontent in Chiapas, since many of them were politically leftist after suffering three decades of US-backed military dictatorship, wanted to deport them but for humanitarian reasons couldn't. Instead, after Guatemalan troops entered Chiapas in 1984 and killed eight refugees at El Chupadero, Mexico decided to start moving the 46,000 recognised refugees to other camps in Campeche and Quintana Roo.

Meanwhile people from El Salvador, fleeing their own civil war, had also been streaming into Mexico for several years. Together with other Guatemalans who weren't recognised as refugees, they amounted by 1987 to an estimated 300,000 extra Central Americans in Mexico. Mexico treats most of them as illegal immigrants and claims to have deported over 100,000 in 1986. Whereas the Salvadorans are scattered around Mexico and some go on to the USA, most of the Guatemalans remain near the border – some in improvised camps, others in villages or the jungle, nearly all in very poor conditions.

Geography & Climate

Chiapas' 74,000 square km fall into five distinct regions, all roughly parallel to the Pacific coast and each other, running north-west to south-east. Along the coast is the hot, fertile plain known as the Soconusco, 15 to 35 km wide, with quite heavy rainfall from June to October, especially in July and August. Inland from there and parallel to the coast is the Sierra Madre de Chiapas mountain range, mostly between 1000 and 2500 metres but higher in the south where the Tacaná volcano on the Guatemalan border reaches 4092 metres. The Sierra Madre continues on into Guatemala, where it throws up several more volcanoes.

Inland from the Sierra Madre is the wide, warm, fairly dry Grijalva River valley, also called the Central Depression of Chiapas, at 500 to 1000 metres high. Three big artificial reservoirs stretch along the Grijalva – the Angostura in the south-east, the Malpaso or Nezahualcóyotl in the north-west, the Chicoasén in between. The state capital, Tuxtla Gutiérrez, lies towards the west end of this central valley.

Next are the Chiapas Highlands, or Sierra Norte de Chiapas, known to locals simply as Los Altos, mostly 2000 to 3000 metres high and also stretching down into Guatemala. San Cristóbal de las Casas, in the small Jovel Valley in the middle of these uplands, is cool with temperatures between high single figures and the low 20°Cs year-round. Rainfall in San Cristóbal is negligible from November to April, but about 110 cm falls in the remaining half of the year. The Chichonal volcano at the north-west end of these highlands erupted in 1981, displacing thousands of Zoque Indians.

In the north and east of the state is one of Mexico's few remaining areas of tropical rainforest, shrinking but still extensive at around 13,000 square km, 17% of the

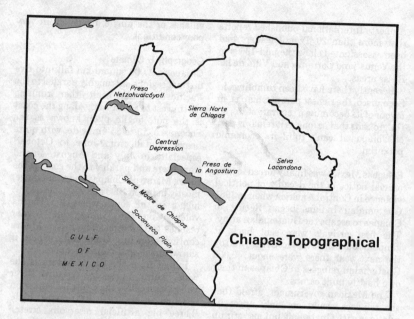

Chiapas Topographical

whole state. The eastern portion is known as the Selva Lacandona.

As elsewhere in Mexico, the season of highest rainfall in all Chiapas' different zones is May to October.

Economy

Chiapas has little industry but is second only to Veracruz among Mexican states in value of agricultural output. It produces more coffee (120,000 tonnes a year, 39% of the national total) and bananas (410,000 tonnes, 25%) than any other state. Only one state (Tabasco) exceeds it in cacao production, and only two in maize. Chiapas also has around 3.5 million cattle, more than any state except Veracruz.

The fertile Soconusco plain and adjacent mountain slopes are the richest part of Chiapas and the source of most of the coffee, bananas and cacao. Tapachula is the chief commercial centre of the Soconusco. Oil was found in north-west Chiapas in the 1970s but the state as a whole derives little benefit from it. Similarly, the Grijalva River which flows through the centre of the state generates more electricity than any other river in Mexico at huge dams like La Angostura, Chicoasén and Malpaso (also called Nezahualcóyotl), but much of the power they produce goes elsewhere; Chiapas is one of only two states where less than half the homes have electricity (the other is Oaxaca).

Ironically, Chiapas stands to gain economically from the refugee problem: the national government has injected large amounts of cash into Chiapas to head off any discontent arising from the refugee presence.

Indians

Of Chiapas' approximately 2.5 million people, an estimated 20% – 500,000 – are

Indians, the pure-blood successors of the peoples who were here before the Spanish came, many of them descended from outlying Mayan groups. The Chiapa are second-class citizens in economic and political terms, with the least productive land in the state. Some are forced by the poverty of their land – or the lack of it altogether – to work for paltry pay on mestizo-run coffee estates. Others have emigrated into Chiapas' eastern jungle to clear new land for farming, or to cities further afield in search of jobs.

Problems of another sort have been caused among some Indian peoples by North American Protestant and Seventh-Day Adventist missionaries. When these people have succeeded in converting some members of a community but not others, rifts have often followed. Hundreds of Tzotzils were expelled from Chamula after being converted by the Protestants of the Summer School of Linguistics; they now live on the periphery of nearby San Cristóbal de las Casas. The Zoques are another group divided by different forms of Christianity.

Despite these problems the traditional culture fostered by festivals, costumes, crafts, religious practices and languages have helped Indian self-respect survive. Also still important among many groups is the *cargo* system, under which each year a different individual takes on the task of organising important community activities such as festivals. This task is expensive but brings high esteem.

Not surprisingly, some Indians remain suspicious of outsiders, and are resentful of any interference in their lives – especially in their religious practices. Many particularly dislike having their photos taken, so ask if you're in any doubt. A tale circulating for some years goes that two tourists were killed for taking photos in the church at Chamula, a Tzotzil village near San Cristóbal de las Casas. Whether or not it's true, it's certainly evidence of the hostility that can be aroused by insensitivity to Indian ways.

Nevertheless many Indians are also friendly and polite, particularly if you treat them with due respect, and an encounter with some of these intriguing cultures is one of the most exciting aspects of a visit to Chiapas. Spanish is no more than a second language to the Indians and in some villages only a few people speak it.

Belief in supernatural beings called *naguales* is shared by several Chiapas Indian peoples. Precise notions of *naguales* vary but if a person – often elderly – has a *nagual* he or she can usually take on other human or animal forms and commit either harmful or protective deeds. Disease is widely believed to result either from the actions of *naguales* or from failure to pay homage to a particular deity (as among most Mexican Indians, older religious beliefs survive alongside Christianity). *Curanderos* cure illness by ritual and herbal methods.

Among the most important festivals are those of the patron saint of each village, Carnival, Semana Santa, the Day of the Dead (2 November) and the day of the Virgin of Guadalupe (12 December).

Choles Around 80,000 Choles live on the remote northern side of the Chiapas Highlands and the lower-lying areas beyond, to the east, west and south-west of Palenque, with a further 20,000 or so over the state border in Tabasco. Tumbalá, Tila and Salto de Agua are three of their main settlements. Many Choles have to leave their homes to work in towns for at least part of the year. The Corpus Christi festival in June brings thousands of people to honour the Black Christ image in the church at Tila.

Chujes & Jalaltecs These two peoples are mainly Guatemalan but small groups settled in Mexico in the late 19th century – Chujes around Tziscao in the Montebello Lakes area, Jalaltecs around Frontera Comalapa near Ciudad Cuauhtémoc. According to the 1980 census there were 700 Chujes and 1000 Jalaltecs in Chiapas, but they have probably since been joined by many others fleeing the fighting in Guatemala.

Lacandones For centuries the Lacandones were Mexico's most untouched Indian people, the last true inheritors of ancient Maya traditions. Living deep in the eastern Chiapas rainforest, most of them simply disappeared when the Spanish came to conquer or convert. But the past four decades have wrought more changes in their way of life than the previous four centuries: 100,000 land-hungry settlers have arrived in the forest, and North American missionaries have succeeded in converting some Lacandones to Christianity. With these newcomers have arrived radios, watches and aeroplanes.

The Lacandones are probably descended both from Chol-speakers who inhabited the forest when the Spanish came and from Mayans who fled there later. Their language is related to Yucatán Maya and the Lacandones themselves call it 'Maya'. A few Lacandones were moved by the Spanish in the 16th century to towns like Ocosingo but others stayed on in the forest, left to themselves to farm and hunt until timber-cutters and chicle-seekers encountered them late in the 19th century. Diseases brought by these outsiders cut into Lacandón numbers until they were in danger of extinction. Today only 300 to 400 Lacandones remain, but at least they have held their own numerically for the past 20 years or so. Swiss anthropologist Gertrude Duby-Blom has conducted a long campaign to save not only the Lacandones but also the forest they inhabit.

The Lacandones are in two main groups. Those of the south are in and around Lacanjá near Bonampak and have been evangelised by US missionaries of the Summer School of Linguistics. In the north, the Lacandones of Naja have yet to succumb to Christianity, though families at Metzabok have converted to Seventh-Day Adventists.

Mames & Motozintlecs An estimated 20,000 Mames live near the Guatemalan border between Tapachula and Ciudad Cuauhtémoc, including some on the slopes of Tacaná volcano. Many more Mames – around 300,000 – are Guatemalans and some of these are almost certainly among the Guatemalan refugees in Mexico. Mame numbers in Mexico are often underestimated because many of them now speak Spanish as a first language.

Also in south-west Chiapas, around 4000 Motozintlec-speakers (also called Mochós) live in the municipalities of Motozintla and Tuzantán de Morelos, the former in the Sierra Madre, the latter in Soconusco. Like the Mames, to whom they are related, some Motozintlecs now speak Spanish first, so their numbers may be higher than 4000. Also like the Mames, the Motozintlecs spread over into Guatemala.

Tojolabals Around 25,000 Tojolabals – also called Chañabals – live in south-east Chiapas in the Comitán-Las Margaritas-Altamirano area, which includes tropical forest, dry plains and cool highlands. Along with the Christian God they pay homage to the sun as creator and protector (represented by fire), and to the moon, which rules life and agriculture and is associated with water.

Tzeltals After the Tzotzils, the 220,000-strong Tzeltals are the Indian group that travellers are most likely to come across in Chiapas. They inhabit the region east, north-east and south-east of San Cristóbal de las Casas. Amatenango del Valle, Aguacatenango, Tenejapa, Cancuc, Oxchuc, Abasolo, Bachajón, Chilón and Yajalón are all Tzeltal villages. Some Tzeltals also live in Ocosingo and in the Selva Lacandona. Each village has its own strong identity and Tzeltals tend to regard themselves primarily as Tenejapanecos, Oxchuqueros or whatever rather than simply as Tzeltals. Thanks partly to their large numbers, tradition is strong among the Tzeltals.

Tzotzils Most of the Indians round San Cristóbal de las Casas are Tzotzil but like the Tzeltals they are strongly differentiated from place to place. You'll notice this most obviously in the strikingly different costumes: for instance men from Zinacantán wear pink while those of Chamula go for woolly black or white tunics. Tzotzil textiles are among the most varied, colourful and elaborately worked in Mexico.

Total Tzotzil population is around 140,000 and their homeland stretches from Venustiano Carranza in the south to Simojovel in the north, with San Cristóbal roughly in the middle. Some have moved to the Selva Lacandona in search of land.

Like the Tzeltals, the Tzotzils have been among the most oppressed of Mexican Indians but their relatively large numbers have enabled them to maintain their group pride. They guard their traditions fiercely; approach them with respect.

Zoques In 1980 around 25,000 Zoques inhabited west and north-west Chiapas, with a few thousand more over the state border in Oaxaca. But in 1981 an eruption of the Chichonal volcano near Pichucalco wrought such havoc on their lands that thousands were forced to move to camps or out of the area altogether, and Zoque identity was severely threatened. Some have started to move back to the area, though, and there are hopes that the damage is not irreversible. The main Zoque settlements now include Coapilla, Copainalá, Tecpatán, Tapilula, Pichucalco, Tapijulapa, Ocozocoautla and Berriozábal, but Zoques have long been despised by mestizos and are usually confined to the edges of towns.

TUXTLA GUTIÉRREZ
Population: 250,000

Many travellers simply change buses in Chiapas' state capital as they head straight through to San Cristóbal de las Casas. But if you're not in a hurry this surprisingly lively modern city has several things worth stopping for. Among them are probably Mexico's best zoo (devoted solely to the fauna of Chiapas), a good new museum and, a few km outside Tuxtla, the 1000-metre-deep Sumidero Canyon through which you can take an exhilarating boat ride. Unfortunately cheap accommodation in Tuxtla is mainly on the rough side, though there are plenty of decent middle-range places. If the canyon is all you're after, you can stay in the smaller, quieter riverside town of Chiapa de Corzo, jumping-off point for the boat trips.

Tuxtla Gutiérrez is 532 metres high, towards the west end of Chiapas' warm central valley. Its name comes from the Nahuatl *tuchtlan*, meaning 'where rabbits abound', and from Joaquín Miguel Gutiérrez, a leading light in Chiapas' early 19th-century campaign not to be part of Guatemala. There's little of historic interest in Tuxtla, which was of minor importance until it became state capital in 1892, apparently because San Cristóbal de las Casas (the previous capital) was considered too hostile to the national dictator, Porfirio Díaz. Since the 1970s Tuxtla has benefited from the oil discovered in north-west Chiapas.

Orientation
The centre of Tuxtla Gutiérrez is the large Plaza Cívica or zócalo, surrounded by modern hotels, official buildings and, on its south side, the cathedral. The city's main east-west artery runs across the south of the zócalo, in front of the cathedral. At this point it's called Avenida Central. Further west the same road becomes Boulevard Dr Belisario Domínguez; to the east it becomes Avenida 14 de Septiembre, then Boulevard Ángel Albino Corzo.

Calle Central runs down the west side of the zócalo, and its junction with Avenida Central is the central point for Tuxtla's street-naming system. This system is simple by comparison with some Mexican

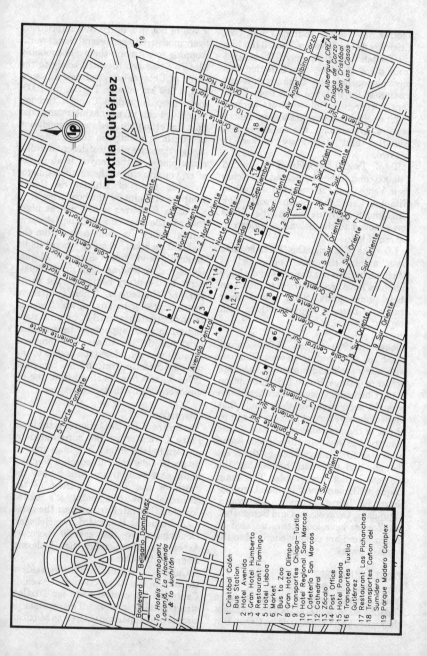

Tuxtla Gutiérrez

1 Cristóbal Colón Bus Station
2 Hotel Avenida
3 Gran Hotel Humberto
4 Restaurant Flamingo
5 Hotel Lisboa
6 Market
7 Bus to Zoo
8 Gran Hotel Olimpo
9 Transportes Chiapa-Tuxtla
10 Hotel Regional San Marcos
11 Cafetería San Marcos
12 Cathedral
13 Zócalo
14 Post Office
15 Hotel Posada
16 Transportes Tuxtla Gutiérrez
17 Restaurant Las Pichanchas
18 Transportes Cañon del Sumidero
19 Parque Madero Complex

cities, but still potentially confusing. East-west streets are called Avenidas, north-south streets are Calles. Avenidas are called 1 Sur, 2 Sur, etc as you go south from Avenida Central, and 1 Norte, 2 Norte, etc going north. Calles are 1 Pte, 2 Pte and so on going west from Calle Central; 1 Ote, 2 Ote, etc going east.

Where it all gets a bit complicated is with the addition (sometimes) of secondary names: each Avenida is divided into a Pte part (west of Calle Central) and an Ote part (east of Calle Central) – thus 1 Sur Ote is the eastern half of Avenida 1 Sur. Likewise Calles have Norte and Sur parts: 1 Pte Norte is the northern half of Calle 1 Pte. The address 1 Pte Norte 412 would be on the northern part of Calle 1 Pte, close to the corner of Avenida 4 Norte.

The Cristóbal Colón (1st class) bus station is at the corner of 2 Norte and 2 Pte, one block north and two west of the zócalo's north-west corner. The main 2nd-class bus station, Transportes Tuxtla Gutiérrez, is on 3 Sur Oriente just west of 7 Ote Sur, which from the south-east corner of the zócalo is four blocks east, two south, then half a block west.

Most cheap accommodation is south-east of the zócalo. More expensive hotels are dotted all round the central area.

Information

Tourist Office There are two helpful tourist offices but both are out in the west of the city on Belisario Domínguez/Avenida Central. Take any colectivo along this road to reach them. People at the federal tourist office (tel 2-45-35, 2-55-09) at Avenida Central Pte 1498, just east of the Hotel Bonampak, usually speak better English. It has information on other parts of Mexico as well as Chiapas and is open 8 am to 8 pm Monday to Friday, 10 am to noon Saturday.

The Chiapas state tourist office (tel 3-48-37) is on the 2nd floor of the Edificio Plaza de las Instituciones, a tall yellow building beside Bancomer opposite the Hotel Bonampak. It's open Monday to Friday, 9 am to 8 pm.

Post & Telegraph The post office and telégrafos are in an alley running off the middle of the east side of the zócalo. The post office is open 8 am to 6 or 9 pm Monday to Saturday for all services, and 9 am to 12 noon Sunday for stamps only.

There are Lada (long-distance phone) casetas at the corners of 1 Sur and 2 Ote and at 4 Sur Ote 234, both open 9 am to 10 pm.

Other Laundromats include one at Ángel Albino Corzo 1508, three blocks from the CREA Youth Hostel.

Zoo

Chiapas, with its huge range of environments, claims the highest concentration of animal species in North America – among them several varieties of big cat, 1200 types of butterfly and 641 bird species. You can see a good number of them in Tuxtla's excellent Zoológico Miguel Alvárez del Toro, where the creatures are kept in relatively spacious enclosures in an unspoiled hillside woodland area just south of the city. Also pleasing about this zoo is its evident concern for conservation; most species are accompanied by charts showing their range of habitat and chances of avoiding extinction. (Whether this message has sunk in with all Chiapas citizens is doubtful: shortly after visiting the zoo I was invited to join a jaguar shoot by a hotel manager.)

Among the creatures you'll see are ocelot, lynx, jaguar, puma, polecat, tapir, red macaw, boa constrictor and some mean-looking scorpions and spiders. And there's a special display of 'the most dangerous species, destroyer of nature and probably of itself'.

To reach the zoo take a 'Cerro Hueco' bus (10c) from the corner of 1 Ote Sur and 7 Sur Ote. They leave about every 20 minutes and take 20 minutes to get there.

Alternatively, a taxi from downtown costs US$0.50, and taxis are also quite easy to pick up coming back.

The zoo is open 8 am to 5.30 pm daily except Monday, and entry is free. It has a bookshop and a restaurant – try *taxcalate*, a maize-based chocolate-cinnamon drink.

Parque Madero Complex

This is a new museum-theatre-park area north-east of the city centre, located around the junction of 5 Norte Ote and 11 Ote Norte. If you don't want to walk, take a colectivo along Avenida Central/14 de Septiembre/Ángel Albino Corzo to Parque 5 de Mayo at the corner of 11 Ote, then a combi north along 11 Ote.

The Museo Regional de Chiapas is the highlight of the complex, with fine archaeological exhibits, colonial history, costume and craft collections all from Chiapas, plus often interesting temporary exhibitions. It's open 9 am to 4 pm, daily except Monday. Next door is the 1200-seat Teatro de la Ciudad.

Nearby there's a shady botanical garden, with many species labelled and a solitary, sad manatee in a shallow pond in the middle (it'll probably be dead by the time you get there). The garden is free and open 9 am to 2 pm and 4 to 6 pm except Monday.

Also in Parque Madero are a public swimming pool (25c) and an open-air children's park, the Centro de Convivencia Infantil, which 'adults' may enjoy too. It has models and exhibits on history and prehistory, a mini-railway, pony and boat rides and mini-golf (children's park open 9.30 am to 8.30 pm Tuesday to Friday, 9.30 am to 9.30 pm Saturday, Sunday and holidays; games and rides open from 3.30 to 8 pm Tuesday to Friday, 9.30 am to 8 pm Saturday, Sunday and holidays).

Sumidero Canyon

The best way to see this natural spectacle is by boat along the Grijalva River, which flows through the canyon from Chiapa de Corzo. You can stay in Chiapa, or easily do the trip in a day from Tuxtla (see separate section). If you want to see Sumidero from the top, you can get combis from Tuxtla to some of the *miradores* (look-out points) on the canyon edge. They're operated by Transportes Cañon del Sumidero (tel 2-06-49) at 1 Norte Ote 1121, 7½ blocks east of the north-east corner of the zócalo. Fare is US$0.50 and they run from about 8 am to 3.30 pm daily. Vehicles saying 'La Atalaya' (the restaurant at the last of the five *miradores*) or 'Sumidero' are the ones you want.

El Aguacero

This is a waterfall on the La Venta River where, if you're keen, you can swim. If not, it might make an off-the-beaten-track day trip – though it's reportedly busy with local sightseers and picnickers at weekends. A three-km road leading to the falls goes north off Highway 190, 53 km west of Tuxtla between Ocozocoautla and Cintalapa. At the end of the road you walk down a path that has 800 steps. Rodulfo Figueroa buses from 6 Sur Pte between 3 and 4 Pte will get you to the road junction.

Places to Stay – bottom end

Cleanest place in this category is the *Albergue CREA Youth Hostel* (tel 3-34-05) at Ángel Albino Corzo 1800, about two km east of the centre. For a bed in one of the small, separate-sex dormitories you pay US$2 and you don't need a Youth Hostel card. There's a small area out back where you can pitch a tent for US$1.50. Breakfast is available for US$1, lunch and dinner for US$1.50 each. To get there from the city centre take a colectivo east along Avenida Central/14 de Septiembre/Ángel Albino Corzo. The hostel is on the right beside a yellow footbridge, just before the black statue of Ángel Albino Corzo on a white base in the middle of the road. Coming from San Cristóbal, you could get off your bus here and save the trek back from downtown.

Two downtown bargains, both quite close to the Transportes Tuxtla Gutiérrez bus station, are small and often full. One is the *Casa de Huéspedes Ofelia* on 2 Sur near the corner of 5 Ote. Rooms are well kept, the management is friendly and the place has its own restaurant, but bathrooms aren't too clean and the mosquitoes can be vicious. Best thing is the price: US$1 per person. The other place is the *Hotel Posada* at 1 Sur 555. Rooms here are round a small courtyard, the family is friendly and rooms with bath are US$1.75.

The *Gran Hotel Olimpo* (tel 2-02-95), in the same part of town at 3 Sur Ote 215, is a large, absolutely-no-frills place where the bathrooms are cleaned and the sheets changed probably after every second occupant. Still, it's fairly cheap. Singles/doubles with fan but no hot water are US$3/4.

A couple of travellers have recommended the *Hotel Fernando* (tel 3-17-40) at 2 Norte Ote 515, where singles are US$3.25, doubles US$5.

Just outside the Cristóbal Colón bus station, on 2 Norte between 1 and 2 Pte, are the *Hotel Santo Domingo* (tel 3-48-39) and the *Hotel María Teresa* (tel 3-01-02) – both dingy and ill-kept. The Santo Domingo charges US$3/4 for singles/doubles, the María Teresa a dollar more in each case.

The *La Hacienda Hotel* (tel 2-79-86) at Belisario Domínguez 1197 at the west end of town has a 20-space trailer park with swimming pool, cafeteria and all hook-ups.

Places to Stay - middle

Hotel Avenida on Avenida Central about 1½ blocks west of the zócalo has only a few rooms but they're decent value at US$4.50/5.50 for singles/doubles – quite big and clean, with fans and private baths. *Hotel Regional San Marcos* (tel 3-18-87, 3-19-40) at 2 Ote Sur 176, on the corner of 1 Sur, is also reasonable value – US$5.50/6.75 for small, clean rooms with private bath in a modern building.

The *Hotel Lisboa* (tel 2-38-26) on 2 Pte Sur 428, between 3 and 4 Sur, has bright, clean but not huge rooms for US$5 to US$5.75 single, US$6.25 to US$7 double. At the *Hotel Esponda* (tel 2-00-80) at 1 Pte Norte 142 you pay US$5 for singles, up to US$8.50 for doubles.

Places to Stay - top end

The *Gran Hotel Humberto* (tel 2-20-80) at Avenida Central Pte 180, a block west of the zócalo, has big, bright, spotless rooms with air-con, TV, phone, large showers, even a bottle-opener fixed to the bathroom wall. Singles are US$11; doubles are US$12.75 with one bed, US$13.50 with two – which all adds up to good value for this downtown location. There's underground car parking, a restaurant and a bar.

The *Posada del Rey* (tel 2-29-11), on the north-east corner of the zócalo at 1 Ote Norte 310, is a little cheaper but not as good. Rooms are light and clean, and some overlook the zócalo, but they could be bigger and need some new plaster. Singles/doubles are US$9.75/12.25.

At Belisario Domínguez 180 in the west of town the *Hotel Bonampak* (tel 3-20-47, 3-20-50) is comfortable and modern with air-conditioned singles/doubles at US$11/13.75, plus 15 bungalows, three suites and two swimming pools. There's a reproduction of the famous Mayan prisoner mural from Bonampak in the lobby, and a pleasant restaurant and cafeteria. Still further west is the *Hotel Lacanjá* (tel 2-34-13, 2-34-85) at Belisario Domínguez 1380. Here clean, decent-sized rooms with TV and phone cost US$11/13.75 and there is a swimming pool, a disco and a couple of restaurants.

Tuxtla's most luxurious hostelry is also out west. It's the 119-room *Hotel Flamboyant* (tel 2-93-63, 2-92-59) at Belisario Domínguez Km 1081 and it certainly lives up to its name. The ultimate in modern Arabic architecture is draped in hanging foliage and the rooms are set round a large swimming pool. There are tennis courts, restaurants and bars. The Disco 'Sheik' (get it?) out front looks like a mosque. Singles/doubles are US$21.25/26.25; you'd pay five times as much for the same in Cancún.

Places to Eat

Many visitors find themselves sitting sooner or later at one of the cafés and restaurants alongside the cathedral. These aren't the cheapest but they're a good place to sample the city's atmosphere. The *Cafetería San Marcos* is always busy.

It's well worth making the short trek out to the *Restaurant Las Pichanchas* (tel 2-53-51) at 14 de Septiembre Ote 857 (look for the sign with a black pot on a pink background and the words *Sientase Chiapaneco*). This is an open-air restaurant round a small plant-filled courtyard with live marimba music, a menu of local specialities several pages long – and hardly anything over US$2. Friendly and efficient waiters will explain it all for you. Try the *chipilín*, a cheese-and-cream soup on a maize base; and for dessert *chimbos*, made from egg yolks and cinnamon. In between you could go for any of six types of tamales, among other things. There are lots of snacks too. Las Pichanchas is open until midnight.

For good quick tacos (25c) and tortas (US$0.50), go to *La Esquina* on the south-west corner of the zócalo where Avenida Central meets Calle Central. *El Pollo Viajero* on 3 Ote a few doors north of Avenida Central is usually busy doling out roast chicken portions (US$1.25), queso fundido and other quick eats.

The *Restaurant Flamingo*, a few yards down a passage at 1 Pte 17, is a quiet, air-conditioned, slightly superior place with good food and service. Tacos or enchiladas are US$1.50, meat dishes around US$3. The long menu also includes salami, snapper and lobster. The *Restaurant London* (tel 3-19-79) at the corner of 4 Pte and 2 Norte is recommended by locals for a slap-up meal.

If you're visiting the tourist offices or the Instituto de la Artesanía Chiapaneca on Belisario Domínguez, you can get a decent meal in the cafeteria of the nearby *Hotel Bonampak*. Spaghetti costs US$1 to US$1.50, tamales Chiapanecos US$1.50; there are also grilled food, sandwiches and antojitos. The hotel has a fully-fledged restaurant too.

Chamula's Grill in the Hotel Lacanjá, further from the city centre at Belisario Domínguez 1380, is a video and live music bar which does good food at middling prices – fish and seafood US$1.50 to US$4, meats US$2.50 to US$2.75, a few Mexican specialities at US$1.50 to US$2.50.

There's a small vegetarian restaurant at 4 Ote Norte 232.

Entertainment

There's live music in the zócalo every Sunday night. Other nights, you can look for live music in the hotels. *Saadas* night spot in the Hotel Regional San Marcos had a synthesiser band when we were last there. *Chamula's Grill* in the Hotel Lacanjá is a pop-video bar which also had a folk duo – or try a disco if the mood takes you; the *Disco Sheik* at the Hotel Flamboyant is reputed to be the best. Entrance costs US$1.75 but it's only open a few nights a week. There's also *El Ron Ron* disco at the Hotel Lacanjá. La Hacienda Hotel has a 'pub'.

Things to Buy

Tuxtla's main market occupies the block bounded by Calles Central Sur and 1 Pte and Avenidas 3 and 4 Sur.

The Instituto de la Artesanía Chiapaneca has a Chiapas crafts exhibition and shop in the Edificio Plaza de las Instituciones out west on Belisario Domínguez. It's the yellow building beside Bancomer opposite the Hotel Bonampak.

If for some reason you're hankering for back issues of magazines like *Rolling Stone, Mad, House & Garden* or *Dirt Rider*, go to Al Caravan Bazar, a small shop on 2 Ote between 1 and 2 Sur.

Getting There & Away

Air Aeroméxico (tel 2-21-55, 3-10-00) is at 1 Sur Pte 1489. Mexicana (tel 2-00-20, 2-54-02) is at Avenida Central Pte 206. Mexicana has direct flights to and from Mexico City most days of the week. Aeroméxico links Tuxtla direct with Mexico City and Tapachula daily, and Villahermosa six days a week.

Planes can also be chartered from a smaller airport, Terán, nearer the city – contact the tourist offices for details – but at the time of writing there were no flights to San Cristóbal de las Casas.

Road Tuxtla Gutiérrez is on Pan-American Highway 190, 263 km east of Juchitán and 540 km east of Oaxaca. East of Tuxtla on this road, San Cristóbal de las Casas is 81 km, Comitán 167 km and Ciudad Cuauhtémoc on the Guatemalan border 248 km. Villahermosa is 289 km away; you head north on Highway 195, which turns off Highway 190 about 30 km east of Tuxtla. From Tuxtla to Tapachula, in the south-west corner of Chiapas at the end of the coastal Highway 200, it's 400 km. A road heads south off Highway 190, 100 km west of Tuxtla, to meet Highway 200 at Arriaga.

Bus Cristóbal Colón (1st class, tel 2-16-39) is at the corner of 2 Norte and 2 Pte. There are buses to San Cristóbal de las Casas (US$1) and Comitán (US$2) 13 times daily; Ciudad Cuauhtémoc (US$3.25) once; Arriaga and Tonalá (US$2.25) 13 times; Tapachula (US$4.75) 16 times; Villahermosa (US$3.75) six times; Acayucan (US$5.25) and Coatzacoalcos (US$6) twice; Salina Cruz (US$3.75) once; Oaxaca (US$6.50) three times; Tuxtepec and Córdoba four times each; Puebla (US$11.50) once; and Mexico City (US$13) six times.

Approximate 1st-class journey times: San Cristóbal de las Casas two hours, Comitán 3½ hours, Tapachula seven hours, Tehuantepec five hours, Oaxaca nine to 10 hours, Acayucan seven to eight hours, Mexico City 19 hours.

For the 20-minute trip to Chiapa de Corzo, it's easiest to take a Transportes Chiapa-Tuxtla combi (20c) from 3 Ote Sur, near the corner of 3 Sur Ote. They run from 5 am to 7 pm.

Transportes Tuxtla Gutiérrez (tel 2-02-30) is on 3 Sur Ote, half a block west of 7 Ote Sur. Some buses are labelled '1st class' but don't be fooled. Departures include about eight daily to Comitán (US$2); five just to San Cristóbal de las Casas (US$1); six to Arriaga (US$1.75); five to Tonalá (US$2); four to Tapachula (US$4.50); three to Palenque (US$3.50) via Ocosingo (US$2); three to Juchitán (US$3) and Oaxaca (US$6); two to Villahermosa (US$2); and one each to Mérida (US$10.50), Chetumal (US$9.75) and Ciudad Cuauhtémoc. Other destinations include Simojovel, Pichucalco, Venustiano Carranza and Motozintla. One traveller wrote to say that colectivos to San Cristóbal also run from the TTG station.

Rodulfo Figueroa (tel 2-28-21) at 6 Sur Pte 440, between 3 and 4 Pte, is a small bus line serving places like Ocozocoautla (US$0.50) and Cintalapa (US$1).

Getting Around

Airport Transport Tuxtla airport is several km west of the city. Transportes al Aeropuerto runs combis (US$1.75 per person) to and from the airport which will pick you up or drop you at hotels in the city. Contact them in the Hotel Jass (tel 2-15-54) at Calle Central 665 or the Gran Hotel Humberto (tel 2-20-80).

Local Transport All colectivos (10c) on Belisario Domínguez-Avenida Central-14 de Septiembre-Ángel Albino Corzo run at least as far as the tourist offices and the Hotel Bonampak in the west, and 11 Ote in the east. Taxis are abundant.

Car Rental Budget (tel 2-55-06) is at Belisario Domínguez 2510, Gabriel Rent-a-Car (tel 2-07-57) is at Belisario Domínguez 780, Renta de Autos Badia (tel 2-92-59, ext 174) is in the Hotel Flamboyant at Belisario Domínguez Km 1081. Dollar (tel 2-89-32) is also on Belisario Domínguez.

SUMIDERO CANYON & CHIAPA DE CORZO

The Cañon del Sumidero is a daunting fissure in the countryside a few km east of Tuxtla Gutiérrez, with the Grijalva River (also called the Río Grande de Chiapas) flowing along its bottom. Since the Chicoasén Dam was completed at the canyon's northern end in 1981, the waters are now deep enough for fast passenger launches to make the 35-km trip through the canyon, whose near-sheer walls rise to somewhere between 900 and 1200 metres high (no one's quite sure of the exact height!). The two-hour ride costs around US$2.50 – a bargain for a crocodile's-eye view of some of Mexico's most awesome scenery. You can also see the canyon from above by travelling out from Tuxtla to one of several look-out points (see under Tuxtla Gutiérrez).

Highway 190, going east from Tuxtla Gutiérrez, crosses the mouth of the canyon at Cahuaré, shortly before the colonial town of Chiapa de Corzo (population about 25,000); you can embark for the boat trip at either Cahuaré or Chiapa de Corzo. Either way the outing can be done in an easy day from Tuxtla Gutiérrez – but since Chiapa de Corzo is an interesting little place in its own right, most people start from there. You can even stay in Chiapa's single small hotel as an alternative to Tuxtla.

History

Chiapa de Corzo, on the east bank of the Grijalva, has an eminent place on the archaeologist's map of Mexico because it has been occupied almost continuously since about 1500 BC. Though it never reached great heights and the ruins today are less than spectacular, its uninterrupted sequence of different cultures – in a cross-roads area where Olmec, Monte Albán, Mayan, Kaminaljuyú and Teotihuacán influences were all felt – makes it invaluable to specialists trying to trace pre-Hispanic cultural developments.

In the couple of centuries before the Spanish arrived, the warlike Chiapa – most dominant of the peoples in western Chiapas at the time – had their capital, Nandalumí, a couple of km downstream from Chiapa de Corzo, on the opposite bank of the river and near the canyon mouth. The first Spanish expedition to the area, under Luis Marín in 1524, was aided in its conquest of Nandalumí by the Chiapa's Zapotec slaves, who supplied canoes for the Spanish to cross the river and fought off the Chiapa when they attacked in midstream.

On that occasion the Spanish didn't stay to occupy the area, but a second, more serious expedition under Diego de Mazariegos arrived in 1528. This time the Chiapa, seeing that defeat was inevitable, apparently hurled themselves by the hundreds – men, women and children – to death in the canyon rather than surrender.

Mazariegos then founded Chiapa de Corzo – called Chiapa de los Indios in its early days – but a month later (March 1528) he transferred his headquarters and most of the settlers to a second new settlement, Villa Real de Chiapa (now San Cristóbal de las Casas), where the climate and the natives were less hostile. The Chiapa Indians rebelled in 1532 and 1534 but that didn't stop Dominican monks from settling in Chiapa de Corzo in the 1540s. Their monastery was built between 1554 and 1572.

In 1863 Chiapa de Corzo was the scene of the decisive battle for control of Chiapas between anti-clerical liberals, supporting national president Benito Juárez, and pro-church conservatives, supporting the French invasion of Mexico. The conservatives, led by Juan Ortega, had already taken San Cristóbal de las Casas, but their defeat by forces from Chiapa de Corzo and Tuxtla Gutiérrez,

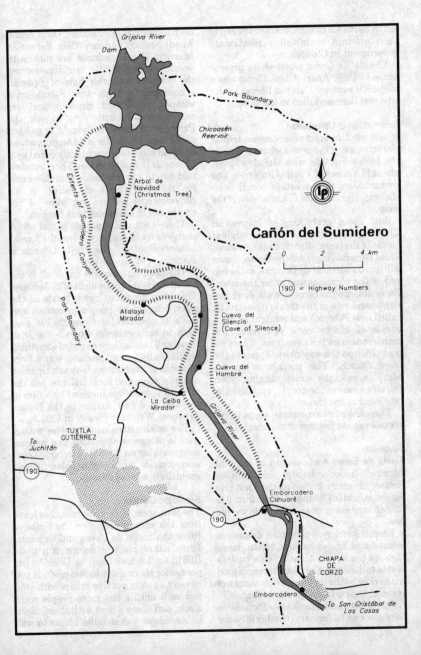

led by Salvador Urbina, marked the end of their attempt to install a reactionary government in Chiapas.

Chiapa de Corzo received its present name in 1888; Ángel Albino Corzo was a mid-19th century Chiapas liberal leader who was born and died in the town.

Information & Orientation

If you want to start your canyon trip at Cahuaré, get off your bus where it crosses the bridge over the wide Grijalva River, about 11 km out of Tuxtla Gutiérrez. The *embarcadero* (embarkation point) is by the bridge, on the west (Tuxtla) side of the river.

Just about everything of interest in Chiapa de Corzo itself is within a couple of blocks of the large, slightly sloping zócalo, Plaza General Ángel Albino Corzo. Buses will let you out on 21 de Octubre, at the top end of the zócalo as you enter the town. For boats into the canyon, walk down the right-hand side of the zócalo (the street's called 5 de Febrero) and straight on for a couple of blocks until you reach the embarcadero on the river front. There's a post office on the way down, opposite the large church. The market is on La Mexicanidad, the street running down the other side of the zócalo, opposite the other end of the church.

There are a few artesanías' shops in the portales at the bottom of the zócalo.

Festivals

Fiesta de Enero A succession of some of Mexico's most colourful and curious fiestas, generally known as the Fiesta de Enero, is held in Chiapa de Corzo from 9 to 22 January every year. The main events are:

From 9 January, young men dressed as women and known as *las Chuntá* dance through the streets nightly. This custom is said to derive from a distribution of food to the poor by the maids of a rich woman of colonial times, Doña María de Angulo.

Processions and dances of *los Parachicos* take place on 15 January (the day of Señor de Esquipulas), 17 January (San Antón Abad) and 20 January (San Sebastián Martir). The Parachicos are men with wooden masks and ixtle 'hair', representing the features and fair hair of Spanish conquistadors. They wear Saltillo-style sarapes, shake tin *maracas* and are accompanied by little girls. In part, the Parachico tradition is thought to go back to the same Doña María de Angulo, whose crippled son was miraculously cured by a Chiapa de Corzo *curandero*. The *curandero* told her to provide some entertainment for the boy *(para el chico)* in his convalescence, so she got some of her employees to shake maracas for him.

There's a musical parade of just about everyone on 19 January, when the formal announcement of the Fiesta Grande is made.

The most renowned event of all is the Combate Naval on the night of 21 January. This is an hour-long mock battle on the river, enacted by people in canoes and hosts of spectacular fireworks. It goes back to early colonial times – the Irish traveller Thomas Gage recorded something similar in 1626 – and probably stems from waterborne encounters between Spanish conquistadors and local Indians, but the modern version was inspired by a film of the battle of Port Arthur in the Russo-Japanese War, seen locally in 1905.

The celebrations usually close with a parade of *carros alegóricos* and general merrymaking on 22 or 23 January. Local women dress up in highly colourful and exquisitely worked dresses.

Sumidero Canyon

The fast, open, fibre-glass launches leave from the embarcaderos on the Grijalva River at Chiapa de Corzo and Cahuaré. From either place a return trip costs US$15 for a whole boat, or US$2.50 per person for six or more in one craft. If you haven't already got five others with you, just wait until a few more people come along, and share a boat with them. Even on weekdays, you shouldn't have to wait more than an hour or so if you get there by, say, 10 am. Chiapa de Corzo is busier than Cahuaré. From both places the launches operate between roughly 7 am and 4 pm. They travel pretty fast so take a layer or two of warm clothing.

It's about 35 km from Chiapa de Corzo to the Chicoasén Dam at the far end of the canyon, and the return trip takes about two hours. The sides of the canyon start to rise once you pass Cahuaré and soon they're beetling up an amazing 1000 metres above you. Along the way you'll see a great variety of bird life – herons, egrets, cormorants, vultures, kingfishers – plus probably a crocodile or two. The boatmen point out a few odd formations of rock or vegetation, including one cliff face covered in a growth of thick, hanging moss so it resembles a gigantic Christmas tree.

At the end of the canyon the fast brown river opens out into the broad reservoir behind the Chicoasén hydroelectric dam. The water beneath you is 260 metres deep.

Zócalo
There are several points of interest around Chiapa's zócalo.

Spanish Fountain Called La Pila, this fine eight-sided mudéjar structure at the bottom end of the zócalo was built in 1562. It's said to be inspired by the Spanish royal crown.

Lacquer Museum The Museo de Laca faces the zócalo on 5 de Febrero. It's dedicated to the craft of lacquered wooden objects or gourds (*jícaras*). Exhibits explain the practical and symbolic importance of gourds (the *Popol Vuh* says the sky is a big, blue, upside-down gourd), and there are examples of lacquerwork from other centres like Uruapan, Pátzcuaro and Olinalá, showing the variety of styles and techniques and the influence of Asian motifs going back to the 18th century. The museum also has masks of the type used in Chiapa's January festivities. You might see some of the fine woodcarving of local master Francisco Jiménez. Hours are Tuesday to Sunday 9 am to 7 pm, Monday 1 to 4 pm; admission is free.

Palacio Municipal On La Mexicanidad, the opposite side of the zócalo from the Museo de Laca, the stairway of the town hall has a map of the battle of 1863 and a mural of local history culminating in the same battle.

Church A block beyond the bottom end of the zócalo, the large church of Santo Domingo dates from the mid-16th century. Part of the adjacent ex-monastery has been converted into a Casa de la Cultura. One of the church towers has an enormous gold, silver and copper bell of famed sonority, made in 1576 (one of the earliest in Latin America).

Other Churches
Three churches crowning small hills around the top of the town were fortified by the liberals as defence points in 1863. You can get good views from all of them. They are shown in the Palacio Municipal mural.

Pre-Hispanic Ruins
Though important to archaeologists, these will interest only the most enthusiastic of visitors. You can reach one small restored pyramid, Montículo 32, by going about a km east along 21 de Octubre (the road which forms the top side of the zócalo – go to the right if facing uphill on the zócalo). It contained a tomb and is located where the road from the town centre meets the bypass.

There are some other stone-faced pyramids and stairways, mostly dating from 100 BC to 200 AD, through some back-streets south-east of here. Ask for *las ruinas*.

Places to Stay
There's just one hostelry in Chiapa de

Corzo – the *Hotel Los Angeles* (tel 6-00-48) on La Mexicanidad at the bottom corner of the zócalo. It's nothing special but it's clean and the rooms, round a courtyard where you could park a car, are quite sizeable. Hot water is intermittent and mosquito nets would be a distinct improvement. Cost is US$5 per room.

Places to Eat

There are several restaurants by the embarcadero but more appealing is the friendly *Restaurant Jardines de Chiapa*, in a garden off the La Mexicanidad side of the zócalo. The menu is limited (and tamales are only available at night) but the fare isn't bad. Sopa Fiesta (US$0.60) contains macaroni, egg, avocado and chicken. *Pollo entomatada* (chicken in tomato sauce) is US$2.

Getting There & Away

Some buses between Tuxtla Gutiérrez and San Cristóbal de las Casas pass through Chiapa de Corzo, but from Tuxtla it's easier to take a Transportes Chiapa-Tuxtla combi (see 'Tuxtla Gutiérrez' section).

Chiapa de Corzo's bus terminals are on 21 de Octubre, the street running east from the top end of the zócalo. Seats on 1st-class buses to San Cristóbal are sometimes in short supply, so book ahead if you can. Alternatively, you could go back to Tuxtla first. Cristóbal Colón (1st class) is a block from the zócalo on 21 de Octubre. There are three buses each morning to San Cristóbal (US$1, 1½ hours) and Comitán. Transportes Tuxtla Gutiérrez is a little further up the same street. It runs buses half-hourly to San Cristóbal; to Palenque via Ocosingo three times daily; and to Villahermosa, Comitán and Motozintla.

SAN CRISTÓBAL DE LAS CASAS

Population: 50,000

For years now San Cristóbal ('cris-TOH-bal') has been one of the most-loved travellers' haunts in Mexico. This tranquil Spanish-built town, high in a temperate pine-clad valley, doesn't have a long list of postcard-type 'sights' but it's surrounded by distinctly mysterious Indian villages, is endlessly intriguing to explore and is full of good food, accommodation and company. Beyond that, it has a unique, even magical, atmosphere that seeps into many people after a few days, something to do perhaps with the smell of wood smoke, the unrivalled clarity of its light, or the Indians padding quickly across the zócalo in their pink, turquoise, black or white costumes. Perhaps it even has something to do with the incongruous range of music which plays softly through the zócalo loudspeakers (where else would you hear muted Black Sabbath at 8 am, followed by Strauss waltzes, Bob Dylan, marimbas, Sergeant Pepper, Glenn Miller and Bob Marley?). Ask anyone who knows the place a little, and they can probably come up with a completely different list of favourite San Cristóbal images.

Not surprisingly the town has changed a bit since the first foreigners 'discovered' it a few decades ago. Budget travellers started stumbling across it in the 1960s on their way from Oaxaca to Yucatán or Guatemala. Today there are many more visitors, hotels, restaurants and craft shops than even five years ago – but the town has assimilated them happily (except perhaps in the banks where waits can be *very* long). Road approaches have improved too, but San Cristóbal is still very much a small, remote, highland town; the airport functions only intermittently, and the town is too far off the beaten track for all but a few tour coaches.

One of the pleasures of San Cristóbal is simply walking its streets and discovering its hidden corners. Another is getting out into the fine countryside and the villages of the Tzotzil and Tzeltal, some of the most traditional of Mexico's Mayan-descended Indians (see Around San Cristóbal).

Distant though it is from the rest of

Mexico, San Cristóbal is by far the most central staging-post in Chiapas. It's only two hours east of Tuxtla Gutiérrez yet a world away in environment and atmosphere. The road from Tuxtla seems to climb endlessly into the clouds before descending slightly into the small valley of Jovel where San Cristóbal lies, 2110 metres high. Agua Azul and Palenque to the north of San Cristóbal, and the Montebello Lakes and Guatemala to the south, are just a few hours away by bus. The little-known Mayan site of Toniná is near Ocosingo, 100 km from San Cristóbal on the Palenque road.

History

Traces of early hunters and collectors have been found in the Jovel Valley, and Moxviquil Hill on its north side has some minor Mayan ruins from about the 8th and 9th centuries. By the early 16th century there were three main Tzotzil centres in the area, all fortified: Chamula and Zinacantán to the north-west and Huixtán to the east. Relations between the three were often hostile and while the last two reputedly sent gifts to the Spanish who arrived in Chiapas in 1524, the invaders had to subdue Chamula by force. Bernal Díaz del Castillo, author of a famed first-hand chronicle of the Spanish conquest of Mexico, was apparently the first Spaniard to enter Chamula, for which he was awarded the place as his *encomienda*.

The Spanish didn't settle in the area until four years later, when Diego de Mazariegos founded San Cristóbal (at first called Villa Real de Chiapa) as their regional headquarters. The same year Mazariegos persuaded another Spanish force, which had entered Chiapas from Guatemala and founded a settlement near what's now Comitán, to withdraw. Some of this second Spanish group went to settle at San Cristóbal too, making a total Spanish presence of perhaps 200 in the early days.

The Spanish occupied the area round the zócalo, known as El Recinto, around which was El Barrio, where Indians and mestizos lived. There were also special barrios for Indian allies who had arrived with the Spanish; Aztecs, Tlaxcalans and Oaxacans settled in the Mexicanos, Tlaxcala and San Antonio barrios, Guatemalans in San Diego and Cuxtitali. A sixth barrio, El Cerrillo, was founded by freed Tzotzil slaves in 1549. The outlying villages were taken as *encomiendas* and, later, haciendas by the Spanish.

For most of the colonial era San Cristóbal was a neglected outpost governed ineffectively from Guatemala. Its Spanish citizens made their fortunes – usually from wheat – at the cost of the Indians, who suffered loss of their lands, diseases, taxes and forced labour. They rose up several times, the most famous occasion in colonial times being the Cancuc rebellion of 1712 by the Tzeltal people, provoked by taxes levied to build a church and hospital in San Cristóbal.

Earlier in the Spanish period, the church had been more a force for protection of the Indians against the excesses of other colonists. Dominican monks first arrived in Chiapas in 1545 and made San Cristóbal their main base. Bartolomé de las Casas (after whom the town is now named), who was appointed bishop of Chiapas the same year, and Juan de Zapata y Sandoval, bishop from 1613 to 1621, are the most fondly remembered prelates.

San Cristóbal remained the chief Spanish town in Chiapas throughout colonial times, and in 1778 its population count including the Indian barrios was 4812, of whom 564 were Spanish. It became the state capital when Chiapas joined recently independent Mexico in 1824.

During the French intervention in Mexico the town was briefly occupied in 1863 by pro-church and French forces, but these were decisively defeated the same year at Chiapa de Corzo, and Chiapas remained in liberal hands. Then, soon

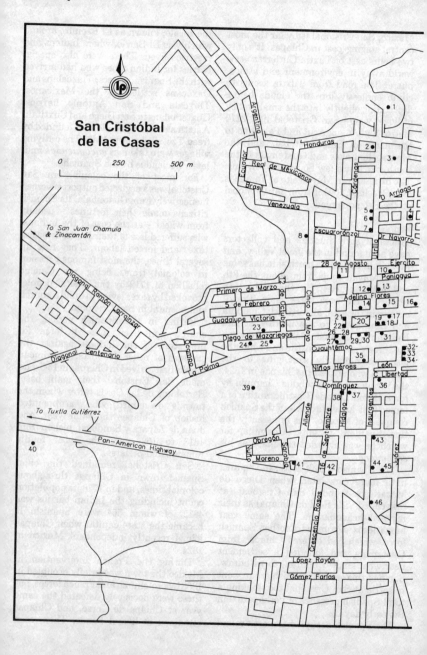

San Cristóbal
de las Casas

0   250   500 m

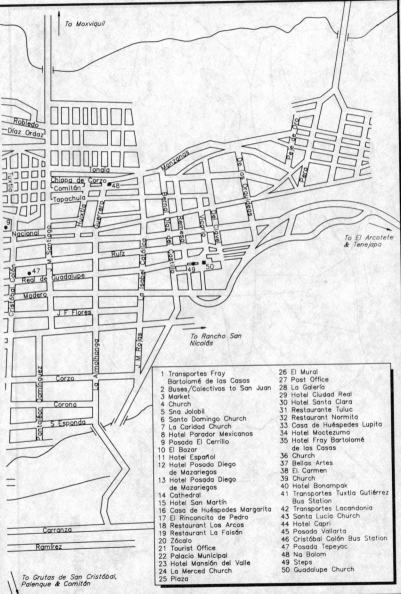

1 Transportes Fray
   Bartolomé de las Casas
2 Buses/Colectivos to San Juan
3 Market
4 Church
5 Sna Jolobil
6 Santo Domingo Church
7 La Caridad Church
8 Hotel Parador Mexicanos
9 Posada El Cerrillo
10 El Bazar
11 Hotel Español
12 Hotel Posada Diego
   de Mazariegos
13 Hotel Posada Diego
   de Mazariegos
14 Cathedral
15 Hotel San Martín
16 Casa de Huéspedes Margarita
17 El Rinconcito de Pedro
18 Restaurant Los Arcos
19 Restaurant La Faisán
20 Zócalo
21 Tourist Office
22 Palacio Municipal
23 Hotel Mansión del Valle
24 La Merced Church
25 Plaza

26 El Mural
27 Post Office
28 La Galería
29 Hotel Ciudad Real
30 Hotel Santa Clara
31 Restaurante Tuluc
32 Restaurant Normita
33 Casa de Huéspedes Lupita
34 Hotel Moctezuma
35 Hotel Fray Bartolomé
   de las Casas
36 Church
37 Bellas Artes
38 El Carmen
39 Church
40 Hotel Bonampak
41 Transportes Tuxtla Gutiérrez
   Bus Station
42 Transportes Lacandonia
43 Santa Lucia Church
44 Hotel Capri
45 Posada Vallarta
46 Cristóbal Colón Bus Station
47 Posada Tepeyac
48 Na Bolom
49 Steps
50 Guadalupe Church

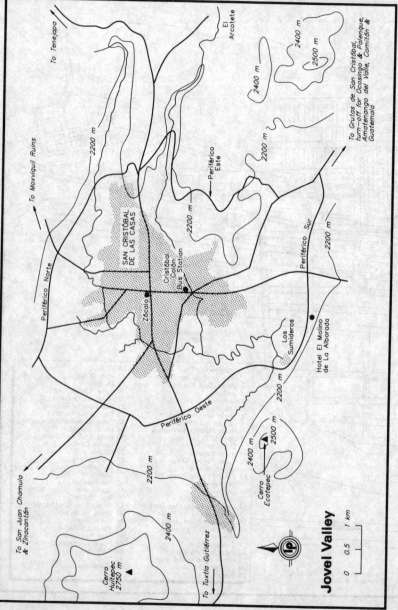

Jovel Valley

0   0.5   1 km

afterwards, began the curious train of events which ended in the famous Chamula rebellion of 1869-70.

One day in 1867, at a place called Tzajalhemel, a Chamula girl called Agustina Gómez Checheb found three pieces of obsidian which seemed to talk. She entrusted them to a local Indian official, Pedro Díaz Cuzcat, who said they woke him at night with their noise inside a wooden box. Tzajalhemel rapidly became an Indian pilgrimage centre where Agustina and Díaz would interpret the 'oracles' of the stones and of a clay figure to which Agustina had allegedly given birth. Díaz even baptised 12 Indians as saints of the new cult, which soon had more followers than the Catholic Church in many Tzotzil and Tzeltal villages north of San Cristóbal. This alarmed the church and civil authorities and in December 1868 the pair were imprisoned in San Cristóbal.

At this point, enter the revolutionary Ignacio Fernández Galindo. Identifying himself with San Salvador or the Tzotzil god Cul Salik, he came from San Cristóbal to rouse the Chamulas to win back their lands and stop burdensome taxes. In June 1869 the schoolmaster and the Catholic priest in Chamula were murdered and the rebels went through the countryside killing more mestizos. Arriving at San Cristóbal, they successfully demanded the release of Agustina and Díaz but were persuaded to leave Galindo and his wife as hostages.

When the hostages were not released, Díaz led a new attack on San Cristóbal, joined by many other Tzotzil villagers, but the authorities had enough time to gather reinforcements and the rebels were beaten – though resistance lingered a bit longer in the northern area round Simojovel. Galindo was sentenced to death, and other rebels were shot or deported to remote parts of Mexico. Díaz survived to lead a further short-lived uprising of hacienda servants in 1870.

San Cristóbal was replaced as state capital by Tuxtla Gutiérrez in 1892. Explanations for this vary, but the most plausible is that it was too hostile to the national dictatorship of Porfirio Díaz. One effect was that it remained isolated: the first paved road from Tuxtla Gutiérrez didn't arrive until the 1940s. Only in the 1970s was a tunnel built to provide adequate drainage for the Jovel Valley and stop the floods which had periodically struck the town since its founding.

San Cristóbal's mostly mestizo population has been swelled in recent years by Tzotzils expelled from Chamula for turning Protestant (a result of the missionary efforts of the Summer School of Linguistics from the USA). Other Indians come into the town mainly to buy and sell. They keep their distance from the mestizo population, the result of centuries of exploitation at Spanish hands and treatment as second-class citizens – a state of affairs which even today is changing slowly. Though shy, Indians can also be friendly and humorous once they get talking, and they can be hard bargainers if you're trying to buy something. Above all, they have a quiet dignity which contributes much to the town's atmosphere.

Names San Cristóbal de las Casas is the town's eighth official name. The others were: 1528-29, Villa Real de Chiapa; 1529-31, Villaviciosa de Chiapa (after the birthplace of its first Spanish judge); 1531-36, San Cristóbal de los Llanos de Chiapa; 1536-1829, Ciudad Real de Chiapa; 1829-1848, San Cristóbal; 1848-1934, San Cristóbal las Casas; 1934-1943, Ciudad las Casas. It has also had two popular names: Jovel and, to distinguish it from Chiapa de los Indios (now Chiapa de Corzo), Chiapa de los Españoles.

Orientation

San Cristóbal is a small place, easy to find your way round, with straight streets rambling up and down several gentle hills. The Pan-American Highway passes along the south side of town, and just off it are the main bus stations. From these terminals, walk north (slightly uphill) to reach the zócalo (Plaza 31 de Marzo), which has the cathedral on its north side. From Cristóbal Colón it's just six blocks up Insurgentes to the zócalo; from Transportes Tuxtla Gutiérrez it's five blocks up Allende, then two to the right along Mazariegos.

Places to stay and eat are scattered all round town, but there are clutches of hotels and *casas de huéspedes* on Insurgentes and on Real de Guadalupe at the north-east corner of the zócalo.

Information

Tourist Office This is at the north end of the Palacio Municipal on the west side of the zócalo. It's open 8 am to 8 pm Monday to Saturday, 9 am to 2 pm Sunday, give or take a few minutes (tel 8-04-14). Some of the staff speak good English and have a lot of information on hand, but how much they'll tell you depends on how busy they are and how energetic they feel.

Money There are several banks on and near the zócalo. Most of them only do foreign exchange from 10 am to 12 noon, though Bancomer on the zócalo continues until 12.30. If you're in anything like a hurry, get in line before 10 am.

Post & Telephone The post office is on Cuauhtémoc between Hidalgo and Crescencio Rosas, one block south and one west of the zócalo's south-west corner. It's open 8 am to 7 pm Monday to Friday, 9 am to 1 pm Saturday, Sunday and holidays. For telegrams go to Diego de Mazariegos 19, 2½ blocks west of the zócalo. There's also a public telex office near the post office. Phone calls to the outside world often involve long waits and you'll have to be very patient to place a call to another country. You can attempt to make them at the farmacía on the south side of the zócalo.

Books Interested outsiders can use the library at Na Bolom at certain hours. It has 14,000 books including one of the world's biggest collections on the Mayas, and many more on other aspects of Chiapas and Central America. Bellas Artes library also has a big collection of books in English. (See Na Bolom and El Carmen sections, below.)

Librería Soluna on Real de Guadalupe, less than a block from the zócalo, has some books in English and a good selection of novels, local interest and anthropology in Spanish. You can also find the interesting Chiapas current affairs magazine *Perfil del Sureste* here. Café El Mural at Crescencio Rosas 4 has some English and Spanish books and magazines for sale, plus several daily newspapers to browse through.

San Cristóbal de las Casas, Chiapas, Mexico, City and Area Guide by Mike Shawcross is an excellent little guidebook in English. First written in 1978, it's now unfortunately hard to find, but still very informative if you're lucky enough to come across a copy. The author is an Englishman who has spent many years in Chiapas and Guatemala.

Also worth seeking out if Chiapas grabs your interest are the historical novels of Rosario Castellanos (1925-74). They're mainly set in the state and at least one, *Balún Canán* (1957), has been translated into English (as *The New Watchmen*). It tells of a landowner who is reluctant to give up his property under the Cárdenas reforms of the 1930s. *Ciudad Real* (1960) is set in San Cristóbal this century, and *Oficio de Tinieblas* deals with Indian religion.

Professor Prudencio Moscoso is a retired teacher and local historian with a large personal library who will happily answer your questions (in Spanish) or let you look at his books in his home at 16 de Septiembre 29 (the white and red house on the corner of Escuadrón 201). Go between 4 and 7 pm Monday to Friday, or call 8-09-50 for an appointment. He doesn't ask for anything in return except perhaps some foreign stamps for his collection!

The Centro de Investigaciones Ecológicas del Sureste, at the corner of Cuauhtémoc and Crescencio Rosas, also has a library and a good collection of large-scale maps of Chiapas. It's open 3 to 7 pm Monday to Friday, 10 am to 1 pm Saturday.

Other The nearest Guatemalan consulate is in Comitán.

Festivals

San Cristóbal's calendar has a plentiful sprinkling of festivals – some involving just one barrio, others the whole town. Processions, parades and fireworks feature in most of them. Ask at the tourist office for what's on while you're there. In spring there's a two-week-long fiesta period covering Semana Santa (the week leading up to Easter) and the Feria de la Primavera y de la Paz (Spring and Peace) the following week. Semana Santa includes processions on Good Friday and the burning of 'Judas' figures on Holy Saturday. The second week features more parades, bullfights, and so on. Sometimes the celebrations for the anniversary of the town's founding (31 March) fall in the midst of it all too!

Other fiestas can go on several days before and after the specific date in question. Look out for events celebrating the feast of San Cristóbal (17-25 July), the anniversary of Chiapas joining Mexico in 1824 (14 September), National Independence Day (15 and 16 September), the Day of the Dead (2 November), the feast of the Virgin of Guadalupe (10-12 December) and preparations for Christmas (16-24 December).

Festivals are also a feature of life in the Indian villages outside the town – see the Around San Cristóbal section.

The Zócalo

Officially called Plaza 31 de Marzo, this is the old Spanish centre of the town, also used as a marketplace until early this century. Today it's a fine place to sit and watch the life of the town happen around you. The steps on the east side are a favourite evening gathering-place for locals and Indians from outlying villages. The cathedral, on the north side, was begun in 1528, but was completely rebuilt in 1693. Its gold-leaf interior has a baroque pulpit and altarpiece. The south-east corner of the zócalo is taken up by the former house of Diego de Mazariegos, the Spanish conqueror of Chiapas. This building, now the Hotel Santa Clara, is one of the few non-ecclesiastical examples of the plateresque style in Mexico. The Palacio Municipal on the west side of the square is a 19th-century neoclassical structure.

Santo Domingo

This is the most beautiful of San Cristóbal's many churches – especially when its pink façade is floodlit at night. Santo Domingo is in the north-west of town opposite the corner of Lázaro Cárdenas and Real de Mexicanos. Together with the adjoining monastery, it was built from 1547 to 1560. The church's baroque façade (on which can be seen the double-headed Hapsburg eagle, symbol of the Spanish monarchy) was added in the 17th century. There's plenty of gold inside and on the ornate pulpit.

Just south of Santo Domingo, La Caridad church dates from 1712. Taxes levied on Indians for the building of La Caridad and an adjoining hospital for the poor sparked off the Tzeltal rebellion of Cancuc the same year.

Sna Jolobil

This is the best place to see Chiapas Indian textiles. Sna Jolobil – it means 'Weavers' House' in Tzotzil – is in the old monastery buildings next to Santo Domingo church. It's an organisation of 650 women backstrap-loom weavers from 20 Tzotzil and Tzeltal villages, aimed at fostering this important folk art both as an

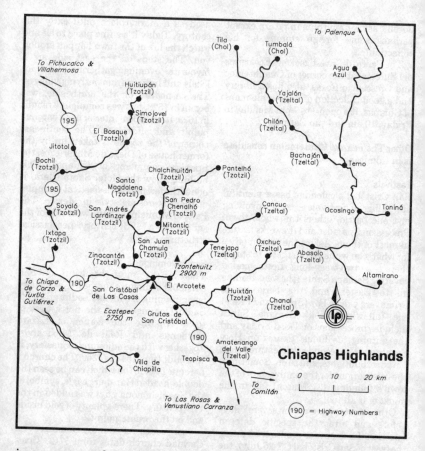

Chiapas Highlands

190 = Highway Numbers

income-earner and to preserve Indian identity and tradition. Founded in the late 1970s, Sna Jolobil's aims include the revival of forgotten techniques and designs, and development of natural dyes. One important revival is brocading, in which the decorative motifs are worked in while the fabric is woven, as opposed to embroidery where decoration is added to pre-woven cloth.

Each village in the Chiapas highlands has its own distinctive dress, and modern Western garb is much rarer than among most Mexican Indians. The designs and

techniques are derived from many stages of their history. Most seemingly abstract designs are in fact stylised snakes, frogs, butterflies, dog paw-prints, birds, people, saints and so on. Some go back to pre-Hispanic times: for instance the rhombus shape on some huipiles from San Andrés Larráinzar is also found on the garments of one of the figures on Lintel 24 from Yaxchilán. The shape represents the old Mayan universe, in which the earth was cube-shaped and the sky had four corners. Some designs can still perform a religious-magical function: scorpion motifs, for example, can be a symbolic request for rain, since scorpions are believed to attract lightning. The sacredness of traditional costume is shown by the dressing of saints' images in old and revered garments at festival times.

The typical men's costume from Chamula – long-sleeved shirt, wool tunic, belt and long trousers – stems from the Spanish, who objected to the relative nudity of the loincloth and cloak that Chamulan men used to wear. Other patterns have been invented or re-invented more recently as an expression of Indian identity. The square, coloured patch on men's costumes from Cancuc and Oxchuc was originally an Aztec motif, brought to the area by the Aztec allies of the 16th-century Spanish conquistadors. Early this century these villages lacked any special costume, but they used the Aztec idea, which had survived among Chamulans, to help create one.

At the time of writing, Sna Jolobil's gallery/saleroom (open daily except Sunday, 9 am to 2 pm and 4 to 7 pm) had moved temporarily across the road to Lázaro Cárdenas 42. Here you can see a fine range of huipiles, generally priced at about US$14 but going up to US$775 and US$1160 for the finest ceremonial garments from Santa Magdalena and Santa Rosario.

Na Bolom

A visit to this fascinating house on Guerrero, at the corner of Chiapa de Corzo six blocks north of Real de Guadalupe, should be high on anyone's list in San Cristóbal. For several decades it has been the home of Swiss anthropologist and photographer Gertrude (Trudy) Duby-Blom and, until his death in 1963, of her husband, Danish archaeologist Frans Blom.

The pair shared a passion for Chiapas and particularly its Indians. While Frans explored, surveyed and dug at ancient Mayan sites including Toniná, Chinkultic and Moxviquil, Trudy has devoted much of her life to studying and campaigning for the tiny Lacandón Indian population of eastern Chiapas. One building at Na Bolom is reserved for Lacandones to use when they visit San Cristóbal.

In Europe Trudy Blom had been a socialist journalist who survived a Nazi concentration camp. Her energy has continued into old age, with recent emphasis on campaigning to save the endangered Lacandón rainforest and starting a tree nursery for Indian villagers.

The house – whose name is Tzotzil for 'Jaguar House' as well as a play on the owner's name – is full of photographs, archaeological and anthropological relics and books, and is a treasure-trove for anyone with an interest in Chiapas. Visits are by guided tour (US$0.30), but these are some of the least formal, most open-ended guided tours you'll find anywhere. They are conducted in English and Spanish daily except Monday at 4.30 pm by volunteers from several countries, who spend a year at Na Bolom and are happy to chat with visitors. The house also has an artist-in-residence programme. The 14,000-book library, including one of the world's biggest Mayan collections and a wealth of other material on Chiapas and Central America, is open separately from 9 am to 1 pm Tuesday to Saturday and 2.30 to 6 pm Monday.

If you're interested in the sorts of things Na Bolom offers, you can stay here (US$34 double) – or just dine with the assembled company.

El Carmen & Bellas Artes

El Carmen church lies at the corner of Hidalgo and Hermanos Domínguez. Formerly part of a nunnery, it has a distinctive tower resting on an arch. The nunnery was built in 1597, the tower in 1680 to replace one destroyed by floods 28 years earlier. Near it is the Casa de Cultura, containing art galleries, a library with a good English collection, and the Bellas Artes auditorium where regular musical and theatrical performances are held.

La Merced
Located on Diego de Mazariegos 3½ blocks west of the zócalo, La Merced was largely reconstructed this century, but there's a pleasant plaza in front of it.

Centro de Investigaciones Ecológicas del Sureste
There are displays on the vegetation, geology and ecology of Chiapas at this centre on the corner of Cuauhtémoc and Crescencio Rosas – plus a library and a good local map collection. Open Monday to Friday 3 to 7 pm, Saturday 10 am to 1 pm.

Museo Zul-Pepen
This is a private butterfly and archaeological museum (!) at Guadalupe Victoria 47. It's open daily except Monday from 4 to 8 pm and costs US$1. The butterfly collection contains many incredibly colourful (if dead) specimens from all over the world. The archaeological section features pieces from several pre-Hispanic cultures but no particular treasures. Compulsory and enthusiastic guided tours in Spanish increase the interest of the displays if you've got the stamina.

Steam Baths
Yes, steam baths. You can have an hour's Turkish bath for US$0.70, or an hour's plain steam for US$0.60, at Baños Mercedarios at Primero de Marzo 55 (open 6.30 am to 8 pm Monday to Saturday, 6.30 am to 6 pm Sunday).

Hills
The most prominent of the several small hills over which San Cristóbal undulates are the Cerro de San Cristóbal in the south-west quarter of town, reached by steps up from Allende, and the Cerro de Guadalupe, seven blocks east of the zócalo along Real de Guadalupe. Both are crowned by churches and afford good views over the town – but there have been reports of attempted rapes on the Cerro de San Cristóbal.

The Cerro de Moxviquil, about 1½ km north of the town, has some Mayan ruins which were excavated by Frans Blom but have now been grown over again. They lie about 200 metres above the Ojo de Agua on the unpaved Periférico Norte (northern ring-road). If you want to look for them, ask in Na Bolom or elsewhere for directions. The ruins themselves apparently require imagination if they're to provide much interest, but the walk is said to be pleasant.

There are many other possible walks of a few hours on the hills around the town. If you're lucky enough to find a copy of Mike Shawcross' San Cristóbal guide, it gives detailed directions for several of them. If not, ask. Cerro Ecatepec is south of the town and a trail leads up it from Los Sumideros, which are the caves that drain the Jovel Valley's small rivers. Los Sumideros are on the Periférico Sur, about two km west of its junction with the continuation of Insurgentes south of the Pan-American Highway. A tunnel made in the 1970s to increase Los Sumideros' drainage capacity and prevent flooding also starts near Los Sumideros. You can ascend Cerro Huitepec (2750 metres), west of the town, either from the church in the south-western barrio of San Felipe or by striking up from the western Periférico, between the Pan-American Highway and the road to Chamula. Cerro Tzontehuitz, 10 km north-east of the town, is the highest point in the Chiapas Highlands at 2900 metres.

El Arcotete
This natural limestone arch over the Río Quinta lies in pleasant country seven km east of the town, which is a popular local outing. Follow Madero east from the town centre and continue along the Tenejapa road. About 4½ km from the town centre a

sign points to El Arcotete down a dirt road. From the end of the road a path leads a further ¼ km to El Arcotete.

Grutas de San Cristóbal

This is a single huge cavern nine km south-east of San Cristóbal, whose first, quite narrow, 350 metres (about 10% of its full length) are paved and lit. You can enter it for US$0.30 from 9 am to 5 pm daily, and though the cave itself doesn't take long to visit, there are some walking trails in the lovely country beyond. Take a Comitán bus and ask for 'Las Grutas' (20c). The half-km track to the cave leads south from the Pan-American Highway about 10 minutes out of town. Alternatively, you can go on horseback (see the Getting Around section).

Places to Stay – bottom end

The *Casa de Huéspedes Margarita* (tel 8-09-57) at Real de Guadalupe 34, 1½ blocks from the zócalo, has long been one of the most popular budget travellers' halts in Mexico – and justifiably so. It's a fine single-storey courtyard house where the *señora* and her family live in the back while about 18 rooms in the front are let to visitors. The rooms are bare but clean, and the beds are comfortable. Each room takes two, three or more people; if you're alone ask for a *dormitorio* bed, or find other travellers to share with you (usually easy). A double room costs US$3.50, a triple US$4.75. Bathrooms are communal but very clean and have 24-hour hot water – a distinct bonus in San Cristóbal's sometimes ultra-cool nights. The place is run by a squad of amiable local boys and has its own good restaurant. There's a notice board where lifts are sometimes offered, and if you have mail sent here it will be held for you. The Margarita sometimes gets full towards evening.

A block further up Real de Guadalupe is the *Posada Tepeyac* (tel 8-01-18) at No 40. It's basic but clean, a rambling place where the rooms at the back are lighter. Singles with communal bath are US$2, singles/doubles with private bath US$2.50/3.

A cheaper but also good budget place is the small *Posada El Cerrillo*, on Belisario Domínguez just north of Ejercito Nacional, four blocks from the zócalo. It's clean and bright with a pleasant little courtyard. Rooms cost US$1.50 with one double bed, US$2 with two singles, US$2.50 with two doubles. Bathrooms are communal.

The *Casa de Huéspedes Lupita* at Juárez 12, between León and Felipe Flores, charges US$1.50 per person (singles available). The rooms aren't huge and need a coat of paint but the place is clean (including the communal bathrooms) and friendly. *Posada Jovel* at Flavio Paniagua 28 charges US$1.25 per person in rooms for up to three people. Baths are communal. For an extra 25c you can use the kitchen.

Many hostelries line Insurgentes but the cheaper ones are mainly of the dingy, uncared-for variety. The better ones include the *Posada Vallarta*, actually off Insurgentes at Hermanos Pineda 10 (the first street to the right as you go up Insurgentes from the Cristóbal Colón bus station). It's clean and modernish; singles/doubles with private bath are US$3/4. The friendly *Posada Insurgentes* (tel 8-24-35) at Insurgentes 73 two blocks from the bus station is clean, has newer beds and furnishings than the others on the street, and has plenty of hot water. Singles/doubles with clean common baths are US$2.25/2.75. The *Posada Lupita* at No 46, with doubles only at US$2, is also basically clean.

There are several self-catering places in San Cristóbal, well worth considering for a stay of more than a couple of days. One of the most popular is the *Posada Morales* at Allende 17, whose three-bed bungalows (US$5 a day) look out from the lower slopes of the Cerro de San Cristóbal. They have kitchen/dining rooms, fireplaces and hot water. Another is the *Rancho Harvard* (tel 8-14-13) on Calzada Roberta in the north-west of town, where you get a large cooking/sitting/eating room (with fridge) and two bedrooms for US$100 to US$150 a month.

Also worth considering for a longer stay is the *Posada El Cubito* at Juárez 92, half a block off the Pan-American Highway. Rooms in small bungalows at the end of a tree-lined drive cost US$4.50 a night but just US$20 for 15 nights.

Camping The *Rancho San Nicolás* camping and trailer park (tel 8-00-57) is in the east of town, two km from the zócalo: continue east along León for a km after it becomes a dirt track. Cost is US$1 per person whether you're in a tent or a vehicle. There's hot water, showers and other hook-ups. The *Hotel Bonampak* (tel 8-16-21), on the Pan-American Highway about a km west of the Cristóbal Colón station, also has a trailer park (US$4.75 per vehicle).

Places to Stay – middle

Several places in this range are on Insurgentes. Just up from the Cristóbal Colón bus station, the *Hotel Capri* (tel 8-00-15) at No 54 has modern, clean, quite bright rooms round a narrow but flowery courtyard for US$4.50/5.75. Further up at No 33, the *Hotel D'Mónica* (tel 8-13-67, 8-29-40) is good value. Its clean, modern, well-kept rooms with TV and fireplaces are US$4.50 single, US$5.75 for a double bed, US$6.75 for two beds.

The *Hotel Fray Bartolomé de las Casas* (tel 8-09-32) at the corner of Insurgentes and Niños Héroes, two blocks from the zócalo, is one of the most characterful places in this range. It's a fine old house with a lovely pillared courtyard (used for parking); clean, well-kept, quite big singles/doubles with private bath cost US$5/6.75. The hotel has its own restaurant.

A block further up Insurgentes at the corner of Cuauhtémoc, the *Hotel Posada San Cristóbal* is much plainer and less comfortable with rooms at US$3.50/4.50.

On the zócalo itself, the *Hotel Santa Clara* (tel 8-11-40) on the corner of Insurgentes was the home of Diego de Mazariegos, the Spanish conqueror of Chiapas. Rooms are mostly big and comfortable and there's a pleasant courtyard brightened by some red macaws (in cages), plus a restaurant (food apparently awful) and a large bar/lounge. Singles/doubles are US$7.75/9.75. A couple of doors along the zócalo, the *Hotel Ciudad Real* (tel 8-18-86) is another Spanish mansion but slightly less spacious. The central courtyard is covered and functions as the dining room. Rooms are clean, neat and well decorated but a bit on the small side; singles/doubles cost US$6.50/8.25.

Hotel Moctezuma (tel 8-03-52), three blocks from the zócalo at the corner of Juárez and León, is another pleasant place with a flowery courtyard, but more modern than the pair on the zócalo. Singles/doubles (clean but some small) are US$6.50/8 and the hotel has its own restaurant.

The *Hotel San Martín* (tel 8-05-33) on Real de Guadalupe, half a block from the zócalo, used to be cheaper but now charges US$4/5 for its plain but bright and clean rooms. A few doors away, the *Hotel Real del Valle* (tel 8-06-80) is similar, and identical in price.

Over in the north-west of town the *Hotel Parador Mexicanos* (tel 8-00-55), on Cinco de Mayo just south of Escuadrón 201, has a few clean, quite modern rooms for US$6.50/8.25. Attractions are a tennis court and its location in an ordinary street in the Mexicanos barrio, where Aztec allies of the early Spanish conquerors settled.

Places to Stay – top end

The *Hotel Posada Diego de Mazariegos* (tel 8-18-25, 8-05-13) is an elegant colonial place occupying two fine buildings with courtyards on Adelina Flores either side of the corner with Utrilla, one block from the zócalo. Singles/doubles are US$10.75/

13.50. The hotel has a restaurant, bar, cafeteria, crafts store, etc. This is the main locale in town for coach tour groups.

The *Hotel Español* (tel 8-04-12) at Primero de Marzo 15 (near the corner of 16 de Septiembre) is another quieter, old place. Its lovely central garden has Talavera tiles and a fountain. Rooms are comfortable but a little dark and moderately sized. Fires are lit when it's cold. Singles/doubles are US$9.75/12.

The *Hotel Mansión del Valle* at Diego de Mazariegos 39, 3½ blocks west of the zócalo, is new, clean and comfortable but rooms could be bigger. Singles/doubles are US$11/13.50. The *Hotel Bonampak* (tel 8-16-21, 8-16-22) is down on the Pan-American Highway about a km west of the bottom of Insurgentes. Rooms are spacious and modern, with singles/doubles at US$10.75/13.50 (TV US$1.25 extra).

The *Hotel El Molino de la Alborada* (tel 8-09-35), also in the top price bracket, gets good reports. Accommodation is in 11 cottages under a wooded hillside south of the airport, on the unpaved Periférico Sur (southern ring-road). To get there from the town centre, follow Insurgentes south, straight on over the Pan-American Highway and past the airfield on the right, until it meets the Periférico. Then turn right.

Places to Eat

Tired of tortillas, tamales and tacos? San Cristóbal will bring you relief. It has one of the best ranges of small restaurants and cafés to suit all kinds of Western palates in Mexico.

To start with, as you walk up from the bus station you could call at the *Plaza 1899* shop at Insurgentes 19 to buy some good whole-wheat bread (*pan integral*) or banana or carrot cake. Then you could pick up a tasty pastry from women selling them on the steps on the east side of the zócalo.

After that, you'll need a few days to sample some of the excellent sit-down establishments. One of the most popular is *La Galería* (tel 8-15-47) upstairs at Hidalgo 3, a few doors from the zócalo. Service is slow but the fare is good. This is a meeting-place, with English magazines and chess to pass the time. Whole-wheat sandwiches are US$0.75 to US$1, granola with bananas and milk US$0.75, potato salad US$1, delicious apple strudel US$0.50. Also offered are breakfasts, yoghurt and good strong coffee.

Another excellent coffee house is *El Mural* at Crescencio Rosas 4, half a block south of Diego de Mazariegos. A speciality here is the crepes – try banana and rompope (US$1). Plenty of succulent cakes too, including superbly gooey lemon meringue pie. Mint and cinnamon tea are available, and the *licuado de frutas revueltas con leche* is a treat (ask for it, it's not on the menu). El Mural is open until 10 or 11 pm (later than most places in San Cristóbal) and has a bookstall and newspapers to read.

Two coffee-and-chess places popular with townsfolk as well as visitors are the *Cafetería El Rinconcito de Pedro* on Real de Guadalupe half a block from the zócalo, and the *Central* on Madero, also within a block of the zócalo.

Among restaurants (as opposed to cafés), the little *Restaurante Tuluc* (tel 8-20-90) comes high on most people's list. It's at Madero 9, just up from the zócalo, and uses herbs as well as anywhere in Mexico. Roquefort salad (US$0.75) is a delight – a plate of very lightly boiled potatoes, beetroot and carrots, with fresh tomato and Roquefort cheese on top. The French onion soup (US$0.50) comes with real Parmesan, parsley and other herbs in seemingly bottomless bowls, and the filete Tuluc (US$2) is a steak wrapped in bacon and stuffed with cheese and green vegetables. Spaghetti (US$0.50) is in four varieties – Italiano, Francés, Argentino and Caruso – which inspired the following memorable exchange with an otherwise helpful waiter:

'What's spaghetti Caruso?'
'Like spaghetti Argentino.'
'What's spaghetti Argentino?'
'It's how they make it in Argentina.'
The Tuluc's only drawback is the compulsory 10% service charge – but bread rolls and butter are free!

The *Casa de Huéspedes Margarita* at Real de Guadalupe 34 has a popular little restaurant serving everything from Mexican standards to egg breakfasts and oats porridge *(avena)*, yoghurt *(leche bulgara)*, pan integral and peanut butter *(crema de cacahuate)*. It's open until 10.30 pm.

El Bazar at Paniagua 2, half a block east of Utrilla, is an open-air place inside the building marked 'Plaza San Cristóbal'. They have over a page of breakfast ideas including yoghurt, granola, fruit and honey for US$0.50, plus typical Mexican dishes at US$1 to US$2 and about 20 types of coffee – some with liqueurs.

Another good-value breakfast place is *La Peñita* on Insurgentes, 2½ blocks up from the Cristóbal Colón station. Prices are around US$0.75. Travellers have also recommended the *Cafetería y Lonchería Palenque* just down the road.

For excellent pizza go to the *Unicornio Restaurant* at Insurgentes 33A. Pizza prices here range from US$1 to US$3.25 but five *chicas* feed at least six people. There are other Mexican and Western foods on the menu including steaks and some seafood. The *Trattoria y Pizzería I Balconi* also does good pizza and its spaghetti Bolognese (US$1) is great. It's on Primero de Marzo, two blocks north of the zócalo.

Good Mexican food is served at the *Restaurant Normita*, open until 10 pm on the corner of Juárez and J F Flores. *Pozole* – a soup of maize, pork, cabbage, radishes and onions (US$1.25) – and enchiladas both go down well. Comida corrida (US$1.25) is served from 1 to 3 pm.

El Trigal at Primero de Marzo 13B, just off 20 de Noviembre, is a mainly vegetarian restaurant. A sample comida corrida (US$1.75) is vegetable soup, brown rice, potato tacos filled with soya meat, fruit salad with cream and a melon licuado.

The *Restaurant La Faisán* at Madero 2, just off the zócalo and opposite the Restaurante Tuluc, used to be a cheap hangout where you could make a lemon tea last for several games of chess. Now it's glassed-in and tarted up but still friendly, with good huevos Mexicanos and other mainly Mexican snacks and meals at US$0.75 to US$2. Next door, the *Restaurant Los Arcos* is also quite popular. Pollo frito and carne asada are US$1.50, tacos US$0.50 an order, and there are long lists of breakfasts and cool drinks. One traveller wrote in particular praise of its talking parrot: 'A pleasure to just sit there and listen to it'.

The Hotel D'Mónica restaurant at Insurgentes 33 has eight good-looking breakfast combinations at US$1 to US$1.50, plus some German items.

La Parrilla, on Belisario Domínguez just beyond Ejercito Nacional, stays open later than most restaurants, serving carnes and quesos al carbón.

Entertainment

San Cristóbal's an early-to-bed town, and conversation in cafés, restaurants or rooms will occupy many of your evenings.

Otherwise, there are regular musical and theatrical performances at the *Casa de Cultura/Bellas Artes* at the corner of Hidalgo and Hermanos Domínguez. *La Galería* and *El Bazar* cafés sometimes have live music in the evenings. *El Paredón d'Scorpio* at Obregón 5, between Insurgentes and Hidalgo, is a bar with live groups, open until midnight. The *Hotel D'Mónica* restaurant at Insurgentes 33 has Latin American music on Friday nights. There are two discos – the *Palace* and the *Princess* – down near the Pan-American Highway (to the left from the bottom of Insurgentes). Entry to either costs US$1.50; Friday, Saturday and Sunday are the busy nights.

Festival dress

Things to Buy

San Cristóbal's market is between Utrilla and Belisario Domínguez, eight blocks north of the zócalo. It has indoor and open-air sections. Many of the traders are Indian villagers, and fresh food is the main stock-in-trade. One local speciality is cream cheese. It functions daily except Sunday, when markets are held in outlying villages.

Chiapas' Indian crafts are justifiably famous and there are now hosts of shops in San Cristóbal selling them. The heaviest concentrations are along Real de Guadalupe (where prices go down as you go away from the zócalo) and Utrilla (towards the market end). Other places to look include the shop beneath La Galería at Hidalgo 3, and the Plaza San Cristóbal on Paniagua between Utrilla and Belisario Domínguez.

Textiles – huipiles, rebozos, blankets – are the outstanding items, for Tzotzil weavers are some of the most skilled and inventive in Mexico. To see the very best and compare the styles of different villages (and get an idea of prices), go to the Sna Jolobil weaving cooperative near Santo Domingo church (see the Sna Jolobil section). Indian women also sell textiles in the plaza around Santo Domingo.

You'll also find some Guatemalan Indian textiles and plenty of the appealing – and inexpensive – pottery from Amatenango del Valle (animals, pots, jugs, etc) in San Cristóbal. Leather is another local speciality.

Always bargain unless prices are labelled (though there's no harm in trying even then), and don't imagine that apparently meek Indians are any softer than anyone else when it comes to haggling.

Getting There & Away

Air San Cristóbal has an airport, south of the Pan-American Highway, but at the time of writing it was out of use as the only local airline, Aero Chiapas, had ceased operations. There are plans, however, to form a pilots' cooperative to start flying charters again to Tuxtla Gutiérrez, Palenque, Yaxchilán, Bonampak, etc. A few charters, which can be booked in San Cristóbal, operate from the airstrips at Comitán and Las Margaritas, 17 km east of Comitán (see the Tours section under Getting Around).

Road San Cristóbal is on Pan-American Highway No 190. South-east by this road it's 86 km to Comitán and 166 km to Ciudad Cuauhtémoc on the Guatemalan border. West, it's 81 km to Tuxtla Gutiérrez. The road to Ocosingo (100 km from San Cristóbal), Agua Azul junction (155 km) and Palenque (210 km) turns north off the Pan-American 12 km south-east of San Cristóbal. It's paved most of the way and in decent shape all the way. For Villahermosa (300 km), you turn north off the Pan-American on to Highway 195, 50 km west of San Cristóbal.

Casa de Huéspedes Margarita has a notice board where long-distance rides are sometimes offered.

Bus First-class buses to and from San Cristóbal aren't as frequent as you might hope; wherever you're coming from or going to, even Oaxaca, book ahead.

In San Cristóbal, Cristóbal Colón (1st class, tel 8-02-91) is at the junction of Insurgentes and the Pan-American Highway. There are 13 services a day to both Comitán (US\$1) and Tuxtla Gutiérrez (US\$1). Other buses go to Ciudad Cuauhtémoc (US\$2) twice daily, and to Arriaga (US\$3), Tonalá (US\$3.25), Tapachula (US\$6, via Arriaga), Villahermosa (US\$4), Juchitán, Acayucan (US\$6.25), Coatzacoalcos (US\$7), Tehuantepec, Oaxaca (US\$7.75), Tuxtepec (US\$8.25), Córdoba (US\$10), Puebla (US\$12.50) and Mexico City (US\$14.25) daily.

Approximate 1st-class journey times: Comitán 1½ hours, Ciudad Cuauhtémoc three hours, Tuxtla Gutiérrez two hours, Villahermosa seven hours, Tapachula (via Arriaga) nine hours, Oaxaca 12 hours, Mexico City 21 hours.

Transportes Tuxtla Gutiérrez (2nd class, tel 8-05-04), on Allende half a block north of the Pan-American Highway, has the only buses to the Agua Azul junction (four km from the falls) and Palenque. There are four of these daily, via Ocosingo, but only the 6 am departure can be booked on the previous day. For all other TTG buses, you can buy tickets half an hour before departure. The five-hour trip to Palenque costs US\$2.50. Don't bother with the service via Villahermosa to Palenque – it's about twice as far. Other TTG buses go to Tuxtla Gutiérrez 24 times daily, Comitán 14 times, Ciudad Cuauhtémoc nine times, Motozintla four times, Arriaga three times, Tonalá and Tapachula once each, Venustiano Carranza twice, plus Yajalón and Comalapa.

For buses to Indian villages in the San Cristóbal area, and other services to Ocosingo, see the Around San Cristóbal section.

If you're heading for Guatemala, leave as early as you can for Ciudad Cuauhtémoc; that gives you a good chance of getting on to a destination inside Guatemala before nightfall.

Buses to Tapachula all take the Tuxtla Gutiérrez-Arriaga route. For the other route, via Ciudad Cuauhtémoc, Motozintla and Huixtla, you have to change buses at least once, probably twice or more, and are unlikely to save time.

Getting Around

For buses to the Indian villages near San Cristóbal, see the Around San Cristóbal section. Taxis are fairly plentiful – one stand is on the north side of the zócalo.

Car Rental Rental cars are in high demand and short supply in San Cristóbal, which means prices are high and waiting lists often long. There's just one agency in town – Budget (tel 8-05-13, 8-06-21) in the Hotel Posada Diego de Mazariegos at the corner of Utrilla and Flores. For a Volkswagen sedan, they charge US\$18.50 a day plus 10c per km. They wanted a deposit of US\$300 when we enquired.

Horses *Casa de Huéspedes Margarita* at Real de Guadalupe 34 offers guided rides to Chamula or the Grutas de San Cristóbal for US\$6 (book the previous day), but it's also possible to hire your own nag for less from the stables used by the Margarita. The stables are somewhere down near the Pan-American Highway at the west end of town. José Hernández (tel 8-10-65) at Elías Calles 10, in the northeast of the town off Huixtla just north of Chiapa de Corzo, also advertises horses for hire.

Tours A few travel agencies in San Cristóbal offer tours to nearby Tzotzil villages or the remote Mayan sites like Yaxchilán and Bonampak. The local village tours don't usually go anywhere you can't reach by ordinary bus, but if you're planning a long or hectic itinerary round several villages, an agency might be able to arrange a special trip. Try Agencia de Viajes las Casas (tel 8-27-27) at Real de Guadalupe or the others mentioned below – though car rental is probably a better bet.

Making your own way to remote, jungle-bound Yaxchilán, Bonampak or Lacandón Indian settlements is an infinitely less practical proposition. There's a frequently impassable road from Palenque to Bonampak – and according to Hilary Bradt and Rob Rachowiecki's guide *Backpacking in Mexico & Central America* you can even take a 10-day walk from Montebello Lakes to this road at certain times of year. However, most people either fly in or take escorted river-road-foot tours.

Both the latter choices can be arranged in San Cristóbal and they're only marginally dearer than from Palenque. Viajes Pakal (tel 8-28-18, 19) at the corner of Hidalgo and Cuauhtémoc, and Amfitriones Turísticos in the Hotel Posada Diego de Mazariegos, both offer the day-trip flight option. Pakal gives you two hours at Yaxchilán and 1½ hours at Bonampak; prices range from US$80 per person, with five in the party, up to US$135 each if there are only two. The flights go from Las Margaritas near Comitán if the San Cristóbal airport is out of action. Amfitriones supposedly gives you 30 minutes less at Bonampak and 30 minutes more at Yaxchilán, for US$97 per head (minimum four people), and its flights go from Comitán. In both cases transport to and from the airfield is included.

Pakal in San Cristóbal also offers a two-day trip starting from Palenque for US$82 per person (five or six people), US$115 each (three or four), US$214 each (one or two). The itinerary: ride from Palenque to the Lacandón settlement of Caribal Lacanjá by car, take a two-hour walk to Bonampak (stay 1½ to two hours), walk back to Caribal Lacanjá and sleep in a Lacandón house. Next morning, travel by car to Frontera Echeverría, then boat along the Usumacinta River to Yaxchilán (stay three hours), and return to Palenque by boat and car.

AROUND SAN CRISTÓBAL

The Tzotzil and Tzeltal Indians of highland Chiapas are among Mexico's most traditional, with some distinctly pre-Hispanic elements in their nominally Catholic religious life, and Spanish very much a second language. Their costume, too, marks them as the inheritors of ancient Mayan traditions (for more on costume see Sna Jolobil in the San Cristóbal section). Their ancestors may have moved to this highland area after the collapse of lowland Mayan civilisation in places like Yaxchilán and Palenque over 1000 years ago.

Today most of these Indians are poor. Many men from San Juan Chamula and Mitontic, for instance, have to spend half the year away from home working on Soconusco coffee plantations. Others leave to work rented land in other lowland areas.

Men hold the community leadership positions, often in the form of traditional 'cargos' or temporary posts which bring prestige but cost a lot, making it very difficult for individuals to accumulate wealth. Senior cargo-holders among the Tzotzil are called *mayordomos* and are responsible for the care of saints' images in the churches. These saints are often identified with pre-Hispanic deities, and their saint's days are marked by important ceremonies. The cargo of an *alférez* (plural *alfereces*) involves organising and paying for these fiestas. Of lower rank are the *capitanes*, whose job is to dance and ride horses at fiestas. *Principales* are men who have carried out important cargos and entered the ranks of 'village elders'.

Women are generally restricted to domestic work, including weaving. In some cases increased sales of textiles have recently enabled them to bring in cash and improve their status.

Very roughly, the Tzotzils occupy an area about 50 km from east to west and 100 km from north to south, with San Cristóbal at its centre. Tzeltal territory is similarly sized and shaped, immediately east of the Tzotzil area. Most of the people live in the hills outside the villages, which are primarily market and ceremonial centres.

In some villages, particularly those nearest San Cristóbal, you may be greeted with wariness or lack of enthusiasm, the result of centuries of Spanish oppression and the desire to preserve traditions from outside interference. Cameras are at best tolerated – sometimes not even that, especially in churches and at festivals. If in any doubt, ask before taking a picture. The tourist office in San Cristóbal displays a sign stating where and when photography is banned. There's a tale that two tourists were killed for taking pictures in the church at Chamula; even if it's not true, it's a warning.

Festivals often give the most interesting insight into Indian life, and there are plenty of them. Apart from fiestas for a village's saints (of which the most important is its patron saint), occasions like Carnival (for which Chamula is famous), Semana Santa, the Day of the Dead (2 November) and the day of the Virgin of Guadalupe (12 December) are celebrated almost everywhere.

You can find basic accommodation in some villages. Market day in most of them is Sunday; proceedings start very early and wind down by lunch time.

Getting There & Away

Road There are paved roads to San Juan Chamula, Zinacantán, and most of the way to Tenejapa. Amatenango del Valle, Huixtán, Oxchuc and Abasolo lie just off main highways. The routes to the following highland villages mentioned involve long stretches of pretty rough dirt track, but buses make it along them and so can a Volkswagen Beetle (slowly).

Bus Always double-check schedules before leaving San Cristóbal. The last buses back to the town often leave surprisingly early.

Buses and colectivos to the villages nearest San Cristóbal leave from Utrilla, a block north of the town's market. They leave for San Juan Chamula and Zinacantán every 20 minutes or so and run up to 5 pm; the cost is 20c. They leave for Tenejapa hourly, take an hour to get there and cost US$0.50. Return services from Tenejapa start getting scarce after 12 noon.

From San Cristóbal to Amatenango del Valle, take a Comitán bus from the Transportes Tuxtla Gutiérrez terminal down near the Pan-American Highway. The fare is US$0.50.

Two other 2nd-class bus companies concentrate on services to Ocosingo and along the rough tracks to the remoter outlying villages. Not surprisingly, their vehicles are even older and less comfortable than TTG's. Transportes Lacandonia (tel 8-14-55) is on the Pan-American Highway in San Cristóbal, between Hidalgo and Crescencio Rosas (that's 1½ blocks west of Cristóbal Colón on the same side of the highway – go through the red gate between two small restaurants). It has about 12 buses daily to Ocosingo (US$0.60), one to Villahermosa, and others to Tila, Yajalón, Tenango, Mesbiljá, Sitalá and Tumbalá.

Transportes Fray Bartolomé de las Casas is on the north side of town. Go along Utrilla past the market and the local village bus terminus, over a small bridge and round a corner. The station's on the right. From here there are buses – slightly more comfortable than Lacandonia's – to Ocosingo (US$0.80) three times daily, San Andrés Larráinzar (US$0.50) and Bochil once at 2 pm (the return bus leaves Bochil at 4 am and San Andrés at 7 am), Chenalhó (US$0.50, 2½ hours) four times, Pantelhó (US$1) three times, Cancuc (US$0.75, five hours) once at 1.30 pm, and others to Yajalón, Oxchuc and Mesbiljá.

A different way of reaching some villages close to San Cristóbal is by horse – see the Getting Around section under San Cristóbal. Or you can walk.

San Juan Chamula

The Chamulans have always defended their independence fiercely: they put up strong resistance to the Spanish in 1524 and launched a famous rebellion in 1869 (see the History section under San Cristóbal). Today they are one of the most numerous of the Tzotzil groups – 40,000-strong – and their village 10 km north-west of San Cristóbal is the centre for some very 'pagan' religious practices. Cameras are forbidden in the church and at festivals.

The centre of the village (usually known just as Chamula) is at the bottom of a hill leading down from the paved road from San Cristóbal. The church stands on the far side of a large plaza. A sign on its door tells visitors to ask at the 'tourist office', also on the plaza, for permission to enter. People stand or kneel on the ground amid thick clouds of incense, sometimes chanting rhythmically, their faces to the floor. Candles, often hundreds of them, seem to burn incessantly. The floor may be carpeted with pine branches, and saints' images are surrounded with mirrors and dressed in sacred garments.

The Chamulans believe that Christ rose from the cross to become the sun. Christian festivals are interwoven with older ones: the pre-Lent Carnival celebrations, which are among the most important and last several days in February or March, also mark the five 'lost' days of the ancient Mayan Long Count calendar, which divided time into 20-day periods (18 of these make 360 days, which leaves five more to complete a full year).

Market day is Sunday. If you get there not long after dawn, you'll see people streaming in from the hills for this most regular Chamulan gathering. There's little of great interest on sale – mostly the locals' basic needs – and not much to do except wander around and imbibe the atmosphere. Apart from Carnival, festivals include ceremonies for San Sebastián (mid-late January); Semana Santa; San Juan, the village's patron saint (22-25 June); and the annual change of cargo (30 December to 1 January).

On some of these occasions a strong alcoholic brew called *posh* is drunk and

you may see groups of men, carrying flags and in ceremonial attire, moving slowly round in tight, chanting circles. At Carnival troops of strolling minstrels wander the roads strumming guitars and wearing sunglasses (even when it's raining) and pointed 'wizard' hats.

More usually, men wear white tunics; those holding cargos have black ones. Chamula women make many of the wool skirts which are used by other villages as well as themselves. The area is also the source of most of San Cristóbal's vegetables.

Zinacantán

This Tzotzil village, centre for the roughly 15,000 Zinacantecos, is 11 km north-west of San Cristóbal. The road to it forks left off the Chamula road, then down into the valley where the village lies. It has two churches. Like the Chamulans, the people here are particularly sensitive about photographs; make sure you ask the village authorities if you want to take any.

The men wear very distinctive red-and-white striped tunics (which appear pink), and flat, round, beribboned palm hats. Unmarried men's hats have longer, wider ribbons. Zinacantán isn't a major market centre like Chamula because the market is usually held only at fiesta times. The most important celebrations are for the patron saint, San Lorenzo, between 8 and 11 August, and for San Sebastián (January).

Zinacantecos have been known as traders since before the Spanish came and today they transport most of the salt consumed in highland Chiapas. They also grow many types of flowers. The geranium is particularly venerated and along with pine branches is offered in rituals to bring a wide range of benefits.

You'll probably notice many crosses dotting the Zinacantán countryside. These usually mark entrances to the abodes of the important ancestor gods or of the Señor de la Tierra (Earth Lord), all of whom have to be kept happy with offerings at the appropriate times.

In addition to the temporary cargo-holders, there are groups of people with more permanent prestige, including the *sacristanes*, who teach the sacred incantations to *mayordomos*, and the *músicos*, who preserve the knowledge of the duties of *alfereces*.

Tenejapa

This is a Tzeltal village 28 km north-east of San Cristóbal, in a pretty valley with a river running through it. There are about 20,000 Tenejapanecos in the surrounding area.

A quite busy market fills the village's main street (round behind the church) early on Sunday mornings. More interesting than what's on sale are the people's costumes, particularly those of the village authorities, who wear wide, colourfully beribboned hats and chains of silver coins round their necks. The women wear brightly brocaded or embroidered huipiles. According to tradition they were taught to brocade by women from Larráinzar and Chenalhó after several Tenejapanecas dreamt that Santa Lucía, the patron saint of weavers, asked them to make her a brocade costume.

At the entrance to the village, just before the church, is a women's weaving cooperative. The range of items on show and sale was disappointingly small when we visited; a sign on the wall attributed this to financial problems arising from a lack of credit and threats by caciques.

Tenejapa has a few comedores in the main street and one basic posada – the *Hotel Molina* – but it's not always open. The main festival is for the village's patron saint, San Ildefonso, on 23 January.

Cancuc, another Tzeltal village, is about 25 km beyond Tenejapa.

Amatenango del Valle

The women of this Tzeltal village, 37 km from San Cristóbal down the Pan-American Highway towards Comitán, are renowned potters. What's different about Amatenango pottery is that it's still fired by the pre-Hispanic method of burning a wood fire around the pieces, rather than putting them in a kiln. In addition to the pots, bowls, urns, jugs and plates that the village has turned out for generations, young girls in the last 15 years or so have made *animalitos* (little animals) which find a ready market with tourists. These are small, appealing and cheap, if fragile. If you visit the village, expect to be surrounded within minutes by girls selling them – and persuade them to bring some better examples, as they'll try to get rid of their worst pieces first. Many of the better ones are sold to shops in San Cristóbal.

Tenejapanecas

Amatenango pottery is made from clay, sand and *bash*, a harder stone-like material, all found locally. These are mixed with water, shaped, dried in the shade, painted, dried again in the sun, fired, and finally covered with *atole*, a maize-based liquid which strengthens the product.

The women wear white huipiles embroidered with red and yellow, wide red belts and blue skirts. Amatenango's patron saint, San Francisco, is fêted on 4 October.

San Andrés Larráinzar

This is a hilltop Tzotzil village, also with a mestizo population, 28 km north-west of San Cristóbal. Sometimes (confusingly) it's called San Andrés Chamula. It's 18 km beyond San Juan Chamula (where the road ceases to be paved and becomes pretty rough in parts). A turn-off uphill to the left, 10 km after San Juan Chamula, leads through some spectacular mountain scenery to San Andrés.

A Sunday market is held in the square in front of the church, and the people seem less reserved towards outsiders than those of San Juan Chamula and Zinacantán. Men wear a red, black and white combination of tunic, long-sleeved shirt and cotton trousers with colourfully ribboned palm hats. Women have white blouses with red and black brocaded patterns, red belts and dark blue wool skirts.

The women of Santa Magdalena (also called Magdalenas), Santa Marta and Santiago – three more villages a few km north of San Andrés – are also known for their brocading. Santa Magdalena's superb ceremonial huipiles are probably the finest of all Chiapas Indian garments. People from these villages attend the San Andrés market.

It's not possible, as far as we could discover, to get to San Andrés and back by bus from San Cristóbal in one day. Local elders didn't offer any helpful suggestions when we asked about accommodation.

But if you're stuck, there's almost sure to be a place.

San Andrés' patron saint's day is 30 November. Carnival celebrations are pretty lively here, too, with plenty of *posh* going down the men's throats. Santa Magdalena's patron saint's day is 22 July.

Mitontic

This is a small Tzotzil village a few hundred metres up to the left off the road to Chenalhó, 23 km beyond San Juan Chamula. There's a picturesque, ruined 16th-century church at one end of the plaza, and a more modern one in use on the left of the plaza.

Cargo-holders can be recognised by their white hats with multicoloured ribbons. The patron saint, San Miguel, is honoured from 5 to 8 May.

San Pedro Chenalhó

This is a Tzotzil village of about 1300 people in a valley with a stream running through it, 37 km north of San Cristóbal. It's the centre for about 14,000 people in the surrounding area. Go to San Juan Chamula and then on up the same road for another 27 km. Chenalhó is 1500 metres high, which means quite a descent from Chamula.

There's a weekly Sunday market and though the bus from San Cristóbal takes about 2½ hours, one of Chenalhó's advantages is that it has at least three accommodation possibilities, making it a good destination if you want more than a day out of San Cristóbal. One is a pink house with green pillars, opposite a green house with pink trimmings, along the street which forks right at the three crosses as you enter the village. The same house also serves meals (eggs, rice and tortillas US$0.75). A second is Señora Consuelo Aguilar Gordillo's house, on the corner of the third street on the left along Avenida Central (the grandly named main street – don't fork right at the three crosses). Señora Gordillo charges about US$1 for a bed.

If neither of these places can take you, look up the friendly priest, Padre Miguel Chanteau, a Frenchman with a St Bernard dog who has been here since 1965. His house is immediately to the right of the church in the main square, and it has a dormitory where he says travellers can stay. If you get the chance to chat with Padre Chanteau, he's a fascinating source of information on the area. As well being the priest, he acts as the village pharmacist, and even brings parties of French schoolchildren over to Chenalhó.

Chenalhó men, if they haven't turned to Western styles, wear black tunics, leather belts, white trousers and sometimes ribboned hats. The main fiestas are for San Pedro (27-30 June), San Sebastián (16-22 January) and Carnival.

It's a further 25 to 30 km up the road to Pantelhó, another Tzotzil village. The turn-off to the left to Chalchihuitán is about one-third of the way to Pantelhó.

Huixtán

This is the centre for the roughly 12,000 local Tzotzils, just to the left of the San Cristóbal-Ocosingo road, 32 km from San Cristóbal and 20 km from the turn-off from the Pan-American Highway. It was one of the main pre-Hispanic Tzotzil centres and has a 16th-century church.

Women wear attractive white shawls with delicate floral patterns. Some men still wear the village's characteristic extremely baggy white trousers, sometimes pulled up to the thighs and tied with a red belt, as well as wool tunics, embroidered cotton shirts and red-banded hats.

A number of mestizos also live in Huixtán. The patron saint is San Miguel Arcángel, whose day is celebrated in late September.

Oxchuc

Here, 20 km beyond Huixtán on the Ocosingo road and 52 km from San Cristóbal, you're in Tzeltal country. The small town, which also has a mestizo population, is dominated by the large colonial church of its patron saint, Santo Tomás.

The local costume leans heavily toward pink and red. Women generally wear very long white huipiles adorned with coloured rectangles and stripes. The men's costume, when they wear it, is a knee-length cotton tunic, with a square of colour on the chest and coloured stripes on the arms. Holes in the armpits enable them to bare their arms and let the sleeves hang loose in hot weather!

Celebrations for Santo Tomás are on 21 December.

Other Villages

Ixtapa, Soyaló and Bochil are Tzotzil centres on Highway 195, which winds northwards to Villahermosa from a junction on the Pan-American Highway 50 km west of San Cristóbal. Beyond Bochil another road branches north-east to El Bosque, Simojovel and Huitiupán, three more remote Tzotzil settlements. It's possible to get a Transportes Fray Bartolomé de las Casas bus cross-country from San Cristóbal to Bochil (five to six hours), which would be an interesting if not-too-comfortable way of starting out for Villahermosa.

Venustiano Carranza, 63 km south of Amatenango del Valle in Chiapas' central valley, is a Tzotzil settlement with some highly individual costumes. Women have extremely colourful embroidered or brocaded skirts and huipiles, while the men's fiesta costume includes baggy 'harem'-type pants brocaded with tiny figures of eight, and colourful cloths wound turban-like round the head. The village is noted for marimba-making. Over the years it has seen more than its fair share of political trouble between Indians and the mestizo authorities, with a number of killings of Indians reported.

Twenty-one km north of Ocosingo on the Palenque road, a road leads off north-west to the remote Tzeltal settlements of

Bachajón, Chilón and Yajalón, and the Chol villages of Tumbalá and Tila.

SAN CRISTÓBAL TO PALENQUE

This 210-km journey – 12 km south-east down the Pan-American Highway from San Cristóbal, then north – is dotted with interesting stopovers. After the Tzotzil and Tzeltal villages of Huixtán and Oxchuc, there's Ocosingo (100 km from San Cristóbal), jumping-off point for the little-known Mayan ruins at Toniná. The turn-off for the superb waterfalls of Agua Azul, four km off the road, is 55 km beyond Ocosingo. Another fine waterfall, Misol-Ha, is two km off the road 36 km after Agua Azul.

Only 2nd-class buses travel the route, taking about five hours from San Cristóbal to Palenque if you don't stop over.

OCOSINGO & TONINÁ

Ocosingo is a small mestizo and Tzeltal valley town on the San Cristóbal-Palenque road, 100 km from San Cristóbal and 110 km from Palenque. It's a friendly, easygoing place but of no particular interest except as an access point for the Mayan ruins of Toniná, 14 km east.

Toniná gets few visitors but that's partly because it's relatively hard to reach. It doesn't compare with Palenque for beauty or importance but it's a sizeable hillside site with some big structures, and fine country roundabout.

Information & Orientation

Ocosingo spreads downhill to the east of the main road. Avenida Central and Avenida 1 Sur run straight down from the main road to the zócalo. Most of the bus stations are on Avenida 1 Norte, parallel to Avenida Central and one block north. Everything is within five minutes' walk of the zócalo. To orient yourself on the zócalo, remember that the church is on the east side and the Hotel Central is on the north side. For the market (open mornings only), go south from the church,

then three blocks along the first street on the left, Avenida 1 Sur. None of the banks in town will change travellers' cheques. Nor, at the time of writing, would the Restaurant La Montura, which apparently used to.

Places to Stay

The Hotel Central on the north side of the zócalo has good clean rooms with fans and private bath for US$3.50 single, US$4 double. The Hotel Margarita (tel 3-00-74, 3-00-48) at Calle Central 6, half a block along the street which leaves the middle of the north side of the zócalo, has quite big rooms (all with private bath, some with fan) but they could be a bit cleaner. Singles are US$4.75, doubles US$6. In a similar price range the Posada Agua Azul at 1 Ote Sur 127, two blocks south of the church, was under reconstruction when we visited, but would be worth checking out. Rooms are medium-sized round a courtyard which has a tiny swimming pool and a few tightly caged creatures including anteaters, hawks and macaws.

At the cheaper end there's the Hospedaje La Palma on the corner of Calle 2 Pte and Avenida 1 Norte, just down the hill from the Transportes Tuxtla Gutiérrez station. It's a basic but clean family-run place, with pleasant flowery courtyard. Singles/doubles are US$0.75/1.50 and bathrooms are communal. The Hospedaje San José is at Calle 1 Ote 6, half a block north of the north-east corner of the zócalo. Rooms are dark and small but it's clean enough. Prices range from US$1 for a single with common bath to US$2.50 for a two-bed room with private bath. Hotel San Jacinto at Avenida Central 13, half a block east of the north-east corner of the zócalo, has singles/doubles for US$1.25/2 with common bath, US$1.75/2.50 with private bath, but it badly needs cleaning and some paint.

Places to Eat

Ocosingo is famous for its queso amarillo (yellow cheese), which comes in three-layered one-kg balls. The two outside layers are like chewy Gruyére, the middle is creamy. If you miss the market, a ball costs US$3.25 at Mini Super Los Portales on the north-east corner of the zócalo.

Restaurant La Montura has a prime location on the north side of the zócalo, with tables on an outside terrace as well as indoors. It has a sizeable menu and is good for breakfast (ham omelette and bolillo US$0.75).

Restaurant/Steakhouse Pesebre's, on the upper floor of the Hotel Margarita at Calle Central 6, offers antojitos for US$0.50 to US$1, beefsteak at US$2 to US$2.50. *Restaurant El Paladino, Steakhouse* at the north-west corner of the zócalo has a long menu and comida corrida for US$1.50. Half a block away from the zócalo on the same street (Avenida Central), the *Restaurant San Cristóbal* also offers a US$1.50 comida corrida. A sample is beefsteak with chips, sopa de arroz, tortillas, frijoles, salad and refresco.

Back on the zócalo there are also the *San Jacinto* and *Los Portales* restaurants.

Getting There & Away

All buses are 2nd class. Transportes Tuxtla Gutiérrez is on Avenida 1 Norte, one block west of the zócalo, one north, then half a block uphill. It has locales to Palenque (US$1.50, 1½ hours), San Cristóbal (US$1.25, 2½ hours) and Tuxtla Gutiérrez (US$2.25, 4½ hours) at 6 am, plus four de pasos to Palenque and seven in the other direction daily, as well as two daily buses to Yajalón.

Transportes Lacandonia (cheaper, older, less comfortable than TTG) is on the same street a little higher up. It has 12 daily buses to San Cristóbal (US$0.75), five to Yajalón, one to Villahermosa (US$3.50, six hours), and others to Tila, Tumbalá and Sitalá.

Transportes Fray Bartolomé de Las Casas (in between the previous two companies for price and comfort) is on the far side of the main road at the top of Avenida 1 Norte. It has five daily departures to San Cristóbal for US$1. Autotransportes Maya, on the main road at the top of Avenida 1 Sur, goes to Palenque (US$1.50) three times daily.

TONINÁ RUINS

Toniná was probably a city-state independent of both Palenque and Yaxchilán, though it declined at the same time as they did, around 800 AD. Dates found at the site range from 500 to 800 AD but, like Palenque and Yaxchilán, it was at its peak in the last 100 years or so of that period. Guillermo Dupaix, Count Waldeck, John L Stephens and Frederick Catherwood all visited Toniná in the first half of the 19th century. Intermittent excavations go on today but a lot remains covered and only limited restoration has been done – which gives the place a 'lost in the jungle' feel compared to more renowned sites.

At the ticket office the keeper may be prepared to go round the site with you and explain it (in Spanish), which would be helpful since there are very few labels. The track goes past the small museum (the keeper will open this for you at the end of your visit), over a stream and up a bank to come out in a flat area, from which rises the terraced hillside that supports the main structures. If you're facing this hillside, behind you in a field are an overgrown outlying pyramid and the main ball court.

The flat area at the foot of the hillside contains a small ball court and fragments of limestone carvings. Some of them appear to show prisoners holding out offerings, with dates and other glyphs on the reverse sides. Three large round stones are probably calendar-related.

The two lowest levels of the terraced hillside have some unremarkable mounds. The most interesting part of the site is at the right-hand end of the third and fourth levels. The stone facing of the wall rising from the third to fourth levels here has a zig-zag x-shape, which may represent Quetzalcóatl and is also flights of steps. To the right of the base of this are the remains of a tomb, with steps leading up to an altar. Behind and above the tomb and altar is a rambling complex of chambers, passageways and stairways, at the third and fourth levels, believed to have been Toniná's administrative centre.

Over towards the centre of the hillside are remains of the central stairway, which went much of the way up the middle of the hillside.

One level higher than the top of the 'Quetzalcóatl' wall you come upon a grave covered in tin sheeting, which you can lift to see the stone coffin beneath. Here were found the bodies of a ruler and two others. To the left on the same level is a shrine to Chac, the rain god. To the right at the foot of a crumbling temple, a carving shows the earth god, labelled *monstruo de la tierra*. Higher again and to the left are two more mounds. Farthest to the left, the pyramid of life and death, may have supported the ruler's dwelling. At the very top of the hill rise two more tall pyramid-temple-mounds.

The unrestored state of the site makes it hard to envisage what most of these structures were like in their heyday, but if you have already visited other Mayan lowland sites like Palenque or Yaxchilán, you can use your imagination to envisage a similar splendour. Many of the stone facings and interior walls were originally covered in plaster, coloured paint or frescoes.

The museum contains many of the better carvings found at the site, including statues, bas-reliefs, altars and calendar stones – all unfortunately unlabelled.

Getting There & Away

The site is 14 km east of Ocosingo along a sometimes rough dirt road. The trip is through pleasant ranch land with lots of colourful birds. In late February and early March 1987, for the first time in living memory, thousands of migrating swallows checked in nightly around 6 pm at a farm on this road – an awesome spectacle, and if they make it a habit, it would be well worth trying to synchronise your visit to Toniná with their arrival.

If you have your own vehicle, follow Calle 1 Ote south from the Ocosingo church. Before long it curves left and you pass a cemetery on the right. At the fork a couple of km further on, go left. At the next fork, the site is signposted to the right. Finally a sign marks the entry track to Toniná at Rancho Guadalupe on the left. From here it's another km to the site itself. Stop at the 'Alto Boleto' sign to pay your 5c entry fee. The house opposite the ticket office sells refrescos. The ruins are open from 9 am to 4 pm daily.

Without your own vehicle, you have the option of a taxi (about US$8 one way), walking, hitching (maybe six vehicles an hour pass Toniná), trying to pick up one of the passenger trucks that head that way, or the buses of Unión de Vehículos de Pasaje y Carga Mixta Ocosingo, which go from Calle 1 Ote, 3½ blocks south of the zócalo. It's hard to establish this company's schedules but it appears to have buses to Guadalupe (near the ruins) at 7.30 am, 11 am and 3 pm. The trip costs US$0.50 and takes about 45 minutes. If you can't get back to Ocosingo before nightfall, the Rancho Guadalupe sometimes puts people up for the night or allows them to camp.

AGUA AZUL

Agua Azul Cascades are among the wonders of Mexico and should not be missed. Just 61 km south of Palenque, scores of dazzling turquoise waterfalls tumble over white limestone surrounded by jungle. Beyond the rapids, numerous pools of tranquil water offer a refreshing respite from the rainforest's sticky humidity.

One place for good, safe swimming is near the restaurant. Use your judgement and avoid the more rapid areas of the waterfalls. Crosses set in the upper part of the cascades show where the unlucky met their end. During the height of the rainy season, the once brilliant blue waters can turn brackish with brown silt.

A trail above the falls takes you over some swaying, less-than-stable foot bridges and up through jungle. Women trekking here should consider taking a male companion. An experienced female traveller reported that she was attacked above the falls, escaping only through a strategically aimed kick to the groin. When she reported the assault to the local authorities, they said they knew the man and that he had jumped tourists before. They did nothing about it, implying that she was to blame for being out on her own in the bush.

Places to Stay

Unless you have a tent or hammock, Agua Azul is likely to be a day trip. There are a few filthy, spartan wooden rooms in a shack where you're provided with a blanket and nothing else for the outlandish sum of US$3.50. You'd do better to string a hammock outside the shack for US$0.35; or you could rent a hammock from the proprietor for US$1 per night. Those with tents are charged US$0.35 per night.

Whether you have come here for the day or are overnighting, watch your gear – several travellers reported rip-offs at Agua Azul. The gatekeeper will try to overcharge the government admission fee. Right now it's 20c per person, US$0.50 per vehicle. Stand firm with the current price and he isn't likely to persist.

Places to Eat

There is a small restaurant here, but the food is overpriced and pretty awful. You are much better off packing a picnic from Palenque.

Getting There & Away

It's 155 km, about 3½ hours by bus, from San Cristóbal to the Agua Azul turn-off. From Palenque village it's 55 km. There are two means of public transport to the falls and each has its drawbacks.

For US$4, colectivo vans leave the same Palenque colectivo station that runs tourists to the ruins. The colectivos depart at 9.30 am daily, make a 15-minute stop at Misol-Ha and then move on to Agua Azul, where you stay 90 minutes to two hours. The colectivos have you back in Palenque town between 2.30 and 3 pm. If you want to stay longer, you can try to hitch-hike back.

You could also catch a southbound bus originating from Palenque to a stop four km from the falls. Or you can hop the San Cristóbal-Ocosingo bus headed for Palenque. The bus will drop you at the *crucero* (cross) where the highway intersects with a dirt road running to Agua Azul.

Although the walk down isn't so bad, the steep walk back up is a killer in the heat. When you arrive back at the *crucero* to catch a bus bound for either Palenque, San Cristóbal or terminating at Ocosingo, you will most likely have to stand as all seats are generally filled when the bus reaches your crossroads. Some travellers have hitched from the *crucero*, but don't count on this.

Your best means of spending several hours at Agua Azul is to catch a ride with a private car. Ask fellow travellers at La Cañada's Restaurant on the outskirts of Palenque or the Maya Restaurant near the zócalo if you can share a ride and petrol expenses. For those who don't wish to spend much time at Agua Azul, the colectivo is a much better choice than the bus.

MISOL-HA CASCADES

About 22 km from Palenque, a waterfall rushes nearly 35 metres into a pool safe for swimming. The cascades and jungle surroundings are spectacular enough to be the setting for an Arnold Schwarzenegger epic. Although there are no campgrounds here, an adequate restaurant is open sporadically.

Getting There & Away

The colectivo from Palenque (see Getting

There under Agua Azul) stops here briefly. Buses bound south for Ocosingo and San Cristóbal, and those headed north to Palenque, will stop at a dirt crossroads from where you walk about two km to the falls.

PALENQUE RUINS

Surrounded by emerald jungles, Palenque is justifiably the favourite site of antiquities for budget travellers. Although not as expansive or massive as Chichén Itzá and Uxmal, Palenque's architecture is exquisite and its stucco figures of royalty and prominent priests are superb.

Using a mixture derived from tree and clay bark to make the stucco dry more slowly, Mayan sculptors were able to create intricate details. Archaeologists and artists alike say that the carved stonework of Palenque's ruins stands unparalleled among Mayan sites in Mexico. Everything you see was achieved without metal tools, pack animals or the wheel.

History

Today, one can see the influence of Palenque's architecture in the ruins of the Mayan city of Tikal in Guatemala's Petén region and in the pyramids of Comalcalco (near Villahermosa). Interestingly, while evidence from pottery fragments indicates that Palenque was occupied over 1500 years ago, it only reached its height of development for about 200 years, from 600 to 800 AD. But what a glorious two centuries!

Palenque first rose to prominence under Pakal, a club-footed king who reigned from 615 to 683. Archaeologists have determined that Pakal is represented by hieroglyphics of sun and shield. From these they deduced that Pakal lived to a ripe old age, possibly 80 to 100 years.

During Pakal's reign, many plazas and buildings, including the superlative Temple of the Inscriptions, were constructed within the 20 square km of the city. The structures were replete with delicately sloping roofs and stucco sculptures. Hieroglyphic texts at Palenque state that Pakal's reign was predicted thousands of years prior to his ascension and would be celebrated far into the future. Pakal was succeeded by his son Chan-Balum, symbolised in hieroglyphics by the jaguar and the serpent.

Chan-Balum continued Palenque's political and economic expansion as well as development of its art and architecture. He completed his father's crypt in the Temple of the Inscriptions and presided over the construction of the Plaza of the Sun temples, placing sizeable narrative stone stelae within each.

Not long after Chan-Balum's death, Palenque started on a precipitous decline. Whether this was due to ecological catastrophe, civil strife or barbarian invasion is disputed, but after the 10th century Palenque was largely abandoned. Situated in an area receiving the heaviest rainfall in Mexico, the ruins were overgrown with vegetation and lay undiscovered until the latter half of the 18th century.

Rediscovery of Palenque It is said that Hernán Cortés came within 40 km of the ruins without any awareness of it. In 1773, Mayan hunters told a Spanish priest that stone palaces lay in the jungle. Father Ordonñez y Aguiar led an expedition to Palenque and wrote a book claiming that the city was the capital of an Atlantis-like civilisation.

An expedition led by Captain Antonio del Río set out in 1786 to explore Palenque. Not just content to report his findings, del Río destroyed some of the ruins. Although his report was lost in Madrid's tangled archives, a copy of it was acquired by a British resident of Guatemala who was sufficiently intrigued to have it published in England. This led a host of adventurers to brave malaria in their search for the hidden city.

Among the most colourful of these adventurers was the eccentric Count de

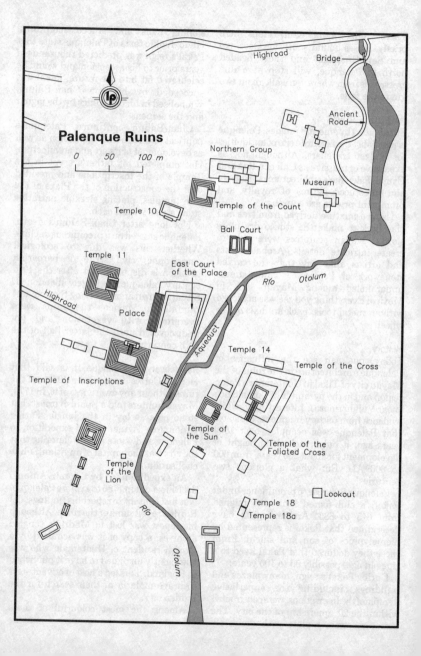

Palenque Ruins

0   50   100 m

Highroad

Bridge

Ancient Road

Northern Group

Museum

Temple of the Count

Temple 10

Ball Court

Temple 11

East Court of the Palace

Río Otolum

Highroad

Palace

Aqueduct

Temple of Inscriptions

Temple 14

Temple of the Cross

Temple of the Sun

Temple of the Foliated Cross

Temple of the Lion

Río Otolum

Lookout

Temple 18
Temple 18a

Waldeck who, in his 60s, lived atop one of the pyramids for two years (1831-1833). He wrote a book complete with fraudulent drawings which made the city resemble great Mediterranean civilisations, causing all the more interest in Palenque. In Europe, Palenque's fame grew and it was mythologised as a lost Atlantis or extension of ancient Egypt.

Finally, in 1837 a man of integrity and archaeological knowledge, the American John L Stephens, reached Palenque with an artist named Frederick Catherwood. Stephens wrote insightfully about the six pyramids he started to excavate and the city's aqueduct system. His was the first truly scientific investigation and paved the way for research by other serious scholars.

Exploring the Ruins

Today, only 34 of Palenque's nearly 500 buildings have been excavated. As you explore the ruins, try to picture the grey edifices as bright red; at the peak of Palenque's power, the entire city was painted vermilion. One of the prime times to visit the site is just after it opens (Palenque's hours are 8 am to 5 pm, admission 10c) when the fog rises from the jungle's floor to ensnare Palenque in a mysterious mist.

Temple of Inscriptions

The magnificent pyramid you will see on the right after you enter is the tallest and most prominent of Palenque's buildings. Constructed on eight levels, it has a central staircase rising some 23 metres to a temple which crowns the structure. On the temple's rear wall are glyphs recounting its history. From these it appears that the edifice was either completed or dedicated in 692 AD.

Ascend the steep 69 steps to the top, both for a magnificent vista of Palenque and surrounding jungle and for access to stairs down to the tomb of Pakal. This crypt lay undiscovered until 1952 when the archaeologist Alberto Ruz, who had

been excavating the staircase, found a sealed stone passageway upon which were seated several skeletons. These victims of religious sacrifice were intended to serve Pakal in death and were buried with clay pots, jewellery and tools for his journey to the next world.

Although Pakal's jewel-decked skeleton and jade mosaic death mask were taken to Mexico City and the tomb re-created in the Museum of Anthropology, the stone sarcophagus lid remains here. The death mask was stolen from the museum in 1985. The carved stone slab protecting the sarcophagus includes the image of Pakal encircled by serpents, mythical monsters, the sun god and glyphs recounting Pakal's reign. Carved on the wall are the nine lords of the underworld. Between the crypt and the staircase, a snake-like hollow tube theoretically connected Pakal to the realm of the living.

Although this was the sole crypt found in Mayan pyramids, it gave rise to wild speculation linking the Mayas with Egypt. However, the theory that this crypt is an exception and that pyramids were built in Mesoamerica to bring the priests closer to heavenly bodies still holds sway among most archaeologists. The crypt remains, to date, unique in Mayan ruins.

The steep staircase leading to the crypt is open only from 10 am to 12 noon and 2 to 4 pm. These hours have been altered over the years so check them upon your arrival. If you're tired, there is a path from the temple at the top of the pyramid to the forested hillside behind. You can reach the Temple of the Foliated Cross from this path.

The Palace

Diagonally opposite the Temple of Inscriptions, lying in the centre of Palenque's plaza, is the Palace, an important block of buildings linked by a maze of open-air patios and underground corridors. If you walk up to what is believed to be an astronomical observatory (restored in 1955), you will see fine stucco reliefs on the walls. On the northern interior wall are imposing monster masks. Contemporary archaeologists and astronomers believe that the tower was constructed so that the Mayan royalty and priest class could observe the sun falling directly into the Temple of the Inscriptions during the 22 December winter solstice. Some archaeologists believe that like the sun, Pakal was deified and the Mayas thought he would also rise again.

Within the tower's courtyard, you will see a singular well-preserved stone known as the Oval Tablet. Engraved on it is Pakal's mother, Zac-Kuk, handing her son the ceremonial headdress of ruler. She ruled for three years until Pakal was sufficiently mature at 12½ to take over.

On the northern (left) section of the palace are some interesting carved stucco figures, on the piers facing the stairs. They apparently depict war; one warrior brandishes an axe over the head of his victim. Within the courtyard, nine substantial stone figures are shown kneeling, possibly awaiting sacrifice or rendering tribute. Another theory suggests that they represent the nine gods of the night.

There is much to explore in the subterranean passageways and courtyards of the palace. In the eastern patio stand three-metre-tall statues of warriors thought to be worshipping a god. At the base of the tower are thought to have been steam baths and toilet drains. The subterranean tunnels harbour stucco carvings best appreciated if you bring a flashlight (torch).

Temples of the Cross

Although Pakal had only the Temple of the Inscriptions dedicated to him during his 70-year reign, Chan-Balum had three buildings dedicated to him, known today as the Temples of the Cross. If you follow the path leading between the palace and the Temple of Inscriptions, you will come first to the Temple of the Sun. It contains

narrative blocks dating from 642, replete with scenes of offerings to Pakal, the sun-shield king. The Temple of the Sun has the best preserved roofcomb of all the buildings at Palenque. The smaller, less well-preserved Temple XIV next door also has tablets showing ritual offerings – a scene commonplace in Palenque. Here a woman makes an offering to a 'dancing man' believed to be Chan-Balum.

Keep following the path and you will come to the largest of the buildings in this group, the Temple of the Cross. Inside are sculpted narrative stones (some tablets have been taken from this relatively poorly preserved temple to the National Museum of Anthropology). One archaeologist suggests that Chan-Balum may be buried under this temple, as the symbolism all over it is similar to that on the sarcophagus lid of Pakal. One particularly fine stucco carving shows a priest smoking a sacred pipe.

To the right of the Temple of the Sun, seemingly cut out from the jungled hillside, sits the Temple of the Foliated Cross. Here, the deterioration of the façade lets you appreciate the architectural composition, with arches fully exposed. A well-preserved tablet carving shows a king with a sun-shield (most likely Pakal) emblazoned on his chest, corn growing from his shoulder blades and the sacred quetzal bird atop his head. One interpretation of this tablet is the Mayan reverence for the life force of the god of maize. The symbol of the sacred ceiba tree's branched cross reflects the Mayan sense of the intersection of the heavens and the underworld to produce life as they know it. Little wonder the Mayas were so vulnerable to the teachings of Christianity with its prominent symbol of the cross.

Other Ruins & Museum

Heading north from the Temple of the Inscriptions, you may make out what used to be a ball court to the north of the palace. Across from it stands the Northern Group of poorly preserved temples. The crazy old

Count de Waldeck who studied the ruins from 1831 to 1833 lived atop one of these – hence its name, Temple of the Count. It is one of Palenque's oldest trademark slope-roofed buildings, constructed in 647 under Pakal.

Just beyond the Northern Group to the east lies Palenque's small museum. While there are some interesting artefacts housed here, there are no descriptions. The museum is open from 10 am to 1 pm and 3 to 5 pm. There is an admission charge of 10c.

Jungle Walks

You can hike on jungle paths just outside the ruins; perhaps you'll encounter the howler monkeys often heard roaring in trees overhead. It's best to bring mosquito repellent for any jungle trek. A short walk on a path just down from the museum brings you to waterfalls known as the Queen's Bath. Although you are not supposed to swim here, many travellers beat the heat with the falls' refreshing shower.

PALENQUE
Orientation

Most travellers visiting Palenque stay in the nearby town of Santo Domingo. So prominent are the ruins in the town's economic scheme of things that these days even locals call Santo Domingo 'Palenque'.

The town is small both in population (about 25,000) and area. It is easy to walk around the town and all hotels recommended are within 10 minutes' walk of either bus station. If you come here by train it will be necessary to take a taxi into town at about US$2. The taxi tariff from the zócalo to the restaurants near the Mayan statue on the outskirts of town is roughly US$1.

Information
Tourist Office Located just off the zócalo in part of the Palacio Municipal, the tourist office has English-speaking staff but no adequate map of either the ruins or the town. The office is open Monday to Saturday 8 am to 2 pm and 5 to 8 pm, Sunday 9 am to 12 noon.

Money There is a Bancomer three blocks west of the zócalo on Juárez which changes money between 10 and 11.30 am Monday to Friday. A Bánamex four blocks west of the zócalo changes money from 10.30 am to 12 noon Monday to Friday. The town's hotels and better restaurants will also change money, though at less favourable rates.

Australians have a favourite ditty about the horrors of a 'pub with no beer', but Palenque was the first place I came across a 'bank with no money'. I stood in the line of gringos for about 20 minutes before the news filtered back from the front of the line that the money had run out. There was a quick exodus to the other bank only to discover that the money shortage was catching. Enquiries revealed that more money was on its way from Villahermosa and should be there within the hour. Some nervous hopping from bank to bank followed as rumours bounced back and forth about where the ready would be delivered first. Finally the truck rolled up at bank number one, followed by a mob of cash-short gringos, only for another half hour to pass while the loot was carefully counted. We got our pesos in the end but it was a uniquely Mexican experience.

– Tony Wheeler

Post The town's post office is just off the zócalo on the left side of the Palacio Municipal. It's open Monday to Friday 8 am to 1.30 pm and 4 to 6 pm, Saturday 8 am to 12 noon.

Places to Stay – bottom end

Although there is some budget to moderate accommodation close to the ruins, staying near or in the town is recommended for access to restaurants and entertainment. Generally speaking, the town's hotels are cheaper and it is easy to catch the frequent colectivos for the short hop to the ruins.

Almost always full is the *Hotel La Croix* (tel 5-00-14) at Hidalgo 10. Its location is

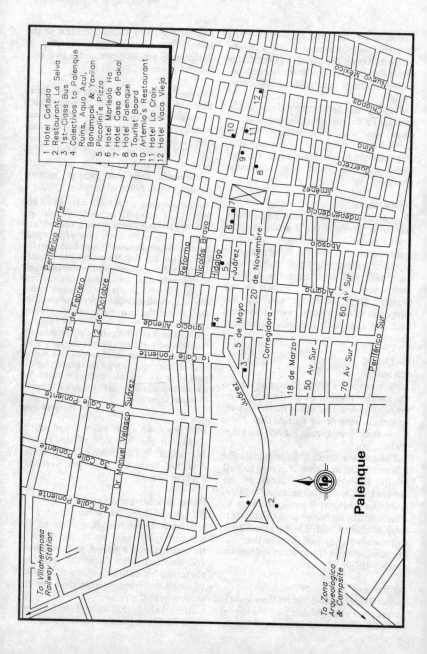

1 Hotel Cañada
2 Restaurant La Selva
3 1st-Class Bus
4 Colectivos to Palenque Ruins, Aqua Azul, Bonampak & Yaxilan
5 Piccolini's Pizza
6 Hotel Marisolo Ha
7 Hotel Casa de Pakal
8 Hotel Palenque
9 Tourist Board
10 Artemio's Restaurant
11 Hotel La Croix
12 Hotel Vaca Vieja

Palenque

To Villahermosa Railway Station

To Zona Arqueologico & Campsite

both a blessing and a curse. Conveniently situated on the left side of the zócalo opposite the church, La Croix has ground-floor rooms facing the zócalo. It can be a bit noisy but with its pretty interior plaza, potted tropical plants and adequate rooms with fan and bath, La Croix's prices are right. Singles and doubles are a mere US$5.

Just opposite the 2nd-class bus station, the *Hotel Avenida* (tel 5-01-16) at Juárez 183 lets you hear every bloody unmuffled bus. In addition to lack of sleep, you may have to contend with broken bathroom fixtures. A single with bath costs US$5.75, a double US$6.75. The *Hotel Regional* on Juárez at Aldama, between the bus station and the zócalo, may seem to be a good deal; singles with bath are US$4, doubles US$5, but the rooms are less than clean and the toilets don't always work.

Camping Campers and mushroom lovers can string a hammock or pitch a tent at the *Mayaber* or *María del Mar* trailer parks for about US$1.50. The María del Mar, about three km from the ruins, appears slightly better maintained than the Mayaber, which is two km from the ruins. Both have shower and toilet facilities. Watch your gear around here. If you want to find 'shrooms to sample, it's best to ask gringo hippies rather than a local, who can reap a reward for turning you in to the authorities.

Places to Stay - middle
The top moderate choice is just out of town, a 10 to 15-minute walk from the zócalo. *Hotel La Cañada* (tel 5-01-02) is worth the walk and in reality is nearly as close to the colectivo station for the ruins and the bus depots as the hotels near the zócalo. To reach La Cañada, walk on the main street away from the zócalo. Pass the 2nd-class bus station and keep going until you are on the outskirts of town where the road forks at the ugly Mayan statue. Take the right fork and you will see a sign for the hotel situated to the right on a dirt road.

La Cañada has a pleasant tropical environment and consists of cottages surrounded by jungle. Most of the cottages are air-conditioned and all come with baths; they cost US$10.25 single and are well worth the US$12.50 for a double. La Cañada has a good, romantic outdoor bamboo restaurant and you are also close to the superb La Selva Restaurant.

If you wish to spend less and stay closer to the zócalo, an excellent choice is the *Vaca Vieja* (tel 5-03-77). Located a short three-minute walk beyond the zócalo, this well-maintained hotel has pleasant rooms with fan and tiled bathrooms priced at US$7 single, US$9.50 double. The origin of its curious name: the proprietor used the proceeds from the sale of his cattle herd to fund the construction of the hotel. To reach the Vaca Vieja, face the zócalo with your back to the town, walk to the right through the zócalo and pass the big Hotel Palenque. After a couple of blocks you will see the hotel on the left at Avenida 5 de Mayo 42 (at the intersection of Calle de Chiapas).

In town on the main street – Avenida Juárez – just before you reach the zócalo is the basic but clean *Misol-Ha* (tel 5-00-92). Another good budget choice, the Misol-Ha has decently maintained rooms with fan and bath. The proprietor says that if you show him the listing of his hotel in this book, he will reduce the price from US$9.25 to US$6.75 for a single and from US$10 to US$7.75 for a double.

Those wishing to stay on the zócalo and spend more for the luxury of a swimming pool might consider the *Hotel Palenque* (tel 5-01-88) at 5 de Mayo 15. Some rooms of this old hotel which once had luxury status are well refurbished, while others leave something to be desired. See your room before you register and if it is not to your liking, ask to look at another. Singles with fan and bath cost US$8.50, doubles US$10.50. Air-conditioning is about US$2 extra.

The *Hotel Casa de Pakal* near the zócalo on Avenida Juárez has air-conditioning.

When I stayed there the toilet wouldn't flush and little effort was made to fix it. Singles with air-conditioning, TV and bath cost US$10, doubles US$12.50.

If you want to stay closer to the ruins, consider *Hotel de las Ruinas* (tel 5-03-52) about 1.5 km from the site. The hotel is clean, and the rather damp and very threadbare rooms are built around a pleasant swimming pool. Rooms with fan and bathroom cost around US$12 but unfortunately the proprietor is far from friendly.

Places to Stay – top end

The *Hotel Chan-Kah* (tel 5-00-43), three km from the ruins, offers attractive sizeable cabins of stone and wood which include pleasant porches fronting on the jungle. There is a good restaurant on the premises. Fan-cooled cabins cost US$25 to US$40.

A few km south of the town on the road to San Cristóbal is the *Hotel Nututum* (tel 4-01-00), in a jungle setting. The major attraction is swimming in the adjacent Río Usumacinta. Large, air-conditioned rooms cost US$16 to US$20 single, US$24 to US$30 double. The food is good if a mite overpriced – but if you can afford to stay here, you can afford to eat here.

Places to Eat

The town's two best restaurants are 10 to 15 minutes' walk from the zócalo. Follow the main street, Avenida Juárez, away from the zócalo until you come to the Mayan statue (about three minutes from the 2nd-class bus station). The left fork will soon bring you to *La Selva*. Beneath its elegant thatched roof, La Selva's pleasant waiters serve some superb Chiapan chicken, beef and pork dishes at moderate (US$2 to US$5) prices. Take a break from beer and try one of the decent local wines (US$5 to US$7) which La Selva stocks. Excellent Chiapan musicians occasionally play here.

Take the right fork at the statue and turn right down a dirt road where you will see the sign for *Hotel La Cañada*. Here in a jungle setting is the hotel's thatch-roofed restaurant, where grilled meats are the speciality. The restaurant seems to attract travellers interested in archaeology, who stay long into the evening discussing the ruins over drinks poured generously by the bar.

In town, just off the zócalo, the *Restaurant Maya* is a real meeting place for travellers. The food is *típico*, the prices a trifle high, but the good company brings many budget overlanders back. Since the portions are skimpy, the comida corrida is a better deal. *Artemio's Restaurant*, near Hotel La Croix on the left side of the zócalo, is less popular, but has better food and portions for the money than the Maya.

The Hotel Vaca Vieja's little *Restaurant Yunuen*, roughly three blocks behind the right side of the zócalo on 5 de Mayo at Chiapas, has good breakfasts and reasonably priced *típico* meals. The Hotel Casa de Pakal's *Restaurant Castellano* also serves OK and moderately priced food. For delicious though not-cheap pizza, walk a short distance down Juárez from the zócalo to *Piccolini's Pizza* – surprisingly good.

If you're hungry at the ruins the small *Shaman-Ek* restaurant by the colectivo stop is OK for a sandwich or a drink.

Entertainment

Entertainment consists of the wonderful noises of the jungle and socialising at restaurants with fellow travellers – particularly *La Cañada* and *Maya's*. There's also a disco near La Cañada. *La Selva Restaurant* frequently entertains its diners with Chiapan folk musicians.

Things to Buy

Lacandonian Indians in traditional garb usually sell arrows at the ruins. In town, there are inferior, over-priced Indian crafts – wait to buy them in San Cristóbal.

Getting There & Away

Air There are no regular flights into Palenque's small airport, but you can fly to Villahermosa from Mérida and other centres and travel from there by land.

Bus It's not a good idea to take the train between Palenque and the Yucatán. There are no *dormitorios* to lock on board, and a couple of notorious *bandido* outfits operate between Palenque and Mérida. So take the bus – it's quicker and you are not as likely to lose your gear. Only 2nd-class buses run between Palenque and Mérida (once a day as of this writing), but if you buy your ticket a day in advance, you will be certain of a seat and the bus is reasonably comfortable. While there has been less thievery on the bus than on the train, some travellers have reported goods stolen. Don't leave anything of value in the overhead rack, and stay alert.

To be sure of a seat between Palenque and San Cristóbal, buy your 2nd-class ticket (there is also no 1st class on this route) a day in advance. It's about five hours by bus between San Cristóbal de Las Casas and Palenque (Transportes Tuxtla Gutiérrez, 2nd class, four times daily, US$2.50).

From Villahermosa, there are three 1st-class departures. Again, try to buy your ticket in advance as 1st class also fills up. From Agua Azul to Palenque, you probably have to stand because the buses are usually full when they reach the crossroads.

Returning from Palenque, you can get to Tuxtla Gutiérrez either via San Cristóbal (2nd class only) or Villahermosa (1st class).

Conveniently, both 2nd and 1st-class bus stations – within a few blocks of one another – have baggage checks where you can keep your luggage while scouting for a hotel or waiting for a bus.

Getting Around

All of the hotels listed in town are within two to 10 minutes' walk of both bus stations. The train station is north of the town and a taxi is generally necessary.

The town is quite small and you should be able to get about on foot. If you wish to take a taxi between the zócalo area and the restaurants near the Mayan statue at the fork on the outskirts of town, it should not cost much more than US$1.

The best way to get to the ruins is via the colectivo vans which run regularly from the colectivo station a few blocks from the zócalo. To find the station, turn right off Avenida Juárez at Calle Allende, and walk about a block to where it intersects with Hidalgo. The price is about 25c and the ride takes 10 to 15 minutes. The colectivos will pick up and drop off passengers at any point along their route between the ruins and Palenque. The same colectivo station is the departure site for vans running daily to Agua Azul at 9.30 am. They will also stop at the Misol-Ha waterfalls and bring you back to Palenque at about 3 pm.

NAJA & LACANJA

Truck-buses run sporadically from Palenque to Lacandonian towns on the periphery of the rainforest. Because they may not run every day, be prepared to bring either a tent or a hammock to string in a local's house after paying the owner. Mosquito repellent is essential.

Visitors searching for 'pure' Lacandonian culture may be disappointed here. The influence of the outside world is substantial and while some locals still wear a vestige of traditional dress, Hispanic clothing is the norm and a focus on things material a growing obsession. Christianity is supplanting animist beliefs, although they still prevail beneath the surface.

RÍO USUMACINTA

The magnificent Río Usumacinta divides Mexico from Guatemala. Here you'll see spectacular rainforests on either bank and beautiful bird life. Some adventurous though possibly ill-informed travellers make the journey between the two countries by boat along the San Pedro River, a tributary of the Usumacinta which flows into it north of Tenosique. However as of this writing, guerrilla activity and the Guatemalan military's response to it makes such a venture very risky. Some travellers are said to have simply 'disappeared'.

The situation could change, making this a fascinating way to cross the border. Be certain to ask your consulate first what the present story is – US consulates are particularly well informed on such matters. For full details of the river route to Guatemala, see the section on Tenosique, Tabasco.

BONAMPAK & YAXCHILÁN RUINS

For the adventurous, the ruins of Bonampak – famous for its frescoes – and the great ancient city of Yaxchilán may be visited from Palenque via two-day camping ventures or by chartering an aircraft from either Palenque, San Cristóbal or the Tabasco town of Tenosique.

Don't be worried if you are disappointed by Bonampak. Yaxchilán will more than reward you, and the 10-km hike through the jungle to Bonampak will in itself be satisfying.

Information

Some things to consider if you visit these ruins: Bonampak and Yaxchilán have neither food nor water, so make certain you are well supplied. It's buggy in these parts – bring insect repellent. Don't leave your gear unattended, as thefts have been reported on previous trips. Finally, carry a flashlight (torch) to better see dark parts of the ruins and for any camping emergencies.

Bonampak

Lying about 155 km south-east of Palenque near the Guatemalan frontier, Bonampak was hidden from the outside world by dense jungle until 1946. A young WW II conscientious objector named Charles Frey fled the draft and somehow wound

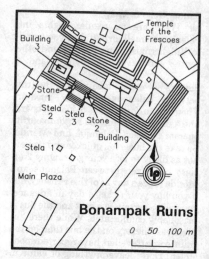

Bonampak Ruins

0   50   100 m

up in the Lacandonian rainforest. There he was virtually adopted by local Indians and shown what the Indians told him was a sacred site of their ancestors. Impressed by what he saw, Frey enthusiastically revealed his findings to Mexican officials and archaeological expeditions were mounted. Frey died in 1949 trying to save an expedition member from drowning in the turbulent Usumacinta River.

The ruins of Bonampak lie around a rectangular plaza. Only the southern edifices of the plaza are preserved; the rest is little more than heaps of stone. It was the frescoes of a temple in the Southern Group, today designated Building 1, that excited Frey and the archaeologists who followed. They saw three rooms covered with paintings depicting ancient Mayan ways. Painted in profile are warriors decked with quetzal feathers, kings and royal families, priests, shamans, dancers, musicians and war captives. The details of costumes themselves reveal much about Mayan life, and the murals are complete with glyphs.

The murals' original colours were brown, green and vermilion, with the

Top: Tziscao Village, Lagos de Montebello (JN)
Left: Hotel Ciudad Real, San Cristóbal de las Casas (TW)
Right: Popcorn Stall (TW)

Top: The Palace, Palenque (JL)
Bottom: Temple of the Inscriptions, Palenque (TW)

figures outlined in black. Unfortunately, the 12 centuries of weather deterioration were accelerated when the first expedition attempted to clean the murals with kerosene. On the plus side, some restoration has been undertaken and you can see recent duplications reproduced from the original murals. Generally the murals are so difficult to decipher that you may wonder what all the fuss was about. If you look closely (or view the reproductions), though, you may think you are looking at portraits from ancient Egypt, despite the fact that no evidence links this part of the New World with Egypt.

Some of the murals depict the victory of the Mayas over the Olmecs. One panel shows dancing at a celebration, another prisoners waiting to be sacrificed, and a third the giving of thanks to the gods for victory. To best see what these faded frescoes originally looked like, check the Bonampak reproduction in the National Museum of Anthropology in Mexico City. There's another reproduction at the CICOM Museum in Villahermosa, and Tuxtla Gutiérrez's Hotel Bonampak has a full reproduction of the central room's mural in its lobby.

Other than some narrative stelae at the foot of the hill leading to Building 1, the Temple of the Frescoes, the eight other buildings of the Southern Group are not in sufficient repair to warrant noting.

Yaxchilán

When you reach Yaxchilán (by boat on the Río Usumacinta if you have not chartered a flight), you will be fully rewarded for the rigours of your journey. Set above the jungled banks of the Usumacinta, Yaxchilán was first inhabited about 200 AD. However, the edifices that have been excavated have glyphs dated 514 to 807. Although not as well restored as Palenque, the ruins of Yaxchilán are larger, and who knows what further excavation will yield?

Unfortunately, the Mexican government is still considering a dam over the Río Usumacinta which would flood both Yaxchilán and some Guatemalan ruins. Fought by anthropologist Trudy Blom (see the section on Na-Bolom under San Cristóbal) along with archaeologists and environmentalists worldwide, plans to construct the dam have at this writing been temporarily halted. Only continued international pressure will keep the dam from being erected. So if you are awed by what you see here, write the Mexican government to express your opposition to the dam.

Yaxchilán rose to the peak of its prominence in the 8th century under a king whom the glyphs call Escudo Jaguar, or 'Shield Jaguar'. His carvings in the form of the great jungle cat appear on many of the site's buildings and stelae. The city's power expanded under Escudo Jaguar's son, Pájaro Jaguar, or 'Bird Jaguar' (752-770). His glyph consists of a small jungle cat with a bird superimposed on his head and feathers on his back.

Built with a still beautiful roofcomb, Building 33 on the south-western side of the plaza has some fine religious carvings over the northern doorways. At the front base of the temple are narrative carvings of a ball game.

The central plaza holds statues of crocodiles and jaguars. Building 20 has the strange lintel of a dead man's spirit emerging from the mouth of a man discussing him, and stelae of Mayas making offerings to the gods. In front of Building 20 are exceptional stelae of Mayan royalty.

Be certain to walk to Yaxchilán's highest temples, which due to the encroachment of the jungle are not visible from the plaza. Building 41 is the tallest of these and if you climb it you will be able to appreciate just how expansive Yaxchilán is. The view from the top is one of the highlights of the visit. Some tour guides do not want to make the effort to show you Building 41 – insist on it!

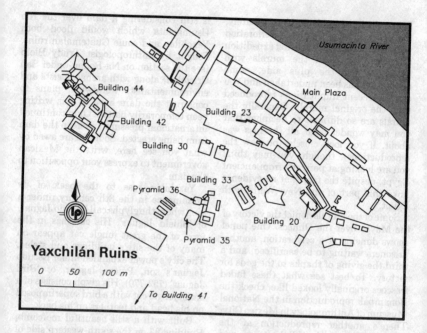

Yaxchilán Ruins

0   50   100 m

To Building 41

Getting There & Away

Air Those in a hurry and with lots of money might consider chartering a four-seater aircraft to Bonampak and Yaxchilán from either Palenque, San Cristóbal or the Tabasco town of Tenosique. Negotiate with your pilot for more time than he says he will allot, especially in Yaxchilán.

In San Cristóbal de Las Casas, flights and tours to Yaxchilán and Bonampak can be arranged through Viajes Pakal (tel 8-28-18, 19) at the corner of Hidalgo and Cuauhtémoc, or Amfitriones Turísticos in the Hotel Posada Diego de Mazariegos. The flight option, with a scheduled total of 3½ hours at the two sites, costs from US$80 per person with five in the party up to US$135 each if there are only two. The flights go from Comitán or Las Margaritas (near Comitán) if San Cristóbal airport is out of action; transport to and from the airstrip is included.

Contrary to rumour, it is not worthwhile

to bus over to the Tabascan backwater, Tenosique, to catch a cheaper flight, as the savings are not all that substantial. No matter where the flight originates, try to bargain down the air fare.

Road Despite what you may hear, it is possible to drive to Bonampak and the trip doesn't even require four-wheel drive – although the local car-rental company might not be too pleased if they know where you intend to take their Volkswagen Beetle. A full tank of fuel might just barely get you from Palenque to Bonampak, Yaxchilán and back but you'd be safer carrying some additional fuel. The round trip is a bit over 300 km.

The Bonampak turn-off is about 10 km south of Palenque on the Ocosingo and San Cristóbal road. It's marked 'Chancalá', not 'Bonampak', and it's wise to ask directions. It takes about three hours from the main road turn-off to the Bonampak turn-off and the road is passable, although it tends to be dusty and you must beware of rocks and potholes. Eventually you reach the Bonampak turn-off to the right and the road deteriorates to a rougher one-lane track. After about 10 km a sign indicates Bonampak to the left. Despite what the sign may say, the distance is about 15 km.

There's a campsite close to this junction and from here it's wise to walk, particularly if it has been raining, although a Volkswagen can make it in good weather. There are several stream-beds and shaky bridges to be crossed, so be careful if you try to drive all the way to the site.

To continue to Yaxchilán you have to drive on to Frontera Echeverría, a border town to Guatemala which is on the Usumacinta River upstream from Yaxchilán. From the Bonampak turn-off from the road it's about 20 km to where a sign indicates the direction to the border, from there you travel another 30 km of rough track. Boats can be hired from this sprawling village to the ruins; you might be asked around US$40 for a complete boat but should be able to knock that down. Yaxchilán is about 20 km downstream, and while you get there quite fast, the return trip against the swift current can take over two hours. Come prepared for the fierce sun.

The public dining room in a comedor (informal eating house) above the river in Echeverría is good for dinner or breakfast. Buses occasionally come down the road from Palenque as far as the Bonampak turn-off and sometimes all the way to Echeverría.

Tours The proprietor of La Cañada Hotel and various travel agencies in Palenque run two-day land and river tours to Bonampak and Yaxchilán, as does the town's tourist office. The cheapest rate is about US$70 for the two-day venture, including transportation and all meals. A four-wheel drive vehicle will take you within 10 km of Bonampak and you walk the rest of the way. Tents are provided for overnighting. The next morning, you are driven to the Río Usumacinta, where an outboard motor boat takes you for an hour through the jungle to Yaxchilán.

Pakal, which also has an office in Palenque, offers the following two-day trip for US$82 per person (five or six people), US$115 per person (three or four), or US$214 per person (one or two): drive to Palenque to the Lacandón settlement of Caribal Lacanjá by car, take a two-hour walk to Bonampak (stay 1½ to two hours), walk back to Caribal Lacanjá and sleep in a Lacandón house, next morning travel by car to Frontera Echeverría, then boat along the Usumacinta River to Yaxchilán (stay three hours), return to Palenque by boat and car.

Walking According to Hilary Bradt and Rob Rachowiecki's guide *Backpacking in Mexico & Central America*, during the dry season the very intrepid can walk from the Montebello Lakes to a point on the Palenque-Echeverría road 45 km from Bonampak; the walk takes 10 days.

COMITÁN
Population: 50,000

This is a pleasant enough town, 85 km south-east of San Cristóbal de Las Casas on the Pan-American Highway, but the only real reason to come here is because it's the jumping-off point for the Montebello Lakes and the last place of any size before the Guatemalan border at Ciudad Cuauhtémoc.

The first Spanish settlement in the area, San Cristóbal de los Llanos, was set up in 1527. It was from Comitán that the Plan de Chiapas Libre, a successful campaign for Chiapas to be allowed to decide its own political future in the turbulent years following independence from Spain, was launched in 1823. Today the town is officially called Comitán de Domínguez, after Belisario Domínguez, a local doctor who was also a national senator during the presidency of Victoriano Huerta. Domínguez had the cheek to speak out in 1913 against Huerta's record of political murders and was himself murdered for his pains.

Comitán is a commercial centre for local maize, banana, forestry and livestock output. It's 1630 metres high, with hilly streets.

Orientation

The 1st-class Cristóbal Colón bus station is out on the Pan-American Highway, which passes through the west edge of the town, about 20 minutes' walk from the town centre. To reach the zócalo, turn left out of the bus station along the highway, take the first right down a hill, then the sixth left (Avenida Central Sur) and go three blocks.

Transportes Tuxtla Gutiérrez (2nd class) is at the corner of 4 Sur Pte and 3 Pte Sur; for the zócalo go left out of the entrance on 4 Sur Pte for 3½ blocks, then three blocks to the left. Buses for the Lagos de Montebello go from 2 Pte Sur between 2 and 3 Sur Pte; from Cristóbal Colón follow the directions from there to the zócalo but take the fourth left (not the sixth) and go 1½ blocks. From TTG go 1½ blocks left and then turn left for another 1½ blocks.

The wide and attractive zócalo is bounded by Calle Central on its north side, Avenida Central on the west, Calle 1 Sur on the south and Avenida 1 Ote on the east.

Information

Tourist Office There's a tourist office (closed Saturday and Sunday) in the Casa de la Cultura on the east side of the zócalo. The Casa de la Cultura also has a small museum, an art gallery and an auditorium. The adjacent church, Santo Domingo, dates from the 16th century.

Other The post office (open Monday to Friday 8 am to 7 pm, Saturday 8 am to 1 pm) is on Avenida Central Sur

between 2 and 3 Sur, 1½ blocks south of the zócalo. The Guatemalan Consulate (tel 2-15-40) is at 6 Norte Pte 17B. Bancomer is on the south side of the zócalo, Bánamex is at the corner of 2 Sur and 1 Ote Sur.

Places to Stay

Comitán has quite a few hotels since a lot of people pass through en route to or from Guatemala. The *Hotel Delfín Pensión* on the west side of the zócalo is one of the better-value places. Its spacious rooms have private baths (hot water intermittent) and those at the back are modern and overlook a leafy courtyard. Singles/doubles are US$2.50/4.

The *Hotel Morales* (tel 2-04-36) on Avenida Central Norte, 1½ blocks north of the zócalo, resembles an aircraft hangar with rooms perched round an upstairs walkway. Small singles/doubles with private bath but in need of paint are US$3.25/4.

Comitán also has several cheap posadas with small, often dingy rooms – most of them OK for a night. *Hospedaje San José* on Avenida 1 Pte Sur, two doors south of Calle 2 Sur, has bigger rooms than most. Doubles are US$3 and the rooms and common bathrooms are clean. *Posada Las Flores* at 1 Pte Norte 15, half a block north of Calle 2 Norte, has rooms round a quiet courtyard; singles/doubles are US$1.50/2. The *Posada Panamericana*, on the corner of 1 Pte Norte and Calle Central Pte, charges US$2/2.50 with private bath, US$1/2 without. The rooms upstairs at the back are on a balcony and get more breeze. A few doors down 1 Pte Norte from the Panamericana, the *Casa de Huéspedes Río Escondido* has its own restaurant and singles/doubles for US$1/2.

There are two upper-end places in the central area. The *Hotel Internacional* (tel 2-01-10), a block south of the zócalo at the corner of Avenida Central Sur and Calle 2 Sur, has clean, bright singles/doubles for US$5.75/6.50, plus its own restaurant.

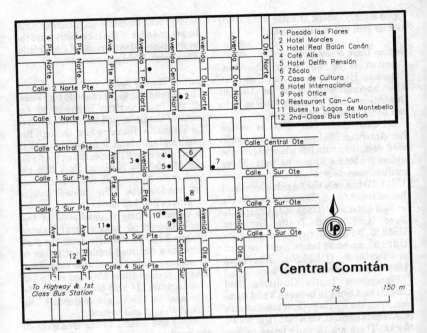

1 Posada las Flores
2 Hotel Morales
3 Hotel Real Balún Canán
4 Café Alis
5 Hotel Delfín Pensión
6 Zócalo
7 Casa de Cultura
8 Hotel Internacional
9 Post Office
10 Restaurant Can-Cun
11 Buses to Lagos de Montebello
12 2nd-Class Bus Station

Central Comitán

0   75   150 m

To Highway & 1st Class Bus Station

The *Hotel Real Balún Canán* (tel 2-10-94), at Avenida 1 Pte Sur No 5 between Calle Central and Calle 1 Sur Pte, is the top place, with a touch of elegance. Prints of Catherwood's 1844 drawings of Mayan ruins line the stairs; the comfortable modern rooms have fridge and phone and cost US$7.50/10.

Places to Eat
Several reasonable cafés line the west side of the zócalo. *Café y Lonchería Alis* does a comida corrida for US$1, antojitos for US$0.50 to US$1.25 (the quesadillas are boring), chicken and meat dishes for US$1 to US$1.25, hotcakes or 'pantcakes' (yes) for US$0.50. The *Acuario* next door is also popular.

For more Western fare, the *Restaurant Nevelandia* on the north-west corner of the zócalo has hamburgers for US$1 and spaghetti for US$1.25, as well chicken and

meat dishes (US$1.25 to US$4) and antojitos from US$1, including a plate of Chiapas cheeses for US$1.75. *Helados Danesa* next door serves up good ice cream. The *Restaurant Can-Cun* on 2 Sur Ote, half a block west of Avenida Central Sur, offers a long list of main courses for US$1.25 to US$2, and soups for around US$0.75.

At the *Rosticería El Pollito* on Avenida Central Sur, half a block south of the zócalo, you can pick up a half or whole chicken, roasted over an open fire, for US$1.50/3.

For a more expensive meal amid international-style surroundings go to the Hotel Real Balún Canán, where *El Escocés Restaurant* is open until 11 pm and the *Grill Bar* until 1 am.

Entertainment
The *Hotel Real Balún Canán* has a disco

(open nightly except Monday until 1 am) and its grill bar has live music.

Getting There & Away

Comitán is 85 km down the Pan-American Highway from San Cristóbal. The international border at Ciudad Cuauhtémoc is 80 km south. It takes 1½ to two hours to either place by bus.

Cristóbal Colón (1st class) is on the Pan-American Highway: from the zócalo head west, then turn left when you hit the highway, about a 20-minute walk. There are three buses daily to Ciudad Cuauhtémoc (US$1.25) but only the 6 am is a local and the last is at 9.50 am. Ten buses daily leave for San Cristóbal (US$1.25), Chiapa de Corzo (US$2) and Tuxtla Gutiérrez (US$2.25, 3½ hours); two for Mexico City (US$9.50, about 22 hours); and one each for Tuxtepec (US$9.50), Acayucan (US$7.25) and Puebla (US$13.50).

Transportes Tuxtla Gutiérrez (2nd class) is on 4 Sur Pte between 3 and 4 Pte Sur. From the zócalo go three blocks south on Avenida Central, then turn right for 3½ blocks. There are 16 daily buses to San Cristóbal and Tuxtla Gutiérrez, with two going on round to Arriaga, one of which continues to Tapachula. Southwards there are 13 buses to Ciudad Cuauhtémoc (US$1), some of which continue on to Motozintla.

Buses and combis for Chinkultic and the Lagos de Montebello leave from 2 Pte Sur between 2 and 3 Sur Pte. From the south-west corner of the zócalo go two blocks west, then 1½ blocks south.

LAGOS DE MONTEBELLO

The temperate forest along the Guatemalan border south-east of Comitán is dotted with about 60 small lakes – the Lagos or Lagunas de Montebello. The area is beautiful, refreshing, not hard to reach, quiet and eminently good for hiking. Some Mexican weekenders come down here in their cars, but the rest of the time you'll see nobody except the few resident villagers and a small handful of visitors. There are

two very basic hostelries and a campground. And at one edge of the lake district are the rarely visited Mayan ruins of Chinkultic. What more could you ask for?

Getting There & Away

The paved road to Montebello turns east off the Pan-American Highway 16 km south of Comitán, just before the town of La Trinitaria. Running first through flat ranch and *ejido* land, it passes the track to Chinkultic after 27 km, entering the forest and Montebello National Park five km further on. At the park entrance (no fee) the road splits. The paved section continues four km ahead to the Lagunas de Colores, where it dead-ends at two small houses 50 metres from Laguna Bosque Azul. To the right from the park entrance a dirt road leads past tracks to several more lakes, then to the village and lake of Tziscao (nine km) and on to Los Dos Lagunas (14 km) before leaving the lake area for the village of Santa Elena (about 45 km) and beyond.

Buses and combis to the area go from the yard of Linea de Pasajeros Comitán Lagos de Montebello on 2 Pte Sur between 2 and 3 Sur Pte in Comitán. One or another form of transport leaves every hour or half-hour up to about 5 pm. They have a number of different destinations so make sure you get one that's going your way. Most people head initially for Chinkultic, Doña María's (La Orquidea), Lagunas de Colores, Laguna de Montebello or Tziscao. Combi and bus fares are pretty well identical; it's US$0.60 to the Chinkultic turn-off, Doña Maria's or Lagunas de Colores, US$0.75 to Tziscao. By bus it's an hour to Doña María's, 1¾ hours to Tziscao. Combis are quicker.

Returning to Comitán, the last bus from Tziscao leaves about 4.30 pm, the last combi from Lagunas de Colores at 4 pm.

There's a steady trickle of vehicles through the lakes area, and hitching is possible. The many little-used vehicle tracks through the forest provide some excellent walks.

Lagos de Montebello

1 Laguna Bosque Azul
2 Laguna Encantada
3 Laguna Ensueño
4 Laguna Esmeralda
5 Laguna Agua Tinta
6 Laguna de Montebello
7 La Cañada
8 Laguna Pojoj

0   1   2 km

Chinkultic

These dramatically sited ruins lie two km along a track leading north off the La Trinitaria-Montebello road 27 km from the Pan-American Highway at the village of Hidalgo. A sign 'Chinkultic 3' marks the turning. Doña María at La Orquidea restaurant, half a km further along the road, has a map and book on Chinkultic.

Chinkultic is on the extreme western edge of the ancient Mayan area, but is regarded as a Mayan site. Dates carved by ancient inhabitants here extend from the equivalent of 591 to 897 AD – the last of which is nearly a century after the latest dates at Palenque, Yaxchilán and Toniná. These years no doubt span Chinkultic's peak period, but occupation is thought to have started in the late Pre-Classic (around 200 AD) period and continued until after 900. It was a sizeable place – some 200 mounds are scattered over a wide area – but only a few parts have been cleared. These are well worth the effort.

The track from the road brings you first to a gate with a hut on the left. Here take the path to the left, which curves round to the right. On the overgrown hill to the right of this path stands one of Chinkultic's major structures, called simply E23. The path leads to a long ball court where several stelae lie on their sides under thatched shelters. Other stelae – some carved with Mayan-looking human figures – lie in the vicinity.

Follow the track back to the hut and turn left, passing what could be a car parking area, soon after which you can spot a few stone mounds in the undergrowth to the right. The hillside ahead of you shortly comes into full view and on it the partly restored temple called El Mirador. The path goes over a stream and steeply up to El Mirador, from which there are good views of the surrounding lakes and a smaller cenote.

The Lakes

Lagunas de Colores The paved road straight on from the park entrance leads through the Lagunas de Colores, so called because their colours range from turquoise to deep green. The first of these, on the right after about two km, is Laguna Agua Tinta. Then on the left come Laguna Esmeralda followed by Laguna Encantada, with Laguna Ensueño on the right opposite Encantada. The fifth and biggest of the Lagunas de Colores is Laguna Bosque Azul, on the left where the road ends. One of the two small houses here sells drinks and food, and there's a lakeside campsite.

Two paths lead on from the end of the road. Straight on, 800 metres brings you to the *gruta* - a cave shrine where locals make offerings to ward off illness and so on (take a flashlight with you). To the left, you reach Paso de Soldado, a picnic site beside a small river after 300 metres. The track goes on; according to an old man who was sitting beside it, it reaches a village called Ojo de Agua after '1½ leagues'.

Laguna de Montebello About three km along the dirt road towards Tziscao (which turns right at the park entrance), a track leads 200 metres left to Laguna de Montebello. This is one of the bigger lakes, with a flat, open area along its shore where the track ends. About 150 metres to the left is a stony area which is better for swimming than the muddy fringes elsewhere.

Cinco Lagunas A further three km along the Tziscao road another track leads left to these 'five lakes'. Only four of them are visible from the road, but the second, La Cañada, on the right after about 1½ km, is probably the most beautiful of all the Montebello Lakes - nearly cut in half by two rocky outcrops. The track eventually reaches the village of San Antonio and, amazingly, is a bus route.

Laguna Pojoj A further km along the Tziscao road, a track to the left leads to this lake a km off the road.

Laguna Tziscao This comes into view on the right a further km along the road. Continue on to the junction for Tziscao village on the right. The village has pleasant grassy streets, friendly people and a hostel (see Places to Stay).

Beyond Tziscao

The road continues five km to Los Dos Lagunas on the edge of the national park, then on east to Santa Elena, a village about 30 km from Tziscao. Yet remoter villages lie north of Santa Elena; *Backpacking in Mexico & Central America* (see Books in the Facts for the Visitor chapter) describes a 10-day hike through these villages and plenty of jungle to the Palenque-Bonampak road 45 km from Bonampak. Buses certainly go from Comitán to Santa Elena; trucks or buses may now go beyond it.

Places to Stay

Half a km past the Chinkultic turn-off, you can camp or rent a cabin at *La Orquidea*, a small restaurant on the left of the road. The owner is Señora María Domínguez de Castellanos, better known simply as Doña María, a remarkable woman who with help from Amnesty International bought a nearby farm and turned it over to Guatemalan refugees. She also has a map and book on Chinkultic. For the small cabins, which have electric light but no running water, you pay US$1.

Inside the national park, camping is officially allowed only at Laguna Bosque Azul, the last and biggest of the Lagunas de Colores, where the paved road ends. There are toilets and water here.

Tziscao village has a hostel - the *Albergue Turístico* - where you pay US$1 per person for a dormitory bunk or a wooden cabana. You can also camp for 25c. The hostel lies on the shore of one of the most beautiful lakes and Guatemala is just a few hundred metres away. To reach the hostel, turn off the 'main road' and into the village. Soon after you come level with the small church on the hill on the right, turn right beside a store on the corner and follow this track down towards the lake, then round to the left. At the hostel you can rent a rowboat for 25c an hour. The señora will cook up eggs, frijoles and tortillas (US$0.75) and there's a fridge full of refrescos, but if you want any variety in your diet, bring it with you. When we visited, the toilets were in bad need of a good clean – apparently that was the señor's job and he wasn't around.

CIUDAD CUAUHTÉMOC

This 'city' is just a few houses and a comedor or two, but it's the last/first place in Mexico on the Pan-American Highway. Comitán is 80 km north, San Cristóbal 165 km. There are several buses a day to and from both these places (mostly Transportes Tuxtla Gutiérrez, 2nd class, but also a couple by Cristóbal Colón, 1st class). In 1st class it takes 1½ hours and costs US$1.25 to Comitán, three hours and US$2.25 to San Cristóbal. In 2nd class it takes a bit longer and costs a bit less.

Another road from Ciudad Cuauhtémoc runs 69 km south-west to Motozintla. There are 2nd-class buses to Motozintla, and from there buses run to Huixtla (about three hours away) on the Chiapas coastal plain north of Tapachula, providing an unusual but spectacular route across the Sierra Madre.

The Mexican border post – where you must hand in your tourist card – is at Ciudad Cuauhtémoc, the Guatemalan one a good three km south at La Mesilla. If your bus from Comitán or San Cristóbal isn't going on to La Mesilla, there are combis (25c) to take you across the no-man's-land.

Travellers have reported that you can get Guatemalan visas/tourist cards at La Mesilla, but these things have a way of changing and you might prefer to get your paperwork sorted out in advance at the Guatemalan consulate in Comitán or even the embassy in Mexico City.

The Guatemalan border post is officially open from 9 am to noon and 2 to 6 pm. You can usually go through outside these hours but will probably have to pay an extra US$1, on top of the regular US$0.50 for your customs inspection.

There's no bank at this border. Individual money-changers operate here but they give you fewer quetzals than a bank would. Try to get some in Mexico before you head for the border.

Guatemalan buses depart La Mesilla for main points inside Guatemala like Huehuetenango (80 km), Quezaltenango (also known as Xela) and Guatemala City. Lake Atitlán and Chichicastenango both lie a few km off the Huehuetenango-Guatemala City road. Before boarding a bus at La Mesilla, try to find out when it's leaving and when it reaches your destination. This could save you several hours of sitting in stationary buses.

ARRIAGA

The usual reason for travellers going to the small town of Arriaga is to leave. It's where the Juchitán-Tapachula road meets the Tuxtla Gutiérrez-Tapachula road and you might have to change buses here. Coming from Oaxaca or Tuxtla Gutiérrez, Arriaga is the first place you reach on the hot coastal plain of Chiapas known as the Soconusco.

Orientation

Until the new Central de Autobuses is completed on Highway 200 at the edge of the town, the bus stations are on 2 Ote, between the highway and the zócalo. Should you need food or a bed, there are several places within a couple of blocks.

Places to Stay

For the better places in town, first go two

blocks towards the centre (away from the highway) from Cristóbal Colón. A left turn here takes you to the clean *Hotel Colón* (tel 2-01-20) at 3 Norte No 8, where singles/doubles cost US$3.25/4 with private bath, US$2 with common bath. A right and then a left bring you to the *Hotel Albores* (tel 2-03-96) and the *Hotel Panamericana* (tel 2-03-57), both clean, on opposite sides of 4 Ote. The Panamericana is friendly and slightly better kept though the rooms have less light. Singles/doubles with private bath are US$3/3.50 in both places.

Slightly cheaper is the *Colonial* (tel 2-08-56) in Callejón Ferrocarril, the narrow street running down beside the Transportes Tuxtla Gutiérrez bus station. Small but clean rooms with private bath cost US$2.50 with one bed, US$3 with two beds. Across the street is the *Viajero* (tel 2-06-19).

The only upper-end place is the *Hotel El Parador)* (tel 2-01-64, 2-01-99), a motel at the edge of town on the Tonalá road at Km 467.

Places to Eat

Several reasonable café-restaurants line 2 Ote in the bus station area. *Restaurant Lupita*, opposite the Cristóbal Colón station, offers fish or seafood for US$1 to US$1.25, meat dishes for US$0.75 to US$1, plus eggs, tacos, enchiladas and good flan. Slightly grander is the *Restaurant Barkly* – to reach it from Cristóbal Colón, go a block away from the highway, then take the first right. It's on the right. Chicken soup, a plate of rice, a chile relleno, a refresco and coffee cost US$1.75.

The *Hotel El Parador* restaurant has an international menu.

Getting There & Away

Road By Highway 200, Juchitán is 145 km west of Arriaga, Tonalá is 23 km south-east and Tapachula 245 km south-east. Another paved road strikes 42 km north to meet the Pan-American Highway (No 190) between Tuxtla Gutiérrez (142 km from Arriaga) and Juchitán.

Bus A new Central de Autobuses is being built on the highway on the west side of town, but in the meantime the bus stations are on 2 Ote, about three blocks from the zócalo. Quite a few buses, for some reason, end their runs in Arriaga – which is probably why you're here. Happily, the same number start their runs here, increasing your chances of getting a seat leaving the town – though it's pretty likely to be 2nd class. To Tonalá, buses (US$0.30) by one company or another and colectivo taxis leave every 20 to 30 minutes from 2 Ote.

Cristóbal Colón (1st class) has two locales and many more de paso services daily to Tapachula (US$3, about four hours) and Tuxtla Gutiérrez (US$2, about three hours); locales to Mexico City (US$11.75, about 17 hours) three times and Puebla (US$10.50) once; plus two de pasos to Juchitán (US$2, about three hours) and Oaxaca (US$5.25, about eight hours). Cristóbal Colón (2nd class), from the same building on 2 Ote, has services to Tonalá and Tapachula about hourly; plus locales to Mexico City (four daily), Coatzacoalcos (three daily), Salina Cruz (twice) and Veracruz (once) as well as other de paso services.

Transportes Tuxtla Gutiérrez (2nd class), over the street from Cristóbal Colón, has 15 buses daily to Tapachula, about 20 to Tuxtla Gutiérrez, six to Juchitán and four to Oaxaca.

Fletes y Pasajes/Autotransportes México-Istmo (2nd class), 1½ blocks towards the highway from Cristóbal Colón, has some buses to Juchitán plus one or two daily to Tuxtepec, Córdoba, Veracruz, Orizaba, Puebla and Mexico City.

Rail Trains from Arriaga are slow, 2nd class and very unreliable. For the masochistic or the incurable railway buff, the station is just a couple of blocks from the bus stations. From Cristóbal Colón, go two blocks towards the town centre, then turn left. Theoretically, there are departures at 1.30 and 10 am for Tapachula (US$1.50, eight hours) and at 10 pm for Veracruz (16½ hours), but even station staff don't pretend to expect any train until they see it.

TONALÁ

Twenty-three km south-east of Arriaga on Highway 200, Tonalá has only marginally more intrinsic appeal but is the jumping-off point for the laid-back beach spot of Puerto Arista and other places on the lagoon-studded nearby coast. A tall pre-Hispanic stela in the Tonalá zócalo appears to depict Tláloc, the central Mexican rain god. There's also a small regional museum at Hidalgo 77, with some archaeological pieces found in the region. Neither is likely to keep you in the town long; if like most people you've come to Tonalá to get to the nearby beaches, you can do so until about 8 pm.

Information & Orientation

Highway 200 runs north-south through the middle of Tonalá under the name Avenida Hidalgo, forming the west side of the zócalo or parque central. Bus stations are at each end of the town on this road.

Tourist Office The tourist office on the ground floor of the Palacio Municipal, on the Hidalgo side of the zócalo, is knowledgeable and helpful, and can even tell you the advantages and disadvantages of the various nearby beaches. It's open 9 am to 3 pm and 6 to 8 pm Monday to Friday, and 9 am to 2 pm Saturday.

Money Bancomer and Bánamex both have branches on Hidalgo a few doors from the zócalo.

Post The post office is a block north of the zócalo at Hidalgo 148.

Places to Stay

Tonalá has no great accommodation

deals. Get to Puerto Arista if you can. The best place in Tonalá centre is the *Hotel Galilea* (tel 3-02-39) on the south side of the zócalo. Rooms are clean but a bit overpriced at US$6.50 single or double with private bath. In a similar bracket but slightly better value is the *Hotel Grajandra* (tel 3-01-44) at Hidalgo 108 near the Cristóbal Colón bus station.

The *Hotel Tonalá* (tel 3-04-80) at Hidalgo 89, roughly halfway from Cristóbal Colón to the zócalo, has decent doubles for US$6, but the singles (US$5) are either grotty or hideously close to the roaring of the heavy trucks which grind through Tonalá all night.

A block down from the west side of the zócalo at 6 de Septiembre No 24, the *Hotel Farro* (tel 3-00-33) is in desperate need of a scrub, some paint and some care. Barely tolerable rooms are US$3/4 with private bath, US$2/3 without.

Places to Eat

The *Hotel Galilea* on the south side of the zócalo has a restaurant with quite a long menu. On the opposite side of the zócalo, at the corner with Hidalgo, the *Café Samborns* is no relation to the up-market restaurant chain of a similar name, but it serves respectable chicken al carbón and seafood. *Filete de pescado empanizado* (fish filet fried in breadcrumbs) with salad costs US$2. Don't expect tranquillity here; they fail to drown out the traffic noise even when they turn the TV to full volume.

Several cafés and small restaurants line Hidalgo as it heads north from the zócalo towards the Cristóbal Colón bus station.

Getting There & Away

Bus If you're heading for Tapachula, it's often easier to wait in the zócalo for a bus – they come every half-hour or so – rather than make your way out to one of the bus stations, though you're a bit less likely to get a seat this way. You can also get off buses in the zócalo.

Cristóbal Colón (tel 3-05-40) is on

Hidalgo six blocks north of the zócalo. It has six 1st-class locales daily to Tapachula (US$2.75, 3½ to four hours), five to Tuxtla Gutiérrez (US$2.25, 3½ hours), two each to Mexico City (US$12, 17 hours) and Villahermosa, and one each to Oaxaca (US$5.50, eight hours) and Puebla (US$10.25), plus numerous de paso services, as well as buses to Juchitán (US$2), Tehuantepec (US$2.50), Acayucan (US$4), Coatzacoalcos (US$4.75) and Tuxtepec (US$6). Second-class buses go to most of the same places plus Salina Cruz (US$2.50, twice daily), for about 10% less. Second-class services to Tapachula are hourly between 5.30 am and 9 pm.

Transportes Tuxtla Gutiérrez (2nd class) has about 15 buses daily to Tapachula from its station on Hidalgo several blocks south of the zócalo, plus about five to Tuxtla Gutiérrez and others to Arriaga, from where there are more frequent services to Tuxtla Gutiérrez, Juchitán and Oaxaca. There are also colectivo taxis from Tonalá to Arriaga.

For transport to the beaches near Tonalá, see the following section.

Rail Yes, there's a railway station (tel 3-05-87, 3-02-32) in Tonalá, at the corner of Madero and Carranza, but no, the trains aren't any more frequent or reliable than at Arriaga. Add or subtract 40 minutes from the Arriaga schedules to find out when they're supposed to leave Tonalá.

BEACHES NEAR TONALÁ
Puerto Arista
This is a half-km collection of palm shacks and a few more substantial buildings in the middle of a 30-km grey beach, where the food's mostly fish, they say there are scorpions, you get through a lot of refrescos, and nothing else happens except the crashing of the Pacific waves while the batteries on your Walkman go down with the sun . . . until the weekend, when a few hundred Chiapanecos cruise in from the towns, or until Semana Santa and Christmas, when they come in the thousands. Then every second palm hut becomes a restaurant or lodging, or both, and the residents make their money for the year.

The rest of the time, the most action you'll see is when an occasional fishing boat puts out to sea, or a piglet breaks into a trot if a dog gathers the energy to bark at it. The temperature's usually sweltering if you stray more than a few yards from the shore, and it's humid in summer.

The sea is clean here but don't go far from the beach: there's an undertow, and currents known as *canales* can sweep you a long way out in a short time.

Puerto Arista is 18 km south-west of Tonalá. The paved road forks right off Highway 200, three km south-east of Tonalá, then passes through some flat but pretty farmland before crossing a lagoon area inhabited by birds and reportedly a few alligators. The landmark is the lighthouse, where the Tonalá road meets Puerto Arista's only street, running parallel to the shore.

Places to Stay & Eat Turn left at the lighthouse, then take the first right and you come to the *Restaurante Playa Escondida*, one of the few places with year-round accommodation. Palm-roof mud cabanas with mosquito nets cost US$2 (shower and toilet separate) or US$4 (private bath). The family is friendly and will serve up salad or vegetable soup, or sometimes beefsteak, as well as usually excellent fish. You can also sling your own hammock here for about US$1.

A few other places are open for sleeping and eating when the crowds are away. Two blocks in the opposite direction from the lighthouse, then left towards the sea, *Las Brisas del Mar* has rooms with two double beds and common baths for US$4.

Alie's Restaurant (right at the lighthouse if coming from Tonalá, then the first right) does good Spanish omelettes for US$2

Puerto Arista

with shrimp, US$1.25 without, plus a variety of seafood.

Boca del Cielo

About three km before Puerto Arista, a road turns left to this little fishing settlement at the mouth of an *estero* (estuary) 17 km away. There's a small seafood restaurant and you can take a launch across the estuary to a sandspit on the ocean front.

Paredón

Twelve km west of Tonalá on the large, nearly enclosed lagoon called the Mar Muerto, this is another fishing settlement with plenty of small seafood restaurants. The water immediately around is pretty dirty, but according to the Tonalá tourist office you can rent boats to a clean, quiet beach not far away.

Getting There & Away

Buses, colectivo taxis and private taxis from Tonalá provide the options unless you have your own vehicle. The Paulino Navarro company runs 2nd-class buses from Tonalá market to Puerto Arista and Boca del Cielo. To reach the market go a block west (downhill) from the Hidalgo side of the zócalo, then turn left a few short blocks along Independencia. You hit the market at the corner of Independencia

and Matamoros. The buses start from the opposite corner of the market (Juárez and 5 de Mayo). To Puerto Arista (30 minutes, 25c) they leave about hourly until around dark; to Boca del Cielo (US$0.50, about 1¼ hours) they're erratic but supposedly leave at 5 and 11 am and 3 pm. The last stays overnight at Boca del Cielo.

For Puerto Arista, colectivo taxis are faster, not much dearer and probably more frequent. They're also likely to operate an hour or two after the last bus. They go from the Independencia side of the market, leave when they're full and cost US$0.50. A private taxi from Tonalá zócalo costs around US$3 to Puerto Arista, US$6 to Boca del Cielo. From Puerto Arista to Boca del Cielo it's US$4.

To Paredón, there are buses and colectivos from the corner of Madero and Allende, a few blocks north-west of the Tonalá zócalo.

TAPACHULA

Most travellers come to Mexico's southern-most city only because it's a gateway to Guatemala, though for ruin buffs Izapa, 11 km east, is worth a visit. The proximity of Guatemala is quickly apparent from the abundance of quetzals (banknotes, not birds) and strange vehicle number plates. Guatemalans hop over the border for three main purposes: business (which

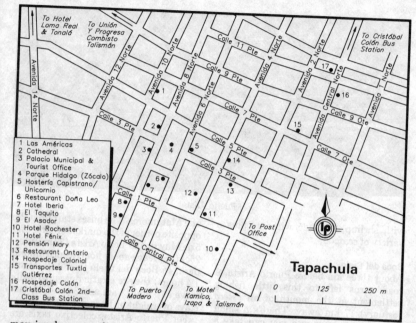

1 Las Américas
2 Cathedral
3 Palacio Municipal & Tourist Office
4 Parque Hidalgo (Zócalo)
5 Hostería Capistrano/Unicornio
6 Restaurant Doña Leo
7 Hotel Iberia
8 El Taquito
9 El Asador
10 Hotel Rochester
11 Hotel Fénix
12 Pensión Mary
13 Restaurant Ontario
14 Hospedaje Colonial
15 Transportes Tuxtla Gutiérrez
16 Hospedaje Colón
17 Cristóbal Colón 2nd–Class Bus Station

Tapachula

0   125   250 m

may involve smuggling), shopping, and refuge from the fighting in their own country. Tapachula's population in 1980 was around 100,000 but refugees (some from El Salvador) have greatly swelled that number, leading among other things to local complaints of increased crime and prostitution.

As well as being a border city, Tapachula is the 'capital' of the Soconusco, Chiapas' coffee and banana-growing coastal plain, and a busy commercial centre. You'll notice quite a few blonde Mexicans and Chinese names in Tapachula; these are mostly the descendants of German immigrants from a few decades ago and Kuomintang supporters who fled the Chinese revolution in the 1940s. All this, plus the heat, give the place a livelier atmosphere than most Chiapas towns; even women go around in shorts, a rarity in Mexico outside beach resorts.

Tapachula is overlooked by the 4092-metre Tacaná volcano to its north-east,

the first of a chain of volcanoes stretching down into Guatemala. The village of Unión Juárez, 40 km from Tapachula, reportedly provides good views of the volcano, and the surrounding country has hiking possibilities.

Tapachula holds an international feria in late February and early March each year.

Orientation

Tapachula's street grid is aligned more or less with the four compass points. The key axes are Avenida Central running north-south and Calle Central (east-west). Avenidas run north-south, are even-numbered west of Avenida Central, odd-numbered east of it, and have the suffix Norte or Sur depending on whether you're north or south of Calle Central. Calles run east-west and are even-numbered south of Calle Central, odd-numbered north of it, with the suffix Ote or Pte depending on whether east or west of Avenida Central. Tapachula's large zócalo, the Parque Hidalgo, is between Avenidas 6 and 8 Norte, with Calle 5 Pte on its north side. Bus stations are scattered north-east and north-west of the zócalo.

Information

Tourist Office The tourist office (tel 6-35-43) is in the Palacio Municipal on the west side of the zócalo. It's open 8 am to 8 pm daily. There's also the small, intermittently open Museo Regional del Soconusco in the same building, with some archaeological exhibits.

Money There are several banks around the city centre where you can change dollars and quetzals. If you're going to Guatemala try to get some quetzals in Tapachula; rates at the borders are usually lower. Outside bank hours, some shops and restaurants in Tapachula will accept cash dollars or quetzals at a lower rate than you'd get in banks. You can change travellers' cheques (losing about 5%) at Estanquilla La Unión on Calle 6 half a block south of the zócalo.

Post The post office is several blocks from the centre at the corner of Calle 1 Ote and Avenida 9 Norte. It's open 8 am to 6 pm Monday to Friday, 8 am to 12 noon Saturday.

Consulate The Guatemalan Consulate (tel 6-12-52) is at Calle 1 Ote 33. Aeroméxico (tel 6-20-50) is at Avenida 2 Norte No 6.

Izapa

If this site was in a more visited part of Mexico it would have a constant stream of visitors, for it's not only important to archaeologists as a link between the Olmecs and the Mayas (see the History section at the beginning of this chapter) but interesting to walk around. It flourished from approximately 200 BC to 200 AD.

Northern Area Most of this part of the site

has been cleared and some restoration has been done. There are a number of platforms, a ball court, and several of the stelae and altars whose carvings provide Izapa's main interest for archaeologists. The platforms and ball court were probably built some time after Izapa was at its peak.

Southern Area This is less visited than the northern area. Go back about ¾ km along the road towards Tapachula and take a dirt road to the left. Where the vehicle track ends, a path leads to the right. There are three areas of interest and you may have to ask the caretaker to find and explain them, as they are separated by foot trails that are less than obvious. One is a plaza with several stelae under thatched roofs. The second is a smaller plaza with more stelae and three big pillars topped with curious stone balls. The third has just one item – a carving of the jaws of a jaguar holding a seemingly human figure.

Getting There Izapa is 11 km east of Tapachula on the road to Talismán. You can reach it by the combis of Unión y Progresa from Calle 9 Pte, a block west of Avenida 12 Norte in Tapachula. The main (northern) part of the site is marked on the left of the road. A second (southern) part lies about ¾ km back towards Tapachula on the other side of the road.

Puerto Madero

This not very attractive beach resort is 25 km south-west of Tapachula. There are plenty of palm-roofed seafood restaurants, but an undertow restricts swimming to just a few areas (the best one is reportedly north of the town, near the last rock jetty). There's some accommodation at Puerto Madero but it's not inviting and the beach is said to be dangerous at night because of refugees who sleep on it. If you're desperate for a beach, head for Puerto Arista, a few hours up the coast.

Transportes Tuxtla Gutiérrez runs

fairly frequent buses (US$0.50, 30 minutes) from Tapachula to Ciudad Madero.

Places to Stay – bottom end

In the lower bracket, Tapachula has little except the functional and over-priced. It may be worthwhile to spend some extra pesos for the quiet and comfort of the *Hospedaje Colonial* (tel 6-20-52), which is better than some middle-range places. It's at Avenida 4 Norte 31, half a block north of Calle 3 Pte and just 1½ blocks from the zócalo. Clean, bright rooms with private baths line an upstairs balcony round a garden full of plants. Singles are US$4. Doubles are US$7 with one double bed, US$8 with two beds. Ring the bell to enter.

Travellers have recommended *Las Américas* (tel 6-27-57) at Avenida 10 Norte 47. A single with fan and private bath is US$2.50. *Pensión Mary* at Avenida 4 Norte 28, half a block south of Calle 3 Pte, charges US$2 per person in clean rooms with communal baths, and serves meals too, but is often full.

The *Hospedaje Colón* on Avenida Central Norte, a couple of doors north of Calle 9 Ote, is clean and provides fans in its medium-sized rooms, but prices are silly: US$4 for a single with common bath and traffic noise. The *Hotel Iberia* on Avenida 8 Norte half a block south of the zócalo offers grubby singles/doubles with private bath but no fan for US$2.50/3. A step up, with its own restaurant but overpriced, is the *Hotel Don Miguel* on Calle 1 Pte between Avenidas 4 and 6 Norte.

Places to Stay – middle

The *Hotel Santa Julia* (tel 6-31-40) at Calle 17 Ote No 5, next door to the Cristóbal Colón 1st-class bus station, has good, clean singles/doubles with TV, telephone and private bath for US$6.50/8.

The *Hotel Fénix* (tel 5-07-55), at Avenida 4 Norte 19 near the corner of Calle 1 Pte, has spacious rooms and open courtyards with plants. It's slightly run-down but pleasant. Rooms with private bath are US$6.50/8, US$1.50 more for air-conditioning.

Places to Stay – top end

The two top hotels, both with air-conditioned rooms and swimming pools, are the *Motel Kamico* (tel 6-26-40 to 48) on Highway 200 east of the city (singles/doubles US$17.75/21.50) and the *Hotel Loma Real* (tel 6-14-40 to 45) just off Highway 200 on the west side of town, where singles/doubles are US$18/22. There is also the *Hotel Don Miguel* (tel 6-11-43 to 49) at Calle 1 Pte 18, where rooms are US$11/14, and the *Hotel San Francisco* (tel 6-14-54) at Avenida Central Sur 94, with the same prices.

Places to Eat

Machacado – chopped fruit with ice, water and sugar – is a popular, refreshing drink in steamy Tapachula. Another cooler is frozen yoghurt (*helado de yoghurt*).

Several restaurants line the south side of the zócalo. *Restaurant Doña Leo* specialises in roast chicken and salad (US$2 for a quarter-bird, US$2.75 for half a bird) and does a US$1 breakfast of eggs with ham, frijoles, orange juice, coffee and sweet bread.

On Avenida 8 Norte at the south-west corner of the zócalo, *La Parrilla* has quicker service than most places in the centre, offering antojitos US$0.75 to US$1, carnes US$1.75 to US$3, tacos, queso fundido US$1 – plus *tortas ultrasónicas siglo XXI*.

For minor pretensions to style go to the *Hostería Capistrano/Unicornio* (tel 6-24-69), overlooking the east side of the zócalo at the corner of Avenida 6 Norte and Calle 3 Pte. It serves wine plus Italian and other food. Good pizzas of various sizes are US$3 to US$4.50, sandwich with salad is US$2. Decoration consists of some framed posters and enormous red plastic bows. Imitation Sades, Paul Youngs and

Springsteens thump out of the ghetto-blaster. The entrance is unimposing; go through the red gate beside a Coca-Cola sign and up two floors.

The *Mandarin*, a Chinese restaurant on the zócalo, has also been recommended by travellers.

For cheaper chicken, grilled this time, try the very busy *El Taquito*, a block south of the zócalo at the corner of Avenida 8 Norte and Calle 1 Pte. A quarter-bird goes for US$1.25, a half for US$1.75. Also busy is *El Asador*, a few doors down Avenida 8 Norte at No 6. Tacos (US$0.75 a helping) are the stock-in-trade.

The *Restaurant Ontario*, at Calle 3 Pte 12A between Avenidas 2 and 4 Norte, is popular for its range of reasonably priced breakfasts and meals. Tacos here are US$0.60.

Getting There & Away

Transport to the Guatemalan border is covered in the Talismán & Ciudad Hidalgo section.

Air Aeroméxico has daily non-stop flights to both Oaxaca and Tuxtla Gutiérrez, both with connections for Mexico City.

Road Tapachula is near the south end of Highway 200, 222 km from Tonalá, 245 km from Arriaga, 410 km from Tehuantepec and 660 km from Oaxaca. To Tuxtla Gutiérrez, for which you branch north-east off Highway 200 at Arriaga, it's 400 km.

The road to Guatemala heads 20 km east past the Izapa ruins to the border point at Talismán Bridge. A branch south off this road leads to another border crossing at Ciudad Hidalgo (38 km from Tapachula). From Huixtla, 40 km north of Tapachula on Highway 200, a road heads east across the Sierra Madre to Motozintla and Ciudad Cuauhtémoc.

Bus Cristóbal Colón (1st class) is at the corner of Calle 17 Ote and Avenida 3 Norte. From the entrance go west (left) two blocks, then six blocks south (left) and

three more west (right) to reach the zócalo. There are 20 buses daily to Tonalá (US$2.75) and Arriaga (US$3), most of them leaving on the hour. There are 15 buses to Huixtla (US$0.50); 18 to Tuxtla Gutiérrez (US$4.75); eight to Tuxtepec (US$8.75) and Mexico City (US$14.75); three to Córdoba (US$10.50); two each to Coatzacoalcos (US$7.50) and Villahermosa (US$8.50); and one each to San Cristóbal de las Casas (via Tuxtla Gutiérrez, US$6), Oaxaca (US$8) and Puebla (US$13).

Approximate 1st-class journey times: Tonalá 3½ hours, Arriaga four hours, Tuxtla Gutiérrez seven hours, San Cristóbal de Las Casas (via Tuxtla) nine hours, Juchitán six hours, Oaxaca 11 hours, Acayucan 10 hours, Mexico City 21 hours.

Cristóbal Colón (2nd class) is at the corner of Calle 11 and Avenida Central Norte. There are fairly frequent services to Tonalá, Arriaga, Juchitán and Tehuantepec, plus two or three daily each to Salina Cruz (US$4.75, seven hours), Oaxaca, Coatzacoalcos and Mexico City.

Transportes Tuxtla Gutiérrez (2nd class) at Calle 7 Pte No 5, just west of Avenida Central Norte, has four buses daily to Huixtla, Tonalá, Arriaga and Tuxtla Gutiérrez, and one via Tuxtla to San Cristóbal de Las Casas and Comitán.

Buses to Motozintla depart from Huixtla and take about three hours. There are buses from Motozintla to Ciudad Cuauhtémoc, Comitán, San Cristóbal de Las Casas and Tuxtla Gutiérrez, but this route won't save time except to Ciudad Cuauhtémoc and possibly Comitán. Going from Guatemala to central Chiapas, it's much better to cross the frontier at Ciudad Cuauhtémoc.

Rail The station lies just south of the intersection of Avenida Central Sur and Calle 14. Theoretically, 2nd-class trains leave at 1.15 pm for Ciudad Hidalgo (1¼ hours) and at 6.10 am and 3.10 pm for

Tonalá (7½ hours), Arriaga (8¼ hours), Juchitán (10 to 11 hours) and Ixtepec, with the latter train going on to Veracruz (23 hours).

Getting Around
Airport Transport Tapachula airport is south of the city off the Puerto Madero road. Combis Aeropuerto (tel 6-12-87) charges US$1.25 to the airport and will pick you up from any hotel in Tapachula.

TALISMÁN & CIUDAD HIDALGO
There are two crossing points into Guatemala near Tapachula. Talismán is 20 km east, Ciudad Hidalgo is 38 km south. The Guatemalan border posts on the other side are called El Carmen and Ciudad Tecún Umán respectively. Bridges span the river at both frontier points but it's a long walk at Ciudad Hidalgo. There's more public transport on both sides of the border from Ciudad Hidalgo/ Ciudad Tecún Umán, but many travellers head for Talismán/El Carmen, which is nearer to Tapachula, has a few long-distance bus connections into Mexico and has a more direct road link (via San Marcos) with Quezaltenango inside Guatemala. Some buses from El Carmen take the longer route to Quezaltenango via Coatepeque, joining the road from Ciudad Tecún Umán in any case.

A bus all the way through from Talismán to Guatemala City takes about five hours and costs US$2.75. If you're heading for Lake Atitlán or Chichicastenango, take a bus that's following the highland route via the Pan-American Highway to Guatemala City, not the lowland route via Escuintla. Los Encuentros is the junction on the Pan-American where the roads for Atitlán and Chichicastenango head off south and north

respectively. You can get connections for these places in Quezaltenango if there isn't one from the border.

At the time of writing it was possible for travellers (including British) to obtain Guatemalan visas at the border, but check in advance to see whether this has changed. There's a Guatemalan Consulate (tel 8-01-84) at Central Norte 12 in Ciudad Hidalgo, as well as in Tapachula. The Guatemalan border posts usually charge US$0.50 for customs inspection and may add US$1 if you're going through outside their 'regular' hours of 9 am to 12 noon and 2 to 6 pm. They may also insist on being paid in quetzals; try to get some before you leave Tapachula.

If you're leaving Guatemala at Talismán, you pay US$2 for various formalities plus any charge for 'irregular hours'.

Getting There & Away
From Tapachula there are six Cristóbal Colón 1st-class buses daily to Talismán (25c). Unión y Progresa on Calle 9 Poniente, a block west of Avenida 12 Norte, also runs frequent combis (25c) to Talismán. A taxi from Tapachula to Talismán takes 20 minutes and costs US$2. Transportes Tuxtla Gutiérrez covers the 45-minute journey to the frontier at Ciudad Hidalgo (US$0.50, every 15 minutes).

There are three daily Cristóbal Colón 1st-class buses from Talismán to Mexico City (US$15).

Ciudad Hidalgo is also the southern terminus of the Mexican railway from Juchitán, Arriaga, Tonalá and Tapachula. It's possible to get a train from Ciudad Hidalgo all the way to Veracruz but it's 2nd class only, unreliable and very slow.

The Yucatán Peninsula

Travellers through Mexico will experience a delightful bit of culture shock on entering the Yucatán. The peninsula is distinctly unique – its terrain, seas, climate, cuisine and most particularly its people. You will find attitudes more open and the atmosphere more relaxed than elsewhere in Mexico and female travellers will appreciate the fact that Mayan men are considerably less *macho*.

So while you may have come to the peninsula to soak up the sun on white beaches or to explore the extraordinary Mayan ruins, you will soon discover that touring the Yucatán is like visiting another country. The Mayan people and their culture are the reason, the product of geographical isolation and a fascinating past.

History

The Yucatán Peninsula consists of Campeche on the Gulf coast, Quintana Roo on the Caribbean and the state of Yucatán in the middle. This chapter includes the bordering state of Tabasco because many travellers moving between Palenque and the Yucatán pass through its capital, Villahermosa, and because the beginnings of the great Mayan civilisation lay substantially in the achievements of early Tabasco's Olmec people.

Early Cultures The popular concept of the Olmecs as the 'Mother Culture' of the Mayas seems an apt characterisation, as that ancient society flourished during the Pre-Classic period from 1500 BC to 300 AD. For more on the Olmecs, see the History sections in the Facts about the Country and Veracruz chapters. Archaeologists have found evidence of Mayan religious life in the Yucatán as far back as 8000 BC. While their Mayan relatives in the jungles of Guatemala and Belize flourished, building great cities like Tikal during the

Early Classic period, the Late Classic epoch from 600 to 900 AD shifted the development of Mayan culture into the Yucatán Peninsula.

The early Olmecs and later Guatemalan Mayas were not the only influences in the remarkable architecture, art and astronomy exhibited by Mayan cities in the Puuc Hills like Uxmal and Kabah. It is believed that Putun Mayan traders who peddled their goods by both land and sea (and are often compared to the Phoenicians) enriched the settlements of the Yucatán with the ideas and arts of central Mexico.

Chichén Itzá Although the Puuc settlements declined by the 10th century, an extraordinary city called Chichén Itzá rose to prominence. Until recently, prevailing archaeological theory held that a Toltec invasion and conquest was responsible for imparting to the priests and artisans of Chichén Itzá the religious philosophy and arts of central Mexico. However, a few years ago, after finding central Mexican influences in Mayan ruins long before the alleged Toltec invasion, some archaeologists offered a new theory. They maintained that it was the Mayas themselves who conquered central Mexico and subsequently brought that region's influences to their Yucatán settlements.

Whichever theory you prefer, there is no doubting the intellectual and artistic brilliance embodied in Chichén Itzá from 900 to 1200 AD. Today at the site you can appreciate the awesome stone architecture and carvings, constructed without metal tools, pack animals or the wheel. Also astounding is the astronomical observatory which, like its predecessors, linked Mayan life to celestial movement. The Mayan calendar proved more exact than its later European counterpart.

Chichén Itzá, like other great Mayan

cities, was ultimately abandoned. It's not known why these sites declined, but there is no shortage of theories. Some archaeologists say that barbarian invaders throttled the Mayan aesthetic and intellectual impulse. Other theorists believe catastrophes like drought, plague, or overpopulation and subsequent famine were to blame. Another hypothesis holds that the majority of Mayas, who were peasant farmers, rebelled against their economic support of the intellectual, royal and religious classes, uprooting their cities in the process.

Whatever the reason, by the time Chichén Itzá was abandoned and the city of Mayapan had become dominant in the region militarily, Mayan civilisation was in eclipse. Strife between Mayan settlements marked the history of the Yucatán from that point until the coming of the Spaniards.

The Colonial Era Among the early Spanish accounts of Mayan life at the time of the conquest, the most prominent was written in the 16th century by Franciscan friar Diego de Landa. He described communal harvests and successful hunts, and related with admiration the hospitality he saw extended to guests of the Mayas. He himself was often offered food and shelter.

While Mayan generosity impressed him, de Landa was horrified by the tales he heard of human sacrifice, with the still-beating hearts of victims ripped from their chests by Mayan high priests. He was also appalled by the Mayan sense of beauty and what they did to achieve it. Pressuring devices were applied to infants' heads to flatten them. Parents induced their children to become cross-eyed. Other beautification techniques included tooth-filing and skin mutilation to create tattoos for the women, and burning off beards with hot cloths for men.

Unfortunately, Friar de Landa was more than a mere observer. Feeling that

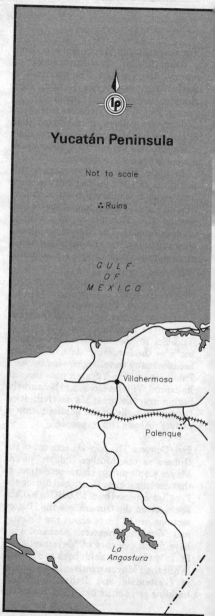

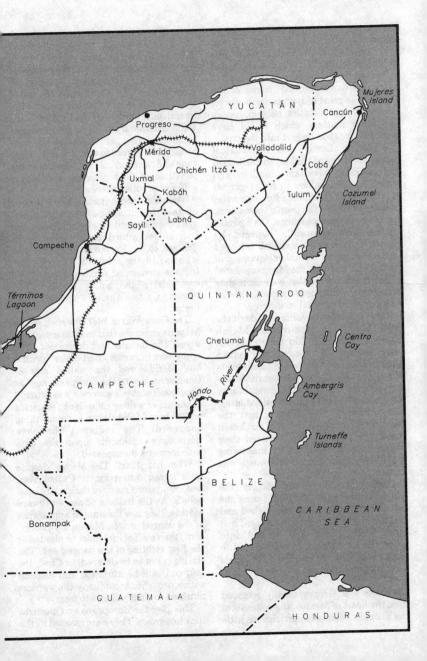

the carvings of Mayan deities were an intolerable affront to his God, he and other priests had hundreds of what were doubtless wonderful works of art smashed or burned. In 1562, in the Mayan town of Mani, de Landa burned 'works of the Devil' – the great Mayan codex books on astronomy, mathematics, religion, history and other matters which would have provided priceless insight into the past.

While de Landa and his clerical colleagues destroyed the Mayan intellectual and aesthetic inheritance, and by and large forced the Indians to either convert or die, their conquistador comrades brutally exploited the people themselves. For the next three centuries, the Spanish settlers were constantly besieged by pirates who coveted the wealth achieved by the Europeans' virtual enslavement of the Indians. Initially, the Mayas mounted a fierce resistance but they were ultimately worn down by European diseases, superior weaponry and internal strife.

It was this internal strife that dealt the death blow to a 16th-century Mayan rebellion. A Mayan Xiu tribe chieftain permitted himself to be baptised to help forge an alliance with the Spaniards in his war against his Cocom Mayan rivals. He even adopted the name of his conquistador ally, calling himself Francisco de Montejo Xiu. Although this alliance met the converted chief's goal, defeat of his Cocom rivals, the conquistadors thanked their Mayan comrade-in-arms by murdering him. With that, Indian resistance was broken.

Chafing at their virtual slavery, the Mayas occasionally revolted during the colonial era, only to be vanquished and brutalised with even greater vigour. Their lands were stolen and turned into haciendas on which they were forced to work, and the Mayas' labour made Spanish plantation owners rich.

The Caste War Geographically removed from the heart of Mexico, the colonists of the Yucatán Peninsula participated little in the War of Independence. Even though the Yucatán joined the newly liberated country, its long isolation gave it a strong sense of independence, and the peninsula desired little subsequent interference from Mexico City. Meanwhile, the end of Spanish rule meant that the Crown's few liberal safeguards that had afforded the Indians minimal protection from the most extreme forms of exploitation were abandoned. Forced to work tobacco, sugar cane and henequen plantations under the servitude of debt peonage, the Mayas suffered in sullen silence.

Then the land barons made a serious mistake. In initiating a separatist movement for independence from Mexico, the *hacendados* armed their Indian serfs. Trained to use European weaponry and schooled in the colonists' strategy, the Indians envisioned a release from their own misery and boldly rebelled. The bloody Caste War of Yucatán had begun.

The Caste War of 1847 saw such strong Mayan vengeance that in little more than a year the Indians had driven out their oppressors from every part of the Yucatán but Mérida and the walled city of Campeche. Seeing the European cause as hopeless, Yucatán's governor was actually in the act of writing an order to evacuate whites from Mérida when a curious thing happened. The Indians, who were relentlessly advancing upon the city, withdrew and disappeared.

What happened? The Mayas, despite their forced conversion to Catholicism, had maintained many of their traditional beliefs. As the Indians advanced toward Mérida, they saw the annual appearance of the winged ant. In Mayan mythology, corn (their staff of life) must be planted at the first sighting of the winged ant. The sowing is not to be delayed, or Chac, the rain god, will be affronted and respond with a drought. Accordingly the warriors returned to their villages to farm.

This gave the Europeans and mestizos time to regroup. They were assisted by the

Mexican national government with which they were now realigned. Their retaliation against the Mayas was without quarter, brutal in the extreme. Between 1848 and 1855, the Indian population was cut in half.

Some Mayan combatants sought refuge in the jungles of Quintana Roo. There they were inspired to continue fighting by a religious leader working with a ventriloquist who made a sacred cross appear to 'talk' (the cross was an important Mayan religious symbol long before the coming of Christianity). The talking cross convinced the Mayas that their gods had made them invincible. The Indians raided the plantations, enslaving in turn the whites who had exploited them for so long.

The isolation of Quintana Roo led the Mexican government to virtually ignore this Indian-controlled region for nearly half a century as the heavily armed Mayas, given arms by the British in Belize in return for timber rights, ran their own show for years. Finally, about the turn of the century, the Mexican army's superior firepower restored peace to the region but because the Mexicans had experienced such difficulty in pacifying Quintana Roo and wished to avert future trouble, they granted the Mayas a good deal of autonomy in the subsequent settlement. Underscoring both the isolation of Quintana Roo and the power of the Indians there, the region was only declared a Mexican 'territory' in 1936 and did not become a state until 1974.

Henequen & the Economy In the states adjacent to Quintana Roo – Campeche and Yucatán – the export economy based on henequen (a crop used to make rope) thrived in the latter half of the 19th century. By WW I it was said that Mérida had more millionaires per capita than any other city in the world. The plantation owners acted as a Yucatecan aristocracy and built opulent mansions which may still be seen in Mérida today, decorated these homes with the artistic treasures of the world and sent their children off to the best schools of Europe.

The plantation owners were not the only Europeans who became rich and powerful. Their supporters in the hierarchy of the Yucatecan Catholic Church profited handsomely as well, with Mérida's priests riding in jewelled buggies and living as lavishly as potentates.

The henequen boom was not enjoyed by most Yucatecans, and the Mayas, roped into a debt peonage system, cultivated the henequen for long hours under a brutal sun for next to no pay. According to the rules of the system, they had to spend their pitiful earnings at food stores run by the plantation where the cost of even their corn dietary staples was ridiculously high. To feed his family, a Maya had to buy on credit from the plantation store and therefore was never able to extricate himself from the debt continuously incurred; the term 'wage slave' was never more appropriate.

The Mexican Revolution somewhat changed this system of exploitation. Supported by the Yucatán's progressive governor, Felipe Carrillo Puerto, peasant unions grew in strength. They staged successful strikes and negotiated better working conditions; some peasants were given land from haciendas no longer being worked. Although their champion Carrillo was assassinated, probably by a conspiracy of plantation owners, the reforms continued. In the post-revolutionary period some of the plantation lands were redistributed among the peasantry, the economic power and political influence of the Catholic Church was curtailed, and schools were constructed for Indian children.

The Yucatán Today Although the post-WW II development of synthetic fibres led to the decline of the henequen industry, it still employs about a third of the peninsula's workforce. The slack has been more than picked up by the oil boom in

Tabasco, the fishing and canning industries of the peninsula, and the rapid growth of tourism in the past decade.

Relative to the rest of Mexico, the peninsula is doing rather well economically, although it too has been hard hit by the fall of the peso and galloping inflation. Nevertheless, while the declining worth of the peso has hurt the Mexican economy in general, it has also lured many tourists to the Yucatán's sunny shores, providing employment and an important source of foreign reserve.

A good number of Mayas till the soils as their ancestors have done for centuries, growing staples like corn and beans. Subsistence agriculture is little different than it was at the time of the great Mayan civilisations, with minimal mechanisation utilised to date. Other Indians, who worked the henequen plantations or were given henequen lands after the Revolution, have had a had a tough time since that crop's economic decline. This has precipitated a movement to the cities in search of employment in light industries or service-related jobs.

Many traditions live on in the Mayas of today. Most are bilingual, speaking both Spanish and Mayan dialects. Many residents of the Yucatán Peninsula are of pure or nearly pure Indian blood, as intermarriage was discouraged during the colonial era.

Women, particularly in the countryside, wear beautiful woven huipiles – white dresses with intricate, colourful embroidery. In the rural areas Mayas still build oval huts, topped with thatch and walled with whitewashed wattle-and-daub. To beat the heat, many Mayas sleep in the ventilated comfort of hammocks, which expose them to air movement from all sides.

Mayan religion remains a fusion of traditional animism and Christianity. Not surprisingly, since many Mayas continue to till the soil, the deities of agriculture remain important, especially Chac, the rain god. The sacred ceiba tree is still revered as its branches link the three worlds of Mayan cosmology: the heavens, life in the here-and-now and the dark underworld. The intersection of these three worlds, symbolised by a cross, made the Christian cross immediately recognisable, thereby powerfully assisting in the conversion of the Mayas to Catholicism.

The ceiba tree's sacred cross was not the only correspondence the Mayas found between their animist beliefs and Christianity. Both traditional Mayan animism and Catholicism have rites of baptism and confession, days of fasting and other forms of abstinence, religious partaking of alcoholic beverages, burning of incense and the use of altars. Today, the Mayan practice of Catholicism is a fascinating fusion of animist and Christian ritual.

The traditional religious ways are so important that often a Maya will try to recover from a malady by seeking the advice of a religious shaman rather than a medical doctor. Use of folk remedies linked with animist tradition is widespread in the Yucatán.

Thanks to the continuation of their unique cultural identity, the Mayas are proud without being arrogant, confident without the requisite *machismo* seen so frequently elsewhere in Mexico, and kind without being servile. And with the exception of those who have become jaded by the tourist hordes of Cancún, the Mayas retain a sense of humour and sunny disposition which is certain to make you want to return to the Yucatán in the future.

Tabasco

All too often denigrated by guidebooks, the state of Tabasco and its capital Villahermosa offer some attractions worth at least a day trip from Palenque. Villahermosa's Parque-Museo La Venta is one of Mexico's great archaeological

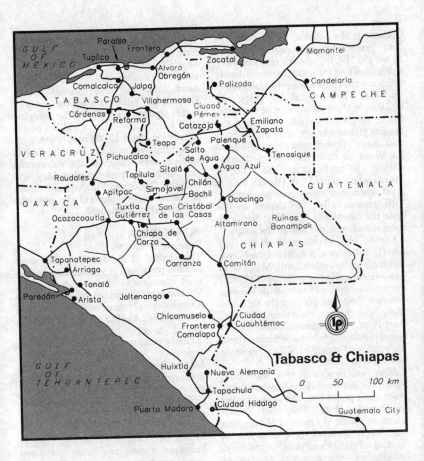

Tabasco & Chiapas

0   50   100 km

Guatemala City

exhibits, with its Olmec stone heads and other impressive artefacts.

Villahermosa also has a fine archaeological museum. Just a short bus ride from the state capital sits the ancient Mayan city of Comalcalco, complete with a formidable pyramid and temples constructed with mortar made from oyster shells.

Outside Villahermosa, travellers can relax at beach sites like El Paraíso, El Limón, Pico de Oro and Frontera. Although not on the Caribbean Sea, these beaches are pleasant enough and nearly completely free of gringo tourists. The town of Teapa, an hour from Villahermosa, offers cave exploration, river swimming and a sulphur spa.

For those intrepid (or foolish) enough to enter Guatemala via a Usumacinta River journey, the Chiapas town of Tenosique the jumping-off point. Some travellers charter aircraft for the Mayan sites of Bonampak and Yaxchilán from Tenosique's airport.

History

Tabasco is the home of the Olmecs, the first great Mesoamerican civilisation (1200-400 BC), whose religion, art, astronomy and architecture would deeply influence the civilisations that followed in its wake. Their capital, La Venta, was situated in the western part of the state. Major artefacts, including some of the famous gigantic heads, were moved from that site to Villahermosa's Parque-Museo La Venta to save them from damage during oil exploration. The Chontal Mayas who followed the Olmecs built a great ceremonial city outside present-day Villahermosa called Comalcalco. By the time the Spaniards landed, it had long been abandoned and lost in the jungle.

Cortés, who disembarked on the Gulf coast in 1519, initially defeated the Mayas and built a city called Santa María de la Victoria. The Mayas regrouped, offering stern resistance until Francisco de Montejo defeated them and pacified the region by 1540. Nonetheless, the tranquillity was short-lived. The depredations of pirates forced the capital to be moved inland from the coast and renamed Villahermosa de San Juan Bautista.

After independence was won from Spain, various feudal land barons tried to assert their power over the area, causing considerable strife. The 1863 French intrusion during the reign of Maximilian was deeply resisted here and led to regional solidarity and political stability. Nonetheless, the economy languished until after the Revolution when exports of cacao, bananas and coconuts began to grow. Then US and British petroleum companies discovered oil, and Tabasco's economy began to revolve around the liquid fuel. During the 1970s Villahermosa became an oil boom town and the state's export of its agricultural crops added to the good times. This new found prosperity has fostered a sense of energy that cuts right through the tropical heat, stamping Tabasco as different from neighbouring Chiapas and Campeche.

Geography & Climate

Tabasco's topography changes from flat near the seaside to undulating hills as you near Chiapas. Due to heavy rainfall – about 150 cm annually – there is much swampland and lush tropical foliage. Outside of Villahermosa, the state is rather sparsely populated for Mexico, with a little more than a million people inhabiting about 25,000 square km.

Be prepared for sticky humidity in this tropical zone. Much of the substantial rainfall here occurs between May and October. Outside of Villahermosa, it can be quite buggy (particularly near the rivers), so bring repellent.

VILLAHERMOSA

Population: 250,000

The capital of Tabasco has had some terrible press and if you were to believe what you read in some guidebooks, Villahermosa should be visited only for its archaeological museums or avoided entirely. Well, the burgeoning oil centre is indeed muggy, has some ugly new concrete edifices and is somewhat more expensive than many other parts of Mexico, but the people of this boom town are surprisingly friendly and the centre of the city is rather attractive. There are some nice walking streets, verdant plazas, engaging views of the Río Grijalva and - of course - the archaeological site, Parque-Museo La Venta. If you are as close as Palenque, a mere two hours away, and even if you have only one day, Parque La Venta in itself justifies a visit here. If you have more time, there are other archaeological sites of note and various day trips to parts of Tabasco.

History

Tabasco's original capital, Santa María de la Victoria, founded by Cortés on the Gulf coast in 1519, was subjected to numerous pirate assaults so the settlement was moved inland. Renamed Villahermosa de San Juan Bautista, Tabasco's capital on the banks of the Río Grijalva remained

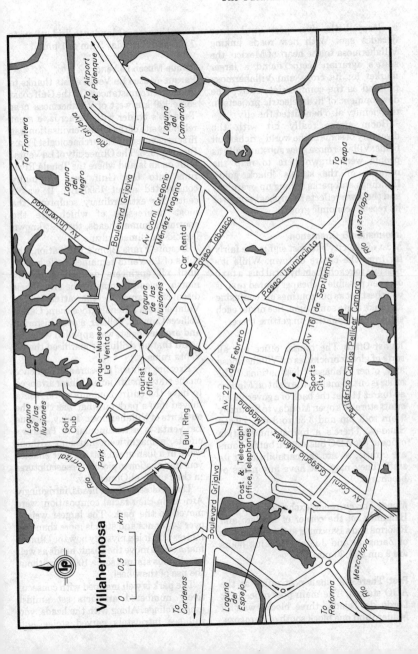

Villahermosa

0   0.5   1 km

To Frontera

To Airport & Palenque

Río Grijalva

Laguna del Camarón

Boulevard Grijalva

Av Corel Gregorio Méndez Magaña

Car Rental

Paseo Tabasco

Laguna del Negro

Av Universidad

Laguna de las Ilusiones

Parque-Museo La Venta

Tourist Office

Laguna de las Ilusiones

Golf Club

Río Carrizal

Park

Bull Ring

Av 27 de Febrero

Magaño

Paseo Usumacinta

Río Mezcalapa

Av 16 de Septiembre

Periférico Carlos Pellicer Cámara

Sports City

To Teapa

Gregorio Méndez

Av Coral

Boulevard Grijalva

Post & Telegraph Office, Telephones

To Cardenas

Laguna del Espejo

To Reforma

Río Mezcalapa

To Teapa

a sleepy little river port until three decades ago. With new roads linking Villahermosa to the heart of Mexico, the state's agrarian sector found a larger market for its crops and Villahermosa profited as the commercial centre. The development of hydroelectric projects in the vicinity also benefitted the city.

Boom times really hit with the discovery of some of the world's richest oil fields. Villahermosa grew substantially as people were drawn here to reap the rewards of the state's 'black gold'. Buildings and parks sprang up overnight and the town reflects the upbeat tempo of its recent economic growth.

Information & Orientation

Most of the city's tourist sights are fairly far from the centre of town. While it's possible to reach them by local bus, a taxi, or when possible a cheaper shared taxi, is your best bet as bus routings are confusing and take quite some time. See under each sight for information on getting there.

Tourist Office The tourist office has all sorts of glossy brochures on Villahermosa and other Tabasco destinations. The office is on the mall to the right off Madero at Juárez 111, at the back of a government crafts store. It's open Monday to Saturday 9 am to 3 pm and 3.30 to 8 pm, closed Sunday. There's a tourist information office at the ADO bus station but its hours are erratic, as are the capabilities of its staff. They may not have any maps or brochures.

Money For currency exchange, there's a Bánamex on the corner of Madero and Reforma and a Bancomer at the intersection of Zaragoza and Juárez. Banking hours are 9 am to 1.30 pm.

Post There's a small post office at the ADO station. The main post office is at Lerdo de Tejada, three blocks west of Madero and one block south of Zaragoza.

Postal hours are Monday to Friday 8 am to 7 pm and Saturday 9 am to 1 pm.

Parque-Museo La Venta

Parque-Museo La Venta exists thanks to unusual circumstances. Off the Gulf coast some 129 km west of Villahermosa near Tabasco's border with Veracruz, a great religious site of the Olmec civilisation was first excavated by the archaeologist Frans Blom in 1925. The Olmec city of La Venta, built on an island where the Tonalá River runs into the Gulf, was originally constructed about 1500 BC. It was a centre for extraordinary sculpture, the most impressive of which are the enormous human heads, the best-known legacies of Olmec culture.

Despite Frans Blom's excavation, the ruins of La Venta remained little known until oil engineers drained a nearby marsh, revealing more of the city. Their discovery came to the attention of Villahermosa's Renaissance man, Carlos Pellicer Cámera. Pellicer, a poet, historian and archaeologist, was appalled when he heard that oil drilling jeopardised the La Venta ruins.

Exerting political pressure and influence on the state's politicians, Pellicer arranged to have the entire contents of La Venta moved into a park on what was then the outskirts of Villahermosa. Today, Parque La Venta is a testimonial to Pellicer's efforts, a magnificent museum without walls in a lush green setting that enables your imagination to picture these sculptures in their original Olmec city.

Three colossal Olmec heads, intriguingly African in their facial composition, were moved to the park. The largest weighs over 24 tonnes and stands more than two metres tall. It is a mystery how the Olmecs managed to move the basalt heads as well as religious statues some 100 km without the use of the wheel.

The park is well mapped with consecutively numbered artefacts set amidst jungle foliage. Along with the heads, you will see intricately carved stelae and

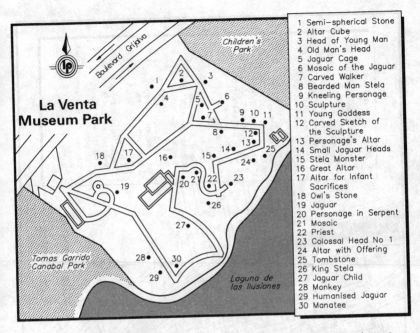

La Venta
Museum Park

1 Semi-spherical Stone
2 Altar Cube
3 Head of Young Man
4 Old Man's Head
5 Jaguar Cage
6 Mosaic of the Jaguar
7 Carved Walker
8 Bearded Man Stela
9 Kneeling Personage
10 Sculpture
11 Young Goddess
12 Carved Sketch of
   the Sculpture
13 Personage's Altar
14 Small Jaguar Heads
15 Stela Monster
16 Great Altar
17 Altar for Infant
   Sacrifices
18 Owl's Stone
19 Jaguar
20 Personage in Serpent
21 Mosaic
22 Priest
23 Colossal Head No 1
24 Altar with Offering
25 Tombstone
26 King Stela
27 Jaguar Child
28 Monkey
29 Humanised Jaguar
30 Manatee

sculptures of manatees, monkeys and, of course, the jaguar. The influence of the Olmecs on future civilisations throughout Mesoamerica was substantial. As well as an artistic influence, the divine jaguar represented in statues and even by the thick lips of the huge heads was a major spiritual force imparted to those societies which came later. A number of the great monuments exhibited here were actually found buried, and are thought by some archaeologists to be sacrificial offerings to the jaguar god.

When you visit Parque-Museo La Venta, you'll wonder why other museums haven't placed their non-perishable artefacts in such attractive outdoor settings rather than behind drab walls and alienating glass. Built on the banks of the Lagunas de las Ilusiones, the park also has free-ranging deer, monkeys, armadillos and coatimundis, as well as caged crocodiles and jaguars. Admission is about US$0.60

and the excellent self-guidance brochure costs about 15c at the gate (free at the tourist office). There's another good booklet available for about US$3.50 with descriptions of each piece and some rather confused numbering. The park's hours are daily 8.30 am to 5 pm, closed Wednesday, with a good sound & light show nightly except Wednesday. There is a small charge for both admission and the sound & light. Carry mosquito repellent at all times.

To reach Parque La Venta, some three km from the zócalo, you can catch buses running from near the centre of Madero which are designated 'Circuito 1', 'Parque Linda Vista', 'Tabasco 2000' or 'Foviste'. Regardless of their nameplate, be sure to ask the driver if they really go to Parque La Venta. More convenient collective taxis charge about US$1.25 to get to the park from the centre of town or the bus station.

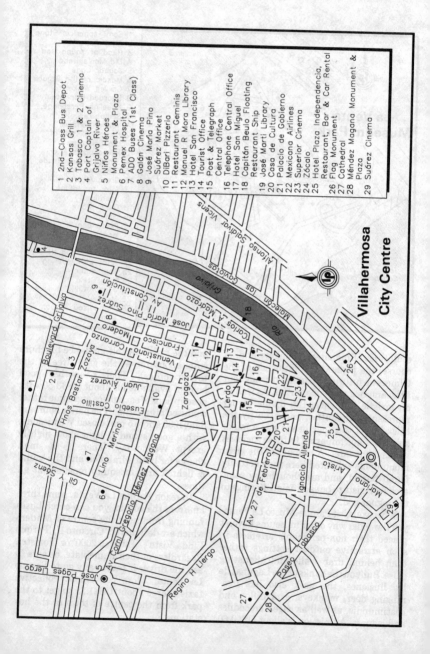

1 2nd-Class Bus Depot
2 Kansas Grill
3 Tabasco 1 & 2 Cinema
4 Port Captain of
  Grijalva River
5 Niños Héroes
  Monument & Plaza
6 Pemex Hospital
7 ADO Buses (1st Class)
8 Galán Cinema
9 José María Pino
  Suárez Market
10 DiBari Pizzeria
11 Restaurant Geminis
12 Manuel R Mora Library
13 Hotel San Francisco
14 Tourist Office
15 Post & Telegraph
   Central Office
16 Telephone Central Office
17 Hotel San Miguel
18 Capitán Beulo Floating
   Restaurant Ship
19 José Martí Library
20 Casa de Cultura
21 Palacio de Gobierno
22 Mexicana Airlines
23 Superior Cinema
24 Zócalo
25 Hotel Plaza Independencia,
   Restaurant, Bar & Car Rental
26 Flag Monument
27 Cathedral
28 Méndez Magana Monument &
   Plaza
29 Suárez Cinema

**Villahermosa
City Centre**

CICOM

The Museo Regional de Antropología & Teatro Esperanza Iris translates as the Centre of Investigation into the Cultures of the Olmecs and Mayas; it's much easier to say CICOM! The museum is dedicated to Carlos Pellicer Cámera, the scholar and poet responsible for preservation of the artefacts in Parque La Venta.

On the top floor is an exhibit devoted to Pellicer as well as excellent maps of Olmec and Mayan sites. Although the museum's explanations are all in Spanish, they are often accompanied by photos, maps and diagrams.

The 3rd floor offers representations of artefacts drawn from prominent Indian civilisations of all parts of Mexico. The most interesting are the 'smiling faced' Totonac masks and homages to Cocijo, the rain god. The 2nd floor contains some local pieces from the Olmec and Mayan cultures with photos, maps and diagrams of sites. The ground floor holds the most sizeable Olmec and Mayan artefacts and travelling modern exhibits. If you are going out to Comalcalco, it's worthwhile to see the site's artefacts and photos here.

The museum is open Tuesday to Sunday from 8 am to 8 pm, with a 25c admission charge. Also in the CICOM complex are archaeological and cultural classrooms and labs. From Wednesday to Saturday, dance, theatre or comedy is presented in the Teatro Esperanza Iris at 7 and 9.30 pm. There's a bookstore and a crafts shop – not cheap.

CICOM is at least a half-hour's walk west along the river; better yet, take a taxi or local bus designated 'CICOM' or 'No 1' from the centre of town, and tell the driver you want to go there. If you are coming from Parque La Venta, the taxi price should be about US$0.50.

Parque La Choca & Tabasco 2000

Parque La Choca and the Tabasco 2000 are two minor sites which those with time might consider visiting. You can walk here from Parque La Venta by going left on Boulevard Grijalva and then right on Paseo Tabasco. Parque La Choca, just beyond the Tabasco 2000 complex, is the site of a state crafts festival in May. It is also a pleasant place to picnic, has a swimming pool and is open Monday to Saturday from 7 am to 9 pm.

The Tabasco 2000 complex is a testimonial to the prosperity the oil boom brought to Villahermosa, with the all-new Palacio Municipal, chic boutiques in a gleaming mall, a convention centre and pretty fountains. There's also a planetarium, whose Spanish-only shows are presented Tuesday to Friday at 4, 5.30, 7 and 8.30 pm. Admission is US$0.75, half-price for students. If you are coming from the centre of the city, take the Tabasco 2000 bus.

Casa de Cultura

Back in downtown Villahermosa, the Casa de Cultura on 27 de Febrero, a block

Olmec figure

and a half from the city's centre, has local arts and crafts exhibits open Monday to Friday, 9 am to 2 pm and 5 to 8 pm. There are crafts for sale, but they are pricey.

Museum of Popular Art

Set in a picturesque old house also on 27 de Febrero at the intersection of Juárez is the minuscule Museum of Popular Art. Exhibits of folk culture depend on the time of year you visit, especially religious holidays. You will be accompanied by a guide (who speaks little English) through re-creations of everyday rural Tabasco life. The museum is open daily except Monday from 9 am to 2 pm and 5 to 8 pm. There is a small admission charge.

Market

Iguana, alligator, peccary and other delicacies wait here for local gourmets.

Places to Stay – bottom end

The *Hotel San Miguel* (tel 2-15-00), in the mall off Madero at Lerdo 315, is the best of the cheapies. Given its price and well-maintained rooms, the San Miguel fills up regularly – so get here as early as possible. Singles with fan and bath cost only US$4.25, doubles US$7. Nearby at Lerdo 303 is *Hotel Caballero* (tel 2-14-55) where basic singles with fans and bath cost US$4.25, doubles US$7.

For budget rooms with air-conditioning try *Hotel San Francisco* (tel 2-31-98) at Madero 604. Spartan singles with bath cost US$4 and doubles only US$4.75 but the place could be cleaner. A few blocks away at Madero 301, *Hotel Madero* (tel 2-05-16) has air-conditioned doubles for US$7.50. Basic single rooms with fan and bath cost US$4, doubles US$5.50.

Camping It might be possible to set up a tent or trailer at the *Ciudad Depotiya* in the southern part of the city. Ask at the field-house adjacent to Olympic Stadium during the day. The Tamolte bus runs out here.

Places to Stay – middle

Villahermosa's best deal for moderately priced lodging is the well-located *Hotel Miraflores* (tel 2-00-54) just off Madero at Reforma 304. Its nicely appointed air-conditioned rooms with bath cost US$14 single, US$18 double.

Also quite nice, and about a five to seven-minute walk from the ADO station, is the *Hotel Ritz* (tel 2-48-59) at Madero 1013. Air-conditioned singles with bath and TV cost US$10.25, doubles US$11.50.

Places to Stay – top end

As an oil boom town, Villahermosa has no shortage of luxury lodges for those with the capital. Consider the pretty *Villahermosa Viva* (tel 2-55-55), 1½ km north on Highway 180, where singles are US$29 to US$35 and doubles US$35 to US$52. Nearby on Highway 180 is the modern *Exelaris Hyatt* (tel 2-84-33), charging US$40 for singles and US$46 for doubles.

The *Maya Tabasco* (tel 2-11-11), eight blocks north of the Plaza de Armas on Highway 180, has singles from US$23 to US$29 and doubles from US$35 to US$46. All these hotels have swimming pools.

Places to Eat

Villahermosa's high humidity is actually good for something. It's likely to take the edge off your appetite, fortunately, for Villahermosa has little in the way of exceptional cuisine. A couple of places on Madero do offer filling, reasonably priced comidas corridas.

Try *Restaurant Gemenis* on Madero (no discernible number) between Méndez and Magallanes. Alleged to serve wild game, the Gemenis had good *típico* cuisine when I ate there. In the same league, at Madero 610 between Méndez and Zaragoza, is *Los Pepes*. Also cooled by overhead fans, Los Pepes serves up good portions of Mexican standards.

For OK breakfasts check out the *Café Su Casa* beneath the 'Cabal' sign, where Madero, Suárez and Reforma intersect.

Top: Ghost town of Real de Catorce, San Luis Potosí (JN)
Left: Lagos de Montebello (JN)
Right: Sumidero Canyon, Chiapa de Corzo (JN)

Top: Quadrangle of the Nuns, Uxmal (JL)
Left: Governor's Palace, Uxmal (JL)
Right: Platform of Venus, Chichén Itzá (TW)

For fast food, try *DiBari Pizza* at Méndez 712 and *Pollo La Texas* at Méndez 207.

If you're willing to spend more, carnivores will like the *Kansas Grill* at Alvarez 803. Close to Parque La Venta is a decent seafood restaurant, *Las Blancas Mariposas*, open afternoons, closed Monday.

For a splurge you can cruise the Río Grijalva while eating so-so cuisine on the *Capitán Buelo*. Departing from a dock at Lerdo de Tejada (tel 3-57-62 for reservations), the *Capitán Buelo* is most interesting during the day when you can observe life on the river. Evenings you see little, but those who enjoy dinner cruises may find it romantic. Sailings are scheduled daily except Monday at 1.30, 3.30 and 9 pm.

Entertainment

Teatro Esperanza Iris at the CICOM complex offers folkloric dance, theatre or comedy Wednesday to Saturday at 7 and 9.30 pm. Call the tourist office for details.

The planetarium at Tabasco 2000 has shows at 4, 5.30, 7 and 8.30 pm, admission US$0.75, half-price for students. Parque La Venta has sound & light shows nightly except Wednesday at 7, 8 and 9.15 pm for a few pesos admission.

Discos can be found in the Villahermosa *Viva*, *Hyatt* and *Maya Tabasco* luxury hotels. For other cultural goings-on, call the Instituto de la Cultura (tel 2-79-47) or check their bulletin of events distributed to the museums and bigger hotels.

Things to Buy

There are plenty of craft stores, but quality seems low for the price in Tabasco. There are more interesting crafts in Chiapas, Yucatán and Quintana Roo.

Getting There & Away

Air There are regular flights from Villahermosa to Mexico City, Mérida, Tuxtla Gutiérrez and Oaxaca.

Bus There are 1st-class buses to Palenque that take about two hours; the cost is US$2.50. Because these often fill up, try to buy your tickets several hours in advance. Ditto for buses bound for Campeche (six hours, US$7) and Mérida (eight hours, US$9.50). There are also buses to Mexico City (15 hours, US$16) and Caribbean destinations such as Chetumal and Cancún.

While there is no *guardería* for your luggage, you might be able to tip a baggage handler to watch your gear for a few hours. Second-class buses run from another terminal on Grijalva, which may be reached by local buses from the zócalo.

Rail The nearest railhead to Villahermosa is 58 km away at the town of Teapa and it's just as well, as the slow trains through Tabasco are frequently held up by *bandidos*.

Getting Around

Airport Transport The colectivo minibuses charge about US$1.50 per person, a whole taxi costs about US$6. They operate on a ticket system from a counter in the terminal.

Local Transport From the 1st-class ADO bus station, it's generally about 15 to 20 minutes' walk to the recommended hotels (those closer are noted). Ordinarily we'd suggest that you do the journey on foot, but Villahermosa's heat and high humidity may make taking a taxi (figure around US$1 in the cheaper Volkswagen Beetle taxis) or a local bus for about 2c worth considering.

As you exit the front of the ADO station, go left for two blocks to the corner of Mina and Zozaya, where buses stop en route to the zócalo and Madero, the main thoroughfare. If you are walking, go out the ADO station's front door, cross Mina and follow Lino Merino five blocks to the principal plaza, Parque de la Paz on Calle Madero.

Although the major sights listed are far from the centre, there is local bus service to them. See each particular listing for the appropriate bus destination. Again, given the heat, you might wish to opt for the convenience of taxis – the yellow Volkswagen Beetles tend to be cheaper, as are the colectivos.

AROUND VILLAHERMOSA
Comalcalco Ruins
If you have the time and are interested in archaeology, a day trip to the ruins of Comalcalco from Villahermosa is worth your while. Comalcalco was constructed during the late Mayan Classic Period between 500 and 900 AD, when the region's agricultural productivity prompted population expansion. The principal crop which brought Indian peasants from Palenque to this region was the cacao bean, still the chief cash crop (the Comalcalcoans traded it to other Mayan settlements).

Although Comalcalco resembles Palenque in architecture and sculpture in many ways, it is unique in its composition. Because stone was in short supply, the Mayas made bricks from clay, sand and – ingeniously – oyster shells. Mortar was provided with lime obtained from the oyster shells. This unique mortar was also used to help sculpt elaborate stucco façades with multicoloured reliefs, grotesque masks, and human and animal representations. Comalcalco is thought by archaeologists to be among the first cities built of brick.

Due to the passage of time, you will have to look carefully to see some of the stucco sculpture. The government has simplified the task of finding the best carvings by erecting thatch roofs to shelter them. As you enter the ruins, the substantial structure to your left may surprise you, as the pyramid's bricks look suspiciously like the bricks used in construction today. Look on the right side of the pyramid and you will see some remains of the stucco sculptures which once covered the pyramid. Then walk through the plaza to the main Acropolis area where, particularly on the northern section, you will find the remains of fine stucco carvings.

Although the west side of the Acropolis once held a crypt comparable to Palenque's Pakal, the tomb was vandalised before the area was known to the outside world; the sarcophagus was stolen. Continue up the hill to the ruin called the Palace, and from this elevation enjoy the breeze while you gaze down on unexcavated mounds.

Since all the structures are built of stucco and brick, you don't want to assist the erosion process by climbing on them. The *No Subir* signs are also for your safety; a tourist broke a leg here not long before I visited the site.

Getting There & Away
Admission is just 25c and Comalcalco is open daily from 8 am to 5 pm. There are daily 1st-class buses here from the ADO station in Villahermosa, and the 55-km journey takes about an hour. Ask the bus driver when buses return from Comalcalco.

TABASCO BEACH TOWNS
Those seeking gleaming beaches and sparkling waters are advised to save their time and money for the Caribbean coast. It's not that Tabasco's beaches are bad, it's simply that they are mediocre, and visits to coastal towns like El Paraíso, El Limón, Puerto Ceiba, Frontera, Miramar and Pico de Oro (all accessible by bus) should be undertaken only if you're desperate for surf or curious about Tabascan seaside life.

The scenery from Villahermosa to the coastal region is rather pretty, with luxuriant tropical foliage. En route, you will pass banana, cacao and copra plantations. All the towns mentioned have cheap hotels or places to hang your hammock.

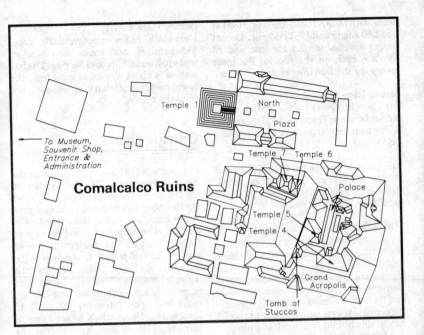

To Museum, Souvenir Shop, Entrance & Administration

Comalcalco Ruins

Temple 1

North Plaza

Temple 7   Temple 6

Palace

Temple 5

Temple 4

Grand Acropolis

Tomb of Stuccos

TEAPA

If for some reason you go to Teapa to catch the train (buses are faster from Villahermosa and far less prone to banditry) or are convinced by the glossy tourist brochure to visit the town, there are a few attractions.

Las Grutas Cocona

You can take a 2nd-class bus or walk four km to explore Las Grutas Cocona. These caves, lit by artificial light, are not a bad place to spend some time while waiting for a train, as at least they are cool. Tours, in Spanish only, start at 11 am, 1 pm and 3 pm. There are sporadic 'sound & light' shows in the caves, which are closed Monday.

Agua Sulfre Spa

Another way to keep cool and kill time is to visit Agua Sulfre Spa, about five km from the zócalo. Although some buses

bound for Pichucalco may stop here, it might prove quicker to hitch back to town or take a taxi for about US$3. If you don't like Teapa's accommodation, consider spending US$10 to US$15 for a room – quite clean – at the spa. There are two gigantic pools here, one of sulphur 'enhanced' water, the other fresh.

River Swimming

If you prefer to relax in a more natural setting, take a Tacotalpa-bound bus to the Río Puyacatengo, about four km from Teapa, and tell the driver to let you off at the bridge. The spot is tropical and pretty, the waters cooling. If you decide to camp here, watch your gear – *bandidos* are infamous in these parts.

Places to Stay & Eat

The *Hotel Jardín* at the Plaza Independencia 123 is the best of a bad lot of budget abodes. Mildewed and barely adequate rooms with fan and bath are overpriced at US$2.50 single and US$3 double. Decent budget eateries are *La Piragua* and *El Jocolito*, both on the zócalo. For more luxury try the *Don José* or *Pino Suárez*.

Getting There & Away

Bus There is regular 1st and 2nd-class bus service between Teapa and Villahermosa, taking a bit more than an hour and costing US$1.

Rail There is service between Teapa and Mérida or Mexico City but as noted, trains in this region are frequently subject to robbery. Take the bus.

TENOSIQUE

If you are considering a visit to Tenosique, in Chiapas, specifically because you have heard that flights to Yaxchilán and Bonampak Ruins are cheaper when chartered here, save your time and trouble and fly from Palenque or San Cristóbal – the saving is not enough to warrant a special trip to this humid nonentity of a town.

A few brave (or ignorant) souls leave for Guatemala via the San Pedro River, a tributary of the Río Usumacinta, with Tenosique as the jumping-off point. As noted earlier in the Río Usumacinta section, guerrilla activity and the Guatemalan military response to it could jeopardise your life. Ask about the status of the situation at your consulate (particularly the US Consulate) at the time you are considering crossing the border from here. One way is to take a bus (1½ hours, US$0.50) to the riverside town of La Palma. From there you can take a boat (four to five hours) to the border town of El Naranjo where buses run sporadically to Flores.

Places to Stay & Eat

The best budget hotel is the *Hotel Azuleta*, on Pino Suárez where singles with fan and bath are US$3, doubles US$4.50. There are cheap restaurants around the zócalo.

Getting There & Away

First-class buses run regularly from Villahermosa, and trains stop here en route to Mexico City and Mérida. The bus station is about a one-km walk from the town; the train station is also about a km from the zócalo.

Campeche

Campeche is the least-visited state on the Yucatán Peninsula. This is a blessing for the traveller who wants to get away from the Caribbean tourist mobs and explore a richly historical region relatively free of gringos. The impressive walled city of Campeche with its ancient fortresses propels the visitor back to the days of the buccaneers. Those who explore the region's ancient Mayan Chenes-style ruins of Edzná, Dzibilnocac and Hochob may find they have the sites all to themselves. Campeche's minor ruins of Chicanna, Becan and Xpujil, near the border with Quintana Roo, are discussed in the Around Chetumal section.

History

Campeche houses several important ceremonial centres of the great Mayan civilisation (see the introduction to the Yucatán chapter for a history of the Mayas).

Once a Mayan trading village called Ah Kin Pech, Campeche was invaded by the conquistadors in 1517. The Mayas resisted, and for nearly a quarter of a century the Spaniards were unable to fully pacify the region. Finally by 1540 the conquistadors gained sufficient control, under the leadership of Don Francisco de Montejo, to found the settlement of Campeche.

The name Campeche is the Spanish bastardisation of Ah Kin Pech, Mayan for 'serpent' and 'tick'. Some of the buildings from which Montejo planned forays into

territories controlled by Mayans still stand.

The settlement soon flourished as the major port of the Yucatán under the careful planning of Viceroy Hernández de Córdoba. Timber, chicle and dyewoods were major exports to Europe, as were gold and silver mined from other regions and shipped from Campeche. Such wealth did not escape the notice of vicious cutthroats who roamed the high seas.

For two centuries, the depredations of pirates terrorised Campeche. Not only were ships attacked, but the port itself was invaded, its citizens robbed, its women raped, its buildings burned. In the buccaneers' Hall of Fame were the infamous John Hawkins, Diego the Mulatto, Lorencillo Graff, Barbillas and the notorious 'Pegleg' himself, Pato de Palo. In their most gruesome of assaults, in early 1663 the various pirate hordes set aside their jealousies to converge upon the city as a single flotilla, massacring many of Campeche's citizens in the process.

It took this tragedy to make the Spanish monarchy take preventive action five years later. Starting in 1668, with construction taking 18 years to complete, 3½-metre-thick ramparts were built; in all a 2½-km hexagon incorporating eight strategically placed fortresses would ultimately surround the city. A segment of the ramparts extended out to sea so that ships literally had to sail into a narrow fortress, now easy to defend, to gain access to the city.

With Campeche nearly impregnable, the pirates turned their attention to ships at sea and other ports. In response, the brilliant naval strategist Felipe de Aranda started attacking the buccaneers in 1717 and in time made the Gulf safe from piracy.

Originally part of the state of Yucatán, Campeche became an autonomous state of Mexico in 1863. Although its port had become perhaps the most protected in the western hemisphere, in the 19th century it fell into an economic decline brought on by the demise of mineral shipments to Spain. Independence, the freeing of Indians from plantation slavery, the devastation wrought by the Caste War and overall isolation wreaked havoc with the port's prosperity.

Without highways to link Campeche to the rest of the country, the state's economy languished until the 1950s, when road and communication networks were finally built. Today, the hardwood lumber and fishing industries are thriving, and the discovery of offshore oil has led to a mini-boom in the city of Campeche. Tourism remains at a modest level here, something which travellers with a yen to avoid the gringo trail will appreciate.

Geography & Climate

The very north of Campeche is quite arid and flat. Immediately south of Campeche's border with Yucatán state, the land turns lush with rainforests abundant in the south-eastern sections of the state. The Gulf coast inlets produced excellent harbours frequently surrounded inland by rugged hills. The state's better than 50,000 square km are inhabited by about 370,000 people.

CAMPECHE

Population: 160,000

For a real respite from the touristy Caribbean coast, Campeche is the place. Tranquil, cheap and filled with historic buildings, Campeche is a worthwhile stop-over between Mérida and Villahermosa.

Information & Orientation

See the Getting Around section for details on how to get to the centre from the bus or train stations. Once in the town's compact centre, virtually all sights are within walking distance.

Tourist Office A friendly tourist office is located nearly on the water between Avenida 16 de Septiembre and Avenida Ruíz Cortínez on the Plaza Moch-Couoh. The only entrance faces the sea. Its hours are 8 am to 2.30 pm and 4 to 8.30 pm, closed Sunday.

Money For currency exchange, there are three banks all open Monday to Friday from 9 am to 1 pm: Bancomer across from Baluarte de la Soledad on Calle 59 2A at Avenida 16 de Septiembre, Banco de Atlántico at Calle 50 406 and Bánamex on Calle 10 15.

1	Santiago Fortress
2	Plaza del 4 Centenario
3	Archaeological Museum
4	Plaza Principal
5	Cathedral
6	Puerta de Mar (Sea Gate)
7	Hotel Castelmar
8	San Pedro Fortress
9	Museo de Campeche
10	Museo Regional de Campeche
11	San Francisco Fortress
12	Alameda
13	Santa Rosa Fortress
14	San Juan Fortress
15	Bus Terminal
16	Railway Station

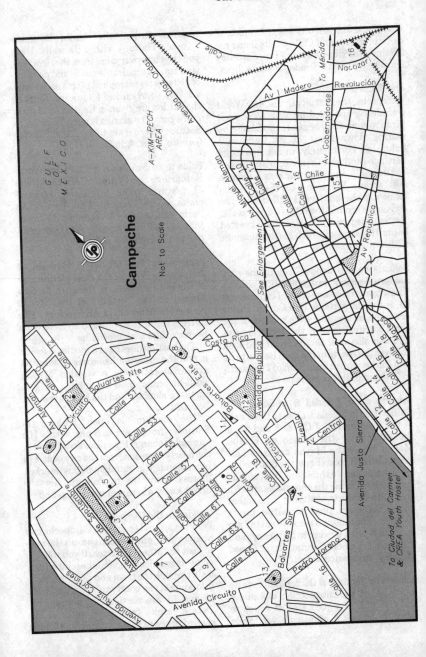

Post The main post office is at Avenida 16 de Septiembre and Calle 53. Its hours are Monday to Friday 8 am to 7 pm, Saturday 8 am to 1 pm and Sunday 8 am to 2 pm.

The Baluartes

Campeche, the first city in the New World completely encircled by walls to prevent pirate plundering, began to modernise by tearing down some of its impressive baluartes. Fortunately, in homage to its heritage (and also to lure tourists), seven of the walls and their fortress bulwarks still stand. You can see them all by following the boulevard called Circuito Baluartes around the city – quite a walk. Better, relegate yourself to the suggested baluartes, some of which house museums within their bastions.

Baluarte de San Carlos Close to the ugly modern Palacio de Gobierno, a stone's throw from the intersection of Calles 8 and 63, is the Baluarte de San Carlos. Inside are some interesting scale models of the city's fortifications in the 18th century. You can also visit the dungeon and look out over the sea from the roof. Baluarte de San Carlos is open from 9 am to 1 pm and 5 to 7.30 pm daily; there is no charge.

Baluarte de la Soledad & Museum The Baluarte de la Soledad, close to the zócalo at the intersection of Calles 8 and 57, is the setting for the Museo de Estelas Mayas. While the Mayan artefacts here are not in such good shape, the bastion has an interesting exhibition of colonial Campeche. Among the antiquities are 17th and 18th-century seafaring equipment and armaments used to battle pirate invaders. The museum is open 9 am to 2 pm and 3 to 8 pm Tuesday to Saturday, and 9 am to 1 pm on Sunday. It is closed Monday. Admission is free.

Baluarte de Santiago & Garden Baluarte de Santiago, at the intersection of Calle 8 and Calle 51, is a good spot at which to relax. It houses a minuscule yet lovely tropical garden, the Jardín Botánico (Xmuch Haltun) within its walls. Here you can ease your mind from the rigours of your travels amidst the shade and perfume of 250 species of tropical plants set around a lovely courtyard of fountains. Tours of the garden are given in English at 12 noon and 4 pm. The garden is open Tuesday to Saturday from 9 am to 8 pm and Sunday 9 am to 1 pm. Admission is 10c.

Baluarte de San Pedro & Crafts Exposition Baluarte de San Pedro on Calle 18 at Calle 51 features some interesting regional crafts in its bastion. This Exposición Permanente de Artesanías is open Monday to Friday from 9 am to 1 pm and 5 to 8 pm. Admission is free.

Baluarte de San Miguel & Museum of Archaeology Perhaps the most picturesque of the old fortresses is Baluarte de San Miguel on the outskirts of the city. It houses the Museum of Archaeology. The fortress has a moat alleged to have once been stocked with crocodiles.

The bastion does have a medieval feel to it and the museum has some interesting artefacts, including a wooden Mayan skull-deformer used on infants to give them the sloping head the Mayas thought beautiful.

The museum is open Tuesday to Saturday from 9 am to 5 pm, with a 10c admission charge. If you don't wish to walk the nearly three km from the city centre to here, catch the municipal bus marked 'Lerma' from the market and let the driver know where you want to get off.

Walking in Old Campeche

Walking around the rest of Campeche can be enjoyable, and you can consult the map to visit the other baluartes. If you want to enjoy magnificent colonial architecture, walk through the town and peer discreetly into some of the courtyards. Calles 55, 57, 59 and 61 are particularly noteworthy. Take a respite from your walks at the shaded green of the Alameda on Avenida

República at Circuito Baluartes. The Alameda's Bridge of Dogs with its colonial carved stone canines was named for Dominican missionaries' dogged dedication to conversion.

The Franciscan cathedral, whose construction began during the year of Campeche's founding in 1540 (it was completed in 1705), is the Yucatán's oldest church. It is located on the zócalo. For a view of the city, though quite a walk, go north on Gobernadores, left on Cuauhtémoc, left on Calle 101 and right on Calle 7. There you will find Fuerte San José el Alto with its magnificent view of the environs. Nearby stands one of the oldest lighthouses in the New World, circa 1864. Next to it a former church is now a museum-cum-souvenir shop.

A good 20 minutes' walk from the centre of Campeche stands the San Francisco Convent built in 1546 and alleged to have been the site of the first mass held in Mexico. Close by is the Pozo de la Conquista where Hernández de Córdoba's soldiers supposedly first found water in 1517.

Museo Regional de Campeche

The best of the city's artefacts are displayed in the Museo Regional de Campeche. Located in a former mansion of the Spanish royal governor, the museum may be found at Calle 59, between Calles 14 and 16.

You will see a model of the colonial city close to the entrance and pre-Hispanic artefacts and paintings on the 1st floor. There's quite a good re-creation of Mayan life here, through the use of models and antiquities. On the upper level you will find an excellent exhibition of colonial life. The Museo Regional is open Tuesday to Saturday from 9 am to 8 pm and Sunday 9 am to 1 pm. There is no admission charge.

Museo de Campeche

Less intriguing for its representation of the past than for its exhibitions of contemporary Mexican art is the Museo de Campeche at the intersection of Calles 63 and 10. The building is the refurbished San José Church (built in 1640). The modern displays change regularly. The museum is open daily from 10 am to 1 pm and 5 to 9 pm; admission is free.

Beach

If you must visit a beach, the Playa Bonita can be reached by the Lerma-Playa Bonita bus from the zócalo (it's nine km west of town). Be forewarned that it is crowded on hot days and frightfully littered, and that its seas are a most uninviting gloppy yellow-green.

Places to Stay – bottom end

Campeche has a good *CREA Youth Hostel*, but because there are reasonably priced hotels in town, you may prefer to stay at one of them rather than take the 25-minute walk (or bus) to the hostel. If you are walking from the centre of town, trek along the shore until you hit Agustín Melgar (Avenida Cortínez becomes Avenida Resurgimiento), where you will take a left to the hostel. Alternatively, take the bus designated 'Lerma' from the zócalo area. As CREA Youth Hostels go, this one is quite nice with clean, segregated dorms, a swimming pool and inexpensive cafeteria. A dorm bunk costs US$1.75, breakfast US$0.60, lunch and dinner about US$1.

There are a number of good hotels at reasonable prices. The well-located *Castelmar* (no phone) at Calle 61 2 between Calles 8 and 10 has clean rooms with fan, bath and (sometimes) balcony for only US$4 a single, US$5.50 double. If you are willing to spend a bit more for air-conditioning (although not all rooms have it), the *Hotel López* (tel 6-33-44) at Calle 12 189 between Calles 61 and 63 offers spotless rooms with bath at US$8 for singles, US$9.50 for doubles and US$11 for three in the room.

Two decent hotels with bath and fan are the *Hotel America* (tel 6-45-88) at Calle 10

252 between Calles 59 and 61; and *Hotel Colonial* (no phone) at Calle 14 122, between Calles 55 and 57. Both charge US$6 for a single and US$7.50 for a double. Rooms at the America are somewhat larger but it is popular and often filled. The Colonial is close to the zócalo and well maintained.

Even if you've arrived late at the bus station and think you're too tired to move much further, resist the temptation to crash across the street at the *Hotel Central*. It's pricey and not all that clean – better to take a taxi to one of the hotels in town.

Camping About 2½ km from the zócalo, *Trailer Park Campeche* has sites for trailers and tents. Follow the coastal road south and make a left on Melgar. Or ask at the tourist office if you can pitch a tent near them.

Places to Stay – top end
Hotel El Presidente (tel 6-22-33) is the cheapest of this luxury chain, offering a swimming pool and views of the Gulf. It's well located at Avenida Ruíz Cortínes 51. Rooms with refrigerators and TV run US$29 for singles and US$37 for doubles.

Nearby at Ruíz Cortínes 61 is the older *Hotel Baluartes* (tel 6-39-11). There is a pool here too, and rooms with Gulf views have air-conditioning and TV for US$23 single, US$27 double.

Places to Eat
Campeche has some good, reasonably priced seafood – particularly its shrimp (*camarones*). Two moderately priced restaurants are the *Restaurant del Parque* on the zócalo at Calles 8 and 57, and the *Miramar* at Calles 8 and 61. The Miramar is famous in Campeche for its seafood, while the Restaurant del Parque offers particularly good value for its comida corrida.

Another good restaurant in the centre is *La Parroquia* at Calle 55 9 between Calles 8 and 10. La Parroquia is a good place to try typical Campechan dishes, especially breakfast. Inexpensive for quick lunches is *Cafetería Nevería* on Calle 8 at Calle 61. The Nevería has inexpensive, so-so, but filling fare. Near the Youth Hostel on the coastal highway, try the palapa-thatched roof café *Balneario Popular*. Especially good are its *camarones empanizadas* – fried shrimp.

Entertainment
In the Plaza Moch-Couoh near the tourist office, there's an interesting production of folkloric music and dance called Estampas Turísticas. It is presented free, weather permitting, on Friday evening at 8 pm. Another folkloric show is put on at the *Puerta de Tierra* on Calle 18 at Calle 59 every other Saturday at 8 pm.

On weekend evenings in the zócalo, there are sometimes performances of regional music and dance. Ask at the tourist office. Campeche's most popular discos are at the luxury *El Presidente* and *Baluartes* hotels. Local cinemas sometimes have English-language films with Spanish subtitles.

Getting There & Away
Bus There are almost hourly 1st-class buses to and from Mérida, taking about 2½ hours and costing about US$2.50. First-class buses also run regularly to Villahermosa, six hours, US$6. There are three daily buses to Chetumal and two to Mexico City.

Rail Trains should be avoided as there is considerable banditry in these parts and, in any event, the trains to and from Campeche are extremely pokey.

Getting Around
Most travellers arrive by bus and have about a 25-minute walk to the centre of town. Local buses, designated either 'Gobernadores' or 'Centro' to the zócalo, depart from in front of the bus station; or take a taxi, they're cheap in Campeche. From the bus station, taxi fare is about

US$1.25 to the centre of town. The train station is about two km out of town, and buses departing from a stop to the right (west) as you leave the station will take you to the zócalo.

If you wish to do the 25-minute walk from the bus station, turn left on Gobernadores and walk until you reach Baluarte San Pedro. Bear left on the boulevard Circuito Baluartes and continue for three blocks, turning right on Calle 57 which in four blocks will bring you to the zócalo. Once you're in the town's compact centre, virtually all sights are within walking distance.

AROUND CAMPECHE

Edzná

About 20 km south-east of Campeche lie the ruins of Edzná, including the impressive, appropriately named Pyramid of Five Storeys. Built in the region's Chenes style, the structure is huge, with a base measuring 61 by 59 metres and a height of 30 metres from the base to the top. You fully appreciate the enormity of the pyramid by walking the 65 steps to the five-room temple at the crest. The temple is topped by a crown-like 'comb', once covered with stucco carvings which have eroded away.

This pyramid, known to the Mayas as the 'House of Grimaces' for the stucco masks that adorned the comb, affords a striking view of the plazas and largely unexcavated mounds below. You can use your imagination to envision the extraordinary irrigation-canal system constructed entirely by hand, as the Mayas had neither metal building implements nor the wheel.

As you descend the pyramid from the top, remind yourself that you are walking past four increasingly larger levels believed at one point to house the local Mayan religious hierarchy. The priests were thought to have lived higher up, 'closer to heaven'.

The Pyramid of Five Storeys is on the eastern edge of the site. On Edzná's western side, you might visit the recently restored Paal u'na, or Temple of the Moon. You can also see some of the finely carved 19 stelae dating back to the 7th century. Most of the rest of Edzná, which flourished for nearly 700 years until it was inexplicably deserted, has yet to be excavated.

Getting There & Away As of this writing, a 2nd-class bus departs Campeche at 8 am, takes 1½ hours to reach the site, and returns to Campeche between 11.30 am and 12 noon. Obviously this doesn't give you much time at the site, but for ruins buffs without their own transport it will have to do. Forget about the 2.30 departure from Campeche. Unless you catch a ride with a private car – and few tourists visit the site – you will be faced with no bus back to Campeche. Be certain to bring a canteen of water; there's no refreshment stand at this isolated site.

Alternatively, expensive guided tours are set up by the luxury hotels if they have enough people. Your best bet if you want to move at your own pace and not spend too much money is to take your own vehicle or, if you are extremely lucky, hitch-hike back. The site is open daily from 8 am to 5 pm.

Isla Jaina

Of interest to true archaeological buffs, an island roughly four hours' sail from Campeche was discovered to be the site of the most substantial Mayan burial ground on the peninsula. Isla Jaina was used for centuries as the final resting-place for the Mayan religious and political hierarchy. In 1950 archaeologists found skeletons in burial jars along with weaponry, jewellery, food and anything else it was thought the deceased Mayas might need en route to another life. Also buried with the Mayas were extraordinary clay figurines.

The Zacpool and Sayasol pyramids were built from a base of limestone brought from the mainland to serve as a foundation over the fragile coral.

Getting There & Away As Isla Jaina is virtually deserted, the only way to get to the island is to have one of the luxury hotels, travel agencies or the tourist office (provided there are enough people) charter a boat and provide a guide. The quoted price is about US$9 per person. Ask the tourist office what a fair price should be.

CIUDAD DEL CARMEN

Very few travellers come to this fishing and oil town on the coast of Campeche, south of the town of Campeche. Those who do either want to fish or try the undulating tropical route from Villahermosa. The route is exceedingly slow because of numerous ferry crossings over estuaries. Ciudad del Carmen was once a pirate headquarters (1558-1717) and today lives off the oil industry, shipbuilding, fishing and canning.

Things to See & Do

If you wish to swim, don't expect the crystalline waters of the Caribbean coast. The best beaches are Playa Benjamín and El Playon. The tiny Archaeological Museum at Liceo Carmelita has some regionally excavated artefacts on display. There is a small admission charge of about 10c. Band concerts are held in the zócalo on Thursday and Sunday evenings.

The town's major festival is dedicated to its patron saint the Virgen del Carmen, and is joyously celebrated the last two weeks of July.

Places to Stay

The *Hotel Zacarias* (tel 2-01-21) at Calle 24 58 is the best hotel for your money. It has clean rooms with fan and bath for US$8 single and US$10 double.

Places to Eat

Two three-star hotels, the *Isla del Carmen* at Calle 20A 9 and the *Lli-Re* at Calle 32 23, have excellent fish dishes, though they're not cheap. There are plenty of taquerías and little marisco stands around the market on Calles 39 and 20.

Getting There & Away

If you are coming from or going to Villahermosa, start early in the day because the journey requires several ferry crossings. There is regular bus service to Campeche (three hours), Villahermosa, Escárcega and Mérida.

ESCÁRCEGA

Population: 11,000

There is little reason to stop in this town at the junction of highways 186 and 261, south of Campeche. A few travellers are exhausted enough to overnight here, and some stop to change buses in Escárcega en route to Palenque. The Mayan ruins of Chicanna, Becan and Xpuhil, located east of Escárcega near the Quintana Roo border, are described in the Around Chetumal section.

Places to Stay

Although you can find cheaper, the *Hotel Akim-Pech* on the Escárcega-Villahermosa road and the *María Isabel Hotel* at Avenida Justo Sierra 127 offer the best lodging for your money. They have clean singles with fan and bath for US$8 and doubles for US$10.

The *Escárcega* on Avenida Justo Sierra 86 and the *San Luis* in front of the zócalo have doubles at less than US$5 but are not well maintained.

Places to Eat

Both the *María Isabel Hotel* and the *Hotel Akim-Pech* have decent *típico* fare at reasonable prices.

Getting There & Away

Bus There is a regular service to Palenque originating at the 2nd-class bus station on Justo Sierra and Calle 31. If you are arriving or departing by 1st-class bus, the

ADO station is at the junction of Justo Sierra and Highway 261. Here you will find buses bound for Campeche, Mérida and Villahermosa. If bound for the Caribbean coast, head for the Caribe bus depot, three blocks west of the zócalo on Perez Martínes. There is a regular service to Chetumal.

Rail The train station is north of Avenida Méndez and services Campeche and Mérida, as well as Mexico City.

MÉRIDA TO CAMPECHE – SHORT ROUTE

The short route to Mérida from Campeche is what most travellers without their own vehicles will take, as 1st-class buses ply the 193 km on Route 180 direct. You can catch 2nd-class buses to Pomuch, 69 km from Campeche, where present-day inhabitants build their houses from debris of Mayan ruins. You might also catch a 2nd-class bus 76 km north of Campeche to the Museo Arqueológico del Camino Real, where you will find some Jaina burial artefacts as well as ceramics and jewellery from relatively recently excavated sites. The museum is closed Sunday and Monday and open Tuesday to Saturday, 9 am to 6 pm, for 2c admission.

Ruins Near Hecelchkan

In Hecelchkan you can rent a jeep and guide for remote sites off dirt tracks but this will set you back US$75 to US$100 for the day. The sites include the ruins of Almuchil, Holactum and Xcalumkin.

Calkini & Becal

Moving north on the short route, about 100 km from Campeche you will find the town of Calkini, site of a 16th-century monastery. On the Campeche state side of the border with Yucatán is the town of Becal, famous as the home of the original Panama hat which is still the chief industry of the village. For a small tip (actually it's hard to avoid paying them), local guides will take you to underground workshops where palm-tree leaves are made into the hats. They are woven underground to maintain consistency of temperature so that they will retain their shape.

MÉRIDA TO CAMPECHE – LONG ROUTE

The long route to Mérida from Campeche should be undertaken with your own car. This 254-km trip via Route 261 is recommended because of the isolated ruins accessible to you. If you are trying to get about by bus, most of the sites have no public transport and you might be stuck for several days at some of them unless you plan to make your way out on foot. The ruins closest to Campeche, Dzibilnocac, Hochob and the Grutas of Xtacumbilxunaan, will be described here. The Puuc sites of Sayil, Xlapak and Labra and the Grutas of Loltún, closer to Mérida, will be covered in the Around Mérida section.

Dzibilnocac

The first two temples you encounter may make you wonder why you have ventured off the beaten track to come here. The third temple will reward you. With its rounded base and delicately narrow design, it is unique. Climb the edifice and see primitive cave paintings on the way up. On the upper level, you will see in full detail a stunning if frightening carving of Chac, the rain god. Looking down, you'll see how little has been excavated around here.

Getting There & Away If you are trying to get here by bus, prepare to spend at least one night in the town of Dzibalchén – in other words, bring a hammock and insect repellent. Take a bus from Campeche to Dzibalchén village (change at Hopelchen if necessary). From Dzibalchén village, there might be a bus to the town of Iturbide; they don't run every day. You can walk to the site from Iturbide.

To drive to the Dzibilnocac ruins, take Highway 261 to the town of Hopelchen, then take the road south to Dzibalchén. Turn left at the zócalo and follow the road to the village of Iturbide. Bear to the right past Iturbide's zócalo on a rugged dirt track (make sure your car has fairly high clearance) to the ruins.

Hochob

Even harder to reach without a car than Dzibilnocac, Hochob rewards the off-the-beaten-track traveller with exceptional ruins. Hochob's central ceremonial plaza, where the only real excavation has been done to date, sits on a hill overlooking the rainforest.

The building on the right of the plaza is festooned with some fine Mayan stucco carvings of geometric designs. Most impressive, although you will have to use your imagination a bit, the façade of the structure was constructed in the image of a gigantic mask of the rain god Chac, with the sizeable door serving as an angry mouth. Though eroded (there's a full reconstruction of the building at the National Museum of Anthropology in Mexico City), the face of Chac in this isolated jungle setting is spooky enough to let the viewer imagine secret Mayan ceremonial rites.

Opposite Hochob's entrance, you will see another edifice bearing Chac's image. To the right is a steep pyramid which is the site's tallest building. Although Hochob has a dirt track running to other mounds, they are yet to be excavated and the path is worth pursuing to get a sense of the enormity of the site. Who knows what splendid ruins wait to be unearthed from the jungles here?

Getting There & Away To reach Hochob by car, drive within a km of the town of Dzibalchen. Take the road to the left where you see the sign for Chencoh, a village nine km from this turn-off. You will need high clearance for this road, which during part of the rainy season may be washed out. At Chencoh, take the second left and after you have passed a farm, make another left onto a mud track which will take you about four km into the rainforest. Turn left at the fork and you will soon see the ruins.

Without your own vehicle it's harder to get here than to the ruins of Dzibilnocac. Take a 2nd-class bus to Dzibalchen from Campeche (with a transfer at Hopelchen if there is no direct bus). From Dzibalchen, walk back about a km on the road to Campeche, and where you see the Chencoh sign start hitching the nine km to that village. You will probably have to walk the four km to Hochob from Chencoh. Once you're at the ruins, there is nothing or no one to stop you from camping here. Just bring plenty of insect repellent.

Grutas (Caves) of Xtacumbilxunaan

About 30 km past the village of Hopelchen on Highway 261, you will see a sign marking the one-km side road to the Grutas de Xtacumbilxunaan (Mayan for 'Caves of the Hidden Woman'). For a tip, a guide will take you through the caves. They are not without interest, but save your energy for the caverns of Loltún.

Yucatán

The state of Yucatán has a treasure trove of attractions for the visitor. Its hub is Mérida, the capital, with colonial architecture, savoury Yucatecan cuisine, and a relaxed atmosphere for a major Mexican city. Its port, Progreso, permits the visitor to experience a truly Mexican beach free of the gringo mobs frequenting parts of the Caribbean coast. Charming Valladolid is a tranquil Mayan town, also removed from the tourist hurly-burly. For those interested in colourful bird life, the flamingo sanctuaries of Río Lagartos and Celestún are certain to delight you.

Best of all, travellers are drawn here by the ruins of the great Mayan civilisation. The archaeological sites of Chichén Itzá and Uxmal bring visitors from all over the world, who come to admire the magnificent

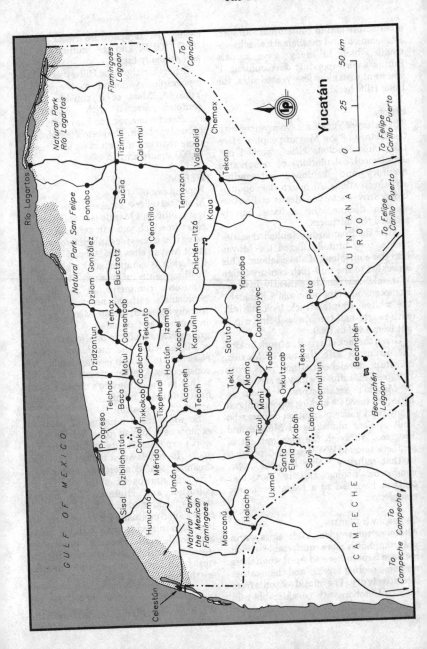

architecture and to contemplate artistic, astronomical and mathematical achievements which in many ways surpass Europe's corresponding development. If you want to explore less-visited sites, the Puuc Hills beckon.

History

The history of Yucatán is synonymous with the history of the Mayan peoples. Here they built fabulous cities, worked out astrological calculations of remarkable accuracy and fashioned outstanding artistic creations. Although the conquistadors arrived after the Mayas' civilisation was in decline, the Indians fiercely resisted the intruders.

After the Spaniards established settlements, they brutally forced the Mayas into the equivalent of slave labour. This abuse led to the mid-19th-century Caste War which saw the Mayas nearly drive the Europeans out of the peninsula. Ultimately, the whites' counterattack took its toll, with nearly half the Mayas being wiped out from 1846 to 1850.

Given the lack of a road network linking the peninsula with the rest of Mexico, Yucatán developed strong ties with Europe. This influence may be seen today in Mérida's architecture. A boom in henequen (used for making rope) produced many millionaire plantation owners who built opulent mansions in Mérida and Progreso. Although the development of synthetics around WW II led to a depression in that industry, other tropical crops, commerce, fishing and in particular tourism have led to a recent economic resurgence.

Geography & Climate

Although the tropical Yucatán is warm year round, it is more comfortable to visit between September and April when there are some cooling breezes and the weather is relatively dry. The humid season is from May to October, with considerable rain and a cloying mugginess. July and August can be extremely sticky, with many days seeing the temperature hover around 40°C (100°F) and the humidity is also exceptionally high.

Other than the Puuc Hills, there is little topographic variation in the state of Yucatán. Most of it consists of flat contours covered with a tangle of rainforest wherever the Mayas have not burned the bush. The state's population is more than one million in an area close to 40,000 square km.

MÉRIDA

Population: 600,000

Most travellers escape cities to find tranquillity but Mérida is one of those rare cities in which you can genuinely relax, using it as a base for exploring some of the great Mayan sites (see Around Mérida).

Mérida is compact and while it is a bustling centre of business, the hub of Yucatán's commerce, it is also the peninsula's cultural heart. People are friendly here and, despite Mérida's growth in tourism, not so jaded as to see every gringo as a mark to rip off. Because this is a Mayan city, the *machismo* present elsewhere in Mexico is considerably less conspicuous. Another attraction of Mérida is that as one of Mexico's oldest cities it has retained much of its colonial architectural charm.

So while it's a jumping-off point for excursions to Mayan ruins, Mérida is also worth exploring for its architecture and crafts. Its hotels are a budget traveller's dream: clean, comfortable and cheap. The only drawbacks of the city are its pollution and climate. The narrow streets, bounded by buildings and constructed originally for horse-carts, are less than pleasant with today's heavy automobile traffic. Because summers are steaming, with heavy showers in late spring and early summer, winter months are the best time to visit Mérida.

History

When the conquistadors landed here in the early 16th century, they saw a major Mayan

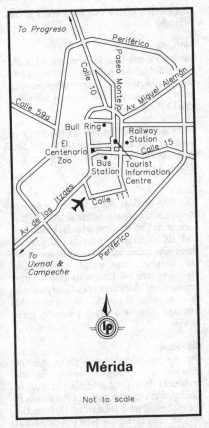

Mérida

Not to scale

the periphery were also worked by Indian slave labour. This gross inequity resulted in the Caste War.

Ultimately the Spaniards, some mestizos and a few Mayas would prosper in Mérida, as it became the centre for the state's tobacco and sugar industries. Later the city became the heart of the henequen trade. By WW I the demand for rope made from the henequen plant gave Mérida more millionaires per capita than any other city in the world. Today you can see the henequen barons' splendid mansions off Mérida's Paseo Montejo.

Currently Mérida flourishes, with light industries producing sisal goods, beer, flour and fine wooden furniture. It remains a commercial centre for the surrounding agrarian sector, serving as the distribution point for henequen, fruit, timber, tobacco and beef. Tourism has also added income.

Orientation

Once you get the hang of it, Mérida's numbered grid system makes it easy to find your way around. The zócalo, or Plaza Mayor, is your easiest reference point. It is bounded by Calles 60, 62, 61 and 63. Odd-numbered streets run east to west, while even-numbered streets run north to south. Numbers on street addresses rise or fall slowly. This means, for example, that between 300 and 400 on a given street, you may have to walk 10 blocks or more.

Tourist Office There is a tourist information booth in the Palacio Municipal off the zócalo, opposite the cathedral. It's open Monday to Saturday from 8 am to 8 pm and Sunday 8 am to 5 pm. There's another convenient office in the Teatro Peon Contreras on Calle 60 between Calles 57 and 59. Its hours are Monday to Friday 8 am to 9 pm, Saturday 9 am to 4 pm and Sunday 9 am to 12 noon. There are other tourist offices in the airport and 1st-class bus station, but they are not as helpful and have less information.

settlement of lime-mortared stone which reminded them of Roman architectural legacies in Mérida, Spain. The Indians of the village resisted and it wasn't until 1542, after nearly 14 years of war, that the Spaniards under the Montejo family were able to take the city, renaming it after its Spanish likeness.

While the Spanish flourished, using Mérida as the peninsula's commercial centre (which it had also been under the Mayas), the enslaved Indians built churches, colonial seats of government, mansions and plazas. The plantations on

Money A casa de cambio in the Palacio Montejo on the zócalo offers higher rates than the banks. Otherwise try Bánamex in the zócalo or the banks in the vicinity of Calle 65 between Calles 62 and 60. Banking hours are 9.30 am to 1.30 pm Monday to Friday.

Post The main post office is on Calle 65 between Calles 56 and 56A. It is open Monday to Friday 8 am to 7 pm and Saturday from 9 am to 1 pm. You can buy stamps at the airport and the 1st-class bus station on weekdays. There is an American Express office which holds mail for clients at the Hotel Los Aluxes, Calles 60 and 44.

Consulates A number of countries have consulates in Mérida. The American Consulate (tel 25-50-11) is at Paseo de Montejo 453 at the corner of Avenida Colón. The Canadian Consulate (tel 25-62-99) is at Calle 62 309-D-19. The British Vice-Consulate (tel 21-67-99) is at Calle 53 489 on the corner of Calle 58. You can get information about travel in Belize at the British Vice-Consulate, weekday mornings from 9.30 am to 12 noon.

Travel Agencies Although there are numerous travel and car-rental agencies in Mérida, those associated with Miguel Escalante Moreno are highly recommended. 'Mike', as Miguel calls himself, speaks fluent English and is a scholar of Mayan antiquities. Moreover, he is scrupulously honest. His agencies include T'ho in the Hotel Reforma and run all the tours to ruins and light shows. Worth considering if you are not renting a car is his tour to the Puuc sites of Sayril, Kabah, Xlapak and the Loltún Caves. The agencies also sell air tickets – ask Escalante about his tours of Cuba. Mérida is the cheapest embarkation point for flights to Havana.

Laundry There's a good laundry on Calle 59 between Calles 72 and 74. They do same-day service and a full load costs about US$1.60.

Festivals
Carnival Prior to Lent in February or March, Carnival features colourful costumes and non-stop festivities. It is celebrated with greater vigour in Mérida than anyplace else in the Yucatán.

Cristo de las Ambillas During the first two weeks in October, the Christ of the Blisters statue is venerated with processions and religious good cheer.

Zócalo
The most logical place to start a tour of Mérida is the zócalo, or Plaza Mayor. It is surrounded by ancient colonial buildings, and its vegetation provides shade for those who come here to relax or socialise. On Sunday, the zócalo's adjoining roadways are off-limits to traffic, and hundreds of Méridans take their *paseo* in this municipal park. If you speak Spanish, this is a good place to meet locals.

Cathedral
On the east side of the plaza, on the grounds of a Mayan temple, is the cathedral. In a quintessential example of Christian arrogance, some of the stones of the cathedral were taken directly from the Mayan temple. Ground for the cathedral was broken in 1561, the church completed in 1598.

Walk into the chapel and look to the left of the principal altar for Mérida's most famous religious artefact, a statue of Jesus called Cristo de las Ambillas, or the Christ of the Blisters. Local legend has it that this statue was carved from a tree in the town of Ichmul. The tree, hit by lightning, supposedly burned for an entire night yet showed no sign of fire. The statue carved from the tree was placed in the local church where it alone is said to have survived the fiery destruction of the church. Charred and blistered, it was venerated and moved to the Mérida Cathedral in 1645. The faithful still make pilgrimages here in its honour.

The rest of the church's interior is drab and relatively empty of ornamentation. The bulk of its riches were pilfered by angry peasants at the height of anti-clerical feeling during the Revolution. The plundering was retribution for the Church's longtime alliance with those who exploited the Indians in these parts.

Palace of the Archbishop

The former Palace of the Archbishop sitting south of the cathedral became a military post during the Revolution. Today it remains an army headquarters in conjunction with some touristy shops.

Palacio de Gobierno

On the north side of the plaza, the Palacio de Gobierno contains murals completed by local painter Fernando Castro Pacheco in 1978 – the culmination of 25 years of work. In vivid colours, the murals portray a symbolic history of the Mayas and their interaction with the Spaniards. Over the stairwell is a painting of Mayan sacred corn, their 'ray of sun from the gods'. Overall, the murals suggest that despite the brutal intrusion of the Europeans, the spirit of Mayan culture lives on. The palace is open Monday to Saturday from 8 am to 8 pm and Sunday from 9 am to 5 pm. On the upper level, you will find the History Chamber Library housing some rare books on the colonial era.

Palacio Municipal

Across from the cathedral, the Palacio Municipal functions as the City Hall, crowned by a clock tower. Originally built in 1542, it has twice (in the 1730s and 1850s) been refurbished. Intended as the town hall, it served as a jail in the 18th century.

Casa de Montejo

Set on the south side of the zócalo, this present-day Bánamex was (until the 1970s) a mansion occupied by the Montejo family. It was constructed for the conqueror of Mérida, Francisco de Montejo, by his son in 1549. Walk in during the bank's business hours and you will see in full measure the contempt and brutality of the Spanish toward the Indians. Carved above the doorway are triumphant conquistadors, their feet atop the heads of the defeated Mayas.

Museo de Antropología

It's about a 20-minute walk from the zócalo to the Museo de Antropología on Paseo Montejo at the intersection of Calle 43. Once a mansion built for a former Yucatán governor, the anthropological museum is administered by the National Institute of Anthropology & History. There are some fascinating artefacts here, accompanied by anthropological interpretations examining every facet of Mayan daily life. Unfortunately they're in Spanish, but the museum is worth a visit anyway for its exhibits.

Among the exhibits are macabre head-flattening devices which the Mayas applied to their babies' skulls to beautify them with sloping foreheads. In a more aesthetic vein, there are sculptures and fine pottery. The museum's gift shop has some good crafts and inexpensive guide-books to various Mexican archaeological sites. Buy them here; they are cheaper than at the sites themselves.

To get to the museum take Calle 60 and make a right on Calle 43 to Paseo Montejo. Hours are Tuesday to Saturday 8 am to 8 pm and Sunday 8 am to 2 pm. The gift shop closes weekdays at 3 pm. Admission to the museum is about 25c.

Paseo Montejo & Local Mansions

The Paseo Montejo was an attempt by Mérida's affluent to create a sense of the Champs Elysées. This French influence and some of Mérida's architecture are by-products of the city's trade with Europe while geographically cut off from most of

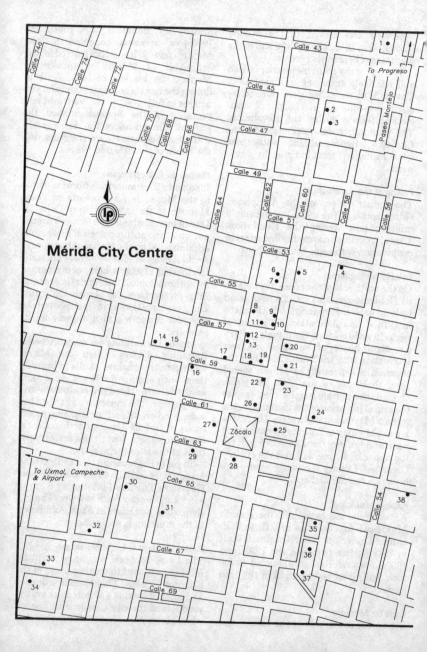

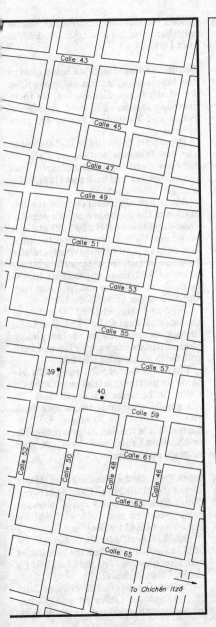

1 Museo de Antropología
2 Santa Ana Church
3 Santa Ana Square
4 British Vice-Consulate
5 Vegetariano La Guaya
6 Santa Lucia Church
7 Santa Lucia Park
8 Hotel Trinidad
9 Wini
10 Mérida Mision
11 Pop Café
12 Hotel Colonial
13 Yannig Restaurant
14 Hotel del Gobernador
15 Cedro de Libano
16 Central Telephone Office
17 Avis Car Rental
18 Hotel Reforma
19 Pizzaria de Vito Corleone
20 Tourist Information Centre
21 Iglesia de Jesús
22 Café Restaurant Express
23 Hotel Caribe
24 Mexicana Airlines
25 Cathedral
26 Palacio de Gobierno
27 Palacio Municipal
28 Palacio Montejo
29 Hotel Lord
30 Hospedaje Bowen
31 Hotel Maria Teresa
32 Posada del Ángel
33 Hotel San Jorge
34 Bus Station
35 Post Office
36 Municipal Market
37 Arts & Crafts Bazaar
38 Hotel Dolores Alba
39 Restaurant Los Almendros
40 Museo Regional de Artesanías

Mexico. The city was also influenced by French merchants who settled in Mérida while conducting trade with their homeland.

Mansions of henequen barons may be seen off the Paseo. A romantic but somewhat expensive way to see the mansions is to rent a *calesa*, a horse-drawn carriage. Bargain hard – you should get 90 minutes for less than US$10. Try to avoid taking a *calesa* Sunday night when locals on their day off provide plenty of business, driving prices up.

Keep walking along the Paseo Montejo and you will come to Monumento a la Patria. Nearby, Parque de las Américas contains trees from every country in the western hemisphere.

On your way back from Paseo Montejo toward the zócalo on Calle 60, you will pass many colonial structures and pleasant little parks. At Calle 59 you will see Hidalgo Park and its 17th-century Jesuit church, Iglesia de Jesús, between the Plaza Hidalgo and Parque de la Madre. Nearby on Calle 59 is the Cepeda Peraza Library housing rare books from the colonial era. Between Calles 59 and 57 the Italian-designed Teatro Peon Contreras, made with beautiful marble, is now a tourist office. On the west corner of Calle 57 stands the 19th-century University of Yucatán. Just beyond is the Parque Santa Lucia, a pleasant place to relax where on Thursday at 9 pm local musicians sometimes play.

Museo Regional de Artesanías

On Calle 59 between Calles 48 and 50, close to the popular Los Almendros restaurant, it's easy to overlook this little-publicised museum. The excellent exhibits are well displayed and offer a good variety of fine items from all over the country. Don't miss it.

Places to Stay – bottom end

North of the Zócalo One of the best deals in this area is the *Hotel Trinidad* on Calle 62 between Calles 55 and 57, which pleasant owner Manolo Riviera, who speaks some English, also runs as an art gallery. Some rooms have private baths, and the shared bathroom is quite clean. Singles here are only US$3.25, doubles US$5.50 – quite a deal but the proprietor is refurbishing the hotel and prices will rise accordingly.

The pleasant *Hotel del Parque* (tel 24-78-44) is at Calle 60 495, at Calle 59. The somewhat small rooms are clean and well

priced for this neighbourhood. Singles with bath and fan cost US$6.25, doubles cost US$7.75.

Bus Station Area Most of the hotels close to the 1st-class bus station are over-priced for what you get. Nonetheless, for those travellers staggering in tired, Posada del Ángel and Hospedaje Bowen are good choices.

Posada del Ángel (tel 23-27-54) close to the 1st-class bus station on Calle 67 between 66 and 68 is quiet and nice. Clean rooms with fan and bath cost US$7.50 for a single, US$9 double.

About half the distance from the bus station to the zócalo is a superb pensión, *Hospedaje Bowen* (tel 21-81-12) at Calle 66 501 near Calle 65. Family-run, the quiet Bowen has a pretty garden courtyard nice to lounge in; purified water is thoughtfully provided and most appreciated in the heat. Rooms with fan and bath cost only US$4.50 single, US$5.25 double.

The *San Pablo* (tel 21-69-74) is close to the bus station at Calle 70 543C at Calle 69, but its small rooms are marginally clean. Spartan singles with fan and bath cost US$3.50, doubles US$4.50.

The sole benefit of *San Jorge* (tel 24-91-44) is its proximity to the bus station on Calle 69 between Calles 68 and 70. Marginally acceptable rooms with bath and fan cost US$5.50 single, US$7.75 double. While the San Jorge is preferable to the San Pablo, you don't get your money's worth here.

South-West of the Zócalo *Hotel María Teresa* (tel 21-10-39) on Calle 64 between Calles 65 and 67 offers quiet, pleasant rooms with fan and bath at US$5 for singles and US$6 for doubles.

The *Hotel Sevilla* (tel 21-52-58) at Calle 62 511 near Calle 65 offers the bare basics with telephone, fan and bath for US$5.50 single, US$6.25 double.

The *Hotel Oveido* (tel 21-36-09) at Calle 62 515 between Calles 65 and 67 has spartan accommodation for those with limited funds. Single rooms with fan and bath cost US$4.75, doubles US$5.50.

South-East of the Zócalo The *Hotel Peninsular* (tel 23-69-96) at Calle 58 519 between Calles 65 and 67 has basic, reasonably kept rooms with fan and bath costing US$6 single and US$7.75 double.

Hotel Mexico (tel 24-70-22) at Calle 60 525 between Calles 65 and 67 has adequate but none-too-plush rooms with fan and bath priced at US$4.75 single and US$5.50 double.

Last and certainly least, for those down to their last dollar, *Hotel D'Farahon* (tel 21-91-92) will provide a marginally acceptable place to flop. If you are desperate enough to find it, you are desperate enough to stay there. Go into the clothing shop at Calle 65 468 between Calles 54 and 56. Walk up the stairs and you will find this warren of a hotel. Spartan singles with fan but no hot water cost US$3, doubles US$4.

Places to Stay – middle
North of the Zócalo For convenience and comfort, these hotels can't be beat. Although they are not the cheapest, you do get real value for your money.

The *Hotel Colonial* (tel 23-64-44) offers sizeable, fully air-conditioned rooms a few blocks from the zócalo at Calle 62 476 at the corner of Calle 57. Manager Leticia Guerrero Zetina speaks English and is most informative. Each room has a telephone and TV, and some rooms have a sink area separate from the shower – a convenience for those sharing a double. There is a minuscule swimming pool adjacent to the bar. Singles cost US$12.75, doubles US$15.

The *Hotel Caribe* (tel 21-92-32) is well-located just a block from the zócalo at Calle 59 500 near Calle 60. Because it offers great value for money it is nearly always full. If you hope to stay here, book your room early in the day. Situated back from the street in a pleasant plaza, the Caribe has both a decent restaurant next

to its lobby and a café in the plaza for breakfasts, snacks and coffee. The hotel has a small rooftop pool and a deck overlooking the plaza. The cheaper rooms have telephones, fans and bath; singles cost US$9.25 and doubles US$11.50.

The *Hotel Reforma* (tel 24-79-22), set back from the street with a tranquil, tiled courtyard, is an older hotel with atmosphere. Located a short hop from the zócalo at Calle 59 between Calles 60 and 62, the Reforma has tropical shrubbery in its lobby and a pool that was empty on each of our two visits to Mérida. Well-maintained rooms have high ceilings. Prices are moderate; singles with bath and fan cost US$8.25 or US$9 with air-conditioning, doubles with bath and fan cost US$9 or US$10 with air-conditioning.

South-West of the Zócalo *Hotel Lord* (tel 23-96-77) on Calle 63 between Calles 62 and 64 is extremely good value for those seeking a double room. Well-maintained rooms with fan, radio, telephone and bath cost US$9.25.

South-East of the Zócalo *Hotel Dolores Alba* (tel 21-37-45) on Calle 63 is a wonderful older hotel, with rooms set above a quiet courtyard containing a swimming pool. Helpful owner Ángel Sánchez speaks English and can book reservations at his family-owned hotel near Chichén Itzá's ruins. Singles with fan and bath at the Dolores Alba cost US$8, doubles US$10. There are some air-conditioned rooms priced a bit higher.

Places to Stay – top end
The Holiday Inn (tel 25-68-77) is Mérida's most luxurious establishment, complete with US satellite TV, swimming pool and tennis courts. It's well-situated, off the Paseo Montejo behind the American Consulate at the intersection of Avenida Colón and Calle 60. Air-conditioned rooms cost US$50.

The *Hotel Casa del Balam* (tel 24-88-44) at Calle 60 488 at the intersection of

Calle 57 has a small swimming pool and neo-colonial atmosphere. Air-conditioned rooms with TV cost US$37.

Del Gobernador (tel 23-71-33) at Calle 59 535 is a reasonable deal, but is architecturally motel-like. The air-conditioned rooms have balconies overlooking the swimming pool and can sometimes be noisy from the street traffic. Rooms are just US$15 double.

Posada Toledo (tel 23-22-56) at Calle 58 487 near Calle 57 offers colonial surroundings at surprisingly low prices (budget travellers might consider a splurge here). The furniture lends a tasteful touch of the past and the roof deck is a splendid place to view the city and relax. Singles with air-conditioning cost US$17, doubles US$21.

Mérida Mision (tel 3-95-00) is centrally located on the corner of Calles 57 and 60. There's lots of old-world charm in this fine hotel. It has a pleasant outdoor restaurant. Rooms are about US$30; suites cost from US$40.

Places to Eat

Reflecting the cultural diversity of the city and external influences, Mérida has a wealth of excellent restaurants ranging from Yucatecan to Lebanese to French to East Indian-vegetarian. There are also plenty of eateries serving *típico* fare at modest prices.

Snacks & Light Meals A centrally located pizza joint, *Pizzeria de Vito Corleone*, serves decent pizza even the Godfather would enjoy. It's an easy walk from the zócalo at Calle 59 between Calles 60 and 62.

American hamburgers and delicious desserts can be had at the *Wini Cafetería*. Wini has two restaurants, one at Calle 60 491 and the other at Paseo Montejo 466. Breakfast here is good, around US$0.75 to US$1.25 for most items.

Típico dishes at low cost are served at *Le Louvre* and *Cafetería Erik*, north off the zócalo on Calle 62. They are right next to one another at 499 and 499A respectively. You can fill up at both places for US$1 to US$1.50. Le Louvre offers some good combination plates and a substantial comida corrida; Cafetería Erik's specialities are fried sandwiches called *tortas* filled with meat or cheese.

There are also tasty tortas at the aptly named *Las Mil Tortas* on Calle 62 between Calles 57 and 55. Close to the University of Yucatán, this is a good place to meet students. Calle 62 between Calle 53 and the zócalo has a host of other cheap eateries. Just use discretion so your stomach doesn't incur the Mayan Revenge.

Slightly pricier than Calle 62's cheapies are three restaurants popular with travellers and locals alike in the vicinity of Hotel Caribe. A good place for spicy fare of considerable diversity, or just for coffee or breakfast, is the *Café-Restaurant Express* across from the Hotel Caribe and the park at Calles 60 and 59. It's crowded but service is prompt by Mexican standards. At the entrance to Hotel Caribe, you will see some outdoor tables belonging to the little *El Mesón Café*. It's pleasant to sit here in the park sipping El Mesón's coffee, and the café is a good place to come for breakfasts or light lunches. Inside *Hotel Caribe*, you will find a restaurant which serves decent Yucatecan cuisine (although not on a par with Los Almendros) at moderate prices.

Nearby at Calle 57 between Calles 60 and 62 is the modern breakfast and sandwich café, *Pop*. In this clean if a bit too plastic café, you can get good egg breakfasts, hamburgers (about US$1) and decent desserts. The more affluent students from the university tend to hang out here.

If it's pastries you want for breakfast, you can get good rolls and Danishes cheaply just off the zócalo at *Panificadora Montejo*, at the intersection of Calles 63 and 62.

For delicious desserts right on the zócalo on Calle 61 try the *Dulcería y Sorbetería Colón*. If you have lost weight en route to Mérida and wish to regain it, this is the place. Enjoy the café's mouth-watering home-made ice cream, cakes and pastries.

Restaurants When in the Yucatán, why not dine as the Yucatecans do? For only US$2 to US$3 for a full meal, you can enjoy the *haute cuisine* of the Yucatán at one of the best restaurants in all of Mexico. *Los Almendros*, within walking distance of the zócalo at Calle 50 493 between Calles 57 and 59 along the Plaza Mejorada, evolved from its original and still thriving little eatery in the town of Ticul to a status which draws gourmets from all over the world. Try *pavo relleno negro* (grilled turkey with hot peppered pork stuffing), *papadzules* (tacos filled with egg smothered in a fiery sauce), *sopa de lima* (chicken in lime broth) or Los Almendros' most famous dish, the zingy onion-and-tomato pork dish *poc-chuc*. All meals are served with piping-hot hand-made tortillas. For those who don't read Spanish, there is a photo-menu of each dish.

Due to geographic isolation, Mérida traded more over the years with Europe than with the rest of Mexico, so it was a magnet for Lebanese traders. Today, more than 25,000 Lebanese are said to live in Mérida and excellent Middle Eastern cuisine can be found here. The best of the Lebanese restaurants and the most centrally located is *Cedro de Libano* at Calle 59 529 between Calles 64 and 66. In this unpretentious restaurant you can enjoy at moderate prices *shish kebab kaftas*, *berehena frito* (fried eggplant), *tijini* (tahini), *tabule*, *kibi* and a garlic-and-yoghurt dip eaten on hot Lebanese flying saucers (pita bread). Vegetarian dishes are less than US$2, meat dishes US$2 to US$3.

If you've been on the road for a while and have been dreaming of French cuisine while subsisting on *típico* taco fare, let your dreams become reality at the *Yannig Restaurant*. The chef, trained in

Paris, serves both traditional Gallic cuisine (from garlic soup to *coq au vin*) as well as imaginative French-Yucatecan concoctions. It's a splurge here, with dinners from US$5 to US$7 without wine. The restaurant is only open for dinner Monday to Saturday from 5.30 to 11.30 pm, but is open Sunday from 1 to 10 pm. Yannig is at Calle 62 480 between Calles 57 and 59.

Vegeteriano La Guaya is close to the Parque Santa Lucia at Calle 60 472 between Calles 55 and 53. The vegetarian cuisine includes some alleged East Indian dishes which, while not exactly traditional subcontinent fare, are tasty creations and a godsend for non-carnivores. You can get a full meal here for about US$2.

If you are around Paseo Montejo, visit *El Farolito de Michin* at the Paseo and Calle 37 for Argentinian grilled meat dishes. It's fairly reasonable, considering the neighbourhood. From this alfresco restaurant you can watch the sons and daughters of Mérida's elite make their *paseos*.

Pancho Villa's at Calle 59 493 between Calles 60 and 62 serves pretty good Mexican fare in a disco-like atmosphere with frequent live entertainment. Try their *coctails al flambe*.

Neither *Patio Español*, serving good Spanish dishes alfresco on Parque Hidalgo near Calle 60, nor *La Casona*, at Calle 60 435 near Calle 47 offering tasty pasta and other Italian dishes, is ultra-cheap, but their moderate prices shouldn't deter the budget traveller tired of Mexican fare. On the other hand, there is a limit to the quality of Mérida's diverse cuisines: *Kon-Tiki*, a Cantonese restaurant on Avenida Colón at Calle 14 serves bland, mediocre Chinese food worth neither the price nor the walk.

Entertainment

Proud of its cultural legacies of the past and attuned to the benefits of tourism, the city of Mérida offers nightly folkloric events put on by local performers of considerable skill. The performances are free to the public. All but Sunday events begin at 9 pm.

Monday A regional *Vaquería* features the city's Folkloric Ballet accompanied by the local Jarana Orchestra; it is staged in the back of the Municipal Palace in the Garden of the Composers.

Tuesday A city band plays music from the past and present. Performances are in Santiago Park, at the intersection of Calles 59 and 72.

Wednesday Mérida's string ensemble plays semi-classical music in Santa Ana Park at Calles 60 and 47.

Thursday Traditional Yucatecan folkloric dancers and troubadours entertain in the Parque Santa Lucia at Calles 60 and 55.

Friday Local theatre is presented in the Garden of the Composers at the back of the Municipal Palace. Also, in the university's patio in a building at the intersection of Calle 60 and 57, entertaining folkloric dances and music are performed. Highly recommended.

Sunday The weekly Arts & Crafts Bazaar is held from 10 am to 3 pm in Parque San Lucia.

Other cultural events are presented free at the university or other sites. Because they vary by time and day, it's best to ask about them at the tourist office.

Various travel agencies promote the 'Mayan Spectacular' presented at Tulipanes Restaurant at Calle 42 462-A. In my estimation, the show is tacky and the food not all that good. If you want to see for yourself, the admission charge is US$6 – not including dinner.

On a more traditional note, a good Mayan ballet folklorico (including Spanish dances) is presented most Sunday mornings at 11 am at the *Teatro Peón Contreras* on Calle 60 near Calle 57.

Students enjoy *Zac Nha*, a popular disco open Friday and Saturday nights at Avenidas Reforma and Colón. Some of the luxury hotels like the Holiday Inn have discos with live music.

Many English films, some of fairly recent release, are screened in Mérida with Spanish subtitles. Buy your tickets before show-time and well in advance on weekends. The popular *Cine Cantarell* and *Cine Fantasio* are near the Hotel Caribe on Calles 59 and 60.

Things to Buy

From standard shirts and blouses to Mayan exotica, Mérida is *the* place on the peninsula to shop. If your aged underwear is suffering from fallout and your threads are threadbare, you can resuscitate your basic backpacker's needs at low cost. For everyday pants, dresses, underwear, blouses, shirts and socks, try either the department stores near the zócalo or in the market area.

For more exotic goods and a sense of what's available, check out locally made crafts at the Museo Regional Artesanías on Calle 59 between Calles 50 and 48. The work on display is superlative, but the items for sale are not as good. It's free to the public and open Tuesday to Saturday from 8 am to 8 pm and Sunday 9 am to 2 pm, closed Monday. For superb quality though fairly high prices, visit La Casa de la Cultura at Calle 63 513 between Calles 64 and 65. La Casa's exhibits of fine local handiwork are in themselves worth a look.

You're now ready to shop at the famous Mérida market. The market more or less sprawls south-east of the zócalo in the sector roughly between Calles 62 and 54 and Calles 63 to 69. The old market is adjacent to the post office at Calles 65 and 56.

Kary's on Calle 64 sells a good selection of traditional Yucatecan *guayaberas* with button-down pockets at reasonable prices. Women's huipiles, the beautifully embroidered Mayan dresses, are sold virtually everywhere. You will find guayaberas, huipiles, rebozos and the famous Panama hat (woven from jipijapa plant leaves and manufactured largely in the Campeche town of Becal) along with a plethora of other local handicrafts at Tejidos y Cordeles Nacionales. A store famous for its Panama hats is appropriately named Becal, and is located at Calle 56 522.

For hammocks, you can save a little if you bus out to the nearby village of Tixcocob to watch them being woven. The bus runs regularly from the Progreso bus station south of the zócalo at Calle 62 524 between Calles 65 and 67. If you don't want to expend the effort to go out there, prices are excellent in Mérida.

No matter where you buy, be careful to check for quality. Make sure the hammock has a tight weave – you shouldn't be able to put your finger through it. Check out the loops at the ends; they should be taut. Be certain the hammock is the right length for you. Hammocks come in several sizes; ranging from smallest to largest, they are *sencillo, doble, matrimonial* and *matrimonial especial*. Because hammocks fold up small, and the larger are more comfortable (though more expensive), consider the bigger sizes.

You will probably be approached on the street by vendors with great deals on hammocks. Even though the prices may sound good, the quality usually isn't. Visit a shop with a good reputation instead. La Poblana at Calle 65 492 between Calles 58 and 60 is famous for its quality and diversity of hammocks. Here you are welcome to ask questions and are not rushed into a purchase. In theory, prices are set, but some travellers report a small measure of success with bargaining. One of La Poblana's attributes: they will mail your purchase for you, saving you the typical post office hassle. Some travellers report slightly cheaper prices for good quality at El Aguacete, Calle 58 604 at Calle 73. Tejidos y Cordeles Nacionales and El Campesino at Calle 58 548 between Calles 69 and 71 are cheaper but provide less guidance – so you should really know what you are looking for or you might get taken.

Finally, for true ruins fans with cash to spend, superb temple rubbings are sold at Originales Patric, a taxi ride from the zócalo at Calle 16 104.

Getting There & Away

Air There are international flights to Mérida from Miami, Los Angeles, Houston, San Francisco and New York with connections from other US cities. Flights from Europe can connect with the US departure points noted. Some Europe-originating travellers fly first to Havana, and after a Cuban stopover take a Mexicana flight direct to Mérida.

Aeroméxico and Mexicana have regular domestic service to Mérida via Mexico City, Oaxaca, Villahermosa, Cancún and other points with connecting flights. To book flights domestic or international, travel agencies to trust are T'ho Travel Agency in the Hotel Reforma and Molica Tours in the Hotel Caribe. These agencies also run tours from Mérida to Havana.

Bus There is 1st-class service between Mérida and most major Mexican cities as well as to the more prominent ruins in the vicinity. There is frequent service between Mérida and Campeche (2½ hours, US$2.50), Cancún (five hours, US$5), Valladolid (three hours, US$3) and Villahermosa (eight hours, US$8.50). There are several buses daily between Mérida and Mexico City, Chetumal, Puerto Juárez (for Isla Mujeres or via Cancún) and Playa del Carmen.

As for the ruins, there are both 1st-class and 2nd-class buses to Chichén Itzá and 2nd-class service to Uxmal and Kabah. Watch your gear on the all-night to Palenque, leaving Mérida at 11.30 pm. While this bus is far safer than the train, travellers have reported gear stolen from overhead racks.

If you are going to points on the north coast, a bus stop about 1½ blocks south of the zócalo at Calle 62 524 between Calles 65 and 67 is the frequent departure point for buses to Dzibilchaltún, Progreso and the hammock-weaving village of Tixcocob.

Those heading to the Celestún flamingo region or Oxkutzcab (in the region of the Labna, Xlapak and Sayil ruins) can choose from several departures a day from the Autotransportes del Sur station at Calle 50 531 at Calle 67. If you are going to Río Lagartos or San Felipe you will find Autotransportes del Noroeste buses departing three times daily from Calle 52 between Calle 63 and Calle 65.

Rail In the Yucatán Peninsula, buses are preferable to trains in that they are considerably faster and infinitely safer; rail robberies in some areas (between Mérida and Campeche in particular) have reached epidemic proportions. There are no *dormitorios* to lock on trains travelling the peninsula – just vulnerable 1st and 2nd-class seating. Even some government tourist offices try to deter tourists from train travel.

If you still want to get between Mérida and other points by rail, a train with no diner departs at midnight for Campeche, Palenque and ultimately Mexico City (two days' journey). The station is at Calle 55 between Calles 46 and 48, about nine blocks north-east of the zócalo. Tickets should be bought several hours in advance.

Getting Around

Airport Transport If you are arriving from the airport, colectivo minibuses will take you to your hotel for about US$1.75 – half the cost of a private taxi. The cheapest transport into town is by bus No 79. Although it costs less than 10c, its schedule is sporadic.

Local Transport Mérida's grid system, with odd-numbered streets running east to west and even-numbered north to south, makes finding your way around quite easy. While streets of this city are easy walk around and to figure out, the local bus system is not. If you must take a bus, be sure to ask if it is going near your destination rather than assume that just because it is going in a given direction it will continue to do so. Fortunately taxis are cheap, and if you are here in the hot season they're worth taking to save you

some misery. Hotels will call cabs for you.

The town centre and the zócalo are within walking distance of the 1st-class bus station on Calle 69 between 68 and 70 (six blocks south-west of the zócalo). To walk from the 1st-class bus station to the zócalo, take a right as you leave the depot on Calle 69. Keep going until you see a church and a little plaza called San Juan de Díos between Calles 64 and 62. Take a left on Calle 62 – it's three blocks from here to the zócalo. Taxis to the zócalo area cost about US$1 from the 1st-class bus station. Second-class buses occasionally stop at Calle 50 between 65 and 67 – it's also six blocks to the zócalo from here.

If you're arriving by train, the station is at Calle 55 between Calles 46 and 48, nine hot blocks' walk from the zócalo. Take Calle 48 from the station and make a right on Calle 62, passing under the archway. In six blocks you will reach the zócalo. Taxis from the station cost about US$1.35 to the centre of town.

Car Rental Miguel Escalante Moreno's agencies rent cars at competitive prices. Contact Escalante at T'ho Travel Agency in the lobby of Hotel Reforma (tel 24-79-22) on the corner of Calles 59 and 62, or at Molica Tours in the lobby of Hotel Caribe (tel 24-90-22) on Calle 59 500 near Calle 60.

UXMAL

The magnificent ruins of Uxmal are an easy day trip from Mérida. Comparable to the great cities of the Greek and Roman empires, Uxmal features some of the most intricately constructed façades of any of the Mayan ruins, and its stucco masks are awesome.

As at the other Mayan sites, opening hours are 8 am to 5 pm and admission is about 25c. Entry is free on Sunday, when the small museum is closed. There is a sound & light show in the evening which costs about US$1.50.

History

Set in the Puuc Hills, which lent their name to the architectural patterns in this region, Uxmal was the central city during the Late Classic period (600-900 AD) of a region which encompassed the satellite towns of Sayil, Kabah, Xlapak and Labna. Although Uxmal means 'Thrice Built' in Mayan, it was actually reconstructed five times.

That a sizeable population flourished at all in this area is a mystery, as there is precious little water in the region. The Mayans built a series of lime-lined reservoirs and cisterns to cache water during the dry season, which apparently sufficed.

First occupied in about 600 AD, the town is influenced by highland Mexico in its architecture, most likely through contact fostered by trade. This influence is reflected in Uxmal's serpent imagery, phallic symbols and columns. The magnificently proportioned Puuc architecture is unique to this region, with intricate, geometrically patterned mosaics sweeping across elongated upper façades.

Given the scarcity of water in the Puuc Hills, Chac the rain god was of utmost importance and his image is in abundant evidence here, with stucco monster-like masks protruding from the ancient edifices. Unfortunately, many of the finely carved lintels (horizontal crosspieces built over doors) brought to the US by the archaeologist John L Stephens were destroyed in a fire. Overall, you will find that the Mayan sense of the ornate reached its apogee in Uxmal.

There is much speculation as to why Uxmal was abandoned about 900 AD. Drought conditions may have reached such proportions that the inhabitants had to relocate. One widely held theory suggests that the rise to greatness of Chichén Itzá drew people away from the Puuc Hills.

The first written account of Uxmal by a European came from the quill of the priest López de Cogulludo in the 16th century.

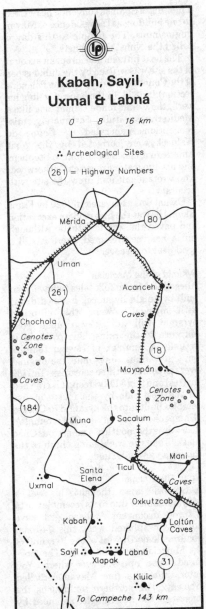

Kabah, Sayil, Uxmal & Labná

0   8   16 km

∴ Archeological Sites

(261) = Highway Numbers

Mérida

Uman

Acanceh

Caves

Chochola

Cenotes Zone

Caves

Mayapán

Cenotes Zone

Muna

Sacalum

Mani

Santa Elena

Ticul

Caves

Uxmal

Oxkutzcab

Kabah

Loltún Caves

Sayil

Xlapak

Labná

Kiuic

To Campeche 143 km

Thinking of Spanish convents, he referred to one building as the residence of Mayan virgins/nuns. The temple to this day is called the Nuns' Quadrangle.

The next influential European account of the site was written by the dubious pen of the Count de Waldeck (see the Palenque section) in 1836. In the hope of selling his work, the Count made Uxmal look like a Mediterranean ruin. Fortunately, misconceptions generated by Count de Waldeck were corrected by the great American archaeologist John L Stephens and his illustrator Frederick Catherwood, who wrote about and drew the site with accuracy.

Uxmal was excavated in 1929 by Frans Blom. His was the first modern excavation and paved the way for others. Although much has been restored, there is still a good deal to discover.

Pyramid of the Magician

Alleged in Mayan folk tales to have been built overnight by an egg-hatched dwarf with magical powers, this elliptical pyramid will amaze you upon your entrance to the ruins. The pyramid is actually a complex of several temples built at various times onto the original over the course of three centuries. Tall (39 metres) and incredibly steep, it is crowned on the west side by the fourth of five temples built into the pyramid in Chenes (Campeche area) style. This temple's doorway is the mouth of a monstrous Chac mask. Take the frightening climb to the top for a view of Uxmal.

Nuns' Quadrangle

A Spanish priest thought this was a Mayan nunnery due to its resemblance to a European convent. Archaeologists have not yet deciphered what this 74-room quadrangle north-west of the Pyramid of the Magician was utilised for. The long-nosed Chac appears everywhere. You enter through a fine Mayan corbelled archway. The northern building is the longest of the quadrangle, balanced by temples at each end. Symbolic friezes gave the left flank the name 'Venus Temple'.

The outlines of a snake on the roof of the west building were believed by some archaeologists to have been brought late in the city's history by Toltec invaders, who introduced the cult of Quetzalcóatl to this region. The theory is contested, as Uxmal was said by other archaeologists to have been abandoned during the Toltec invasion.

Ball Court

Just outside the corbelled arch entrance to the Nuns' Quadrangle lies rubble which once served as a ball court. Walls had high rings through which a ball was supposed to be hit. Some of the debris is thought to be the spectators' stone seats.

Governor's Palace

Across the ball court from the Nuns' Quadrangle sits the Governor's Palace. Perhaps the quintessential work of Puuc style, it sits atop three man-made terraces literally heightening its grandeur. This long (more than 100 metres) edifice with corbelled arches at either end is highlighted by the rich frieze of the upper façade – a gently undulating mosaic of thousands of stones set in geometric patterns, festooned with Chac masks.

Death mask

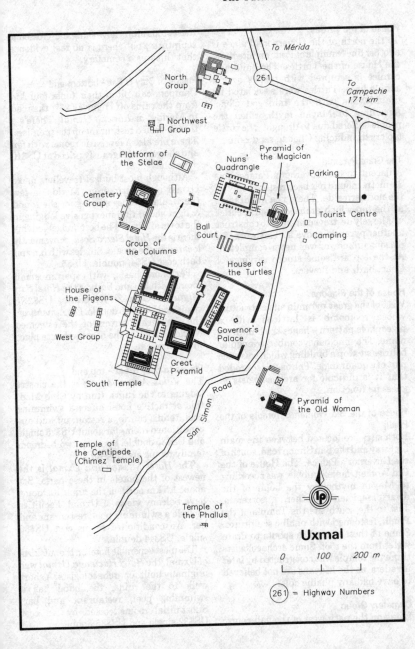

To Mérida

261

To Campeche
171 km

North Group

Northwest Group

Platform of the Stelae

Cemetery Group

Nuns' Quadrangle

Pyramid of the Magician

Parking

Tourist Centre

Camping

Ball Court

Group of the Columns

House of the Turtles

House of the Pigeons

West Group

Governor's Palace

Great Pyramid

South Temple

Pyramid of the Old Woman

San Simon Road

Temple of the Centipede (Chimez Temple)

Temple of the Phallus

Uxmal

0   100   200 m

261 = Highway Numbers

House of the Turtles

To the north of the Governor's Palace is another fine example of Puuc architecture, the House of the Turtles. The building's cornice is sculpted with turtles over a simple base. Turtles were associated by the Mayans with the rain god Chac. According to Mayan myth, when the people suffered due to drought, the turtle too cried, inducing Chac to send rain.

The Great Pyramid

Adjacent to the Governor's Palace, this 32-metre mound has been restored only on the northern side. There is a quadrangle at the top which archaeologists theorise was largely destroyed in order to construct another pyramid above it. This work, for reasons unknown, was never completed. At the top are some stucco carvings of Chac, birds and flowers.

House of the Pigeons

West of the great pyramid sits a structure whose roofcomb is latticed with a pigeonhole pattern – hence the building's name. The nine honeycombed triangular belfries sit atop a building which was once part of a quadrangle. The base is so eroded that it is difficult for archaeologists to guess its function.

House of the Old Woman & Temple of the Phalli

Both sites are located between the main highway and the San Simon road, south of the Governor's Palace. The House of the Old Woman, largely rubble, was according to Mayan mythology the home of the dwarf magician's mother, a sorceress. Just to the south sits the Temple of the Phalli, festooned with phallic sculptures. Some of these served as spouts to drain water from the roof. Some archaeologists think the temple was constructed by later invaders, as the Mayans are not believed to have had any phallic cult.

Cemetery Group

Lying on the path west of the ball court, these stone altars have skull-and-crossbone sculptures, but there is no real evidence that this was a cemetery.

Places to Stay & Eat – bottom end

Campers can pitch their tents four km from the ruins off Highway 261, the road to Mérida, at *Rancho Uxmal*. There's a thatch-roofed restaurant on the premises. There are also a few basic rooms with fan and shower, outrageously priced at US$10 a double.

Although most budget travellers make Uxmal a day trip from Mérida, a few (particularly those staying for the sound & light show) find inexpensive lodging in the town of Ticul. The best budget lodging there is the *Hotel Sierra Sosa*, conveniently located on the zócalo. Singles with fan and bath cost US$4, doubles US$5.

Far more basic, with spartan small rooms with fan and bath, is the *Hotel San Miguel* at Calle 28 195 costing US$2.75 single and US$3.25 double. *Los Almendros*, the first headquarters of the esteemed Mérida outlet, is the best moderate place in Ticul to eat.

Places to Stay & Eat – top end

The *Villas Arqueológicas* is the closest lodging to the ruins. Run by Club Méd, this attractive hotel offers a swimming pool, tennis courts, a restaurant and air-conditioned rooms for about US$25 single and US$35 double. Spacious two-bedroom family rooms are US$40.

The *Hotel Mission Inn Uxmal* is the newest of the hotels in these parts. Set about 1.5 km north of the ruins, its rooms have balcony views of Uxmal. Facilities include a swimming pool, restaurant and bar. Air-conditioned rooms cost US$36 single, US$44 double.

The most venerable hotel on the outskirts of Uxmal, the *Hotel Hacienda Uxmal* was originally built for archaeologists. A short walk to the ruins, the hotel has a swimming pool, restaurant and bar. Substantial rooms cooled by fan cost US$32 single and US$35 double.

Getting There & Away

There is only 2nd-class bus service between Mérida and Uxmal. Buses leave the main Mérida terminal daily at 7 and 9 am, 12 noon, 3 and 5 pm; the trip takes about 90 minutes and costs about US$1. This bus continues on to Kabah and Campeche. Buses return to Mérida from the front of the Hotel Hacienda Uxmal at 9 am, 12 noon, 3, 6 and 7.30 pm. There is also bus service between Uxmal and Campeche.

Because the buses do not originate from the Hotel Hacienda Uxmal, flag them down to be certain they will stop. In the late afternoon there will likely be standing room only. Occasionally, an enterprising individual will cart travellers in his private combi to Mérida for the same price as the bus.

PUUC ROUTE

To fully appreciate the expanse of the Puuc Hills Mayan civilisation at the height of its greatness, a visit to the ruins of Kabah, Sayil, Xlapak, Labná and the Loltún Caves will prove truly rewarding. Ironically, one of the benefits of seeing the ruins is also its curse. Few tourists and even fewer locals visit these sites, so not only is there no public transportation other than to Kabah, but the scarcity of cars to these ruins makes hitch-hiking difficult.

Your alternatives are to rent a private car or to go with a tour. The T'ho Travel Agency in the lobby of the Hotel Reforma (tel 24-79-22) and Molica Tours in the lobby of the Hotel Caribe run excellent tours out of Mérida; but no matter how you visit these sites, your time and money will be well spent. Those who take the time to look around the jungles near Sayil, Xlapak and Labná will find some spectacular bird life.

KABAH

Situated 22 km south-east of Uxmal, Kabah consists of ruins on either side of the road. The site is open from 8 am to 5 pm; admission is 12c.

Codz Pop Temple

Coming south from Mérida, you will see the remarkable Codz Pop Temple with its façade festooned with about 270 masks of Chac, the rain god. If you wondered about concerns for rain in this region, have a look at this temple. Each of these mosaic masks consists of about two dozen carved stones. The noses are thought to have once had handles for lanterns which, set aflame, created a fiery wall of Chacs.

The name Codz Pop means 'Coiled Mat', because to some observers the steps conjure up that image. The ornate façade of the Chenes style blends well here with the Puuc architectural input more common in this region.

Other Kabah Ruins

To the right of the Codz Pop as you face the road is a small pyramid. Behind the Codz Pop (away from the road) is a Temple of Columns in the Greek-like Puuc columnar style. The columns are particularly well preserved at the back of the building.

Cross the highway and you will see three paths. The track to the left brings you to a temple called the Witches' House, a name from now lost Mayan mythology. The path to the right takes you to a rubble of ruins on a mound which was once called Teocalli, or Great Temple. Your best bet is to take the sacbe, or cobbled elevated path, straight ahead until you come to a statuesque arch. It is said that from the arch a sacbe avenue runs all the way to Uxmal, terminating at a smaller arch.

Getting There & Away

There are a few buses a day between Mérida and Kabah (one hour and 45 minutes, US$1.15), and between Campeche and Kabah. Buses running south from Mérida continue on to Campeche. Be forewarned that not all buses stop for your return from Kabah, particularly if they are full. The

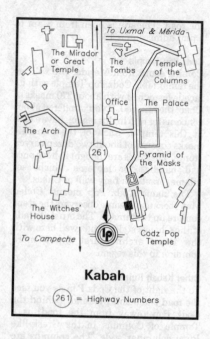

Kabah

261 = Highway Numbers

El Mirador

If you take the path south from the palace you will come to the temple El Mirador, with its interesting rooster-like roofcomb once painted a bright red. Just beyond El Mirador is a huge phallic stela.

Views of Sayil

Across the road from the entrance you can take a steep, slippery road to the summit of the hill where you will find a well-worn temple. Note the human head carved above its doorway. More impressive than the temple itself is the fine view it affords of the Puuc Hills.

Getting There & Away

Get there by car, hitch-hiking or guided tour.

XLAPAK

The site of Xlapak ('shla-PAK') is 5.5 km from Sayil. In Mayan, Xlapak means 'Old

alternatives are renting a car, taking a tour, or (difficult) hitch-hiking.

SAYIL

If you are driving, go about five km south of Kabah and take a left turn-off (east) to Sayil. The ruins are open from 8 am to 5 pm for about 10c.

El Palacio

Sayil is best known for its Greek-like El Palacio, built in 730 AD. This great palace containing more than 50 chambers has an ornate sculpted 2nd storey of Chac masks and diving gods accentuating its simple columned base. A less gaudy 3rd storey completes the harmonious design. If you look to the north-west side of the building, you will see one of the many *chultunes*, brick water-collectors, in the Puuc region. It is said that this *chultune* can hold more than 30,000 litres of rainwater.

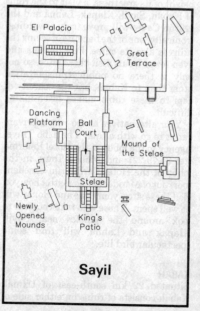

Sayil

Walls'. Although there is only one partially restored building here, it is worth a quick look if you have time. The ornate palace is decorated with Chac masks and fretted geometric latticework in the Puuc style. To the right is the rubble of what were once two smaller buildings.

If you trek along the remnant of an old four-wheel drive road behind the palace, you may be rewarded with the sight of some brilliantly coloured tropical birds. The long-tailed *moc-moc*, or well-named 'clock bird', is here in good number. Xlapak is open from 8 am to 5 pm for 5c admission.

Getting There & Away
The site is accessible via car, hitch-hiking (difficult) or guided tour.

LABNÁ
A three-km drive from Xlapak brings you to the ruins of Labná. The site is open from 8 am to 5 pm and there is an admission charge of a few cents.

The Arch
Labná is best known for its magnificent arch, once part of a building but now resembling a gate, which links two small plazas. The corbelled structure, three metres wide and six metres high, is well preserved and stands close to the entrance of Labná. The mosaic reliefs decorating the upper façade have a Grecian feel.

If you look at the ornate work on the north-eastern side of the arch, you will make out mosaics of Mayan huts. At the base of either side of the arch are rooms of the no longer existing building, including upper lattice patterns constructed atop a serpentine design. Archaeologists believe a high roofcomb once sat over the fine arch and its flanking rooms.

El Mirador
Standing on the opposite side of the arch, and connected to it by the cobbled avenue which the Mayans called a *sacbe*, is a pyramid with a temple atop it called El Mirador. The pyramid itself is poorly preserved – largely stone rubble. The temple with its five-metre-high roofcomb, true to its name, looks like a watchtower. According to 19th-century archaeologist John O Steffens' reports, the roofcomb was once decorated with painted stucco carvings of ball players and ominous skulls. This perhaps served as a testimonial to the seriousness of the game, as well as to the fate of the losing captain.

Palace & Chultune
Archaeologists believe that at one point in the 9th century, some 3000 Mayas lived at Labná. To support such numbers in these arid hills, water was collected in catch basins called *chultunes*, each capable of holding up to 30,000 litres of rainwater. At Labná's peak there were some 60 *chultunes* in and around the city. Today you can spot one of these cisterns on the 2nd storey of the palace which sits near the entrance to

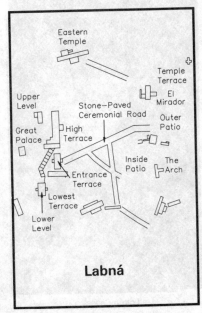

Labná

Labná. This one is particularly well preserved and you will see others in various degrees of deterioration around the site.

The palace, the first edifice you come to at Labná, is connected by a *sacbe* to El Mirador and the arch. One of the longest buildings in the Puuc Hills, its design is not as impressive as its counterpart at Sayil. There's a ghoulish sculpture on the eastern corner on the upper level – a serpent gripping a human head between its jaws. According to Mayan mythology, crocodile jaws symbolised the entrance to the underworld. Close to this carving is a well-preserved Chac mask.

Getting There & Away

Get here by car, guided tour or hitch-hiking.

LOLTÚN CAVES (GRUTAS DE LOLTÚN)

Loltún Caves are among the most intriguing caverns in Mexico and are

Loltún Caves

certainly the most interesting *grutas* in the Yucatán. If you are driving the Sayil-Labná route, they are 18 km east of Labná. Or you may reach the caves more directly from Mérida by driving first to the town of Oxkutzcab (via Ticul), then going seven km west.

More than just a fine subterranean realm for spelunkers, Loltún provided a treasure trove of data for archaeologists studying the Mayas as well as some impressive artefacts. Carbon dating has provided evidence that the caves were first utilised by humans some 2500 years ago, perhaps seeking shelter or looking for water. The caves contain spectacular stalactite and stalagmite formations.

To explore the 1.5-km labyrinth, slippery (bring good shoes), steep and narrow in places, it is necessary to take a tour with a local guide. Tours are scheduled at 9.30 and 11.30 am, and at 1.30 and 3 pm and may be organised at other hours if you offer enough money. Occasionally there is a guide on the premises who speaks English – ask for him specifically. Admission to the caves costs about 15c and the guides, who are not paid by the government, merit a tip for their two-hour tour.

Within these awesome caverns (distractingly illuminated by coloured lights) you will see both spectacular natural formations and those carved over the years by the Mayas. In a chamber where soot on the walls makes it apparent the Indians cooked there, are ancient Mayan stone *metate* or corn grinders.

In the Gallery of the Five Chultunes Chamber, a carved eagle and a monster overlook the startlingly realistic, naturally formed head of a dolphin (the product of erosion) dropping water into cisterns. The Mayas believed water in this cave was sacred and used it in their religious rituals.

As you walk through the various underground caverns, it takes little imagination to see other formations resembling animals and humans which were carved by the forces of erosion. Among the more obvious are camels, jaguars and, toward the tour's end, the carved petals which made the Mayas name the cave 'Flower of the Rock'.

Among the highlights of this subterranean world is a grand cavern appropriately called The Cathedral. The Mayas held major religious ceremonies in this immense grotto, where stalagmites and stalactites create the sense of a stone forest.

In another chamber erosion has opened its roof to the sun, permitting a huge tree and other vegetation to grow. Tropical birds link the underworld with the heavens.

In the last cave you come to is the ladder that takes you back to the sunlight. A smaller ladder takes you to a site where a mastodon's fossils were found; the bones are in the National Museum of Anthropology in Mexico City.

Getting There & Away

Your best bet is to rent a car or take a tour to Loltún and the other Puuc sites. If this is not possible, take a bus from Mérida to the town of Oxkutzcab. Pay about US$3 for a taxi running the scant seven km from the zócalo; or catch a *camión*, a ridiculously crowded mini-truck which runs from Oxkutzcab every hour or so. Flag the camión down at the crossroads up from the zócalo. The fare should be 15c.

The alternative is hitch-hiking, but be warned that there simply aren't that many tourists. While you are waiting for transport back, you can have a meal at the *Restaurant El Guerrero* near Loltún's entrance. The *típico* fare is tasty, but the tariff a bit steep for what you get.

MAYAPAN RUINS

Although some popular historians have written that Mayapan ruled a union of Mayan states which included Uxmal and Chichén Itzá, in reality the great cities were already in eclipse by the year 1200. From 1200 to 1450, Mayapan was the last

dominant city of the mighty Mayan empire.

The crudeness of Mayapan's architecture is indicative of the civilisation's decline. Although excavation of this walled site is somewhat minimal, with most of Mayapan's 3600 buildings covered by jungle, true ruins buffs might find a visit to this once-powerful capital worthwhile.

Getting There & Away

To reach the ruins of Mayapan, do not confuse it with the contemporary village of the same name. Catch a country bus bound for Las Ruinas de Mayapan or a bus to the nearby town of Telchaquillo (to do this you might have to transfer in the village of Acanceh).

TICUL

Ticul is a centre for fine huipile weaving – the embroidery on these dresses is extraordinary. For both quality and price, Ticul is a good place to buy the traditional Mayan costume. While you are here, you can pay homage to the best Yucatecan cooking by dining at the original *Los Almendros Restaurant*, whose most famous branch is in Mérida.

On the outskirts of Ticul, be certain to visit the re-creations of Mayan sculptures by the artist Wilbur González. Private tours and collectors come to the González Gallery for good reason: his sculptures are accurate to the most minor detail. Ask to see González' private collection and his pet jaguar. Ticul also seems to be a centre for shoe-making; the town has a phenomenal number of *zapaterías* or shoe shops.

Places to Stay

The *Hotel Sierra Sosa*, on the zócalo, has clean basic accommodation with fan and bath for US$4 single, US$5 double. More spartan is the *Hotel San Miguel* at Calle 28 195. Singles at the San Miguel cost US$2.75 with fan and bath, doubles US$3.50.

Getting There & Away

To reach Ticul, you can either come direct from Mérida or via Mayapan. From Ticul, you can move on by bus to the ruins of Uxmal.

PROGRESO

Population: 20,000

If Mérida's heat is getting to you, then do as the locals do and relax at the seaside town of Progreso. If you have come from the Caribbean or think you will find turquoise waters here you might be disappointed, as Progreso's seas are gritty green. Nonetheless, the beach is nice and the waters cooling, and you'll see a Mexican beach town enjoyed by locals rather than by pasty tourist hordes.

The beach slopes so gradually into the sea that you can walk a good half km into the calm waters without having to swim. When you have had enough sun and sea, walk along the malecón facing the beach to see some magnificent mansions built by millionaire henequen barons.

If it's not a holiday or summer, Progreso is a sleepy little town. However, come summer it seems as if all of Mérida is here, particularly on Sunday. If you come to Progreso in summer, walk six km east along the palm-fringed beach to the tiny village of Chicxulub, a pleasant escape from the crowds. Alternatively, if you walk about five km west of Progreso, you will find the little fishing village of Yucalpeten whose new harbour is stealing some of the thunder from Progreso's business. Progreso's two-km stone wharf, said to be the world's longest when it was constructed nearly a century ago, has seen

Woman weaving

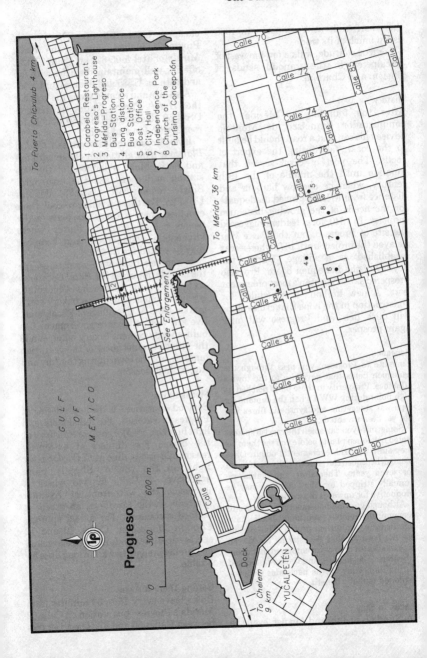

Progreso

To Puerto Chicxulub 4 km

GULF
OF
MEXICO

To Mérida 36 km

To Mérida 36 km

See Enlargement

Dock

To Chelem
9 km

YUCALPETÉN

Calle 79

0   300   600 m

1 Carabela Restaurant
2 Progreso's Lighthouse
3 Mérida–Progreso
   Bus Station
4 Long distance
   Bus Station
5 Post Office
6 City Hall
7 Independence Park
8 Church of the
   Purísima Concepción

Calle 70
Calle 72
Calle 74
Calle 76
Calle 78
Calle 79
Calle 80
Calle 77
Calle 82
Calle 84
Calle 86
Calle 88
Calle 90
Calle 81
Calle 83
Calle 85
Calle 87

the wharf built at Yucalpetén in 1968 usurp much of its trade.

For true solitude, walk a few km west of Yucalpetén to the tranquil sands of Chelem and Churbna.

History

After the founding of Mérida, the conquistador Francisco de Montejo advised his son that a road should be built to the coast, facilitating the export of goods. The port of Sisal served that function until the middle of the 19th century, when its shallow harbour and distance from Mérida proved inadequate for the needs of the growing henequen industry. In 1840, local leaders suggested the site of Progreso, but the Caste War delayed the project until 1872 when it was established as a village. During the heyday of the henequen boom, Progreso prospered as the Yucatán's most prominent port. A new harbour is scheduled for construction in the hope that cruise ships will dock here and Progreso will once again prosper.

Henequen

En route to Progreso, you pass through the henequen fields that gave rise to the town's affluence. Prosperity in these parts reached its high point during WW I when the demand for rope was staggering and synthetic fibres had not yet been invented.

Sometimes you can smell the greyish spikey-leafed henequen plants before you see them, as they emit a putrid, excremental odour. Once planted, henequen can grow virtually unattended for seven years. Thereafter, the plants are annually stripped for fibre. A plant may be productive for upwards of two decades.

Although growing henequen for rope is still economically viable, synthetic fibres have significantly diminished profits. This decline has not been all that devastating for Mayan peasants, as the crop never employed that many labourers to begin with, and those who worked during its heyday on the haciendas were too exploited to really benefit.

Places to Stay

On Sundays in July and August, even the cheapest hotels fill up. The best of Progreso's budget inns is the *Hotel Miralmar* (tel 5-05-62) on Calle 77 124, offering well-maintained singles with fan and bath for US$5 and doubles for US$6.

Also nice and located along the beach is the *Hotel Playa Linda*. It charges US$4.50 single and US$5.50 double for rooms with fan and bath.

If you are extremely low on cash, the *Río Blanco* is a bit grotty but cheap with fan and bath. Make a left out of the bus station and then take the first right. Single rooms cost US$3.75, doubles US$4.25. For those wishing to cook their own food, there is a very nice place on the beach called *Tropical Suites* where kitchenette, living room and bedroom may be rented for US$10.

In summer those who want to escape the crowds put up at the *Hotel Cocoteras* six km east along the beach at Chicxulub. If you get hungry there is a bakery and a market here. At the village of Yucalpeten, five km west, the state government has built an ugly cement luxury hotel. While the village is quiet most of the year, rich families jam the town during the July and August high season.

Places to Eat

Seafood – surprise – is the best offering at Progreso's eateries. For breakfasts and light lunches, try *Morgan's* or *Rawlito's* at the beach. For dinners at extremely reasonable prices, dine at *El Cordobes* set right on the zócalo. Slightly more expensive, at Calle 69 146 where it intersects the waterfront at Avenida Malecón, is the *Carabela*, an excellent seafood restaurant. For a real splurge, *Capitán Marisco* at Calles 10 and 12 serves superb seafood; in high season and on Sunday prepare to wait in long lines for a table.

Getting There & Away

Buses leave every 15 to 30 minutes from Mérida's Progreso bus station on Calle 62 between Calles 65 and 67. The trip takes

45 minutes to an hour. It is a brief walk to the sea from Progreso's bus station and the town is very easy to walk around.

DZIBILCHALTÚN RUINS

Unless you are a true ruins freak or have lots of free time around Mérida, the ruins of Dzibilchaltún are not worth your while. On the other hand, the largely unexcavated, little visited archaeological site has historical appeal in that it was the longest continuously utilised Mayan administrative and ceremonial city, serving the Mayas from 2000 BC until the European intrusion.

Xlacah Cenote

The city's cenote, Xlacah, its clear water some 44 metres deep, was made famous when a 1958 National Geographic expedition of divers brought up valuable artefacts which the Mayas must have ritually tossed into these sacred waters. You can see some of the artefacts at the museum here. It's open daily from 8 am to 5 pm.

Temple of the Seven Dolls

Dzibilchaltún's sole restored edifice is the Temple of the Seven Dolls. While not particularly striking from a distance, the temple grows in appeal as you examine its graceful proportions up close. To date, it is the only Mayan religious site found with windows. Archaeologists excavating the temple came across seven malformed clay dolls which they believe were used in sacred ceremonies to ward off illness. Some of the figurines may be seen in the museum here.

Getting There & Away

Buses leave from Mérida's Progreso bus station on Calle 62 between Calles 65 and 67. Buses come here direct, taking about 30 minutes, four times daily. Or take a Progreso-bound bus and ask to get off at the off-road to the ruins, a four-km walk. If you wish to go from the ruins to Progreso, bus, walk, or hitch the four km to the main highway and hail the frequent Progreso-bound buses running north from there.

CELESTÚN

Famed as a bird sanctuary, Celestún is about a 1½-hour bus journey from Mérida. Although this region abounds in anhinga and egrets, most bird-watchers come here to see the flamingoes. If you have the time, flamingoes are far more numerous near Río Lagartos. Celestún, good for a day trip, is a little spit of land which sits on the estuary formed by the Río Esperanza and the Gulf. Two drawbacks to coming here: the beach is so-so, and on some days fierce afternoon winds swirl choking dust through the town. The dust makes the sea silty and therefore unappealing for swimming in the afternoon.

Given the winds, the best time to see birds is in the morning. Hire a boat from the bridge where launches are docked about one km from the town. The rental should run to about US$5 per 1½ hours.

Places to Stay

The *Hotel Gutiérrez* at Calle 12 22 is the top budget choice, with well-kept rooms with fan and bath costing US$5. Cheaper and not as nice is the *Hotel San Julio* (tel 1-85-89) at Calle 12 92, where singles with fan and bath cost US$3.50 and doubles US$5.

Places to Eat

For good food and variety, dine at *La Playita* on the shore. *Restaurant Celestún* also serves reasonably good seafood.

Getting There & Away

Buses run from Mérida's Autotransportes del Sur depot on Calle 50 531 at the intersection of Calle 67. They depart hourly, mornings and afternoons until 2 pm and every two hours thereafter until 10 pm. The trip takes about 1½ hours.

IZAMAL

Population: 20,000

Izamal is a town whose past reflects the history of the peninsula and whose present is worth a venture to see a largely unvisited Yucatecan town.

Convent of St Anthony de Padua

When the Spaniards conquered Izamal, they destroyed the major Mayan temple and built from its stones a substantial structure which would become one of the oldest convents in the hemisphere, the Convent of Saint Anthony de Padua. The convent's ground was broken in 1533 and it was built on the base of the former Mayan Popul-Chac pyramid.

When you enter the immense 12-metre-high church today, you may observe implements from the 16th century, including a candle mould still in use. This complex of buildings, constructed with no fewer than 75 architectural arches, is an impressive sight. The town's plaza and adjacent buildings lend a further sense of the colonial past. Their yellowish colour led the town to be dubbed Ciudad Amarilla, or the Yellow City.

Pyramid of Kinich Kakmo

Izamal was once a population and ceremonial centre of the Mayas. If you look across the plaza from the convent, you will see a largely unrestored pyramid built in homage to the sun god Kinich Kakmo. Climb it to the top (but be careful in the upper portion, as the staircase has crumbled) and you will see scores of mounds yet to be excavated from the ubiquitous jungle.

Places to Stay & Eat

Few travellers overnight here, but if you do, you will find basic rooms at the hotels *Toto* and *Kabul* near the plaza. They charge US$4 for a single with fan and bath and US$5 for a double.

Getting There & Away

There are direct buses from Mérida; other buses require a transfer at Hoctun. There is also a slow narrow-gauge train.

CHICHÉN ITZÁ

The most famous and best restored of Yucatán's Mayan sites, Chichén Itzá will awe the most jaded of ruins visitors. Unfortunately, a site of this calibre, between the tourist centres of Cancún and Mérida, is overrun by milling mobs of tourists between 11 am and 3 pm. To better appreciate the ancient city, it is highly recommended that you overnight nearby and do your exploration of the site either early in the morning or late in the afternoon.

By overnighting in the vicinity, you can enter at 8 am, explore the site for three hours, and take a siesta during the tourist peak. Return at 3 pm and stay until the 5 pm closing. In the evening you can attend a somewhat hokey historical sound & light show utilising coloured spotlights – Spanish version, 7 pm, US$0.75; English version, 9 pm, US$1.50. The light is probably better than the sound.

History

Chichén Itzá had two periods of greatness and was abandoned between those epochs. Still the subject of much debate is the question who was responsible for the superior civilisation that flourished here.

Most archaeologists agree that Chichén Itzá's first major settlement, during the Late Classic period between 550 and 900 AD, was pure Mayan. At Uxmal you can see the Puuc-style architectural similarities between that site and the older buildings of Chichén, particularly La Casa Colorada (the Red House). About the 10th century, the city was largely abandoned for unknown reasons.

The city was resettled about 1100 AD. Shortly thereafter, according to what archaeologists at one point believed almost unanimously, Chichén was invaded by the Toltecs who had moved down from their central highlands capital of Tula.

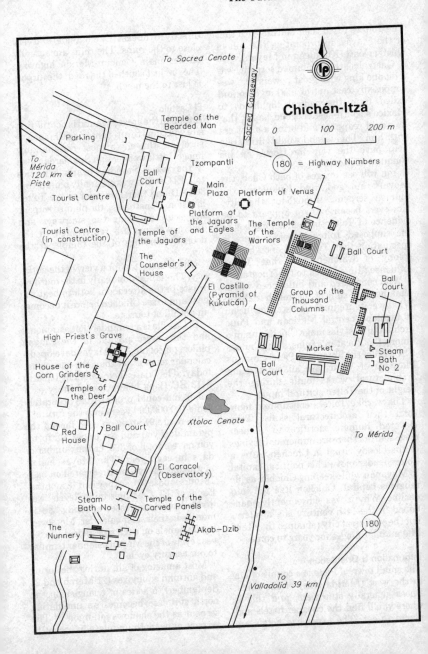

Chichén-Itzá

0   100   200 m

(180) = Highway Numbers

To Sacred Cenote

Temple of the Bearded Man

Parking

To Mérida 120 km & Piste

Tourist Centre

Tourist Centre (in construction)

Ball Court

Sacred Causeway

Tzompantli

Main Plaza

Platform of Venus

Platform of the Jaguars and Eagles

The Temple of the Warriors

Temple of the Jaguars

The Counselor's House

Ball Court

El Castillo (Pyramid of Kukulcán)

Ball Court

Group of the Thousand Columns

High Priest's Grave

House of the Corn Grinders

Temple of the Deer

Market

Ball Court

Steam Bath No 2

Red House

Ball Court

Xtoloc Cenote

To Mérida

El Caracol (Observatory)

Steam Bath No 1

Temple of the Carved Panels

The Nunnery

Akab-Dzib

To Valladolid 39 km

The Toltecs fused their culture with that of the Mayas, incorporating the cult of Quetzalcóatl (Kukulcán in Mayan).

Quetzalcóatl, the plumed serpent, was a blonde king with great powers who was supposedly cast out of his kingdom and exiled from the central highlands to Mexico's south-east. Legend had it that he would reappear and bring a great era with him. This legend would ultimately help pave the way for Cortés in his conquest of Mexico.

You will see images of both Chac, the Mayan rain god, and Kukulcán, the plumed serpent, throughout the city. However, because there appears to be evidence of Toltec influence long before the supposed Toltec invasion, there is speculation that Tula had once been a colony of Chichén and that Toltec influence filtered back to the Yucatán.

Who conquered and influenced whom remains the subject of much debate. Whatever its origin, the substantial fusion of highland central Mexican and Puuc architectural styles make Chichén unique among the Yucatán's ruins. The fabulous El Castillo, the Temple of Panels and the Platform of Venus are all outstanding architectural works built during the height of the Toltec cultural input.

The warlike Toltecs contributed more than their architectural skills. They elevated human sacrifice to a near obsession, for there are numerous carvings of the bloody ritual in Chichén. After a Toltec leader moved his political capital to Mayapan while keeping Chichén as his religious capital, Chichén Itzá fell into decline. Why it was subsequently abandoned in the 14th century is a mystery, but the once great city remained the site of Mayan pilgrimages for years to come.

Information & Orientation

The small town of Piste is a couple of km to the west (Mérida side) of the ruins. Buses generally stop here, and this is where you'll find the cheaper hotels and places to eat. The expensive hotels are directly to the east (Cancún side) and very close to the ruins. The ruins are actually off the main Cancún-Mérida highway. They're just south of the road; the airport is just to the north.

El Castillo

Although the great pyramid is not the first site you come to after entering Chichén, it surely is the city's most commanding image. Little wonder that Spaniards called it 'the castle'. Standing nearly 25 metres tall, El Castillo was originally built before 800 AD and therefore prior to the Toltec invasion. Nonetheless, the plumed serpent was sculpted along the stairways and Toltec warriors are represented in the doorway carvings of the temple at the top.

Climb to the top for a view of the entire city. This is best done early in the morning or late in the afternoon, both to beat the heat and to see Chichén before it becomes an anthill of tourists.

El Castillo is a reminder that astronomy and time were pivotal in the Mayan philosophy of life. The Mayas developed a calendar more exact than the one we use today. They date their calendar back to 3113 BC (long before their history as a tribe) and could project time accurately some 100,000,000 years into the future!

There are 91 steps on each face of the pyramid; if you add the upper platform, you have a total of 365, or the number of days in each year. The Mayas had a mathematical system predicated on base 18 (ours is base 10), so they had 18 months. Each of El Castillo's nine levels was divided by a staircase reflecting the 18 months in their solar calendar. Moreover, the 52 panels on each side reflect the 52-year cycle of the Mayan calendar (similar to our century cycle).

Most amazing of all, during the spring and autumn equinoxes (21 March and 21 September), a series of triangles on the north staircase becomes an undulating serpent as the shadows fall upon it! The serpent appears to undulate in ascent in

March and descent in September. This incredible display lasts three hours and 22 minutes.

Not astounded yet by El Castillo? Well, there's more: a pyramid *inside* El Castillo. When archaeologists opened it, they found a brilliant red jaguar throne with inlaid eyes and spots of shimmering jade. The inner sanctum also holds a Toltec chac-mool figure, even though it was built before the Toltec intrusion. Did the Toltecs place the figure there? Or does it support the newer theory that it was the Mayas who initially colonised the Toltecs at Tula?

The inner pyramid is only open from 11 am to 1 pm and 4 to 5 pm. The dank air inside can make climbing the stairs a sweltering experience.

Principal Ball Court

Just after you enter Chichén, walk to your left (or north-west of El Castillo) and you will see the best-preserved and largest ball court in all of Mexico. This principal ball field is only one of the city's eight courts, indicative of the importance the games held here. The field is flanked by temples at either end and bounded by towering parallel walls with stone rings cemented up high.

There is evidence that the ball game may have changed over the years. Some carvings show players with padding on their elbows and knees, and it is thought that they played a soccer-like game with a hard rubber ball, precluding the use of hands. Other carvings show players wielding bats; it appears that if a player hit the ball through one of the stone hoops, his team was declared the winner. It's thought that during the Toltec period the losing captain, and perhaps his team-mates as well, were sacrificed.

Along the walls of the ball court are some fine stone reliefs, including decapitations of losing players. Acoustically the court is amazing – a conversation at one end can be heard 135 metres away at the other end and if you clap, you hear a resounding echo.

Temple of the Bearded Man & Temple of the Jaguars

The structure at the northern end of the ball court, known as the Temple of the Bearded Man and named for a carving inside it, has some finely sculpted pillars and reliefs of flowers, birds and trees. See also the temple at the end of the court facing out on El Castillo. This Temple of the Jaguars (the south-eastern corner of the ball court) has some rattlesnake-carved columns and jaguar-etched tablets. Inside are faded mural fragments depicting a battle, possibly between the Toltecs and the Mayas.

Tzompantli – Temple of Skulls

The Tzompantli, a Toltec term for Temple of Skulls, is between the Temple of the Jaguars and El Castillo. You can't mistake it because the T-shaped platform is festooned with carved skulls and eagles tearing open the chests of men to eat their hearts. In ancient days this platform held the heads of sacrificial victims.

Platform of the Jaguars & Eagles

Adjacent to the Temple of Skulls, this platform's carvings depict jaguars and eagles gruesomely grabbing human hearts in their claws. It is thought that this platform was part of a temple dedicated to the military legions responsible for capturing sacrificial victims.

Platform of Venus

Near the path to the Sacred Cenote, looking north from El Castillo and east from Tzompantli, you will find the Platform of Venus. Rather than a beautiful woman, the Toltec Venus is a feathered serpent bearing a human head between its jaws. The platform is decked with feathered snake figures. Some maps refer to this as the Tomb of Chac-Mool because a figure of the reclining god was found within the structure.

Sacred Cenote

Near the Platform of Venus, you will see a 300-metre dirt path running north to the huge sunken well that gave this city its name. Chichén Itzá means 'Well of the Itzá' (the Mayas of this city were called 'the Itzá'). The Sacred Cenote is an awesome natural well, some 60 metres in diameter and 35 metres deep. The walls between the summit and the water's surface are beautifully ensnared in tangled vines and other vegetation.

Although some of the guides enjoy telling visitors that virgins were sacrificed by throwing them into the cenote to drown, divers in 1923 brought up the remains of men, women and children. Whether they were drowned here for religious or other reasons is not known.

Skeletons were not all that was found in the Sacred Cenote. Around the turn of the century, Edward Thompson, a Harvard professor and US consul to the Yucatán, bought a hacienda which included Chichén for US$75. It was his decision to have the cenote dredged. Artefacts as well as valuable gold and jade jewellery from all parts of Mexico were recovered; these were given to Harvard's Peabody Museum, which later returned much of it. The artefacts' origins show the far-flung contact the Mayas had (there are some items from as far away as Colombia). It is believed that offerings of all kinds, human and otherwise, were thrown into the Sacred Cenote to please the gods. Subsequent diving expeditions sponsored by the National Geographic Society in the 1960s turned up hundreds more of the valuable artefacts.

Group of the Thousand Columns

Comprising the Temple of the Warriors, Temple of Chac-Mool and Sweat House or Steam Bath, this group takes its collective name from the copious number of pillars in front. The platformed temple greets you with a statue of the reclining god, Chac, as well as stucco and stone-carved animal deities. The temple's roof caved in long ago; columns entwined with serpents once served as roof supports. If you have been to Tula, you will see some similarities between its Toltec temple and this one.

A 1926 restoration revealed an edifice inside the Temple of the Warriors, constructed prior to it – the Temple of Chac-Mool. You may enter via a stairway on the north side. The temple walls have largely deteriorated murals of what is thought to be the Toltecs' defeat of the Mayan defenders here.

Just east of the Temple of the Warriors sits the rubble of a Mayan sweat house, with an underground oven and drains for the water. The sweat houses were regularly used for ritual purification.

Market

If you walk south from the Temple of the Warriors, you will come to some colonnaded chambers once thought to house Chichén's elite. Nearby is a remnant of what may have been an area of walled market stalls. None of these structures are in good shape.

Ossuary

The Ossuary, otherwise known as the Bonehouse or High Priest's Grave, is a deteriorated pyramid, the first building you come to as you take the dirt path south from El Castillo. As with most of the buildings in this southern section, the architecture is more Puuc than Toltec, adding to the belief that when the Toltecs took control they moved the focus of the city north. During excavation of the Ossuary, the remains of a man believed to be a high priest were found in a natural grotto over which the pyramid was built. Archaeologists are thinking about fully restoring this edifice in the near future.

La Casa Colorada

La Casa Colorada or 'The Red House' on the right fork leading from the Ossuary was named by the Spanish, who saw the red paint of the deteriorating mural on its doorway. This building has little Toltec influence and its design shows largely a pure Puuc-Mayan style. Referring to the stone latticework at the roof façade, the Mayas named this building Chichén-Chob, or House of Small Holes. What was thought to be a Toltec ball court to its rear has now been carbon dated to three centuries prior to the Toltec invasion, adding to the debate over who originally conquered whom.

Temple of the Deer

Until it deteriorated in the 1920s, the mural of a deer gave this classical little Mayan structure its name. The only reason to see this edifice is to go to the back of the building and climb to the top for a nice view of the surrounding ruins.

El Caracol (Observatory)

Take the path to the left from the Ossuary to reach Chichén's observatory. Called by the Spanish 'El Caracol' (giant conch snail) due to its interior cylindrical staircase, the Observatory is one of the most fascinating and important of all of Chichén Itzá's buildings. Its circular design resembles some central highlands structures, although, surprisingly, not those of Toltec Tula. In a fusion of architectural styles and religious imagery, there are Mayan Chac rain god masks over four external doors facing the cardinal directions.

The windows in the observatory's dome are aligned with the appearance of certain stars at specific dates. From the dome the priests decreed the appropriate times for rituals, celebrations, corn-planting and harvests. The observatory was built over several centuries and is a product of Toltec times, though its base was undertaken earlier.

Nunnery & Annex

Thought by archaeologists to have been a palace for Mayan royalty, the Nunnery with its myriad of rooms resembled a European convent to the conquistadors, hence their name for the building. The Nunnery's dimensions are imposing: its base is 60 metres long, 30 metres wide and 20 metres high. The construction is Mayan rather than Toltec, although a Toltec sacrificial stone stands in front. A small building added onto the west side is known as the Annex. These buildings are constructed in the Puuc-Chenes style, particularly evident in the lower jaw of the Chac mask at the opening of the Annex. There are several other Chac statues on the façade of the Nunnery.

The Church

Near the Annex sits a relatively small building, notable only for upper façade masks alternating Chac with animal gods called *bacabs* – crab, turtle, snail and armadillo – which Mayan mythology claims hold up the sky.

Akab-Dzib

On the rough path east of the Nunnery, the Akab-Dzib is thought by some archaeologists to be the most ancient structure excavated to date here. The central chambers date all the way back to the 2nd century. Akab-Dzib means 'Obscure Writing' in Mayan, referring to the south-side annex door whose lintel depicts a priest with a vase etched with hieroglyphics. The writing has never been translated, hence the name. Note the red fingerprints on the ceiling, thought to symbolise the deity Zamna, a sun god from whom the Mayas sought wisdom.

Chichén Viejo – Old Chichén

Chichén Viejo, or Old Chichén, are the largely unrestored, basically Mayan ruins (some have Toltec additions). Here you'll see a pristine part of Chichén without much archaeological restoration.

Although visiting Old Chichén is best done with a guide, if you wish to go there yourself take the path which runs from the south-west corner of the Nunnery. Follow this for about 20 minutes until you come to some thatched huts. Take the trail behind the smallest hut and you will first reach a group of ruins labelled by archaeologists 'the Date Group'. A date lintel here (879 AD) explains the name; it's set over two columns of a former temple which is now largely rubble. Nearby, the House of the Phalli is well preserved and named for the phalli set in the edifice's chambers.

Beyond the House of the Phalli, take the trail another 20 minutes to the Lintel Group. Of these, all are poorly preserved except for the restored Temple of the Three Lintels. Built in traditional Puuc-Chenes style with rain god masks adorning the building's corners, the temple is named for its three dated lintels. There are other ruins in the vicinity, best located with the help of a guide.

Places to Stay – bottom end

Posada Novela is a decrepit motel-like building at the end of Piste nearest the ruins. The rooms are spartan, but basically acceptable. Singles with fan and bath cost US$4, doubles US$5.

Another basic budget place is the *Hotel Cunanchen* west of the zócalo's bus stop (the Mérida end of town). Marginally acceptable rooms cost about US$4 single, US$6 double. There may not be water at night.

Camping

Camping at the *Piramide Inn & Trailer Park* on the edge of town closest to the ruins is a good deal. For slightly less than US$2 per person, you can pitch a tent and enjoy the Piramide Inn's pool. There are hot showers and clean, shared toilet facilities here.

Places to Stay – middle

Hotel Dolores Alba is run by the family which operates the hotel of the same name in Mérida at Calle 63 464 (you can make reservations in Mérida by calling 21-37-45 for the Chichén Itzá lodgings). Although not in Piste, this hotel five km east of the ruins is highly recommended. They will transport you to the ruins, but you must take a taxi, bus or walk back. The hotel is a truly amicable place with a swimming pool, pleasant rooms and an excellent moderately priced restaurant. Singles with fan and bath cost US$7, doubles US$9. There are a few air-conditioned rooms for about US$1.50 extra. If you are coming here by bus, remind the driver to drop you off.

The *Piramide Inn* (tel Piste 5) on the ruins side of Piste has a swimming pool and pretty gardens. Its well-maintained, substantial rooms are air-conditioned and cost US$12.50 single, US$15.50 double. You can make reservations in Mérida by calling 24-04-11.

Places to Stay – top end

The expensive hotels at Chichén Itzá are pleasant places to stay and have the great advantage of being very close to the ruins. You can leave the ruins any time the crowds or the heat get too much and zip back to your hotel in minutes for a swim in the pool or a drink from the bar. In fact if you are going to splurge on just one expensive hotel in Mexico, this is a good place to do it.

Hotel Mayaland (tel Piste 4) has a good restaurant-bar and a swimming pool. Most of the rooms have private balconies. Singles are US$40, doubles US$50.

The *Hotel Villa Arqueológica* (tel 6-28-30) is Club Méd-managed with a restaurant, tennis courts and swimming pool. Rooms are fairly small, costing US$30 for singles and US$40 for doubles, but there are also pleasant two-bedroom suites at US$50, ideal for families. Apart from being architecturally attractive with its lushly vegetated courtyard and swimming pool, the hotel is decorated with numerous glass showcases holding fine Mayan sculptures and pottery pieces.

The *Hotel Hacienda Chichén* (tel 21-92-12 in Mérida) close to the ruins has cottages used some time ago by archaeologists. There is a swimming pool in this very pleasant hotel and you will also find a good restaurant on the premises. Singles cost US$40, doubles US$45.

The *Hotel Misión Chichén* has a swimming pool, children's zoo, restaurant and bar. Singles cost US$43, doubles US$56.

Places to Eat

The *Nicte-Ha* and *Parador Maya*, both in the centre of Piste, have so-so *típico* fare at prices relatively inexpensive for this tourist-trap of a town. *El Carousel* is a bit up-market but the food is only OK for standard Mexican cooking.

If you are willing to spend the money, the *Restaurant Xaybe* opposite the Misión Inn has excellent cuisine, sometimes served buffet style for the tour bus clientele. Figure US$4 for lunch, US$6 for dinner. If you eat here you can use the swimming pool; if you don't, you can still swim for about US$1. The luxury hotels all have restaurants, with the Club Méd-run *Villas Arqueológica* serving particularly distinguished cuisine. Count on around US$25 to US$35 for dinner for two at the Villa, including a bottle of wine and the tip. Snacks like burgers are around US$6.

Entertainment

Other than the mediocre sound & light show at the ruins, there is a disco called *Tavares* adjacent to the Piramide Inn.

Getting There & Away

Air There's a small airstrip close to Chichén Itzá.

Bus First and 2nd-class buses run from both Mérida and Cancún to Piste. Whether or not they stop at the ruins 2½ km from Piste seems to be at the caprice of the driver. To the ruins from Mérida takes about two hours (US$2); from Cancún figure roughly three hours (US$3). If you're travelling by 2nd-class bus, add about 30 to 45 minutes. If you want to stay in Valladolid, there is fairly frequent bus service to Piste and the ruins.

GRUTAS DE BALANKANCHE

Mayas residing near Chichén Itzá had long believed that there was something sacred from the past buried in the region. This was borne out in 1959 when a guide to the ruins was exploring a cave on his day off. Pushing against one of the cavern's walls, he is said to have broken through into a larger subterranean opening. Archaeological exploration revealed a path that runs some 300 metres past carved stalactites and stalagmites, terminating at an underground pool.

Discovered in the caves and exhibited today were offerings left to Tlaloc, the Toltec central Mexican god of rain (similar to the Mayan Chac). Among the offerings were incense burners carved with the image of Tlaloc and some miniature *metates* used for grinding corn. These are found principally in two places: a large domed cavern called The Throne where you'll find a fused pillar of stalactites and stalagmites (Balankanche means 'Hidden Throne' in Mayan), and the subterranean pool area.

While artificially lit, the cave is still dark in places and newcomers find it easy to get lost; a tour is therefore compulsory. The escorted tours of three or more visitors leave Monday to Saturday at 9, 10 and 11 am, and at 2, 3 and 4 pm, at a cost of 15c. On Sunday the tours are free, departing at 8, 9, 10 and 11 am only.

It's slippery and cool inside the cave and so narrow in a few spots that you will have to get down on all fours and crawl. It's a good idea to do your exploring in trousers rather than shorts. The dark, narrow passageways are not recommended for the claustrophobic.

Getting There & Away

The caves are about six km east of the ruins of Chichén Itzá and only two km from the Hotel Dolores Alba on the road toward Cancún. You can get here by buses running east from Chichén or by taxi.

VALLADOLID

Population: 40,000

Valladolid is a taste of the colonial in the heart of Mayan country. Here amidst the splendour of colonial architecture, huipile-clad Mayan women hawk their wares. If you have just explored Chichén Itzá, Valladolid is a good place to relax.

Some travellers visiting Chichén Itzá choose to stay 40 minutes away in Valladolid for its pleasant atmosphere and inexpensive hotels. Other travellers come here from the Caribbean coast for a few days' respite from the tourist trail. At the very least, those journeying between the Caribbean and Mérida should spend a few relaxing hours here, as Valladolid is a good place to break the five-hour bus trip between Cancún and Mérida.

History

Although the initial attempt at conquest by the conquistador Montejo was thwarted by fierce Mayan resistance in 1543, Montejo the Younger ultimately subdued the Indians and took the town. What until then had been the Mayan ceremonial centre of Zaci became the Spanish settlement of Valladolid.

During much of the succeeding colonial era, Valladolid's humidity and surrounding rainforests kept it isolated and thus relatively autonomous of royal rule. With the French and US revolutions as a catalyst, local leaders in 1809 plotted a rebellion which was discovered and quashed. Nonetheless, the seeds of future unrest were sown. The next uprising would be by the Indians.

Brutally exploited and banned along with the mestizos from even entering the settlement of pure-blooded Spaniards, the Mayas in the Caste War of 1847 made Valladolid their first town of attack. Later during the 1910 Revolution, the Indians attempted to take the town.

Today, Valladolid is a marketing centre for agricultural products and crafts sent from here to either the Caribbean coast or Mérida. Although it may appear sleepy,

Valladolid is a prosperous seat of agrarian commerce, and is the principal city of the Peninsula's midsection.

Orientation

Because this compact town has streets on a numbered grid, Valladolid is easy to find your way around. Odd-numbered streets run east-west, even-numbered streets north to south. Recommended hotels are within a short walk of the zócalo or just off it. The zócalo is bounded by Calles 39, 40, 41 and 42.

If you have arrived by bus, to reach the zócalo from the depot's Calle 39 and 46 locale, simply walk left on Calle 39 and in two lengthy blocks you will be at the heart of Valladolid.

Information

Tourist Office The tourist office in the zócalo's Palacio Municipal has city maps. Its hours are erratic but you can also find maps at any of the major hotels on the zócalo.

Money For currency exchange, banks on the zócalo are open Monday to Friday from 9 am to 1.30 pm. Some of the bigger hotels and restaurants will also change money if you need pesos after banking hours.

Post The post office is just beyond the bus terminal at Calle 40 195A. Its hours are Monday to Friday from 8 am to 6 pm, Saturday 9 am to 1 pm.

Festivals

On 3 June the struggle against the dictator Porfirio Díaz is celebrated to mark the 1910 revolt in these parts.

Church of San Bernardino de Siena & Convent of Sisal

Although Valladolid has a number of interesting colonial churches, the Church of San Bernardino de Siena and the Convent of Sisal three blocks south-west of the zócalo on Calle 41A at the corners of

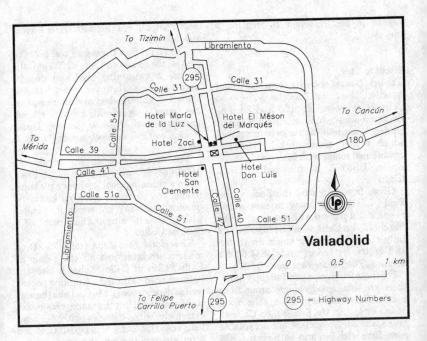

Calles 41 and 46 are said to be the oldest Christian structures in the Yucatán. Constructed in 1552, the complex was designed to serve a dual function as a fortress, given the enmity of the Indians toward the Spaniards.

If you venture inside, apart from the miracle-working Virgin of Guadalupe on the altar, the church is relatively bare of ornamentation. During the uprisings of 1847 and 1910, angry Indians responded to the clergy's links with landowners by rifling the church of decorative materials. Outside the church a 17th-century horse-drawn well is being renovated for contemporary use.

Other Churches

Other churches of note are the Cathedral of San Gervasio which sits with its pretty garden on the zócalo, San Roque at Calles 41 and 38 with its exhibition hall of Mayan artefact photographs, Santa Ana at Calles 41 and 34, La Candelaria at Calles 44 and 35, San Juan Iglesia at Calles 49 and 40, and Santa Lucía at Calles 40 and 27.

Cenotes

It can get really sticky in Valladolid so consider taking a dip in an ancient cenote. The Cenote Zaci, on Calle 36 near Calle 39 a three-block walk from the zócalo, is one place to cool off, but some visitors are put off by its scummy-looking waters. Zaci is open from 8 am until dark, with an admission price of 15c. Near the cenote is a small regional ethnographic museum worth a brief look.

For cleaner waters, pedal a bike west out of town on Calle 41 past the Coca-Cola plant until you come to the highway. Make a left at the highway and another left when you see the sign for Dzitnup Cenote. Given its distance from town, the cenote is best reached by renting a bicycle.

Places to Stay

The best budget choice in town is, without question, the *Hotel Zaci* (tel 6-21-67) on Calle 44 between Calles 37 and 39. The Zaci's rooms are built around a pleasant garden, complete with a swimming pool which is not always filled. Nice air-conditioned rooms with bath cost US$3.50 single, US$5.75 double and US$7.50 triple.

Given how delightful the Zaci is, you would have to be crazy to save a few pennies and put up with the bugs at the *Hotel Lilly* on Calle 44 across from it. The Lilly charges US$3 for singles with fan and grotty bathroom and US$4.50 for doubles. The roaches are free.

For those willing to spend slightly more, there are some good choices around the zócalo. The cheapest of these is the *Hotel María de la Luz* (tel 6-20-70) on Calle 42 near Calle 39. An ancient but acceptable room here with fan and bath costs US$4 single, US$6 double. The swimming pool was filled, but not just with water – avoid swallowing.

The *Hotel San Clemente* (tel 6-22-08) just off the zócalo on Calle 42 206 at Calle 41 has a swimming pool and decent-looking rooms. However, when I stayed there the toilet leaked and there was no hot water. Singles with air-conditioning and bath cost US$6.50, doubles US$8. Rooms with TVs cost about US$0.50 extra.

The nicest hotel on the zócalo, *El Mesón del Marqués* at Calle 39 203 has a clean swimming pool and very pleasant rooms. You pay a bit more but given the quality, some say it's worth it. Singles with air-conditioning and bath cost US$9, doubles US$10.

The *Hotel Don Luis* (tel 6-20-24), a modern structure just off the zócalo at Calle 39 191 at Calle 38, has a pleasant palm-shaded patio and swimming pool as well as decent rooms. Maybe I was there at the wrong time, but the management was extremely surly. Singles with fan and bath cost US$5, doubles US$6.50. If you want air-conditioning, the price goes up about US$1.

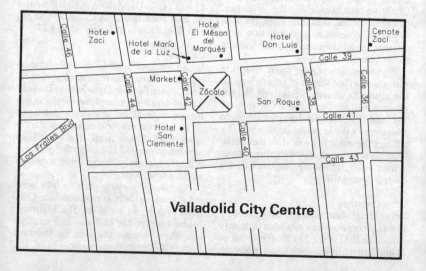

Valladolid City Centre

Places to Eat

For those willing to spend a bit more, *Casa de los Arcos* on Calle 39 between Calles 38 and 40 serves superb Yucatecan cuisine. It's not all that expensive and the comida corrida at about US$2 is quite a good deal. Another restaurant serving good food is the dining room of *Hotel Mesón del Marqués*, Calle 39 203 on the zócalo. The food is somewhat pricey, but of good quality and served in pleasant surroundings.

The dining room of *Hotel María de la Luz*, on the zócalo (Calle 42 at Calle 39) overlooking the plaza, has decent food at reasonable prices. For good Yucatecan food, try *Cenote* on Calle 36. You dine under a thatched roof and the prices are moderate.

For cheap yet acceptable fare, try the tiny mall of shops and restaurants in the Bazar Municipal next to the Hotel Mesón del Marqués on the zócalo. Here you can fill up cheaply at *El Amigo Panfilo* and *Doña María's* or enjoy OK pizza served at *Sergio's*. If you are waiting for a morning bus, you can get a cheap breakfast across from the station at the *Mendoza Taurino*.

Things to Buy

There are some beautiful huipiles on sale cheaply in shops and in the market. Hammocks are also cheaper here than on the Caribbean coast (see the Things to Buy section under Mérida for details on buying hammocks).

Getting There & Away

There is frequent service to Mérida by either 1st-class (three hours, US$3.50) or 2nd-class (3½ hours, US$3) bus and most of these will stop at Chichén Itzá if you remind the driver (30 to 45 minutes, US$0.50). There is also regular service to Cancún/Puerto Juárez (two to 2½ hours, US$2), but early-morning buses may be jam-packed with commuters.

A quicker, more comfortable way to Cancún is the shared taxis parked outside the bus station – US$5 per person. The taxis leave when they fill their seats. Buses also run frequently to Tizimín (about an hour, US$0.75) where those going on to Río Lagartos transfer. If you are going to Isla Holbox, there are three Chiquila-bound buses daily.

Getting Around

Given Valladolid's grid-numbered streets and compact size, walking everywhere but Dzitnup Cenote is a snap. For Dzitnup, rent a bike at the shop on Calle 44 between Calles 41 and 39. It's the cheapest place in town with bikes for about US$0.30 per hour, but it's only open from 8 am to 1.30 pm.

To reach the zócalo from the bus station, walk left out the entrance on Calle 39 and within about five minutes you will reach the main plaza.

TIZIMÍN

Many travellers bound for Río Lagartos or San Felipe will change buses in Tizimín, the second largest city in the state of Yucatán. There is little to warrant an overnight stay, although Tizimín is relatively free of tourists.

The zócalo is pleasant, the nearby convento on Calle 51 a fairly interesting colonial structure and the adjacent Los Reyes Church has a skilfully carved altar. Keep going five lengthy blocks on Calle 51 and you will come to a modest zoo, the Parque Zoológico de la Reina.

Information & Orientation

The city is laid out in an easy-to-navigate numbered grid. Maps are available at the Chamber of Commerce (Cámara del Comercio) one block west of the plaza mayor at the end of the mall. To get to the zócalo from the bus station, go north a block on Calle 47, turn left on Calle 50 and walk a block west.

Places to Stay

The *Hotel San Jorge*, conveniently located on the zócalo at Calle 52, has basic

502 The Yucatán Peninsula – Yucatán

rooms with fan and bath for US$4 single, US$5 double.

Places to Eat
The market, between the bus station and the zócalo, has cheap street fare. An excellent though moderately expensive restaurant is *Los Tres Reyes* on the corner of Calles 52 and 53. You can eat very well here for US$2 to US$3.

Getting There & Away
There are 1st and 2nd-class buses between Tizimín and Mérida with frequent daily departures. Eight 2nd-class buses run between Valladolid and Tizimín. For Río Lagartos there are three 1st-class departures and five daily 2nd-class buses which continue on to San Felipe.

Getting Around
All the recommended sights are easily accessible on foot.

RÍO LAGARTOS
For those interested in the most spectacular flamingo colony in Mexico, it is worth going out of your way to this little fishing village 104 km from Valladolid and 50 km from Tizimín. In addition to thousands of flamingoes, the estuaries are home to snowy egrets, red egrets, great white herons and snowy white ibis. Although Río Lagartos (Alligator River) was named after the once-substantial alligator population, don't expect to see any of the reptiles as hunting has virtually wiped them out.

The town of Río Lagartos itself, with its narrow streets and multi-hued houses, has a bit of charm, but if it were not for the flamingoes, you would have little reason to come here. Although the state government has been making noises about developing the area for tourism, this has not happened yet.

Flamingoes
The Hotel Nefertiti takes most bird-watchers on flamingo boat tours. The hotel offers different options, among them a three-hour boat tour to the flamingo sanctuary at Las Coloradas for five passengers at US$5 per person; or a two-hour boat trip to San Felipe costing US$3.50 per person in a boatload of five.

If you can't get enough people together to make the trip affordable, go out to the docks near the Nefertiti and hire a boatman to take you to see small flamingo nesting grounds for about US$5. The trip takes less than an hour.

The Spanish word *flamenco*, which means 'flaming', makes sense in terms of the bird's name as you approach a horizon of hundreds of brilliantly hued, flaming red-pink birds. When the flock takes flight, the suddenly fiery horizon can make you think you're hallucinating.

Bird-Watching on Foot
If you walk some of the 14 km along the beach from the lagoon out to Punta Holohit on the sea, you will most likely see colourful bird life. Among the species common here are egrets, herons, flamingoes, ibis, cormorants, stilts, pelicans and plovers. Wear some decent footwear that you can get wet as well as clothes that you can go in the water with. You might be able to arrange with Hotel Nefertiti to have a boat pick you up at Punta Holohit for your return if you walk all the way.

Beaches & Springs
The only beach around Río Lagartos must be reached by boat. The Hotel Nefertiti will take you there for about US$0.75 per person in a boat carrying five passengers. However, the beach is not all that nice; there are no palms to shelter you from the sun and the water is brackish. Some visitors prefer Chiquilá Spring, a one-km walk from the Nefertiti.

Places to Stay
Unfortunately, the *Hotel Nefertiti* (tel 14-15) is the only hotel in town. Given its monopoly, the hotel takes little care to keep up its rooms, which are basic and OK but overpriced. You will spot the Nefertiti

easily on the shore: it's the sole multi-storied edifice in town. Rooms with fan and bath cost US$7 single, US$8.50 double.

An option is to go to the pink-and-white building off the zócalo on Calle 10 and ask if you can either hang a hammock or rent a room. If you can strike a bargain for a room in this private house, it will be cheaper than the Nefertiti.

Camping is a pleasant alternative if you are equipped for it. Walk about one km along the shoreline east of Hotel Nefertiti to a pretty cenote. Nobody will bother you here at night, but pack up your gear during the day when the cenote is invaded by local kids.

Places to Eat

The best restaurant in Río Lagartos is *Los Flamingos Restaurant* at Hotel Nefertiti, although it's not cheap (US$3 to US$4 for dinner). There's decent, reasonably priced seafood at *Los Negritos'* 2nd-floor dining room off the zócalo. Across from the Nefertiti is the *Restaurant Económica*, whose food – as the name implies –is cheap. Unfortunately, it is also lousy.

Entertainment

The Hotel Nefertiti's *Los Flamingos Restaurant* turns into a disco later in the evening.

Getting There & Away

If you are coming from Valladolid, there is frequent service to Tizimín (eight daily 2nd-class buses) for the 54-km, one-hour journey. You must transfer here to another bus bound for Río Lagartos; with three 1st-class and five 2nd-class departures for the 50-km, one-hour journey, you should have no problem getting there. There are 1st-class bus between Mérida and Río Lagartos, two a day when this was written.

Getting Around

Río Lagartos is small and everything is within walking distance. See the section on flamingoes for boat-tour information.

SAN FELIPE

Population: 300

This tiny fishing village of painted wooden houses on narrow streets makes a nice day trip from Río Lagartos. While the waters are not Caribbean turquoise and there's little shade, in spring and summer scores of visitors come here to camp. Other than lying on the beach, bird-watching is the main attraction as just across the estuary at Punta Holohit there is abundant bird life.

Places to Stay

There are no hotels in San Felipe, but the proprietor of La Herradura grocery store near the pier will tell you about inexpensive house rentals. Spartan rooms are sometimes available for rent above the Cínema Morufo. Campers are ferried across the estuary to islands where they pitch tents or set up hammocks.

Places to Eat

The town's sole eatery, *Restaurant El Payaso*, is cheap and quite good for seafood.

Getting There & Away

Buses from Tizimín which run to Río Lagartos continue on to San Felipe and run a return service. The 12-km ride takes about seven minutes.

ISLA HOLBOX

Fed up with the tourist hordes of Cancún, Isla de Mujeres, and Cozumel? Want to find a beach site virtually devoid of gringos? In that case Isla Holbox might appeal to you, but before you make haste for the island note that there are no finished hotels as yet and the most basic facilities are in short supply. To enjoy Isla Holbox, you must be willing to rough it.

The 25-km by three-km island has sands that run on and on, as well as tranquil waters where you can wade out quite a distance before the sea reaches shoulder level. Moreover, Isla Holbox is magic for shell collectors, with a galaxy of shapes and colours. The fisher-families of the island are friendly, unjaded by encounters with pushy tourists or the relatively frenetic pace of the Mexican mainland.

As to drawbacks, the seas are not the translucent turquoise of the Quintana Roo beach sites, because here the Caribbean waters mingle with those of the darker Gulf. Seaweed can create silty waters near shore at some parts of the beach. While there are big plans to one day develop Isla Holbox, as of this writing there is only one partially finished hotel. Most travellers camp or stay in spartan rooms rented from locals.

Places to Stay

The unfinished and as yet unnamed hotel will rent rooms without electricity for about US$3.50 per night. For less than US$1, locals will rent you rooms or provide hammock hooks at their houses.

Places to Eat

So far, the only eatery on the island is the *Joany Restaurant*. The Joany offers inexpensive seafood and *típico* fare. For prepared goods, there is a small selection at the *Tienda Dinorio*.

Otherwise, you do the cooking with fish caught by locals or yourself and the sparse selection of items sold in the market. Some of the locals who rent rooms will cook for a small sum. There is a decent little *panadería* at the east side of the zócalo, but if you want fresh bread get to the bakery before 8 am as it goes fast.

Getting There & Away

To reach Isla Holbox, you take the ferry from the port of Chiquilá. Buses make the 2½-hour trip three times a day from Valladolid, and in theory the ferry is supposed to wait for them. However, it may not wait for a delayed bus or may even leave early (!) should the captain feel so inclined.

It is therefore recommended that you reach Chiquilá as early as possible. The ferry is supposed to depart for the island at 8 am, 11.30 am and 3 pm and make the trip in about an hour. Ferries return to Chiquilá at 5, 6.30 and 10 am and 2 pm. The cost is US$0.50.

If you are going from Isla de Mujeres or Cancún to Isla Holbox, you don't have to change buses at Valladolid because there are buses to Chiquilá from Puerto Juárez.

Try not to get stuck in Chiquilá, as it is a hole of a tiny port with no hotels and little camping space. Its only restaurant, *El Viento*, serves poor-quality food and you are advised to bring food just in case.

Quintana Roo

This sizeable state of more than 50,000 square km has a relatively small population of about 175,000 and agriculturally it is not all that productive. These facts are in good measure due to the state's geology – the jungle-covered topsoil is simply too thin to support much farming – but equally important, they are a result of Quintana Roo's unique history.

Recently a new factor has led to an economic boom in some areas, with more likely to come: tourism. Quintana Roo has spectacular beaches, a balmy tropical climate and teeming tropical reefs, enticing thousands of sun-worshippers and aquatic sports aficionados to come here annually. Cancún, Cozumel and Isla Mujeres resort hot-spots attract international visitors; for those seeking a less social scene, Quintana Roo offers a bevy of unspoiled beaches between Cancún and Tulum. And for those fascinated by Mayan antiquities, the seaside ruins of Tulum and the luxuriant jungle setting of Cobá provide a unique sense of the great civilisations which occupied this region long before the coming of Europeans.

Two Warnings At peak North American holiday periods the beach resorts of

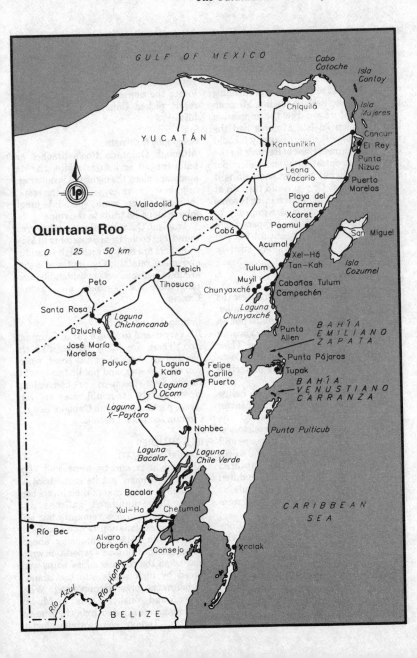

Quintana Roo can be very crowded. If you turn up at Cancún or anywhere along the coast around Christmas or New Year, better have a reservation or be prepared to camp out.

Also, the coast suffers from overwhelming tourist hyperbole. From reading Mexican tourist literature you'd get the impression that Garrafon on Isla Mujeres had the world's best snorkelling; actually it could be in the Guinness Book of Records for the greatest concentration of snorkellers per square metre, but greatest snorkelling it certainly is not. Or you could turn up at Xel-Ha thinking you were coming to some secluded inlet ideal for a swim, only to find 20 bus-loads of day-trippers there ahead of you. Xel-Ha is beautiful, but you have to wait for the midday rush to subside in order to see it.

History

The conquistadors arrived long after the great Mayan cities of this state had fallen into decline. Although the Indians put up staunch resistance, here as in Yucatán and Campeche, they were defeated. Their numbers greatly reduced by the Caste War, many Mayas fled to the protective jungles of Quintana Roo.

In what is now the town of Felipe Carrillo Puerto, a rebel chief, a Mayan priest and a ventriloquist rallied the Indians to continue their resistance. Inspired, they drove most Europeans and mestizos out of Quintana Roo. The scores of Europeans the Indians captured suffered the fate the Mayas had endured for three centuries under Spanish rule, as this time it was the whites who were enslaved.

Given Quintana Roo's distance from the rest of Mexico, as time went by the Indian rebellion was largely ignored by the Mexican government. A delicate détente ensued until about the turn of the century when peace was finally negotiated. Nonetheless, Quintana Roo's isolation and Indian influence kept it a territory and it was not admitted as a state of

Mexico until 1974. By then, educated Mayas began to see the economic possibilities of tourism, as did affluent developers with close ties to the federal government. A computer programmed to locate the perfect spot for a Caribbean resort picked Cancún, and the rest is history.

Geography & Climate

Although Quintana Roo's beaches are palm-fringed and sugar white, the flat landscape along the highways is unvarying rainforest. However, Cobá, in the state's interior, offers some splendid jungle foliage along its trails to the ruins.

Tropical Quintana Roo is sultry year round, but cooler from September to May. Summers are sticky, with high humidity and more rainfall. The southern region around Chetumal gets considerably more rain than the northern area around Cancún.

Getting Around

It's very useful to have a car in Quintana Roo. There are many places, like the beaches and bays along the coast, where you want to stop, and public transport is rarely very frequent or convenient. Unfortunately car-rental rates are very steep, particularly from Cancún. See the Cancún section for details.

ISLA MUJERES

Population: 13,000

Although it is said by some that 'The Island of Women' got its name because Spanish buccaneers kept their lovers here while they plundered galleons and pillaged ports, a less romantic but still intriguing explanation is more probably accurate. In 1519, a chronicler aboard Hernández de Córdoba's expedition wrote that when the conquistadors' ships were forced by high winds into the island's harbour, the crew reconnoitred. What they found onshore was a Mayan ceremonial site filled with clay figurines of females. Today, some archaeologists

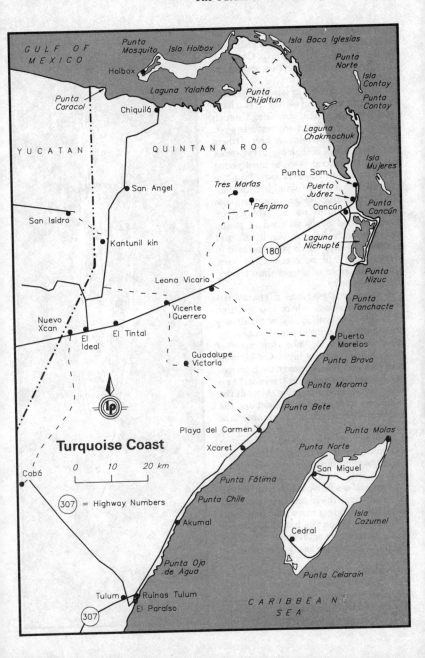

Turquoise Coast

0   10   20 km

(307) = Highway Numbers

believe that the island was a stopover for Mayas en route to worship their goddess of fertility, Ixchel, on the island of Cozumel. The clay idols are thought to represent the goddess.

The chief attribute of Isla is its relaxed social life in a tropical setting. If you have been doing some hard travelling through Mexico, you will find many travellers you met along the way relaxing here. Others make Isla the site of their one to two-week holiday. It's a good place to meet young travellers and sun-seekers away from the high-rise alienation of Miami-like Cancún. The surrounding waters are turquoise blue and bathtub warm. Women are rarely hassled by locals used to seeing topless *gringas*. In sum, Isla is safe and relatively clean; if this is your first visit to Mexico, you will be comfortable here. Many visitors have a hard time tearing themselves away.

However, not everyone is enamoured of Isla. The village where you will find virtually all the available lodging is already built-up and growing beyond its capacity. By day there's the non-stop noise of jackhammers and by night the blare of radio rock-and-roll. Moreover, the principal beach is rather small and the island as a whole not all that attractive. Most of the palm trees were killed in a blight and the part of the island not built-up consists of Yucatán scrub bush. The ballyhooed snorkelling at the island's Garrafón National Park is overrated. Prices, while not outrageous like in Cancún, are higher than you will find in most of Mexico.

Come and see for yourself. Even critics get caught up in the island's easy pace and social life, spending more time here than anticipated. When you have had enough of Isla, the more tranquil shores of beaches south of Cancún are easily accessible.

Orientation

The island's town, where you will doubtless be staying, is tiny and in next to no time you will know its few streets well. That the streets are often unmarked will

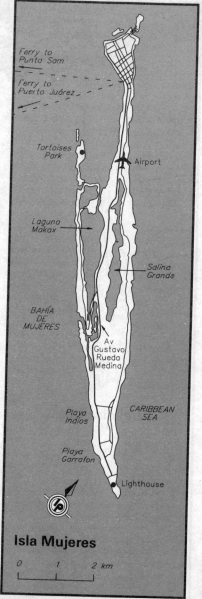

Isla Mujeres

0   1   2 km

not pose much of a problem – just ask someone for directions.

Isla Mujeres has two separate visitor populations. Those who stay here are in large part budget travellers of a variety of nationalities. The day-trippers are predominantly American and Canadian package tourists from Cancún. Attractions like Garrafon attract lots of visitors, so try to do your sightseeing early in the day.

Information
Tourist Office Located on Guerrero one block west of Hotel Isleno and just past Hotel Carmelina is the island's tourist office. They have crude map hand-outs, and will change money at a not-so-great rate after banking hours as well as make international collect calls for a fee. Hours are theoretically 9 am to 2 pm and 5 to 7 pm Monday to Saturday, although the office is sometimes closed during these hours. The clerk is one of the few islanders who speaks no English!

Money The bank at Juárez 5 is so packed that many travellers change at a lower rate at the grocery store or tourist office. Some hotels will change dollars at a poor rate. Travellers who want the bank rate justify the lines as another Isla opportunity to meet people.

Post The post office on Guerrero at the intersection with López Mateos is at the north-west end of town close to the Poc-Na Youth Hostel.

Festivals
A Caribbean-wide music festival is held in February. Carnival is celebrated here prior to Lent (it's more colourful in Mérida).

Garrafon National Park
Although the waters are translucent and the fish abundant, Garrafon is one of the most overrated of all snorkelling sites. For starters, it's teeming most of the time with hordes of day-trippers from Cancún, so

you are more often ogling fellow snorkellers than aquatic life. Furthermore, the reef is virtually dead, which makes it less likely to inflict cuts but reduces its colour and the intricacy of formations. The water can be extremely choppy, sweeping you into jagged areas. When the water is running fast here – not an unusual occurrence – snorkelling is a hassle and dangerous for non-swimmers. Those without strong swimming skills should be advised that the bottom falls off steeply quite close to shore; if you are having trouble, you might not be noticed amidst all those bobbing heads.

Garrafon is open daily from 8 am to 5 pm, and the earlier you get here (see the Getting Around section), the more time you will have free of the milling mobs from Cancún. Admission is US$0.75, but you might avoid paying if you walk to the park via the sea wall at the adjoining property just to the north. There are lockers for your valuables – recommended as a safeguard – for about US$1. Snorkelling equipment can be rented for the day at US$3. Garrafon also has a small aquarium and museum.

In my opinion, the free snorkelling off the pier at the Hotel El Presidente is superior to Garrafon's.

Playa Los Cocos
Walk five to 10 minutes north along the shore from your hotel and you will see Playa Los Cocos, the village's principal beach. The waters are chest-high far from the shore, translucent and calm. However, the beach is relatively small for the number of sun-seekers and while there are some palapa-thatched-roof huts for shelter from direct rays, there are no trees. Try to come early in the morning or later in the day – at mid-day, Playa Los Cocos can be awfully crowded. If you can't tear yourself away from the beach, there are a couple of restaurant palapas selling over-priced food, beer and soft drinks.

Along the northern edge of Playa Los Cocos at the pier adjacent to Hotel El

Presidente the clear water and colourful aquatic life make for good snorkelling and it's infinitely less crowded than El Garrafon. There is no admission charge for these waters and you can also rent snorkelling gear in town cheaper than at El Garrafon.

Playa Lancheros

As you head to Garrafon, four km from the town and 1.5 km from Garrafon you will see Playa Lancheros. This is where the bus from town terminates and down by the beach is a distressing spectacle. Captive in a water pen are two enormous sea turtles. Some sick tourists actually get a charge out of climbing on their gigantic backs and getting a ride from the helpless behemoths while their friends photograph them. Equally pathetic, in the watery enclosure next to the turtles, a Mexican wrestles a lethargic shark for some pesos. The beach adjoining these cages is not particularly nice.

Mayan Ruins

If you are bored with beaches, there are some minor Mayan ruins just past Garrafon National Park. Initially seen by Hernández de Córdoba when his ships were forced by high winds into Isla's waters, this temple was built in honour of the goddess of fertility, Ixchel.

There's really little left to see here other than a fine sea view and in the distance, Cancún. The clay female figurines were pilfered long ago and a couple of the walls were washed into the Caribbean. The remaining walls have window slits used by Mayans to observe the stars.

You can easily stroll to the ruins from Garrafon or take a taxi, although that's hardly necessary. They're beyond the lighthouse at the south end of the island.

Fortress of Fermin Mundaca

The story behind the ruins of this house and fort are more intriguing than what remains of them. A slave-trading pirate, Fermin Antonio Mundaca de Marechaja, fell in love with a visiting Spanish beauty. To win her, the rogue built a two-storey mansion complete with gardens and graceful archways as well as a small fortress to defend it. While Mundaca built the house, the object of his affection's ardour cooled and she married another islander. Broken-hearted, Mundaca died, and his house, fortress and garden fell into disarray.

The Mundaca fort is off the main road near Playa Lancheros.

Marine Biology Research Station

North of Playa Lancheros is a marine biology research station where during working hours on weekdays visitors are welcome to see preserved turtles and shellfish. You may also speak with researchers regarding the aquatic ecology of this part of the Caribbean.

Deep-Sea Fishing

To charter a boat for deep-sea fishing, ask around the dock for an official of the Boatmen's Cooperative. Equipment and food may be provided for an all-day outing. Among the game fish you might land are sailfish, marlin, red snapper and barracuda.

Scuba Diving

Scuba diving to see sunken galleons and beautiful reefs in the crystalline waters of the Caribbean is possible and equipment and boats can be rented. Inquire at the dive shops in town and remember to bargain – scuba is expensive here with costs from US$35 up for the equipment alone.

Some dive shops take their patrons to the Sleeping Shark Caves, where the otherwise dangerous creatures are alleged to be lethargically non-lethal due to the low carbon dioxide content of the caves' waters. Veteran divers say it's foolish to test the theory: you could become shark bait. Far better, explore the fine reefs off

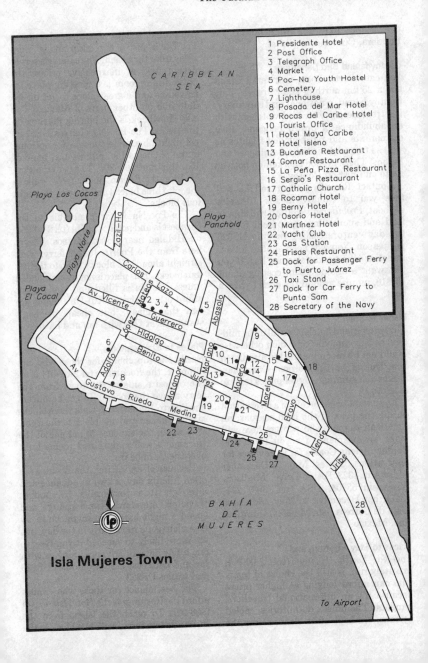

CARIBBEAN SEA

Playa Los Cocos

Playa Panchold

Playa Norte

Playa El Cocal

1 Presidente Hotel
2 Post Office
3 Telegraph Office
4 Market
5 Poc–Na Youth Hostel
6 Cemetery
7 Lighthouse
8 Posada del Mar Hotel
9 Rocas del Caribe Hotel
10 Tourist Office
11 Hotel Maya Caribe
12 Hotel Isleno
13 Bucañero Restaurant
14 Gomar Restaurant
15 La Peña Pizza Restaurant
16 Sergio's Restaurant
17 Catholic Church
18 Rocamar Hotel
19 Berny Hotel
20 Osorio Hotel
21 Martínez Hotel
22 Yacht Club
23 Gas Station
24 Brisas Restaurant
25 Dock for Passenger Ferry to Puerto Juárez
26 Taxi Stand
27 Dock for Car Ferry to Punta Sam
28 Secretary of the Navy

Lazil–Ha
Carlos Lazo
Av Vicente
López
Guerrero
Hidalgo
Benito
Adolfo
Gustavo
Rueda
Medina
Matamores
Juárez
Abasolo
Marigno
Madero
Morelos
Bravo
Allende
Uribe

BAHÍA DE MUJERES

Isla Mujeres Town

To Airport

the island like Los Manchones, La Bandera, Cuevones or Chital.

Contoy Island Bird Sanctuary

You can charter boats to a small island about 25 km north of Isla Mujeres. Tiny Contoy Island, a national bird sanctuary, is a treasure-trove for bird-watchers with an abundance of brown pelicans, olive cormorants and red-pouched frigates as well as frequent visits by flamingoes and herons. There is good snorkelling both en route and just off Contoy.

Contact Ricardo Gaitan and he will take you to Contoy in his 10-metre sailboat, *Providencia*. Gaitan will supply food and snorkelling equipment for the two-day venture costing roughly US$25 per person. You will need suntan lotion, insect repellent and a sleeping bag. If you just want a one-day trip, costing about US$16, inquire around the dock to hire a boat.

Places to Stay

The better island hotels often fill up by mid-day, so accommodation which otherwise would not be recommended is also listed here. During the high seasons – Christmas, Easter and summer – hotel prices tend to escalate.

If you want to be certain of a reservation during the peak of the high seasons, an American woman who winters here will make arrangements for you for a fee. Contact Arlene Coates far in advance for reservations. Coates' May to December address is 1322 Foster Drive, Madison, Wisconsin 53704, USA (tel (608) 244-4341); her December to May address is Lista de Correos, Isla Mujeres, Quintana Roo, Mexico.

Places to Stay – bottom end

Poc-Na Youth Hostel (tel 2-00-90), privately run, is still the choice of many who can afford lodging at higher prices because it's an international travellers' hangout. The unisex dormitories, cooled by fans, are kept quite clean, as are the communal toilets. Another advantage, Poc-Na is just a hop, skip and a jump away from the beach. The cafeteria serves decent food at inexpensive prices; the patio dining room is a meeting place for travellers and a great place to get up-to-date info on other parts of Mexico. The only drawback is the blaring jukebox on the patio. The Poc-Na charges US$1.80 per night plus a one-time fee for optional rental of sheets 15c, pillows 15c, blanket 15c, thin mattress 20c. To get to the Poc-Na from the Puerto Juárez ferry, walk to the left three blocks and then to the right four blocks.

The Poc-Na is far preferable to the cheapest island hotel, *Xul-Ha* (tel 2-00-75), on Hidalgo near López Mateos. To get here from the Puerto Juárez ferry, walk straight ahead two blocks, then to the left four blocks. This place is not recommended unless Poc-Na is filled and you cannot afford other lodging. Xul-Ha's rooms are less than clean, but cheap by Isla's standards at U$5 with fan and bath.

Places to Stay – middle

Easily the top choice for those who can afford it, the *Rocamar* (tel 2-01-01) is on the opposite side of the town from the ferry above the zócalo. To get here from the Puerto Juárez ferry, walk three blocks straight ahead and one block to the right. It is worth the expense to get one of the Rocamar's well-maintained rooms built over the Caribbean.

Because of its setting, the Rocamar is often filled a day or two in advance and although it is expensive by budget travellers' standards, some splurge and spend a night here. You might be lucky enough to get a room early in the day, but are more likely to succeed if you reserve one a few days in advance. Singles with fan and bath cost US$17, doubles US$20 and triples US$23.

The best choice for those who cannot afford the Rocamar is the *Hotel Isleno* (tel 0-08-03). To reach the Isleno from the Puerto Juárez ferry, walk one block to the left and three blocks to the right (it will be on the corner on your right). Immaculately maintained, this freshly painted two-storey hotel is managed by the delightful and most helpful Cecilia, who is fluent in English. Here large rooms with a big ceiling fan and two beds cost US$10. Although the rooms share sinks, showers and toilets with three others, it's less of a drawback than you might think as maids constantly keep things clean. More expensive rooms cost US$12 with private bath and there is a room which can sleep three with private bath for US$15. The one drawback of the Isleno is that some of the rooms are on the level of a noisy street intersection. Ask Cecilia for a quiet room but note that the Isleno fills up early.

If you want a room with private bath for US$10, single or double, the following three hotels on the same street are good choices.

The *María José* (2-01-30) has nice rooms with fan and bath, a few with balconies and sea views. It's conveniently located across from the dock, but that street can be noisy from time to time. To get here from the Puerto Juárez ferry, walk one block to the left and you will see it across the street.

The *Hotel Martínez* (2-01-54) just up the street from the María José is well-maintained. A drawback is that the puritanical proprietor does not allow visitors in the rooms and has a strict 11 pm curfew.

On the same street a block above the María José and the Martínez is the *Hotel Osorio* (tel 2-00-18). This older hotel has huge, clean rooms with fan and bath and is popular, often filling up in the morning.

For those willing to pay a bit more for a newer hotel, up the street from the Osorio is *Hotel Maya Caribe* (tel 2-01-90). From the Puerto Juárez ferry, go left one block and right for 2½ blocks. Modern single rooms with fan and bath cost US$14.50, doubles US$16.50, triples US$18.50.

Rooms at the *Berny* (tel 2-00-25) are built over a patio with a small swimming pool. Rooms with air-conditioning and bath for one or two people cost US$20. Triples cost US$22. To reach the Berny, walk two blocks to the left from the Puerto Juárez ferry and half a block right.

The *Rocas del Caribe* (tel 2-00-11) is particularly worth considering if you get a room overlooking the sea (not all the rooms have sea views). Rooms cost US$16 to US$20 and they're comfortable and clean although not always in good repair. Walk one block left from the Puerto Juárez ferry and four blocks to the right.

The *Autel Carmelina* (tel 2-00-06) is reached by walking left one block from the Puerto Juárez ferry and three blocks to the right. You will see it on the left. The outside of the Carmelina is ugly and motel-like, and there can be considerable street noise, but the rooms are adequate, equipped with fan and bath. Singles cost US$7.50, doubles US$8.50.

The cheaper *Las Palmas* (no phone) offers spartan, less-than-clean rooms with fan and bath for US$8 single and US$10.50 double. It is recommended only if there are no alternatives. To reach Las Palmas from the Puerto Juárez ferry, walk left three blocks, right three blocks and left for another block. It is opposite the post office.

Cheaper still, yet preferable to Las Palmas, is *Posada San Jorge* (tel 2-00-52). Its bare basic rooms are old, and acceptably clean and inexpensive for Isla Mujeres. Singles with fan and bath cost US$6.50, doubles US$8.50. To get to Posada San Jorge, walk one block straight from the Puerto Juárez ferry and then to the left four blocks.

Places to Stay – top end

If you are willing to spend US$40 to US$50 per night, the *Posada del Mar* (tel 2-01-98), across from the dock four blocks left of the Puerto Juárez ferry, has a pleasant garden and quasi-colonial surroundings preferable to the antiseptically modern architecture of El Presidente. The Posada del Mar is not on the beach but you don't have to walk far to reach the sands.

El Presidente (tel 2-01-22) has a pool and a superb location right on the beach. On one side there's a shallow lagoon ideal for kids, while the sea beats the rocky shore on the other side. At the end of the headland there's a pier and some good snorkelling. Singles/doubles cost US$50/60.

Places to Eat

Most restaurants on the island are overpriced by Mexican standards, even for seafood which you would think cheap here. While shrimp is often US$2 to US$3, lobster may have US prices or higher. Nonetheless, many of the restaurants are pleasant for leisurely dining, and some offer musical entertainment.

Poc-Na Youth Hostel on Matamoros and Carlos Lazo has a cafeteria that is cheap and serves decent standard fare. Breakfasts are good; try the French toast. For dinner the *chile relleno* is recommended. Or just come here for coffee and meet budget travellers from all over the globe.

Two pleasant places above the zócalo next to the Rocamar on Guerrero are *Sergio's* and *La Peña*. *Sergio's* offers good breakfasts and tasty Mexican dinners. In the evening, strolling singing guitarists make the rounds and there's a happy hour (two drinks for the price of one) from 6 to 7 pm. A piña colada costs US$1.50, a beer US$0.75. The upstairs balcony area looking out over the square is an enjoyable place to sit.

La Peña is a good place for a drink as it has a terrace at the back which overlooks the sea. In the evening rock or salsa bands entertain here, and as at Sergio's there's a two-for-one happy hour. La Peña serves seafood and pizza; there are mixed reports about the pizzas but the *helados* desserts are great.

Somewhat more expensive, *Gomar's* on Hidalgo at the corner with Madero serves excellent seafood and chicken dishes. A huge VCR shows movies; when I ate there

the feature was *Zulu*. There are tables outside on the verandah and good snacks (sandwiches for US$1.50), although the service can be slow and erratic, particularly late in the evening.

Peregrino's does a pretty good job of preparing Mexican fare and seafood at relatively inexpensive prices. It's adjacent to the Carmelina on Guerrero. For US$2 to US$3, crowded *Rolandi's* (near Gomar's) serves the best pizza on the island, though their pasta leaves much to be desired.

For cheap seafood and so-so *típico* fare, try *Carnitas Estilo Michoacán* on Hidalgo near Abasolo. While the restaurant's sign is difficult to read, you can recognise the eatery by the coconuts and tropical vegetation.

Some of the little seaside cafés near the ferry serve shrimp at reasonable prices. Check to see which are offering the best deals – the quality is generally comparable.

At the upper end, *Ciro's* on Matamoros and Guerrero, the *Bucañero* on Hidalgo, and the restaurants at the *Posada del Mar* and *El Presidente* are overpriced for what you get. Big spenders from Cancún and well-heeled visitors to Isla splurging for a night dine at *María's Kan-Kin Restaurant Française* near Garrafon. The prices for continental *haute cuisine* are high, but the food is said to be good.

For breakfasts, your best bet is to be early for pastries and coffee at the *panadería* one block from the waterfront on Madero. If you are waiting for a ferry and want to be in air-conditioning near the waterfront, *Martitas* across from the dock is good.

Entertainment

There are two discos on the island: *Calipso* at the end of the dock at the beach, and *Buno's* off the beach at Carlos Lazo. There is often a rock or salsa band at *La Peña* and strolling guitarists at *Sergio's*. *El Presidente Hotel* and *Posada del Mar* sometimes offer live music. Otherwise, tourists organise their own parties on this highly social isle.

Things to Buy

Crafts from many parts of Mexico may be purchased from the plethora of gift shops on the island. Unfortunately, prices are far higher and quality sometimes lower than you would find at their point of manufacture. If you are going to other regions of Mexico – Mérida for hammocks and huipiles, Oaxaca for leather and woven goods, San Cristóbal de las Casas for Indian arts, don't buy on Isla. Casa del Arte Mexica on Avenida Hidalgo does have some interesting limestone bas-relief carvings and other items.

For everyday needs there are two food markets, Super Bertino on the zócalo and Mirtita at Juárez 14. Film is sold expensively at a number of shops in town. Pharmaceutical needs may be met at the drugstore at Juárez 2. Occasionally, English-language magazines and newspapers are sold at the corner of Bravo and Juárez, but you are more likely to find *Time* and *Newsweek* at Cancún.

Getting There & Away

There are two points of embarkation from the mainland by ferry to Isla Mujeres. Punta Sam is the base for car ferries (2c), taking 30 to 40 minutes. These offer greater comfort on their spacious decks than the Puerto Juárez passenger ferries (30c), which take 45 to 50 minutes and are small and often crowded. On the passenger ferries the crossing can be surprisingly rough and if you sit up front you're likely to get wet.

The Punta Sam car ferry leaves Punta Sam at 8.30 and 11 am, and at 1.30, 5.45, 8.30 and 11 pm. Departures from Isla Mujeres are at 7.15 and 10 am, and at 12.15, 4.30, 7.30 and 10 pm. The Puerto Juárez passenger ferry leaves Puerto Juárez at 8.30, 9.30, 10.30 and 11.30 am, and at 1.30, 3.30, 5.30 and 7.30 pm. From Isla Mujeres departures are at 6.30, 9.30 and 11.30 am, and at 1.30, 3.30, 5.30 and 7.30 pm. The schedules are subject to change and you should check them upon arrival.

From points out of town other than Cancún, there are some buses direct to Puerto Juárez from Mérida and Valladolid. Most buses from other cities will take you to Cancún. From Cancún, either bargain for a taxi or take the Ruta 8 Puerto Juárez bus, which you can flag down at stops along the Avenida Tulum. The Ruta 8 stops at both Puerto Juárez and Punta Sam. Conversely, there is usually a Ruta 8 bus which will meet the ferry to take you to Cancún. It takes about 20 minutes and costs pennies.

Airport From the airport, the government runs five-seater vans at set prices to Puerto Juárez, US$5 total, and Punta Sam, US$7 total. Cheaper if you are alone, for those with time, is the colectivo bus dropping off tourists at the Cancún luxury hotels. Ask to be dropped off near the Cancún bus station at some point on Avenida Tulum. From Avenida Tulum, catch a Ruta 8 bus to Puerto Juárez or Punta Sam. This can take quite a while, giving you a tour of the high-rise luxury of Cancún in the process. It will make you appreciate Isla Mujeres.

The cheapest way to get back to the airport is to take a Ruta 8 bus to Cancún and bargain for a taxi from there. This is suggested because avaricious taxi drivers fix outrageous prices from Puerto Juárez and Punta Sam with little bargaining possible. If you find other passengers to share the taxi with from the mainland docks direct to the airport, it will save you the hassle of stopping first in Cancún.

Whichever way you go to the airport, allow time, as taxi and bus tyres have been known to blow out and the airport is anything but efficient. Furthermore, don't count on the airport's bank to have dollars when you want to convert your pesos upon departure. If the bank has no dollars or is closed, get cash at a none-too-great rate at one of the airport's car-rental desks.

Getting Around

The village of Isla Mujeres is tiny and all sites in the town are within walking distance. If you arrive with heavy luggage, little boys will wheel it on push-bikes to your hotel.

The best way to reach other parts of this flat island is by bicycle. At about US$1 a day, bikes (some in poor condition) may be rented from the Hotel María José on Madero, Bicicletas Ernesto on Juárez and the Carmelina on Guerrero.

Motorbike rentals are also a popular way to tour the island. Of the rental shops visited, the best deals were from Moto Rent Ciro's on Guerrero between Mateos and Matamoros, near the Poc-Na Youth Hostel. They quoted prices of US$1.75 per hour with a US$17 deposit. Count on around US$10 a day. Other rental places for mopeds are Moto Servocop Joaquín at Avenida Juárez 7-B and Gómez Castillo at Bravo and Hidalgo.

By local bus from the market or dock, you can get within 1.5 km of Garrafon; the terminus is Playa Lancheros. The personnel at Poc-Na Youth Hostel can give you an idea of the bus's erratic schedule. (Locals in league with taxi drivers may tell you the bus doesn't exist.)

If you walk to Garrafon, bring some water – it's a hot two to three-hour's 5.5-km walk. Those taking a taxi will be better off price-wise if they share the ride with others – it costs about US$1.20 for a taxi to Garrafon, less than US$1 to Playa Lancheros.

CANCÚN

Population: 115,000

The beaches here have fine white sand and the waters are a warm, tranquil turquoise; and while prices are higher than in most of the rest of Mexico, you don't have to be affluent to stay in this resort. But before you succumb to the exhortations of the Mexican tourist office and plan your vacation in Cancún, consider whether it really is for you. You might fly here just for Isla Mujeres and the less-visited beaches south of Cancún, or use it as an arrival point for the Yucatán Peninsula.

Cancún is a long 'island' connected to the shore by a land-bridge, bounded by beaches and within day-tripping range of major Mayan ruins. If you want luxurious, high-priced hotels, sanitary – some would say sterile – environs, and scads of gringos blowing their two-week-a-year vacation wads, Cancún is the place. If not, and you still want the tropical amenities and social life but amidst budget travellers,

1	Ferry Service Office
2	Plaza de Toros Bull Ring
3	Post Office
4	Cultural Centre
5	Hotel Bahía de Mujeres
6	Club Verano Beat
7	Hotel Playa Blanca
8	Hotel Bojorquez
9	Hotel Carrousel
10	Hotel Calinda Cancún
11	Tik Tak Restaurant
12	Hotel Casa Maya
13	Club Nautico 3
14	Club Nautico 2
15	Villas Takul
16	Hotel Maya Caribe
17	Hotel Dos Playas
18	Tennis Club
19	Hotel El Presidente
20	Hotel Cancún Viva
21	Hotel Fiesta Americana
22	Hotel Boniti Beach
23	Convention Centre
24	Museum
25	Hotel Camino Real
26	Hotel Kristal Cancún
27	Mexican Airlines Office
28	Hotel Playasol
29	Hotel Aristos
30	Fishing Club
31	Hotel Meson
32	Pok Ta Pok Golf Course
33	Hotel Hyatt Cancún Caribe
34	Villas Verano Beat
35	Cancún Sheraton
36	San Miguelito Archaeological Site
37	El Rey Archaeological Site
38	Club Méditerranée

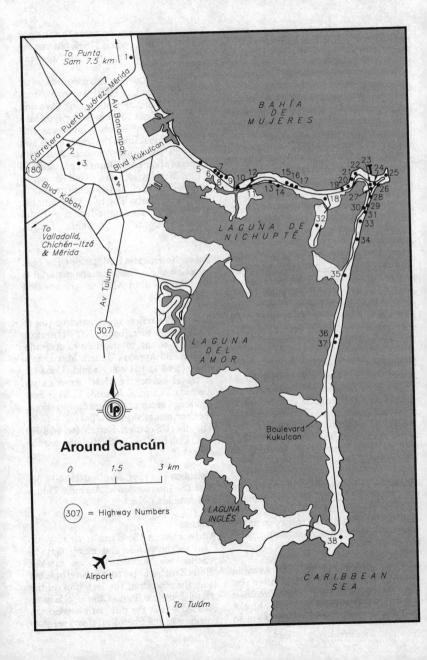

BAHÍA
DE
MUJERES

LAGUNA DE
NICHUPTÉ

LAGUNA DEL
AMOR

Boulevard
Kukulcan

Around Cancún

0   1.5   3 km

(307) = Highway Numbers

LAGUNA
INGLÉS

CARIBBEAN
SEA

Airport

To Tulúm

To Punta
Sam 7.5 km

Carretera Puerto Juárez–Mérida

Av Bonampak

Blvd Kukulcan

180

Blvd Kabah

To
Valladolid,
Chichén–Itzá
& Mérida

Av Tulum

307

move to Isla Mujeres. If you prefer isolated beach life, bus an hour away to Playa del Carmen or the more isolated beaches to its south.

Orientation

With the exception of the Youth Hostel, hotels and lodging in the Zona Hoteles are priced far beyond the means of the budget traveller– stick to Cancún City.

For the inexpensive hotels and restaurants in Cancún City, stay off Avenida Tulum for the most part and patronise the establishments on Avenida Yaxchilán. There are a few cheap eateries on Avenida Sun Yax Chén as well. Avenida Yaxchilán runs parallel to Avenida Tulum and is one long block north of it.

While Cancún City is close to the coast on the mainland, the Zona Hoteles is more or less one road running out from the city on the narrow sandspit and then turning south to encircle the lagoon. Construction has worked its way right along the northern arm and is now heading south on the seaward side.

Information

Tourist Office There are tourist kiosks dispensing maps and other information at various points on Avenida Tulum. Luxury hotels also have maps. The free monthly magazine *Cancún Tips* actually has better maps than the tourist kiosks and will let you know what is going on entertainment-wise.

Money Banks on Avenida Tulum are open from 9 am to 1.30 pm. Otherwise, many casas de cambio, travel agencies, hotels and the Youth Hostel (poor exchange rate) will change money, but shop around to get the best rate.

Post The main post office is on Avenida Sun Yax Chén. Make a right after you reach the intersection on Avenida Yaxchilán and Sun Yax Chén and walk a few blocks to the post office. Its hours are 9 am to

7 pm daily. If someone wants to write you here, the postal code is 77500, but you are better off receiving mail at American Express.

Cancún's American Express office (tel 4-19-99) is next to Hotel America. From the bus station, walk along Avenida Tulum for about 10 minutes until you hit a traffic circle where Tulum intersects with Avenida Cobá. Cross the traffic circle and you will see Hotel America. American Express's hours are 10 am to 1 pm, and 3 to 5 pm, Monday to Friday. Call American Express to check as the hours appear to change regularly. The telephone number is 4-19-99, the mailing address is c/o Hotel America, Suite A, Avenida Tulum, Cancún.

Books, Newspapers & Magazines The best selection of English-language material is at Librería Don Quijote at Avenida Tulum 27.

Airlines The offices of Aeroméxico (tel 4-27-28) and Aerocaribe (tel 4-12-31) are in a complex at the intersection of Avenida Tulum and Avenida Uxmal. Mexicana's office (tel 4-12-65) is at Avenida Cobá 13. A travel agency in Hotel America on Avenida Tulum at Avenida Cobá is now handling Continental's Cancún operations. For Continental's airport office call 4-25-40. The other US carriers, Eastern (tel 4-28-70) and United (tel 4-28-58), are at the airport.

Consulate The US Consulate (tel 4-14-38) is at the intersection of Avenida Tulum and Avenida Cobá.

Beaches

All beaches in the Cancún vicinity are open to the public and many may be reached via municipal buses marked 'Hotel Zone'. The best of the hotel beaches is at the Sheraton, the last stop on the 'Hotel Zone' bus. Playa Chacmool is more isolated – take the dirt path beyond the entrance of the Sheraton. If you want to bathe in the buff, walk out to Club Méd's beach. Those who want the company of young Mexican and gringo sun-worshippers should try the Youth Hostel's beach.

Beach Activities

Snorkelling Most snorkellers who wish to explore reefs pay a visit to nearby Isla Mujeres – see that section for information. If you just want to see the sparser aquatic life off Cancún's beaches, you can rent snorkelling equipment for about US$4 from most luxury hotels. The bigger hotels and travel agencies also can book you on boats which take snorkellers to La Bandera, Los Manchones, Cuevones and Chital reefs.

Scuba This expensive sport is all the pricier in equipment rental and boat transport from Cancún. Veteran divers might prefer nearby Cozumel's justly famous Palancar Reef. Nonetheless, agencies and hotels rent gear and provide passage to some fine reefs in the vicinity. Los Manchones and Cuevones reefs, situated between Cancún and Isla Mujeres, afford diving depths of 10 to 15 metres.

Fishing The luxury hotels in the Zona Hoteles will charter virtually every kind of deep-sea fishing excursion your heart desires, so long as your pocketbook is bottomless. Far cheaper is to simply fish from the Nichupte bridge.

Other Water Sports The luxury hotels will either lend you the equipment or put you in touch with the sources for sailing, wind-surfing, water-skiing and virtually any other known water sport. Just so long as you know it's for a price. For wind-surfing lessons phone the Cancún wind-surfing school at 4-20-23.

For cheaper rentals for aquatic equipment, try the Verano Beach Hotel next to the Youth Hostel. Say you are a student.

Mayan Ruins

There are Mayan ruins in Cancún, and while not that impressive they are quite nice. El Rey Ruins between the Sheraton and Club Méd date from somewhere between 1200 and 1500 AD. You'll see a portion of a small temple and a number of ceremonial platforms. The dirt path signposted beyond the Sheraton Hotel will take you down to the ruins on the lagoon side of the road. There are lots of mosquitoes, so bring repellent and look for the huge lizards which inhabit the site. There is a small admission charge for these meagre ruins – after all, this is Cancún. Hours are 8 am to 5 pm.

Museum

The Museo de Antropología e Historia, next to the Convention Center in the Zona Hoteles, has a limited collection of Mayan artefacts. Although most of the items are from the Post Classic period (1200-1500 AD), including jewellery, masks and skull deformers, there is a Classic period hieroglyphic staircase inscribed with dates from the 6th century as well as the stucco head which gave the local ruins site its name, El Rey ('the king'). The museum is open Tuesday to Sunday, 10 am to 2 pm and 5 to 8 pm. Admission is US$0.30.

Golf

The Pok-Ta-Pok Golf Course has a unique hazard on its 12th hole, a menacing Mayan ruin. It is suggested you drive around it, or the gods might seek revenge for a gringo intrusion.

Aviary

Since Cancún is home to over 200 species of birds, you might enjoy seeing some of them close at hand at the Mauna Loa Complex close to the Convention Center. There are some beautiful long-tailed *mot-mot* (known to some as the 'clock bird' due to its pendulum-like tail), pretty parrots, frigate birds, osprey and herons.

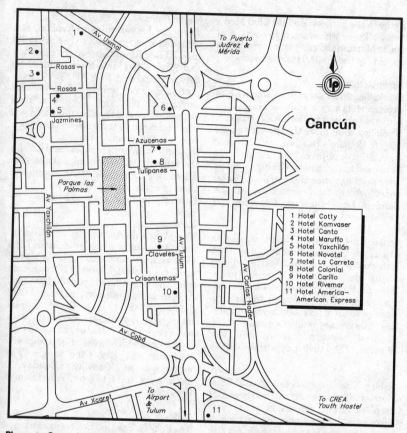

Cancún

1 Hotel Cotty
2 Hotel Komvaser
3 Hotel Canto
4 Hotel Maruffo
5 Hotel Yaxchilán
6 Hotel Novotel
7 Hotel La Carreta
8 Hotel Colonial
9 Hotel Carillo
10 Hotel Rivemar
11 Hotel America–
    American Express

Places to Stay – bottom end

CREA Youth Hostel (tel 3-13-37) makes a stay in Cancún possible for even the most penny-conscious traveller. Its dorms are right on a beautiful beach and it even has a swimming pool. A dorm bunk will cost you slightly more than US$2.50. Use the hostel's lock-up for your valuables. You can also beat the high cost of Cancún's restaurants by eating at the Youth Hostel's cafeteria. Breakfasts served from 8 to 9.30 am cost less than US$1. Lunches served from 2 to 3.30 pm and dinners served from 7.30 to 9 pm cost US$1.25.

To reach the Youth Hostel from Cancún City (it's about five km from the bus terminal), take local bus Ruta 1, called 'Zona Hoteles', and ask the driver where to get off. If he doesn't know the term 'CREA', keep your eyes peeled for a sign on the beach side of the road that says 'Albergue de la Juventud'. The YH's full address is Paseo Kukulkán – Km 3.2, Apdo, Cancún, Quintana Roo.

If you are really short on cash and don't want to stay in a dorm bunk, the alternative is less than appealing. *Hotel La Carreta* (no phone) next to El Pirata Restaurant on Calle Azucenas, a small side street that runs off Avenida Tulum near its intersection with Avenida Uxmal, has very spartan rooms with bath (no hot water) for US$5 single or double. The rooms are not particularly clean.

Places to Stay - middle

Fortunately, if you avoid the Zona Hoteles luxury sector and Avenida Tulum in town, there are a number of good, moderately priced hotels on or near Avenida Yaxchilán.

The *Hotel Komvaser* (tel 4-16-50) at Yaxchilán 15 offers a swimming pool and well-kept air-conditioned rooms with hot plates for cooking. Singles with bath cost US$18, doubles US$20, triples US$21.

One block up Yaxchilán from the Komvaser near Avenida Sun Yax Chén is an excellent deal, the *Hotel Canto* (tel 4-13-24). Singles with air-conditioning and bath cost US$12, doubles US$14.

The *Hotel Marrufo* (tel 4-13-34) on a little side street off Avenida Yaxchilán, Calle Rosas, offers basic rooms with refrigerator, fan and bath at US$6 for singles and US$10.75 for doubles.

Also cheap and quite acceptable is the *Hotel Yaxchilán* (tel 4-13-24), at Avenida Yaxchilán 41-43. Singles with TV, fan and bath cost US$8.50, doubles US$9.30, triples US$11.50.

On Uxmal near Yaxchilán, you will find the motel-like *Cotty* (tel 4-13-19). Basic rooms with air-conditioning, TV and bath cost US$9, doubles US$10.

The best deal in the moderate price range on Avenida Tulum is the *Novotel* (4-29-99), near the intersection with Avenida Uxmal. Architecturally a combination of the colonial and contemporary, the Novotel offers rooms with fan and bath at US$18 single and US$21 double. Its air-conditioned rooms cost US$29 single, US$30 double.

A decently priced hotel on Avenida Tulum is the *Colonial* (tel 4-15-35), just off the main street at Tulipanes 22. Its location and well-kept rooms costing US$18 single or double would be

recommended but we've had one report of theft from a room here.

If you want to stay on Avenida Tulum, the *Hotel Rivemar* (tel 4-17-08) near Calle Crisantemas charges US$17.50 single or double for air-conditioned rooms with bath. *Hotel Carrillo's* (tel 4-12-27) just off Tulum on a side street called Claveles also offers air-conditioned rooms with bath for US$20 single, US$24 double.

Places to Stay - top end

The top-end hotels at Cancún are all along the beach front around the lagoon. Many of them are part of international chains (like Best Western, Hyatt or Sheraton) or the major Mexican hotel chains. All of them are expensive – there's not much under US$100 a night and many are much more than that. You can slap 15% IVA tax on top of their quoted prices as well. It's easy to tell they're going to be expensive since so many quote their prices only in US dollars. Some of them are terrible value, especially for a country where labour costs are low – enormous profits are being made here!

The big hotels obviously have trouble with bill disputes, as some of them get you to sign not only the registration and credit card forms, etc, but also a form stating that you agree the nightly tariff is really US$x! The Krystal Cancún makes the veiled threat that if you're not careful you might sit around arguing over your bill rather than catch your flight.

Food and other costs are also often extremely high; anybody who has spent some time travelling around Mexico will find a US$10 breakfast bill rather absurd. The hotels' one major advantage is that almost all of them are on the beach. All have pools, restaurants, bars and other facilities. Satellite TV reception picking up US stations is another Zona Hoteles norm.

Avenida Kukulcán runs right around the lagoon. Along the northern stretch of beach the water is calmer. The beach running north-south from Punta Cancún to Punta Nizuc is better but the sea here can sometimes be rough. Starting from Cancún City and working round the lagoon, hotels include:

Verano Beat Cancún (tel 3-07-22) is closest to town of the hotels in the Zona Hoteles. This smaller hotel has less than 100 rooms.

Playa Blanca (tel 3-03-44) is a smaller hotel with a pleasant garden but the beach here is not the best and the hotel's booking system is unreliable. Rooms are around US$90.

Club Caribe Cancún (tel 3-08-11) is a smaller hotel with a generally pleasant design marred by amazingly cheap and shoddy construction. Around US$100 a night is a lot for dark corridors, paint-splattered tiles and a general air of penny-pinching.

Carrousel (tel 3-05-13) is another smaller hotel with 111 rooms with balconies overlooking the sea.

Calinda Cancún Quality Inn (tel 3-16-00) has its own restaurant and is a real package-tour place complete with entertainment directors and paranoia about their guests not paying bills. There are 280 rooms, all facing the ocean.

Casa Maya (tel 3-05-55), five km from the city, has three pools, tennis courts and restaurants plus over 300 rooms.

Villas Tacul (tel 3-08-00) close to the Convention Center has pleasant gardens and 200-plus rooms.

Club Lagoon Caribe (tel 3-11-11) has an unusual location on the lagoon side of the road and has 91 'bungalow-style' rooms.

Dos Playas Suites (tel 3-05-00) has 67 suites.

El Presidente (tel 3-02-00) is part of the Mexican hotel chain. There are 337 rooms in this well-placed hotel but overall it's rather featureless and the pool/garden area can be crowded.

Viva Cancún (tel 3-08-00) is close to the Convention Center and has 200-plus rooms with the usual facilities.

Fiesta Americana (tel 3-14-00) on Paso Cancún is constructed to look like a Mediterranean village. It is close to the Convention Center with tennis courts, multiple restaurants, and rooms with US TV and bar.

Camino Real (tel 3-01-00) is an architectural pyramid with two beaches and a man-made mini-lagoon. It has three restaurants, a disco, tennis, a swimming pool and scuba instruction.

Exelaris Hyatt (tel 3-15-20) is a luxurious 14-storey high-rise offering boat rental, movies, night tennis, and rooms with US TV, bar and refrigerator.

Krystal Cancún (tel 3-11-33) offers tennis courts, boat rentals, racquetball courts, a health club and an immense swimming pool backed by what looks like Grecian columns. The dull rooms could belong to a generic five-star hotel anywhere in the world. At around US$160 they're very expensive, particularly if you get a room with cracked washbasin and toilet. The restaurant is good though, and the endless swimming pool is superb.

Aristos (tel 3-00-11) is near the Convention Center. Recently renovated, this was one of the first hotels at Cancún.

Mison Miramar (tel 3-17-55) has about 200 rooms plus the usual restaurants, bars and swimming pools.

Hyatt Cancún Caribe (tel 3-00-44) has 200-plus rooms facing the ocean along a fine stretch of beach.

Flamingo Cancún is a smaller hotel with less than 100 rooms, with views over both the lagoon and the ocean.

Sheraton Cancún (tel 3-19-88), situated on the nicest of the hotel beaches, offers indoor and outdoor pools, night tennis courts, miniature golf and a whirlpool. There are two restaurants, a bar and a disco on the premises of this big and decidedly deluxe hotel.

Brisas Cancún (tel 4-16-43) has 200-plus rooms looking towards the sea or the lagoon.

Club Méditerranée (tel 250-41-99), way down at the southern end of the beach, is secluded and well away from everywhere. There are 300 rooms and a minimum booking period of one week.

Places to Eat

CREA Youth Hostel has an inexpensive cafeteria in its grounds. You don't have to stay at the Hostel to eat there.

Otherwise, you can eat decently in Cancún City at reasonable prices so long as you stay off Avenida Tulum. The key streets for dining on the cheap are Avenida Yaxchilán and streets that run off it – particularly Avenida Sun Yax Chén.

For excellent Yucatecan specialities at low cost, eat at *Rincón Yucateco* on Avenida Uxmal halfway between Avenida

Tulum and Avenida Yaxchilán. A tasty and filling comida corrida is served for US$1.25.

Another place for good Yucatecan food is *Restaurant Peregrina* on Yaxchilán 28 in front of Hotel Canto. If you are hankering for decent cheap Mexican grilled-meat dishes, *La Parrilla* at Avenida Yaxchilán 51 will satisfy you.

For so-so but filling Chinese, Indian or Thai dishes, try the US$2.50 to US$3.50 main courses at *O'Lian Restaurant* near Hotel Yaxchilán on Avenida Yaxchilán.

If you haven't tried *Los Almendros'* Yucatecan specialities in Mérida, or you want to enjoy them again, make the long trek to its Cancún branch on Avenida Bonampak at Sayil.

There are cheap *taquerías* on Avenida Cobá and Avenida Sun Yax Chén. If you are dreaming of the joys of the *panadería*, there are two good bakeries: *Los Globos* on Tulipanes, a side street just off Avenida Tulum; and *Panificadora Covadonga* on Avenida Tulum near Avenida Uxmal.

Around the Zona Hoteles most people will eat in their hotels, although there are numerous restaurants, most of them far from cheap! Near the museum, *Pizza Otto* is a pleasant little pizza place where you can count on US$4 to US$7 for a pizza. Back towards Cancún City, *Pietro Pizza* near the Plaza Nautilus is a little cheaper and also good.

Entertainment

There are discos at most of the luxury hotels in the Zona Hoteles. *Carlos 'n Charlie's* has a raucous atmosphere – a gringo university bar scene. On the more classical side, a mediocre *Ballet Folklorico* (the companies in Mexico City are far superior) performs at the Convention Center at 7 pm Monday to Saturday for a US$21 tariff which includes dinner. (The dancers come on at 8.30 pm.)

The Convention Center also presents a 'Polynesian' (?!) cultural dance show at the *Mauna Loa* (where else?). The Convention Center's *La Cantina* has live

'romantic' Spanish guitarists. You can enjoy music without outlandish cover charges at the *Hotel El Presidente*, where a band plays nightly except Monday. The *Lone Star* on Avenida Yaxchilán has country and western music. *Casa Salsa* on Plaza Caracol Mall features reggae and salsa (after 11 pm).

If you want to see a bullfight, they are held each Wednesday from December until June in the ring adjacent to the Pemex station on Paseo Kukulkán in Cancún City.

Things to Buy

There are gift shops and touts everywhere in Cancún, with crafts from all over Mexico at sometimes exorbitant prices. Save your shopping for other Mexican destinations. If you hanker for a hammock, buy it in Mérida. Still, window-shopping in Cancún's air-conditioned and often extremely luxurious shopping centres is good fun. Have a wander around the Plaza Nautilus with its art galleries and boutiques. Don't miss the amazing 'sculptures' of Sergio Bustamante.

Getting There & Away

Air There are flights with Aeroméxico, Mexicana, Continental, Eastern and United from US cities like Miami, Houston, New Orleans, New York, Chicago, Los Angeles and San Francisco, with connecting flights from major US cities. There are also charter flights (some very cheap from Minneapolis if you live in that part of the Midwest – check around at travel agencies).

There are regularly scheduled domestic flights between Cancún and Mexico City, Cozumel, Villahermosa and Mérida with connecting service to other major Mexican cities.

Bus First and 2nd-class buses ply the streets between Cancún's depot (where Avenida Tulum intersects Avenida Uxmal) and destinations throughout the Yucatán Peninsula. Some major destinations with journey duration and 1st-class fares: Mérida, five hours, US$4.50; Valladolid, two hours, US$2; Chichén Itzá, three hours, US$3. There is 1st and 2nd-class service to Playa del Carmen costing less than US$1, taking about an hour. There is also 1st and 2nd-class bus service to Tulum (US$2, two hours) and Chetumal (US$6, seven hours).

Local buses (Ruta 8) take about 20 minutes from stops on Avenida Tulum to the Puerto Juárez and Punta Sam ferry docks if you're going to Isla Mujeres.

Getting Around

Airport Transport Getting into Cancún from the airport is relatively reasonable, with set-priced comfortable collective buses costing only US$1.50 to US$2. If you are going to the cheaper accommodation in Cancún City it might take a while, as the bus will drop people off first at the expensive beach-front hotels in the Zona Hoteles. Getting back to the airport is more expensive as you have to bargain with taxis. The tariff will likely be US$3 to US$4.

The reason that there are collective buses in from the airport but only taxis back out is a deal between the government and the taxi drivers. The government at first didn't want tourists put off immediately by outrageous taxi fares and was going to run set-price buses and vans both coming and going from the airport. The taxi drivers' union complained that they were being deprived of their livelihood, and a compromise was reached. Government transport would take tourists into Cancún and taxis would take tourists back to the airport. Therefore going to the airport might cost you double the fare you paid to get to town.

Local Transport Although you can walk everywhere in Cancún City, the Zona Hoteles generally requires a 'Ruta 1, Zona Hoteles' local bus or a taxi. The buses only cost a few cents and run along Avenida Tulum. Buses for the Puerto Juárez and

Punta Sam ferries bound for Isla Mujeres (Ruta 8) are equally inexpensive.

There are plenty of taxis around Cancún and, as long as you make sure to agree on the fare beforehand, they're quite economical. A taxi between Cancún City and the museum would be about US$1 to US$1.50, a taxi to Puerto Juárez (for the Isla Mujeres ferry) from Cancún City would be about US$1.50. There seems to be a minimum fare of around US$1 no matter how short the trip.

Car Rental The automobile rental agencies have some of the greediest, least honest personnel you will meet in Mexico. They see so many rich tourists that they will try to squeeze high prices from you for vehicles sometimes in sorry shape.

The agencies in Cancún, even the smaller places, charge ridiculous rates. However, there are many agencies at the airport; you are likely to get a better deal if you bargain here within earshot of these competitors. If you are willing to play hard-ball, say to one agency, 'Your competitor at the next desk offered me a car for this amount; I will consider a better offer from you.' Then move on to another agency at the next desk and you will eventually get a cheaper rate.

As of this writing, Volkswagen Beetles were going for at best US$30 a day with unlimited mileage and Volkswagen sedans for US$35. At peak tourist times you may end up paying US$10 to US$20 a day more. Before you sign the contract, make certain everything you have bargained for has been factored into the cost on paper with no room for add-ins after you have returned the car and are about to pay. One trick agencies often employ is to tell you the price includes everything and to add in the 15% IVA government tax just when you are about to pay. Check the condition of the car as well. Does it have a spare wheel? A jack? Can you open the trunk lid?

It's possible to arrange one-way rentals usually for an additional charge of around

20c a km for the distance back to the starting point. You could, for example, rent a car in Cancún and drive it down the coast to Tulum, inland to Cobá and Chichén Itzá and on to Uxmal and the Puuc Hills sites before leaving it in Mérida, 320 km from Cancún.

Wherever you drive in Quintana Roo, be wary of the limited number of gas (petrol) stations. Maps usually show where they can be found.

Tours It's silly to take a tour to Garrafon National Park on Isla Mujeres. Take the public ferries (see Getting There under Isla Mujeres). They are infinitely cheaper and actually more comfortable than many of the tour boats. Virtually any other tour you might wish is available from Cancún: trips to ruins like Chichén Itzá, Cobá and Tulum; snorkelling at Xel-Ha; glass-bottom boats and scuba/snorkelling expeditions. Enquire at the luxury hotels or the many agencies.

The glass-bottom boat *Manta* (tel 3-16-76) embarks from near the Club Caribe Cancún. Another glass-bottom boat, the *Fiesta Maya* (tel 3-03-89), has a bar and a band on board for dancing. It departs daily except Monday for a four-hour cruise which takes in Garrafon.

COZUMEL
Population: 32,000

Cozumel is a resort island with crystalline, teeming waters which attracts scores of tourists. Its legendary Palancar Reef was made famous by Jacques Cousteau and is a lure for divers the world over. Scuba is not an inexpensive sport and Cozumel attracts tourists better heeled than those staying at Isla Mujeres or Playa del Carmen. Nonetheless, the island is not solely geared to the jet-set crowd like Cancún and while prices are not cheap by Mexican standards, you can stay and eat at Cozumel on a moderate budget.

Because the beaches at the mainland ferry departure point of Playa del Carmen are actually prettier than those on Cozumel, most budget travellers come here to scuba and snorkel. You can either ferry over just for the day or overnight in a hotel.

History
Measuring 53 km long and 14 km wide, Cozumel is the largest of Mexico's islands. Mayan settlement here has been traced by archaeologists back to 300 AD. During the Post Classic period, Cozumel flourished both as a commercial centre and as a major ceremonial site. Mayas sailed here on pilgrimages to pay homage to shrines dedicated to Ixchel, the goddess of fertility.

Cozumel's Mayan name was Ah Cozumil-Petén, 'Place of the Swallows'. The island reached its height after the eclipse of the great Mayan cities. Nonetheless, its commercial prominence is believed to have given the island's inhabitants a high standard of living.

Although the first Spanish contact with Cozumel in 1518 by Juan de Grijalva was peaceful, it was followed by the Cortés expedition in 1519. Cortés, en route to his subsequent conquest of the mainland, laid waste Cozumel's Mayan shrines. While the Mayas offered staunch military resistance until they were conquered in 1545, the Spaniards introduced smallpox. The disease decimated the Indians' substantial population so that by 1570 only 300 Mayas and Spaniards remained on the island.

While the island remained virtually deserted into the late 17th century, its coves provided sanctuary and headquarters for several notorious pirates such as Jean Lafitte and Henry Morgan. Pirate brutality led the remaining populace to move to the mainland and it wasn't until 1848 that Cozumel began to be resettled by Indians fleeing the viciousness of the Caste War.

At the turn of the century, the island's population – which was now largely mestizos – grew thanks to the craze for chewing gum. Cozumel was a port of call

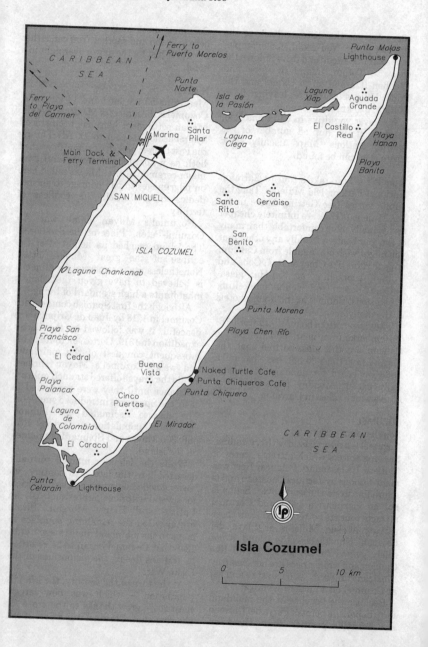

CARIBBEAN SEA

Ferry to Puerto Morelos

Punta Mojas Lighthouse

Ferry to Playa del Carmen

Punta Norte

Isla de la Pasión

Laguna Xlap

Aguada Grande

Marina

Santa Pilar

Laguna Ciega

El Castillo Real

Playa Hanan

Main Dock & Ferry Terminal

Playa Bonita

SAN MIGUEL

Santa Rita

San Gervaiso

San Benito

ISLA COZUMEL

Laguna Chankanab

Punta Morena

Playa San Francisco

Playa Chen Río

El Cedral

Buena Vista

Naked Turtle Cafe

Punta Chiqueros Cafe

Playa Palancar

Cinco Puertas

Punta Chiquero

Laguna de Colombia

El Mirador

CARIBBEAN SEA

El Caracol

Punta Celarain

Lighthouse

Isla Cozumel

0   5   10 km

on the chicle export route and locals harvested chicle on the island. Although chicle was later replaced by synthetics, Cozumel's economic base expanded with the building of a US Air Force base here during WW II. However, when the US Army Corps of Engineers built their airstrip they destroyed many of the Mayan ruins.

When the US military departed, the island fell into an economic slump and many of its people departed. Those who stayed fished for a livelihood. Then in 1961, Jacques Cousteau raved about Cozumel's reefs and a resort was born.

Fortunately, Cozumel never could become as developed as Cancún due to its scarcity of water. Cancún's proximity has kept development here more modest than the island's Mexican speculators would like. As it now stands, there may be too many tourists on the island for the tastes of many travellers.

Orientation

It's easy to make your way around the island's sole town, San Miguel, where the budget lodging can be found. Moving east to west, Avenida Juárez runs direct from the ferry dock through the centre of town. Avenida Juárez is intersected by various avenidas running north to south. These avenues are numbered in multiples of five. They are termed 'Norte' if located north of Juárez or 'Sur' if south of Juárez.

Calles run parallel to Avenida Juárez. Those termed 'Norte' are assigned an even number; those called 'Sur' are assigned an odd number. Avenida Rafael Melgar is the boulevard which runs along the waterfront.

Confused? This will sort itself out when you walk the town or look at a map – the best is *The Brown Map of Cozumel & San Miguel*, about US\$1.25. It includes a key for virtually every establishment in the town.

Information

Tourist Office The tourist office is a little booth off Avenida Melgar in the main plaza. In theory it's open from 8 am to 1.30 pm and 5.30 to 8 pm, but the hours are really at the caprice of the clerk. If the booth is closed you're not missing much as they're not particularly well informed.

Money For currency exchange, Bancomer and Banco Atlántico off the main plaza change money only from 10 am to 12.30 pm. Most of the major hotels, restaurants and stores will change money at a less advantageous rate when the banks are closed.

Post The post office is south of Calle 7 Sur on the waterfront just off Avenida Melgar. Its hours are Monday to Friday from 9 am to 1 pm and 3 to 6 pm, and Saturday 9 am to 12 noon.

Touring the Island

Except for Chankanab Bay, in order to see most of the island you will have to rent a moped or bicycle, or take a taxi (see Getting Around). The following route will take you south from the town of San Miguel first.

Chankanab Bay Beach

This bay of clear water and fabulously coloured fish is the most popular on the island. It is nine km south of the town.

You used to be able to swim in the adjoining lagoon, but so many tourists were fouling the water and damaging the coral that Chankanab Lagoon was declared a National Park and declared off-limits to swimmers. Don't despair – you can still snorkel in the sea here and the lagoon has been saved from destruction.

Snorkelling equipment can be rented. Divers will be interested in a reef offshore; there is a dive shop, and scuba instruction is offered.

If you get hungry, there is a restaurant and snack shop on the premises. The beach has dressing rooms, lockers and showers, which are included in the US$2 admission price to the National Park, open 9 am to 5 pm daily. The park also has a botanical garden with 400 species of tropical plants.

Getting There & Away There's one daily local bus which leaves San Miguel at 11 am, returns at 5 pm and costs US$0.50. If you use the El Presidente bus, you can be dropped off a km from the beach. The taxi fare from San Miguel to Chankanab Bay is about US$5.

San Francisco & Palancar Beaches

San Francisco Beach, 14 km from San Miguel, and Palancar Beach, a couple of km south of it, are the most magnificent of Cozumel's sands. San Francisco's white sands run for more than three km, and rather expensive food is served at its restaurant. If you want to scuba or snorkel at Palancar Reef you will have to take a tour or charter a boat.

El Cedral

To see these small yet oldest of Mayan ruins on the island, take a paved road slightly after San Francisco Beach for about 3½ km. Although El Cedral was thought to be an important ceremonial site, its minor remnants are not well preserved. The surrounding area is the agricultural heart of Cozumel.

Punta Celarain

The southern tip of the island has a picturesque lighthouse on a dirt track four km from the highway. To enjoy truly isolated beaches en route, climb over the sand dunes. There's a fine view of the island from the top of the lighthouse. Fried fish and beer are served here on Sunday.

East Coast Drive

The wildest part of the island, the eastern shoreline, is highly recommended for beautiful seascapes of rocky coast. Unfortunately, except for Punta Chiquiero,

Chen Río and Punta Morena, it is ill-advised to swim on Cozumel's east coast due to a potentially lethal undertow. There are small eateries at both Punta Morena and Punta Chiquiero and a hotel at Punta Morena. Some travellers camp at Chen Río.

El Castillo Real & San Gervaiso Ruins

Beyond where the east coast highway meets the cross-island road that runs to town, intrepid travellers may take the sand track about 17 km from the junction to the Mayan ruins known as El Castillo. They are not very well preserved and you need a four-wheel drive to navigate the road.

If you are a real ruins buff, there is an equally unimpressive ruin called San Gervaiso on a bad road from the airport. Four-wheel drives can reach San Gervaiso from a track originating on the east coast, but some insurance policies do not cover this rough dirt road. The jungle en route is more interesting than the ruins.

Punta Molas Lighthouse

There are some fairly good beaches and minor Mayan ruins in the vicinity of the north-east point, accessible only by four-wheel drive.

Beach Activities

Scuba Diving Because of Cozumel's magnificent reefs and incredibly clear waters, divers the world over come here. For equipment rental, instruction and/or boat reservations, there are numerous dive shops on Avenida Melgar along San Miguel's waterfront. Generally, a two-tank, full-day scuba trip will cost US$35 to US$45 and an introductory scuba course in the neighbourhood of US$50.

Among the more prominent scuba destinations are the five-km-long Palancar, whose stunning coral formations and 'horseshoe' of coral heads in 70-metre visibility offer some of the world's finest diving; Maracaibo Reef, for experienced divers only, a challenge due to its current and aquatic life; Paraiso Reef, famous for its coral formations – incredible brain and star coral here; Yocab Reef, shallow yet vibrantly alive and great for beginners.

For a map complete with depth chart of Cozumel's reefs, see *Chart of the Reefs of Cozumel Mexico* prepared by Ric Hajovsky. It is sold in many of the dive shops.

Snorkelling You can go out on a boat tour for US$20 to US$25 or, far cheaper, rent your gear and snorkel at the following places: Chankanab Bay, San Francisco Beach, La Ceiba Beach (where a plane was purposely sunk for the film *Survive*), El Presidente Hotel and Palancar.

Snor Caribe Tours has a 10 am to 4 pm day trip which visits four coral reefs for snorkelling. Lunch is included in the US$25 price.

Glass-Bottom Boat If you don't want to snorkel, in fact if you don't want to even go in the water, you can enjoy the coral formations and aquatic life by taking a glass-bottom boat. The craft are supposed to leave the dock every day at 10.30 am, 12.30 pm and 2.30 pm, but generally wait until they are filled. They cost US$5 up, but if you don't come to Cozumel at the height of the tourist season you might try to bargain for a lower price.

Fishing There's great fishing off the coast of Cozumel, with marlin, tuna, bonito, tarpon, red snapper, barracuda and – most prized of all – sailfish. Game fish supposedly run at their height in these waters from late February to late June. Unfortunately, like much else on Cozumel, chartering a deep-sea fishing craft is very expensive and you are unlikely to get off with paying less than US$125 per day for the smallest of sea-going boats.

Places to Stay – bottom end
Posada Letty (no phone) at Calle 1 Sur and Avenida 15 Sur is the cheapest Cozumel accommodation and looks it.

Marginally acceptable rooms with bath and fan cost US$4.25 for one or two people.

The *Hotel Yoli* (tel 2-00-24) on Calle 1 Sur one block from the plaza slightly up from Avenida 5 Sur is family run and though the rooms are a bit dingy, they are marginally clean. Basic singles with fan and bath cost US$5, doubles US$6.

Places to Stay – middle
Hotel Saolima (tel 2-08-86) on Adolfo Salas 268, between Avenida 10 Sur and Avenida 15 Sur, is without question the best deal in town. The Saolima has clean, pleasant rooms in a quiet locale, with fan and bath, for only US$8 single and US$9.50 double.

The *Hotel Pirata* (tel 2-00-51) on 5a Avenida Sur 3-A near the plaza is another good deal, particularly for those who want air-conditioning. The Pirata offers decent singles or doubles at US$10 with fan and bath, US$14 with air-conditioning.

The *Hotel Flores* (tel 2-01-64) at Adolfo Salas and Avenida 5 Sur has very basic but adequate rooms with fan and bath costing US$8 for one or two people and US$10 for a triple.

The *Hotel López* (2-01-08) on Calle 1 Sur near the plaza has so-so rooms in a good location. Singles with fan and bath cost US$9 and doubles are overpriced at US$15.

For those willing to pay more for the luxury of air-conditioning and a swimming pool, the *Hotel Aguilar* (tel 2-03-07) on Avenida 5 Sur at Calle 3 Sur has sizeable rooms in a pleasant environment costing US$17 single and US$20 double. The hotel has touts working the docks. Don't believe their rates; they get a commission if they bring you here and you pay extra for it. Simply find the Aguilar on your own and the rates will be cheaper.

The *Hotel Pepita* (tel 2-00-98) on 15a Avenida Sur at the intersection of Calle 1 Sur offers well-maintained air-conditioned rooms and a delightful garden in a tranquil part of town. Rooms, some with

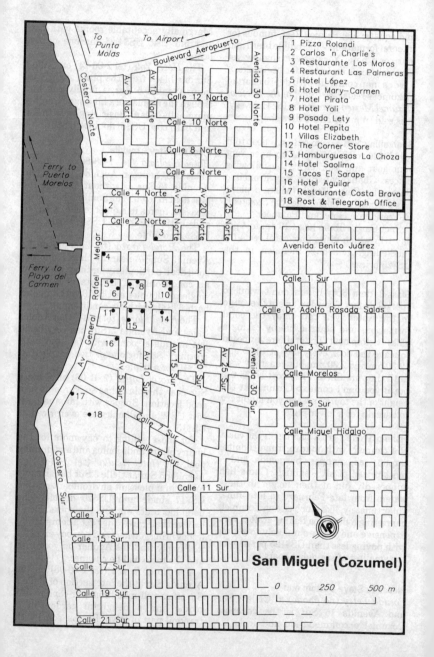

To Punta Molas
To Airport
Boulevard Aeropuerto

Costera Norte

Ferry to Puerto Morelos

Ferry to Playa del Carmen

1 Pizza Rolandi
2 Carlos 'n Charlie's
3 Restaurante Los Moros
4 Restaurant Las Palmeras
5 Hotel López
6 Hotel Mary-Carmen
7 Hotel Pirata
8 Hotel Yoli
9 Posada Lety
10 Hotel Pepita
11 Villas Elizabeth
12 The Corner Store
13 Hamburguesas La Choza
14 Hotel Saolima
15 Tacos El Sarape
16 Hotel Aguilar
17 Restaurante Costa Brava
18 Post & Telegraph Office

Calle 12 Norte
Calle 10 Norte
Calle 8 Norte
Calle 6 Norte
Calle 4 Norte
Calle 2 Norte

Av 5 Norte
Av 10 Norte
Av 15 Norte
Av 20 Norte
Av 25 Norte
Avenida 30 Norte

Avenida Benito Juárez
Calle 1 Sur
Calle Dr Adolfo Rosada Salas
Calle 3 Sur
Calle Morelos
Calle 5 Sur
Calle Miguel Hidalgo
Calle 7 Sur
Calle 9 Sur
Calle 11 Sur
Calle 13 Sur
Calle 15 Sur
Calle 17 Sur
Calle 19 Sur
Calle 21 Sur

Av Rafael Melgar
Av General

Av 5 Sur
Av 10 Sur
Av 15 Sur
Av 20 Sur
Av 25 Sur
Avenida 30 Sur

Costera Sur

San Miguel (Cozumel)

0   250   500 m

refrigerators, cost US$15 single and US$21 double.

At the high end of the moderate scale, but worth it for exceptional surroundings and comfortable air-conditioned rooms, is the *Hotel Mary-Carmen* (tel 2-04-56) on 5a Avenida Sur 4 close to the main plaza. Large rooms built around a courtyard cost US$23 single or double and US$29 triple. Another fine choice for those willing to part with a bit more is the *Villas Elizabeth* (tel 2-03-30) on Adolfo Salas 3A not far from the dock. Some of the rooms here are particularly good deals: a kitchen, refrigerator and air-conditioning are included at US$21 single or double and US$25 triple.

Places to Stay - top end

El Presidente (tel 2-03-22), 10 km south of town, is said to be one of the best of this luxury chain. It's on a good beach with waters fine for snorkelling, a well-praised restaurant and tennis courts. Singles and doubles cost US$80.

The *Hotel Sol Caribe* (tel 2-17-11), about seven km south of town, has good snorkelling and diving, night tennis, movies and two restaurants. Singles or doubles cost US$100 and up.

La Ceiba (tel 2-03-79) about seven km south of San Miguel is on a beach offering fine snorkelling. The resort has tennis, a swimming pool, a sauna and a good restaurant. There are boat rentals on the premises. Singles cost US$70, doubles US$80.

Places to Eat

It's touristy and overpriced by Mexican standards, but *Restaurant Las Palmeras* across from the dock is interesting for the wide range of visitors who dine here. For *típico* Mexican fare or excellent charcoal-broiled hamburgers (US$2.50), the prices aren't overly outrageous and the food is good.

If you are willing to walk a bit, you will find food reasonably priced for Cozumel at *Restaurante Costa Brava* on Avenida Melgar just south of Calle 7 Sur. Filling breakfasts cost US$1 and steaks are only about US$1.50.

Hamburguesas La Choza is on Adolfo Salas at Avenida 10 Sur. At US$2, they are huge and delicious.

Restaurante Los Moros on Juárez and Avenida 10 Norte is known for its grilled chicken dishes at fairly reasonable prices. It's loud and busy, but good.

While *Pizza Rolandi's* local outlet on Avenida Melgar, four blocks north of the plaza beyond Calle 6 Norte, is expensive relative to its Isla Mujeres restaurant, its pizza is quite good. Stay away from the lousy pasta dishes.

Tacos El Sarape on Avenida 5 Sur near Adolfo Salas is a good cheap local taquería. It's only open in the evenings from 7 pm on.

Put together your own healthy meals at *The Corner Store & Fruit Bar* on Adolfo Salas at Avenida 5 Sur. Delicious honey, granola and other health foods are sold here.

For cheap *típico* street fare, try the market on Adolfo Salas between Avenida 20 Sur and Avenida 25 Sur. There's an excellent bakery, *Panificadora Cozumel*, just off the waterfront on Calle 2 Norte.

Entertainment

Nightlife in Cozumel is extremely expensive, but if you want to dance, the most popular disco in town is *Disco Neptuno* on the southern end of Avenida Melgar. Another hot spot is *Disco Scaramouche* at the intersection of Avenida Melgar and Adolfo Salas. Figure US$2 to US$3 cover charge and then premium prices for watered-down drinks. Far more expensive are discos like *Morgan's* off the plaza and *Grip's* near the dock.

Also on Melgar there's a raucous bar that is the local version of the Carlos 'n Charlie's chain. The luxury hotels *El Presidente, Sol Caribe* and *La Ceiba* have discos. *The Forum* presents mariachi bands nightly at a cover charge of US$7, which also entitles you to two drinks. Far cheaper than live entertainment are the town's two cinemas which often screen English-language films with Spanish subtitles. *Cine Borgues* is on Avenida Juárez and Avenida 35, *Cine Cozumel* is on Avenida Melgar and Calle 4 Norte.

Things to Buy

There are scores of costly boutiques whose prices have been driven up by affluent tourists and cruise-ship passengers. So while there are quality items for sale here from all over Mexico, the cost may be outrageously high. The major locally made item, black coral jewellery, is a good buy. Roberto's, off the plaza at Avenida 5 Sur, is one of the better boutiques for black coral. For folk crafts, check out La Concha also near the plaza on Avenida 5 Sur. For leather goods, visit El Sombrero near the dock.

Getting There & Away

Air There are international flights on Continental (tel 2-02-51), United (tel 2-02-63) and American (tel 2-08-99) from Houston, Chicago and Dallas respectively, with connections to other US cities. Aeroméxico (tel 2-02-51) also has a flight from Houston, and Mexicana (tel 2-02-63) has flights from Miami. Domestically, both Aeroméxico and Mexicana have flights here from Mérida and Mexico City as well as flights from other Mexican cities which connect with these.

From Playa del Carmen, Aero Cozumel has flights virtually every two hours to Cozumel. These seven-minute flights, costing only US$6, offer an alternative for those prone to seasickness.

Ferry The cheapest way to come to Cozumel is by ferry from the mainland port, Playa del Carmen. The ferry costs slightly more than US$1 and takes about one hour and 15 minutes. It leaves Playa del Carmen at 6 am, 12 noon and 6 pm. For the return trip it leaves Cozumel for Playa at 4 am, 9.30 am and 4 pm. If you're

prone to seasickness beware of the ferry when the weather is rough.

For those willing to pay a bit more, hydrofoils cost US$3 and take 20 minutes between Playa and Cozumel. These 'water-jets' leave Playa at 7 am and 3.30 pm, and depart Cozumel at 6 am and 2.30 pm. There is also a hydrofoil service between Cozumel and Cancún with water-jets leaving Cancún daily at 10 am and 7 pm and leaving Cozumel at 8 am and 5 pm. The price is about US$15.50.

If you wish to bring your car to Cozumel, there are car ferries leaving Puerto Morelos (about 26 km south of Cancún) at 6 am. These leave Cozumel for Puerto Morelos at 12 noon. There are no Monday ferries. The car ferry leaves Cozumel at the International Pier in front of the Hotel Sol Caribe. Fares are US$0.40 per passenger, US$0.50 per motorcycle and US$1.75 per car. The trip takes about 2½ hours.

Getting Around

Airport Transport It costs about US$0.75 to take a minibus from Cozumel's airport into the heart of the town. Once in San Miguel, it is easy to find your way around the compact city's street grid. Most budget travellers will lodge in San Miguel.

Local Transport There is a hotel bus which runs south (8 am to 10 pm) on the hour from the north coast hotel zone to El Presidente Hotel on the south coast. Heading back to the north coast, the bus departs El Presidente hourly from 8.40 am to 9.40 pm. Unfortunately the taxi drivers' union has recently managed to make this bus a 'hotel employees only' vehicle. If you wish to take a local bus to Chancanab Bay Beach, a single bus leaves daily from near the tourist booth in town (near the ferry) at 11 am, costing US$0.50. It returns at 5 pm. The walk from El Presidente south to Chancanab is about one km.

For other points on the island there is no public transportation, so you will have to rent a car or a moped or take a taxi. Taxi fares average US$2.25 for every 15 minutes of travel, and pricey auto rentals correspond to rates charged throughout the tourist belt of Mexico's Caribbean. Little wonder, then, that for those who want to explore Cozumel, the moped is extremely popular. At this writing, Ruben's just off the south side of the plaza was offering the best rates of US$8 for 24 hours. Also offering good deals was Villas Elizabeth near the dock at Adolfo Salas 3A. Check your moped carefully before you take it on the road – some are in bad shape.

Cheaper still, for those with the energy, is to tour the island by bicycle. Ruben's rents bikes for US$2.50 a day, as does the Hotel Saolima at Adolfo Salas 268, and Hotel Aguilar on Avenida 5 Sur at Calle 3 Sur.

Car Rental For automobile rentals, figure at least US$30 per day for a Volkswagen Beetle and a higher rate for sedans. Bargain hard for the best deal and make sure everything is in the contract before you sign.

PLAYA DEL CARMEN

Travellers who want serene tropical sands without Cancún's resort feeling, Isla Mujeres' tiny beach and over-developed town, or Cozumel's costs, have a hard time understanding why Playa del Carmen gets relatively few of Mexico's Caribbean tourists. One logical answer is that most tourists either don't know 'Playa', as it is affectionately called, or see it simply as the ferry port for Cozumel. Nonetheless, word of Playa's tropical tranquillity and good beach is getting out and in a few years it is likely to have all the trappings of a resort. Those who come now have a treat in store for them.

The Beach

The beach runs on and on, with palms shading the sands and bathtub-warm waters. You can walk out quite a distance in the quiet seas without the water reaching your shoulders.

Playa has one of the few nude beaches in Mexico. Go north from the Blue Parrot Inn around the point and you will see the beach. It's long enough to let you stake out some isolated sands.

If you want to snorkel, walk to the north end of the nude beach where there's a small reef. Or take a day trip to Cozumel for snorkelling and scuba. Since Playa has beaches superior to Cozumel's and is cheaper, many budget travellers prefer to stay in Playa and make occasional day trips to Cozumel.

If you stay in Playa, the dive shop of the Cueva Pargo Cabañas, located on the beach, will rent you snorkelling equipment, as will some of the hotels. Huacho Corrales, owner of the Cueva Pargo, takes tourists aboard his 36-foot mahogany-and-teak sailboat for scuba and snorkelling expeditions or longer cruises to points off the coast of Belize.

Places to Stay – bottom end

CREA Youth Hostel is a new facility and the cheapest clean lodging in town, but it has its disadvantages. The hostel is quite a walk to the beach, and you sleep in single-sex dorm bunks. On the positive side, the hostel is clean, has a basketball court and is cheap at US$2.50. The hostel also has an inexpensive café serving breakfast for about US$1 and lunch and dinner for US$1.50. To reach the hostel from the bus stop, walk up the main street, Avenida Principal, away from the beach. After five blocks, make a right when you see Lubricantes International. Take the dirt road one km and make another left. Figure the hostel to be a good 20 to 25-minute walk from the beach. At night, be certain to take a flashlight (torch) as the dirt road is potholed and unlit.

Fortunately, there are a couple of good cheap hotels as alternatives. The best is the *Posada Lilly*. Although it's located across Avenida Principal from the bus

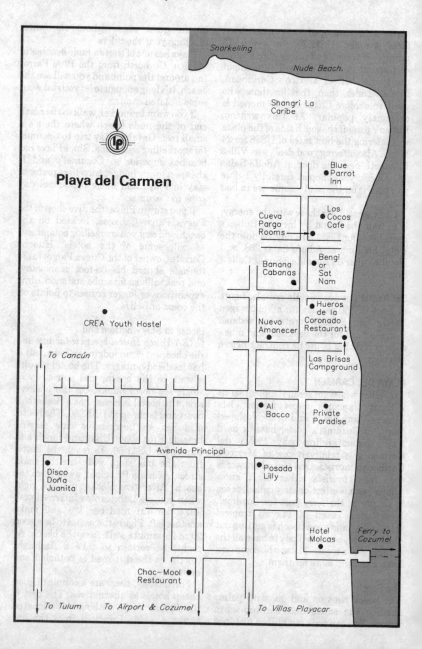

Playa del Carmen

Snorkelling

Nude Beach

Shangri La Caribe

Blue Parrot Inn

Cueva Pargo Rooms

Los Cocos Cafe

Banana Cabanas

Bengi or Sat Nam

CREA Youth Hostel

Nuevo Amanecer

Hueros de la Coronado Restaurant

Las Brisas Campground

To Cancún

Al Bacco

Private Paradise

Avenida Principal

Disco Doña Juanita

Posada Lilly

Hotel Molcas

Ferry to Cozumel

Chac–Mool Restaurant

To Tulum

To Airport & Cozumel

To Villas Playacar

station, it is surprisingly quiet, particularly at the back. Here spotlessly clean, large rooms with fan and bath cost US$6 single, US$8 double. Also quite nice on the main road but a bit more expensive is the *Hotel Playa del Carmen*. A couple blocks east of the bus station (toward the highway), this hotel has decent rooms with fan and bath costing US$8 single, US$10 double.

There are a couple of good, basic cheapies on the road above the beach. The *Sian Kihn* charges US$6 for a single with fan and bath, US$10 for a double. *Posada Flores* offers basic rooms with fan and bath for US$8.

Camping Stay away from *Las Ruinas Campground*. It's filthy and a lot of theft has been reported. Preferable is *Las Brisas Campground* which is better maintained and watched. You can pitch a tent at Las Brisas for US$2. There are showers and cooking facilities on the premises. Las Brisas also has spartan wooden shack cabins for about US$5; those who stay there use the same communal showers and toilets as the campers.

Places to Stay – middle

The following places may seem expensive by Mexican standards for those travelling on the cheap, but the cabañas are so inviting that you might consider a splurge. Unless noted otherwise, all of the listings are on or near the road just above the beach. If you are coming here during the holidays, write for reservations.

In the grounds of *Nuevo Amanecer* the proprietress Arlene King has installed a hot tub. (Arlene is from – surprise – California.) There are pool tables on the premises and each of the cabañas is thoughtfully equipped with a hammock. Comfortable rooms with fan and bath cost US$20 for the smaller cabañas and US$25 for the larger. To find Nuevo Amanecer, walk north along the beach for two blocks and make a left. For reservations write to Arlene King, Apto Postal 1056, Cancún, Quintana Roo, Mexico.

Want a thatch-roofed cabaña in a tropical setting just a stone's throw from the beach? *Cueva Pargo* is run by a helpful couple, Huacho and JoAnne Corrales, and has a variety of cabañas and costs. Prices include good breakfasts served in the cabañas' Sailorman Pub next door on the beach. A cabaña with (clean) shared bath costs US$18 single, US$21 double; a cabaña for two with private bath costs US$28. A beach house costs US$50 and there is a large cabaña for four costing US$55. The Cueva Pargo also has a sailboat for day-long or month-long snorkelling/scuba excursions. To make reservations, write to Cueva Pargo, Box 838, Cancún, Quintana Roo, Mexico.

If you're willing to spend more to be right on the beach, the *Blue Parrot Inn's* cabañas provide a touch of paradise. The thatched-roof cabañas, set on a pretty stretch of sands, are well maintained and the setting is a beachcomber's delight. Run by former Florida resident Rick Jones and his Japanese wife, the Blue Parrot also has a terraced restaurant serving some of the best food in Playa. If you make reservations or are extremely lucky, there is one small cabaña with shared bathroom for US$20 for one or two people. Other beach-front cabañas cost US$30 to US$50, depending on facilities. For reservations, write to the Blue Parrot Inn, PO Box 652737, Miami, Florida 33265, USA.

Next to a tropical garden is the popular *Banana Cabañas*. Run by the friendly ex-Oklahoman Sam Beard and his wife Martha, the cabañas are reasonably priced at US$15 for one or two people. Larger cabañas sleeping up to four cost from US$18 to US$21. A cabaña with a kitchenette costs US$20. Banana Cabañas is on the road above the beach.

Follow Avenida Principal to the block above the beach and you will come to a fence behind a dentist's office signposted *Private Paradise*. Set in a courtyard, these cabañas are run by an American named Christine who provides a family-like setting for her guests. Cabañas cost about US$18.

On the road above the beach is the pleasant and reasonably priced *Calypso House*, where cabañas for one or two with shared bath cost US$12.

Just above the beach across from the Cueva Pargo is a hotel of curious East Indian design known as both the *Bengi* and the *Sat Nam*. Yoga is taught here. The rooms are small for the price, but if you like the locale, singles with shared bath cost US$10 and doubles US$12.

Places to Stay – top end

If you want to really get away from it all, north of the town along the nude beach is the newly built *Shangri La Caribe*. Run by the helpful English-speaking Adolfo, these pretty cabañas have a swimming pool, recreation room and restaurant. Doubles cost US$72. The snorkelling area is close by and the Shangri La rents equipment.

Those seeking luxury lodging in town will find the *Villas Playacar* to their liking. Cabañas have kitchens, and tennis, water skiing and scuba trips are offered. During the high season, prices range from US$110 to US$250; during the low season (summer) they range from US$70 to US$150.

Built above the ferry dock with pretty seaside views, the *Hotel Molcas* charges US$60 to US$80 for its double rooms.

Places to Eat

Los Cocos Café, right on the beach before you get to the Blue Parrot, serves delicious seafood at reasonable prices. The American chef here is truly inspired and Los Cocos will remain a tiny seaside café of high quality as long as he works there.

If you want good seafood in a pleasant setting and are willing to pay a bit more, dine at the *Blue Parrot Inn* restaurant. Set on a terrace overlooking the Caribbean, it couldn't have a more romantic setting.

If you can't afford the food, come by for coffee or a drink at sunset.

Al Bacco serves some of the better Italian food on the Mexican Caribbean at moderate prices. Their veal dishes and pasta are superb. To get to the Al Bacco, walk one block north along the road above the beach and make a left. The *Mascaras Restaurant* just above the beach on Avenida Principal is recommended only for its pizza – the pasta is lousy. Also, avoid the quasi-Chinese restaurant near the Mascaras which has awful versions of the Mexican notion of Cantonese.

Those interested in trying Yucatecan specialities at reasonable prices should check out the *Chac-Mool Restaurant*, two blocks south off Avenida Principal on the road to the airport. *El Capi*, on Avenida Principal a couple of blocks from the highway, has decent, cheap *típico* Mexican fare.

For good, inexpensive seafood, try *Doña Juanita's Restaurant* on the road above the beach two blocks north of the bus terminal. Their shrimp dishes are particularly tasty. Also good for seafood a little further north on the same road is *Hueros de la Coronado*.

Good places for breakfasts are the *Sailorman's Pub*, *Banana Cabañas*, *Los Cocos* and the *Blue Parrot*. There is also a good bakery in Playa. Beware of *El Zorro Bar & Restaurant* on the beach, which has a less than wonderful reputation.

Entertainment

Generally entertainment consists of you, your companions, the beach and the stars, but if you must have a disco, try the *Doña Juanita* on Avenida Principal just off the main highway to Cancún.

Getting There & Away

Air There are flights every two hours between Cozumel and Playa, taking seven minutes and costing only US$6.

Road If you start early enough in the day, it is fairly easy to hitch to Playa from other points along the Caribbean between Cancún and Tulum.

Bus Don't turn up your nose at 2nd-class buses running along the Carribean coast. They are slightly cheaper than 1st class, have more frequent schedules and may not be much slower. Playa has regular 1st and 2nd-class service to Cancún and other points along the Caribbean as well as Cobá and Valladolid. Furthermore, it's easy to take a bus from virtually any part of Mexico to Cancún and transfer to a Playa-bound bus from there. Playa is only an hour from Cancún.

The following schedules are subject to change and are included to give you a sense of frequency. First-class buses leave Cancún for Playa at 7 and 9.30 am, 12 noon, 5.30 pm and midnight. They take roughly an hour and cost about US$1. Buses move on from Playa to Akumal, Xel-Ha, Tulum, Puerto Felipe Carrillo, Bacalar and Chetumal. Second-class departures from Cancún to Playa and from there on to the same destinations are at 8 and 10.30 am, 1.15 and 4.30 pm. Buses leave Playa for Cobá and Valladolid at 5.15 and 10.45 am.

Ferry The cheapest way to get between Cozumel and Playa is by ferry – it costs slightly more than US$1 and takes about 1¼ hours. The ferry leaves Playa at 6 am, 12 noon and 6 pm. It leaves Cozumel for Playa at 4 am, 9.30 am and 4 pm. When the weather is rough, passengers who don't have strong sea-stomachs may suffer. The hydrofoils are more expensive and more comfortable, costing US$3 and taking 20 minutes to whisk passengers between Cozumel and Playa. These 'water-jets' leave Playa at 7 am and 3.30 pm, returning from Cozumel to Playa at 6 am and 2.30 pm.

Getting Around
If you are leaving Playa for the airport, ask your bus driver if he will drop you near the road linking the airport to the highway.

There you might be able to catch a cheap taxi.

BEACHES ALONG THE COAST
Some of the world's most beautiful beaches lie between Cancún and Tulum. If you want a beach of your own in tropical splendour, away from the tourist throngs of Cancún and Isla Mujeres, this stretch of Caribbean coast will make your dreams come true.

Privacy does come at a bit of a cost. Several of the beaches have either no lodging or only expensive hotels. If you have a tent, hammock and mosquito netting, you will be rewarded for roughing it.

Another reason that relatively few tourists overnight at these beaches is the lack of transportation. Although buses run sporadically between Cancún and Tulum during the day, 1st class is invariably full and will usually not stop. Even if 2nd class is not full, all of the seats may be and the bus may not stop if there is no standing room. You'll have to stand with your pack because time is rarely taken to put it underneath in the luggage compartment. To figure out when a bus is likely to be heading south, extrapolate from the times given in the Getting There sections for Playa del Carmen and Tulum, or get up-to-date information in Cancún. During the day, Caribbean coastal buses tend to run at roughly two-hour intervals.

While you are waiting for the bus to get you between beaches, try hitch-hiking. Every day, scores of gringos who have rented cars in Cancún go day-tripping down the coast. Beachcombers find it relatively easy to catch a ride if they start out early enough. Bus fare between beaches is generally less than US$1 so don't bother hitching just to save money.

The highway is generally a km or more back from the beach and you have to turn off the road to find it. Not all beach off-roads are signposted by name but the sites will correspond to the numbered km signs listed below for each beach. The road itself is straight and dull; dense vegetation spills back from the road on both sides and there's little sign of habitation.

The best way to get to the Caribbean's isolated beaches is to rent a car in Cancún. This is expensive, but if you want to splurge for one day, car rentals will save walking in from the highway along the off-roads, which can be time consuming and exhausting if it's hot. Try organising a group of travellers to share the rental costs.

Be sure to bring snorkelling equipment. Few beaches have gear for rent, and those that do may charge outlandish prices.

Puerto Morelos (Km 328)

Puerto Morelos, 32 km south of Cancún, is a sleepy fishing village known principally for its car ferry to Cozumel. There is a good budget hotel and travellers who overnight find it refreshingly free of tourists.

There are some small Mayan ruins in the vicinity. Very little has been excavated and they are not well preserved. The ruins include sites for docking Mayan canoes which took the Indians on pilgrimages to Cozumel to worship the goddess of fertility, Ixchel.

Beach Activities

A splendid reef sits 600 metres off Puerto Morelos but you need a boat to reach it. Half or full-day snorkelling trips may be arranged through the Hotel Playa Ojo de Agua's dive shop a block north of the zócalo.

The reef and the wreck of a Spanish galleon seven km to the north-east make Puerto Morelos a popular destination for scuba fans. The infamous Sleeping Shark Caves are eight km to the east. You may book a trip and rent necessary equipment from the Hotel Playa Ojo de Agua's dive shop one block north of the zócalo.

You can fish off the pier for red-mouthed grunt, known locally as *chac-chi*. The dive shop of the Hotel Ojo de Agua is the place to make reservations for deep-sea fishing expeditions.

Places to Stay

For good basic budget lodging, stay at the *Posada Amor*. Family run, the Posada's guests are treated with the loving care implied by the name. Rooms with fan and a clean shared bathroom cost US$9, single or double.

The *Hotel Playa Ojo de Agua*, a block north of the zócalo, has a swimming pool, restaurant and bar. Divers receive a special rate if they make use of the hotel's dive-shop excursions and equipment rental. Rooms and three meals run US$65. For reservations and information write to Nery Vada, Apto Postal 299, Cancún, Quintana Roo, Mexico.

La Ceiba Beach Hotel, on the beach north of Puerto Morelos, has a restaurant, small swimming pool and dive shop which runs scuba excursions. Rooms come with refrigerators and have balconies overlooking the beach. Singles or doubles cost about US$50, with a discount for divers. For reservations, write to the hotel, Apto Postal 1252, Cancún, Quintana Roo, Mexico.

Places to Eat

For cheap *típico* meals off the main plaza, try the *Casa Martín* or the *Restaurant Doña Zenaida*. The thatch-roofed restaurant of the *Posada Amor* may offer only one or two dishes but they are very good; Yucatecan specialities cost US$2 to US$3. For those willing to spend more, the food at the *Hotel Playa Ojo de Agua* and the restaurant of *La Ceiba Beach Hotel* is excellent.

Getting There & Away

All 2nd-class and many 1st-class buses stop at Puerto Morelos coming from, or en route to, Cancún. Buses generally come by every couple of hours during the day – extrapolate from the timetable given for Playa del Carmen. It takes about 45 minutes to get here by bus from Cancún.

Hitch-hiking south from Puerto Morelos is generally pretty good if you start out early in the day. If you are driving, the Pemex station here is the last fuel you will find until Tulum.

The Cozumel Car Ferry leaves Puerto Morelos daily except Monday at 8 am and returns from Cozumel at 12 noon. Locals say it is best to be at the dock two to three hours early; car boarding at Puerto Morelos begins at 6 am. If leaving from Cozumel, be at the dock in front of the Hotel Sol Caribe a couple of hours early.

You don't have to have a car to take the ferry. Fares are US$0.40 for each passenger, US$0.50 for motorcycles and US$1.75 per car. The passage takes 2½ hours and seas can be rough. If you can keep it down, food is served on board. The ferry tends to change its hours every few months, so find out current departure hours in advance.

Punta Bete (Km 298)

This is a beautiful swimming beach fringed by coconut palms with four km of white sand lapped by turquoise waters. Although some parts of the tranquil seas here have rocky bottoms, you can avoid the sharp outcroppings because the water is translucent. Generally, deeper blue patches indicate that there is something on the bottom causing shadows. The one area to stay away from is the sea between the Cabañas Blue Marlin and the Lafitte resort, as the bottom is carpeted with jagged outcroppings and spiny sea urchins.

Beach Activities Snorkelling is particularly good between Xcalacoco Campgrounds and Kai Luum Camptel, provided that you watch out for rocks and sea urchins. Snorkelling off the Blue Marlin is also good, but there are more rocks on the bottom there.

Cabañas Lafitte resort has a reef off its beach accessible by the resort's skiff (which you must pay to use unless you are a guest of Lafitte). There is an exquisite array of coral here, including brain coral. The dive shop at Cabañas Lafitte will take you on scuba excursions and rents all necessary equipment. It can also arrange deep-sea fishing expeditions. From shore,

the fishing is said to be best at the north end of the resort where you can catch pampanos.

You can trek south 12 km through six bays to Playa del Carmen. Wear good shoes as in spots there is sharp coral along the shore.

Places to Stay - bottom end Because there is no worthwhile cheap accommodation on this beach, camping is the way to enjoy Punta Bete cheaply if you are more than day-tripping. *Xcalacoco Campgrounds* ('shkala-CO-co') have reasonably well-kept showers and toilets and it's a lovely place for tent or hammock, but don't forget mosquito repellent. Camping sites cost about US$1.50 and because fires are against the rules, you must cook on a camping stove. Xcalacoco has a couple of cabañas at US$7 a double but they are so spartan that you're better off outdoors.

If you want camping with everything provided at outrageous prices, *Kai Luum Camptel* is for you. Here you sleep on beds in large tents shaded by palapa-thatched roofs. 'Maid service' is provided (!) and the food is good, served in the evenings under candlelight, as Kai Luum has no electricity. The cost for two in a tent is US$32, including breakfast and dinner; lunch is offered at about US$5 a head. For reservations write to Camptel Ventures, Box 2664, Evergreen, Colorado 80439, USA.

Places to Stay - middle Not far from Xcalacoco Campgrounds are some pretty cabins known as *Cabañas Marlin Azul*. They face the beach and are equipped with electricity, hot water and fans. The restaurant serves seafood at moderate cost. A double with private bath costs US$20.

Places to Stay - top end *Cabañas Lafitte* resort, which has its own entrance road from the highway, is a great place for those with the money who wish to get away from it all. Situated on a good beach, Lafitte's cabañas have hot water, fans and private bath. The resort has a swimming pool, ping-pong table and fine restaurant. Given the setting and the friendly atmosphere, guests return here year after year.

Doubles cost US$65 including breakfast and dinner. You can make reservations through the same address as the Kai Luum Camptel.

Xcaret (Km 290)

Until you reach the beach, the land here is part of a privately owned turkey farm. There is a small admission charge (about 25c). At this unusual Caribbean site you will find, just beyond a couple of small Mayan ruins, a path taking you past limestone water-filled caves harbouring colourful fish. It is said that you can scuba-dive quite some distance through these grottoes, although most tourists just go for a dip in the cool cave waters.

Just beyond the caves is a *caleta* (small inlet) alive with tropical fish. Although the small lagoon is rocky, with little sand for sunning, the fine snorkelling is the principal reason for coming here.

At this time Xcaret is strictly a day trip as there are no facilities for camping. A rather noisy restaurant has recently opened.

Pamul (Km 274)

Although Pamul's small rocky beach does not have long, languorous stretches of white sand like some of its Caribbean cousins, the palm-fringed surroundings are inviting and if you walk only about two km north of Pamul's little hotel, you will find an alabaster sand beach to call your own. If you're collecting coral, try the shores just south of Pamul. The least rocky section is the southern end, but watch out for spiked sea urchins in the shallows offshore.

Beach Activities The waters here are calm and the best snorkelling is a bit of a swim away from the shoreline.

There are a few beaches like Malaysia's famous Rantau Abang, where gigantic sea turtles annually come to lay their eggs. Why they return to the same beach every year is a mystery not understood by zoologists. Pamul is one such beach and if you are here in July or August you may be lucky enough to observe a huge sea turtle lumbering ashore to lay her eggs. This tends to happen at night, so bring a flashlight (torch).

Places to Stay & Eat *Hotel Pamul* offers basic but acceptable rooms with fan and bath for US$6 single and US$12 double. There is electricity in the evenings until 10 pm. The friendly family that runs this somewhat scruffy hotel and campsite also serves breakfasts and seafood at their little restaurant for reasonable prices.

Camping The fee is US$3 for two people per site. There are showers and a communal toilet here.

Yal-ku Lagoon (Km 256.5)

One of the secrets of snorkelling aficionados, Yal-Ku Lagoon is not even signposted. Its dirt road turn-off is across from a stone-walled house with a windmill. The tiny lagoon is a good place to snorkel, filled with a phantasmagoric array of aquatic life. Best of all, you may have the lagoon to yourself.

Yal-Ku is basically for day trips, as there is little shade and not much in the way of decent places to pitch a tent. Bring your own refreshments and snorkelling gear.

Akumal (Km 255)

Like Pamul, Akumal is a beach where gigantic turtles come ashore in summer to lay their eggs – the name means 'Place of the Turtles' in Mayan. Unlike Pamul and other beaches north between here and Cancún, Akumal is strictly a resort for the affluent. Nonetheless, its excellent snorkelling and beach of cinnamon sands, festooned with shady palm trees, make

Akumal a worthwhile day trip for the budget traveller.

Akumal Bay was once a coconut plantation, which went out of business in 1925. The following year Akumal became briefly known to the world when the *New York Times*-sponsored Mason-Spinden expedition along Quintana Roo's coast noted how picturesque the bay was. Thereafter, Akumal lay forgotten by the outside world until 1958 when a Mexican diving organisation investigating the wreck of a Spanish galleon publicised the beauty of this bay. At the time, the only way to get here other than on foot was by boat from Cozumel. In 1964 a road was built and developers' pesos financed the resorts in evidence today.

Don't despair; the beach is large enough to give you a measure of privacy. A reef teeming with multicoloured fish breaks the waves, making the waters calm.

Beach Activities There are two dive shops here where you can rent snorkelling gear. The best snorkelling is at the north end of the bay; or try Yal-Ku Lagoon, 1.5 km north of Akumal.

World-class divers come here to explore the Spanish galleon *Mantancero* which sank in 1741. You can see artefacts from the galleon at the museum at nearby Xel-Ha. The dive shops will arrange all your scuba excursion needs but it won't be cheap. Beginners' scuba instruction can be provided for less than US$90; if you want certification, the dive shops offer three-day courses. They will also arrange deep-sea fishing excursions for those willing to pay the price. Make your reservations in advance.

Places to Stay The least expensive of this resort's three hotels is the *Villas Mayas*, where basic air-conditioned cabañas with bath and the amenities of tennis and basketball courts cost US$48 double. The Villas Mayas also has condo suites with two bedrooms, two bathrooms, a living room and kitchen for US$125. These can sleep six people. For reservations write to Akutrame, Box 1976, El Paso, Texas 79950, USA.

The *Hotel Ina Yana Kin Akumal Caribe* on the south end of the beach is an attractive two-storeyed modern lodge with swimming pool, boat rental and night tennis. Spacious air-conditioned rooms equipped with refrigerators cost US$65. On the north side of the beach you will find the cabañas of *Las Casitas Akumal* consisting of a living room, two bedrooms, two bathrooms and a refrigerator. Bungalows start at US$70. For reservations write Las Casitas, PO Box 714, Cancún, Quintana Roo, Mexico.

Places to Eat Even the shade-huts near the beach are expensive for light lunches and snacks. Just outside the walled entrance of Akumal is a grocery store patronised largely by the resort workers; if you are day-tripping here, this is your sole inexpensive source of food. The store also sells tacos and other *típico* food.

For those willing to splurge, both the *Zasil Restaurant* next to Las Casitas on the north side of the shore and the *Lol Ha* (ask for the specials) next to the dive shop on the beach have a reputation for fine cuisine. Somewhat cheaper is the restaurant owned by the *Ina Yana Kin*.

Entertainment One or another of the three hotels will have live entertainment nightly and sometimes a band for dancing.

Things to Buy Although Akumal's two boutiques offer quality crafts, the prices are outrageous. If you are visiting any other part of Mexico, do your shopping there.

Getting There & Away If you are day-tripping, either come here by bus and let the driver know where you wish to get off, or else hitch-hike. Hitching earlier in the day is easier – after sundown it can prove difficult. If you are driving, it takes about an hour to Cancún. If coming from the airport, you can take a taxi here but it is expensive.

Las Aventuras (Km 250)

The well-heeled patronise this resort, including divers who make arrangements with Yucatán Diving Adventures. The beautiful *Aventuras Akumal* hotel has double rooms for about US$45; all rooms face the sea and each has a balcony looking out on the fine stretch of beach. There's some coral just offshore and the resort also has a pool and bar. The resort's *Los Tucanas* restaurant is pleasant, and dinner for two with beer, dessert and coffee will cost about US$25. The turn-off is about three km south of Akumal.

Chemuyil (Km 248)

This is a beautiful alabaster sand beach shaded by coconut palms. There is good snorkelling in the calm waters with exceptional visibility, and fishing from the shore is said to be good.

Chemuyil is just starting to be developed, with some condos already built. During winter's high season there are a fair number of campers here, but it's worth a stop before it really becomes developed.

Places to Stay If you camp toward the south end of the shoreline, you will avoid those who have come just for the day and enjoy the isolation and tranquillity.

The only accommodation is spartan screened shade-huts with hammock hooks. Enquire about availability at the bar; they cost US$4, and showers and toilets are communal.

Places to Eat Unless you have the equipment and goods to cook for yourself, the only option is the *típico* fare prepared at the bar, including some seafood.

Xcacel (Km 247)

Xcacel ('shah-SELL') has no lodging other than camping, no electricity and only a small restaurant stall. This is actually fortunate, because if Xcacel was more developed, the most magnificent of Mexico's Caribbean beaches would be overrun. As it stands, you can enjoy this patch of paradise in relative privacy.

Beach Activities For fine fishing and snorkelling, try the waters north of the campground. The rocky point leads to seas for snorkelling, and the sandy outcropping is said to be a good place to fish from. The waters directly in front of the campground are not the best to swim in as there is no reef to break the waves. Swimming, like snorkelling, is best from the rocky point to the north end of the beach.

Xcacel offers good pickings for shell collectors, including that aquatic collector the hermit crab. There are also some colourful and intricate coral pieces to be found. When beachcombing here, wear footgear.

Take the old dirt track which runs two km north to Chemuyil and three km south to Xel-Ha, and you may spy parrots, finches or the well-named clockbird *(mot-mot)* with its long tail.

Places to Stay For beachcomber tranquillity, camp at the south end of the beach. There is a charge of US$1 per person for camping and a small day-use charge of about US$0.40. There are showers and a toilet but bring mosquito repellent.

Xel-Ha Lagoon (Km 245)

This lagoon was designated a national park to preserve it, but how can the government protect it when every day hordes of tourists wearing polluting suntan oils inundate Xel-Ha? Moreover, to facilitate access to the lagoon, concrete has been poured around the periphery.

Is it worthwhile to visit Xel-ha ('SHELL-ha')? Definitely, so long as you come either very early in the day or very late to avoid the tour buses. At least there are no hotels as yet; people come here simply to snorkel. Just don't get the impression that this is some secluded little inlet. With 20 or 30 tourist buses lined up in the parking lot it's certainly not a place for peace and quiet.

Snorkelling Xel-ha is a feast for the eyes, with parrot, angel and butterfly fish among the nearly 50 species in residence. It's best to bring snorkelling equipment. A stand rents it here, but the prices are high (US$4) and some of the masks have been worn to the point of no longer being watertight. If a rented mask is not suitable for you, ask for another no matter how much the unpleasant vendor tells you that the mask is fine and you are to blame for not snorkelling correctly. If you snorkel during tour-bus time you'll see plenty of arms and legs, churned-up debris and waters fouled by those feeding the fish.

Xel-ha is open from 8 am to 5 pm daily. The admission charge is US$0.40.

Museum The small maritime museum contains artefacts from the wreckage of the Spanish galleon *Mantancero*. The galleon sank in 1741 just north of Akumal, and in 1958 Mexican divers started their salvage operation. On display are guns, cannons, coins and other items. There are also items from some more recent wrecks as well as Mayan artefacts but the museum is not worth the 25c admission.

Places to Eat There's a café here, but the food is grossly overpriced and lousy to boot. It's better to bring food if you are staying any length of time. You can buy a refreshing coconut from a vendor, who will open it with his machete.

Things to Buy With so many gringos on hand, there's a gift shop of Mexican crafts on the premises but the goods are inferior and the prices steep. Make your purchases elsewhere.

TULUM

The ruins of Tulum, though well-preserved, would hardly merit rave notices if it weren't for their setting. And what a setting! Here the grey-black buildings of the past sit on a palm-fringed beach, lapped by the turquoise waters of the Caribbean.

While Tulum literally means 'City of the Dawn' in Mayan, a looser translation is 'City of Renewal'. For those travellers who are 'ruined out', the dramatic environs of Tulum will renew their desire to explore antiquities.

Like Chichén Itzá, Tulum's proximity to the tourist centres of Cancún and Isla de Mujeres make it a prime target of tour buses. To best enjoy the ruins, visit them either early in the morning or late in the day. The ruins are open from 8 am to 5 pm and there is a 20c admission charge. Around mid-day, when Tulum's fortress city is besieged by bus-loads of tourists, it is best to make use of either the ruin's beaches or the sands south of here. After a siesta, you'll be refreshed enough to return to the largely abandoned ruins in the late afternoon.

History

Although a stela has been found at Tulum dated 546 AD, most archaeologists believe the stone was moved much later to the site and that Tulum was actually settled during the decline of the Mayan civilisation in the Decadent or Post Classic period (700-1500). The city-fortress may have been built as late as 1200. In fact, Tulum was probably still occupied after first contact with the Spaniards, as a mural found here depicts Chac, the rain god, riding a four-legged animal. Since horses were unknown until the conquistadors brought them to the New World, some archaeologists conclude that Tulum was still settled at the time of initial European intrusion.

The ramparts that surround three sides of Tulum (the fourth side being the sea) leave little question as to its strategic function as a fortress. Averaging nearly seven metres in thickness and standing

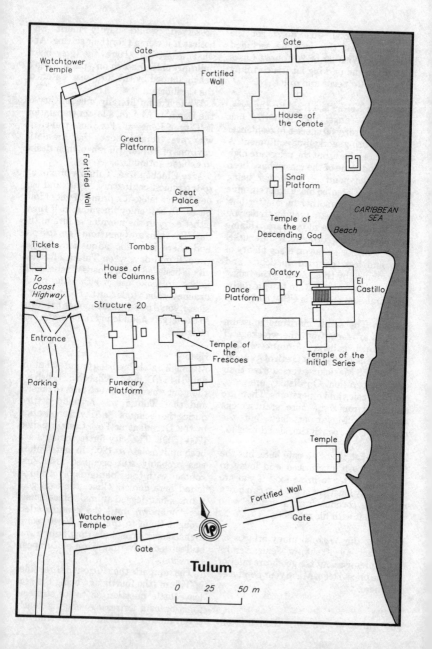

Tulum

0   25   50 m

Top: Day of the Dead, Mérida (TW)
Left: Yucatán Folk Dance, Mérida (JL)
Right: Juice Vendor, Puerto Juárez (TW)

Top: Temple of the Warriors, Chichén Itzá (TW)
Left: La Iglesia De Jesús, Mérida (TW)
Right: The Church, Cobá (TW)

three to five metres high, the walls have an interior walkway from which Tulum's defenders could throw spears or chuck rocks at invaders. There is evidence of considerable strife between Mayan city-states during the Decadent Period. Another theory holds that the wall separated the priest class and nobility living within the city from the peasant huts built outside.

When Juan de Grijalva's expedition sailed by Tulum in 1518, he was amazed by the sight of this walled city with its buildings painted a gleaming red, blue and white and a ceremonial fire flaming atop its seaside watchtower. The city was abandoned about three-quarters of a century after the conquest. Mayan pilgrims continued to visit over the years and Indian refugees from the Caste War took shelter here from time to time.

In 1842, archaeologist John L Stephens and his illustrator Frederick Catherwood visited Tulum by boat. They made substantive drawings and notes which, published in 1848, piqued the curiosity of the outside world. Subsequent expeditions were mounted, the most important being the 1916-1922 investigations by the Carnegie Institute. If you look north along the coast, you will see beyond the walls the huts of archaeologists working here today.

Don't come to Tulum expecting majestic pyramids or anything comparable to the architecture of Chichén Itzá or Uxmal. The buildings here, decidedly Toltec in influence, were the product of Mayan civilisation in decline. Nonetheless, the dramatic setting and well-preserved structures give a tranquil sense of the past.

Information & Orientation

Don't confuse the ruins of Tulum with the town of Tulum. The ruins lie a few minutes' walk from the main highway off an access road. The town of Tulum, a couple of km south of the ruins on Highway 307, offers nothing in the way of lodging or restaurants. Hotels and eateries are found either at the crossroads to the ruins or south of them along the beach. Ask the bus driver to drop you at the crossroads (crucero) to the ruins rather than the town.

Structure 20 & the Funerary Platform

As you enter the city gate, look to the first building on your right, Structure 20. The roof caved in about 1929, making it a bit difficult to envision what once was a royal palace. Painting fragments remain on the walls. Just to Structure 20's right is a Funerary Platform with a cross-shaped grave in its centre. Here archaeologists found skeletons and animal offerings, the latter to provide sustenance for the deceased on the journey to the next world.

Temple of the Frescoes

If you walk straight toward the sea from Structure 20, you will come to the relatively well-preserved Temple of the Frescoes. Thought initially to have been built about 1450, the temple has been added to on several occasions. Here you will see a carved figure very much in evidence at Tulum, the diving god. Equipped with wings and a bird's tail, this fascinating deity has been linked by some archaeologists with the Venus morning-star symbol of Quetzalcóatl. Others believe it bears some relation to the Mayan god of the bee, honey being a valued sweetener and a major Yucatecan trade product. On the western façade are stucco masks thought to symbolise Quetzalcóatl in another form.

Inside the temple the best-preserved of the greenish-blue on black murals may be seen through protective bars. The mural is painted in three levels demarcating the three realms of the Mayan universe: the dark underworld of the deceased, the middle order of the living and the heavenly home of the creator and rain gods. Look closely at the middle level and you will see a god astride a four-legged beast – an image probably indicating knowledge of the conquistadors' horses.

The Great Palace

To the left of the Temple of the Frescoes, as you face the sea, is the Great Palace. Smaller in size only to El Castillo, this largely deteriorated site contains a fine stucco carving of a diving god.

El Castillo

Look straight toward the sea from the Temple of the Frescoes and you can't miss Tulum's tallest building, a watchtower fortress overlooking the Caribbean, appropriately named El Castillo by the Spanish. Over the years, El Castillo was built as a series of additions. It started as a palace-like base, upon which a staircase and a crowning temple were constructed.

Note the serpent columns of the temple's entrance, with rattlers' tails supporting the roof and their heads adjoining the floor. Chichén Itzá's Temple of the Warriors has a similar columnar design influenced by the Toltec plumed serpent. Atop the entrance columns of El Castillo's temple is a fine carving of the diving god.

Take the pyramid-like staircase to the summit's temple for the view. On one side you'll see the luminous Caribbean shimmering in the tropical sun and on the other the antiquities of Tulum. This watchtower guarded the city against sea invasion. Picture how surprised the Mayas of Tulum must have been to spy the sails of the first Spanish ships along this coast.

Look down to the north from El Castillo and you will see a good small beach, great for sunning and a refreshing dip. There's a bit of an undertow here, so swim with caution.

Temple of the Descending God

Facing north (left as you face the sea) from the front of El Castillo, you will see the Temple of the Descending God. True to its name, there is a good stucco carving of a diving god atop the door. If you ascend the inner staircase, you will see paint fragments of a religious mural.

Temple of the Initial Series

At the south flank of El Castillo stands a restored temple named for a stela now in the British Museum, which was inscribed with the date 564. At first this confused archaeologists, who had evidence that Tulum was not settled until some time later. Today, scholars believe that the stela was moved here from a city founded much earlier. This temple has a handsome arch and windows on three sides.

Places to Stay – bottom end

Conveniently located at the crossroads of the main highway and the road which runs one km to the ruins is the appropriately named *El Crucero Motel*. It's a seven to 10-minute walk to the ruins from here. El Crucero has an inexpensive restaurant and small grocery store. Simple rooms with fan and bath cost US$5 single, US$7 double and US$8 triple.

If you want to stay cheaply on the beach, it is roughly a 20-minute walk from the ruins to the *Santa Fe* and *El Mirador* cabañas and campgrounds and just a couple of minutes further down the road to the *Zaacil Kin* cabañas and campgrounds. All of these bare basic bungalows are similar, with tiny Mayan huts containing hammocks for sleeping. Each hut costs US$2.50 per night. There are communal showers and (filthy) pit toilets. Alternatively, camping with tent or hammock costs about US$0.85 per person. Whether you stay in a cabaña or outside bring mosquito repellent, as the beasties are voracious.

All three cabañas have little outdoor restaurants. Overall, budget travellers seemed the happiest at Zaacil Kin. About a km beyond it lies *El Paraíso* cabañas, grossly misnamed as the disrepair of the cabañas and the unkempt facilities have turned 'paradise' into a pigsty.

To reach the seaside cabañas, you can either cut your time in half by walking from the ruins' parking lot on a trail signposted for the Santa Fe Cabañas or stick to the main road until you reach the signposts. If taking the trail at night, be sure to carry a flashlight.

Places to Stay – middle

To reach the following cabañas it is best to have a vehicle, as there are no buses on the road to Boca Paila and few cars, making hitch-hiking difficult. All have simple restaurants.

About 4.5 km south of the ruins is *Cabañas Chac-Mool*, where basic thatch-roofed cabañas with shared hot-water shower and toilet cost US$14. You may also arrange to camp here. About 5½ km south of Cabañas Chac Mool lie the *Cabañas Los Arrecifes*. Here you have a choice of a bamboo-and-thatch Mayan hut sleeping two with a shared bath for US$8, a cottage with private bath costing US$15, or a cottage on the beach with private bath for US$20. Los Arrecifes has a superlative beach and a horse you can rent. Six km south of Los Arrecifes you will find *Cabañas Tulum*. Here basic thatch-roofed bungalows cost US$18 double with bath.

Places to Eat

All the recommended beach-front places have reasonably priced restaurants. *El Crucero Motel* serves inexpensive *típico* Mexican fare. Opposite the Pemex station is a so-so vegetarian restaurant called *Alexandros*. The best restaurant at the crossroads is *El Faisan Y Venado*, featuring hunter's game; prices are moderate.

If you take the beach road south just beyond the end of the pavement, a sign on a tree on the beach side of the road announces 'restaurant'. Their *comida del día*, meal of the day, is superb.

There are cheap taco stands across from the ruins. El Crucero Motel sells food at its mini-store. The town of Tulum has small grocery stores.

Things to Buy

Small shops selling tourist souvenirs and T-shirts cluster around the car park by the ruins. Have a look at Gilberto Silva's stall in the corner. He has some beautiful limestone bas-reliefs of Mayan subjects – very fine work and rather expensive.

Getting There & Away

During the day, buses coming north from Chetumal and south from Cancún stop at the Tulum crossroads about every two hours. If you are venturing between Tulum and points north along the Caribbean coast, try hitch-hiking while you are waiting for the bus as there are many gringos going to or from the ruins in rental cars. Note that 1st-class buses, if filled, may not take you aboard and are reluctant to drop you between Tulum and Akumal. No problem with 2nd class, other than the possibility that you will have to stand if all seats are taken. There are shared long-distance taxis, but they are exorbitant for fares between Tulum and Cancún.

If you are moving on to Cobá, buses leave the *crucero* at 6 am and 12 noon. Buses running south to Tulum stop en route to Chetumal at approximately 6.30, 8 and 10 am, 12 noon, 1.30, 4 and 6 pm. Buses coming north to Tulum en route to Cancún stop at 6.30, 10 and 11.30 am, 12 noon, 2.30, 4 and 4.30 pm and sometimes 7 and 8.30 pm. These schedules vary so be certain to check when you reach this coast. Again, buses that are filled may not stop.

When you arrive at Tulum's crossroads, it's an easy seven to 10-minute walk to the ruins.

BOCA PAILA TO PUNTA ALLEN

If you think you might find a tourist-free paradise by taking the unpaved road to land's-end some 57 km south of Tulum at Boca Paila, forget it. The scenery en route is the typically monotonous flat Yucatecan terrain. Furthermore, the beaches are far from spectacular, though there's no doubt you will find plenty of privacy.

You ultimately meet land's-end at the lobster-fishing village of Punta Allen. While not without some charm, its beaches are less attractive than, say, the sands around Cabañas Los Arrecifes just a short drive from Tulum.

It's important to gas up in Tulum because there is no Pemex station on the Tulum-Punta Allen road.

Places to Stay

One of the two hotels on the road to Punta Allen is *La Villa de Boca Paila*, where luxury cabañas complete with kitchens cost about US$90 per double, including two meals. The clientele is predominantly affluent American fisherfolk. For reservations write to PO Box 159, Mérida, Yucatán, Mexico. Boca Paila is 25 km south of the ruins.

Ten km south of Boca Paila you cross a rickety wooden bridge. Beyond it is *El Retiro Cabañas* where you can hang hammocks or camp for a few dollars.

Punta Allen does have some rustic lodgings. The *Curzan Guest House* has cabañas with hammocks for about US$20 a double. The couple who run it prepare breakfast and lunch at a cost of US$5 per person and charge US$10 for dinner. They can arrange snorkelling and fishing expeditions, or visits to the offshore island of Cayo Colibri, known for its bird life. To write for reservations, the address is Curzan Guest House, c/o Sonia Lillvik, Box 703, Cancún, Quintana Roo, Mexico.

If you wish to camp on Punta Allen's beach, simply ask the Maya in front of whose house you would be sleeping for permission.

COBÁ

Perhaps the largest of all Mayan cities, Cobá – whose grounds extend at least 50 square km – offers the chance to explore nearly pristine antiquities set deep in tropical jungles. Prepare to do some walking on jungle paths and dress for humidity, wear decent footgear and cover yourself with repellent because the rainforest here can be thick with mosquitoes. It's also a good idea to bring a canteen of water because it's hot and the refreshment stands are outside the main gate. Avoid the heat of mid-day.

Don't let all this put you off; no site in the Yucatán Peninsula offers such an opportunity to play at being an archaeologist. The estimated 5% that has been unearthed will reward you by letting you walk the *sacbeab* (avenues) of one of the Mayas' greatest cities.

Cobá is worth visiting for other reasons. On jungle walks, you are likely to see tropical birds, butterflies, reptiles and insects. The ruins are open 8 am to 5 pm and entry is about 25c.

History

Cobá was settled earlier than Chichén or Tulum, its heyday dating from 600 AD until the site was abandoned about 900 AD. Cobá's architecture is a mystery; its towering pyramids and stelae resemble the architecture of Tikal, several hundred km away, rather than that of Chichén Itzá and other sites of northern Yucatán a quarter of that distance.

While there is not yet a definitive explanation, some archaeologists theorise that an alliance with Tikal was made through marriage to facilitate trade between the Guatemalan and Yucatecan Mayas. Stelae appear to depict female rulers from Tikal holding ceremonial bars and flaunting their power by standing on captives. These Tikal royal females, when married to Cobán royalty, may have brought architects and artisans from Guatemala with them.

Archaeologists are also baffled by the network of extensive stone-paved avenues or *sacbeob* in this region, with Cobá as the hub. The longest runs nearly 100 km from the base of Cobá's great pyramid Nohoch

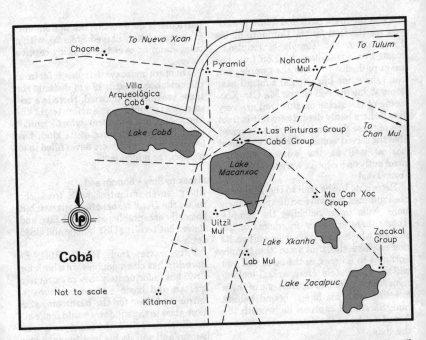

Mul to the Mayan settlement of Yaxuna. In all, some 40 *sacbeob* passed through Cobá. Why did the Mayas build such an extensive road network if they had no pack animals to traverse the wide (some measuring 10 metres across) straight roads? The best guess is that they held both a ceremonial and trade route function.

Archaeologists believe that this vast city once held 40,000 Mayas. They don't know why it was abandoned. The small populace presently inhabiting the region raises the question of what happened to all the people.

The first excavation was by the Austrian archaeologist Teobert Maler. Hearing rumours of a fabled lost city, he came to Cobá alone in 1891. There was little subsequent investigation until 1926 when the Carnegie Institute financed the first of two expeditions led by J Eric Thompson and Harry Pollock. After their 1930 expedition not much happened until 1973, when the Mexican government slowly began to finance excavation. Archaeologists now estimate that Cobá contains some 6500 structures of which just a small percentage have been excavated and restored.

Cobá Group

Soon after you enter the ruins, you will see a right fork designated 'Cobá Group'. Take this path past unexcavated mounds and the rubble of ruins until you come to the enormous pyramid called the Temple of the Churches. Climb to the top of this steep edifice for a view of the Nohoch Mul pyramid to the north and shimmering lakes to the east and south-west. If you continue along this path you will ultimately come to Lake Cobá.

Las Pinturas Group

From the Temple of the Churches, come

back to the main path and follow it until you see the sign for the Conjunto de las Pinturas, or the Temple of Paintings, located on a trail branching off from the main path. En route to the temple, you can take a one-km circular subtrail past some stelae dubbed Grupo Ma Can Xoc. Some of the stelae on this trail are very fine, others badly deteriorated. It is from one of these that archaeologists theorised that the carved woman with the ceremonial bar as well as the woman standing arrogantly on a captive were royal females from Tikal.

Returning to the trail to the Temple of the Paintings, you will find disappointingly bare walls upon reaching the temple. Today there are mere fragments of the murals which once gave this edifice its name. Take the trail from the temple entrance to a break in the bush and you will see a huge stela. Here, a regal-looking man stands over two figures, one of them kneeling with his hands bound behind him. Sacrificial captives lie beneath the feet of a ruler at the deteriorating base of the stela.

Nohoch Mul – The Great Pyramid

Return to the main trail and follow the signs to Nohoch Mul. It's about a 1.5-km walk through lush, humid jungle and though you may be hot and tired at this point, the trek is well worth the effort. At a splendid 42 metres high, the great pyramid is the tallest of all Mayan structures in the Yucatán Peninsula. Climb the 120 steps for a majestic view of the surrounding jungle, observing that the Mayas carved shell-like forms where you put your feet.

There are some diving gods carved over the doorway of Nohoch Mul's temple at the top, similar to the sculptures at Tulum. Apparently this temple at the summit was added onto the pyramid long after it was constructed.

From the great pyramid's face, look to the right in the plaza and you will see Temple 10. The building itself is not

particularly noteworthy, but in front of it is the exquisitely carved Stela 20, with a ruler standing over two kneeling captive slaves.

There are unexcavated ruins as far from the entrance as Ixtil, 19 km distant. For those seeking the unusual, there is a tri-storeyed pyramid near Kucilan (eight km south of Cobá's centre) which, unlike other Mayan structures of its kind, has lower storeys which were never filled in to support the added level.

Places to Stay – bottom end

About seven minutes' walk from the ruins, the *Hotel Isabel* offers spartan but basically acceptable rooms with fans and shared bath costing US$3 single and US$5 double.

Fifty metres from Hotel Isabel, *El Bocadito* has clean doubles with bath for US$6 but unfortunately they're extremely spartan and basic – some furniture, a mirror and door for the bathroom, and more glass in the windows would make all the difference! Still, the manager is very helpful and will do his best to make you comfortable.

Places to Stay – top end

Run by Club Méd, *Villa Arqueológica Cobá* is a gathering spot for archaeologists and those interested in antiquities. There is a library here with the focus on Mayan culture and history, and a study of Mexican, Guatemalan and Honduran archaeological sites. The very pleasant hotel has a swimming pool and good restaurant. Air-conditioned doubles cost about US$50.

For reservations if you are based in the US, phone (800) 528-3100; or when in Mexico City call 203-38-86. You can supposedly make bookings through the travel agent at the Hotel Antillan lobby in Cancún. He's a helpful guy but there's no guarantee that you'll actually find a room reserved for you when you arrive in Cobá! If there's no room available in Cobá they may let you sleep in the library or fix you up with a room in the employees' quarters.

Places to Eat

For *típico* fare, the restaurant of *Hotel Isabel* and the nearby *El Bocadito* are both reasonable. El Bocadito's very helpful manager will go out of his way to make sure you eat well. For a real splurge, figuring close to US$10 without wine, the *Villa Arqueológica Cobá* prepares fine continental cuisine.

Getting There & Away

From Tulum, buses leave the *crucero* for Cobá at 6 am and 12 noon, taking 1½ hours and costing about US$1.35. From Valladolid, buses leave inconveniently for Cobá at 4 am and 2 pm. If you want to come here from Cancún or Puerto Juárez, you will have to transfer at X-Can to catch the bus from Valladolid. No matter which bus you take, tell the driver where you want to disembark or he may not stop.

From Tulum's ruins, you can arrange for a long-distance taxi but it will cost at least US$6 one way. If you start out early enough, and are willing to be patient, you may have some luck hitching as some gringos who rent cars drive between Tulum and Cobá.

If you're driving on from Tulum to Valladolid and Chichén Itzá, don't be fooled by the maps which show a direct road to Chemax. Actually you have to go north to intercept the Cancún-Valladolid road at Nuevo-X-Can.

FELIPE CARRILLO PUERTO

Population: 17,000

Set at the intersection of coastal Highway 307 between Cancún and Chetumal, and Highway 184 heading west to Mérida via Ticul (with an easy side-trip to Uxmal), Felipe Carrillo Puerto has little to offer the tourist. Nonetheless, at 153 km from Chetumal and 247 km from Cancún, some travellers take a pit stop or overnight here. Although not particularly noteworthy for anything else, Felipe Carrillo Puerto is the historic site of the 'Talking Crosses' that inspired Mayan rebels during the Caste Wars. The site is signposted.

Places to Stay

Near the plaza, you will find the *Hotel Esquivel* with clean rooms with fan and bath costing less than US$5, single or double. Just off the plaza is the *Hotel Chan Santa Cruz*, which offers basic rooms with fan and bath at US$5.50, single or double. There are a few US$9 rooms here with air-conditioning.

Places to Eat

One of the chain eateries you might have enjoyed in Tulum, *El Faisan y El Venado*, is situated near the traffic circle. Its speciality is game meats and its prices are moderate. If you want to enjoy air-conditioning and good food in this steaming inland town, try the *Zona Maya*, great for roast chicken and pizza at reasonable prices. It's down the street from El Faisan.

Getting There & Away

Buses running south from Cancún en route to Chetumal stop here, as do buses moving north from Chetumal. There are also buses between Felipe Carrillo Puerto and Mérida. If you want to visit Uxmal, go to the town of Ticul and transfer to an Uxmal-bound bus.

CHETUMAL

Population: 50,000

Chetumal is the undistinguished capital of Quintana Roo state, but there are reasons not to simply pass through here en route to Belize and Guatemala. Bacalar with its beautiful Laguna de Siete Colores (Lake of Seven Colours), the Cenote Azul and Laguna Milagros are within easy range for day trips. If you have your own transportation (or are willing to rent a car or pay for an expensive taxi), there are some ruins – Kohunlich in particular – which archaeology buffs will find of interest.

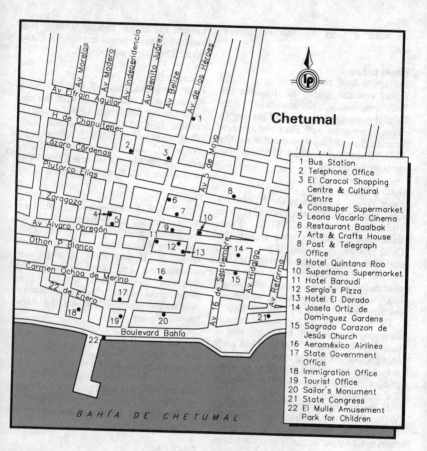

Chetumal

1 Bus Station
2 Telephone Office
3 El Caracol Shopping Centre & Cultural Centre
4 Conasuper Supermarket
5 Leona Vacario Cinema
6 Restaurant Baalbak
7 Arts & Crafts House
8 Post & Telegraph Office
9 Hotel Quintana Roo
10 Superfama Supermarket
11 Hotel Baroudi
12 Sergio's Pizza
13 Hotel El Dorado
14 Josefa Ortiz de Dominguez Gardens
15 Sagrado Corazon de Jesús Church
16 Aeroméxico Airlines
17 State Government Office
18 Immigration Office
19 Tourist Office
20 Sailor's Monument
21 State Congress
22 El Mulle Amusement Park for Children

History

Before the conquest, Chetumal was a Mayan port for shipping gold, feathers, cacao and copper from this region and Guatemala to the northern Yucatán. After the conquest, the town was not actually settled until 1898 when it was dubbed Payo Obispo. In 1936, the name was changed to Chetumal.

Chetumal was virtually obliterated by the 1955 Hurricane Janet, which is why the present buildings look so new. Many houses are built of the mahogany or rosewood abundant in the area (the Mayas called the settlement 'Place of Hard Wood'); as in Belize, many are built on stilts.

The potpourri of people here include black Belizians engaged in trade, British expatriates from Belize, Mayas, and Mexicans from all over the country who come to enjoy Chetumal's status as a duty-free port. Mexicans pay only 6% tax on imports, relative to the 15% tacked on elsewhere.

Information & Orientation

Everything you need in town is within

walking distance. The bus station is not far from the hotels – just follow the Avenida de Los Héroes into town.

Chetumal is hot all year and excruciatingly sticky during the summer months. In winter and early spring, the humidity abates somewhat.

Tourist Office The Palacio Municipal is located where Héroes runs into the bay. The tourist office is on its 2nd floor. The personnel here are helpful and some speak English. The tourist office is open Monday to Friday from 8 am to 2.30 pm and 6 to 10 pm; it's closed on the weekend.

Money For currency exchange, there's a Bancomer at Héroes 6 and a Bánamex at the intersection of Obregón and Juárez. Banking hours are 9.30 am to 1 pm.

Post The post office is three blocks south and two blocks east of the bus station at Plutarco Elias Calles 2A.

Visas Belize requires no visas for entry. There is a Guatemalan Consulate at Obregón 342 (tel 2-13-65). It's open from 9 am to 2 pm Monday to Friday and offers quick visa service.

Things to See
Most of what's worthwhile in the area is outside of Chetumal (see Around Chetumal) but check out the market and the duty-free stores near the bay. If you are really desperate, there's a zoo on the outskirts. Be careful when walking in isolated areas at night, as rip-off artists from Belize City have been known to take advantage of gringos passing through Chetumal.

If you want to go out to a beach, catch a bus either at the terminal or on Avenida Héroes for a 15 to 20-minute, six-km ride to Calderitas Bay. Palapas (thatched roofs) here shelter you from the sun and there are refreshment stands. If you wish to pitch a tent, there's a campsite. Try to avoid Sunday, when the beach is packed with locals and their families on their day off.

Places to Stay – bottom end
Try to find a room early, as budget lodging tends to fill up with people plying the duty-free trade. The *CREA Youth Hostel* is the cheapest place in town, but it is less attractive than other budget lodging because of its inconvenient location quite a walk from the centre of town, its 11 pm curfew and the fact that you have to lodge in single-sex dorm bunks. To get here from the bus station, walk five blocks south and then six blocks east to the hostel at the intersection of Obregón and Calzada Veracruz. The cost is US$1.50 for a dorm bunk with shared bath. Breakfasts are US$0.75 and dinners about US$1 at the hostel's cafeteria.

The *Hotel Baroudi* (tel 2-09-92) on Obregón east of Héroes, a five-block walk from the bus station, is a good budget choice. Clean rooms with fan and bath cost about US$4 single, US$5 for two people sharing a bed, US$6 for two beds. The *Hotel María Dolores* (tel 2-05-08) at Obregón 206 west of Héroes has tiny, stuffy rooms but they are reasonably clean and cheap at US$4 single and US$5.25 double with fans and bath.

If you are exhausted when you get to town, there are two hotels close to the bus station. The *Hotel Ucum* (tel 2-07-11) a block north of the bus station and off to the right at M Gandhi 167 is a good place to know about; when other hotels are filled, this lodge may still have vacancies. It's pretty decent with rooms equipped with fan and bath costing US$5, single or double. *Hotel Tulum* (tel 2-05-18) just above the bus terminal is much less pleasant, with considerable noise from the buses and their patrons. Although Hotel Tulum is cheaper at US$4 for singles, US$5.50 for doubles, Hotel Ucum is preferable.

If you desire a place that's a bit fancier, try *El Dorado* (tel 2-03-15) on Avenida 5 de Mayo 21 (a block east of Héroes between Obregón and O Blanco). Here you will find large immaculate rooms with either fan or air-conditioning for US$6 single and US$8 double.

Places to Stay – middle

At Obregón 193 (also slightly east of Héroes) is the *Hotel Quintana Roo*. Pleasant rooms with fan and bath at this well-managed hotel cost US$9.

Near the bus station, on Calle Belize 186, is the *Hotel Real Azteca*. To find it, walk out the terminal's front door, make a left and walk past the market. Make another left (you'll see a CFE plant on the right) and walk a block to Calle Belize. Make a right and you will see the Hotel Real Azteca. Here air-conditioned singles/doubles with bath cost US$10/12.

Places to Stay – top end

El Presidente (tel 2-05-42) on Avenida Héroes has a swimming pool and restaurant. Air-conditioned rooms with TV cost US$35 to US$40. Across the street from the bus stop, the *Hotel Continental Caribe* (tel 2-04-41) features a couple of swimming pools, restaurant and bar. Air-conditioned rooms run US$27 single, US$30 double.

Places to Eat

The *Restaurant Baalbak*, on Héroes between Plutarco Elias (9a Calle) and Zaragoza, is run by a Lebanese. It has decent *típico* and Middle Eastern fare at moderate prices. Another OK restaurant owned by a Lebanese, the *Restaurant Hadad* on Héroes 42, serves savoury shish kebab. You can get a good exchange rate for dollars here after banking hours.

If you are based near the bus station, *Restaurant Pantoja* next to Hotel Ucum on M Gandhi 164 has good inexpensive Mexican fare. Down on the river bank amid wooden buildings is the newly built *Restaurant Chetumal*; it's on Calle 5 de Mayo a block north-west of Avenida Héroes. At least you get some breeze here

while enjoying excellent Mexican cuisine at moderate prices.

For the cheapest eats, there's a good bakery next to the Hotel María Dolores on Obregón and so-so fare at *Restaurant Milagros* on Zaragoza at Héroes. There are plenty of cheap food stalls in the market near the bus station.

Entertainment

There's a disco at *Hotel El Presidente* and a band plays nightly at *Hotel Continental Caribe*.

Getting There & Away

Air There are a few flights from major Mexican cities to Chetumal's relatively new airport, but to date the service is limited. It is said more flights will be added – so check the schedule. You can fly from here to Mérida.

Bus There are 1st-class buses running north from Chetumal to Cancún at 7 am, 1 pm and 6 pm. (See under Cancún for buses to Chetumal.) These northbound buses can drop you at prominent Caribbean points en route like Tulum, Akumal and Playa del Carmen. There is also a frequent bus service to Mérida and a regular service to Villahermosa. If you are going to Palenque, your best bet is to take a bus to Escárcega and transfer there to a 2nd-class bus for Palenque. There is also service to Mexico City and Campeche, and one daily bus to Tuxtla Gutiérrez.

To Belize & Guatemala Batty Bros Bus Service runs buses from Chetumal to Belize City at 5, 6, 6.45 and 10 am, at 12 noon, and at 1, 1.30 (express), 3 and 5 pm. The run to Belize City takes three to five hours at a cost of about US$4. Change money at the border during customs inspection if you want Belizian currency – the money-changer's rates are comparable to the bank's rates. On Batty Bros 5 and 6 am buses, you can continue with the same bus on to the Guatemalan border (seven hours, US$6) at the town of San Ignacio.

If you are only going to Belize City, the Venus Bus Line also makes the run at the same cost as Batty Bros, departing Chetumal at 8 and 11 am, 2, 4 and 6 pm.

AROUND CHETUMAL
Bacalar
This small town sits on the banks of beautiful La Laguna de Siete Colores – The Lake of Seven Colours – and also has a fortress.

The Lake The lake is well named; depending upon how the sun hits it, the hue may change dramatically, ranging in extremes from violet to vermilion. With its smooth limestone bottom, warm temperature and clear waters, Bacalar is superb for swimming.

The Fortress Bacalar's fortress was built over the lagoon to protect citizens from raids by pirates and Indians. It served as an important outpost for the whites in the Caste War. In 1859, it was seized by Mayan rebels who held the fort until Quintana Roo was finally conquered by Mexican troops in 1901.

Today, with formidable cannon still on its ramparts, the fortress remains an imposing sight. It houses a museum exhibiting colonial armaments and uniforms from the 17th and 18th centuries. The museum is open daily from 8 am to 1 pm and has a small admission charge of 8c.

Places to Stay & Eat Although most travellers stay in Chetumal and make Bacalar a day trip, there is a *Youth Hostel* in the town charging slightly less than US$2 for a dorm bunk with shared bathroom. Its cafeteria provides inexpensive meals. Across from the fort, there is a sporadically open casa de huéspedes charging about US$2.50 per person for a room with fan and shared bath.

For camping there's the *Laguna Milagros Trailer Park* near Hotel Las Lagunas. The rate is less than US$2 to pitch a tent, and facilities include communal showers, toilet, an alfresco café for *típico* fare and a tiny grocery store for provisions.

The *Hotel Las Lagunas*, constructed on a precipice which provides a grand view of the lagoon below, has a swimming pool which is filled during high season and a diving board built over the lake. Pleasant rooms with fan and bath cost US$12 single, US$15.50 double. There is a moderately priced outdoor restaurant on the premises.

Getting There & Away The most comfortable and quickest means to go the 36 km from Chetumal to Bacalar by public transport is to take a combi leaving every 20 minutes or so from a stop on Avenida Cristóbal Colón, two blocks north of the bus depot between Avenida Belize and Avenida Héroes. The first van starts out for Bacalar at 5 am and the last departs Bacalar at 7 pm. The ride takes about a half hour at a cost of about US$1. Cheaper but less comfortable, less punctual and slower are local buses leaving the bus terminal almost every hour and costing about 25c.

Cenote Azul
Only a few km from Bacalar, Cenote Azul offers swimming in a natural well. There is an excellent but expensive restaurant next to the cenote.

Getting There & Away Take the Bacalar combi or bus and get off at the cenote a couple of km from Bacalar.

Laguna Milagros
Although not as picturesque as the lake at Bacalar, Laguna Milagros is still pretty and virtually free of visitors on week days. Bird life can be seen around the lake.

Getting There & Away From Chetumal, you

can find combis running regularly to Laguna Milagros at a stop on Calle M Gandhi between Avenida Belize and Avenida Juárez. The combis are designated 'Xul-ha'.

Xcalak & Chichorro Reef

Xcalak fishing village is accessible via a two-hour boat charter from Chetumal or a rugged drive if you have your own vehicle – take the dirt track running off Route 307 at Limones for 118 km. This village is the little-visited jumping-off point for beaches, good snorkelling and Chinchorro Reef. Chinchorro, about 16 km off the coast, has excellent visibility and divers enjoy exploring the hulks of four galleons sunk around the reef. Xcalak has no hotels but the town has some small stores for provisions.

Kohunlich Ruins

These ruins, dating from the early Classic period (250-600 AD) and largely unexcavated, contain the impressive Pyramid of the Masks. At the end of the main plaza and built in homage to the Mayan god of the sun, the pyramid is carved with three-metre masks of the solar deity. Examination of the facial features reveals Olmec influence, particularly in the thick-lipped mouth.

The hydraulic engineering used at the site was a great achievement; nine of the site's 21 hectares were cut to channel rainwater into Kohunlich's once enormous reservoir.

Kohunlich is largely unexcavated, its nearly 200 mounds covered with vegetation. The surrounding rainforest is thick. Kohunlich's caretaker, Señor Ignacio Ek, may offer you a tour for a few dollars if he is around.

Getting There & Away At this writing, there is no public transport running the 65 km to the site from Chetumal. If you take a bus heading west from Chetumal, you could get off at the small road to the ruins and walk nine km to the site. Then you would have to try to flag down a bus from the main highway back to Chetumal or points west, or hitch-hike (no easy feat here).

Alternatively, you could organise a group of travellers and rent a taxi from Chetumal, but this would be extremely expensive. You'd be better off renting a car with a group.

Chicanna, Becan & Xpuhil Ruins

Unfortunately, visiting these minor yet interesting ruins near the Campeche-Quintana Roo border is difficult without a car. The pristine, mostly unexcavated sites, largely free of tourists, will fascinate true ruins buffs, but be forewarned that those expecting restored ruins like Uxmal and Chichén Itzá are likely to be disappointed.

A few travellers, with camping equipment in case they get stuck, flag down buses or hitch west of Chetumal to visit the ruins; most come by car. Bring insect repellent because the surrounding jungles are insect-infested.

Chicanna, which wasn't discovered until 1967, is about 130 km west of Chetumal. If you arrive by bus, the turn-off road is only a half-km walk to the ruins.

On some doorways of Chicanna's buildings, constructed in Chenes-style, you'll see sculptures of ferocious-faced animals. Also impressive are the twin towers of the restored pyramid, the temple designated Building 2 with a serpent-monster mask reflecting the city's Mayan name, 'The House of the Snake's Mouth'.

The largest of the three sites, Becan (2.5 km east of Chicanna) means 'Path of the Snake' in Mayan. It is well named, as a two-km moat ringing the entire city was built to protect the site from prevalent 2nd-century tribal conflicts. Becan was occupied from 550 BC until 1000 AD.

Yet to be excavated from Becan's profuse jungle cover are subterranean channels linked to religious ritual. Archaeologists have dug up some artefacts from Teotihuacán here, but still must determine whether they got here through trade or conquest.

Six km east of Becan, you will see from the highway the three latticed towers of Xpuhil's pyramid. This temple is the only truly excavated building on the site. It is built in this region's unique Río Bec style with solid towers and extremely steep and narrow steps. There are two sculpted masks carved into the rear of the pyramid. The ruins of Río Bec nearby are accessible only by four-wheel drive when the dirt track is dry.

Veracruz

Civilisation in the Americas probably dawned in the state of Veracruz more than 3000 years ago. Two and a half millennia later, Hernán Cortés established his first base here, bringing face-to-face the two utterly different cultures whose forced marriage created modern Mexico. Today this 600-km-long, 100-km-wide coastal strip has a wide variety of life styles and landscapes.

Veracruz has tropical coast and 5000-metre highlands, traditional Indian societies, one of Mexico's liveliest cities, substantial remains of several intriguing pre-Hispanic cultures, a museum bettered only in Mexico City and famous festivals, lakes and beaches. Yet few visitors spend more than a couple of days here; the main attractions are scattered across the state, so that Veracruz loses out to other, more compact regions. Strongly in its favour, though, is that it's on the way from Mexico City to the Yucatán.

The three outstanding destinations are: the city of Veracruz, Cortés' first beachhead and for four centuries Mexico's biggest port, which today has the country's liveliest zócalo and most exciting spring carnival; El Tajín, the well-preserved centre of a little-understood but sophisticated ancient culture, where Totonac Indians 'fly' from the top of a 30-metre pole in re-enactment of a pre-Hispanic rite; and Jalapa, the hill-country state capital, whose museum's impressively displayed, superb collection includes finds from Mexico's first civilisation, the Olmec.

Also attractive is the green, hilly Los Tuxtlas area in the south, where pleasant Catemaco is a low-key lakeside resort. There are, too, some other ancient sites worth visiting, a town famed for its flowers (Fortín de las Flores), and a number of beach spots – though none of the latter rival the Pacific or Yucatán coasts.

History

Veracruz has literally hundreds of archaeological sites, ranging in time from the Olmecs of 1000 BC to the Aztecs of 1500 AD, but, with the notable exceptions of El Tajín and Zempoala, few of them have been explored and even fewer restored. While enthusiasts may also find trips to San Lorenzo, El Zapotal and some other sites worthwhile, there's more to interest most of us in the state's museums – notably at Jalapa (a must) but also Santiago Tuxtla and Tres Zapotes. For Olmec fans the La Venta collection in a park in Villahermosa, Tabasco, is also a must. Elsewhere, the Mexico City Anthropology Museum has fine collections from all Veracruz cultures, while the Rufino Tamayo Museum in Oaxaca and the Anahuacalli Museum in Mexico City have some good pieces from Classic Veracruz.

Olmec There's evidence of a hunting, fishing and gathering village at Santa Luisa, on the northern Veracruz coast, from as early as a few thousand years BC. Much more importantly, it was in the hot, wet far south of the state, at San Lorenzo, that the first great centre of Central America's first true civilisation, the Olmec, flourished from about 1200 to 900 BC.

This may well have been the first civilisation in the Americas – in South America the Chavín culture of Peru is thought to have begun a little later. The name 'Olmec', which means 'people from the region of rubber' in Nahua, was given in the 1920s to the makers of various ancient objects in a distinctive style which had apparently come from southern Veracruz and neighbouring Tabasco. Typical of the style are representations of 'were-jaguars' – figures which combine the features of human babies and jaguars, probably the mythical offspring of a human female and a jaguar. Also famous are the 'Olmec heads' – basalt sculptures of human heads, probably rulers, up to nearly three metres high with grim, flat, pug-nosed features, wearing curious helmets. Judging by the snarls, sneers and pitiless blank gazes on most of the Olmec faces, it was a society held together by fear of terrifying gods, priests and rulers.

The name 'Olmec' still refers as much to the art style as to any particular group of people, although there were obviously very strong connections between the different places which worshipped the same group of gods and produced carvings in such a unique style. The style persisted for perhaps 1500 years in southern Veracruz and Tabasco; its influence spread far and wide.

After the fall of San Lorenzo, La Venta in Tabasco was the main centre of Olmec power until it too was violently destroyed about 400 BC. Olmec culture lingered on, gradually being influenced from elsewhere, for another 400 years or so at Tres Zapotes, west of San Lorenzo in Veracruz. Given their influence on later art and religion, the Olmecs are now recognised as Mexico's ancestral culture.

After the Olmec decline, the Mayas to the east, the Zapotecs in Oaxaca to the south, and Teotihuacán in the Valley of Mexico all developed major civilisations in what is known as the Classic period (300 to 900 AD). In Veracruz, the main centres of civilisation moved west and northwards. Cerro de las Mesas, a site about 60 km south of Veracruz city, peaked around 400 to 600 AD and, according to different experts, shows influences from the Olmecs, the Mayas, Teotihuacán, Oaxaca and Izapa (in Chiapas), which formed a bridge in time and style between the Olmecs and Mayas.

Classic Veracruz In central and north Veracruz during the Classic period, there arose a number of power centres which were politically independent but shared religion and culture. Surprisingly little is known of this culture despite its wealth of sites and finds, and it is known simply as the Classic Veracruz civilisation. Its

hallmark is a unique, abstract-type carving in which pairs of parallel lines are curved and interwoven to resemble nothing so much as works from the Bronze and Iron ages in China.

The most important centre of Classic Veracruz, El Tajín near Papantla in the north of the state, was at its height about 600 to 900 AD and contains at least 11 ball courts as well as the mysterious Pyramid of the Niches which had, it is thought, 365 small square openings around its sides. Other main centres were Las Higueras near Vega de Alatorre, close to the coast south of Nautla, and El Zapotal near Ignacio de la Llave, south of Veracruz city. These and others were probably politically independent of each other, and El Tajín at least appears to have been a place where ordinary people lived, as well as a ceremonial centre.

Classic Veracruz, like other pre-Hispanic Mexican cultures, didn't exist in isolation. Its influence is apparent at Teotihuacán and Cholula, for instance, and Veracruz sites show Mayan and Teotihuacán influence. Exports to central Mexico of products like cotton, rubber, cacao and vanilla grown in fertile Veracruz helped the region develop.

Totonacs, Toltecs & Aztecs El Tajín was abandoned about 1200 AD, possibly destroyed by nomadic Chichimecs from the north. By this time the Totonacs, a people who may have occupied El Tajín in its later years, were establishing themselves from Tuxpan in the north to beyond Córdoba in the south. North of Tuxpan was the Huastec civilisation (see the chapter on North-East Mexico).

According to various accounts, the Totonacs had originated either in northern Veracruz or at Chicomoztoc near Zacatecas and then participated in the great era of Teotihuacán, where they helped build the great pyramids. From there they moved east some time after 450 AD, first establishing a centre at Mixquihuacán, near Zacatlán in mountainous north

Puebla, then – perhaps prompted by Chichimecs – pushing on into Veracruz. Here they developed a number of small independent groups.

The era from 900 to 1521 is known as the Post-Classic. The warrior-like Toltecs who dominated Central Mexico in the early Post-Classic age occupied the Huastec centre Castillo de Teayo in north Veracruz, and Toltec architecture or objects have been found at two important Totonac sites in central Veracruz, Zempoala and Isla de los Sacrificios.

Later, the Aztecs too turned their sights east. Between 1440 and 1469 they subdued most of the Totonac and Huastec areas. The remains of Totonac centres near Veracruz city like Zempoala, Isla de Sacrificios and Quiahuiztlán all show Aztec influence.

When Hernán Cortés turned up in Veracruz with his 11 ships and 550 men in 1519, he found that the Aztecs controlled virtually all of the region and were exacting costly tribute of goods and sacrificial victims from the Totonacs and from the Popolocas to their south. They were also maintaining garrisons to control the frequent revolts by these subject peoples.

Colonial Era The situation was tailor-made for the Machiavellian Cortés, who aimed to conquer the Aztec empire and grab the fabulous hordes of gold and silver which earlier Spanish expeditions had heard about. For a description on his tactics see the 'History' section in the 'Facts About the Country' chapter.

Cortés set up a small settlement called Villa Rica de la Vera Cruz (Rich Town of the True Cross), north of the present city, and appointed town officials who duly elected him their leader. Most of what is now the state of Veracruz came into Spanish hands with the fall of the Aztec empire. Cortés sent out a force which secured the far south of the state by 1522, and the north was subdued by a series of expeditions culminating in Cortés' own expedition to the Huasteca in 1523.

Control of Veracruz harbour became essential for anyone trying to govern Mexico. The fate of Mexico turned on events here many times – but for most of the locals in the hot, damp state life was pretty miserable.

The Indian population was drastically reduced in the 16th century by a combination of diseases which had long plagued it and new ones like smallpox brought by the Spanish. The case of Zempoala, which declined from about 30,000 people in 1519 to eight families in 1609, was not unusual.

In addition to the famous names who came and went through Veracruz, large numbers of black slaves also arrived here, contributing a sizeable element of the racial mix that is Mexico today. By 1600 there were about 140,000 blacks and people of part-black ancestry in Mexico.

Apart from Veracruz itself, the chief Spanish towns were founded on the cooler, healthier inland slopes: Orizaba in the 16th century as a garrison on the Veracruz-Mexico City road; Córdoba in 1618; and Jalapa, which became a trade centre in the 18th century, on the site of an Indian town.

19th & 20th Centuries The Veracruz coast was so uninviting that the population of Veracruz city actually decreased during the first half of the 19th century. However, Mexico's first railway linked Veracruz, Córdoba, Orizaba and Mexico City in 1872, and some industries developed towards the end of the century under dictator Porfirio Díaz. As elsewhere in the country, a little industrialisation was accompanied by a lot of repression.

In 1906 textile workers' leaders in Veracruz state began to organise in the Gran Círculo de Obreros Libres (Great Circle of Free Workers), and workers in the Río Blanco textile mills near Orizaba complained to Díaz about their 12-hour day, miserable wages, censorship of what

they read and the fact that they had to pay for depreciation of the mill machinery. Díaz supported the mill owners and the workers went on strike (which was not allowed). Women were refused credit at the workers' shop, fighting and shooting started, the shop was burnt down, troops arrived and shot into the crowd, the workers dispersed and came back later to collect the bodies and were shot at again. An estimated 100 died. This was one of the main incidents leading to the revolution against Díaz a few years later.

At that time the state of Veracruz had about one million people, the sixth highest population in Mexico. Today it has over six million and is the third most populous state – a growth partly attributable to its oil wealth. The north of the state has been an oil industry centre since early this century and, following the later discovery of new fields in the south, by the 1980s Veracruz had half Mexico's petroleum reserves and one-third of its refining capacity.

The state's diverse climatic zones yield a huge range of agricultural products – from coffee and orchids in the hills to cotton and maize in the coastal lowlands and wood and rubber in the southern tropical forests. Sugar refining and fishing are also major industries.

Despite wages in the industrial centre of Orizaba being as high as in Mexico City or Monterrey (around US$1.25 an hour), the state in general is a poor one. This is probably due to the dominance of agriculture – 38% of the Veracruz workforce are on the land or in fishery, against a national average of 26%. Today Veracruz has more people in the lowest pay brackets, more illiterates (34%), more one-room dwellings (38%) and more homes without access to piped water (49%) than most states in Mexico.

Geography & Climate

The Veracruz coastline curves 684 km along the Gulf of Mexico (about 575 km from end to end). The state spreads inland for 40 to 140 km, giving a total area of 71,699 square km. Most of it is below 500 metres in altitude, but the Sierra Madre Oriental protrudes into parts of the north-west, and Mexico's central volcanic belt stretches well into central Veracruz. The country's highest mountain, the 5700-metre Pico de Orizaba, is here, on the border of Veracruz and Puebla.

The state receives warm wet winds from the Atlantic in summer and autumn, and cooler winds from the north, usually dry but sometimes bringing drizzle, in winter and spring. Nevertheless it's warm and humid most of the time: hotter along the coast, wetter in the mountains, hottest and wettest of all in the low-lying south-east. Two-thirds or more of the rain falls between June and September.

The city of Veracruz receives about 165 cm of rain a year, with temperatures well into the 30s (°C) in the wet months and falling into the teens at night only from December to February. Tuxpan, on the northern coast, is a little drier, a little hotter in summer and a fraction cooler in winter. Córdoba, on the inland slopes, has around 230 cm of rain a year, with temperatures rarely reaching the 30s and sometimes sinking into single figures. Coatzacoalcos, on the southern coast, gets 300 cm of rain a year and is a couple of degrees warmer than Veracruz city.

As you travel across the hot dry highlands from Mexico City or Puebla towards Jalapa or Orizaba, you often notice thick bands of cloud stretching across the horizon ahead. These mark the top of the slope down from the central highlands to the Veracruz coast, and immediately you start to descend this slope you enter a different climatic world. It's remarkable to notice how the brown aridity of the highlands suddenly gives way to thick green vegetation within a few hundred metres of the start of cloud cover.

More than 40 rivers, running down from the Sierra Madre, the volcanic belt and the mountains of Oaxaca and Chiapas in the south, cross Veracruz. In the south-east they help create the low-lying, jungly, marshy area prone to flooding which gave rise to the Olmec civilisation 3000 years ago.

People

You'll probably notice quite a few people with a negroid touch to their features in coastal Veracruz – these are the descendants of African slaves brought in by the Spanish and of immigrants from Cuba. The state's six million-plus population also includes about 400,000 Indians.

Totonacs Eastern Mexico's most famous pre-Hispanic rite, the *voladores* (fliers), is now performed regularly for tourists at El Tajín, Papantla and Zempoala. Five men in highly colourful costumes climb to the top of a 20-metre-high free-standing pole. Four sit on a tiny wooden platform, each tying a rope to one ankle, while the fifth dances, bangs a drum and plays a whistle on an even tinier platform above them. Suddenly he stops and the others jump off into thin air. Upside down, arms outstretched, they slowly revolve round the pole and descend to the ground as their ropes unwind.

This 'dance' is full of symbolism but almost everyone you ask will give a different account of its meaning. One version is that the five men are the sun and the four seasons, and that the four fliers each circle the pole 13 times. This gives a total of 52 revolutions, which is not only the number of weeks in the modern year but also an important number in pre-Hispanic Mexico which had two calendars. One calendar corresponded to the 365-day solar year, the other to a ritual year of 260 days, with a day in one meeting a day in the other only every 52 solar years.

You may also be told that the four fliers are connected with the compass points and the fifth man is the centre of the universe, or that the whole thing is a maize fertility rite, or that the dancers represent macaws (their costumes are bright enough) which in turn symbolise the sun.

In pre-Hispanic times the ceremony was widespread, particularly in eastern Mexico. Today it's practised mainly by Totonacs, but also sometimes by their Otomí, Nahua and Huastec neighbours in north Puebla and north-west Veracruz.

The Totonacs dominated most of north and central Veracruz in the centuries before the Spanish conquest, but from the mid-15th century came under the repressive domination of the Aztecs. The Totonacs of Zempoala in the centre of the state became Hernán Cortés' first allies in Mexico, seeing the Spanish as an opportunity to throw off the Aztec yoke. But since the early colonial days they have fared no better than other Indian groups. Totonac rebels occupied Papantla briefly in 1836.

The territory occupied by modern-day Totonacs is shared with mestizos and other Indians and extends from Tecolutla on the Veracruz coast inland to the southern Sierra Madre Oriental in northern Puebla. There are about 80,000 Totonacs in Veracruz and 60,000 in Puebla. Traditional beliefs and customs are stronger in the remoter mountain areas. The chief Totonac gods are their ancestors, the sun (which is also the maize god) and St John (also the lord of water and thunder). Venus and the moon are identified with Qotiti, the devil, who rules the kingdom of the dead beneath the earth.

The Catholic religious calendar is superimposed on more ancient practices: the Day of the Holy Cross (3 May) coincides with ceremonies for the fertility of the earth and new seeds, the Day of St John the Baptist (24 June) is the traditional beginning of the rainy season. Some Totonacs apparently believe that the world is flat, the sky is a dome, and the sun travels beneath the earth at night.

Tepehuas This small group of quite traditional Indians, numbering about 7000, is scattered around the foothills of the Sierra Madre west of Poza Rica where the states of Veracruz, Puebla and Hidalgo meet. About 5000 of them are in Veracruz, in and around San Pedro Tlilzacuapan and Pisaflores near Ixhuatlán de Madero, and Chintiapan near Tlachichilco. A road from Tuxpan to Alamo, Ixhuatlán and Tlachichilco gives access to this region, known as Chicontepec.

Tepehua women wear white blouses and skirts embroidered with animal designs. The old Tepehua religion is still strong: the sun god is believed to control human lives, while the moon is a malign male being and the stars have to stand guard over the sun while it rises. The Tepehua also believe in witchcraft and in gods of natural things like trees, hills and rivers.

Other Indian Groups About half of Veracruz's 400,000 Indians are Nahua, many of whom live in the state's western highlands. There are also about 50,000 Huastecs in the far north, 15,000 Otomíes in the north-west, 20,000 Popolucas in the south-east, and around 15,000 Zapotecs. For more on the Nahua, Huastecs and Otomíes, see under Puebla state, North-East Mexico and Hidalgo state respectively.

VERACRUZ

Population: 400,000

As a coastal resort, the port city of Veracruz has less to offer than most places on the Pacific or Yucatán coasts (though its relative cheapness makes it a favourite among Mexicans). But it's one of the liveliest truly Mexican cities, with a tropical port atmosphere, a zócalo that swings late into the evening, and the biggest carnival between Rio de Janeiro and New Orleans. An hour away are the Totonac ruins of Zempoala.

The people of Veracruz, known as Jarochos, are fairly relaxed and the café life is good here. The harbour, close to the city centre, is still busy, though these days overshadowed by oil ports to the north and south like Tampico, Coatzacoalcos and Ciudad del Carmen. Nevertheless Veracruz maintains a strong sense of self-sufficiency.

People from Mexico City flood down here at weekends and holiday times. At Christmas, Carnival (the week before Ash Wednesday), and Semana Santa (the week before Easter) hotel prices tend to go up, and the city and nearby beaches are jam-packed with visitors. It's well worth booking accommodation and transport in advance if you're going to be in Veracruz at these times.

History

From the day Cortés landed here in 1519 until the coming of the aeroplane, Veracruz was Mexico's main gateway to the outside world. Foreign invaders and pirates, past and future rulers of Mexico, governments in exile, rebels, settlers, silver, saints, slaves – all these came and went to make the city a linchpin in the country's history, second to none except the capital.

The Spanish Anchoring off San Juan de Ulúa on Good Friday, 21 April 1519, Cortés reconnoitred what is now downtown Veracruz the following day, made his first contact with Moctezuma's envoys, and baptised the place Villa Rica de la Vera Cruz (Rich Town of the True Cross). But it wasn't here that he set up the settlement of the same name, his first on Mexican soil. That seems to have been originally at Quiahuiztlán, a Totonac settlement north of Zempoala, and later at La Antigua, between Zempoala and Veracruz. It was finally established on the present site of Veracruz in 1598. San Juan de Ulúa, however, remained the most important anchorage and was fortified from as early as 1535.

Until 1760 Veracruz was the only port allowed to handle trade with Spain. Tent cities blossomed here for trade fairs when the annual fleet from Spain arrived, but despite its importance Veracruz was never one of Mexico's biggest cities. Even in the second half of the 19th century it had only about 10,000 people. This was partly due to its unhealthy coastal climate, with malaria and yellow fever rampant (even the trade fair was moved to healthier Jalapa between 1720 and 1777), and, in the early days, to frequent foreign raids which made it a dangerous place to live.

Other Europeans The English and the French challenged Spain's control of the Caribbean and in 1567 an English fleet under John Hawkins sailed into Veracruz harbour with the intention of selling some black slaves. The nine English ships were trapped by a Spanish fleet arriving with a new viceroy and only two escaped. One of them, however, carried Francis Drake, who went on to harry the Spanish mercilessly in a long career as a sort of licensed pirate.

The most vicious attack on Veracruz came in 1683 when 600 pirates under a Frenchman called Lorencillo stormed its fortifications, held the 5000 citizens in the parish church with little food or water, killed any who tried to escape, piled the Plaza de Armas with loot, got drunk, raped many of the women, threatened to blow up the church unless the people revealed where their secret stashes were hidden, and left a few days later 600,000 pesos richer.

Santa Anna At Veracruz in 1822 a young officer in the army of newly-independent Mexico, Antonio López de Santa Anna, took the first step in an opportunistic career which saw him, despite countless personal and national disasters, become a popular hero, surviving numerous wars and rebellions, and dominating Mexican politics for three decades. Santa Anna was commander of the force charged with driving the Spanish from their last Mexican toehold, San Juan de Ulúa. The new self-proclaimed emperor, Agustín Iturbide, suspected him of planning to turn Veracruz over to the enemy and

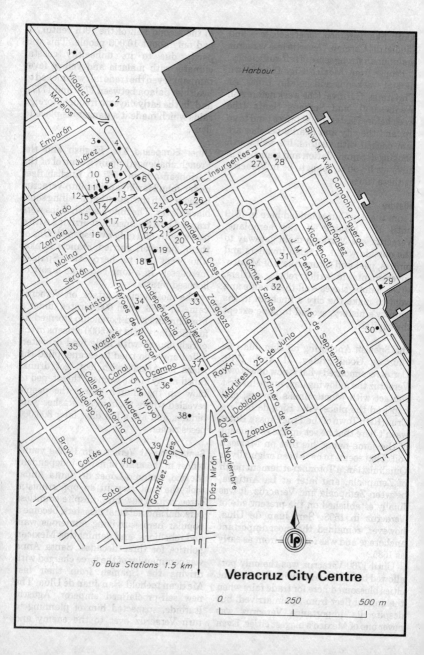

Harbour

Veracruz City Centre

0   250   500 m

To Bus Stations 1.5 km

1	Railway Station
2	Post Office
3	Hotel Rex
4	Plaza de la República
5	Buses to San Juan de Ulúa
6	Hotel Oriente
7	Hotel Rias
8	Hotel Concha Dorada
9	Hotel Colonial
10	Bar Palacio
11	Hotel Imperial
12	Hotel Prendes
13	Palacio Municipal & Tourist Office
14	Plaza de Armas (Zócalo)
15	Gran Hotel Diligencias
16	Gran Café de la Parroquia
17	Cathedral
18	Plaza de la Campana
19	Hotel La Carmelita
20	Hotel Santillana
21	Hotel Amparo
22	Restaurant-Bar La Gaviota
23	Buses to Mocambo & Boca del Río
24	Hotel Vigo
25	Hotel Puerto Bello Centro
26	Gran Café de la Parroquia (Insurgentes Branch)
27	Hotel Emporio
28	Carranza Museum
29	Hotel Mar Y Tierra
30	Hotel Villa Rica
31	Hotel Baluarte
32	Baluarte de Santiago
33	City Cultural Museum
34	Cocina Económica Elia
35	Hospedaje Hatzín
36	Café Catedral
37	La Merced Café
38	Parque Zamora
39	Hotel México
40	Mercado Hidalgo

ordered him back to Mexico City. Instead, Santa Anna proclaimed a republic and, joined by independence heroes like Guerrero and Guadalupe Victoria, ousted Iturbide.

Fourteen years later Santa Anna, now president, was back in Veracruz to renounce his promises to the Texans who had just defeated him in the north. In 1838, so the story goes, Santa Anna, under bombardment from a French fleet during the 'Pastry War', fled the city in his underwear – only to make a heroic return, driving the invaders from the city and losing his left leg in the process.

Santa Anna was in Mexico City during the Mexican-American war when the 10,000-strong invading army of Winfield Scott turned up at Veracruz in 1847. The city surrendered after a week-long bombardment which killed over 1000 Mexicans including many civilians. Fittingly, it was through Veracruz that Santa Anna left Mexico when finally deposed in 1855.

Occupation A few years later the city was host to the liberal government of Benito Juárez during the Reform War, an internal Mexican affair. Here in 1859 the liberals scored an important victory in that war and promulgated their reform laws, nationalising church property and putting education into secular hands.

Events took an international turn again in 1861. Juárez, having won the Reform War, said Mexico couldn't pay its foreign debts. Encouraged by his conservative opponents, a joint French-Spanish-British force occupied Veracruz. The British and Spanish planned to take over only the Veracruz customs house and recover what Mexico owed them, but Napoleon III of France was looking for an empire, and planned to conquer Mexico. Realising this, the British and Spanish went home. The French marched inland to begin their five-year intervention. When their puppet ruler of Mexico, Maximilian, arrived at Veracruz with his wife Carlota in 1864, they received such a cool welcome that Carlota was reduced to tears.

All these hostilities, added to the ever-present yellow fever and malaria, did little for Veracruz's popularity and during the first half of the 19th century its population shrank by half to about 7000. The country's first railway linked Veracruz with Mexico City in 1872, but the port was by then so silted up that the town's abandonment was considered.

Under the dictatorship of Porfirio Díaz, investment was poured into the city and the harbour was improved, but Díaz's lack of popularity in the rest of the country was such that he was ousted in the revolution of 1910-11 and departed for exile – via Veracruz.

The 20th Century After Díaz's departure, new civil wars brought American troops back to Veracruz. President Woodrow Wilson, meddling in Mexican affairs and opposed to the conservative dictator Victoriano Huerta, ordered occupation of the city in April 1914 to stop a delivery of German arms for Huerta. Even Huerta's revolutionary and reform-minded opponents denounced the US intervention after heavy Mexican casualties, including civilians, but they took advantage of the sidetracking of Huerta's forces and he was forced to resign the same year. Soon afterwards his victorious opponents fell apart in quarrels, and for a while Veracruz was the capital of the Constitutionalist faction led by Venustiano Carranza.

Veracruz is now officially titled 'four times heroic', referring to the final expulsion of the Spanish in 1825, the triumph over the French in the Pastry War and the resistance to the Americans in 1847 and 1914.

Orientation

Downtown Veracruz is between and around two plazas about 700 metres apart, linked by the street Independencia running roughly north-south. Many of the streets in this area are restricted to pedestrians-only. The centre of the city's action is the more northerly Plaza de Armas, or zócalo, which has the cathedral, Palacio Municipal (city hall), and numerous cafés and restaurants. The harbour is half a km east of here.

The other plaza is Parque Zamora, which is a multiple road junction with a wide green area in the middle. Near here is the main market. Two km south along Díaz Mirón are the 1st and 2nd-class bus stations.

The post office and rail station are on Plaza de la República, half a km north of the zócalo.

Information

Tourist Office The city and state tourist office (tel 32-99-42) is on the ground floor of the Palacio Municipal, facing the zócalo. The staff are well-informed (even about city buses), helpful and usually English-speaking. Hours are 9 am to 9 pm daily. The office has information on exhibitions, concerts and other cultural events in the city. There's also a national tourist office (tel 32-16-13) which deals with problems and complaints but gives information too; it's close by at Zaragoza 20 (entrance in No 24).

Money Banks include Bánamex and Bancomer on Independencia one block north of the zócalo.

Post The post office (tel 32-20-38) is at Plaza de la República 213 and is open 8 am to 8 pm Monday to Friday, 8 am to 1 pm Saturday. The lista de correos keeps mail for 10 days only, but the poste restante holds it for a month.

Consulates The American Consulate (tel 31-01-42, 36-12-78) is at Juárez 110. The city tourist office has details on at least 11 other consulates in the city.

The Zócalo

This square, also called the Plaza de Armas, Plaza Lerdo and Plaza de la Constitución, is the hub of the city for Jarochos and visitors alike. It has palm trees, a fountain, the fine 17th-century Palacio Municipal on one side and the 18th-century cathedral, also known as the *parroquia* (parish church), on another.

People are the main attraction. One side of the zócalo is lined with cafés designed for sipping beer or coffee while people-watching. Here in the space of a few minutes you might see a man selling a two-metre-long model of a sailing ship, prostitutes meeting Korean sailors, a middle-class family trying to control its children, a visiting band of New England folk dancers, another man selling leaping foam-rubber lizards with flashing eyes – all to the accompaniment of wandering mariachis, marimba-players, trumpeters and guitarists vying to be heard above each other. The zócalo is busy and noisy every night into the early hours, especially at weekends.

Harbour

Ferries no longer run across the harbour to San Juan de Ulúa, but you can stroll along Insurgentes (also called Paseo del Malecón) and view the ships and derricks across the water. Near the corner of Insurgentes and Figueroa is a monument to the defenders of the city against the Americans in 1914.

San Juan de Ulúa

This fortress, once on an island, is linked to the mainland by a causeway across the north side of the harbour. The island was named in 1518 by Juan de Grijalva who landed here during an exploratory voyage along the Mexican coast from Cuba: He found four priests at a shrine to Tezcatlipoca, the Aztec smoking mirror god. The next year Cortés also landed here and it became the main entry point for early Spanish newcomers to Mexico. The Franciscan chapel is thought to have been built in 1524. The first fortifications went up in the 1530s but what we see now was mostly built between 1552 and 1779. San Juan de Ulúa was the last bit of Mexico to become independent from Spain; the Spanish garrison here refused to surrender until 1825, four years after the last viceroy had recognised Mexican independence.

The fortress was not only a garrison and defence for the harbour but also a prison – most notoriously under Porfirio Díaz who reserved three stinking dungeons known

as Las Tres Potrancas (The Three Fillies) or El Purgatorio, La Gloria and El Infierno (Purgatory, Glory and Hell) for political prisoners. These cramped cells were in the central part of the fortress called the Fuerte San José (San José Fort) and were so damp that stalactites formed. Many of the prisoners died of yellow fever or tuberculosis. Díaz himself bade farewell to Mexico from San Juan de Ulúa, but wasn't consigned to one of his own dungeons.

From 1916 to 1960 the fortress was an ammunition factory. Today it's an empty, romantic ruin of passageways, battlements, bridges and stairways, which you can wander round between 9 am and 5 pm Tuesday to Sunday (entry fee 11c, except Sundays and holidays when it's free).

To get there, take a 'San Juan de Ulúa' bus (8c) from in front of the souvenir shops on Landero y Coss near the corner of Lerdo. They depart about every half-hour. The last bus back to town leaves at 5 pm.

Museums

Carranza Lighthouse On Insurgentes between Xicoténcatl and Hernández stands the Carranza Lighthouse. There is a statue of revolutionary hero Venustiano Carranza in the front and inside is the small Carranza Museum, containing pictures and documents of the life of the man whose government was based in Veracruz for a time. One room is preserved as it was when Carranza and others formulated the Mexican constitution here in 1914-15. The museum is open from 9 am to 1 pm and 4 to 6 pm Tuesday to Friday, 10 am to 2 pm and 5 to 7 pm Saturday, Sunday and holidays. Entry is free.

Baluarte de Santiago Of the nine forts which once surmounted a defensive wall round the city, Baluarte de Santiago is the only survivor. It was built in 1526 and now houses small exhibitions. At the corner of Canal and 16 de Septiembre, it is open daily from 10 am to 7 pm and admission is free.

City Cultural Museum The Museo Cultural de la Ciudad, at the corner of Zaragoza and Morales, has pre-Hispanic artefacts from the Veracruz region and displays on its history and Indian cultures.

Beaches & Lagoons

Isla de los Sacrificios – where in 1518 Juan de Grijalva found the bodies of two sacrificial victims with the hearts torn out – used to be a popular island beach but is now closed to the public for conservation purposes. The cleanest and least crowded beaches are south of the city at Costa de Oro and Mocambo.

Mocambo, 10 km south of the city centre, is easier to reach and has palm sunshades, public swimming pools and paddling pools in front of the big Hotel Mocambo. To get there take a 'Boca del Río – Mocambo' bus from Serdán between Zaragoza and Landero y Coss.

Beyond Mocambo the road crosses the mouth of the Río Jamapa at Boca del Río. The left fork just over the bridge continues along the coast to Isla del Amor and Mandinga (21 km from Veracruz), both of which have a few seafood restaurants and boats for hire to explore the lagoons behind them.

Carnival

Veracruz breaks into a nine-day party before Ash Wednesday (February or March) each year. Starting the previous Tuesday, there are brilliantly colourful and imaginative parades through the city every day, beginning with one devoted to the 'burning of bad humour' and ending with the 'funeral of Juan Carnaval'. Other organised events include fireworks, traditional and modern dances and music (plenty of salsa and samba), children's parades, a mini-marathon, and handicraft, food and folklore shows. The informal side of the proceedings is equally attractive, with most people hell-bent on having as

good a time as possible and a festive atmosphere taking over the whole city. It's easy to pick up a programme of events when you're there.

Places to Stay

Hotel prices in Veracruz are reasonable, though they go up at peak periods like Christmas, Carnival and Semana Santa. There's a clutch of good-value places around the zócalo; you pay more on the seafront but there are a couple of decent deals there too. There are also some cheap but decent hotels around the bus stations and a few more places near the market. In the cheapest places you may not get hot water.

Places to Stay – bottom end

Zócalo Area Right on the zócalo at Lerdo 153, the *Hotel Imperial* (tel 31-16-41) is an ancient fort-like building with coats of arms on the walls and an antique caged lift rising from the middle of a cavernous lobby. It hasn't been decorated for years but somehow that adds atmosphere. Rooms are slightly musty but clean enough and have fans and private baths. Singles/doubles are US$4.25/5.25 with a balcony and zócalo view, US$3.25/3.75 without.

A few doors along the zócalo, the *Hotel Concha Dorada* (tel 31-31-21) at Lerdo 77 has singles/doubles (some air-conditioned) for US$3/4, as well as two-person suites for US$5. Round the corner from here at Morelos 359, the *Hotel Rias* (tel 32-42-46) is basic with singles/doubles at US$2.50/3 including fan and private bath. The *Hotel Rex* (tel 32-54-36), a block further up Morelos at 226, is a crumbling, shabby ex-convent with lots of cats, friendly if eccentric staff, wide walkways, beautiful tiles and two church domes rising behind an untidy pillared courtyard. The rooms are big, with bathrooms, fans and peeling paint, and front onto a noisy road. Singles/doubles are US$2/3.

A block south-east of the zócalo at Molina 56 on the corner of Landero y Coss, the *Hotel Vigo* (tel 32-45-29) has basically clean rooms, most with fans, for US$3 single or double. Rooms on the street get more light but are noisier.

A little further south at Landero y Coss 209, the *Hotel Santillana* (tel 32-31-16) has clean, quite big rooms with tile floors, green walls and blue-and-white striped bedspreads. Singles are US$3.25, doubles with one bed US$4.25, doubles with two beds US$5.75. The *Hotel Amparo* (tel 32-27-38) at Serdán 482, between Trigueros and Zaragoza, has exactly the same colour scheme as the Santillana but the private bathrooms are a little smaller. Doubles are the same price, singles US$0.50 less.

One of the cheapest places in Veracruz is the *Hotel La Carmelita* (tel 32-26-08) in a narrow pedestrian alley 2½ blocks south of the zócalo at Plaza de la Campana 42. Rooms could be cleaner but have fans and usually small private baths. Singles/doubles are US$1.50/2.50.

The *Hospedaje Hatzín* (tel 32-15-71) is as near to Parque Zamora as to the zócalo, but not too far from either at Callejón Reforma 6 between Arista and Morales. It's

clean and the owner is friendly. Singles/doubles cost US$2.50/3.25. The rooms are small but those on the upper floor are breezier and there's an open walkway outside them. All rooms have fans, some have private baths and the communal bathrooms are clean.

Bus Station Area Opposite the 2nd-class bus station at Lafragua 1100 the *Hotel Rosa Mar* (tel 37-07-47) is clean and friendly, and has parking space. Rooms are sizeable, with private bath and fan. Singles cost US$3.75; doubles cost US$5.25 with one bed, US$6.25 with two beds.

The *Hotel Impala* (tel 37-01-69), half a block away at the corner of Lafragua and Orizaba, is also clean, with similar-size rooms at US$3.75 single, US$5.75 for two people in a double bed.

Hotel Cheto (tel 37-42-41) at 22 de Marzo 218, on the corner of Orizaba, is a pink bungalow with a small yellow courtyard and a friendly owner. All rooms have fans, and private baths which could be cleaner. Singles/doubles (one bed) are US$3.50/4.25.

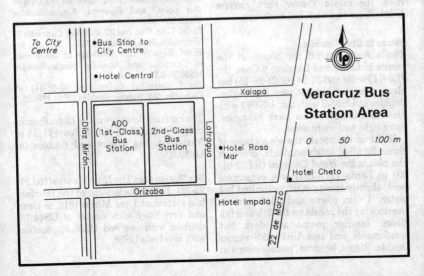

Market Area The *Hotel México* (tel 32-48-31) at González Pages 77, next to the south-east corner of the market, has very minor pretensions to style in an unlikely part of town. Some rooms have fans and balconies with table and chair overlooking a busy street, others have carpets and antiquated air-con. All cost US$2.75 single, US$4.25 double.

The *Hotel La Palma* (tel 32-47-31) at González Pages 330, a block south of the junction with Hidalgo, has tolerably clean rooms with private bath and hot water for US$2.75 single, US$3.75 double.

Boca del Río Thirteen km south of the city centre, this quiet riverside town known for its seafood has the *Hotel Boulevard* at Calle Zamora 211 or 304. Tolerably clean, medium-sized rooms cost US$3 for one double bed, US$3.75 for two.

Camping There are two trailer parks in Mocambo, 11 km south of the city centre. Both are on the main road, Carretera Mocambo-Boca del Río. *Parador Los Arcos* (tel 37-40-75) charges US$3 for two people per day with full hook-ups. Next door, the *Fiesta Trailer Park* charges US$1.75 for two with full hook-ups.

Places to Stay – middle
Zócalo Area Just off the zócalo at the corner of Lerdo and Landero y Coss, the *Hotel Oriente* (tel 31-24-90, 31-26-15) has clean, pleasant but not very big singles/doubles at US$5/6 with fan, US$6/7 with air-con. Outside rooms have balconies, more light and more noise.

Right on the zócalo there's a choice of three dignified establishments, of which the pick is the *Hotel Colonial* (tel 32-01-93) at Lerdo 117. There's a swimming pool, slightly snooty staff, unlimited hot water, TV in rooms and tiled terraces overlooking the zócalo on the 5th and 6th floors. Interior rooms are dark but comfortable and cost US$7.25/8 single/double. Bigger, brighter, noisier rooms at

the front are US$7.75/9.25. There are also suites from US$13.25.

The *Hotel Prendes* (tel 31-02-41) at the corner of Lerdo and Independencia has very comfortable air-conditioned rooms with a phone, colour TV and sometimes windows from US$8/9.75. The *Gran Hotel Diligencias* (tel 31-21-16), facing the zócalo at Independencia 1115, has 134 bright, spotless, air-conditioned modern rooms for US$9/11, most of them decorated with attractive sketches of Indian costumes.

Seafront Area Four blocks from the sea and away from the zócalo, the *Hotel Baluarte* (tel 36-08-44) is in a quiet part of town opposite the Baluarte de Santiago, at Canal 265 on the corner of 16 de Septiembre. It's clean, modern and very well kept. Rooms have TV, phone and air-con and cost US$6.50/7.50.

The seafront road, Camacho, is dotted with hotels for several km south from the harbour. These include, in the first 1½ km and in north-to-south order:

Hotel Mar y Tierra (tel 31-28-66) at the corner of Camacho (also called Paseo del Malecón at this point) and Figueroa. Singles/doubles US$5.50/7.50.
Hotel Villa Rica (tel 32-48-54) at Camacho 7. Singles/doubles US$4.75/6.75.
Hotel Royalty (tel 36-10-41) at the corner of Camacho and Abasolo. Singles/doubles US$5.75/6.75.
Hotel Cristóbal Colón (tel 32-38-44) at Camacho 681. Singles/doubles US$4.75/6.25.

Ten km from downtown, the *Hotel Posada de Cortés* (tel 37-99-99), at Suárez 1314 in Mocambo, has singles and doubles for US$9.50.

Bus Station Area The *Hotel Central* (tel 37-22-22), half a block north of the 1st-class bus station at Díaz Mirón 1612, is clean and very busy with singles at US$4.75, doubles with one bed US$6.75, doubles with two beds US$8.

Places to Stay - top end

With a couple of exceptions on Insurgentes/ Paseo del Malecón overlooking the harbour, all the most expensive places are on Camacho or actually south of Veracruz proper, in the beachside suburbs of Mocambo (10 km from downtown) and Boca del Río (13 km).

The *Hotel Emporio* (tel 32-00-20 to 24) is the most lavish downtown hotel, towering over the harbour at the corner of Insurgentes and Xicoténcatl. An outside lift soars above three swimming pools, and the hotel claims to have more jacuzzis than any other in the world. It has boutiques, a roof garden, a discotheque and several restaurants and cafeterias. The 202 rooms range from 'standard' singles/doubles (which could be bigger) for US$19.25/21.75 to a 'presidential' suite for US$55.75. Make sure you get a room with a view if you stay here!

The slightly more modest *Hotel Puerto Bello Centro* (tel 38-00-88, 32-55-24) points skyward (it is literally arrow-shaped) at Insurgentes 458. The rooms aren't huge but are bright and clean, with balconies and excellent views from the upper floors. Singles/doubles are US$13.25/ 14.50, suites from US$16.

Heading down the seafront, places you'll come to include, in north-to-south order:

Hostal de Cortés (tel 32-00-65) at the corner of Camacho and Las Casas, 103 rooms, swimming pool, singles and doubles US$24.
Hotel Villa del Mar (tel 32-02-27), on Camacho opposite Villa del Mar beach, swimming pool, rooms and bungalows from US$14.
Hotel Torremar (tel 35-21-00), Avenida Ruíz Cortínes 4300 near Mocambo, 190 rooms, singles/doubles US$20/21.50.
Hotel Playa Paraíso (tel 37-83-06), on Ruíz Cortínes near Mocambo, bungalow-style singles/doubles US$18.50/22.75.
Hotel Mocambo (tel 37-15-00), on Carretera Veracruz-Mocambo in Mocambo, singles and doubles US$24.50. This is a big, famous place.
Suites Mediterráneo (tel 86-03-10) at Km 12, Boulevard Mocambo-Boca del Río, 60 rooms,

100 suites, singles/doubles from US$7/14.25.
Hotel Costa Sol (tel 86-00-75) on Avenida Veracruz in Boca del Río, singles/doubles US$19.75/22.75.

Places to Eat

Veracruzana sauce is usually found on seafood. It's made from onions, garlic, tomatoes, olives, green peppers and spices.

Downtown Veracruz is surprisingly poor value for seafood, but Boca del Río, 13 km south, is renowned for it. *Pardino's* in the centre of the village is the biggest and best-known restaurant, but there are several more by the riverside, where typical prices are US$1.50 for two stuffed crabs, US$2 for octopus, US$1.50 for oysters, US$2 for *filete Veracruzana relleno de camarones* (fish in Veracruzana sauce, stuffed with shrimp).

Mandinga, about eight km further along the coast from Boca del Río, is known for its seafood (especially prawns) and has a clutch of small restaurants. AU buses go from Boca del Río to Mandinga. There are also a few seafood spots in Mocambo, three km north of Boca del Río, and some more expensive ones dotted along Camacho as it winds its way from Veracruz to Mocambo.

In Veracruz the zócalo cafés are popular more for their beer (US$0.50), coffee and surroundings than for their food. The *Bar Palacio* and the *Salon Regas* (there's no sign but it's next door to Bar Palacio) are two of the busiest.

Just off the zócalo, at the corner of Independencia and Zamora, is a famous café that others all over the country have been named after. The *Gran Café de la Parroquia* is a big, efficient, convivial café that is the city's favourite meeting place. It echoes with the customers' traditional clinking of spoons on coffee glasses to speed up the waiters. The menu is quite extensive: fish and meat are between US$2.50 and US$2.75 (the *ración de pavo* is five large slabs of turkey breast in gravy with a bowl of jalapeño peppers), enchiladas US$0.75, eggs around US$1, and also available are thick juicy hamburgers and 'sandwinches'. It's open from 6 am to 1 am and is packed most of the time. There's a newer, even bigger place with the same name and menu on Insurgentes.

For a decent comida corrida near the zócalo, go to the *Restaurant-Bar La Gaviota* at Molina 78, just off Zaragoza. US$1 will buy you consommé with chunks of potato and carrot, bolillo, spaghetti with ham pieces, milanesa and cucumber, and pear crumble. There's also a regular menu and it's open 24 hours.

There are a few seafood restaurants – the kind where they call out to you as you walk by – at the corner of Insurgentes and Landero y Coss. But if *El Chato Moyo* is anything to go by, they're overpriced and make 'mistakes' on the bill; and at 9.30 on a Sunday night the *huachinango* (snapper) wasn't fresh either.

A bit further down Landero y Coss is the municipal fish market, with a line of stalls selling seafood cocktails for US$0.50 and up. There's another clutch of stalls in the main market (Mercado Hidalgo) near Parque Zamora. Try the *Ostionería Playa Azul* where prices range from US$0.40 for shrimp cocktail to US$1.50 for vuelve a la vida.

La Merced, on the corner of Rayón and Clavijero, is Parque Zamora's answer to the Gran Café de la Parroquia, complete with clinking glasses. Comida corrida is US$1.50 and the regular menu includes fish (US$2 to US$3) and meats (US$2.25). Just over the road at the corner of Rayón and Prim, *El Chief* does 'executive breakfasts' of juice, café con leche, eggs and hotcakes for US$0.45. The nearby *Café Catedral*, on Ocampo half a block west of Independencia, is similar to La Merced and is popular day and night.

At Independencia 1520 between the zócalo and Parque Zamora, *Cafetería Emir* is a slick place. The fried chicken with salad and French fries (US$2.50) is a bit disappointing, but there are good-looking antojitos (around US$1.25) and licuados. A large plate of fruit salad costs US$1.

For comida corrida you could also try *Cocina Económica Elia* on Héroe de Nacozari, a pedestrian street half a block west of Independencia between Morales and Arista, or the *Café La Parrilla* in one of the two arcades between Ocampo and Parque Zamora. Both are popular and reasonably priced.

Things to Buy

There are all manner of seaside knick-knacks in stalls near the corner of Insurgentes and Landero y Coss. You'll find hammocks, coral, shells, pearls, sailor caps, Veracruz T-shirts, embroidered dresses and candies.

The main market is the Mercado Hidalgo, a block south-west of Parque Zamora between Cortés and Soto. Street stalls spread south-west along Soto. This is the place where ordinary Jarochos shop for their daily needs. Shops are on Independencia and on the streets to its west.

Getting There & Away

Air Aeroméxico (tel 32-93-56, 32-75-42) is some distance from downtown in the Hotel Puerto Bello at the corner of Camacho and Iturbide. Mexicana (tel 32-22-42, 36-15-76) is more central, at the corner of Serdán and 5 de Mayo. There are between two and five Mexicana flights daily to and from Mexico City.

Bus The main bus stations (centrales de autobuses) are back to back, just off Díaz Mirón, two km south of Parque Zamora. The 1st-class side (almost exclusively reserved for ADO) is at Díaz Mirón 1698 by the corner of Xalapa. The entrance to the 2nd-class side is one block back from Díaz Mirón, on Lafragua. The 2nd-class station has a guardería (left-luggage office), open from 6 am to 2 pm and 3 to 10 pm.

ADO (tel 37-55-22, 37-57-88) has buses

to Mexico City and just about everywhere in east and south-east Mexico: Mexico City, 29 services daily, US$5.50; Jalapa, 38 daily, US$1.50; Córdoba, 13 daily, US$1.50; Orizaba, nine daily, US$1.75; Puebla, eight daily, US$3.75; Tehuacán, three daily, US$2.50; Alvarado, 15 daily, US$0.85; Tlacotalpan, six daily, US$1.25; Santiago Tuxtla, nine daily, US$1.75; San Andrés Tuxtla, 23 daily, US$2; Catemaco, two daily, US$2; Acayucan, 12 daily, US$3; Juchitán, two daily, US$6.75; Tehuantepec, two daily, US$7; Salina Cruz, three daily, US$7.25; Tuxtepec, four daily, US$2.25; Oaxaca, two daily, US$6.25; Coatzacoalcos, 15 daily, US$3.75; Villahermosa, 10 daily, US$5.75; Campeche, two daily, US$11.25; Chetumal, two daily, US$12.75; Mérida, two daily, US$13.50; Cancún, one daily, US$17; Ciudad Cardel, 25 daily, US$0.50; Zempoala, five daily, US$0.75; Nautla, six daily, US$2; Papantla, three daily, US$4.75; Poza Rica, 10 daily, US$5; Tuxpan, six daily, US$5.50; Tampico, five daily, US$8.75; Reynosa, one daily, US$16.

Approximate ADO journey times: Mexico City 6½ hours, Puebla four hours, Jalapa 2½ hours, Córdoba two hours, Cardel 30 minutes, Papantla five hours, Tuxpan six hours, Tampico 10 hours, San Andrés Tuxtla three hours, Villahermosa eight hours, Mérida 18 hours.

The Cuenca de Cosamaloapan line (tel 2-02-02) also runs from the 1st-class station to San Andrés Tuxtla, Tuxtepec, Valle Nacional, Cosamaloapan, Tierra Blanca, Tres Valles and Loma Bonita.

AU (tel 37-57-32) is the main 2nd-class line. Its direct long-distance services, which are almost as good as 1st class, go to Mexico City 13 times daily; Jalapa 12 times daily; Puebla, Córdoba and Orizaba 13 times daily; Tehuacán three times daily; Tuxtepec twice daily; Salina Cruz twice daily; Juchitán, Tehuantepec and Arriaga once daily. There are also ordinary stopping services to most of those places plus Cardel (US$0.40, every

20 minutes), Alvarado, Santiago Tuxtla, San Andrés Tuxtla, Catemaco, Acayucan, Villahermosa, Tlacotalpan and Poza Rica. Prices are about 10% lower than in 1st class.

Other 2nd-class lines include Autobuses Sotavento (to Tierra Blanca, Loma Bonita, Tuxtepec, Tlacotalpan and Cosamaloapan) and Lineas Unidas del Sur (hourly to Acayucan and Coatzacoalcos, half-hourly to Alvarado, San Andrés Tuxtla and Catemaco).

Rail Veracruz railway station (tel 32-25-69, 32-33-38) is at the north end of Plaza de la República. The overnight sleeper, 'El Jarocho', is quite a popular way of travelling between Veracruz and Mexico City. It leaves Mexico City at 9.32 pm, Veracruz at 9.30 pm, and passes through Córdoba, Fortín de las Flores and Orizaba. The full trip takes 10 hours. Roomettes to or from Mexico City cost US$8.75 for one person, US$13 for two. Bedrooms are US$14.50 for two, US$19.50 for three, US$24.50 for four. There are also 1st-class seats (US$3 unreserved, US$6.50 reserved) and 2nd-class seats (US$1.75) on this train. For reserved seats or sleepers, book as far ahead as you can, particularly for weekend travel.

Daytime trains on the same route leave Mexico City at 7.34 am and Veracruz at 8 am. They take 11 to 12 hours and have 1st and 2nd-class seats. There are also trains to Córdoba and Orizaba at 12.45 pm, and to Mexico City via Jalapa at 7.25 am.

The curious and unhurried might like to try a train between Veracruz and Tapachula, 885 km away near the Chiapas-Guatemala border. The daily service has 1st and 2nd-class seats and takes an alleged 23 hours, passing through Papaloapan, Juchitán, Arriaga and Tonalá, but down the line in Chiapas station staff say these trains can turn up any time of day or night. It's certainly cheap: fares to Tapachula are US$3.50 2nd class, US$6 1st class. Departure from Veracruz is scheduled for 4.30 pm.

Getting Around

Airport Transport Veracruz airport is about 12 km from downtown off Highway 140, the old road to Jalapa. El Gallo taxi service (tel 32-35-20) runs combis to the airport for US$1 per person. They will pick you up from your hotel.

Bus All rides within the city are 8c. Bus 'Díaz Mirón' goes downtown from half a block north of the ADO station on Díaz Mirón. For the zócalo, get off at the corner of Madero and Lerdo and walk two blocks to the right along Lerdo. Returning to the bus station, pick up the same bus on 5 de Mayo. 'PZ' buses from the same stop near the ADO go to Parque Zamora.

The bus marked 'Mocambo – Boca del Río', from the corner of Zaragoza and Aquiles Serdán, goes to Parque Zamora, then down the seafront along Camacho to Mocambo and Boca del Río (25 minutes, 16c).

For San Juan de Ulúa, take a 'San Juan de Ulúa' bus from in front of the souvenir shops on Landero y Coss near the corner of Lerdo. They depart about every half-hour. The last bus back to town leaves at 5 pm.

AU buses go to Isla del Amor and Mandinga.

Car Rental Hertz (tel 31-25-68) is at Serdán 14. Budget (tel 32-34-75) is at the corner of Díaz Mirón and Alacio Pérez. Auto Rentas Fast (tel 36-14-16) is at Lerdo 241. Autos Laurencio (tel 32-57-52) is at Serdán 3.

VERACRUZ TO PAPANTLA

There are several places worth brief stops on or close to Highway 180 as it heads north to Papantla, 231 km away, hugging the coast most of the way. Some of them are easy day trips from Veracruz. Swimmers should watch out for undertow on this coast.

La Antigua

This riverside village 23 km north of Veracruz, about a km east of the highway, is where Cortés is thought to have scuttled his ships. It was one of the sites of Villa Rica, the Spanish settlement that preceded Veracruz, and boasts a house that was supposedly occupied by Cortés, and a very early church (the Ermita del Rosario, probably dating from 1523). Small seafood restaurants here are popular with day-trippers from Veracruz.

Zempoala

The ruins of this important pre-Hispanic Totonac town stand in a modern town of the same name (sometimes spelt Cempoala) 42 km north of Veracruz. After El Tajín, these are the most impressive ruins in the state. *Voladores* perform here most days around noon to 2 pm.

History The site was probably occupied before 1000 AD but started to become an important centre for the Totonacs from about 1200 as they were pushed eastward by the Toltecs or Chichimecs. Zempoala may have been the leader of a 'federation' of southern Totonacs. It became subject to the Aztecs in the mid-15th century along with most of the rest of Veracruz, and many of the buildings are in Aztec style.

The town had a system of defensive walls, underground pipes for water and drainage and, by the time the Spanish arrived here in May 1519, about 30,000 people. As Cortés approached the town one of his horsemen rode ahead and, his imagination on fire, came back to report that the buildings were made of silver – but it was only the white plaster or paint gleaming in the sun.

The Totonac chief of the town, a portly man called Chicomacatl, is known to history as 'the fat cacique' from a description by Bernal Díaz del Castillo. Eager for protection against the Aztecs, he struck up an alliance with Cortés, offering hospitality and, among other things, eight women. But he wasn't able to stop the Spanish from smashing the statues of the Zempoalans' gods and

Top: Pyramid of the Niches, El Tajín (JN)
Bottom: Bus in Catemaco (JN)

Top: Voladores, El Tajín (JN)
Left: Voladores, El Tajín (JN)
Right: The Palace, Sayil (TW)

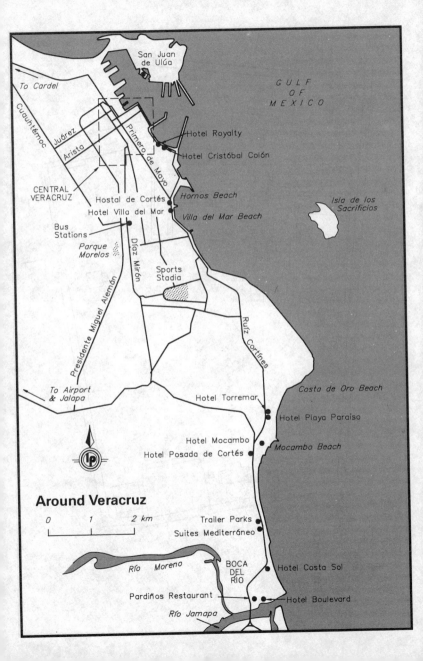

Around Veracruz

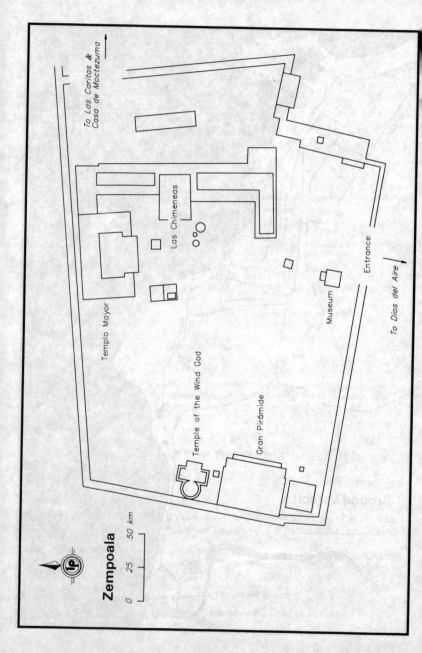

Zempoala

0   25   50 km

To Las Caritas &
Casa de Moctezuma

Templo Mayor

Las Chimeneas

Temple of the Wind God

Gran Pirámide

Museum

Entrance

To Dios del Aire

lecturing them on Christianity. Zempoalan carriers went with the Spaniards when they set off for Tenochtitlán in August 1519, going as far as Tlaxcala and Cholula.

At Zempoala Cortés defeated the 1520 expedition under Pánfilo de Narváez, sent by the governor of Cuba to arrest him.

By the beginning of the 17th century Zempoala had virtually ceased to exist. Its population, devastated by new diseases, was down to eight families and soon afterwards it was abandoned. The present town dates from 1832.

The main ruins are at the end of a short track to the right as you enter Zempoala, where a sign says *Bienvenidos a Cempoala*. They're open daily from 8 am to 6.30 pm. The entrance fee is US$0.50 except on Sunday, when it's free.

Ruins The site is attractive, with lines of palms, mountains in the background and a baseball field in the middle. There's a small museum at the entrance whose collection includes a white-painted model skeleton, some Remojadas-type pottery and parts of a fresco.

Most of the buildings are faced with smooth, rounded riverbed stones and are constructed as a series of narrow platforms. Their typical feature is the battlement-like 'teeth' called *merlons* (locally, *almenas*) on top of many of the walls.

Straight ahead from the entrance is the Templo Mayor (Main Temple), an 11-metre-high, 13-platform pyramid on a base 65 by 40 metres. Originally it was plastered and painted. A 27-metre-wide staircase ascends the front. On top are the remains of a three-room shrine. It was probably this building which Pánfilo de Narváez occupied as his HQ in 1520 and which Cortés' men captured by setting fire to the thatched roof of the shrine on top.

To the right is the building known as Las Chimeneas (The Chimneys), where Cortés and his men were lodged on their first visit to Zempoala. Its name comes from the hollow columns at the front, which were once filled with wood. It has seven platforms and probably held a temple on top.

In the plaza in front of the Templo Mayor and Las Chimeneas is a platform that was probably an altar and two circular structures whose purpose is something of a mystery.

On the far (west) side of the site the two main structures are known as the Gran Pirámide (Great Pyramid) and the Temple of the Wind God. The Great Pyramid has three platforms, with two stairways climbing them in typically Toltec and Aztec style. It faces east and was probably devoted to the sun god. The Temple of the Wind God is similar to temples dedicated to Ehecatl, a wind god, in central Mexico in Aztec times. It's circular, with a rectangular platform and ramps in front.

In the sugar-cane fields behind Las Chimeneas are a few more buildings. If you cross the irrigation channel and keep going with Las Chimeneas behind you, a building called Las Caritas (The Little Heads) is on your right. It once held large numbers of small pottery heads in niches. Further along the same path, a structure called La Casa de Moctezuma is behind some trees to the right.

There are other pre-Hispanic buildings in the village. A large wind god temple, simply known as Dios del Aire, is reached by going back down the site entrance road, straight on over the main road, and round the corner to the right.

Getting There & Away Zempoala is three km west of Highway 180. The turn-off is by a Pemex station eight km north of Cardel. There are five ADO buses daily from Veracruz to Zempoala (US$0.75), or you can take one of the frequent buses to Cardel (US$0.50 by ADO, US$0.40 by 2nd-class AU), followed by a green-and-white colectivo taxi (US$0.30) or another bus (15c) from the Cardel bus stop on to Zempoala. Total journey time from

Veracruz to Zempoala is about one hour. There are also three buses daily from Mexico City's eastern bus station (TAPO) to Zempoala for US$5.

Villa Rica & Quiahuiztlán

Sixty-nine km from Veracruz, this is where Cortés probably founded the first Spanish settlement in Mexico. There are traces of a fort and church on a hill called Cerro de la Cantera.

Not far south are some remains of pre-Hispanic Quiahuiztlán, a Totonac town which Cortés moved on to after his first visit to Zempoala and probably where the Aztec tribute-collectors were imprisoned. All you see now are two groups of miniature temples about one metre high, looking a bit like bee-hives and thought to have been a cemetery. They stand west of Highway 180, near the top of a hill just north of a higher rocky outcrop visible from the road, about 1½ km south of the Villa Rica turn-off.

The site of Mexico's first nuclear-power station is at Laguna Verde, about 10 km north of Villa Rica, east of the road. Construction started in the early 1970s and, after a string of problems and delays, opening was scheduled for mid-1987, by which time the initial budget of US$450 million had grown to US$3 billion. A belated campaign for a national referendum on whether it should be opened seems unlikely to bear fruit.

Nautla

This is a small fishing town between road and sea 150 km north of Veracruz, with a handful of cheap but respectable hotels and a long beach nearby where you can eat seafood. For 20 km north of Nautla, the narrow strip between Highway 180 and the beach is liberally sprinkled with attractive parking bays. There's a range of hotels and restaurants as well as three trailer parks. The most northerly trailer park looks the best.

Tecolutla

Reached by heading a few km north-east from Highway 180 at Gutiérrez Zamora, 201 km from Veracruz, Tecolutla is a minor seaside resort with a palm-fringed beach and a few hotels. It's on the north side of the mouth of the Río Tecolutla and, if you like sea air, you could use it as a base for visiting El Tajín and Papantla. There are ADO (1st class) and Transportes Papantla (2nd class) buses to and from Papantla.

Northern Veracruz

The north of the state is mostly flat or rolling plains, lying between the southern end of the Sierra Madre Oriental and the Gulf coast. The chief attraction is the ancient site of El Tajín. Tuxpan is a pleasant river-mouth town. From northern Veracruz you can travel south to Veracruz city, west across the Sierra Madre to central Mexico, or north to Tampico.

PAPANTLA

Set on a hillside among the low outliers of the Sierra Madre Oriental, at an altitude of 290 metres, Papantla is the nearest and best base for visiting El Tajín and an interesting place in its own right. It has some decent accommodation but is not touristy, and Totonacs in traditional costume are a common sight. The men wear baggy white shirts and trousers, the women embroidered blouses and *quechquémitls*. *Voladores* perform here regularly, including during the Corpus Christi festival which is in late May or early June.

Orientation

Papantla lies on Highway 180, which runs almost due east-west on this stretch between Poza Rica and the coast at Tecolutla. The centre of town, with the cathedral and the Hotel Tajín (which has a flashing red neon sign at night), is uphill (south) from the main road. To get from the ADO bus station to the centre, turn left out of the bus station entrance, walk up to the main road, cross it and go straight on up Juárez. At the top of Juárez turn right on Enríquez to reach the central plaza, officially called Parque Tellez.

To go from the ADO to the local bus station (for El Tajín), walk up to the main road as above, then turn right along it until you reach the big Hotel Totonacapan on the left. Go up 20 de Noviembre, the street beside the hotel. The bus station is a couple of blocks up on the left.

If you carry on up 20 de Noviembre past the bus station you come out on the main plaza. On the south side of the plaza is the cathedral, on the west the Palacio Municipal.

Information
Tourist Office There's a tourist office in the Palacio Municipal (upstairs at the back) but it appears to be devoted to bureaucracy rather than to helping visitors.

Other The post office (closed Saturday afternoons and Sundays) is at Juárez 102. For money exchange, Bancomer is quicker than Bánamex. Both are on Enríquez, the street which runs from the top of Juárez to the main plaza.

Central Plaza
The south wall of the plaza, which supports the cathedral above, is decorated with a 50-metre-long concrete mural by local artist Teodoro Cano depicting Totonac and Veracruz history. A serpent (probably Quetzalcóatl) stretches along most of the mural. In the middle can be seen the Pyramid of the Niches and Remojadas pottery, at the far left the Totonac death god whose statue is also at El Tajín. You can also pick out *voladores*, a pre-Hispanic stone carver and the modern oil industry. The roof of the kiosk in the middle of the plaza has a painting on a similar theme. Inside the Palacio

Municipal are copies of carvings from the southern ball court at El Tajín.

The plaza really comes alive on Sunday, when *voladores* usually perform in the cathedral yard at about 11 am (their pole is a permanent fixture there), and when cultural events such as traditional dances are held in the early evening.

Festivals
Corpus Christi At the end of May or the beginning of June, Papantla is thronged by people who come for the Corpus Christi parades and dances. *Voladores* (whose act apparently used to be reserved exclusively for this festival) perform two or three times a day, and other dances are called Los Negritos, Los Huehues (The Old Men) and Los Quetzalines. The main procession is on Sunday.

San José Espinal, 27 km south of Papantla, is the scene of a fair and dances for San José on 18 March, including *voladores* and a dance depicting a battle between Moors and Spaniards.

San Andrés Coyutla, about 30 km beyond Espinal in the fringes of the Sierra Madre, performs numerous dances around a cross dedicated to San Andrés on his day, the first Sunday in December.

Places to Stay
There are three hotels in central Papantla which are all quite good value. *Hotel Papantla* (tel 2-00-80) on the main plaza at Enríquez 103 has big clean rooms, some overlooking the plaza, at US$3.75 for one double bed, US$7.50 for two beds. *Hotel Pulido* (tel 2-00-36) at Enríquez 205 has smaller and not quite so clean rooms round a central parking area. Singles cost US$3.25; doubles cost US$3.75 for one bed, US$5 for two beds.

Choicest of the three is the *Hotel Tajín* (tel 2-01-21) at Nuñez 104. Rooms may have fans, air-conditioning, TV or balconies with views over the town. All have mosquito screens on the windows, and the same price – US$4.75 for singles, US$6.50 for doubles. The rooms need a touch of paint but there is a pleasant lobby and upstairs sitting area. To get there from the main plaza, walk a few metres up the street at the left-hand end of the big mural.

Places to Eat

All food is strictly Mexican in Papantla, with an emphasis on meat in this cattle-raising area. The restaurant of the *Hotel Tajín* is one of the most popular places. Portions aren't huge but they're not too expensive either. Various beefsteak 'filetes' (US$1.25) are served: *tampiqueño* is strips of beef with fried bananas, small tortillas, guacamole, frijoles, salad and cheese; *al carbón* is charcoal-grilled meat with French fries, frijoles and salad. Eggs cost US$0.35 to US$0.90, chicken US$1, enchiladas Suizas US$0.75. There are also tacos, quesadillas and *bocoles*, another member of the tortilla family, which comes wrapped around frijoles and another filling.

Also popular is the small, nameless place over the road from the Hotel Tajín. Comida corrida is US$1.25; breakfast is good too.

The *Restaurant Terraza*, at the top of 20 de Noviembre in a corner of the main plaza, has a good upstairs location overlooking the plaza but deafening music (an organist at night, tapes during the day). Fish costs US$1.25, beefsteak US$1.50. Portions of chicken and French fries (US$1.25) aren't huge but at least the tortillas keep coming. Go through the 'Foto Felipe' door to enter the Terraza.

For straight tacos, you'll find cheaper and better fare at stalls like *2 Hermanos* and *Mary*, on the upper floor of the market at the top of 20 de Noviembre (north-west corner of the main plaza), than in the *Restaurant Sorrento* at Enríquez 105, the other end of the plaza.

Things to Buy

The Juárez market on 20 de Noviembre has Totonac costumes (some of them quite pretty), good baskets and vanilla. Papantla is in one of Mexico's leading vanilla-growing areas and you can buy it in extract form, in the original pods or in *figuras* – pods woven into the shape of flowers, insects, etc. There's another small market, the Mercado Hidalgo, selling mainly food; it's just off the south-west corner of the main plaza.

Getting There & Away

Bus If you're travelling by bus direct from Mexico City to Papantla, you have to leave from the northern, not the eastern, bus station in the capital.

In Papantla, ADO (1st class, tel 2-02-18) is at Juárez 207. It's usually worth booking ahead on buses from here because often only a few seats are available, since the bus routes originate elsewhere. There are nine services a day to Poza Rica (US$0.25); eight to Jalapa (US$3.25); four to Veracruz (US$4.75); three each to Mexico City (US$3.75) and Ciudad Cardel (US$2.75); two each to Tuxpan (US$1), Villahermosa (US$10.75) and Acayucan (US$7.75); and one each to Nautla (US$1.25), San Andrés Tuxtla (US$6.75) and Tecolutla (US$0.50).

Approximate ADO journey times: Poza Rica 20 minutes, Tuxpan one hour 10 minutes, Tampico 5½ hours, Veracruz five hours, Jalapa six hours, Mexico City five hours.

From the 2nd-class bus station on 20 de Noviembre, blue-and-white Transportes Papantla buses depart frequently but very slowly to local villages, Poza Rica (US$0.25), Tecolutla, Jalapa, Puebla and Veracruz.

See the 'El Tajín' section for getting from Papantla to El Tajín.

EL TAJÍN

One of the least visited and understood of Mexico's major archaeological sites lies among hills covered in tropical vegetation

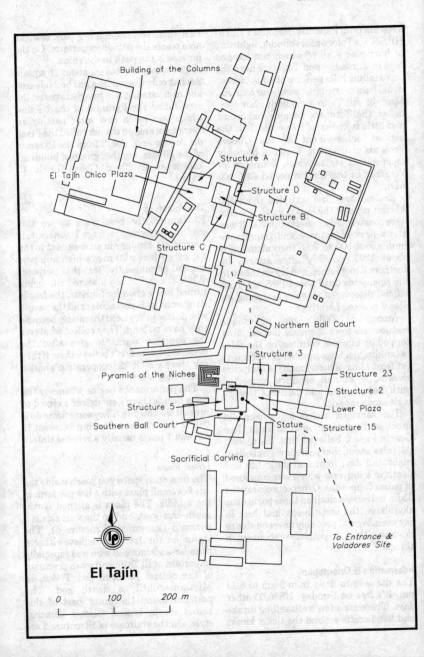

Building of the Columns

Structure A

El Tajín Chico Plaza

Structure D

Structure B

Structure C

Northern Ball Court

Pyramid of the Niches

Structure 3

Structure 23

Structure 2

Structure 5

Lower Plaza

Southern Ball Court

Structure 15

Statue

Sacrificial Carving

To Entrance & Voladores Site

El Tajín

0   100   200 m

a few km from Papantla. Its name ('El Ta-HEEN') is Totonac for thunder, lightning or hurricane – all of which can happen here in summer – and Totonacs from the surrounding hills perform their *voladores* ritual here every day, usually for tourists. Most of El Tajín was built, however, before the Totonacs became important and little is known of its people. It is the highest achievement of the Classic Veracruz civilisation, a web of probably independent states which flourished in Veracruz in the Classic period (300-900 AD).

El Tajín was first occupied about 100 AD but most of the buildings visible now were constructed around 600 or 700. It was at its peak of activity and importance from about 600 to 900, then abandoned about 1200, possibly after attacks by northern Chichimecs, and lay unknown to the Spaniards until about 1785, when an official discovered it while searching for illegal tobacco plantings.

Among El Tajín's rare or unique features are rows of square niches, often topped by unusual cornices, on the sides of buildings, a huge number of ball courts (at least 11 have been found), a sculpture showing a human sacrifice connected with the ball game, and the use of 'Greek'-style stone mosaics.

The Mexican archaeologist who did much of the excavation at El Tajín, José García Payón, believed that the mosaic patterns and niches somehow symbolised night and day, light and dark, life and death in a universe which was composed of pairs of opposites. Other sources say the Tajín universe contained three parts – the sky above, the earth below and here in between. We will probably never be able to do more than hypothesise about such things.

Information & Orientation

The site is open daily from 9 am to 5.30 pm. It's free on Sunday, US$0.60 other days. There are a few stalls selling drinks and handicrafts around the ticket kiosk.

Past that, you reach a car park and the area where the *voladores* perform. On the far side is the path to the ruins.

The whole site covers about 10 square km but only the nucleus has been cleared and excavated. It's in two main parts: the area round the Pyramid of the Niches, which you reach first after passing an overgrown area on the left called the Plaza del Arroyo and, uphill from the Pyramid of the Niches, another group of buildings known as El Tajín Chico (Little El Tajín).

The Voladores

El Tajín is the best place to see this exciting performance, since Totonacs do it every day for money in an area next to the car park where a 20-metre-high iron pole stands permanently for the purpose. While it's sad to see a sacred rite being turned into a show for tourists, the feat is dangerous and spectacular and the people who do it say they need the money because they have no land. They collect whatever the audience wants to give after the performance, so don't believe them if they say there's a US$2 'cooperation charge' before they start.

The performance begins whenever the fliers decide there's enough of a crowd to make it worthwhile. They sometimes do it two or three times a day, but between 11 am and 1 pm is usually a reliable time.

Lower Plaza

The first open space you reach inside the site is a small plaza with a low platform in the middle. The plaza is aligned north-south-east-west, and on the west side is a pyramid (known as Structure 5). The statue on the 1st level depicts either a thunder-and-rain god who was especially important at El Tajín and was a precursor of the central Mexican god Tláloc, or Mictlantecuhtli, a death god. The patterns round the lower part of this statue are in typical Classic Veracruz style. On the staircase of Structure 5 are traces of the buildings' original blue and red paint.

On the north side of the plaza is another pyramid, Structure 3, with traces of blue paint. To the right of Structure 3 is a plainer pyramid, Structure 23, and on the east side of the plaza is long, low Structure 15 with a wide central staircase. All these structures were probably originally topped by small temples, since this was part of El Tajín's main ceremonial centre.

Southern Ball Court

Between the left (south) side of Structure 5 and the adjacent mound (Structure 6) is this 60-metre-long court, one of Mexico's most famous because of six sculptures, dating from about 1150, which decorate its walls.

North Corners The panel on the north-east corner (immediately on the right as you enter from the Lower Plaza) is the easiest to make out. Three ball-players wearing knee-pads are in the centre. One, seated, has his arms held by the second while the third is about to plunge a knife into his chest in the ritual sacrifice which followed the ball game. A skeletal death god on the left and a presiding figure on the right look on. Another death god hovers over the victim. The panel at the far (north-west) end of the same wall is thought to represent a ceremony which preceded the ball game. Two players face each other, one with crossed arms, the other holding a dagger. Speech symbols emerge from their mouths. To their right is a figure with the mask of a coyote – the animal which conducted sacrificial victims to the next world. The death god is on the right.

South Corners The south-west panel seems to show part of the initiation of a young man into a band of warriors associated with the eagle. A central figure lies on a table; to the left another holds a bell. Above is an eagle-masked figure, possibly a priest. On the south-east panel one man offers a bunch of spears or arrows

to another, possibly part of the same ceremony.

Central Panels These are devoted to the ceremonial drinking of *pulque*, a kind of cactus-beer. In the northern panel, a figure holding a drinking vessel signals to another person leaning on a *pulque* container. Quetzalcóatl sits cross-legged beside Tláloc, the fanged god of rain, water and lightning. On the south panel Tláloc, squatting, passes a gourd to someone in a fish mask who appears to be in a *pulque* vat. On the left is the maguey plant, from which *pulque* is made.

The top sections of both these panels represent two dancing figures and, in the middle, a laughing drunken face with its tongue out. The two dancing figures may symbolise the 'doubling' effect of *pulque*, which induces a sacred 'second' state. Maguey is not native to this part of Mexico, which points to influences from central Mexico (possibly Toltec) at this late stage of El Tajín.

Pyramid of the Niches

El Tajín's best-known building is just off the Lower Plaza, by the north-west corner of Structure 5. It's a 35 square-metre structure, aligned with the compass points, which was built on top of an earlier pyramid. The six lower levels reach a height of 18 metres and each is surrounded by rows of small square niches. The wide staircase on the east side was a later addition, built over some of the niches.

There were originally 22 niches on the lowest level on each side, 19 on the next level up, then 16, 13, 10 and seven. Some archaeologists reckon the temple on top, of which little remains, had five niches on three sides plus two on its east side – making a total of 365, the number of days in a year. This suggests that the building could have been used as a kind of religious calendar. The insides of the niches were painted red, and their frames blue. The view that they held statues of gods is now out of favour.

Pyramid of the Niches

The only similar known building in Mexico is a seven-level niched pyramid at Yohuallichán near Cuetzalán, 50 km south-west of El Tajín in northern Puebla. This was probably an earlier site than El Tajín and didn't reach the same artistic heights, but it was clearly the product of a connected culture.

In front of the Pyramid of the Niches, projecting from the north side of Structure 5, is Structure 2. This was built over an earlier structure which is visible if you climb to the top of Structure 2 and look down inside.

Northern Ball Court

A path leads north towards El Tajín Chico from the plaza between the Pyramid of the Niches and Structure 3. On the right after a few metres is the Northern Ball Court, which is smaller and earlier than the southern one, and also has carvings on its sides.

El Tajín Chico

Continuing uphill you reach El Tajín Chico, thought to have been the administrative centre of El Tajín. Here many of the buildings have the interesting geometric stone mosaic patterns known as Greco (Greek). It's extremely unlikely that they had anything to do with Greece; they bear more resemblance to decorations in Mitla, Oaxaca, than anywhere else.

The main buildings at El Tajín Chico are on the east and north sides of a small plaza, and are probably from the 9th century. On the east side of the plaza (the right-hand side as you approach) is, first, Structure C, with three levels and a staircase on the plaza side. This building was originally painted blue. Next to it, Structure B was probably living quarters for priests or officials. Behind Structure B and off the plaza, Structure D has a large lozenge-design mosaic. On its top was a chamber (probably a shrine) open on the east side where three columns stood. A passageway runs under this building from east to west.

On the north side of the plaza, Structure A has a façade that resembles a Mayan roofcomb with a stairway leading up through an arch in the middle. The construction of the arch, with the stones on each side jutting further and further towards each other until they are joined at the top by a single slab, is known as 'corbelled' and is typical of Mayan architecture – yet another piece in the jigsaw of influences between ancient Mexican cultures. At the top of the stairway you come out in a corridor which goes all the way round the building, with rooms on all four corners. Some of the lower mosaics in the corridor resemble swastikas.

Uphill to the north-west of El Tajín Chico plaza, hidden by vegetation, is the unreconstructed Building of the Columns, with large staircases that were probably only decorative. Some of its columns, carved with warriors, priests and deities, now lie next to the car park. The Building of the Columns originally had an open patio inside and, with its adjoining structures stretching over the surrounding hillside for nearly 200 by 100 metres, was one of the most important buildings.

Getting There & Away

See the 'Tuxpan' and 'Poza Rica' sections for how to reach El Tajín from those places. From Papantla, take a blue 'Jaloapan' or 'Agua Dulce' bus for 13c from the 2nd-class bus station to the road junction village of El Chote, and from there a 'Poza Rica' bus (15c) to the El Tajín entrance road (clearly marked by a huge Coca-Cola sign tagged *Bienvenidos a la zona arqueológica del Tajín*'. Buses run every few minutes on both sections of this route. It takes about half an hour to get from Papantla to the entrance road, then 15 minutes by foot to the ruins themselves.

POZA RICA

Population: 200,000
The only reason to stay overnight in Poza Rica – easy access to El Tajín – has evaporated since the bus station was moved to the edge of town, far from the hotels. This is an oil town and not much else. Nodding donkeys are at work within the urban area and gas burn-offs light up the night sky. Papantla, 16 km away, is a much more pleasant and convenient base for visiting El Tajín. Poza Rica is the nearest town to a lesser archaeological site, Castillo de Teayo, but Tuxpan is almost as practicable a base.

Poza Rica lies at an altitude of 60 metres, among low hills which are the final eastward fling of the Sierra Madre Oriental. West of Poza Rica, in northern Puebla state and eastern Hidalgo, the remote mountainous country is home to several Indian groups. The roads across this area would be interesting routes between the Gulf coast and central Mexico (see the introduction to this chapter and under Puebla and Hidalgo states for more on this area and its peoples).

Orientation

The bus station is on the far north-west side of town. If you're coming in from the south-east (eg Papantla), you enter Poza Rica on a street named Central Oriente, which passes along the southern edge of the central area, to your right. If you're heading for the centre, it's best to get off the bus at or near the large Plaza Cívica 18 de Marzo, on the right of the road coming from Papantla.

If you want to get back downtown from the bus station, white local buses outside the bus station will take you. Central Poza Rica is bounded on the south by Highway 180, called Central Oriente on the south-east (Papantla) side of town and Cárdenas after it crosses a roundabout, going west. Boulevard Ruíz Cortínez, the other major street, strikes north-east from Cárdenas just west of the roundabout. Between Ruíz Cortínez and Central Oriente is an area of grid-plan streets named 2, 4, 6, etc Norte (Nte) and 2, 4, 6, etc Oriente (Ote).

Information

Tourist Office Amazingly, there's a helpful tourist information desk in the ADO section of the bus station.

Money There are banks around Plaza 18 de Marzo.

Post The post office is by the Parque Juárez, six blocks up Ruíz Cortínez from Cárdenas.

Airlines Aeroméxico (tel 2-61-42, 2-88-77) is in the Edificio Geminis (Geminis building) facing Parque Juárez at the north end of Avenida 8 Norte.

Places to Stay
Hotel Cárdenas (tel 2-66-10) at the corner of Bermúdez and Zaragoza has singles/doubles for US$1.75/2.25. To reach it from Cárdenas, walk one block up Ruíz Cortínez, and take the right-hand one of the two streets that meet Ruíz Cortínez on the left here. This is Bermúdez; Zaragoza is now the fifth street on the right. Also on Bermúdez, *Hotel Colonial* charges US$2.75 per person. *Hotel Fénix*, on Avenida 6 Norte, one block west of Plaza 18 de Marzo, has singles/doubles at US$3.50/4.50.

Hotel Juárez at Ruíz Córtínez 133 (one block north of Cárdenas) has singles/doubles for US$4/6. *Hotel Poza Rica* (tel 2-02-00), three blocks further up Ruíz Cortínez at the corner of Avenida 2 Norte, charges US$4 per person. The large *Hotel Salinas* (tel 2-07-06), even further up Ruíz Cortínez at No 1000, has parking, a restaurant, and singles/doubles for US$4.50/5.25.

Hotel Robert Prince (tel 2-07-68) is at the corner of Avenida 6 Norte and 10 Oriente (Ote), one block west and four north of Plaza 18 de Marzo. Singles/doubles cost US$6/7.50. On the road to Papantla, 4½ km out of Poza Rica, the 160-room *Hotel Poza Rica Inn* is the luxury place at US$11.75/13.75 singles/doubles.

Getting There & Away
Air From Poza Rica airport, south of the town, Aeroméxico flies to Ciudad Victoria and Mexico City three times a week.

Road Highway 180 heads north to Tuxpan (56 km) and Tampico (246 km), southeast to Papantla (16 km) and Veracruz (254 km). Highway 130 heads west through the Sierra Madre in northern Puebla state to Huauchinango and Tulancingo (152 km), after which Highway 132 branches left to Teotihuacán and Mexico City (250 km). For more on Highway 130, see under Puebla and Hidalgo states.

Bus If you're travelling by bus direct from Mexico City to Poza Rica, you have to leave from the northern, not the eastern, bus station in the capital.

Poza Rica is a surprisingly important communication centre and its big new Central de Autobuses is divided into two parts – one for ADO and one for the rest.

ADO's services (1st class) include 32 a day to Tuxpan (US$0.75), 21 each to Mexico City (US$3.75) and Tampico (US$3.75), 17 to Papantla (25c), 16 to Veracruz (US$5), 12 to Jalapa (US$3.75), nine each to Nautla (US$1.75) and Villahermosa (US$10.75), eight to Acayucan (US$8), five to Puebla (US$3.75), four to Ciudad Cardel (US$3), two each to Matamoros (US$11) and Reynosa (US$11.25), and one each to Córdoba (US$6.50) and Orizaba (US$6.75).

Omnibus de México, also 1st class but a few pesos cheaper than ADO, operates from the other part of the terminal, with three buses a day to Mexico City, four to Tuxpan and one each to Guadalajara, Querétaro and Celaya.

Estrella Blanca (2nd class) runs 23 buses daily to Mexico City (US$3.25). Transportes Frontera/Mexico-Tuxpan-Tampico (2nd class) serves Puebla (US$3.25) via Tlaxcala (US$3) 11 times a day; Nuevo Laredo (US$12.25) via Ciudad Victoria (US$6.75) and Monterrey (US$9.75) four times; plus Tampico (US$3.50, five direct services daily), Tuxpan (US$0.50), Reynosa (US$10.25, twice daily), Matamoros (US$10, once daily) and Pachuca.

Transportes Papantla (2nd class, tel 2-56-66) goes to El Tajín (25c) 10 times a day (the buses have different destinations, including Agua Dulce), Papantla (23c) every 10 minutes, Tecolutla every 40 minutes, Veracruz 11 times a day, Jalapa twice a day.

Approximate 1st-class journey times are: Papantla 20 minutes, Tuxpan 50 minutes, Tampico 5¼ hours, Veracruz five hours, Mexico City five hours. To El Tajín, 2nd class takes 30 minutes.

CASTILLO DE TEAYO

This small town lies 38 km from Poza Rica. Beside its main plaza is a steep 13-metre-high pyramid topped by a small temple. Castillo de Teayo was occupied from about 800 AD as one of the southernmost points of the Huastec civilisation, but the pyramid, now restored, is in the style of the Toltecs. It was probably built during a period of domination or occupation of the area by the Toltecs between 900 and 1200.

Around the base of the pyramid are some stone sculptures found in the area. These are believed to be the work of both the Huastecs and of the Aztecs, who controlled the area for a few decades before the Spanish conquest. Some of them are in a unique combination of Huastec and Aztec styles.

The very bumpy 23-km road to Castillo de Teayo lies west off the Poza Rica-Tuxpan road 15 km from Poza Rica.

COATZINTLA

Totonacs, some representing Roman soldiers, re-enact the Crucifixion on Good Friday in this town a few km south of Poza Rica on the El Tajín road. On Easter Saturday effigies of Judas Iscariot are burned. The festival of Santiago Apóstol (St James) is celebrated with a fair and dances, including the *voladores*, during the last week of July.

TUXPAN

Population: 70,000

Tuxpan (sometimes spelt Tuxpam) is a fishing town and minor oil port near the mouth of the Río Tuxpan, 348 km north of Veracruz and 190 km south of Tampico. It has something of a holiday atmosphere, mainly thanks to the beach 12 km east which unfortunately is now being ruined by the construction of a power station. There's little to see in Tuxpan but it's the liveliest coastal town between Tampico and Veracruz, with a tropical feel, a fine wide river, a few pleasant little parks and several decent hotels. Tuxpan is also a possible base for visiting Castillo de Teayo, 64 km away, and El Tajín, 70 km away – though Papantla is much more convenient for El Tajín.

History

Tuxpan was originally a Huastec settlement and the area was later ruled by Toltecs and then Aztecs. The Spanish subdued the nearby coastal region and inland highlands by 1523, within four years of their arrival in Mexico. In 1813 and 1814, during the independence war, the town received a commercial boost when merchants who were unable to move their goods inland from Veracruz transferred them to Tuxpan.

After independence, a Spanish force of 3000 landed at Cabo Rojo (80 km north of Tuxpan) in 1829 in a feeble attempt to regain Mexico. The invaders occupied Tampico, which had been evacuated, but surrendered to Santa Anna soon afterwards.

Tuxpan made its greatest leap forward with the discovery of oil fields in its hinterland at the turn of this century. La Barra de Tuxpan, on the nearby coast, was the scene of a battle in 1914; revolutionaries defeated conservative Huertistas and made Tuxpan, for a few glorious weeks, the Constitutionalist capital of Veracruz.

Orientation

The main landmark in Tuxpan is the

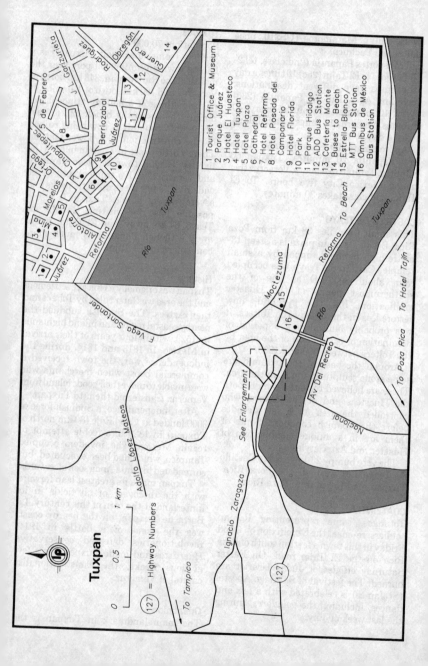

Tuxpan

127 = Highway Numbers

0   0.5   1 km

To Tampico
To Poza Rica
To Hotel Tajín

Río Tuxpan

Río Tuxpan

To Beach

Reforma

Moctezuma

Av Del Recreo

Nacional

Ignacio Zaragoza

Adolfo López Mateos

E Vega Santander

See Enlargement

1 Tourist Office & Museum
2 Parque Juárez
3 Hotel El Huasteco
4 Hotel Tuxpan
5 Hotel Plaza
6 Cathedral
7 Hotel Reforma
8 Hotel Posada del Campanario
9 Hotel Florida
10 Park
11 Parque Hidalgo
12 ADO Bus Station
13 Cafetería Monte
14 Buses to Beach
15 Estrella Blanco/ MTT Bus Station
16 Omnibus de México Bus Station

Garizurieta
Rodríguez
Obregón
Guerrero
5 de Febrero
J L Garizurieta
Chapultepec
Ortega
Morelos
Mina
Alatorre
Berriozábal
Juárez
Juárez
Reforma

bridge spanning the east-flowing Río Tuxpan. The centre of town is on the north side of the river, spreading five or six blocks west (upstream) from the bridge. Hotels, restaurants, banks and post office are all in this area. Reforma, the riverfront road, passes under the bridge and continues 12 km east to the beach. A block back from Reforma is Juárez, with many of the hotels. Parque Juárez, at the west end of Juárez, functions as a small zócalo.

Information

Tourist Office There's a tourist office (tel 4-01-77) on the west side of Parque Juárez. It's open 9 am to 7 pm Monday to Thursday and 1 to 7 pm Saturday and Sunday. The staff are friendly, the director speaks English, and they have reams of information (in Spanish) on local history, but there's not much in the way of tourist attractions for them to tell you about. The office is part of a small museum which includes Totonac pottery figures, a stone carving of Tlascolteotl (the Huastec love, birth and harvest god), a Totonac *quechquémitl*, and copies of pre-conquest paintings which appear to show tribute payments to the Aztecs.

Money There are several banks along Juárez.

Post The post office (closed Saturday afternoon and Sunday) is at Morelos 12.

Festivals

Tuxpan holds a carnival in late April with a procession of allegorical floats and the crowning of a clown king and queen. A big fishing tournament brings hundreds of visitors in late June or early July, and festivities for the Assumption of the Virgin Mary on 15 August go on for a week afterwards with folk-dancing contests, bullfights and fireworks. The Totonac *voladores* usually perform.

Places to Stay – bottom end

The *Hotel Posada del Campanario* (tel 4-08-55), at 5 de Febrero 9, isn't particularly welcoming to foreigners but the rooms are good value at US$2/2.50 for quite clean, sizeable singles/doubles with private bath and fan. Many of them have windows opening on to a small inner garden.

Much more basic is the *Hotel Colón* (tel 4-12-99, 4-08-21) at Juárez 14. This is a friendlier but dirtier and noisier wooden place where singles/doubles with private bath go for US$1.50/2. The entrance is through the Taquería Colón.

Places to Stay – middle

Best value in this range, though at the higher end of it, are the upper floors of the 77-room *Hotel Florida* (tel 4-02-22, 4-06-02) at Juárez 23. The big, not-quite-spotless rooms have superb river views for US$5.25/7.75 single/double with fan, or US$7.75/11.25 with air-con. There are also wide balconies/sitting areas and a lift.

Hotel Tuxpan (tel 4-41-10) at the corner of Juárez and Mina is popular, with 30 rooms (fans only) at US$3.75/4.50 for singles/doubles. Some rooms have big windows overlooking the street. Rooms in the *Hotel El Huasteco* (tel 4-18-59) at Morelos 41 are smaller and darker but the place is clean and friendly. One double bed costs US$4.50, two beds US$7, air-conditioning an extra US$0.75.

Places to Stay – top end

The *Hotel Reforma* (tel 4-02-10, 4-06-18) at Juárez 25 has a slight edge over the *Hotel Plaza* (tel 4-07-38, 4-09-38) at Juárez 39. Both are clean, air-conditioned and characterless, with TV in rooms, but the Reforma has slightly bigger rooms and a sitting area in a covered courtyard said to be 200 years old. Singles/doubles in both places are US$7.75/11.25. The Reforma also has some more expensive suites.

On the Tampico road at the edge of town, the *Hotel Plaza Palmas* (tel 4-38-

47) is a new luxury place with 104 rooms and suites with air-conditioning and colour TV. Singles/doubles are US$13/14.50. There's a restaurant, bars, swimming pool and tennis courts.

The very top place in Tuxpan is the *Hotel Tajín* (tel 4-21-51, 4-22-60) on the south side of the river a couple of km east of the bridge. Here you pay about US$16/18 singles/doubles.

Places to Eat

The restaurants of the Hotels *Plaza*, *Reforma* and *Florida*, all on Juárez, are the busiest of the smarter places in town. They serve Mexican and international fare with a heavy bias towards seafood. Most of it's pretty tasty, but you pay for the clean, orderly surroundings as well as the food.

At the Hotel Florida's restaurant fish soup costs US$1.60, seafood soup US$2.50, shrimp salad US$3. Other more expensive dishes include stuffed crab, squid or octopus cooked in wine, and vuelve a la vida, as well as enchiladas (US$1.60) and sizeable hamburgers (US$1 to US$1.75). At the Reforma's restaurant, the dearest of the three, you pay US$1.75 for enchiladas Suizas, US$3 for fish filet and US$4 for steak or shrimp; the special fish filet (with shrimp, garlic butter, rice and bread) isn't as big a plateful as you'd expect for US$4.

Among cheaper places, the *Cafetería Monte* at the corner of Obregón and Rodríguez does a thriving trade in enchiladas, fried bananas, and *bocoles* and *chalupas* (two members of the tortilla family with meat, chicken or bean fillings and piquant sauce). You can take away or eat in – but the tables are often full. For seafood try *Los Guayos* by the small waterfront Parque Hidalgo between Pipila and Azueta, or the *Restaurant Pereda* 1½ blocks west, also on the waterfront. Or go to the beach (see 'Around Tuxpan').

For cakes and coffee *Pastelisimo*, by the cathedral between Juárez and the waterfront, looks inviting. There's an open-air cafeteria in Parque Juárez.

Entertainment

There are a few sleazy bars, some with live music, on the eastern part of Juárez and the waterfront. The *Hotel El Tajín* has a disco.

Getting There & Away

Bus If you're travelling by bus direct from Mexico City to Tuxpan, you leave from the northern, not the eastern, bus station in the capital.

Tuxpan has three main bus stations. ADO (1st class) is on Rodríguez, half a block north of the river. From here buses go to Mexico City (US$4.25, 11 times daily), Tampico (US$3.25, 21 times), Veracruz (US$5.75, 10 times), Villahermosa (US$11.50, seven times), Poza Rica (US$0.75, 24 times), Papantla (US$1, five times), Acayucan (US$8.50, five times), Jalapa (US$4.25, five times) and San Andrés Tuxtla (US$7.50, three times). They go once or twice a day to Matamoros (US$10.25), Reynosa (US$10.50), Puebla, Córdoba, Orizaba and Tamiahua. Only a few of these services are direct, so it's worth checking the timetable and booking ahead.

Omnibus de México (also 1st class) is under the bridge and has buses to Mexico City (US$4.25, three times daily direct), Guadalajara (US$10.75, twice), Poza Rica (US$0.75, four times), Querétaro (US$6.75) and Tamiahua (eight times). Buses run once each to San Juan de los Lagos, Lagos de Moreno, León, Irapuato, Salamanca and Celaya.

Estrella Blanca and México-Tuxpan-Tampico (2nd class) are at the corner of Constitución and Alemán, two blocks north of the river and two blocks east of the bridge. They run three direct locales to Mexico City daily. Ordinary buses leave for Tampico every hour or half-hour, Poza Rica every 10 minutes, Ciudad Victoria and Monterrey four times daily, Reynosa and Nuevo Laredo twice daily, and

Matamoros, Tamiahua, Tlacolula and Huejutla daily.

Approximate 1st-class journey times: Tampico 4½ hours, Poza Rica 50 minutes, Papantla one hour 10 minutes, Matamoros 11 hours, Jalapa five to seven hours, Veracruz six hours, Mexico City six hours.

For El Tajín, go to Poza Rica or Papantla, then take a half-hour trip on local buses. Ten buses a day leave Poza Rica bus station for El Tajín. Going via Papantla involves a 10-minute walk between bus stations in Papantla and then two more buses, but these services are far more frequent than those from Poza Rica. See the 'Poza Rica' and 'Papantla' sections for details.

Getting Around

You can get a ferry across the river from the little park in front of the cathedral for 2c.

AROUND TUXPAN
Tuxpan Beach

A wide strip of sand stretches 20 km north along the shoreline from the mouth of the Río Tuxpan, 12 km east of the town, but its joys have been severely reduced by a power station being constructed two km north of the river mouth. Construction traffic trundles behind the strip of seafood shack-restaurants which lines the first km, then turns onto the beach itself for the rest of the trip to the site.

Places to Stay & Eat Dedicated beach-goers might still find Tuxpan Beach worth a visit – the water appears clean enough for the moment and the food prices are low. Typical costs are US$1 for fish soup; US$1.50 for seafood soup or red snapper; US$2.25 for a large oyster or shrimp cocktail, or octopus or shrimps with rice.

One or two places here rent basic rooms. The only slightly substantial place is the decaying *Hotel Playa Azul*, about 1½ km from the river mouth, where rooms with fan and bath go for US$3.50 (one double bed) or US$5 (two beds). The owner is so disgruntled by the nearby construction that he advises visitors to go north to Tamiahua instead!

Getting There & Away Those with plenty of time or their own vehicles could try going on up the beach past the power station. It's reportedly safe for camping.

To reach Tuxpan Beach from the town, take a 'Playa' bus (15c) from the Superbodega shop on Reforma, half a block east of Guerrero. It appears to be going the wrong way but does a quick circle of the town centre before heading out to the beach, where it drops you just north of the river mouth. Coming back, it's easy to pick up a colectivo taxi (25c) at the beach bus stop.

The road from town to beach passes several seafood restaurants and some docks with surprisingly big ships. Shortly before reaching the coast it crosses the mouth of the Tampamachoco Lagoon, which stretches about 10 km north from the Río Tuxpan.

Tamiahua

Tamiahua, 43 km from Tuxpan by paved road, is at the southern end of the 90-km-long Laguna de Tamiahua. It has a few seafood shack-restaurants and you can rent launches for fishing or trips to the lagoon's barrier island.

Western Veracruz

The slopes and valleys which rise from the coastal plain to the central highlands hold several old and sizeable towns. Jalapa is the most important and interesting. Córdoba, Fortín de las Flores and Orizaba lie close together further south, on Highway 150 from Veracruz. The area, known for its coffee, tobacco and flower cultivation, can be subject any time of

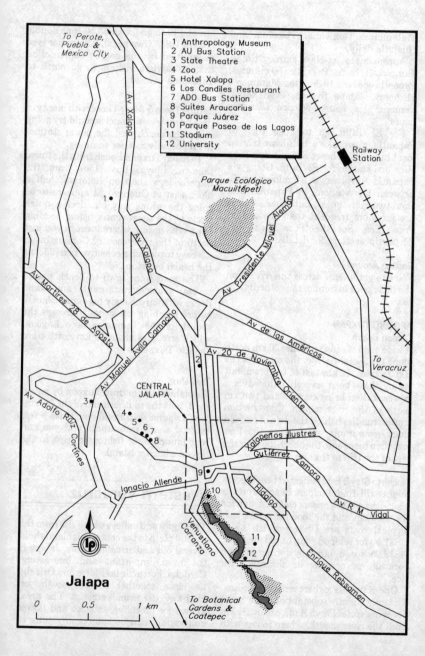

1 Anthropology Museum
2 AU Bus Station
3 State Theatre
4 Zoo
5 Hotel Xalapa
6 Los Candiles Restaurant
7 ADO Bus Station
8 Suites Araucarius
9 Parque Juárez
10 Parque Paseo de los Lagos
11 Stadium
12 University

To Perote,
Puebla &
Mexico City

Railway
Station

Parque Ecológico
Macuiltépetl

Av Xalapa

Av Xalapa

Av Presidente Miguel Alemán

Av Martires 28 de Agosto

Av Manuel Avila Camacho

Av de los Américas

To Veracruz

Av 20 de Noviembre Oriente

CENTRAL
JALAPA

Av Adolfo Ruiz Cortines

Xalopeños Ilustres

Gutiérrez Zamora

Ignacio Allende

M Hidalgo

Av R M Vidal

Venustiano Carranza

Enrique Rebsamen

Stadium

University

Jalapa

0   0.5   1 km

To Botanical
Gardens &
Coatepec

year to a persistent drizzle known as *chipichipi*.

JALAPA
Population: 250,000

The state capital of Veracruz (sometimes spelt Xalapa, always pronounced 'Ha-LAP-a') is an intriguing colonial city, 1427 metres high on the slope between the coastal plain and Mexico's central highlands, with some fine parks and excellent mountain views.

Jalapa's main attraction is its superb anthropology museum, but it's also the cultural capital of the state in a wider sense. Sometimes called the Athens of Veracruz, Jalapa has been home to the Universidad Veracruzana (University of Veracruz) since 1944. There are frequent concerts, exhibitions, theatre and dance performances, and some cafés and restaurants with live music. Most visitors come just for the museum but often leave wishing they had more time to get to know the place. If Jalapa appeals to you, try enquiring about the university's summer courses for foreign students.

History
A pre-Hispanic town here became part of the Aztec empire around 1460. Cortés and his men passed through in 1519. After the Spanish conquest Jalapa didn't take off until the annual trade fair of goods arriving from Spain was held here from 1720 to 1777. In 1847 at Cerro Gordo, 30 km east, the invading American troops of Winfield Scott routed Mexicans under Santa Anna (who was baptised in Jalapa) in the only resistance the Americans encountered on their way from Veracruz to Mexico City.

Today, as well as a government and cultural centre, Jalapa is a commercial hub for the coffee and tobacco grown on the mountain slopes, and is well known for its flowers. It has wealthy modern areas as well as some narrow winding colonial streets.

Orientation
The main road into Jalapa from Puebla and Mexico City changes names three times as it goes through the city centre and out the other side. Entering from the north as Avenida Xalapa, it passes the anthropology museum on the right, 3½ km from downtown. Then it becomes Camacho, curving right to approach the central area and passing the 1st-class (ADO) bus station on the left. When it reaches the city centre it is called Enríquez.

Here the Parque Juárez, a small formal garden on the right, is more or less the middle of the city. Just past Parque Juárez is the cathedral, dating from 1772, on the left. About 300 metres beyond Parque Juárez, Enríquez divides into Gutiérrez Zamora and Xalapeños Ilustres.

Central Jalapa is on a hillside, with Enríquez running roughly east-west across it. Hotels are on Enríquez, Gutiérrez Zamora, Zaragoza (parallel to Enríquez and one block south of it), and Revolución which runs uphill beside the cathedral to the 2nd-class (AU) bus station.

Information
Tourist Office There's a tourist office (tel 7-30-30) on the corner of Zaragoza and Bravo. It's closed on Saturday afternoon and Sunday.

Post The post office is in the Palacio Federal on Gutiérrez Zamora, two blocks east of where Enríquez divides to become Gutiérrez Zamora. It's closed on Saturday afternoon and Sunday.

Market The market is in the block bounded by Revolución, Altamirano and Dr Lucio.

Anthropology Museum
Jalapa's Museo de Antropología (tel 5-49-52, 5-07-08) is devoted to the archaeology of the state of Veracruz and is one of the best museums in Mexico – not only for its

large, exciting collection but also for its spacious, attractive lay-out. With its excellent models and explanatory displays (in Spanish), the museum is a textbook example of how a lesser-known area of Mexican archaeology can be made interesting. Some English-speaking staff are happy to answer questions.

To reach the museum from the city centre take a 'Tesorería' bus (4c) from Revolución 3¼ blocks north of Enríquez. The museum is a long, low grey building with a fountain, on the west side of Avenida Xalapa in the north of the city. It's open from 10 am to 5 pm daily except Monday. The entrance fee is 25c (free on Sunday).

Parks

Jalapa's luxuriant vegetation and hillside setting have enabled it to create some of Mexico's loveliest parks. The central Parque Juárez is a formal one on a terrace overlooking the town and valley below. Just a block south is the beautiful Parque Paseo de los Lagos, which winds a km along either side of a lake, with the campus of the University of Veracruz above it on one side. It's a peaceful place for an early morning stroll. At its northern end is the Casa de Artesanías (open 9 am to 7 pm Monday to Friday, 9 am to 1 pm Saturday and Sunday), where local handicrafts are shown and sold; look out for brass, embroidered dresses, reed furniture and curios carved from coffee plants. There's a park with a small zoo on the north side of Camacho by the Hotel Xalapa. In the north of the city, Calle Guadalajara leads 700 metres east off Avenida Xalapa nearly opposite the anthropology museum to the Parque Ecológico Macuiltépetl, laid out around an extinct volcano.

Botanical Garden The Jardín Botánico Francisco Javier Clavijero, 3½ km south of the Parque Juárez along Allende and then Bolivia, is a small area of the region's original forest, with a path winding through it and some labelled trees.

Places to Stay - bottom end

The *Hotel Continental* (tel 7-35-30) at Gutiérrez Zamora 4 is a friendly place with two internal courtyards (one roofed) and bigger rooms than other places in the same price range. Look at a few rooms before choosing – some are a lot better than others. They're all bare but clean. Singles/doubles are US$3.25/3.75 and the only drawbacks are the plastic sheets beneath the real one and a disinfectant smell in some rooms. Beware the bizarre logo on some of the bedclothes, which may be a singing nun but could give anyone a nasty turn in the morning half-light.

The *Hotel Limón* at Revolución 8 has small tiled rooms and a rectangular tiled courtyard with a fountain and trees. It's clean and rooms have private bath and hot water. Singles are US$2.25; doubles are US$2.75 with one bed, US$3.50 with two. The man at the desk is gruff but probably friendly beneath the surface.

Places to Stay - middle

Hotel México (tel 8-80-00) at Dr Lucio 4, near the corner of Enríquez, has 69 carpeted, basically clean but slightly

1	Market
2	Hotel Limón
3	Cathedral
4	Restaurant Terraza Jardín
5	El Agora
6	Hotel México
7	Restaurant Emir
8	El Escorial
9	Hotel Continental
10	Palacio Federal, Post Office
11	Tourist Office
12	Hotel Salmones
13	La Casona del Beaterio
14	Café La Parroquia
15	Restaurant Monroy
16	Hotel María Victoria
17	Casa de las Artesanias
18	Parque Los Berros

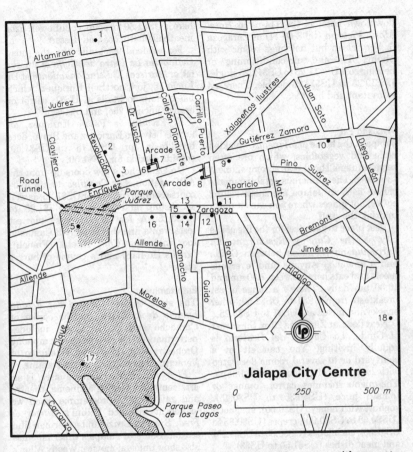

Jalapa City Centre

0   250   500 m

damp rooms for US$4 single, US$4.50 double with one bed, and US$5.25 double with two beds. The central courtyard is also a car park.

Suites Araucarius (tel 8-12-11, 7-34-33) at Camacho 60 next to the ADO bus station offers clean rooms with TV, fridge and cooking facilities. Singles are US$4.50, doubles with one bed US$5.25, doubles with two beds US$6.25.

Hotel Salmones (tel 7-54-31 to 35) is at Zaragoza 24 on the corner of Bravo, unmistakable because of its salmon-pink paint. It has a small garden, big lobby, restaurant and rooms with carpets, phones and sometimes TV. Singles/doubles are US$6.25/7.25.

Places to Stay – top end

Top place in town is the modern, plush 202-room *Hotel Xalapa* (tel 8-22-22, 7-72-18) on Victoria 1½ blocks uphill from Camacho. The central part is built round a swimming pool and there are bars, a restaurant, cafeteria, disco and glass-fronted convention hall. Air-conditioned singles/doubles are US$16/17.75.

Its predecessor as the number-one

downtown hotel is the 114-room *Hotel María Victoria* (tel 8-60-11) at Zaragoza 6. Very clean but not huge rooms with phone, TV and air-conditioning or heating cost US$11.25 to US$12.25 single, US$13.25 to US$14.25 double. There's a restaurant and bar too.

Places to Eat

Jalapa is the home of *jalapeños* – pickled chile and vegetables, which are often served in a small bowl as an accompaniment to meals. The numerous establishments called 'café' in Jalapa are shops selling coffee, not places where you can sit down to drink the stuff.

Best place to get a feel for the life of the city is the *Café y Restaurant La Parroquia* on Zaragoza between Guido and Camacho. Anyone and everyone meets and eats here between 7.30 am and 10.30 pm daily. There's a range of set breakfasts from US$1 to US$2.50; other snacks and meals are US$1 to US$3.25.

Next door, at Zaragoza 20 on the corner of Guido, *La Casona del Beaterio* is equally inviting. You can sit in a courtyard or in several rooms decorated with hundreds of photos of old Jalapa. The menu includes carrot, orange or tomato juice (US$0.35 to US$0.45), yoghurt with honey (US$0.50), spaghetti (US$0.60 to US$0.90), crepes (US$0.85 to US$1.50), enchiladas (US$0.80 to US$1.25) and meat dishes (US$1.50 to US$3).

A couple of doors in the other direction along Zaragoza from the Café y Restaurant Parroquia, the clean *Restaurant Monroy* does antojitos; a four-course comida corrida costs US$1.25. You'll find a bigger and better comida corrida for US$2.25 in the *Restaurant Terraza Jardín*, the biggest and brightest of the city's modern cafeteria-style places, on Enríquez overlooking the Parque Juárez.

Restaurant-Café-Bar Emir, in the arcade between Enríquez and Dr Lucio behind the Hotel México, is another popular modern place. Comida corrida here is US$1.50 for soup, cauliflower, fish/meatballs/barbacoa and dessert.

For seafood cocktails try the busy *Ostionería La Ostra del Golfo* at Juárez 59, or *Mariscos El Estacionamiento* at Dr Lucio 15, just north of Enríquez, which has shrimp cocktails at US$1, carrot or orange juice at 25c, and tortas.

El Escorial in Pasaje Enríquez, an arcade between Enríquez and Bravo, does breakfasts for US$0.75 to US$1.50, comida corrida for US$1.50.

On Camacho, a few doors up from the ADO station, *Los Candiles* does a four-course comida corrida for US$1.25, as well as shrimp and steak for US$1.25 to US$2.25. A few of Jalapa's smartest restaurants line this stretch of Camacho too, including *Chez Apetit* (French), *Luigi's* (Italian) and a couple of burger places.

Entertainment

The state theatre *(Teatro del Estado Ignacio de la Llave)*, at the corner of Camacho and De la Llave, includes performances by the Jalapa Symphony Orchestra and the Ballet Folklórico of Veracruz University in its programme.

El Agora, in the Parque Juárez, is an arts centre containing a cinema, theatre and gallery. The programme when we visited it included Fellini's *Ginger & Fred, Bye Bye Brazil* and a German film season. Some of Jalapa's other cinemas also show unusual movies: Woody Allen's *Hannah & Her Sisters* was on at the Cine Pepe, where Camacho becomes Avenida Xalapa.

The *Café y Restaurant La Parroquia* has a notice board of what's on, including theatre, exhibitions, rock and classical music. *El Escorial* restaurant sometimes has live rock music in the evenings. There's a disco (the *Paladium*) in Callejón Diamante (also called Rivera) off Enríquez between Dr Lucio and Carrillo Puerto.

Getting There & Away

Air The nearest airport is at Veracruz. ADO runs buses there to connect with flights.

Road Jalapa is 175 km from Puebla by the good Highway 140 via Perote. To Veracruz, it's 99 km by Highway 140, or a bit further if you turn left off Highway 140 on to Highway 125 for Cardel and then down Highway 180 to Veracruz. A paved mountain road winds south through Huatusco to Fortín de las Flores (121 km), Córdoba and Orizaba. Northwards, Highway 127 is also mountainous for most of the 110 km to Martínez de la Torre, from where it's 39 km by Highway 130 to the coast near Nautla.

Bus The 1st-class bus station is at Camacho 84. ADO buses go to Veracruz (US$1.50) every 20 or 30 minutes from 5.30 am to 9.30 pm; Cardel (US$0.75) 16 times daily; Mexico City (US$4) 22 times; Poza Rica (US$3.50) 11 times; Coatzacoalcos (US$5) and Orizaba (US$2.50) nine times each; Córdoba (US$2.25) eight times; Papantla (US$3.25) seven times; Tuxpan (US$4.25), Puebla (US$2.50) and San Andrés Tuxtla (US$3.25) six times each; Veracruz airport (US$3.50) and Villahermosa (US$7.25) five times each; Zempoala (US$1), Nautla (US$2.25) and Tuxtepec (US$3.25) three times each; Tampico (US$7.25), Santiago Tuxtla (US$3.25), Mérida (US$15), Campeche (US$12.50) and Chetumal (US$14.25) twice each; Catemaco (US$3.50) and Cancún (US$18.75) once each; and Alvarado, Acayucan, Misantla, Tantoyuca, Huamantla, Huatusco and Tlacotalpan.

Approximate ADO journey times: Puebla 2½ hours, Veracruz 2½ hours, Tuxpan five to seven hours, Papantla four to six hours, Mexico City 4½ hours, Villahermosa eight to nine hours.

Estrella Azul 1st-class buses go eight times daily to Huatusco, Fortín de las Flores and Córdoba; twice daily to Orizaba.

The AU (2nd class) bus station (tel 5-01-44, 5-01-57) is on the corner of Revolución and Julian Carrillo. Services – some direct, some stopping – include 16 daily to Veracruz (US$1.50), 12 to Mexico City (US$3.75), every half-hour from 6 am to 7 pm to Cardel, four to Papantla (US$3) and Poza Rica, two to Villahermosa (US$6.75), and others to Nautla and Tehuacán.

Rail Jalapa has a railway station, way out in the north of the city four blocks east of the junction of Avenida Cárdenas and Avenida Alemán, but there's only one slow train a day each way to Mexico City and Veracruz. The 3.30 pm departure for Veracruz takes four hours, the 11.40 am train for Mexico City takes eight hours. Fares to Mexico City are US$2.25 in 1st class, US$1.25 in 2nd class.

AROUND JALAPA
Cofre de Perote

Cofre de Perote is a 4282-metre-high volcano south-west of Jalapa. The name means 'coffer', a reference to the mountain's shape. It's also called Nauhcampatépetl (square mountain). A rough dirt road (initially called Calle Allende) leading from the town of Perote, climbs 1900 metres in 24 km to just below the rocky summit 50 km west of Jalapa along Highway 140. There are radio and TV masts around the top.

Coatepec

This village 15 km south of Jalapa is known for its locally grown coffee and orchid gardens. The María Cristina orchid garden, on the main square, is open daily. Orchid wreaths are prominent in the church decorations for the festival of San Jerónimo (30 September).

Huatusco

Huatusco, 70 km south of Jalapa on the Fortín de las Flores road, has a procession and traditional dances for the festival of San Antonio on 13 June, and a procession of pilgrims from the surrounding area early in the morning of 12 December to the shrine of the Virgin of Guadalupe. Not far from Huatusco is the Totonac site of Quauhtochco, with a four-level pyramid.

Naolinco

Naolinco, 26 km north of Jalapa on the Martínez de la Torre road, re-enacts the crucifixion on Good Friday, has a fair with dances for San Mateo on 21 September, and holds the traditional celebrations for the Day of the Dead on 2 November. A paved road leads five km north to a lookout (*mirador*) to an 80-metre waterfall.

CÓRDOBA

Population: 150,000

This town at 924 metres has a long colonial history but nowadays it's less important than it used to be. If you're looking for somewhere to stop between Veracruz (126 km away) and Mexico City, Córdoba ('CORR-do-ba') is pleasant and relaxed enough but there's nothing of major appeal to see or do. Jalapa (though it involves a bit of a detour) and Puebla are much more interesting stopovers between coast and capital.

History

Named after the city in Andalusia, Spain, Córdoba was founded in 1618 by 30 Spanish families in order to stop attacks by escaped black slaves on transport travelling between Mexico City and the coast. Known as La Ciudad de los Treinta Caballeros (City of the 30 Knights), it has long been the first place of any size on the main route from Veracruz to Puebla and Mexico City. By the late 18th century it was also an important sugar industry centre, with more than 50 mills.

In 1821 royalist forces were beaten at Córdoba in the last significant battle of the independence war, and later the same year the Treaty of Córdoba finalised Mexican independence from Spain. Mexico's first railway, completed in 1872, passed through Córdoba en route from the capital to Veracruz. Today the city is quite a prosperous commercial and processing centre for the sugar cane, coffee and tobacco grown on the surrounding

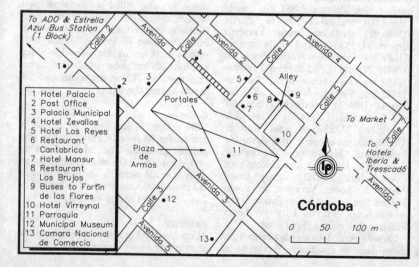

1 Hotel Palacio
2 Post Office
3 Palacio Municipal
4 Hotel Zevallos
5 Hotel Los Reyes
6 Restaurant Cantabrico
7 Hotel Mansur
8 Restaurant Los Brujos
9 Buses to Fortín de las Flores
10 Hotel Virreynal
11 Parroquia
12 Municipal Museum
13 Camara Nacional de Comercio

To ADO & Estrella Azul Bus Station (1 Block)

Portales

Plaza de Armas

To Market

To Hotels Iberia & Tresscad6

Córdoba

0   50   100 m

hillsides, and for fruit from the lowlands to the east. But its importance as a way-station has declined with the spread of the internal combustion engine, which removes the necessity for an overnight stop between Mexico City and the coast.

Orientation

Everything of importance in Córdoba is within a few blocks of the central Plaza de Armas, also called Parque 21 de Mayo, which is rectangular with several colonial buildings. The parroquia (parish church) occupies its south-eastern half. The central streets are on a grid plan, with Avenidas running north-west to south-east, and Calles at right angles to Avenidas.

Information

Tourist Office The Cámara Nacional de Comercio (National Chamber of Commerce, tel 2-11-47, 2-81-77) at 308 Calle 5, between Avenidas 3 and 5, gives out maps and a booklet on the city and can answer some questions. It's open 9 am to 1 pm and 4 to 7 pm Monday to Friday, and 9 am to 1 pm Saturday.

Post The post office, at 3 Avenida 3 just north-west of the Plaza de Armas, is open 8 am to 8 pm Monday to Friday and 9 am to 1 pm Saturday and Sunday.

Market & Shops The market, particularly busy on Saturday and Sunday, is bounded by Calles 7 and 9 and Avenidas 8 and 10. Shops are in the blocks south-east of the Plaza de Armas.

Hotel Zevallos

This is not a hotel but the former family home of the Condes (Counts) of Zevallos or Ceballos, built in 1687. It's on the north-east side of the Plaza de Armas (near the top end, entered through an archway). Plaques in the courtyard record that in this building Juan O'Donojú and Agustín de Iturbide met after mass on 24 August 1821 and agreed on Mexico's independence

from Spain. O'Donojú was the incoming Spanish viceroy, apparently a liberal, who had concluded that it was useless for Spain to try to cling to its colony; Iturbide was the leader of the anti-imperial forces, a former royalist general who had changed sides and issued the Plan de Iguala with independence movement leader Vicente Guerrero.

The plan called for independent Mexico to be a constitutional monarchy with the King of Spain or another European prince as nominal head of state, but the Treaty of Córdoba between O'Donojú and Iturbide allowed for a Mexican to hold that office. Iturbide went on to a brief reign as Emperor Agustín I.

Other Sights

Córdoba's municipal museum at 303 Calle 3 is an appallingly displayed one-room collection including some *palmas* from the Classic Veracruz period and earlier. The building that houses it is 17th century.

La Parroquia de la Immaculada Concepción, in the Plaza de Armas, is Córdoba's impressive late 18th-century parish church, which has two towers and loud and famous bells. At the top (north-west) end of the Plaza de Armas is the 19th-century neoclassical Palacio Municipal (town hall) which was the seat of the state government briefly in 1917.

Places to Stay

There are three good deals on and around the Plaza de Armas. The *Hotel Virreynal* (tel 2-23-77), opposite the parroquia at the corner of Avenida 1 and Calle 5, has spacious and clean but bare rooms with tiled floors, private bath, telephone and no fans for US$3 single, US$4.50 double. The hotel also has a good restaurant.

A bit more comfortable but a few blocks from the centre is the *Hotel Iberia* (tel 2-13-01, 2-42-76). It's at 919 Avenida 2, two blocks downhill from the Virreynal, then one block to the left and half a block to the right. It has pleasant modern rooms with TV, telephone and pointed-arched windows, around a long courtyard with trees. Singles are US$3.25, doubles US$3.75 or US$5.25.

For a spot of luxury try the *Hotel Mansur* (tel 2-60-00), on the Plaza de Armas at the corner of Avenida 1 and Calle 3. Rooms aren't enormous but are well kept and the lobby is very elegant. Singles/doubles with TV, phone and air-conditioning are US$6.50/8.

Elsewhere, the *Hotel Tresscadó* (tel 2-23-66) at 909 Avenida 2 is very bare and a bit smelly but basically clean. Singles are US$1.75, doubles US$2 to US$2.50. Hot water is limited to five hours a day and some of the fans don't work. *Hotel Los Reyes* (tel 2-25-38) at 10 Calle 3 has singles for US$2.75, doubles for US$3.75 or US$5.50. Rooms have fans and the staff are friendly but the rooms need paint and a good scrub and airing.

The *Hotel Palacio* (tel 2-21-88) at the corner of Avenida 3 and Calle 2, recently remodelled, has big and pleasant air-conditioned singles/doubles with TV for US$7.50/10.25. It has its own restaurant.

Places to Eat

The restaurant of the *Hotel Virreynal* is popular at breakfast and also for its excellent comida corrida (US$2), of which an example is vegetable soup, two enchiladas, rice, beef with bananas, and jelly or flan.

Restaurant Los Brujos at 306 Avenida 2, reached from the Plaza de Armas by an alley between the hotels Mansur and Virreynal, is a reasonably priced local favourite. It does a four-course comida corrida for US$1, as well as meat, chiles rellenos or fish (*mojarra frito* is tasty) for US$1.50.

The portales on the north-east side of the Plaza de Armas are lined with cafés and restaurants where you can drink the local coffee in a variety of ways. *Restaurant El Cordobés* at 111 Avenida 1 has cappuccino and chamomile and cinnamon (*canela*) tea as well as a long

food menu which includes meats (US$1.75 to US$3.50), chicken (US$1.50), spaghetti (US$1) and seafood (cocktails US$1 to US$2). At 101 Avenida 1, the top of the portales, *El Tabachín* is renowned for its freshwater prawns (*langostinos*).

Just off the Plaza de Armas the *Restaurant Cantabrico* at 11 Calle 3 is a tasteful slightly up-market restaurant with piped-in music and a long menu of fish and meat in the US$1.50 to US$2.75 range as well as Mexican snacks.

Getting There & Away

Road A toll autopista (Highway 150-D) heads west from Córdoba, by-passing Fortín de las Flores and Orizaba en route to Puebla. Highway 150, the road up from Veracruz, continues through those towns, then turns south-west for Tehuacán.

Bus ADO and Estrella Azul (1st class, tel 2-03-90, 2-18-30) are at the corner of Avenida 3 and Calle 4.

There are hourly ADO buses to Mexico City (US$4), 21 daily to Orizaba (25c), 19 to Villahermosa (US$7.50), 17 to Puebla (US$2.50), 15 to Veracruz (US$1.50), 13 to Coatzacoalcos (US$5.50), nine to Jalapa (US$2), eight to San Andrés Tuxtla (US$3.25), seven to Acayucan (US$4.75), five to Tehuacán (US$1), four to Oaxaca (US$5) and three to Tuxtepec (US$1.75). Two each go to Huajuapan (US$2.50), Tamazulapan (US$3), Nochixtlán (US$3.50), Campeche (US$12.75), Mérida (US$15) and Playa del Carmen (US$18.25). One each goes to Cancún (US$19), Papantla (US$6.25) and Tuxpan (US$7.25). There is also service to Cosamaloapan, Tierra Blanca, Loma Bonita and Tres Valles.

Estrella Azul has eight buses a day to Jalapa (US$2). Approximate 1st-class journey times are: Veracruz two hours, Mexico City four hours, Puebla two hours.

AU (2nd class, tel 2-18-42) is at the corner of Avenida 7 and Calle 9. It has services (with stops) to Orizaba (25c) and

Tehuacán every 20 minutes from 4.20 am to 9 pm. It runs 21 direct buses a day to Mexico City (US$3.75); 18 to Puebla (US$2.25); 10 each to Veracruz (US$1.50) and Tuxtepec (US$1.75); nine each to Acayucan (US$4) and Coatzacoalcos (US$4.75); six to Cosamaloapan (US$2); three each to Alvarado (US$2.25), San Andrés Tuxtla (US$3) and Catemaco (US$3.25); two each to Santiago Tuxtla (US$3), Villahermosa (US$6.75) and Tehuacán (US$1); and services to Tierra Blanca, Tres Valles, Playa Vicente and Loma Bonita.

Lineas Unidas México-Istmo runs 2nd-class buses from the AU station to Juchitán (US$5.50) three times daily, Arriaga twice, Tehuantepec (US$5.75) and Salina Cruz (US$6) once each.

Buses for Fortín de las Flores (12c) leave from Avenida 2 between Calles 3 and 5, opposite the Los Brujos restaurant.

Rail Córdoba railway station (tel 2-09-13) is at the corner of Avenida 11 and Calle 33 in the south of the town. The most important trains are the night sleepers between Mexico City and Veracruz, which stop at Córdoba. The 9.32 pm from Mexico City reaches Córdoba at 4.20 am and Veracruz at 7 am. The 9.30 pm from Veracruz arrives at Córdoba at 11.41 pm and Mexico City at 7.37 am. These trains have the full range of accommodation. Fares to Mexico City are: 2nd-class seat US$1.25, 1st-class seat US$2.25, 1st-class reserved seat US$5, roomette for one US$6.75, roomette for two US$10, bedroom for two US$11.

There are also three other trains daily to Fortín and Orizaba (one hour), two each to Veracruz (2½ to three hours) and Mexico City (seven to nine hours), three to Tierra Blanca (two to three hours), and one to Papaloapan and Coatzacoalcos (nine hours). Of these, the 1.55 and 10.25 am to Orizaba and Mexico City, the 3 am to Tierra Blanca, Tres Valles, Papaloapan and Coatzacoalcos, and the 4.27 pm to Veracruz also have 1st-class seats.

FORTÍN DE LAS FLORES
Population: 16,000

The only reason for visiting Fortín ('Forr-TEEN') de las Flores (altitude 1010 metres) is indicated by its name, which means Fortress of the Flowers. In April, May and June the town's many gardens, *viveros* (nurseries) and plazas blossom with a riot of lovely, colourful flowers including gardenias, orchids, camellias and azaleas. In these months Fortín is a lovely place to stop between the highlands and the coast. Emperor Maximilian and his wife Carlota had a pad here, the Hacienda de las Ánimas, but it's now private property surrounded by a high wall.

Two km west of Fortín on the autopista to Rizaba, the road crosses the Barranca (Canyon) de Metlac, 164 metres below.

Information & Orientation
Fortín is seven km from Córdoba and 11 km from Orizaba. It has a big open plaza, the Parque Central, with the Palacio Municipal (town hall) and library in the middle and a church at the south end. Avenida 1 is the main road running through the town across the north side of the Parque Central, Avenida 3 goes across the middle of the parque, Avenida 5 forms its south side. Calle 1 runs down the west side of the parque, Calle 3 down its east side.

There's a market area a block south of the parque and a couple of blocks east.

Places to Stay & Eat
Posada La Marina, on the north-east corner of the Parque Central at the junction of Avenida 1 and Calle 3, has clean, bright, big rooms with private bathrooms for US$2.75 per person.

Hotel Bugambilia at the corner of Avenida 1 and Calle 7 has singles/doubles for US$3.25/5.25.

Hotel Fortín de las Flores (tel 3-00-55, 3-01-08), on Avenida 2 between Calles 5 and 7, is a well-kept top-end hotel. It has 130 rooms, gardens, table tennis and a swimming pool with bar and tables. All rooms have fans, some have air-conditioning, but you'd expect them to be bigger at US$10.50/13.25 singles/doubles.

Posada Loma (tel 3-06-58) is one km out of town, set back above Highway 150 towards Córdoba. The rooms are in bungalows in big gardens; singles/doubles cost US$9.50/11.25. Facilities include swimming pool, billiards, squash and table tennis.

There are a few restaurants along Calle 1, both on the Parque Central and north of it.

Getting There & Away

Bus The ADO station is about three blocks west of the Parque Central along Avenida 1. There are five direct buses daily to Mexico City (US$4), and services to Veracruz.

There are frequent local buses to and from Córdoba and Orizaba. To Córdoba

(12c) they leave from Avenida 1 a block east of Fortín's Parque Central. The trip takes 15 minutes.

Rail There's a train station two blocks north of the north-west corner of the Parque Central on Calle 1 Norte. There are three trains daily in each direction (Córdoba and Veracruz one way, Orizaba and Mexico City the other), plus one a day to Tierra Blanca and Coatzacoalcos, and another just to Orizaba. One-way fares to Mexico City: 2nd class US$1.25, 1st class US$2.25, 1st-class reserved seat US$5.

ORIZABA
Population: 150,000

Orizaba is an industrial and transport centre. It's 144 km from Puebla, 271 km from Mexico City, 16 km from Córdoba and 142 km from Veracruz and lies at an altitude of 1284 metres. Mexico's highest mountain, the 5700-metre Pico de

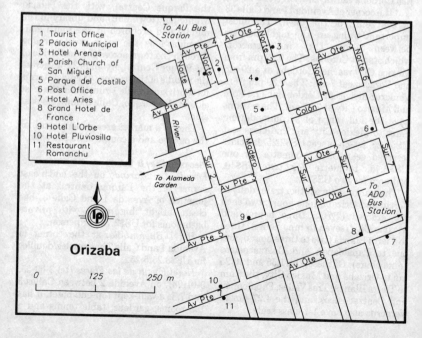

1 Tourist Office
2 Palacio Municipal
3 Hotel Arenas
4 Parish Church of San Miguel
5 Parque del Castillo
6 Post Office
7 Hotel Aries
8 Grand Hotel de France
9 Hotel L'Orbe
10 Hotel Pluviosilla
11 Restaurant Romanchu

Orizaba

0   125   250 m

Orizaba, is often visible to the north-west, though the climbing approaches are from the far side. Orizaba has a few colonial buildings, some dating back to the 17th century, and lots of church domes rising above its streets. It's quite a lively, pleasant town, but like the slightly more affluent Córdoba has no compelling attractions.

History

There was an Aztec garrison here after the area became subject to the Aztec empire in the mid-15th century. Later the Spanish founded a town to guard the Veracruz-Mexico City road. In the 1860s Maximilian and Carlota had a retreat at the Hacienda de Jalapilla, three km south of Orizaba (now private property). Orizaba developed as an industrial centre in the late 19th century, and an international industrial and scientific fair was held here in 1880. Some of the area's factories were early centres of the unrest that eventually led to the unseating of dictator Porfirio Díaz.

Today Orizaba has a big brewery and cement, textile and chemical factories. It's also a centre for the surrounding fertile, agricultural area.

Orientation

Orizaba has a strong claim to Mexico's most confusing street name system. The central square, called the Parque del Castillo, has the parish church of San Miguel on its north side. Madero, running down the west side of the parque, is the town centre's north-south axis, and Colón along the south side of the parque is the east-west axis. Beyond that, things get more difficult.

Follow this if you can: streets east of and parallel to Madero are called Calle Norte 2, Calle Norte 4, Calle Norte 6, etc while they're north of Colón, but they become Calle Sur 3, Calle Sur 5, Calle Sur 7, etc when they get south of Colón. Thus Calle Norte 2 and Calle Sur 3 are different stretches of the same street. Streets west

of and parallel to Madero are on a similar 'system': one block west is Calle Norte 3/Calle Sur 2, two blocks west is Calle Norte 5/Calle Sur 4, etc.

East-west streets are called Avenidas and change their names and numbers when they cross Madero: the first street south of and parallel to Colón is Avenida Poniente (Pte) 3 when it's west of Madero, and Avenida Oriente (Ote) 2 when it's east of Madero. The next one south is Avenida Pte 5/Avenida Ote 4. The first street north of and parallel to Colón is Avenida Pte 2/Avenida Ote 3, the next one up is Avenida Pte 4/Avenida Ote 5.

The market is in the block east of Madero and north of Ote 5.

Information

Tourist Office There's a tourist office in the Casa Consistorial, on Calle Norte 1 between Avenidas Pte 2 and 4, behind the town hall. Its opening hours are 10 am to 1.30 pm and 5 to 7 pm Monday to Friday, and 10 am to 1.30 pm Saturday. At the time of writing there was no telephone in the office but questions were answered at 4-36-77.

Post The post office is at the corner of Sur 7 and Ote 2.

Town Hall

The Palacio Municipal, off the north-west corner of the Parque del Castillo, is made entirely of iron and steel. Originally the Belgian pavilion at the Paris International Exhibition in the late 19th century, it was bought by Orizaba for 105,000 pesos, dismantled, shipped across the Atlantic, and rebuilt.

Churches

San Miguel, the parish church on the north side of the Parque del Castillo, is a large mainly 17th-century construction with several towers and some Puebla-style tiles. Orizaba has several other colonial churches, including the 18th-century La Concordia, El Carmen and

Santa Gertrudis, all with churrigueresque façades.

Mural

The Centro Educativo Obrero (Workers' Education Centre), a neoclassical building on Colón between the Parque del Castillo and the Alameda, has a mural by José Clemente Orozco.

Gardens

Alameda Garden is a formal park four blocks west of the centre along Colón.

Topiary The garden of the Fundación Mier y Pesado, on Ote 6 a few blocks east of the ADO station, has bushes spectacularly cut into the shapes of soccer players, birds, etc.

Brewery

You can arrange to tour the big Cervecería Moctezuma at Pte 7 and Sur 10 by calling 5-11-50, 5-13-07 or 5-10-38 in advance.

Places to Stay

Best value in town is the *Hotel Arenas* (tel 5-23-61) at 169 Norte 2, half a block south of Ote 5. It's family-run, friendly, and has a well-cared-for tropical garden in its central courtyard. Spotless rooms with bath cost US$2.75 single, US$3.75 or US$4.75 double.

Hotel San Cristóbal (tel 5-11-40) at 243 Norte 4, half a block north of Ote 5, has clean rooms with bath for US$2.75 single or double. *Hotel Colonial* (tel 5-01-57) at 262 Sur 2 is basic with small rooms with bath at US$2.50 single or double.

The *Grand Hotel de France* at the corner of Ote 6 and Sur 5 is a decaying place with an imposing tiled staircase and sizeable singles/doubles for US$4.75/6.50.

Top-end places include the *Hotel L'Orbe* (tel 5-53-44) at 33 Pte 5, with 72 air-conditioned rooms with TV from US$8.25 single, US$10 double. The *Hotel Pluviosilla* (tel 5-52-65, 5-53-00) at 163 Pte 7 has rooms round a central courtyard

where you can park a car. Singles/doubles are US$6.75/7.25. *Hotel Aries* (tel 5-37-69) at 265 Ote 6 is modern and soulless and the rooms are clean but dark. Singles/doubles are US$6.75/8.75. Only the suites (more expensive) receive much daylight.

Places to Eat

Most of the restaurants are along Madero Sur, Sur 3 and Pte 7/Ote 6; they usually close by 8.30 pm. One of the best is the *Restaurant Romanchu* opposite the Hotel Pluviosilla on Pte 7. The Hotel Pluviosilla has its own restaurant, *La Borda*, where meals are not cheap (breakfast from US$1.75, dinner US$2.25 to US$3) but are quite substantial.

Restaurant Capricornio, attached to the Hotel Aries, has a long menu including moderately tasty pizza at prices ranging from US$1 for a small cheese pizza to US$3 for a large Napolitana.

Getting There & Away

Road An autopista (Highway 150-D) by-passes Orizaba, heading east to Córdoba and winding its way westward up to 2385 metres on the way to Puebla. Highway 150 runs south-west from Orizaba to Tehuacán, 65 km away, from where it's a further 246 km to Oaxaca.

Bus The ADO bus station (1st class, tel 4-27-23) is at 577 Ote 6 between Sur 11 and 13. There are 28 buses daily (16 locales) to Mexico City (US$4), about 50 to Córdoba (25c), 15 (six direct) to Veracruz (US$1.75), 12 (four locales) to Puebla (US$2.25), eight to Jalapa (US$2.75) and four to Tehuacán (US$0.80). There are three each to Oaxaca (US$4.75), Tuxtepec (US$2), Coatzacoalcos (US$5.75) and Villahermosa (US$7.75); and one each to Tuxpan (US$7.50), San Andrés Tuxtla (US$3.75), Catemaco (US$4), Acayucan (US$5), Campeche (US$13) and Mérida (US$15.25), as well as buses to Tlacotalpan, Cosamaloapan, Tres Valles, Tierra Blanca and Huajuapan.

Approximate journey times are: Córdoba

30 minutes, Mexico City four hours, Veracruz 2½ hours.

The AU (2nd class, tel 5-05-40, 5-19-55) bus station is at 425 Zaragoza Pte. To reach the town centre from here, turn left out of the exit, take the first fork right and head for the church domes which you can see two or three blocks ahead. From Orizaba AU has frequent services to Córdoba (25c). It also runs 18 direct buses daily to Puebla (US$2); 10 to Veracruz (US$1.75); eight to Coatzacoalcos (US$5); seven to Mexico City (US$3.50); four to Tuxtepec (US$2); three each to Alvarado (US$2.50), Acayucan (US$4.50) and Villahermosa (US$7); two each to San Andrés Tuxtla (US$3.25) and Catemaco (US$3.50); and one to Arriaga (US$7). There are also services to El Seco (US$1.25, for Tlachichuca and the Pico de Orizaba), Tierra Blanca, Tres Valles, Playa Vicente, Loma Bonita and Cosamaloapan.

Rail Orizaba is on the Mexico City, Córdoba, Veracruz line with three trains a day in each direction to Veracruz (three to four hours) and Mexico City (six to eight hours), plus one to Córdoba and Coatzacoalcos. The station (tel 5-24-90) is south of the central area at the corner of Pte 19 and Sur 10.

AROUND ORIZABA
Tuxpango
Five km east of Orizaba on Highway 150, there's a two-km side road south to the Tuxpango dam and reservoir on the Río Blanco and a cable railway which drops steeply and rapidly 800 metres to the dam and the village of Tuxpango. The cable car makes 10 trips up and down a day – the first descent is at 6.40 am, the last ascent at 11.15 pm.

Zongólica
Zongólica is a Nahua village 37 km south of Orizaba where Nahua dances are performed on 3, 9 and 10 May for the festival of the Señor de los Recuerdos (the

Lord of Remembrance). It's also a centre for celebrations of the Day of the Virgin of Guadalupe, with processions and dances on 11 and 12 December.

Southern Veracruz

This flat, hot, wet region is crossed by many rivers flowing down from the mountains of Oaxaca and the central highlands, but is broken by hills only where the volcanic Sierra de los Tuxtlas rise to above 1800 metres, then sweep down to the sea about 150 km from Veracruz city.

The green, fertile area around the Sierra de los Tuxtlas has several lakes and waterfalls; the early 19th-century traveller Alexander von Humboldt called it the 'Switzerland of Veracruz'. His comparison was far-fetched but the area, more commonly known as Los Tuxtlas, is one of the best-looking and most agreeable parts of Veracruz, with a more comfortable climate than the surrounding lowlands. It has a small lakeside resort (Catemaco), a quiet coastline and an easygoing 'capital' (San Andrés Tuxtla). Catemaco apart, it's off the beaten tourist track – locals will often greet foreigners warmly or gape in surprise.

Los Tuxtlas is also the western fringe of the ancient Olmec heartland, with two interesting museums in and near the little town of Santiago Tuxtla. The basalt for the huge Olmec heads of San Lorenzo, 60 km south of Los Tuxtlas, was quarried from Cerro Cintepec in the east of the Sierra de los Tuxtlas, then transported probably by roller and raft to its destination. Tres Zapotes near Santiago Tuxtla is an important late or post-Olmec site, and Laguna de los Cerros, south of the Sierra near Covarrubias, was an early Olmec centre, probably contemporary with San Lorenzo. Unfortunately there's nothing to interest non-specialists at either site now.

On the far eastern slopes of the Sierra de los Tuxtlas and in the plains just south live a few communities of Popoluca and Nahua Indians. The 20,000 or so Popolucas here are the only ones of their kind; their language is spoken nowhere else. Remote San Pedro Soteapan, 40 km north of the Acayucan-Coatzacoalcos road, is their biggest settlement. Hueyapan de Ocampo, near Covarrubias between Catemaco and Acayucan, is the second biggest. The Nahuas, whose ancestors probably came to the area in the 8th century, are the easternmost members of Mexico's biggest Indian group, which is scattered over much of the central part of the country.

South of Los Tuxtlas the town of Acayucan, with San Lorenzo nearby, is the northern gateway to the low-lying Isthmus of Tehuantepec, the narrowest part of Mexico. In the far east of the state the broad Río Coatzacoalcos approaches the Gulf of Mexico, passing through the industrial towns of Minatitlán and Coatzacoalcos.

Roads Highway 180 goes all the way from Veracruz through Los Tuxtlas to Acayucan, Coatzacoalcos and Villahermosa. At Acayucan, 246 km from Veracruz, Highway 185 branches south across the isthmus to Juchitán, 195 km away. A more westerly route south off Highway 180 is Highway 175 (narrow in parts) which goes through Tlacotalpan and up the Papaloapan Valley to Tuxtepec (117 km from Highway 180), then twists and turns over the mountains to Oaxaca (215 km from Tuxtepec).

VERACRUZ TO LOS TUXTLAS
Archaeological Sites
Highway 180, heading south-east from Veracruz, ducks a few km inland after

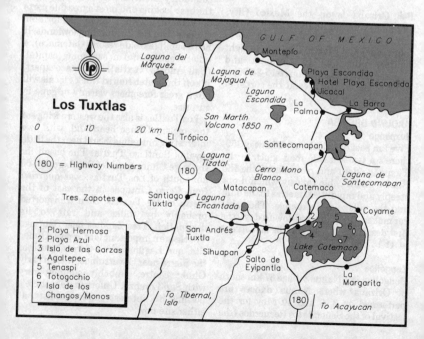

Boca del Río. A side-road to the south, 28 km from Veracruz, leads to the small towns of Tlalixcoyan and Ignacio de la Llave (58 km from Veracruz). Near Ignacio de la Llave are two minor archaeological sites.

El Zapotal This was a late Classic Veracruz or Totonac centre which flourished from about 600 to 900 AD. Excavations since 1971 have revealed that a 30-metre-high mound was the tomb of about 400 women. From the mound 22 well-sculpted, life-size clay statues have been unearthed. Most of them are of half-nude women, probably goddesses. There's a small museum on site but otherwise not much to see now.

Cerro de Las Mesas (Hill of the Altars) This lies between Ignacio de la Llave and Piedras Negras to the west. This was an important transitional site after the decline of the Olmecs, and flourished between about 400 and 600 AD. There are hundreds of mounds, some of which were pyramids. The greatest find here was a collection of 782 carved jade pieces buried under a staircase – possibly a treasure-trove or an offering to the gods. These and some stone carvings have been moved to museums elsewhere.

Alvarado

This busy fishing town is 67 km down Highway 180 from Veracruz. It stands on the narrow spit of land separating the Gulf of Mexico from the Laguna de Alvarado, meeting point of several rivers including the Papaloapan. East of the town a long road bridge crosses the channel which joins the lagoon to the sea.

Alvarado has a few hotels, and the restaurant in the Port Authority building has a reputation for superb seafood at very good prices. The parish church was built in the 18th century. Carnival celebrations here are timed to start immediately after the Veracruz carnival finishes. The other main festival is around the day of the Holy Cross (Santa Cruz) on 3 May. You can hire boats here for trips on the lagoon or up the river to Tlacotalpan (about two hours).

Tlacotalpan

This quiet, little-visited old town beside the wide Río Papaloapan is reached by a road which heads 10 km south from Highway 180, 16 km east of Alvarado. Tlacotalpan has some very pretty streets, churches and plazas and two small hotels – the *Posada Doña Lala* and the *Hotel Reforma* – on Carranza, the main street. The Museo (Museum) Salvador Ferrando, open 10 am to 3 pm and 5 to 7 pm daily except Monday, is mainly devoted to the late 19th century, and includes displays of furniture and women's costumes of that time. You can rent boats in Alvarado for the journey upriver to Tlacotalpan, or in Tlacotalpan for other trips.

Tlacotalpan's lively Candelaria festival, in late January and early February, features bull-running in the streets and several river-based events. In one of these an image of the Virgin is carried along the river and is followed by a flotilla of small boats.

SANTIAGO TUXTLA

Here, 140 km from Veracruz and 14 km from San Andrés Tuxtla, you are in the rolling green foothills of the volcanic Sierra de los Tuxtlas, where lots of maize and cattle are raised. Santiago is a small, pretty valley town with a river running through it, 285 metres high and founded in 1525, which makes it the oldest Spanish settlement in the area. Its few visitors today come mainly because of its Olmec associations. There's an Olmec head and a museum in the town square, and an important Olmec site and another museum at Tres Zapotes, 23 km away. After a day of visiting these relics, don't be surprised if the modern-day locals take on Olmec facial features too!

Santiago celebrates the festivals of San Juan (24 June) and Santiago Apóstol (St James, 25 July) with processions and

Tlacotalpan

dances including the Liseres, in which the participants wear jaguar costumes. It's also noted for its Christmas and New Year festivities.

Information & Orientation

Buses arriving in Santiago drop you at Morelos, a street just off the highway. Calle Ayuntamiento runs off Morelos at right angles to the central square and its clock tower. The post office is in the central square. There's a Multibanco Comermex here too, but the nearest place to change travellers' cheques is San Andrés Tuxtla.

Cobata Head

The Olmec head in the central plaza is known as the Cobata head, after the place where it was found on the Cerro (hill) de Vigía, west of Santiago. It's thought to be a very late or even post-Olmec production, but is the biggest of all the Olmec heads found so far and is unique in that its eyes are closed.

Museum

Along one side of the central square stands the Santiago museum, with several more Olmec pieces. Unfortunately labelling is scarce, but the man at the desk is knowledgeable and helpful. Among the Olmec exhibits (all carved in stone) are a colossal head from Nestepec west of Santiago, a rabbit head from Cerro de Vigía, a toad or frog, and a copy of Monument F or 'El Negro' from Tres Zapotes which is an altar or throne with a human form carved into it. The museum also has some interesting anthropology exhibitions. It's open 9 am to 7 pm Tuesday to Saturday (9c), and 9 am to 3 pm Sunday (free).

Places to Stay & Eat

Hotel Castellanos (tel 7-02-00, 7-03-00), on the main square at the corner of 5 de Mayo and Comonfort, has a swimming pool and 48 bright, clean, air-conditioned rooms of varying sizes. Singles/doubles are US$6.25/6.75. It also has a pleasant restaurant where eggs cost US$0.50, meat or chicken US$1 to US$1.75 and seafood a bit more.

Hotel Morelos (tel 7-04-04) has Morelos 12 as its address but it's actually on

Obregón, a small street running off Morelos almost opposite the Autotransportes Los Tuxtlas bus station. Rooms have fans and private bath with hot water but aren't very big, and some are brighter than others. Singles/doubles are US$3/4.75.

From the main square you can reach a small mariscos restaurant by going down the hill and over the river, and then left a few metres.

Getting There & Away

Bus ADO, AU and Cuenca del Papaloapan are all next to each other where Morelos meets the highway. Autotransportes Los Tuxtlas is a short way along Morelos from the highway.

ADO (1st class) has a few services each day to San Andrés Tuxtla (20c), Catemaco (US$0.30), Acayucan (US$1.50), Coatzacoalcos (US$2), Alvarado (US$1), Veracruz (US$1.75), Jalapa (US$3), Puebla (US$5.25) and Mexico City (US$7).

Cuenca (2nd class) has about nine buses daily to San Andrés Tuxtla; others to Tlacotalpan, Cosamaloapan, Tuxtepec (US$2) and Tierra Blanca (US$2.50); and two to Oaxaca (US$4.75, 10 hours).

AU (2nd class) has two or three buses daily to San Andrés Tuxtla, Catemaco, Acayucan (US$1.25), Coatzacoalcos (US$1.75), Veracruz (US$1.50), Jalapa (US$2.50), Córdoba (US$3), Orizaba (US$3.25), Puebla (US$5) and Mexico City (US$6.50).

The cramped, suspension-free buses of Autotransportes Los Tuxtlas depart every few minutes to San Andrés Tuxtla (15c) and Veracruz (US$1.50), slightly less often to Catemaco and Acayucan. They're also supposed to leave for Tres Zapotes (US$0.50) every 1½ hours from 5.45 am to 2.45 pm but some buses don't turn up.

Journey times are only about 15 minutes less than those to San Andrés Tuxtla.

TRES ZAPOTES

This village 23 km across the plains west of Santiago Tuxtla would be left in rural obscurity if it wasn't close to one of the most important centres of the late Olmecs. The ancient site itself is now just a series of mounds in maize fields, but there's a museum in the village where many interesting finds are displayed.

History

Tres Zapotes was probably first occupied while the great Olmec centre of La Venta in Tabasco still flourished. It carried on after the destruction of La Venta in about 400 BC, in what archaeologists now regard as an 'epi-Olmec' phase when the spark had gone out of Olmec culture, and other civilisations – notably Izapa – were also leaving their mark here. Most of the finds are from this later period.

The Olmec head now in the Tres Zapotes museum was the first to be discovered in modern times; it was found by a hacienda worker in 1858. An equally important find was made here in 1939 when Matthew Stirling, the first great Olmec excavator, unearthed Stela C, a chunk of basalt with an epi-Olmec were-jaguar carving on one side and, on the other, a series of bars and dots apparently giving part of a date in the Mayan Long Count dating system. Stirling calculated the date as 3 September 32 BC – which meant that, if he was right, the Olmecs had preceded the Mayas, who at that time were believed to have been Mexico's earliest civilisation. Much archaeological controversy followed but other finds over the next decades supported Stirling. In 1969 a local farmer came across the rest of the stela, which bore the missing part of Stirling's date.

Museum

Tres Zapotes museum is open daily 9 am to 5 pm. Entry is 10c (free on Sundays and holidays). The objects are arranged on a cross-shaped platform. On the far side is the Tres Zapotes head, dating from about

100 BC. On the nearest side, opposite the head, the biggest piece is Stela A, on which you can make out three human figures in the mouth of a jaguar. This originally stood on its end. To the right of Stela A are what may have been a sculpture of a captive with hands tied behind its back ('fingers' are visible at the base) and another piece with a toad carved on one side and a skull on the other. Beyond Stela A is an altar or throne carved with the upturned face of a woman, and beyond that, in the corner, the less interesting part of the famous Stela C (the part with the date is in the Mexico City museum but there's a photo of it on the wall of the museum building here).

The museum attendant is happy to answer questions (in Spanish), is full of interesting details about the collection, and refuses tips.

The site these objects came from is about a km away. Walk back past the Sitio Olmeca, left at the end of the road past the small village square (where you can get drinks at a small café), on over the bridge and along the road.

Getting There & Away

Autotransportes Los Tuxtlas runs buses (US$0.70) from San Andrés Tuxtla to Tres Zapotes. They supposedly leave San Andrés every 1½ hours from 5.30 am to 2.30 pm and call at Santiago Tuxtla 15 to 20 minutes later, taking about an hour from San Andrés to Tres Zapotes, but the schedule is highly unreliable. The last return buses from Tres Zapotes to Santiago supposedly leave at 2 and 4 pm.

A much quicker alternative is the green-and-white colectivo taxis (US$0.50) which run between Calle Morelos in Santiago and Tres Zapotes. A sign ('zona arqueológica') on Highway 180 as it enters Santiago from San Andrés, points the way to Tres Zapotes. Eight km down this road, you fork right onto a decent dirt track for the last 15 km to Tres Zapotes. It comes out at a T-junction on what's probably the village's main street, next to a taxi stand called Sitio Olmeca. From here you walk to the left, then turn left again to reach the museum.

SAN ANDRÉS TUXTLA

Population: 50,000

The 'capital' of the Los Tuxtlas region, 154 km from Veracruz, is at an altitude of 365 metres among the rolling hills which typify the area. Foreigners are rare enough here for locals to utter a friendly 'goodbye' as you pass them on the street. (Don't take this as a thinly veiled hint to get out of town quick; the Spanish adiós, usually translated as 'goodbye', is used as a greeting too.)

North of San Andrés is the San Martín volcano, at an altitude of 1850 metres high. The town was founded after its eruption in 1664. Dormant now, it's not quite the highest peak in the Sierra de los Tuxtlas – that honour goes to Cerro Cumbres Bastonal, between Lake Catemaco and Coatzacoalcos, which is 1879 metres high. The country around San Andrés grows maize, bananas, beans, sugar cane, fruit, cattle and good-quality tobacco, which is turned into cigars (puros) in the town.

The Mexican TV soap opera Como Duele Callar ('How it hurts to keep quiet') was being filmed on location in San Andrés when we visited the town, and the normally tranquil pace of life was shattered by scenes reminiscent of Beatlemania. For days on end crowds of teenagers besieged the Hotel Del Parque, where stars Graciela Mauri and Enrique Rocha were staying. The hotel's receptionist described it all as an escándalo!

There's not much to do in San Andrés, but it's a pleasant, town, relatively free of tourists, and a convenient base for the Los Tuxtlas area, with good transport connections and cheaper accommodation than Catemaco. Santiago Tuxtla is 14 km west and Catemaco is 12 km east.

Information & Orientation

San Andrés' bus stations (except for Autotransportes Los Tuxtlas) are on Juárez, which runs downhill from Highway 180 on the west side of town. To reach the centre, walk down the hill, over the bridge and straight on to the main plaza with its church, a couple of blocks beyond. The building immediately on your right as you enter the plaza is the Palacio Municipal (town hall). Most places to stay and eat are on or near Juárez or the plaza.

The post office is on Lafragua; head down 20 de Noviembre directly over the plaza from the Palacio Municipal and follow it round to the left. To reach the market from the plaza, walk down Rascón (between the Hotel Del Parque and the Canada shoe shop) for three blocks.

Salto de Eyipantla

This 50-metre-high, 40-metre-wide waterfall is a favourite day-trip for locals. A perpetual cloud of mist is thrown up by the spray and the gorge walls are covered in moss and other plants which thrive in the dampness. A staircase of 242 steps leads down to a lookout point and there's also a cafeteria. Autotransportes Los Tuxtlas buses (25c) run about half-hourly to Eyipantla. The trip takes about 40 minutes. The falls are 12 km from San Andrés; follow Highway 180 east for four km to Sihuapan, then turn right down a dirt road.

Laguna Encantada

The 'Enchanted Lagoon' is one of the best-known lakes of Los Tuxtlas, because of its odd habit of rising in dry weather and falling when it rains. It's in a small volcanic crater three km north-east of the town. A dirt road goes there but no buses.

Matacapan

At Cerro del Gallo near Matacapan, just east of Sihuapan, there is a pyramid from the early Classic period (300-600 AD) in a style typical of Teotihuacán, the great Classic culture in central Mexico. This site may have been on the route to Kaminaljuyú in Guatemala, the farthest-flung Teotihuacán outpost.

Places to Stay - bottom end

There are three reasonably priced hotels on Pino Suárez. To reach them, turn left when you hit the main plaza coming from Juárez. Pino Suárez is the second street on the right. The *Hotel Catedral* (tel 2-02-37) at the corner of Pino Suárez and Bocanegra is probably the best of the three. Large, quite clean rooms with fan, private bath and 24-hour hot water cost US$1.50 single, US$2.50 double.

A bit further up the street, the *Hotel Figueroa* at the corner of Belisario Domínguez also has clean rooms with fan, private bath (not always so clean) and hot water. Some have more light or are bigger than others, and some open onto the balcony-walkway above the street. Singles/doubles are US$1.50/3. Opposite the Figueroa, the *Hotel Colonial* is grubbier and worse kept than the other places in the street. Singles and one-bed doubles are US$1.50, two-bed doubles US$1.75.

Places to Stay - middle

If you can get a room, the very friendly *Posada San José* (tel 2-10-10, 2-20-20) at Belisario Domínguez 10 is probably the best value in town. To reach it, follow directions for Pino Suárez as above and turn left at the end of Pino Suárez. There are 30 good clean rooms round a covered interior courtyard, all with private bath and most with fan. Some of them have balconies. Singles/doubles are US$3.25/4.25.

Hotel San Andrés (tel 2-06-04) at Madero 6 (turn right when you hit the plaza from Juárez) is also recommended by travellers. It has 31 rooms with TV but they're often all full. Singles with fan are US$6.50, singles with air-con and doubles with fan are US$7.75, doubles with air-con are US$9.25. A little further along Madero at No 10, the *Hotel Zamfer* (tel

2-02-00) is one of those 'modern' places that is already ageing: electrical sockets hang from the walls, the 'hot' water is lukewarm, ventilators direct little air but a lot of noise, and the paint needs a scrub. The staff are friendly but it's not a good deal at US$4/4.50 single/double.

Places to Stay - top end
Top place in town is the 48-room *Hotel Del Parque* (tel 2-01-98) at Madero 5 on the plaza. Singles/doubles with TV and phone are US$12/13.50.

Places to Eat
San Andrés has a superb corner seafood restaurant that you'd probably walk past without noticing if you didn't know it was there. It's *Mariscos Chazaro* at Madero 12, next to the Hotel Zamfer. Surroundings (apart from a cartoon of the owner as the 'alchemist of the sea') are nothing special, even a bit fly-blown, but each order is prepared before your eyes with multiple ingredients and great care by Señor Chazaro and the results are delicious. Sopa de mariscos (US$1.75) is a tasty meal in itself.

Of the two cafés on the plaza, opposite the Canada shoe shop, *Café Los Portales* is busier and much better than the *Cafetería Catedral*. You can get good cappuccino for 25c, huevos rancheros for US$0.50, four tacos for US$0.75, meat or chicken for US$1.25 to US$2.

The Hotel Del Parque restaurant has slick service but the food's no better than average (eggs US$0.75 to US$1, meat or chicken US$2.25 to US$3, seafood US$3.50).

Along Juárez, *Caperucita* at No 106, on the right moving away from the plaza, is an open-air, semi-fast-food place patronised mainly by middle-class teenagers. Unappetizing pizzas are US$1.50, *tortugas* (buns filled with ham, salami and cheese but surprisingly tasteless) are US$0.75. There are also tortas (US$0.40) and burgers.

Just over the bridge on the left the *Lonchería Guadalajara de Noche* at

Juárez 212 doesn't look like much from the outside, but inside it's an Aladdin's cave of hanging plants, a fish tank, cart wheels, Olmec heads, faces carved in coconut shells, pistols and a picture of the Virgin inside an enormous plastic garland. As for the food, four quesadillas with guacamole are tasty but cost US$1 and don't dent your appetite. Other potentially more interesting items such as queso fundido al carbón were unavailable when we were there one evening – but it may be worth trying at lunch time. There are also meats, and vegetable salad.

A little further up Juárez at No 229, *Antojitos La Bahia* is the best bet on the street. It has blue doors, red-and-white striped walls and yellow plastic tablecloths, and does very good cheap snacks and licuados. For 25c you get three tasty *entomatadas* (tortillas with cheese, chicken and chile in tomato sauce). Eggs (Mexicanos, scrambled or with ham) are also just 25c.

Things to Buy
For cigars, go to the Santa Lucia factory (tel 2-12-00) at Boulevard 5 de Febrero 10 (actually Highway 180 – turn right for a few metres at the top of Juárez). They have a wide variety of good short, fat, long or thin cigars at factory prices. Even if you don't want to buy any, the sights and smells of the cigar-making process are interesting.

Getting There & Away
Bus ADO (1st class) is at the top of Juárez, where it hits Highway 180. Services include 18 buses daily to Veracruz (US$2); 16 to Coatzacoalcos (US$2); 11 to Mexico City (US$7.25); 10 to Villahermosa (US$4); seven to Jalapa (US$3.25); five to Santiago Tuxtla (20c); four each to Catemaco (15c), Tampico (US$10.50), Córdoba (US$3.50) and Mérida (US$11.50); three each to Puebla (US$5.75) and Campeche (US$9.25); and two to Chetumal (US$10.75). Approximate ADO journey times: Veracruz three hours, Mexico City

nine hours, Acayucan 1½ hours, Villahermosa six hours, Mérida 15 hours.

AU (2nd class), a couple of blocks down Juárez towards the town centre, has six buses daily to Acayucan (US$1) and Coatzacoalcos (US$1.75); five each to Alvarado (US$1), Córdoba (US$3) and Orizaba (US$3.25); four each to Santiago Tuxtla (15c), Catemaco (15c) and Puebla (US$5.25); and two each to Mexico City (US$6.50), Veracruz (US$1.75), Jalapa (US$3) and Villahermosa (US$3.50).

Cuenca del Papaloapan (2nd class) is next door to AU. Its buses go to Tlacotalpan and Cosamaloapan (US$1.50) about 10 times daily, Tierra Blanca and Oaxaca (US$5, about 10 hours) twice each and Tuxtepec (US$2.55) daily.

Getting Around

Autotransportes Los Tuxtlas (2nd class) uses cramped, bumpy, sometimes ancient buses but it's often the quickest way of getting to local destinations. Its buses leave from the corner of Independencia and Rafael Solana Norte in San Andrés. To get there from the main plaza head down Rascón, between the Hotel Del Parque and the Canada shoe shop, for three blocks to the market; then turn right and take the first left. There are services to Santiago Tuxtla (15c), Veracruz (US$1.75) and Catemaco (15c) every few minutes; to Acayucan (US$1) about every 20 minutes; plus (unreliably) every half-hour to Salto de Eyipantla (25c) and every 1½ hours between 5.30 am and 2.30 pm to Tres Zapotes (US$0.70).

CATEMACO

Population: 25,000

This small, untidy, friendly town on the western shore of a beautiful lake makes most of its living from fishing and from Mexican tourists who flood into it in July, August, and particularly around Christmas and Semana Santa (the week before Easter). The rest of the year it's a quiet, economical place to stay where you can take boat trips on the lake, walks or bus trips around it; or visit the little-known nearby coast. Catemaco is 12 km from San Andrés Tuxtla, 166 km from Veracruz, 80 km from Acayucan and 312 km from Villahermosa. The town is at an altitude of 370 metres.

Lake Catemaco, surrounded by volcanic hills, is roughly oval-shaped, 16 km long and on the average about six km wide. It has several islands; on the largest one, Tenaspi, Olmec sculpture has been found. Streams flowing into the lake are the source of Catemaco and Coyame mineral water. The country round the lake holds four smaller lakes and, to the east, the mountain of Santa Marta. Cerro Mono Blanco (White Monkey Hill) north of the town is reputed to be an annual meeting place of *brujos* (witch-doctors), and Catemaco numbers a well-known herbal healer, Gonzálo Aguirre Pechi, among its citizens.

Orientation

Catemaco, small though it is, is slightly confusing to get around owing to the curves of the lake shore. From the AU bus station, walk downhill towards the church to reach the main plaza. The lake shore is then two blocks to your right. From the ADO, walk uphill to the church and plaza. If you're in the plaza, over the road and facing the Hotel Catemaco, the lake is two blocks behind you. The road going to your left divides after two blocks; the right fork goes to AU and Highway 180, the left fork goes to the Autotransportes Los Tuxtlas station.

The road heading east round the lake starts where the rutted town streets end; go down Hidalgo (to your right if facing Hotel Catemaco) and ask. The road passes Playa Hermosa on the right after about 1½ km. About four km out of town a left turn takes you on to the rough dirt road that goes to Sontecomapan and the coast.

Information

Money You can change cash and travellers'

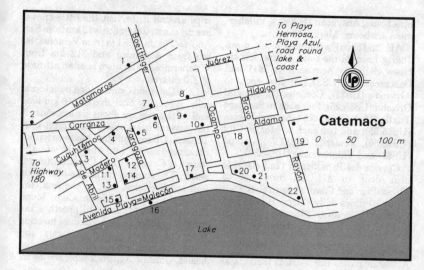

1   Hotel San Francisco
2   AU Bus Station
3   Transportes Los Tuxtlas Bus Station
4   Restaurant Alfredo's
5   Posada Vicky
6   Hotel Las Brisas
7   Hotel Acuario
8   Hotel Catemaco
9   Zócalo
10 Church
11 Hotel Los Arcos
12 Market
13 Mariscos El Tegogolo
14 Las Brisas
15 La Luna Restaurant
16 Restaurant La Ola
17 Hotel Julita
18 ADO Bus Station
19 Post Office
20 Hotel Del Brujo
21 La Suiza Restaurant
22 Los Sauces Restaurant

cheques at Multibanco Comermex on the zócalo.

Post The post office is on Aldama, two blocks down from the zócalo.

Market The market is on Madero, 1½ blocks from the plaza.

Church
The pretty domed and towered church of the Virgen del Carmen in the plaza is a pilgrimage centre for a couple of days leading up to 16 July.

Boat Trips
There are always plenty of boats ready to take people out from the moorings just down from the plaza. Prices for different destinations are posted, but you could try bargaining, especially out of season. The price is per boat, not per person, so the more the cheaper.

One of the most popular trips is to Tanaxpillo Island, better known as Isla de los Monos or Isla de los Changos (Monkey Island). Around 60 red-cheeked Macaca Arctoides monkeys, originally from Thailand, live here. They belong to the University of Veracruz which uses them for study purposes. Despite pleas from the university to leave the animals alone, boat operators bring food for them so that tourists can get close-up pictures. Posted price for the half-hour trip to Monkey Island and back is US$5.75. Sometimes there are also colectivo boats for US$2 per person.

Boat tours to other destinations are offered, or you can devise your own itinerary for US$9.50 an hour.

Lake Walk
The lake-front road turns into a path at the eastern edge of the town for a pleasant hour's waterside stroll which takes you as far as the big Motel Playa Azul. On the way you pass a grotto topped with a blue cross where the Virgin is believed to have appeared in the 19th century. Further on is Playa Hermosa, less a beach than a narrow strip of grey sand. The water's a bit murky but not too cold.

East of the Lake
If you want to explore the villages and country to the east of the lake, take a local bus going to La Margarita. They leave every hour or two from the corner of Juárez and Rayón. The friendly people in the Tienda La Surtidora del Sur on the corner carry the timetable in their heads. Some locals say La Margarita buses also go from the plaza.

Places to Stay
Catemaco has accommodation across the price range, but add 30-50% at the peak periods.

Places to Stay - bottom end
Hotel Acuario (tel 3-04-18), on the plaza at the corner of Carranza and Boettinger, is excellent value. Large, comfortable singles/doubles with private bath are US$2/3. Some rooms are brighter than others, and those upstairs are in slightly better condition. *Hotel Los Arcos* (tel 3-00-03) at Madero 7 on the corner of Mantilla is also a good bet. The clean, bright rooms have fans and private baths and there are wide balcony-walkways. Singles/doubles are US$3/4.25.

Going down a bit in price, the *Hotel San Francisco* (tel 3-03-98) at Matamoros 26 has fair-sized rooms with fan and private bath for US$2 single or double. There's a bit of damp on the walls but otherwise it's quite well kept. *Hotel Julita* at Avenida Playa 10, near the waterfront just down from the plaza, has some basic but clean rooms with fan and private bath for US$1.50/3 single/double.

Posada Vicky at Zaragoza 56 is approached by very poky stairs but the rooms are reasonably clean at US$1.50/2 single/double. Some have private bath, some have balconies. *Hotel Gallardo*, next door, is a bit better. Singles/doubles with private bath are US$2/3.25.

Camping *Restaurant Solotepec* at Playa Hermosa 1½ km east of town has a small camping area/trailer park close to the lake. *Hotel Canarias*, about 180 km out of town on Highway 180 to Acayucan, also has a trailer park.

Places to Stay - top end
Probably the best place is 2½ km east of town by the lake. It's the *Motel Playa Azul* (tel 3-00-01, 3-00-42) where 100 bright, clean, modern rooms are set in single-storey blocks around a garden. Singles/doubles are US$11.25/13.50 and there's a swimming pool, restaurant, volleyball court, boat rental and disco (in season). There's also the *Hotel La Finca* (tel 3-03-22), two km out of town on the Acayucan road, where the air-conditioned rooms all have balconies and lake views, at prices similar to the Playa Azul. La Finca has a pool and restaurant too.

Back in town, the *Hotel Del Lago* (tel 3-01-60, 3-04-31) is on the lake-front road, Avenida Playa, at the corner of Abasolo (two or three blocks to the right if you go down to the lake from the main plaza). Rooms are clean but not very big - you're paying for the lake-front setting. Singles/doubles are US$9/10.25. There's a restaurant and small swimming pool.

The *Hotel Catemaco* (tel 3-00-45, 3-02-03), right on the plaza, charges US$11.50/

13.50 for air-conditioned singles/doubles with TV. It has a restaurant, video bar (beer US$0.70) and pool.

Places to Eat

The lake provides the specialities here, among them the *tegogolo*, a lake snail reputed to be an aphrodisiac and best eaten in a sauce of chile, tomato, onion and lime; *mojarra* (a type of perch); and *anguilas* (eels). *Changocon* (monkey meat), which used to be another local 'delicacy', is now very rare – not because of an outbreak of mercy but because of the forests where the monkeys and numerous other mammals used to live have nearly all been cut down. *Chipalchole* is a soup with shrimp or crab claws.

The town waterfront is lined with good restaurants where you can dine from lake, sea or land. The two best-known are *La Ola* and *La Luna*, a few metres apart on opposite sides of the lakeside road (turn right when you reach it from the main plaza). Mojarra in both places costs US$1.50 to US$2. In the other direction along the waterfront is a clutch of slightly cheaper but good places, first *La Suiza*, then *Los Sauces* and *El Cacique*. The last-named is probably the best; try its *mojarra al tachogobi* (in a hot sauce) or eel with raisins and hot chile. Most of these places are closed by 7 pm out of season.

Mariscos El Tegogolo, at the bottom of Mantilla, does delicious shrimp, oyster, octopus, crab and sea snail cocktails for US$0.85 (small) or US$1.70 (large); also vuelve a la vida (US$2.25).

For antojitos, *Restaurant Alfredo's*, on Cuauhtémoc near the junction with Carranza, is a relaxed little place with friendly young staff, tapes of Western rock music and good tacos (12c each) of beefsteak or *cochinita pibil* (Yucatán-style pork). It also does a four-course comida corrida and stays open until midnight every night. *Restaurant y Tortería Yesi* on Zaragoza just off Carranza is another good snack place. An order of entomatadas or enfrijoladas costs just US$0.35, and they serve enchiladas too.

Of the hotel restaurants, the *Hotel Catemaco* serves quite good food but you pay for the smart surroundings (spaghetti US$1.75, meat dishes US$1.75 to US$3.75).

Entertainment

There's sometimes live music in the *La Luna* restaurant. On Sunday nights the town holds an open-air dance to tropical music on the plaza. Entry is (US$2.50).

Getting There & Away

Bus ADO (1st class) is on Aldama, a block down from the plaza. There are four buses daily to San Andrés Tuxtla (15c) and Alvarado (US$1.25); three to Santiago Tuxtla (US$0.30) and Veracruz (US$2); two to Mexico City (US$7.50); and one each to Acayucan (US$1), Coatzacoalcos (US$1.75), Villahermosa (US$3.75), Jalapa (US$3.50), Córdoba (US$3.50) and Puebla (US$5.75).

AU (2nd class) is at the junction of Carranza and Matamoros, on the way out of town to Highway 180. It has six buses a day to Acayucan (US$0.90) and Coatza-coalcos (US$1.50); five each to San Andrés Tuxtla (15c) and Alvarado (US$1); four each to Santiago Tuxtla (US$0.30), Córdoba (US$3.25), Orizaba (US$3.25) and Puebla (US$5.25); and two each to Veracruz (US$2), Jalapa (US$3.25), Mexico City (US$6.75) and Villahermosa (US$3.50).

Autotransportes Los Tuxtlas is on Cuauhtémoc near the corner of 2 de Abril. Its buses are scheduled to go to San Andrés Tuxtla (15c), Santiago Tuxtla and Veracruz (US$2) every 10 minutes; Acayucan (US$0.90) every 20 minutes; and Sontecomapan (US$0.50), Playa Escondida (US$0.55) and Montepío (US$0.90) every 1½ hours from 6 am to 3 pm.

Journey times are about 20 minutes different from those to San Andrés Tuxtla.

Getting Around

If you can't be bothered to walk to Playa Hermosa, get an Autotransportes Los Tuxtlas 'Montepío' bus (see 'Getting There & Away') or a local 'La Margarita' bus (see 'East of the Lake').

El Timbre on Madero rents bikes for 25c an hour.

THE COAST NEAR CATEMACO

A badly rutted dirt road heads north off the Coyame road and about four km out of Catemaco to a little-visited part of the Gulf coast. Autotransportes Los Tuxtlas buses (see 'Getting There & Away') bump, grind and lurch along it as far as Montepío, traumatising the numerous piglets by the roadside. The buses take 1½ hours to Playa Escondida, the most worthwhile destination. The last returning buses supposedly leave Montepío at 2 and 4 pm, but you can hitch a lift easily enough. This is mainly ranch-land, horses are a common form of transport, and the countryside is superb, with green hills rolling right down to parts of the shore.

Sontecomapan, the first potential stop, is 18 km from Catemaco at the head of a lagoon. You can hire boats to take you out on the lagoon or to the small fishing settlement of La Barra at the lagoon mouth. To La Barra and back costs about US$6. There are also a couple of restaurants at Sontecomapan, which is a popular day trip for Mexicans.

After Sontecomapan the track climbs over the shoulder of a hill, with a superb view of the lagoon below. After about nine km it reaches a small junction where a half-hidden sign points to 'Playa Escondida, El Eden de Dios 2 km'. The walk down this track takes you past the long, sweeping grey-sand beach of Jicacal, with another small, poor fishing village, then up onto a promontory where the *Hotel Playa Escondida* stands. This unassuming establishment has basic rooms (shower but no hot water) for US$3.25 and a small restaurant. Its attraction is its position high on a forested headland with great views down to Playa Jicacal on one side and the smaller Playa Escondida on the other. It's that rare thing in Mexico – a rural retreat. A steep path leads down from the hotel to Playa Escondida.

Back on the 'road' you soon reach a biological research station which is next to one of the few tracts of unspoiled rainforest left on the Gulf coast. The station reportedly welcomes visitors and may be able to point you to paths through the forest. The end of the road is at Montepío, about seven km on from Playa Escondida. Two rivers enter the sea here and there's a beach with a small restaurant.

ACAYUCAN

Population: 30,000

This is a road-junction town at the north end of Highway 185, the main route across the Isthmus of Tehuantepec. The once-great Olmec site of San Lorenzo is only 35 km away. On Highway 180, Villahermosa is 235 km east, Catemaco 80 km north-west and Veracruz 246 km north-west. Juchitán is 195 km south by Highway 185. If you're thinking of driving across the isthmus from Acayucan, be warned that around La Ventosa shortly before Juchitán, the road is sometimes swept by very strong winds which can blow high vehicles off the road.

Information & Orientation

If you need to stay in Acayucan there are a few decent hotels around the central Plaza de Armas. From the bus stations on the east side of town, go back to Hidalgo, the road you've just turned off, turn left, and walk six blocks to reach the Plaza de Armas with its dovecot in the middle, modern church on one side and town hall on the other.

Bancomer on Hidalgo, just down the hill from the Plaza de Armas, changes travellers' cheques.

Places to Stay

Hotel Ritz (tel 5-00-24), on the road between the bus stations and the central plaza at Hidalgo 7, has quite big, reasonably clean singles/doubles for US$2.50/3 at the back, US$3/3.25 at the front. Rooms have fan and private bath. If you continue on to the corner of Hidalgo and Bravo, one block beyond the Plaza de Armas, then go left for 1½ blocks, you reach the *Hotel Ancira* (tel 5-03-03, 5-00-48) at Bravo 2, which has sizeable rooms with new beds, tile floors and good clean bathrooms. Singles/doubles are US$3/3.75 with fan, US$3.50/4.25 with air-conditioning.

Back on the plaza, the *Hotel Joalicia* (tel 5-08-77, 5-13-88), at Zaragoza 4 on the corner of Victoria, used to be Acayucan's top hotel. That honour now goes to the new Hotel Kinaku, so the Joalicia has kept its prices down to stay competitive – which makes it good value. Clean, large rooms with private bath, balcony, fan, reading light and telephone (for all those long-lost friends you want to look up in Acayucan) cost US$3.25 single, US$5.25 double.

The *Hotel Kinaku* (tel 5-04-10, 5-04-66) is at Ocampo Sur 7, a block from the plaza in the street behind the church. Its spacious rooms have air-conditioning and TV; singles/doubles cost US$11/14.

Places to Eat

The *Restaurant Prince's* in the Hotel Joalicia is a good place to eat. Tacos, enchiladas, etc are US$0.60 to US$0.85, mole Poblano with rice is US$1.50, meats are US$1.50 to US$2, and you can get a large plate of French fries *(papas Francesas)* for 25c. Comida corrida is US$0.85. There are also a few restaurants along Hidalgo in the Plaza de Armas – *La Parrilla* looks the best. The restaurant in the *Hotel Kinaku*, open 7 am to 11 pm, seems to be the smartest place in town.

Getting There & Away

The three bus stations are all together, by the market, off Hidalgo six blocks east of the Plaza de Armas.

ADO (1st class) has buses to Coatza-coalcos (US$0.75) every hour; 19 daily to Veracruz (US$3); 13 to San Andrés Tuxtla (US$1.25); 12 to Villahermosa (US$2.75); 10 to Mexico City (US$8.50); eight to Jalapa (US$4.50); seven each to Córdoba (US$ 4.50) and Puebla (US$6.75); four each to Alvarado (US$2.25) and Orizaba (US$4.75); three each to Santiago Tuxtla (US$1.25), Tuxpan (US$8.50) and Tampico (US$11.50); two each to Catemaco (US$1) and Tuxtepec (US$2); and one each to Campeche (US$8.25) and Chetumal (US$9.75).

Cristóbal Colón (also 1st class) goes to Juchitán, Tehuantepec and Salina Cruz each three times daily; to Villahermosa, Tuxtla Gutiérrez, Arriaga, Tonalá and Tapachula twice each; and Oaxaca once.

Approximate journey times are: Juchitán three hours, Tapachula 10 hours, Tuxtla Gutiérrez seven to eight hours, Catemaco 1½ hours, Veracruz five hours, Mexico City 11 hours, Villahermosa four hours, Campeche 11 hours, Chetumal 13 hours.

AU (2nd class) serves Coatzacoalcos (US$0.70) 10 times daily; Orizaba (US$4.25) eight times; Mexico City (US$7.50) seven times; Córdoba (US$4) six times; Catemaco (US$0.90), San Andrés Tuxtla (US$1) and Puebla (US$6.25) five times; Santiago Tuxtla (US$1.25) and Villahermosa (US$2.50) four times; and Veracruz (US$2.75) and Jalapa (US$4) twice.

SAN LORENZO

The site of the first great Olmec ceremonial centre is about 35 km from Acayucan. There are plans for some restoration as well as development of the small museum to make San Lorenzo a worthwhile destination for visitors, but at the time of writing there was little to see. Most of the main finds are in museums elsewhere, and excavations often mean that the site's closed anyway. If you're interested, contact the Jalapa Anthropology Museum (tel Jalapa 5-49-52, 5-07-08) to find out the latest situation.

Locals in Acayucan say you can reach San Lorenzo by taking a bus to Texistepec (south of the Coatzacoalcos road), then another to San Lorenzo, a total journey of 1½ to two hours. San Lorenzo proper is three km south-west of the village of Tenochtitlán. Finds have also been made at Tenochtitlán and at Potrero Nuevo, three km south-east of San Lorenzo.

The main structure at San Lorenzo is on a small plateau about 1¼ km long rising about 50 metres above the surrounding land. Some of the plateau was artificially heightened by the Olmec and there are hand-made ridges jutting from its sides which may have been meant to produce a bird-shaped ground plan.

Eight Olmec heads have been found here, and other large stone objects have been detected underground. Some very heavy stone thrones, with figures of rulers carved in the side, were also found, as well as thousands of smaller items including butchered and burnt human bones which indicate cannibalism, and tools made of the black volcanic glass, obsidian, which must have been imported from Guatemala or the highlands of Mexico. Such wide contacts, added to the labour involved in building the site and transporting the basalt for the heads and thrones from the Sierra de los Tuxtlas, shows how powerful the rulers of San Lorenzo were. San Lorenzo also had an elaborate stone-pipe drainage system. It flourished as a ceremonial centre from about 1200 to 900 BC. During its dramatic destruction most of the big stone carvings were mutilated, dragged onto the ridges and covered with earth.

MINATITLÁN & COATZACOALCOS

These two towns, 50 and 70 km east of Acayucan, mushroomed to nearly half a million people each as they grew into transport and refining centres in the oil boom of the late 1970s. The area is now an industrial wilderness and Minatitlán became one of the world's most polluted places, where people living by the river had to set fire to its surface to get rid of the poisonous fumes from pollutants. The 1980s have seen some efforts to clean up the area – and a fall in population resulting from the oil-price slump.

One thing that doesn't seem to have been cleaned up is the narcotics business in southern Veracruz: in November 1985, 22 police were killed in an ambush by a drug gang 25 km south of Coatzacoalcos. Marijuana is extensively cultivated in this area and in neighbouring Oaxaca.

Coatzacoalcos, until a couple of decades ago an easygoing fishing town and small port, retains its pleasant central plaza and has an impressive new bridge over the river that it's named after. There are plenty of hotels here for the oil-people but there's nothing to make anyone else want to stay. If you're driving and don't want to push on to Villahermosa or Los Tuxtlas, you could try the reportedly good *Hermanos Graham* trailer park, 37 km east of Coatzacoalcos. Full hook-ups for two people cost US$5, and it has a restaurant.

The North-East

This huge area, stretching nearly 1000 km from north to south and 500 km from east to west, means three things to travellers: the US border; the major inland cities of Monterrey, Saltillo and San Luis Potosí; and the coast down to the port city of Tampico. Between these points are large tracts of often rugged and awesome, but empty, country which offer only a few points of real interest unless you're a confirmed wilderness-seeker.

Some travellers speed straight through the whole region en route to more famous destinations in central Mexico and Veracruz.

But Monterrey, Saltillo and San Luis Potosí are three intriguing cities and all state capitals – Monterrey young and industrial; Saltillo quieter and older; and San Luis with a fine colonial centre surrounded by plentiful evidence of 20th-century progress. There are, too, some interesting trips to be made into the country around these cities. Elsewhere,

the mountain ghost town of Real de Catorce, between Saltillo and San Luis Potosí, is a highlight; the coast offers a few remote beaches and lagoons; and the Huasteca country west of Tampico is verdant and subtropical with a substantial Indian population.

Although distant from Mexico City and close to the USA, the north-east is far from being a no man's land to be crossed before you reach the 'real' Mexico. On the contrary, it is an independent-minded region with a high degree of local pride and a good deal of antagonism towards the politicians and bureaucrats in the capital.

Geography

The north-east is dominated by the Sierra Madre Oriental (Eastern Sierra Madre) mountain chain, which runs 1200 km south-south-east from northern Coahuila until it meets the volcanic belt that stretches across central Mexico. Sometimes

pine-forested it is cut in places by deep, steep valleys. The Sierra Madre rarely rises above 2000 metres north of Monterrey and Saltillo, but to their south there are large tracts above that height and several peaks around 3600 metres.

On its east side the Sierra Madre slopes down to the Gulf coast plain, which ranges in width from nearly 300 km along the Rio Grande valley just south of the US border (one of Mexico's most fertile areas, largely thanks to irrigation) to as little as 20 km further south, where the Sierra's outliers come close to the coast. Down here, the coastal plain is surprisingly arid in parts. Lagoons stretch along a lot of the coast, but some of the marsh behind them has been reclaimed.

West of the Sierra Madre Oriental is the high, dry plateau known as the altiplano central, 1500 to 2000 metres high, itself broken by a number of smaller mountain ranges. Cactus and yucca are the predominant vegetation here. The altiplano stretches across central north Mexico until it reaches the Sierra Madre Occidental range, paralleling the Sierra Madre Oriental down the west side of the country.

The border between north-east Mexico and Texas is formed by the Rio Grande (called the Río Bravo by Mexicans), which flows roughly north-west to south-east to reach the sea near Matamoros, opposite Brownsville, Texas. Going upstream, the other main border towns are Reynosa (opposite McAllen), Nuevo Laredo (opposite Laredo), Piedras Negras (altitude 220 metres, opposite Eagle Pass) and Ciudad Acuña (opposite Del Rio).

Monterrey is set under the eastern edge of the Sierra Madre, at the head of a gradual slope up from the coastal plain/Rio Grande valley. Saltillo is on the western side of the range, where it meets the altiplano central. San Luis Potosí is in a valley in a rugged, narrow part of the altiplano, with both Sierra Madres not far away. East of San Luis Potosí is one of the major breaches in the Sierra as the Río Verde descends a series of plateaux and valleys to the Huasteca. This is a fertile region where the Gulf coast plain meets forested outlying hills. On the coast itself is the other major city of the region, Tampico.

Climate

The Tropic of Cancer crosses the region about 150 km north of Tampico and San Luis Potosí. The coast and coastal plain are normally warm and humid, though surprisingly chilly north winds – known as *nortes* – can quickly turn the weather from steamy to cold, particularly between November and March. Temperatures along the coast reach well into the 30s (°C) during the day from April to October, though on winter nights the mercury sometimes falls below 10°. At Matamoros, in the north, there's about 75 cm of rain a year; further south around Tampico you get around 130 cm, while Tamazunchale in the Huasteca sometimes gets over 200 cm a year.

Inland, it gets drier and, until you cross the Sierra Madre, hotter. Nuevo Laredo, Saltillo and San Luis Potosí have less than 50 cm of rain a year, while Monterrey has 70 cm. Monterrey is one of the hottest places in Mexico in summer, often hitting the 40s between May and September and rarely falling to single figures in winter. Across the Sierra, in summer Saltillo hits the 30s and San Luis Potosí reaches the high 20s, but in winter the temperatures are often in single figures at night. Further west it's equally cool in winter, even hotter in summer.

All over the region the wettest months are June to October, when more than half the annual rain falls. September is usually the wettest month.

Four States

The north-east encompasses the whole of three states – Tamaulipas, Nuevo León and San Luis Potosí – and about half of a fourth, Coahuila.

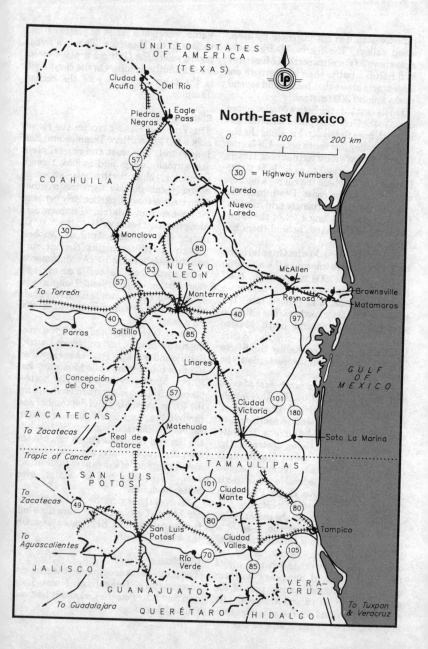

Tamaulipas This state stretches down the coast from the US border and also has a long finger of territory running inland up the Rio Grande Valley. It covers 79,000 square km and has a population of 2.2 million. Ciudad Victoria (population 170,000) is its capital city, but Tampico-Ciudad Madero, the port and oil city in the south, is the biggest with around 600,000 people.

The main border towns – Matamoros, Reynosa and Nuevo Laredo, each with about 300,000 people – derive some income from tourism but more important are commerce and industry, for which their location so close to the USA is ideal. Reynosa has oil refineries and petrochemical plants. The low-lying lands behind the Rio Grande are major livestock and large-scale agricultural areas. Maize, sugar cane, cotton and wheat are all important crops. The Falcón Dam between Reynosa and Nuevo Laredo has provided irrigation and electricity for a large area since 1953.

Plenty of smuggling also helps the border economy – not least the traffic in Mexicans who flock northwards in the hope of entering the US to work illegally. Others, attracted by the relatively good employment prospects in the border towns themselves, have helped Tamaulipas' population to more than quadruple since the 1940s.

Tamaulipas is about average on the wealth scale of Mexican states: 20% of its work force is in manufacturing and construction, and 18% in agriculture and fishing. It has 1.2 million cattle and is Mexico's biggest producer of sorghum (a grain). Soybeans, tobacco and coffee are among its other main crops. The coastal lagoons give a good harvest of shrimp, and the Gulf waters yield shrimp, red snapper and trout.

Nuevo León Inland from Tamaulipas, Nuevo León is dominated by Mexico's third biggest city, the sprawling industrial giant Monterrey. The state covers 65,000 square km and is rich by Mexican standards. Wages and supplies of electricity and piped water are higher than average, illiteracy and numbers of one and two-room dwellings are lower. This is thanks not only to industry but also to successful agriculture, particularly in the north, which is irrigated from the Rio Grande. Livestock raising, maize, sugar cane and cotton are all important. In the south, citrus fruit is grown.

Nuevo León has been greatly affected by the migration of Mexicans to the northern border, and Monterrey itself has exerted an enormous pull on rural people in search of work. Since 1940, Nuevo León's population has mushroomed from 541,000 to over three million (more than two-thirds of them in Monterrey).

San Luis Potosí Curving round like a misshapen banana from the altiplano in the north to the Huasteca in the south-east, San Luis Potosí is one of Mexico's poorer states. Despite oil finds in the Huasteca early this century and the growth of San Luis Potosí city, the state capital, into a major industrial centre, only 14% of workers in the state are in manufacturing or construction. Wages are lower than the national average, one-third of the population cannot read or write, and nearly half the households lack electricity and piped water.

The state's population has grown much slower than in other north-eastern states, having increased by only 2½ times (to 1.85 million) since 1940. Uniquely among the north-eastern states, this population includes a sizeable number of Indians. There are about 50,000 Huastecs (see the 'Huasteca' section in this chapter), 130,000 Nahua and 11,000 Pames.

The Nahua are Mexico's most numerous and widespread Indian group, with 1.4 million people scattered from east to west across the middle of Mexico. Some Nahua, originally from the centre of the country, were settled in San Luis Potosí by the Spanish as reward for their help in the Chichimec War, a decades-long conflict in the 16th century between the Spanish and the warlike tribes of north-central and north-west Mexico. Today they occupy the same south-eastern part of the state as the Huastecs.

The few thousand Pames in San Luis Potosí are the only remnants of an apparently peace-loving Chichimec group that in pre-Spanish times spread from Saltillo as far south as the states of Guanajuato and Querétaro. Today they live in a few villages and towns in dry mountainous zones in the south-east of the state between Ciudad Valles and Río Verde, notably Santa Catarina, Ciudad del Maíz and Tamasopo. They have abandoned their traditional dress but keep their own language and some elements of their traditional religion.

Coahuila This is the third biggest state in Mexico at 150,000 square km. Much of the state lies in the arid altiplano, but like Nuevo León, it has a productive irrigated agricultural zone in the north, where livestock are raised and maize, sugar cane and cotton are grown. Wine and brandy are produced in the south. There are also several sizeable industrial cities: Torreón, Monclova (population about 140,000), the state capital Saltillo (about 300,000) and Piedras Negras (about 80,000) which is the centre of a coal-mining area. Thanks to these economic pluses, Coahuila is one of Mexico's richer states. Since 1940 its population has more than trebled to 1.8 million.

The North-East Border

Several hundred thousand visitors enter north-east Mexico from the USA every year. The border formed by the Rio Grande has divided the countries since 1848.

The north-east border towns are not among Mexico's most exciting, having been quietened down and cleaned up since the US prohibition and post-war years when they attracted thousands of Americans interested in drinking, gambling and sex. But they retain a little of the low life and shady goings-on that gave them their outlaw image and, like all international borders, yield the first experience of a new culture to those entering though them. Mostly they're untidy, sprawling, functional places.

Many visitors go straight through the border towns deeper into Mexico and it's quite possible to push on to Monterrey or Saltillo or down the Gulf coast on the same day. You can even get direct buses to Mexico City if you're prepared for an overnight haul.

All border towns have good transport links with the south. But if you're not in a hurry or want a break before moving on, the border towns generally provide an easy transition from North to Latin America and have years of experience in catering to 'gringos' – though prices tend to be higher than in the interior. Especially if it's your first time in Mexico, boredom isn't likely to be a problem.

Today many of the towns are geared toward the Texan tourist trade. Americans hop over the border for a day or a weekend of bargain-priced eating, drinking, shopping, even visiting the dentist, as well as a watered-down dose of Mexican atmosphere. The border towns are the least 'Mexican' in Mexico. Most of the local people have visited the USA or had contact with it, many speak at least some English, and American products, TV programmes and other influences are ever-present. While their experience of Americans makes border Mexicans generally more understanding of northern ways, some are brusquely nationalistic, having seen the rough side of life in the States as migrant workers.

The three main border towns – Nuevo Laredo, Reynosa and Matamoros – are all in the state of Tamaulipas.

History

Primitive cultivation started as early as 3400 BC in the Sierra de Tamaulipas in the south central part of that state, but never gave rise to any advanced cultures such as that of the Huastecs, which arose later in the low-lying zone only a little further south. When the Spanish arrived in Mexico the borderlands and all of Tamaulipas except its south were inhabited mainly by semi-nomadic groups.

This was the last part of Mexico to be colonised by the Spanish. It wasn't until the 1740s that the authorities in Mexico City decided to start some settlements in Tamaulipas – and then only in order to protect their claim to the territory against the French, who had taken over Louisiana, and the British, who were on the Atlantic coast of North America. Tamaulipas was then called Nuevo Santander: it stretched inland from the coast between Altamira, just north of Tampico, and the River Nueces in Texas, 240 km up the coast from the Rio Grande.

The border really started to make history after Mexico won its independence from Spain in 1821. Coahuila and Texas became a single state of the new Mexican republic – an enormous area inhabited by just 49,000 people. To help populate Texas, Mexico started allowing English-speaking Roman Catholics from North America to settle there, and by 1835 30,000 of these immigrants, attracted by cheap land and tax exemptions, outnumbered Mexicans by nearly four to one. (They were probably the first North Americans to head 'south of the border' in search of a bargain!)

Tension grew between the two groups; the newcomers resented being governed by a Mexican-dominated state legislature in Saltillo, they were rarely true Catholics, and they were angered by the banning of slavery in Mexico in 1829. Encouraged by chauvinists inside the United States, the Texans declared themselves independent.

President Santa Anna of Mexico led an army north and on reaching San Antonio, Texas, in March 1836, he found a Texan force – which included Davy Crockett – inside an old mission called the Alamo. After a few days' siege, Santa Anna launched a full assault. Several hundred Mexicans died, but so did all the defenders.

Three weeks later 365 Texans captured at Goliad, south-east of San Antonio, were executed on Santa Anna's orders, and news of this act sent men and supplies pouring in from the United States to help the Texans. In April Sam Houston routed Santa Anna's army in half an hour at the San Jacinto River. Santa Anna himself fled but was captured two days later. He agreed to keep Mexican forces south of the Rio Grande, and to prepare the ground for Texan independence back in Mexico City. But opposition to the idea at home was so strong that he couldn't keep his promise. The dispute smouldered on, with independent Texas recognised by the US but not by Mexico, until in 1845 the US Congress voted to annex Texas.

Scorning half-measures, US President Polk sent an envoy to Mexico City with the message that he wanted not only all land north of the Rio Grande, which meant the whole of Texas, half of New Mexico and half of Colorado, but also California and, for good measure, the rest of New Mexico. A few million dollars were graciously offered for some of this territory. The Mexicans told the envoy where to go, but in May 1846 a skirmish between troops led by General Zachary Taylor and a Mexican force north of the Rio Grande gave the US the excuse to start the Mexican-American War.

Three American armies were sent out. One took New Mexico and California with barely a shot fired, another sailed via Matamoros and Tampico to Veracruz, which it took before moving inland to capture Mexico City. The third, 6000 men under Taylor, defeated the Mexicans at Matamoros, then moved inland to take Monterrey and Saltillo.

When the shooting was over, the treaty

of Guadalupe Hidalgo (1848) ceded Texas, California and New Mexico territories to the United States, and the present north-eastern boundary of Mexico was set.

The border towns have mushroomed since the turn of this century, when they had only a few thousand people each, and particularly since WW II when many Mexicans were allowed to work legally in the US – the beginning of a great movement of Mexicans to the border that continues today. The population of the main border towns has grown by more than 20 times since 1940 and today Matamoros, Nuevo Laredo and Reynosa all have around 300,000 or more inhabitants.

From the 1960s the government has spent money on roads, housing, schools and so on along the border in an effort to ease the effects of the rush to the north. In the past decade it has also tried to cope with and at the same time make use of this flood of people by allowing some businesses to import raw materials and export finished products with little customs duty. This enables American companies to take advantage of relatively cheap labour, Mexican workers to earn relatively high wages, and extra dollars to cross into Mexico.

By 1985 these *maquiladoras*, as the factories are known, were employing 186,000 people in towns along the whole border – two-thirds of them in motor vehicle, electrical and electronic goods assembly plants. Recently even Japanese companies have been getting in on the act as a way of exporting cheaply to the US.

One curious side of the *maquiladoras* is that most of the jobs go to women, and male unemployment for a time even increased, doubtless wreaking havoc with many a macho ego.

Despite the government's efforts, the borderland has suffered with the rest of Mexico from the economic crisis of the 1980s. This, combined with the greater wealth and political freedom that Mexicans

see across the Rio Grande, has led to discontent. There has been strong support in the area for the right-wing opposition party, PAN – along with strong protests when the government appeared to be manipulating election results. In December 1984, when PAN claimed 16 victories out of 38 seats at local elections in Piedras Negras but was only awarded a few, protesters set fire to the city hall.

MATAMOROS
Population: 350,000

This is the most interesting and least hybrid of the three main crossing points. It has fewer tourists entering than the other two, a town centre with a real Mexican feel to it, an interesting museum and a reasonable beach 37 km away.

First settled during the Mexican colonisation of Tamaulipas in the mid-18th century, Matamoros used to be called Congregación de Nuestra Señora del Refugio. It was renamed after Father Mariano Matamoros, a hero of the independence war. The scene of fierce fighting against Zachary Taylor's American invasion force in 1846 and of other clashes in Mexico's succession of 19th-century wars, it received the title 'Heroic, Loyal and Unconquered City of Matamoros' – a misnomer since Taylor's troops had occupied it.

The city profited from the American civil war as the nearby port of Bagdad became a key cotton-exporting and arms-importing post for the Confederates, whose own ports were blockaded by the Unionists. Bagdad, however, was destroyed by a hurricane in 1880 and you'd have to dig to find traces of it now.

Today Matamoros is much bigger than it appears from its low-key centre. It's a manufacturing and commercial centre for a large agricultural hinterland where cotton and sugar cane are major crops. Tanneries, cotton mills and distilleries are among its main industries.

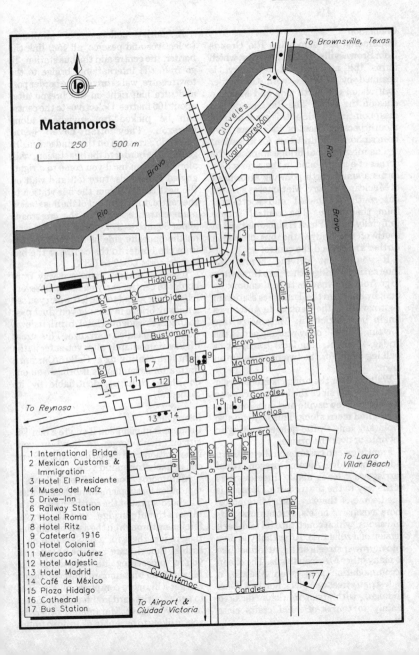

Matamoros

0   250   500 m

To Brownsville, Texas

Río Bravo

Río Bravo

Claveles

Álvaro Obregón

Avenida Tamaulipas

Hidalgo

Iturbide

Herrera

Bustamante

Bravo

Matamoros

Abasolo

González

Morelos

Guerrero

To Reynosa

To Lauro
Villar Beach

Calle 10

Calle 9

Calle 8

Calle 7

Calle 6

Calle 5

Calle 4

Calle 3

Calle 2

Calle 1

Carranza

Cuauhtémoc

Canales

To Airport &
Ciudad Victoria

1 International Bridge
2 Mexican Customs &
   Immigration
3 Hotel El Presidente
4 Museo del Maíz
5 Drive-Inn
6 Railway Station
7 Hotel Roma
8 Hotel Ritz
9 Cafetería 1916
10 Hotel Colonial
11 Mercado Juárez
12 Hotel Majestic
13 Hotel Madrid
14 Café de México
15 Plaza Hidalgo
16 Cathedral
17 Bus Station

Orientation

Matamoros lies across the Rio Grande from Brownsville, Texas. The river, which forms the international boundary, is spanned by a bridge with US border controls on the north side and Mexican ones on the south. The Rio Grande is a disappointing trickle at this point near its mouth because most of its waters have been siphoned off upstream for irrigation.

The international bridge stands at the corner of a sharp bend in the river which forms a small north-pointing arrowhead of Mexican territory. Matamoros spreads out south, south-east and south-west from the bridge. The central square (officially called Plaza Hidalgo) is two km south of the bridge, the bus station a further km beyond the centre.

If you're not driving across the international bridge, there are three ways to go from Brownsville to Matamoros: by taxi; by bus from the Trailways station in Brownsville to the Central de Autobuses (main bus station) in Matamoros (see 'Getting There'); or by walking across the bridge, then catching local transport or walking again for the two or three km to town.

Walking over the bridge is much easier than it sounds since the bridge is close to downtown Brownsville and only a couple of hundred metres long. This way you also avoid any long traffic queues waiting to get onto or over the bridge.

From Mexican customs on the southern side of the bridge, Álvaro Obregón, a dual carriageway, leads about three-quarters of the way to the town centre. Obregón is lined some of the way with Matamoros' more expensive hotels, restaurants, bars and shops, which constitute its laid-back version of a zona rosa. After that you dive into narrower streets on a grid format like so many other Mexican towns. The cheap accommodation area is on Abasolo, a pedestrian street one block north of Plaza Hidalgo, with two markets devoted mainly to tourist-oriented crafts close by.

A motley collection of minibuses (colectivos and peseros, all 15c) link the border, the centre and the bus station. To go from the international bridge to the town centre, walk through the border post and turn half-right on to Obregón after about 100 metres. Colectivos to the centre can be picked up anywhere along Obregón. They often have 'Sexta-Mercado' scrawled on the windscreen. To go from the border to the bus station, walk along Obregón until you come to a right-angled crossroads, turn left and wait on the next corner. From the bus station to the centre, turn right out of the bus station main entrance, walk to the crossroads about 50 metres away, turn left and wait on the opposite side of the road. A taxi from the border to the centre or the bus station costs US$2 to US$3.

If you're making your own way from border to centre, carry on along Obregón, following it round to the left when you see a railway bridge in front of you. Just past the big El Presidente Hotel, turn left down Calle 5, also called Carranza. This street divides immediately after you enter it, the right fork continuing as Calle 5/Carranza until after seven blocks it brings you out on Plaza Hidalgo, identifiable by its cathedral.

Information

Customs & Immigration If you're a non-US citizen, don't forget to hand in your immigration card as you leave the US – no one is likely to remind you.

Matamoros border officials have a reputation for supplementing their salaries. The border post at the southern end of the international bridge usually waves foreigners through on the assumption that they're just there for a day's shopping or eating, though cars may be checked. If you're proceeding further south into Mexico from Matamoros, however, things can get a bit more complicated. You need to get a tourist card and have it stamped before you leave Matamoros, otherwise you're likely to be sent back to do so from a further checkpoint about 20 km down the road.

There's an immigration section in the border post which theoretically should do this for you, but it's often uninhabited. If that's the case, or if you're going to be leaving Matamoros by bus, the Central de Autobuses also has an immigration post which performs the same function and is more frequently staffed.

Relaxed, leather-clad and gun-carrying, the officer amiably repeated that here in Matamoros tourist cards of more than 30 days' validity were never issued.

'That's funny, your consulate in Houston told me at least 90 days is normal.'

'Never more than 30.'

'But 30 is not enough – I want to see a lot of your country, to travel to Mexico City and the south. That is why I need more.'

'We cannot give more than 30 days. You could come back tomorrow and see another officer.'

'That would be a waste of my time, to come here twice. Is there a charge for tourist cards of more than 30 days?'

'No, no, there is no charge.'

'OK, I'll come back tomorrow and talk to another officer.'

'Come inside my office.'

(inside his office)

'I can give you 180 days. You can see all of Mexico.'

'I don't need 180 days, I only want 120.'

'I will give you 180. How much will you give me?'

'Five dollars.'

'You have many dollars. This is a poor country. Twenty.'

'I need my dollars to live on. Ten.'

'It is little.'

But he accepts the proffered ten, stamps the card, writes 180 on it and, deal done, we go on our way.

Tourist Office Matamoros has two tourist offices. One is in the border building and has a variety of leaflets but is as rarely open as the immigration office in the same building. The other is in a shack on the right-hand side of the beginning of Obregón; staff are there more often, are happy to answer questions (in Spanish) but have no printed give-aways.

Money Matamoros has several banks which will change cash or travellers' cheques; they are on Plaza Hidalgo and Calle 6 or both. Often you get a better rate for cash dollars in the casas de cambio dotted round the central area, mostly on Calle 6 north of Plaza Hidalgo and on Abasolo. These stay open in the afternoons after the banks close but don't usually accept travellers' cheques. One which does change travellers' cheques is Casa de Cambio Astorga on Calle 7 between Bravo and Matamoros. Running a casa de cambio is not, it seems, a very secure occupation; the owner of one on Abasolo was shot dead one morning when we were in Matamoros.

There are also casas de cambio on International Boulevard in Brownsville, the road running straight ahead from the north end of the international bridge. Some of them are open 24 hours a day.

Other There are post offices at Calle 6 No 214, between Herrera and Iturbide, and in the Central de Autobuses. The Central de Autobuses has left-luggage lockers, which are sometimes full. The American Consulate (tel 2-52-50, 2-13-09) is at Calle 1 No 232.

Museums

Museo del Maíz Apart from a bit of atmosphere and the markets, Matamoros offers only one real attraction, the Museo del Maíz (Museum of Maize), also called the Casa de Cultura, at the corner of Calle 5 and Avenida Constitución, about seven blocks north of the main square. This well-thought-out museum, with lots of imaginative displays, is devoted to one subject – maize, the plant which has always been the basis of Mexican civilisation – but uses that subject to convey a powerful political message about *la lucha que aún no termina – latifundistas frente a la posesión comunal* (the fight which still goes on – big landowners against communal ownership). As in most

Mexican museums, all explanatory material is in Spanish.

The first sections deal with the beginnings of maize cultivation in Mexico, which gave rise to the first settled agricultural communities, and with the spread of the cultivated plant over much of the world. There are numerous pre-Hispanic objects on display. The continuing uses of maize, including in religion, magic and folk medicine, are covered, and there's a section on its role in the history of Tamaulipas, where it has been grown since at least 3400 BC.

Further displays deal with land ownership issues in Mexico, showing that much of the country is still in the hands of big landowners who use the land for cash crops or livestock grazing, with a lot of the produce being exported. The same land could make Mexico self-sufficient in maize which, with beans, has been the country's staple diet for millennia; the grazing of one cow occupies an area which could grow enough maize for eight to 10 people. The land distribution records of Mexico's past presidents are listed and, it is claimed, uneven access to credit and technical resources make things even more unjust for the peasants. No alternative points of view are presented.

A chart shows that Mexico, self-sufficient in maize until 1965, had to import 2½ million tons of it in 1975 and 3½ million tons in 1980. In that year Mexico produced 11 million tons and consumed 15 million, while the USA produced 169 million tons and consumed 113 million. Maize, one display purports, is the 'secret food of the modern world', being the raw material of hundreds of food and industrial products made by multinational companies.

The museum displays culminate in a life-size model of protesting peasants, complete with sound-effects! Entry is free and it's open every day except Monday from 9.30 am to 5 pm.

Casa Mata At the corner of Guatemala and Santos Degollado, this old fort was the scene of fighting in the Mexican-American War. It now contains some memorabilia of the Mexican revolution and a few Indian artefacts. Entrance is free. To reach this museum from Plaza Hidalgo, head east on Morelos as far as Calle 1, turn right, go five blocks to Santos Degollado, then two blocks to the left.

Beach
Matamoros' beach, known as Lauro Villar Beach or Washington Beach, is in fact 37 km east of the town on Highway 2, but it's empty and clean enough to attract a few Texans. It has a few beachside seafood restaurants. The 'Playa' bus from the corner of Abasolo and Calle 11 in downtown Matamoros goes there.

Places to Stay – bottom end
There are one or two dingy places near the bus station but better value is to be found on or near Abasolo, a pedestrianised street running east-west, one block north of Plaza Hidalgo. Since Matamoros is a border town, prices here are a bit higher than you will pay for similar accommodation further south.

There's nowhere outstanding but the *Hotel Majestic* (tel 3-36-80) at Abasolo 89, between Calles 8 and 9, is marginally the pick of the bunch. The management is friendly and helpful. Rooms with private bathroom (US$3.75 for one person, US$4.75 for two) are basically clean, and bigger and brighter than in comparable establishments. A range of antiquated furniture gives the rooms a modicum of atmosphere and the hot water works, but some of the beds sag alarmingly in the middle.

The *Hotel México* (tel 2-08-56) at Abasolo 807, also between Calles 8 and 9, is more expensive but not significantly better at US$6/8. The *Hotel Continental*, between Calles 7 and 8 on Abasolo, is a grubby place with a balcony full of old Coke crates and rooms at US$4.25/5.50.

On González, west of Plaza Hidalgo

between Calles 8 and 9, the *Hotel Madrid* is as well-kept as you could expect for the price in Matamoros, but rooms are none too big or airy. Here you pay US$4.75/6. One block north of Abasolo, at the corner of Matamoros and Calle 6, the *Hotel Colonial* is friendly and a bargain of sorts if there are more than two of you. Prices range between US$4.25 and US$5.50 for one to four people, but interior rooms are gloomy with signs of damp while those on the street have a traffic-noise problem.

Places to Stay – top end

There's a lack of places in the middle bracket in Matamoros. For a step up from the budget places, go to the *Hotel Ritz* or the *Hotel Roma*, both only a few blocks from the centre.

The Roma (tel 3-61-76, 6-05-73), on Calle 9 between Matamoros and Bravo, is the cheaper of the two. It's modern, clean and friendly but for US$16/17.50 its 30 rooms are neither as big nor as bright as they should be, even though they have TV, telephone and carpeting. The Ritz, on Matamoros between Calles 6 and 7, is altogether bigger, brighter and better with a large attractive lobby and rooms at US$16/20.

The very top place in Matamoros is the *Hotel El Presidente* (tel 3-94-40) at Álvaro Obregón 249. The 120 air-conditioned rooms with colour TV go for US$36/37.25. For this you also get gardens and a swimming pool.

Places to Eat

The town has a pleasant range of eating places, from small cafés to the expensive haunts of visiting Texans and wealthier locals. Of the town centre places, the clean *Café de México* (tel 2-50-23) on González between Calles 8 and 9 is popular from morning to evening, and the food isn't bad either. Four enchiladas with salad, or an omelette with frijoles and tortillas, cost US$1. Other dishes go up to US$2.25 and beer is US$0.50. Decor is basic – this is really just a friendly, slightly up-market

'eating hall'. There are numerous cheaper small places of varying quality in the area: the *Cafetería Lety* on Calle 9 beside the Juárez market looks like one of the better bets.

Also popular, the *Cafetería 1916* on Calle 6 between Matamoros and Bravo pays more attention to atmosphere and cuisine than the Café de México and is a bit more expensive. A big three-course lunch goes for US$2.75, a large chicken salad for US$1.75.

Slightly further up the scale there's the *Restaurant y Bar Piedras Negras* at 175, Calle 6, half a block north of the main square. Favoured by better-off Mexicans and a few gringos, it'll offer you a large serving of four tacos (cheese, meat, avocado or chicken) with salad, rice and frijoles for US$2.25. Seafood dishes cost up to US$4, meat or steak up to US$4.25.

If you're after American-style food, try the *US Bar & Restaurant* (tel 2-14-75) on Plaza Hidalgo at the corner of Calle 5 and González. Here, in genuine steak-house surroundings, Mexico comes about as close to the USA as it ever does, with efficient waiters, a tinkling piano and a separate cocktail area. Steaks or seafood with trimmings cost between US$5 and US$10. There are also salads at US$4 to US$5.50, enchiladas at US$2.75. A beer will set you back US$0.85.

Elsewhere, there's *El Fandango* (tel 2-50-14) at the corner of Abasolo and Calle 5, with some outdoor tables. They specialise in charcoal grills from around US$4 upwards. *La Hacienda* (tel 3-94-40), attached to the El Presidente Hotel, charges around US$10 to US$15 for a meal. The dreadfully named *Drive-Inn* (tel 2-00-22) on Hidalgo near the corner of Calle 6 is one of those spots that attract Texans in search of a bargain gourmet experience. Seafood and meat are equally attractive, with prices similar to La Hacienda's.

Entertainment

There's not much. Abasolo is a good street for people-watching, with no traffic, lots of shops and itinerant musicians. There's live music in the *La Hacienda* restaurant of the El Presidente Hotel, and dance music in the *Drive-Inn* restaurant.

Things to Buy

Matamoros has two central tourist-oriented craft markets and a few interesting but expensive folk art-type shops along Obregón. The larger of the two markets, the Mercado Juárez, is on Abasolo between Calles 9 and 10. A lot of the stuff is second-rate – including blankets, hats, pottery and glass – but you may find something appealing. Vendors also set up on the pavement outside and some of them sell attractive-looking leather belts. You'll have to bargain hard to beat prices down to levels that you'd get further south. The second market, selling similar goods, is on Bravo between Calles 8 and 9. *Piñatas* (hollow clay vases decorated with colourful papier-mâché, paper and ribbons to represent people or animals, which are filled with gifts and smashed open at festival times) seem to be on sale almost year-round, including at a shop on the corner of Matamoros and Calle 8. Not the handiest item to stuff in a backpack, but if you're on the way home to the USA, Matamoros would be one of the least inconvenient points to pick one up.

Out on Obregón, Barbara's has interesting clothes, rugs, ceramics, brass and copperwork, and lovely near-life-size papier-mâché animals (the zebra and giraffe are snips at US$1100 and US$1200 respectively!). Mary's is another shop worth looking into if you have money you want to get rid of.

Getting There & Away

Air Matamoros has an airport (tel 2-20-56) 17 km out of town on the road to Ciudad Victoria. There is a direct Aeroméxico flight from and to Mexico City every afternoon and an extra one each way on Tuesday and Saturday mornings. Aeroméxico also flies Matamoros/Ciudad Victoria/Mexico City and vice-versa on Wednesday, Friday and Sunday mornings. The Aeroméxico office (tel 3-07-01) in Matamoros is at Obregón 21.

Road For information on routes south from Matamoros, see the 'South from Matamoros or Reynosa' section.

Bus Matamoros is linked by bus with almost everywhere in Mexico. Both 1st and 2nd-class buses run from the bus station (Central de Autobuses) (tel 2-01-81) on Canales near the corner of Aguiles. The bus station has a 24-hour restaurant, a post office and left-luggage lockers (in the restaurant).

Three of the better 1st-class bus lines, Transportes del Norte, Omnibus de México and ADO, all serve Matamoros. Transportes del Norte goes to Mexico City (US$13) via San Luis Potosí four times a day; to Durango (US$11.50), to Tampico (US$6.50) and to Guadalajara (US$13.25) via Monterrey daily.

Omnibus de México has 10 buses a day to Monterrey (US$4), four to Guadalajara (US$13), three to Durango (US$11.25) via Torreón (US$8.50), and one each to Mexico City (US$13) and Chihuahua (US$14).

ADO serves the Gulf coast, with two departures daily for Tampico (US$6.50), Tuxpan (US$10.25) and Veracruz (US$16), and one for San Andrés Tuxtla (US$17.75) and Villahermosa (US$21.75).

Tres Estrellas de Oro, also 1st class, goes to Reynosa (US$1.25), Monterrey (US$4) and Saltillo (US$5) once daily; to Ciudad Victoria (US$3.75) and San Luis Potosí (US$8) four times; to Guadalajara (US$13.25) twice; to Querétaro (US$10.25) and Mexico City (US$13) twice; to Tepic, Mazatlán (US$19.50), Culiacán (US$22.50), Los Mochis, Guaymas, Hermosillo (US$31), Mexicali (US$39.50) and Tijuana (US$41.50) once; also to

Lagos de Moreno, San Juan de Los Lagos, León, Irapuato, Salamanca and Morelia.

Transportes Monterrey-Cadereyta-Reynosa runs 16 1st-class and seven 2nd-class buses daily to Reynosa and Monterrey. Fares in 1st class are US$1.25 to Reynosa, US$4 to Monterrey; in 2nd class they're US$1 and US$3.50 respectively.

Autotransportes Ciudad Mante runs 2nd-class buses to Ciudad Valles (US$6) nine times a day, Tampico (US$6.50) 15 times, and Ciudad Victoria (US$3.50). Oriente, also 2nd class, goes to Guadalajara (US$11) seven times daily, San Luis Potosí (US$7) three times, Ciudad Victoria (US$3.50) five times, Tampico (US$6.50) 15 times and to Querétaro and Rio Verde. Transportes Frontera is another 2nd-class line running to Mexico City (US$11.75) six times a day, Tampico (US$6.50) and Tuxpan (US$9.50) daily; also to Ciudad Victoria, Ciudad Valles, Querétaro, Celaya, León, Irapuato and Morelia.

Journey times by 1st class are about two hours to Reynosa, six hours to Monterrey, seven hours to Saltillo, eight hours to Tampico, 18 hours to Mexico City, a bit longer in 2nd class.

Rail Matamoros railway station (tel·2-02-55) is on Hidalgo, eight blocks north of González along Calle 10. There's one service a day in each direction between Matamoros and Monterrey, via Reynosa, but though cheap it's neither quick nor reliable. The 6.50 am departure from Matamoros is scheduled to arrive in Reynosa at 8.43 am and Monterrey at 1.55 pm. In the other direction, the train leaves Monterrey at 6 am and Reynosa at 10.50 am, reaching Matamoros at 1.05 pm. The fare between Matamoros and Monterrey is about US$2 in 1st class, US$1.30 in 2nd.

To/from Brownsville, Texas If you're going straight through Matamoros deeper into Mexico, or out of interior Mexico into the US, it's worth considering the buses run by the Mexican lines Tres Estrellas de Oro (1st class) and Autotransportes Ciudad Mante (2nd class) between the Trailways station in Brownsville and several cities inside Mexico. They may save you effort – but they certainly lose you money and possibly time. Prices are about 50% higher than to or from Matamoros and these buses can take up to two hours to get over the international bridge, through customs and immigration, and into and out of Matamoros bus station.

Trailways in Brownsville (tel 546-7171) is at 1165 Saint Charles on the corner of 12th St. Facing into the USA from the north end of the international bridge, walk left (west) on Elizabeth, then two blocks south on 12th. The Tres Estrellas de Oro departures from here are to Ciudad Victoria, San Luis Potosí, Querétaro and Mexico City (US$20.75) twice daily; to Monterrey, Saltillo and Guadalajara once; and to Ciudad Victoria, San Luis Potosí, Lagos de Moreno, León, Irapuato, Salamanca and Morelia once. Autotransportes Ciudad Mante runs to Tampico (US$9.50) three times a day; to Ciudad Victoria and Ciudad Valles twice.

Most of these buses will also take you between Brownsville Trailways and Matamoros bus station for US$1.75. But it's cheaper and probably quicker to walk over the international bridge, which is close to downtown Brownsville, and take local transport between the border and downtown Matamoros.

Trailways and Valley Transit Company/Greyhound link Brownsville with the rest of the USA. Both their terminals are only a few minutes' walk from the international border. VTC/Greyhound has four buses a day going in the direction of Corpus Christi (3½ to four hours) and Houston (nine to 10 hours) with connections to Galveston, New Orleans, New York and Miami. It has five a day to San Antonio (about eight hours) for Austin, Dallas, Tulsa, Kansas City, St Louis (Missouri), Chicago, El Paso, Phoenix and Los

Angeles. The terminal (tel 546-2264) is at 1305 Adams. Walk two blocks straight ahead from the north end of the international bridge, then turn left on 13th St to reach it.

Trailways has several direct services a day to San Antonio, Corpus Christi and Houston, and connections to Austin, Dallas, Oklahoma City, Wichita, Kansas City, Little Rock, Memphis, St Louis (Missouri), Chicago, Amarillo, Denver, El Paso, Tucson, Phoenix and Los Angeles.

Brownsville has an airport a few km east of town. Buses (US$0.50) run hourly between the airport and the town terminal on 12th St, 1½ blocks north of Elizabeth (the street running west from the north end of the international bridge). Transtar (tel 544-2828 in Brownsville or (800) 882-2828 toll-free) is one airline with services most days (sometimes several times a day) between Brownsville and Austin (off-peak one-way fare US$82), Houston (US$45), Los Angeles (US$128), Miami (US$138), New Orleans (US$108), San Antonio (US$82), San Diego (US$128) and Tampa/St Petersburg (US$138).

Getting Around

Matamoros is served by buses and a variety of minibuses known as colectivos or peseros. The fare on any of these is 15c. You can stop them on almost any street corner. They usually have their destinations painted on the front windscreen but check before getting in; the town centre is 'Centro', the bus station 'Central de Autobuses' and the international bridge 'Puente Internacional'.

From the border to the bus station, walk along Obregón until you reach a right-angled crossroads, turn left and wait on the next corner for a pesero.

From the border to downtown, pick up a pesero (usually saying 'Sexta-Mercado') on Obregón. Most transport to downtown runs along Morelos; get off at Calle 6 or 7 for Plaza Hidalgo. From the bus station to downtown, get a bus from directly opposite the main bus station entrance, or a pesero by turning right out of the entrance, left at the nearby crossroads and waiting on the other side of the road.

From downtown to the border, buses and peseros ('Carranza-Claveles') run north along Calle 6, then east along Hidalgo and north on Obregón, before taking a back street called Claveles to reach the border post. From the centre to the bus station, pick up a green 'Canales' bus at the corner of Abasolo and Calle 11.

Walking from the bus station to downtown, turn right out of the bus station entrance, walk to the first crossroads, turn right on Calle 1 and walk about eight blocks to Morelos, where you turn left and go four blocks to the main square. To get to Lauro Villar Beach, 37 km from Matamoros, take a 'Playa' bus from Abasolo and Calle 11.

There are plenty of taxis in Matamoros, as in other Mexican towns. From the border to downtown or the bus station costs US$2 to US$3.

REYNOSA

Population: 350,000

Across the Rio Grande from the small settlement of Hidalgo, Texas, with the bigger US town of McAllen nine km away, Reynosa is one of north-east Mexico's most important industrial towns. It has oil refineries, petrochemical plants, cotton mills and distilleries. Pipelines from here carry natural gas to the USA and Monterrey. It's also the centre of a big cattle-raising, cotton, sugar cane and maize-growing area.

More important as a border crossing than Matamoros, less so than Nuevo Laredo, Reynosa has a pleasant enough town centre (altitude 90 metres) on a small hill not far from the international bridge, some distance from the industries which have grown up on the southern side of town. It's as good as any border town for

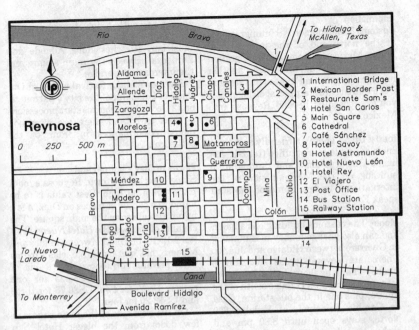

Reynosa

0   250   500 m

1 International Bridge
2 Mexican Border Post
3 Restaurante Sam's
4 Hotel San Carlos
5 Main Square
6 Cathedral
7 Café Sánchez
8 Hotel Savoy
9 Hotel Astromundo
10 Hotel Nuevo León
11 Hotel Rey
12 El Viajero
13 Post Office
14 Bus Station
15 Railway Station

onward transportation into Mexico and is well geared to the Texan tourist trade.

Reynosa was founded in 1749 as Villa de Nuestra Señora de Guadalupe de Reynosa, 20 km from its present location, during the Mexican colonisation of Tamaulipas. Flooding forced the move to the present site in 1802. Reynosa was one of the first towns to rise up in the independence movement of 1810.

Orientation

Reynosa's central streets are laid out on a grid pattern aligned north, south, east and west. The wide and airy central square, with a cathedral, a cinema, a few hotels and restaurants, sits on top of a small hill less than a km south-west of the international bridge. Between the bridge and the centre lies a zona rosa with the town's most expensive restaurants and bars. Cheaper accommodation is a couple of blocks south of the square. The bus

station is 1½ km south-east of the bridge and centre.

The walk from bridge or bus station to town centre takes about 15 to 20 minutes. From the bridge, walk straight ahead off the exit ramp, crossing one road to reach a desolate-looking three-way junction, where you take the right fork. This street is Zaragoza, and you can see the central square at the top of the hill a few blocks straight ahead. From the bus station, turn left out of the main entrance, and walk to the end of the block to another desolate-looking junction. Turn left here on to Colón and walk about six blocks until you reach Hidalgo or Díaz, where a right turn and three blocks uphill bring you to the square.

Ramshackle but frequent local buses and colectivos (15c or 20c) link the bridge, centre and bus station (see 'Getting Around').

Information

Customs & Immigration US immigration is at the north end of the international bridge. Mexican customs and immigration are at the south end, and there's another immigration post in Reynosa bus station. Get a tourist card stamped at either post if you're proceeding beyond Reynosa into Mexico.

Tourist Office There's a friendly and quite knowledgeable tourist office (tel 2-11-89) inside the customs and immigration building on the Mexican side of the international bridge. Some of the staff speak English.

Money The customs building has a bank. You can also change money in Bánamex, on Guerrero between Hidalgo and Juárez. There are several casas de cambio (money-changing shops) in the downtown area, particularly on Hidalgo south of the square, plus one in the bus station. Casa de Cambio Principal, at Hidalgo 820 Norte, stays open until 8.30 pm and cashes travellers' cheques. Some shops also change money at competitive rates.

Post The post office is on the corner of Díaz and Colón.

Airlines Aeroméxico (tel 2-11-15, 2-24-40) is at Guerrero 1510, on the corner of Portes Gil about a km from the town centre. Its telephone number at the airport is 3-00-40. Travel agents in the centre are more convenient for booking flights; one is Vibrasa (tel 2-56-88) at Zaragoza Ote 555 between Hidalgo and Díaz, half a block from the main square.

Things to See

Apart from a stroll round the pleasant, open main square, there's little specific to do in Reynosa. Hidalgo is pedestrianised for a couple of blocks south of the square. There's a basic market a few blocks further south bounded by Hidalgo, Juárez, Colón and the railway tracks. The zona rosa, with a few tourist-oriented craft shops, restaurants, bars and the odd musician, stretches along Allende and Zaragoza between the main square and the international bridge.

Reynosa's major festival is that of Our Lady of Guadalupe, the city's patroness, on 12 December. Pilgrims start processions a week early and there are afternoon dance performances in front of the cathedral.

Places to Stay – bottom end

Since it's a border town, Reynosa's room prices are a bit high. Best value is to be found in a couple of places on Díaz, a few minutes' walk from the main square. The cheaper of the two, the *Hotel Nuevo León* (tel 2-13-10) on Díaz between Méndez and Madero, has quite sizeable, clean rooms with private bathrooms and a bit of newish furniture at US$3.25 for one person, US$5 for two, US$6.75 for three and US$8.25 for four.

On the west side of the main square, a few doors from the bigger Hotel San Carlos, the *Hotel Plaza* has rooms from US$4.75 for one, US$5 for two. The *Hotel El Dorado*, at the corner of Aldama and Chapa, charges US$5.50/8. The *Hotel San Miguel* on Colón, 2½ blocks from the bus station, is OK if you can't be bothered to go into town, with rooms at US$7/9.

Steer clear of *Mike's*, at the bottom of Zaragoza, where small grubby wooden cells go for US$7.50/10.75 a night but are probably more often let by the hour.

Places to Stay – middle

The *Hotel Rey* on Díaz between Méndez and Madero, a couple of doors down from the Hotel Nuevo León, has clean, bright rooms with TV at US$8 for one person, US$9 for two, US$10.25 for three and US$11.25 for four. It's very popular and may not have a room if you arrive late.

On the edge of the small zona rosa at Zaragoza 885 Ote, at the corner of Canales, the *Hotel Avenida* (tel 2-05-92) has rooms at US$9/10.75.

Just south of the main square at Juárez 860, the pleasant *Hotel Savoy* (tel 2-00-67) has rooms at US$10.25/14 and is often full.

Places to Stay – top end

The *Hotel San Carlos* (tel 2-12-80), on the main square at Hidalgo 970 Norte, is a step towards the luxury bracket with clean, bright, air-conditioned rooms with TV at US$13/15.25 or US$15.25/17.50 (king-size). It has its own restaurant and parking.

The top downtown place is the *Hotel Astromundo* (tel 2-56-25) on the corner of Juárez and Guerrero. It has clean, spacious rooms with TV, plus swimming pool, parking facilities and restaurant. Room prices are US$15.75/19.25.

The *Motel Virrey* (tel 3-10-50) at the corner of Boulevard Hidalgo and Avenida Balboa, on the Monterrey road about three km from central Reynosa, has rooms with balconies, air-con and TV for US$15/20. It also has its own restaurant and swimming pool.

Places to Eat & Nightlife

Proximity to the international border means that many restaurants in Reynosa stay open until 11 pm or later. *El Viajero* (tel 2-61-00) is at Díaz 520 Norte, just down the street from the hotels Nuevo León and Rey. It's friendly and either air-conditioned or heated, depending on the season. The food is good and reasonably priced, with a long menu of international and Mexican dishes up to US$2.50, or comida corrida for US$2.25.

Half a block from the main square at Morelos 575, the *Café Sánchez* is a restaurant-cafeteria-type place popular with locals and slightly cheaper than El Viajero. The *Café San Carlos*, in the Hotel San Carlos, is a little dearer but also busy.

Places in the zona rosa have prices appropriate for the day-tripping Texans who make up a lot of their clientele, but in the evenings the *Restaurant Carrusel/ Hostelería del Bohemio* on Zaragoza Ote is filled with mostly young local people enjoying live Mexican music in a convivial atmosphere. Here a helping of tacos costs US$1.25, a steak US$2.75. The liveliness of the other music places and discos in the zona rosa depends on the season and day of the week. On a Monday in February you'd probably die of agoraphobia but Fridays or Saturdays around Christmas, Easter, July or August are fun.

Getting There & Away

To/From McAllen, Texas The nearest Texas transport centre, McAllen, is nine km from the border. Valley Transit Company (VTC) runs buses both ways between McAllen and Reynosa bus station for US$1 one way, every 20 minutes between 6 am and 7 pm. There are three later services, with the last leaving Reynosa bus station at 11 pm. Coming from McAllen, you can get off these buses at the Greyhound office on the US side of the border and walk over the international bridge and into Reynosa town, if you don't want to go straight to the bus station. Leaving Mexico, you can walk over the bridge and pick up the buses at the same Greyhound office (fare still US$1).

Valley Transit Company runs a co-ordinated service with Greyhound in the US. It has connections from McAllen to San Antonio (about 5½ hours) and Houston eight times daily and to Laredo twice. Trailways also has services from McAllen to San Antonio.

The Mexican bus line Transportes Monterrey-Cadereyta-Reynosa also runs between Reynosa's Central de Autobuses and McAllen.

McAllen has an airport, from which Continental (tel 383-8101) flies direct to Houston four or five times daily. In Reynosa, taxis wait on Allende to take passengers to McAllen; they leave when they're full.

Air Reynosa airport is eight km out of town, off the Matamoros road. There are two Aeroméxico flights direct to Mexico

City daily except Saturday, when there is only one. On Tuesday, Thursday and Saturday afternoons Aeroméxico also flies to and from Guadalajara via Saltillo. See the earlier 'Information' section for where to buy flight tickets.

Road For information on routes south from Reynosa, see the 'South from Matamoros or Reynosa' section.

Bus Both 1st and 2nd-class buses run to almost anywhere you'd want to go in Mexico from Reynosa's Central de Autobuses on the eastern side of town, next to the big Blanco supermarket.

Transportes del Norte (1st class) goes twice daily to Ciudad Victoria (US$4), San Luis Potosí (US$8), Querétaro (US$10.50) and Mexico City (US$13); four times to Monterrey (US$2.75) and Saltillo (US$3.75); twice to Torreón (US$7.25) and Durango (US$10.50); twice to Matamoros; and twice to San Luis Potosí, Zacatecas, Aguascalientes and Guadalajara.

ADO (1st class) departs for Tampico (US$6.75), Tuxpan (US$10.50), Veracruz (US$16) and Villahermosa (US$21.75) twice a day.

Omnibus de México (1st class) runs to Matamoros eight times daily; to Mexico City (US$13) twice; to Monterrey (US$2.75), Saltillo (US$3.75), Chihuahua (US$12.50) and Ciudad Juárez (US$17) once; to Guadalajara (US$11.75) three times; to Zacatecas (US$8.25) once; also to Tepic, Durango, San Juan de Los Lagos, Torreón and Aguascalientes.

Tres Estrellas de Oro (1st class) goes twice a day to Ciudad Victoria (US$3.75), San Luis Potosí (US$8), Querétaro (US$10.50) and Mexico City (US$13); twice to Guadalajara (US$12); and once to Monterrey (US$2.75) and Saltillo (US$3.75).

Transportes Monterrey-Cadereyta-Reynosa has 1st-class direct departures to Monterrey (US$2.75), Saltillo (US$3.75), Torreón (US$7.25) and Matamoros (US$1.25). Transportes del Noreste runs six daily direct 1st-class buses to Monterrey, and four to San Luis Potosí.

Second-class lines include Transportes Frontera/Estrella Blanca, which goes to Mexico City (US$12) four times a day; to Ciudad Victoria (US$3.50) five times; and to Ciudad Valles (US$6), Tampico (US$6.75), Tuxpan (US$9.75), San Luis Potosí, Querétaro, León, Irapuato and Celaya.

Autotransportes Mante (2nd class) goes to Ciudad Valles four times a day, Tampico three times, Ciudad Victoria six times. Oriente (2nd class) has numerous services to Ciudad Victoria and Ciudad Valles; six a day to Guadalajara, Lagos de Moreno and San Juan de Los Lagos; and eight each to San Luis Potosí and Tampico.

Approximate 1st-class journey times: to Matamoros two hours, Monterrey four hours, Saltillo five hours, Mexico City 16 hours.

Rail Reynosa railway station is at the southern end of Hidalgo, six blocks from the main square. You probably wouldn't know it was a station if it weren't next to the railway tracks. There's one slow train daily in each direction. The 8.45 am departure arrives at Monterrey at 1.55 pm; the 10.50 am departure reaches Matamoros at 1.05 pm. The fare to Monterrey is about US$1.50 in 1st class, US$1 in 2nd class.

Getting Around
Airport Transport The airport is eight km out of town, off the Matamoros road. Buses don't go all the way to the airport. A taxi from town costs US$4 to US$5.

Local Transport Hundreds of decrepit buses and minibuses (colectivos) rattle their way round Reynosa's rutted one-way streets, providing an effective if bone-jarring urban transport system. All fares are 15c or 20c.

From the international bridge to the

bus station (Central de Autobuses), take No 14, or catch a free ride on one of the Valley Transit Company or Transportes Monterrey-Cadereyta-Reynosa coaches coming from McAllen. The latter will pick you up as they pull out of the Mexican border building; they're not officially supposed to take you but usually will.

If you don't feel like the short walk from the bridge to the town centre, walk down the bridge exit ramp and straight over the first road, and wait on the next corner (a three-way junction). Most buses going right from here, including '17 Obrera', run close to the central square.

From the centre to the bridge, most buses or colectivos running along Guerrero, a one-way street, will get you there. The corners of Díaz and Hidalgo are convenient places to pick them up. From the centre to the bus station, catch the '17 Obrera' from Madero, at the corner of Díaz or Hidalgo.

From the bus station to the centre, turn left out of the bus station main entrance, walk to the end of the block, turn left, and catch a '17 Obrera' on the next corner (Colón and Rubio).

SOUTH FROM MATAMOROS OR REYNOSA

You have the choice of going west to Monterrey, or south by Ciudad Victoria or Tampico. Tampico's the place to head for if you're aiming for Veracruz and the south; Ciudad Victoria is en route to San Luis Potosí and Mexico City.

Roads

From Matamoros Highway 2 – patrolled by Green Angels – goes west to Reynosa, 98 km away. Highway 101 is not as good as the other main arteries leading south from the border, but it is the start of the shortest way from the border to Mexico City (1016 km). From Matamoros to Ciudad Victoria by Highway 101 is 312 km.

For Tampico, Highway 180 (rougher but still adequate) branches off Highway 101, 183 km south of Matamoros. It's another 315 km to Tampico from the intersection, making 498 km from Matamoros to Tampico. After Tampico, Highway 180 carries on south to Veracruz. A longer but better road from Matamoros to Tampico is Highway 101 to Ciudad Victoria, then Highway 85 south to Ciudad Mante, then Highway 80 east to Tampico.

From Reynosa Highway 40, a good road patrolled by Green Angels, goes west to Monterrey (225 km). At China, 109 km from Reynosa, Highway 35 branches south-west off Highway 40 to meet Highway 85 running south from Monterrey to Ciudad Victoria (which is 402 km from Reynosa). East of Reynosa, Highway 2 goes to Matamoros (98 km), with Highway 97 branching south a few km out of Reynosa to meet Highway 101 coming south from Matamoros to Ciudad Victoria (322 km from Reynosa to Ciudad Victoria this way but the roads are inferior).

Matamoros to Tampico

The 498 km of this road are mostly 30 to 40 km inland from the coast, crossing several rivers but passing mainly through flat drab lowlands – though there are stretches where the outliers of the Sierra Madre Oriental come close to the coast. For the first 183 km the route follows Highway 101 to Ciudad Victoria, then turns off along Highway 180. There are basic hotels in San Fernando (137 km from Matamoros), Soto La Marina (269 km) and Aldama (381 km).

Drivers can make detours to a few villages on the often wild coast in at least four places where it's possible – and reportedly safe – to set up a vehicle for the night (though there are no specific camping facilities). There's a lot of bird life in this area.

If you're interested in exploring this or any other part of Mexico's Gulf coast in detail, check out Donald Schueler's excellent *Adventuring Along the Gulf of Mexico* (Sierra Club Books, San Francisco), which gives a full coverage of the ecology and wildlife.

El Mesquital This is a small fishing village with lighthouse and beach, on the long, thin spit of land that divides the Laguna Madre (biggest of the lagoons on this stretch of coast) from the Gulf of Mexico. The road to El Mesquital leads about 60 km off the highway from a little south of Matamoros airport.

La Carbonera This is another fishing village, on the inland side of the lagoon. You can get a boat out to the lagoon barrier island, where there is quite good surf and porpoises can sometimes be seen. A road leads here from San Fernando.

La Pesca Forty-eight km from Soto La Marina, La Pesca has a long beach that attracts a few American surfers, plus some fishermen for the Laguna de Morales or the Río Soto La Marina. It was near the mouth of this river that the idealistic Spanish guerrilla leader, Francisco Javier Mina, landed with four ships in 1817 with the aim of helping the Mexicans in their fight for independence. Mina moved inland to help the revolutionaries near Zacatecas; the fort he left behind at Soto La Marina was captured the next year but the expedition was a big morale-booster for the Mexicans. Among the captives when the fort surrendered was Fray Servando Teresa de Mier, who crops up in Mexican street names as Padre Mier. He was a champion of independence and introduced the printing press to Tamaulipas.

Barra del Tordo From Aldama, 117 km from Tampico, a road goes through the eastern fringes of the Sierra de Tamaulipas to Barra del Tordo, another hamlet with a beach and good fishing.

Ciudad Victoria

About 40 km north of the Tropic of Cancer, the capital of Tamaulipas (population about 170,000, altitude 333 metres) has no special attractions, but the central Plaza Hidalgo is pleasant with one middle-range and two expensive hotels on it, if you want to stop overnight.

Ciudad Victoria is quite a big transport centre, a five-way highway junction and the first major town south of Monterrey, Matamoros and Reynosa.

Forty km north-east of Ciudad Victoria, Lago Guerrero is a huge reservoir which attracts Mexicans and North Americans for bass-fishing and duck, goose and dove-hunting.

Places to Stay *Hotel Everest* (tel 2-40-50) and *Hotel Sierra Gorda* (tel 2-22-80) both cost from US$15/20 with air-con, TV in rooms and restaurant. The *Hotel Los Monteros*, next door to the Sierra Gorda, is cheaper only because it doesn't have air-conditioning. There are also motels north and south of town on Highway 85 and a few cheaper hotels on Juárez, close to the centre.

The *Victoria Trailer Park Resort* on the north-eastern side of town, off the intersection of Highway 85 to Monterrey and Highway 101 to Matamoros, charges US$6 (electric, water and sewerage hook-ups included) for two people.

Getting There & Away Ciudad Victoria has an airport, east of town off the Soto La Marina road.

There are three Aeroméxico flights a week to and from Matamoros, and daily ones to and from Mexico City, some of which stop at Poza Rica.

The Aeroméxico office (tel 2-87-97, 2-97-40) in town is at Morelos 155B on the corner of Hidalgo.

From Ciudad Victoria, you can continue south-west to San Luis Potosí (346 km away) by Highways 180, 80 and 57. For Mexico City, Highway 85 south via Ciudad Mante and Ciudad Valles is the most direct.

About 60 km south of Ciudad Victoria there's a climb (200 metres in five km) up to the Mesa de Lera.

First-class buses to Mexico City cost US$9 and take about 13 hours; Tampico US$3, about 3½ hours; Matamoros or Reynosa US$3.75, five hours; Monterrey US$3.50, four hours; San Luis Potosí US$4.25, 5½ hours; Ciudad Valles US$3, 3½ hours.

Tula

This small town is noted for its leather goods and festivals. It lies about 100 km south-west of Ciudad Victoria on Highway 101. Traditional dances are performed on 3 May, El Día de la Santa Cruz (Day of the Holy Cross). On 13 June, El Día de San Antonio de Padua, folk plays called Pastorelas are put on, with angels, devils and Indians as the main characters. The Danza del Patriarca (Dance of the Patriarch) is performed. There are also dances to celebrate El Día de la Virgen del Carmen on 16 July.

NUEVO LAREDO

Population: 300,000

More foreign tourists enter Mexico through Nuevo Laredo than any other town on the US border, and the untidy collection of low-rise buildings that greets you on the south side of the international bridge over the Rio Grande fits the traditional border-town image better than Reynosa or Matamoros to the south-east. Nuevo Laredo has more restaurants, shops and hotels catering to the US tourist trade than anywhere else on the north-east border, but prices are if anything less suited to budget travellers.

The original Mexican settlement (1755) at this point of the Rio Grande was on the north side, with the name Laredo de San Agustín. Occupied by US troops in the Mexican-American war, the town became US territory under the Treaty of Guadalupe Hidalgo (1848) at the end of that war, which fixed the Rio Grande as the boundary between the two countries. Most of the Mexican inhabitants then moved over the river to expand the small settlement on the south side, which was given the name Nuevo Laredo. Nearly wiped out by cholera the next year, it survived to register a population of 1283 in 1876, and about 9000 in 1910, as a border post of growing importance and a commercial centre for its cattle-rearing hinterland, boosted by railway links to the USA and Monterrey.

Prohibition in the US started Nuevo Laredo on its tourist trail. Today cattle and agricultural trade remain important, with the surrounding area having been irrigated in the 1950s, and the town is a centre of natural gas production and other border industries. On the other bank of the river, Laredo is now an important Texan city; its Hilton, visible from Mexico, is an appropriate symbol of the more-than-geographical difference between the two sides of the river.

Nuevo Laredo is at an altitude of 128 metres.

Orientation

Drivers can avoid most of Nuevo Laredo and head on south by crossing the border on a new road bridge to the east. The old bridge brings you into Mexico at the north end of Guerrero, Nuevo Laredo's main street, which stretches straight ahead for two km. The downtown area spreads along either side of Guerrero for the first km. Its main plaza, with a kiosk in the middle, the government palace on the east side, and a few hotels and restaurants around it, is seven blocks along Guerrero from the bridge. Most accommodation, restaurants, bars and the tourist shops and markets are near this plaza or between it and the bridge, a couple of blocks either side of Guerrero.

Street numbers on Guerrero tell you how far they are from the bridge: 109 would be in the block nearest the bridge, 509 in the fifth block down, 2009 would be 20 blocks from the bridge, etc. Other north-south streets, parallel to Guerrero, are numbered in the same way. The most important of these are Matamoros, Juárez, Ocampo and Galeana. The

1	Mexican Border Post & Tourist Office
2	Town Bus Station
3	Cadillac Restaurant
4	Hotel Sam's
5	Hotel Calderón
6	Café Quinto Patio
7	Hotel Meson del Rey
8	Main Plaza
9	Hotel Reforma
10	Café Almanza
11	Motel Don Antonio

numbers on east-west streets are confusing but appear to get higher as you go from east to west, with blocks 28 and 29 straddling Guerrero. Thus, 2809 and lesser numbers would be east of Guerrero (to the left if you have the international bridge behind you), 2909 and higher would be to the west.

Nuevo Laredo's Central Camionera, the arrival and departure point for long-distance buses, is way out on the southern side of town. Local buses run between it and the town bus station, which is on Matamoros, two blocks south and one block west of the international bridge. The railway station, also linked by bus with the town bus station, is 10 blocks south on Guerrero from the bridge, then 10 blocks west on Gutiérrez.

Information

Customs & Immigration Mexican immigration and customs are in the border post at the south end of the international bridge. Get a tourist card stamped here if you're going on south beyond Nuevo Laredo.

Tourist Office There's a small but helpful tourist office (tel 2-01-04) in the border building, with a copious selection of leaflets on Nuevo Laredo and northern Mexico. When it's open (9 am to 3 pm and 'sometimes' in the evening) there's usually at least one English-speaker on duty.

Money Bánamex/Euromex has a casa de cambio on Guerrero between Canales and Mina, which is the only bank or casa de cambio in town that will change travellers' cheques. Its rate for cash is better than the other casas de cambio, a few of which are on Guerrero just south of the international bridge.

Post The post office is on the corner of Reynosa and Dr Mier.

Airlines Mexicana (tel 2-20-52, 2-22-11) is at Heroes de Nacataz 2335.

Consulate There's an American Consulate (tel 4-05-12) in Nuevo Laredo.

Places to Stay - bottom end

There's only one worthwhile place in the cheaper bracket but it's one of the better deals to be found in any border town. Nothing special – just cheap, popular with Mexican families, and clean and friendly enough. This is the *Hotel Calderón* (tel 2-00-04) at Juárez 313, just a few blocks from the international bridge. There's no sign outside but it's the only building on this part of Juárez that could be a hotel. Rooms with shower, and furniture and decoration that were once

quite homely, cost US$4 for one person, US$4.25 for two people in one bed, US$4.50 for two people in two beds.

Elsewhere, *Hotel Ajova*, on Hidalgo half a block west of Guerrero, is modern but already shoddy with rooms from US$5.50. *Hotel Sam's* (tel 2-59-32), a few doors away at Hidalgo 2903, is friendlier and slightly better at US$5.50 for one bed, US$6.50 for two. *Hotel Texas* (tel 2-18-07) at Guerrero 837 is dingy and grubby with rooms at US$4.25 for one double bed, US$6.50 for two double beds. *Hotel Reno* on the corner of Ocampo and Belden is similar and costs US$5.50 for one or two people.

Places to Stay - middle

Motels provide some of the best value in this range. *Motel Don Antonio* (tel 2-11-40) at González 2435 is good value with big clean rooms, large comfortable beds, and US stations on TV in the room for US$8.50 (one person), US$10 (two people), US$11.50 for three, US$13 for four. Like all motels, it's a bit soulless, though the young staff are friendly enough. It's four blocks along González going east (left if you're coming from the international bridge) from Guerrero. *Motor Hotel Fiesta* (tel 2-47-37) at Ocampo 559 is sparkling clean and a bit brighter than the Don Antonio at US$11.25 for one or two people.

The *Hotel Reforma* (tel 2-62-50) at Guerrero 822 is a busy town-centre hotel with its own restaurant, a pleasant lobby and comfortable rooms costing US$12.50 for one, US$14.75 for two. It's often full.

The *Hotel Alameda* (tel 2-50-50) at González 2715 has adequate rooms for US$9/10.75.

Places to Stay - top end

Hotel Mesón Del Rey (tel 2-63-60) at Guerrero 718 on the main plaza is comfortable enough but not as luxurious as you'd expect for US$16.75/18. *Hotel Palacio Del Rio* (tel 2-24-83) at Ocampo 101 is as close as you can get to the Rio

Grande (turn left immediately off the international bridge) but the view's nothing special, the rooms could be cleaner, and despite the swimming pool, restaurant and disco on Friday, Saturday and Sunday, it's grossly overpriced at US$40 and up.

If you're looking for US-style luxury, best bets are two of the many motels which dot Guerrero and Avenida Reforma on the way out of town to the south. *El Río* (tel 4-36-66) at the corner of Reforma and Toluca has a pool, restaurant, bar, etc and costs US$31/34.50. The *Hacienda* (tel 4-46-66), two km further south at Reforma 5530, has similar facilities; rooms for one or two people cost US$32.

Places to Eat

Avoid the places on Guerrero for the first few blocks south of the bridge if you want value for money.

On the north side of the main plaza, at the corner of Dr Mier and Ocampo, *Café Quinto Patio* is a serviceable, friendly, but not especially clean café-restaurant with ordinary Mexicans making up its clientele. Chicken tacos, or chicken enchiladas with mole sauce, cost US$1, meat from US$1.50, egg dishes up to US$1.

On the opposite side of the plaza at the corner of Ocampo and González, the *Café Almanza* is a small, cosy, family-run place, cleaner and more cared-for than the Quinto Patio and only slightly more expensive. The menu includes fish, soups and breakfasts, and it's open from 7 am to midnight.

Two places very popular with the townsfolk lie a km or so down Guerrero from the international bridge. The *Río Mar* (tel 2-91-94) at Guerrero 2403 is small and unassuming but packed out at night with people tucking into seafood at bargain prices between US$1.75 and US$3. It's closed on Monday. A few blocks north, at Guerrero 2114 between Venezuela and Lincoln, *El Rancho* (tel 4-87-53) is a not-so-poor person's taco-and-beer hall,

offering a long list of different types of taco.

Several Texan-oriented restaurants are scattered around the streets close to the bridge, of which the best-known is the *Cadillac* (tel 2-91-24) on the corner of Belden and Ocampo. Proudly proclaiming 'Since 1926', it's a saloon-style place with tinkling piano, white-coated waiters and sepia-tint photos of Prohibition-era American drinking clients on the walls. The stand-up bar is still there but the Cadillac is more of a restaurant these days. The menu offers quail and frog's legs at US$9 and lobster tails at US$14.50, but there are also less expensive items, including Mexican food. Young Texans form a large part of the Cadillac's customers.

Other classy eateries include *The Winery* (tel 2-08-95) at Matamoros 308, and *La Fittes* (tel 2-22-08) at the corner of Matamoros and Victoria, which specialises in seafood.

Entertainment

Nuevo Laredo has horse and greyhound racing at the *Hipódromo-Galgódromo* on the south side of town. Signposts point to it. Dates and times are irregular but at the last count the horses ran on Sunday afternoon, the dogs on Saturday at 6 pm and on Sunday at 1 pm. You can usually bet with US dollars. Nuevo Laredo also has a bull ring.

Nightlife boils down to some very sleazy bars in the streets near the bridge or music of various kinds, live and recorded, in the tourist restaurants. The *Cadillac* has a piano player, or try *The Winery* or *O'Henry's* on Matamoros about three blocks south of the bridge. The *Lion's Den* is a disco on the same part of Matamoros.

Nuevo Laredo holds an agricultural, livestock, industrial and cultural fair during the second week of September.

Things to Buy

The less you buy the better if you've got your travelling ahead of you, but if you're on the way home it may be worth a browse round some of the shops and markets for the odd souvenir. Much of the stuff is mass-produced but there are a few shops selling good collections of handicrafts from all over Mexico. There's a craft 'market' on the east side of Guerrero half a block north of the main plaza, another one on the west side of Guerrero half a block south of Hidalgo, and a small mall on the west side of Guerrero between Hidalgo and Belden, as well as lots of individual shops all along this northern section of Guerrero. Items on sale range from pottery, textiles and saddles to brass giraffes and enormous clay eagles. Local products include wrought iron, glass and ceramics.

Getting There & Away

To/From Laredo, Texas Transportes del Norte and Transportes Frontera run buses between Laredo, Texas and cities inside Mexico including Mexico City, Guadalajara and Mazatlán, but these are dearer than their services between Nuevo Laredo and the same Mexican cities. You can use these buses to go between Laredo and Nuevo Laredo bus station – though it's cheaper and often quicker to walk over the international bridge and use a town bus in Nuevo Laredo. Transportes del Norte (1st class) has 10 buses a day between Laredo Greyhound station and Nuevo Laredo bus station (fare US$2), and Transportes Frontera (2nd class) has eight a day between Laredo Trailways station and Nuevo Laredo bus station (US$1.75). Heading from the US into Mexico, you're only supposed to use these buses if you're going south beyond Nuevo Laredo.

Both Greyhound and Trailways link Laredo with other US cities. It's a three-hour ride to Corpus Christi or San Antonio, eight or nine hours to Houston and about 13 hours to Dallas.

Laredo has an airport. Flights include two or three daily each way between Laredo and Houston by Continental (tel toll free (800) 282-3125 in the US).

Air Nuevo Laredo airport is off the Monterrey road, 14 km south of town. Mexicana has one or two direct flights to and from Mexico City every day except Tuesday, and one to Guadalajara on Tuesday, Thursday and Sunday, returning on Monday, Wednesday and Friday.

Bus Nuevo Laredo bus station (Central Camionera) is about three km from the international bridge on the southern side of town. It has a left-luggage section and restaurant, and 1st and 2nd-class buses to every city in the northern half of Mexico.

Transportes del Norte (1st class) goes to Querétaro (US$11.75) and Mexico City (US$14.50) nine times a day, San Luis Potosí (US$9.25) eight times, Saltillo (US$3.75) four times, Guadalajara (US$12) three times and Mazatlán (US$15) once, as well as to Monterrey, Aguascalientes, Zacatecas, Lagos de Moreno, San Juan de Los Lagos, Durango, Tampico, Ciudad Victoria and Toluca.

Tres Estrellas de Oro, also 1st class, runs direct to Monterrey (US$3) five times a day; to San Luis Potosí (US$9.25), Querétaro (US$11.75) and Mexico City (US$13.50) four times; and to Saltillo (US$4), Guadalajara (US$12), León, Irapuato, Salamanca, Morelia, Celaya and Uruapan (US$15) once each.

Transportes Frontera (2nd class) has services to Saltillo (US$3.50) and San Luis Potosí (US$8.50) every one or two hours; to Guadalajara (US$10.75) seven times daily (twice direct); and to Matehuala (US$6.25), Querétaro (US$10.50), Monterrey, Guanajuato, Aguascalientes, Zacatecas, Celaya, León, Salamanca, Toluca and Morelia.

The Tamaulipas-Zuazua line (2nd class) has eight services a day to Monterrey (US$2.50). Autobuses Blanco (2nd class) serves Ciudad Victoria,

Ciudad Valles, Tampico, Tuxpan, Monterrey, Saltillo and Guadalajara.

Transportes del Noreste goes to Piedras Negras (US$2.50) four times a day and Reynosa (US$3) six times.

Approximate 1st-class journey times: Monterrey three hours, Saltillo four to 4½ hours, Tampico 12 hours, Mexico City 16 hours.

Rail Nuevo Laredo railway station is on Avenida César López de Lara, at the western end of Gutiérrez, 10 blocks from Guerrero. The timetable seems to change every year but, especially if there are sleeping carriages, the trains from here can make a comfortable if slower alternative to a long bus haul south.

At the time of writing there were two daily departures for Mexico City by way of Monterrey, Saltillo and San Luis Potosí. 'El Regiomontano', with sleeping accommodation and a restaurant car, leaves Nuevo Laredo at 2 pm. 'Aguila Azteca', with nothing other than 1st-class reserved seats, departs at 6.55 pm. El Regiomontano is quicker – about four hours to Monterrey, six to Saltillo, 12 to San Luis Potosí and 19 to Mexico City. The Aguila Azteca takes 24 hours to Mexico City and also stops at San Miguel de Allende and Querétaro. The returning Regiomontano leaves Mexico City Buenavista station at 6 pm and the return Aguila Azteca leaves Mexico City at 8 am.

You can reserve 1st-class seats as far ahead as you like – advisable around Christmas, New Year and Easter, and in June, July and August, when 1st class can get fully booked. Make advance reservations for trips from Nuevo Laredo by telephoning (or writing a month ahead) to the local National Railways of Mexico commercial agent, Señora Guadalupe Contreras de López. Her telephone number is Nuevo Laredo 28097 and her address is PO Box 595, Laredo, Texas 78042, USA. She will let you know the price and you then send a bank cheque or bank draft within a specified time to confirm the reservations.

For Regiomontano reservations you can also phone Nuevo Laredo 20134.

For trips from Mexico City, go through the same procedure with Señor Javier Sánchez Méndez, the chief of the passenger traffic department, National Railways of Mexico, Buenavista Grand Central Station, 06358 Mexico DF (tel Mexico City 547-89-72).

First-class reserved seats from Nuevo Laredo cost US$19 to Mexico City, US$4 to Monterrey, US$14 to San Miguel de Allende. First-class unreserved seats are a little less than half, 2nd-class seats about a quarter. Roomettes to Mexico City are around US$25 single, US$28 double; a double bedroom is US$32.

Getting Around

Frequent city buses (15c) make getting around Nuevo Laredo easy enough. From the international bridge or downtown to the bus station, take a No 48 from the town centre terminal on Matamoros, two blocks south and one west of the bridge. You can also pick it up on the main square at the corner of Galeana and Dr Mier, or Galeana and González. The same No 48 brings you into town near the bridge from the bus station: pick it up directly over the road as you walk out of the bus station's main entrance.

To get to the railway station from downtown, catch a blue-and-white 'Arteaga González' bus from the town centre terminal.

South from Nuevo Laredo

It's mostly cacti and eagles all the way along Highway 85 to Monterrey, with occasional cattle. The town of Sabinas Hidalgo, halfway, has a few motels and restaurants. Forty km west of Sabinas Hidalgo are the Bustamante Caves, a series of chambers three km long. At present you need a guide to visit the caves, but they are being developed for visitors.

You can go past Monterrey and push on to Saltillo, 98 km beyond, by the excellent Highway 40. This Saltillo route is now the main one from Nuevo Laredo to Mexico City (1223 km away). It's possible to cover the 773 km from Nuevo Laredo to San Luis Potosí in one very long day's driving. From Nuevo Laredo to the Gulf coast, going via Monterrey is most direct if you're heading for Ciudad Victoria, Tampico and points south. If your destination is north of Ciudad Victoria, Highways 2 and 97 via Reynosa are shorter.

Green Angels patrol Highway 85 from Nuevo Laredo to Monterrey, Ciudad Victoria and Ciudad Valles, and Highway 40 from Monterrey to Saltillo.

FROM PIEDRAS NEGRAS/CIUDAD ACUÑA

It's a seven or eight-hour bus ride through the state of Coahuila to Saltillo or Monterrey. Highway 57 south from Piedras Negras to Saltillo (445 km) is a good road, fairly straight and level, with only isolated towns and villages. Along the way, 25 km south of Monclova, Highway 53 branches south-east to Monterrey instead of Saltillo (there are no gas stations on Highway 53).

The Saltillo route is the main one from Piedras Negras to Mexico City (1340 km away). It's patrolled by Green Angels all the way. The main route to the Gulf coast is via Monterrey.

A faintly possible alternative to the bus is the train (2nd class only) which leaves Piedras Negras at 9 am, arriving in Saltillo at 7.10 pm (it doesn't go to Monterrey).

Kikapoo Indians

Near the town of Múzquiz, about 30 km west of Nueva Rosita on the Piedras Negras-Saltillo road, is a settlement of about 500 Kikapoos. Members of their tribe driven south from Wisconsin and Illinois by white colonists were originally given permission in 1775 by Charles III of Spain to settle in the Spanish province of Coahuila and Texas, on condition that they helped resist the raids of other North American Indians such as the Comanches

and Lipanes. (Comanches travelled south almost every September between 1700 and 1850 in search of horses and buffalo – nowadays their principal trail is the Coahuila/Chihuahua border.)

The Kikapoos were still hunters and gatherers at the beginning of this century, but today most of them spend half the year as agricultural workers in the US and most families have four-wheel drives. They retain their own language, religion and many customs, although their traditional homes – huts made of wood and reed with curved roofs in summer, tepee-like structures in winter – are being replaced by modern materials and designs. Every home keeps a sacred fire burning in a central hearth.

Monclova

A little over halfway from Piedras Negras to Saltillo is the city of Monclova, 586 metres high with the extreme temperatures of the altiplano central. It's an industrial centre with one of the biggest iron and steel works in the country, and was one of the earliest settlements in this part of Mexico, dating from 1644. It was here that the independence heroes Hidalgo and Allende were finally ambushed and arrested in 1811. There are one or two reasonable hotels near the centre of Monclova if you need to stay. The *Hotel Olimpia* (tel 3-62-11) at Hidalgo Norte 203, and the *Hotel Ludivina* (tel 5-38-11) at the corner of Veracruz and Boulevard Juárez, are two of the better ones. There are others on Cuauhtémoc.

The town of Escobedo, near Monclova, achieved fleeting renown in 1984 when supporters of the PAN political party, angry at apparent election fraud, kidnapped the mayor, stripped him naked and left him tied to a post.

Monterrey & Saltillo

These two inland cities, capitals of Nuevo

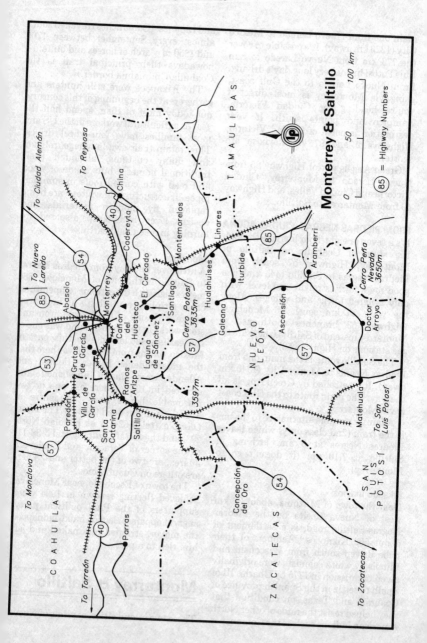

Monterrey & Saltillo

0 — 50 — 100 km

(85) = Highway Numbers

León and Coahuila states respectively, are less than 100 km apart but a world away from each other in atmosphere. Monterrey is Mexico's third biggest city and second biggest industrial centre, new, hectic, noisy, polluted but exciting – a unique place that makes an impression on everyone who visits it. There are some worthwhile side trips into the surrounding mountains and forests.

Saltillo contains industry too but it's a much smaller city. It lies 1000 metres higher in the arid Sierra Madre and has some fine views over the mountains. Its quiet central area has a small-town feel and some lovely colonial buildings that make it a pleasant place to stop on the way to or from the US border. Like Monterrey, it has excellent transport links with the rest of Mexico.

NUEVO LEÓN & COAHUILA
History
It was the search for silver (not found) and slaves, and the desire of missionaries to spread their word, which first brought the Spanish north to this sparsely inhabited region. Saltillo was founded in 1577. In 1579 Luis de Carvajal was commissioned to found Nuevo León, designated as an area 200 leagues north and west of the mouth of the Río Pánuco at Tampico. He set up abortive settlements in Monterrey and Monclova but also fought with the Spanish governors of the Pánuco region. Eventually arrested as a lapsed Jew, he died in prison in Mexico City.

Monterrey and Monclova were refounded successfully in 1596 and 1644 respectively. The Spanish used friendly Indians from Tlaxcala and other places to the south to help them settle these regions. It was from Nuevo León and Coahuila that Texas was first settled in the late 17th century.

Slowly, ranching became viable around the small new towns, despite raids by hostile Chichimecs which continued into the 18th century. Nuevo León had an estimated 1.5 million sheep by 1710. Huge empty areas could be taken over by a few people, laying the foundations of the enormous landholdings whose owners came to dominate the area. One southeast Coahuila holding of 89,000 hectares in 1731 (bought from the crown for 250 pesos) grew to 5.87 million hectares by 1771, becoming the Marquesado de Aguaya which was protected by a private cavalry. Still, the altiplano central remained largely unpopulated right up to the end of the 19th century.

In the early years of Mexican independence after 1821, Coahuila and Texas were one state of the new republic, but Texas was lost in 1848 after the Mexican-American war. As the 19th century progressed, ranching and industry (especially in Monterrey) grew, helped by the arrival of railways. By 1900 Nuevo León had 328,000 inhabitants, Coahuila 297,000.

Coahuila produced two leading lights of the Revolution, Francisco Madero and Venustiano Carranza. See the 'History' section in the 'Facts about the Country' chapter for more about them. The stabler climate of the post-Revolution years brought electricity, irrigation and more industry to the states, helping to put them among Mexico's wealthiest. But the 1980s economic crisis has struck here as elsewhere in the country and there is now wide support for the opposition right-wing party, PAN.

MONTERREY
Population: 2.18 million
Everything else comes second to industry in Monterrey. It's Mexico's ultimate 'muck and brass' city, with plenty of both. Young, unfettered by the past, it pursues profit with a single-mindedness unique in the country. Factories belch dirt and noise on the edges of the city; buses do the same just about everywhere. Only the downtown area and the extensive wealthy suburbs are screened from the immediate effects of Monterrey's sources of lucre. But it's also a grand city with one of the world's biggest plazas, a few relics of the early Spanish

years and a partly pedestrianised downtown area of towering hotels, chic restaurants and shops – all surrounded by dramatic mountains.

Life is faster and everything is more efficient here than anywhere else in Mexico. Monterrey's people – known as *Regiomontanos* – have a reputation for tight-fistedness (though they seem to have enough time to point the way in friendly fashion to enquiring visitors). Extremes of poverty and wealth rub shoulders: you can see a man stagger into a café and gobble up leftovers at empty tables; then, a few minutes later, see another man carry his poodle to keep its feet from getting dirty.

All of which gives the place a raw energy unequalled in the country. Monterrey is an assault on the senses – not a place to relax but a fascinating, extreme example of urban Mexico. Even its civic architecture is exciting: several entire blocks have been demolished to open up the enormous Gran Plaza and vistas of the dramatic mountains which circle the city, including the distinctive saddle-shaped Cerro de la Silla (1740 metres). In the plaza, towering over a delicate colonial cathedral, stands a tall, thin, orange concrete block, from which green laser beams sweep over the entire city at night.

At an altitude of 538 metres, with a population of officially 2.18 million but in reality probably a few hundred thousand more, Monterrey and the villages it has swallowed sprawl 30 km from east to west. The surrounding country offers caves, canyons, lakes and waterfalls, but most of the foreign visitors here are business people or American vacationers who come for shopping, eating and the top-end hotels. Almost as many tourists enter Mexico by flying to Monterrey as come overland through Matamoros.

For budget travellers Monterrey's disadvantage is that cheaper accommodation is mainly in a seedy area near the bus station, a good 20 minutes' ride from the downtown area, and that some of the out-of-town sights are hard to reach by public transport.

History

Monterrey had to be founded three times before it got off the ground. The first attempt was in 1577, the second (by the ill-fated Luis de Carvajal) in 1592, and the third (successful) effort in 1596 by Diego de Montemayor, who christened his 34-person settlement Ciudad Metropolitana de Nuestra Señora de Monterrey, after the Conde de Monterrey who was viceroy of Mexico at the time.

The early inhabitants subsisted on a diet that was supplemented by roots and Monterrey struggled on as a remote northern outpost. It slowly became the centre of a sheep-ranching area, often at odds with the Chichimec Indians who already lived in the area. Its importance grew with the colonisation of Tamaulipas in the mid-18th century, since it was on the trade route to the new settlements. In 1777, when it had about 4000 inhabitants, it became the seat of the new bishopric of Linares.

In 1824 it was made capital of the state of Nuevo León in newly-independent Mexico, and for its pains was occupied by Zachary Taylor's troops in the Mexican-American War – but only after three days' fierce fighting by Mexicans led by General Pedro de Ampudia. The city was occupied again in the 1860s by French troops, who were driven out by Benito Juárez's forces in 1866.

Monterrey's location close to the US gave it advantages in trade and smuggling: in the American Civil War it was a staging post for cotton exports by the blockaded Confederates. It began to emerge as an industrial centre in the 1860s and by 1910 was one of Mexico's biggest cities, its population having jumped from 27,000 in 1853 to about 80,000. Railways had come to Monterrey in 1881, and tax exemptions for industry under state governor Bernardo Reyes during the 'Porfiriato' period had attracted Mexican, American, British and French investment, including some by the Guggenheim family.

The city was the site of the first heavy industry in Latin America – the iron and steel works of the Compañia Fundidora de Fierro y Acero de Monterrey. In 1890 José Schneider founded the Cervecería Cuauhtémoc, which became Mexico's biggest brewery, soon starting to make glass, cartons, and bottle caps as well. Other industries – furniture, clothes, cigarettes, soap, cement, bricks – sprang up and today they have been joined by innumerable others. Two intermarried families, the Garzas and the Sadas, came to dominate business, building a huge empire – the Monterrey Group – that included many of the city's biggest companies.

Monterrey grew steadily through the 20th century and especially since the 1940s, when the spread of electricity enabled hundreds of new industries to set up. Little planning went into the city's growth, and the environment and the poor were mainly left to look after themselves, but education was promoted by the Garza Sadas and today Monterrey has four universities and a famous Technological Institute.

Economic success and distance from the national power centre in Mexico City have given Monterrey an independent turn of mind, and relations between its leaders and Mexico City are marked by suspicion, sometimes even hostility. Monterrey resents 'meddling' in its affairs by the central government, which in turn sometimes accuses the city of being too capitalistic or, even worse, too friendly with the USA.

Relations reached their lowest point under the left-leaning Mexican President Echeverría in the early 1970s. After the ageing head of the Monterrey Group, Eugenio Garza Sada, was murdered (apparently by left-wing guerrillas) in 1973, it was alleged that Echeverría had been trying to pressure the old man into turning his enormous steel company HYLSA over to the government.

Echeverría's supporters blamed the Garza Sadas for Mexico's economic problems of the time; and the family was accused of starting rumours that Echeverría was planning a coup to stay in power beyond his normal six-year term. The Garza Sadas, perhaps in fear of wholesale nationalisation, broke the Monterrey Group into two parts – the Alfa Group and the VISA Group.

President López Portillo, Echeverría's successor, fostered better relations with the powers of Monterrey. In 1978 the city was responsible for more than one-third of Mexico's exports, the production of its 14 biggest companies was worth US\$4 billion, and Alfa was number 403 on *Fortune* magazine's list of the world's biggest non-US companies.

But the economic crisis of the 1980s struck hard at the city. The Alfa Group went broke; the city government ran short of money; in 1986 a government-owned steel mill was closed, adding a further 8800 to the list of jobless. Monterrey is surviving, pulling through by hard work – but it's not surprising that there's support for the right-wing opposition party, PAN.

Orientation

Downtown Monterrey focuses on the zona rosa, an extensive area of pedestrianised streets and the more expensive hotels, shops and restaurants. On the eastern edge of the zona rosa is the huge Gran Plaza, round which stand the cathedral, government buildings, a theatre and so on. South of the zona rosa and the Gran Plaza is the nearly dry bed of the Río Santa Catarina, which cuts across the city from west to east. The bus station and most of the cheap accommodation are 2½ km north-west of downtown, the rail station 3½ north-west. Frequent if extremely noisy buses run all over the city (see 'Getting Around').

In the downtown and bus station areas

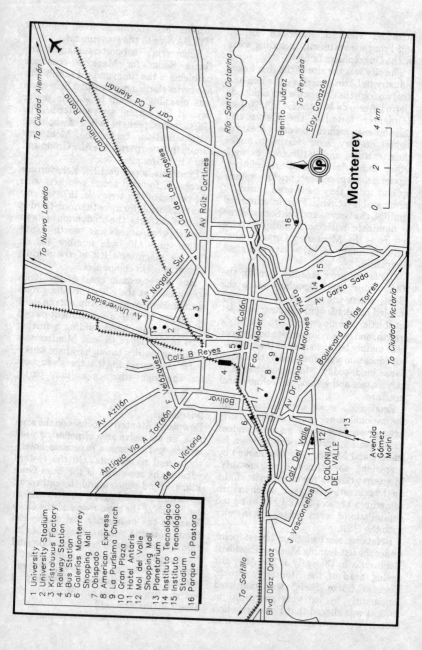

Monterrey

0   2   4 km

To Ciudad Alemán
To Reynosa
To Eloy Cavazos
To Nuevo Laredo
To Ciudad Victoria
To Saltillo

Río Santa Catarina
Benito Juárez
Corr A Cd Alemán
Camino A Roma
Av Cd de Los Ángeles
Av Rúiz Cortines
Av Nogalar Sur
Av Universidad
Calz B Reyes
E Velázquez
Av Aztlán
Antigua Via A Torreón
Bolívar
P de la Victoria
Av Colón
Fco I Madero
Av Dr Ignacio Morones Prieto
Boulevard de las Torres
Av Garza Sada
Avenida Gómez Morin
Calz Del Valle
COLONIA DEL VALLE
J Vasconcelos
Blvd Díaz Ordaz

1   University
2   University Stadium
3   Kristaluxus Factory
4   Railway Station
5   Bus Station
6   Galerías Monterrey
    Shopping Mall
7   Obispado
8   American Express
9   La Purísima Church
10 Gran Plaza
11 Hotel Antaris
12 Mol del Valle
    Shopping Mall
13 Planetarium
14 Instituto Tecnológico
15 Instituto Tecnológico
    Stadium
16 Parque la Pastora

streets are on a grid aligned roughly north-south-east-west. The corner of Juárez and Aramberri, roughly halfway between downtown and the bus station, is the centre of town as far as addresses are concerned. North-south streets have the suffix 'Norte' or 'Nte' if they are north of Aramberri, 'Sur' if they're south. East-west streets are 'Poniente' or 'Pte' if west of Juárez, 'Oriente' or 'Ote' east of Juárez. Numbers get higher as they move further away from the intersection.

Information

Tourist Office Monterrey has a friendly, modern tourist office called Infotur (tel 45-08-70, 45-09-02) at the corner of Matamoros and Zaragoza underneath the Gran Plaza. Staff speak fluent English, are knowledgeable about both Monterrey and the state of Nuevo León, and have lots of leaflets to hand out, including good maps of Mexico and street-directory maps of Monterrey. They can also tell you about cultural and entertainment events in the city. Unfortunately they know as little as anyone else about Monterrey's bus system. The office is open 10 am to 5 pm on Saturday and Sunday, 9 am to 1 pm and 3 to 7 pm Monday to Friday.

Money Numerous downtown banks change cash and travellers' cheques. There are a couple of casas de cambio on Ocampo, between Galeana and Juárez, downtown, which are usually open until 6 pm and on Saturday morning. Casa de Cambio Trebol, on Padre Mier between Escobedo and E Carranza, is open until 6 pm Monday to Friday and to 1 pm on Saturday, but doesn't change travellers' cheques.

American Express (tel 44-52-41) is at Padre Mier Pte 1424, on the corner of Bravo.

Post The central post office (tel 42-40-03) is on Zaragoza between Washington and Cinco de Mayo, just north of the Gran Plaza. It's open 8 am to 8 pm Monday to Friday, 9 am to 1 pm Saturday and Sunday.

Consulate The US Consulate (tel 43-06-50, 46-06-50) is at Constitución Pte 411, not far from the downtown area.

Festivals

Independence Anniversary Monterrey's biggest celebrations are held on 15 and 16 September, with a big parade on the 16th.

Spring Fair There are many festivities during the spring fair, which begins on Palm Sunday.

Festival of Our Lady of Guadalupe Held on 12 December, this festival draws thousands of pilgrims and worshippers for several days previously to the Santuario de Guadalupe, a big modern church south of the Río Santa Catarina, visible from the Gran Plaza. The same festival is also celebrated in a big way in Abasolo, a village about 25 km from Monterrey off the Monclova road, where there are pilgrimages, a fair, a parade of floats and horseback-riders, and folk-dancing.

Gran Plaza

This block-wide, km-long plaza (sometimes called the Macro Plaza) is a monument to Monterrey's ambition. Carved out within the past few years by the demolition of several entire blocks, it is surrounded by the best of the city's old and new architecture, has well-planned vistas of the surrounding mountains, and offers respite from the noise and bustle of streets nearby.

At the southern end, nearest the Santa Catarina River, is the Palacio Municipal (city hall), a modern building raised up on concrete legs. A hundred metres north, facing each other across a part of the Gran Plaza known as the Plaza Zaragoza, are the baroque-façaded cathedral, built between 1600 and 1750 except for the bell tower which was added in 1851, and the old city hall built in 1853 around a 16th-century courtyard. A few metres further on is the stunning Faro del Comercio (Lighthouse of Commerce), a tall, thin orange concrete block designed by the architect Luis Barragán. Green laser beams from the top sweep over the city at night. It couldn't be in greater contrast to the adjacent cathedral.

Continuing northwards, there is the Fuente del Comercio (Fountain of Commerce), the Obreros de Nuevo León (Workers of Nuevo León) statue, and the Fuente de la Vida (Fountain of Life) with a Neptune-like character riding a chariot in the middle. Beyond this the City Theatre and State Congress building face each other on opposite sides of the plaza. The state library is on the right, with the Bosque Hundido (Sunken Forest), a favourite spot for couples, in front of it.

Down some steps you come to the Esplanada de los Héroes (Esplanade of the Heroes), also called the Plaza Cinco de Mayo, with statues of various national heroes and, facing back down the length of the Gran Plaza, the Palacio de Gobierno (Government Palace), built of pink stone in 1908 with imposing inner stairs and courtyard. If you go behind the Palacio de Gobierno you find the 1930s post office, yet another architectural contrast.

Zona Rosa

This is the area of top hotels, restaurants and shops just west of the south end of the Gran Plaza bounded roughly by Padre Mier on the north, Ocampo on the south, and Juárez on the west, with a westward extension along Hidalgo. Many of the streets are pedestrians-only and it's usually a bustling place worth taking a look round for window shopping and something to eat or drink, if nothing more. Plaza Hidalgo, tucked away at the back of the old city hall off Zaragoza between Morelos and Hidalgo, is small and the restaurants around it are enclosed, making it a far cry from the traditional Mexican town square.

The Obispado

The former bishop's palace stands on a hill 2½ km west of the zona rosa, along Matamoros, and gives fine views over the city and surrounding mountains. Built in 1786-87, it also served as a fort (during the US attack on Monterrey in 1846, the French intervention of the 1860s, and confrontations between local Constitutionalists and the forces of Pancho Villa in the Revolution years) and a yellow-fever hospital before becoming what it is now – the Regional Museum of Nuevo León. You can trace the history of the state through exhibits and displays, which include remains of a mammoth found locally. All explanatory material is in Spanish. The Obispado is closed on Monday.

Cuauhtémoc Brewery & Museums

This curious complex features an art gallery, a sports museum, a baseball hall of fame, brewery tours and . . . free beer! It's in the gardens of the Cervecería Cuauhtémoc, the maker of Bohemia, Carta Blanca and Tecate beer, and is a km north of the bus station at Avenida Universidad 2202.

The art gallery (Museo de Monterrey, tel 72-48-94) has a not-very-interesting permanent collection but some excellent visiting exhibitions, which have included Picasso, Siqueiros, Miró, Giacometti and Moore. The baseball hall of fame (salon de la fama) has pictures, memorabilia and facts and figures on Mexican baseball. American fans can spot not only Mexican players who later made names for themselves in the USA but also Americans whose careers made more headway south of the border. The sports museum (Museo Deportivo de Monterrey) features boxing, bullfighting, rodeo and soccer.

Brewery tours are at 11 am, noon and 3 pm, Tuesday to Friday. You don't have to go on one to get the free beer, which is served outdoors to all who visit any of the exhibits, which are also free. The complex is open from 9.30 am to 5.30 pm Tuesday to Friday, 10.30 am to 6.30 pm on

Saturday and Sunday. There's also a café set among old brewing vats, where tasty sweet pastries are served.

Colonia del Valle & Chipinque

Colonia del Valle, six km south-west of downtown, used to be Monterrey's most exclusive suburb. It's still one of them, but the richest people have now moved a km or two south, up the slopes of the Mesa de Chipinque, which rise to 835 metres above the city. The whole area is called Garza García and gives a glimpse of the way Mexico's wealthy live – in big houses behind high walls, with satellite TV dishes sprouting like mushrooms.

Colonia del Valle contains the Mol del Valle shopping mall and other areas of classy shops in the streets off Calzada del Valle. The Planetarium (tel 78-58-19), at Avenida Gómez Morin 1100, is a science and technology museum too and is open from 3 to 7 pm, Tuesday to Sunday. Colonia del Valle also has lots of restaurants. There's an automobile museum at the corner of Vasconcelos and Río Suchiate.

Mesa de Chipinque, several km up the hill from Colonia del Valle, offers fine views back over the city and woodland walks as well as the luxury Hotel Chipinque, where there are horses for hire. Unfortunately you need a taxi or your own vehicle to get there since buses don't run beyond Colonia del Valle (see 'Getting Around').

A good landmark in Colonia del Valle is the roundabout where six roads meet next to the Mol del Valle, which is serviced by buses. A sculpture containing a lot of pipes stands in the middle of the roundabout. Calzada del Valle runs west, past the right-hand side of Mol del Valle, for three km from here; Avenida Gómez Morin runs south to the Planetarium (about 1½ km away) and on towards the Mesa de Chipinque.

Other City Sights

La Purísima Church About a km west of downtown by a pleasant little park at the corner of Hidalgo and Peña, this church is a fine example of modern architecture, built in 1946 and designed by Enrique de la Mora. It is constructed around several parabola-shaped arches. The statues on the façade are of the 12 disciples.

The Alameda This is a park occupying several blocks a km north-west of downtown, bounded by Pino Suárez, Aramberri, Villagrán and Washington. It has a zoo on the west (Villagrán) side, and sometimes Sunday-morning concerts.

Parque La Pastora This has a bigger zoo, woodlands and canoe rides, but it's five km east of downtown, off Avenida Eloy Cavazos.

Technological Institute The Instituto Tecnológico, in the south-east of the city on Avenida Garza Sada between Pernambuco and Avenida del Estado, is one of Mexico's best-regarded higher-education schools. It has fine facilities, including a stadium which hosted World Cup soccer games and a library with a huge collection of different editions of *Don Quixote*.

Art Galleries Monterrey has several, including the Museo de Monterrey. Another, the Casa de Cultura on the corner of Colón and Escobedo, is more interesting for the curious building that houses it (a gothic-style ex-railway station) than for the temporary shows inside, which are not usually of high quality. Among the commercial galleries, a good one concentrating on modern work is Arte Actual Mexicano at Río Bravo 210 in Colonia del Valle.

Lead Crystal Workshop You can see artisans turning lead crystal into jugs, glasses, etc at the factory of Kristaluxus (tel 51-98-69, 51-93-93) in the north of the city at J M Vigil 400, between Zuazua and E Carranza, Colonia del Norte. Tours are

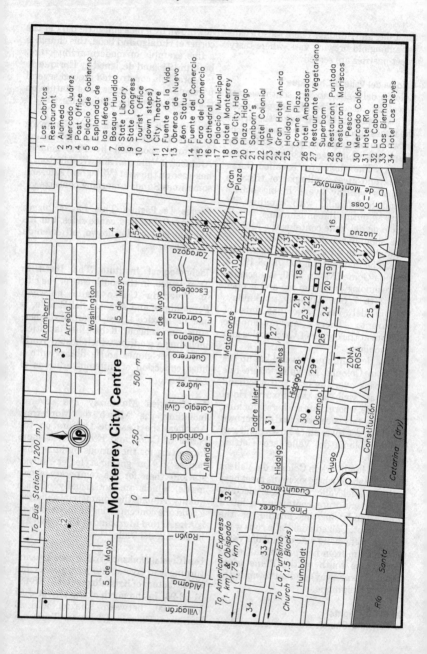

Monterrey City Centre

1 Los Cabritos Restaurant
2 Alameda
3 Mercado Juárez
4 Post Office
5 Palacio de Gobierno
6 Esplanada de los Héroes
7 Bosque Hundido
8 State Library
9 State Congress
10 Tourist Office (down steps)
11 City Theatre
12 Fuente de la Vida
13 Obreros de Nuevo León Statue
14 Fuente del Comercio
15 Faro del Comercio
16 Cathedral
17 Palacio Municipal
18 Hotel Monterrey
19 Old City Hall
20 Plaza Hidalgo
21 Sanborn's
22 Hotel Colonial
23 VIPs
24 Gran Hotel Ancira
25 Holiday Inn
26 Crowne Plaza
27 Restaurante Vegetariano Superbom
28 Hotel Ambassador
29 Restaurant Puntada
30 Restaurant Mariscos la Pesca
31 Mercado Colón
32 Hotel Río
33 La Cabana
34 Das Bierhaus
35 Hotel Los Reyes

available at 10.30 am Monday to Friday (telephone first) and there's a showroom where you can buy the products.

Places to Stay

Nearly all the cheaper hotels are within a few blocks of the bus station, where a room away from the street and the growling buses is a decisive plus. There's middle-range accommodation in this area and in the zona rosa, while the top-end places are nearly all in the zona rosa.

Places to Stay – bottom end

Some of the best value is on Calle Amado Nervo within two blocks of the enormous bus station. If you leave the bus station and stand facing the dual carriageway (Avenida Colón) immediately outside, with more of the bus station to your right than your left, Amado Nervo is the street running straight ahead on the far side of Colón.

The first place you come to, at Amado Nervo 1138, the *Hotel Posada* (tel 72-39-08) has clean, recently modernised rooms with fans, plenty of hot water in the shower, and even peepholes in the doors for the suspicious. Prices are US$4.25 for one person, US$5 for two people in a double bed, US$5.50 for two people in two beds. Some rooms on the upper floors have views over the city. For an extra fee you can have TV in the room. In winter the rooms can be cold because there's no heating.

Half a block further down at Amado Nervo 1007, the *Hotel Nuevo León* (tel 74-19-00) is also clean and fairly modern, with plenty of hot water. The interior rooms are pretty quiet for this part of town but don't have very much light. Singles/doubles are US$4.75/5.50.

The *Hotel Amado Nervo* (tel 75-46-32) at Amado Nervo 1110 has smaller, dingier rooms for US$4.50/5.50, and the *Hotel Virreyes* (tel 74-66-10) at Amado Nervo 902 has larger but tattier rooms for US$3.75/4.25.

Two other cheap places in the bus station area are the *Hotel Roosevelt* (tel 75-76-02), Universidad 1295 at the corner of Gutiérrez, where rooms vary considerably and cost from US$3.25 single or double (many of them are grubby); and the *Hotel Madero* (tel 75-54-71) at Madero Pte 428, between Cuauhtémoc and Jiménez, where singles/doubles which could be much cleaner cost US$3.75/4.75.

A step up in class but a bit further from the bus station is the *Hotel Patricia* (tel 75-07-50) at Madero Ote 123, between Juárez and Guerrero, where clean, quite pleasant rooms with air-conditioning cost from US$6.25. The hotel has a parking lot.

If you arrive at the railway station late at night, the nearest hotel is the *Hotel Estación* at Victoria 1450, the street running straight ahead as you walk out of the right-hand exit road of the station. It's very basic but probably tolerable for a night, with singles/doubles at US$2.75/3.75.

Places to Stay – middle

The middle range in Monterrey goes up to US$15 because there are so many places above that price. But there are several where quite comfortable rooms go for US$8 or US$9.

Bus Station Area Paying three or four extra dollars above the cheap end can make a big difference in comfort and ambience in this part of town. One such place is the big new *Fastos Hotel* (tel 72-32-50, 74-14-68), over the road from the bus station at Colón Pte 956, on the corner of Villagrán. The hotel's *económico* rooms are modern, quite big and comfortable and cost US$8.50/9; better rooms with air-con, heating, TV, etc, are US$15. Fastos has its own restaurant and bar.

The *Hotel 5a Avenida* (Quinta Avenida, tel 75-65-65) at Madero Ote 234, between Guerrero and Galeana, has comfortable air-conditioned rooms with TV for US$7.75/8.75. It also has its own clean, modern restaurant.

Hotel Jandal (tel 72-46-06, 72-36-36) at the corner of Cuauhtémoc Nte 825 (corner of Salazar) has spotless, air-conditioned, comfortable singles/doubles with TV for US$12.25/14.50; there's parking and a restaurant. Despite its name it doesn't appear to have any New Zealand connections (actually it's pronounced 'han-DAL'). Nearer the bus station the *Hotel Son Mar* (tel 75-44-00) at Universidad Nte 1211, close to the corner of Colón, has slightly bigger, equally comfortable rooms for US$14 single or double. The Son Mar has its own restaurant and parking.

Downtown On the western edge of the zona rosa at Hidalgo Pte 543, the slightly ageing *Hotel Los Reyes* is the nearest thing to a downtown bargain with big, clean, air-con doubles for US$9.75/10.75.

The *Hotel Colonial* (tel 43-67-91 to 96) at Hidalgo Ote 475 is very centrally placed and has air-conditioning, but it should be better-kept at US$13.50 single or double. Also close to the centre is the modern 120-room *Hotel Jolet* (tel 40-55-00 to 09) at Padre Mier Pte 201, where singles/doubles with air-con and TV cost US$14.75/17.25.

Elsewhere Near neither the bus station nor downtown but somewhere between the two is the towering *Gran Hotel Yamallel* (tel 75-35-98) at Zaragoza Nte 912. Modern in style, it offers parking and TV but in fact it's slightly decrepit. The only real reason to stay here is the view over the city from the upper floors. Singles and doubles cost US$9.50.

Places to Stay – top end
Downtown You have the pick of a clutch of places in the US$17 to US$34 bracket. At all of them you can expect restaurants and bars, and carpeted rooms with air-conditioning, TV and phone. For atmosphere none rivals the *Gran Hotel Ancira* (tel 43-20-60) at the corner of Escobedo and Plaza Hidalgo. It's been

going since 1912, which gives it several decades over other Monterrey hotels. During its early years, it is said, Pancho Villa once rode into the lobby, which is now a sitting area with piano player and hovering waiters, a restaurant and shops. Big rooms and plenty of old-fashioned elegance go for US$30.75 single or double.

The *Hotel Royalty* (tel 40-98-00) at Hidalgo Ote 402 has singles/doubles for US$17/18.50. The 200-room *Hotel Monterrey* (tel 43-51-20) fronts on to the Gran Plaza at Morelos Ote 574, has an electric band in its lobby bar, is one of the more popular top-end places and charges US$26 for singles or doubles.

The enormous *Hotel Río* (tel 44-90-40, 44-95-10) occupies a whole block between Morelos and Padre Mier; its address is Padre Mier Pte 194. It has a swimming pool and its 400 rooms cost from US$25.50 single or double. The *Hotel Ambassador* (tel 42-20-40) at the corner of Hidalgo and E Carranza has 241 rooms at US$33 single or double. The new *Holiday Inn Crowne Plaza* (tel 44-93-00), at Avenida Constitución Ote 300, is a huge 390-room place with blue-lit elevators gliding up and down above a cavernous restaurant/lounge where a rock band plays in the evenings. Singles and doubles are US$39.75.

Elsewhere Out in the wealthy suburb of Garza García, the *Hotel Antaris* (tel 78-99-66) at Río Danubio Ote 400 is probably Monterrey's most exclusive place – a very elegant modern hotel with just 34 rooms. Further out of town in roughly the same direction there's the equally plush *Hotel Chipinque* (tel 78-11-00), up on the Mesa de Chipinque.

In the north of the city, on the road heading in from Nuevo Laredo, the *Holiday Inn Norte* (tel 52-42-00, 52-33-90), at Avenida Universidad Nte 101, has a swimming pool and charges US$33 single or double. Cheaper is the *Motel Royal Courts* (tel 76-27-10) at Avenida Universidad Nte 314, also with a pool, where singles/doubles are US$19.25/19.75.

Places to Eat

Downtown Every block of the zona rosa seems to have one or more restaurants/cafés. There's a wide range of prices and types of food, but real value-for-money is hard to come by at either end of the scale. The cheapest places of all are the comedores (informal eating houses) in the markets – benches and tables set up around a couple of gas rings where the cooks turn out local staples.

Best value among the cheaper restaurants is on Hidalgo. *Restaurant Mariscos La Pesca* at Hidalgo Ote 126, between Juárez and Galeana, does a variety of fish dishes for around US$1.25 and shrimp several ways for US$1.50 to US$2.50. But its *comida especial* is a real bargain at US$1 for tasty fish soup followed by fish fillet, rice, French fries and salad – with a refresco and bread thrown in.

Over the road at Hidalgo 123 Ote, *Restaurant Puntada* has a long menu of Mexican items with nothing above US$0.85 and is always packed.

More expensive but with a pleasant atmosphere is *La Cabana* on Matamoros between Pino Suárez and Cuauhtémoc. It's a kind of large but comfortable log cabin where you can just drink beer or eat seafood, meat, chicken enchiladas with mole sauce, or soup at prices between US$0.75 and US$4.25.

Vegetarians will find a haven at *Restaurante Vegetariano Superbom* (tel 45-26-63) upstairs at the corner of Padre Mier and Galeana. There's quite a long menu of genuine vegetarian food, with nothing dearer than US$1.25. Try the yoghurt with puréed beetroot. The Superbom is open from 8 am to 8 pm Monday to Thursday, 8 am to 4 pm on Friday, and 10 am to 6 pm on Sunday. Other vegetarian restaurants are on Escobedo, half a block north of Padre Mier, and at the corner of Ocampo and Cuauhtémoc.

A few blocks west of the zona rosa proper, *Das Bierhaus* at the corner of Hidalgo Pte and Rayón is a quite pleasant German-style beerhouse where you can down mugs while perching on stools at high tables, or sit in a bit more comfort and eat. Beer from the barrel costs US$0.50 (with free peanuts); food is in the US$1 to US$4.75 range except for shrimp, which go for US$8.

If you fancy sampling the atmosphere of the *Gran Hotel Ancira*, a coffee at a table in the lobby costs only 25c.

For fast food, *Picos* on Plaza Hidalgo is reasonable value. Burgers go for US$1, chicken tacos for US$1.25, and scrambled eggs with ham and frijoles for US$0.85. There's also one of the more expensive *VIPs* chain at the corner of Hidalgo and E Carranza. Spinach salad with bacon and mushrooms costs US$1.50; spaghetti bolognese US$2.25; enchiladas, tacos or burritos US$2.25 to US$2.75; pollo frito VIPs US$3.50; and shrimp US$5.50. Still in American style but in classier surroundings is *Sanborn's* on the corner of Morelos and Escobedo.

For the best meals you have to pay the highest prices. Two well-known places on Plaza Hidalgo are the *Luisiana* (tel 43-15-61) where the food is international and a meal will cost you about US$12 to US$18, and *El Regio* (tel 43-62-50) where the tables are set in slightly intimidating long straight rows but the Mexican food has a good reputation and a meal is around US$7 to US$10.

Bus Station Area Ordinary Mexican eateries in this part of town are pretty poor. For instance *Cafetería y Mariscos Flores* at Colón 860, directly opposite the bus station, serves chicken that is mostly bones and doesn't tell you that the prices on the menu are out of date until you get the bill. Fortunately there's one excellent restaurant in the area devoted solely to a regional speciality, and a few reliable American-style places too.

El Pastor at Madero Pte 1067 near the

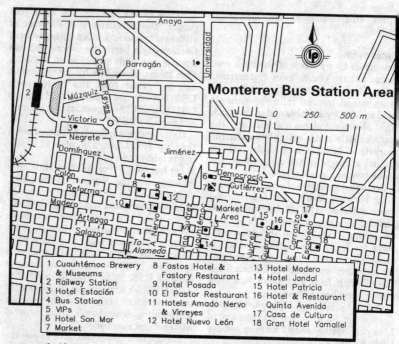

Monterrey Bus Station Area

0   250   500 m

1 Cuauhtémoc Brewery
  & Museums
2 Railway Station
3 Hotel Estación
4 Bus Station
5 VIPs
6 Hotel Son Mar
7 Market

8 Fastos Hotel &
  Fastory Restaurant
9 Hotel Posada
10 El Pastor Restaurant
11 Hotels Amado Nervo
   & Virreyes
12 Hotel Nuevo León

13 Hotel Madero
14 Hotel Jandal
15 Hotel Patricia
16 Hotel & Restaurant
   Quinta Avenida
17 Casa de Cultura
18 Gran Hotel Yamallel

corner of Alvárez serves nothing but *cabrito*, which is kid and a speciality of this part of Mexico. It tastes a bit like lamb. El Pastor does a variety of different parts of the animal, often charcoal-grilled, at prices between US$1 and US$3. Friendly waiters will explain to you (mainly in Spanish) what the different names mean. *Paleta* at US$2.75 is roast shoulder. El Pastor is open from 11 am to 11 pm.

Fastory Restaurant in Fastos Hotel on Colón opposite the bus station is a spic-'n'-span modern place, open 24 hours, with Mexican and Western food. Spaghetti bolognese (no trimmings) costs US$1.50, enchiladas US$1.75, breakfasts up to US$2.50, steaks up to US$3.50. There's a *VIPs* on Pino Suárez, just north of Colón, with the same menu as the downtown VIPs.

A similar style but smaller and slightly cheaper place is the *Restaurant Quinta Avenida*, in the hotel of the same name at Madero Ote 234. Here tacos cost US$1.50, steaks US$1.75 to US$3.25. Comida corrida at the clean and modern *Hotel Jandal* restaurant, on the corner of Cuauhtémoc and Salazar, is US$2.25.

Elsewhere Near the Alameda, *Los Cabritos* at the corner of Aramberri and Villagrán is another place specialising in cabrito. It's slightly dearer than El Pastor. Also popular in this part of town, but not cheap, is the *Café Lisboa* on Aramberri on the north side of the park.

If you find yourself in Colonia del Valle and don't want to hit one of the many expensive restaurants there, *Piccolos Pizza* (tel 78-64-27) on the west side of the Mol del Valle, nearly opposite the Hotel Antaris, is quite good value from US$1.25.

Entertainment

Monterrey has numerous cinemas and an active cultural life including concerts, theatre and art exhibitions. The tourist office can tell you what's on, and posters are placed in strategic spots around town listing events. You might also come across some street theatre in the zona rosa.

There are bullfights and rodeos every Sunday. The bullfights are held in the afternoons at the big covered Plaza de Toros at Universidad 2401 in the north of the city. Rodeos *(charreados)* take place in several different places, usually on Sunday mornings. Two better-known venues are in Guadalupe, on the east edge of the city, and Cryco, 35 km south by Highway 85. Monterrey also has professional soccer and baseball teams.

The city lacks pleasant spots for sitting in cafés and watching the world go by, and live music is to be found mainly in the expensive hotels and restaurants. The *Ancira* and *Ambassador* hotels and the *Luisiana* restaurant have piano bars, and there's live music – usually by electric bands – in the *Monterrey* and *Holiday Inn Crowne Plaza* hotels. A disco popular with the wealthier young is the *Baccaratt* (tel 78-65-48) at Grijalva 50 in Colonia del Valle. Video bars are in fashion too; try *Heaven* (tel 78-10-18) at Orinoco 108, Colonia del Valle.

Things to Buy

Markets Monterrey has several markets, at least three plush shopping areas and some interesting craft shops. There are few distinctive local handicrafts but, as elsewhere in northern Mexico, plenty of leather goods around.

The two main downtown markets are the Mercado Colón, bounded by the streets Morelos, Garibaldi, Ocampo and Juárez, and the Mercado Juárez, bounded by Juárez, Aramberri, Guerrero and Arreola. Both are big, bustling places selling everything ordinary Mexicans need and containing numerous eating houses or comedores – the cheapest places to eat in town. Two markets near the bus station are between Universidad and Jiménez, a block north of Colón, and along Reforma east of Cuauhtémoc.

Shops The zona rosa has plenty of upmarket shops but the two slickest shopping malls are Galerías Monterrey, about three km west of the zona rosa on Gonzalitos between Insurgentes and González Garza, and Mol del Valle by the roundabout where Gómez Morin and Calzada del Valle meet in Colonia del Valle. These are the places where Monterrey's rich spend their pesos in boutiques, jewellers', furniture-makers, ceramics stores, shoe and leather goods shops, restaurants, cafés, etc. Galerías Monterrey contains the 'Liverpool' department store; Mol del Valle has a skating rink. Plaza Dorada, on Hidalgo Pte west of Pino Suárez, is another flashy boutique and shoe-shop complex. There's also an older-established shopping area on Madero between Cuauhtémoc and Zaragoza.

Interesting crafts shops with folk art items from different parts of Mexico – some of them surprisingly cheap – are Carapán at Hidalgo Ote 305, and Tikal at Río Guadalquivir 319 in Colonia del Valle. Casa de las Artesanías near the Gran Plaza at the corner of Coss and Allende has an interesting range of modern art objects influenced by folk-tradition, as well as some clothes.

The only craft product for which Monterrey is particularly known is lead crystal. This isn't cheap but there are sometimes reduced-price offers at the Kristaluxus factory.

Getting There & Away

Air Aeroméxico (tel 40-87-60, 40-87-66 to 69; at the airport 44-77-30, 44-77-40) is at the corner of Padre Mier and Cuauhtémoc. Mexicana has offices at the corner of Zaragoza and Matamoros (tel 45-30-77), Hidalgo Pte 922 (tel 44-11-22), Cuauhtémoc Nte 716 (tel 74-14-74, 74-14-77) and the corner of Hidalgo and Escobedo (tel 45-64-82, 45-64-22). Its airport phone number is 45-08-11, 45-08-71. Continental Airlines (tel 43-70-01, 44-70-25) is at Padre Mier Pte 188.

Aeroméxico has two daily flights each way between Monterrey and Houston, and Continental one. Aeroméxico also flies non-stop to and from Los Angeles daily. Mexicana serves Dallas/Fort Worth non-stop once a day in each direction, San Antonio and Chicago three times a week each.

There are several daily flights (most by Mexicana, a few by Aeroméxico) to and from Mexico City. Aeroméxico flies direct to Chihuahua twice daily; Cancún, Guadalajara, León and Torreón once daily; Durango six days a week; Aguascalientes four days a week; Mazatlán and Toluca three days a week. Mexicana goes to Tampico non-stop daily, to Mazatlán and San Luis Potosí three times a week.

Road For routes to the north-east border, see the North-East Border section earlier in this chapter. Saltillo's the place to head for initially if you're going to the north-west, Mazatlán, Zacatecas or Guadalajara. Head west along Colón or Constitución until you reach the Saltillo road, Highway 40. This is now also the best road to San Luis Potosí (546 km from Monterrey), Querétaro and Mexico City (960 km).

The alternative route south, Highway 85, which passes through Montemorelos, Linares, Ciudad Victoria, Ciudad Mante and Ciudad Valles is not only further to Mexico City (984 km); it's also an inferior road, especially in some of the stretches south of Ciudad Valles. Whereas Highway 40 to Saltillo and Highway 57 from Saltillo to Mexico City are patrolled by Green Angels all the way, there are stretches on Highway 85 south of Ciudad Valles which aren't.

If you're heading to Tampico and points south along the Gulf coast, Highway 85 is the one to follow as far as Ciudad Mante, where you turn east on Highway 80.

Bus Monterrey bus station (Central de Autobuses) occupies three blocks along Colón between Pino Suárez and Reyes. It's a small city in itself, with ticket desks strung out along the whole length. A selection of lines and services follows.

Omnibus de México (tel 75-71-21) (1st class) goes to Reynosa (US$3) and Matamoros (US$4.25) 10 times daily; to Torreón (US$4.50), Chihuahua (US$10) and Ciudad Juárez (US$14.50) four times; to Zacatecas (US$5.50), Aguascalientes (US$7) and Guadalajara (US$9.25) three times; to Durango (US$7.75) three times; to Tampico (US$7) once.

Transportes del Norte (tel 75-42-80) (1st class) goes to Saltillo (US$1) frequently; to San Luis Potosí (US$6.50) 10 times a day; to Mexico City (US$11.50) about 15 times daily; to Nuevo Laredo (US$2.75) about half-hourly; to Laredo, Texas, about 12 times daily; to Reynosa (US$2.75) four times a day; to Ciudad Victoria and Ciudad Valles (US$6.25) four times a day; to Tampico (US$7) eight times daily; also to Matehuala (US$4.25), Matamoros and Mazatlán.

Tres Estrellas de Oro (tel 74-24-10) (1st class) goes to San Luis Potosí (US$6.50) 10 times daily; to Nuevo Laredo (US$2.75) five times daily; and to Saltillo, Mexico City (US$11.50), Reynosa (US$2.75) and Matamoros (US$4).

Autobuses Anáhuac (1st and 2nd class) goes to Matehuala (US$4.25 in 1st class, US$4 in 2nd class) and San Luis Potosí (US$6.50 1st class, US$6 2nd class) 14 times daily; to Querétaro (US$9 1st class, US$8 2nd class) and Mexico City (US$11.50 1st class, US$10.50 2nd class) six times daily; to León (US$8 2nd class), Salamanca (US$9 2nd class) and Celaya (US$9.25 2nd class) at 10.30 pm; to Piedras Negras (US$5.25 1st class, US$5 2nd class) seven times a day; also to Ciudad Acuña (US$6 1st class, US$5.50

2nd class), Zacatecas, Guadalajara, Santa María del Río, San Luis de la Paz, Cuatrociénegas and Monclova.

Transportes del Noreste (2nd class) goes to Matehuala (US$3.75) and San Luis Potosí (US$6) four times daily; to Reynosa (US$2.50) three times.

Estrella Blanca (2nd class) goes to Mexico City about 14 times a day; to San Luis Potosí (US$6) about eight times daily.

Transportes Tamaulipas (tel 75-32-02) (2nd class) goes frequently to Ciudad Victoria (US$3.25) and Ciudad Valles (US$5.75); to Tampico (US$6.50) about eight times daily; to Matehuala (US$3.75) and San Luis Potosí (US$6) about 12 times daily.

Transportes Monterrey-Cadereyta-Reynosa (2nd class) goes to Matamoros (US$4) 13 times daily; to Brownsville, Texas (US$4.75) twice; to Reynosa (US$2.75) and McAllen, Texas (US$3.75) six times a day.

Transportes Frontera (2nd class) goes to Nuevo Laredo (US$2.50) every 30 minutes; to Saltillo 14 times daily; to Matehuala (US$4) and San Luis Potosí (US$6) frequently; to Ciudad Valles (US$5.75) four times a day; to Tampico (US$6.25) 10 times daily.

Linea Verde (2nd class) goes to Aguascalientes, Guadalajara, Fresnillo and Zacatecas.

Autobuses El Aguila (2nd class) goes to Reynosa six times a day.

Approximate 1st-class journey times: Nuevo Laredo three hours, Laredo Texas 3½ hours, Reynosa four hours, McAllen Texas five hours, Matamoros six hours, Brownsville in Texas seven hours, Saltillo 1½ hours, San Luis Potosí six hours, Tampico eight hours, Mexico City 12 hours. Add 10 to 20% for 2nd-class journey times.

Rail Monterrey railway station (tel 75-46-53) is about half a km west of the bus station along Colón, then three blocks north on Nieto.

There are two trains daily to Mexico City. 'El Regiomontano', also known as the Pullman, has sleeping accommodation and a dining car. It leaves Monterrey at 6 pm, reaching Saltillo at 8.10 pm, San Luis Potosí at 1.50 am and Mexico City at 8.45 am. There is no 2nd class on this train. The 11.30 pm departure from Monterrey, the 'Aguila Azteca', has no sleeping accommodation – only 1st and 2nd-class seats, with 1st class reservable. It reaches Saltillo at 2.35 am, San Luis Potosí at 10.05 am, San Miguel de Allende at 1.09 pm, Querétaro at 2.42 pm and Mexico City at 7.20 pm.

A 1st-class ticket to Mexico City costs US$6.75 or US$15 with a reserved seat; a roomette costs US$18.50 for one person, US$28.25 for two people; a bedroom is US$31.50 for two, US$42.50 for three, US$53.50 for four. Second-class fare is US$3.75.

Northward, the Regiomontano leaves Mexico City at 6 pm, reaching Monterrey at 9 am, while the Aguila Azteca leaves Mexico City at 8 am and arrives in Monterrey at 2.20 am. Both trains go on to Nuevo Laredo – a further four or five hours. First-class reserved fare to Nuevo Laredo is US$4, 1st-class unreserved US$1.75, 2nd class about US$1.

Other trains from Monterrey include the 6 am to Reynosa (arrival 10.50 am, fare US$1.75 in 1st class, US$1 2nd class) and Matamoros (arrival 1.05 pm, 1st class US$2, 2nd class US$1.25); the 8 am to Tampico (about 11 hours) via Ciudad Victoria; and the 8.10 am to Torreón.

For advance reservations from Monterrey go to the station, or telephone Señora Juanita Garza (754604), or phone or write to Señor Javier Sánchez Méndez (tel Mexico City 547-89-72), Chief of Passenger Traffic Department, National Railways of Mexico, Buenavista Grand Central Station, 06358 Mexico DF. Allow at least a month if you're ordering reservations by mail.

Getting Around

Airport Transport Monterrey airport is off the road to Ciudad Alemán (Highway 54) north-east of the city, about 15 km from the city centre. There is no shuttle service to the airport. A taxi costs about US$4.50.

Bus Buses (10c) are noisier when you're outside them than inside, and they go just about everywhere in Monterrey frequently, but often by roundabout routes. Unfortunately there's no centralised source of info on which ones go where. People on the street often know how to get from where you are to where you want to go; if they don't, ask a bus driver.

A few useful numbers follow. Don't worry if they appear to be going in the opposite direction to the one you want; their routes are sometimes extremely convoluted.

Bus Station to Downtown Buses 17 and 18, from the corner of Amado Nervo and Reforma, go to the edge of the zona rosa, then do a dogleg around it. For the Gran Plaza, best place to get off is the corner of Juárez and 15 de Mayo. For the zona rosa, get off at the corner of Juárez and 15 de Mayo, or on Pino Suárez at the corners of Padre Mier, Hidalgo or Ocampo.

Downtown to Bus Station No 39 (orange) can be picked up on Juárez at the corners of Ocampo, Hidalgo, Morelos or Padre Mier. It takes you to Colón. No 17, going north from the corner of Cuauhtémoc and Padre Mier, also goes to Colón.

Bus Station to Obispado, La Purísima & Downtown No 1 from the corner of Amado Nervo and Reforma goes within a few blocks of the Obispado, passes La Purísima church, then goes along Ocampo to Zaragoza.

Downtown to Obispado No 4 from the corner of Padre Mier and Garibaldi goes west along Padre Mier. For the Obispado, get off when it turns left at Degollado, walk straight up the hill, turn left at the top of the steps, then take the first right (10 minutes of walking).

Downtown or Bus Station to Cuauhtémoc Brewery No 1 'San Nicolás-Tecnológico' goes up Juárez from downtown and passes the corner of Cuauhtémoc and Colón (near the bus station) on its way up Universidad to the brewery. No 1 'Universidad' goes north up Cuauhtémoc from Padre Mier to Colón, then on up Universidad to the brewery.

Cuauhtémoc Brewery to Bus Station & Downtown Nos 17 and 18 go south along Universidad, then right along Colón and left down Amado Nervo before heading downtown.

Downtown to Colonia del Valle/Garza García Bus 'San Pedro' from the corner of Ocampo and Pino Suárez goes to the big roundabout in Colonia del Valle (where Gómez Morin, Vasconcelos and Calzada del Valle meet), then heads west along Vasconcelos.

Downtown to Technological Institute Take No 1 from the corner of Padre Mier and Pino Suárez.

Car Rental Avis (tel 40-22-20) is at Ocampo 370 and at the airport (tel 44-47-23). Hertz (tel 44-70-83) is at Garibaldi 814.

Tours A company called Osetur runs sightseeing-and-shopping tours to places in and out of the city in small coaches. Destinations covered depend on the day of the week but include the Gran Plaza, the Cuauhtémoc Brewery complex, the Planetarium, the Kristaluxus lead crystal factory, Galerías Monterrey shopping mall, craft shops, a rodeo, Mesa de Chipinque, Grutas de García and Horsetail Falls. A morning city tour which is basic and covers two or three destinations costs US$3.25. Osetur (tel 43-66-16, 44-68-11) is based in Colonia Loma Larga south of the Río Santa Catarina, but tours leave from downtown at the corner of Escobedo and Ocampo. Telephone first or ask the tourist office where the tour goes on a particular day.

AROUND MONTERREY

Don't go looking for the cable car up Cerro

de la Silla – it was closed after an accident a few years ago.

Grutas de García

A 2½-km-long lighted route leads through 16 chambers in this cave system high in the Sierra del Fraile, approached by a 700-metre cable-car ascent 43 km west of the city. There are lots of stalactites and stalagmites, as well as petrified seashells. Each chamber has a different name such as 'The Eagle's Nest', 'Chamber of Clouds', 'The Eighth Wonder'.

The caves were formed about 50 million years ago and discovered by the parish priest in 1843. This is a popular weekend outing among Monterrey people. Sunday is the only day you can get a bus there; it's operated by Transportes Monterrey-Saltillo and leaves Monterrey main bus station at 9, 10 and 11 am and at noon, returning in the afternoon (US$1 for the round trip). On other days the same line runs buses every half-hour to Villa de García, nine km from the caves, where if you're very keen you could try hiring a donkey.

The caves and cable car are open from 9 am to 4.30 pm, Tuesday to Sunday. Entrance fee (including cable car) is US$1.25. A sign points the way to the caves 25 km out of Monterrey on Highway 40 to Saltillo.

Cañón de la Huasteca

On the western edge of Monterrey, 16 km from the centre, this canyon ('wass-TEK-a') is 300 metres high with some dramatic rock formations. Unfortunately the shanty town at one end of it and children's playground in the middle reduce its wildness. Reach the mouth of the canyon by taking a 'Santa Catarina/Huasteca' bus (10c) from the corner of Padre Mier and Juárez, or Cuauhtémoc and Madero, in downtown Monterrey. The same bus brings you back to the city centre. The town of Santa Catarina, at the north end of the canyon, celebrates the festival of the Virgin of San Juan de Los Lagos with dances and fireworks from 10 to 15 August.

Cascadas Cola de Caballo

This 25-metre waterfall, whose name means Horsetail Falls, is six km up a rough road from El Cercado, a village 35 km south of downtown Monterrey by Highway 85. It is on private land and open from 8 am to 6 pm, Tuesday to Sunday. Like many Mexican 'beauty spots', it has its share of hawkers and food stalls. Horses and donkeys can be hired from a car park about one km before the falls. Autobuses Monterrey-Villa de Santiago-El Cercado go to El Cercado from Monterrey bus station. The village of Santiago, close to El Cercado, is the scene of some of the region's biggest celebrations of the apple harvest – the Fiesta de la Manzana – in the second half of August.

On the way to El Cercado you pass close to the Rodrigo Gómez Dam, known as La Boca – an artificial lake where Regiomontanos go swimming, sailing and water-skiing.

If you have your own vehicle, you can drive 33 km up a rough road from El Cercado to the Laguna de Sánchez, a mountain lake surrounded by pine forests.

MONTERREY TO CIUDAD VICTORIA

The 287 km of this road pass through Mexico's most important citrus-growing area, centred on the towns of Allende, Montemorelos, Hualahuises and Linares. The Sierra Madre rises to the west. There are hotels in Montemorelos and Linares. Montemorelos is the centre for celebrations of the orange harvest (Fiesta de la Naranja) in November.

Linares

This small city has an 18th-century cathedral, the 18th-century church of La Misericordia and a small museum containing some of the ancient rock paintings found in the area. Its best-known festival is the Fiesta de Villaseca in

August, which celebrates the arrival of the Cristo de Villaseca, a wooden copy of a Spanish sculpture of Christ, in Guanajuato a few centuries ago. Cock fights, music, dancing and the running of cats are the chief attractions.

Sierra Madre

From Linares a scenic road (Highway 58) heads west up into the Sierra Madre to the towns of Iturbide (44 km from Linares) and, with an eight-km northward detour, Galeana (72 km from Linares), climbing 1000 metres from the valley. Highway 58 continues west down on to the altiplano central, where it meets Highway 57 between Saltillo and Matehuala, 98 km from Linares.

Iturbide This area has several caves, canyons and waterfalls. There's a hotel in town where you can hire horses to reach some of them. Nine km before Iturbide a giant bas-relief, *Los Altares*, dedicated to road builders, stands beside the road.

Galeana High on a wheat-producing plateau, Galeana is a centre for hand-loomed wool shawls and blankets. The town celebrates the festival of San Pablo with fireworks and processions from 20 to 25 January. Seven km north is a 15-metre-high natural bridge called the Puente de Dios, over which a local road passes. The 3635-metre peak of Cerro Potosí, one of the highest in the Sierra Madre Oriental, is 35 km west of Galeana.

SALTILLO

Population: 300,000

Set 1599 metres high in the Sierra Madre, Saltillo was founded in 1577 and is the oldest city in the north-east. It's on the main road and rail routes south from the north-east border and is a very pleasant place to break a journey. It is a city with the confidence, even stateliness, of old capitals, as well as having new shops and housing that give it a prosperous air.

The pace of life is much slower than in Monterrey – the people of Saltillo even seem to speak at a more comprehensible speed! A few mariachi bands hang around the downtown area at night, blowing on their trumpets and hoping for customers. Here you'll find both the first gem of colonial architecture and the first reasonably priced colonial-style hotel on this route south.

History

The search for slaves and silver brought the Spanish to the area, but they stayed to ranch sheep and grow wheat despite the threat of raids by Chichimec tribes. During Saltillo's first two centuries, Indians from Tlaxcala were brought to help the Spanish stabilise the area, and they set up a colony beside the Spanish one at Saltillo. The Tlaxcalans' skill on the treadle-loom and the abundance of wool in the area led to the development of a unique type of sarape, for which Saltillo became famous in the 18th and 19th centuries.

Work on Saltillo's cathedral started in 1746, and the city's growth was helped by the colonisation of Tamaulipas over the following decade, since it was on the trade route to that area. Saltillo was made capital of the province of Coahuila later that century but by 1800 it still had less than 7000 people.

Capital of the state of Coahuila and Texas after Mexican independence in 1821, it was occupied by US troops under Zachary Taylor in 1846 during the Mexican-American War which was sparked off by the dispute over Texas. Ten km south of Saltillo, at Buenavista, the 20,000-strong army of General Santa Anna was repulsed by Taylor's men in 1847, the decisive battle for control of the north-east during that war.

President Benito Juárez came to Saltillo during his flight from the invading French forces in 1864 and the city was occupied again by foreign troops before being freed in 1866. During the

Porfiriato (1876-1910) agriculture and ranching prospered in the area, and the coming of the railway helped trade and the first industries in the city, but Monterrey was by this time fast overtaking Saltillo in size and importance.

Nevertheless the two cities, although only 85 km apart, are separated by the Sierra Madre and are in distinct regions. Today Saltillo in no way lives in the shadow of its more famous neighbour. It has its own industries – flour and textiles among them, as well as big Chrysler and Pemex plants – and is a commercial and communications centre for a large livestock and agricultural area. With a population of about 300,000, it has also been outgrown by the modern south-west Coahuila city of Torreón but is still the capital of the state.

Orientation

Downtown Saltillo is on a slightly higgledy-piggledy grid format, with two plazas as the main landmarks. The Plaza de Armas, with the cathedral on its east side and fine colonial buildings around the other sides, is the more monumental of the two. Hidalgo, an important street, runs across the east side of the plaza, in front of the cathedral. The dividing point for Saltillo's street addresses is the junction of Hidalgo and Juárez at the south-west corner of the cathedral. With your back to the main façade of the cathedral, up the hill on Hidalgo (to the left) is south (Sur), downhill to the right is north (Nte), behind you is east (Ote), in front of you is west (Pte).

If you leave the Plaza de Armas on the opposite side to the cathedral (west) and walk one block further, you come out on another main thoroughfare, Allende. A right turn here (northward) and three or four blocks down the hill brings you to the Plaza Acuña with the market building on its north side. Most places to stay and eat, and almost all the city's activity, are within five minutes' walk of these two plazas. The busiest street is Aldama,

running down to the west from Plaza Acuña. Victoria, parallel to and south of Aldama, has a number of more up-market shops.

The bus station is way out on the south-west side of town – a good 15-minute bus ride. The railway station is a 20-minute walk from the centre; from Plaza Acuña, walk up the hill on Allende three blocks, turn right on Victoria, go down Victoria and straight across the Alameda park at the bottom. One more block straight on brings you to a crossroads where you turn left on E Carranza (named not after revolution hero Venustiano Carranza but Emilio Carranza, who made the first non-stop flight from Mexico City to New York). After three long blocks you see the station on your right.

Information

Money You can change cash and travellers' cheques at either the banks or a casa de cambio on the north side of the Plaza de Armas up to 6 pm, Monday to Friday.

Post The post office, open Monday to Saturday plus Sunday morning, is at Victoria Pte 223, a few doors down from the Hotel Urdinola.

Airlines Aeroméxico (tel 4-10-11, 4-10-66; at the airport 8-04-39, 8-06-99) is at Allende Nte 815.

Festivals

Día del Santo Cristo de la Capilla On 6 August, the Day of the Holy Christ of the Chapel, brings dance groups from different parts of Coahuila to Saltillo to honour a holy image. The best-known group is the Matachines.

Feria Anual The city holds its annual fair in mid-August.

Feria de la Uva Parras, a small town 150 km west of Saltillo off the Torreón road in a wine and brandy-producing area, has a week-long grape fair in early August. It

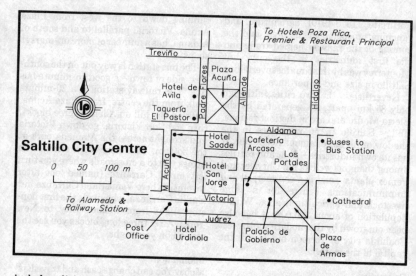

Saltillo City Centre

0   50   100 m

To Alameda & Railway Station

To Hotels Poza Rica, Premier & Restaurant Principal

Treviño

Plaza Acuña

Hotel de Avila

Taquería El Pastor

Padre Flores

Allende

Hidalgo

Hotel Saade

Cafetería Arcasa

Los Portales

Buses to Bus Station

Aldama

M Acuña

Hotel San Jorge

Victoria

Cathedral

Juárez

Post Office

Hotel Urdinola

Palacio de Gobierno

Plaza de Armas

includes religious celebrations on Assumption Day and traditional dances by descendants of early Tlaxcalan settlers. Parras has some colonial buildings, a house where Francisco Madero lived and several hotels.

Festival of San Nicolás Tolentino Ramos Arizpe, about 10 km north of Saltillo on the Monterrey road, has dances by the Matachines from before dawn on 10 September and a parade at about 5 pm.

Plaza de Armas
In contrast to the bustling Plaza Acuña, the Plaza de Armas is spotlessly clean and relatively tranquil, with street vendors seemingly banished.

Cathedral Built between 1746 and 1801, the cathedral of Santiago dominates the plaza and has one of Mexico's finest churrigueresque façades, its columns of elaborately carved pale grey stone in pristine condition. It's particularly splendid when lit up at night. Inside, the transepts (side-arms of the cross-shaped ground plan) are full of gilt ornamentation – and

no, the human figure perched on a ledge at the top of the dome, seemingly about to fall, isn't real! You can go up the smaller of the two towers if you ask the man in the religious goods shop underneath. At the top of the stairway you come out among the bells, with good views over the city and surrounding mountains.

Palacio de Gobierno On the opposite side of the plaza to the cathedral is the state government headquarters. You are free to wander into the elegant building, which has a fountain in its inner courtyard.

Los Portales (The Portals) This is the open-air covered section behind the arches on the north side of the plaza. It harbours a couple of café/restaurants and a video-games parlour.

Art Gallery This courtyard-and-fountain building on the south side of the plaza contains an art gallery.

The Alameda
The park, full of shady trees and pathways like all other parks of the same

name in Mexico, has a children's playground and is a favourite spot for young couples. A pond at the southern end is alleged to be shaped like Mexico, but the resemblance is far from obvious.

Plaza México

Also known as the Fortín de Carlota (Carlota's Fortress), this spot in the south of the city offers the best views over Saltillo and the surrounding country. It's a 10-minute bus ride from downtown (see 'Getting Around').

Places to Stay – bottom end

Best choice in this category is *Hotel Saade* (tel 3-34-00) at Aldama Pte 397, one block west of Plaza Acuña. It's modern and clean with quite spacious rooms that cost US$4.25 for one person, US$6.50 for two in a double bed and US$7 for two in two beds.

Of the two cheaper downtown possibilities, *Hotel Poza Rica* (tel 3-65-96) at Allende Nte 436 has none-too-clean bathrooms but is tolerable value for US$3.75/4.25 single/double. *Hotel De Avila* (tel 3-72-72), at Padre Flores 211 in the north-west corner of Plaza Acuña, is marginally cleaner at US$4.75 for one or two people.

There are two hotels over the road from the bus station. The *Hotel Central* is much the better of the two, at US$5.50 for a double bed. The poky *Hotel Siesta* charges US$3.75.

Places to Stay – middle

Best value of any hotel in Saltillo is the *Hotel Urdinola* (tel 4-09-40) at Victoria Pte 207. From Plaza Acuña, walk south up the hill on Allende three blocks and turn right on Victoria. The hotel is about 200 metres along on the left. There's a glamorous lobby with a couple of model knights-in-armour standing at the bottom of a wide white stairway that sweeps upward to a stained-glass window. Rooms at the back are around a long courtyard with a fountain. For big, clean rooms with

TV you pay US$7.50 for one person, US$8.50 for two. The hotel also has a pleasant, if not cheap, dining room and very friendly and helpful staff. The only minor drawback is that they sometimes ask for a deposit of more than a night's lodging when you check in (any balance refundable).

The *Hotel Premier* (tel 2-10-50) at Allende Nte 566 is comfortable enough but without the atmosphere of the Urdinola. Singles/doubles are US$10.25/ 10.75.

Places to Stay – top end

The top downtown establishment is the *Hotel San Jorge* (tel 3-06-00) at M Acuña Nte 240. From Plaza Acuña, go west down Aldama one block, then turn left onto M Acuña. This hotel has recently been upgraded; it has a restaurant and swimming pool, and clean, quite big rooms with TV go for US$18.75 single, US$20.75 double.

Other top-end places are on the main roads leading out of town. All of these have restaurants and swimming pools. Some offer tennis and discos. The most expensive is the *Camino Real Motor Hotel* (tel 4-15-15), seven km from Saltillo centre at Boulevard Los Fundadores 2000 on Highway 57 to San Luis Potosí and Mexico City. Here single/double suites are US$29.50/34.25. Also on Highway 57 are the *Motel La Fuente* (tel 2-20-90, 2-23-05) at Fundadores Km 3, where singles and doubles cost US$19.75; and slightly further out of town the *Motel La Torre* (tel 2-10-10), a bizarre building that looks like an overgrown water-tower, where doubles are US$27.

Hotel Rancho El Morillo (tel 2-63-00, 4-46-57) is a small (14 rooms) colonial-style place in the woods off the south-western bypass at Calzada Antonio Navarro Km 2. It charges US$15.75/17.50 for singles/ doubles. *Motel Huizache* (tel 2-83-55), 1½ km north of the city centre at Boulevard V Carranza 1746, where Highway 40 to Torreón meets Highway 57 going north to Monclova, has doubles at US$15.25.

Places to Eat

Saltillo is short on inviting restaurants but has several good snack places and fast-food joints.

Among the restaurants, *Cafetería Arcasa*, on Allende two blocks up the hill from Plaza Acuña, does pretty average Mexican and Western food. Tacos and enchiladas cost around US$1, chicken and steaks from US$2 to US$2.75. It has a selection of local and national newspapers to help you pass the time.

Restaurant Principal (tel 4-33-84) at Allende Nte 710, four blocks down the hill from Plaza Acuña, specialises in *cabrito* (kid), a regional speciality. If neither of these places grabs you, try the more expensive restaurants in the hotels Urdinola or San Jorge.

Pastelería y Cafetería Daisy Queen (tel 3-33-49) at Allende Nte 515A does cakes as well as yoghurt with fruit (25c small size, US$0.50 large – but beware undefrosted strawberries). Its tacos are small and overpriced.

Much better for tacos – in fact one of the best places in northern Mexico, as its never-ending stream of customers proves – is *Taquería El Pastor* on Plaza Acuña at the corner of Aldama and Padre Flores. Delicious *tacos al pastor* (beefsteak) are 10c each, *tacos de lengua* (tongue) are 15c each. There's another place with the same name, menu and prices two blocks down Aldama from the plaza.

At the bottom (west) end of Victoria, near the Alameda, are a couple of places selling mostly yoghurt. *Hugos La Juerta – La Casa del Yoghurt*, half a block up Victoria from the Alameda, does a bewildering variety of forms and flavours of yoghurt and a huge range of things to mix with it. You can try yoghurt licuados (liquidised), *nieve* (mixed with ice cream) or cocktails. A block further up the hill, the less imaginatively named *Yoghurt* is similar but with a slightly smaller menu; you can add jam, raisins, candies, chocolate, etc to a variety of flavours for a total cost of US$0.30 to US$0.60.

Next door to Yoghurt is another popular shopfront-stall, this one dedicated to *nachos* (corn chips) with maize, cream and chile.

Things to Buy

Saltillo used to be so famous for its sarapes that a certain type was known as a 'Saltillo' even if it was made elsewhere in Mexico. The technique involves leaving out colour fixatives in the dyeing process so that the different bands of colour *se lloran* (merge, or literally weep) into each other. The finest ones would have silk or gold and silver threads woven into them. Nowadays the local workshops have sadly stopped making all-wool sarapes and seem to be obsessed with jarring combinations of bright colours. But you can still get ponchos and blankets in more 'natural' colours, some of which are pure wool.

Shops where you can see these and other handicrafts include El Saltillero (tel 4-11-36) at the corner of Victoria and M Acuña, and the Sarape Factory on Hidalgo a couple of blocks up the hill from cathedral. In the latter you can watch people at work on treadle looms.

Getting There & Away

Air Saltillo airport has Aeroméxico flights non-stop to Mexico City daily except Sunday, and three times a week each to Reynosa and Guadalajara.

Road Saltillo is the junction of five major (good) roads. Highway 40 heads north-east to Monterrey, Highway 57 north to Monclova and Piedras Negras. To the west, Torreón is 277 km away by Highway 40, on the way to Mazatlán, Chihuahua and the north-west border. To the south-west, Highway 54 crosses high, dry plains towards Zacatecas (363 km) and Guadalajara (680 km). Highway 57 to the south is the road to Mexico City (852 km).

Outside Saltillo it climbs to over 2000 metres, then descends gradually along the altiplano central to Matehuala (260 km) and San Luis Potosí (451 km) through barren but often spectacular country.

Bus Saltillo's modern bus station is way out on a bypass on the south-west edge of town, but it's clearly a matter of some pride to the city since you can buy postcards of it. It has no left-luggage section. First-class lines have their ticket desks to the right-hand end of the booking hall as you enter, 2nd class to the left.

Lots of buses serve Saltillo but few start their journeys here. This means that on 2nd-class buses in particular, you often can't buy a ticket until the bus has arrived and the ticket clerk knows how much room there is for new passengers. It also means that on 2nd-class buses you may have to stand for a while. Whatever, it pays to buy your ticket early and board the bus first – if you can.

Transportes Del Norte (1st class) goes to San Luis Potosí (US$5.50), Querétaro (US$8) and Mexico City (US$10.50) six times daily; to Guadalajara (US$8) three times; to Aguascalientes (US$6) five times; to Monterrey (US$1), Nuevo Laredo (US$3.75), Torreón (US$3.50), Durango (US$7) and Mazatlán (US$11) several times; to Chihuahua (US$9) five times; to Reynosa (US$4) and Matamoros (US$5) three times; to Zacatecas (US$4.75) twice; to Ciudad Victoria once; also to Ciudad Juárez (US$13.50) and Tampico (US$8.25).

Omnibus de México (1st class) goes to Mexico City (US$10.50) twice daily; to Torreón (US$3.50), Reynosa (US$3.75) and Matamoros (US$5) frequently; to Zacatecas (US$4.25) and Aguascalientes (US$6) three times daily; to Guadalajara (US$8) five times; to Durango (US$6.50) three times; to Ciudad Juárez (US$13.25) twice; to Tepic (US$10.75) twice; to Tampico once.

Tres Estrellas De Oro (1st class) goes once a day to San Luis Potosí (US$5.50),

Querétaro (US$8), Uruapan (US$11.25), Reynosa (US$3.75) and Matamoros (US$5).

Anáhuac has both 1st and 2nd-class services. Its 1st-class buses go to Mexico City (US$10.50) 10 times daily; to Matehuala (US$3.25), San Luis Potosí (US$5.50) and Querétaro (US$8) four times; to Piedras Negras (US$5.25) seven times; to Ciudad Acuña (US$6) four times; to Concepción del Oro (US$1.50), Zacatecas (US$4.50) and Guadalajara (US$8) once.

Anáhuac 2nd-class serves the same destinations for fares about 10% lower, plus Aguascalientes (US$5.50), Durango and Torreón.

Transportes Monterrey-Saltillo and Transportes Coahuila-Zacatecas run 1st and 2nd-class buses to Torreón, plus 2nd-class buses to Concepción del Oro, Zacatecas, Monterrey, Mazatlán (US$10), Ciudad Juárez (US$12.25) and Durango (US$6).

Transportes Frontera/Blancos/Linea Verde (2nd class) go to Matehuala hourly; to Concepción del Oro (US$1.25) and Zacatecas (US$4) hourly from 6.30 am; to San Luis Potosí (US$5) 13 times daily; to Querétaro (US$7.25) 10 times; to Guadalajara (US$7.25) eight times; to Mexico City (US$9.50) five times; to León (US$7.25) and Celaya (US$8.50) four times; to Fresnillo (US$4.50), Toluca (US$9.25) and Morelia (US$9.50) three times; to Aguascalientes five times.

Autobuses Saltillo-Parras (2nd class) goes to Parras (US$1.75) four times a day.

Approximate 1st-class journey times: Nuevo Laredo 4½ hours, Matamoros seven hours, Monterrey 1½ hours, Matehuala four hours, San Luis Potosí five hours, Guadalajara nine hours, Tampico 10 hours, Mexico City 11 hours.

Rail Saltillo railway station (tel 3-55-84) is just off E Carranza, south-west of the city centre. 'El Regiomontano' (the Pullman)

is the best train; it has sleeping accommodation and a dining car and leaves at 8.25 pm for San Luis Potosí (5½ hours away) and Mexico City (12½ hours); and at 6.50 am for Monterrey (2½ hours) and Nuevo Laredo (7½ hours).

The Aguila Azteca, with nothing less than 1st-class reservable seats, leaves at 12.13 am for Monterrey (two hours) and Nuevo Laredo (seven hours); and at 3 am for San Luis Potosí (seven hours), San Miguel Allende (10 hours), Querétaro (11½ hours) and Mexico City (16½ hours).

There are also trains to Monterrey at 3.35 pm, San Luis Potosí at 12.40 pm, Piedras Negras at 8.05 am and Margaritas (Zacatecas) at 7.30 am.

The station is open for advance ticket sales from 11.30 am to 12.30 pm and 3 to 3.30 pm; also for Pullman sales from 6 to 7.30 pm. Fares to Mexico City: 1st class US$6; 1st-class reserved seat US$13.25; roomette US$16.50 for one person, US$25.25 for two; bedroom US$27.75 for two. You can also make advance reservations from Saltillo by telephoning Señora Juanita Garza (Monterrey 75-46-04) – allow a month.

Getting Around

Most of Saltillo's activity is within a few minutes' walk of the two central squares, the Plaza de Armas and the Plaza Acuña.

To reach the city centre from the bus station, walk out of the entrance of the bus station and you will see minibuses waiting to your right, past the end of the bus station. No 9 (10c) takes you downtown. Convenient points at which to get off are the cathedral (easily recognised as you pass it on the right coming down Hidalgo) or the main downtown bus stop at the corner of Allende and Treviño (from where you walk one block uphill on Allende to reach Plaza Acuña). Returning to the bus station from downtown, pick up No 9 at the corner of Aldama and Hidalgo.

To reach downtown from the railway station, walk 200 metres straight ahead out of the station, cross a single-track railway line, and go left down the road (E Carranza) for three blocks until you meet Madero, where you turn right. Walk straight across the Alameda park which you reach after one block on Madero, then straight on up Victoria, which meets Allende at the top. Three blocks to the left brings you to Plaza Acuña; one to the left then one to the right brings you to Plaza de Armas.

To reach Plaza México take bus 'Zapoliname' (10c) from Aldama and Hidalgo.

CONCEPCIÓN DEL ORO

This small town (known locally as 'Conche') is in the Sierra Madre southwest of Saltillo, on the road to Zacatecas. It's described in tourist literature as a gold-and-silver-mining centre which is accessible by train on a day trip from Saltillo. Trains in fact only run to a place called Margaritas, which is said to be 20 minutes by bus from Concepción del Oro. More reliable if you want to check out the town is the bus, which goes through some dramatic country en route – wild and hilly, with immense vistas populated almost exclusively by tall cactus trees.

According to locals in Concepción, gold, silver and other stones are mined in the hills around the town, but unless you're determined and know something about minerals and gems, you're not likely to find a bargain. The only stones for sale that we found were coloured crystals offered by a man in a dark room down a side street. He claimed they were malachite, pyrite, calcite and rock crystal.

The town is a bleak industrial place harbouring, it seems, more than its fair share of drunks. The *Restaurant Anáhuac* just up the road from the Transportes Frontera bus station does comida corrida for US$0.75 (chicken-neck soup, chile relleno, frijoles and spaghetti).

Getting There & Away

Bus Transportes Frontera (2nd class) runs hourly during the day from Saltillo bus station to Concepción del Oro. The fare is US$1.25; journey time is 1½ hours. From Concepción, Transportes Frontera goes to Saltillo and Monterrey 14 times daily; to Zacatecas (US$3) six times; to Matehuala (US$2.25) and San Luis Potosí (US$4.25) twice each. The buses leaving Concepción are often crowded.

Rail The train from Saltillo to Margaritas leaves at 7.30 am, costs US$0.50, and takes 3½ to four hours. Coming back, it leaves Margaritas at 2 pm. Trouble is, no one in either Saltillo or Concepción seems really sure how far it is from Margaritas to Concepción, or whether there really are buses between the two places.

San Luis Potosí

The state of San Luis Potosí ('Pot-o-SEE') has two of the most interesting destinations on the way south from Mexico's north-east border: the mountain ghost town of Real de Catorce and the city of San Luis Potosí itself, steeped in history and the first major colonial town reached on this route into Mexico. The eastern part of the state (see 'Tampico & the Huasteca' in this chapter) is home to about 50,000 Huastec Indians, descendants of an advanced pre-Hispanic civilisation.

History

Before the Spanish conquest of Mexico in 1521, western San Luis Potosí was inhabited by hunters and collectors known as Guachichiles (the Aztec word for sparrows), from their custom of wearing little but loincloths and sometimes pointed bonnets resembling sparrows. The Guachichiles, like other Chichimec tribes, were warlike; they often sacrificed their prisoners. One of their settlements, Tangamanga, is believed to have been on

the site of the present city of San Luis Potosí.

A couple of religious missions entered the south-west of the state in the 1570s and 1580s, but it was the discovery of silver in the Cerro de San Pedro mountains that really awakened Spanish interest. The city of San Luis Potosí was founded near the silver deposits in 1592. Cattle ranchers moved into the area in the 1590s too. Indians from further south – Tlaxcalans, Tarascans and Otomíes – were brought to work the mines and haciendas.

Yields from the San Pedro mines declined from the 1620s but other mineral finds, the expansion of ranching, and missionary activities led to the founding of more Spanish towns in the 17th century. Among them were Santa María del Río, Río Verde, Charcas and Matehuala.

In the 18th century the area was noted for maltreatment of Indians, partly because a number of parishes were transferred from the hands of the Franciscans, who did their best to protect the Indians, into the control of the secular (non-monk) clergy. In 1767 there was an uprising sparked by the appalling conditions in the mines and discontent over the expulsion from all Spanish territory of the Jesuits, who ran the best schools in Mexico and managed their estates relatively well.

An administrative reform in 1786 divided New Spain into 12 local government *intendencias*, one of which was based at San Luis Potosí and included what are now the states of San Luis Potosí, Tamaulipas, Nuevo León, Coahuila and Texas. But such power lasted only until Mexican independence: in 1824 the state of San Luis Potosí was formed with its present area.

In the 19th century the contrast between the wealth of San Luis Potosí city and the poverty of many in the countryside became even more marked. There were several uprisings, including one at Ahualulco in 1846 provoked by landowners

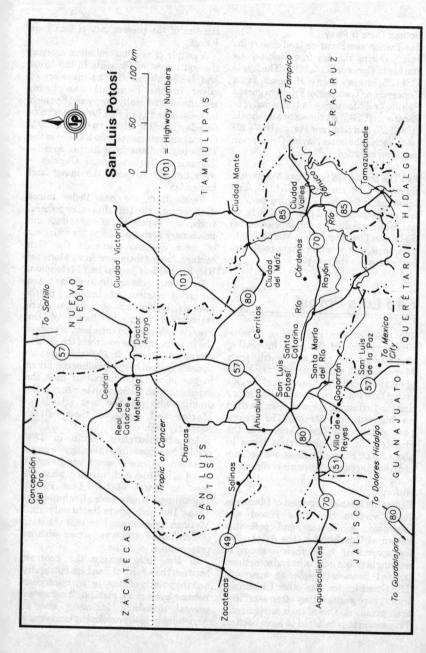

San Luis Potosí

(101) = Highway Numbers

0   50   100 km

trying to take over communal lands. The Sierra Gorda uprising of 1848 was led by an ambitious soldier called Eleuterio Quiroz who demanded land distribution, the dissolution of the army and controls on political activity by the church.

The most recent attempt at an army coup in Mexican history was led against Lázaro Cárdenas' government by his former agriculture minister Saturnino Cedillo in San Luis Potosí in 1939.

Dance

Some dances which you may see at festivals in San Luis Potosí have their origins in pre-Hispanic rituals designed to thank or beseech the gods. For those which originated in the Huasteca, see 'Tampico & the Huasteca'.

Los Chichimecas This dance comes from the Salinas region in the far west of the state. Sometimes it goes on for days as a kind of act of penitence by the dancers, who wear masks and palm crowns decorated with feathers and mirrors. Its three parts are called El Venadito, El Meco and El Bautizo. The music comes from a violin and a drum.

MATEHUALA

Population: 50,000

The only town of any size on Highway 57 between Saltillo and San Luis Potosí, Matehuala ('Ma-te-WAL-a') is an unremarkable but pleasant and quite prosperous place 1600 metres high on the altiplano central. Matehuala was founded in the 17th century, and its winding central streets give it a colonial air, but the main reason for going there is because it's the major jumping-off point for Real de Catorce. Matehuala is 203 km from Saltillo, 191 km from San Luis Potosí, and about halfway from the border at Piedras Negras or Nuevo Laredo to Mexico City. The Tropic of Cancer is about 20 km south.

Orientation

Central Matehuala lies between two squares about 400 metres apart – the formal Plaza de Armas with a kiosk in the middle, and the bustling Placita del Rey to the north, in front of the large concrete church. Cheaper hotels and the town's restaurants are in this area; motels are on Highway 57 as it by-passes the town to the east.

The bus station is about two km south of the centre. To walk to the centre from the bus station, turn left out of the entrance, then go straight along the road (5 de Mayo) for about 1½ km until you reach the corner of Guerrero, where you turn left. Guerrero ends after a few blocks when it meets Morelos. The Plaza de Armas is a few metres to the left along Morelos. To the right, Morelos divides after a few metres. The left fork becomes Bustamante and leads on to the Placita del Rey. None-too-frequent local buses also run between the bus station and the centre (see 'Getting Around').

Festivals

Fiesta del Cristo de Matehuala Held the first two weeks of January, the festival includes religious ceremonies and processions, fireworks, folk dances, rodeos and cock fights. The main day is 6 January.

Founding of Matehuala From 8 to 16 July a feria celebrates the founding of the town.

Places to Stay

In Town The place with the most atmosphere is the *Hotel Matehuala* (tel 2-06-80) at the corner of Bustamante and Hidalgo. The departure point for buses to Real de Catorce is only a few doors away. The hotel has a large central courtyard with rooms on two levels around it. Rooms are basic and there's no hot water but the place has a pleasant atmosphere and friendly staff. Upstairs singles/doubles are US$2.25/3.25 and you must use the

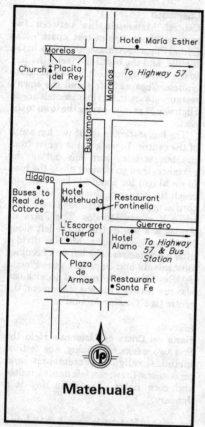

Matehuala

The *Hotel María Esther* is a step up, a family-run place where rooms with private bath cost US$3.25 single, US$4.25 for two people in a double bed, US$4.75 for two beds. For rooms with common bath you pay US$1.75 single, US$2.25 double.

Motels Several motels dot Highway 57 as it passes Matehuala to the east. They include, in north-south order, the *Hacienda* (tel 2-00-65) where singles or doubles are US$16; *Las Palmas* (tel 2-00-02) where singles/doubles are US$14.50/17; and *El Dorado* (tel 2-01-74) with singles/doubles at US$9/10.50. The first two, at least, have their own restaurants.

Places to Eat

Restaurant Santa Fe, one of a few places on the Plaza de Armas, is clean, friendly and reasonably priced, and serves generous portions of good plain food. For US$1.50 you can get three good pork chops with French fries, frijoles and tortillas, and a big plate of salad with ham, two types of cheese, avocado, lettuce, onion and Russian dressing. At breakfast a ham omelette with *bolillo* (bread roll), frijoles, salad and French fries will cost you US$1.

On the opposite corner of the Plaza de Armas from the Santa Fe, *L'Escargot* serves up a variety of excellent tacos to eat in or take out at 15c per taco made with maize or wheat flour. They're sometimes served with a scowl but don't let that put you off.

Restaurant Fontinella (tel 2-02-93), at Morelos 618 round the corner from the Hotel Matehuala, does a reasonable-value four-course comida corrida plus coffee for US$1.50.

Getting There & Away

Bus From the bus station at the south end of town there are fairly frequent services north and south but, like Saltillo, Matehuala is mid-route for most buses so you can usually buy tickets only when the bus arrives.

common bathrooms, which are clean. Downstairs you pay US$3.25/4.25 and get your own bathroom but these can be very damp. Rooms away from the street are much quieter.

Elsewhere, the *Hotel Alamo* on Guerrero near the Morelos end is dingy and grubby with singles/doubles at US$2.25/2.75. There are also a few places on the northern section of Morelos which you reach by walking along Bustamante from the Hotel Matehuala, past the church, and turning right at the traffic lights. Here the *Hotel Primavera* is shabby, with singles/doubles at US$1.75/3.25 with bathroom.

Transportes del Norte (1st class) runs to San Luis Potosí (US$2.25), Querétaro (US$4.75) and Mexico City (US$7.50), Saltillo (US$3.25), Monterrey (US$4.25) and Nuevo Laredo (US$7).

Autobuses Anáhuac runs both 2nd-class and less frequent 1st-class buses. The last of its many daily services to San Luis Potosí (US$2.25 1st class, US$2 2nd class) leaves at 8 pm. There are nine buses a day to Querétaro (US$4.75/4.25) and Mexico City (US$7.50/6.75); 16 to Saltillo (US$3.25/2.75) and Monterrey (US$4.25/3.75); two to Piedras Negras (US$8.50/7.50); three to Ciudad Acuña (US$9 1st class); three to Reynosa (US$5.25 1st class); two to Linares and Montemorelos. Transportes Frontera runs 2nd-class buses to Saltillo (US$2.75), Monterrey (US$3.75), Nuevo Laredo (US$6.25), San Luis Potosí (US$2.25), Querétaro (US$4.75), Mexico City (US$6.75), Guadalajara (US$6), Guanajuato (US$4.50), León, Toluca and San Juan de Los Lagos.

Transportes Tamaulipas has 2nd-class buses (which for some obscure reason it describes as 1st class) to Monterrey (US$3.75) 13 times daily, to San Luis Potosí direct (US$2.25) four times; to Reynosa (US$5.25) twice; and to Linares.

Approximate 1st-class journey times: Saltillo four hours, San Luis Potosí 1½ hours, Mexico City seven hours.

Getting Around

Orange buses marked 'Centro' run from the bus station to the town centre but aren't very frequent. It's often quicker to make the 25-minute walk.

Buses for Real de Catorce leave at 8 am, 12 noon and 4 pm from Hidalgo, a few doors from the Hotel Matehuala. One-way fare is US$0.75. Get to the office an hour ahead to buy your ticket.

REAL DE CATORCE

Population: 800

This is a place with a touch of magic. High in an offshoot of the Sierra Madre Oriental, Real de Catorce was a wealthy and important silver-mining town of 40,000 people until early this century. Today it's almost deserted, its paved streets lined with decaying or boarded-up stone houses, its mint a ruin. Thirty km north-west of Matehuala and reached by a 2⅓-km road tunnel through former mine shafts, the town lies in a narrow valley at 2756 metres, with spectacular views westward to the plain below.

Its remaining 800 or so souls now eke an existence from old mine workings and from pilgrims who come to pay homage to the figure of Saint Francis of Assisi in the town's church. The festival of St Francis (San Francisco) is on 4 October, and between 100,000 and 200,000 people flock into and out of the tiny settlement between 25 September and 12 October.

The rugged mountains surrounding the town are a source of the hallucinogenic mushroom peyote. The Huichol Indians, who live 400 km away on the Durango-Nayarit-Jalisco-Zacatecas borders, believe that their peyote and maize gods live here. Every May or June they make a pilgrimage to the hills around Catorce, known to them as Wírikuta, for rituals involving peyote.

You can visit Real de Catorce on a day trip by bus from Matehuala, or stay in one of its few hostelries to soak up the mountain air and strange, peaceful atmosphere – which have attracted a tiny handful of Americans and Europeans to make this place home.

History

The name Real de Catorce literally means 'Royal of 14': the '14' probably comes from 14 soldiers killed by Indians in the area about 1700. The town was founded in the mid-18th century and the church built between 1783 and 1817.

The mines had their ups and downs: during the independence war years (1810-1821) some of the shafts were flooded and in 1821-22 an Englishman called Robert Phillips made a year-long journey from London to Catorce bringing a 'steam machine' for pumping the water from the mines.

Real de Catorce reached its peak in the late 19th century when it was producing an estimated US$3 million in silver a year, and had a theatre, a bull ring and shops selling imported European goods. Numbers of large houses still standing today bear witness to this period of opulence for some of its citizens. The dictator Porfirio Díaz journeyed here from Mexico City in 1895 to inaugurate two mine pumps bought from San Francisco, California. Díaz had to travel by train, then by mule-carriage, then on horseback to reach Catorce.

Quite why Catorce was transformed into a ghost town within three decades is a slight mystery. Locals in the town will tell you that during the revolution years (1910-20) *bandidos* took refuge here and scared away the other inhabitants. The official state tourist guidebook explains, perhaps more plausibly, that the price of silver slumped after 1900.

Orientation

The bus from Matehuala drops you at the end of the 2⅓-km Ogarrio tunnel, from where the town spreads out before you. A rough street, Lanza Gorta, leads straight ahead (west) to the church, which is roughly the centre of town.

Parish Church

This is quite an impressive neoclassical building but it's the reputedly miraculous image of St Francis of Assisi on one of the side altars that is the attraction for thousands of Mexican pilgrims. A cult has grown up this century around the statue, whose help is sought in solving problems. Some believe it can cleanse their sins. Also in the church are numerous grateful offerings from people whom St Francis has helped, including paintings of 'miraculous' incidents attributed to him.

Casa de la Moneda

Opposite the main entrance of the church, the old 'House of Money' is now empty and crumbling. Coins were minted here for a few years in the 1860s. A friendly old fellow who usually hangs around on the steps of the mint is full of stories about the town's past and has the key to the cockpit (see below). He doesn't ask for money but you may want to give him some coins!

Plaza Hidalgo

Further west along the street that leads from the bus halt to the church and mint, you reach this small plaza raised above the right side of the street. This was constructed in 1888 with a fountain in the middle; the kiosk you see now replaced the fountain in 1927.

Palenque de Gallos & Plaza de Toros

A block or so north-west of the plaza lies this monument to the town's heyday, a cockpit built like a Roman amphitheatre. It was restored in the 1970s and now hosts occasional theatre or dance performances. It's normally locked – the man on the steps of the mint has the key and will open the cockpit for you. Further up the hill (Zaragoza) past the cockpit, you soon reach the edge of the town. Here, opposite the graveyard, is the bull ring (Plaza de Toros), also recently restored.

Museum

In the bowels of the church, with its entrance on Lanza Gorta, is a small museum containing photos, documents and whatever else has been rescued from the crumbling town that pertains to its heyday – including a rusting, ancient car, said to be the first to reach Catorce.

Places to Stay & Eat

Real de Catorce has three middle-range hostelries and a couple of cheap casas de huéspedes, all catering mainly to pilgrims.

El Real, up the hill to the right off Lanza Gorta one block after the church, is an old house restored to provide a few quite comfortable bedrooms at US$7.50 double. The communal bathroom is clean. It also serves Italian and other food in its restaurant; main dishes are US$2 to US$3, two cups of coffee and two bolillos cost US$1. There is an excellent Huichol yarn picture on the dining-room wall.

At the bottom of the same street, where it meets Lanza Gorta, the *Mesón de la Abundancia* has a few more rooms but was closed (apparently temporarily) when we visited Catorce in January.

If you go up Zaragoza, the street running uphill to the north from Plaza Hidalgo, you soon find yourself on the edge of the town. Here, near another church, is the modern *Quinta La Puesta Del Sol* with superb views down the valley to the west, where rooms with TV and private bath cost US$4.75.

There are a few casas de huéspedes and food stalls along Lanza Gorta and near the bus halt. *Casa de Huéspedes La Providencia* on Lanza Gorta has basic but cleanish rooms for US$2.25.

Things to Buy

There are one or two craft shops in the town selling silver and gold jewellery.

Getting There & Away

Bus Three buses a day make the journey from Matehuala to Real de Catorce and back. One-way fare is US$0.75 and the journey takes 1¼ hours. In Matehuala the buses leave at 8 am, noon and 4 pm from Hidalgo, a few doors from the Hotel Matehuala. It's advisable to get there an hour before departure if you want a seat. You can buy return tickets.

Road The road up the hill to Catorce is mostly well-paved. The Ogarrio tunnel is only wide enough for one vehicle; men stationed at each end with telephones control traffic. If you're driving south down Highway 57 you can turn off through Cedral to reach Catorce, rather than going to Matehuala and then back northwards again.

SAN LUIS POTOSÍ

Population: 500,000

The capital of the state named after it, this town has played a succession of important roles in Mexican history, first as a major silver-producing centre, later as host to a line of governments-in-exile and revolutionaries. Today its main importance is as a regional capital and centre of industry, including brewing, textiles and metal foundries (the Industrial Minera México company claims the highest chimney in Latin America). But the colonial heart of the city, which is an architectural feast of nearly every different Mexican style, has been preserved from the onslaught of industry, and its plazas, markets, cafés, restaurants, churches, museums and other buildings make it a very attractive halt between Mexico City and the north-east.

San Luis, 1878 metres high, is far enough (424 km) from Mexico City to maintain an independent, self-assured air and its 500,000 people take as much pride in being Potosinos as in being Mexicans. It has a university and a fairly active cultural life.

History

Diego de la Magdalena, a Franciscan friar, started a small settlement of local Guachichil Indians about 1585 on the approximate site of the university building in what is now the city's Plaza de los Fundadores.

Another early leading light was Miguel Caldera, a mestizo who had spearheaded the Spanish side in the later part of the Chichimec War and carried out the ultimately successful policy of giving the Chichimecs food and clothing in return for peace. Caldera came to Mexquitic, 23 km north-west of San Luis, for this purpose in 1587 and a Franciscan monastery was set up there in 1590. As in other northern settlements, the Spanish used trusted Tlaxcalan Indians in San Luis and Mexquitic to help them 'civilise' the local Chichimecs.

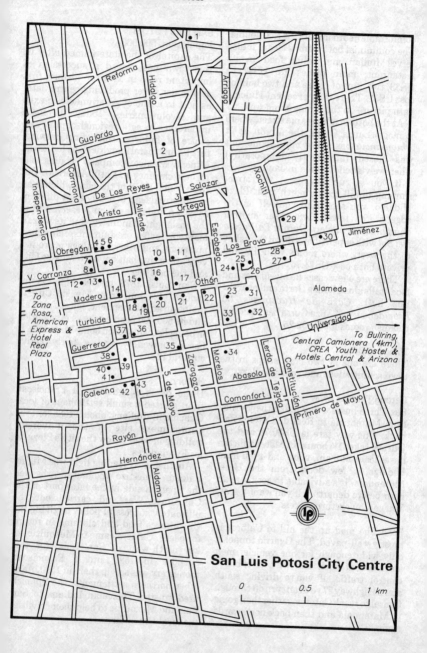

San Luis Potosí City Centre

0   0.5   1 km

1	Market
2	Mercado Hidalgo
3	Post Office
4	Capilla de Loreto
5	La Compañía Church
6	University Building
7	Ipiña Building
8	Restaurant-Bar Ipiña
9	Plaza de los Fundadores
10	Restaurant Posada del Virrey
11	Restaurant Tangamanga
12	Hotel Panorama
13	Restaurante La Parroquia
14	Caja Real
15	Palacio de Gobierno
16	Plaza de Armas
17	Cathedral
18	Restaurant-Bar Castillo
19	Hotel de Gante
20	Hotel Plaza
21	Tourist Office
22	Hotel Concordia
23	Plaza del Carmen
24	Hotel Principal
25	Hotel Nápoles & María Cristina
26	Hotel Royal
27	Cafe Tokio
28	Hotel Jardín Potosí
29	Hotel Anáhuac
30	Railway Station
31	Iglesia del Carmen
32	Teatro de La Paz
33	Mask Museum
34	Iglesia de San Agustín
35	Hotel Filher
36	Hotel Progreso
37	El Bocolito Restaurant
38	Museo Regional de Artes Populares
39	Plaza San Francisco
40	Iglesia de San Francisco
41	Museo Regional Potosino & Capilla de Aranzazú
42	Iglesia del Tercer Orden
43	Iglesia del Sagrado Corazón

A Guachichil told the head of the monastery about the existence of silver in the area, and Caldera sent out prospecting parties. They found silver in the Cerro de San Pedro, 20 km east of the present city, in March 1592; the city was officially founded near Magdalena's village and its

springs in November the same year. It was named Real de Minas de San Luis Potosí – the 'Potosí' coming from the immensely rich Bolivian silver town of the same name, which the Spanish hoped San Luis would rival.

It didn't; yields from the mines started to decline in the 1620s, but the city was by then well enough established as a ranching centre to ensure its continued importance. It became a communications, trade and government centre too and was the major city of north-east Mexico for three centuries – which makes it an interesting contrast to Monterrey, the upstart that overtook San Luis by sheer economic power at the turn of this century.

San Luis was one of the first cities to fall to the forces of Hidalgo and Allende in 1810 at the beginning of the independence war. In 1846 Santa Anna trained his army here before heading north in an unsuccessful effort to throw the invading Americans out of Mexico. During the French intervention of the 1860s, Mexican President Benito Juárez set up his government in San Luis twice – once when he was fleeing before French forces, once when he was on the way back to oust Emperor Maximilian.

Later in the century San Luis was renowned as one of Mexico's most ostentatiously rich cities, known for its lavish houses and luxury goods imported from the USA and Europe. It also played an important part in national politics. But it became, too, a breeding ground for the liberals who started the campaign to remove dictator Porfirio Díaz.

A national liberal convention here in 1901 was the first gathering of anti-Díaz elements. In 1910 Francisco Madero, the liberal candidate running against Díaz in that year's election, spent polling day, 21 June, in jail in the city. Bailed out by his family, Madero hatched a strategy in San Luis with other colleagues who had avoided jail. Then he went to San Antonio, Texas, where in October 1910 he announced the Plan de San Luis Potosí: this declared the recent election illegal, named Madero as provisional president, and designated 20 November as the day for Mexico to rise in revolution.

Since the revolution years San Luis has made steady progress as an industrial centre, helped initially by the arrival of widespread electricity supplies in the 1940s. It's a fairly prosperous city, with a laid-back kind of zona rosa and some luxury suburbs – but there's discontent too. In April 1987 three women went on a hunger strike in the kiosk of the central Plaza de Armas demanding to see 24 'disappeared prisoners', including eight members of the Revolutionary Workers' Party (PRT). According to one press report the women were told by a state justice official that if they wanted to discuss the case with the authorities, they would have to give up their fast, at least for the imminent Semana Santa holiday week, because they were making a bad impression on tourists.

Orientation

Central San Luis Potosí is a compact area, easy to walk around and centred on four plazas. It stretches two km from the railway station and Alameda park (adjacent to each other) in the east to the Plaza de los Fundadores in the west. Between these extremes lie the Plaza del Carmen, surrounded by a clutch of fine buildings a block west of the Alameda, and the Plaza de Armas or zócalo, a block east of the Plaza de los Fundadores. A couple of blocks south-west of the Plaza de Armas is the Plaza San Francisco, site of the main museums. Hotels and restaurants are mainly in this central area, with cheaper lodgings concentrated close to the railway station. There is also a Youth Hostel and a couple of more expensive hotels near the bus station, which is out on the eastern edge of the city. Most shops and markets are in the streets north of the Plaza de Armas.

A small zona rosa, with some scattered up-market restaurants and shops, stretches a couple of km along Carranza, west of the Plaza de los Fundadores.

Information

Tourist Office San Luis has a friendly and informative tourist office (tel 2-31-43, 4-29-94). Some English is spoken and there's a wealth of leaflets and booklets available on the city and state. The office is upstairs at Othón 130, half a block east of the Plaza de Armas, and is open from 9 am to 8 pm Monday to Friday, 9 am to 2 pm Saturday.

Money Numerous banks change cash and travellers' cheques but they often close at noon. There are some casas de cambio, where rates are usually lower than in the banks but which stay open later. One is Casa de Cambio La Imperial at Morelos 300 near Pasaje Ortega. American Express is at Carranza 1077 in a curious Arabic-style building.

Post The post office (tel 2-27-40) is at Morelos 235, on the corner of Pasaje Ortega, three blocks north and one east of the Plaza de Armas. It's open from 8 am to 7 pm Monday to Friday, 9 am to 1 pm Saturday. There's another post office in the 1st-class hall of the bus station.

Consulate There's a US consular agent (tel 4-87-05) at Carranza 766.

Festivals

In addition to its spring arts festival (see 'Entertainment'), San Luis has a number of religious fiestas, many of them concentrated in particular barrios or neighbourhoods.

San Sebastián For 10 days up to 20 January there are processions and pilgrimages to the shrine of San Sebastián in the barrio named after the saint.

Semana Santa This brings a silent procession through the city on Good Friday.

Santiago Apóstol Celebrations take place in the Santiago area of the city on 25 July.

San Luis Rey The second half of August sees celebrations of the city's patron saint's day on the 25th with processions of floats and holy images in the Tlaxcala and Montecillo barrios. The Feria Nacional Potosina (Potosino National Fair) is also held around this time, with commercial, agricultural, industrial and cultural exhibitions.

Virgen de los Remedios This fiesta is held the first week of September in the Tequisquiapan barrio, with fireworks.

San Miguel Arcángel This festival on 29 September features processions and dances in front of the church of San Miguelito.

Virgen de Guadalupe Dances and fireworks take place on 12 December in the barrio of San Juan de Guadalupe.

Plaza de Armas
Also known as the Jardín Hidalgo, this is the city's main square, popular with Potosinos for chatting and watching the world go by from the seats dotted around it. There are several cafés and restaurants around the plaza. The kiosk in the middle is inscribed with names of Mexican musicians.

Palacio de Gobierno This neoclassical building constructed between 1798 and 1816 occupies the entire west side of the square. Numerous Mexican VIPs have lodged here, including presidents Iturbide and Santa Anna, but its most illustrious occupant was Benito Juárez – first in 1863 when he was fleeing from invading French forces, then in 1867 when he confirmed here the death sentence of Emperor Maximilian, who had been installed by the French. You can visit the rooms he occupied, upstairs inside, which contain life-size models of Juárez and, kneeling before him, Princess Salm-Salm, an American who had married into Maximilian's family and came to San Luis to make one last plea for the emperor's life. The rooms are open from 8 am to 3 pm, Monday to Friday (entry free).

The Cathedral This stands on the east side of the Plaza de Armas. When originally completed in 1710, this three-nave baroque building had only one tower. The northern (left-hand) one was added this century and is an exact copy of the other. The marble statues of the apostles on the façade are copies of ones in a church in Rome.

Treasury The old royal treasury (*Caja Real*) is behind the Palacio de Gobierno on the corner of Madero and Aldama. It's a pretty 18th-century baroque building. Above the typical Potosino balcony on the façade stands a stone statue of the Virgin, given to the city by Charles III of Spain. Between the Treasury and the Plaza de Armas is the house, Madero 175, where in 1910 Francisco Madero and others worked out their revolutionary manifesto, the Plan de San Luis Potosí.

Plaza del Carmen
Iglesia del Carmen This is the most spectacular building in San Luis, a churrigueresque church built between 1749 and 1764. The vividly carved stone façade has the upside-down pyramid-shaped pillars known as *estípites* which are a hallmark of the churrigueresque style. Perching and hovering angels show the influence of Indian artisans. The Camarín of the Virgin is to the left of the main altar inside. The entrance and roof of this chapel are a riot of small plaster figures. The main altar is by neoclassical architect Eduardo Tresguerras.

Teatro de la Paz The Peace Theatre stands next to the Iglesia del Carmen. The neoclassical building, constructed between

1889 and 1894, contains a concert hall and exhibition gallery as well as a theatre.

National Mask Museum The Museo de la Máscara (tel 2-30-25), on the south side of the plaza, has an interesting collection of about 1500 masks used in folk celebrations throughout Mexico, plus a few from other countries, with explanatory material in Spanish. The bulk of the collection was donated by a San Luis engineer, Moya Rubio. The building is late 19th century. Hours are Tuesday to Friday 10 am to 2 pm and 4 to 6 pm; Saturday and Sunday 10 am to 2 pm.

Iglesia de San Agustín This church, a block south of Plaza del Carmen down Escobedo, is an amalgam of architectural styles. It has a 17th-century baroque façade, an 18th-century churrigueresque tower and a neoclassic interior.

Plaza San Francisco
Dominated by the red bulk of San Francisco church, this quiet square has several places of interest.

Museo Regional de Artes Populares The Regional Museum of Popular Art (tel 2-75-21) to the right of the church displays and sells good-quality crafts from San Luis Potosí state, including rebozos from Santa María del Río, woodwork and pottery. It's open from 10 am to 2 pm and 4 to 6 pm Tuesday to Saturday, 10 am to 2.30 pm on Sunday, and 10 am to 3.30 pm on Monday.

Iglesia de San Francisco The church has a baroque façade. The interior was remodelled this century but the sacristy (priest's dressing room), reached by a door to the right of the altar, is original 18th century with a fine dome and carved pink stone. The room through the arch at the south end of the sacristy is called the Sala De Profundis and has a stone fountain carved by Indians. Above the room's entrance is a painting of the life of Santa Clara by

Miguel Cabrera, Mexico's best-known 18th-century artist.

Museo Regional Potosino This museum (tel 2-51-85) is at Galeana 450, along the street to the left of San Francisco church. It has a good collection of archaeological finds, mostly from the pre-Hispanic Huastec civilisation in the west of the state, as well as colonial art, displays on the state's surviving Indian cultures, and other materials relating to the state's history. The museum is in former monastery buildings attached to San Francisco church and gives access to the lavishly decorated 18th-century churrigueresque Capilla de Aranzazú. Open Tuesday to Friday 10 am to 1 pm and 3 to 6 pm, Saturday 10 am to noon, Sunday 10 am to 1 pm.

Iglesias del Tercer Orden & del Sagrado Corazón These two small churches, both formerly part of the monastery, stand together at the south end of the plaza. The Tercer Orden church, on the right, was finished in 1694 and restored in 1959-60. Sagrado Corazón dates from 1728-31.

Plaza de los Fundadores
The Founders' Plaza is where the city started. On the north side is a 1653 building with a courtyard which is now part of the Potosino University. To the left (west) of this is the church of La Compañía, also called del Sagrario, built in the 17th century with a baroque façade. Further to the left is the Capilla de Loreto, a 1700 Jesuit chapel with picturesque twisted 'Solomonic' pillars. The west side of the plaza is occupied by the Ipiña building, a neoclassical edifice started in 1906 and never quite finished because of the Revolution.

Parks
The Alameda This is behind Del Carmen church and used to be the vegetable garden of the monastery attached to the church. Today it's a popular park with shady paths and a small pond with an island.

Tangamanga Park A few km south-west of the centre, near the corner of Diagonal Sur and Avenida Tatanacho, lies this new 4.1 square km park, officially called the Centro Cultural y Recreativo Tangamanga. It has two lakes, sports fields and a huge theatre; 600,000 trees have been planted.

Places to Stay – bottom end

The *CREA Youth Hostel* (tel 2-66-03) is on Diagonal Sur just a block and a half from the bus station. For US$1.75 per person you get a bunk in a clean four or six-person single-sex dormitory. The bathrooms, with plenty of hot water, are clean too. Meals are served to groups only. A Youth Hostel card isn't needed. From the 2nd-class hall in the bus station turn right out of the entrance, walk to the main road, then go 1½ blocks left to reach the hostel. From the 1st-class hall, go left out of the entrance and walk 1½ blocks.

Most other cheap-end accommodation is within a couple of blocks of the Alameda and railway station. Best value is probably the *Hotel Anáhuac* (tel 2-65-04 to 05) at Xochitl 140. Plain, but basically clean with tiled floors and quite bright, it charges US$4/4.75 for singles/doubles and US$5.50 for three.

The *Hotel Jardín Potosí* (tel 2-31-52) at Los Bravo 530 is also basically clean, with 57 rooms mostly facing onto an inner courtyard with a few plants and more light than you'd expect. It needs a drop of paint, though. Singles/doubles with bath are US$4.50/5. There are also rooms for three and four at US$6.75 and US$7.50 but only families or women are allowed in these.

Another possibility is the *Hotel Principal* (tel 2-07-84) at Juan Sarabia 145 opposite the big Hotel María Cristina. The Principal was in a state of chaos when we visited it, owing to heavy renovation work – which could make it into the best value of all the cheap places. Singles/doubles are US$2.75/4.50.

Right on the Plaza de Armas at Jardín Hidalgo 22, the *Hotel Plaza* (tel 2-46-31) is also worth a look. The 28 rooms are neither light nor large but there's a brighter landing/sitting area. Singles, doubles and triples are US$4, US$4.75 and US$5.50.

Going down a rung, the basic *Hotel Royal* (tel 2-42-93) is half a block north of the Alameda at Constitución 220. It has dark rooms and ancient furniture but is more or less clean. For a double bed and private bath you pay US$3.75. There are also rooms without private bath at US$2.25 single, US$2.75 for two in a double bed and US$4.50 for two beds, but the communal bathrooms need paint and better ventilation. Interior rooms look on to a small court and have less traffic noise.

Even more basic is the *Gran Hotel* at Los Bravo 235. Singles/doubles are US$2.25/2.75 with private bath, US$1.75/2.25 with common bath. The paint's flaking, the beds are lumpy, and there's a strong smell of disinfectant.

Camping The *Motel Cactus*, one km south-east of the Juárez roundabout heading out on Highway 57 to Mexico City, has a one-hectare trailer park (tel 2-18-71) where full hook-ups cost around US$7 for up to four people. You can use the motel's swimming pool and restaurant.

Places to Stay – middle

The best all-round value of any place in town is the *Hotel Progreso* (tel 2-03-66) at Aldama 415, half a block from Plaza San Francisco, which some of its rooms look onto. It's antiquated and quaint, but sizeable singles/doubles with private bath, comfortable beds, wooden floors and old furniture cost US$5.50/6.50. Some of the doubles have bathtubs and separate miniature sitting rooms, but above all the Progreso is spotlessly clean. The staff are friendly too. Street-facing rooms are brighter but of course noisier. Beware the horrifically Heath Robinsonian electrical system.

More expensive, but cheap for what it

offers, is the *Hotel Filher* (tel 2-15-62) at Universidad 375 on the corner of Zaragoza, three blocks south of the Plaza de Armas. It's a modern place with a touch of luxury; the rooms are round a huge internal well which gives a very spacious feel. For big, bright, clean singles/doubles with photos of old San Luis on the walls you pay US$8.25/9.75.

The *Hotel de Gante* (tel 2-14-92 to 93), just off the Plaza de Armas at 5 de Mayo 140, has wide corridors and bright, large-ish singles/doubles with bathtubs and fairly modern furniture for US$6.75/7.75. It recently received the coat of paint it desperately needed.

Near the bus station, the *Hotel Central* (tel 2-47-20) at Las Torres 290 has singles/doubles for US$7.75/8.75. To reach it, turn left out of the 2nd-class hall of the bus station, then take the first right.

Places to Stay – top end

Two big, comfortable, modern hotels tower side by side on a small street called Juan Sarabia, off Los Bravo. The *Hotel Nápoles* (tel 2-84-18 to 19) at Juan Sarabia 120 has 84 rooms at US$11.50/13.50 for singles/doubles. The *Hotel María Cristina* (tel 2-94-08) at Juan Sarabia 110 has 74 rooms at US$11, US$13, US$14.75 and US$16.75 for singles, doubles, triples and quadruples; it's often full. Three meals a day cost an extra US$5.50 in the María Cristina. Both places have TV and telephone in rooms, parking and restaurants. Get a room on one of the top floors for the view.

Similar in price and a bit nearer the Plaza de Armas is the *Hotel Concordia* (tel 2-06-66) at the corner of Morelos and Othón. For the same facilities as at the Nápoles and María Cristina you pay US$11, US$13, US$15 and US$17 for singles, doubles, triples and quadruples.

The most luxurious downtown place is the 10-storey *Hotel Panorama* (tel 2-17-77) at Carranza 315, half a block west of the Plaza de los Fundadores. It's 23 years old but appears brand new. The 127 big,

bright rooms have sparkling bathrooms with bathtubs, colour TV and in some cases balconies and great views. The hotel also has a bar, pizzeria, cafeteria, swimming pool, disco and music in the elevator! Of course you pay for it: singles/doubles are US$19/23, with suites from US$27 to US$43, but children under 12 pay nothing if they share a room with their parents.

Several blocks further west, the *Hotel Real Plaza* (tel 4-69-69) at Carranza 890 has singles/doubles for US$12.75/14.75.

Directly opposite the exit to the 2nd-class hall of the bus station is the *Hotel Arizona* (tel 4-47-80) at J G Torres 158, where singles/doubles are US$11/13.

Numerous motels border the main roads on the edges of the city. Heading south on Highway 57 to Mexico City, you come first to the *Motel Cactus* (tel 2-18-71 to 72) shortly after the big Glorieta Juárez roundabout, where accommodation ranges from US$15/16.75 singles/doubles to US$42 for a four-person master suite. A bit further down Highway 57 is the *Hotel Real de Minas* (tel 4-70-10, 4-70-25) where singles/doubles are US$16.75/18. Beyond that is the *Sands Motel* (tel 2-74-87) with 50 rooms at US$11/13 for singles/doubles, and even further out the very plush *Hostal del Quijote* (tel 8-13-12, 8-12-99) where you pay US$40 or more.

On the west side of the city, on Avenida de las Poétas which is also Highway 80 to Guadalajara, is the *Motel Tuna* (tel 3-12-07) with singles/doubles from US$12/15. It's near the Othón monument.

Places to Eat

San Luis has a good collection of cafés and restaurants. Pride of place goes to the unassuming *El Bocolito* on Plaza San Francisco at the corner of Aldama and Guerrero. There's no sign showing its name outside, but it serves some of the tastiest and best-value Mexican food in the north. The menu consists mainly of local specialities with names like *zarape*, *gringa* and *pelangocha*, but the friendly waiters will list all the ingredients for you. They're combinations of things like bacon, pork or beef lightly fried up with chile, herbs, onion, tomato or green pepper, often with melted cheese on top, and cost US$1.25 to US$1.50 for a very filling plateful. *Chile queso* (US$0.75) is a big, not very piquant chile filled with melted cheese and served with frijoles and grated cheese on top. There are also egg dishes and mountains of tortillas. El Bocolito is run by the Cooperativo de las Casas José Marti, an organisation which provides housing and funds for Indian students, and the waiters and cooks are all young Indians.

Plaza de Armas The *Restaurant Posada del Virrey*, on the north side, is the smartest place on the plaza but it's still a relaxed café-style spot, particularly popular in the evenings. You can sit over a coffee or beer or eat an avocado or shrimp cocktail (US$0.75/1.25), fish (US$1.50), chicken (US$1.75), a banana split (US$0.75) or ice cream (US$0.35).

The *Tangamanga* at the north-east corner of the plaza, where Los Bravo meets Hidalgo, is a modern-style restaurant with good service and a good comida corrida for US$1.25. Other dishes go up to US$2. The comida corrida in the *Hotel Plaza* on the south side of the plaza is US$1.25 and also filling but a bit less appetising – thick bean soup, rice, chile relleno, sweet and coffee.

Just off Plaza de Armas at Madero 125-145, the *Restaurant-Bar Castillo* is a coffee-and-drinks place where you can also eat eggs (US$0.75), enchiladas (US$0.75 to US$1.75), or chicken or meat (US$1.50 to US$1.75). For a Margarita, Bloody Mary, Tom Collins, Sangría or vodka and tonic you pay US$1.

Plaza de los Fundadores & Avenida Carranza On the south side of the plaza, at the corner of Carranza and De León, the *Restaurante La Parroquia* is a large clean place serving mainly Mexican food. It's popular at all times of day, including breakfast time. Enchiladas, chilaquiles and tacos cost around US$1, fish US$1.50, meat US$1.25 to US$2.25, seafood cocktails US$0.75 to US$1.25. Also served are *cabrito* (kid), *barbacoa* (meat slowly baked in an oven), *pozole* (maize soup with meat and vegetables) and pizza.

On the Carranza/Carmona corner of the plaza the slick, pot-planted, new *Restaurant-Bar Ipiña* combines Mexican dishes with tempting North American ideas. Meat, chicken and fish cost US$1.50 to US$3.75, hamburgers US$1.50, salads US$1, fruit salad (a whole plateful) US$0.75. There are also waffles (US$0.75), crepes (US$1.25), yoghurt granola and honey (US$1), and desserts ranging from hot fudge sundae (US$0.75) through mango sundae and pear melba (US$1) to banana split (US$1.25). The Ipiña is open until 11 pm daily.

West of the plaza, Carranza forms an embryonic zona rosa for a couple of km, with a few up-market restaurants scattered along it. These include *Los Cazadores Potosinos* at No 700 which specialises in meat (US$2.25 to US$3); a steak house and a pizzeria in the 900 block just past the Hotel Real Plaza; and the *Tiberius*, with Italian food, at No 1047.

Alameda Area Fronting the north-west corner of the Alameda, the *Café Tokio* at Othón 415 is a huge eating hall, popular with everybody including families. It does a comida corrida for US$1.25, or if you're slightly less hungry the crisp enchiladas Potosinas come with frijoles, guacamole, salad and cheese for around US$1. There are also tortas (25c to US$0.40), fish (US$1 to US$1.25) and meat (US$0.75 to US$2).

On the corner of Los Bravo and Constitución, the *Café Pacífico* is clean, popular, modern and quite similar to the Restaurante La Parroquia. Comida corrida is US$1.75.

Entertainment

San Luis has several downtown cinemas and a fairly active cultural life. Ask in the tourist office for what's on and keep your eyes on the posters around town for concerts (popular and classical) and exhibitions. The Teatro de la Paz has something on most nights. The city also hosts a big 10-day spring arts festival in mid-May with contemporary, traditional and classical dance, concerts, theatre, films, opera and exhibitions.

Bullfights take place at the Plaza de Toros on Universidad, east of the Alameda. There's also a bullfighting museum here.

There are a few discos in town and in the motels on the outskirts. *La Jaula del Jacal*, in the Hotel Panorama, costs US$2.25 to enter. The *Dulcina*, north of the city on Highway 57, is reputed to be one of the best.

Things to Buy

Markets The Mercado Hidalgo is five blocks north of Plaza de Armas along Hidalgo. It sells mainly food and flowers and has some comedores (informal eating houses). Street markets extend north from the Mercado Hidalgo along the pedestrian street Alhóndiga. Leather boots and belts, baskets and pottery are among the most attractive items here. There is another big market on the other side of Reforma, which crosses the north end of Alhóndiga.

Shops The main area of shops lies between Mercado Hidalgo and the Plaza de Armas. There are also a number of more expensive boutiques, furniture, shoe, antique, etc shops along Carranza, west of the Plaza de los Fundadores in the zona rosa. The excellent bookshop chain Librería de Cristal has a branch at Carranza 765.

For local crafts, go to the Museo Regional de Artes Populares on Plaza San Francisco, or try Tlaxcalilla at Escobedo 1030 on the Plaza del Carmen, Artesanías Potosinas at Miguel Barragán 345, La Perla del Bajío at Hidalgo 370, or Artes Nacionales at Morelos 630.

Getting There & Away

Air Mexicana Airlines (tel 4-11-19, 4-12-33) is at the corner of Madero and Uresti, six blocks west of the Plaza de Armas. There are daily Mexicana flights to and from Mexico City, and three a week non-stop to and from Monterrey.

Road The excellent Highway 57 runs 413 km south to Mexico City; northward it goes to Matehuala (192 km) and Saltillo (260 km). Highway 45 goes north-west to Zacatecas (196 km). To the east, Highway 70 goes to Ciudad Valles (268 km) and Tampico (409 km). Highway 70 also continues west of San Luis Potosí to Aguascalientes (168 km). For Guadalajara (348 km from San Luis), take Highway 70 west until just after the small town of Ojuelos de Jalisco, where you branch left on Highway 80 through Lagos de Moreno.

Bus The Central Camionera (tel 2-74-11) lies on the corner of J G Torres and the south-eastern bypass, just south of Glorieta Juárez roundabout and several km east of the centre. It's a gigantic place with separate halls *(salas)* for 1st, 2nd and 3rd class and a multitude of lines serving virtually everywhere in the northern half of Mexico. There's a post office in the 1st-class hall and a *guardería* (left-luggage office) at the 2nd-class Transportes Frontera ticket desk.

Fares on 1st-class services vary only insignificantly between lines. Transportes del Norte (1st class, tel 2-40-61) runs to Nuevo Laredo (US$9.25) 11 times daily; to Matehuala (US$2.25), Saltillo (US$5.50) and Monterrey (US$6.50) 10 times; to Reynosa (US$8) and Matamoros (US$8) twice; to Ciudad Victoria (US$4.25) three times; to Mexico City (US$5.25) 23 times; to Querétaro (US$2.50) 21 times; to Guadalajara (US$4.25) seven times; to

San Luis Potosí Bus Station Area

Zacatecas (US$2.25) and Torreón (US$7) twice. You can also buy Greyhound tickets from Laredo, Texas to San Antonio (US$23), Austin (US$34), Houston (US$51) and Dallas (US$62) as well as a seven-day Greyhound Ameripass (US$99) here.

Omnibus de México (1st class, tel 2-60-93) goes to Casas Grandes (US$17.75) twice daily; to Ciudad Juárez (US$17) three times; to Chihuahua (US$12.50) six times; to Durango (US$5.75) five times; to Torreón eight times; to Querétaro and Mexico City 16 times; to Saltillo, Reynosa, Celaya (US$3) and Guadalajara once.

Tres Estrellas de Oro (1st class, tel 2-49-94) goes to Mexico City 11 times daily; to Monterrey 11 times; to Nuevo Laredo seven times; to Guadalajara four times; to Matamoros three times; to Reynosa three times; to Ciudad Victoria six times; to Ciudad Valles (US$3.25) and Tampico (US$5) twice; to Morelia (US$5) four times; to Uruapan (US$6) twice; to San Juan de los Lagos (US$2.50) four times; to Tijuana (US$33) once; also to Mazatlán (US$10.50), Culiacán (US$13.75), Los Mochis (US$16.50), Guaymas (US$20.75), Hermosillo (US$22.25) and Mexicali (US$30.75).

Chihuahuaenses (1st class, tel 26252) has locales to Zacatecas, Fresnillo (US$3), Torréon, Chihuahua and Ciudad Juárez 11 times daily; and 10 services a day to Querétaro and Mexico City.

Autobuses Anáhuac (1st class, tel 2-41-42) has frequent buses to Matehuala and Saltillo; to Monterrey four times daily; to Ciudad Acuña (US$11.25) twice; to Piedras Negras (US$10.75) twice; to Lagos de Moreno, León (US$2.25), Irapuato, Salamanca and Celaya (US$3.50) six times; to Querétaro and Mexico City 11 times.

Second-class bus prices also show no price variation between different lines. Flecha Amarilla (tel 2-78-74, 2-20-77) services include trips to Dolores Hidalgo (US$1.75) 10 times a day; to San Miguel de Allende seven times; to Guadalajara (US$3.75) once; to Guanajuato (US$2.50) five times; to Celaya (US$2.75) 10 times; to León (US$2) every 40 minutes from 9 am to 8.30 pm; to Morelia (US$4.25) 16 times; to Pátzcuaro (US$5) eight times; to Querétaro (US$2.25) 12 times; to Uruapan (US$5.75) five times between 4.30 and 9.40 am; to Toluca (US$4.50) twice.

Estrella Blanca (tel 2-43-77) has 21 direct and 19 other buses to Mexico City (US$4.75); plus buses to Guadalajara (US$4) four times daily; to Aguascalientes (US$2) 16 times; to Chihuahua (US$11.25) and Ciudad Juárez (US$15.25) three times; to Mazatlán (US$8.75) once; to Torreón (US$6.25) 10 times; to Durango (US$5.25) six times; to Zacatecas (US$2) and Fresnillo (US$2.75) 19 times; to Matehuala (US$2.25) and Monterrey (US$6) eight times; to Nuevo Laredo (US$8.50) three times.

Transportes Frontera (tel 2-43-77) has a continuous 24-hour service to Matehuala, Saltillo (US$5) and Monterrey. It has buses to Matamoros (US$7.25) six times daily; to Reynosa (US$7.25) seven times; to Querétaro and Mexico City 17 times daily; to Dolores Hidalgo and Guanajuato once; to Toluca twice; also to Nuevo Laredo, Ciudad Victoria (US$3.75), León and Morelia.

Autobuses Anáhuac 2nd class (tel 2-59-91) has buses to Piedras Negras (US$10.25) and Ciudad Acuña once each; and 10 locales to Matehuala, Saltillo and Monterrey.

Omnibus de Oriente/Transportes Reynosa (tel 2-42-02) run 'expresses' to Reynosa three times daily; to Tampico (US$5) six times; to Guadalajara five times; to Matamoros twice; also to Ciudad Valles and Ciudad Mante. Its ordinario services (same price except for Guadalajara which is US$0.40 cheaper by ordinario than by express) go to Guadalajara 31 times daily; Tampico via Ciudad Valles 21 times; Tampico via Ciudad Mante nine times; Reynosa 13 times; Mexico City twice; and Matamoros nine times.

Third-class buses from San Luis are like city buses but travel to outlying towns and cities. Transportes Vencedor (tel 2-40-42) runs what it calls 1st and 2nd-class buses but are really 2nd and 3rd class. They go to Tamazunchale (US$4.50 '1st', US$4 '2nd'); Tampico (US$4.25 '2nd'); Ciudad Valles (US$3 '2nd'); and Río Verde (US$1.75 '1st', US$1.50 '2nd').

Autobuses Rojos goes to Santa María del Río hourly from 6.30 am to 11.30 pm. Autobuses Potosinos (tel 2-01-50) also goes to Santa María.

Altiplano Tamaulipas (tel 2-14-49, 4-01-40) has a few services to Matehuala,

Monterrey and Reynosa at normal 2nd-class prices.

Approximate journey times by 1st-class bus: Saltillo five hours, Monterrey six hours, Reynosa eight hours, Tijuana 42 hours, Mexico City five hours. To San Miguel de Allende by Flecha Amarilla (2nd class) takes 4½ hours.

Rail San Luis railway station is on Othón, on the north side of the Alameda, at the eastern edge of the city centre. The most important trains are 'El Regiomontano' and the 'Aguila Azteca'.

The southward El Regiomontano leaves at 2.05 am, arriving in Mexico City at 8.46 am; northward it departs at 1.01 am, reaching Saltillo at 6.34 am, Monterrey at 9 am and Nuevo Laredo about 1 pm. This train has sleeping accommodation, a dining car and no 2nd-class carriages. You can make reservations for it at 6 pm.

The southward Aguila Azteca leaves at 10.35 am, reaching San Miguel de Allende at 1.09 pm, Querétaro at 2.42 pm and Mexico City at 7.20 pm. Northward it departs from San Luis at 5.45 pm, reaching Saltillo at 11.53 pm, Monterrey at 2.20 am and Nuevo Laredo at 7.20 am. It has 1st and 2nd-class seats only (1st class reservable 1½ hours before departure).

Other trains depart for Monterrey at 7.15 am, Tampico at 7.50 am and Aguascalientes at 10 am.

Fares to Mexico City: 2nd class US$2; 1st class US$3.50; 1st-class reserved seat US$7.50; roomette for one US$9.50, for two US$14.25; bedroom for two US$15.75.

Getting Around

Airport Transport San Luis airport is off the Saltillo road, north of the city. Mexicana (tel 4-11-19, 4-12-33) runs a colectivo (US$3.25 per person) for arriving and departing flights which will pick you up/drop you anywhere in the central area of the city. But for two or more people a taxi (US$4.50) is cheaper for the half-hour trip.

Local Transport From the bus station to downtown, exit the bus station from the 2nd-class hall and turn left. The buses wait on the first corner. Get off immediately after passing the Alameda park on your right, then walk four blocks west (left) to reach the Plaza de Armas. A taxi from bus station to city centre costs US$0.75. Buses returning to the bus station from downtown are marked 'Central' and run along Iturbide, one block south of the Plaza de Armas.

For Tangamanga park, take a yellow 'Perimetral' bus from the west side of the Alameda and get off at the Monumento a la Revolución (Revolution Monument).

Car Rental National (tel 2-55-44) is in the Hotel Real de Minas, Odin (tel 2-32-20) at Carranza 710, Rente del Centro (tel 2-12-48) at Carranza 757.

SANTA MARÍA DEL RÍO

Fifty km south of San Luis Potosí city, just off the Mexico City road, this small town is famed for its excellent hand-made rebozos. They are usually made of synthetic silk called *artisela*, in fairly simple patterns which appear to involve some tie-dyeing, with garish colours less in evidence than in many Mexican textile centres. It takes about two weeks to make one, and prices in Santa María are lower than in San Luis.

You can see and buy the rebozos at the Escuela del Rebozo (Rebozo School) on the central Plaza Hidalgo, and in a few private workshops. There's a smart motel and restaurant, *La Puesta del Sol*, at the entrance to Santa María from the highway. The buses of Flecha Amarilla, Autobuses Rojos and Autobuses Potosinos link the town with San Luis Potosí.

About 12 km east of Santa María, at the village of La Labor del Río, is the thermal spring of Lourdes whose waters are supposed to help cure kidney problems. There's a hotel here too.

GOGORRÓN

This is another hot springs, allegedly beneficial for rheumatism and arthritis, whose waters reach 40°C. It may be visited on a day trip from San Luis Potosí. It's about 50 km from San Luis, reached by taking Highway 57 south for 24 km, then turning right on to Highway 37 towards Villa de Reyes. A hacienda around the springs has been turned into the *Centro Vacacional Gogorrón* (tel 4-66-55) with rooms, restaurant, etc. The publicity leaflet speaks for itself:

Gogorrón is one of the most important resort located in the centre of the country. It has been remodelated for the confort of ower visitors.

The natural view of beauty convine wiht. The confort and best service. The cabage wiht roman tubes for pleasure and relax of ower visitor's.

Restaurant we can serve international and mexican dishes (Kitchen) Video-Bar, Plus, Discoteque and after you have a full day of joy, in the Swiming poll with warm water we recomed for curatives purpes, jump springs at 40 degrees . . . .

It counts wiht huge green areas specialy for having sport in the on side like volley ball and reading hourses for the security of children we have special games . . . .

Come with us to have a good time full of hapiness . . . .

We wait for you any time you wish it!

You can use the pools or the hotter Roman baths for US$1 an hour and stay overnight in comfortable single/double rooms for US$9.25/12.50 without meals, or US$13.50/21 with meals. Accommodation without meals isn't available at weekends and holidays, but there are discounts for children. Enquire or book at the Gogorrón desk in the tourist office (tel 2-36-36) in San Luis Potosí, or telephone the centre direct.

Flecha Amarilla's 'San Felipe' bus runs from San Luis Potosí bus station to the Gogorrón entrance every half hour. Fare is US$0.75 and the trip takes about 50 minutes.

RÍO VERDE

Population: 35,000

Located 131 km east of San Luis Potosí on the Ciudad Valles road, Río Verde has a few hotels and restaurants. Sixteen km south by rough road is a small lake, Laguna de la Media Luna, from which a mammoth's bones and pre-Hispanic pottery vessels containing small figures have been recovered. The waters are warm and clear except during the rainy summer months, and the lake attracts divers. It's sometimes possible to rent equipment in the town.

Tampico & the Huasteca

About 400 km down the Gulf coast from the US border, at the mouth of the River Pánuco, is the double city of Tampico-Ciudad Madero, not one of Mexico's most thrilling towns but a place where travellers can spend a tolerable day or so on the way north or south. Tampico is a scruffy, bustling place, Mexico's busiest port and a communications hub, while Ciudad Madero is the processing centre for the country's oldest-established oil fields.

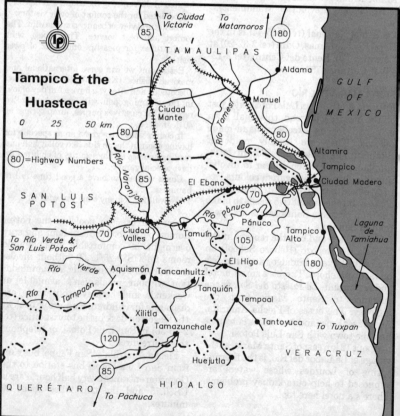

Stretching inland from Tampico is the fertile region where the Gulf coast plain meets the fringes of the Sierra Madre Oriental. It's called the Huasteca ('wass-TEK-a'), after the Huastec people who have populated it for about 3000 years and reached considerable heights of civilisation well before the Spanish arrived. The Huasteca, spread over southern Tamaulipas, eastern San Luis Potosí and northern Veracruz, is an often beautiful region where some of the Huastecs still live a traditional life style. Highway 85, one of the main routes from the north-east border to Mexico City, goes through the middle of the Huasteca, which for most people is a more interesting place to break a journey than Tampico.

History

Pre-Hispanic The Huastecs probably arrived in the area between 1500 and 1000 BC, by which time settled agriculture had already begun in the Sierra de Tamaulipas on the northern edge of the region.

The Huastec language is classified as one of the Mayance family. Since other languages in this family in Mexico are spoken only in the south-east – including by the Tzotzils, Tzeltals and Lacandones of Chiapas and the Mayas of the Yucatán – it has been theorised that they all stem from a language which was once spoken all down the Gulf coast. One suggestions is that the Huastec language split from the rest of the Mayance family about 900 BC – which could be explained by the rise of the Olmec culture, probably non-Mayance-speaking, in the intervening area around that time.

Between 800 and 200 BC the Huastecs were constructing circular buildings and growing maize, beans and squash. From about 200 BC to 800 AD – a period known to archaeologists as Pánuco III – they started to make rectangular buildings, produced some fine pottery and carved stone and bone, and were beginning to dominate the Huasteca.

Emigrant Huastecs may have founded the great Teotihuacán civilisation in central Mexico; stories taken down by the Spanish in the 16th century speak of 'inhabitants of Pánuco' who 'took themselves to Teotihuacán, where they raised the hills in honour of the sun and moon'. Central Mexican civilisations adopted gods which were probably of Huastec origin; Quetzalcóatl was worshipped at Teotihuacán and by the Toltecs, Tlazoltéotl by the Aztecs.

The Huastecs' greatest period was roughly 800-1200 AD. Organised under a number of independent rulers, they built many ceremonial centres, practised phallic fertility rites, occasionally sharpened their teeth, were Mexico's chief cotton producers, and expanded as far west as north-east Querétaro and Hidalgo.

The Huastecs developed great skill in pottery and in stone and shell-carving.

Bone figure

There are unfortunately no spectacular Huastec sites to visit; the two most interesting are Castillo de Teayo (see the Veracruz chapter) and Tamuín. As a result Huastec archaeology is still in its infancy and relatively little is known of this most northerly pre-Hispanic civilisation.

Spanish Conquest In 1518 a Spanish ship commanded by Juan de Grijalva passed along the Huastec coast in the first of several visits over the next few years by Spaniards keen to make the area their own domain. In 1523 Cortés marched an army from Mexico City to defeat the Huastecs and founded a colony called San Estéban, now Pánuco. During the next two years Cortés prevailed over not only the rebellious Huastecs – about 400 of whose leaders were apparently burnt to death by his sidekick Gonzálo de Sandoval – but also the Spanish governor of Jamaica, Francisco de Garay, who arrived with a royal commission to govern the Pánuco area. Cortés used threats to persuade him to withdraw.

Nuño de Guzman, an enemy of Cortés and friend of the governor of Cuba, was appointed royal governor of the Pánuco area in 1527 but spent most of his time pillaging and slaughtering in western Mexico – though he did have time to organise a few slave-catching raids north of the Pánuco. At the time 80 Indians could be sold for one horse. Eventually Guzman's misdeeds caught up with him and he was sent back to Spain.

Conversion of the Huastecs to Christianity began at a mission at Tampico in the 1530s. The area came back under rule from Mexico City in 1534 and several monasteries were set up despite occasional further Huastec rebellions. But attacks from the north by Chichimecs, provoked by more slave raids, kept the Spanish from expanding north of the Huasteca for nearly two centuries. The most important Spanish towns were Pánuco, Tampico and Ciudad Valles. Meanwhile slavery and imported diseases reduced the Huastec population from an estimated one million to probably less than 100,000 during the 16th century. There were further Huastec rebellions in the 19th century, provoked by filching of their lands.

Oil Tampico, destroyed by pirates in 1684, was refounded in 1823 by families from Altamira to the north. Through the 19th century it remained a minor port. It was occupied by the 3000-strong Spanish force which landed down the coast in 1829 in a feeble bid to regain Mexico (the Spanish were defeated by yellow fever and a siege by Santa Anna), and again by the Americans in 1846 and the French in the 1860s.

Suddenly, with the discovery of oil in the area by US and British companies from 1901, Tampico became the world's biggest oil port, rough, tough and booming. Luckily outside the main combat zones of the Mexican Revolution, the area was producing a quarter of the world's output in the early 1920s. But the oil and its profits remained under foreign control until a strike by oil workers in Tampico in 1938 led to its nationalisation by President Lázaro Cárdenas. Mexico's second oil boom, in the 1970s, took place mainly further south along the Gulf coast, but the area around Tampico-Ciudad Madero remains important. Pipelines and barge fleets bring oil from fields north and south, onshore and offshore, to its refineries and harbour, and Ciudad Madero is the HQ of the very powerful oil workers' union, the STPRM.

The Huastecs Today
About 100,000 Huastecs live south of Ciudad Valles in San Luis Potosí state and east of Tantoyuca in Veracruz. More than 80% speak Spanish as well as Huastec. They are Christian but still practise a few other ceremonies – particularly dances – to help ensure the fertility of the land. *Curanderos* (curers) and shamans are important in matters of bodily and

spiritual health. Diseases are often thought to be caused by curses or witchcraft; traditionally the affected part of the body is sucked and smoked with a resinous twig which enables the curer to diagnose the problem.

Huastec women still wear *quechquémitls* colourfully embroidered with traditional designs like trees of life, animals, flowers and two-armed crosses. With this go a black skirt and coloured ribbons which are wound into the hair to keep it on top of the head.

Huastecs generally live in one-room houses of wood and palm, and practise a basic agriculture in which maize, beans, squash, rice, peanuts and coffee are important – the last three mainly for trading. Their most important craft products are hats, mats and bags made from palm.

Dance Two interesting Huastec dances, which you may see if you attend one of their festivals, are Las Varitas and Zacamson.

Las Varitas (The Little Twigs) is danced mainly in honour of San Miguel Arcángel and the Virgen de Guadalupe. One of its homes is the Tancanhuitz area. The dancers, wearing white shirts and shorts and carrying a knife in one hand and bells and coloured ribbons in the other, imitate the movements of animals such as bats or butterflies to the accompaniment of a flute or violin.

Zacamson (*zacam* means 'small', *son* means 'music') comes especially from around Aquismón. The dancers, wearing white shorts and shirts with squares of coloured material attached to their backs and heads, again imitate animals to music from a harp, fiddles and sometimes

Quechquémitl and bag

a guitar. The full performance has more than 75 parts, danced at different times of day and night. It's accompanied by much drinking of sugar-cane alcohol, some of which is thrown on the earth – which produced it – before the dance starts.

TAMPICO

Somewhat faded since its heyday in the 1920s, Tampico is still a lively, untidy town where the many bars and cantinas stay open late and lots of marimbas are heard on the streets. It lacks any outstanding attractions but has some of the atmosphere you'd expect from a tropical port. Together with Ciudad Madero, which adjoins it to the north-east, it has a population of about 600,000, which makes it Mexico's eighth biggest city.

Orientation

Tampico's bus station is in the north of the city, beyond the Laguna del Carpintero, one of many lakes which dot this low-lying, marshy region round the mouth of the Pánuco River. If you walk out on to the road from the bus station, you'll see a line of decrepit Chevrolets apparently queueing up to get into a wrecker's yard. These are in fact the colectivos which will take you to the city centre *(centro)* for 15c.

Downtown Tampico is centred on two wide plazas just a couple of blocks apart. One is the zócalo or Plaza de Armas, with the cathedral (dating from 1823 but remodelled this century) on its north side and the Hotel Inglaterra on the south side. The other – one block south and one east of the zócalo – is the Plaza de la Libertad. Numerous hotels and restaurants of all grades are within a few blocks of these two plazas. Down a gentle hill south of either plaza you come to a bustling area which contains the market, the railway station and the riverside docks.

Addresses on east-west streets usually have the suffix Ote (east) or Pte (west), while those on north-south streets are Nte (north) or Sur (south). The dividing point

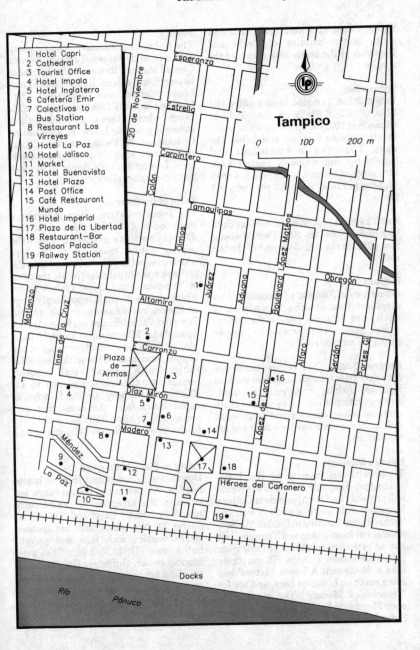

1 Hotel Capri
2 Cathedral
3 Tourist Office
4 Hotel Impala
5 Hotel Inglaterra
6 Cafetería Emir
7 Colectivos to
  Bus Station
8 Restaurant Los
  Virreyes
9 Hotel La Paz
10 Hotel Jalisco
11 Market
12 Hotel Buenavista
13 Hotel Plaza
14 Post Office
15 Café Restaurant
   Mundo
16 Hotel Imperial
17 Plaza de la Libertad
18 Restaurant–Bar
   Saloon Palacio
19 Railway Station

Tampico

0   100   200 m

between east and west and north and south is the meeting of Colón and Carranza at the north-west corner of the zócalo.

Information

Tourist Office Tampico tourist office (tel 12-00-07, 12-26-68) is on the zócalo at Olmos Sur 102. Go up one block of stairs beside Helados Chantal and follow the signs. The office is enthusiastic and helpful but unfortunately doesn't have very much of interest to tell you. It's open Monday to Friday 9 am to 2 pm and 5 to 7 pm.

Post The main post office is on Plaza de la Libertad at Madero 309. There's also a post office in the 2nd-class part of the bus station.

Festivals

Anniversary of Tampico's Refounding This event is celebrated with a procession on 12 April from Altamira (where the settlers came from); the procession passes through Tampico zócalo.

Semana Santa This brings numerous Miramar Beach-based activities such as regattas, fishing tournaments, windsurfing competitions, sand-sculpture contests, music, dancing and bonfires, as well as other events like book fairs and art exhibitions.

Huastec Museum

Those with an interest in the little-studied pre-Hispanic culture of the region will probably find the Museo de la Cultura Huasteca well worth a visit. It's in the Technological Institute in Ciudad Madero, several km from downtown Tampico, but has an extensive collection of finds from this little-known culture. To get there take a 'Boulevard A López Mateos' bus going north on López de Lara, and ask for 'Tecnológico Madero'. The museum is open Monday to Friday 10 am to 5 pm and Saturday 10 am to 3 pm. Entry is free.

Beach

The 10-km-long Miramar Beach is about 15 km from downtown Tampico, beyond Ciudad Madero. Its waters are reported to be surprisingly clean. Buses 'Boulevard A López Mateos' and 'Recreativo' from López de Lara will take you to a part of the beach where there's a hotel with a swimming pool and, nearby, a miniature Chapultepec Park with a small zoo. There are several small seafood restaurants here. During Semana Santa a series of festivities takes place.

South of the River

The 'Isleta' colectivo, which goes from a block south of the Plaza de la Libertad, diagonally across a smaller plaza from the railway station, takes you to the ferry which crosses the Pánuco River. From the far bank you can get colectivos to the town of Tampico Alto, about 12 km away, where there's a small, appallingly kept archaeological museum on the zócalo. Tampico Alto celebrates the festival of the Señor de las Misericordias around 6 to 13 May. Nearby, on the northern edge of the Laguna Tamiahua, is the settlement of La Ribera, with several small seafood restaurants. Colectivos also run to La Ribera from the ferry landing. Lanchas or motor boats from the same spot can apparently be hired for trips up the river to the town of Pánuco or south to the lagoon.

Places to Stay – bottom end

Downtown Tampico isn't short of hotels but few of those in the budget range are enticing. An exception is the recently remodelled *Hotel Capri* (tel 2-26-80) at Juárez 202 Nte, where basic but spotless singles/doubles with fans and private baths cost US$2.75/3.75. The very friendly owner, Guillermo Galván, has a beautiful pet ocelot and is a keen amateur archaeologist who often makes trips to the little-known Huastec sites in the area.

A very cheap possibility is the *Hotel Buenavista* (tel 2-29-46) at Héroes del

Cañonero 112 Ote, near the corner of Colón. Rooms with one double bed cost US$1.75 with common bath, US$2.25 with private bath. For two beds and private bath you pay US$4.50. Some of the rooms have a bit of a view over the town; they're fairly clean and not bad value for the price.

Places to Stay – middle

Prices in the middle and top ranges are inflated by the oil business.

Two modern 40-room hotels under the same management offer a touch of air-conditioned comfort in the rather sleazy area down near the market and river docks. The *Hotel Jalisco* (tel 12-27-92, 12-29-24) at La Paz 120 has clean but not huge air-con rooms for US$5.50 single, US$6 or US$6.25 double. Rooms with fan only are US$1.25 cheaper. About a block west, the *Hotel La Paz* (tel 40-03-82) at La Paz 307 Pte has similar accommodation and identical prices. To reach these hotels from the zócalo, go two blocks south along Colón, down a flight of steps, then one block more and turn right on La Paz.

The *Hotel Imperial* at López de Lara 101 Sur, near the corner of Carranza, has seen better days. Some renovation was going on when we were there, and if this doesn't put the prices up the place will be reasonable value. Large and basically clean but dingy rooms cost US$4.50 single, US$6.75 double. Some have carpets and traffic noise, others have linoleum tiles and a view of a rubbish-strewn courtyard. None have fan or air-conditioning.

The *Hotel Plaza* (tel 4-16-78) at the corner of Madero and Olmos has clean, comfortable, sizeable rooms which are good value for Tampico at US$8.25/9.50. For that reason it's sometimes full.

Places to Stay – top end

Two luxurious downtown places are the *Hotel Inglaterra* (tel 12-56-78) on the zócalo at Díaz Mirón Ote 106, where singles/doubles are US$25/26.50; and the *Hotel Impala* at Díaz Mirón 220 Pte, 1½ blocks west of the zócalo, where you pay US$16/18.

There are more top-end hotels along Avenida Hidalgo, going north-west from the city centre out towards the airport.

Places to Eat

Seafood is of course the thing to look for in Tampico. Its crabs in particular are renowned for their size and flavour. *Carne asada Tampiqueña* is beefsteak marinated in garlic, oil and oregano and usually served with guacamole, strips of chile and totopos (maize chips).

Two popular places are *Cafetería Emir* and *Café-Restaurant Mundo*. The Emir, at Olmos 107 Sur half a block south of the zócalo, does fish for US$1.75 to US$2.25, meat for US$2.25 to US$2.75, quesadillas and enchiladas for around US$1.50. The Mundo, at the corner of López de Lara and Díaz Mirón, is a little cheaper and also does big sandwiches with salad for US$1 to US$2.

Popular for seafood is the *Cafetería y Nevería Elita* on Díaz Mirón half a block east of the zócalo, where you can get two stuffed crabs for US$2, shrimp kebab for US$2.25, snapper for US$2.75 to US$3. *Helados Piter* on Aduana, half a block north of Díaz Mirón, is a busy cafeteria and ice-cream place.

Restaurant Los Virreyes at the corner of Colón and Obregón, a block south of the zócalo, is open until midnight and serves decent fare. Seafood (including crab) is mostly in the US$2 to US$3 bracket, meat dishes are US$1.75 to US$3.75, chicken is US$1.75, hamburgers around US$1, egg dishes and breakfasts US$1 to US$2.

Down on the Plaza de la Libertad at the corner of Aduana and Héroes del Cañonero, the *Cafetería y Restaurant El Sol* is an echoing place with a booming jukebox, red-and-white striped walls and a bit of a harbour low-life atmosphere. Beer isn't sold to women and a sign forbids customers from chatting with the cashier.

The food is average. Fried fish is US$2, shrimp a bit more. The *Restaurant-Bar Saloon Palacio*, over the road, is classier.

The best food downtown is probably to be found in the big hotels like the Inglaterra and the Impala. There are also several places on Avenida Hidalgo, out towards the airport.

Getting There & Away

Air The Mexicana airline office (tel 13-08-04, 13-25-20) is at Díaz Mirón 106 Ote. Mexicana has three or four flights daily to and from Mexico City, and one most days to and from Monterrey.

Road See earlier in this chapter for roads to Matamoros (498 km), Ciudad Victoria and Monterrey. To the west, by the fairly rough Highway 70, Ciudad Valles is 141 km and San Luis Potosí 409 km. Thirty-seven km along this road from Tampico, another road heads off south through Pánuco, El Higo, Tempoal and Huejutla towards Pachuca and Mexico City (see the 'Near Mexico City – North & West' chapter for more on this route).

To the south, it's 182 km to Tuxpan by Highway 180. Until the new road bridge over the Pánuco River at Tampico is completed, drivers going south have the choice of the passenger ferry (hard to find, but it's near the new bridge) or a detour 12 km upstream east to the nearest bridge.

Bus If you're travelling to Tampico from Mexico City, buses leave from the northern terminal in the capital.

Tampico bus station (tel 13-40-93, 13-41-82) is out on Calle Zapotal, about four km north of downtown. See 'Getting Around' for transport to and from the bus station. First class is on the right side of the bus station as you enter, 2nd class on the left. There are post and telégrafo offices on the 2nd-class side, and cafeterias in both parts.

ADO (1st class) mainly serves the Gulf coast area, with five buses daily to Acayucan (US$11.75), three to Jalapa

(US$7.25), 12 to Veracruz (US$8.75), 13 to Mexico City (US$7.50), two each to Reynosa (US$6.75) and Matamoros (US$6.50), eight to Tuxpan (US$3), four to Villahermosa (US$14.50). It also offers service to Poza Rica (US$3.75), San Andrés Tuxtla (US$10.75), Pachuca (US$6.25), Papantla (US$4), Coatzintla, Huejutla, Tantoyuca and Cardel.

Transportes del Norte (1st class) goes to Ciudad Victoria (US$3) and Monterrey (US$7) seven times daily; Nuevo Laredo (US$9.75) twice; and Matamoros, Mexico City, Saltillo (US$8.25) and Torreón once each.

Omnibus de México (1st class) has a few buses to Reynosa, Matamoros, Monterrey, Huejutla, Mexico City, Ciudad Valles, Tamazunchale, Celaya, Torreón and Chihuahua (US$17.25).

Tres Estrellas de Oro (1st class) serves San Luis Potosí (US$5) and Guadalajara (US$8.75) twice daily; and Mexico City, Mazatlán (US$15.50), Culiacán (US$18.75), Los Mochis (US$21.25), Hermosillo (US$27.25), Mexicali (US$35.75) and Tijuana (US$38) once each.

Omnibus de Oriente has 1st-class buses to Reynosa (six daily); Matamoros and San Luis Potosí (four each); Guadalajara (two); and Ciudad Victoria, Querétaro (US$6.75) and Celaya (one each). It also has 2nd-class services to most of the same places.

Approximate 1st-class journey times: Tuxpan 4½ hours, Veracruz 10 hours, Ciudad Valles two hours, San Luis Potosí 6½ hours, Ciudad Victoria 3½ hours, Monterrey eight hours, Saltillo 10 hours, Matamoros eight hours, Nuevo Laredo 12 hours, Mexico City 10 hours.

Second-class buses are about 10% cheaper and more frequent but slower and less comfortable. Transportes Frontera goes to Nuevo Laredo six times daily; Ciudad Victoria and Monterrey 11 times; Poza Rica seven times; Reynosa twice; and Ciudad Valles, Mexico City and Matamoros once each.

México-Tuxpan-Tampico has five limited-stop, numbered-seat services daily to Mexico City via Tuxpan, Poza Rica or Huejutla, and numerous other buses to the same places plus Tantoyuca.

Sistema Vencedor Golfo y Omnibus de Oriente Golfo has numerous daily services to Reynosa, Matamoros, San Luis Potosí, Ciudad Victoria, Ciudad Valles and Guadalajara, plus less frequent ones to Tamazunchale, Ciudad Mante, Río Verde, Celaya and Querétaro.

Transportes Mante/Transportes Tamaulipas goes to Matamoros 14 times daily, Ciudad Victoria 15 times, Reynosa five times and Monterrey eight times.

Rail Tampico railway station (tel 12-11-79, 12-03-34) is two blocks south of the Plaza de la Libertad at the corner of Aduana and Héroes de Nacozari. There's one daily train each to and from Monterrey (about 11 hours) and San Luis Potosí, with limited 1st-class seating.

Getting Around
Airport Transport Tampico airport is about 15 km north of downtown. For airport transport, contact Transportes Aeropuerto Tampico (tel 13-36-14).

Local Transport Decrepit old colectivo taxis wait outside the bus station to take you downtown (15c). Returning from downtown to the bus station, take a 'Perimetral-Central Camionera' colectivo from Olmos, a block south of the zócalo. The bus marked 'Boulevard A López Mateos', going north on López de Lara from the corners of Madero, Díaz Mirón or Carranza, will get to the Huastec museum or Playa Miramar.

CIUDAD VALLES
This town on Highway 70, 141 km from Tampico and 268 km from San Luis Potosí, is the main centre of the Huasteca Potosina (the part of the Huasteca which lies in San Luis Potosí state). Commerce in cattle and coffee are among the most important activities.

This major road junction lies approximately halfway along the road from Matamoros (541 km away) to Mexico City (477 km). The town itself has few particular attractions, although it's pleasant enough, but it would make a good base for exploring the Huasteca, an area of both flat farmland and forested hills with plenty of rivers, waterfalls and caves.

About 50,000 Huastec Indians live in the area between Ciudad Valles and Tamazunchale to the south. This area also has some of the main pre-Hispanic Huastec sites, though none remotely rivals the great sites of central, eastern and southern Mexico. There's a small Museo Regional in Ciudad Valles. Figures quoted for Ciudad Valles' population range from 23,000 to the 220,000 inscribed on a sign outside the town itself. Around 80,000 is a good guess.

Information & Orientation
The bus station is way out on the eastern edge of town. Local buses wait outside and drop you close to the central square. For part of their run they go along Highway 85 before turning left to approach the town centre. Hidalgo is the main street linking the central square and Highway 85, about seven blocks away to the east.

Places to Stay
If you're on a very tight budget and looking for nothing more than a bed, you could try the *Posada del Golfo* on the approach road to the bus station. It doesn't look like much but it advertises air-conditioning, hot water and 24-hour service.

In town there are two perfectly adequate places with little difference between them. *Hotel Rex* (tel 2-03-45) at Hidalgo 418 is 3½ blocks from the main plaza, clean and unspectacular. Singles/doubles with bath are US$4/4.75. *Hotel Piña* (tel 2-01-83) at Juárez 210, a little closer to the plaza, is also clean and slightly more modern but the rooms, around a courtyard where you can park, are no bigger. Prices are identical to the Rex's. Juárez is parallel to Hidalgo, one block north.

The *Hotel San Fernando* (tel 2-01-84) is on Highway 85 where it passes through the town, half a block north of the junction with Juárez. Its address is Boulevard 5 or 17 (take your pick). Singles/doubles are US$5/6.25. It's not as clean as the Piña or the Rex and isn't worth the extra cash.

A km north of the town along Highway 85, the *Hotel Valles* (tel 2-00-50) is a luxurious air-conditioned motel with singles/doubles around US$11/21. It has a swimming pool and a steakhouse-type restaurant as well as a 25-site campground/trailer park where full hook-ups cost around US$5.

Places to Eat

Pizza Bella Napoli next to the Hotel Piña at Juárez 210 does excellent spaghetti (US$1 to US$1.25) and pizzas (US$1 to US$3.50). For Mexican food, including comida corrida, try the *Restaurant Malibu* at Hidalgo 109, a few doors from the central plaza.

Getting There & Away

Road The 265 km west to San Luis Potosí are spectacular as the road rises from the edge of the coastal plain, across part of the Sierra Madre, to the altiplano central. But the road is twisting with a sometimes poor surface and takes about 4¼ hours' driving time. East to Tampico the road is in the same condition but straighter – the 142 km takes about two hours.

To the north, Ciudad Mante is 96 km away by Highway 85, and Ciudad Victoria 232 km. Southward on Highway 85, Pachuca (383 km away) is the only sizeable town before Mexico City. After Tamazunchale (105 km from Ciudad Valles) the road climbs to over 2000 metres to cross the Sierra Madre, exceeding 2500 metres shortly before

Pachuca (see the 'Near Mexico City – North & West' chapter). Ciudad Valles to Pachuca is about eight hours' driving time.

Bus Ciudad Valles is quite an important communications centre so it has reasonable services to most of the north-east quarter of Mexico from its Central de Autobuses on the east edge of town. There are few locales (buses which start their journeys here), however.

Transportes del Norte (1st class) has one direct service to Mexico City (US$5.75) daily, plus a bus to Ciudad Victoria (US$3), Monterrey (US$6.25) and Nuevo Laredo (US$9).

Omnibus de México (1st class) has three buses a day to Mexico City (US$5.75); four to Tampico (US$1.75); one each to Guanajuato (US$5.75) and Querétaro (US$5.50); and others to Tamuín (US$0.30), Dolores Hidalgo and Celaya.

Tres Estrellas de Oro (1st class) goes to Río Verde and San Luis Potosí (US$3.25) and to Tampico (US$1.75) twice daily; to Tepic, Mazatlán (US$13.50), Culiacán, Los Mochis, Hermosillo, Mexicali (US$32.25) and Tijuana (US$36.75) daily; and also to Guadalajara (US$7.50).

Oriente (2nd class) goes to Tampico (US$1.50) 25 times a day; Guadalajara (US$6.75) 12 times; San Luis Potosí (US$3) 17 times; Matamoros (US$6) six times; Reynosa (US$6) five times; Querétaro 22 times. It also goes to Tamuín (US$0.30), Río Verde (US$1.50) and Ciudad Victoria (US$2.50).

Vencedor Golfo (2nd class) goes to Tampico 34 times daily, to San Luis Potosí 19 times, to Guadalajara twice, also to Tamazunchale.

Flecha Roja (2nd class) goes to Mexico City (US$5.25) via Zimapán, Ixmiquilpan, Actopan and Pachuca 13 times a day.

Transportes Frontera (2nd class) has one local direct bus to Mexico City (US$5.25) each day and five other daily services via Tamazunchale and Actopán;

plus one bus daily to Matamoros (US$6); two each to Tampico (US$1.50) and Nuevo Laredo (US$8.25); four to Monterrey (US$5.75); and six to Ciudad Victoria (US$2.50).

Autotransportes Mante (2nd class) includes services to Matamoros (US$6), Monterrey (US$5.75), Ciudad Victoria (US$2.50) and Reynosa (US$6).

Approximate journey times: Mexico City 10 hours, Ciudad Victoria 3½ hours, Tampico 2½ hours, San Luis Potosí 4½ hours.

HUASTEC ARCHAEOLOGICAL SITES
Tamuín
This site lies seven km from the town of the same name, which is 28 km east of Ciudad Valles on Highway 70. The ruins are neither spectacular nor in very good condition, but this was one of the more important Huastec centres (it flourished from about 700 to 1200 AD) and is one of the few sites worth visiting at all. To reach it, go about one km east of the town on Highway 70, then turn south on a road marked 'San Vincente' for 5½ km. From a small sign indicating the zona arqueológica, it is about an 800-metre walk to the ruins.

The whole site spreads over about 170,000 square metres but the only cleared part is a plaza with platforms made of river stones on all four sides. In the middle of the plaza is a small platform, from the east side of which extends a low bench with two conical altars. The bench and altars, now covered with a palm roof, bear the remains of frescoes which may represent priests of Quetzalcóatl and probably date from the 8th or 9th century AD.

Buses run to Tamuín town from Tampico and Ciudad Valles. From there you have to walk or take a taxi.

Ebano
Here, 51 km east of Tamuín along Highway 70, only 62 km from Tampico, is a circular mound nearly 30 metres wide

dating from the Pánuco I and II periods (350 BC to 200 AD). It was probably a temple.

SOUTH OF CIUDAD VALLES
This south-east spur of the state runs into the eastern side of the Sierra Madre Oriental and has a high proportion of Nahua and Huastec Indians in its population. See the 'Near Mexico City – North & West' chapter for more on the road south from the Huasteca to Mexico City.

Tancanhuitz
Also called Ciudad Santos, this small town is in the heart of the area inhabited by the modern-day Huastecs. It's set in a narrow, tree-covered valley 52 km south of Ciudad Valles, three km east off Highway 85. There's a lively market on Sunday. Tancanhuitz and nearby Aquismón are major centres for the festivals of San Miguel Arcángel and the Virgen de Guadalupe on 28 and 29 September and 12 December respectively. There are some pre-Hispanic Huastec remains near Tampamolón, a few km east of Tancanhuitz.

Aquismón
A Huastec village 11 km north-west of Tancanhuitz, Aquismón holds its market on Saturday. In the wild country roundabout is the 105-metre Cascada de Tamul, the highest waterfall in the state, which reaches 300 metres wide in flood, and the Sótano de las Golondrinas (Pit of the Swallows), a 300-metre-deep hole in the ground which is home to tens of thousands of swallows and parakeets. Neither is accessible by vehicle.

Tamazunchale
This town of about 20,000 people, 95 km south of Ciudad Valles on Highway 85, is in a low-lying area of luxuriant tropical vegetation and renowned for its bird and butterfly life. There are a few hotels and restaurants here and a Sunday market. For the Day of the Dead (2 November) the

people spread confetti and marigold petals on the streets, leading to altars built by families for their dead.

Other Huasteca Festivals

Dances are held in Axtla, halfway between Tancanhuitz and Tamazunchale, for the festival of Santa Catalina on 24 November, and in Tanquián, 49 km east of Tancanhuitz, for San José on 18 March. Matlapa, 12 km north of Tamazunchale, holds a procession and dances for the festival of San Pedro on 28 June. In Xilitla, a hilltop village 16 km west of Axtla, an image of San Agustín is honoured with pilgrimages and dances on 27 August.

Central Mexico

THE CENTRAL OVERLAND ROUTE
El Paso/Ciudad Juárez to Mexico City

Unless you are starting your journey from the south-western region of the US, are heading to Chihuahua to catch the Copper Canyon train, or are intent on getting as quickly as possible to the Bajío Silver Cities, alternative routing is recommended for those travelling overland to Mexico City. The central route from El Paso/Ciudad Juárez to Mexico City is considerably less attractive than Mexico's Pacific coastal highways and takes substantially longer than the road from the Gulf coast. Nonetheless, if you decide to come this way, the central route has certain attributes.

South from Ciudad Juárez, the towns along the central route are good places to get away from gringos. You are certain to sharpen your Spanish, as there are few tourists in this region and relatively few locals speak English.

For scenic splendour, the train ride through the Copper Canyon is among the world's more spectacular rail trips. Cutting through majestic mountain scenery, the train runs between Chihuahua and the Pacific coastal port of Los Mochis.

As you wend your way south along the central route, you'll enter the heart of *caballero* (cowboy) country. This region, Mexico's 'Wild West', features men in cowboy hats as a colourful part of local dress; in the countryside, many of them are indeed cowpokes. In local politics the inheritance of Pancho Villa seems to live on, particularly in the rebellious state of Chihuahua where dissent against the ruling national political party, PRI, is strong. In the state capital, Chihuahua, it's easy to strike up conversations concerning grievances against the government.

Finally, as you near Mexico City, the Bajío's Silver Cities of Zacatecas and Guanajuato will awe you with their fine colonial architecture. Culturally rich and proud of their identity, the friendly citizens will make you feel welcome. As you walk amidst the architectural legacies of the colonial past, you will feel Mexico's turbulent yet vibrant history surround you – for unlike the tourist-oriented coastal zones, this is the real Mexico.

CIUDAD JUÁREZ
Population: 1,100,000

If you reach the El Paso/Ciudad Juárez (Texas/Mexico) border early enough, there is little reason not to immediately catch a southbound bus or train. While El Paso is a truly Hispanic city – in some areas you will need to begin acquiring your Spanish-language skills even before leaving the US as many residents speak no English – there is little to interest the visitor.

Although Ciudad Juárez is not as dull as El Paso, its allure for certain gringos lies in its cheap dental work and other dubious services. It's one of those frontier towns where inhabitants do what they can to survive while grafting onto their culture the worst aspects of gringoland across the border. It's not a pretty picture.

Nor is the climate all that hospitable. Ciudad Juárez is insufferably hot in summer; in winter wind may swirl off the desert, sweeping stinging sands in its wake. On the day I entered Juárez it started raining during a dust storm, thereby creating a mud storm! In a matter of moments, huge chunks of mud turned my rucksack from blue to grey.

Don't let this put you off Mexico. Just to the south, the atmosphere is far friendlier, the scenery more *simpático* and the climate relatively mild.

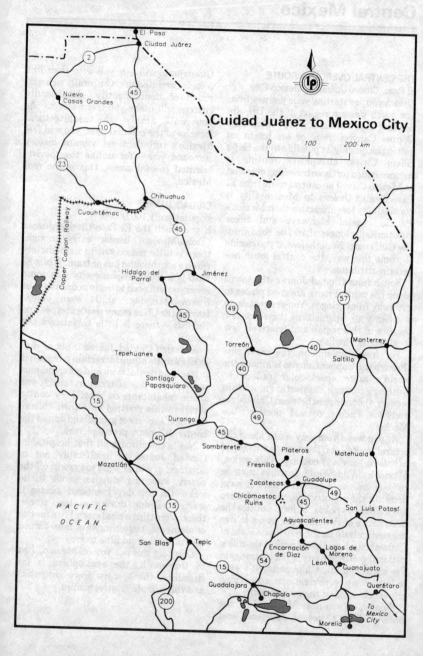

Cuidad Juárez to Mexico City

0   100   200 km

History

There is little left in Ciudad Juárez that reflects its colourful history. Because of its unique geographical location as part of the only easily traversable pass in the northern Sierra Madre mountains, Juárez was first settled as an Indian commercial centre situated along a major trading route. Enter the Spanish conquistadors. They too appreciated the strategic setting, building first a fortress and then a town here. The conquistadors called their outpost Paso del Norte. In the mid-19th century, when Benito Juárez's rebels were forced north by the legions of Maximilian, they briefly made the settlement their seat of government, changing its name to Juárez in the process.

Juárez continued to play a prominent historical role. In 1913 Pancho Villa pulled a Trojan Horse ruse, clandestinely bringing 2000 rebels in by train and taking the town. Based here on the border, Villa imported arms and ammunition from the US. Hence, Juárez became crucial to the ultimate success of the Revolution.

Today, most of Juárez's growth into the fourth largest Mexican city, with slightly more than a million inhabitants, is due to its proximity to the US. Its people provide a source of cheap labour, both for industries within the city churning out goods for export and for illicit employment across the border.

Orientation

Coming in from the El Paso airport, to reach downtown El Paso and bus connections to Ciudad Juárez you need not take an expensive taxi (approximately US$10) if you have the time and energy to walk to the bus stop. As you leave the airport, go straight out the door heading south. Walk past the Hilton Hotel and after a long, 1.3-km walk, you will see the Marriott Hotel. Keep walking to the main intersection, Montana St, and turn right, where you will spot a bus stop. Take any bus (they run every 20 to 30 minutes) for

US$0.75 and ask the driver to let you off at San Jacinto Park.

A block south of San Jacinto Park, just beyond the J C Penney Department Store, you will find the Camión Rojo (red) buses which for US$1 will transport you across the border to Ciudad Juárez. Or, if you want to save a dollar, walk south 30 minutes from San Jacinto Plaza and cross the Rio Grande into Mexico via either the Stanton St or Santa Fe St bridges; immigration is at the end of the Stanton St bridge. There is a 5c charge to enter Mexico on foot.

Information

Immigration As long as you don't venture more than 32 km south of Juárez, you won't need a tourist card. Travellers may move freely between El Paso and Juárez (although to return to the US you must be able to show proof of US citizenship or a visa for non-nationals).

For those moving deeper into Mexico, a stop at the immigration office at the foot of the Stanton St Bridge on the Mexican side is required to secure your tourist card. If you want the 180-day maximum, be prepared to show sufficient funds to cover your stay. The immigration office is open 24 hours a day (I entered at night and had to coax a reluctant bureaucrat away from his card game). If you are a US citizen and experience some tourist card problems, call the American Consulate at 13-40-48.

Tourist Office Information brochures and maps of El Paso are available at the airport, the Civic Center's Visitors Bureau next to the Trailways bus station and a tourist office across from the Greyhound bus depot on Santa Fe and Mills Sts. The Gardner Hotel at 311 East Franklin St also has a map.

In Ciudad Juárez, you will find the government tourist office near the immigration checkpoint on Malecón between Juárez and Lerdo. Look for it in the basement of the high-rise government building. Although the staff aren't

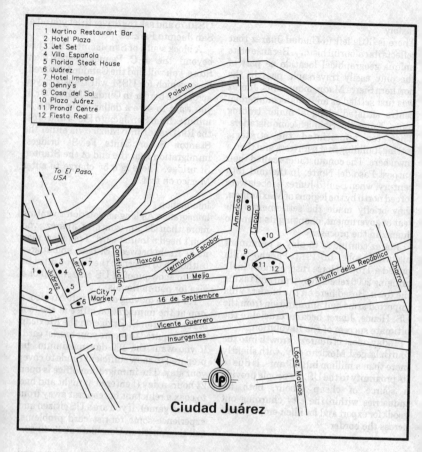

1 Martino Restaurant Bar
2 Hotel Plaza
3 Jet Set
4 Villa Española
5 Florida Steak House
6 Juárez
7 Hotel Impala
8 Denny's
9 Casa del Sol
10 Plaza Juárez
11 Pronaf Centre
12 Fiesta Real

Paisano

To El Paso,
USA

Constitución

Tlaxcala

Hermanos Escobar

I Mejia

Américas

Lincoln

P Triunfo della República

Charro

City
Market

16 de Septiembre

Vicente Guerrero

Insurgentes

López Mateos

Ciudad Juárez

particularly knowledgeable and their English is limited, they will give you a city map complete with hotel and restaurant listings. The office is open Monday to Friday from 9 am to 2 pm, and 4 to 7 pm.

Money There are banks on Avenida 16 de Septiembre as well as close to the bus station, but they are only open Monday to Friday, 9 am to 1 pm. If you can't make banking hours, there are plenty of casas de cambio in the tourist area and their rates are not too much lower than at the banks.

Post The post office is at the intersection of Lerdo and Ignacio Peña. Hours are 8.30 am to 7.30 pm Monday to Saturday.

Consulate If you are having tourist card/visa problems and are an American citizen, call 13-40-48. For other emergencies, phone (915) 525-6060.

Things to See
There's frankly little of note to see in Ciudad Juárez. Most visitors are here on day trips for cheap dental care, shopping, track betting or prostitution. If you are going anywhere further south, you will find better-quality crafts at significantly lower prices.

Museo Chamizal
Museo Chamizal is known to many locals by its old name, Museo Arqueológico. It's in Parque Chamizal and, given Juárez's impossible-to-decipher bus system, best reached by taxi. Admission is 5c but the artefacts on exhibit don't warrant a visit unless you have absolutely nothing else to do with your time. Although there are some ancient statues and pottery on display, the museum has more copies than originals. Hours are 9 am to 6.30 pm daily.

Pronaf Museum
The Pronaf Museum in the heart of Juárez's Pronaf gringo shopping centre has even fewer artefacts of interest than Museo Chamizal. It too is best reached by taxi (ask for Museo Pronaf). The museum's hours are 10 am to 7 pm, closed Monday.

Old Municipal Palace
The Old Municipal Palace on 16 de Septiembre is the last vestige of colonial architecture in Ciudad Juárez, the rest of the structures falling into the category of modern hideous.

Places to Stay - bottom end
The *Juárez* (tel 2-99-85) at 143 North Lerdo charges US$6 single, US$7 double. The *Hotel Plaza* (tel 2-68-61) at downtown's Cathedral Square is slightly preferable at about US$7 single, US$8 double.

Places to Stay - middle
El Paso Although the Impala in Ciudad Juárez offers better accommodation for the money, the *Gardner Hotel* (tel 532-3661) is the top budget choice for those who do not want to overnight in Juárez. Located at 311 East Franklin near the intersection of Stanton, it's well situated, a few blocks from the major bus terminals and an easy walk to the Camión Rojo buses bound for Ciudad Juárez. The seedy-looking exterior of the Gardner, a building listed on the El Paso Historic Register, gives credibility to the claim that the notorious bank robber of the 1930s, John Dillinger, stayed here shortly before he was nailed by the FBI in Tucson. But don't let the outside put you off; the hotel's interior is quite clean.

The Gardner's dorms, US$8.50 with shared bath, have earned the hotel the status of an American Youth Hostel (you don't need a card). When I was there the dorms were empty and most of the hotel's residents were senior citizens staying in private rooms. Clean rooms without bath cost US$14 single, US$18 double. Rooms with private bath run US$16 single, US$20 double. The management has a safe to lock up your valuables.

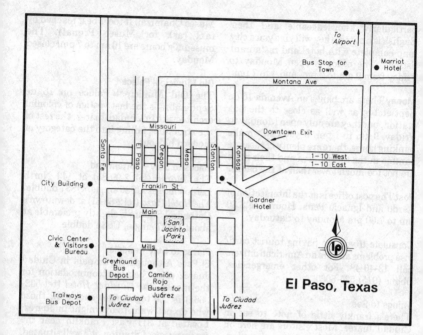

El Paso, Texas

Ciudad Juárez Far and away your best choice for moderate-priced comfort and safety in Juárez is the *Hotel Impala* (tel 2-04-18), two minutes' walk from immigration and the Stanton St Bridge in the first block of Lerdo 828. Proprietor Virginia Campbell is most helpful and all of the 38 rooms have air-conditioning, hot water and TV. Each floor of the hotel has a purified-water dispenser. Singles cost US$10, doubles US$12.

Places to Stay – top end
Those seeking luxury accommodation in Juárez should consider two of the hotels in the Pronaf shopping area: the *Fiesta Real* right at the Pronaf Center (tel 3-00-47) or the *Plaza Juárez* (tel 3-13-10) on Lincoln at Coyoacan. Both have swimming pools, restaurants and bars. Air-conditioned rooms with colour TVs cost US$35 single, US$40 double at each hotel.

Places to Eat
In El Paso, the only cheap eateries are the typical US fast-food emporiums such as the ubiquitous *McDonald's* and *Burger King*. In Juárez, the café of the *Hotel Impala* offers good, inexpensive Mexican and gringo fare. Near Lerdo, at 184 González, you'll find reasonably priced Mexican dinners and breakfasts at *Antojitos La Herradura*. There's a clean *Denny's* at 1345 Lincoln Avenue (catch a taxi from the Pronaf Center).

There are cheap *taquerías* everywhere in Juárez, but exercise discretion if you are just entering Mexico. It's best to build up some immunity to new bacilli for a few days before you become adventurous with street fare.

For those willing to spend more money, there are high-gloss eateries on Avenida Juárez Norte like *Martino Restaurant* at 412, *Villa Española* nearby where Juárez intersects Colón, *Florida Steak House* at 301 and *Jet Set* at 668. If you are shopping at the Pronaf and willing to spend the bucks, *Casa Del Sol* offers Mexican and Continental cuisine accompanied by strolling mariachis.

Entertainment

The Plaza de Toros, four km from the city's centre, stages bullfights on an irregular basis, but usually on Sundays or US holidays. Ask at the tourist office if one is being held while you are in town. Every Sunday, the Charrería holds rodeos at the stadium on Charro near República. Wednesday to Sunday, the Juárez Racetrack on Vicente Guerrero holds dog and (weather permitting) horse races.

There are plenty of bars on Avenida Juárez exhibiting what border towns are infamous for. Watch your wallets.

Things to Buy

The primary shopping emporium, the Pronaf Center, is about three km from the Mexican side of the border. Reminiscent of a US shopping mall, Pronaf boasts some quality crafts amidst its sea of junk, but at prices significantly higher than elsewhere in Mexico. Unless this is your last stop and you must bring back a knick-knack for Aunt Tilly, don't waste your time here.

Getting There & Away

Border See the 'Orientation' section for transport from El Paso airport and the border crossing.

Air There are connecting or direct flights to El Paso, just across the border in Texas, from almost all major US cities.

Bus Buses connect virtually all urban centres of the US with El Paso. Both the Greyhound and Trailways bus depots are within a few blocks' walk of the Camión Rojo buses running regularly to Juárez. While it is possible to go directly from the El Paso Greyhound station to Chihuahua

via the Transportes Chihuahenses bus company, there's the small risk that a delay at Mexican immigration might lead to your bus departing without you. An alternative is to catch your southbound bus from Juárez's bus station.

Heading for points south, the two main 1st-class bus companies in north central Mexico are Omnibus and Transportes Chihuahenses. There are advantages and drawbacks to each line. Omnibus is faster, but also (according to some Mexicans), less safe. On the other hand, while Omnibus rarely picks up standees en route, Chihuahenses often does, making for a longer, hotter ride.

Because Juárez's local bus system is so difficult to figure out, it is recommended that you bargain for a taxi to take you to the long-distance bus station at Triunfo de la República and López Mateos. This should cost about US$3. If you're well-versed in Spanish you might be able to

Caballero

catch a local bus to the Central de Autobuses from Avenida 16 de Septiembre near the market. From the Central de Autobuses, buses run regularly to Chihuahua (every 20 to 30 minutes, US$5), Nuevo Casas Grandes (six daily, US$4), Mexico City (eight daily, US$26) and virtually every other major centre in Mexico.

Rail Juárez's train station is an easy walk from the Mexican side of the Stanton St Bridge. Just keep walking straight on Lerdo some 11 blocks, but note that Lerdo's name changes to Corona. You will find the Ferrocarriles Nacionales station at the intersection of Corona and Insurgentes.

Getting Around
Unless your Spanish is superb – and even then – the Juárez bus system is impossible to understand in this spread-out city. Bargaining for taxis the short time you are here will save you much time and trouble. A taxi should cost you no more than US$3 from the Mexican side of the border to the long-distance Central de Autobuses.

CASAS GRANDES & NUEVO CASAS GRANDES
Although Nuevo Casas Grandes, four hours south-west of Ciudad Juárez, is a more comfortable place to stay your first night in Mexico than Juárez, the city of Chihuahua is on a more direct route to Mexico City and may be a preferable first stop for those in a hurry. The only reason to visit Nuevo Casas Grandes are the ruins of Paquimé, adjacent to the small town of Casas Grandes. While Paquimé is the region's major archaeological site, it is hardly in the league of the spectacular sites to the south.

Information & Orientation
Set in a green valley certain to delight your eyes after the desolation of the surrounding desert, Nuevo Casas Grandes is a modern town where it is relatively easy to get around on foot. Although there is no

tourist office, you will easily find your way about.

Money Change money at the International, open from 9 am to 1.30 pm, at the intersection of Obregón and 5 de Mayo.

Post You will find the post office a block from 5 de Mayo at 16 de Septiembre and Madero.

Paquimé Ruins
Buses running to the start of the Casas Grandes trail to the ruins leave from a stop on Constitución a block from where it intersects 5 de Mayo. The buses run every half hour when the ruins are open, daily from 9 am to 5 pm. They may be distinguished by a 'Casas Grandes/Col Juárez' sign on their sides. The eight-km journey takes about 15 minutes.

You will be let off at old Casas Grandes' zócalo where a sign will direct you for the 10-minute walk to the ruins. Before leaving old Casas Grandes, sit in the tranquil town's zócalo to enjoy a spell of Mexican small-town life. This tiny town is a good place to wind down after hard travelling.

The walk to the ruins is unshaded, so consider bringing a hat. While you are supposed to pay a few pesos admission at the site, you may find that Paquimé's caretaker is either absent or asleep.

Set beneath the attractive backdrop of the Sierra Madre, Paquimé was the major Indian trading settlement in northern Mexico between 1000 and 1200 AD. Agriculture flourished here as well and poultry (largely turkeys) was raised in adobe cages to protect the fowl from harsh climatic extremes.

Two major cultural influences shaped the architecture of Paquimé. The initial settlement had adobe structures similar to Pueblo structures of the US Southwest. As the city grew in prominence, it was influenced through trade by southern Indian civilisations, particularly the Toltec. This contact introduced the

Panquimé Ruins

inhabitants of Paquimé to Toltec architectural designs of religious, sporting and agricultural structures. You may see here today this interesting legacy of religious step pyramids, a *pelota* (ball) court, and part of the network of canals that once made the area fertile.

Despite fortified walls and unique interior water systems, including hidden cisterns, Paquimé fell prey to outside invaders (some say Apaches) in 1340. The city was sacked, burned and abandoned, and its once great structures were left alone for more than 600 years. Unfortunately, after the site was partially excavated in the early 1970s, exposure to the elements led to erosion of the structures; during your visit you may see work crews patching Paquimé with adobe.

Paquimé's inhabitants were great potters and jewellers. While some of their finest works are displayed in Mexico City's National Museum of Anthropology, you may see some of the exceptional animal-shaped Casas Grandes pottery with striking red, brown or black geometric designs over a cream background on

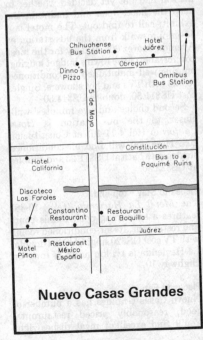

Nuevo Casas Grandes

exhibit at Nuevo Casas Grandes' Motel Piñon (see 'Places to Stay').

Places to Stay – bottom end

Hotel Juárez (tel 4-02-33) has a convenient location a few doors from the bus depot at Obregón 110, but that's its only attribute. The place is fairly decrepit and overpriced. Singles cost US$5, doubles US$6. Showers may only occasionally be hot and there's no extra charge for the *cucarachas*.

Places to Stay – middle

In Nuevo Casas Grandes moderately priced hotels are your best bets, with the *Motel Piñon* (tel 4-06-55) at the top of the list. The late Luis Piñon was a dedicated collector of Paquimé's artefacts until the government took control of the site in 1970. Señor Piñon displayed his fine collection in a small museum next to his motel. Shortly after Señor Piñon's death, his son had not yet decided whether to keep the hotel open and maintain the exhibit; call to find out. The motel is a 15-minute walk from the bus station at Avenida Juárez 605. It is by far the most comfortable of the town's budget lodging, offering well-maintained air-conditioned rooms with TVs and hot showers. Singles cost US$11.50, doubles US$14.50

Second choice and five minutes' walk closer to the bus station is *Hotel California* (tel 4-11-10) at Constitución 209. Here you will find air-conditioned singles with bath at US$11.25 and doubles at US$22.50.

Places to Stay – top end

The *Motel La Hacienda* (tel 4-10-48) features a swimming pool, tennis court and restaurant. Its air-conditioned rooms with TV cost US$20 single, US$24 double. La Hacienda is 1½ km north of town on Highway 10.

Places to Eat

Nuevo Casas Grandes has a number of good, reasonably priced restaurants. You'll find excellent meat dishes right next to Motel Piñon at *México Español*. The owners are from Argentina; their specialities are grilled meats. Good standard Mexican fare is available at the *Constantino*, across the street and two blocks toward 5 de Mayo from Motel Piñon.

If your tastes run slightly to the exotic, try the little Mormon-run *La Boquilla Restaurant* at 5 de Mayo 111b (look closely or you'll miss it – it's not far from Avenida Juárez). La Boquilla serves up shrimp and turtle (!) tacos. Those with more conventional palates will find *Dinno's Pizza* at the intersection of 5 de Mayo and Obregón convenient to the bus depots. For those watching their pesos more than their palates, there are a host of cheap *taquerías* on Obregón around the bus station.

Entertainment

Other than standard Mexican film fare, there's little entertainment in Nuevo Casas Grandes. On Friday and Saturday, you may engage in a bit of contemporary anthropology by observing youthful interactions at the *Discoteca Los Faroles*, across from Motel Piñon at Juárez 604.

Getting There & Away

Bus Buses run regularly to and from Ciudad Juárez (about four hours, US$3.50) and Chihuahua (about 4½ hours, US$4.75). Omnibus is generally faster than Chihuahenses.

Rail Trains do run to Nuevo Casas Grandes, but they are too slow to consider as an alternative to the bus because they stop in every dry-gulch pueblo in the desert.

CHIHUAHUA

Population: 800,000

Although Chihuahua is a comfortable, prosperous city, most travellers find little purpose in staying here other than to catch the Barranca del Cobre train or to overnight during their journey to points south. Nonetheless, there are a few sights

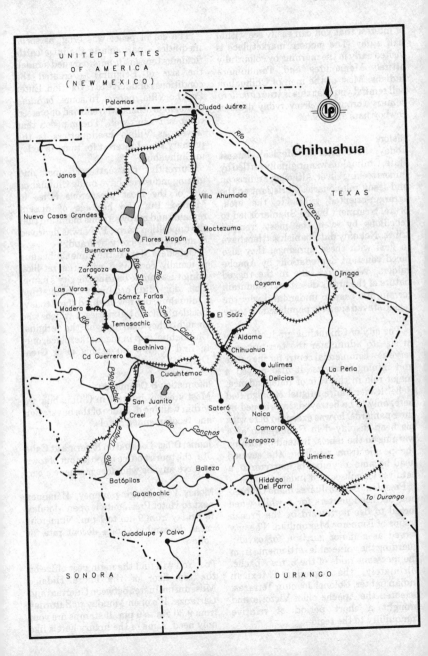

of interest that you can easily see within half a day. The modern marketplace is visited early in the morning by colourfully attired Mennonites and Tarahumara Indians. Most of the men of Chihuahua will remind you that this is true *caballero* country through their everyday dress of cowboy hats and boots.

History

Today the capital of Mexico's largest state, Chihuahua was originally settled by miners seeking silver. Although Franciscan and Jesuit missionaries Christianised the agrarian-oriented tribes in the area, brutal treatment by the Spaniards led to rebellions by even the most tranquil tribes. Not only did Spanish settlers have to deal with these uprisings, they also faced constant depredations by Apache raiders. When you take in the rugged nature of the area's desert and mountain terrain, it's easy to understand why the region stayed sparsely populated for some time.

The city of Chihuahua gradually grew in size to administer the territory and serve as a commercial centre for the cattle and mining interests. It also played a major role in the War of Independence. Rebel leader Padre Miguel Hidalgo fled here, only to be betrayed. Imprisoned by the Spaniards, he was executed here with his head displayed in Guanajuato as a warning to the rebels. Instead of turning the people from rebellion, the severed head became a symbol of martyrdom, a catalyst for subsequent independence.

President Benito Juárez made Chihuahua his headquarters for a while when forced to flee northward by the French troops of Emperor Maximilian. The city served as a major garrison for cavalry guarding the vulnerable settlements from the incessant raids of the fierce Apache. Ultimately, the legendary Mexican Indian fighter, Colonel Joaquín Terrazas, defeated the Apache chief Victoria and brought a short period of relative tranquillity to the region.

The era of peace was brief, as social inequities – particularly the huge cattle fiefdoms (one *latifundista* owned a ranch the size of Belgium) – created the conditions conducive to revolution. Enter Pancho Villa, patriot to some, *bandido supremo* to others, who enlisted oppressed *campesinos* in revolt. The mansion that served as Villa's headquarters is the primary site of interest for tourists today in Chihuahua.

Currently, the cattle, timber and mining industries have made Chihuahua one of the most prosperous cities in Mexico. But the heritage of dissent remains and many citizens maintain that the opposition party, PAN, was deprived of an election victory by fraud.

Outside of Mexico, the name Chihuahua is usually correlated with the rat-like, miniature canine bearing the city's name. The dog did originally come from Chihuahua, but few are bred there today. Residents like to tell stories of gringos who thought they had bought the 'original Chihuahua' pup in the marketplace, only to find it grow up as big as a Great Dane.

Information & Orientation

Most areas of interest in Chihuahua are within walking distance of the bus station and recommended hotels.

Tourist Office Located on Reforma at Calle 31a, the tourist office is too far out of town to serve anyone who does not have a car.

Money For changing money, Bánamex next to Hotel Presidente is open Monday to Friday from 9 am to 1 pm. Numerous casas de cambio give a decent rate for dollars.

Post You will find the main post office on the top floor of the Padre Hidalgo Museum on Juárez between Guerrero and Carranza. It's open Monday to Saturday from 9.30 am to 6 pm. If stamps are your only need, some of the luxury hotels like

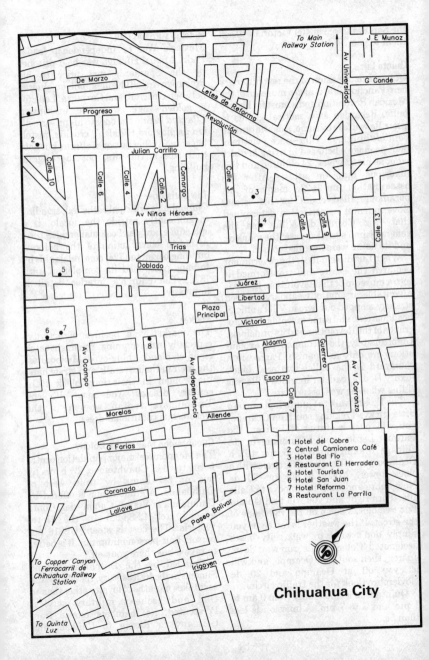

1 Hotel del Cobre
2 Central Camionera Café
3 Hotel Bal Flo
4 Restaurant El Herradero
5 Hotel Tourista
6 Hotel San Juan
7 Hotel Reforma
8 Restaurant La Parrilla

Chihuahua City

the San Francisco at 409 Victoria will sell them to you.

Quinta Luz

Quinta Luz, mansion of the revolutionary hero Pancho Villa, is also a museum of the Mexican Revolution and a must for history buffs. Regarded as a tactical genius in guerrilla warfare by some, a charlatan and *bandido* by others, Villa – once a victim of debt peonage – believed in living *la dulce vida*, as his 22 wives, 24 children and this luxurious mansion attest. After his assassination in 1923, many of his paramours filed claim for his estate. Governmental investigation determined that Luz Corral de Villa was the generalissimo's legal spouse; the mansion and its name were awarded to her.

When Luz died in 1981, the government acquired the estate and transformed it into a museum of the Revolution. Inside is a veritable arsenal of weaponry, penned strategy mapped out here in Villa's official headquarters, and some exceptional photographs of the Revolution and its principals. Unfortunately, the accompanying explanations are only in Spanish. Parked in a courtyard is the bullet-spattered black luxury Dodge roadster in which Villa was riding when he was assassinated.

The 1½-km walk to Quinta Luz can be a little tricky. Trekking south on Ocampo, you will pass a statue of Bolivar, the Parque Lerdo and a monument to Ojinaga. Making sure that you are still on Ocampo, you will see a traffic circle with a clock tower. Make a left on 20 de Noviembre and walk two blocks to Calle 10a. Turn right and you will find Quinta Luz two blocks down on the right side of the street. If the weather is rotten or you simply don't want to walk, city buses designated 'Colonía Dale' run west down Juárez, then south on Ocampo, and will let you off at Ocampo and 20 de Noviembre (look for the traffic circle).

Quinta Luz is open daily from 9 am to 1 pm and 3 to 7 pm. Admission is less than 5c.

Hidalgo's Prison Cell

Mexico's War of Independence leader Padre Miguel Hidalgo was held prisoner by the Spaniards just prior to his execution in 1811, in a jail on Juárez between Guerrero and Carranza. Look for a golden eagle with the inscription *Libertad* to find the door to his prison cell. On display are Hidalgo's crucifix, pistol, letters and other personal effects, but note that this is the site, not the original building.

The Cathedral

Chihuahua's principal cathedral, standing magnificently astride the zócalo, is a splendid example of colonial architecture. Although construction of the baroque building began in 1724, continual raids by Indians postponed its completion until 1826. The church's interior detail is impressive.

Market

The market is a beehive of activity, especially in the morning. You might catch sight of blonde, blue-eyed Mennonites, the men in their overalls and straw hats, the women in their long black 19th-century dresses. You may also spy Tarahumara Indian women in the picturesque traditional dress.

Cuauhtémoc Mennonite Colony

The Mennonites' major population centre is the town of Cuauhtémoc, 2½ hours by bus or 3½ hours by train west of Chihuahua. A guided tour is offered by Chihuahua's Viajes Cañon del Cobre agency (tel 12-88-93) in the Hotel Victoria. The cost is steep: US$16 per person, four-person minimum. It is better to take a bus there yourself.

Founded by the Dutchman Menno Simonis in the 16th century, the Mennonite sect takes no oaths of loyalty other than to God and eschews military service. Persecuted, its members moved from Germany to Russia to Canada, and thousands settled in the tolerant, post-revolutionary Mexico of the 1920s.

In Cuauhtémoc, you will see Mennonites in traditional dress, driving their horse-drawn buggies and speaking their own dialect of German. They lead a spartan existence, speak little Spanish, and marry only amongst themselves. Their substantial population increase in Mexico has led many to emigrate to Paraguay and Brazil. The Mexicans praise the Mennonites' hard work and cheese and meat products (especially sausage), but find the austere life style and work ethic hard to fathom.

Places to Stay - bottom end

By far the best of the cheapies is Hotel San Juan (tel 2-81-67) at Victoria 823. An older hotel with a courtyard, the San Juan is heated and offers singles with bath for US$7.25 and doubles for US$8.50. The proprietor, Señor José Talámes, speaks some English and is helpful. The San Juan is less than 15 minutes' walk or a US$0.75 taxi ride from the bus station.

If you are absolutely exhausted after arriving by bus, the Hotel del Cobre (tel 5-17-58) across from the bus station on Calle 10a at Progreso offers clean singles with air-conditioning, TV and bath for US$6.50 single, US$8 double.

The Hotel Tourista at Juárez 817 has small, basic but clean singles with bath for US$5.50 and doubles for US$7.25.

If you're really hurting for cash, Hotel Reforma (tel 2-58-08) at Victoria 814 is marginally acceptable. Here spartan rooms run US$3 single and US$3.75 double.

Places to Stay - middle

The Hotel Bal Flo (tel 16-03-00) at the intersection of Niños Héroes and Calle 5a 702 offers pleasant air-conditioned rooms with bath, charging US$9.50 for singles, US$13 for doubles and US$17 for triples. Television in the room is US$1 extra. The Bal Flo is owned by Balthazar Flores, who speaks English fluently and can tell you a good deal about Chihuahua. The hotel is a 15-minute walk or US$0.75 taxi ride from the bus station.

Places to Stay - top end

Chihuahua's deluxe hotel is the Hyatt Exelaris (tel 6-60-60) at Niños Héroes and Independencia. Other three-star hotels are the Castel Sicomoro (tel 3-54-45) at Ortiz Mena 411, El Presidente (tel 6-06-06) at the zócalo-Libertad 9, and the San Francisco (tel 6-75-50) at Victoria 504. All of these hotels are in the US$40 to US$50 range.

Places to Eat

For good standard breakfasts and Mexican fare, try the cafeterias of the hotels Bal Flo, San Juan and Del Cobre. Surprisingly good, especially for breakfasts, is the Central Camionera café. This is a real cafeteria where you stand in line - the service is good, the food cheap and filling. Two other spots for decent breakfasts are the Comedor Familiar at Victoria 830 and Mí Café at Victoria 807. Or try Lonchería Jiménez just outside the train station.

There are two excellent places for meat dishes. Near the Bal Flo is El Herradero on Calle 5a between Trias and Niños Héroes. A short walk from Hotel San Juan is La Parrilla at Victoria 420, known for its barbecued meats. Vegetarians and those in the mood for pizza will find Dinno's Pizza on Independencia across from the Hyatt to their taste.

Entertainment

For bullfights, go on Sunday to the Plaza de Toros at the intersection of Canal and Cuauhtémoc. Some Saturdays and Sundays, you will find rodeos scheduled at the Lienza Charro in the western part of the town. Evenings, there are discos at the Hyatt, El Presidente and Victoria.

Things to Buy

For Tarahumara Indian crafts, ponchos, sweaters and silver jewellery, visit the Museo de Artes y Industrias Populares at Reforma 5 (closed Monday), and Arte

Popular Mexicano at Aldama 710. For jewellery, try Artesanías y Gemas Naturales de México at Calle 10 3019.

Getting There & Away

Bus Buses link Chihuahua with virtually every part of Mexico. There are regular departures to Juárez (five hours, US$5), Nuevas Casas Grandes (4½ hours, US$4.75) and Mexico City, among other destinations, by the nine companies that share the Camionera Central.

Rail There are two train stations. The Barranca del Cobre Station is off Ocampo nearly two km south-west of the zócalo, a block from the prison. To get to the station, take a 'Col Rosalía' or 'Sta Rosa' bus and get out at the prison – it looks like a medieval castle, you can't miss it. Walk behind the prison to the station. To make certain of getting a ticket the morning of your departure, you might consider taking a taxi. The domed Vistatrens leave daily at 7 am. The regular Mixto train departs at 7.20 am on Monday, Wednesday and Friday.

The regular Ferrocarriles Nacionales Juárez-Mexico City station is accessible via Granjas Colón or Villa Colón buses running from the centre. Since you can't see the station from the road, ask the driver to let you know when you have reached it. If you are headed by rail south to Zacatecas, there is a nightly 11.25 pm departure.

Getting Around

All of the recommended sites and hotels are only a walk from the hotels and bus stations. There is good city bus service when you need it, and taxi fares are reasonable if you bargain.

SOUTH FROM CHIHUAHUA

Ciudad Jiménez

Some travellers driving south from El Paso spend a long day on the road, overnighting in the small town of Ciudad Jiménez, 220 km (138 miles) south of Chihuahua.

At Jiménez, the highway branches into Highway 49, the more direct route for Zacatecas and Mexico City, and Highway 45, a longer route south which leads to Durango. If you are travelling Highway 49, there's little reason to stop in the towns of Torreón or Gómez Palacio, whose hideous contemporary architecture resulted from destruction during the Revolution.

Places to Stay Although Jiménez has little to interest the visitor, its modern, moderately priced *Motel Florido* offers pleasant air-conditioned singles for US$8.50, doubles for US$10.50. Or camp here for US$3 per vehicle. The Motel Florido also has a reasonably priced restaurant.

Hidalgo del Parral

For those en route to Durango, Hidalgo del Parral is a town rich in revolutionary history. Believing that the infamous revolutionary Pancho Villa would sooner or later pass by a house on Calle Gabino Barreda in his 1919 Dodge, nine conspirators staked it out for 103 days. On 20 July 1923 Villa approached the house with his six bodyguards, and the assassins opened fire. While five of his bodyguards lay mortally wounded, Villa, bleeding profusely from 17 bullet wounds, crawled alongside his black automobile. With his last gasp, he took aim and shot one of his assassins.

Seven conspirators escaped into the desert. Their leader, Jesús Salas Barraza, calmly gave himself up to Parral's authorities, saying he had planned the assassination because he cared about Mexico's future and believed Villa was only out for his own gain with dictatorship in mind. Apparently the revolutionary government concurred, for although Salas was sentenced to 20 years, he was released from jail a few months after the trial.

The *campesinos* of the state of Chihuahua, many of whom Villa had led into battle, saw the *generalissimo* as a great advocate of the people. A few *caballeros* can recall that 30,000 mourners attended Villa's funeral in Parral, where Villa remains a folk hero. It's easy to find his grave in the town's cemetery because it's the only one without a cross.

Parral was best known for centuries as a mining centre where enslaved Indians in the 16th century, and later their descendants, mined the rich veins of silver, copper and lead. As a measure of thanks for the area's mineral wealth, the people of the region contributed funds for the building of the Church of Our Lady of Fatima – Iglesia de Nuestra Señora de Fatima. Appropriately, the church was constructed right down to the pews with locally mined minerals: silver, lead, gold, zinc, manganese and copper.

Another Parral church worth noting is the Church of the Virgin of the Thunderbolt – Iglesia de la Virgen del Rayo. It has intriguing gargoyles on its roof and is festooned with figurines in its niches.

Parral was occupied by the army of Napoleon III during the interventionist period. Students of Mexican history can find the site of a fort once occupied by French troops on El Cerro de la Cruz.

Places to Stay Few travellers overnight in Parral, most moving on to Durango. Those who choose to stay will find cheap, marginally acceptable lodging at the *Centro Viajero* (tel 2-01-48) at Coronado 4. Spartan singles cost US$5, doubles US$6.50.

DURANGO

Population: 340,000

Don't be too put off by the modernisation you will see as you come by bus from the outskirts of the city. Proceed immediately to Durango's delightful old central plaza, where you'll discover fine colonial architecture. Some 14 km from the city's centre you can visit the sets of many Westerns, some of which starred John Wayne and were directed by the legendary John Ford.

In summary, given its superb architecture and relaxed atmosphere, Durango is a good place to break a journey.

History

Founded in 1523 by the conquistador Don Francisco de Ibarra, and named after the Spanish city of his birth, Durango became prominent thanks to the mineral wealth in the region. Just north of the city, the Cerro del Mercado – a mountain of iron – is one of the world's largest iron deposits. The Río Tunal's capacity to irrigate soils also encouraged Durango's growth. Farmers reap excellent harvests of wheat, corn, cotton and barley.

More recently, the city's prosperity has increased due to the timber industry's harvest of paper products from the forested slopes of the Sierra Madre. Also, the dusty 'Western' scenery in the vicinity leads Hollywood to construct 'Wild West' towns here for its movies. When films are in production, numerous local craftspeople, carpenters and extras are employed.

Information & Orientation

Virtually all sights are within walking distance of each other.

Tourist Office To reach Durango's tourist office from the principal plaza, walk three blocks west down 5 de Febrero and then look left on Zaragoza. However, the staff do not speak English.

Money For currency exchange you will find a Bancomer just off the Plaza de Armas, open Monday to Friday from 9 am to 1.30 pm.

Post To reach the post office, go four blocks north of the plaza to Constitución 213. Hours are Monday to Friday from 8 am to 8 pm.

Festivals

Feria Nacional Every 8 July, the celebration of Durango's 1563 founding has become what is said to be one of the most exciting

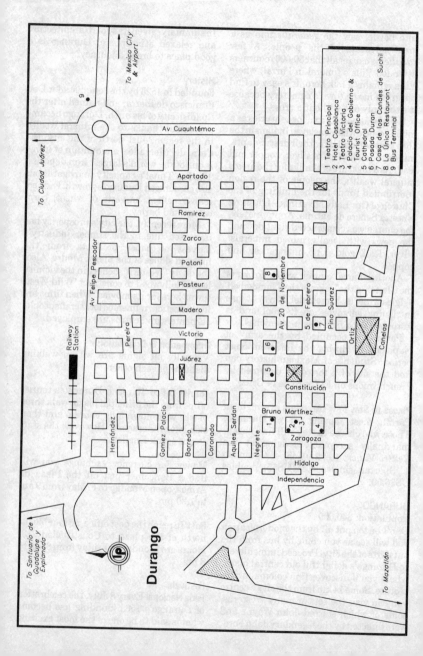

To Mexico City & Airport

To Ciudad Juárez

Av Cuauhtémoc

Apartado

Ramirez

Zarco

Patoni

Pasteur

Madero

Victoria

Juárez

Constitución

Bruno Martínez

Zaragoza

Hidalgo

Independencia

Av Felipe Pescador

Railway Station

Hernández

Gomez Palacio

Barreda

Coronado

Aquiles Serdan

Negrete

Av 20 de Noviembre

5 de Febrero

Pino Suarez

Ortiz

Conelos

Pereira

To Santuario de
Guadalupe y
Esplanada

Durango

To Mazatlán

1 Teatro Principal
2 Hotel Casablanca
3 Teatro Victoria
4 Palacio del Gobierno &
   Tourist Office
5 Cathedral
6 Posada Duran
7 Casa de los Condes de Suchil
8 La Única Restaurant
9 Bus Terminal

festivals in Mexico. The fiesta brings some of the country's most famous musicians, bands and dancers to perform against a colourful backdrop of local industrial, agrarian and artistic exhibits. All hotels are booked in advance, so if you hope to spend the night, make reservations early.

Cathedral

On the principal plaza, the Plaza de Armas, stands the town's baroque cathedral. Under construction from 1695 to 1750, the cathedral's twin domed bell towers dominate the plaza. Although the interior decor cannot compare with the exterior architecture, the cathedral is a fine example of northern Mexican colonial construction. Facing the cathedral on Sunday, musicians perform on the plaza's bandstand while locals promenade.

Teatro Principal

From the cathedral, walk down 20 de Noviembre and on your right you will see a beautifully constructed 19th-century Teatro Principal which has succumbed to cultural hard times and now functions as a movie theatre.

Palacio del Gobierno

From the Teatro Principal, go south on Bruno Martínez and beyond the Teatro Victoria, on the north side of another plaza, you will see the Palacio del Gobierno. Built on the estate of a Spanish mine owner, the Palacio was expropriated by the government following the War of Independence. Inside are colourful murals depicting state history and the economic activities of local residents.

University of Durango

On the west side of the plaza is the University of Durango. Once a Jesuit monastery, the university is a good place to meet young people, some of whom enjoy exchanging political ideas.

Casa de los Condes de Suchil

From the university, take 5 de Febrero back to the Casa de Los Condes de Suchil. This mansion is a striking example of early 17th-century Hispanic colonial architecture. Its detail and carvings have been well cared for and you can easily picture it housing the Spanish governor of Durango, the Conde de Suchil. For a time the mansion's ornate façade fronted the region's local court of Inquisition. Today the mansion serves a more commercial function, in addition to its landmark status; the Casa has a portion of its courtyard given over to upscale boutiques.

Market

The town's main market is easily reached by continuing down 5 de Febrero from the Casa de los Condes.

University Museum

Worth avoiding is the University Museum at the intersection of Pasteur and Aquiles. Its collection of antiquities is meagre.

City View

If you want to relax in a pastoral setting, take a city bus designated 'Remedios/Parque Guardiana' from a stop near the cathedral. It will take you to a park where you may hike to the Iglesia de los Remedios at the crest of a hill. From here, all of Durango is visible.

Western Movie Towns

To visit Hollywood sets constructed as 'Western' towns, you must have a car or take a tour generally organised only on Saturday and Sunday by the tourist office. The sets are located 14 km north of the city on Highway 45. The more elaborate of the two, Villa del Oeste, was used in two of John Wayne's more mediocre efforts, *Big Jake* and *Chisum*. Chupaderos is more decrepit, yet ironically some of its structures shelter impoverished local families.

Places to Stay - bottom end

The *Hotel Reyes* (tel 1-50-50) at 20 de Noviembre 220 is basic but well-maintained; singles are US$4.25 with bath, doubles US$5.75. It's too easy to walk past the Reyes – look up to the 3rd floor for its sign.

Places to Stay - middle

Without question, for location, atmosphere and price you can't do better in Durango than *Hotel Posada Duran* (tel 1-24-12) just east of the Plaza de Armas at 20 de Noviembre 506. The Posada Duran's inner courtyard is tastefully constructed around a romantic fountain, and many of the rooms overlook the plaza. Rooms in the fine old colonial mansion cost US$8 singles with bath, US$10 doubles.

For plush yet reasonable accommodation try the *Hotel Casablanca* (tel 1-35-99), a convenient two blocks from the plaza at 20 de Noviembre 811. Large, well-appointed rooms with air-conditioning and bath cost US$13 for singles, US$16 for doubles.

Places to Stay - top end

The *Hotel Presidente* (tel 11-04-08), a km east of the plaza at the intersection of 20 de Noviembre and Apartado, is a colonial-style building with swimming pool and restaurant. Air-conditioned rooms with phones and TV cost US$30 single, US$33 double.

Places to Eat

If you arrive late and are hungry, walk three blocks from the plaza down 20 de Noviembre until it intersects with Pasteur. There you will find a cheap, filling *carne* place, *La Única*, where a fine mariachi band plays until midnight. For excellent, low cost *típico* cuisine, try *Fil-Bet's*, also on 20 de Noviembre at 212 Ote. Their inexpensive comida corrida is substantial and good.

If you are hankering for decent pizza and willing to spend a bit more, try the outdoor patio of *Restaurant La Terraza* on the 2nd floor of a building on 5 de Febrero overlooking the plaza. Pizzas here cost US$2 to US$4. For those willing to spend a bit for continental cuisine, the *Café Neveria La Bohemia* at 20 de Noviembre 907 serves decent spaghetti and German dishes like sausage with cabbage for US$1.50 to US$5. Their Mexican food is cheaper and their afternoon comida corrida at less than US$2 is a good deal.

Getting There & Away

Bus There are four 1st-class bus companies providing direct or connecting services to virtually every part of Mexico. There is a regular service from Durango to Mexico City (nearly hourly), Guadalajara and Mazatlán via a scenic mountain road. There is frequent service to Zacatecas; the trip takes 4½ hours at US$4. There is also 1st-class service to Durango from most urban centres. To reach Durango from Chihuahua by bus takes 11 hours and costs about US$10.

The Central Camionera is far from the centre of town, which may be reached in 15 minutes by local buses designated 'Centro'. In the other direction, to reach the bus station take a bus marked 'Central Camionera' from the market near the plaza. There are slightly more expensive colectivo vans to the bus station from near the plaza. Most convenient of all, taxis are reasonably priced – bargain down to about US$1.

Rail Train service to and from Durango is slower than 1st-class bus. If you are coming from the north and wish to avoid 11 hours of less than electrifying scenery, consider an overnight sleeper. It's slow but at least you will sleep through the tedium. From the train station, take a bus in front of the station directly to the main plaza via Constitución; or walk some seven blocks down Martínez to the intersection of 20 de Noviembre, turn left and walk one block to the plaza.

ZACATECAS

Population: 165,000

If you've come from the north, welcome to the first of Mexico's justly fabled Silver Cities. If you've been visiting Silver Cities like Guanajuato in the south, don't hesitate to journey a few hours further, as Zacatecas is particularly fascinating.

In fact, at 2445 metres Zacatecas literally takes your breath away. The town is carved between the slopes of the Cerro de la Bufa, a mountain whose silhouette resembles a Hispanic wineskin or *bufa*. As you climb stone-stepped streets, you will see some of Mexico's finest colonial buildings, including what may be the most beautiful baroque church in Mexico. The historic, friendly town is all the more to be appreciated for its lack of tourists.

History

Long before the first conquistadors arrived, the Zacateco Indians were mining silver here. Then an Indian gave a piece of the fabled metal to a conquistador.

After subduing the Indians, the Spaniards moved in, founding a settlement and starting mining operations here in 1548. Caravan after caravan of silver was sent off to Mexico City. While some treasure-laden wagons were raided by nomadic Indians, enough silver reached its destination to create fabulously wealthy silver barons. Agriculture and ranching developed to serve the rapidly increasing populace of the town.

Thanks to Zacatecas' mineral wealth, the city and Crown prospered. In the first quarter of the 18th century, Zacatecas' mines were producing 20% of the colony's silver. However, in the 19th century the volatile course of political events somewhat diminished the flow of silver as various forces fought to control the city. In 1871, Benito Juárez decisively defeated local rebels here. Although silver production later improved under Díaz, the Revolution disrupted it. In 1914 Pancho Villa, through brilliant tactics, defeated a stronghold of 12,000 soldiers loyal to the self-seeking General Huerta. This may have led to Villa's undoing, as he violated the orders of the man who would become Mexico's first post-revolutionary president, Carranza.

After the Revolution, Zacatecas continued to thrive due to silver. To this day it remains a mining centre, with the 200-year-old El Bote mine still productive.

Orientation

The major sites are all within walking distance of the centre. To keep your bearings in this colonial city of twisting, inclined streets, take note of the two major thoroughfares, Hidalgo and Juárez. When you get lost, as you invariably will, just have a local point you back to one of the main streets. Hidalgo becomes González Ortega at points south-west of its intersection with Juárez.

Take it easy when walking the cobblestoned streets of this steeply inclined city, because you'll need time to acclimatise to the altitude. Walking to the major points of interest at 2500 metres can lead to exhaustion. Also, at this elevation it can be quite cool. Carry a sweater or jacket for morning and late afternoon chilliness.

Information

Tourist Office The tourist office is easy to find; it's next to the cathedral on the Plaza Hidalgo. Unlike the Durango office, the helpful staff here speak English and offer plenty of brochures describing Zacatecas' attractions (although these are in Spanish). It's open Monday to Friday from 8 am to 3.30 pm, closed weekends.

Money For currency exchange, you will find two banks at the intersection of Hidalgo and Callejón de la Caja, open Monday to Friday from 9 am to 1.30 pm.

Post The post office is conveniently located just off Hidalgo, one block north-east of Juárez at Allende 111. Its hours are

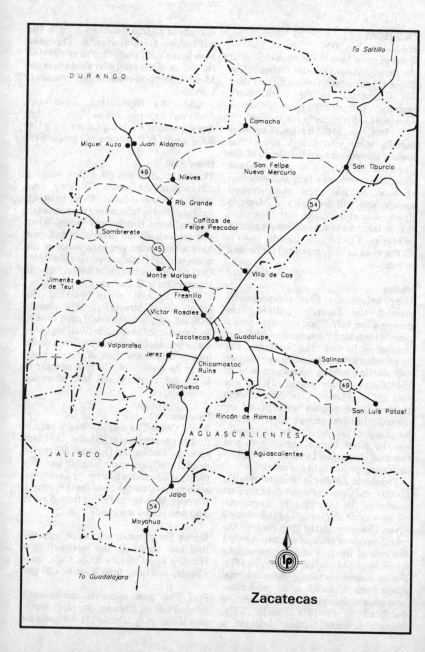

To Saltillo

DURANGO

Camacho

Miguel Auza   Juan Aldama

(49)

Nieves

San Felipe
Nuevo Mercurio

San Tiburcio

Río Grande

(54)

Cañitas de
Felipe Pescador

Sombrerete

(45)

Jiménez
de Teul

Monte Mariana

Villa de Cos

Fresnillo

Victor Rosales

Valparaíso

Zacatecas   Guadalupe

Jerez

Salinas

Chicomostoc
Ruins

(49)

Villanueva

Rincón de Romos

San Luis Potosí

AGUASCALIENTES

JALISCO

Aguascalientes

Jalpa

(54)

Moyahua

To Guadalajara

Zacatecas

Monday to Friday from 8 am to 7 pm and Saturday from 9 am to noon.

Festivals

Zacatecas holds a fiesta from late August into September. On the principal day, 27 August, a battle between Moors and Christians is re-created atop the Cerro de la Bufa. Renowned *toreadores* are imported to fight the famous bulls bred in this region.

Cathedral

The cathedral is one of the true masterpieces of colonial Mexican architecture, with its carved pink sandstone façade. Although ground was broken in 1612, the cathedral was not completed until 1752, and in this city of affluent silver barons no expense was spared. The interior was once festooned with elaborate gold and silver ornaments and adorned with tapestries and paintings. However, in the course of the country's turbulent history, the cathedral's wealth was plundered. The towers and façade laced with baroque carvings still make it worth a trip to Zacatecas.

Palacio del Gobierno

Looking north from the cathedral, you will see the Palacio del Gobierno on the Plaza Hidalgo. It was originally built in 1727 as a mansion for the silver baron Count Santiago de la Laguna, and was acquired by the state. In the city hall portion of the building, you will see a fine mural of the region's history which was painted in 1970 by Antonio Rodríguez.

Mercado González Ortega

Walking south away from the cathedral on Hidalgo, you will come to a colonial structure, the Mercado González Ortega. On the upper level, fronting Hidalgo, an upscale shopping mall complete with restaurants has replaced the old market. The lower level opens onto Tacuba St and if you follow Tacuba you will come to Zacatecas' lively daily marketplace.

Teatro Calderón

Across Hidalgo from the Mercado González Ortega is the beautiful 19th-century Teatro Calderón, an ornate example of colonial architecture.

Santo Domingo Church

Perched atop a steep street looking down upon the cathedral, the Santo Domingo Church displays a heaviness ungraceful in contrast to the cathedral. Inside, however, are some fine gilded paintings and ornate decor.

Museo Pedro Coronel

Next to the Santo Domingo Church is the Museo Pedro Coronel. An affluent Zacatecan artist bequeathed to his home town this collection of artefacts from all over the world and a group of ritual masks arguably among the world's finest. The museum's collection of Mexican Indian masks is memorable. Coronel also amassed works by Picasso, Roualt, Chagall, Hogarth, Daumier and Goya as well as artwork from the Orient.

Although this is only a regional museum, it is truly special. Allow extra time to fully enjoy it. Admission is free; hours are Tuesday to Sunday from 10 am to 5 pm.

University & Mint

If you want to talk with Mexican students, you will find the Universidad Autonoma de Zacatecas nearby on the same street as the museum. Just beneath the university, on Calle de Hierro, you will see the building that housed Zacatecas' mint, the Casa de la Moneda. Inside is a display of early coins.

Church of San Agustín

Walk further along and you will come to the partially restored Church of San Agustín. Built in the 18th century, this finely constructed church functioned for a time as a casino. Its major relief depicts the life of St Augustine. The church's visiting hours are Monday to Saturday, 8

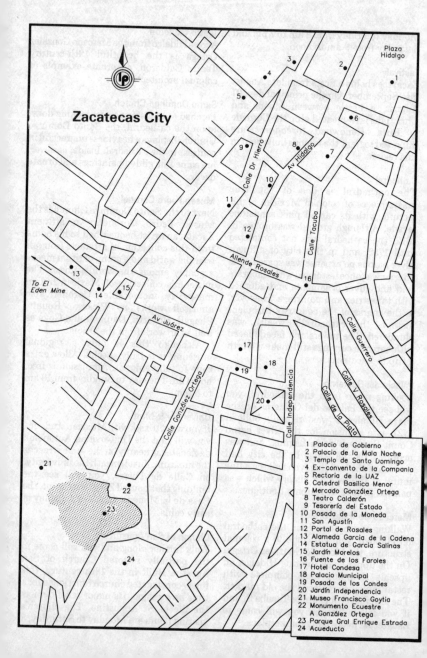

Zacatecas City

Plaza Hidalgo

To El Eden Mine

1 Palacio de Gobierno
2 Palacio de la Mala Noche
3 Templo de Santo Domingo
4 Ex-convento de la Compania
5 Rectoría de la UAZ
6 Catedral Basílica Menor
7 Mercado González Ortega
8 Teatro Calderón
9 Tesorería del Estado
10 Posada de la Moneda
11 San Agustín
12 Portal de Rosales
13 Alameda García de la Cadena
14 Estatua de García Salinas
15 Jardín Morelos
16 Fuente de los Faroles
17 Hotel Condesa
18 Palacio Municipal
19 Posada de los Condes
20 Jardín Independencia
21 Museo Francisco Goytia
22 Monumento Ecuestre
   A González Ortega
23 Parque Gral Enrique Estrada
24 Acueducto

am to 2 pm, and 4 to 5 pm; closed on Sunday. Admission is free.

Cable Car

For a view of the city, ride Zacatecas' cable car; its departure station is close to the Motel del Bosque. Taking the teleférico tram to the top of the Cerro de la Bufa (about US$0.50 each way), you will be treated to the spectacle of the city spread out beneath you. When it's too windy, the cable cars stop running. The hours of operation are Tuesday to Sunday, 12.30 to 7.30 pm.

Museo de la Toma de Zacatecas

Atop the Cerro de la Bufa there are some places of interest. Near the cable car station is the Museo de la Toma de Zacatecas, commemorating the victory of Pancho Villa's revolutionaries over the Federales in 1914. Some historians say that Villa's taking of Zacatecas insured his victory. The museum is open daily from 10 am to 6 pm. On the day I visited, the staff closed the museum from 2 to 4 pm. Although the tourist office says this happens irregularly, it's best to visit at other hours. Admission is free.

La Capilla

Adjacent to the Museo de la Toma de Zacatecas is La Capilla de la Virgen del Patrocinio. Named for the patron saint of the city, the 18th-century chapel has a portrait of the virgin said to be capable of healing the sick. On the cliffside near the church is a meteorological observatory.

Mausoleo de los Hombres Ilustrios de Zacatecas

Behind La Capilla is the Mausoleo de los Hombres Ilustrios de Zacatecas. Here, with a commanding view of the city, are the graves or memorials of Zacatecan revolutionaries.

El Eden Mine

La Mina El Eden, once one of Mexico's richest mines, is a 'must' for visitors to Zacatecas for the dramatic insight it gives into the source of wealth in this region – and the terrible price paid for it. Digging for what proved to be a fabulous yield of silver, gold, iron, copper and zinc, enslaved Indians, many of whom were between eight and 10 years old, worked under horrific conditions. As your guide will tell you, each day at least eight mining slaves met their doom.

As you take a miniature mine train into the middle level of the mine and are guided along lit walkways over treacherous shafts below, it is easy to see why so many lost their lives to accidents and diseases like silicosis and tuberculosis. Although the guide speaks only Spanish (telephone 2-30-02 to ask when an English-speaking guide is available) a visit is still worthwhile. After you disembark from the train, you are led along creaky wooden boards through dark passageways and over subterranean pools. Visible beneath are water-filled lower shafts whose flooding due to a miscalculated explosion ultimately closed the mine.

At the tour's end, you will naturally be taken to a gift store within the shaft where there is some surprisingly reasonable jewellery and samples of the minerals of La Mina. There is a disco in the mine Thursday to Sunday from 9 pm to 2 am.

To reach the mine, in theory you can enter from a point near the cable car's lower embarkation station. When I attempted this, there was no one operating the elevator. For more certain success, walk up Avenida Juárez and stay on it after its name changes to Avenida Torreón at the Alameda Park until you see the huge Seguro Social Hospital. Make a right here and a short left on Calle de la Loma, and you will be at the entrance to La Mina. Or take a bus from Jardín Independencia up Juárez to the hospital. Tours are offered from 12.30 to 7.30 pm, Tuesday to Sunday; closed Monday. Admission is US$0.70. From the mine, you can reach a point near the cable-car departure station by asking the guide to take you up in the elevator.

The excellent guides here make US$26 a week; some are university students working their way through school. Consider a tip in order.

Museo Francisco Goytia

The Museo Francisco Goytia, a gallery of painting and sculpture, is worth visiting. Set above the pleasantly pastoral Cerro de Alicia park (great for picnics) where part of the city's ancient aqueduct system remains intact, the museum has ground-floor exhibits of the works of the great early 20th-century painter Goytia (1882-1960). Goytia was a Zacatecan whose paintings of Indians are particularly good. The upper floor of the former governor's mansion is given over to the works of local artists and exhibits on tour.

The museum hours are 9 am to 1.30 pm and 5 to 8 pm Tuesday to Sunday, closed Monday. Admission is free. To reach the Museo Francisco Goytia, follow Hidalgo south to Juárez where its name changes to Avenida González Ortega. Follow it up the steep hill until you see Cerro de Alicia park. The museum is behind the park.

Convento de Guadalupe

To visit one of Mexico's most beloved religious sites, the Convento de Guadalupe, you must take a local bus about eight km to the town of Guadalupe. To catch the bus, walk from the Plaza de Independencia past the old bus station and make a left on the Callejón de Tampico. Just past the overhead passenger walk you will see an alley where the Guadalupe bus is parked. The fare is 8c and buses depart every 15 minutes for the 20-minute ride.

Ask the bus driver to let you off near the Convento; you'll see the unequal towers of a church topped with a dome. As you enter the tree-shaded courtyard with the church directly in front, you'll see the entrance to the right of the museum.

Founded in the early 18th century, the convent served as an educational centre

for Franciscan monks preparing to proselytise in what is now northern Mexico and the US Southwest. You may visit the convent's interior on your own or wait for a tour guide. Inside, the walls are covered with some of the finest religious paintings in colonial Mexico. Walk to the top of the convent and ask to be admitted to the Coro Alto, a choir overlooking the interior of the ornate church.

After you leave the convent, walk to the left and ask if you can have a guide show you (for a few pesos) the decorated interior of the Capilla de Napoles, its golden dome shimmering with 22-carat gold.

The convent/museum is open daily from 9 am to 1 pm and 3 to 5 pm. Admission is 10c every day except Sunday when it is 5c.

Places to Stay - bottom end

The basic but clean *Hotel Colón* (tel 2-04-64) is a 15 to 20-minute walk from Plaza de la Independencia, at López Velarte 508. A room here with private bath costs US$5 single, US$6.25 double. Another acceptable cheapie is the *Hotel Río Grande* (tel 2-53-49), offering clean rooms with shared bath for US$1.60. From the old bus station, go over the road bridge and then left 150 metres up the hill to the hotel at Calzada de la Paz 313.

Places to Stay - middle

For a slight splurge, the top choice in Zacatecas is the *Posada de los Condes* (tel 2-10-93), conveniently located near the intersection of Hidalgo and Juárez at Juárez 18. The building itself, over three centuries old, is a national landmark. You have a choice of two kinds of nicely refurbished rooms with bath, telephone and TV (one US channel is received). The rooms with French doors which open onto balconies above the street are fine for people-watching and romantic, but tend to be a bit noisy. For those who appreciate quiet, the management will provide clean, fan-ventilated interior rooms upon request. Singles cost US$8.70, doubles

US$11.15. The hotel's proprietor, Manuel López, speaks English and is most helpful.

A good second choice is the *Posada de la Moneda* (tel 2-08-81), a block south of the cathedral at Hidalgo 413. Singles with bath, telephone and hot water cost US$7.60, doubles US$9.50.

Across the street from the Posada de los Condes is the less attractive but cheaper *Hotel Condesa* (tel 2-11-60) at Juárez 5. Adequate rooms with sporadic hot water, telephones and TVs cost US$6 for singles and US$7.50 doubles.

Places to Stay – top end
Hotel Aristos (tel 2-17-88), located on the periphery of town at the Lomas de la Soledad, has a good view of Zacatecas as well as a fine restaurant and swimming pool. Singles here are US$28, doubles US$32.

The *Calinda Zacatecas* (tel 2-33-11) at López Mateos and Callejón del Barro is the best luxury hotel in town. Singles are US$20, doubles US$23.

Places to Eat
There are good comidas corridas in the restaurant of the *Posada de los Condes* for less than US$1.50, inexpensive breakfasts at the café of the *Hotel Condesa* and adequate Mexican standards at the restaurant of the *Posada de la Moneda*.

A terrific place to snack and meet students just south of the cathedral is the *Café y Nevería Acropolis*. Great coffee (rare in Mexico), burgers, fries, all sorts of sodas and desserts are inexpensive and the decor itself is worth a stop. Students decorate their white saucers with intricately arranged coffee grounds; the proprietor hangs the best of these elegant leavings on the café's walls.

For cheap roast chicken dishes, try the little 2nd floor *Rosticería El Pastor*, across from the library at Plaza Independencia 214 (look up to see it). For less than US$1 you can fill up on chicken and chips. Notice the sign out front commemorating this residence as the birthplace of the first journalist in America.

For cheap Mexican meat dishes, try the *Mesón La Mina*, conveniently located at Juárez 15 near Hidalgo. You can also get beer and decent coffee here. Another aptly named cheap meat café is *El Carnerito* at Juárez 105.

Those hankering for pizza will enjoy the fare at *Pizzeria Bambinos* at Juárez 205. If you are willing to spend US$4 to US$5 for good seafood, dine at *Villa del Mar*, Ventura Salazar 340.

Entertainment
The bizarrely situated disco in *El Eden Mine* features a rock-and-roll club complete with light show Thursday to Saturday from 9 pm to 2 am. For a pretty place to dance, with a romantic view of the city, try *El Elefante Blanco Disco* next to the Motel del Bosque. The luxury hotels *Aristos* and *Calinda* have their own nightly discos.

Things to Buy
Zacatecas is famous for its fine leatherwork, colourful sarapes and wood and stone carvings. Bargain at shops in and around the old market on Tacuba and Hidalgo.

Getting There & Away
Bus There is frequent 1st-class bus service between Zacatecas and Mexico City (about US$9, nine hours), Guadalajara (about US$4, four hours), Durango (US$4, 4½ hours) and Aguascalientes (US$2, two hours).

Rail Zacatecas is on the main rail route to Mexico City and Ciudad Juárez.

Getting Around
Although the modern bus station is far from the city centre, reaching the centre is neither expensive nor difficult. Buses charging less than 10c run regularly for the 15-minute trip. If you are in a hurry, you can bargain a taxi down to about US$1.

The train station, too, has buses and taxis running regularly to the centre. Once you are in town, the major sites are all within walking distance, but allow extra time to reach your destinations because of the high altitude and steep streets.

CHICOMOSTOC RUINS

The Chicomostoc Ruins, also known as Quemada Ruins, lie in a valley some 56 km from Zacatecas. Due to the difficulty in getting here, unless you have a car or are a true ruins buff a visit is not worth the effort.

If you've been to Monte Albán near Oaxaca, you'll see some similarity in the design of the pyramids here. Only the largest, known as The Temple, has been fully restored. Some archaeologists say the site, founded during the late 12th century, served as a fortress for the Nahuatlacas Indians during the pre-Aztecan empire period; others believe it was a religious site for local royalty and the priestly class.

Getting There & Away

Buses no longer run directly to the Chicomostoc Ruins. Second-class buses stop at the village of La Quemada (US$0.50), an hour's walk from the ruins, but you might find a driver willing to let you off on the road about 25 minutes' walk from Chicomostoc. Catching transport back may be even chancier. It may be easier to catch a bus first to Villanueva and then another back to Zacatecas.

Alternatively, pricey tours may be booked in Zacatecas from the luxury Hotel Aristos (tel 2-17-88) and the Turismo Marxal travel agency (tel 2-11-60) in the lobby of the Hotel Condesa on Avenida Juárez 5.

AGUASCALIENTES

Population: 450,000

Aguascalientes, named for its hot springs, is a booming, prosperous, industrial city with just enough colonial legacies to justify a brief visit. It's the capital of the state of Aguascalientes, which is one of Mexico's smallest. Travellers with limited time would do best to move on to one of the Bajío's more interesting silver cities.

History

Before the conquistador invasion, indigenous people built a labyrinth of catacombs which made the first Spaniards here dub Aguascalientes *La Ciudad Perforada* – the perforated city. Archaeologists still have no explanation for the tunnels, which are off limits to visitors.

Cortés dispatched Pedro de Alvarado to subdue the tribes in this region. When Alvarado reached Aguascalientes in 1522, a fierce attack by Indians forced him to retreat. Although King Philip II decreed Aguascalientes a city in 1575, continual raids by the Chichimecs limited settlement for years. The city was initially a fortress from which soldiers protected outlying miners, silver convoys from Zacatecas and cattle drovers. As the Indians were suppressed, the city grew.

According to legend, a kiss planted on the lips of dictator Santa Anna by the attractive wife of a prominent local politician brought about the creation of Aguascalientes state, independent of Zacatecas. Aguascalientes has prospered and is more than double the size of its rival capital.

Today, more than half of the state's population lives in the city, where industry, textile crafts, and the region's ranches, vineyards and orchards provide employment. While this has benefited the people of Aguascalientes, urban expansion has significantly diminished the former colonial charm of the city. Nonetheless, there are some sights of interest here within walking distance of the centre.

Information & Orientation

Tourist Office The tourist office (tel 6-01-23) is inconveniently located way out at Avenida las Américas 502. Hours are Monday to Friday 8 am to 3 pm and 5 to 7 pm, closed weekends. The staff, while not

Aguascalientes

1 Plaza de Toros San Marcos
2 Hotel Rosales
3 Hotel Imperial & Cafetería Cathedral
4 Cafetería & Bar Cielo Vista
5 Chicken & Pizza Palace
6 Las Bugambilias Restaurant
7 Palacio del Gobierno
8 Palacio Municipal
9 Hotel Senorial
10 Hotel San José
11 Museo de Aguascalientes
12 El Greco Restaurant
13 Hotel Moser
14 Restaurant El Pastor

unfriendly, seemed preoccupied with reading comic books and didn't speak English. A better bet for maps and brochures is the tourist desk of the 1st-class Hotel Francia, located right on the Plaza Principal.

Money There are several banks off the Plaza Principal. Their hours are Monday to Friday, 9 am to 1.30 pm.

Post You will find the main post office on Calle Hospitalidad. Hours are Monday to Friday 8 am to 7 pm, and Saturday 9 am to noon.

Festivals
Feria de San Marcos This is held in late April and early May.

Feria de la Uva This festival celebrates the grape harvest in mid-August.

Palacio del Gobierno
The most noteworthy example of colonial architecture in Aguascalientes is the Palacio del Gobierno on the main plaza. The building, once the mansion of the feudal baron the Marqués de Guadalupe, was originally constructed in 1665 and refurbished on numerous occasions. Built of red sandstone, tezontle (porous rock) and pink cantera quarried stone, the palace opens into a striking courtyard of arches, pillars and a staircase. Its mural, painted in the 1960s by the Chilean Oswaldo Barra (no surprise that his mentor was Diego Rivera), is a compendium of the historic and economic forces that forged Aguascalientes.

Palacio Municipal
Next to the Palacio del Gobierno is the similarly styled but more contemporary Palacio Municipal housing a mural of Zapata.

Cathedral
Also on the central square is a less-than-magnificent 18th-century baroque cathedral. Although its exterior may be disappointing, the interior is another matter. Inside is the renowned *Last Supper* by the great colonial Zapotecan Indian artist, Miguel Cabrera, as well as other excellent 17th and 18th-century religious paintings.

Teatro Morelos
Alongside the cathedral is the Teatro Morelos, which in 1914 played host to a revolutionary convention in which Pancho Villa suggested to supporters of his rival Carranza that the two leaders resolve their differences and save the Revolution by having the state execute them both! The wily Villa was hardly serious, knowing that Carranza would not even show up at the convention, let alone entertain the idea.

Jardín de San Marcos
This pretty, enclosed park on Avenida Carranza is a good place to relax.

Museo de José Guadalupe Posada
Walk four blocks from the plaza to the corner of Pimental and Chavez, and you will come to the Museo de José Guadalupe Posada. Aguascalientes' most famous patriot, Guadalupe Posada was a fine artist whose political engravings and cartoons lampooning the dictator Porfirio Díaz spurred on the local impulse to revolt. The museum's hours are Tuesday to Sunday, 10 am to 2 pm and 4 to 7.30 pm; closed Monday.

Temple of El Encino
Next to the museum is the Temple of El Encino. Some believe that the temple's black statue of Jesus is growing and that when it *eventually* reaches an adjacent column, a worldwide calamity will ensue.

Museo de Aguascalientes
The Museo de Aguascalientes may be reached from the plaza by taking Avenida Madero and then making a left on

Zaragoza. While its collection of regional artefacts is not exceptional, there are some decent exhibits of local arts.

Church of San Antonio

Next to the Museo de Aguascalientes is the Church of San Antonio, a crazy-quilt of architectural styles by the local self-taught (some say his work shows it) architect, Refugio Reyes. You'll either love it or loathe it.

San Marcos Winery & Hacienda Las Bovelas

If you have your own vehicle you can go a few km north on the highway to Zacatecas for a tour of the San Marcos Winery. It's open to the public 9 am to 3 pm weekdays, and 9 am to noon on Saturday. The brandy made here is cheap and surprisingly good. Go a little further north and you may visit the region's most famous bull-breeding ranch, Hacienda Las Bovedas. If you don't have a car, you might get the Valladolid bus from Avenida López Mateos to stop here. Tell the driver where you want to get off.

Thermal Springs

The best known of Aguascalientes' thermal springs is the Ojo Caliente, whose relaxing waters are better characterised as 'warm' rather than hot. To get there, take the bus marked 'Emiliano Zapata' from Avenida López Mateos or a taxi (bargain down to less than US$1). The admission price varies from US$0.50 for the big public pool to US$5 for individual pools.

Twenty-one km further out of town, but more attractive, are the Balneario Valladolid springs. Admission starts at US$0.80 and escalates according to your needs. Public transport to these springs is the 'Valladolid' bus running from Avenida López Mateos.

Places to Stay – bottom end

If you are too exhausted to continue on to the centre of town upon arrival by bus, next to the Central Camionera you will find the *Hotel Continental* (tel 5-55-42) adequate at US$5 for a single with bath, US$5.50 for a double. Nearby on the Circunvalación is the less spartan *Hotel Gómez* (tel 7-04-09), offering singles with bath for US$6 and doubles for US$7.50.

The centre of town offers better choices for your money. Four blocks from the main plaza is the *Hotel Maser* (tel 5-35-62), at Montoro 303 where it intersects with 16 de Septiembre. This extremely pleasant hotel offers rooms built over a pretty courtyard. Singles with bath cost US$5.50, doubles US$6.50. Also adequate, inexpensive and well located is the *San José* (tel 5-51-30), a block closer to the plaza than the Maser at Hidalgo 207. Basic rooms cost US$5 with bath for singles and US$6.25 for doubles. If you want to be only a block from the plaza and don't mind tiny but reasonably maintained rooms, try the *Hotel Rosales* (tel 5-21-65). Dig the Rin Tin Tin poster and the hotel's labyrinth layout. The Rosales' postage-stamp rooms, some with TVs, cost US$5.50 for singles with bath, US$6.25 doubles.

Places to Stay – middle

If you want to stay right on the plaza and are willing to spend a little more, the *Hotel Imperial* (tel 5-16-64) across from the cathedral offers rooms with balconies and a view of the plaza at US$8 single with bath, US$10 double. The Imperial has a few interior rooms which while smaller, may be quieter than those with balconies and are substantially cheaper; singles with bath cost US$4.50, doubles US$5.75 – you must ask for these. Another excellent choice across from the cathedral is *Hotel Senorial* (tel 5-16-30). Here you will find pleasant, clean rooms with balconies at US$7 single with bath, US$9.50 double.

Places to Stay – top end

The sole 1st-class hotel in the centre of town is the *Hotel Francis* (tel 5-60-80) right on the plaza at Avenida Madero.

Air-conditioned singles cost US$18, doubles US$22.

Places to Eat

If you arrive absolutely famished, there's a reasonable restaurant in the *Hotel Continental* next to the bus station and plenty of cheap *taquerías* in the vicinity. For better quality, there are more appealing restaurants closer to the centre; *El Greco* at Madero 434 near Zaragoza offers filling meals for US$1 to US$1.50.

Close to the plaza, a stone's throw from the Hotel Imperial at the intersection of Moctezuma and 5 de Mayo, is the inexpensive *Cafetería Cathedral*. A good place to watch life go by in Aguascalientes, this café serves inexpensive sandwiches, desserts and decent coffee. For heartier fare in the vicinity, try the restaurant of

the Hotel Río Grande, *Las Bugambilias*. You spend more here for the pleasant atmosphere, but the food is good and the prices are not outrageous.

The nicest restaurant I ate at in Aguascalientes, *El Pastor* at López Mateos 314 not far from the plaza, may be a bit pricey for some. Continental dishes like chateaubriand cost US$4.50 and other European dishes slightly less. Still, you can enjoy the well-named El Pastor's tranquil garden atmosphere and not break the bank by ordering typical Mexican fare for around US$2.

For a really good deal, quantity-wise, try the *Chicken & Pizza Palace* on Mateos Pte 207. From 1 to 5 pm, an all-you-can-gorge buffet offers pastas, pizzas and various salads for less than US$2.

Evenings, enjoy the romantic atmosphere

Refrescos van

of *Cafetería & Bar Cielo Vista*, adjacent to the plaza at Plaza Principal 101. Although prices are a bit steep, you can listen to an excellent guitarist while sipping coffee and sampling pastries.

Entertainment

Evenings, enjoy the guitarist at the *Cielo Vista*. There's a disco at the luxury *Las Trojes Hotel* on the highway to Zacatecas. On some Sundays, there are rodeos near the Parque Centenario – enquire at the Hotel Francia.

Things to Buy

The Centro de Diseño out on Avenida López Mateos is the scene of local craftspeople engaged in excellent weaving and pottery with designs traditional to this area. While the crafts are not all that cheap, the quality is high. Less pricey but often somewhat shoddy are the goods sold at the market between 5 de Mayo and Juárez.

Getting There & Away

Buses run regularly from and to Zacatecas, Guanajuato and Mexico City. The 1st-class buses are substantially faster than the train.

Getting Around

The Central Camionera and railway station are some distance from the city centre, but frequent local buses will take you to the Plaza Principal from the depots.

The Bajío

The Bajío ('ba-HEE-oh'), once an important source of silver, is of great historic interest. Visitors today reap the legacy of the area's rich past in the magnificent colonial architecture of Guanajuato, San Luis Potosí and Querétaro; the important historical sites so abundant in Querétaro; and the picturesque mountain village of San Miguel de Allende where gringos come to study Spanish. For a dazzling sense of Mexico's history, there can be no more rewarding journey than to the Bajío.

History

In pre-Hispanic times the Bajío was inhabited mainly by Otomíes and semi-nomadic Chichimecs. During the 15th century the Aztecs from the Valley of Mexico and the Tarascans from the west both extended their dominance into the area. The names of both states are Tarascan: Guanajuato means Frog Hill,

Querétaro means Place of the Ball Game.

The Spanish conquered the Otomíes and Chichimecs around Querétaro in 1531 and settled the state over the next few decades. The Guanajuato area, including the most important settlement at Yuriria-púndaro, had been subdued by the infamous Nuño de Guzman in the late 1520s but only after the discovery of silver in the mid-16th century did the Spanish take a serious interest in settling it. Local Otomíes under Nicolás de San Luis Montañez, their chieftain who had taken a Spanish name, helped in the subjugation of the semi-nomadic Chichimecs further north.

After silver was found in Zacatecas, Spanish prospectors combed the rugged lands north of Mexico City and were rewarded by discoveries of mineral wealth. Here in abundance were gold, iron, lead, zinc, tin and, in the most

1 San Luis Potosí
2 Zacatecas
3 Aguascalientes
4 Jalisco
5 Guanajuato
6 Querétaro
7 Hidalgo
8 Veracruz
9 Michoacán
10 Mexico

spectacular of veins, silver. The richest mines were worked in Guanajuato, where for two centuries 30 to 40% of the world's silver was mined. Guanajuato city became one of the three greatest silver-mining centres in the Americas, along with Zacatecas and Potosí in Bolivia. Silver barons in the wealthy mining cities lived opulent life styles at the expense of Indians who worked the mines first as slave labour and then as wage slaves.

Mexico's criollo middle class – people of Spanish blood but born in New Spain – were generally no less prejudiced against Indians and mestizos than were the peninsulares, New Spain's Spanish-born ruling caste. But, while not excluded from the corridors of colonial power (they were particularly strong in the armed forces, for instance), they came to resent the peninsulares' dominance in the colony and, perhaps no less importantly, their arrogance. Until at least the 1790s, however, criollos who advocated independence from Spain were mainly regarded as nutcases. Most criollos were doing well enough under the colonial system.

Two things changed matters. One was the arrival in 1794 of a corrupt new viceroy, the Marqués de Brancaforte, to replace the popular Conde de Revillagigedo. At least three independence conspiracies were thwarted in the next seven years but their perpetrators were still regarded as something of a lunatic fringe.

What really lit the spark was the occupation of much of Spain by Napoleon Bonaparte's troops in 1808. This gave rise to three alternative governments in Spain: Napoleon's brother Joseph, the imprisoned King Ferdinand VII, and a Spanish resistance government in Cádiz. The current viceroy in New Spain, José de Iturrigaray, saw the confusion back home as a chance to make himself emperor of Mexico and allowed the criollos to form a *junta* or temporary ruling body while the overall situation remained unclear. Peninsulares in Mexico City couldn't accept this and sent Iturrigaray into exile, arresting some leading criollos too. Provincial criollos, more independent-minded than those in the capital, were incensed by this and some began to draw up plans for rebellion while they met as 'literary societies'.

The house of Miguel Domínguez, a member of one such group in Querétaro, was raided on 13 September 1810. Three days later his colleague, Miguel Hidalgo, declared independence in Dolores. San Miguel de Allende was the first town to fall to the rebels, Celaya the second, Guanajuato the third. Sometimes called simply 'La Independencia', this part of the Bajío is proud to have given birth to Mexico's most glorious moment and is visited almost as a place of pilgrimage by people from far and wide.

After the successful War of Independence, the Bajío continued to serve as a stage upon which Mexico's history was forged. Following a brief war with the US, an infamous treaty was signed at Querétaro in 1848 surrendering half of Mexico's territory to the US. In 1867, Emperor Maximilian was captured and executed at Querétaro. And in 1917, Mexico's revolutionary constitution, still the law of the land, was written at Querétaro.

Geography

The Bajío lies immediately north of Mexico's central volcanic belt, where the southern end of the altiplano central is broken by a number of low ranges. This fertile area stretches almost from coast to coast and is between 1500 and 1800 metres high. Broadly speaking it encompasses the states of Guanajuato and Querétaro, apart from their mountainous north-eastern fringes.

People & Economy

Today Guanajuato has about 3.5 million people, Querétaro about 900,000. There are about 20,000 Otomí Indians in each state. At Misión de Chichimecas, near San Luis de la Paz in northern Guanajuato,

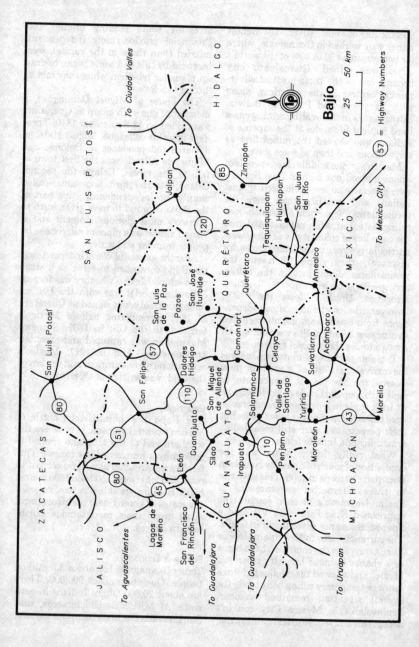

Bajío

0   25   50 km

57 = Highway Numbers

there's a small group of about 1500 people still known as Chichimecs.

Guanajuato has some important industrial centres like León (shoes, saddles, other leather goods, steel, textiles and soap) and Salamanca, which has a big oil refinery. Still Mexico's fourth largest silver producer, it's also an important source of gold and fluorspar. Guanajuato has traditionally been Mexico's granary and today produces 10% of the country's wheat, 8% of its barley, 5% of its maize, 29% of its sorghum and 17% of its alfalfa.

Querétaro turns out opals, mercury, zinc and lead, and industry is developing around Querétaro city. The state can claim nearly one pig per person and is a major breeding ground for fighting bulls. Other animals are important in both states; between them they produce about 700 million litres of milk a year, 10% of Mexico's total output. Wealth levels are about average for predominantly agricultural regions in Mexico.

GUANAJUATO

Population: 90,000

Welcome to one of the country's outstanding destinations. Subterranean passageways serve as the town's streets and houses are crammed onto the steep slopes of a ravine once thought by Indians to be habitable only by frogs. The impossible topography was settled because the silver and gold mines of Guanajuato were among the richest in the world. The colonial structures built from this wealth remain intact through much of the city, making Guanajuato what the government calls a 'colonial monument' to a prosperous, turbulent past.

History

One of the hemisphere's richest veins of silver was uncovered at the La Valenciana Mine in 1558. For 2½ centuries, the excavation of what is now the periphery above the city produced 20% of the world's silver. Colonial barons benefiting from this mineral treasure were infuriated when King Charles III slashed their share of the wealth in 1765. The King further enraged the city with his 1767 decree banishing Jesuits from Latin America for their anti-monarchical stance. Both the wealthy barons and the poor Indian miners who held allegiance to the Jesuits were alienated from Spanish rule.

This anger found a focus in the War of Independence. In 1810, rebel leader Father Hidalgo led a successful conquest of Spain's Alhóndiga fortress with the assistance of Guanajuato's citizenry. When the Spaniards retaliated, furious that locals had lynched royalist prisoners, they retook the city. In the infamous 'lottery of death', names of Guanajuatan citizenry were drawn strictly at random and the unlucky 'winners' were tortured and hanged.

The rebels won, freeing the silver barons to acquire mineral wealth with which mansions, churches and theatres were built. To this day, Guanajuato remains a conservative – some would say reactionary – bastion of faith and the past.

Information

Tourist Office The tourist office is just one block east of the bus station at Juárez and 5 de Mayo. Its hours are Monday to Friday from 8.30 am to 7.30 pm, and weekends from 10 am to 2.30 pm and 5 to 7.30 pm. Opening hours don't always adhere to this schedule. In the park across from the office a tourist information booth may be open when the main office is closed. The tourist office will provide you with a relatively useless map (it's not their fault – the city is impossible to map) and up-to-date hotel rates, and will also book some worthwhile tours.

Money For currency exchange, you will find a number of banks along the Plaza de la Paz and Juárez. Their hours are 9 am to 1.30 pm Monday to Friday. When the banks are closed, some of the larger hotels

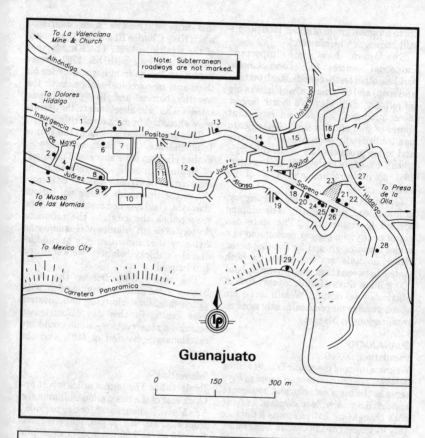

Guanajuato

0   150   300 m

1	Hotel Alhóndiga	
2	Bus Station	
3	Hotel El Insurgencia	
4	Tourist Office	
5	Hotel Murillo	
6	Plaza Alhóndiga	
7	Alhóndiga de Granaditas	
8	Hotel Central	
9	Hotel San Francisco	
10	Market	
11	Jardín de la Reforma	
12	Plazuela San Fernando & Pizza Piazza	
13	Museo Y Casa de Diego Rivera	
14	Museo del Pueblo de Guanajuato	
15	University of Guanajuato	
16	Post Office	
17	Plaza de la Paz	
18	Hotel Posada de la Condesa	
19	Hotel Casa Kloster	
20	Hostería del Frayle	
21	Café Valdez	
22	Café El Retira	
23	Jardín de la Unión & Hotel Posada Santa Fe	
24	Hotel San Diego	
25	Iglesia de San Diego	
26	Teatro Juárez	
27	Teatro Principal	
28	Iglesia de San Francisco	
29	Monument al Pipila	

will change your money at slightly less advantageous rates.

Post You will find the main post office near the university at Ayuntamiento 25. It's open Monday to Friday from 8 am to 8 pm and Saturday from 9 am to 1 pm.

Festivals

Cervantes Festival *Entremeses*, dramas along with internationally renowned music and dance groups, are performed during Guanajuato's Cervantes Festival. Held in late September or early October, the festival attracts talent and tourists worldwide so tickets and hotels should be booked in advance. If you can't find a hotel, plenty of buses run between Guanajuato and not-so-distant destinations like Querétaro, San Miguel de Allende, Dolores Hidalgo, León and Irapuato.

While some events are held in Teatro Juárez, the most spectacular of *entremeses*, with galloping horses and medieval costumes, are performed in the ancient setting of the Plazuela San Roque. If your visit to Mexico coincides with the festival dates, don't miss it.

Feria de San Juan This is held from 22 to 26 June, at the Presa de la Olla Park with dances, costumes and fireworks.

Día de la Cueva The festival is held on 31 May.

Philip II's Gift The 9 August festival celebrates Philip II's gift of the jewelled wooden Virgin now adorning the basilica.

Museo de las Momias

Museo de las Momias is the quintessential example of Mexico's obsession with death, to say nothing of commercial possibilities. The Museum of the Mummies attracts visitors from far and wide, who come to see scores of corpses dug up from the public cemetery.

Nearly a century ago, when some poor Mexicans could no longer pay the authorities' rent to keep their relatives' bodies buried in the public cemetery, the remains were disinterred. To the horror of the authorities and the relatives of the dead, what they unearthed were not skeletons but flesh mummified in grotesque forms and facial expressions. The soil's chemical content combined with the region's atmospheric conditions to preserve the flesh in this unique way.

Not all of the bodies are the originals exhumed in 1896. When the city officials thought about it, they decided that they had one blockbuster of a tourist attraction and over the years the bodies of the impoverished continued to be dug up. The most 'expressive' were put on display here, the others cremated.

Admission is 25c, with an additional 25c for cameras – flashes are permitted. The museum is open daily from 9 am to 6 pm and your tour guide will expect a tip. To reach the museum, either take a tour, or at the north-western side of town take the Panteón/La Rocha bus to the entrance. It's a long, steep walk for those who want to hoof it.

Alhóndiga de Granaditas

The Alhóndiga de Granaditas – originally the site of a major rebel victory in the War of Independence – is today an important art museum funded by the state. A massive grain-and-seed storehouse for 13 years, the Alhóndiga in 1810 became a bailiwick for Spanish troops and royalist leaders who barricaded themselves in the granary when 20,000 rebel troops under Padre Hidalgo attempted to conquer the city. The substantial structure allowed the outnumbered Spaniards to hold out and it looked like they would be able to defend their fortress, until a young Indian miner named Pipila rushed the gates, setting them afire before he succumbed to a hail of bullets. While the Spaniards choked on smoke, the rebels advanced and took the Alhóndiga.

The Spaniards later took their revenge: the heads of four leaders of the rebellion, including Hidalgo who was executed in Chihuahua, were hung from the four corners of the Alhóndiga from 1811 to 1821. Instead of intimidating the locals, the display for a decade reminded rebels of their martyrs, spurring them on to eventual independence. Inside are the metal cages in which the heads were displayed. The hooks on which the martyrs' heads hung may still be viewed.

Today, the venerable building has become a fine state museum. On the ground floor are good examples of regional crafts as well as exhibits of pre-Hispanic artefacts. Don't miss the murals of Guanajuato's history painted by Chavez Morado. On the upper floor are rooms of artefacts, lithographs and photographs of Guanajuato's history. A fine art gallery houses a permanent collection and some travelling exhibits.

Opening hours are Tuesday to Saturday, 9 am to 2 pm and 4 to 6 pm; sundays 10 am to 4 pm. The museum is closed on Monday. Admission is 9c; half price on Sunday. There is a 5c charge for photography. The Alhóndiga is a block's walk from the tourist office.

Museo y Casa de Diego Rivera

The birthplace of Diego Rivera, today a museum of some of his paintings, is to the right of the university at Positos 47 (close to the Alhóndiga). In reactionary Guanajuato, where Catholic influence prevails (in the late 1920s the city was a bastion of support for the attempted counter-revolution led by the church), the Marxist revolutionary Diego was *persona non grata* for years. Ultimately, profits prevailed over principle and Guanajuato now honours its once blacklisted native son with a small collection of his work in the house where he was raised.

The museum's 1st floor contains the Rivera family's 19th-century antiques and fine furniture. On the 2nd and 3rd floors are some 90 paintings and sketches by the master, including Indian and peasant portraits and puppets crafted for carnivals. Also on exhibit are sketches from some of Rivera's memorable murals. The museum is open Monday to Saturday from 10 am to 2 pm and 4 to 7 pm, closed Sunday. Admission is 2c.

Museo del Pueblo de Guanajuato

Right next to the university at Positos 7 is the relatively new Museo del Pueblo de Guanajuato. Located in a former church and opened in 1979, it has a permanent collection of impressive pre-Hispanic pottery as well as excellent ceramics by contemporary potters from the region.

While there are some religious paintings from the colonial period, what really catches the eye are the paintings of regional artists José Chavez Morado and Olga Costa. See in particular Chavez Morado's mural in the former chapel – a three-fold history of Guanajuato from exploitation of Indian miners to the Revolution. Some Sundays chamber music concerts are performed in the chapel. The museum is open Tuesday to Sunday from 10 am to 2 pm and 4 to 7 pm. Admission is 2c.

Colonial Architecture

The best way to enjoy the colonial legacies that make this city unique is literally to lose yourself in it. This is not hard no matter how good your sense of direction, because the labyrinth of cobbled alleys and subterranean passageways in the ravine are as confusing as they are colourful. Explore the steep stairways supporting pastel-hued homes decked with flowers, walk across medieval brick bridges that once served as aqueducts, and saunter beneath subterranean walls of greenstone along picturesque passageways where a lazy river once flowed until its waters were diverted by the colonists.

You may choose to follow Ruta 2 on the tourist office map, which takes in among other sights the ballyhooed Callejón del Beso. The well-named 'Alley of the Kiss' is so narrow at points that stories are told of lovers clandestinely expressing their passion from balconies on either side of the alley.

Even though this route and other tourist-map walks are sporadically signposted, you are certain to get lost. Moreover, you may encounter tour groups covering the same ground. To get away from the crowds just keep walking, and when you get really lost ask one of the friendly locals to direct you to a major sight. In this highly concentrated city, you won't have to walk far.

Plazuela de los Ángeles & Plaza de la Paz

Walking toward the centre of town from the bus station on Juárez, you will see the first of many pleasant gardens, Plazuela de los Ángeles (the Callejón del Beso is just off this plaza). Keep walking along Juárez and you will come to the Plaza de la Paz. Around the plaza are some magnificent mansions built by Guanajuato's silver barons.

Basilica de Nuestra Señora de Guanajuato

This church on the Plaza de la Paz contains a jewel-covered image of the Virgin, patroness of Guanajuato. The wooden statue was supposedly hidden in a cave from the Moors for 800 years. Philip II, in thanks for the riches which accrued to the Crown, gave the statue to Guanajuato in 1557.

Jardín de la Unión

At the centre of town is the pretty Jardín de la Unión. This zócalo, the social heart of the city, is surrounded by cafés and shaded by trees. Late afternoons and early evenings, itinerant guitarists serenade those taking their ease here. Band concerts are frequently held on Tuesday, Thursday and Sunday evenings from 7 to 10 pm.

Teatro Juárez

Across from the Jardín Unión sits the magnificent Teatro Juárez, built in 1903. It was inaugurated by the dictator Díaz, whose lavish yet refined tastes are reflected in the interior. The outside is festooned with columns, lamp-posts and statues; inside, the motif is Moorish, with the bar and lobby walls and ceiling gleaming with carved woods, stained glass and precious metals.

Admission is about 1c. During the Cervantes Festival, plays and concerts are performed here. The Teatro is open Tuesday to Sunday from 9.45 am to 1.45 pm and 5 to 7.45 pm.

San Diego Church

Right next to the Teatro is the overrated San Diego Church. While its baroque exterior may be of some interest, the interior of this Franciscan edifice is not all that noteworthy and its ill-cared-for religious paintings are in an alarming state of decay.

La Compañía de Jesús Church

A short walk from the Jardín Unión will bring you to the tranquil Plazuela del Baratillo, highlighted by a fountain presented to Guanajuato by Maximilian. Nearby is the Teatro Principal, the post office and La Compañía de Jesús Church. A Jesuit church constructed in 1747, it was the largest of its order when completed. The church was part of a Jesuit seminary which now is the site of the University of Guanajuato. You can easily walk up to the university from the church.

University of Guanajuato

The university, whose medieval green ramparts are visible above much of the city, is considered one of Mexico's finest schools for music and theatre. If you want to meet students, wander around the university grounds or have coffee at any of the city's popular cafés geared to young people.

City Parks

For some real peace and quiet amidst greenery, continue walking a half-hour from Jardín Unión (Juárez's name will change to Sospena and later Paseo de la Presa) to the parks Presa de la Olla and Presa de San Renovato. Or catch local buses designated 'Presa' or 'Olla' on the subterranean level beneath San Diego Church if you're leaving the Jardín Unión area. These peaceful parks have reservoirs and at Presa de Olla you can rent rowboats for about 35c an hour, daily until 6.30 pm.

Places to Stay – bottom end

In Guanajuato, there is no question concerning the top choice for budget lodgings. The *Casa Kloster* (tel 2-00-88) on Alonso 32 is owned by a feisty and venerable gent. Señor Jesús Perez, who runs the pensión with his wife, is every traveller's surrogate papa. The hard-working couple make Casa Kloster one of the best deals in Mexico. Arranged around a courtyard with birds and flowers, the clean rooms with shared bath and toilet cost just US$2.50. The señor will pour you tequila, tell you stories and make you feel at home. To reach the pensión, walk 15 minutes from the bus station along Juárez. As you near the basilica, you will see an alleyway sign-posted 'Callejón de la Estrella'. Turn right here and you will come out on Calle Alonso.

A distant second choice for rock-bottom lodging is the *Hotel Posada de la Condesa* (tel 2-14-62) at Plaza de la Paz 60. The hotel is just off the bottom of the hill from Juárez beneath the basilica, 12 minutes' walk from the bus station. It can be noisy here, but the rooms are basically clean. Singles with bath are US$3.25, doubles US$6.

Places to Stay – middle

The following places are a five-minute walk from the bus station on Avenida Juárez.

The *Hotel San Francisco* (tel 2-20-84) on Juárez at Gavira offers comfortable, well-maintained rooms at good prices.

Ask for the quietest rooms – those in the interior, not off the balcony. Singles with bath cost US$6.25, doubles US$8.

The *Hotel Central* (tel 2-00-80) at Juárez 111 is also a good deal, offering pleasant singles with bath for US$6.75 and doubles US$8.

El Insurgencia (tel 2-22-94) at Juárez 226 very close to the bus station is clean enough, but its rooms are overpriced at US$12 single with bath, US$14 double.

To reach the following hotels from the bus station, walk one block east and take the street branching left from the front of the tourist office building.

Hotel Alhóndiga (tel 2-05-25), at Insurgencia 49 five minutes' walk from the bus station offers very nice, clean rooms with bath. Singles cost US$6.50, doubles US$10.

Hotel Murillo (tel 2-18-84) at Insurgencia 9 five minutes' walk from the bus station is a good deal; clean singles with bath are US$6, doubles US$10.

Hotel El Minero has tastefully appointed rooms and an indoor pool (scummy water). Singles are US$7 with bath. Doubles are a good deal at US$8.25.

Places to Stay – top end

The striking *Posada Santa Fe* (tel 2-00-84), conveniently located on the Jardín Unión, is an old building dating from 1863 with real charm. The Posada has all the amenities plus a romantic sidewalk café (you don't have to stay here to visit it). Singles cost US$25, doubles US$30.

Hotel San Diego (tel 2-13-00) is another 1st-class hotel on the Jardín Unión. Singles cost US$21, doubles US$26. If you are going to spend this kind of money, the Posada Santa Fe is worth the little bit extra.

The *Hostería del Frayle* (tel 2-11-79) at Sopena 3 is a good three-star hotel for the money. Singles cost US$15, doubles US$18.

Places to Eat

The *Pingus Restaurant* across from the

Posada Santa Fe at the Jardín Unión has no name on the outside, but is an excellent place for economical breakfasts and coffee. The best place for substantial and economical *típico* meals is the *Café El Retiro* opposite the Teatro Juárez at Sopena 12. Also across from Teatro Juárez and almost as good a deal as the Retiro is *Café Valadez* at Jardín Unión 3. For US$2, try the Valadez's excellent *pollo mole*.

If you are around the university between 12 noon and 4 pm, their cafeteria serves good, cheap food. Just a block to the left of the basilica is the *Centro Nutricional Vegetariano* at Ponciano Aguilar 45. Inexpensive and tasty, this is one of the best vegetarian restaurants for budget travellers in northern Mexico.

When near the post office, try *Las Palomas* at Calle de la Campana 19. This art gallery-cum-restaurant is a pleasant place for reasonably priced Mexican cuisine as well as some Italian dishes. Speaking of Italian, there are two excellent *Pizza Piazza* restaurants serving spaghetti and pizza with good Mexican beer. Good places to meet students, one Pizza Piazza is located in Plazuela San Fernando, the other to the back of the Jardín Unión in an alleyway. If you are staying on Insurgencia, the student hangout *Cocina Económica* at No 26 serves very cheap breakfasts and comidas corridas. Those really watching their pennies can risk their innards at food stalls near the bus station and around the Mercado Hidalgo.

Entertainment

A good *peña* or nightclub with folkloric singers in spiffy cowboy hats and regional outfits is *Rincón del Beso*, close to Casa Kloster at Alonso 21A. There's no cover charge and drinks are pretty reasonable. For rock and salsa, try *Sancho's Disco* at the Plazuela de Cata. Those seeking more classical entertainment should check with the tourist office about performances at Teatro Juárez or Teatro Principal.

On various weekends throughout the year, *entremeses* or short 1½-hour plays are presented in the Plazuela de San Roque. Performed by the University of Guanajuato's theatre department, these performances are worth seeing if only for the costumes and special effects (they are in Spanish). The tourist office knows the dates of performances; try to buy your tickets in advance from either the tourist office or Teatro Juárez.

Things to Buy

The Mercado Hidalgo, about one long block from the tourist office as you head toward the centre of town on Juárez, is a less-than-attractive iron grillwork structure whose two floors teem with sellers hawking mediocre pottery, some nice woollen and leather goods, and regional specialties ranging from touristy junk to well-made crafts. Mercado Hidalgo, even its food stalls, is uncommonly clean and uncluttered for Mexico and worth a stop.

Although more modern, far more typically Mexican is the Mercado Gavira next door, with the usual chaos. It's good fun. In either market, the multitude of food stalls may be cheap but should be chosen with discretion, or you risk the Guanajuatan gripe.

Getting There & Away

Bus There are a dozen daily Flecha Amarilla buses running to and from San Miguel de Allende, taking less than two hours at slightly more than US$1. There is regular 1st-class service to and from Mexico City (12 buses daily, about US$5), Querétaro (12 buses daily, US$1.50) and Guadalajara (16 buses daily, about US$5).

Rail Train service to Guanajuato is painfully pokey and is ill-considered in view of the frequent and far faster 1st-class bus service.

Getting Around

Most of Guanajuato's principal sights are within easy walking distance of the centre, as are the recommended hotels which may be reached on foot from the bus station. In fact part of the enjoyment of a visit here is exploring this medieval-style city and its colonial splendour on foot.

To reach the outer sights, consider a tour, or get there by local buses described under the individual sites. If you are tired upon arrival by bus and wish to stay at a hotel like Casa Kloster, 15 minutes' walk from the bus station, taxis are cheap – about US$1 if you bargain.

Tours For sights on the outskirts of Guanajuato, a 3½-hour tour, your choice of morning or afternoon departure, costs a mere US$2.50. Although the tour guide speaks only Spanish, the convenience of a direct ride to the sights justifies the expense.

You can buy your tickets from major hotels like the San Diego opposite Jardín Unión or from Transportes Turísticos de Guanajuato, which has an office down the street from the basilica. A minibus will take you to the following sights, affording some good views of the city en route: the Pipila Monument, La Valenciana Church and Mine, and of course the infamous mummies.

AROUND GUANAJUATO

The Pipila Monument, La Valenciana Mine and La Valenciana Church are most easily reached via the tour described earlier. If you have the time you can also visit these sights by public transport.

Pipila Monument

The monument honours the Indian miner whose daring enabled rebels to initially defeat the Spanish at the Alhóndiga de Granaditas. While the monument is somewhat less than impressive, the view from the site above the city makes up for it.

To get to the monument, take a bus designated 'Pipila', or walk along the Calle Sopena from Jardín Unión, making a right on Callejón de Calvario (you will see the sign-post 'Al Pipila'). The climb to the monument is steep but worthwhile, since you pass some interesting homes hanging over the cliffside. For a few pennies, you can go inside Pipila's statue and walk to the top, but it is really not worth the climb because the view is no better than from the monument's base.

La Valenciana Mine

To reach La Valenciana Mine and La Valenciana Church, take a bus designated 'Valenciana' that leaves hourly from a street directly beneath the Alhóndiga. The mine, which for 250 years produced 20% of the world's silver, was shut down after the Revolution. Reopened in 1968 and cooperatively run, the mine still yields some silver, nickel and lead. Today, miners may be seen descending an immense main shaft. The seemingly bottomless pit is carefully screened off to protect bystanders.

La Valenciana Church

More interesting than the mine is nearby La Valenciana Church. It was said that the silver baron of La Valenciana, Conde de Rul, tried to atone for exploiting the miners by building the ultimate in churrigueresque-style churches. Ground was broken in 1765, the church completed in 1788. La Valenciana's façade is spectacular and its interior dazzling with golden retablos, stained glass and filigree carvings.

LEÓN & IRAPUATO

The industrial towns of León and Irapuato, north-west and south-west of Guanajuato respectively, have little to offer the visitor. Guanajuato city is close enough to overnight in instead; buses depart at all hours.

Founded in 1576, León has a few remnants of the colonial past like its Palacio Municipal and cathedral, but industrial and population growth to a million inhabitants have completely robbed the city of its charm. Perhaps the only reason to briefly stop here is to pick up a cheap pair of shoes in Mexico's foremost *zapato*-manufacturing centre. If for some reason you must overnight here, take a local bus from the station to the city centre; Avenida Juárez has inexpensive hotels like the *Paris* or *America*.

Other than its famed strawberries, industrial Irapuato has no visitor attractions. If you are stuck here for a few hours, make a brief stop at the baroque Iglesia del Hospital built in 1713 and the Templo de San Francisco.

SAN MIGUEL DE ALLENDE
Population: 40,000

San Miguel is proof that Mexico and the USA can be friends. A colonial town in a beautiful setting, it's also home to a big colony of artistically inclined North Americans. If you squirm at the notion of 3000 or so gringos congregated in one small Mexican town, reserve judgment until you've been there – for both cultures manage to show themselves in their best light in San Miguel.

The Americans' dollars help make them welcome, of course, and the place

León

certainly has its neo-colonial aspect (count the number of Mexicans in any smart restaurant), but relations between the two communities are distinctly friendly. Some long-time foreign residents are fully involved in the town's life, and there are voluntary and co-operative organisations which help promote goodwill. The type of American attracted to San Miguel also helps – generally they're the sort who are likely to be sensitive to local feelings and culture. For the Mexicans' part, they are inordinately addicted to festivals, which makes the place even more colourful.

The physical beauty of San Miguel stems from the hillside setting of its many lovely old buildings and streets, which give vistas over plains and low ranges of hills far into the distance. It's particularly beautiful in March when multitudes of jacaranda trees sprout mauve blossoms. Set 1910 metres high, the place has a very agreeable climate (a few degrees hotter than Mexico City and never too much rain) and superbly clear light, which is one reason it attracts artists. Along with the artists come musicians, writers, language or arts students and others just looking for a pleasant place to hang out. Some foreigners have lived here for decades, others return year after year; nearly all find it easy to feel at home. Many of them are middle-aged or older. San Miguel is also a good base for visiting Guanajuato, Querétaro, Dolores Hidalgo and other places in the area.

On the debit side it's not, in general, cheap by Mexican standards; there are only a few bottom-range hostelries and most of the central eating places are in the upper bracket. This is a result of San Miguel's popularity among older and better-heeled North Americans. Peak tourist period in San Miguel is January to March. April, May, October and November are the quietest months.

The 'de' in San Miguel's name is often left out, so it's usually pronounced 'san mig-ELL a-YEN-deh'.

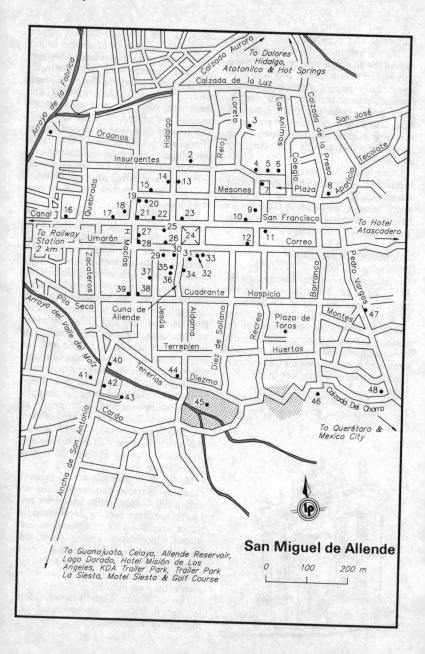

San Miguel de Allende

0   100   200 m

To Dolores
Hidalgo,
Atotonilco & Hot Springs

To Hotel
Atascadero

To Railway
Station
2 km

To Querétaro &
Mexico City

To Guanajuato, Celaya, Allende Reservoir,
Lago Dorado, Hotel Misión de Los
Angeles, KDA Trailer Park, Trailer Park
La Siesta, Motel Siesta & Golf Course

Nine km south of the town, near the Celaya road, is the Ignacio Allende dam and reservoir, opened in 1978.

History

San Miguel, the story goes, owes its founding to a few hot dogs. These hounds were dearly loved by a Franciscan monk, Fray Juan de San Miguel, who started a mission near an often-dry river five km from the present town in 1542. One day they wandered off from the mission and didn't come back. A search party found them reclining at the spring called El Chorro in the south of the present town, presumably enjoying its refreshing waters. This site was so much better than the original that the mission was moved.

Fray Juan was a courageous barefoot friar who had already spent a decade among the Tarascans of Michoacán before being sent as abbot to a monastery in Acámbaro, between Celaya and Morelia, in 1540. From there he moved to Querétaro to push missionary work northwards. San Miguel was the most northerly Spanish settlement in central Mexico when it was founded. Tarascans and Tlaxcalans were brought to help pacify and convert the Otomíes and Chichimecs of the surrounding area.

The Chichimecs were not easily subdued and San Miguel only just survived until 1555, when a Spanish garrison was established here to protect the new road to the silver centre of Zacatecas. By the end of the 16th century the town had forsaken its previous names of San Miguel El Viejo and San Miguel de los Chichimecas to become San Miguel El Grande. Spanish cattle and crop growers settled in the surrounding area and San Miguel grew into a thriving commercial centre known for its sarapes, knives and horse tackle, and home for some of the wealthy Guanajuato silver barons.

San Miguel's greatest son, Ignacio Allende, was born here in 1779. He became a fervent believer in the need for Mexican independence and, despite being in the colonial army, was one of the leaders of a conspiracy which set 8 December 1810 as the date for armed uprising.

When the plan – and some weapons – were discovered by the authorities in Querétaro on 13 September, a messenger rushed to San Miguel. Allende was not there but Juan de Aldama, another conspirator, was. Aldama sped north to Dolores where, in the early hours of 16 September, he found Allende at the house of the local parish priest Miguel Hidalgo, also one of the coterie.

A few hours later Hidalgo proclaimed rebellion from his church. Within a few days – according to some accounts, the same night – San Miguel was in rebel hands, its local regiment having joined forces with the band of insurgent criollos, mestizos and Indians which had already grown to several hundred. The Spanish population of the town was locked up and some of the rebels set about looting it. Allende was only partly able to restrain them. Moving on to further victories at Celaya, Guanajuato (where there was a bloody massacre of the Spanish), Zacatecas, San Luis Potosí and Valladolid (now Morelia), the rebel army grew to about 80,000 and defeated the Spanish at Las Cruces near Mexico City. Against Allende's advice, Hidalgo decided not to attack the city itself, fearing an appalling massacre of its citizens. Instead he went west to occupy Guadalajara and was defeated by the army of General Félix Calleja at Puente de Calderón in January 1811.

The initial surge of the rebellion was spent – desertions weakened the rebel force and in March Hidalgo and Allende were captured in an ambush near Monclova in Coahuila and taken to Chihuahua. Allende was executed almost immediately, Hidalgo four months later having been found guilty of heresy and treason by the authorities. It was only after 10 more years of struggle that Mexico finally achieved independence.

In 1826 San Miguel was rechristened San Miguel de Allende. It began to take on its current character with the founding of the Escuela de Bellas Artes (School of Fine Arts) in 1938 and the Instituto

Allende in 1951, both of which attracted many foreign students. San Miguel has been declared a national monument, which means that new building is restricted to preserve its colonial character.

Orientation

San Miguel's main bus station has moved several times in recent years, but at the time of writing it's a dusty yard near the small river called Arroyo de la Fábrica which skirts the west side of town. The streets which meet at the top corner of the bus station are Organos (going east, up the hill) and Beneficencia. It's about 800 mildly uphill metres to the town centre. Go three blocks up Organos until you can't go any further, then to the right along Hernández Macías for three blocks. Immediately after you pass the yellow bulk of the Centro Cultural Ignacio Ramírez on the right, turn left uphill along Canal for one block. You are now in the zócalo, called the Plaza Allende or Plaza Principal, with the parroquia (parish church) towering on one side.

From here the town continues a bit steeper uphill to the east, falls away gently to the south, and is roughly level with the north. Many hotels and restaurants are within a couple of blocks of the plaza, but in any case San Miguel is a compact town and very few places cannot be reached on foot.

Information

Tourist Office The office (tel 2-17-47) – helpful and knowledgeable, excellent big maps of the city if you ask nicely – is at the Correo corner of the zócalo. It's open 10 am to 2.45 pm and 5 to 7 pm Monday to Friday, 10 am to 1 pm Saturday, 10 am to 12 noon Sunday.

Money Of the two banks on San Francisco half a block from the zócalo, Multibanco Comermex is much quicker. There's another bank on the west side of the zócalo. San Miguel must have the world's most beautiful bank buildings. Unfortunately the hours when they're prepared to change dollars can be short and early (eg 9 to 10 am only) and queues long. The Hotel Posada San Francisco on the zócalo will change cash dollars at close to the bank rate when banks are shut. Also try some of the shops in the streets round the zócalo – they may even give a better rate than the banks for cash. The casa de cambio at Mesones 5 only takes cash.

Post The post office is one block up Correo from the zócalo. It's open (including lista de correos) 8 am to 7 pm Monday to Friday, 9 am to 1 pm Saturday. Queues are often long.

Books El Colibri bookshop on the Umarán corner of the zócalo has lots of English-language books. Lagundi in Plaza Colonial on the corner of Canal and Hernández Macías has a few. The Biblioteca Pública (Public Library) at Insurgentes 25 has thousands to be borrowed, plus magazines. It's open daily except Sundays and holidays from 10 am to 2 pm and 4 to 7 pm. On Thursday from 10.30 am to 1 pm there's a bring-and-buy sale of books and other things here. Bellas Artes has a good bookshop.

Newspapers & Noticeboards The expatriate community puts out a Friday newspaper in English called *Atención San Miguel* (20c). It's full of what's on and the comings, goings and doings of the longer-stayers and their friends, plus lots of small ads offering rooms, apartments, or houses to sell, rent or exchange; furniture sales; house-sitter jobs; classes in yoga, Spanish, art or dance; Alcoholics Anonymous in English; easels for sale; meditation sessions in hot springs. You can buy the paper at the Biblioteca Pública, El Colibri bookshop and the Sánchez and Supervinos supermarkets on the zócalo; and at Lagundi and La Dolce Vita in Plaza Colonial on the corner of Canal and Hernández Macías.

Noticeboards in the Biblioteca Pública and the Autotienda shop on the west side of the zócalo offer the same sort of things. There are also noticeboards in Bellas Artes (what's on) and in hotels.

Courses The reputation of San Miguel's art schools has fallen a little since the heady 1940s when Siqueiros was taking mural-painting courses at Bellas Artes. In part this is due to the many amateurs who come to pursue artistic hobbies rather than careers. It works to the advantage of most people, since there are many easy-to-join courses which demand only enthusiasm. Language courses – group or private – are numerous; some of them are listed here, or just ask around. Most courses run almost year-round with just a three-week break in December.

Instituto Allende (tel 2-01-90), in an old mansion on Ancha de San Antonio, offers courses in fine art, crafts and Spanish. Art and craft courses can be joined at any time, usually involve nine hours of attendance a week and cost between US$110 and US$225 a month. They can often count for credits in North American college courses. Spanish courses begin about every two weeks and range from conversational (50 minutes a day, US$70 for four weeks) to total impact (individual tuition, three hours a day, US$410 for a month). Write to Instituto Allende, San Miguel de Allende, Guanajuato 37700, Mexico for details.

Bellas Artes (tel 2-02-89), also called the Centro Cultural El Nigromante or Centro Cultural Ignacio Ramírez, is at Hernández Macías 75 on the corner of Canal in a beautiful old monastery. Courses in art, dance, crafts and music here are aimed primarily at Mexicans, are usually in Spanish and cost around US$5 a month for nine hours a week.

The Academía Hispano Americana (tel 2-03-49 or 2-23-33) at Mesones 4 runs combined Spanish-language and Mexican-culture courses at US$240 a month. It aims to 'prepare serious students for a life among the peoples of Latin America'. Write for more information.

Other language schools include Casa de la Luna at Cuadrante 2 (small classes, US$2 an hour, at least 10 hours a week), which was highly recommended by one traveller, and Inter-Idiomas (tel 2-21-77) at Mesones 15.

Walking Tours A tour of some of the lovely houses and gardens in San Miguel which are otherwise closed to the public departs at 11.30 am every Sunday except in December from the Biblioteca Pública. You pay a few dollars. Another walking tour goes from the San Miguel Writing Centre at Hernández Macías 101 on Friday at 9.30 am – call 2-04-35 for information and reservations.

Riding Club Pegaso (tel 2-02-55) at Huertas 19 is run by two North Americans and offers trail riding, jumping or dressage courses.

Consulate The US Consulate (tel 2-23-57 or in emergencies 2-00-68, 2-09-80) is at Hernández Macías 72, behind La Dolce Vita restaurant in Plaza Colonial on the corner of Canal and Hernández Macías. It's open 9 am to 1 pm Monday and Wednesday, and 4 to 7 pm Monday to Thursday.

Other There's a nine-hole golf course about 1½ km out of town on the Guanajuato road, and a laundromat at Local J in Pasaje Allende, open 8 am to 8 pm except Sunday.

Festivals

Being so well endowed with churches and patron saints (it has six – San Miguel, San Juan Bautista, the Virgins of Guadalupe and Loreto, La Inmaculada and San José), San Miguel has a multitude of festivals every month of the year. You'll probably learn of some by word of mouth – or the sound of fireworks – while you're there. Some of the more important ones:

Blessing of Animals This happens in several churches including the parroquia on 17 January.

Allende's Birthday On 21 January various official events celebrate this occasion.

Candelaria Seeds are blessed in the parroquia on this day, 2 February, as a plea for good crops.

Cristo de la Conquista This image in the parroquia is fêted on the first Friday in March.

Semana Santa Events begin two weekends before Easter with a pilgrimage carrying an image of the Señor de la Columna (Lord of the Column) from Atotonilco, 14 km north, to the church of San Juan de Díos in San Miguel on Saturday night or Sunday morning.

On the Friday before Palm Sunday people visit each others' homes, where images of the Virgin Mary are decorated and surrounded by flowers and young wheat plants.

During Semana Santa itself, the week before Easter, the many activities include a lavish procession of silence on Good Friday and the burning or exploding of images of Judas Iscariot on Easter Day. Families build brightly decorated altars in their homes.

Las Yuntas (The Yokes) This unusual festival traditionally happens on 31 May outside the town on the old road to Mexico City. Oxen are dressed in lime necklaces and painted tortillas, and their yokes are festooned with flowers and fruit. One beast carries on its back two boxes of 'treasure' (bread and sugar) and is surrounded by characters in bizarre costumes on horses or donkeys. A mock battle between 'Indians' and 'Federales' follows. A wizard appears to heal the 'wounded' and raise the 'dead'.

Corpus Christi This moveable feast in June features dances by children in front of the parroquia. One is called Los Hortelanos (The Gardeners).

Independence The anniversary of the beginning of the independence movement features several days of festivities leading up to a parade on 16 September.

San Miguel Arcángel Celebrations honouring the town's chief patron saint take in the weekend before or after the actual saint's day on 29 September. There are cockfights, bullfights and reportedly a running of bulls through the streets, but the hub of a general town party is provided by traditional dancers from several states who meet at Cruz del Cuarto, on the road to the railway station. Wearing bells and costumes which include feather head-dresses, scarlet cloaks and masks, groups carry flower offerings called *xuchiles*, and some play lutes made of armadillo-shell. They then walk in procession to the zócalo and the parroquia. The roots of these performances probably go back to pre-Hispanic times.

Dances continue over a few days and include the Danza Guerrera in front of the parroquia, which represents the Spanish conquest of the Chichimecs. The dancers also make processions to cemeteries.

Day of the Dead An unusual local touch to this fiesta at the beginning of November is the making of candies from orchid bulbs.

Christmas This starts on 16 December, the first of nine nights of *posada* (inn) parties in which families traditionally get together to sing carols, re-enact Joseph and Mary's search for an inn, and break *piñatas* – clay pots filled with gifts and decorated with tissue paper to form animals, people, stars, pineapples, etc. The nine nights represent the nine-day journey of Joseph and Mary from Nazareth to Bethlehem.

Buildings

Part of the joy of San Miguel is just wandering the streets – around every second corner you come upon another fine old building or new vista. Some of the most interesting buildings are described here in an order you can follow on foot. For more detail on these and others, pick up a copy of the INAH guide to San Miguel Allende (in English).

Parish Church The parroquia – or rather its pink 'sugar-candy' tower – dominates the zócalo. This strange structure, all soaring pinnacles, is gothic in impact but really belongs to no architectural school at all. It was designed by an untutored local Indian, Zeferino Gutiérrez, in the late 19th century. He reputedly instructed the builders by scratching plans in the sand with a stick. Most of the rest of the church dates from the late 17th century.

The *camarín*, a chapel beside the main altar which contains ceremonial clothing for saints' images, was designed by Mexico's best-known neoclassical architect, Eduardo Tresguerras, around 1800. The crypt contains the remains of a 19th-century Mexican president, Anastasio Bustamante. In the chapel to the left of the main altar is a much-revered image of the Cristo de la Conquista (Christ of the Conquest), made by Indians in Pátzcuaro from cornstalks and orchid bulbs, probably in the 16th century.

The church to the left of the parroquia is San Rafael, founded in 1742, which has also undergone gothic-type alterations.

Museo Casa de Allende Over the road from the parroquia at the Cuna de Allende corner of the zócalo stands the house where Ignacio Allende was born, recently turned into a museum dedicated to the man and the independence movement he was instrumental in starting. An inscription on the façade says *Hic natus ubique notus* – Latin for 'Born here, known everywhere'. Another plaque points out that the better-known independence hero, Miguel Hidalgo, only joined the movement after being invited by Allende. The museum is open 10 am to 4 pm Tuesday to Saturday, 10 am to 2 pm Sunday.

Casa de los Perros The 'House of the Dogs', so-called because of the carved canines supporting its main balcony, is at Umarán 4. Here lived one of San Miguel's many independence heroes, Juan de Umarán. Today it's occupied by the Galería Maxwell shop.

Casa del Mayorazgo de Canal This is one of the most imposing of San Miguel's colonial residences. It's private property but the exterior gives a good idea of the splendour in which the Canal family lived. The entrance is at Canal 4 and it stretches above the arcade on the west side of the zócalo. The neoclassic building has some late baroque touches. The façade on Canal has Corinthian columns and, above, an image of the Virgin of Loreto.

San Francisco This church on the north side of a small garden at the corner of San Francisco and Juárez has an elaborate late-18th-century churrigueresque façade. An image of San Francisco de Assisi is at the top, and the Crucifixion appears below it with Our Lady of Sorrows and San Juan on either side. The tower and interior are mainly neoclassical.

Tercer Orden This chapel on the west side of the same garden was built in the early 18th century and like San Francisco church was part of a Franciscan monastery complex. The main façade shows San Francisco and symbols of the Franciscan order. On the side of the building can be seen San Diego and the two-armed cross of Lorraine.

Oratorio de San Felipe Neri This multi-towered and domed church, built in the early 18th century, stands at the corner of Insurgentes and Llamas. The main façade is baroque with Indian influence. Five niches hold statues of San José, San Juan Bautista, San Felipe, San Pedro and San Pablo. A passage to the right of this façade leads to the east wall, which has an Indian-style doorway with an image of Our Lady of Solitude that dates from an earlier church on the site. The adjacent filled-in doorway is topped by a medallion of San Felipe and a cross of Lorraine. You can also see into the cloister from this side of the church.

Inside the church there are 33 oil paintings showing scenes from the life of San Felipe Neri, the 16th-century Florentine who founded the Oratorio Catholic order. In the east transept is a painting of the Virgin of Guadalupe by Miguel Cabrera. The altars are primarily neoclassical but the main one has some older paintings on mirrors.

In the west transept of the church are two pairs of twisted baroque pillars at the entrance to a very lavishly decorated chapel, the Santa Casa de Loreto, built in 1735. It's a replica of a chapel in Loreto, Italy, legendary home of the Virgin Mary. If the chapel doors are open you can see tiles from Puebla, China and Valencia on the floor and walls, gilded cloth hangings and images above the tombs of chapel founder Manuel de la Canal and his wife María de Hervas de Flores. The altar has an image of the Virgin of Loreto in a glass case. Behind the altar, the *camarín* has six more altars – mostly very elaborate gilded baroque. In one is a reclining wax figure of San Columbano which contains the saint's bones.

La Salud This is the church with the big shell carved above its entrance, just east of San Felipe Neri. The façade is early churrigueresque. Above the door is a figure of La Inmaculada, at the sides are San Joachim and Santa Ana, and below are San Juan Evangelista and El Sagrado Corazón (Sacred Heart). The dome, covered in blue and yellow tiles, has a prickly-pear-shaped lantern. The church's paintings include San Javier by Miguel Cabrera.

Colegio de Sales Next door to La Salud, which used to be part of it, this was once a college run by the order of San Felipe Neri. Founded in the mid-18th century, it counted among its alumni many of the 1810 revolutionaries. The local Spaniards were locked up here when the rebels took San Miguel.

Bellas Artes This education and cultural centre at the corner of Canal and Hernández Macías is housed in the beautiful former monastery of La Concepción, started in the mid-18th century. The cloister is neoclassical and so is the dome of the monastery church, added in the late 19th century by the versatile Zeferino Gutiérrez, who was possibly inspired by pictures of Les Invalides in Paris.

One room in the cloister is devoted to an unfinished mural by David Alfaro Siqueiros, done in 1948 as part of a course in mural painting for US war veterans. The subject of the work – though you wouldn't guess it – is the life and work of Ignacio Allende. More accessible murals in Bellas Artes were done by Pedro Martínez in the early 1940s. They include *La Cantina, Los Tejedores* (The Weavers) and *El Fanatismo del Pueblo – la caza del vampiro* (The Fanaticism of the People – the vampire hunt).

Inquisition Jail This is at the corner of Cuadrante and Hernández Macías. The cross carved on the corner of the building is an Inquisition emblem. Over the road is a house occupied by Inquisitor Victorino de las Fuentes in 1815.

Instituto Allende Begun in 1735 as the home of the Conde de la Canal who paid for the Santa Casa de Loreto chapel in the Oratorio de San Felipe Neri, this later became a Carmelite convent before eventually taking on its present role in 1951. Located at Ancha de San Antonio 4, it's a large, pleasant building with several patios and an old chapel. Above the entrance is a carving of the Virgin of Loreto, patroness of the Canal family. Cardo, the first street going east of Ancha de San Antonio beyond the Instituto, leads to the cool Parque Benito Juárez.

Famous Names
Partly thanks to its key role in the independence movement, San Miguel has more than its fair share of homes of the famous. Ones not already mentioned include those of Juan and Ignacio de Aldama (independence) at San Francisco 10; Luis Malo (independence) at Cuna de Allende 5; Francisco de Lanzagorta (independence) at Correo 4; El Pipila, the man who burned down the door of the Guanajuato Alhóndiga to begin the massacre of the Spaniards inside, at Barranca 90; Mariano Escobedo, leader of the Mexican forces which drove out the French in the 1860s, at Mesones 85; and Ignacio Ramírez, a leading mid-19th century liberal thinker known as El Nigromante (The Sorcerer) at Umarán 28. These are not generally open to the public.

Lookout Point & Park
One of the best views over the town and surrounding country is from the Mirador up on Calle Real de Querétaro past the Posada La Ermita in the south-east of the town. If you take Calzada del Chorro, the street leading directly downhill from here, and turn left at the bottom, you reach El Chorro, the spring where the town was founded. Today it gushes out of a fountain built in 1960. A bit further down the hill is the shady Parque Benito Juárez.

Hot Springs & Atotonilco
An exhilarating short trip out of San Miguel is to the hot springs of La Gruta, close to the important shrine of Atotonilco. La Gruta (open daily 9 am to 5 pm, entrance US$1.50) consists of three small swimming pools into which the waters of a

thermal spring have been channelled. The hottest pool is in a cave entered through a tunnel and lit by a single shaft of sunlight. You can have a shoulder massage from the hot water as it gushes from the cave roof. Take your swimming gear and towel with you.

Buses to La Gruta supposedly leave every hour from in front of the Oratorio de San Felipe Neri in San Miguel, but in practice are highly irregular. A taxi costs US$3, or you could try getting one of the frequent Dolores Hidalgo buses from the bus station to drop you. La Gruta is 13 km north of San Miguel on the Dolores road, a few metres from signs saying 'Manantiales de La Gruta' on the left of the road or 'Parador del Cortijo' on the right. Returning to San Miguel, flag down any of the buses that speed past going south. One will stop before very long.

The track past La Gruta leads to the hamlet of Atotonilco, about a km away, dominated by the *santuario* (sanctuary) founded by Father Luis Felipe Neri de Alfaro in 1740 as a spiritual retreat. Here Ignacio Allende was married in 1802; eight years later he returned with Miguel Hidalgo and the band of independence rebels en route from Dolores to San Miguel to take the shrine's banner of the Virgin of Guadalupe as their flag – a clever move which drew the support of Indians who have a special reverence for the Virgin of Guadalupe.

Today Atotonilco is a goal of pilgrims and penitents from all over Mexico. It's also the starting point of an important and solemn procession two weekends before Easter, in which the image of the Señor de la Columna is carried to the church of San Juan de Dios in San Miguel. Inside, the sanctuary has six chapels and is vibrant with statues, folk murals and other paintings. Outside you can pick up a booklet called *El Venerado y Histórico Santuario de Atotonilco, Guanajuato* by José Mercadillo Miranda, a parish priest who did much to preserve and explain the works of art in the shrine. Indian dances

are held here on the third Sunday in July.

There's another hot spring at Taboada, eight km north of San Miguel on the Dolores road, then two km west along a side-road. The three swimming pools here (one of them Olympic-size) are filled with thermal waters. Entry is US$1.50. There's also the luxurious *Hacienda Hotel Taboada* (tel 2-08-50), where rooms cost upwards of US$30. Buses are supposed to go to Taboada from the Oratorio de San Felipe Neri in San Miguel at 9 and 11 am, and at 1 and 3 pm.

Places to Stay

Most of the cheaper places in San Miguel would be in the middle range in most Mexican towns. Many of the best-value places are often full. Book ahead if you can. If you can't, you'll find a room somewhere but may have to pay more. The tourist office will ring round for you if you like. Some hotels give discounts for long-term guests. The places listed here include private bathrooms.

If you're planning to stay in San Miguel a few weeks or more, consider renting your own place or house-sitting for someone. There are plenty of places available; check the newspapers and noticeboards.

Places to Stay – bottom end

The dingy *Hotel Hidalgo* (tel 2-02-75) at Hidalgo 22 has 15 small rooms at US$2 per person.

One of San Miguel's best-value places and therefore often full is the *Parador de San Sebastian* (tel 2-07-07) at Mesones 7. It's family-run, with plain but pleasant rooms on two levels round an arcaded courtyard, and great views from the roof. Singles/doubles are US$4/5.

Also good value is the *Hotel Quinta Loreto* (tel 2-00-42), which has 31 good rooms round a big garden at Calle de Loreto 15 (the entrance is opposite No 48). There's also a tennis court, swimming pool, plenty of parking space and a popular restaurant. It's only a few blocks from the zócalo but is in a part of town where few tourists go. Singles/doubles are US$4.75/6. Weekly rates are US$30/39 without meals, US$53/85 with two meals a day. Monthly, you pay US$120/156 without meals, US$213/340 with two meals a day.

The *Hotel Vista Hermosa* (tel 2-00-78, 2-04-37) at Cuna de Allende 11, just off the zócalo, has 16 rooms round a three-storey courtyard at US$3.75/4 for singles/doubles. Good value but often full. Over the road the *Posada Allende*, built into the side of the parroquia, has five dilapidated and overpriced rooms but is run by an eccentric and friendly old lady. Singles/doubles are US$3.75/5.50 in a one-bed room, doubles/triples are US$6.50/8.50 in a two-bed room.

Camping The *Lago Dorado KDA Trailer Park* (tel 2-23-01) advertises a swimming pool, lounge, laundromat and all hook-ups. To reach it from the town, turn right off the Celaya road after three km at the Hotel Misión de los Angeles, then continue for two km, crossing a railway en route. Its postal address is Apartado Postal 523, San Miguel de Allende, Guanajuato. The *Trailer Park La Siesta* (tel 2-02-07) is on the grounds of the Motel La Siesta, on the Celaya road two km out of town. You can use the motel facilities such as swimming pool and tennis court. The postal address is Apartado Postal 72. Both places have about 70 sites and charge around US$4 for two people.

Places to Stay – middle
The *Posada Carmina* (tel 2-04-58) at Cuna de Allende 7, next door to the Hotel Vista Hermosa, has a nice courtyard and just 10 fair-sized, clean rooms. Singles/doubles are US$6.75/8. The postal address is Apartado Postal 219.

The very friendly and comfortable *Hotel Mesón de San Antonio* (tel 2-05-80) is at Mesones 80 near the corner of Hernández Macías. There are just 14 double rooms round two courtyards, all at US$12. Some have a sitting room as well as a bedroom; all are well furnished, some beautifully. Meals are available but pets and children are banned.

The convivial *Hotel Central* (tel 2-08-51), at Canal 19 just down from the zócalo, has clean, sizeable rooms round two courtyards (a fountain in one). Quite a few language students and other medium-term stayers use it. For US$9 single or US$14 double you also get breakfast. Some of the downstairs rooms are a bit damp. There are some bigger rooms – suitable if you're staying a while – on the roof.

Posada de las Monjas (tel 2-01-71) at Canal 37 is a rambling place with good, clean rooms of varying sizes, patios to sit in, parking space and a cafeteria. Singles are US$9 to US$10.75, doubles US$10.75 to US$12.50.

Places to Stay – top end
The *Posada San Francisco* (tel 2-00-72, 2-14-66), on the zócalo at Plaza Principal 2, has 48 big, well-furnished rooms round two courtyards (the front one has a fountain). The upstairs rooms have better views. There's a TV lounge too. Singles/doubles are US$13.75/15.25. The postal address is Apartado Postal 40.

Huéspedes Féliz, out towards the Instituto Allende at the corner of Calle del Codo and Ancha de San Antonio, has comfortable doubles for US$15 including breakfast.

Behind the Instituto at Ancha de San Antonio 30, the *Hotel Aristos San Miguel* (tel 2-01-49 or 2-02-92) has a big garden and singles/doubles for US$14.75/17.75. There are also some bungalows at US$350 a month but they're booked for up to four years ahead!

Hard to beat for a longer stay in the top bracket is *La Mansión del Bosque* (tel 2-02-77) at Aldama 65. American Ruth Hyba has turned her home into a superb guest house around several patios. Each of the 23 very comfortable, well furnished and beautifully decorated rooms is completely different from the others. All the paintings in the rooms have been given by guests. Some rooms have good views over the rooftops to the countryside, some have private terraces, all have a gas or open fire. Most have bathtubs as well as showers. There is a dining room/bar and a big lounge/library too. Rates include two meals a day; singles are US$25 to US$32, doubles US$50 to US$55. Discounts are offered in April, May, October and November if you book ahead. Reservations by the beginning of August are advised if you're planning to visit in January, February or March, when one month is usually the minimum stay. The postal address is Apartado Postal 206. Most of the guests are women.

Opposite the Instituto, the *Posada La Aldea* (tel 2-10-22, 2-12-96) at Ancha de San Antonio s/n has 66 rooms, about half of them overlooking an enormous garden/courtyard with a fountain in the middle. There's a big dining room, swimming pool, lounge, games room and TV room. Singles/doubles are US$17.25/21.75.

Posada La Ermita (tel 2-07-77), a former coaching inn at Pedro Vargas 64 some way uphill from the zócalo, has 24 fine suites with fireplaces, big bedrooms, sitting rooms and terraces. Some have superb views. There's a swimming pool, bar and dining room. Singles/doubles are US$22.75/27.25, but you can fit five people in a suite for US$37.

The *Hotel Sierra Nevada* (tel 2-04-15) in three colonial houses at Hospicio 35 is the top place in town at US$60 to US$130 for a double.

Outside the town, there's the *Hotel Misión de los Angeles* (tel 2-10-26), three km south on the Celaya road. It has a swimming pool and singles/doubles are around US$22/27. More expensive is the *Hotel El Atascadero* (tel 2-02-06), a converted hacienda (turn off the Querétaro road at the sign 1½ km out of town).

Places to Eat

Some of the best food in town – at good prices too – is to be found at the little *Fonda La Mesa del Matador* on Hernández Macías between Canal and Umarán. Spaghetti a la Mesa, prepared at your table with shrimp and wine, is US$2. The place also specialises in chicken dishes; *pollo suprema Parmesana* (sliced chicken breast dipped in Parmesan cheese and fried, served with beetroot, carrots and French fries) is just US$2.25.

The *Hotel Quinta Loreto* restaurant at Loreto 15 is popular and reasonably priced (soup US$0.50, roast pork or hamburger US$1.50). It also does a good-value comida corrida.

El Trigal on the corner of Umarán and Hernández Macías has just a few tables and the fare is mainly vegetarian. A three-course vegetarian comida corrida costs US$2. Also try stuffed tomatoes (US$1.25), ensalada chef (US$1.75), burgers (vegetarian US$1.50, with ham or bacon US$2), granola and yoghurt with fruit (US$1), or carrot juice (US$0.30).

Café Colón (tel 2-09-89) at San Francisco 21, near the corner of Juárez, isn't bad value for San Miguel with a range of salads from US$1.75 to US$2.50, burgers or four enchiladas at US$2.50, and lots of egg options. Iced tea comes hot – you pour it over ice.

The small *Tuti Fruti* on Hidalgo between Mesones and Insurgentes does a four-course comida corrida for US$1.75, also breakfast for US$1, hamburger with chips or enchiladas US$1.50, and a great Tuti-Fruti mixed-fruit juice for US$0.75.

La Dolce Vita is a smarter café inside the Plaza Colonial on the corner of Canal and Hernández Macías. It specialises in great pastries, cakes and ice cream. A croissant with ham and cheese will set you back US$1.

For a treat, go to *Señor Plato* (tel 2-06-26, closed Monday) at Jesús 7. Tables are spaced around a greenery-filled courtyard and the fare is delicious – *camarones cerveza* (shrimp in beer) are US$7.25, *medallones a limón* (beef medallions in lemon sauce) or *huachinango* (snapper)

Rockefeller US$5, spaghetti al burro US$2.25, oyster cocktail US$2.50. And you can fill up on the free titbits before you even start what you've ordered!

Restaurant Mama Mia (tel 2-20-63) at Umarán 8, in a beautiful pink-pillared courtyard, is packed most nights with people eating, drinking and listening to excellent live music. The food's good but there should be more of it for the price. Lasagne is US$2.50, fettucine or spaghetti is US$1.50 to US$2, *pollo pechuga Florentine* (chicken breast in spinach) comes with salad and baked potato and costs US$3.75, Irish coffee is US$3.50. Mama Mia is open at lunch-time too.

On Insurgentes near the corner of Hernández Macías, a street stall sells half a chicken and potatoes for US$1 late into the night.

Entertainment

San Miguel has, as you would expect, a thriving cultural and entertainment scene. Keep an eye on the noticeboards or buy a copy of *Atención San Miguel* to find out what's on. Some events are held in English.

Mama Mia restaurant on Umarán has good live music (flamenco guitar, pan pipes, etc) nightly and at lunch-time. A separate bar on the premises sometimes features rock or local bands. *La Fragua* restaurant on Cuna de Allende has a Mexican folk band. *Pancho & Lefty's* on Mesones between Hidalgo and Hernández Macías has rock videos and sometimes live bands. Tuesday and Wednesday are quieter nights, when some places close.

El Ring (tel 2-19-98) on Hidalgo between Mesones and Insurgentes is the most popular disco. *Laberinto's* (tel 2-03-62) at Ancha de San Antonio 7, almost opposite the Instituto Allende, is a bit cheaper. There's also *Los Topos* (tel 2-04-89) at Hidalgo 96.

Bellas Artes is a major venue for exhibitions, theatre and concerts, some featuring international names, and holds an annual chamber music festival in August. The *Instituto Allende* also has exhibitions. The *Teatro Angelo Peratta* on Mesones near the corner of Hernández Macías holds regular concerts with old-fashioned instruments. The *Café-Teatro Athanor* at Mesones 5 has drama or puppet theatre on Friday and Saturday nights.

Good art galleries include *Galería San Miguel* at Umarán 1 for contemporary art, and *Galería Atenea* at Mesones 83 on the corner of Hidalgo.

Things to Buy

San Miguel has several markets. The main one is just off Canal about six blocks downhill from the zócalo. Another market on Colegio behind the Colegio de Sales offers fruit, vegetables, flowers, shoes and clothes. There's also a good fruit and vegetable market by La Salud church.

Local crafts include tinware (especially lamps), wrought iron, silver, brass, leather and sarapes. Most of these are products of long traditions going back to the 18th century; it is even said the sarape was invented here. Some of the best handicrafts and folk art from elsewhere in Mexico, and even further afield, also find their way to San Miguel, where numerous shops sell them – at a price. You can find almost anything; if the shop you're in hasn't got a Huichol yarn painting or a Guatemalan huipil, ask where to go. Casa Maxwell, which runs right through from Canal to Umarán half a block down from zócalo, has a huge stock of crafts and there are many other shops within a few blocks.

Beckmann on Hernández Macías half a block south of Cuadrante has a good selection of silver. So does the more expensive Joyería David (tel 2-00-56), at Zacatecas 53. A pottery shop at Mesones 85 on the corner of Hidalgo sells pretty Talavera tiles about seven cm square made in Dolores Hidalgo for 10c each. Casa Canal (tel 2-04-79) at Canal 3 on the corner of Hidalgo has women's clothes by Josefa, the Mexican international designer.

A hand-embroidered skirt and jacket would set you back about US$60.

Getting There & Away

Road San Miguel is 30 km west of Highway 57 from Querétaro to San Luis Potosí. Paved roads from the highway approach San Miguel from the north-east and south-east. San Miguel is 58 km from Querétaro, 172 km from San Luis Potosí. Other decent roads lead north to Dolores Hidalgo (41 km) and south to Celaya (50 km). For Guanajuato you can go to Dolores, then west for 54 km; or take a rougher but still paved road west from the Celaya road 11 km out of San Miguel. Mexico City is 270 km from San Miguel.

Bus San Miguel has worse bus connections than almost any comparable town in Mexico. The services are frequent enough, but most are 2nd class and timetables are scarce and unreliable. You can never be sure when a bus is leaving until it's pulling out of the dusty yard that currently serves as a bus station at the corner of Organos and Beneficencia. You can get a rough idea by asking there beforehand (English is rarely spoken).

Tres Estrellas de Oro runs two 1st-class buses a day each way between San Miguel and Mexico City (US$3.75, four hours). Flecha Amarilla and (better) Herradura de Plata, both 2nd class, do the same trip every hour in about the same time for US$3.25. To or from Querétaro (US$0.75, 1¼ hours) there's just one 1st-class bus daily, run by Omnibus de México, and 2nd-class buses by Flecha Amarilla and Herradura de Plata every half-hour or so.

Flecha Amarilla (tel 2-00-84) also has buses to Guanajuato (US$1) seven times a day, San Luis Potosí (US$2.25, four hours) six times, Aguascalientes (US$2.75) three times, León (US$1.75) 11 times, Celaya (US$0.75) and Dolores Hidalgo (US$0.50) frequently, Morelia twice and San Juan de los Lagos once.

Rail San Miguel railway station is about two km west of the town. Take a taxi or walk into town. The Aguila Azteca leaves at 1.09 pm on its way to Querétaro (arrival 2.42 pm) and Mexico City (7.20 pm); northward, it departs at 2.35 pm, reaching San Luis Potosí in 2½ hours, Saltillo 9¼ hours, Monterrey 12 hours and Nuevo Laredo 17 hours. Sleepers are available on this train. First-class fare to Mexico City is US$2.25, plus an extra US$2.75 if you reserve a seat. Second-class fare is US$1.25.

Getting Around

Car Rental Gama (tel 2-08-15) at Hidalgo 3 is the only place in town. For a Volkswagen Beetle you pay US$16.25 a day plus US$0.75 per km and your own petrol; or US$114 a week with the first 500 km free, plus your own petrol. Their cars often get fully booked up a week or more ahead.

DOLORES HIDALGO

This is where the Mexican independence movement began in earnest. On 16 September 1810 Father Miguel Hidalgo, the parish priest, rang the bells to summon people to church earlier than usual and issued the *Grito (Cry) de Dolores*, whose precise words have been lost to history but which boiled down to 'Viva Our Lady of Guadalupe! Death to bad government and the *gachupines*!'

Gachupines was the derisive name for Mexico's Spanish overlords, against whom a powder keg of resentment finally exploded in this small town. Miguel Hidalgo, Ignacio Allende and other conspirators, alerted to the discovery of their plans for an uprising in Querétaro, decided to launch their rebellion immediately from Dolores. After the *Grito*, they freed prisoners in the town jail and, at the head of a growing band of criollos, mestizos and Indians, set off for San Miguel on a campaign that would bring their own deaths within a few months but ultimately led to Mexican independence. Today Hidalgo is the

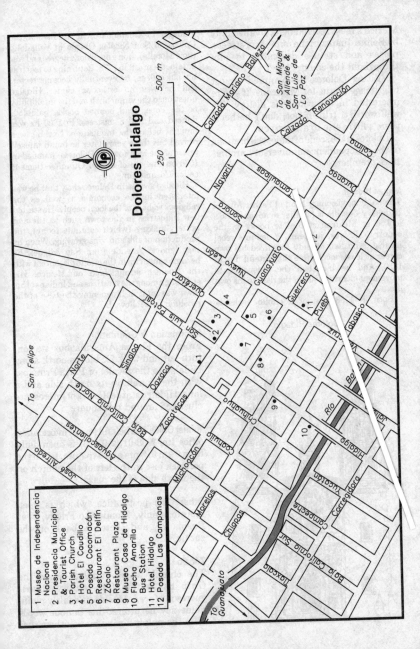

Dolores Hidalgo

1 Museo de Independencia
  Nacional
2 Presidencia Municipal
  & Tourist Office
3 Parish Church
4 Hotel El Caudillo
5 Posada Cocomacán
6 Restaurant El Delfín
7 Zócalo
8 Restaurant Plaza
9 Museo Casa de Hidalgo
10 Flecha Amarilla
   Bus Station
11 Hotel Hidalgo
12 Posada Las Campanas

To San Felipe

To San Miguel
de Allende & San Luis de
La Paz

To Guanajuato

0   250   500 m

Mexico's most revered hero, rivalled only by Benito Juárez in the number of streets, plazas and statues dedicated to him throughout the country.

Visiting Dolores has acquired almost pilgrimage status for Mexicans. If you're interested in the country's history, it's well worth a trip. If not, don't bother – there's little else to attract you.

Dolores is the scene of major celebrations of the independence anniversary around 16 September.

Miguel Hidalgo

The balding, visionary head of Father Miguel Hidalgo y Costilla is familiar to anyone who's looked at Mexican statues or books on the country. He was, it seems, a genuine rebel idealist, who had already sacrificed his own career at least once before that fateful day in 1810. And he launched the independence movement clearly aware of the risks to his own life.

Born in 1753, son of a criollo hacienda manager in Guanajuato, he studied at the College of San Nicolás Obispo in Valladolid (now Morelia), won a bachelor's degree and was ordained a priest in 1778. Returning to teach at his old college, he eventually became rector. But he was no orthodox cleric: Hidalgo questioned the virgin birth and the infallibility of the Pope, read banned books, gambled, danced and had a mistress. In 1800 he was brought before the Inquisition. Nothing was proved but three years later he found himself priest of the hick town of Dolores – founded in 1570 on the site of an old Otomí settlement called Cocomacán.

Hidalgo's years in Dolores show that he was interested in the economic as well as the religious welfare of the local people. He started new industries in the town such as tile and pottery-making (which continue today), the production of silk and vine growing. When he met Ignacio Allende from San Miguel, he became caught up in the criollo discontent with the Spanish stranglehold on Mexico. His standing among the mestizos and Indians of his town was vital in broadening the base of the rebellion that followed.

Dolores Hidalgo

Information & Orientation

From the Flecha Amarilla bus station, turn left and walk 2½ blocks north along Hidalgo to the zócalo, or Plaza Principal with the church on its north side and a large Hidalgo statue. Points of interest are clustered around this square.

Tourist Office The helpful tourist information office (tel 2-08-01, 2-01-93) is open daily from 9 am to 3 pm and 5 to 7 pm. It's in the portales just to the left of the church on the north side of the plaza.

Other The post office, which is open mornings only, Monday to Friday, is at Puebla 22, and there's a bank on the zócalo.

Zócalo

The church where Hidalgo issued the *Grito* has a fine 18th-century churrigueresque façade. Inside, it's fairly plain. Some say he uttered his famous words from the pulpit during mass, others that he spoke at the church door to the people gathered outside. To the left of the church is the Presidencia Municipal, with two murals on the independence theme. The zócalo contains a huge statue of Hidalgo and a tree which, according to a plaque beneath it, is a sapling of the Tree of the Noche Triste, under which Hernán Cortés is said to have wept when he and his men were driven out of Tenochtitlán in 1520.

Museo de la Independencia Nacional

Half a block west of the zócalo along Zacatecas, this museum has few relics but plenty of information on the independence movement and its roots. It charts, for instance, the appalling decline in Mexico's Indian population between 1519 (an estimated 25 million) and 1605 (one million), and lists 23 Indian rebellions between 1524 and 1800 as well as several criollo conspiracies in the years leading up to 1810. There are lurid paintings and some details on the heroic last 10 months of Hidalgo's life. Hours are Monday to Friday 9 am to 2 pm and 4 to 7 pm, Saturday and Sunday 9 am to 3 pm. Entry is 10c.

Museo Casa de Hidalgo

This house, where Hidalgo lived and where (with Ignacio Allende and Juan de Aldama) he decided in the early hours of 16 September 1810 to launch the uprising, is something of a national shrine. A continuous trickle of visitors wanders through it with hushed voices. One large room contains a big collection of memorials, wreaths and homages to Hidalgo, as well as the verses dedicated to his guards which he wrote on his cell wall on the eve of his execution in Chihuahua on 30 July 1811. Of interest is an enormous Metepec tree of life on the independence theme.

Other rooms contain Hidalgo's bed and dining table, documents of the Revolution, and furniture and objects from the period. There's a display of ceramics dating back to the 17th century, similar to those made in the pottery centre which the priest started in Dolores. The house is at the corner of Hidalgo and Morelos, between the zócalo and the Flecha Amarilla bus station. Hours are Tuesday to Saturday 10 am to 6 pm (US$0.40), Sundays and holidays 10 am to 5 pm (free).

Places to Stay

Dolores is near enough to San Miguel de Allende and Guanajuato to be visited in a day, but if you want to stay, there are a few choices.

Most basic is the *Hotel Hidalgo* (tel 2-08-52) at Veracruz 5. Walk one block east from the zócalo along Guerrero, then turn right. Rooms are bare but sizeable and reasonably clean. Singles are US$2.75; doubles are US$3.75 for one bed, US$4.75 for two beds. *Hotel El Caudillo* (tel 2-01-98) at Querétaro 8, half a block north of the zócalo, has its own restaurant and is cleaner, but has smaller rooms and some electrical fittings hanging out of the wall. Singles are US$4.25; doubles are US$5.25 with one bed, US$5.50 with two beds.

The *Posada Cocomacán* (tel 2-00-18), on the zócalo at Plaza Principal 4, has 34 clean rooms with ageing furniture round a courtyard for US$4.75 (one bed) or US$6.50 (two beds). The most up-market place in Dolores is the *Posada Las Campanas* (tel 2-04-27) at Guerrero 15, 2½ blocks east of the zócalo. There are 40 moderate-size rooms, 25 of them with TV, at single/double rates of US$6/8. Those on the ground floor can be damp.

Places to Eat

Restaurant Plaza (tel 2-02-59), on the south side of the zócalo at Plaza Principal 17B, does comida corrida for US$1.50 (noodle soup, rice and bananas, fried chicken and coffee), eggs and frijoles for US$0.75, burritos for US$0.50. The witty manager is apt to exclaim *No gritos aquí!* to noisy children.

Also popular are the restaurant of the *Hotel El Caudillo* at Querétaro 8 and the *Restaurant El Delfín* on Guerrero, half a block east of the zócalo.

Things to Buy

Dolores is a bit of a pottery-making centre; in particular it turns out cheap, pretty Talavera tiles in a bastardised Puebla style. A number of shops sell these and other crafts.

Getting There & Away

Dolores is 40 km north of San Miguel de Allende by Highway 51, 55 km east of Guanajuato by Highway 110, and 158 km south of San Luis Potosí by highways 110 and 57.

Bus Unfortunately Dolores has to rely almost solely on Flecha Amarilla (tel 2-06-39), one of Mexico's worst 2nd-class bus lines. Its vehicles are old, slow, dilapidated and prone to breakdowns, and if they stick to timetables it's pure coincidence. But they get you there in the end. The bus station in Dolores is on Avenida Hidalgo, 2½ blocks south of the zócalo.

Between Dolores and San Miguel de Allende there are Flecha Amarilla buses about every 20 to 30 minutes. The trip takes about an hour and costs US$0.50. There are 28 buses daily each way between León, Guanajuato and Dolores, also 15 daily to/from Querétaro and Mexico City (US$3.50, five hours), 10 to/from Celaya, 11 to/from San Luis Potosí, three to/from Aguascalientes.

Flecha de Oro runs 2nd-class services every half-hour to Celaya and to San Luis de la Paz.

POZOS

Once a flourishing silver and copper mining centre, Pozos is now more or less a ghost town. A couple of thousand people live on among abandoned houses and mine workings in what, 80 or so years ago, was a town of about 50,000. Many of them make a living from textile handicrafts. If you've time to spare, Pozos might make a side-trip from San Miguel de Allende, Querétaro or Guanajuato.

Unfortunately it's not too easy to reach unless you have a car. The most frequent buses are from San Luis de la Paz, 11 km north, which has a few hotels, mostly on Niños Héroes. There are also some from San José Iturbide, 28 km south. Both San Luis and San José are about seven km east of Highway 57 from Querétaro to San Luis Potosí. From San Miguel de Allende with your own vehicle, take the Querétaro road, turn left off it after four km towards Dr Mora, follow that road for 35 km crossing Highway 57 on the way, and proceed left at a crossroads from which Pozos is 14 km away

QUERÉTARO

Population: 260,000

Two and a half hours from Mexico City, yet free of its pollution, crime and chaos, close to San Miguel de Allende yet not inundated with that city's burgeoning gringo population, Querétaro is worth a brief stop. Here you will find some monuments and colonial architecture which, while not spectacular like that of Guanajuato and Zacatecas, still warrants at least a half-day's visit. If you're interested in Mexico's past, don't miss Querétaro, as it has played an important role in Mexican history.

History

First settled by the Otomí Indians who in the 15th century became absorbed into the Aztec empire, Querétaro was conquered by the Spaniards in 1531. Franciscan monks used the settlement as a base for sending out missionaries to what is now the US Southwest as well as Central America. Later, Querétaro became the site of intrigue, with creole patriots plotting to free Mexico from the yoke of Spanish rule. Conspirators, including Padre Miguel Hidalgo, met secretly at the house of the woman who would become known as La Corregidora, Josefa Ortiz - seen by Mexicans as the catalyst for revolt.

When the conspirators were about to be captured, the mayor locked his wife, Doña Josefa, in a room in the Palacio

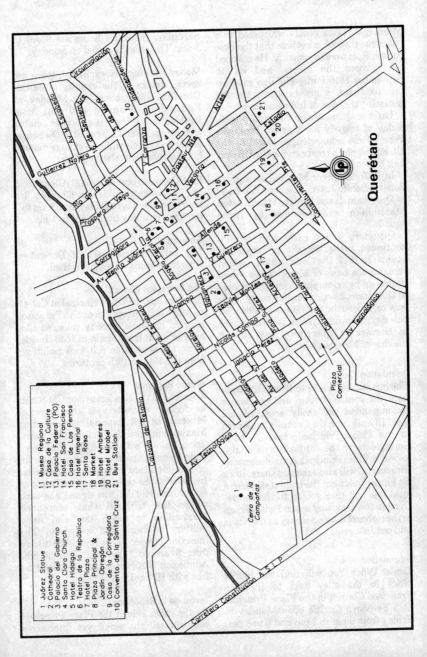

Querétaro

1 Juárez Statue
2 Cathedral
3 Palacio del Gobierno
4 Santa Clara Church
5 Hotel Hidalgo
6 Teatro de la República
7 Hotel Plaza
8 Plaza Principal &
  Jardín Obregón
9 Casa de la Corregidora
10 Convento de la Santa Cruz
11 Museo Regional
12 Casa de la Culture
13 Palacio Federal (PO)
14 Hotel San Francisco
15 Casa de Los Perros
16 Hotel Imperial
17 Santa Rosa
18 Market
19 Hotel Amberes
20 Hotel Mirabel
21 Bus Station

Municipal. Doña Josefa whispered to a colleague through a keyhole that their co-conspirators were in jeopardy. He galloped off, warned the rebels, and on 16 September 1810 Padre Hidalgo gave his famous *Grito*, a cry to arms, thereby initiating the War of Independence.

Later in Querétaro on 2 February 1848, a day of tragedy for Mexico, President Pena y Pena acknowledged defeat by the US and signed a treaty giving the US over half the country.

In 1867, Emperor Maximilian surrendered to Benito Juárez's General Escobedo at Querétaro. It was here that the ill-fated Maximilian was executed by firing squad.

Querétaro in the early 20th century continued to be the site of important events. In 1917, the Constitution – which remains the basis of Mexico's law – was drawn up by triumphant revolutionaries in Querétaro. Mexico's ruling party, PRI, was organised in Querétaro in 1929. To this day, prominent politicians come here in homage to Querétaro's role in the making of Mexican history.

Orientation

The bus station is a 10 to 15-minute walk from the centre of town and the hotels recommended are easily accessible on foot. To walk from the Central Camionera to the Plaza Principal, take Avenida Corregidora to the Jardín Obregón, also known as Plaza Principal. A bus designated 'Burocrata' will also take you there. It's a bit longer trek from the train station, so a local bus will take you in to the centre. Once in town, getting around with a map to the sights of interest is easy as the city is laid out in a grid.

Information

Tourist Office You will find the tourist office in the alley next to the San Francisco Church in the Plaza Principal at 5 de Mayo 61. It's open Monday to Friday from 9 am to 2 pm and 5 to 8 pm.

Saturday, the office hours are 9 am to 1 pm. The office is closed on Sunday.

Money For currency exchange, there are several banks in the vicinity of Jardín Obregón. Their hours are Monday to Friday from 9 am to 1.30 pm. After banking hours, there is a casa de cambio at E Montes Sur 33. Several of the bigger stores and hotels will also change money, but the rates are relatively low.

Post The main post office is at Allende Sur 14, 1½ blocks from Jardín Obregón. Its hours are Monday to Friday from 8 am to 7 pm and Saturday from 9 am to 1 pm.

Festivals

The entire second week of December, Querétaro holds its major festival.

San Francisco Church

Situated on the Plaza Principal at Calle 5 de Mayo is the magnificent San Francisco church. Its dome's pretty coloured tiles were brought from Spain in 1540. Inside, there are some fine religious paintings from the 17th to 19th centuries.

Museo Regional

Adjacent to the San Francisco Church in its former monastery is the Regional Museum. In 1861, imperialists supporting Maximilian used this building as a fort. Today, along with some fine European and colonial paintings, the museum houses important historical memorabilia. Included is the table where the Treaty of Guadalupe Hidalgo was signed, the desk where the tribunal that sentenced Maximilian to death sat, and early military uniforms and weaponry. The museum is open Tuesday to Saturday from 9 am to 1 pm and 3 to 5 pm. Admission is 10c; students are admitted free with ID card.

Teatro de la República

On the other side of the Plaza Principal you will see the small yet impressive

Teatro de la República where in 1867 a tribunal decided to execute Maximilian. Revolutionaries wrote a part of the present constitution here in 1917. In 1929, politicians met to organise Mexico's ruling party, PRI, in this theatre. It's free and open daily from 10 am to 3 pm and 5 to 9.30 pm.

Casa de la Corregidora

On the Plaza Independencia sits the Casa de la Corregidora, where Doña Josefa Ortiz informed rebel leaders of the attempt to arrest them. The colonial structure is now the Palacio Municipal. It is open to the public Monday to Friday from 8 am to 9 pm and Saturday from 1 to 8 pm. Nearby is the Casa de la Cultura, where fine local crafts are exhibited.

Commercial District

In Querétaro's commercial centre at the corner of Allende and Madero is the pleasant Fountain of Neptune, designed by the great Mexican architect Tresguerras in 1797. Go inside the Santa Clara Church next to the fountain for an ornate bit of baroque. Nearby in the old cloister Mesón de Santa Clara, plays are put on by the University of Querétaro drama department on Friday and Saturday nights.

Follow Madero further past the rather mundane Palacio del Gobierno and the 18th-century cathedral. Turn back to Calle Guerrero to visit the Palacio Federal, also housing a post office. Once an Augustinian monastery, the ornate mansion is carved with bizarre and beautiful gargoyles and beasts of religious symbolism. The gargoyles are allegedly saying 'Hail Mary' in sign language. Around the corner from the Palacio Federal stands the Casa de los Perros. There are some notable carvings of ferociously ugly, unworldly dogs on the house's exterior.

At the intersection of Arteaga and Montes stands the Santa Rosa de Viterbos church with its pagoda-like bell tower and impressively gilded, magnificently marbled interior. The great architect Tresguerras remodelled the church with tiles for the dome and a tower holding what some say is the first four-sided clock built in the New World.

Convento de la Santa Cruz

Only about 10 minutes' walk from the centre of the town is one of Querétaro's most interesting sights, the Convento de la Santa Cruz. A monastery built on the battleground where the alleged miraculous appearance of St James led Otomí Indians to surrender to the conquistadors and Christianity, the Convento also functioned as a fortress. A Spanish force retreated here toward the end of the War of Independence, and Maximilian for a time established a bastion in the Convento. After his surrender and subsequent death-sentence, the emperor was jailed here while he awaited the firing squad.

An excellent English-speaking guide will provide insight into the Convento's history and artefacts. He'll show you sundials, an ingenious water system and unique ways of colonial cooking and refrigeration. The guide will also relate several of the Convento's miracles, including the legendary growth of a tree from a walking stick stuck in the earth by a pious friar. The thorns of the tree appear in the pattern of a cross.

From the Convento you can see some 76 towering arches of an aqueduct system which still brings water about 12 km to the city.

Site of Maximilian's Execution

At the north-west end of the city is the Cerro de las Campañas, the site of Maximilian's execution by firing squad. It's a good 35-minute walk; from the Jardín Obregón, go north a few blocks on Corregidora and make a left on General Escobedo. Where Escobedo dead-ends at Tecnológico, cross the street and make a right. The emperor's family constructed a chapel on the site. Next to it is a statue of Benito Juárez.

Places to Stay – bottom end

Hotel Hidalgo (tel 2-00-81), conveniently located just a block north of Jardín Obregón, is a good deal for the money. Rooms, which are built around a quiet inner courtyard, include singles with bath for US$3.50 and doubles for US$4.25. Also an excellent deal and well situated near the Jardín Unión at Juárez Norte 23 is the *Hotel Plaza* (tel 2-11-38). For pleasant rooms with bath, the Plaza charges US$3.80 for a single (two people for the same price if they share a bed) and US$7 for a double with two beds.

Also cheap, but not as nice as the hotels Hidalgo and Plaza, is the *Hotel San Francisco* (tel 2-05-58) two blocks south of Jardín Obregón at Corregidora Sur 114. Basic, reasonably maintained rooms with bath run US$4 single, US$5 double.

Places to Stay – middle

If you have just arrived by bus, are too tired to seek out the above lodgings near the centre, and are willing to fork out a bit more, consider the following places.

Turn left as you walk out the front door of the bus station and you will see the modern *Hotel Mirabel* (tel 4-35-35) at Constituyentes 2 Oriente. Comfortable singles with TV and bath cost US$9.50, doubles US$16.

You'll find well-appointed rooms at cheaper prices a block's walk from the bus station. The *Hotel Amberes* (tel 2-86-04) is on Corregidora Sur 188; to reach it make a left as you leave the front entrance of the bus station and a right at the first intersection on Corregidora Sur. You will see Amberes halfway down the block. Rooms with TV and bath cost US$7.75 single, US$9.50 double.

Another excellent hotel further down Corregidora at Colón 1, opposite the Alameda (near the intersection of Corregidora and Zaragoza) is *Hotel Impala* (tel 2-25-70). This big, relatively new hotel has private rooms with TV and bath for US$7 single, US$8.75 double.

Places to Stay – top end

The *Jurica Querétaro* (tel 2-10-81), about 10 km north of the city on Highway 57, is a magnificent converted 17th-century hacienda with pool, golf course and tennis courts. Singles cost US$40, doubles US$47. The *Holiday Inn*, on Highway 57 a km north of the 45 and 45D interchange, has a pool and tennis courts. Its rooms cost US$35 single, US$40 double.

Places to Eat

The top choice for excellent food at moderate prices is *La Flor de Querétaro* at Juárez Norte 5. The comida corrida is filling and inexpensive here. A good place for paella and a substantial comida corrida is the *Restaurant Café Viena* at 16 Septiembre Pte 8.

For a taste of the high seas at low-tide prices, try *Figón Pirata* at Pasteur Norte 37. Those craving home-made ice cream will find nirvana at *Nevería Galy* at 5 de Mayo 8. If you are staying at the *Hotel San Francisco*, its restaurant serves adequate Mexican food at low prices.

Entertainment

Sit in the *Jardín Obregón* Sunday evenings to watch local families enjoying band concerts. The *Academia de Bellas Artes* at the intersection of Juárez Sur and Independencia is often the site of classical music, ballet and theatrical performances. Those craving disco can try *L'Opera* at Circuito Jardín Sur 1 or *Disco Emiliano's* at Tecnológico 140.

Getting There & Away

Bus Until the government finally opens its rapid electric rail service between Mexico City and Querétaro, you will save up to two hours by taking the bus. The frequent bus service is also the best transport between Querétaro and other major centres like Guadalajara, Juárez and San Miguel de Allende.

Buses running to or from Mexico City (two hours, US$2) and destinations north of the capital tend to stop at Querétaro en route. To San Miguel de Allende, there's one 1st-class bus daily by Omnibus de México and 2nd-class buses about half-hourly by Herradura de Plata and Flecha Amarilla. The trip takes 1¼ hours and costs about US$0.75.

There's a guardería (left-luggage office) in the bus station. It charges 10c per item for each 24 hours.

Getting Around
Querétaro is a compact city and you will easily reach most major sights on foot. There are buses from both the Central Camionera and the train station to the centre. If you want to take a local bus to the Cerro de las Campañas, look for buses with 'Carrillo ISSSTE' or 'Satellite ISSSTE' signs.

SAN JUAN DEL RÍO
Just east of Highway 57, 56 km south of Querétaro and 170 km north of Mexico City, San Juan del Río is something of a craft centre. It is known particularly for its gems and jewellery – a business based on local opals but including the polishing and setting of gems from elsewhere; basket-weaving and furniture are also important industries. The town has a pleasant colonial centre and produces good wine and cheese.

Places to Stay & Eat
For meals, try the Centro Vasco on the zócalo. There are other restaurants (such as Las Corceles) on the main street, Juárez. Cheaper hotels in the central area include the Hotel La Paloma (tel 2-01-01) at Juárez 92 Pte and the Hotel Jalisco (tel 2-04-25) at Hidalgo 15 Sur. More expensive are the Hotel Hostería del Virrey (tel 2-23-12) at Hidalgo 41 Norte, the Hotel Villa de los Reyes (tel 2-16-23 or 2-11-621) at Juárez 9 Pte, the Hotel Misión del Río San Pascual (tel 2-12-44 or 2-16-40) at Abasolo 6, and the Hotel O'Puente (tel 2-05-68) at Juárez 25 Pte.

Two resort-hotels in old haciendas to the west of town are used mainly by people from Mexico City for a spot of none-too-cheap relaxation. Tennis, riding, golf and swimming are included in the facilities at both. Rooms in the Hotel Estancia de San Juan (tel 2-01-55, 2-07-38, 2-01-20) are around US$30 to US$45. At the Hotel La Mansión Galindo (tel 2-00-50) rooms are in the US$50 to US$80 range.

Getting There & Away
There are frequent buses to and from Querétaro (US$0.75) by several lines, mostly 2nd class. You can also get 2nd-class buses cross-country to Pachuca (four hours, US$2) through Ixmiquilpan and Actopan. Some Mexico City-Querétaro buses stop at San Juan.

TEQUISQUIAPAN
This small town ('teh-kiss-ki-AP-an') 26 km north-east of San Juan del Río is famed for its radioactive hot springs, and more than 20 hotels have sprung up to turn it into a sizeable resort-retreat from Mexico City. Many of the cobbled streets are free of traffic and it makes a peaceful spot for relaxation at any time but few hotels are in the budget range. Many of the springs are channelled into swimming pools – some on hotel grounds, some (usually cheaper) open to the general public.

'Tequis' has a busy crafts market, particularly on Sunday. In late May and early June the town holds a Feria Nacional de Queso y Vino (National Cheese & Wine Fair), with plenty of free tastings and other celebrations. There's a tourist office at the corner of Morelos and Andador Niños Héroes near the town centre. To get to Tequisquiapan by bus, you have to change at San Juan del Río. Highway 120 from San Juan continues 263 km north-east from Tequisquiapan across the Sierra Madre to come out on the Pan-American Highway, No 85, between Tamazunchale and Ciudad Valles. About 160 km from Tequisquiapan, there's a fork north to Río Verde.

Places to Stay

Cheaper hotels include the *Posada Mejía* (tel 3-02-36) at Guillermo Prieto 8, the *Posada Los Mezquites* at Centenario 2 Norte and the *Hotel La Esperanza* (tel 3-07-12) on Paseo de la Media Luna.

More expensive are the *Hotel Las Delicias* (tel 3-01-80) on Prolongación Cinco de Mayo, which has a thermal swimming pool in big gardens, and the *Hotel La Plaza* (tel 3-02-89) in the town centre.

At the very top end, with rooms generally above US$30, are the *Hotel Las Cavas* (tel 3-08-04, 3-07-04) at Paseo de la Media Luna 8 and the *Hotel La Querencia* (tel 3-01-11, 3-01-25) on Carretera Estación Bernal.

Michoacán & the Central Highlights

The state of Michoacán (population three million) is a beautiful mountainous region of 59,928 square km that extends over part of the Sierra Madre Occidental range in west-central Mexico. One of the mountains in the Tancitaro sub-range near Uruapan, Paricutín, became volcanic, blew its top on 24 February 1943 and spewed lava until 1952. Today, it is a favourite destination for hikers. Average temperatures are 23°C (high), 13°C (low).

Between the mountains are the river watersheds of Lerma and Balsas and a spiderweb of tributaries spread across the state. The Río Balsas forms most of the state's southern border with Guerrero, while the Río Lerma, which flows into the eastern end of Lake Chapala, delineates part of the border with the states of Guanajuato and Jalisco. The state of Querétaro borders a small portion of Michoacán's north-east corner. The state of México borders Michoacán between the states of Guerrero and Querétaro.

Along the north-western edge, the Río Coahuayana divides Michoacán from the small state of Colima. Michoacán's border with Jalisco runs jaggedly south from about the middle of Lake Chapala to the Río Coahuayana.

The last border is the coastline, a narrow extension of the plain along the coast of Guerrero. Unlike the mountainous regions to the north, this area becomes hot and humid, especially in the summer.

Morelia, the state capital, with its well-preserved colonial architecture, is a good starting point if you are coming up Highway 15 from Mexico City. Seventy km south-east along a well-surfaced two-lane highway is another architectural gem, Pátzcuaro, which, before the arrival of the Spaniards in the early 16th century, was capital of the Tarascan Indian kingdom. Lake Pátzcuaro is known for its fisherfolk with their traditional butterfly nets, and also for the Isla de Janitzio, the largest of five islands.

The road from Pátzcuaro winds around the lake and heads north to Tzintzuntán and the remains of a great Tarascan city with structures unlike any others in Mesoamerican architecture. From there the road continues to the town of Quiroga, known for its wooden trays, and intersects Highway 15.

Farther west, Highway 15 crosses Highway 37 at the Indian town of Carapan Highway 37 goes south through the picturesque town of Paracho, world famous for its hand-made guitars and wooden furniture, and then passes the road to Angahuan, the town nearest the now-extinct volcano of Paricutín. Another 18 km south is the city of Uruapan, known for fine lacquered bowls and pitchers and nearby waterfalls created by the Río Cupatitzio. Highway 37 continues south along a serpentine route through the mountains and down past the immense artificial lake created by the Infiernillo Dam. About 20 km after the road winds away from the lake, the views of the Sierra Madre Occidental are magnificent. When you reach the village of Arteaga, 74 km further south, you'll see tropical vegetation such as banana trees and coconut palms. The highway ends near the small coastal resort of Playa Azul and the industrial city of Lázaro Cárdenas.

Highway 200 runs west along the coast of Michoacán, passing several small beaches and villages, but there are few hotels and the area is reputedly unsafe for overnight camping. Only the area around Playa Azul and Lázaro Cárdenas is considered safe.

MORELIA

Population: 400,000
Morelia, the capital of Michoacán, lies in the north-western part of the state, 309

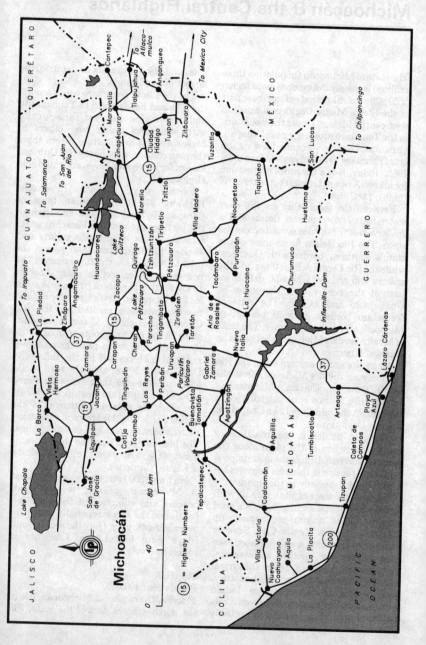

Michoacán

km west of Mexico City, 340 km south-east of Guadalajara, and 70 km north-east of Pátzcuaro. It has an altitude of 1951 metres and an average temperature of 23°C.

Morelia was officially founded in 1541, although a Franciscan monastery had been in the area since 1537. New Spain's first viceroy, Don Antonio de Mendoza, named it Valladolid in honour of the Spanish city by the same name and encouraged several families of 'noble' Spaniards to move there. The families remained and maintained Valladolid as a very Spanish city, at least architecturally, until 1828. By that time, New Spain was the independent republic of Mexico and hatred of the Spanish was great. The state legislature changed the city's name to Morelia to honour one its native sons, José María Morelos de Pavón, a key figure in Mexico's independence movement.

Today, with its downtown streets lined by colonial-style buildings, Morelia still looks as Spanish as it probably did before independence. City ordinances now require that all new construction be done colonial-style with arches, baroque façades and carved pink stone walls.

Orientation

In the fairly compact city almost everything of interest is within walking distance of the zócalo, except the aqueduct and the Juárez Park & Zoo. The aqueduct runs parallel to Avenida Acueducto at the eastern end of the city and, if you are arriving from Mexico City, it's one of the first things you see when you enter the city limits. Avenida Acueducto runs west and then north-west until the end of the aqueduct at the Fuente de las Tarascas (also known as the Fuente de Villalongin), just after the Museo de Arte Contemporáneo and a pleasant park.

From the fountain, Avenida Madero from the north-east continues into Morelia and becomes a main street for the downtown area. Several hotels, historic sites and government offices are on or just off this street, including the cathedral and zócalo (also called the Plaza Central, Plaza de los Mártires or Plaza de Armas). Other important streets run parallel to (east-west) Madero or intersect it (north-south).

Information

Tourist Office The state tourist office (tel 3-26-54), Nigromante 79 in the Palacio Clavijero, can be extremely helpful if you speak Spanish; the staff speak limited English. A few brochures are available in English. Hours are 9 am to 8 pm daily.

Money Casas de cambio at Pino Suárez 166 and Aquiles Serdán 65A are open from 10 am to 2 pm and 4 to 7 pm Monday to Friday, 10 am to 2 pm Saturday. Banks are plentiful in Morelia, particularly on and around Madero, but you can only change money until 1 pm.

Post The main post office is at Madero Oriente (East) 369 and is open from 8 am to 8 pm Monday to Friday and 9 am to 1 pm Saturday. Lista de correo mail can be obtained until 5 pm Monday to Friday.

Telephone Calls There's a 24-hour caseta de larga distancia for long-distance calls in the bus station and on Madero across from the cathedral.

Laundromat Lavandería Sandy is at two locations – Corregidora 787 and Aldama 425 (corner of Nicolás Bravo). Both are open from 8 am to 8 pm Monday to Saturday and 9 am to 2 pm Sunday. Lavandería Automática Ivonne is at Plaza de las Americas and Lavandería Automática Rebullones is at Plaza Rebullones.

Festivals

Country Fair Agricultural, livestock and handicrafts exhibits are featured at this fair 1 to 21 May.

Founding of Morelia The town's anniversary

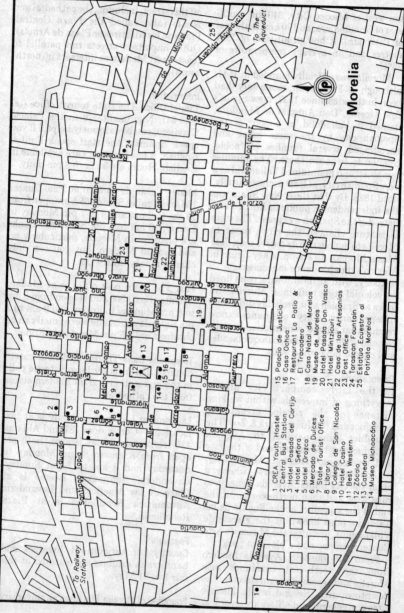

Morelia

1 CREA Youth Hostel
2 Central Bus Station
3 Hotel Posada del Cortijo
4 Hotel Señora
5 Hotel Orozco
6 Mercado de Dulces
7 State Tourist Office
8 Library
9 Colegio de San Nicolás
10 Hotel Casino
11 Best Western
12 Zócalo
13 Cathedral
14 Museo Michoacáno
15 Palacio de Justicia
16 Casa Ochoa
17 Restaurant Lo Patio & El Tracadero
18 Casa Natal de Morelos
19 Museo de Morelos
20 Hotel Posada Don Vasco
21 Hotel Mintzicuri
22 Casa de las Artesanias
23 Post Office
24 Tarascan Fountain
25 Estatua Ecuestre al Patriota Morelos

and International Organ Festival take place on 18 May.

Don José María Morelos y Pavón's Birthday

This is celebrated on 30 September.

Christmas Fair From 13 December to 4 January traditional Christmas items, handicrafts and manufactured goods produced in Michoacán are promoted.

Walking Tours

The most efficient way to see the city is to take one of the two-hour walking tours offered by the state tourist office daily at 10 am, noon and 4 pm. The average charge is US$1.35 per person.

If you decide to proceed on your own, the zócalo or Plaza Central is a good starting point. As mentioned in the orientation section, this plaza is also known as Plaza de los Mátires (Plaza of Martyrs) and Plaza de Armas. It is bordered on the east by the cathedral and on the other three sides by long shopping arcades with arches and pillars. The zócalo is well-kept with several large trees, a fountain, a gazebo in the centre and benches for relaxing in the shade.

Cathedral

The cathedral overlooking the zócalo is a combination of baroque, neoclassical and herreriano (a classical Spanish style) architectural styles. Its twin 70-metre towers are a prime example of this combination – classical linear bases, baroque mid-sections and multi-columned neoclassical tops. Inside, much of the baroque relief work was replaced in the 19th century with more balanced and calculated neoclassical pieces. Fortunately, however, one of the cathedral's interior highlights was preserved – a sculpture of the Señor de la Sacristía made from dried maize and topped with a gold crown from the 16th-century Spanish King Philip II. There's also a large organ with 4600 pipes.

Museo Michoacáno

Just off the zócalo at Allende 305 and Abasolo is the Michoacán Museum. Housed in the late 18th-century baroque-style palace of Isidro Huarte, the museum displays a great variety of pre-Hispanic artefacts, contemporary paintings by local artists, 17th and 18th-century paintings and Spanish colonial furniture, and has exhibits on the geology and fauna of the region. One of the museum's highlights is a mural on the stairway by Mexican painter Alfredo Alce divided in left and right halves portraying those who have had a positive (right half) and negative (left half) influence on Mexico. The Tarascan stone throne in the pre-Hispanic section is also worth checking out. Other exhibits describe French and American intervention in Michoacán. Hours are 9 am to 7 pm Monday to Saturday and 9 am to 3 pm Sunday. Admission is free.

Palacio de Justicia

Located across from the zócalo and the Museo Michoacáno the Palacio was built between 1682 and 1695 to serve as the town hall. Its façade is an eclectic but well-done mix of French and baroque styles. Inside, a dramatic mural of the first Court Tribunal here by Agustín Cárdenas graces the courtyard.

Casa Natal de Morelos

Morelos was born in this house at Corregidora and García Obeso on 30 September 1765. Two centuries later, the state government declared it a national monument and made it a museum. Morelos memorabilia fills two rooms; a public library, auditorium and projection room occupy the rest of the house. An eternal torch burns next to the projection room. When crowds aren't streaming through for one of the many cultural events offered here, the rose garden between the museum and the torch is a pleasant place to take a break from sightseeing. Morelia's Cine-Club organises a variety of small-scale international film festivals here with three showings weekly at 1 pm on Tuesday, Wednesday and Thursday. Arrive well before 1 pm because admission is free and the seats disappear quickly. Museum hours are 10 am to 2 pm and 4 to 9 pm daily. Admission is 5c.

Museo de Morelos

If the Casa Natal de Morelos didn't satisfy your curiosity about this native son, visit the Morelos Museum around the corner at Morelos 323. Morelos bought the house in 1801 and added a second storey in 1806. Exhibits describe his rise to power in Mexico and his military campaigns during the struggle for independence. Various mementoes are displayed including documents, uniforms, the table where the declaration of independence was signed and even Morelos' bed. Hours are 9 am to 7 pm daily. Admission is 5c.

Estatua Ecuestre al Patriota Morelos

This statue of Morelos on horseback trotting to battle is on Glorieta Morelos, a plaza between Calzada Fray Antonio de San Miguel and Avenida Acueducto at the east end of Morelia. Commissioned by the Porfirio Díaz government, the statue was built and erected by Italian sculptor Giuseppe Ingillieri between 1910 and 1913.

El Acueducto

Although it looks much older, the aqueduct was built between 1785 and 1788 to satisfy the city's growing water needs. With 253 arches stretching two km, it is an impressive yet unexpected sight right through the city. Visit at night for a spectacular sight when spotlights illuminate the arches and the Tarascan fountain in the park at the end of the aqueduct.

El Fuente de las Tarascas

The Tarascan fountain is a 1960s replacement of a fountain that mysteriously disappeared sometime in 1940. It is mainly comprised of a bevy of half-naked Tarascan women in stone. The effect is strangely beautiful at night.

La Casa de las Artesanías

The House of Arts & Crafts occupies the Ex-Convento de San Francisco at Plaza de Valladolid, Calles Vasco de Quiroga and Humboldt three blocks east of the cathedral. It's both a museum and a market for contemporary crafts from all over Mexico. Each showcase is arranged by state. Sometimes artists can be seen working here on everything from copperware, weaving and carving to pottery and lacquerware.

El Palacio Clavijero

The Clavijero Palace was established in 1660 as a Jesuit school by its chief patron, Fray Javier Clavijero. After the Jesuits were expelled in 1767, the building served alternately as a warehouse and prison until 1970 when it was renovated for use as public offices, including a library and the state tourist office. The public library is attached to the palace.

Be sure to visit the arcade on the western side of the palace (Calle Valentín Gómez Farías) to see and taste some of the goodies for sale at the Mercado de Dulces (Candy Market). Long rows of tables, counters and boxes piled high with brightly coloured sweets are too tempting to pass up. Try the *moreliana*, a local speciality of burnt milk and sugar pressed into a disk shape. Crafts are also sold in the arcade, but you can probably find the same items for less in the Casa de las Artesanías.

Juárez Park & Zoo

The Juárez Park and Zoo is three km south of the zócalo on Calzada Juárez, which is an extension of Calles Galeana and Nigromante. Picnicking is possible on the zoo grounds.

Places to Stay

The state tourist office determines how

many stars a hotel rates and thus how much it can charge:

*	US$5.40
**	US$9.00
***	US$15.00
****	US$24.30
*****	US$45.20

Though several of the hotels listed below in the 'Places to Stay – bottom end' section don't qualify for even a one-star rating, this doesn't necessarily mean that the hotel's standards aren't up to par. It does mean that a star-less hotel can't legally charge more than a one-star rate.

Places to Stay – bottom end

Morelia's CREA Youth Hostel (tel 3-31-77), Chiapas 180 at Oaxaca south-west of downtown, is comfortable and clean with single-sex dormitory rooms and bunk beds. Simple, inexpensive meals are available: breakfast is US$0.35, lunch is US$0.50 and dinner is US$0.50. IYHF members pay US$1 per night for accommodation.

The Hotel Posada del Cortijo (tel 2-96-97), Eduardo Ruíz 673 near the bus station, didn't earn any stars with the state tourist office probably because the smudged walls and bare bulbs dangling from precarious cords wasn't their idea of comfort. Check more than one room though. Singles, doubles and triples are high for what you get at US$7.20, US$9 and US$11.

The Hotel Plaza (tel 2-30-95, 2-18-46), Valentín Gómez Farías 288 near Eduardo Ruíz and the bus station, has clean, simple rooms with cold tiled floors. Most of the rooms don't have views. Singles/doubles are US$7/9.

The Hotel Concordia (tel 2-30-52), Valentín Gómez Farías 328, is conveniently located near the zócalo and bus station with very clean, quiet rooms, antique telephones and tiled floors. There's a restaurant next to the lobby. At US$7.20/9 for singles/doubles, it's a good deal.

The Hotel Mintzicuri (tel 2-06-64), Vasco de Quiroga 227, is one of the best deals in the bottom-end price range. It's a fairly modern hotel with a lobby decorated with an imitation Orozco mural, new bathrooms and bright red carpeting. Each room is named after a different city. Singles/doubles are US$6/7.50. Breakfast is US$0.50 to US$0.60.

The Hotel Posada Don Vasco (tel 2-14-84), Vasco de Quiroga 232, is a bit old, but still a pleasant place to stay, with plants in every hall and portraits of Vasco de Quiroga on every wall. Rooms are clean and carpeted. Singles/doubles are US$4/5.

The only redeeming aspect of the Hotel Valladolid (tel 2-00-27), Portal Hidalgo 241, is its location right across from the zócalo. Rooms are dark and dank, and even at US$4/5.15 singles/doubles seem overpriced.

The Hotel Orozco (tel 2-28-78), Avenida Madero Poniente 507, is not much better than the Valladolid with dark rooms and grey halls and a sulphurous gas leak near the stairway. The bathrooms are clean though. Singles/doubles are US$5.50/6.10.

The Hotel Vallarta (tel 2-40-95), Avenida Madero Poniente 670, is supposedly a two-star hotel, but it seemed like a dive with paint and plaster chipping off the walls. Singles/doubles are US$4.50/5.20.

Places to Stay – middle

The Hotel Real Victoria (tel 3-23-00), Guadalupe Victoria 245, has very comfortable rooms with huge showers, globular lamps, televisions, green carpeting and yellow bedspreads. At US$15/18.75 for singles/doubles, it's overpriced compared to Mexico City rates.

The Hotel Catedral (tel 3-07-83), Ignacio Zaragoza 37, has light and cheery rooms arranged around a courtyard of columns. Each room is carpeted and has huge bathrooms. Singles/doubles are US$14.60/18.50. A café attached to the hotel serves decent espresso, but don't eat here.

The *Hotel Casino* (tel 3-10-03), Portal Hidalgo 229, has clean rooms with green carpeting, bright orange bedspreads, telephones and straw crucifixes on the walls. Rooms away from the street are quieter. The centre court of the 1st floor is comprised of thick slabs of glass that form a skylight for the ground-floor restaurant. Since a few slabs have begun to crack, visions of guests crashing through the floor aren't unreasonable. Singles are US$10.20, doubles US$12.50, triples US$16.

Places to Stay – top end

The colonial-style *Best Western – Hotel Virrey de Mendoza* (tel 2-06-33), Portal de Matamoros 16, is one of the best hotels in Morelia. Most of the rooms have hanging lamps, great four-poster beds, antique telephones, TVs, and cabinets full of snacks and drinks. Arches and columns surround the courtyard just off the lobby and a suit of armour graces the stairway. Singles/doubles are US$22/25.

The *Hotel Alameda* (tel 2-20-23), Avenida Madero Poniente and Guillermo Prieto, is a beautiful four-star hotel with a deluxe lobby bar and restaurant placed around a colonial-style courtyard and fountain. Every room has a TV, telephone and small cabinet of snacks and liquor. Singles are US$18.75, doubles US$23, triples US$27.

Places to Eat

Morelia is known for certain Michoacán specialities and typical Mexican dishes served Michoacán style:

corundas maize bun containing meat, wrapped in a corn husk; similar to a tamale

huchepos sweet-tasting soft maize

atole de sabores thick, creamy, corn-based drink served with various flavourings

enchiladas red tortillas rolled around meat or cheese, wrapped in leaves and sprinkled with potatoes, carrots and onions. A piece of fried chicken is usually served with these

pozole red stew made with boiled corn kernels or hominy, chicken or pork and served with avocados, onions, lettuce, radishes, a squirt of lemon and a pinch of oregano

gorditas fried corn dough similar to a pancake, topped with potatoes or meat and chile sauce

tamales Michoacán-style tamales are hard and salty, usually made with a small piece of pork or beef in the centre, and topped with cheese

buñelos flattened wheat-dough patties fried until crisp and served plain or topped with sweet sauces

ates Morelianos sweetened jellied fruit served as dessert

sopes con carne literally soup with meat, but more similar to gorditas served in a bowl of fried dough

Pizza Real, Madero Oriente 75 near the Tarascan Fountain, serves pizza of many sizes and combinations ranging in price from US$0.95 for a small to US$3.50 for a 'super'.

Restaurant Vegetariano La Fuente, Avenida Madero Oriente 493B, is the city's only vegetarian restaurant. Try the jicama salad, vegetable soup or tortilla soup.

Restaurant Las Costillas de Don Luis, across from the cathedral, is a popular local hang-out where meat dishes are served with guacamole and refried beans for US$1.50 to US$2.10. A full meal can be had for US$2.45.

Restaurant Hostería del Laurel, Vasco de Quiroga 232 attached to the Hotel Posada Don Vasco, does a popular comida corrida for US$0.85. It's so popular that even when crowded, the room is quiet because everyone is busy eating.

Restaurant Don Quijote, Portal Hidalgo 229 attached to the Hotel Casino, serves a filling breakfast for US$1.90 to US$3.70. For lunch and dinner they serve various national and regional specialities such as pollo en mole, pescado blanco de Pátzcuaro (white fish of Pátzcuaro) and enchiladas placeras.

Getting There & Away

Bus Several inter-city bus companies operate between Morelia and destinations in Michoacán and other states. The Central Camionera (bus terminal) is at Eduardo Ruíz and Valentín Gómez Farías two blocks north of Madero.

Tres Estrellas (1st class) has buses to Pátzcuaro (US$0.75) and Uruapan (US$1.85) four times daily, Lázaro Cárdenas (US$5.25) three times daily, Nuevo Laredo (US$14.70) twice daily, Monterrey (US$12) via Querétaro once daily, Manzanillo (US$7) and Colima (US$4.25) daily, Mexico City (US$4.10) via Toluca 10 times daily, express to Mexico City's Terminal del Norte twice daily and Tijuana (US$36) five times daily.

Flecha Amarilla (2nd class) has buses to Mexico City (US$3.75) every 10 to 15 minutes all day, Guadalajara (US$3.80) every 20 minutes, San Luis Potosí (US$1.60) via León 10 times daily and via Querétaro nine times daily, Manzanillo (US$6.30) twice daily.

Norte de Sonora (2nd class) regularly runs buses to Guadalajara, Tepic, Mazatlán, Los Mochis, Guaymas, Mexicali, Tecate and Tijuana.

Rail There are three trains daily in each direction between Uruapan and Mexico City with stops at Morelia and Pátzcuaro. The trains to Mexico City depart Morelia at 10.33 am, 6.03 pm and 11 pm and arrive nine hours later. The last train is a sleeper (US$7.30) and the others are 1st class (US$3).

For information about trains from Mexico City to Morelia, see the 'Getting There & Away' section for Mexico City.

From Morelia to Pátzcuaro and Uruapan, trains depart at 6.22 am, 10.20 am and 5.32 pm. To Pátzcuaro the trip takes one hour and 20 minutes and costs 22c; to Uruapan the trip takes four hours and costs US$0.60. Both fares are 1st class.

From Morelia to Guanajuato or Celaya the trip takes five hours and costs US$0.60 for a 1st-class seat.

The train station (tel 2-02-93, 2-10-68) is on Avenida Periodisimo south-west of the zócalo. Taxi fare to the zócalo is US$0.40.

Getting Around

Almost everything is within walking distance of the zócalo, but for places too far to walk, take a taxi. You shouldn't have to pay more than US$0.75 for most destinations within the Morelia area.

PÁTZCUARO

Population: 38,000

Once the capital of a mysterious Purépechan Indian empire and then the seat of the bishopric of Michoacán, Pátzcuaro is now a beautiful city with the atmosphere of an Indian village and the regal splendour of Spanish architecture. It stands on the south-east shore of Lake Pátzcuaro along Highway 14, about 70 km south-west of Morelia and 67 km north-east of Uruapan.

The Purépechans mysteriously appeared along Lake Pátzcuaro in the early 14th century. Anthropologists and archaeologists are still uncertain where they came from because they are not linked to any other peoples in the Americas. Their language does, however, resemble Zuñi (spoken in the American Southwest), a Mayan-Totonac dialect (once spoken in southern Mexico) and Quechua (spoken in Peru). The Spanish supposedly began calling the Purépeche Indians 'Tarascans' because the Indians often used a word that sounded like tarasca.

In 1400, with the death of Purépechan King Tariácari, the kingdom was divided into three parts – Pátzcuaro, Tzintzuntzán and Ihuatzio – ruled together as a league. They remained a league until the Spanish

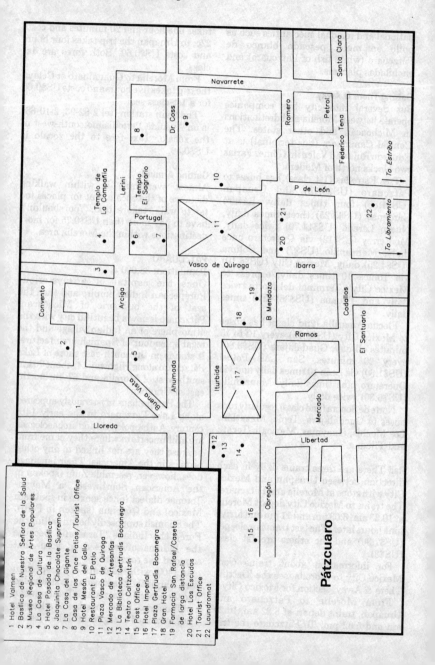

Pátzcuaro

1 Hotel Valmen
2 Basílica de Nuestra Señora de la Salud
3 Museo Regional de Artes Populares
4 La Casa de Cultura
5 Hotel Posada de la Basílica
6 Joaquinita Chocolate Supremo
7 La Casa del Gigante
8 Casa de los Once Patios/Tourist Office
9 Hotel Mesón del Gallo
10 Restaurant El Patio
11 Plaza Vasco de Quiroga
12 Mercado de Artesanías
13 La Biblioteca Gertrudis Bocanegra
14 Teatro Caltzontzín
15 Post Office
16 Hotel Imperial
17 Plaza Gertrudis Bocanegra
18 Gran Hotel
19 Farmacia San Rafael/Caseta de larga distancia
20 Hotel Los Escudos
21 Tourist Office
22 Laundromat

arrived first in 1522 and later in 1529 with soldiers and colonists who either killed the Indians or forced them into slavery for work in the mines. The Spanish soldiers led by conquistador Nuño de Guzman burned the Purépechan chief alive in their quest for gold.

Guzman's inhumanity to the Indians was so severe that the Catholic Church and the colonial government sent a bishop named Vasco de Quiroga to straighten out the mess. Quiroga arrived in 1540 to establish a bishopric and community of villages based on the humanistic ideals of Sir Thomas More's *Utopia*. To escape the cruelties of local Spanish mining lords and landowners, Quiroga successfully encouraged each village around Lake Pátzcuaro to establish their own craft specialities, a tradition that continues today. Not surprisingly, Quiroga is venerated for his work; streets, plazas, restaurants and hotels in Michoacán are named after him.

Pátzcuaro's altitude is 2174 metres. The average temperature is 16°C. Rainfall is heaviest from June (20 cm) to September (22 cm).

Orientation

Although Pátzcuaro is relatively small, finding your way may be confusing if you don't know that the downtown area lies in a hilly region five km south of the lake front. Most places of interest and services are downtown, while boats to Janitzio (the largest of the islands in Lake Pátzcuaro), the train station and *pescado blanco* restaurants are at or near the lake.

From Morelia the highway parallels the train tracks all the way to the lake and almost to the station. The road to downtown Pátzcuaro veers south from the highway, just before the junction to the station, and becomes Avenida Lázaro Cárdenas and then Calle Ahumada as it winds downtown. When it reaches Calle Lloreda, Plaza Gertrudis Bocanegra – the smaller of Pátzcuaro's two plazas – is two

blocks to your right. Two open-air markets (one for food and the other for crafts), the library and a theatre are on this plaza. Plaza Vasco de Quiroga, the other plaza, is only a block away (see map) with several hotels, restaurants and historical buildings around it. Everything of interest in Pátzcuaro is only a block or two from either plaza. Watch the street names – some change with every block.

Information

Tourist Office There are two tourist offices in Pátzcuaro, one at Portal Hidalgo 9 (tel 2-18-88) on Plaza Vasco de Quiroga, and a smaller one on the 2nd floor of the Casa de los Once Patios (tel 2-12-14), down the street from the basilica and around the corner from Plaza de Vasco Quiroga. Both are open 9 am to 2 pm and 4 to 7 pm daily and are usually staffed by people who know some English. They can help you find a hotel room.

Post The post office is at Obregón 13, half a block north of Plaza Gertrudis Bocanegra, near the theatre. Hours are 9 am to 6 pm Monday to Friday, 9 am to 1 pm Saturday and Sunday.

Telephone Calls Casetas de larga distancia can be found in the Farmacia San Rafael on Mendoza between Plaza Vasco de Quiroga and Plaza Gertrudis Bocanegra, and in the Hotel San Agustín at Iturbide 1 less than a block from Plaza Gertrudis Bocanegra. Hours for the latter are 8 am to 8 pm daily.

Laundromat The lavandería at Jesús Terán 14 not far from Plaza Vasco de Quiroga is open from 9 am to 2 pm and 4 to 8 pm Monday to Friday, 9 am to 2 pm Saturday.

Festivals

Las Pastorelas Processions in honour of the 'three wise men' take place on 6 January.

San Antonio del Abad Traditionally called

'the blessing of the animals', 17 January is the day people dress up their animals and bring them to the basilica.

Procesión del Silencio Christ's death is mourned in a silent procession around Pátzcuaro on Good Friday.

Día de los Muertos The Day of the Dead celebrations on 2 November are held in veneration of the dead from sunset until sunrise the following day on the island of Janitzio in Lake Pátzcuaro. The candlelight procession, music and dances are world famous.

Nuestra Señora de la Salud Celebrations on 8 December honour the Virgin of Health with a colourful procession of Tarascan pilgrims and dancers. The traditional dances performed include Los Reboceros, Los Moros, Los Viejitos, Los Panaderos and Los Mojigangas. Pátzcuaro's biggest celebration, La Feria Artesanal y Agrícola (Arts, Crafts & Agricultural Fair), also begins on this day with the state's finest exhibition of Michoacán crafts, most of which are for sale.

Mercado de Artesanías

Bishop Vasco de Quiroga left his mark on several sites in Pátzcuaro. More than four centuries later, the effects of his efforts in encouraging Lake Pátzcuaro villages to develop crafts specialities can be seen in the Mercado de Artesanías along a passageway next to the Biblioteca Gertrudis Bocanegra on the plaza by the same name. Some of the crafts sold here include thick, hand-woven wool sweaters, grotesque Tócauro masks, intricately carved wooden forks and knives from Zirahuén, and pottery. Bargaining is the rule though prices are already low.

La Biblioteca Gertrudis Bocanegra

The Gertrudis Bocanegra Library, named in honour of a woman who was executed by a firing squad in Plaza Vasco de Quiroga for her support of the independence movement, occupies the former Church of San Agustín. Colourful Juan O'Gorman murals covering the inside walls depict the history of Michoacán from pre-Hispanic times to the 1910 Revolution. A great selection of paperbacks in English at the back is testimony to the large number of gringos passing through.

Teatro Caltzontzín

Next door to the library, this theatre was a convent attached to the church before 1936. Movies and occasional cultural events are presented here. Murals in the main hall colourfully remind movie-goers of traditional Purépechan farming and dancing, including the renowned Purépechan Danza de los Viejitos (Dance of the Elders).

The Dance of the Elders is often performed at the Café Cayuco, Cuesta Vasco de Quiroga 3A near Plaza Vasco de Quiroga, on Friday and Saturday at 8 pm. The dance features performers in traditional Tarascan garb (wide-brimmed hats with coloured ribbons, black, red and white shawls and embroidered shirts) and wide-eyed masks of old men. The exaggerated expressions on the masks and in the dancers' steps are meant to mock old age.

Mercado

As you leave the theatre, the city's busy mercado or public market is to your right starting at the corner of Obregón and Libertad. Stock up on various local fruits, vegetables and herbal remedies, or look for the man who walks leashed piglets here every day.

La Casa del Gigante

On Plaza Vasco de Quiroga, visit this 17th-century mansion, a well-preserved example of colonial architecture. It was built in 1663 for a count and countess.

La Casa de los Once Patios

The House of 11 Courtyards, just off Calle Lerini and up a nameless cobblestoned street from Calle José María Coss, is also known as the Casa de las Artesanías and the Museo de Arte Contemporáneo, which means the house's various rooms are filled with arts and crafts. When Vasco de Quiroga had the house built, it was used as one of Mexico's first hospitals; later, Dominican nuns moved in and made it into a convent. Today, the house's well-preserved colonial-style buildings are used for an arts & crafts museum, gallery and crafts shops. One of the shops specialises in wooden musical instruments such as guitars and violins, made in the Michoacán highlands near Uruapan. Hours are 10 am to 7 pm daily.

Museo Regional de Artes Populares

After visiting the Casa de los Once Patios, turn left on Calle Lerini and walk a couple of blocks to the two-storey Museo Regional de Artes Populares. The museum was originally founded by Vasco de Quiroga in 1540 as the Colegio de San Nicolás Obispo. Today it is probably Mexico's most comprehensive museum of Michoacán arts and crafts. If you plan to shop for Michoacán handicrafts, it is a good idea to stop here first for an overview of the best items available. Exhibits include delicate white rebozos from Aranza, hand-painted pottery from Santa Fe de la Laguna, copperware from Santa Clara del Cobre and clay pots from Tzintzuntzán. One room is set up as a typical Michoacán kitchen with a tremendous brick oven. Hours are 10 am to 1 pm and 3 to 6 pm, Tuesday to Sunday. Admission is 15c.

La Casa de Cultura

Across the street from the museum is La Casa de Cultura, which in the 17th century served as the Hospital of Santa María. At the time of writing it was closed for renovation as the Museum of Don Vasco de Quiroga.

Basílica de Nuestra Señora de la Salud

The basílica is one block north of the Museo Regional de Artes Populares and was originally intended as Vasco de Quiroga's grand contribution to the people of Pátzcuaro. He wanted a church that would be three times as large as Notre Dame of Paris, big enough for 30,000 worshippers, but this was ambitious. The basílica was finished in the early 19th century. Its most interesting sight is the figure of the Virgen de la Salud (Virgin of Health) made by local Tarascan Indians for Vasco de Quiroga in 1546. Miraculously, the figure, which is made from a corn cob and honey paste called *tatzingue*, has survived more than four centuries of earthquakes and vandalism. Ever since Quiroga labelled the figure with the Latin words *salus infirmorum* (healer of the sick), pilgrims have come from all over Mexico on the eighth day of every month to ask the Virgin for a miracle. As with the Basílica de Guadalupe in Mexico City, the pilgrims crawl on their knees across the plaza to the basílica.

Isla de Janitzio

Although many tourists visit the island of Janitzio, the largest in the lake, both the boat ride from Pátzcuaro's docks and a two-hour stroll around the island are worthwhile. The 20-minute boat trip (US$0.95) offers great views of the other towns along the shore and often boatside demonstrations of Tarascan fishermen's famous butterfly-shaped fishing nets. The *pescado blanco* (white fish) they catch is considered *the* regional speciality. In addition to restaurants, the island has an abundance of souvenir shops, pigs and a huge Stalinistic statue of Morelos on the highest point. You can venture inside the statue to see a set of murals depicting Morelos' life.

Boats leave approximately every 20 minutes between 7 am and 6 pm from the docks.

Places to Stay – bottom end

The *Hotel Los Escudos* (tel 2-12-90), Portal Hidalgo 73, is a wonderful place

Lake Pátzcuaro

To Zamora
97 kms

To Morelia
45 kms

San Jerónimo

San Andrés

Chupícuaro

Santa Fe

Quiroga

Lake Pátzcuaro

Tzintzuntzán

Pacanda

Puacuaro

Yunuen

Ihuatzio

Erongaricuaro

Tecuen

Janitzio

Uricho

Jaracuaro

Arocutin

Uranden

Tocuaro

San Pedro

Huecorio

Tzurumutaro

San Bartolo

Pátzcuaro

To Morelia
59 kms

To Uruapan
62 kms

To Santa Clara
18 kms

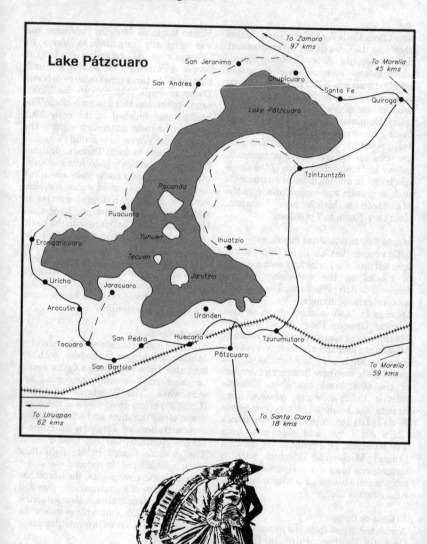

conveniently located right on Plaza Vasco de Quiroga. All of the rooms are arranged around a beautiful stone courtyard full of plants and hanging lamps. Most rooms have fireplaces, hand-carved bed headboards, TVs and carpeting. Singles cost US$7.30, doubles US$12.25, triples US$14.75.

The *Hotel Posada de la Basílica* (tel 2-11-08), Arciga 6 across from the basilica, is a super deal with red tile floors, fireplaces and gilded mirrors in several rooms. When it's open, go to the top of the tower for a fantastic view of Pátzcuaro and the lake. Singles are US$6.70, doubles US$10, triples US$12.25.

The *Hotel Valmen* (tel 2-11-61), Lloreda 34 near the bus terminal, has very clean basic rooms around two colonial-style courtyards. Most rooms have hot showers. Singles, doubles and triples are US$2 to US$4.

The *Hotel Imperial* (tel 2-03-08), Obregón 21 near the post office, has basically clean rooms, though in some the plastered walls are peeling and cracking. Singles are US$4.20, doubles US$6, triples US$6.70.

The *Hotel Concordia* (tel 2-00-03), Portal Juárez 31 on Plaza Gertrudis Bocanegra, has simple, almost crude rooms that are probably the cheapest in town. The courtyard and lack of bugs make this a fair deal. Singles cost US$2.60, doubles US$3.70, triples US$4.75.

The *Gran Hotel* (tel 2-04-43), Plaza Gertrudis Bocanegra 6, is a clean, modern, no-frills hotel with a manager who brags about the hotel's frills. Singles cost US$6.75, doubles US$8.50, triples US$10.10.

Camping This is possible at two trailer parks. The *Trailer Park El Pozo* (tel 2-09-37) is just off the Pátzcuaro-Morelia highway (No 120) across the train tracks on the lake front. There are 20 sites with full hook-ups, a coin laundry, hot showers and a dock. Watch carefully for the sign pointing across the tracks. The cost is US$5 for two per night. Tent camping is possible for a lesser fee.

Trailer Park Don Vasco (tel 2-06-94), Lázaro Cárdenas 450, is a new park attached to the hotel of the same name.

Places to Stay - middle

The *Hotel Misión San Manuel* (tel 2-13-13), Portal Aldama 12 on Plaza Vasco de Quiroga, is a romantic, colonial-style hotel with courtyards and potted plants in the halls. Most of the rooms have beamed ceilings, dark wood panelling and carpeting. Singles cost US$11, doubles US$12.50, triples US$16.25.

The *Hotel Posada de San Rafael* (tel 2-07-70), Plaza Vasco 18, is not as romantic as the *Hotel Misión San Manuel*. The rooms are clean and surround a monastery-like courtyard. Some have wooden floors and beam ceilings. Singles cost US$11, doubles US$13.60, triples US$16.25.

The *Hotel Mesón del Gallo* (tel 2-14-74), Calle Dr Coss 20, is a colonial mission-style place with dark carved furniture from Michoacán in most of the rooms. There are 20 rooms and five suites (each with a small personal bar). A swimming pool, restaurant and two lounges are attached to the hotel. Singles cost US$9, doubles US$11, triples US$13.

The *Hotel Mansión de Iturbide* (tel 2-03-68), Portal Morelos 59, has charming, colonial-style rooms with TVs, dark wood furniture and plants in the hallways. Singles are US$10.25, doubles US$15.30, triples US$18.

Places to Stay - top end

The best place in town is the *Best Western – Posada de Don Vasco* (tel 2-06-94), Avenida Lázaro Cárdenas 450 (also referred to as Avenida de las Américas). The colonial-style motor inn has typical Best Western standards. Singles/doubles are US$26/27.

Places to Eat

Near the docks on Lázaro Cárdenas, *La*

Mansión del Lago serves a variety of fish specialities, including *pescado blanco* and *los chorales*. The latter are sardine-like fish deep-fried and eaten whole from head to tail.

The restaurant at the *Hotel Los Escudos*, Portal Hidalgo 73, and the *Restaurant El Patio*, Plaza Vasco de Quiroga 19, are both known for similar specialities.

The restaurant at the *Gran Hotel*, Portal Regules at the Plaza Gertrudis Bocanegra 6, does a good comida corrida for US$1.60.

The sunny courtyard *Restaurant El Monje* of the Hotel Misión San Manuel, Portal Aldama 12, serves 12 types of soup (US$0.65 per bowl) and a speciality called *chareles* (US$1.60). They also do a decent breakfast for US$1.80.

The *Restaurant El Patio*, Plaza Vasco de Quiroga 19, does a good breakfast (US$1.35): juice or fruit, choice of five types of eggs, and hot chocolate or tea. Their comida corrida (US$2.10) includes soup, Mexican rice, grilled ribs, chile relleno, coffee and dessert. Try the *trucha del lago al gusto – estilo Pátzcuaro*, trout dipped in egg and fried.

The *Restaurant La Basílica*, Arciga 6 across from the basilica on the 2nd floor of the Hotel Posada de la Basílica, serves a filling breakfast (US$1.60 to US$2) of juice or fruit, hotcakes, buttered toast and coffee. At lunch, the comida corrida (US$2.25) includes soup, rice, meat or fish, dessert and tea or coffee. There's a great view of the city and Lake Pátzcuaro.

The *Restaurant Gran Hotel*, Plaza Gertrudis Bocanegra 6, does a good comida corrida (US$2.10) that includes fish or chicken soup, macaroni or rice, fish or meat, dessert, coffee or tea. It offers musical performances from 2 to 5 pm.

Facing the Casa de Cultura at Calle Lerini 38 (also known as Calle Enseñanza) is a small shop called *Joaquinita Chocolate Supremo* run by an old woman who makes very sweet home-made chocolate. A big packet is US$1.75.

Getting There & Away

Bus The Central Camionera (Central Bus Terminal) is at Ahumada 63 near Plaza Gertrudis Bocanegra. Buses to Morelia (US$0.80) depart every half-hour, to Uruapan (US$0.80) every half-hour, to Mexico City (US$3.75) every four hours, to Guadalajara (US$2.75) four times daily – a six-hour trip.

Rail The train station is near the lake at the end of Avenida de las Américas. Buses heading for downtown frequently pass by the station. There are three trains daily from Pátzcuaro to Uruapan and, in the opposite direction, to Morelia and Mexico City. Trains depart Uruapan at 7.15 pm and 6.35 am and arrive at Pátzcuaro at 9.25 pm and 8.45 am; and at Mexico City 7.50 am and 8.50 pm. Trains for Uruapan depart Pátzcuaro at 7.36 am and 6.46 pm; the trip takes about 2½ hours.

Getting Around

To get to the docks from downtown Pátzcuaro, take any bus labelled 'Sta Ana', 'Lago' or 'San Pedro' from the corner of Portal Juárez and Portal Regules in Plaza Gertrudis Bocanegra.

Flecha Amarilla buses go from Pátzcuaro's bus terminal to other cities on Lake Pátzcuaro.

AROUND PÁTZCUARO

Tzintzuntzán

Population: 9100

The town and archaeological site of Tzintzuntzán ('zeen-TSUNE-zahn', altitude 2050 metres) are 15 km from Pátzcuaro along the north-east edge of Lake Pátzcuaro. Tzintzuntzán is a Tarascan name meaning 'Place of the Hummingbirds', though the Tarascan armies that came from here were more like hawks. One of the three cities of the Tarascan League formed in the late 14th century by King Tariácuri to share control of the kingdom, Tzintzuntzán eventually became the capital.

As testimony to their power and

control, the people erected an impressive complex of pyramid temples over a large terrace of carefully fitted stone blocks. Each temple consisted of 12 levels with a stairway leading to a platform on top. Two of the temples have been partially restored and can be visited during daylight hours. Admission is less than 5c. The site is atop a hill one km from town.

In town, craftspeople display hand-painted ceramics and straw figurines (the town's specialities) on Calle Principal, not far from another of the town's principal sites – the 16th-century Franciscan Convent of San Francisco. Olive trees in the church courtyard were supposedly planted by Vasco de Quiroga against the wishes of the Spanish government.

The weeklong Día de Nuestro Señor del Rescate (festival of the Lord of Rescue) begins on 1 February and is essentially a big party in honour of the Lord of Rescue. It was established by Vasco de Quiroga in the mid-16th century as a means of encouraging the Tarascans to accept and practise 'Christian charity'.

Quiroga
Population: 16,000

The town of Quiroga (altitude 2074 metres), 10 km north-east of Tzintzuntzán at the junction of the highway to Morelia and Zamora, was named after Vasco de Quiroga because he was responsible for many of the buildings and traditional handicrafts. Wooden toys and trays are two of the specialities you'll see displayed.

On the first Sunday in July, the Fiesta de la Preciosa Sangre de Cristo (Festival of the Precious Blood of Christ) is celebrated with a long torchlight procession. It's led by a group carrying an image of Christ crafted from a paste of corn cobs and honey.

URUAPAN
Population: 170,000

When the Spanish monk Juan de San Miguel arrived in 1533, he was so impressed with the Río Cupatitzio and lush vegetation surrounding it that he named the area Uruapan ('oo-rue-AH-pahn'), which translates roughly from Tarascan, the local Indian language, as 'fruit and flowers' or 'eternal spring'.

Juan de San Miguel laid the foundations of the town by having a large market square, hospital and chapel built and arranging the streets in an orderly chequerboard pattern. As the Spanish *encomienda* system, a feudal system of land grants to Spanish soldiers and serfdom for the Indians, spread in the surrounding countryside, Uruapan rapidly developed as a major agricultural centre.

Today, its continual water supply and temperate climate have maintained Uruapan's status as one of Mexico's most productive agricultural areas renowned for its high-quality avocados and fruit. In addition, Uruapan's craftspeople are famed for their beautiful hand-painted cedar lacquerware, particularly trays and boxes.

Uruapan's altitude is 1611 metres. Average temperature is 20°C.

Orientation

Uruapan is about 320 km south-east of Guadalajara (approximately 5½ hours by bus), 125 km from Morelia (just over two hours) and 313 km from Playa Azul on the Pacific coast. It is situated in the highlands near the Volcano of Paricutín and at the junction of Highways 14 from Pátzcuaro and 37 from Highway 200 on the Pacific coast.

The city lies on the east bank of the Río Cupatitzio, with most of the streets still arranged in the chequerboard pattern laid down by Juan de San Miguel in the 1530s. Everything of interest to travellers, except perhaps the train station, is within walking distance of the zócalo, which is surrounded by Calles Ocampo, Corregidora, Constitución and Álvaro Obregón. The zócalo is actually three connected plazas, which, from the western end, are Jardín de

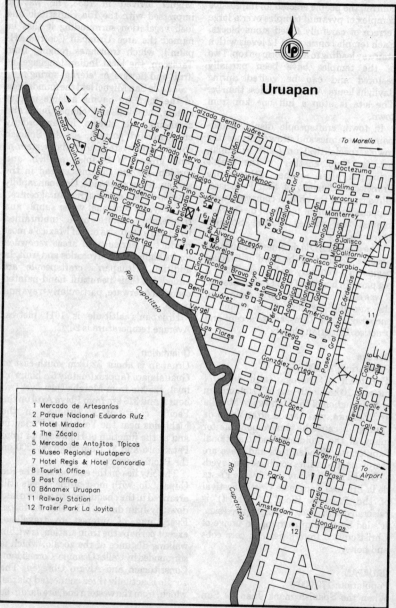

Uruapan

To Morelia

To Airport

1 Mercado de Artesanías
2 Parque Nacional Eduardo Ruíz
3 Hotel Mirador
4 The Zócalo
5 Mercado de Antojitos Típicos
6 Museo Regional Huatapero
7 Hotel Regis & Hotel Concordia
8 Tourist Office
9 Post Office
10 Bánamex Uruapan
11 Railway Station
12 Trailer Park La Joyita

los Mátires, the Plaza Principal and the Plaza Fray San Miguel.

As with many cities in Mexico, watch street names because they often change every few blocks. In Uruapan, Álvaro Obregón is a dividing line with the names of intersecting streets different on each side of it. Obregón itself also changes to Emilio Carranza as it runs north-west and to Francisco Sarabia in the opposite direction. Unfortunately, no one is absolutely certain at which points the streets parallel to Obregón change names.

Paseo Gral Lázaro Cárdenas, one of the major streets in town, runs south-west towards the coast and north-east to intersect the highway to Morelia and the volcano of Paricutín.

Information

Tourist Office The tourist office (tel 2-06-33), Cinco de Febrero 17 in the courtyard of the ex-Hotel Progreso about half a block south-west of the zócalo, has plenty of brochures and leaflets in English and Spanish about sites and activities in Michoacán. The staff's knowledge of English is extremely limited. Hours are 9 am to 2 pm and 4.30 to 7 pm Monday to Friday, and 9 am to 2 pm Saturday.

Money Bánamex is near the zócalo at the corner of Morelos and Cupatitzio. Bancomer is at the corner of Emilio Carranza and 20 de Noviembre. Banco Serfin is at Cupatitzio 13. Comermex Lázaro Cárdenas is at Juan Ayala and Independencia. Banco Internacional is at Cupatitzio 23.

Post The post office is at Cupatitzio 36 about a block south-west of the zócalo. It's open from 8 am to 7.30 pm Monday to Friday and 9 am to 1 pm Saturday and Sunday.

Festivals

Domingo de Ramos Palm Sunday is celebrated with a procession through the city streets. Figures and crosses woven from palm fronds are sold after the procession. There's also a ceramics contest.

María Magdalena The Festival of Saint Mary Magdalene is celebrated on 22 July with a procession of decorated mule and oxen teams and traditional dances on the atrium of the church.

San Juan Apóstol The Festival of Saint James the Apostle venerates the saint on 25 July with traditional dances and musical performances, fireworks and parades.

San Francisco Saint Francis, the patron saint of Uruapan, is honoured on 4 October with colourful festivities and the Canacuas dance by Tarascan women.

Día de la Raza Otherwise known as Columbus Day, 12 October is the day that Christopher Columbus discovered the New World.

Festival de Coros y Danzas The Choir & Dance Festival is a contest of Tarascan dance and musical groups that lasts for three days around 24 October and offers a good opportunity to see and hear a variety of traditional Tarascan dances and music.

Museo Regional Huatapera

For a decent overview of Tarascan crafts, visit the Museo Regional Huatapera (also known as the Museo de la Huatapera) facing the Plaza Principal. The building was erected by Fray Juan de San Miguel in the 16th century to serve as a chapel and the first hospital in the Americas. Hours are 9.30 am to 1.30 pm and 3.30 to 6 pm, Tuesday to Sunday. Admission is free.

Parque Nacional Eduardo Ruíz

The park's main entrance is on Calzada Fray Juan de San Miguel at the end of

Calle Independencia. The Río Cupatitzio begins at the north-western corner of the park where underground springs come to the surface. The river and springs keep the surrounding tropical vegetation lush, which makes for cool picnic grounds or a pleasant afternoon stroll on one of the several paths. The springs used to be a great place for a dunk, but now they're a popular outdoor laundromat. The park is open until sunset.

Places to Stay – bottom end

The *Hotel Mirador* (tel 2-04-73) faces the western end of the zócalo at Ocampo 9 and could probably be considered a bargain basement hotel. Big, dark rooms with dusty wooden floors and hot showers are US$3.15 for singles and US$6.30 for doubles. Some of the rooms have great views of the zócalo and are surprisingly quiet until you open the windows.

The *Hotel Hernández* (tel 2-16-00), Portal Matamoros 8 also on the zócalo near the Hotel Regis, has 75 big rooms with wooden floors, blotched walls, bathrooms and telephones. Singles are US$6.50, doubles US$9.50, triples US$11.25.

Camping This is possible at the southern end of Uruapan on Calle Honduras about two blocks from Paseo Gral Lázaro Cárdenas at the *Trailer Park La Joyita*. It's a small, well-kept park behind a row of shops. The front gate is locked late at night. Electrical and water hook-ups are available for a few vehicles. The bathrooms are spotless and the showers are hot. The fee is US$3.25 for two per night.

Places to Stay – middle

The *Hotel Regis* (tel 3-58-44), Portal Carrillo 12 on the zócalo, has plain, clean, but slightly malodorous rooms that seem overpriced. Singles/doubles are US$7.50/9.50. Although there's an economical restaurant behind the lobby, the hotel's only advantage is its central location.

The *Hotel Concordia* (tel 3-04-00), Portal Carrillo 8 a few doors from the Regis, is one of the best deals for a middle-priced hotel in Uruapan. Clean, comfortable rooms with radios, TVs and bathrooms that even have sterile paper strips over the toilet seats cost US$10 single, US$12.50 double, US$15 triple. Parking is available in a lot about a block away. A restaurant and bar face the lobby and reception area.

Places to Stay – top end

The hacienda-style *Hotel Mansion del Cupatitzio* (tel 3-21-00), at the western end of the Parque Nacional Eduardo Ruíz on Calzada Fray Juan de San Juan Miguel, is considered one of the best hotels in Uruapan. There is a heated pool and coin laundry on the premises. Singles/doubles are US$20/25.

Places to Eat & Drink

The *Café Tradicional de Uruapan* is on Calle Emiliano Carranza about a block north-west of the zócalo. It is practically a bona fide European café complete with a range of coffees that is probably one of the best you'll see in Mexico. The range includes cappuccino, espresso, café Cubano (double espresso), café Uruapan (finely ground coffee made from locally grown beans) and café con leche (coffee with milk).

El Portón del Victoria, Cupatitzio 11, is a favourite with locals. *Típico* dishes are served for US$2.10 to US$3.15.

The *Restaurant La Pérgola*, Portal Carrillo near the Hotel Concordia on the zócalo, is a popular place that does a good comida corrida for US$2.

The *Emperador Restaurant*, Portal Matamoros 18 on the zócalo, specialises in beef dishes (US$3.50 maximum) and cheap but strong coffee (25c per cup).

The *Mercado de Antojitos Típicos*, near the zócalo at the corner of Corregidora and Constitución, has several food stalls serving fast foods and local specialities such as *huchepos* (a sort of corn mash). The stalls are popular with local families.

Things to Buy

Various local specialities such as lacquered trays and boxes can be bought at the Mercado de Artesanías, Calzada Fray Juan de Miguel across from the entrance to the Parque Nacional Eduardo Ruíz.

Getting There & Away

Bus The Central Camionera (central bus terminal) is one km from central Uruapan on the highway to Morelia. *Tres Estrellas de Oro* (tel 3-10-83) has 1st-class buses to Morelia every half-hour from noon to 6.30 pm (US$1.50), Guadalajara three times daily from 11.30 am to 12.30 am (US$3.25), Mexico City four times from 1 to 10 pm (US$7) and Lázaro Cárdenas three times daily from 11.50 am to 10.30 pm (US$3.25).

Autotransportes Flecha Amarilla (tel 2-18-70) has 2nd-class buses to the same destinations for less and with more frequent departures to Mexico City (six times, US$4.50) and Guadalajara (every two hours, 24 hours daily, US$2.60).

Rail The Estación del Ferrocarril (tel 3-13-67) is on Paseo Lázaro Cárdenas at the end of Calle Americas. The schedule for trains running to and from Uruapan follows:

Uruapan-Mexico City

		Train 28	Train 30
departs	Uruapan	7.15 pm	6.35 am
	Pátzcuaro	9.25 pm	8.45 am
	Morelia	10.57 pm	10.22 am
	Toluca	5.37 am	6.00 pm
arrives	Mexico City	7.50 am	8.50 pm

		Train 27	Train 29
departs	Mexico City	9.29 pm	6.55 am
	Toluca	11.56 pm	9.35 am
	Morelia	6.08 am	5.12 pm
	Pátzcuaro	7.36 am	6.46 pm
arrives	Uruapan	10.07 am	9.05 pm

Trains 29 and 30 have only 1st and 2nd-class unreserved coach seats available. Trains 27 and 28 have both coach classes, 1st-class reserved seating, sleeping berths, roomettes and bedrooms.

Getting Around

Since almost everything of interest to travellers is within walking distance of the zócalo except the train station, the only relevant bus line is between the zócalo and the station and vice versa – 'Zapata Revolución'.

AROUND URUAPAN

Tzaráracua Waterfalls

About 10 km south of Uruapan just off Highway 37, the Río Cupatitzio cascades over a 20-metre cliff into a couple of pools and, two km farther upstream, over a smaller cliff. The waterfalls are called Tzaráracua and Tzaráracuita and can be reached by foot or horse (US$2.75 round trip for both falls). There's a frequent bus from the Uruapan zócalo – labelled 'Tzaráracua' – for 5c.

Paricutín

No one expected Paricutín to completely blow its top in 1943, but it did and continued spewing lava for eight years.

During the last week of February 1943 Tarascan Indians in the villages of Paricutín and San Juan de Parangaricutiro left the area when they began to notice strange movements at the top of the mountain. Both villages and everything else within 20 km were soon covered by the lava flow; a church spire can still be seen jutting out of the volcanic rock. The ½-km-wide crater created on the mountain by the eruption can be visited on horseback, although the crater pit steams and sputters a bit.

For a day trip from Uruapan, ride the 'Los Reyes' bus from the zócalo to the village of Angahuan. It's best to catch the first bus, which leaves at 7.30 am, because the trip takes over an hour and you want plenty of time to explore the area around the volcano. Stock up on snacks (fruit and crackers) and water before leaving Uruapan.

Arranging a guide and a horse in Angahuan is no problem because the villagers are accustomed to taking visitors

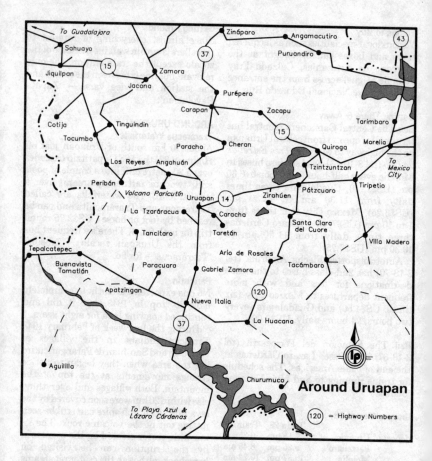

Around Uruapan

(120) = Highway Numbers

to the volcano – for a price, of course. A guide should cost US$5 and the horse US$13. The round trip to the rim takes about six hours; a shorter trip by foot to a hill just outside of Angahuan takes about two hours round trip. The last bus to Uruapan leaves at 7 pm.

Paracho

Paracho is 30 km north of Uruapan on Highway 37. This small town is world-renowned for its hand-made guitars and is worth visiting to watch a few of the world's best guitar-makers at work. They are also known for making high-quality violins and cellos.

LÁZARO CÁRDENAS

Population: 50,000

Lázaro Cárdenas is the largest city on the Michoacán coast. It's named after a reform-minded leader who served as governor of Michoacán from 1928 to 1932 and as president of Mexico from 1934 to 1940. In the late 1960s he encouraged then-President Díaz Ordaz to begin constructing a huge US$500 million Sicartsa iron and steel works and US$40 million port in the village of Melchor Ocampo. The project didn't get under way until after his death in 1970 and during the administration of President Luis Echeverría (1970 to 1976).

Echeverría renamed the village Lázaro Cárdenas and erected what became a slum city around the project, which by this time was slated to cost over US$1 billion. The resulting plant produced steel wire, which Mexico really didn't need, and was run with coal imported from Colombia. The plant cost much more than it could ever earn and greatly contributed to the 450% increase in Mexico's foreign debt, which was more than US$19 billion by 1976.

Today, the plant continues to run, supposedly with injections of British capital, but more emphasis seems to have been placed on the city's burgeoning port facilities. While not as much of an eyesore as it was in the past, the city has nothing of real interest to travellers. Reasons to stop here are to stock up on food and water, change buses, and head for Playa Azul, a beach resort 24 km west of Lázaro Cárdenas.

PLAYA AZUL

Playa Azul is a small beach resort town backed by lagoons formed by a tributary of the Río Balsas. Although it has mostly been a resort for Mexican families, North Americans are gradually being attracted here by the beautiful beach and surfable waves.

Information

Post The post office is five blocks down Calle Carranza from the Hotel Playa Azul. Hours are 8 am to 2 pm and 3 to 6 pm Monday to Friday, and 8 am to 2 pm Saturday.

Telephone Calls Supposedly, long-distance collect calls can now be made from any telephone in town, but if you want

assistance, go to the caseta de larga distancia in a small building near the Hotel Playa Azul's parking lot.

Horses Horses can be hired from the Hotel Delfin for US$4.70 per day.

Places to Stay

The *Bungalows de la Curva* (tel 6-00-58) was closed at the time of writing; it used to be one of the best and most economical places to stay in town. A bungalow that could sleep three cost US$16.50, including access to a swimming pool and restaurant. If it reopens, it'll probably be at the same location near the Pemex station on Avenida Carranza,

Also on Avenida Carranza is the *Hotel Delfin* (tel 2-19-54), next door to the Bungalows de la Curva. Its 25 rooms are clean and simple; most have ceiling fans and look out on a courtyard and a murky green swimming pool. Singles cost US$7.85, doubles US$9.80, triples US$11.75.

The *Hotel Playa Azul* (tel 6-00-24) is down the street from the Delfin. One of the hotel's three-floor buildings collapsed during the 1985 earthquake while, remarkably, the two adjoining buildings were untouched. At the time of writing, the damaged building was being reconstructed. The owner/manager speaks some English and is happy to answer any questions you may have about the hotel or Playa Azul. The rooms are clean and comfortable with air-conditioning in a few and fans in the rest. Singles, doubles and triples in the two three-storey buildings are US$14.50, US$17.30 and US$20.75. The rooms facing the street are cheaper: singles are US$12.50, doubles US$15.10, triples US$17.25.

The *Casa de Huéspedes Silva*, one block from the Hotel Playa Azul, has dungeon-like, slightly malodorous rooms with latches that allow masochistic types to lock themselves in. Fans in each room offer some relief. The rate is US$5 for one or two.

The *Hotel Costa de Oro* (tel 6-00-86) is on Calle Emiliano Zapata, one block towards the centre of town if you are coming from the Pemex station. Just look for the street piled high with coconuts. It is clean and seems worth the price: US$3.60 single, US$4.75 double, US$5.75 triple.

If you have a hammock, you can string it up at one of the *enramadas* (small shade huts or *palapas*) at any of the beach-front restaurants and cafés for a nominal fee or for free.

Camping It is possible to camp at the *Hotel Playa Azul* trailer park. The charge per night is US$2.10 per person including access to electricity, water, the swimming pool and bathrooms.

Places to Eat

The *Hotel Delfin* restaurant will make almost any Mexican dish you want for US$2.60 including tortillas, rice and beans and features service on bright orange table cloths.

The *Casa de Huéspedes Silva* restaurant is actually the kitchen of the attached house. Everything on the menu is under US$1.

Breakfast at the *Hotel Playa Azul* is a filling deal that includes eggs or hotcakes, fruit or juice, tea or coffee and toast for US$2. Those who eat here have free access to the swimming pool, except from July to August and during Semana Santa, the high-season periods.

Getting There & Away

Bus & Combi Buses and Volkswagen combis run approximately every five minutes from 5 am to 9 pm between Playa Azul, La Mira and Lázaro Cárdenas. In Lázaro Cárdenas, catch either a bus or combi on the city's main street, Avenida Lázaro Cárdenas. The buses drop you off in front of the town's Pemex station, while the combis continue past the station and down Calle Carranza. The combis will drop you off anywhere along Carranza. Fares to Lázaro Cárdenas are US$0.40 by combi and 25c by bus.

Inter-city buses do not pass through Playa Azul; instead they will drop you off 1½ km from town at the highway junction.

Several inter-city bus lines run from the Central Camionera in Lázaro Cárdenas near Constitución and Avenida Lázaro Cárdenas including Autobuses del Occidente, Flecha Roja, Tres Estrellas de Oro, Autobuses Galeana and Transportes del Norte de Sonora.

Colima

With an area of only 5455 square km, the state of Colima is Mexico's fourth smallest after Tlaxcala, Morelos and Aguascalientes. Despite its relatively small area, the state is geographically diverse with everything from snowcapped volcanoes to tropical lagoons near Manzanillo. More than three-quarters of Colima is covered with mountains and hills. The climate is equally diverse with higher temperatures and humidity along the coast and cool, sometimes freezing, temperatures in the highlands and mountains farther inland.

Colima borders the state of Jalisco to the north, east and west and the state of Michoacán to the south-east. To the north and west, part of the border is delineated by the Río Cihuatlán. To the south-east and east, the Río Coahuayana, also known as the Río Tuxpan and the Río Naranjo, forms most of the border. The Río Armería, one of the state's largest rivers, flows down from the Sierra de Cacoma mountain range of Jalisco, crosses Colima from north to south and enters the Pacific Ocean through the Boca de Pascuales south-east of Manzanillo.

The history of the state of Colima mostly revolves around the arrival of the Spanish in the area in 1523 and the founding of Colima, the capital city and third Spanish city established in New Spain. Before the Spanish arrived, the area was inhabited by a variety of Indian groups, including the Nahua, Toltecs, Otomíes and Chichimecs. Descendants of these groups still live in the area, but no single group stands out.

There's something of interest for every traveller in Colima. For beach-lovers and fans of tropical paradise, there's plenty of both along the coast, particularly in and around Manzanillo and at the small beach resorts of Cuyutlán and Playa Paraíso. Inland, Colima, the capital, is a quiet place where much of the original colonial-style architecture has been well preserved. Nearby, the white-washed town of Comala has also retained some of its colonial legacy, but today it is better known for its handicrafts, especially hand-carved furniture. Overlooking both places are the steaming Volcán de Fuego de Colima (3960 metres) and the extinct Volcán Nevado de Colima (4330 metres) of the Nevado de Colima National Park, both of which can be climbed by foot, horse or four-wheel drive, but only if you are feeling really adventurous.

COLIMA
Population: 73,000

The area around Colima was first claimed by Spanish conquistador Capitán Gonzálo de Sandoval in 1523. By 1527, Cortés decided that the third city of New Spain, after La Villa Rica de Veracruz and Mexico City, should be built here and named Colima in honour of King Coliman, a past Nahua Indian ruler of the area. Most of the buildings in Colima, however, were not built until after the Spanish left in the early 19th century. Although it was one of the first cities in Mexico, the area wasn't declared a state until 1857 and the city not a capital until a year later. Today, Colima is a pleasant place surrounded by farmland and not often visited by foreigners.

Orientation
Colima sits on a fertile plain surrounded by hills and mountains, the highest ones being the twin volcanic peaks of Nevado de Colima (4330 metres) and Fuego de Colima (3960 metres). Although it's only 45 km from the coast, the city is at a higher elevation and, consequently, cooler and less humid.

Central Colima is demarcated by three plazas that run from west to east

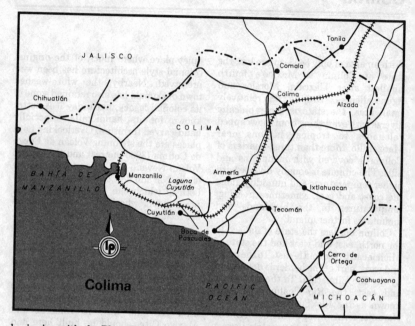

beginning with the Plaza Principal (also known as the Jardín Libertad), the Jardín Quintero behind the cathedral and, three blocks to the east, the Jardín Nuñez.

As with most cities and towns in Mexico, street names change frequently. Along the northern side of the Plaza Principal, Calle Quintero becomes Calle Francisco Madero as it goes eastward. Other examples: Reforma becomes Constitución as it goes north, 16 de Septiembre becomes Hidalgo as it goes east, Ocampo becomes 27 de Septiembre as it goes north. The street name selection seems set on mentioning every one of Mexico's most highly regarded leaders.

Information
Tourist Office The Dirección General de Turismo (tel 2-43-60) is staffed by smiling people who, despite their limited English, can be helpful. Several English-language brochures about Colima (the state and the city) are available. Hours are 8.30 am to 3 pm and 5 to 8 pm Monday to Friday, 9 am to 1 pm Saturday.

Post The post office is at Madero and Revolución and is open daily, except weekends, from 8 am to 6 pm.

Festivals
La Virgen de la Salud The festival of the Virgin of Health on 2 February is celebrated starting nine days before with traditional dance and music performances, bullfights and fireworks.

La Fiesta Brava The bullfights of the Festival of the Virgin of Health on 5 February continue on this day with a parade of costumed riders on horseback and a bullfight open to public participation.

La Feria Regional de Colima The purpose of this fair, held from 25 October to 3 November, is to promote the products and businesses of Colima. Exhibits cover everything from agriculture, industry and tourism to arts and crafts.

La Casa de Cultura

The House of Culture is a government-run centre at Ejército Nacional that includes the Museo de las Culturas de Occidente. The museum houses one of Mexico's best collections of pre-Hispanic artefacts as well as exhibits covering the anthropological history of the Colima area. The exhibits are arranged chronologically beginning with the period from 225 to 850 AD in which an independent culture, evidenced by finds of uniquely grotesque clay figurines, thrived in Colima. Hours are 9 am to 1 pm and 3 to 6 pm. Admission is free.

Museo de la Máscara y la Danza

The Museum of Masks & Dances, part of the Universidad de Bellas Artes at Niños Héroes and 27 de Septiembre, maintains a special collection of hand-carved masks and dance costumes. Hours are 10 am to 1.30 pm Monday to Saturday.

Palacio del Gobierno

The Government Palace is at the western end of the Plaza Principal where, before it was built between 1884 and 1904, Colima's jailhouse once stood. A local artist named Jorge Chávez Carrillo painted the murals on the walls of the stairway inside the palace in honour of independence hero Hidalgo's 200th birthday; they depict Mexican history from the Spanish conquest to the present.

Cathedral

Also on the Plaza Principal is Colima's main cathedral, rebuilt several times since the Spanish first constructed a cathedral here in 1527. The latest reconstruction dates from the 1940s just after the 1941 earthquake. For a commanding view of Colima, ask at the church office for a brief tour to the top of the cathedral's right tower.

Colección de Automóviles Antiguos

Despite its relatively long history, Colima's most famous sight is the Collection of Antique Automobiles crammed in a shaky warehouse behind an auto parts store at Avenida Revolución 79, across from Jardín Nuñez. Ask for Señor Francisco Zaragoza Vázquez, owner of the store and the collection, and he will lead you through a maze of shelves and old parts to the warehouse. Since 1952 he has collected 300 automobiles that date from 1912 to 1950; they included a 1928 Ford Model A, a 1931 Buick and a 1925 Ford Model T. Several horse-drawn carriages probably date back to the late 19th century.

Places to Stay

Colima doesn't have an abundance of places to stay, but you shouldn't have any problem finding a room.

Near the airport, train station and road to Manzanillo is the *Motel Servicio Costeño* (tel 2-19-00). The rooms are very clean and have TVs and a fresh, woody smell. Each room looks out on a grassy area and the swimming pool. Singles/doubles are US$10/12.50.

The *Hotel San Cristóbal* (tel 2-05-15), Reforma 98, has rooms with fans and 'Turkish-style' bathrooms (holes in the ground), all of which were dirty. A single is US$3, overpriced even at that.

The best place in town is the *Hotel Ceballos* (tel 2-13-54) on the north side of the Plaza Principal at Portal Medellín 12. Clean, high-ceilinged rooms with overhead fans and balconies overlooking the Plaza Principal are US$6/11.50 singles/doubles.

The worst and cheapest place in town is the *Casa de Huéspedes Miramar*, Morelos 265. You have to be desperate to stay in one of its dark and dirty rooms. Perhaps by the time this appears in print, they will have cleaned up their act, but they'll first have to get rid of the turtle-like manager. Singles/doubles are US$1.65/3.30.

At the north-east end of town at

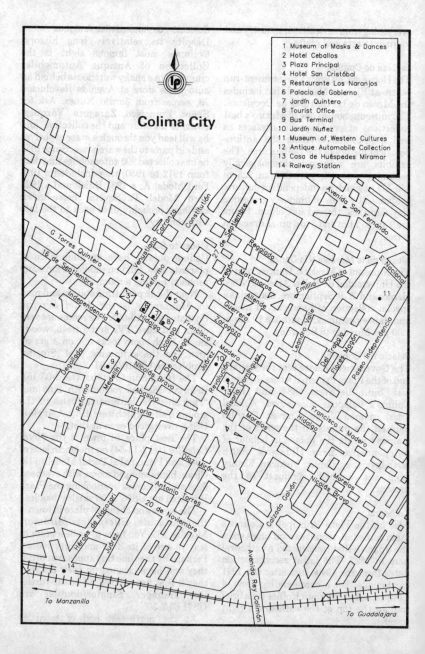

Colima City

1 Museum of Masks & Dances
2 Hotel Ceballos
3 Plaza Principal
4 Hotel San Cristóbal
5 Restaurante Los Naranjos
6 Palacio de Gobierno
7 Jardín Quintero
8 Tourist Office
9 Bus Terminal
10 Jardín Nuñez
11 Museum of Western Cultures
12 Antique Automobile Collection
13 Casa de Huéspedes Miramar
14 Railway Station

To Manzanillo

To Guadalajara

Boulevard Camino Real 51 (Highway 54 to Ciudad Guzmán) is the *Motel Los Candiles*, a clean, American-style motel with 77 rooms, a coffee-shop and a swimming pool. Singles/doubles are US$10/14.

Places to Eat

The Conasupo supermarket next to the tourist office on Hidalgo makes inexpensive licuados and chocolate milk shakes at the back of the store.

Similarly refreshing drinks are available at *Jugolandia*, on Madero across from the Jardín Quintero.

Some travellers claim that the best pizza in Mexico is served at *Giovanni's Pizza*, Zaragoza and Constitución just north of the Plaza Principal. More than 20 types of pizza are available as well as spaghetti. Nothing costs more than US$2.

For local *colimense* dishes such as grilled and spiced filet mignon, try the *Restaurante Los Naranjos*, Barreda 34 just north of the Jardín Quintero.

Getting There & Away

Bus The inter-city bus terminal is near the centre of town on Reforma between Nicolás Bravo and Abasolo. Tres Estrellas de Oro (1st class) buses go to Manzanillo (US$1) every 15 minutes, to Guadalajara (US$2.70) almost every half-hour, to Lázaro Cárdenas (US$3.70) 15 times daily and to Mexico City (US$8) seven times daily. Transportes Norte de Sonora (2nd class) runs buses to these and other destinations for slightly less and probably more frequently.

Rail The train station (estación de ferrocarriles) is on the southern side of town (see map). There's a train to Manzanillo (1st class US$0.65, 2nd class US$0.35, two hours) at 3.30 pm and one to Guadalajara (1st class US$1.75, 2nd class US$0.95, six hours) at 8 am.

AROUND COLIMA

Comala

The small, picturesque town of Comala, nine km north of Colima, is home to La Sociedad Cooperativa Artesanías Pueblo Blanco, a handicrafts centre renowned for its colonial-style hand-carved furniture and ironwork. Although most of the items are shipped to other parts of Mexico, the market next to the centre sells many of them. The centre is one km south of town, just off the road to Colima.

Stop by the *Restaurante/Bar Los Comales* facing the town square for lunch and a beer. You have to order a drink in order to get lunch, which is included in the price and is usually all the tacos you can eat.

To get to Comala from Colima, take any 'Comala' bus from the Central Camionera in Colima. Buses leave every 15 minutes from 5 am to 8 pm and cost US$0.40.

Nevado de Colima National Park

Both volcanoes – Volcán de Fuego de Colima (3960 metres) and Volcán Nevado de Colima (4330 metres) – can supposedly be hiked in a day or two each, if you can start at the base trail/logging road of either one and not from Highway 54. That's the biggest problem because, aside from an occasional logging truck from the nearby paper-mill town of Atenquique and horseback riders from Fresnito, there are very few vehicles trudging up to either summit.

The trail/road from Fresnito is pleasant and begins climbing gradually, but expect to spend about two days hiking to the summit of Nevado de Colima. If you have the time, the hike is worthwhile just for the spectacular view, especially at sunrise, and for the experience of playing in the snow in Mexico. Nevado de Colima usually has snow on its summit year-round. You can spend the night at a rustic cabin called La Joya a few km from the summit, but you must have your own water.

To get to Fresnito, take a bus from

Colima to Tonaya and ask the driver to let you off at the Fresnito junction. Walk or hitch-hike to the village and ask locals for the trail to Nevado de Colima. It's easy to find because it begins as the main road through the village.

If you decide to drive to either summit, you must have a four-wheel drive.

MANZANILLO
Population: 70,000

First and foremost, Manzanillo is a major port and industrial city. Before the Spanish arrived in the early 16th century, Manzanillo had been a port for more than 200 years for galleons shuttling to and from Asia. The urban (some might say squalid) sprawl has a downtown that is a tangle of train tracks, shipping piers and traffic surrounded by stagnant marshy splotches locals call lagoons. Surprisingly, Manzanillo is also a beach resort famous for a few hotels, beaches and marlin fishing.

Orientation
Manzanillo is 325 km south-west of Guadalajara and 101 km west of Colima. It extends for 16 km from north to south, the first five km of which are fingers of land squeezed between the Bahía de Manzanillo and the various lagoons of the Laguna de Cuyutlán. The resort hotels and finest beaches begin on Playa Azul across the Bahía de Manzanillo from the Playa San Pedrito, the closest beach to downtown (about one km). Farther north-west is a rocky outcropping occupied by Las Hadas Resort and sheltering part of the Bahía de Santiago and the beaches of La Audencia, Olas Atlas and Miramar. Just south of Miramar is the Santiago Lagoon.

Downtown Manzanillo is bounded by the Bahía de Manzanillo to the north, the Pacific Ocean to the west, and the Laguna de Cuyutlán to the south-east and south. Avenida Morelos, the principal street, runs along the northern edge of the city, west from Avenida Niños Héroes which

leads to Highway 200. The city centre begins at the zócalo (also known as the Jardín Obregón) on Morelos, and continues southward with major streets such as Avenida México and Avenida Carrillo Puerto criss-crossed from west to east by Allende, Cuauhtémoc, Guerrero and Nuñez.

Information

Tourist Office The tourist office (tel 2-01-81) is 1½ blocks east of the zócalo in the PRI building near the train station. The staff are helpful but disorganised. Hours are 8 am to 3.30 pm Monday to Friday, closed on weekends.

Money Many banks are scattered throughout Manzanillo, including Banco Mexicano on Avenida Puerto Carrillo (next to the Aeroméxico office) and another across from the zócalo at the corner of Morelos and Puerto Carrillo. Most are open for money exchange from 9 to 11.30 am.

Post The post office is east of the zócalo on Calle Cinco de Mayo between Morelos and Juárez. Hours are 8 am to 7 pm Monday to Friday, 9 am to 1 pm Saturday, 9 am to 12.30 pm Sunday.

Telephone Calls There's a caseta de larga distancia on the west side of Avenida México between Calle Cuauhtémoc and Nicolás Bravo/Guerrero (this street changes names as it crosses Avenida México). Hours are 9 am to 9 pm, Monday to Saturday. There's another one facing the east end of the zócalo.

Airlines The Aeroméxico ticket office (tel 2-08-25) is at Avenida Puerto Carrillo 107, between Allende and Calle Miguel Calindo (which becomes Calle Cuauhtémoc as it crosses Avenida México). The Mexicana ticket office (tel 2-33-54) is at Avenida México 382 between Bravo/Guerrero and Nuñez.

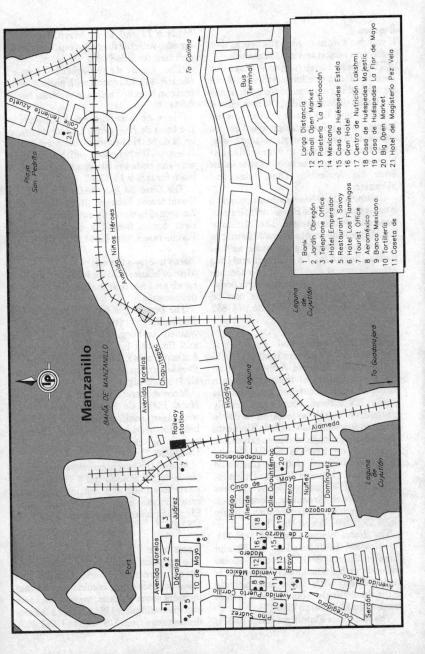

Manzanillo
BAHÍA DE MANZANILLO

1 Bank
2 Jardín Obregón
3 Telephone Office
4 Hotel Emperador
5 Restaurant Savoy
6 Hotel Los Flamingos
7 Tourist Office
8 Aeroméxico
9 Banco Mexicano
10 Tortillería
11 Caseta de

12 Small Open Market
13 Paletería 'La Michoacán'
14 Mexicana
15 Casa de Huéspedes Estela
16 Gran Hotel
17 Centro de Nutrición Lakshmi
18 Casa de Huéspedes Majestic
19 Casa de Huéspedes La Flor de Mayo
20 Big Open Market
21 Hotel del Magisterio Pez Vela

Beaches

If you don't want to go to the beach, then there's no reason to visit Manzanillo.

The closest beach to town is Playa San Pedrito, about one km north-east of the zócalo, but it's too close to the port. Across the Bahía de Manzanillo, the next closest beach – Playa Las Brisas – caters to a few hotels, but it is long enough to not get too crowded. Playa Azul stretches north-west from Las Brisas and curves around to Las Hadas Resort and the best beaches in the area: La Audencia, Olas Atlas and Miramar.

Getting to these beaches from downtown is easy: take any 'Las Brisas' or 'Miramar' bus from the train station. The 'Miramar' bus goes all the way to Playa Miramar in 40 minutes, stopping en route at Las Brisas, Playa Azul, La Audencia and Olas Atlas. Miramar and the last two beaches have waves big enough for surfing or body-surfing. Both types of boards can be rented at Miramar for US\$1.25 to US\$2 per hour.

Places to Stay – bottom end

The *Hotel del Magisterio Pez Vela* (tel 2-11-08), Calle Teniente Azueta 7, is on Playa San Pedrito at the north-eastern corner of town about one km from the zócalo. It's a clean, simple and usually gringo-free hotel associated with a Mexican organisation called Sindicato Nacional de Trabajadores de la Educación – Unidad de Servicio Social Comité Ejecutivo Nacional (roughly translated this means National Trade Union of Educational Workers – Social Services Unit National Executive Committee). Singles, doubles and triples with fans are US\$6.25, US\$8.35 and US\$11.50.

The *Hotel Emperador* (tel 2-23-74), Dávalos 291 (also listed as No 69 and Carrillo Puerto 391), has dark rooms walled in with cinder blocks. Each room is fairly clean with fans and private bathrooms. Singles, doubles and triples range from US\$2.40 to US\$4.75.

The *Hotel Los Flamingos* (tel 2-10-37),

Madero 72 and 10 de Mayo, has clean doubles with tile floors, private bathrooms and fans for US\$8.50.

The *Casa de Huéspedes Estela*, Madero 333, has rooms with peeling walls and can be called a dive. A room for two is US\$4.20.

There are more chickens than people in the *Casa de Huéspedes La Flor de Mayo* on 21 de Marzo between Cuauhtémoc and Guerrero. It's not clean, which is probably why the beds are elevated on blocks. A room for two is US\$2.10.

The *Casa de Huéspedes Majestic*, on Cuauhtémoc between 21 de Marzo and Zaragoza, is similarly run down, but it's right across from the central market. Rooms range from US\$4.20 to US\$6.75.

Places to Stay – top end

Most of Manzanillo's middle and top-end hotels are on or near the beaches outside of downtown.

The best of the top-end hotels is *Las Hadas Resort* (tel 3-00-00), a white-washed Arabian-style project conceived and financed by Bolivian tin magnate Antenor Patino. The film *10* featuring Bo Derek was made here. Rooms start at US\$120 per night.

More moderately priced is the nearby *Hotel Playa de Santiago* (tel 3-00-55) with clean, comfortable rooms that have balconies overlooking the beach. There's a swimming pool. Singles/doubles are US\$20/26.

Also on the beach, but closer to town, is the *Hotel La Posada* (tel 2-24-04), which advertises itself as a seaside lodge with great rooms and a swimming pool. Singles/doubles range from US\$28 to US\$40.

Places to Eat

The popular family-style *Restaurant Savoy*, corner of Puerto Carrillo and Dávalos, does a fine comida corrida that includes soup, chicken, vegetables, tacos and quesadillas for US\$2. Their à la carte dishes range from US\$0.80 to US\$1.60.

Centro de Nutrición Lakshmi, on Cuauhtémoc between Madero and 21 de Marzo, is a 'nutrition centre' and health-food restaurant that serves yoghurt and hamburgers.

The *Paletería 'La Michoacán'* at the corner of Avenida México and Bravo/Guerrero serves a variety of freshly squeezed juices and licuados at economical prices.

The *Chantilly*, corner of Madero and Juárez, serves inexpensive food such as club sandwiches, salads and hamburgers for US$0.75 to US$2.

Getting There & Away

Air Aeroméxico and Mexicana both have daily flights to Manzanillo from most major cities in Mexico. Aeroméxico has direct flights from Los Angeles every day except Tuesday and Wednesday.

Bus The bus terminal is east of downtown Manzanillo on the road to Colima. Several bus companies run between Manzanillo and major cities throughout Mexico. Tres Estrellas de Oro (1st class) has buses six times daily to Guadalajara (US$3.70, six-hour trip), twice to Tijuana via Puerto Vallarta (US$29.40), twice to Mexico City (US$9.15, 14 hours), and frequent departures to Colima (US$1.10), Guaymas (US$18) and Mazatlán (US$8.50).

Transportes Norte de Sonora (2nd class) has a 7.15 am bus to Tijuana (US$26.75) that stops in Puerto Vallarta (US$2.85) and Mazatlán (US$8.30). There's a bus to Mexico City twice daily (US$8.50).

Autobuses de Occidente (2nd class) has buses five times daily to Mexico City (US$8.50) via Morelia, every hour 24 hours daily to Guadalajara (US$3.50), and four times daily to Lázaro Cárdenas. It offers frequent service to Armería, Tecoman, Colima, Toluca and Uruapan.

Rail The train station is at the eastern end of Juárez near the zócalo (see map). The only train daily from Manzanillo to Colima and Guadalajara departs at 6 am.

Getting Around

Bus Public buses run every 20 minutes from the train station to Playa Las Brisas, Playa Azul, Playa La Audencia, Playa Olas Altas and Playa Miramar. You can also flag down the bus anywhere along Avenida Niños Héroes and Highway 200. The fare is 15c.

The 'Centro' bus runs from the bus station to downtown Manzanillo, but takes longer than the 15-minute walk because it stops at practically every street corner.

Taxi Taxis are plentiful in Manzanillo and are the quickest way to get around. A ride from the bus station to downtown costs US$0.50. Set the price before your ride begins because many taxis don't have meters.

AROUND MANZANILLO

The small beach resort towns of Cuyutlán and Paraíso are south-east of Manzanillo off Highway 200. Cuyutlán, the more developed of the two, is near the south-eastern end of the Laguna de Cuyutlán, about 62 km from Manzanillo. There's supposedly a road along the beach that connects Cuyutlán with Manzanillo and, four km to the south-east, Paraíso, but don't count on it.

Both towns have a few hotels and restaurants that are popular mostly with Mexican families and seldom visited by North Americans. Consequently, expect to pay much less here for beach-front accommodation than you would in places frequented by tourists.

Cuyutlán

In Cuyutlán most of the hotels and places to eat are on, or about a block from, the beach.

The *Hotel San Rafael*, Veracruz 46 on the beach, has 35 rooms, most with fans and hot water. An ocean-front restaurant is supposed to open soon; the swimming pool looks like it has been open a long time. Two or three people can squeeze into each room at US$5.25 per person, but if it isn't busy you might make a deal with the management.

The *Hotel Cosmopolita*, Veracruz 26, is a step down from the San Rafael with 47 fan-less rooms that look dirty. Singles/doubles are US$2.10/4.20.

The *Hotel Ceballos*, Veracruz 10, is the best place in town. For US$19 per person you get a clean, comfortable room overlooking the ocean and three meals daily in the hotel's modern concrete pavilion restaurant.

The *Hotel Polima*, Veracruz 22, is an airy, beach-front hotel with cheap but dirty rooms that you should rent only as a last resort. They charge US$1.60 to US$3.25.

The *Hotel Tlaquepaque*, Veracruz 30, has cleaner rooms than most of the others; some rooms have skylights and overhead fans. They charge US$3.25 to US$4.25 per person.

The *Hotel Morelos*, Hidalgo 185, is a spartan, wonderfully clean white-walled place with screens on cinder-block windows, fans and hot showers in every room. They charge US$2.10 per room no matter how many people you want to cram in. However, if you also want food at the adjoining *Restaurant Morelos*, the room and food will cost each person US$6.25. The restaurant does a good seafood comida corrida for US$1.50.

Next to the Restaurant Morelos is the equally good *Restaurant Bucaramanga* where a comida corrida that includes fish, soup, refried beans, coffee and cake costs US$1. Their breakfast of eggs, refried beans, toast and coffee is even less – US$0.75. Fish specialities cost US$1.50 to US$2.

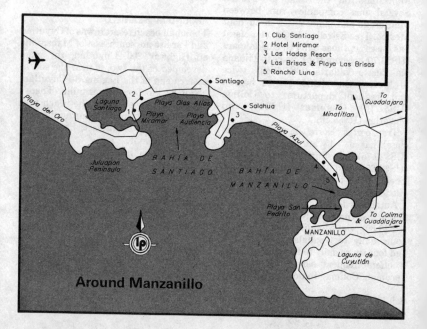

1 Club Santiago
2 Hotel Miramar
3 Las Hadas Resort
4 Las Brisas & Playa Las Brisas
5 Rancho Luna

Around Manzanillo

Aside from a long stretch of relatively isolated beach, Cuyutlán is also known for its green wave in late spring, caused by little green phosphorescent critters.

Cuyutlán's main connection to the rest of the world is a 15-km paved road through coconut groves to the Highway 200 town of Armería, a dusty place sliced by train tracks and splattered with donkey dung. Your only reason for stopping here is to catch the bus that runs to Cuyutlán approximately every hour from 5.30 am to 8.30 pm.

Paraíso

Paraíso is six km south of Cuyutlán and seven km south-west of Armería. There's not much here, which is what makes it appealing and, unfortunately, more popular than Cuyutlán: two hotels, fishing boats, a black-sand beach and several beach-front fish restaurants that are no more than thatched-roof structures called *enramadas*.

The *Hotel Paraíso* (tel 4-29-10) has very clean rooms with fans, window screens, a swimming pool full of kids and a restaurant that supposedly never closes. A double is US$7.25. For the amusement of visitors and to ensure a constant supply of fish, the hotel's owner has built an immense fish-breeding tank at one end of the restaurant. An electric pump sucks sea water into the tank while tubes return the 'used' water to the sea.

Next door is the *Hotel Villa del Mar* with only six rooms, a screaming parrot and bathrooms that could use some cleaning. A room will cost you US$3.75. The restaurant here serves huge seafood meals for US$1.50 to US$2.

The bus between Armería and Paraíso runs about every half-hour from 6 am to 8 pm.

Jalisco

Before independence from Spain in the early 19th century, all of the area that the state of Jalisco now occupies plus parts of the adjoining states of Colima, Michoacán, Nayarit, Zacatecas, Aguascalientes and Guanajuato were named Greater Spain in the early 1530s by the tyrannical Spanish conquistador Nuño de Guzmán. Guzmán hungered for wealth and used Indian slave labour to extract it for him. His

mistreatment of the Indians caused the viceroy of New Spain in Mexico City, Antonio de Mendoza, to boot him out. Mendoza installed Pérez de la Torre in Guzmán's place and the area was renamed New Galicia in honour of the Spanish province of Galicia.

It remained New Galicia until 1821 – after independence from Spain – when most of the territory became the state of

Jalisco. The name 'Jalisco' is derived from 'Xalisco', which means 'the sandy place' and was one of four Chimalhuacán Indian kingdoms that controlled the area before the Spanish bullied their way across in the 1520s and 1530s.

Although parts of Jalisco are indeed 'sandy', that's not an accurate description of this of 80,137 square km in west-central Mexico. Most of the state is dotted with the mountains of the Sierra Madre del Sur and the Sierra Madre Occidental ranges. The mountains along the south-western edge of the state hug the coastline from Puerto Vallarta south almost to the town of La Cumbre before giving way to a wide coastal plain. Then the mountains creep nearer to the coast again, closing off the plain towards Barra de Navidad at the southern corner of Jalisco.

As you travel inland the elevation increases, the air becomes cooler and less humid and, around Guadalajara, the land flattens and becomes the great Central Plateau of Mexico. South of Guadalajara, the Río Lerma flows down out of the Sierra Madre del Sur mountains and along part of the Central Plateau before emptying into 1109-square-km Lake Chapala, Mexico's largest lake.

Because of the area's ideally temperate climate, Lake Chapala has become home to one of the largest groups of Americans outside the USA, mostly retirees. Proximity to the cosmopolitan cultural attractions and large airport of Guadalajara is another reason. Consequently, the area is also popular with travellers.

On the coast, the mega-resort city of Puerto Vallarta has hotels and restaurants for every budget, tropical paradise that hasn't yet completely become touristy, and a variety of easily accessible beaches. Farther south are the less-visited but equally pleasant beach towns of Chamela, Careyes, San Patricio-Melaque and Barra de Navidad.

The inland Jalisco cities of Lagos de Moreno and San Juan de los Lagos are covered elsewhere in this book.

GUADALAJARA

Population: 4 million

Guadalajara was founded in 1542 by Juan de Oñate. Its name was derived from the Arabic for 'valley where water flows over the rocks'. It became the capital of New Galicia in 1560 and quickly grew into one of New Spain's largest and most important cities after Mexico City.

After Mexico won independence from Spain, Guadalajara retained its importance and acquired a reputation as the nation's most 'Mexican' city. Many 'typically' Mexican things and traditions were created here: the Jarabe Tapatío or Mexican Hat Dance, the broad-rimmed *sombrero* hat, *charreadas* (Jaliscan rodeos), mariachi music and tequila, which is often considered the national drink.

Orientation

Guadalajara sits at an altitude of 1552 metres on the edge of Mexico's great Central Plateau, an immense chunk of land that covers almost two-thirds of the total area of Mexico. The city is 574 km north-west of Mexico City and 344 km east of Puerto Vallarta and considered a major transit point because Highways 90, 54 and 15 converge here. The latter two continue northward to the USA border. All three highways combine temporarily in Guadalajara to form a *periférico*, a transit highway that allows you to avoid most of the city.

If you enter the city from the direction of the Miguel Hidalgo International Airport, which is about 16 km south, the intersection of Calzada Lázaro Cárdenas and Calzada Jesús González Gallo in the suburb of Tlaquepaque marks the outskirts of the city. Lázaro Cárdenas runs north-west from the intersection, cutting the main part of the city roughly in half, but it also bypasses the heart of the city, which begins approximately where Gallo ends. It continues through the city, intersecting Avenida Colón, Avenida Mariano Otero and the major south-west

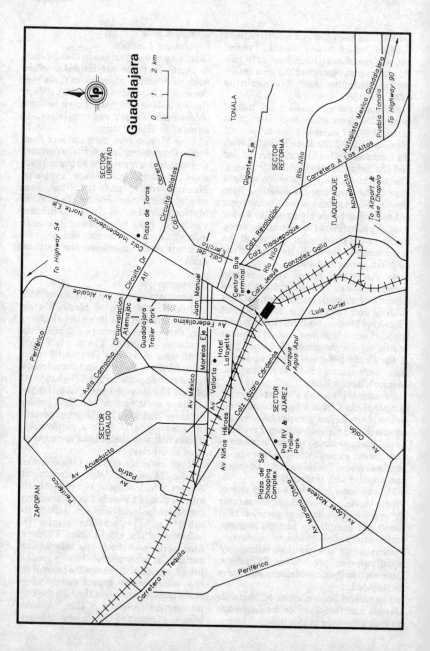

to north-east axis of Avenida López Mateos before merging with Avenida Vallarta and Avenida México and leading to Highway 15 northbound.

Calzada Gallo runs north/north-west from the intersection and ends at the major thoroughfare of Calzada Independencia just after it slices through the Parque Agua Azul, one of Guadalajara's largest parks. Calzada Independencia begins near the south-west corner of the park at the Plaza Juárez and the Monument to Independence. Avenida 16 de Septiembre, another major street leading to central Guadalajara, also begins at this point, but it becomes Avenida Alcade as it enters the heart of Guadalajara.

This area near the monument and park is Guadalajara's main transit and budget-hotel zone. The train station is on the plaza at the beginning of Independencia and 16 de Septiembre; the central bus terminal is near the north-east corner of the park.

The heart of Guadalajara is a series of beautiful plazas laid out between Pedro Loza, one block west of Avenida Alcade, and the Institut Cultural Cabañas, about two blocks east of Calzada Independencia. The first three plazas – Plaza de los Laureles, Plaza de las Armas and Plaza de la Liberación – flank the cathedral to the west, south and east respectively. The Plaza de la Liberación is also surrounded by the Palacio de Gobierno, the Teatro Degollado and the Museo Regional de Guadalajara. One block east of the Plaza de la Liberación and the Teatro Degollado is the 1½-km-long Plaza Tapatía, which is probably the longest plaza in Mexico. About a block south of the Plaza Tapatía and a block east of Calzada Independencia is the immense Mercado Libertad or market.

West of central Guadalajara in an area demarcated by Avenida Juárez/Avenida Vallarta (it changes names) on the north, Avenida Chapultepec on the west and Avenida Niños Héroes on the south, is one of Guadalajara's better neighbourhoods. The University of Guadalajara is in this area at Vallarta/Juárez, Tolsa and López Cotilla. Avenida Chapultepec is the zona rosa.

Information
Tourist Office The state tourist office (tel 14-86-86), Morelos 102 at Plaza de la Liberación, has a variety of brochures and leaflets in English about Guadalajara and the rest of Jalisco. A few of the staff speak English and are happy to answer any questions about the area. They can also tell you where to catch buses for various sights around the city. Hours are 9 am to 9 pm Monday to Friday, 9 am to 1 pm and 3 to 7 pm Saturday.

The federal tourist office (tel 13-16-05) is at Degollado 50 near the state tourist office and is worth visiting only if you want information about travel outside Jalisco.

Money Banks and casas de cambio are plentiful in Guadalajara, but most banks will only exchange money from 9 to 11 am, whereas many of the casas de cambio are open until at least 7 pm, sometimes later. There are several casas de cambio on López Cotilla between Corona and Independencia Sur: Casa de Cambio El Gallo, López Cotilla 207; Casa de Cambio Libertad, López Cotilla 175; Casa de Cambio Monterrey, 16 de Septiembre 427; and Casa de Cambio de Carlos Ortíz Terraza, Corona 181.

Post The main post office is on Carranza between Calzada Independencia and Juan Manuel near the Teatro Degollado.

American Express Money exchange is also possible at the American Express office (tel 30-02-00), López Mateos 447 at the end of the 'Par Vial' bus route. Mail service is offered here as well; they hold mail for about two months. Hours are 9 am to 6 pm Monday to Friday, 9·am to 1 pm Saturday.

Telephone Calls The main caseta de larga distancia is around the corner from the Hotel Internacional on Calle Donato Guerra between Moreno and Juárez. They'll make collect calls for free only if the call is accepted; otherwise you must pay a US$1 service charge. International collect calls can also be made from some pay phones, but be prepared to wait a long time to get through to an operator.

Courses The Foreign Student Studies Center of the University of Guadalajara offers 12 levels of intensive Spanish-language courses ranging from beginning to advanced. If enough students sign up, they also offer courses in history, culture, economics, sociology, literature and art. Cultural activities such as folkloric music concerts and dance performances and excursions to Guanajuato, San Miguel de Allende and Morelia are also available. Lodging is arranged with local Mexican families. Fees average US$200 for tuition and US$300 for lodging; the excursions are a variable expense. For more specific information and an application form, contact them directly by writing to: Centro de Estudios para Extranjeros, Apartado Postal No 1-4521, Guadalajara, Jalisco, CP 44100, México.

The University of Arizona (tel (602) 621-4729) also offers a summer programme in Guadalajara. Contact them for more information by writing to: Guadalajara Summer School, Robert Nugent Building 205, University of Arizona, Tucson, Arizona 85721, USA.

Bookstores A fair selection of books and magazines in English is available at most major hotels in Guadalajara such as the Best Western Hotel Fenix, the Camino Real and the Hotel Fiesta Americana. The Sandi Bookstore, Tepeyac 718, Colonia Chapalita also has a decent selection.

Airlines

Aerocalifornia
  SJC 7 No 1423 (tel 25-60-35)
Aeroméxico
  Vallarta 1458, 8th floor (tel 15-93-42)
Air France
  SJC 5 No 1540 (tel 30-37-21)
American Airlines
  SJC 5 No 1526 (tel 30-03-49)
Mexicana
  SJC 26 No 1896-2 (tel 11-21-91)
Lufthansa
  Circunvalción A Yañez 2895 (tel 15-41-48)
KLM
  SJC 5 No 1390-1005 (tel 25-32-71)

Consulates

Australia
  Mar Negro 1221 (tel 23-07-57) & Circunvalción Providencia 1216-B (tel 23-05-11)
Great Britain
  Lerdo de Tejada 2264-102 (tel 15-14-06)
Belgium
  Plaza de la Amistad (tel 15-01-97, 15-55-55)
France
  López Cotilla 1221 (tel 25-10-52)
West Germany
  SJC 12 No 202 (tel 13-96-23)
USA
  Progreso 175 (tel 25-92-01)

Festivals

La Virgen de Zapopan One of the most important events for Guadalajara is this celebration on 12 October. An image of the Virgin is loudly and colourfully paraded through the streets of Guadalajara with dance and music groups to a shrine in the suburb of Zapopan.

Fiestas de Octubre 12 October also marks the beginning of fiestas that last the rest of the month and include rodeos, art exhibits, folk dances, bullfights and music performances.

Plaza de los Laureles

Because of its central location on Avenida Alcade facing the cathedral, Plaza de los Laureles is a good place to begin a tour of Guadalajara. As its name suggests, much of the plaza is planted with laurels. The cathedral dominates the eastern side of the plaza.

Cathedral

Begun in 1558 and consecrated in 1616, the twin-towered cathedral is almost as old as the city. From a distance it is an impressive structure, but up close you can see the hotchpotch of styles used in constructing it. Exterior decorations, some of which were completed long after the cathedral's consecration, include churrigueresque, baroque and neoclassical styles. The interior includes 11 richly decorated altars given to Guadalajara by King Ferdinand VII (1784 to 1833), Gothic vaults and Tuscany-style pillars.

Plaza de las Armas & Palacio del Gobierno

With the 16th to 17th-century cathedral on the north side and the 18th-century Palacio del Gobierno on the east, the Plaza de las Armas is a pleasant place to sit and imagine how life may have been in colonial times.

The Government Palace was finished in 1774 and, like the cathedral, was built in a combination of styles – in this case, a strange mix of simple, neoclassical features and riotous churrigueresque decorations. The most interesting artistic feature is the huge 1937 portrait of Miguel Hidalgo painted by Mexican muralist Clemente Orozco on one of the stairways (the first one on your right). The mural depicts the Mexican people's struggle for liberty and independence while various political and religious ideologies are being forced on them. The mural can be viewed from 9 am to 6 pm Monday to Saturday.

Plaza de la Liberación
Museo Regional de Guadalajara

East of the cathedral on the former site of several colonial buildings is the large Plaza de la Liberación. The Regional Museum of Guadalajara stands on the north side of the plaza and occupies the former seminary of San José, a late 17th-century baroque-style building with two storeys of arcades and an inner court. The museum, also known as the Museo del Estado de Jalisco y de Hidalgo, has an eclectic collection of exhibits that cover the pre-history and history of western Mexico.

Displays in the ground-floor archaeological section include the almost complete skeleton of a woolly mammoth, arrowheads, jewellery and pottery figurines, some of which date back to the Pre-Classic period (1500 BC to 300 AD).

On the 1st floor, the exhibits include a gallery of paintings from the 17th century to the present, a history gallery covering life and events in Jalisco since the Spanish conquest, and an ethnographical section with displays showing life among various Indian groups in Jalisco and the *charro* or Mexican cowboy. Hours are 9 am to 3.45 pm Tuesday to Sunday. Admission is US$0.40.

Teatro Degollado

Built in the late 1850s and inaugurated by Emperor Maximilian, the neoclassical-style Degollado Theatre stands at the eastern end of the Plaza de la Liberación. Inside on the ceiling, a mural by Gerardo Suárez depicts the fourth canto of Dante's Divine Comedy. The Ballet Folklórico of Mexico is often presented here; ask at the box office or tourist office for the latest schedule and ticket information.

Plaza Tapatía
Instituto Cultural de Cabañas

The Plaza Tapatía, a 1½-km-long pedestrian mall and plaza of shops, restaurants, street performers, fountains and trees, stretches from the Teatro Degollado to the 180-year-old building that now houses the Instituto Cultural de Cabañas.

The building was constructed in 1801 by Spanish architect Manuel Tolsá as the Hospicio Cabañas, an orphanage named after its founder Bishop Don Juan Cruz Ruíz de Cabañas. In addition, it occasionally served as an insane asylum, military barracks and jail. It remained an orphanage until only about a decade ago. All 23 courts and the chapel that Tolsá designed have remained intact. The orphanage acquired an important place in Mexican history when rebel leader Hidalgo arrived here in 1811 to sign a proclamation against slavery.

More than a century later, Mexican muralist Clemente Orozco painted a series of murals in the main chapel that depicts the savagery of the Spanish conquest and the Four Riders of the Apocalypse. Although the murals convey a sense of impending doom, the fiery figure in the centre is a sign of hope that humans will find the path to heaven.

Today the building is occupied by the Instituto Cultural de Cabañas, an art institute, part of which is a museum and the other part a school. The museum features a permanent exhibition of Clemente Orozco's drawings and paintings, and temporary exhibits dedicated to painting, sculpture and engraving. The institute also sponsors dance festivals, theatre performances and concerts.

The building is open to the public from 10 am to 6 pm Tuesday to Sunday for 10c admission.

Plazuela de los Mariachis

The Plazuela de los Mariachis, just south of the Plaza Tapatía near the intersection of Javier Mina and Independencia, is an alley crammed with cheap restaurants, cafés and mariachi bands. The bands charge US$2 per song and are liveliest at night.

Parque Agua Azul
Museo Arqueológico del Occidente

The Blue Water Park is near the southern end of the Calzada Independencia, beginning where Calzada González Gallo runs into Independencia. The park is a quiet refuge from the city and a good place to have a lazy afternoon picnic; there's also a zoo.

The Western Archaeological Museum, just west of the park on Plaza Juárez, maintains a small collection of pre-Hispanic figurines and artefacts from Jalisco and the neighbouring states of Nayarit and Colima. Hours are 10 am to 6 pm Monday to Friday.

Places to Stay – bottom end

Most of the budget hotels are on the noisy streets around the huge bustling bus terminal. If you have the time and the money to look elsewhere for a room, then head closer to downtown.

Downtown The *Hotel Hamilton* (tel 40-67-26), Madero 381, is one of the traditional mainstays for budget travellers. It's clean, centrally located, usually noisy and always inexpensive. Singles/doubles are US$3.70/4.25.

The *Hotel Las Américas* (tel 13-96-22), Hidalgo 76, will probably replace the Hamilton as a favourite among budget travellers because it's quite new and in a great location on the Plaza de la Liberación. Singles/doubles are US$4/5.

Mercado Libertad Area The *Hotel Paris* (tel 13-30-69), Calzada Independencia Norte 73, seems to do a brisk hourly business despite their well-used, dirty rooms. Beware, the walls are thin. Payment is by the bed, not by the person: US$3.25 for one bed and US$5.25 for two beds.

The *Hotel Lisboa* (tel 14-25-27), Huerto 20 south-east of the Plaza de la Liberación, is a cheap and noisy place with dirty walls but clean sheets. Try to get a room away from the street. One-bed rooms are US$3.25, two-bed rooms US$3.75.

The *Hotel Independence* (tel 13-17-98), Grecia 48 near the big Pemex station on Calzada Independencia, is clean, popular and often booked-up. A single or double for two in one bed is US$2.60.

The *Hotel Mexico 70* (tel 17-99-78), Avenida Javier Mina 230, is cheap, dark and dismal. Do not get a room near the street or the noise will practically lift you from your bed. Singles/doubles are US$3.75/4.25.

The *Hotel Imperio* (tel 17-50-42), Avenida Javier Mina 184, has 31 clean, simple rooms and seems to cater mostly to Mexican families. As with all the other hotels in this area, get a room away from the street. Singles/doubles are US$3.75/5.25.

The *Hotel Ana Isabel* (tel 17-79-20), Avenida Javier Mina 164, can be a bit noisy, but the smiling, English-speaking managers run a decent hotel. Muzak is piped in to every room. Soft drinks are sold in the 2nd-floor lobby. Singles/doubles are US$4/6.

Bus Terminal Area The hotels near the bus terminal are some of the worst in the city. A few of the better ones:

The *Hotel Praga* (tel 17-37-60), 28 de Enero No 733A less than a minute's walk from the terminal, is cleaner and less noisy than most of the others in the area. The rooms are simple and comfortable. A parking garage and inexpensive restaurant are attached to the hotel. Singles/doubles are US$3.60/4.25.

The *Hotel Vista Hermosa* (tel 19-46-11) is directly across from the bus station at Calle Doctor R Michel 270. Singles/doubles are US$5.25/6.

The *Hotel San José* (tel 19-27-26), Calzada 5 de Febrero 116, is a sparkling place with an air of luxury and modernity. It has 76 rooms. Singles are US$4.75, doubles US$5.70, triples US$6.35.

The *Hotel Flamingos Guadalajara* (tel 18-00-03), Independencia Sur 725 three blocks from the bus station, is one of the best deals in the area. Most of the rooms have newly tiled floors and modern bathrooms. Singles cost US$4, doubles US$4.60, triples US$5.

Camping This is possible at any of four trailer parks. The *Guadalajara Trailer Park* (tel 23-08-69), on Avenida Alcade (Highway 54) south of Circunvalico Atemajac junction, has 210 sites for camping, most with full hook-ups. Only five km north of downtown Guadalajara, this is the closest campground to the city centre. The park includes a small grocery store, laundry room and swimming pool. The charge is US$6 for two people per night.

On the south side of Guadalajara about 7½ km from the city centre is the *Pal RV & Trailer Park* (tel 21-99-44) at Turquesa 1940 near Mariano Otero and Avenida López Mateos (Highway 15), just east of the Plaza del Sol shopping complex. The park has clean showers and 57 sites with full hook-ups, but it tends to be noisy because Otero is a busy boulevard. They charge US$6.50 for two people.

About eight km south of Pal park is the *San José del Tajo* trailer park with 210 sites, a heated swimming pool, a small grocery store and a laundry room. They charge US$8 for two people.

Places to Stay – middle
The *Hotel del Parque* (tel 25-28-00), Avenida Juárez 845 near the Parque de la Revolución and across from the University of Guadalajara, is clean and comfortable and was recently renovated. Singles/doubles are US$8/10.

The *Hotel Nueva Galicia* (tel 14-87-80), Calle Corona 610, is a place of fading elegance with a uniformed boy working the elevator. The locals claim that the attached restaurant is better than the hotel, which explains why it's often crowded at lunch time. Singles/doubles are US$6.25/8. Air-conditioning costs an extra US$3.25.

The *Hotel Universo* (tel 13-28-15), López Cotilla 161, is a modern concrete-block building with large smoked-glass windows, a pleasant lobby and parking garage. Singles/doubles are US$8/10.50.

The *Hotel Plaza Genova* (tel 13-75-00), Juárez 123, caters to a prosperous, mostly Mexican clientele. It's in a centrally located modern tower building with an elevator, comfortable breakfast lounge and in-house laundry service. A cafeteria and lobby bar are attached to the hotel. Singles cost US$9.50, doubles US$11.50, triples US$13.75.

The *Hotel Internacional* (tel 13-03-30), Moreno 570, is clean, modern and devoid of character, but there is air-conditioning and a TV in each room. A bar and restaurant are attached to the lobby. Singles are US$10.50, doubles US$12.50, triples US$15.25. There's a good bakery across the street.

The *Hotel Fenix Best Western* (tel 14-57-14), Avenida Corona 160 two blocks south of Plaza de las Armas, is a centrally located tourist-class hotel. Most rooms have balconies, refrigerators, telephones and TVs with cable service. A restaurant and three bars are attached to the hotel. Singles/doubles are US$36/38.

The *Hotel Frances* (tel 13-11-90), Maestranza 35 just off Plaza de la Liberación, is one of the best deals in Guadalajara. The hotel was built in 1610 as *El Mezón de San José*, an inn for traders from Mexico City, but fell into disrepair earlier this century. It was renovated and reopened in 1981. Several of the rooms have old paintings on the walls and narrow, wrought-iron balconies overlooking the Plaza de la Liberación. A grand piano, beautiful marble fountain and gold chandelier give the lobby an Old World elegance and grace. Not surprisingly, the hotel was declared a national monument just after it reopened. Try to get a room facing the Palacio de Gobierno. Each room has a double and single bed and colour TV. Singles/doubles are US$13/16 including tax.

The *Hotel Continental* (tel 14-11-17), Avenida Corona 450, used to be called a 'modern' hotel, but it's now a bit worn and aged. The rooms are still clean and comfortable. Singles/doubles are US$8.40/11.50.

The *Hotel Los Reyes* (tel 13-00-76), Calzada Independencia Sur 164, is centrally located and has 176 rooms with air-conditioning, TVs and telephones. The lobby has a cool marble floor. Singles cost US$14.25, doubles US$17.40, triples US$21.

Places to Stay – top end

The *Hotel Lafayette* (tel 30-11-12), Avenida La Paz 2055, is in Guadalajara's financial district close to airline offices and the American Consulate. It's also near the city's best restaurants and nightclubs. All rooms have colour TVs, air-conditioning and telephones. The hotel has a swimming pool, piano bar and restaurant. Singles are US$20, doubles US$27, triples US$32.

The *Hotel Calinda Roma* (tel 14-86-50), Avenida Juárez 170, is a splurge for budget travellers that seems to be popular with American tour groups. It's part of the USA-based Quality Inn hotel chain. The hotel's rooftop swimming pool is supposedly the only one in Guadalajara.

The *Hotel de Mendoza* (tel 13-46-46), Calle Carranza 16 near Plaza de la Liberación, is a popular modern hotel in an old but refurbished colonial building. Most of the rooms have air-conditioning and TV. A heated swimming pool, restaurant and lounge are attached to the hotel. Singles/doubles are US$28/32.

Guadalajara also has a Sheraton, a Holiday Inn and a Camino Real – all of which have standards similar to comparable hotels in the USA.

Places to Eat

The Mercado Libertad has an entire floor of food stalls which range in quality from excellent to poor, the latter only for steel stomachs. One traveller who fell ill from a meal here reports seeing a waitress blow her nose and cough over the food as if blessing it. The following rules should help you find a good, inexpensive meal: take your time and choose carefully. Look for the most crowded stalls because people usually patronise the ones serving consistently good food. Go only at lunch time when the food is fresh and tasty; leftovers are served for dinner.

El Palacio Chino, Avenida Corona 145

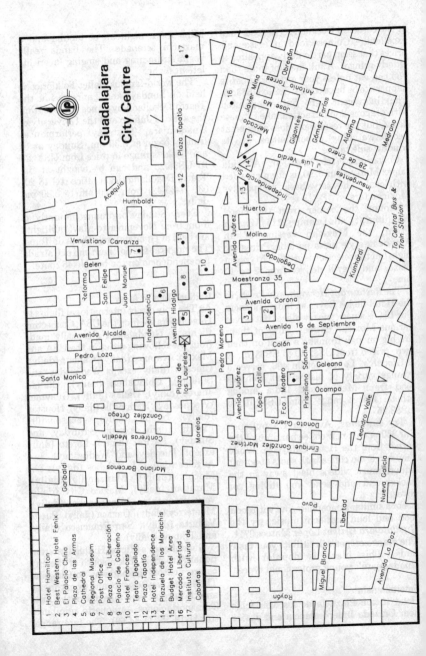

Guadalajara
City Centre

1 Hotel Hamilton
2 Best Western Hotel Fenix
3 El Palacio Chino
4 Plaza de las Armas
5 Cathedral
6 Regional Museum
7 Post Office
8 Plaza de la Liberación
9 Palacio de Gobierno
10 Hotel Frances
11 Teatro Degollado
12 Plaza Tapatía
13 Hotel Independence
14 Plazuela de los Mariachis
15 Budget Hotel Area
16 Mercado Libertad
17 Instituto Cultural de Cabañas

at the corner of Cotilla, serves good – not excellent – Chinese food at reasonable prices that seem particularly appealing to elderly gringos. A full meal of more than you can eat unless your girth or appetite happens to be huge costs US$2 to US$3.75. The fluorescent light fixtures painted with dragons don't exactly make Chinese decor, but the restaurant does offer great people-watching opportunities at its window-side tables.

Carporales (tel 31-41-39), Avenida López Mateos Sur 5290, is often crowded with locals. They serve basic, inexpensive Mexican fare.

Around the corner from the Hotel Hamilton at Calle Ocampo 211 is *Venecia Pizza*, the Mexican version of an American-style pizza parlour. Prices are high, but the selection is great – 35 types of pizza, and they'll deliver from 2 to 10 pm.

The *Restaurant Hermanos de Reyes*, in the Hotel de los Reyes at Independencia Sur 164, is a new, snazzy place that serves various Mexican entrees. Most of them are big enough to make a meal on their own, priced from US$2.10 to US$3.75.

Giovan's, López Cotilla 406, serves a strange variety of dishes that includes food from Mexico and India among others. Prices range from US$2.10 to US$3.25.

Try *Bananas*, Avenida Chapultepec Sur 330, a chic new coffee bar around the corner from the Hotel Lafayette. While they serve you coffee with shots of potent liquor, music videos blast away in the background and send you diving for cover.

For a similar atmosphere, but with good food and loud mariachi music, try the *Guadalajara Grill* at López Mateos 3711. The mango crêpes will titillate your taste buds. This place is popular with Guadalajara's young professional types.

Entertainment

Head to the Plazuela de los Mariachis near Calzada Independencia and Javier Mina for a nightcap of tequila and a mariachi serenade. The bands really begin strumming and singing feverishly late at night.

The world-famous Ballet Folklórico is held on Sundays and Thursdays at the Teatro Degollado by dance troupes from the state of Jalisco and the University of Guadalajara. Thursday performances usually begin at 8.30 pm, Sunday at 10 am. Tickets range in price from US$3.25 to US$6.25 and can be bought at the Teatro Degollado ticket office (tel 18-20-03, 17-30-42) from 9.30 am to 5.30 pm daily.

Every Sunday beginning promptly at 5 pm from November to May, bullfights are held at Guadalajara's Plaza de Toros. The ring is at the northern end of Calzada Independencia on the bus No 45 route.

Getting There & Away

Air The only direct international flights to Guadalajara are from the USA. Connecting flights to Guadalajara are easily made from the following cities in the USA and Mexico: Acapulco (daily), Cancún (daily), Chicago (daily except Wednesday and Sunday), Chihuahua (daily), Ciudad Juárez (daily), Dallas (daily), Guaymas (Wednesday), Hermosillo (daily), Houston (daily), Ixtapa (daily), Jacksonville, Florida (daily except Saturday and Sunday), La Paz (daily), Loreto (daily except Tuesday and Wednesday), Los Angeles (daily), Los Cabos (daily), Los Mochis (daily), Manzanillo (daily), Mazatlán (daily), Mexico City (daily, very frequent), Minneapolis (daily), Monterrey (daily), Oaxaca (daily), Puerto Vallarta (daily), San Francisco (daily) and Tijuana (daily).

Guadalajara's Miguel Hidalgo International Airport is 16 km south of the city centre just off the highway to Chapala. The easiest way to get to and from the city and the airport is to take one of the Auto Transportaciones Aeropuerto minibuses (tel 11-18-55, 11-54-69). The fare ranges from US$2 to US$4 depending upon the number of passengers.

Bus Guadalajara's busy Central Camionera is near the Parque Agua Azul (see map). Almost every major line in Mexico operates to and from this terminal 24 hours daily: Flecha Amarilla, Tres Estrellas de Oro, Transportes Pacífico and Flecha Roja. If you are travelling around Mexico by bus, just show up at the terminal when you want to travel and you probably won't have to wait more than an hour for a bus. Express buses depart hourly for Mexico City and should take about eight hours.

Rail The train station is at the southern end of Calzada Independencia Sur, just a few blocks from the bus terminal. There are two evening trains daily to Mexico City: Train No 12 at 7.30 pm (1st and 2nd-class seats only) and Train No 6 at 8.55 pm (sleeping berths available). Fares are US$2.50, US$1.90 and US$8.25 for 1st class, 2nd class and sleeping berth; the trip takes about 12 hours.

Train No 92 to Colima and Manzanillo departs at 10 am daily (US$6 one way) and arrives at each city at 4.13 and 6.16 pm. The train from Manzanillo to Guadalajara departs at 8 am daily. The trip in either direction takes about 8¼ hours.

Getting Around

Bus Guadalajara has hundreds of regular and electric buses (labelled 'Par Vial') covering everywhere you need to go in the city every five minutes between 9 am and 10 pm. Fares are 10c. The tourist office has a complete list of the 140 bus routes in Guadalajara. Some of them are:

No 18: 16 de Septiembre – Estación Terminal, Lisboa, Monte San Elias, Sierra Leona, Avenida Los Maestros, Mil Cumbres, Avenida Normalistas, Avenida Alcade, Avenida 16 de Septiembre, Estación del Ferrocarril (train station)

No 22: San Juan de Dios – Centro – Plaza del Sol Avenida Colón y 18 de Marzo (Plaza del Sol), Avenida Colón, Pelicano, Avenida 8 de Julio, Washington, Estación del Ferrocarril (train station), Calzada Independencia, San Diego, Baeza Alzaga, San Felipe, Tolsa, Marte, Washington, Mariano Otero, Obsidiana Lapislazuli, Avenida 18 de Marzo, Avenida Colón, Terminal

No 33: Revolución – Centro – Tlaquepaque Terminal Salado Alvarez, Hidalgo, Revolución, Miguel Blanco, González Martínez, Priscilian Sánchez, Calzada Independencia, Revolución, Hidalgo, Santa Rosalía, Salado Alvarez, Terminal

No 34: Río Nilo – Central Camionera – Loma Dorada Loma Dorada sur Río Nilo, González Gallo, Dr Roberto Michel, La Paz, Enrique González Martínez, Prisciliano Sánchez, Calzada Independencia, Revolución, Río Nilo Terminal

No 37: Calzada Tlaquepaque – Centro Terminal Salado Alvarez, Manuel Dieguez, Rosales, Constitución, Boulevard Tlaquepaque, Constancia, Revolución, Calzada Independencia, Miguel Blanco, Enrique González, Priscipiano Sánchez

No 45: San Juan de Dios – Estación del Ferrocarril (train station) – Arquitectura Calzada Independencia, Volcán Zacapu, Volcán Villa Rica, Volcán Popoca, Volcán Bobuya, Real Pelle, Calzada Independencia Norte to Sur, Constituyentes, Avenida 16 de Septiembre, Estación del Ferrocarril, Calzada Independencia Sur to Norte, Volcán Vulcano, Volcanes de China, Volcanes Tuxtla, Calzada Independencia Terminal

Combi & Taxi Combis or minibuses and vans cover almost all the same routes as the buses, but cost 15c and usually run longer hours. Taxis are plentiful in Guadalajara, but don't always trust the taxi meters. Set your fare before the ride begins and don't pay more than about US$3 to go anywhere in the city.

Car Rental Most of the major international car-rental agencies have offices in Guadalajara and offer almost the same cars for the same rates and terms. Avis has two offices: the International Airport (tel 89-02-21) and the Hotel Fiesta Americana (tel 15-48-25, 30-17-50, Aurelio Aceves 225). A Volkswagen Beetle can be rented for US$29 per day plus US$6.50 per day for a collision-damage waiver and a 15% value-added tax. You must be at least 21 years old and have a major credit card. Budget Rent-a-Car has offices at the airport (tel 89-00-20) and at Niños Héroes 934 at the corner of 16 de Septiembre (tel 14-10-53). Hertz Rent-a-Car has offices at the Hotel Camino Real (tel 21-72-17, Avenida Vallarta 5005) and also at the airport (tel 89-01-56). National Car Rental is at the airport (tel 35-34-05) and downtown at Avenida Niños Héroes 961 (tel 14-71-75).

Local agencies such as Alpri Rent-a-Car (tel 14-68-60), Odin Rente Un Auto (tel 14-44-10) and Del Sol Rente Un Auto (tel 13-90-11) offer similar cars at slightly lower rates and better terms. They also have offices in the downtown area and at the airport.

AROUND GUADALAJARA
Tlaquepaque

About five km south-east of downtown Guadalajara, Tlaquepaque ('teh-lah-key-PAH-key') used to be separate town, but Guadalajara spread south-eastward and made it a suburb. The townspeople, who had long been artisans and craftspeople, decided to capitalise on their talents by cleaning and beefing up the central plaza, renaming many of the shops 'galleries' to attract tourist dollars. Fortunately, the throngs of crafts-hungry gringos who have descended on the place have not spoiled the refurbishment of central Tlaquepaque.

Many flowers, small benches and monuments now grace the plaza. The shops are full of ceramics, including bizarre anthropomorphic monsters, papier mâché animals and bronze figures. First visit the Museo Regional de la Cerámica y los Artes Populares de Jalisco at Independencia 237 next door to the Sergio Bustamante gallery to get an idea of the best handicrafts available in Tlaquepaque. The museum is open from 10 to 4 pm. Also visit the glass factory across the street from the museum. Many of the shops are closed on Sunday.

To get to Tlaquepaque, take any purple-and-black bus numbered 110, 111 or 275 from the Mercado Libertad; the trip takes 20 minutes.

Tonalá

The Guadalajara suburb of Tonalá, also an arts centre, is the poorer, less touristy relative of Tlaquepaque. The shops here call themselves 'factories', not galleries – an accurate description considering that many of them manufacture the glassware and ceramics found in Tlaquepaque and other parts of Guadalajara. Unfortunately, there is an overabundance of freakish statues of Mickey Mouse and a pink Jesus Christ. On Thursday and Sunday most of the town becomes a huge street market that takes hours to explore. To get there catch bus Nos 103 or 104 from Moreno in Guadalajara; the trip takes 40 minutes.

Lake Chapala

Less than 42 km south of Guadalajara, Mexico's largest lake is 85 km long and 28 km wide. Low property prices and a near-perfect climate in the northern lake shore towns of Chapala, Ajijic ('ah-hee-HEEK') and Jocotepec have attracted a growing population of American and Canadian retirees. So many have settled in this area that it is now one of the largest communities of American expatriates in the world; estimates vary but 30,000 is frequently mentioned. To ward off homesickness, almost every imaginable North American organisation has been established here, including the Masons, Shriners, Daughters of the American Revolution, Eastern Star, Rotary Club, Lions Club, Salvation Army, Humane Society, Knights of Columbus, Weight Watchers, Alcoholics Anonymous, US

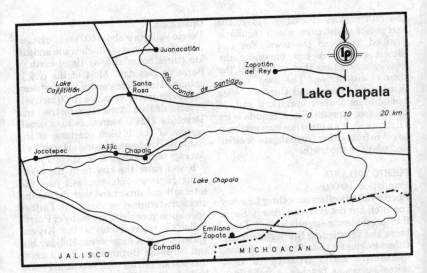

Lake Chapala

0   10   20 km

military veterans' posts and country clubs.

One of Chapala's country clubs, the Villa Montecarlo, was once the country estate of Mexican president Porfirio Díaz, who served as president from the late 1800s to the early 1900s. Later, British author D H Lawrence wrote most of *The Plumed Serpent* while living on Calle Zaragoza in Chapala.

Lake Chapala is beautiful at sunset, the only time you can really enjoy it. The lake is now polluted and clogged with a mass of vegetation that's quickly spreading from the shore.

Although all three towns along the north shore can easily be visited in a day trip, there are several hotels and a trailer park among them. In Chapala, the *Hotel Nido* (tel 5-21-16) and its adjoining restaurant, Madero 202 near the waterfront, are often recommended as *the* budget hotel and restaurant in town – US$7/10 for a single/double and US$3 for a huge comida corrida.

In Ajijic, a good place to stay is the *Posada Ajijic* (tel 5-33-95), on Calle 16 de Septiembre. The small motor inn has

15 rooms facing Lake Chapala; singles/doubles are US$10 to US$22 and most have fireplaces and shower-bath combinations. A restaurant and small swimming pool are attached to the hotel. *Pal Trailer Park* (tel 5-37-64) on the Ajijic-Chapala highway has 110 sites, most with full hook-ups. There's a laundry room, icy swimming pool and recreation room on the premises. They charge US$5 for two persons.

The small town of Jocotepec just a few km west of Ajijic is the least visited and least Americanised of the three towns. Many of the handicrafts sold in the other towns are made here. For a place to stay, try the *Posada del Pescador*; singles/doubles are US$12.

To get to Chapala from Guadalajara, there are several buses daily from the Central Camionera (central bus terminal). From there you'll have to hitch rides to get to the other towns.

Tequila

The town of Tequila, 50 km north-west of Guadalajara on Highway 15, has been home to the liquor of the same name since the 17th century. Fields of *agave*, the cactus-like plant from which tequila is distilled, surround the town. You can almost get drunk just breathing the heavily scented air that drifts from the town's distilleries. The two largest distilleries – Sauza and Cuervo – offer public tours of their operations and, of course, free samples. Since Tequila is on Highway 15, it's a main bus stop and easy to get to from either Guadalajara or cities and towns to the north.

PUERTO VALLARTA

Population: 90,000

Puerto Vallarta offers something for every traveller, but not everyone likes it. Some find its cobblestone streets too full of cars, buses and vacationing North Americans. Others looking for budget accommodation, inexpensive feasts (relative to USA prices), pleasant beaches, a frolic in a tropical paradise, wild disco/bar-hopping or Mexican handicrafts will find more than enough in Puerto Vallarta.

In 1851, the Sánchez family were the first settlers in the area. Corn farmers and fisherfolk followed several years later. By 1918 there were enough people settled around the Río Cuale, which now divides the city, to give it a name on the map. Vallarta was chosen in honour of Ignacio Luis Vallarta, a former governor of the state of Jalisco. It was called Puerto, which means 'port', because farmers had been shipping their harvests by boat from a small port area north of the Río Cuale.

The small fishing and farming village changed when John Huston's film crew came to town to make *Night of the Iguana*. The *paparazzi* of Hollywood arrived to report on every movement of Richard Burton and Elizabeth Taylor for hungry scandal-mongers, and Puerto Vallarta suddenly became world-famous. Tour groups began arriving not long after the film crew left and they haven't stopped coming.

Orientation

Puerto Vallarta is about 400 km (6½ hours' driving time) west of Guadalajara and 210 km (three hours' driving time) north of Barra de Navidad. Most of the city is crammed into a crescent of land between the mountains of Aguacate (1500 metres), Picacho de Palo María (1600 metres) and Torrecilla (1240 metres), and a small portion of the 161-km coastline of the Bahía de Banderas, Mexico's largest bay. Average temperature is 25°C (76°F).

If you enter the city from the north along Highway 200, you will pass the international airport and then the marina and ferry terminal on your right. Farther up, also on your right, are many of Puerto Vallarta's resort hotels – the Krystal Vallarta, Fiesta Americana, Holiday Inn and Sheraton Buganvilias. You'll know that you are getting close to central Puerto Vallarta when Highway 200 becomes the cobblestoned Avenida México, which becomes Avenida or Paseo Díaz Ordaz (known by both names) as it runs along the bay. This area is also known as the *malecón* or levee for the boulders placed below and in front of the palm-studded sidewalk. Shops, restaurants and discos line the other side of the street, which changes names again and becomes Morelos at the seahorse statue and old lighthouse monument.

Three blocks farther south is the heart of the city – the Plazuela Aquiles Serdán (on the right) and the Plaza de Armas and the Parroquia (parish church) de Guadalupe (on the left). A few budget hotels and restaurants are found in this area, but most are on the south side of the Río Cuale and Isla Río Cuale.

Morelos becomes Ignacio Vallarta as it crosses the bridge over the Río Cuale. Just south of the river are the closest beaches to downtown Puerto Vallarta – Playa Olas Altas and Playa de los Muertos. Only the latter is passable because the former was, at the time of writing, too close to beach-front construction sites. On and around Madero, the third street from the river

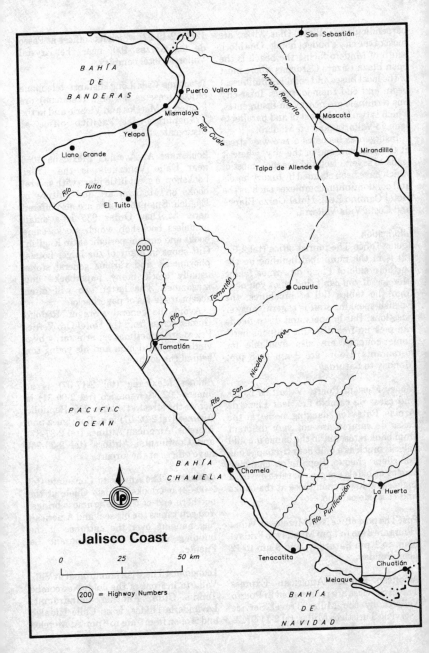

Jalisco Coast

0   25   50 km

(200) = Highway Numbers

perpendicular to Playa Olas Altas, are most of the city's budget hotels. One block south of Madero facing the beach is the open Plaza Lázaro Cárdenas where most of the local buses and combis (minibuses) begin and end their journeys. Inter-city bus terminals are nearby on Insurgentes, which is two blocks east of and parallel to Ignacio Vallarta, and on Madero.

Insurgentes becomes a two-way street at the southern end of the city, where it leads to several isolated beaches, most of which have been claimed by luxury hotels and condominium complexes such as the Hotel Camino Real, Hotel Garza Blanca and Costa Vida Vallarta.

Information

Tourist Office The tourist office (tel 2-02-42) is in the municipal building on the northern side of Plaza de Armas facing Morelos. If you can't find what you need from the tables full of brochures, the English-speaking staff is eager to answer questions. Bar-hoppers and disco fiends can pick up free discount coupons here. Some coupons are also available for restaurants. Hours are 9 am to 8 pm, Monday to Saturday.

Money Most of Puerto Vallarta's banks and casas de cambio are near Plaza de Armas. Rates for changing money at the casas de cambio are not very different from bank rates, but in the banks it could take as much as a half-hour to change one travellers' cheque. Reports on changing money at hotels are mixed; rates are both higher and lower than those at the banks and casas de cambio.

Post The post office is on Morelos at Mina. Hours are 8 am to 7 pm Monday to Friday, 8 am to 1 pm Saturday, and 9 am to 12 noon Sunday.

American Express American Express Travel Services are represented in Puerto Vallarta by the Miller Travel Service (Servicio Turísticos Miller, tel 2-11-97, 2-12-97, 2-13-97) which has offices at Paseo de las Garzas 100, near the Krystal Vallarta Hotel complex.

Telephone Calls Long-distance telephone offices (casetas de larga distancia) are located at Morelos and Vicario and in the Transportes del Pacífico office at Insurgentes 282.

Bookstores At Avenida Mexicana 1056 near Calle Venezuela is the Trilce bookshop, a great little place with several books on Mexican art and culture in English. Spanish classes are also offered here. At Díaz Ordaz 935 is a small nameless bookshop which stocks some books and current periodicals in English. Gift shops in many of the larger hotels, pharmacies and various general stores usually stock many paperbacks and magazines. The latter two will often accept trade-ins of paperbacks.

Avoid the general store on Rodolfo Gómez across from the Hotel Oro Verde. Prices are sometimes set arbitrarily by a vindictive blind man and his young son behind the counter.

Airlines Mexicana (tel 2-17-07) is at Juárez 202. Aeroméxico (tel 2-00-31) is across the street at Juárez 255. Republic Airlines (tel 2-02-67) is at Rodríguez and Morelos. American Airlines (tel 2-37-87) and Continental Airlines (tel 2-30-96) have offices at the airport.

Consulates The American Consulate (tel 2-00-69) overlooks the Isla Cuale at the northern end of the easternmost bridge. You can't miss the big seal and American flag hanging over the entrance of the building next to the Restaurant La Fuente.

Laundromat There is a laundromat at Villa Vallarta in front of the John Newcombe Tennis Club. Another laundromat, Lavandería Hildas, is on Calle Hidalgo and is open from 9 am to 6 pm. At Morelos

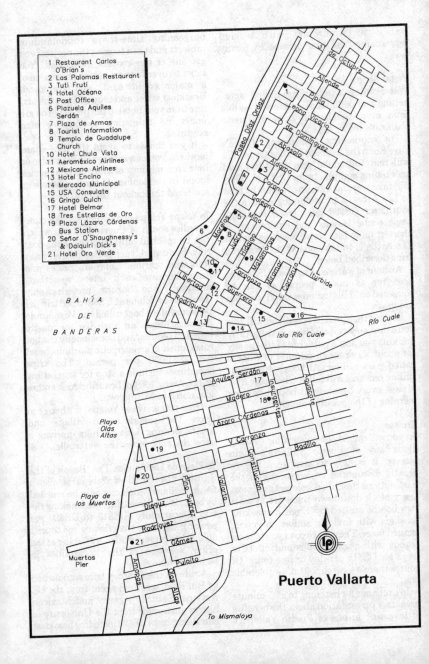

1 Restaurant Carlos
  O'Brian's
2 Las Palomas Restaurant
3 Tuti Fruti
4 Hotel Océano
5 Post Office
6 Plazuela Aquiles
  Serdán
7 Plaza de Armas
8 Tourist Information
9 Templo de Guadalupe
  Church
10 Hotel Chula Vista
11 Aeroméxico Airlines
12 Mexicana Airlines
13 Hotel Encino
14 Mercado Municipal
15 USA Consulate
16 Gringo Gulch
17 Hotel Belmar
18 Tres Estrellas de Oro
19 Plaza Lázaro Cárdenas
   Bus Station
20 Señor O'Shaughnessy's
   & Daiquiri Dick's
21 Hotel Oro Verde

BAHÍA
DE
BANDERAS

Río Cuale

Isla Río Cuale

Aquiles Serdán

Madero

Lázaro Cárdenas

V Carranza

Badillo

Playa
Olas
Altas

Playa de
los Muertos

Dieguz

Rodríguez

Gómez

Pulpito

Muertos
Pier

To Mismaloya

Puerto Vallarta

860 is a laundromat with a sign advertising 'the best service in family wash'.

Water Sports

Water-skiing, windsurfing, diving, snorkelling and pedal-boating are all possible from most beaches in front of Puerto Vallarta's major hotels.

For snorkelling and diving, Chico's Dive Shop (tel 2-18-95) at Díaz Ordaz 772 will rent full scuba gear for US$7 and snorkelling equipment for US$3.75. They will take you and a group of others by boat to Los Arcos, a prime diving spot to the south, for US$30 per person including basic scuba lessons and equipment. A shorter, more inexpensive way to dive at Los Arcos is to take one of the trimaran trips described below.

An hour of water-skiing costs US$40 per boat for as many people as can be squeezed on. This includes water-skis and life vests.

For half that price, a speedboat will give you a bird's-eye view of Puerto Vallarta by yanking you and a parachute into the sky for about six or seven minutes of what is called para-sailing. Although the parasailing hawkers will tell you how safe it is, almost every beach-front hotel has signs warning of the possible dangers.

Cruises

As you will quickly discover while walking along any of Puerto Vallarta's main streets, it is easy to arrange a free or greatly discounted cruise to any of the destinations described below. On almost every block downtown there are at least two booths staffed by English-speaking hawkers with inviting smiles on young, tanned faces. They try to coax you to their stands with sugary hellos and offers of jeeps for US$15 per day or free tours. Of course there's a catch, but it's a tolerable one.

In exchange for listening to a 70-minute breakfast presentation about the benefits of investing in one of Puerto Vallarta's burgeoning time-share condominium projects and then touring the project, you get one of the goodies mentioned. You must be over 25 years old, in possession of a major credit card, and employed. Breakfast is free and they will pay the taxi fare from your hotel to the project. You are under no obligation to buy or sign anything.

If you choose to avoid the time-share hawkers, you can arrange a boat cruise or tour through any of the travel agencies found in the lobbies of the big hotels or scattered throughout the city.

To Yelapa Yelapa is a fishing village-cum-paradise south of Puerto Vallarta which can be reached only by a two-hour boat ride. Boats and 'yachts' depart every day from the marina. Compare prices and deals because each offers something different. The *Sarape* provides only transport to Yelapa at US$8 round trip per person, while a boat called the *Vagabundo* includes lunch, an open bar for mostly beer and tequila, and occasionally the hot salsa music of an energetic marimba band for US$13.50 per person. The trips sometimes include a stop for snorkelling at Los Arcos, a set of beautiful rock arches just north of Mismaloya.

Once you arrive at Yelapa, it's better to leave the pseudo-rustic village and iguana-bearing kids to hike upriver a short distance to see the waterfalls.

To Playa de Las Ánimas The 'Beach of the Spirits' just north of Yelapa is also a fishing village which can only be reached by boat. With three trimarans making the trip almost daily (US$13 to US$20 per person), it seems that fishing for tourist dollars has replaced offshore fishing as the prime vocation of the 12 families in residence here.

A ride on the *Fantasy* trimaran owned by Bill Reid, a retired agent from the US National Security Agency and Mexican history instructor from the University of San Diego, costs US$20 including breakfast on board, lunch at Las Ánimas, an open bar, and Reid's colourful narration about the area and lunch time singing. According to his son Beach Mann (his real name), Reid has written a few books, including the ghost-written autobiography of film producer John Huston. Reid's beach-front house at Las Ánimas was one of Huston's favourite retreats when he was living in Mexico.

Other Local Cruises From the marina, sunset drinking and dance cruises cost US$8 per person. Cruises to the beach of Piedra Blanca to the north cost US$18 per person and to the village of Quimixto to the south US$18 per person. Both villages are similar to Yelapa and Las Ánimas.

Playa de Mismaloya

About 10 km south of Puerto Vallarta is Mismaloya, the site where John Huston directed Richard Burton in *Night of the Iguana*. Several buildings used in the film stand on top of a hill overlooking the beach. Palm-frond shacks along the beach serve meals of lobster (US$9.50) or various types of fish (US$2.75) with rice, enchiladas, salsa and tortillas. If a full meal is too much, you can get a coconut (US$0.35) or a shish kebab of marlin or shrimp (US$0.70).

For an adventurous excursion, head inland from Mismaloya along a dirt road which runs parallel to the river for two km to Paraíso de Chino (Chino's Paradise). This is the site of a decent seafood restaurant with tables set under palapas (shade huts) next to the river as it pours over boulders.

A more exotic locale – Eden de Mismaloya – is two km farther inland and is truly paradise. The film *Predator*, not exactly paradisiacal, was made here; this accounts for the burned-out hull of a helicopter on display next to the restaurant. The Eden de Mismaloya restaurant is similar to Chino's except that the waiters wear white smocks, a parrot follows you to your table and a pet badger wanders between the kitchen and bar waiting for its next bottle of Pepsi.

If you're thirsty and can handle a large, potent drink, try one of the restaurant's speciality drinks. The Piña Surpresa or Pineapple Surprise is a stout concoction of rum, vodka, grenadine, pineapple juice and orange juice served in a carved-out pineapple. The Coco Loco or Crazy Coconut is a numbing mix of vodka, rum, tequila, lemon juice, sugar, orange juice and coconut milk served in a carved-out coconut.

After quenching your thirst, walk upriver a short distance past the restaurant to two small lagoons and stretch out in the sun on the boulders.

Getting to both these places can be difficult if you don't have your own transport. You may be able to hitch a ride, but start early in case you have to walk all the way.

Bullfights

Bullfights are held every Wednesday starting at 5 pm in the bull ring across from the marina.

Horseback Riding

Horses can be hired on the beach in front of the Hotel Buenaventura and a few other hotels for US$5 per hour (subject to bargaining). The most popular excursion is into the tropical jungle of the hills east of Puerto Vallarta, but you should have a guide with you because it's easy to get lost. Organised riding trips can also be arranged through most local travel agencies for US$11 per person.

Museo del Cuale

This 'museum' on Cuale Island barely qualifies as one because it has only a few small temporary exhibits – pre-Hispanic weapons and some clay pots at the time of writing. On the way to the museum, have a look at the makeshift gallery of paintings sometimes on display under the bridge.

BULLFIGHTS IN
Puerto Vallarta, Jal.
BULLRING "LA PALOMA"

(HIGHWAY TO THE AIR PORT RIGHT
AGROSS THE MARINA)

VVednesday December 10,
1986 - At 5:00 p. m.
M A T A D O R S :

RICARDO SANCHEZ
COMPETING WITH

PACO SANTOYO
THEY WILL FACE DEADLY
AT SPANISH STYLE

4   C E R R A L V O   4
BRAVE BULLS

JOHN NEWCOMBE
TENNIS CLUB
VALLARTA

Bullfighting ticket

Places to Stay

Puerto Vallarta has a broad range of places to stay, from the US$3.75-a-night Hotel Chula Vista to the US$115-a-night Camino Real. As a rough rule, most of the tourist-class and resort-style hotels are concentrated to the north and south of central Puerto Vallarta, while mid-range hotels can be found immediately north and south of the Río Cuale in central Puerto Vallarta. The most inexpensive hotels are south of the Río Cuale on or near Madero.

The following break-down by price range is approximate because rates for each hotel, except perhaps the very low-budget hotels, vary greatly according to the season. Rates are highest in December and January and lowest in June and July. In the summer, deluxe and 1st-class hotels become affordable for mid-price-range travellers and even, in certain hotels, for low-budget travellers. Hotel and air-fare packages offered by tour operators in the USA such as Empire Tours are another economical way of staying in Puerto Vallarta.

Places to Stay – bottom end

South of the Río Cuale *Casa de Huéspedes Garcia*, Madero 338, has clean, simple rooms with bathrooms and ceiling fans – five with a shower/bath combination – for US$4.50 for one person and US$5.75 for two.

Hospedaje Hortencias (tel 2-24-84), Madero 336, is a cool, comfortable place to stay. Louvre windows in each room keep the temperature down. Singles cost US$4, doubles US$5, triples US$5.

Hotel Lina (tel 2-16-61), Madero 376, is clean and comfortable with ceiling fans in some rooms, hot-water showers, an open-air courtyard and usually no bugs. Singles/doubles are US$4.50/5.75.

Hotel Belmar (tel 2-05-72), Insurgentes 161 (and Serdán), has rooms with clean bathrooms (including towels). Singles cost US$6, doubles US$6.75, triples US$11.25.

Hotel Bernal (tel 2-36-05), Madero 423, has dark, simple rooms with showers, toilets and sinks all crammed together. The rooms in back are the noisiest while the rooms in front are close to a serenading bevy of dogs and roosters. Singles cost US$5.75, doubles US$8, triples US$9.50.

Hotel Analiz (tel 2-17-57), Madero 429, seems cleaner than the Bernal probably because the rooms face a narrow courtyard and the bathrooms are larger. The potted plants on the 1st floor give this place a cool tropical air. Singles cost US$5, doubles US$8, triples US$10.75.

Hotel Azteca (tel 2-27-50), Madero 473, is one of the best lower-end places to stay if you are looking for a room with a kitchenette. The four rooms with kitchenettes include refrigerators and stoves and cost US$9 for one or two people. The other rooms are singles for US$8.50, doubles for US$10.50, triples for US$12.50. All rooms are arranged around a large airy courtyard and include hot water, fans and towels. You can see Elizabeth Taylor's house from the roof.

Hotel Villa del Mar (tel 2-07-85), Madero 440, is like most of the other budget hotels – clean and pleasant with ceiling fans and a central courtyard. Singles cost US$6.50, doubles US$9.50, triples US$11.50.

North of the Río Cuale Hotel Chula Vista (tel 2-02-90), Juárez 263 near the Aeroméxico office, has 22 clean, simple rooms with bathrooms and fans. Singles cost US$3.75, doubles US$4.75, triples US$5.25.

The *Hotel Océano* (tel 2-10-50) at Galeana 103 across from the old lighthouse monument is a good deal – US$8/10.50 for singles/doubles, some with balconies overlooking the malecón and the bay.

Hotel Marlin (tel 2-09-65), Avenida México 55, has clean rooms around a big open courtyard; some offer ocean views. Rates are US$8.50 single, US$10.50 double, US$12.50 triple.

Camping This is possible at two trailer parks in Puerto Vallarta – *Tacho's Trailer Park* and *Puerto Vallarta Trailer Park*. The latter is on the east side of Highway 200 at Francia 143, behind the Hotel Las Cabañas and across from the entrance to the Hotel Plaza Las Glorias. Spaces have full hook-ups and are shaded by plenty of trees, but the bathrooms and showers can get dismal. They charge US$5 per night per vehicle or tent.

Tacho's is farther outside of town on the road to the Puerto Vallarta suburb of El Pitillal (see map). They have 155 spaces, most with full hook-ups, and charge US$5 per space.

Places to Stay – middle
The *Hotel Encino* (tel 2-00-51), Juárez 115, is near the bridge over the Río Cuale and next to a long-distance telephone office (see map). A swimming pool, restaurant and two bars are part of the hotel. Its 75 rooms are clean and simple with air-conditioning and telephones; some have great views of the Río Cuale and the Pacific Ocean. Doubles are US$13.50 and triples US$16.25.

Hotel Rosita (tel 2-20-93), Paseo de Díaz Ordaz 901, has big, basic rooms, some with great ocean views and high cathedral-style ceilings. Singles/doubles are US$14/16.50; air-conditioning is an extra US$2.

The beach-front *Hotel Oro Verde* (tel 2-15-55) is a 160-room hotel at Rodolfo Gómez and Playa de los Muertos that caters mostly to Canadian tour groups. Before breakfast, hotel guests can be seen staking out prime parcels of sand. Those who wake up too late resort to the swimming pool. A double room costs US$40 per night, but probably goes for less when arranged as part of a package or in the off-seasons (especially June and July).

Places to Stay – top end
If US$46 to US$75 is your price range for a double or suite, the *Molino de '*

at Ignacio and Serdán is a good choice. Most of the rooms surround a garden courtyard and fountain and offer ocean views.

La Casa del Puente offers a deluxe pair of beautifully furnished apartments overlooking the Río Cuale behind the Restaurant La Fuente del Puente and the American Consulate. They charge US$50 for four people, but during the off-season the price can be as low as US$25. This tops the list of Puerto Vallarta's most quiet and romantic little secrets.

At the deluxe end there are several hotels and condominium complexes: the *Hotel Camino Real* (US$115 per night), *Sheraton Buganvilias* (US$60 + per night), *Garza Blanca* (private villas for US$170 per night) and *Fiesta Americana*. All of them offer the opportunity for a luxurious vacation for much less than comparable vacations in Hawaii or other parts of the USA. Travel agents in the USA should be able to provide detailed descriptions of these and other top-notch hotels in Puerto Vallarta.

Places to Eat

The restaurant situation in Puerto Vallarta is similar to the hotel situation – something for every budget. Generally, the cheaper restaurants and food stalls are found near the cheaper hotels, particularly around Madero. Most of the expensive restaurants are attached to 1st-class and deluxe hotels.

South of the Río Cuale At Madero 396 the *Refrescaría* serves great inexpensive juices and milk shakes. It's a good place to sit for a bit and quench your thirst.

Also on Madero at No 340 is the *Restaurant El Corita*, which serves a basic but filling comida corrida of chicken soup, vegetables and chicken for less than US$1. Don't be shocked by the chicken's foot that always comes with the soup.

Los Parados taco stand on the corner of crowntes and Madero, clean and the best in town. A short

1 Marina
2 Holiday Inn
3 Hotel Fiesta Americana
4 Puerto Vallarta Trailer Park
5 Sheraton Buganvilias
6 Hotel Buenaventura
7 Hotel Rosita
8 Hotel Oro Verde
9 Hotel Camino Real
10 Costa Vida Vallarta
11 Hotel Garza Blanca

To Tacho's Trailer Park

BAHÍA DE BANDERAS

Río Cuale

Around Puerto Vallarta

(200) = Highway Numbers

To Los Arcos, Mismaloya, Tomatlán,
Playa Las Ánimas & Yelapa

distance to the south down Insurgentes is another taco stand that locals claim is excellent.

Restaurant Gilmar, Madero 18, serves a fair comida corrida for US$1, a continental breakfast for less than US$0.75 and a full breakfast of juice, hotcakes and tea for US$1.25.

For a refreshing snack try a cold coconut for 25c from any of several coconut stands on Avenida Serdán.

Señor O'Shaughnessy's is owned by an American of Irish descent who displays his Irishness in this ocean-front restaurant. In the evenings Mr O'Shaughnessy roams from table to table with microphone in hand serenading guests with Broadway musical hits while someone at an organ tries to play along.

Next door at *Daiquiri Dick's*, owned by an American named Dick, business is booming. The outdoor restaurant and small bar are usually full of North Americans, perhaps because of the romantic tropical appearance – candlelight, lots of palm fronds and tables overlooking crashing waves. A full dinner for one (enough for two) with a large seafood cocktail *(ceviche)* and entree is US$6.

There are two small beach-front restaurants at Playa de los Muertos at the end of Madero that are good people-watching posts and fair places for a small meal of sandwiches, pizza or soup.

Felippi's Restaurant, atop a hill overlooking Puerto Vallarta from the south, is a romantic place from which to watch the sunset and dine on some of the best seafood in Puerto Vallarta (US$10 to US$15 for a sumptuous meal). Unless you are willing to hike up the hill, you need a car or a cab to get there.

La Perla is a pricey (for Mexico) gourmet restaurant at the Hotel Camino Real. A meal for two costs US$40; the same meal would easily cost more than US$100 in the USA. If you want to spoil yourself, this is one place you could do it.

North of the Río Cuale *Las Palomas Restaurant*, on the malecón at Aldamas and Díaz Ordaz, is one of the few restaurants in Puerto Vallarta that serves pigeon (US$1.75 to US$2.25). They also serve a variety of typical Mexican dishes, including big portions of seafood.

Tuti Fruti, at the corner of Morelos and Corona, is a good place for freshly squeezed juices, sandwiches and all sorts of licuados.

El Viejo Vallarta, on Díaz Ordaz across from the seahorse statue, serves home-style Mexican cooking and is particularly known for its tasty enchiladas (three with chicken, beans and salad for US$2) and inexpensive seafood. A plate of eight grilled shrimp with beans and salad is US$3.50. Breakfast is a bargain here – eggs, ham, rice, beans and tortillas for US$1.35.

Restaurant El Panorama is another place fit for gluttony. A very filling meal for two cooked right at your table costs US$45. It is worth visiting just to see the magnificent view of Puerto Vallarta and the Bahía de Banderas.

Carlos O'Brian's, Díaz Ordaz and Pipila, is a noisy, rowdy gringo hang-out where drinking is more common than eating. There are three bars, two dining rooms and everything including a kitchen sink hanging from the walls and ceilings. A line of people begins forming at the door as early as 4.30 pm. It's open until 2 am.

Fonda La Margarita is a pleasant though touristy courtyard restaurant and bar at Juárez 152. In the evenings, a mariachi band plays until midnight. Speciality dishes include shrimp salad (US$3.50), shrimp and spaghetti (US$7), a Mexican platter (US$7.50), frogs' legs (US$8) and filet mignon (US$6.50).

Tasty roasted chicken on a spit can be bought from a couple of nameless chicken restaurants one block south of the Hotel Buenaventura (Avenida México 1301). It's cheap and filling.

Cheap and usually clean food can be had at the Municipal Market where numerous food stalls serve rice dishes, frijoles, chicken and mole.

On Isla Cuale *Le Bistro* is a French-style jazz place on the island of Cuale often described as 'a charming splurge'. A full meal costs US$4.50 to US$6.

Restaurant Vallarta Cuale, across from the small museum on Cuale island, is a pleasant place to sip Margaritas and watch the sunset. They serve seafood and American food at slightly less than American prices. A strange raccoon-like animal chained to a post near the entrance greets you with a low-pitched scream.

Entertainment
Drinking and dancing are Puerto Vallarta's main forms of night-time entertainment. There are several bars and discos, most of which cater to vacationing North Americans. *Studio 54* next to the Sheraton Buganvilias is a high-tech take-off on its New York City counterpart.

La Jungla or The Jungle is a disco bar at the Hotel Camino Real that has a huge screen for music videos and several rows of bright, flashing lights. This is supposedly one of the best discos in town, though except for a few high-tech innovations like the screen and penetrating sound system, it seemed fairly typical.

The City Dump at Ignacio Vallarta 278 and *Friday López* at the entrance to the Hotel Fiesta Americana are also popular disco bars. Lines form outside both discos on Friday and Saturday nights.

There's always a line outside *Carlos O'Brian's*, a favourite drinking-hole for fun-seeking, rabble-rousing gringos.

Other discos and bars often mentioned by locals are *Capriccio* at Pulpito and Olas Altas, *Ciro's* on Díaz Ordaz and *Isadora's* at the Holiday Inn.

Brazz, Morelos 518, is a popular drinking-hole for Mexicans after work and for gringos after too much sun. A mariachi band plays in the evenings until midnight.

Things to Buy
Shops and boutiques in Puerto Vallarta sell just about every type of craft made in Mexico, but prices are higher than in Mexico City and Guadalajara. Try the Mercado Municipal along the north bank of the Río Cuale between the bridges for haggling on everything from Taxco silver, sarapes and sandals to hand-woven wool wall-hangings and blown glass. The market has 156 shops and stalls and is open from 8 am to 8 pm.

Avoid Aero Boutiques at the airport because their prices are outrageous. Buy everything you need in town. A downtown shop sold a pair of silver earrings at an officially regulated price of US$1 per gram while two airport boutiques refused to sell according to weight and insisted on charging more than three times the price.

Getting There & Away
Air Most flights between Puerto Vallarta and other Mexican cities are handled by Aeroméxico and Mexicana. There are flights daily on both airlines between Puerto Vallarta, Mexico City (one hour and 10 minutes) and Guadalajara. Mexicana also has direct flights between Puerto Vallarta and Chicago, Dallas, Denver and Los Angeles in the USA.

Bus Inter-city bus lines operate from individual terminals on or near Madero and Insurgentes on the south side of the Río Cuale. Tres Estrellas de Oro (tel 2-10-19), Insurgentes 210, has fast 1st-class air-conditioned express buses to Guadalajara three times daily (US$5, six hours); Mexico City five times (US$12, 14 to 15 hours); Manzanillo (US$3, five hours), Tijuana (US$25, 36 hours), Mazatlán (eight to 10 hours), Los Mochis and Hermosillo twice daily (US$16).

Norte de Sonora (tel 2-16-50), Madero 343, also claims to have 1st-class buses but most seem to be 2nd class. Their buses go to almost the same destinations as Tres Estrellas at about the same frequency.

Autobuses del Pacífico has the most frequent service to southern destinations, including hourly departures for Manzanillo for US$4.50.

Ferry In 1987 the ferry system was severely overloaded by the high demand for crossings between Puerto Vallarta and Cabo San Lucas. If the system normalises, departures are scheduled for Tuesday and Saturday at 2 pm aboard the modern Danish ship *Puerto Vallarta*. Fares were reasonable, but were rising rapidly – over 300% in less than a year. Make reservations for on-board accommodation as far in advance as possible. Supposedly you can't make reservations more than 30 days in advance; Scott attempted to make reservations exactly 30 days before his departure and was told that everything except the salon (lowest) class, had filled up already. He found out later that most of the accommodation is reserved for VIPs. The day before departure, lo and behold, their spaces become available to the public, but you must be near the head of the line to take advantage of this. For more information about the ferry system, see the 'Cabo San Lucas' section.

Getting Around
Airport Transport Buses and combis pass by the airport entrance on Highway 200 quite often, but the airport taxi vans are very inexpensive. From the airport to Plaza Lázaro Cárdenas, just south of the budget-hotel area around Madero, costs less than US$2.

Bus & Combi Local buses run from 6 am to midnight every five minutes on most routes (5c for any ride). Plaza Lázaro Cárdenas at Playa de los Muertos is a major station and departure hub for buses that run north through Puerto Vallarta and for combis that run south to Mismaloya. Most buses run from Playa de los Muertos through town up Juárez to El Pitilal at the northern end of the city.

Combis or minivans to Mismaloya depart every 10 to 15 minutes from Plaza Lázaro Cárdenas. Flag one down from the side of the road. Most rides average 20c.

Following are descriptions of each combi route:

Route 1: El Pitillal – Puerto Vallarta El Pitillal, Highway 200, Avenida México, Morelos, Ignacio Vallarta, Carranza, Olas Altas, Lázaro Cárdenas, Insurgentes, Libertad, Juárez, 31 de Octubre, Morelos, Péru, Avenida México, Highway 200, El Pitillal

Route 2: Puerto Vallarta – Mismaloya Olas Altas, Lázaro Cárdenas, Insurgentes, Highway 200 southbound, Playa Mismaloya, Highway 200 northbound, Insurgentes, Carranza

Route 3: El Pitillal – Puerto Vallarta El Pitillal, Avenida Francisco Villa, Avenida México, Morelos, Ignacio Vallarta, Carranza, Olas Altas, Lázaro Cárdenas, Insurgentes, Libertad, Juárez, 31 de Octubre, Morelos, Péru, Avenida México, Avenida Francisco Villa, El Pitillal

Taxi Taxis are the costliest way to get around, but are still inexpensive by American standards. A taxi from downtown to the airport (one of the longest rides you're likely to take) costs US$1.75 to US$2.50.

Car Rental Avis (tel 2-11-12), Hertz (tel 2-04-73) and National (tel 2-11-07) all have branches in Puerto Vallarta and charge about the same prices – US$40 per day for a Volkswagen Sedan. Mexican agencies such as Quick Rent a Car (tel 2-35-05), Odin Rente un Auto (tel 2-28-25) and Alpri Rent a Car (tel 2-06-50) offer comparable rates. Jeeps are the most popular vehicles and probably the most expensive (US$55 per day). They can be rented for US$15 per day by attending one of the time-share presentations described above in the cruise section. This is worthwhile if only to go to Eden de Mismaloya, four km inland from Mismaloya, which is 10 km south of Puerto Vallarta.

CHAMELA

The first major coastal town south of Puerto Vallarta is Chamela, 152 km away. The town is more a community of small settlements scattered along the 11-km shore of the Bahía de Chamela. Much of this shore consists of fine, untouched beaches – perfect escapes. Unfortunately, tourism has begun to creep in and alter the landscape.

At Chamela's Super Mercado a km-long road leads to the beach-front *Villa Polinesia & Camping Club* (Guadalajara tel 22-39-40). From their brochure:

Villa Polinesia & Camping Club Offers:
*12 villas, one with its own private pool
*35 Polinesian huts
*Shaded trailer spaces with full hook-ups
*Security night and day
*Cleanliness throughout
*Neat modern bathrooms and showers
*A small supermarket
*Safe drinking water
*Hot water all the time
*Bar B-Q areas
*Laundry and washing facilities

They charge US$5 per night for a space.

There's another trailer park and motel just north of the turn-off to the Villa Polinesia, which is appropriately named the *Motel Trailer Park*. The camping sites aren't fantastic, just a small grassy area and a few trees. The motel is similarly unspectacular with singles for US$4.25, doubles for US$5 and triples for US$5.75.

SAN PATRICIO-MELAQUE

The small beach resort town of Melaque ('meh-LAH-key) is 60 km south-east of Chamela, just after Highway 80 from Guadalajara merges with Highway 200. Although it is about the same size as its twin resort town of Barra de Navidad two km along the beach to the south-east, it rarely appears on maps. Another oddity is that it's officially known as San Patricio-Melaque, so locals refer to it as San Patricio. This may be because of the

town's renowned Fiesta de San Patricio, a rambunctious Mexican version of Saint Patrick's Day from 10 to 17 March.

Information & Orientation

Everything in Melaque is within walking distance. Most of the hotels, restaurants and public services are concentrated on or near Gómez Farías and López Mateos. Gómez Farías becomes Avenida Las Palmas (also known as Miguel Ochoa) as it follows the shore first west and then south before ending at a once-isolated but now popular beach. Barra de Navidad is accessible via Highway 200 (five km) or the beach (two km).

Tourist Office The tourist office (tel 7-01-00) is near the Hotel Melaque on Avenida Las Palmas, but unless you can speak some Spanish, the staff can't be very helpful. Hours are 9 am to 8 pm Monday to Friday and 9 am to 1 pm Saturday.

Money Bánamex on López Mateos exchanges money from 10 am to noon Monday to Friday.

Post The post office is at Morelos 2 at the corner of López Mateos.

Telephone Calls A caseta de larga distancia at Gómez Farías 203-B is open 8 am to 9 pm Monday to Saturday and 8 am to 2 pm Sunday.

Things to Do

Come to Melaque only if you want to relax and do nothing on the beach or join the drunken festivities during the Fiesta de San Patricio or Semana Santa (Easter week).

Places to Stay

Room rates vary as much as 30% depending on the season (summer is the high season), so it's impossible to classify hotels according to price ranges. Also, it's not unlikely that a hotel of lesser quality

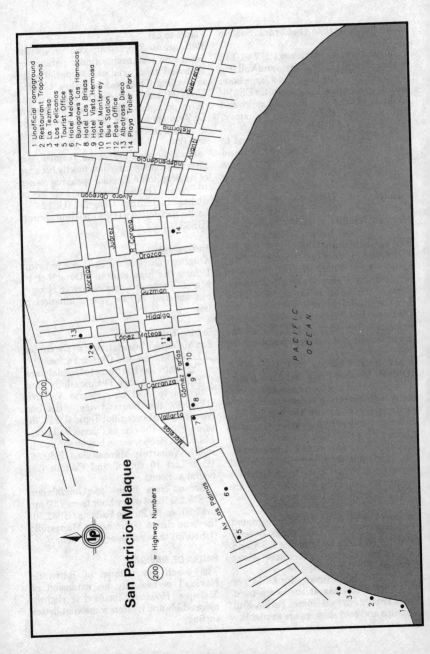

San Patricio-Melaque

200 = Highway Numbers

1 Unofficial campground
2 Restaurant Tropicana
3 La Tezmisa
4 Los Pelicanos
5 Tourist Office
6 Hotel Melaque
7 Bungalows Las Hamacas
8 Hotel Las Brisas
9 Hotel Vista Hermosa
10 Hotel Monterrey
11 Bus Station
12 Post Office
13 Albatross Disco
14 Playa Trailer Park

PACIFIC OCEAN

would cost more than a better one. So shop around!

Bungalows Las Hamacas (tel 7-01-13), at the corner of Gómez Farías and Vallarta one block from the beach, is a large hotel with single/double 'bungalows' for US$10/13. Most of the rooms have balconies and full kitchens that include a stove, refrigerator and dishes.

Hotel Las Brisas (tel 7-01-08), next to Las Hamacas, has 22 rooms with fans and hot-water showers and, out front, a large veranda where you can sit, sip something cool and watch the sunset.

Hotel Vista Hermosa (tel 7-00-02), Gómez Farías 110, is very popular with Mexican families probably because it's one of the best budget hotels in town. Singles/doubles are US$6.75/10.

Hotel Monterrey (tel 7-00-04), Gómez Farías 200, is a dark, simple place with rooms arranged around a small courtyard. Some of the rooms in the main building face the ocean; the ones on the 2nd floor offer the best views. It was recently renovated, but they didn't change the prices much yet: singles/doubles cost US$4.75/6.

The *Hotel Melaque* (Guadalajara tel 14-56-05, 16-00-95), is a 2nd-class resort-style place that has more than 200 rooms, many with balconies facing the bay. It's particularly popular with Mexican families, although they are trying to lure American guests with a flyer that begins 'USA and Mexico – Friends Forever'. A restaurant, bar, swimming pool and miniature golf course are attached to the hotel. Rates for one or two people in a double room are US$11/24 including three meals.

Camping There is an unofficial campground at the end of Avenida Las Palmas. Several recreational vehicles from the USA and Canada have claimed spaces here. Water is available, but nothing else.

You can camp officially for US$4 per night plus a 15% tax at the beach-front *Playa Trailer Park* on Gómez Farías. Full hook-ups and cold showers are available.

Places to Eat

Restaurant Tropicana, one of several beachside restaurants under palapas or thatched roofs, claims to specialise in everything. Their seafood dishes (US$3 to US$4.25) are reputedly the best in town. A few palm-frond doors down from here is *La Tezmisa* where a pig wallowing in the mud and shade grunts a welcome as you enter.

Los Pelicanos, next to La Tezmisa, is a favourite among travellers mostly because of its hospitable English-speaking owner Philomena García. She serves a variety of dishes including lasagna (US$2.75), barbecued chicken (US$1.35) and shrimp (US$3.30).

Entertainment

Albatross Disco is the only one in town. During the high season – December to March – there's a modest cover charge, but the rest of the year admission is free.

Getting There & Away

Bus Melaque's bus station is at the corner of López Mateos and Gómez Farías.

Tres Estrellas has buses to Guadalajara (US$3.60, five hours) 11 times daily from 7.45 am to 1.30 am; Puerto Vallarta (US$2.45, five hours) twice – the bus comes from Manzanillo; Tepic (US$4.75, same bus as the one to Puerto Vallarta); Mazatlán (US$8, same bus as the one to Puerto Vallarta); Manzanillo (US$0.85, 1½ hours) 10 times; and Colima (2½ hours) at noon.

Second-class buses to Guadalajara (US$3.25) leave every hour from 7.20 am to 11.20 pm. To Puerto Vallarta (US$2.30) they run direct 16 times; to Manzanillo (US$0.75) they run every half-hour.

BARRA DE NAVIDAD

The beach resort town of Barra de Navidad is basically an extension of Melaque. However, its food is slightly more edible and it offers somewhat better surfing.

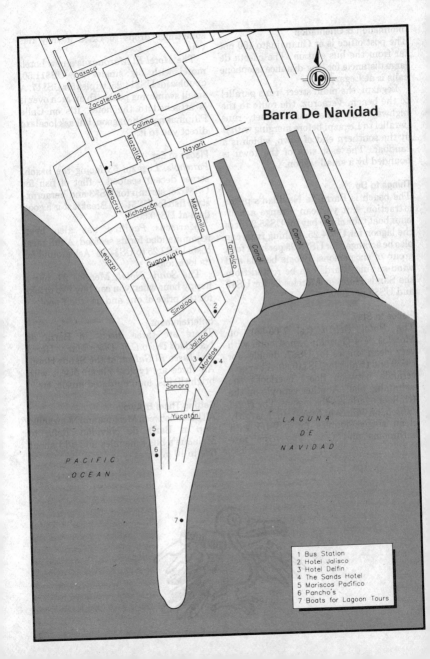

Barra De Navidad

PACIFIC OCEAN

LAGUNA DE NAVIDAD

1 Bus Station
2 Hotel Jalisco
3 Hotel Delfin
4 The Sands Hotel
5 Mariscos Pacífico
6 Pancho's
7 Boats for Lagoon Tours

Information & Orientation

The post office is at Guanajuato 100 not far from the bus station. The caseta de larga distancia for long-distance telephone calls is at Legazpi 117.

Legazpi, the main street, runs parallel to the beach. Veracruz, the route to the highway and other main street, runs parallel to Legazpi before merging with it at the southern end of town, which is a sandbar. The east side of the town is bounded by a small lagoon.

Things to Do

The beach is Barra de Navidad's prime attraction, but you can arrange a half-hour boat tour of the bay for US$5.25 or of the lagoon for US$4.25. Fishing trips can also be arranged for US$5.25 per hour for a group of six persons. Boogie boards and wind-surfing boards can be rented from the Sands Hotel at Morelos 23 for US$2 and US$8 per hour.

Places to Stay

The *Hotel Delfin* (tel 7-00-68), on Morelos, is a German-owned hotel with very clean singles for US$7, doubles for US$9 and triples for US$10.30. A bar on a veranda between floors overlooks the swimming pool. Another veranda on the 4th floor overlooks the lagoon. The *Hotel Jalisco*, on Jalisco at Mazatlán, has fairly clean singles/doubles for US$4/5 with bathrooms and fans. The room rate

sometimes drops to US$3 if they like you.

The *Motel El Marquez* is a new hotel/motel with big singles for US$11.50, doubles for US$14.25, triples for US$17. A small swimming pool with an arch over it is attached to the hotel. It's on Calle Filipinas near the lagoon, but ask locals to direct you to it.

Places to Eat

Pancho's, Legazpi 53 facing the beach, serves decent seafood – filet of fish for US$1.25, shrimp for US$3 and Veracruz-style fish for US$1.25. Breakfast is a good deal at US$0.60.

Mariscos Pacífico has also been recommended for its seafood. A full meal costs US$3.25 to US$4.25. Ask around for its location.

The *Sands Hotel*, Morelos 23, has a happy hour when you can buy two drinks for the price of one and use their pool.

Entertainment

There are three discos in Barra de Navidad: *Disco Giff*, *Disco Mar y Tierra* and *Disco El Galeon* at the Sands Hotel. All three are typical cheap discos with bright lights, loud outdated music, etc.

Getting There & Away

All buses between Melaque and Manzanillo stop at Barra de Navidad. Refer to Melaque's bus schedules and add about five to 10 minutes.

The West Coast – Nogales to Tepic

This chapter covers the 1505-km stretch of Highway 15 from Nogales on the US border to Tepic, capital of the state of Nayarit. From Nogales, a scaled-down version of Tijuana with its share of stereotypical tacky border-town schlock, Highway 15 cuts through the harsh Sonora desert to the boom town of Hermosillo. Part of Hermosillo's prosperity is due to the damming of the Río Sonora; extensive irrigation of the surrounding area made this one of the most productive regions in the country. For travellers, the city is interesting mostly because it's a fairly typical example of a growing Mexican city. Most travellers, however, head straight for the beach, especially during the oppressively hot summer months.

The nearest beaches to Hermosillo are at Old and New Kino on Bahía Kino, 120 km to the west. Unless you want to camp on the beach or in a trailer park, however, there is no budget accommodation in the twin Kinos. Frequent buses between Bahía Kino, Hermosillo and Guaymas to the south make this an easy day trip if you start early enough.

Guaymas is, in a sense, the coastal version of Hermosillo – a growing city that caters more to trade than to tourism. It is also the principal port for the state of Sonora. Most travellers either pass through Guaymas on their way to or from the ferry terminal (ferry to Santa Rosalía, Baja California) or make a day trip from Bahía San Carlos, 20 km to the north. Bahía San Carlos is a predominantly gringo retreat with trailer parks and over-priced hotels. Scenically, both towns are well situated on calm, pleasant bays with beautiful beaches.

After Guaymas the next place worth visiting is the town of Alamos at the edge of the Sierra Madre Occidental mountain range about 55 km south-east of the Highway 15 town of Navojoa. During the 18th and 19th centuries this was a busy silver-mining centre that attracted many wealthy Spanish and, later, Mexican mining magnates who built opulent haciendas here. Today, the restored haciendas are its chief attractions and definitely worth seeing if you want an idea of what life may have been like during that period.

About 160 km south of Navojoa is the relatively young town of Los Mochis in the neighbouring state of Sinaloa. Since its founding in 1893 by an American entrepreneur the town's economic life has revolved around sugar and railroads, although other types of commerce such as agriculture and manufacturing are now equally important. This is the terminus for the train through Copper Canyon and, near-by at Topolobampo, the ferry from La Paz.

If you skip a side-trip to Copper Canyon, then you will miss one of the highlights of any trip through Mexico. From sea level the train winds through the canyon over 85 bridges to an elevation of 2500 metres and a spectacular view of canyons deeper than the USA's Grand Canyon.

Back on Highway 15 travelling south from Los Mochis, you pass through the Pacific lowlands of the Sierra Madre Occidental range, a fairly prosperous area of farms and small ranches, before reaching the bustling beach resort city of Mazatlán ('Mah-zaht-LAHN') 430 km south of Los Mochis.

With a long string of new hotels, condominium complexes and restaurants with menus in English, Mazatlán tries to attract increasing numbers of mainly North American visitors. If fun in the sun and sea, dining, drinking and dancing till dawn are your main objectives, then you'll be pleased with Mazatlán.

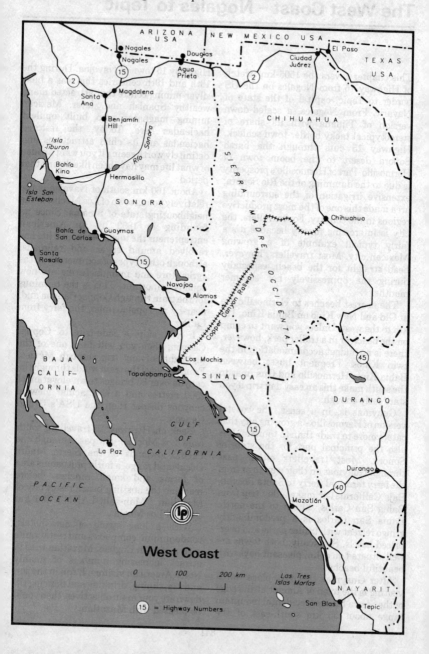

West Coast

```
0        100        200 km
```

15 = Highway Numbers

A more sedate seaside escape can be found 200 km south/south-east at the small town of San Blas. Surrounded by tropical jungle and a lagoon known for its exotic birds, the town is paradise off the beaten path, but still easily accessible by paved road from Highway 15 (36 km).

The last city on this route is Tepic, capital of the state of Nayarit 70 km from San Blas. For travellers there's nothing particularly noteworthy about the place except that it's an important junction. Highway 200 starts here and heads south to Puerto Vallarta. After Tepic, Highway 15 cuts inland towards Guadalajara and Mexico City.

NOGALES

Population: 75,000

Like its border-city cousins Tijuana, Ciudad Juárez, Nuevo Laredo and Matamoros, Nogales (altitude 1120 metres) is a major transit point for goods and people travelling between the USA and Mexico. Just across the border is its twin city by the same name. Both cities were named Nogales (walnuts) because of the many walnut trees that were once in the area.

Today, fruits and vegetables mostly from the highly productive fields of the Mexican states of Sonora and Sinaloa pass through here for transhipment to American supermarkets. The Ferrocarril del Pacífico (Pacific Train) also passes through on its way to and from Mexicali (Baja California) and points south. Several major bus lines, including the USA-based Greyhound lines, begin and end routes in Nogales. As a transit point, you can't beat it as a place to get in and out quickly.

Nogales presents an easier introduction to Mexico than a bustling border city of split personalities like Tijuana, which is trying to shed its tawdry, red-light image and become a modern trading centre. Nogales has everything Tijuana has – curio shops (overflowing with wrought-iron bird cages, tacky felt paintings, plaster renditions of Mickey Mouse), cheap bars and plenty of liquor stores – but all on a much smaller scale.

Information & Orientation

The commercial section of Nogales is only a few blocks in width, being hemmed in on either side by hills. The main street is Obregón, which eventually runs into Highway 15. Almost everything is within walking distance of the border; it's virtually impossible to get lost here.

The bus station is conveniently located on Juárez (next to the Café Olga at No 37) near the border crossing. If you plan to head south, don't forget to get your tourist card validated at the Mexican immigration office after crossing from Nogales, Arizona. If you're driving, be sure to get a vehicle permit from the *aduana* (customs office), next to the immigration office. The border offices are open 24 hours a day.

Places to Stay

There are 13 hotels and motels in Nogales. You might want to continue down the road, since the rates will be high. If you overnight, two recommended hotels are the *Hotel Granada* (tel 2-29-11) at López Mateos and González just east of Avenida Obregón, and the *Hotel Olivia* (tel 2-22-00) at Avenida Obregón 125. Both have air-conditioned rooms with telephones and TVs for US$25 double.

Places to Eat

For food, try the *Café Olga*, Juárez 37 next to the bus station, at any time of the day or night. *The Apolo*, at Km 6 on Highway 15, reputedly serves some of the best turtle soup (called *cahuama*) in northern Sonora. *El Cid*, Avenida Obregón 124 overlooking the street, has an excellent menu but is expensive by Mexican standards (US$4 to US$8). Ask for a table by the window.

HERMOSILLO

Population: 500,000

Founded in 1700 by Juan Bautista

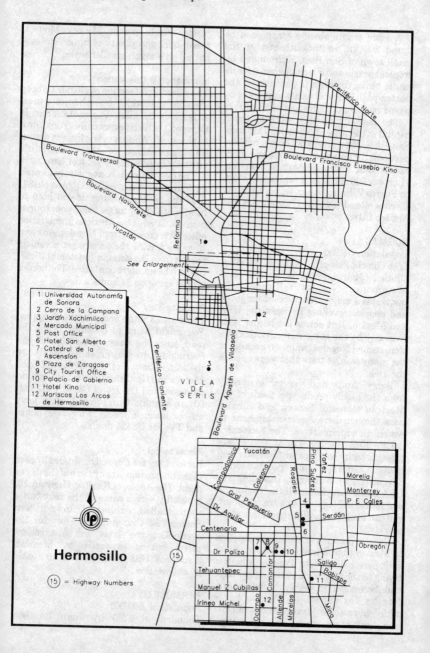

1 Universidad Autonomía
  de Sonora
2 Cerro de la Campana
3 Jardín Xochimilco
4 Mercado Municipal
5 Post Office
6 Hotel San Alberto
7 Catedral de la
  Ascensión
8 Plaza de Zaragosa
9 City Tourist Office
10 Palacio de Gobierno
11 Hotel Kino
12 Mariscos Los Arcos
   de Hermosillo

Hermosillo

(15) = Highway Numbers

Escalante for the resettlement of Pima Indians, Hermosillo is now the capital of the state of Sonora. It's right on Highway 15 approximately 227 km due south of Nogales and *La Frontera* (the international border). Like many cities in Mexico, Hermosillo is quickly industrialising and attracting a large influx of people from the surrounding countryside. In little more than a decade, the city has gone from being primarily an agricultural and administrative centre of 45,000 to a multi-industry city of more than 500,000. Part of this growth stemmed from the completion of a large Ford automotive plant that recently began manufacturing and assembling automobiles here. Most of the autos are destined for US dealerships because they are priced too high for Mexicans.

Hermosillo is often overlooked by travellers intent on reaching the cooler, more glamorous vacation spots on the coast. However, since it is home to the University of Sonora and a number of other educational institutions, Hermosillo has many of the social and cultural amenities of a larger city without the overwhelming commercialism.

Orientation

Highway 15 enters Hermosillo from the north-east and becomes Boulevard Francisco Eusebio Kino, a wide boulevard lined with orange and laurel trees. Kino continues east through the city, curves south-west and becomes first Boulevard Rodríguez, then Boulevard Rosales and Boulevard Agustín de Vildosola before regaining its designation as Highway 15. The major business and administrative sections of town lie on either side of this main thoroughfare and along the Boulevard Transversal which transects it from north/north-west to south-east. The Periférico, a highway artery originally designed to circumscribe the periphery of Hermosillo, has almost become an inner loop due to the city's rapid expansion.

The central section of Hermosillo, which is also the oldest and most charming, lies to the south just after the adjoining community of Villa de Seris. The Cerro de la Campana (Hill of the Bell) is the most prominent landmark in the area and an easy point of reference night or day. The panoramic view from the top is beautiful and well worth the climb.

Information

Tourist Office The city tourist office (tel 7-29-64) is on the ground floor of the Palacio de Gobierno (Government Palace) and offers some information in English and Spanish about Hermosillo and the rest of the state of Sonora.

Money There are several banks on Boulevard Rosales. Casas de cambio are scattered throughout downtown Hermosillo.

Post The main post office is at Rosales and Avenida Serdán and is open 8 am to 7 pm Monday to Friday and 9 am to 1 pm Saturday and Sunday.

Laundromat Lavarama laundromat is at the corner of Yañez and Sonora. Lavandería Automática de Hermosillo is a self-service laundry at Juárez and Periférico 2 Poniente that's open Monday to Saturday from 8 am to 8 pm and Sunday from 8 am to 2 pm.

Plaza de Zaragoza

A visit to the Plaza de Zaragoza is highly recommended, especially at sundown when thousands of yellow-headed blackbirds flock in to roost in the park trees for the night. On the west side is the lovely Catedral de la Ascensión (also called Catedral Metropolitana) that celebrated its bicentennial in 1979. On the east side is the Palacio de Gobierno (Government Palace and municipal offices) with colourful courtyard murals depicting various episodes in the history of Sonora. The cathedral and palace are open daily; free admission.

Museo de Sonora

The Sonora Museum hugs the eastern side of the Hill of the Bell and, by walking clockwise around the hill, you can't miss it. Most of the exhibits cover various aspects of Sonora's history and anthropology. Hours are Wednesday to Saturday 10 am to 5.30 pm and Sunday 10 am to 3.30 pm. Admission is free.

Centro Ecológico de Sonora

The Ecological Centre of Sonora is a wonderful zoo and botanical garden 2½ km south of downtown Hermosillo near the Periférico Sur and just off Highway 15. Many animals and plants indigenous to Sonora and other desert biomes around the world are displayed. It's open Wednesday to Sunday at varying hours.

Universidad Autonomía de Sonora

The Autonomous University of Sonora has a fine arts complex across from the campus at the main traffic circle formed by the intersection of boulevards Rosales (Rodríguez) and Transversal. A variety of theatrical and musical events and art exhibits are presented throughout the year. Check with the university or the tourist office for the latest information.

Places to Stay

If you insist on spending a night here in the summer, you must have a room with air-conditioning that works. Some hotels advertise air-conditioning, but the cool air may blow with barely more force than a whisper. Check the room before you accept it.

Many of Hermosillo's motels and hotels are strung out along Boulevard Francisco Eusebio Kino (Highway 15) in the northeast corner of the city. One of these is the *Motel El Encanto* (tel 4-47-30), Boulevard Kino 901 three blocks west of the Holiday Inn. The rooms are clean and air-

conditioned with tiled floors, telephones and TVs. There's also a swimming pool. Singles/doubles are US$10/15.

Closer to downtown is the *Hotel Kino* (tel 2-45-99), Pino Suárez 151 at the base of the Hill of the Bell right before Suárez merges with Rosales. This no-nonsense hotel is a favourite among Mexican business people. Rooms have private baths, air-conditioning, colour TVs and mini-refrigerators. Singles/doubles are US$12/15.

Nearby is the *Hotel Montecarlo* (tel 2-33-54), at Juárez and Sonora just off Boulevard Transversal. This reasonably priced older hotel has clean, air-conditioned rooms. It fills up quickly each day, so make reservations or show up before sundown. Singles/doubles are US$8.50/9.50.

The *Hotel San Alberto* (tel 2-18-00), Avenida Serdán and Rosales, is an attempt at modern elegance, but it's really just a good mid-priced hotel. Single/double rooms with air-conditioning, cable TV and a complimentary continental breakfast are US$15/19. There's also a swimming pool.

The cheapest and dingiest places to stay are the casas de huéspedes on Sonora between Garmendia and Matamoros, with room rates averaging US$3 to US$5 per night. Most of the rooms seem to be rented out long term to students or short term to hookers. At night the hookers tend to be noisy, so make your selection carefully.

Places to Eat

The state of Sonora is known for both beef and seafood dishes. *Jardín Xochimilco*, Obregón 51 in the adjoining community of Villa de Seris, offers a complete dinner that includes tripe, kidneys, ribs and steak charcoal-broiled in huge ovens for US$4.

Mariscos Los Arcos de Hermosillo, Michel 43, is well known for its excellent but high-priced seafood. Entrees start at US$4 and can easily go over US$15 for two, particularly if you order the *Mariscada*, a feast that includes charcoal-broiled fish and 12 side dishes. Other items on the menu are *ceviche* (sort of a fish cocktail), shrimp, sea turtle and octopus.

The *Restaurant La Huerta*, San Luis Potosí 109, has also been recommended for its seafood.

The *Hotel Kino* restaurant has a reputation for good, moderately priced meals with an excellent comida corrida for under US$2.

Rene's Café on Rosales at Moreno and Michel is a bright, cheery place that also does a good comida corrida.

Some of the cheapest food in town can be bought from any of the numerous street-corner hot-dog carts and cheap food stalls in the *Mercado Municipal*. Not too far away from the plaza, the Mercado is a large indoor market at Suárez and Calles. The tacos here can usually be trusted not to wreak havoc on your innards. The hot dogs are surprisingly good, especially when piled with condiments such as mustard, guacamole, chiles, relish and refried beans. Another street-cart treat is the *pico de gallo*, a delicious mixture of chunks of orange, apple, pineapple, cucumber, jicama, watermelon and coconut – very refreshing on a hot day.

Cantinas

Robert Wheeler, an American who lived and worked in Hermosillo as an English teacher, had this to say about the Hermosillo cantina scene:

This brings me to the subject of the cantinas, as opposed to the tourist hangouts or more exclusive lounges. Here, as an Anglo you will be asked to buy a lot of drinks, or be given the more insistent demand that you keep your wallet in your pocket. Invariably, a man with money will be generous with it, even if it is supposed to go for rent or groceries. A man without money, on the other hand, will not hide his thirst. These drinking establishments offer the male tourist an opportunity to rub elbows with some real

gentlemen, along with the reprobates and con artists. I would not recommend that women visit these establishments, even if they are escorted or intrepid. The women who frequent this type of bar are for the most part prostitutes.

When you enter, you will usually find an unadorned room and a bar that might have a trough at the base of it; the trough was formerly used as a urinal. As often as not, there will be live music played by roving two or three-piece bands, sometimes competing against each other. In Sonora, the music is typically northern *ranchero* style, which is characterised by the guitar, stand-up bass and accordion. It is not unusual for someone to spend considerably more on the music than on the bar bill, neither of which comes cheaply relative to the overall cost of living (a beer or a song cost around 50c each while the daily minimum wage is something over two dollars).

On one of my bar appearances, I got to experience the extremes of Mexican hospitality. I had walked into a cantina around noon, causing some surprise since this was not a place that saw many foreigners. A man got up and offered me his stool, ordered me a pitcher of beer, apologised that he didn't have time to join me, and left. I shared the pitcher with a couple of old men who were immediately at my shoulder. Several other men down the bar ordered me drinks and kept the bands playing non-stop. I myself was low on money and needed to change a travellers' cheque. When I excused myself for that purpose, several of the men expressed doubt that I really intended to return as promised. I got a rousing welcome when I did come back.

Later I got talking to a man about his relatives in California. He then insisted that I meet his family and join them for dinner. I reluctantly agreed, not wanting to offend him. We took a long bus ride to the outskirts of the city through some of the poorest sections. My host was becoming loud and abusive to other passengers and I knew that I had made a mistake.

We finally got off and he took me down some dirt streets until he stopped at a vacant lot. There he asked for a loan so he could get back his typewriter that was being repaired (he knew that I was a writer). He told me it would be best if I waited for him there. I gave him the money, without the least illusion about what was going on. He yelled to me that he would be right back, and I yelled to him that he needn't hurry. At least that's what I hope I said, as I started walking back towards the city.

Things to Buy

If you always wanted to buy a pair of cowboy boots and a ten-gallon hat, you'll probably find what you want in Hermosillo. The city's shops offer one of the best selections in Mexico of these and other cowboy-related paraphernalia.

Getting There & Away

Bus The Central de Autobuses at Boulevard Transversal 400 handles most of Mexico's major bus lines. Tres Estrellas de Oro (tel 3-24-16) is the principal line with 1st-class air-conditioned buses to Agua Prieta six times daily, Mexicali every hour 24 hours daily, Nogales hourly from 2.30 am to 6.30 pm and Guaymas every hour 24 hours daily.

Rail The Ferrocarril del Pacífico train stops at a terminal just off Highway 15 about 2½ km north of central Hermosillo. The train to Los Mochis and other points south departs in the evening while the northbound train departs in the morning.

AROUND HERMOSILLO

Bahía Kino – Old & New Kino

Named for Father Eusebio Kino, a Jesuit missionary who established a small mission here for Seri Indians in the late 17th century, the bay-front town of Kino is divided into old and new parts that are as different as night and day. The old quarter is a dusty, run-down fishing village, while New Kino is a winter gringo-land of trailer parks and condominiums. The twin Kinos are 120 km west of Hermosillo on Highway 16.

If you're on an tight budget, you'll have to camp out at one of the trailer parks for US$5 to US$9 per night or sleep for free under a thatched palapa (shade hut) on the New Kino beach.

You can eat cheaply, though, in the old quarter at any of several open-air restaurants that serve fresh barbecued fish. *La Palapa* restaurant is often recommended.

Buses to Kino run four times daily from Hermosillo (US$1). The last bus from Kino to Hermosillo usually leaves between 4 and 6 pm.

GUAYMAS

Population: 105,000

Founded in 1769 by the Spanish at the site of Yaqui and Guaymas Indian villages, the city of Guaymas today is a principal commercial and manufacturing centre as well as the main port of Sonora. Most of the copper, silver, gold and molybdenum (a by-product of copper used for strengthening alloys) extracted from Sonora's mines is shipped through here. A copper refinery was recently built in Guaymas which increased Mexico's daily copper-processing capacity to more than 33,000 tonnes. The city is also known for one of the largest fishing fleets in Mexico. Seafood processing plants are one of the major industries in Guaymas.

With so much commerce and industry in Guaymas, tourism isn't a priority. The main reasons to stop here are to escape from the oppressive heat of Hermosillo and get to the Bahía de San Carlos resort beaches 20 km north of Guaymas. Since the ferry from Santa Rosalía in Baja California lands here, the city is also a popular transit point. Apart from a small tree-lined plaza, however, the city itself has nothing of great appeal to travellers.

Orientation

Highway 15 becomes Boulevard García López as it passes along the northern edge of Guaymas. Downtown Guaymas and the port area are directly south of López and most easily reached by turning onto Avenida Serdán at the western end of town. Avenida Serdán is the main street; everything you'll need is on or within three blocks of this street.

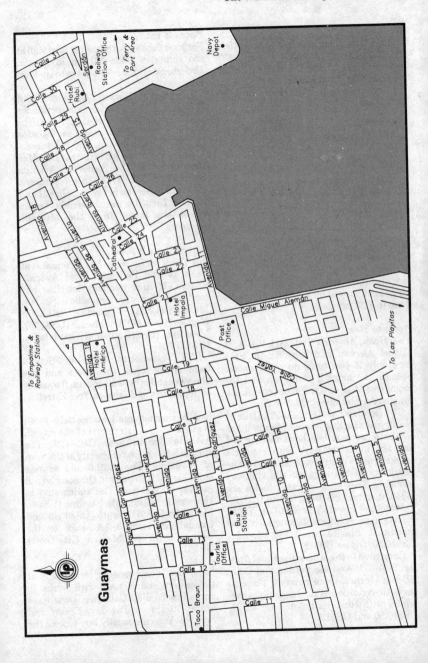

Guaymas

Information

Tourist Office There's a small tourist office (tel 2-29-32) at Avenida Serdán 437 between Calle 13 and Calle 12 with staff who can help you make arrangements for the ferry crossing to Baja. Hours are daily from 9 am to 1 pm and 3 to 6 pm.

Money There are several casas de cambio and banks along Avenida Serdán. Most of the banks are open for money exchange from 8.30 to 11.30 am.

Post The post office is on Avenida 10 just off Calle 20. Calle 20 is also known as Alemán. Hours are 8 am to 7 pm Monday to Friday and 9 am to 1 pm Saturday.

Telephone Calls The Farmacia Santa Marta at Calle 19 and Avenida Serdán has a caseta de larga distancia for making long-distance telephone calls. They'll place a call for you for US$0.40. Hours are 8 am to 8.30 pm daily.

Places to Stay

The *Hotel América* (tel 2-11-10) is at Miguel Alemán and Avenida 18. Stay here only if you have no other choice because the hotel is run-down and the rooms smell like old dark-room chemicals. Singles/doubles are US$5.25/6.25.

The *Hotel Impala* (tel 2-09-22), Calle 21 No 40 just south of Avenida Serdán, has comfortable rooms, but they are overpriced and the halls are hazy with cigarette smoke from an adjoining cantina. The parakeets in the cage on the stairway probably have lung cancer. Singles are US$9, doubles US$10.50, triples US$12.

Motel del Puerto (tel 2-34-08), Yañez 92, has clean, comfortable rooms with few amenities. Singles are US$9, doubles US$10.50, triples US$12.

Compared to the others, the *Hotel Rubi* (tel 2-01-69), Avenida Serdán and Calle 29, is a cleaner, more pleasant place to stay. Air-conditioned singles, doubles and triples with clean bathrooms are US$9, US$10.50 and US$12.

Places to Eat

For good fish tacos, try the big food stall at the corner of Calle 18 and Rodríguez. Unfortunately there's no place to sit down here.

Lonchería Tony's, Calle 20 and Rodríguez, does a big comida corrida for US$1. You can also order a la carte various Mexican specialities such as tostadas (US$0.75), refried beans and fish tacos.

Also recommended are the *Del Mar Restaurant* at the corner of Avenida Serdán and Calle 17, *Pako's Restaurant* on Avenida Serdán between Calles 21 and 22, and *Taco Braun* on Avenida Serdán across the street from the Mercado Zaragoza.

Getting There & Away

Bus The Tres Estrellas bus terminal is at Calle 14 and Rodríguez near Avenida Serdán. It runs frequent 1st-class air-conditioned buses to Hermosillo (US$1.80), Mexicali (US$11), Tijuana (US$13.50), Nogales (US$5.60), Los Mochis (US$4.75), Mazatlán (US$10.50) and Guadalajara (US$17.50).

The Transportes Norte de Sonora terminal is across the street and has almost exactly the same routes, frequency of departures and fares as Tres Estrellas.

Rail The train information office (tel 2-49-80) is at the south-eastern end of the city on Avenida Serdán near Calle 29. The station is 10 km east of the city at the town of Empalme. The southbound express stops here at 9.30 pm and the northbound express at 5.30 am. The trains stop in Hermosillo (US$1.35), Nogales (US$4), Mazatlán (US$7), Tepic (US$9.50) and Guadalajara (US$13). A single on the sleeper train to Mexico City costs US$36.

Ferry The Transbordador terminal is at the eastern end of town with ferries to Santa Rosalía, Baja California. Departures are at 10 am on Tuesday, Friday and Sunday. You can usually buy tickets the

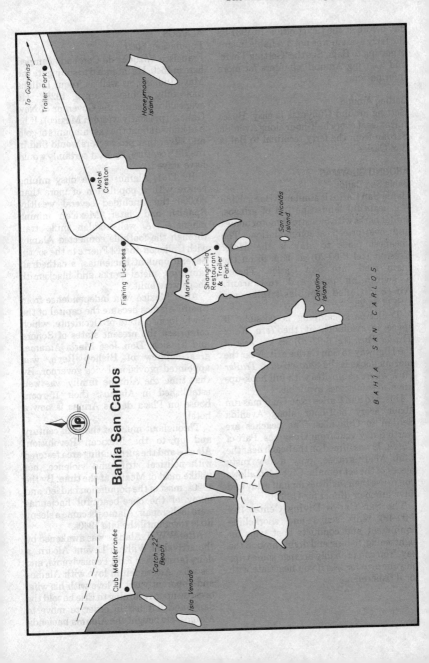

Bahía San Carlos

day before at the ticket office. In 1987-88 the ferry system was not a reliable means of getting to Baja. See the 'Getting There' and 'Getting Around' chapters for more information.

Getting Around
Getting around Guaymas is easy. Buses run at least every half-hour along Avenida Serdán from the ferry terminal to Bahía San Carlos.

AROUND GUAYMAS
Bahía San Carlos
Bahía San Carlos is similar to Bahía Kino – a beautiful landscape full of gringos, trailer parks with monstrous motor homes and over-priced accommodation. The cheapest place to stay is the *Motel Creston* (tel 6-00-20) at Km 15 on the main road into San Carlos. There's a swimming pool and restaurant. Air-conditioned doubles/triples are US$14.75/23.

Trailer-park camping is possible, if space is available, at the *Teta Kawi Trailer Park* (tel 6-02-20) 9½ km west of the Highway 15 San Carlos exit. Near the marina docks is the *Shangri-la & Trailer Park* where campsites with full hook-ups are also sometimes available.

Buses to San Carlos from Guaymas run about every half-hour along Avenida Serdán in Guaymas. The beaches are worth a day visit from Guaymas. Part of *Catch-22* was filmed on the beach near the Club Méditerranée; only a few rusty pieces of the set remain. Club Méd allows you to use their facilities for half a day and have lunch or dinner for US$18.

The San Carlos Diving Center (tel 6-00-49) rents scuba and snorkelling equipment and conducts boat trips for sightseeing, fishing and diving around the bay. You can probably arrange some trips on your own for less if you negotiate with local fishermen.

ALAMOS
Population: 5000
Francisco Vázquez de Coronado camped here in 1540. He intended to subjugate the Mayo Indians, as well as Yaqui Indians (not fully achieved until 1928). He eventually became the Governor of New Galicia (presently western Mexico). If he had known about the vast amounts of gold and silver that prospectors would find in the 18th century, he most certainly would have stayed.

By 1781, Alamos was a busy mining centre with a population of more than 30,000 that included several wealthy Spanish and, later, Mexican mining magnates. A well-trodden mule trail through the foothills connected Alamos with Culiacán and El Fuerte to the south. Several opulent haciendas, a cathedral, tanneries, metal works and blacksmith shops were built.

After Mexico won independence from Spain, Alamos became the capital of the newly formed state of Occidente, which comprised the present states of Sonora and Sinaloa. Don José María Aldama, great-nephew of Bishop Reye, was appointed provisional vice governor. By that time the Aldama family was well established in Alamos; their 15-room house on Plaza de las Armas is now a hotel.

Throughout much of the 19th century and up to the Mexican Revolution, Alamos and the surrounding area festered with political strife and violence, not unlike most of Mexico at the time. By the 1920s, most of the population had left and many of the once-beautiful haciendas were in disrepair. Alamos became a sleepy little town until the late 1940s.

After WW II, Alamos was awakened by the arrival of William Levant Alcorn, a dairy farmer from Erie, Pennsylvania, and his wife. Alcorn fell in love with Alamos and apparently out of love with his wife, because upon returning to Erie he sold the dairy and left her in order to move to Alamos. He bought the Aldama hacienda

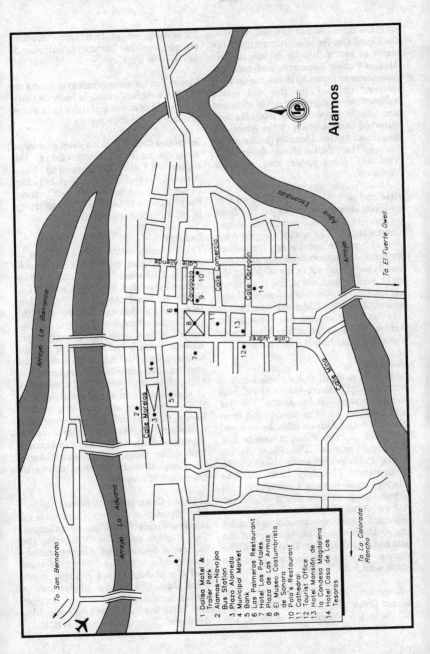

Alamos

To San Bernardo

Arroyo La Aduana

Arroyo La Barranca

Agua Escondido

Arroyo

To El Fuerte Owell

Calle Villaude

Calle Comercio

Zaragoza

Calle Obregón

Calle Juárez

Calle Morelos

Calle Mina

To La Colorada Rancho

1 Dolisa Motel &
  Trailer Park
2 Alamos-Navojoa
  Bus Station
3 Plaza Alameda
4 Municipal Market
5 Bank
6 Las Palmeras Restaurant
7 Hotel Los Portales
8 Plaza de las Armas
9 El Museo Costumbrista
  de Sonora
10 Polo's Restaurant
11 Cathedral
12 Tourist Office
13 Hotel Mansión de
   la Condesa Magdalena
14 Hotel Casa de Los
   Tesoros

on Plaza de las Armas and restored it as the Hotel Los Portales. Alcorn liked the result so much that he decided to buy Alamos's other haciendas and convince Americans to invest in them. He set up a holding company for the real estate transactions, somehow attracted investors and sold 88 properties in 1950. He also attracted the attention of the American media and was written up in the *Saturday Evening Post, Better Homes & Gardens, National Geographic* and *Arizona Highways*.

Alcorn's company and hotel are still alive and well. You can usually find him on most afternoons sitting on the front veranda of his hotel recounting stories about Alamos. The stories are grist for a steamy romance novel or spy thriller: an American father-son duo living in Alamos and flying in and out in the middle of the night loading and unloading mysterious packages, an American 'cowboy' and retired (at age 40) CIA agent who likes to ride his horse around the Plaza de las Armas, and intrigue at the Mars (as in chocolate bars) family's hacienda.

Orientation

Alamos is a small town nestled in the foothills of the Sierra Madre Occidental mountain range 53 km east of Navojoa and Highway 15. The paved road from Navojoa enters Alamos from the west end and leads to the Plaza Alameda and municipal market. The Plaza de las Armas and cathedral are two blocks south of the market. The Arroyo La Aduana (the Custom-house Stream, usually dry) runs along the town's northern edge; the Arroyo Agua Escondida (the Secret Waters Stream, also usually dry) along the southern edge. Both converge at the east end with the Arroyo La Barranca (the Ravine Stream) which runs from the north-west.

Information

Tourist Office The tourist office (tel 8-00-53) is in the Presidencia office at the Palacio Municipal. Hours are 9 am to 3 pm and 5 to 7 pm Monday to Saturday, 9 am to noon Sunday.

Money You can change money at a bank on the Plaza de las Armas. In Navojoa there are several banks along Highway 15 where you can also change money.

Telephone Calls There's a caseta de larga distancia in Polo's Restaurant at the corner of Calle Zaragoza and Calle Allende. Long-distance collect calls can be made for a small fee, but don't expect the proprietor to be thrilled about trying to get an operator for you.

Cathedral

The cathedral is the tallest building in Alamos and also one of its oldest. It dates back to 1783 when Bishop Antonio de los Reyes, appointed by King Carlos III of Spain to head the newly established Bishopric of Sonora, Sinaloa and the Californias, established himself at Alamos. According to a town legend, everyone in Alamos contributed something to the construction of the cathedral. Some of the most unusual contributions included fine china plates that were placed at the bases of the pilasters in the church tower. A three-tiered belfry was built in the tower. Inside, the altar rail, lamps, censers and candelabra were fashioned from silver. All these items were melted down in January 1866 under orders from General Ángel Martínez after he booted imperialist troops out of Alamos.

El Museo Costumbrista de Sonora

The Museum of Sonoran Customs is on the eastern side of the Plaza de las Armas. The displays and exhibits covering the history of Sonora and Alamos include photographs from the 1860s that show that the plaza has not changed much since then. Old mining implements, a sewing machine, horse-drawn carriages and 19th-century clothing are also displayed. Museum hours are erratic.

Activities

A boat ride up the Río Mayo to hot springs and a tropical jungle or treks to the summit of nearby Mt Los Frailes can be arranged through Richard Schneider, an American who lives on the north side of Plaza de las Armas. For more details write to him at PO Box 86, Alamos, Sonora 85760, Mexico; or write Aventuras Sonora, R C Leonard, PO Box 2303, Idaho Falls, Idaho 83401, USA.

Places to Stay

The *Hotel Enríquez*, on the west side of Plaza de las Armas, is in a 250-year-old building with rooms that look just as old. None of the rooms have bathrooms. Singles/doubles are US$3.25/6.25.

The *Hotel Los Portales* (tel 8-02-01), also on the west side of Plaza de las Armas, is in the beautifully restored hacienda of the Aldama family. A central courtyard surrounded by stone arches and cool, comfortable rooms with fireplaces add up to a romantic experience. Singles/doubles are US$17/25.

The *Hotel Mansión de la Condesa Magdalena* (tel 8-02-21), Calle Obregón 2 across from the Palacio de Gobierno, was built as a hacienda in 1685 for one of the region's first major mining families, the Salidos. All 13 rooms have fireplaces and stone floors. There's also a whirlpool and restaurant. Former Mexican President Miguel de la Madrid and his cabinet officers stayed here when they visited on 14 November 1986. Singles/doubles are US$25/35.

The *Hotel Casa de los Tesoros* (tel 8-00-10), Obregón 10, is a 14-room 'inn' built in the 18th century as a convent. Like the other restored buildings converted into hotels, this is an outstanding example of Spanish colonial architecture. Indian dances are presented every Saturday night. Singles/doubles are US$22.50/29.50.

The *Dolisa Motel* (tel 8-01-31), on your left just before you enter town, has clean, basic rooms with air-conditioning for US$8 to US$12.

Camping Tent and motor-home camping are possible at Alamos' two trailer parks. The *Dolisa Motel & Trailer Park* (tel 8-01-31) is on your left just before you enter the town. All of the spaces have full hook-ups and are behind the motel on a well-landscaped lot. Clean bathrooms and hot showers are available. They charge US$5 per night for two people.

The *Acosta Trailer Park* (tel 8-02-46) is just over a km east of the municipal market on a fruit farm at the edge of town. Follow the signs across town. There are 30 sites with full hook-ups, a laundry room and two swimming pools. They charge US$7 per night for two people.

Places to Eat

Some of the cheapest food can be had at the food stalls in the municipal market. The *ceviche tostada*, a seafood tostada, is cheap and filling.

For tacos try the *Taquería Blanquita* across from the Plaza Alameda at the corner of Rosales and the municipal market.

'Home cooking' is offered by *Las Palmeras Restaurant* on the north side of Plaza de las Armas from 7 am to 10 pm. This is a favourite among expatriate residents.

Polo's Restaurant, corner of Calle Zaragoza and Calle Allende just off the Plaza de las Armas, was empty each time we visited – not a good sign. Even the clean white table cloths didn't attract a clientele.

Getting There & Away

The Alamos-Navojoa bus station is on Morelos across from the Plaza Alameda. Buses depart every hour from 6.30 am to 6.30 pm for Navojoa (US$0.65).

LOS MOCHIS

Population: 130,000

The only reason to visit Los Mochis is to

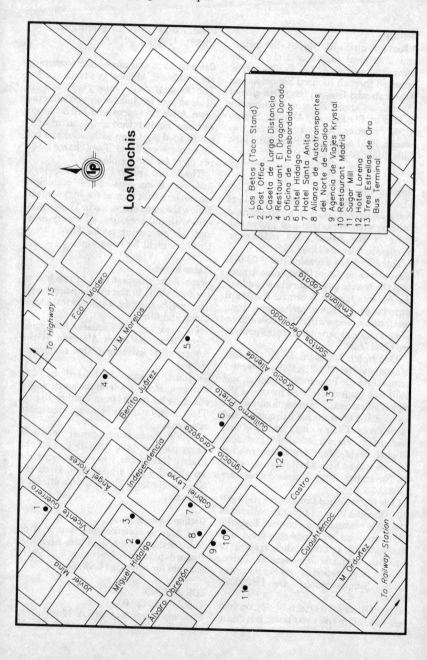

Los Mochis

1 Los Betos (Taco Stand)
2 Post Office
3 Caseta de Larga Distancia
4 Restaurant El Dragon Dorado
5 Oficina de Transbordador
6 Hotel Hidalgo
7 Hotel Santa Anita
8 Alianza de Autotransportes del Norte de Sinaloa
9 Agencia de Viajes Krystal
10 Restaurant Madrid
11 Sugar Mill
12 Hotel Lorena
13 Tres Estrellas de Oro Bus Terminal

catch a train, boat or bus to someplace else. The city traces its origins to an American engineer's 1872 visit to nearby Topolobampo Bay. The engineer, Albert Kinsey Owen, felt that this would be a perfect place to establish sugar-cane plantations, an American colony and a railroad line east to Chihuahua. His work was continued in 1893 by Benjamin Francis Johnston, an American entrepreneur who can probably be credited with officially founding the city of Los Mochis. A huge sugar mill was built by Johnston just after he arrived. The American colony, however, was never completely realised, unless you want to consider the trailer park at the edge of town, which is full of North Americans, a temporary colony. The Chihuahua al Pacífico railroad from Topolobampo through Los Mochis to the Copper Canyon and Chihuahua was completed in 1961 and instantly considered an engineering marvel.

Today, the town's economic life still revolves around sugar and railroads, but other types of commerce such as agriculture and manufacturing have become equally important.

Orientation

Los Mochis is 164 km south of Navojoa and 436 km north-west of Mazatlán in the state of Sinaloa. It's difficult to get lost in Los Mochis because, unlike the streets in many Mexican cities, the streets here don't have more than one name. Avenida Gabriel Leyva, the main street through the city, runs directly south-west from Highway 15. Central Los Mochis can be considered the area that is within two or three blocks of the intersection of Gabriel Leyva and Avenida Álvaro Obregón.

The railroad station for the Chihuahua al Pacífico, not the Ferrocarril del Pacífico that runs north-south (and vice versa), is at the south-eastern edge of Los Mochis two km from downtown. The closest railroad station for the Ferrocarril del Pacífico is 52 km north-east at Sufragio.

The Chihuahua al Pacífico also stops here, but don't count on making a connection; it's better to take a bus to Los Mochis and arrange your ticket there. For more information, see the 'Getting There & Away' section.

Information

Post The post office is on Hidalgo between Vicente Guerrero and Ángel Flores. Hours are 8 am to 6 pm Monday to Friday and 8 am to noon Saturday.

Telephone Calls A caseta de larga distancia can be found on Flores between Independencia and Hidalgo in a casa de cambio next to the Hotel Monte Carlo.

Places to Stay

Los Mochis doesn't have an overabundance of places to stay, but you shouldn't having any trouble finding a room.

The *Hotel Hidalgo* (tel 2-34-56), on Hidalgo between Guillermo Prieto and Zaragoza, is a run-down place with a lobby that's part of a family's shabby living-room. Its central location is the only reason to stay here. Air-conditioned (supposedly) singles are US$3.75, doubles US$4.60, triples US$5.60.

The *Hotel Lorena* (tel 2-02-39), Obregón 186 at the corner of Guillermo Prieto, has plain, comfortable rooms with TVs, air-conditioning, desks and old telephones. A cafeteria/restaurant on the 3rd floor is open daily from 6 to 11 am and 6 to 11 pm. Parking is available in front. Singles are US$8, doubles US$10, triples US$12.

The *Hotel Santa Anita* (tel 5-70-46), Gabriel Leyva and Hidalgo, is one of the best hotels in town and consequently one of the most expensive. Comfortable, air-conditioned singles/doubles with TVs, cable movies and telephones are US$30/48.

Camping The *Los Mochis Trailer Park* (tel 2-00-21), one km west of Highway 15, has 140 spaces with full hook-ups. There are also hot showers, a laundry room and restaurant. They charge US$7 for two per night.

Places to Eat

The *Restaurant Madrid*, at the corner of Gabriel Leyva and Álvaro Obregón, is a simple place with white table cloths and lots of credit-card decals (for show only) on the front window. A filling breakfast is US$1, pork chops US$1.50 and half a roasted chicken US$1.50. All dishes are served with tortillas and refried beans.

The best tacos in Los Mochis are at *Los Betos*, corner of Juárez and Vicente Guerrero. Another decent taco stand is *El Taquito* on Gabriel Leyva between Independencia and Hidalgo.

The *Restaurant El Dragon Dorado*, at Morelos and Zaragoza, is a Chinese restaurant with chop suey but without chopsticks. You can get a fairly good-sized meal here for under US$1.50.

Getting There & Away

Air The Los Mochis international airport is south-west of the city. Aeroméxico has daily flights to Los Mochis from Hermosillo, Mexico City and Tijuana. Aerocalifornia, a much smaller airline, has direct flights daily from La Paz (once a day), Guadalajara (twice) and Tijuana (once).

Bus Since Los Mochis is on a major transit route, every principal bus line stops here. You can catch a bus going to main destinations 24 hours daily. The Tres Estrellas de Oro (1st class) terminal is on Álvaro Obregón just east of Allende and has buses to Mazatlán (US$6.50) every hour from 6 am to 2 pm, Tepic (US$10.50) every half-hour 24 hours daily, Guadalajara (US$13.50) every half-hour 24 hours, Mexico City (US$22) every half-hour 24 hours, Morelia (US$17.60) every half-hour 24 hours, Puerto Vallarta (US$13) twice daily, Navojoa (US$2.10) every half-hour 24 hours, Guaymas (US$4.75) every half-hour 24 hours, Hermosillo (US$6.50) every half-hour 24 hours, Tijuana (US$18) every half-hour 24 hours and Nogales (US$10.25).

Rail The Chihuahua al Pacífico train runs from Los Mochis all the way to Chihuahua with stops along the way at Sufragio (also a stop for the Ferrocarril del Pacífico train) and Creel in the Copper Canyon. There are two trains – the *vista* and the *mixto* – departing daily at 6 and 7 am respectively. The first train costs more, but it's faster, cleaner, more comfortable and usually air-conditioned or heated. It affords better views of the canyon too. Vista tickets (US$8.50 to Chihuahua, US$4.60 to Creel) can be bought the day before departure at the Agencia Viajes Flamingo (tel 2-19-29), Hidalgo 419 around the corner from the Hotel Santa Anita. Otherwise, tickets can be bought at 5 am on departure day, but be prepared to elbow through a crowd to get to the station's only ticket window. Mixto tickets to Chihuahua and Creel are US$4.25 and US$2.30, a good deal only if you're ready for what might be a cold or hot (no heating or air-con), crowded trip that passes the most spectacular scenery in the canyon after sunset when it's too dark to see anything. For more information, see the 'Copper Canyon' section.

Warning: train schedules in Los Mochis that show the vista and mixto trains departing at 7 and 8 am are correct, because all schedule times are on Central Time, which is one hour ahead of Los Mochis. Schedule information for the Chihuahua al Pacífico follows:

departures	vista	mixto	
Los Mochis	7.00 am	8.00 am	(6&7am in Los Mochis)
Sufragio	7.46 am	9.11 am	
El Fuerte	8.28 am	10.04 am	
Temoris	11.12 am	1.24 pm	
San Rafael	1.17 pm	4.03 pm	
Divisadero	1.58 pm	4.46 pm	
Creel	3.20 pm	6.18 pm	
La Junta	5.41 pm	9.05 pm	

Cuauhtémoc	6.29 pm	10.15 pm
Chihuahua	8.43 pm	1.05 am

This schedule is approximate because the trains tend to run late; cargo trains en route cause delays.

The Ferrocarril del Pacífico trains stop at El Sufragio at the following times:

northbound	southbound
arr 12.10 am	arr 8.30 pm
arr 8.55 am	arr 2.10 am
dep 12.20 am	dep 9.00 pm
dep 9.30 am	dep 2.25 am

Ferry The ferry to La Paz departs from Topolobampo, 24 km south of Los Mochis, at 10 am on Monday, Thursday and Friday. Tickets can be bought the day before departure from the Oficina de Transbordador or ferry office (tel 2-00-35) in Los Mochis at Avenida Juárez 125 between Allende and Guillermo Prieto. Office hours are 8 am to 12.30 pm Monday to Friday and 8 am to 1.30 pm Saturday and Sunday.

In 1987 and 1988 the ferry system was not the most reliable way to travel between the Baja California peninsula and mainland Mexico. See the 'Getting There' chapter for more information about the system.

Getting Around

Everything in Los Mochis except the Chihuahua al Pacífico train station is within walking distance of downtown (the area around the intersection of Gabriel Leyva and Avenida Álvaro Obregón). To get to the train station, you can either take a taxi (US$2.50 even at 5 am) or bus (not possible at 5 am when you most need it) from the Café Marino on Zaragoza between Álvaro Obregón and Hidalgo. At 5 am taxis to the train station can always be found in front of the Hotel Santa Anita at the corner of Gabriel Leyva and Hidalgo.

Buses to San Blas (the Ferrocarril Pacífico train station) and Topolobampo (the ferry terminal) leave from two terminals on Álvaro Obregón between Gabriel Leyva and Ángel Flores and across from the Agencia de Viajes Krystal. Buses for Alianza de Autotransportes del Norte de Sinaloa and Transportistas del Valle del Fuerte run from each terminal.

BARRANCA DEL COBRE – THE COPPER CANYON

Scott took the Chihuahua al Pacífico 6 am (Los Mochis time) vista train to Creel:

It's 5 am and chaos reigns in the waiting room of the Los Mochis train station. An army of children is screaming, singing and dancing past me as I try to write this. How the hell can they be so awake at this cold dark hour? All I want to do is get on the train and snooze for an hour or two, but there's no train in sight yet. Only 54 minutes and 25 seconds until it's supposed to arrive. I shouldn't be counting; after all, this is Mexico, a land where no two clocks tell the same time even in the same time zone. The clock in the waiting room is broken.

Sometime later, a whistle blows and a mass of people, suitcases, shopping bags and blankets carries me through the door to the platform. I tighten the shoulder straps of my pack and ready my elbows in anticipation of heavy pushing and shoving to get on the train, but it's remarkably easy. Most of the people are waiting for the cheaper second train and the children are corralled into their own cars.

I settle into my seat, close my eyes and dream that a Mexican elf is dancing through the train offering gringos corn chips for breakfast. The train jolts and begins chugging out of the station. I open my eyes to see a bespectacled schoolgirl across from me digging into a huge crinkly bag of corn chips and noisily stuffing handfuls into her mouth. She offers me some, but it's too early for a corn-chip fix.

As the sun rises, the train passes through flat, gray farmland and gradually begins to climb through fog-shrouded hills. The land takes on the bluish-white hue of dawn until the first rays of sunlight creep over the hilltops and colour everything pale yellow. Like fingers popping up from beneath the desert, dark pillars of cacti become visible.

About three hours from Los Mochis the train passes over the harrowing Río Fuerte bridge and through the first of 88 tunnels. At the head of the car, a young woman in a spiffy skirt and shirt tells us in English that the train will pass over 38 more bridges and that the Copper Canyon is deeper than the USA's Grand Canyon. The entire line from Chihuahua to Los Mochis cost US$90 million and took almost 90 years to build.

The train cuts through small canyons and hugs the sides of cliffs as it climbs higher and higher through the mountains of the Sierra Tarahumara, a sub-range of the Sierra Madre Occidental. The trip becomes a whirlwind of dramatic geological images – sheer craggy cliffs towering above and vertical canyon walls leading to a riverbed far below. Seven hours out of Los Mochis, we stop for 15 minutes at Divisadero for the first and only true view of the Copper Canyon. Along the rest of the trip, the train runs through pine forests skirting the edge of the canyon, but not close enough to see down into it.

Unless you plan to hike into the 2300-metre-deep canyon, the viewpoint at Divisadero is the only chance you'll get to see it. This will also probably be the first time you see some of the Tarahumara Indians who inhabit the canyon. The Indians come up from the canyon to display and sell their handicrafts to visitors.

The *Posada Barranca del Cobre* hotel (Chihuahua tel 6-59-50) is also at Divisadero near the canyon rim. Double rooms with fireplaces, which you'll need in winter, are US$32, including all meals. On the return trip to Los Mochis, a group of elderly Americans who had stayed here complained vociferously that the rooms were too cold and rustic and the meals awful, barely edible. However, these same folks were used to travelling through Mexico in US$50,000 motor homes.

Although the hotel will arrange a guided tour for you into the canyon, you can hire one of the Tarahumara Indians yourself. You must have your own food for the trip; there are two restaurants, but no stores in Divisadero. For US$10 your guide will lead you down 1820 metres to the Río Urique. Carry enough water for

Tarahumara
Indians

the descent and be prepared for a change in climate from very cold – Divisadero is over 2460 metres high – to warm and humid near the river. Fall is the best time to come because flash floods and suffocatingly high temperatures are a problem in the summer.

Topographical maps of the canyon can be obtained from the Dirección General de Geografía del Territorio Nacional, San Antonio Abaz No 124, 5th floor, Mexico City, Mexico DF. The 'San Jacinto map no 6 13-1, Chihuahua' map is recommended. A general map of the Copper Canyon region can be ordered from the International Map Company, 5316 Santa Teresa, El Paso, Texas, USA. Decent topographical maps and the general map can be bought at the Tarahumara Mission Store in Creel, which is the next train stop after Divisadero.

Tarahumara Indians More than 50,000 Tarahumara Indians live in the canyons of the Sierra Tarahumara, including the Copper Canyon. Although the Tarahumara are the second largest Indian tribe north of Mexico City (the largest is the Navajo), they have also been one of the most isolated groups and have therefore been able to maintain many of their traditions.

One such tradition is the *tesquinada*, the object of which is to consume copious amounts of potent *tesquino* or corn beer. Between *tesquinadas* the Indians run non-stop through many km of rough, often vertical, terrain along the canyon sides. Many of them still live in caves, a few of which can be seen near Creel, and subsist on corn tortillas and refried beans.

Catholic missionaries have made some progress improving living conditions for the Tarahumara, but they haven't been entirely successful in converting them to Catholicism. Many of the Tarahumara attend church services, but their ancestral gods are still worshipped, particularly Raiénari, the sun god and protector of men, and Mechá, the moon god and protector of women. Sorcerers are as important as Catholic priests and are the only members of the Tarahumara permitted to consume peyote, a hallucinogen derived from a small cactus. They often take peyote in order to perform a bizarre peyote dance to cure the sick.

CREEL
It's easier to begin a trek into the canyon from Creel because, in addition to maps, you can stock up on staples and catch a bus to Batopilas, a village 140 km away deep in the heart of the canyon and Tarahumara country. Creel is also a convenient jump-off point for an all-day trip to Basaseachic Falls or Cusárare Falls or half-day hikes to nearby lakes.

Information
The Tarahumara Mission Store is open from 9.30 am to 1 pm and 3 to 6 pm. The money earned from selling Tarahumara handicrafts, photographs and books about the Indians goes back to them. The Catholic missionaries who run the store are a fount of knowledge about the Indians and the various canyons and rivers of the Copper Canyon and Sierra Tarahumara.

Money Banco Serfin on the plaza changes money from 10.30 am to noon, Monday to Friday, and charges a varying commission of 1% to 1.5% of the amount being changed.

Post The post office is on the other side of the zócalo in the Presidencia Municipal.

Telephone Calls There's a caseta de larga distancia for making long-distance telephone calls in the Hotel Nuevo, across the tracks from the train station.

Tours
Margarita's (of Casa de Margarita described below) husband, Daniel, offers several trips to the surrounding countryside, a few of which could probably be done on

your own. The following are condensed descriptions of the trips:

Recohuata Hot Springs The day trip begins with a 1½-hour truck ride and then a hike down 607 metres into the canyon to the hot springs. Daniel will only do this trip if a group wants to go.

Lago Arareco Lake Arareco is an easy seven-km hike from town along the graded dirt road to Cusárare. Hitch-hiking is also relatively easy. A few caves inhabited by Tarahumara Indians can be seen along the way. At the lake there's an old log cabin that was used as a set for the filming of a Mexican movie, *El Refugio del Lobo* (Refuge of the Wolf).

Cascada Cusárare The 30-metre-high Cusárare waterfall is 22 km south of Creel near the village of Cusárare. As you get near the town, look for a small roadside shrine and km marker on the right side of the road. Just past that is a small sign that marks the road to the 'Cascada – Waterfall Hotel'. Follow that road to the right for three km, crossing the river three or four times. When the road ends, follow the trail to the top of the waterfall. The trail winds around to the bottom of the falls. Hitch-hiking to the 'hotel' road is usually easy.

San Ignacio & Tarahumara Caves Follow Avenida Mateos south, passing the town cemetery on your left, and continue straight ahead. Caves will appear on both sides of the road before you eventually arrive at the small village of San Ignacio, where there's a 400-year-old mission church.

Valley of the Monks The valley is nine km away and considered a day trip by horse. Ask Daniel about hiring a horse.

Río Urique They claim that this can be done in a day, but on the map it looks longer because it flows along the bottom of the Copper Canyon.

Río Oteros This is considered a day hike; ask before you go.

These and other tours can also be arranged by the Hotel Nuevo and the Motel Parador (tel 75) on Mateos about five blocks from the zócalo. The Parador

offers all-day tours to Basaseachic Falls, 140 km north-west of town, and a general tour of the Copper Canyon. The waters of Basaseachic fall 245 metres, the second highest drop in the world (the first is Ángel Falls in Venezuela), and are worth the bumpy four-hour drive and 1½-hour hike from Creel. Arranging a car and guide on your own will cost US$42 for four people.

One of the best books written about the Copper Canyon trails is Rick Fisher's *National Parks of Northwest Mexico, Volume II*, available for US$11.95 (including postage) from Sunracer Publications, PO Box 40092, Tucson, Arizona 85717, USA.

The village of Batopilas, 140 km south of Creel deep in the heart of the canyon country, is a great starting point for treks into the canyons. There are a few small hotels and guest houses where you can rent rooms, including the hotels *Batopilas, Samachique, Napuchi* and *Parador*.

Places to Stay

At an elevation of 2338 metres, Creel can be cold, even snowy, especially in the winter. Warm rooms are available in town at a few hotels and guest houses.

One of the homiest places to stay is the *Casa de Margarita*, Mateos 11, in a small house on the corner of the zócalo. Margarita's young son usually meets the train each evening to snare any backpackers who need a place to stay and, in the two minutes it takes to walk to his house, to try talking them into hiring horses the next day. Four double rooms in the house and three small 'cabins' at the back are rented out for US$3.50 to US$4 per person, including breakfast and dinner. Both meals are shared with the family and a cast of characters from around the world. While I was there, the cast included a middle-aged woman who had been there for eight months 'resting', a bee farmer from Kansas, a cocky cockney traveller who had just come from southern California where he raised travel money by selling a detergent called 'Sensations' door-to-door, and a British couple who had been travelling for two years. Write to Margarita Quintero de González, Avenida López Mateos y Parroquia 11, Codigo Postal 33200, Creel, Chihuahua, Mexico.

The *Hotel Korachi* has clean log cabin-style rooms with wood stoves and hot-water showers. It's on an unmarked street across from the train station, so ask people to show you the way. Singles are US$2.60 to US$5.20; doubles are US$4.25 to US$8.50.

The *Motel Parador de la Montaña* (Chihuahua tel 15-54-08, 12-20-62) is a favourite with tour groups. It has very comfortable singles US$18.75, doubles US$23.65, triples US$27 with TVs and hot showers. If you want meals included, then rates are US$37.50 single, US$58.50 double, US$79.25.

The *Hotel Nuevo*, across from the train station, has clean, comfortable rooms. Some of them have wood-burning stoves, others have chimneys. Singles/doubles are US$10.50/21.

The cheapest place in town is the *Hotel Ejidal* with cold, basic rooms facing the train tracks next to the Chihuahua bus office. In each room a ceramic bowl and water jug are the only source of water; a bare light bulb hangs from the ceiling. Second-floor rooms are US$1, 1st-floor US$1.60.

Places to Eat

Creel doesn't have many restaurants. *Restaurant Mary* is one of the few that serves passable food – two enchiladas, refried beans and salad for US$0.40.

There are two grocery stores on Mateos where you can buy fruit, vegetables and a few other staples. For some reason, peanuts are available in abundance.

Getting There & Away

Bus There are daily buses from Creel to Chihuahua (US$3.25, five hours) via San Juanito, La Junta and Cuauhtémoc at 7 am, 10 am, 1 pm and 4 pm; the trip takes four hours. The ticket office and departure point is on the other side of the train tracks across from the zócalo.

Buses to Batopilas (US$3.75, seven to 10 hours) leave on Tuesday, Thursday and Saturday at 7 am. The bus departs from a shop one block from the Chihuahua bus office on the second street from the train tracks. There's always a broken-down red-and-white bus in front of the shop. Tickets are sold until 8 pm. The return bus from Batopilas to Creel departs at 4 am on Monday, Wednesday and Friday.

Rail The train schedule from Los Mochis to Chihuahua is the same as in the Los Mochis 'Getting There & Away' section. From Chihuahua to Los Mochis, the schedule is as follows:

departures	vista	mixto
Chihuahua	7.00 am	7.20 am
Cuauhtémoc	9.13 am	10.41 am
La Junta	10.05 am	12.00 pm
Creel	12.16 pm	2.47 pm
Divisadero	1.58 pm	4.35 pm
San Rafael	2.30 pm	5.15 pm
Temoris	4.24 pm	7.32 pm
El Fuerte	7.08 pm	10.48 pm
Sufragio	7.51 pm	11.42 pm
Los Mochis	8.38 pm	12.49 am

Even though El Fuerte, Sufragio and Los Mochis are on Mountain Time, which is one hour behind Central Time, the schedule times above are on Central Time.

If you take the vista train from Los Mochis rather than from Chihuahua, you will probably stand a better chance of seeing the dramatic scenery that has made this trip world famous. The trains are almost always late, so pray that the inevitable delays occur after, not before, you've seen some of the best parts of the landscape. The trains from Chihuahua seem to run late more often and by more hours than the ones from Los Mochis.

Cuauhtémoc

The only point of interest between Creel and Chihuahua is the town of Cuauhtémoc, home to a community of Mennonites. The community dates from 1921 when a group of Mennonites left Canada in protest at government restrictions and bought 92,000 hectares of land around present-day Cuauhtémoc. They have built a prosperous community and managed to maintain their isolation from much of the rest of the world.

MAZATLÁN

Population: 260,000

Mazatlán ('Mah-zaht-LAHN'), a beach resort, is also a port and shrimp-packing city. The Spanish began using the area as a port in 1531 to send off galleons full of Sierra Madre gold. They were the ones who named it Mazatlán, which means 'place of the deer'. Today the only deer in sight are plastered on billboards advertising tobacco. Nor are there any signs of the long-standing Spanish presence here, even in 'old' Mazatlán.

Orientation

Old Mazatlán is concentrated on a wide peninsula at the southern end of the city bounded on the west by the Pacific Ocean and on the east by the Bahía Dársena. Highways 15 and 40 merge before they enter the city from the east and south-east and become Calzada Gabriel Leyva just after passing the train station. If you wish to avoid old Mazatlán, then you can turn right on Calzada Gutiérrez Najera and right again on Avenida Ejército Mexicano (Avenida Juan Carrasco) and follow that north to new Mazatlán or out of the city.

Just after Calzada Gabriel Leyva passes the marina on the left, Avenida del Puerto forks off to the south and continues along the edge of the peninsula, passing shrimp-packing plants, launches to Isla de la Piedra (Stone Island, which is to the south in the Bahía Dársena), cruise-ship docks and the ferry terminal and going right to the lighthouse at the tip. After the terminal, Avenida del Puerto curves around to the Pacific Ocean side of the peninsula and runs along the coast passing two *miradores* (lookout points) and briefly becoming Paseo Centenario. It changes name again to Paseo Olas Altas as it curves around a small cove that was once *the* resort centre of Mazatlán.

Calle Ángel Flores cuts across the peninsula from Olas Altas north-eastward through downtown Mazatlán and almost all the way to the cruise-ship docks on the other side. It passes old Mazatlán's two principal plazas – Plaza Hidalgo and Plaza de la República (also called the zócalo) – and intersects the streets that comprise the city's principal business district. Almost everything of interest to travellers, including budget hotels, can be found from Ángel Flores north/north-westward towards Paseo Claussen (the continuation of Paseo Olas Altas) and Avenida del Mar (continuation of Claussen).

Paseo Olas Altas becomes Paseo Claussen as it passes Calle Ángel Flores and the Cerro de la Nevería (Ice Cream Parlour Hill). It curves around the hill and skirts the edge of Bahía Puerto Viejo and the beginning of Mazatlán's long beach Playa del Norte (North Beach). Somewhere along the way, Paseo Claussen becomes Avenida del Mar, which continues for seven km, becoming the principal street for new Mazatlán or the 'Golden Zone'.

The Golden Zone is a long stretch of resort hotels and time-share condominiums that begins just after the traffic circle junction for Highway 15 (alternate route) across from the Hotel Los Sábalos. Avenida del Mar splits into two streets and changes names to Avenida Camarón-Sábalo (the inland branch) and R T Loaiza (the coastal branch, more commonly known just as Playa Las Gaviotas). This area is rapidly expanding westward (not northward, although that's what you may think), covering the last

Top: Weaver, Puerto Vallarta (SW)
Left: Taxco (SW)
Right: El Templo del Carmen (TW)

Top: Children's Party Shop, Tepoztlán (JL)
Left: Guanajuato (JL)
Right: Bird Seller, Puebla (JN)

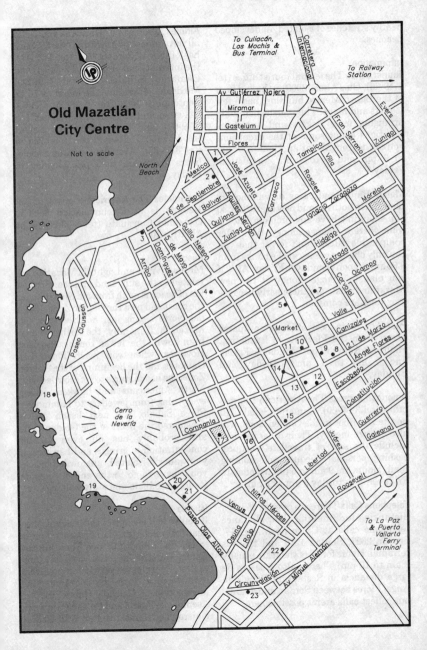

Old Mazatlán City Centre

Not to scale

To Culiacán, Los Mochis & Bus Terminal

To Railway Station

Carretera Internacional

Av Gutiérrez Najera

North Beach

Cerro de la Nevería

Paseo Claussen

Paseo Olas Altas

To La Paz & Puerto Vallarta Ferry Terminal

Market

Miramar
Gastelum
Flores

Mexico
José Azueta
16 de Septiembre
Bolivar
Anjules Velarde
Quijano
Zuniga Vel
Guillo Nelson
5 de Mayo
Dominguez
Arribo

Tampico
Fran Serrano
Villa
Zuniga
Evers
Rosales
Carrasco
Ignacio Zaragoza
Morelos
Hidalgo
Estrada
Ocampo
Canizales
Corona
Valle
21 de Marzo
Ángel Flores
Escobedo
Constitución
Guerrero
Galeana
Juárez
Libertad
Roosevelt

Compañia

Niños Héroes
Venus
Osuna
Rojo
Circunvalación
Av Miguel Alemán

nearby stretches of isolated, undeveloped beaches.

Information

Tourist Office The federal tourist office (tel 1-49-66), Olas Altas 13000 on the 2nd floor of the Banco México building, has a few leaflets and maps. They can be helpful in arranging ferry tickets and answering questions about some of the excursions you can do from Mazatlán. Hours are 8 am to 3 pm and 5 to 7 pm Monday to Friday.

Money Banks and casas de cambio are plentiful in both old and new Mazatlán, so you shouldn't have any problem finding somewhere to change money. Both offer comparable rates. Don't forget that you can only change money at the banks from 8.30 am to noon Monday to Friday. Also, if you plan to change money at the new Mazatlán banks, get there early because long lines are common.

Post The main post office is on Juárez across from the Plaza de la República. Hours are 8 am to 7 pm Monday to Friday and 9 am to 1 pm Saturday and Sunday.

American Express The American Express office (tel 3-06-00), Camarón Sábalo 310 on the 2nd floor in the Golden Zone, will also change money. Their other services include the sale of travellers' cheques, cashing personal cheques and holding mail. Hours are 9 am to 6 pm Monday to Friday and Saturday 9 am to 1 pm.

Telephone Calls There are casetas de larga distancia for making long-distance telephone calls at Cinco de Mayo 117, Serdán 2627, Serdán 1510 and the bus terminal. Hours for all of them are usually 9 am to 10 pm. There's also a caseta de larga distancia in Restaurant Bony's on Ángel Flores between Serdán and Juárez, but collect calls aren't possible here.

Airlines Aeroméxico, Mexicana and Delta all have offices in Mazatlán. Aeroméxico has offices at Serdán 2511 (tel 1-25-14), the international airport (tel 2-34-44) and Camarón Sábalo 310 (tel 4-16-21). Mexicana offices may be found at 16 de Septiembre 443 (tel 1-30-95), Paseo Claussen and Belisario Domínguez (tel 2-79-69), and the international airport (tel 2-57-67). Delta is at the Hotel El Cid (tel 3-54-55), Avenida Camarón-Sábalo; hours are 9 am to 6 pm Monday to Friday.

Consulates The American Consulate (tel 1-29-05) is at Circunvalación 6. The Canadian Consulate (tel 3-73-20) is at Albatros 705.

Beaches

Most activities and sights in Mazatlán are related to the sun, sand and sea. Sixteen km of beach stretch from old Mazatlán up the coast and past the Golden Zone. Playa del Norte begins just north-west of old Mazatlán. Generally, the farther you go from town, the fewer the beach-goers. However, when you reach Playa Las Gaviotas and the beginning of the Golden Zone, the beach starts to get crowded with North Americans and hawkers selling everything from jewellery to hammocks. Playa Sábalo, the next beach up, is considered the heart of the Golden Zone and probably has an even greater concentration of gringos and hawkers. If you want an isolated, uncrowded beach, you'll have to go to the end of Avenida Camarón-Sábalo and start walking.

Islands

If you've had enough of the beaches, then head for one of Mazatlán's islands. Jaunts to Isla de la Piedra (Stone Island) in the Bahía Dársena are the cheapest and easiest. Boats leave every 15 minutes from 6 am to 6 pm from the docks near the intersection of Calzada Gabriel Leyva, Avenida del Puerto and Calzada Gutiérrez Najera. The round-trip fare is US$0.35.

Harbour cruises on the *Yate Fiesta* are offered nearby at the yacht office. Two three-hour cruises are offered daily for US$3 per person.

Trips to Isla Chivas, one of three islands facing the Golden Zone (the other two are Venados and Pájaros), can be arranged from the Aqua Sports shop at the Hotel El Cid on Playa Sábalo. The diving and snorkelling around the island are reputedly some of the best in the area. Equipment can be rented from Aqua Sports. Boats leave the beach every two hours from 9 am to 7 pm; round-trip fare is US$0.50.

Acuario Mazatlán

Mazatlán also harbours a land-locked attraction – though still related to the sea. The Mazatlán Aquarium is on Avenida de los Deportes, just north of the Sands Hotel and about a block from Playa Norte. They claim to have over 200 kinds of fish, including piranhas and marlins, in 51 tanks. Hours are 8 am to 8 pm daily. Admission is US$0.45.

High Divers

When the weather permits, there are high divers in Mazatlán similar to Acapulco's famous La Quebrada high divers. The divers' towers are near the lookout point at the base of the Cerro de la Nevería. The divers perform daily year-round from 9.30 to 11 am and 3.30 to 6 pm.

Places to Stay – bottom end

Most of Mazatlán's bottom-end accommodation is concentrated near the Plaza de la República and the intersection of Serdán and Avenida del Mar.

The *Hotel del Centro* (tel 1-26-73), J M Canizales 18, has several clean, basic singles, doubles and triples with fans for US$6.25, US$7.60 and US$8.75. It's near the cathedral and the corner of Juárez and Canizales.

The *Hotel Milan* (tel 1-35-88), J M Canizales 10, has clean, air-conditioned rooms with telephones and shower/bath combinations. Potted plants and rocking chairs grace the hallways. Singles/doubles are US$5.80/6.75.

The *Hotel Beltran* (tel 2-27-76), Serdán 819, has simple, dormitory-like rooms with fans and hot showers. Singles cost US$4.25, doubles US$5.75, triples US$6.25.

The *Hotel México* (tel 1-38-06), Serdán and México across from the Beltran, is the place to stay only as a last resort. The walls are cracking and full of holes that probably date from the Mexican Revolution. In fact, you could easily imagine Pancho Villa's men staying here. Singles/doubles are US$3/3.75.

The *Hotel San Jorge* (tel 1-36-95), Serdán 2710 across from the beach, has a sign painted on the front window advertising 'absolutely clean' rooms. The 2nd-floor rooms are pink, clean and cheery, but the walls are smudged with a mysterious substance. Singles/doubles are US$4.75/9.25.

The *Hotel Vialta* (tel 1-60-27), Azueta 100, has big, dusty rooms that surround a simple courtyard. They charge US$4.25 per room for any number of people.

The front-desk manager at the *Hotel Morales* (tel 1-31-38), Azueta 145, was very suspicious when we asked for their room prices. She said that they have 'many prices', including singles for US$3.75.

The *Hotel Emperador* (tel 1-24-34), Río Panuco across from the bus terminal, is not the best place to stay – hard beds, clean basic rooms, drab halls and dirty stairs. Singles/doubles are US$4.75/6.

Camping This is possible at any of the trailer parks in the Golden Zone, but expect to pay extortionate rates – US$6 to US$10 per night. These rates aren't too different from those at most trailer parks in Mexico, but the conditions here are much worse. The parks are often packed with motor homes and portable satellite dishes. Since most of the motor homes have their own bathrooms and showers, the park owners rarely, if ever, clean or repair the park's facilities. If you insist on

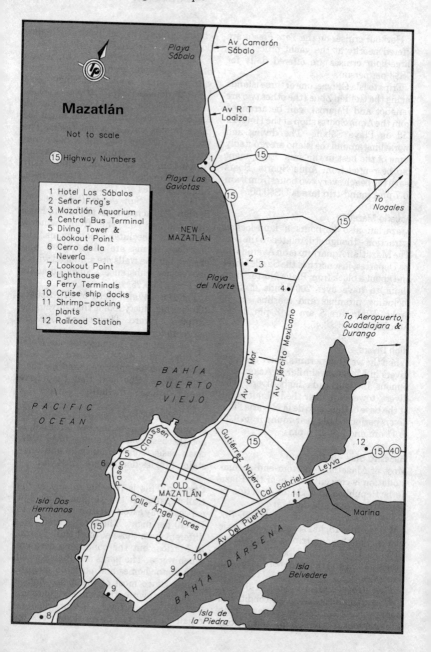

Mazatlán

Not to scale

(15) Highway Numbers

1 Hotel Los Sábalos
2 Señor Frog's
3 Mazatlán Aquarium
4 Central Bus Terminal
5 Diving Tower & Lookout Point
6 Cerro de la Nevería
7 Lookout Point
8 Lighthouse
9 Ferry Terminals
10 Cruise ship docks
11 Shrimp–packing plants
12 Railroad Station

Playa Sábalo

Av Camarón Sábalo

Av R T Loaiza

Playa Las Gaviotas

To Nogales

NEW MAZATLÁN

Playa del Norte

Av del Mar

Av Ejército Mexicano

To Aeropuerto, Guadalajara & Durango

BAHÍA PUERTO VIEJO

PACIFIC OCEAN

Isla Dos Hermanos

Claussen

Paseo

Gutiérrez Nájera

OLD MAZATLÁN

Cal Gabriel Leyva

Marina

Calle Ángel Flores

Av Del Puerto

BAHÍA DÁRSENA

Isla Belvedere

Isla de la Piedra

1	Hotel México
2	Hotel Beltran
3	Mexicana Office
4	Parque Zaragoza
5	Restaurant Hostería De Los Arcos
6	Hotels Vialta & Victoria
7	Casa Familiar Aurora
8	Hotel San Lorenzo
9	Long Distance Telephone Office
10	Hotel Milan
11	Hotel Del Centro
12	Restaurant Bony's
13	Post Office
14	Cathedral & Plaza De La República
15	Restaurant Dony
16	Railway Ticket & Booking Office
17	Plaza Hidalgo
18	Tourist Office
19	High Divers of Mazatlán
20	Federal Tourist Office
21	El Shrimp Bucket
22	Immigration
23	US Consulate

camping, go to the end of Avenida Camarón-Sábalo and find an isolated beach to sleep on.

Places to Stay - middle

Marco's Suites (tel 3-59-98), Avenida del Mar 1234 about halfway between new and old Mazatlán, is a great deal for this price range. Its Icelandic owners, the Arnasons, keep the place super-clean; they live in one of the suites. The suites can accommodate two to four persons and most of them have ocean views and fully-equipped kitchens. They charge US$24 per night for each suite.

The *Hotel Belmar* (tel 1-42-99), Paseo Olas Altas 166, is a big hotel with a labyrinth of halls leading from a reception area covered with blue tiles to old and new wings. Both old and new rooms are clean, large and usually air-conditioned with TVs, hot showers and, in some, views of the ocean. The older rooms are furnished with antique dressers and four-poster beds. New-wing rooms: Singles/doubles near the swimming pool are US$12.50/

14.60; singles/doubles with ocean views are US$14.60/17. Old-wing rooms: singles/doubles without views are US$10.50/12.50; with ocean views US$12.50/14.60.

The *Hotel Siesta* (tel 1-26-40), Paseo Olas Altas 11, is above El Shrimp Bucket restaurant with most of the rooms overlooking a courtyard full of tropical plants and the Bucket's tables. Everything is painted a different shade of green, which amplifies the tropical atmosphere. Singles cost US$15.45, doubles US$19, triples US$23.

Places to Stay - top end

Mazatlán is full of top-end places to stay with rates ranging from US$22/24 for singles/doubles at the *Sands Hotel* (Avenida del Mar, tel 2-00-00) to US$70/75 for singles/doubles at the *Camino Real* (Playa Sábalo, tel 3-11-11).

If you plan to stay in a top-end hotel and want as much as possible for your money, sign up for one of the many package deals offered in Sunday newspaper travel sections in the USA. Most travel agents should also be able to help you. The packages often include 25 to 45% discounts on room rates, a rented car and airport transfers.

Places to Eat

The restaurant attached to the *Hotel del Centro*, J M Canizales 18, serves a decent meal that includes a filet of fish, beans and rice for US$2.

The *Restaurant Hostería de Los Arcos*, on Serdán between Ocampo and Estrada just past the municipal market, serves typical Mexican fare; a full meal costs under US$2. It's popular with Mexican families.

Fresh fish, shrimp and squid can be bought from the street market at the corner of Serdán and Quijano.

The *Restaurant La Faena*, Avenida del Mar and Río Tamazula facing the ocean, is a good place to have an octopus cocktail (US$2) and people-watch. They serve eight types of shrimp dishes (US$6.80) and various fish filets (US$3.75).

Larana Sonriente Restaurant & Bar has been recommended for its variety of seafood cocktails: octopus, seafood mix, shrimp, smashed marlin, garlic octopus and turtle. Unfortunately, we weren't able to find it; try looking on Avenida del Mar near Restaurant La Faena.

Avenida Cafetería & Nevería, Avenida del Mar 880 next to Señor Frog's, is a big sidewalk café renowned for its coffees and freshly squeezed juices.

Señor Frog's, Avenida del Mar next to the Avenida Cafetería & Nevería, is a Mazatlán landmark that's almost always packed to the gills with Americans. They advertise 'lousy food and warm beer', but actually the food is good (just overpriced) and the beer only warm when they can't cool the bottles fast enough to keep up with demand.

El Shrimp Bucket, Paseo Olas Altas 11, is another Mazatlán landmark that's popular with gringos. Founded in 1962, this is the first of 50 El Shrimp Bucket bars and grills established in the USA, Mexico, Spain and South America. The shrimp bucket is their speciality and not cheap – US$11, which would be a bargain in the USA considering the incredible shrimp feast in the bucket. Other dishes include a seafood platter (US$8.75), shrimp cocktail (US$3.50) and Mexican combo platter (US$3).

Entertainment

Mazatlán is full of discos, most of which are in the Golden Zone. Often recommended are *El Caracol* at the Hotel El Cid, the *Tango Palace, Frankie Oh!* and *Oh Baby!*.

Getting There & Away

Air Delta Airlines offers a direct round-trip flight between Mazatlán and Los Angeles daily for US$216 to US$280. Aeroméxico and Mexicana have direct daily flights to Mazatlán from Los Angeles and several Mexican cities including Tijuana, La Paz, Guadalajara and Mexico City.

Bus The central bus terminal is just off Avenida Ejército Mexicano (also known as Avenida Juan Carrasco) and the corner of Avenida de los Deportes about three blocks inland from Playa Norte. Tres Estrellas de Oro (1st class) has frequent departures to many major cities, including Mexico City (US$15.25, 18 hours) five times daily, Guadalajara (US$7, nine hours) twice, Tijuana (US$25, 26 hours) twice, Nogales (US$16.75, 18 hours) and most major points in between twice, Tepic (US$4, four hours) every hour and Puerto Vallarta (US$7, eight hours) twice.

Transportes del Pacífico (2nd class) has more frequent departures to the same cities for less money.

To get into downtown Mazatlán from the bus terminal, go to Avenida Ejército Mexicano and catch a 'Playa Azul' bus going to your right if the bus terminal is behind you. This bus stops in downtown Mazatlán near the municipal market and continues on to the ferry terminal and the lighthouse. The 'Villa Galaxia' bus also goes to the market, but that's as far as it goes.

Rail The train station is at the eastern end where Highways 15 and 40 enter the city. The 'Cerritos-Juárez' and the 'Insurgentes' buses shuttle between the station and downtown. The Ferrocarril del Pacífico trains make daily stops in Mazatlán, northbound at 6.40 pm and southbound at 8.20 am.

Average 1st-class fares for the following destinations are: Guadalajara US$5.75, Mexico City US$8, Hermosillo US$17, Nogales US$11 and Mexicali US$15. Sleeping berths in Pullman cars are available on north and southbound trains for about double the above fares.

Tickets can be bought at the train office in the Hotel Hacienda (tel 2-70-00), Avenida del Mar and Calle Flamingos.

Ferry There are daily ferries between Mazatlán and La Paz, Baja California. The ferry departs at 5 pm from a dock at the southern end of town (see map); the trip averages 17 hours. Hard plastic seats (bolted-down salon seats) and cabins are supposed to be available. For a full description of the salon section and types of cabins available, see the 'Getting There & Away' chapter.

Reservations are necessary for the cabins, but these are practically impossible during holidays, especially Semana Santa (Easter Week) and Carnaval (Mardi Gras). Call the ferry office to make reservations as soon as you arrive in town (tel 1-70-20 to 21). The office is open from 8 am to 3 pm Monday to Friday. Cancellations are sometimes available on the day of departure. Get to the office very early, some recommend 5 am, if you plan to buy your ticket on the day of departure.

Salon seats cost US$2 and cabins (per person) US$4.35 (four-person cabin), US$9.50 (four-person, bathroom and shower in room), and US$18.75 (two-person deluxe suite).

Ferries from La Paz arrive at about 10 am.

The 'Playa Azul' bus runs to the ferry terminal from downtown Mazatlán and Avenida Ejército Mexicano (Avenida Juan Carrasco) almost every 10 minutes from 6 am to 8 pm.

Getting Around
Airport Transport The Mazatlán international airport is 30 km south of the city. There are no buses; you have to take a taxi for US$2.75 from downtown or US$3.25 from the Golden Zone.

Bus The 'Sábalo' bus runs from the municipal market to the beach via Juárez and then continues along Avenida del Mar all the way to the Golden Zone.

The 'Playa Sur' bus runs along Avenida Ejército Mexicano (Avenida Juan Carrasco) near the central bus terminal and through the city to the municipal market and the ferry terminal.

The 'Villa Galaxia' bus follows the same route as the Playa Sur bus, but doesn't continue past the market.

The 'Insurgentes' bus also runs near the bus terminal and through the city to the market, but continues on to the train station.

Pulmonía After buses, *pulmonías* are the cheapest way to get around the city, particularly along the coast from the Golden Zone to Playa Olas Altas. Although *pulmonía* means 'pneumonia', here it means 'golf cart'. You can flag one down almost anywhere along the Mazatlán coast. From the Golden Coast to Serdán costs US$0.50.

Taxi Taxis are the most expensive way to get around, but they're also the easiest way. Set the price before getting in; expect to pay US$2 to go from old Mazatlán to the Golden Zone.

TEPIC
Tepic, capital of the state of Nayarit, has nothing of interest for travellers except a bus terminal and train station. If you have to stop here, catch the next bus or train as soon as possible to Mazatlán, 278 km away, five hours by bus, US$2.75; Puerto Vallarta, 169 km, three hours by bus, US$1.85; Guadalajara, 127 km, five hours by bus because it stops at every small town and village en route; or San Blas, 70 km, approximately one hour, US$0.70.

Norte de Sonora buses to San Blas depart at 6 am, 9 am, 2.15 pm, 4.30 pm, 5.30 pm and 6.30 pm.

Southbound Ferrocarril del Pacífico trains stop here at 11.15 am and 1.45 pm and arrive in Guadalajara at 5.10 and 7 pm. Northbound trains stop in Tepic at 2.05 and 6.30 pm and arrive in Mazatlán at 6.45 pm and 1 am.

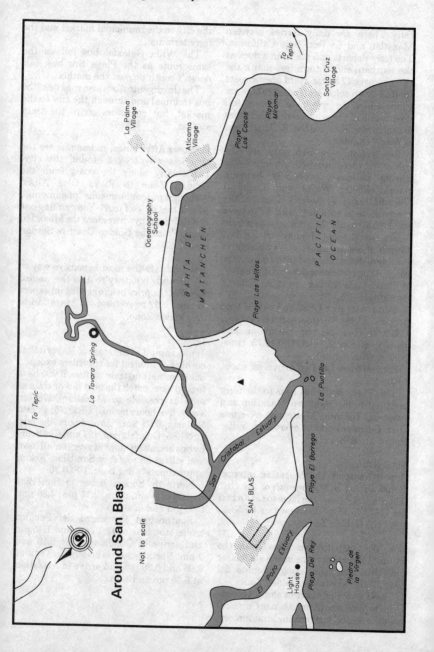

Around San Blas

Not to scale

SAN BLAS

Population: 6000

The small fishing village of San Blas, 70 km north-west of Tepic, was an important Spanish port from the late 16th to the 19th centuries. The Spanish built a fortress here to protect their *naos* (trading galleons) from marauding British and French pirates. Today's visitors come to enjoy a paradise that may seem too good to be true, with isolated beaches, exotic colourful birds, a thick tropical jungle where mango and papaya are plentiful, navigable rivers and an estuary.

The village has been discovered by travellers and has the amenities of a small beach resort town – a few hotels, restaurants, grocery stores, etc. Fortunately, however, it is far enough off the beaten track to have the broken cobblestone streets, muddy potholes and small shops of a wild frontier town.

I suspect, though, that the real reason the village hasn't been developed as a major resort is due to the proliferation of *jejenes* (nicknamed 'no-see-ums' because they're difficult to see) at dusk and dawn. No-see-ums are tiny fly-like creatures with huge appetites for human flesh that aren't deterred from attack by normal window screens or weak insect repellents. These guys slip through all but the finest mesh screening, have their fill and leave you with an indomitable itch.

Orientation

San Blas sits on a tongue of land bounded on the west/south-west by El Pozo Estuary, on the east by the San Cristóbal Estuary, and on the south by Playa El Borrego and the Pacific Ocean. The only road into and out of the village is the 36-km paved road to Highway 15 and onward to Tepic. Just west of the bridge over the San Cristóbal Estuary, the road passes the Cerro de la Contaduría and the ruins of the old Spanish fortress. At the Pemex station, the road splits into three branches with the centre one, Juárez, becoming the main street and leading to the village's small zócalo. Calle Batallón de San Blas runs along the western side of the zócalo and leads south to the beach; this could be considered the village's other main street. From the zócalo, everything in the village is within walking distance.

Information

Tourist Office There's a small tourist office Palacio Municipal on the east side of the zócalo, but it isn't very helpful. You would be better off trying to get your travel questions answered at one of the hotels, such as the Hotel Las Brisas.

Money The only place in town to change money is the Banco Nacional de México on Juárez about a block east of the zócalo. You can change money only from 8.30 to 9.30 am.

Post The post office is on Michoacán near the south-west corner of the zócalo. Hours are 9 am to 1 pm and 3 to 7 pm Monday to Friday, 9 am to 1 pm Saturday.

Telephone Calls The small shop and newsstand on the south side of the zócalo doubles as a caseta de larga distancia with two lines for making long-distance telephone calls. Be patient because it could take more than an hour to reach an operator.

Festivals

Father José María Mercado Every year on 31 January the anniversary of the death of Father José María Mercado is commemorated with a parade, a demonstration march by Mexican marines and fireworks in the zócalo. Mercado lived in San Blas in the early 19th century and helped Miguel Hidalgo with the independence movement by sending him a set of old Spanish cannons from the village.

San Blas Day 3 February is mainly an extension of the festivities begun on 31 January. Dance and musical presentations are also featured.

Beaches

San Blas's best attractions are its natural wonders – the beaches and jungles. The nearest beach is Playa El Borrego at the end of Calle Batallón de San Blas.

The best beaches are south-east of the village around the Bahía de Metanchén, starting with Playa Las Islitas seven km away. A paved road that veers south from the road to Highway 15 passes the dirt road to Playa Las Islitas and continues past an Oceanography School and through the village of Aticama eight km from Playa Las Islitas. Between Playa Las Islitas and Aticama the beach is wonderfully isolated and popular with surfers who claim that the world's longest wave sweeps ashore here. After Aticama, Playa Los Cocos and Playa Miramar have palapas (shade huts) under which you can lounge and drink from a coconut. You can either walk or take a taxi from San Blas to Playa Las Islitas for US$2 one way. There's also a bus three times daily from San Blas to the village of Santa Cruz, just past Playa Miramar.

Jungle Boat Ride

A maximum of six passengers hop in a boat at the Embarcadero a la Tovara, to your left as you cross the bridge into town. The guide steers the boat into the San Cristóbal Estuary and up a river to the freshwater spring of La Tovara. A jungle full of exotic birds and lush, tropical plants and trees surrounds you. Bring your bathing suit because you can swim at La Tovara. The ride costs US$13.25 per boatload; the price is set by the tourist office.

Places to Stay

Considering its small size, San Blas has a fair selection of places to stay. Look at the room before you accept it and be sure that the window screens are without holes or tears.

The *Hotel Las Brisas* (tel 5-01-12), Cuauhtémoc 106, has 32 large rooms with fans and a suite with a full kitchen.

There's a great restaurant, swimming pool and yard full of exotic birds. You can buy ice, soft drinks, snacks and postcards in the reception area. The staff speak English and are extremely helpful. Singles/doubles are US$13.60/18.

Across from the Hotel Las Brisas is the *Hotel Posada Casa Morales* (tel 5-00-23), Cuauhtémoc 197, with clean rooms with fans and good window screens (very important). Some rooms have ocean views. The hotel has a restaurant and bar. Singles are US$8, doubles US$10.50, triples US$13.

The *Hotel Posada del Rey* (tel 5-01-23), corner of Campeche and a short nameless alley (see map), is a simple, relatively modern place with a small swimming pool. Clean rooms have fans and hot-water showers. Singles cost US$4.25, doubles US$8.50, triples US$10.50.

The *Hotel Bucañero* (tel 5-01-01), Juárez 75 one block from the end of Juárez, is full of character. Stuffed crocodiles greet you at the door. Wagon wheels and chunks of an old stone column are scattered around the inner courtyard. The rooms are OK, just a bit too humid and musty even though there are fans. Singles cost US$6.25, doubles US$8.25, triples US$10.

The *Hotel Flamingos*, at the end of Juárez just past the Bucañero, has rooms around a courtyard full of plants with a well in the middle. Singles cost US$6.25, doubles US$8.25, triples US$10.

Camping The *Trailer Park Los Cocos* (tel 5-00-55) is near Playa El Borrego almost at the end of Calle Batallón de San Blas, in a grassy area with lots of trees. Electricity and showers are available. Beware of the hungry mosquitoes that swarm into the bathrooms at sunset.

At Playa Los Cocos there's a trailer park on the beach next to a few palapa (shade hut) restaurants.

Places to Eat

The restaurant at the *Hotel Las Brisas*

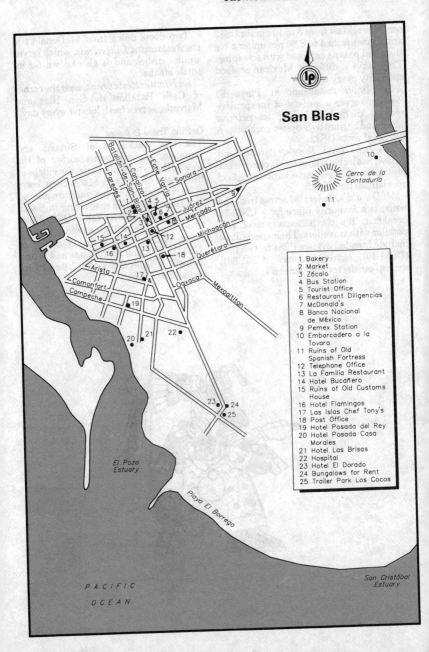

San Blas

Cerro de la Contaduría

El Pozo Estuary

San Cristóbal Estuary

Playa El Borrego

PACIFIC OCEAN

1 Bakery
2 Market
3 Zócalo
4 Bus Station
5 Tourist Office
6 Restaurant Diligencias
7 McDonald's
8 Banco Nacional de México
9 Pemex Station
10 Embarcadero a la Tovara
11 Ruins of Old Spanish Fortress
12 Telephone Office
13 La Familia Restaurant
14 Hotel Bucañero
15 Ruins of Old Customs House
16 Hotel Flamingos
17 Las Islas Chef Tony's
18 Post Office
19 Hotel Posada del Rey
20 Hotel Posada Casa Morales
21 Hotel Las Brisas
22 Hospital
23 Hotel El Dorado
24 Bungalows for Rent
25 Trailer Park Los Cocos

serves breakfast from 8 to 10 am for US$2 and dinner from 4 to 8.30 pm under a big thatched palapa enclosed with screening. They serve a different Mexican seafood speciality every night.

Sí Simon restaurant at Playa El Borrego serves a variety of inexpensive seafood dishes, including an octopus salad and shrimp and oyster cocktails. A full meal costs US$2.

Las Islas Chef Tony's, Paredes and Arista, has a chef whom locals claim is the best in town. They serve various seafood specialities for US$2.

McDonald's, Juárez 36 across from the bank, is a favourite place for a US$0.75 breakfast. It's clean, usually cool and popular with travellers. Their specialities include breaded oysters (US$2), fish filet (US$1.40), oysters 'casino' (US$1.60), shrimp omelettes and shrimp kebabs.

Two doors down from McDonald's is the *Restaurant Diligencias*, which serves similar dishes and is also known for its turtle steaks.

La Familia Restaurant, near the corner of Calle Batallón de San Blas and Mercado, serves fresh lobster every day.

Getting There & Away

The bus station is at Sinaloa and Canalizo, the north-east corner of the zócalo. Buses to Santa Cruz, the village at the far end of Bahía de Matanchén, leave at 9 am, 11 am and 1 pm and turn around to return shortly after arriving in Santa Cruz. Buses depart for Tepic (US$0.75) at 6.30, 7.30, 8.30 and 9.30 am and at 1, 4 and 5 pm. Buses depart for Guadalajara (US$2, six hours) at 7.30 am and 4 pm. Buses from Tepic arrive at 6, 7, 8 and 9 am and at 2 and 6 pm.

Baja California

Northern Baja

Northern Baja is that part of the Baja California peninsula north of the 28th parallel. This parallel is symbolically marked by a tall steel monument just north of Guerrero Negro. Officially, northern Baja is known as the State of Baja California while the southern portion is known as the State of Southern Baja California (Estado de Baja California Sur).

Northern Baja is one of Mexico's fastest-growing regions. Most of its economic growth is occurring in and around Tijuana and Mexicali and along the Pacific coast south to Ensenada. New housing complexes, manufacturing plants and business centres are being constructed. Tourism, state and federal investment and foreign (mainly American and Japanese) business and property investment have all increased dramatically in the last five years. Why this sudden development?

Northern Baja is only three hours' drive from Los Angeles, California, and inexpensive. The value of the Mexican peso has been falling steadily against the American dollar. This depreciation of the peso has been greater than increases in the inflation rate. Consequently, prices do not rise as quickly and Baja has been getting continually cheaper for Americans, large numbers of whom flock to Baja to take advantage of inexpensive liquor, lobster dinners and hotels.

One result has been a tremendous

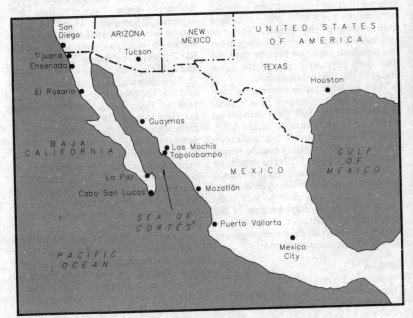

increase in foreign, mainly American, investment in coastal property between Tijuana and Ensenada. Until recently it was illegal for foreigners to own land within 100 km of the Mexican coastline. That meant all of Baja was off-limits to foreign property investors. Then the Mexican government created the *fideicomiso*, a 30-year bank trust. Supposedly, after 30 years a trustee will be able to easily re-negotiate an extension.

An additional attraction is Baja's duty-free status, which allows for the sale of many imported goods at prices lower than those found in the USA. Northern Baja's shop owners have begun to capitalise on this by selling designer jeans, French perfumes and the latest Japanese video recorders.

Baja's duty-free status has also attracted several American and Japanese manufacturers, who have established *maquiladoras* or assembly plants in and around Tijuana. They've discovered that it's cheaper to make television sets, compact refrigerators and stuffed animals in Baja than north of the border. The raw materials can be brought into Baja duty-free and then exported back to the USA with duty payments only on the value added to the original materials.

The new business developments have brought people to Northern Baja from all of Mexico. Many just pass through on their way to opportunities in the USA. The US Immigration & Naturalization Service says 5000 people cross the border illegally every week. With the expansion of business in Tijuana and Mexicali, however, more have settled in these areas. Many migrants who do cross will likely return to Northern Baja because of the recent passage of a stricter US immigration law that makes it illegal for employers in the USA to hire non-residents.

TIJUANA

Population: 1½ million

Tijuana ('tee-WAH-na'), the gateway to Northern Baja California, is a fast-growing city with multiple personalities. For most of its existence it was a tawdry border town where booze and sex flowed. It was also a gaudy place where curio shops overflowed with cheap, wrought-iron bird cages, sombreros and bright multicoloured sarapes. All this still exists, but Tijuana is quickly acquiring the sophistication of a big city, with business deals and housing developments.

The vigorous economy of today's Tijuana is in sharp contrast to its beginnings in 1848 as an innocuous ranchers' settlement at the end of the Mexican-American War. It remained an isolated settlement until 1870, when the Mexican government built a shack at the border and called it a customs depot. Gradually, Tijuana became a bit of a rough and rowdy town.

In 1911 it earned a footnote in the history books when a rebel leader named Ricardo Magón and his associate, a Welsh soldier-of-fortune named Caryl Pryce, advanced across Northern Baja and attacked Tijuana on 8 May. The street battles between local federalist troops and the rebels were observed from across the Río Tijuana by sightseers. The rebels won and held the town for six weeks. Then on 11 June federalist reinforcements arrived and ran the rebels out of town. Magón vanished; Pryce and his band of mercenaries marched across the border and were promptly arrested for violating the USA's neutrality treaty with Mexico.

The brief Battle of Tijuana did not seem to hurt its notoriety with tourists. In fact, everything considered illicit in the USA flourished in Tijuana. Gambling, prostitution, horse-racing, liquor stores and bars were ready to serve anyone with the right amount of cash.

During Prohibition in the USA Tijuana was flooded with thirsty Americans. After Prohibition ended, the Mexican government decided to clean up its image by declaring casinos and prostitution illegal. Today, the only visible reminder of that declaration is the grand casino – now a high school. Otherwise, everything else is still available in one form or another.

Temperatures in Tijuana vary between 36°C (high) and 0°C (low).

Orientation

Tijuana parallels the USA border for about 20 km. It is divided by the Río Tijuana, which flows from inland Baja across the border and into the Pacific Ocean. The streets are well organised in sort of a grid pattern, but street signs are often lacking and several downtown streets have two names. In this book numbered streets will be followed by their names in parentheses the first time they are mentioned.

As you cross the border confusion about the streets might set in. You are only a short distance – 1½ km – from downtown Tijuana. If you are walking across you will come to a big lot full of buses and taxis. All buses with a sign saying 'Central Camionera' will take you downtown (see the 'Getting Around' section) for 25c. Taxi fare to downtown is officially US$1.50, but can run to as much as US$5 for foreigners who don't protest.

If you wish to continue walking, turn right when you get to the lot and follow the sidewalk to the pedestrian bridge. The lot will be on your left as you proceed along the sidewalk. You will cross a street and walk across a plaza-like area before reaching the bridge.

On the other side of the bridge, cross the street and follow the map to Calle 2a (Benito Juárez). This is one of Tijuana's main streets, to the north of which are concentrated most of the sleazy bars and clubs. The more respectable districts lie south and south-east of Calle 2a.

Follow Calle 2a a few blocks to the west and you will come to Avenida Revolución, the main drag. Most visitors buy cheap liquor, imported goods and Mexican handiwork here. It is also the location of the Jai Alai Palace – El Frontón Palacio.

The 'new' centre of Tijuana is directly east of the Jai Alai Palace on both sides of the Río Tijuana. Paseo de los Héroes, Paseo de Tijuana and Vía Oriente are the principal streets in this part of town. All three streets run parallel to the river.

Information

Border Crossing The border – La Frontera or La Linea – at Tijuana is open 24 hours a day. For general information about customs and crossing with your car, see the 'Facts for the Visitor' chapter.

Tourist Office The Tijuana Chamber of Commerce Tourism Office (tel 685-95-20, 685-95-11) is the Tijuana city office. In Spanish it is called Cámara Nacional de Comercio, Servicios y Turismo de Tijuana. You'll find it at the corner of Avenida Revolución and Calle Comercio, the eastern extension of a street also known as Calle 1a and Calle Artículo 123. The helpful staff speak English and will answer any question you have about Tijuana. They stock a wide selection of brochures about Baja California and the rest of Mexico. Any queries specifically about Northern Baja California which they cannot answer should be directed to the state tourism office. Hours are Monday to Friday 9 am to 2 pm and 4 to 7 pm, Saturday 9 am to 1 pm.

If you have legal problems while touring Northern Baja, the Procuraduria de Protección al Turista (tel 684-21-81), in the Government Centre (Centro de Gobierno) at 1-208 Vía Oriente, is the organisation for you. It was established to assist tourists with legal problems and disputes. Its hours are 8 am to 7 pm.

Money Money can be exchanged at banks and casas de cambio. Banks offer better rates, but are much slower and more bureaucratic than the casas de cambio. You may not have to exchange US dollars for pesos in Tijuana because dollars are accepted by almost everyone except bus drivers.

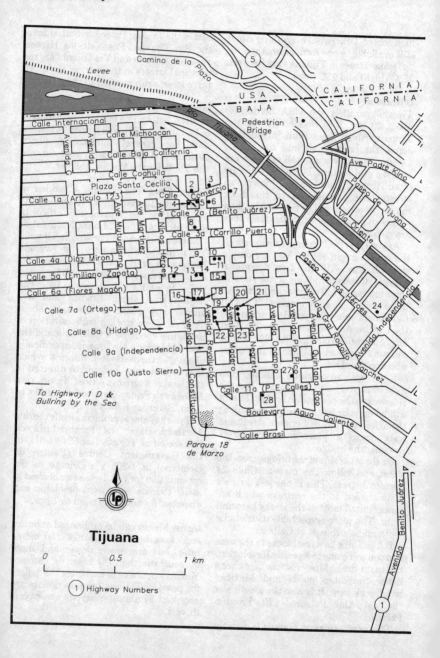

Tijuana

0   0.5   1 km

(1) Highway Numbers

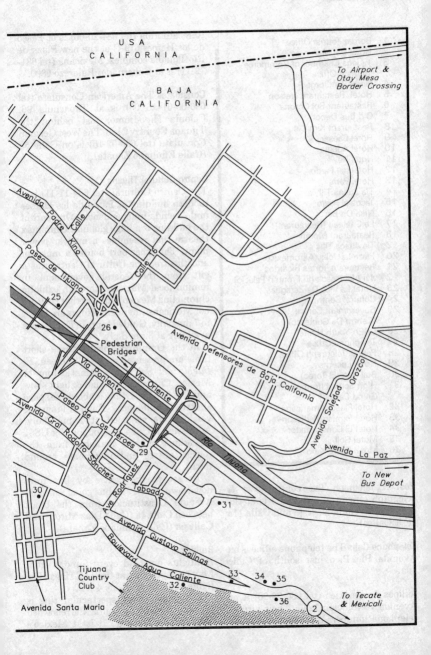

1	Border Tourist Office
2	Hotel Del Mar
3	Tijuana Chamber of Commerce Tourism Office
4	Hotel San Jorge
5	Hotel/Restaurant Nelson
6	Restaurant Bol Corona
7	Old Bus Depot
8	Restaurant Kim Ling
9	Hotel Caesar
10	Hotel Adelita
11	Hotel Rey
12	Hotel del Pardo
13	Hotel Paris
14	Tía Juana Tilly's
15	Tacos al Pastor
16	Nica-Oh Bar
17	Le Château (Restaurant)
18	Restaurant Monin
19	Tia Juana Tilly's
20	Plaza La Jolla/Aeroméxico
21	Restaurant Tortas Ricardos
22	Jai Alai Palace (El Frontón Palacio)
23	Hotel La Villa De Zaragoza
24	Cultural Centre
25	Government Centre (Centro De Gobierno)
26	CREA Youth Hostel
27	Telephone Office
28	Post & Telegraph Office
29	Hotel Lucerna
30	Bull ring (El Toreo)
31	High School (formerly the Grand Casino)
32	Hotel Fiesta Americana
33	Hotel Paraíso-Radisson
34	Hotel El Conquistador
35	Motel Golf
36	Motel Padre Kino

Post & Telegraph The central post & telegraph office (tel 685-26-82) is at the corner of Avenida Negrete and Calle 11a (P E Calles).

Telephone Calls The telephone office is on Avenida Pio Pico just south of Calle 10a.

Airlines Aeroméxico (tel 685-22-30) is at Avenida Revolución 1236. Their airport telephone numbers are 683-27-01 to 05.

Aerocalifornia (tel 684-20-06) is at Paseo de los Héroes 619-C at the new Plaza de Río Tijuana complex. Mexicana (tel 681-72-11) is at Gobernador Balarezo 2800.

Consulates The American Consulate (tel 686-00-01 to 05) is at Tapachula 96, Colonia Hipodromo, just behind the Tijuana Country Club. The West German Consulate (tel 685-52-15) is on Calle 5a (Calle Emiliano Zapata).

Centro Cultural Tijuana

The Centro Cultural (tel 684-11-11) is a modern building at Paseo de los Héroes and Avenida Independencia. One part of the building is a huge globular Omnimax theatre that resembles a nuclear power plant. The other part houses a museum and theatre. The Cultural Centre was a gift from the federal government to remind local Mexicans through exhibits chronicling Mexico's history that they are not Mexican-Americans. Hours are 11 am to 7 pm daily. Guided tours in English are available at 3 pm daily.

In the Omnimax theatre three short films are presented on a 180° screen. *El Pueblo del Sol* is a cinematic tour of Mexico, *Chronos* is a sound & light show and *The Dream is Alive* is about the space shuttle Challenger. English-language versions are screened at 2 pm daily. Admission is US$4.50. Coupons for US$1 off admission are available from the tourist offices and merchants around town.

To get to the centre by bus from downtown, catch any bus going south on Avenida Constitución from the block between Calle 4a (Calle Díaz Mirón) and Calle 5a (Calle Emiliano Zapata).

Bullfights

Bullfights are held every Sunday from May to September at two bull rings. The fights begin at precisely 4 pm.

The larger, more spectacular ring is Plaza de Toros Monumental, the renowned 'bull ring by the sea'. It is at Mexico's north-westernmost corner just a few metres from the border fence. The green US Immigration & Naturalization Service vehicles are usually watching the fence from the other side.

The other bull ring, known as El Toreo, is at Boulevard Agua Caliente 100, between downtown Tijuana and the Agua Caliente Racetrack. Fights are held here from May to August and then at the Monumental ring the rest of the season.

Ticket prices at both rings range from US$4.50 to US$16. They can be bought from Ticketron outlets in the USA, at a ticket kiosk on Avenida Revolución and at the bull rings. For reservations call 685-15-10 or 686-22-10.

Bullfighting tickets

Jai Alai Palace

El Frontón Palacio de Jai Alai (tel 685-16-12) is one of the most prominent buildings on Avenida Revolución. It is between Calle 7a (Calle Ortega) and Calle 8a (Calle Hidalgo). Jai alai originated in the Basque region of Spain. It is a fast-moving game played with two teams of two players each in a long, walled-in court. Players wear a small wicker basket on their arm which is used to catch and throw a hard rubber ball with a tightly-woven goatskin casing. Spectators are allowed to bet on each game. Hours are 7 pm to 1 am nightly except Thursday. Admission is US$2.

Places to Stay – bottom end

The *Hotel del Mar* (tel 685-73-02), Calle 1a No 1948 (Calle Artículo 123) is across the street from the Hotel Nelson. It is conveniently located half a block from Avenida Revolución, but borders a sleazy part of town. A double costs US$7.50. The rooms and even the communal bathroom are kept quite clean. The manager speaks English and is helpful to travellers.

The *CREA Youth Hostel* is a member of the International Youth Hostel Federation. It is part of a sports complex just north-west of the general hospital on Avenida Padre Kino (see map). Although somewhat detached from the rest of the city, it is set in a pleasant park-like area with lots of trees and grass. The hostel is definitely the cheapest place to stay in Tijuana. A bed in a typical single-sex dormitory room costs US$2.50. To get here from the border take any blue-and-white 'Central Camionera' bus and get off when you see the large sports complex on your right. The hostel is open all day from 7 am to 11 pm.

Camping 'Unofficial' free camping is possible on any public beach in the area, but the farther from Tijuana the better because there'll be fewer people. There is a *KOA Trailer Park/Campground* about 20 km south of Tijuana along the coast. It has all of the typical facilities and

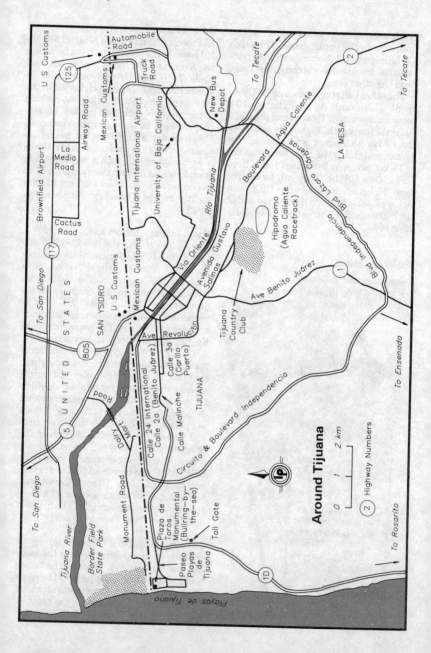

Around Tijuana

0   1   2 km

② Highway Numbers

recreational vehicle hook-ups of KOA campgrounds in the USA. Leave the toll road at the San Antonio del Mar exit. They charge US$11 per night for a space.

Places to Stay – middle

The *Hotel Caesar* (tel 688-05-50) at the corner of Calle 5a (Calle Emiliano Zapata) and Avenida Revolución has lots of character: rooms painted in shades of green, hallways decorated with hundreds of posters and photographs of matadors and bullfights, and a restaurant that created the 'Caesar salad'. Room rates range from US$20 for a single to US$55 for the best room in the hotel.

The *Hotel Nelson* (tel 85-43-03), Avenida Revolución 502, has been a long-time favourite with budget travellers because of its central location and 75 clean, basic rooms. Rates are US$15 single and US$22 double. There is an inexpensive coffee-shop next to the lobby.

The *Hotel La Villa de Zaragoza*, Avenida Madero 1120, is a new brown stucco motel directly behind the Jai Alai Palace. Each room has a TV, telephone, heater and air-conditioning. Rates are between US$20 and US$25 for singles and doubles.

The *Hotel Rey* (tel 685-14-26) at Calle 4a (Calle Díaz Mirón) No 2021, is an older hotel in a great central location. The beds have mattresses that swallow you, but otherwise the hotel is not bad. Rooms cost US$13 per night for either a single or a double.

The *Hotel Adelita* (tel 685-94-95) at Calle 4a (Calle Díaz Mirón) No 2770, is a simple hotel with no amenities other than hot showers. If you are looking for a clean, basic place with no frills, this is it. Rooms cost US$10 per night.

The *Hotel del Pardo* is on Calle 5a (Calle Emiliano Zapata) between Avenida Niños Héroes and Avenida Constitución. Several of the rooms are multicoloured and decorated with graffiti, but otherwise clean and comfortable. Try to get a room away from the kitchen and the cages full of noisy birds in the central courtyard. Rates average US$15 single or double.

The *Motel Padre Kino* (tel 86-42-08), Boulevard Agua Caliente 3, is next to the Tijuana Country Club and only a five-minute walk from the racetrack (Hipódromo). The typical motel-style place is popular with gringos who have cars. A single costs US$13 and a double US$16 to US$19.

Places to Stay – top end

The *Hotel Lucerna* (tel 684-01-15) is at the junction of Paseo de los Héroes and Avenida Rodríguez. The modern hotel primarily caters to visiting businessmen. All rooms have air-conditioning, colour TVs and telephones. There is a restaurant, piano bar and swimming pool. Room rates start at US$40.

The *Hotel Paraíso-Radisson* (tel 81-72-00) is next to the Tijuana Country Club at Boulevard Agua Caliente 1. It used to be part of the USA-based Quality Inn system. All rooms have air-conditioning, colour TVs and telephones. Rates start at US$40. The 'King Jester's Disco' at the hotel is popular with local university students.

The *Hotel El Conquistador* (tel 86-48-01) is across from the Tijuana Country Club at Boulevard Agua Caliente 700. Look for the motel with the colonial-style architecture. All 110 rooms have air-conditioning, colour TVs and telephones. Rates start at US$34 single and US$39 double.

The *Hotel Fiesta Americana Tijuana* (tel 81-71-16 or toll free in the USA (800) 223-2332), Boulevard Agua Caliente 4500, has 430 rooms and charges US$70 per night. It is the best and most prominent hotel in Tijuana. Its shiny 23-storey towers are the two tallest buildings in Tijuana.

Places to Eat

The *Hotel Nelson Restaurant* is a clean coffee-shop-type place next to the Hotel

Nelson at Avenida Revolución 502. They serve very inexpensive Mexican-American food. A breakfast of eggs, toast, frijoles and coffee costs US$1.15. They also serve inexpensive comidas corridas at lunch time.

Restaurant Kim Ling, Calle 3a (Calle Carrillo Puerto) between Avenida Revolución and Avenida Constitución, is a popular lunch-time restaurant which serves good chop suey for US$2.

Tía Juana Tilly's is one of the most popular gringo hang-outs in Tijuana. There are two locations: one next to the Jai Alai Palace and the other at Avenida Revolución and Calle 5a (Calle Emiliano Zapata). The food and drinks seem overpriced, but most people come here for the booze and party atmosphere. A plate of nachos costs US$2.

The *Restaurant Monin* is an economical place for quesadillas, tacos, burritos and omelettes at the corner of Calle 7a (Calle Ortega) and Avenida Revolución. It is clean with a bouquet of paper flowers on every indoor table. Try their Mexican-style eggs with tortillas, beans and salad for US$2.50.

Another economical place near downtown is *Restaurant Tortas Ricardos* at the corner of Avenida Madero and Calle 7a (Calle Ortega). It is popular with the local businesspeople. They serve a 'New York' steak with enchiladas and guacamole for US$4. Their Mexican combination plate is reasonable at US$2.50.

Things to Buy
Avenida Revolución and Avenida Constitución are the principal shopping streets. Since Baja California is a duty-free zone, many great deals on imported goods can be found. Calvin Klein, Ralph Lauren and several other top-name designers have opened stores in Tijuana.

Local handicrafts are plentiful, especially jewellery, wrought-iron furniture, baskets, silver, blown glass, pottery and leather goods. Try the Municipal Market on

Avenida 'C' between Calles '1' and '2'. Bargaining is usual in small shops.

Mexican liquor and beer are also popular 'souvenirs'. US customs regulations allow only one litre of liquor and six bottles of beer per adult (21 years or older) into the country.

Getting There & Away
Air Tijuana International Airport is becoming a popular departure and arrival point. Flights to and from this airport cost less than flights which depart from the USA, especially due to the devaluation of the peso. For example, a flight to La Paz from Tijuana costs US$160.80 round trip, while from Los Angeles it costs US$189.

Aeroméxico, Mexicana and Aerocalifornia are the only airlines operating from Tijuana Airport. Aeroméxico has flights from Tijuana to Acapulco, Cancún, Guadalajara, La Paz, Loreto (Baja California), Los Angeles, Los Cabos (Cabo San Lucas/San José), Los Mochis, Mazatlán, Mexico City and Puerto Vallarta. Mexicana flies from Tijuana to Acapulco, Veracruz and Zacatecas (all mainland destinations). Aerocalifornia (in the USA tel toll free (800) 522-1516, in Tijuana tel 684-20-06) flies from Tijuana to Los Mochis for US$80 (one way) and US$145 (round trip), and from Los Mochis to La Paz for US$27 (one way).

Bus There are old and new bus depots in Tijuana. The old depot is at the corner of Avenida Madero and Calle 1a (Calle Artículo 123, also known as Calle Comercio). All the major companies, including Autotransportes del Pacífico (tel 686-90-45), Autotransportes Tres Estrellas de Oro (tel 686-91-86) and the USA-based Greyhound bus line (in the USA tel toll free (800) 528-0447) operate on more limited schedules out of this depot.

The new depot (Central Camionera) is a cavernous building on the outskirts five km south-east of downtown where Boulevard Lázaro Cárdenas becomes the airport highway. To get there, take any

'Buena Vista', 'Centro' or 'Central Camionera' bus from Calle 2a east of Avenida Constitución. This bus also stops at the border bus lot and the CREA Youth Hostel.

Greyhound operates a daily bus service between San Diego and Tijuana. Fares from San Diego to Tijuana are US$4 one way and US$8 round trip during special-offer periods (which vary each year) and regularly US$7.65 one way and US$14.55 round trip; from San Ysidro to downtown Tijuana (only two miles away, but still probably cheaper than a Tijuana taxi) it costs US$2 one way and US$4 round trip.

Autotransportes de Tres Estrellas de Oro buses travel throughout Mexico and are considered 1st class since most have air-conditioning and toilets. Autotransportes de Pacífico and Autotransportes de Baja California (ABC) operates mostly 2nd-class buses to various destinations on Mexico's Pacific coast and in Baja California respectively. Following is fare and schedule information for a few of the major routes from Tijuana's old bus depot. All fares are for one-way trips; departures are daily. Most of the fares quoted are for Tres Estrellas buses:

La Paz: US$17 to US$20; departs at 10 am, takes 22 to 24 hours. Mexicali: US$2.50; departs every hour between 6 am to 10 pm, takes three hours. Ensenada: US$1.50; departs every hour between 6 am to 10 pm, takes 1½ hours. Mexico City: US$38; departs every hour 24 hours a day, takes 48 hours. The bus usually follows Highway 2 to Highway 15, which it takes to Mexico City. Hermosillo: US$11; departs every hour 24 hours a day, takes 13 hours.

Some fare and schedule information for buses departing from the new bus depot:

Ensenada: ABC 2nd-class buses depart almost every half-hour or hour from 5 am to midnight; the trip takes 1½ hours and costs US$1.15. Tres Estrellas de Oro 1st-class air-conditioned buses stop in Ensenada en route to other destinations farther south. Fare is US$1.25.

Mexicali: ABC buses depart almost every hour from 5.30 am to 10 pm; fares are Tecate US$0.50, Mexicali US$2 and San Luis US$2.65. Tres Estrellas (1st class), Transportes del Pacífico (1st class) and Transportes del Norte de Sonora (2nd class) all, except for certain express buses, stop in Mexicali en route to various mainland destinations (see below for schedule information). Fares average slightly higher than ABC's.

Santa Rosalía: a direct ABC bus departs at 4.30 pm; fare is US$10. Tres Estrellas buses stop en route.

La Paz: an ABC bus departs at 8 am and stops at all major cities and towns. Fare is US$15.75. Tres Estrellas buses depart at 10.30 am, 2 pm, 6 pm and 10 pm for this 22 to 24-hour trip. Fare is US$17.25.

Express to Guadalajara & Mexico City: Tres Estrellas buses depart at 9.30 am, noon, 2.30 pm, 5 pm and 8 pm. The trip to Guadalajara takes 36 hours (US$27); to Mexico City 46 hours (US$33.75).

Other 1st-class Tres Estrellas buses to Mexico City via Guadalajara depart at 11 am, noon, 7.30 pm, 8 pm and midnight and stop at most major cities along Highway 15 from Santa Ana to Guadalajara. After Guadalajara, buses to Mexico City go via Morelia or Querétaro. Sample fares: Hermosillo US$10, Los Mochis US$15, Mazatlán US$20.50, Querétaro US$31.35 and Morelia US$30.75.

Transportes del Pacífico runs 1st-class buses along routes similar to Tres Estrella's. Departures are at 11 am, at 1, 3, 5, 6, 7, 8, 9 and 10 pm and at midnight. Fares are comparable.

Transportes del Norte de Sonora runs 2nd-class buses to Mexico City along routes similar to those above. Fares are lower: Mexico City US$30.50, Guadalajara US$24, Mazatlán US$19, Los Mochis US$14, Hermosillo US$9 and Morelia US$28.

Trolley The San Diego Trolley (tel (619) 233-3004) is one of the cheapest ways to travel between downtown San Diego and the international border at San Ysidro. The trolley stops in San Ysidro on the east side of the border station. You can walk across a pedestrian bridge to enter Mexico. A trolley departs from the stations indicated on the route map about every 15 minutes daily from 5 am to midnight. Fares range from US$0.50 to

US$1.50. Leaflets with full schedule and fare information are available at each station.

Rail Passenger rail service no longer operates from Tijuana. The closest rail service is in San Diego and Mexicali. For information about the train from Mexicali, see the 'Getting There & Away' section under 'Mexicali'.

Amtrak runs daily trains between San Diego and Los Angeles (in the USA tel toll free (800) 872-7245). The San Diego Trolley runs from the San Diego Amtrak station directly to the international border at San Ysidro.

Getting Around
Airport Transport A taxi from downtown Tijuana can be ordered by calling the government-regulated service on tel 683-10-20. Rates are approximately US$6 between downtown Tijuana and the airport for one person. If you share the ride the rate might be lower.

If you are coming from or going to San Diego, then you can arrange your taxi fare and bus ride for a flat rate of US$15 through Mexicoach. Convenience is really the only reason to do this.

Bus Buses are plentiful in Tijuana. From the border almost any bus will take you downtown (near the Jai Alai Palace and Avenida Revolución). Look for the ones marked 'Central Camionera'. Buses going to the border from downtown depart from Calle 2a between Avenidas Constitución and Revolución; these go from west to east.

Taxi Taxi drivers in Tijuana are used to gringos, especially on the five-minute ride from the border to downtown Tijuana. The drivers will ask US$5 per person for a ride that should only cost US$1.50. In general, expect to pay anywhere from US$1 to US$5 for most downtown taxi rides.

ENSENADA
Population: 170,000

At first Ensenada seems quiet and unassuming, almost boring. Everything appears to move in slow motion – people on the sidewalks, boats and trawlers in the harbour, cars and the occasional donkey cart on the street. Beneath this serenity is a city fit for Bacchus, the Roman god of wine and drunken revelry.

Ensenada's altitude is 3½ metres above sea level. Maximum temperature is 40°C; minimum temperature is 4.4°C.

History
Ensenada and the Bahía de Todos Santos (Bay of All Saints) have served as a port for fishing trawlers and cargo ships for more than four centuries. Juan Rodríguez Cabrillo claimed to have discovered the bay on 17 September 1542 during his journey along the coast with the Spanish caravels *San Salvador* and *Vittoria*. Cabrillo and his crew stayed here for about six days and replenished their supply of fresh water. They encountered a small group of Indians who had probably been living in the area for several centuries; not much is known about them.

The next visitors to the bay arrived with a fleet of ships led by Captain Sebastián Vizcaino on 5 November 1602. He sailed into the bay which protects present-day Ensenada and named it Ensenada de Todos los Santos or 'the small bay of all saints'. It was given this name because the bay had an almost saintly beauty to it and, most importantly, All Saints Day was on 1 November. Later, the name was shortened to Ensenada.

For the next 250 years the bay became a frequent port of call for Spanish galleons or *naos* headed to Acapulco from Manila. The *naos* usually passed by once or twice a year loaded with Oriental treasures such as Chinese silks, spices, Japanese artwork and jewels. The last *nao* – the *Magellan* – sailed past in 1815.

In the late 17th century the area around the bay began to attract Spanish missionaries though a mission was never established there because of water shortages; the water that Cabrillo had found more than a century earlier wasn't discovered. Missions were built about 48 km to the north and south.

There were many visitors to Bahía de Todos Santos between Vizcaíno's visit and the end of the 18th century, but the first settlement wasn't established until 1804. That year the Viceroy of New Spain granted land in present-day Ensenada to José Manuel Ruíz. Ruíz set up a cattle ranch which he named Rancho Ensenada and then sold in 1824 to a Spanish sergeant named Francisco Gastelum. The Gastelum family expanded their ranch and established several farms in the area.

Farming and cattle ranching were the mainstays of this small community until 1870 when gold was discovered 35½ km away at Real del Castillo (no longer on maps). Todos Santos was the closest bay and the ranches were the closest food supply. As miners and their families poured into Ensenada, it quickly became a booming port town and shipping centre – in fact, one of the largest ports on the west coast of North America. This initial prosperity earned it the status of capital of Northern Baja from 1882 to 1915 and attracted a variety of investors.

Not much happened in Ensenada until the 1920s when Prohibition began in the USA. Like Tijuana, Ensenada began to cater to Americans hungry for gambling and drunken revelry. The Hotel Playa Ensenada and gambling casino opened in the early 1930s. The hotel and casino had a short life, however, because the Mexican government outlawed gambling in the late 1930s. The hotel was renamed the Riviera del Pacífico and tried to continue functioning as a resort for another decade. Today, the Riviera is a quasi-cultural centre and wedding reception hall. One of the most beautiful buildings in Ensenada,

it's an excellent example of Spanish-style architecture.

As more people began visiting Ensenada, other hotels and restaurants were built. Ensenada became a tourist resort and weekend retreat with more than four million visitors per year – mostly Southern Californians. Today, it is Baja's third largest city.

Orientation

Ensenada is a principal fishing and shipping port 109 km south of Tijuana. The city's Bahía de Todos Santos is an ideal locale for a port: the Punta Banda peninsula juts out to the south-west and protects the bay and the city from high waves and strong winds.

Most hotels and restaurants are concentrated along Boulevard Lázaro Cárdenas, also marked on some local maps as Boulevard Costero west of Riviera del Pacífico. It runs near the waterfront and Avenida López Mateos (also known as Calle 1a). López Mateos is one block inland from and parallel to Lázaro Cárdenas for a short distance.

A few more blocks inland is the business centre, Avenida Juárez (also known as Avenida Benito Juárez). Perpendicular to these streets is Ensenada's 'drinking district'– Avenida Gastelum and Avenida Ruíz – where several bars and cantinas such as Hussong's are located.

Information

Tourist Office The state tourism office (tel 676-22-22) is next to the Fonart Centro Artesanal at Avenida López Mateos 13-B. Many brochures and cards from Ensenada's hotels, motels and restaurants are available; the staff wasn't able to offer much else.

Next door is the Procuraduria de Protección al Turista (tel 676-36-86 or for emergencies 678-22-01), which assists tourists with legal problems. In 1987 they were considering moving this office to the Centro Social, Cívico y Cultural de

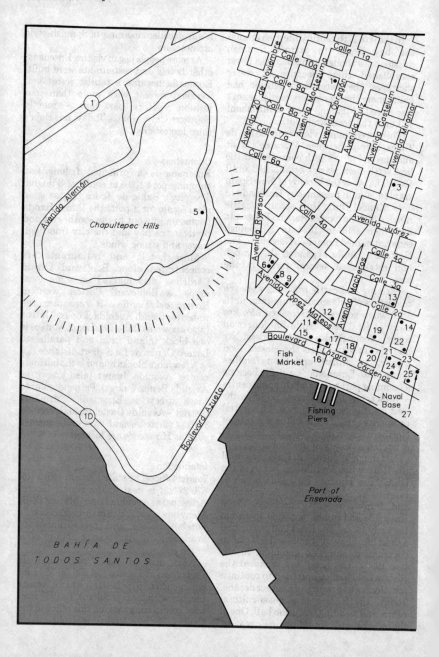

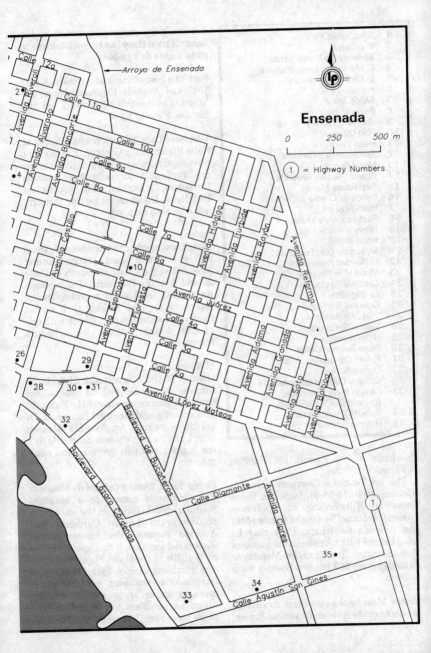

Ensenada

0   250   500 m

(1) = Highway Numbers

1	Telephone Office
2	Bus Depot
3	Bodegas De Santo Tomás
4	El Mercado (Street Market)
5	El Mirador (Lookout)
6	Hussong's
7	Señor Tacos
8	Papas & Beer
9	The Taco Factory
10	Post Office
11	Hotel Plaza
12	Restaurant La Gondola
13	Motel Pancho
14	Charro (Rodeo) Grounds
15	Restaurant Marios
16	Carlos 'n' Charlie's
17	Plaza México
18	Restaurant Via Veneto
19	Henry's Restaurant
20	Hotel Bahía
21	Mesón de Don Fernando
22	El Rey Sol Restaurant
23	Motel Villa Fontana
24	Casamar Restaurant
25	La Baguette
26	Casa del Sol Motel
27	Villa Marina Hotel
28	Misión Santa Isabel
29	Hotel America
30	State Tourism Office
31	Fonart Centro Artesanal
32	Centro Social, Cívico y Cultural de Ensenada
33	Campo Playa Ensenada Recreational Vehicle Park
34	Roberto's Restaurant
35	Haliotis Restaurant

Ensenada in the Riviera del Pacífico building.

The new Tourist & Convention Bureau (Cotuco) (tel 678-28-63) is in the Plaza Comercial Villafontana at Boulevard Lázaro Cárdenas (Boulevard Costero 540) and Avenida Gastelum. They may be more helpful with tourist-related inquiries than the state office. Hours are Monday to Saturday 9 am to 7 pm and Sunday 9 am to 2 pm.

Money Most banks and casas de cambio are on Avenida Ruíz and Avenida Juárez, but don't try exchanging money at the banks. I tried three banks; each told me to go to a casa de cambio.

Post The post office is at Avenida Juárez 1347 and Avenida Espinosa. Hours are Monday to Saturday 8 am to 7 pm and Sunday 8 am to 1 pm.

Telephone Calls The telephone office is at Calle 10a and Calle Obregón. A note about telephone numbers: seven-digit numbers are applicable for calls from outside Ensenada; for local calls dial only the last five digits. If you aren't getting through, ask a local to help you.

Rodeos

Rough and rowdy *charreadas* or Mexican rodeos are held almost every summer weekend at the Charro Grounds at Calle 2a and Avenida Blancarte. The cowboys do typical feats such as riding bulls, roping calves and making their horses dance to mariachi music. Check with one of the tourist offices for schedule information.

El Mirador

On top of the Chapultepec Hills is El Mirador, a scenic lookout where you can get a panoramic view of the Bahía de Todos Santos and the city of Ensenada. To get there go right up Avenida Alemán from Calle 2a in downtown Ensenada. It's the highest point in town, so you can't miss it.

Centro Social, Cívico y Cultural de Ensenada

The Centro is housed in a beautiful Spanish-style building on the waterfront at Boulevard Lázaro Cárdenas and Avenida Riviera. Also known as the Riviera del Pacífico, it first opened in the early 1930s as the Hotel Playa Ensenada and gambling casino. Jack Dempsey, a famous American boxer, was hired as the manager in order to attract wealthy American gamblers to the casino. The place closed in 1938 when the Mexican government outlawed gambling. Today, various cultural events, weddings, conventions, meetings and art exhibitions are held here. Walk in and look around; it is usually open to the public.

Places to Stay - bottom end

Ensenada has several hotels and motels which are inexpensive relative to prices in the USA, but overpriced compared to many places on mainland Mexico. You should expect to pay at least US$10 to US$15 for a room in this category.

The shabby *Motel Pancho* at Avenida Alvarado 211 has the cheapest rooms in Ensenada. The location is great – directly across from the *charro* (rodeo) grounds and bull ring. Clean rooms with either a sagging double bed or twin beds cost US$10.

The *Hotel America* (tel 6-13-33) is a dive across from the Fonart Centro Artesanal and state tourism office, and south of the Ensenada River gully. Single/double rooms average US$15. An Australian couple who stayed here reported that the beds were so bad they ended up sleeping on the floor. Look at the room first.

Camping *Campo Playa Ensenada Recreational Vehicle Park* has over 100 small, grassy spaces for pitching a tent or parking a camper 1½ km south of downtown Ensenada at the corner of Calle Agustín San Gines and Boulevard Lázaro Cárdenas. Full hook-ups are available at most spaces. They had hot showers until the water heater exploded; the owner was supposed to replace it soon. The charge is US$5 per night per space.

There are several 'official' campgrounds and trailer parks north and south of Ensenada. Most offer basic facilities such as toilets, sinks, showers, faucets and electrical outlets. My personal favourites are the trailer parks and campgrounds on Punta Banda and Estero Beach. The parks north of Ensenada seemed too close to the fish cannery in El Sauzal. Rates range from US$5 to US$10 per night.

Places to Stay - middle

The *Motel Villa Fontana* (tel 8-34-34) is at a great central location near the corner of Avenida López Mateos and Avenida Blancarte. Rooms are old with high ceilings and worn floor tiles, but they are clean, airy and spacious. A cheerful English-speaking manager usually works the reception desk and is willing to answer questions about Ensenada. Single/double rooms are US$26.50. A US$25 deposit is required upon check-in and returned when you check out.

Around the corner from the Motel Villa Fontana is the popular *Hotel Bahía* (tel 8-21-01) on Avenida López Mateos. Clean, carpeted single/double rooms with small refrigerators, heaters and balconies are US$23 (during the week) to US$34 (on weekends). Rooms with balconies overlooking the bay are the first ones taken. Suites are US$50 and are a popular deal for groups because the price can be split among as many as six persons.

East of the *Hotel Bahía* at the corner of Avenida López Mateos and Avenida Castillo is the *Misión Santa Isabel*, an old Spanish mission-style motel with arches and red roof tiles. Singles/doubles are US$35/US$37.

Places to Stay - top end

Hussong's Quinta Papagayo Resort (tel 8-36-75, 4-41-55) is a beautifully landscaped complex on Highway 1 about 1½ km north of Ensenada. The rooms are large and airy with balconies overlooking the ocean, macramé wall-hangings, terra-cotta floor tiles and hand-carved furniture. One and two-bedroom apartments are also available. All guests have access to the resort's tennis courts, and there's a great restaurant attached to the complex. Double room rates are US$50 to US$60.

Places to Eat

Take your pick. There are at least 57 restaurants in Ensenada serving everything from from typical Mexican dishes and seafood to Chinese and French cuisine.

Downtown *El Rey Sol Restaurant* at Avenida López Mateos 1000 and Avenida Blancarte is an elegant, Old World-style French-Mexican restaurant that specialises in delicious seafood, chicken and vegetable dishes. Their breakfast omelettes are also tasty. A full meal starts at US$4.

Henry's Restaurant, across from the Hotel Bahía, is the sort of place many gringos frequent because its menu is entirely in English. Don't be tempted; the customer doesn't matter much here. You get to stare at the remains of the previous customer's scrambled eggs for too many minutes until the waitress realises there is someone new at the table.

The *Mesón de Don Fernando* is a good place for breakfast on Avenida López Mateos as long as the music is not too loud. *Huevos rancheros* (ranch-style eggs) served with salsa, refried beans and bacon costs US$3. For lunch and dinner they serve lobster tacos and burritos and several other seafood dishes.

Lobster pizza? Yes, there is a restaurant/pizzeria that serves this – *Restaurant La Gondola* on the north side of Avenida López Mateos between Avenida Miramar and Avenida Macheros. A lobster pizza for one or two people costs US$4. They also serve 12 other types of pizza ranging from US$1.50 to US$4, as well as various Mexican dishes for under US$2. Table cloths and attentive service keep the place clean, comfortable and homey.

For some of the tastiest tacos in town try the *Taco Factory* at the corner of Avenida Gastelum and Avenida López Mateos; and try *Señor Tacos* near the corner of Avenida Ruíz and Calle 2a. Señor Tacos offers 50 types of tacos as well as *quesadillas* (melted cheese and a variety of toppings on a flour tortilla) and tostadas.

Bars & Cantinas

Potent, tasty and inexpensive liquors and beers are one of Ensenada's prime attractions for gringos. On the weekends most of the major bars and cantinas in Ensenada are packed with people from early afternoon to early morning.

Hussong's at Avenida Ruíz 113 is one of the best-known cantinas in the Californias. Bumper stickers and T-shirts bearing the name 'Hussong's' are seen throughout Southern California and Northern Baja. There is even a beer called Hussong's, but it's brewed in Mazatlán. The Hussong family arrived in Ensenada from Germany in the late 19th century. They used their knowledge of traditional German beer-brewing to establish one of Ensenada's first cantinas. Some of its earliest clientele were rough and hardy miners and ranchers. Today, the miners are gone and the ranchers are few; tattooed bikers in black leather, college students and mariachi bands have replaced them. Tourists who have been told that this is *the* place to come in Ensenada sit with their backs against the wall watching the activity around the bar. Poke your head in and catch a glimpse of one of Ensenada's few 'historic' landmarks. Hours are 10 am to 2 am.

Papas & Beer is half a block south-west of Hussong's at the corner of Avenida López Mateos and Avenida Ruíz. They cater mostly to vacationing college students and hardy and hearty party souls. Hours are 10 am to 3 am.

Plaza México is an outdoor 'bar' at the corner of Avenida Macheros and Boulevard Lázaro Cárdenas. This is also a popular gringo hang-out, especially with younger Southern Californians. Their huge Margaritas cost US$2 and are sure to make it difficult for you to walk away. Buy drink tickets from the waiter if you think you'll want more than one drink.

Carlos 'n' Charlie's is on Boulevard Lázaro Cárdenas between Avenida Miramar and Avenida Macheros. Although mostly a bar, it is also a seafood restaurant with one of the most eclectic interiors of any restaurant and bar in Baja California and probably the rest of Mexico. An effigy of President Reagan floats overhead suspended from parachute cords attached to the ceiling. Stuffed animals, colourful flotsam, bricks and hooks also hang from above, layers of graffiti grace the walls, and a King Kong-size wristwatch behind the bar lets you know if you have stayed past your bedtime.

Things to Buy

Many of the items in Tijuana's shops are sold here for slightly less, though the selection is not as extensive.

Baja Californian wine is sold here at a good price because the Santo Tomás Winery is in Ensenada. Liquors and beers from throughout Mexico are also sold here at a discount.

Shops on Avenida López Mateos overflow with colourful sarapes, wrought-iron bird cages, silver jewellery (and cheap imitations), wood-carvings, leather goods and other crafts from all Mexico.

Getting There & Away

Bus The bus depot is at Avenida Riveroll and Calle 11a, 10 blocks north/north-east of Avenida López Mateos. Tres Estrellas de Oro, Tres Estrellas del Norte, Transporte Norte de Sonora and Autotransporte de Baja California are the four main companies operating to and from Ensenada. Both Tres Estrellas companies have 1st-class air-conditioned buses while the latter two have 2nd-class buses.

Following are the schedules and routings of a few lines:

Transportes Norte de Sonora leaves for Tijuana hourly, 5 am to 11 pm, US$15; Mexico City, 5 pm, US$32.75

Tres Estrellas del Norte leaves for Tijuana every half-hour, 6 am to 4 pm, then 5, 5.30, 6, 7 and 7.45 pm, US$1.30; Mexicali, 6.30, 7.30 and 10.30 am, 1, 3.30 and 6.30 pm, US$3.50; Hermosillo US$11.50, Guaymas US$13.15, Los Mochis US$17.15, Mazatlán US$22.75.

Tres Estrellas de Oro leaves for La Paz, 12.15, 4, 8, 9.30 pm and midnight, US$16.50; Loreto, departures as for La Paz, US$12.25; Mulegé,

departures as for La Paz, US$10.65; Santa Rosalía, departures as for La Paz, US$10; San Ignacio, departures as for La Paz, US$9.15; Mexico City via Zacapu, 10.30 am, 11.40 am, 2.30 pm, US$36; Mexico City via Guadalajara, 5 and 7 pm, duration 48 hours, US$36

Autotransportes de Baja California leaves for La Paz, 10 am, US$15; Mulegé, 10 am, US$9.63.

Buses from Tijuana and Mexicali arrive almost hourly in Ensenada. For specific schedule information, see the 'Getting There & Away' sections for each city.

Getting Around

Car Rental Renting a car in Ensenada is only necessary if you need convenient transport to the beaches, Punta Banda peninsula and Agua Caliente (hot springs). There are two local car-rental agencies: Ensenada Rent-a-Car (tel 8-18-96) at Avenida Alvarado 95, and Scorpio Rent-a-Car on Avenida Castillo between Boulevard Lázaro Cárdenas and Avenida López Mateos. Scorpio rents jeeps for US$30 to US$40 per day including insurance. The first 200 km are free and then you are charged 20 to 30c per km. The other agency's rates are similar.

Avis Rent-a-Car has an agency in the TraveLodge at Avenida Blancarte 130.

MEXICALI

Population: 500,000

Mexicali is one of Baja California's largest and fastest-growing cities. It is the capital of the state of Baja California (Northern Baja) and the north-westernmost terminus of the Mexican rail system. Like Tijuana, it is trying to shed its stereotypical border-town image.

A new Civic & Commercial Centre (Centro Cívico-Comercial) has been constructed in the southern part of the city. The centre includes a medical school, bull ring, movie theatres, bus station, hospitals, government offices and restaurants. The restaurant and shopping section of the centre is called the zona

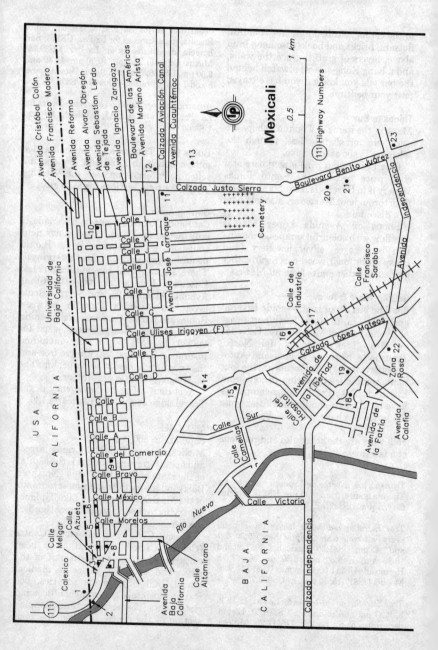

Mexicali

1 km

0.5

0

(111) Highway Numbers

Top: Melons, Tijuana (SW)
Left: Agua Caliente Tower, Tijuana (SW)
Right: Bullfight Poster (SW)

Top: Riviera, Ensenada (SW)
Bottom: Cabo San Lucas (SW)

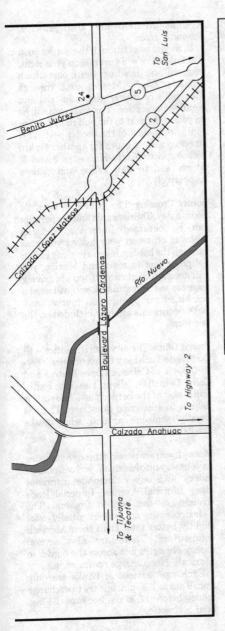

1 US Customs
2 Mexican Customs
3 Hotel del Norte/Restaurant del Norte
4 Parque Chapultepec
5 Post Office
6 Fortín de las Flores Hotel
7 Mariscos Olympo
8 Plaza Hotel
9 State Tourism Office (La Subdirección de Turismo del Estado)
10 Museum (El Museo Regional de la Universidad Autonomía de Baja California)
11 Coca-Cola Bottler
12 La Casa del Patrón
13 Baseball Stadium (Estadio de Beisbol 'Nido de las Aguilas')
14 El Teatro del Estado
15 City Tourism Office (El Comité de Turismo y Convenciones)
16 Motel Azteca de Oro
17 Railroad Station
18 Centro Civico-Comercial
19 Plaza de Toros Calafia
20 El Dragon Restaurant
21 Holiday Inn
22 Bus depot (Central Camionera)
23 Hotel Lucerna
24 La Misión Dragon Restaurant

rosa, probably a parroting of Mexico City's chic zona rosa of European-style cafés and restaurants. Mexicali does not yet have the same calibre of commercialism as Mexico City, but it's trying.

One of the most popular festivals here is the Fiesta del Sol, which celebrates Mexicali's founding in 1903. A variety of events is scheduled from 10 to 26 October, including pop-music groups, cock fights, art exhibitions, theatrical productions and a parade. An exposition of crafts, local industrial products and agriculture is also featured.

Mexicali lies at sea level. The maximum temperature is 46.6°C and the minimum is -2.2°C. Be warned that it is unbearably hot here in the summer.

Information & Orientation

Most of Mexicali's main streets run in relation to the border line. As you pass through the border post, the street on your left leads into Avenida Francisco Madero, which is one block south of and parallel to the border. This avenue passes through Mexicali's central business district. Restaurants, shops, bars and cheap, sleazy hotels are concentrated in this area. The other streets that run parallel to Avenida Madero are also principal shopping areas.

If, as you pass through the border post, you follow the wide avenue on your right, you will be heading south-east down Calzada López Mateos and through Mexicali's relatively new industrial and commercial section. The zona rosa will be on your right next to the bull ring, four km south/south-east of the border post. This street continues south for another 4½ km before splitting into Highways 2 and 5, which lead to San Felipe and Sonora respectively.

Border Crossing The border is open 24 hours a day. Tourist cards and car permits can be obtained from the Mexican customs office on your left as you pass through the border. If you are going to San Felipe or east to mainland Mexico, you will need a tourist card. If you are driving your car to the mainland, you will need a combined car permit and tourist card. Both documents are now included on the one form.

Tourist Office The city tourism office – El Comité de Turismo y Convenciones (tel 7-25-61) – is at Calzada López Mateos and Calle Camelias, about two km south/south-east of the border post. The staff is helpful in answering questions. There is usually someone around who speaks English.

Money If you are passing through Calexico on your way into Mexicali, you can change money and buy automobile insurance along Imperial Avenue. Imperial leads straight to the border crossing. The Calexico casas de cambio usually offer slightly better rates than their Mexicali competitors. There are also several money-changers just across the border in Mexicali. None charge commission.

Exchange services at banks are only from 9 am to 1.30 pm, but try to exchange money before 12.30 pm because the last hour is chaotic.

In Calexico there is a First Interstate Bank with a 24-hour teller machine at 250 East 4th St across from the De Anza Hotel.

El Museo Regional de la Universidad Autonomía de Baja California

This is a small museum at Avenida Reforma and Calle L (tel 2-57-15). It is also called El Museo Hombre, Naturaleza y Cultura. The exhibits cover a number of topics – human evolution, geology, photography and palaeontology. It is open Tuesday to Saturday from 9 am to 6 pm.

Plaza de Toros Calafia

The Plaza de Toros is where some of the best matadors in the world gather to test their courage against some of the biggest, meanest bulls in Mexico. The bull ring is at Avenida Calafia and Boulevard de Los Héroes next to the Centro Cívico y Comercial (tel 7-25-50). The matadors come for *la corrida de toros* (the bullfight) held on alternating Sundays at 4 pm between October and May. Tickets can be bought at the gate or arranged through the tourist office for US$6.

Places to Stay – bottom end

Fortín de las Flores Hotel (tel 2-45-22) at Avenida Cristóbal Colón 612 has somehow earned a one-star rating for its 23 rooms. Air-conditioning and TVs in each room are this hotel's only amenities.

Las Fuentes Hotel (tel 7-15-25) at Boulevard López Mateos 1655 is another one-star wonder. Its 37 rooms all have TVs which you will probably need to muffle the lascivious moans emanating from nearby rooms. This hotel seems to cater to a different clientele every hour.

Places to Stay – middle

The 173-room *Hotel/Motel Castel Calafia* (tel (706) 568-33-11, in the USA (213) 462-6391, (800) 421-0767) is at Calzada Justo Sierra 1495 about 2½ km south-east of downtown Mexicali. The rooms are plain, comfortable and air-conditioned; most

include colour TVs. Singles/doubles are US$20/US$23 per night.

The *Hotel Del Norte* (tel 54-05-75), Calle Melgar 205 at Avenida Francisco Madero, has 52 rooms, some with colour TVs and air-conditioning. Downstairs, the restaurant serves moderately priced Mexican dishes and embarrassingly huge Margaritas for only US$3 – embarrassing because they are so large everyone in the restaurant knows that you will hardly be able to stand up after finishing one. The hotel is conveniently located just across from the border crossing. A single costs US$15 and a double US$18.

Places to Stay – top end

The *Holiday Inn* (tel (706) 566-13-00, in the USA (800) 238-8000) is three km south-east of downtown Mexicali at Boulevard Benito Juárez 2220. It is the best hotel in Mexicali with all the usual amenities of a Holiday Inn. A single or double is US$48 per night.

Places to Eat

Mexicali has a fair selection of good restaurants, including a few excellent Chinese ones. Unfortunately they're scattered around town; buses are available from downtown.

Mexican Food *Cenaduría Selecta* at Avenida Arista 1510 and Calle G serves select dishes of typical Mexican fare such as tacos de carne and burritos. Prices average US$2 to US$3. Hours are 8 am to 11 pm.

La Casa del Patrón at Calzada Aviación 1000 in the Centro Comercial Sol serves mouth-watering charcoal-grilled steaks with salad and tortillas.

Mariscos Olympo, a small seafood restaurant at Calle Melgar 139, serves an octopus speciality. Frankly, I am a bit dubious about seafood restaurants far from the sea.

The *Restaurant del Norte*, a clean, modern, American-style coffee-shop, is part of the Hotel del Norte and offers exceptional value. They serve big, inexpensive meals from morning to night for under US$2. A spicy Mexican omelette costs US$1.60, filet mignon US$4 and T-bone steak US$4.

Chinese Food *El Dragon* is said to be one of Mexicali's best. It is housed in a huge pagoda at Boulevard Benito Juárez 1830 and is open from 11 am to 11.30 pm. A big meal of chop suey, fried rice, won-ton soup and roast duck costs US$3 to US$4. The waiters are an interesting cultural mix of Mexican and Chinese.

This restaurant should not be confused with *La Misión Dragon* which is half a km east of Boulevard Benito Juárez on Boulevard Lázaro Cárdenas. Unlike its more urban counterpart, this 'Dragon' is surrounded by beautiful gardens, fountains and pools. You will get more than enough food for US$2 to US$5 if you order à la carte. This may be the first time you eat Chinese food served by Spanish-speaking Chinese waiters while 'Madonna' tunes pour out from overhead speakers.

Things to Buy

Curio shops selling cheap leather goods and junky souvenirs cum trophies of brief and brave ventures across the border are concentrated on Calle Melgar and Avenida Reforma – easy walking distance from the border. Mexican liquor and beer are, of course, cheaper to buy here than in the USA. US customs regulations limit you to bringing one litre of liquor per person into the USA.

Getting There & Away

Bus The bus companies for inter-city travel are all located under one roof at the central station (Central Camionera) on Avenida Independencia near Calzada López Mateos. They are Autotransportes del Pacífico (tel 7-24-61), Autotransportes Tres Estrellas de Oro (tel 7-24-10), Autotransportes Norte de Sonora (tel 72-42-2l) and Autotransportes de la Baja California (tel 7-24-20).

Some sample fares with Tres Estrellas to destinations in mainland Mexico from Mexicali are: Guaymas US$10, Los Mochis US$14.50, Mazatlán US$20.50, Guadalajara US$27, Querétaro US$32, Manzanillo US$30.

Sample Tres Estrellas and ABC fares to destinations within Baja California are: Tijuana US$2.25, Ensenada US$3.75, Guerrero Negro US$11.25, San Ignacio US$13.25, Santa Rosalía US$14, Mulegé US$15, Loreto US$16.50, La Paz US$25.

The bus to La Paz leaves daily at 4.30 pm. The trip takes about 24 hours.

On the USA side in Calexico the Greyhound bus station (tel 357-1895 or toll free (800) 237-8211) is at 101 First St.

Rail The main station (tel 7-24-44) is at Calle Ulises Irigoyen or Calle F. Passenger service goes from Mexicali to Mexico City via Hermosillo, Guaymas, Los Mochis, Mazatlán and Guadalajara. For fare and schedule information and reservations call 57-23-86 or 57-21-01.

The express departs daily at 8 am and the local at 8.40 pm. One-way Pullman fare all the way to Mexico City is US$43 per person for a double compartment. Express tickets are sold at the station from 5 to 8 am daily. Local tickets are sold at the station from 4 to 8.30 pm daily.

It is recommended that you make reservations in advance for the Pullman compartments. Call the reservations numbers, or write to The Station Chief (El Jefe de Estación), Estación de Ferrocarril, Box 3-182, Mexicali, Baja California, Mexico, or PO Box 231, Calexico, California 92231, USA. Dining facilities are available on the express train. Snack-bar service is available on the local train. The following fares are estimates only:

Getting Around

All local city buses leave from Calle Altamirano two blocks from the border crossing (see map). The 'Justo Serra' bus goes to the museum. Any 'Centro Cívico' bus goes to the state tourism office, the bull ring and the train station. The 'Central Camionera' bus goes to the new civic-commercial centre and the intercity bus station.

28TH PARALLEL

The 28th Parallel splits Baja California into equal halves. It is marked by a 42.68-metre (140-foot) high steel monument which is supposed to resemble an eagle. The monument marks off the State of Baja California (Northern Baja) from the State of Baja California Sur (Southern Baja). It also commemorates the completion of Highway 1 and the unification of Northern and Southern Baja. The time zone changes from Pacific Time in the north to Mountain Time in the south, which is one hour ahead.

Hotel La Pinta Guerrero Negro, one of several La Pinta hotels in Baja, is situated precisely on the 28th parallel. It has 28 very comfortable singles/doubles for US$45/US$47. The hotel includes a restaurant, a bar and, next door, a desolate trailer park. There is a better trailer park in Guerrero Negro.

Southern Baja

GUERRERO NEGRO

The first town south of the 28th parallel, Guerrero Negro is renowned for having the world's largest evaporative salt works and a lagoon that annually becomes the mating and breeding grounds for California grey whales.

The salt works consist of thousands of evaporation pools, each of which is about 83½ square metres and 92 cm deep with sea water. The pools are just south of Guerrero Negro on your left as you enter

km		2nd	regular	single roomette	double roomette	double room
250	Pto Peñasco					
410	Caborca					
480	Trincheras					
534	Benjamín Hill	US$2.00	US$3.75	US$10.75	US$16.00	US$18.00
660	Hermosillo	US$2.50	US$4.50	US$15.50	US$22.50	US$25.25
801	Empalme					
919	Cd Obregón					
987	Navajoa	US$3.75	US$6.75	US$20.00	US$30.00	US$33.00
1126	Sufragio	US$4.25	US$7.75	US$22.50	US$33.75	US$37.50
1186	León Fonseca					
1227	Guamuchil					
1340	Culiacán					
1460	La Cruz					
1559	Mazatlán	US$6.00	US$10.50	US$30.50	US$45.75	US$50.75
1709	Acaponeta					
1776	Ruiz					
1875	Tepic					
2149	Guadalajara	US$8.25	US$14.50	US$40.50	US$61.50	US$68.00
2227	Ocotlán					
2253	La Barca					
2281	Yurecuaro					
2316	La Piedad					
2407	Irapuato					
2468	Celaya					
2513	Querétaro	US$9.50	US$17.00	US$47.75	US$72.25	US$80.00
2758	Mexico City	US$10.50	US$18.50	US$52.50	US$79.50	US$88.00

town on Boulevard Zapata. The water evaporates quickly here because of the intense dry heat of the immense Vizcaíno Desert farther south. After the water evaporates, the salt is scraped from pools with big dredges and then taken by truck to nearby quays. It is then transferred onto barges and taken to Cedros Island where freighters transport it to several countries. The works produce more than 5,512,679 tonnes of salt each year.

The breeding grounds for the grey whale are in Scammon's Lagoon, south of the salt works about 24 km from the junction with Highway 1. The lagoon has been designated a natural park called Parque Natural de Bellena Gris (Grey Whale Natural Park). It is named after Captain Charles Melville Scammon, a mid-19th-century American whaler who discovered the lagoon in the 1850s.

The whales migrate 9677 km each year from the Bering Sea to Scammon's Lagoon where they stay from late January to early March. The warm waters of the lagoon offer an ideal habitat for the grey whales to give birth and rear their offspring. By late March they begin their long journey back to the Bering Sea.

Information

Money A money-changer next door to the Las Dunas Motel offers a fair rate of exchange. There are also a few banks in town.

Places to Stay

Guerrero Negro does not have an abundance of places of stay. The *Motel El Morro* has clean basic rooms with hot showers for US$6 single, US$8 double and US$9.50 triple. It is on the north side of Boulevard Zapata before the huge radio antenna.

Las Dunas Motel is a few doors down from Motel El Morro. All of the rooms have showers and a strong smell of disinfectant. The rates are US$6.60

single, US$8.25 double and US$10 triple.

Cuartos de Sánchez-Smith is the best deal in town. There are showers in some of the rooms. To find it, continue along the main street past the city hall. When you see a park on your right, turn left and ask for directions to Calle Juan de la Barrera, a small street tucked behind a principal shopping street. Rates are US$5 double.

Places to Eat

Located on your right as you enter town, *Malarrimo* is one of the best restaurants in Guerrero Negro. Seafood is their speciality – everything from abalone and shrimp to fish and clams. A full meal costs US$3 to US$4.

Mario's Restaurant & Bar is next door to the Motel El Morro. They serve excellent, inexpensive seafood dishes.

The Mexican family-style *Restaurant Lupita* is on the north side of the main street in town. It can get a bit crowded with locals on the weekends, but their US$2 breakfast deal is worth the wait.

Getting Around

To get to the lagoon, if you do not have your own transport, you can either hike through the desert (not recommended if it is hot), hitch-hike (difficult if you do not see many gringos in the area) or hire a taxi for US$5. The best place to look for a ride is at the Malarrimo Trailer Park, which is just to your right as you enter town from Highway 1. You'll see the sign.

SAN IGNACIO

After the scrub brush and cacti forests of the Vizcaíno Desert, the lush oasis town of San Ignacio is a welcome sight. An underground river which surfaces just outside town appealed to a group of Jesuit priests who visited here in 1728. They decided to build a mission and plant dense groves of date palms and citrus trees, which still fill the arroyo surrounding the town. After the Jesuits were expelled, they were replaced by Dominican missionaries who built a beautiful lava-block church and mission, which continues to dominate the cool, tree-shaded plaza of San Ignacio.

Today, the church still holds services, and the town serves as a supply depot for surrounding ranchos. There are a few small grocery stores, a restaurant, a hotel, a casa de huéspedes and a *tortillería*. If you are coming from the north, this is one of the first places in Baja California where you begin to see vestiges of Baja's Spanish heritage. San Ignacio offers a peaceful break from the bustling development in most other Baja towns.

Information & Orientation

The actual town of San Ignacio is 1½ km from Highway 1. A paved road leads south from the highway junction (known as San Lino) past a small lake and through a jungle of palm trees into the town. The inter-city bus leaves you at the highway junction. You can either walk or hitch a ride into town.

Most of the town's basic services (telephone office, bank and grocery stores) are found around the plaza. Remarkably, international collect calls are quick and easy to make from here – much easier than calls from larger Baja towns.

Misión de San Ignacio

This mission church on the town plaza is one of the most beautiful and best preserved in Baja California. It was completed in 1786 by a Dominican priest named Juan Crisostomo Gómez, but the foundations date back to 1728. The church is well preserved because thick lava stone blocks were used for the walls. Services are still held here.

Places to Stay

The Fischer family's *La Posada Motel* is the only budget place to stay in town. Comfortable but spartan doubles with hot showers cost US$10. With the church behind you and the plaza on your left,

walk straight on until you see a road on your right. Follow this road to the end and turn left. The motel is on your right about one block up the hill.

The *Hotel La Pinta San Ignacio*, on the jungle road (the main road) just before you enter town, is part of the chain of La Pinta hotels in Baja California. At US$45 for a double it is designed more for vacationers than for budget-conscious travellers. The hotel was built to resemble an old Spanish mission with its tiled courtyard and pool set in groves of palms and citrus trees.

Camping This is possible at a trailer park behind the San Lino Pemex station (at the highway junction). Tents are difficult to set up because the ground could be too hard for tent stakes. Full hook-ups are available. Don't be startled by strange grunts and groans in the middle of the night. Local cows, donkeys and goats like to visit the park to munch on delectable weeds. If someone is around to collect money, then one night will cost US$3; otherwise there is no charge.

There are a couple of other campgrounds in the jungle closer to town. One campground is near a rotting pile of coconut shells and the other is beneath a grove of palm trees. Neither is particularly recommended because the bugs tend to be bothersome.

Places to Eat

La Casa Azul (The Blue House) is the home of the tortilla-maker. It is difficult to find, so ask the townspeople to steer you in the right direction. The house is interesting to visit if only to see customers streaming in with dish towels to wrap up fresh corn tortillas. A dozen cost 10c. Bring a towel too if you want to buy some.

Apart from the restaurant in the *Hotel La Pinta*, the *Lonchería Chalita* is about the only place to eat in town. Typical Mexican fare is served at very low prices. Best of all is the atmosphere because it is a small operation run in a family's living room. You eat whatever the family feels like serving that day. The restaurant is on the plaza near the Conasupo market.

The restaurant in the *Hotel La Pinta* also serves typical Mexican food, but the prices are much higher because the hotel caters mostly to gringos on short vacations. They serve lots of beef from the neighbouring cattle ranches.

Getting There & Away

The Tijuana-La Paz bus makes a daily stop at San Lino on Highway 1, the junction with the short road to San Ignacio. To leave San Ignacio buy a bus ticket at the Conasupo market on the town plaza. It is fairly easy to hitch-hike from the market to the Pemex station, where you can ask drivers for rides if you want to hitch-hike between towns and cities.

SANTA ROSALÍA

Population: 14,000

Santa Rosalía is unique among Mexican towns and villages. It was founded in the 1880s by the French-owned El Boleo Copper Company for miners working in nearby copper mines. El Boleo was one of the Rothschild family's many worldwide ventures. The company built the clapboard frame houses and French-style colonial homes that still occupy Santa Rosalía's main streets. They also assembled a pre-fabricated galvanised iron church designed by Alexandre Gustave Eiffel (of Eiffel Tower fame) for the 1889 World Fair in Paris. The church continues to be used for services.

The French operated the copper mine in Santa Rosalía until 1953. Most of the mines closed in 1956, but a few continue to produce ore. Most of the original 19th-century ore-processing plant is still intact. You can't miss it because the road into town passes beneath the plant's old conveyor belt.

Most of the downtown area was built in a small canyon or arroyo. Almost all the

town's shops and services are here while the residential areas are on plateaus on either side of the canyon. The northern mesa was where the French mining officials built their houses. Today, that area is home to the town's municipal authorities and the Hotel Francés.

Places to Stay

The two best hotels in Santa Rosalía are *El Morro Hotel* and the *Hotel Francés*. El Morro Hotel (tel 2-04-14) is 1½ km south of town just off Highway 1. Singles are US$10 and doubles are US$17. The Hotel Francés (tel 2-08-29) is on Calle 11 de Julio. Both are considered 1st-class hotels and have air-conditioned rooms, swimming pools, restaurants and bars. When the French controlled the local mining company the Hotel Francés served French food and wine. Singles are US$7.65, doubles US$10 and triples US$12.50.

The *Hotel Olvera* (tel 2-00-57) is on the 2nd floor of a building at No 14 on the plaza at the eastern end of Avenida Revolución (Avenida Álvaro Obregón). Clean, air-conditioned rooms with bathrooms and showers are US$5.

Camping There is a trailer park just south of town in a beautiful location right on Bahía de San Lucas. Hot showers and clean toilets are available. A space costs US$5. A small seafood restaurant under a thatched palapa (shade) roof serves fair-sized meals (fish tacos and burritos) for US$2.

Places to Eat

The ocean-front *Restaurant Selene* next door to the tourist office serves sumptuous seafood dishes. The port and ferry terminal are too close to the restaurant for a romantic seaside dinner, but at least the food is good. Prices are in the US$5 to US$10 range.

Restaurant El Pollito has chicken specialities but also serves lobster lunches or dinners for US$10 and various meat dishes for US$3 to US$4. *Restaurant Pericos* next door to El Pollito is also recommended; they serve almost the same dishes as El Pollito.

Restaurant Sabina is a family-style place frequented mostly by locals. All of the food is typically Mexican. Plan on US$1 to US$2 for a basic meal.

Restaurant Terraza is a popular Mexican family-style place recommended for its various fish specialities. Ask the locals for the locations.

Try the *Panadería El Boleo* on Avenida Revolución if you want, for delicious French-style breads and pastries. The bakery was started by the French when copper-mining operations were in full swing in the late 19th and early 20th centuries.

Getting There & Away

Bus All Tijuana-La Paz (or vice versa) buses stop daily in Santa Rosalía. One bus usually stops at 11 am (going north) and 9.30 pm (going south). The bus depot is across the highway from the tourist office just south of the Pemex station.

For hitch-hiking try the Pemex station; it's a popular stop for gringos heading north or south.

Ferry Santa Rosalía is the northernmost ferry depot on the Baja peninsula. The ferry sails from here to Guaymas on Tuesday, Thursday and Sunday at 11 pm and arrives at 7 am. It leaves Guaymas at 10 am and arrives in Santa Rosalía at 7 pm on Wednesday, Friday and Monday. The ferry office (tel 852-00-13) in Santa Rosalía is just north of the tourist office and south of the old ore-processing plant. Make reservations at least three days in advance. Even if you have a reservation, get to the ticket office early to buy your ticket. It is essential that you have your tourist card. If you have a vehicle, then the car permit should double as a tourist card.

Ticket prices are US$0.40 for *salon* class (reclining seats), US$0.80 for *turista*

class (bunk in a roomette with two other persons), US$1.80 for *cabina* class (two-person cabin with bathroom) and US$3.50 for *especial* class (deluxe cabins not available on all ships, but definitely worth getting because the experience is incredible). In the winter, ferries are occasionally delayed because they cannot disembark or arrive if the winds are too strong off the coast of Santa Rosalía.

Vehicle prices are US$2.50 for up to five metres; US$2.80 for up to 6½ metres; and US$5.25 for vehicles with trailers up to nine metres. Do not forget your vehicle permit if you are going from Baja to the mainland. You should obtain the car permit in Tijuana. For more information see the 'Facts for Visitor' chapter.

LORETO

Population: 5000

Loreto is 339 km north of La Paz and 136 km south of Mulegé. It is a small, unassuming fishing and farming town with a few mud and cobblestone streets and a restored mission that is a reminder of Loreto's important role in the history of the Californias.

The first permanent European settlement in the Californias, Loreto was founded with the establishment of Misión Nuestra Señora de Loreto on 25 October 1697 by the adventurous Jesuit priest and explorer Juan María Salvatierra. This was the first of several missions established in the Californias for the explicit purpose of converting local Indian inhabitants to Catholicism, settling the land and thus indirectly extending the control of the Spanish Crown in what was then called 'New Spain'. Loreto became the first capital of the Californias and served as a convenient staging point for the expansion of the mission system even after the official expulsion of the Jesuits began in 1767. Father Junípero Serra arrived here in 1769 and trekked northward to present-day California to establish a now-famous chain of missions. Loreto continued to serve as capital of the Californias until

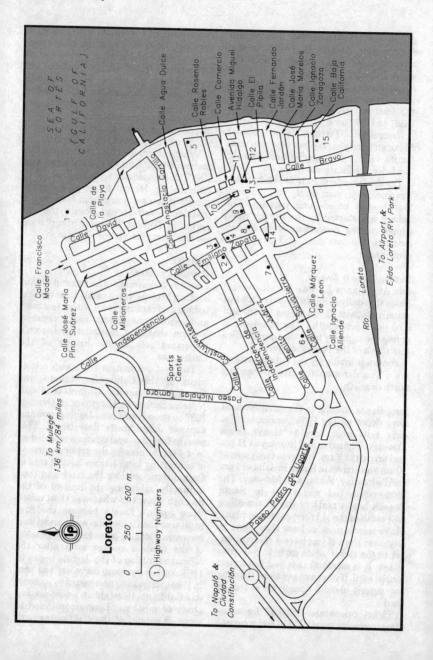

Loreto

SEA OF CORTÉS (GULF OF CALIFORNIA)

Calle Agua Dulce
Calle Rosendo Robles
Calle Comercio
Avenida Miguel Hidalgo
Calle El Pipila
Calle Fernando Jordán
Calle José María Morelos
Calle Ignacio Zaragoza
Calle Baja California

Calle Anastacio Carillo
Calle de la Playa
Calle David
Calle Francisco Madero
Calle José María Pino Suárez
Calle Misioneros
Calle Independencia
Calle

Calle Bravo
Calle Zapata
Calle Emiliano
Calle Salvatierra
Calle Márquez de León
Calle Ignacio Allende
Calle Benito Juárez
Calle Independencia
Calle Héroes de
Calle Constituyentes

Sports Center
Paseo Nicholas Tamara
Paseo Pedro de Ugarte

Río Loreto

To Airport & Ejido Loreto RV Park

To Mulegé 136 km/84 miles

To Nopaló & Ciudad Constitución

1 Highway Numbers

0   250   500 m

1	Hotel La Pinta
2	Pemex Gasoline Station
3	Focandi Department Store
4	Caesar's Restaurant
5	Hotel Misión
6	Motel Salvatierra
7	Public Telephones
8	Dive Shop
9	Misión de Nuestra Señora de Loreto/Museum
10	Post Office/Telegraph Office
11	Plaza Civica (Zócalo)
12	La Casita Restaurant
13	Café Olé
14	Bus Station
15	Hotel Oasis

most of the town was destroyed by a hurricane in 1829. The capital was then moved to La Paz.

Loreto was chosen as the site for a mission and capital because it was believed to be protected from inclement weather by mountains to the west and the long island – Isla del Carmen – offshore. This topography still offers considerable protection from bad weather and was probably a major factor in convincing the Mexican government to begin construction of a major tourist resort here. The climate was another attraction because each year there is an average of 300 days of sunshine and temperatures ranging from 18° to 32°C. Another less obvious factor was that the wife of the governor of Southern Baja California was from Loreto.

Over the last several years Fonatur, the Mexican government tourist development agency which developed major resorts such as Cancún and Ixtapa, has been building a huge resort 6½ km south of Loreto. It is a strange complex in the making because of the order in which things are being built. An 'international' airport was built just outside of town. Streets were laid, lamp-posts erected, and electrical lines strung in this resort complex now called Nopoló, though lots of shrubs and weeds aren't what you'd

expect of a luxury resort. The complex includes an El Presidente Hotel and a 'decoturf' tennis centre that has John McEnroe as the 'touring pro'.

Information & Orientation

At the centre of Loreto is the old mission church, a structure that towers above all else. You can see it as you enter the town from the north on Highway 1. Calle Independencia branches off from Highway 1 and becomes one of the principal roads in town. To reach the church, go 1½ km down Calle Independencia and turn left at Calle Salvatierra. Most of the town's hotels and services are within walking distance of the church.

The bank, post office, and telephone and telegram offices are all near or around the plaza or zócalo, which is 200 metres east of the church at Calle Francisco Madero and Calle Salvatierra.

La Misíon de Nuestra Señora de Loreto

Founded on 25 October 1697 by Father Juan María Salvatierra, this was the first mission and permanent European settlement in the Californias. The floor plan of the church was arranged in the shape of a Greek cross. Most of the building fell into disrepair after a hurricane destroyed much of the town in 1829. It was restored only over the last decade. The beautiful gilded altar and crude old portraits of past resident priests remain intact in the main chapel of the church.

Museum

A small museum set up by the National Institute of History & Anthropology stands next to the church. Several rooms of interesting exhibits and displays chronicle the restoration of the mission, the history of Baja California and the establishment of the mission system. The set of intricately carved leather saddles was presumably used on 19th-century ranches. The museum bookstore sells many books in Spanish about the history of Mexico and Baja California.

Scuba Diving & Snorkelling

Both activities are possible in the beautiful reefs offshore around the islands of Isla del Carmen and Isla Coronado. Carlos Díaz Uroz and his wife own Loreto Divers (tel 3-00-29) at Calle Salvatierra 47 near the mission. They organise various diving trips. From April to November the water temperature is an average 24° to 29°C and visibility depth is 18 to 24 metres. From December to March the water temperature is an average 15° to 21°C and visibility depth is nine to 15 metres. Complete rental equipment is available. A beginner's-level scuba course is offered for US$60 in open water.

Fishing

This is the main reason many people visit Loreto. The fishing zones here are supposedly some of the greatest in the world. Several fishermen will gladly take gringos and anyone else on day-long fishing trips. The fishing near Loreto, however, is not as good as it used to be. Professional shrimp fishermen have overfished the waters by using gill nets, which catch and kill as much as nine tonnes of fish for each tonne of shrimp. The government of Southern Baja California has only recently begun to consider measures to prevent an almost complete depletion of fisheries in the Sea of Cortés. It is highly likely that something will be done soon because of Baja's economic dependency on tourism.

Places to Stay – bottom end

Motel Salvatierra (tel 3-00-21) is on the left side of the main road, Calle Salvatierra, as you enter town from the south on Highway 1. The rooms are clean and have air-conditioning and hot showers, but they look a bit worn. Rates are US$6.50 single, US$7.50 double, US$8.50 triple.

The Casa de Huéspedes San Martín is at Calle Juárez 4. It is the cheapest place in town, but for what you get it still doesn't seem worth the price. A single costs US$5,

a double US$6. Each room has a basic shower that usually has hot water. The place was being renovated, which is probably why it appeared shabby.

Camping The only official camping in the area is at Ejido Loreto RV Park. The park is south-east of town on the other side of the river and right on the beach. The American managers hope to eventually develop a large 'RV village' here. Full facilities and hook-ups are already in place. These include clean bathrooms, hot showers, a laundry room and electricity. They will also arrange seven-hour fishing trips for US$60 and boat trips to Coronado Island. Office hours are 8 am to 1 pm and 2 to 9 pm. The rate is US$7.50 per space.

Unofficial camping is available at the small cove just south of the empty streets of Nopoló.

Places to Stay – middle & top end

The Hotel Misión de Loreto (tel 3-00-48) at Calle de la Playa 1 is on the waterfront east of the plaza. The rooms are comfortable; several have great views of the Sea of Cortés and all are air-conditioned. Rates are US$25 single, US$30 double and US$35 triple. If the hotel really wants your business, they will sometimes offer small discounts. There is a swimming pool and two restaurants on the premises. The hotel manager can arrange a boat for fishing trips for US$70 per day.

Hotel La Pinta Loreto (tel 3-00-25, toll free in the USA (800) 472-2427) is 1½ km north of the plaza. It has 50 rooms, many of which face the Sea of Cortés. Most rooms are new and have air-conditioning, showers, balconies or patios and TVs. There is also a swimming pool, restaurant and bar.

La Siesta Bungalows (tel 3-00-29) are owned by Carlos Díaz, the owner of Loreto's dive shop. He rents two fully furnished beach-front units for US$22 double, and US$4 for each extra person.

He can also arrange a combination of diving trips and accommodation, for example two nights and one day of diving for US$60, three nights and two days of diving for US$95, or four nights and five days of diving for US$195. Contact Señor Díaz at Calle Salvatierra 47, next to the mission.

Places to Eat

Caesar's Restaurant (tel 3-02-03) is across from the Focandi department store near the intersection of Calles Emiliano Zapata and Benito Juárez. A photograph of Señor Caesar strategically placed beneath the skulls of two small animals greets you as you enter. The entire place is under a big palapa (shade hut). The food is some of the best in town. A seafood lunch averages US$3.50; the seafood platter is more than enough for one person. Various meat dishes like carne asada cost US$4 to US$5.

Try *La Casita Restaurant* for inexpensive fast food such as hot dogs, tamales and hotcakes. Prices are US$1 to US$2 for enough to fill your stomach. It is just south of the the plaza on Calle Francisco Madero.

A bakery one block east of Rancho Viejo Restaurant on Calle Benito Juárez sells many types of *pan dulce* (sweet rolls) and breads.

Getting There & Away

Air Aeroméxico has daily flights (except Wednesday) from Los Angeles to Loreto via Tijuana and vice versa. After Loreto the flight goes to Mexico City via Guadalajara. For now these are the only international connections through Loreto's international airport.

Bus The Tijuana-La Paz buses stop daily at the Loreto bus station, located where Avenida Miguel Hidalgo merges with Calle Salvatierra. The buses also usually stop at Nopoló and Puerto Escondido. Buses to La Paz (US$4) depart at 8 am, 10 am, 2 pm and 3 pm. Buses to Tijuana (US$13) depart at 3, 6, 9 and 11 pm.

LA PAZ

Population: 150,000

La Paz is the capital of the state of Baja California Sur or Southern Baja. 'La Paz' means 'peace', a suitable word for the city today. Its altitude is six metres above sea level. Maximum temperature is 42°C; the minimum is 10°C.

Information & Orientation

It is not easy to get lost in La Paz. As Highway 1 approaches the city, it begins to run parallel to Bahía de La Paz (the Bay of La Paz) and is also known as Calle Abasolo. You can skip the downtown area and head straight for Cabo San Lucas by turning right on Calle 5 de Febrero and then following the signs to Carretera al Sur and Cabo San Lucas. After Calle Abasolo (Highway 1) crosses Calle 5 de Febrero and passes four more streets, it is called Paseo Álvaro Obregón and runs along the waterfront. Paseo Álvaro Obregón is also referred to as the corniche or malecón. When you see the Hotel de los Arcos on your right, most of downtown La Paz is within one or two blocks of Paseo Álvaro Obregón. Most points of interest, hotels and restaurants are in this area. The tourist office is on the waterfront after the wharf. If you turn right on Avenida Independencia just after the tourist office and go up approximately four blocks, you will be in the heart of the city at Plaza Constitución.

Immigration The Immigration Office is at Paseo Álvaro Obregón and Calle Muelle. If you plan to travel to the mainland and your tourist card has not yet been stamped, you must visit this office before buying a ferry ticket. You may not be able to buy a ferry ticket if your tourist card has not yet been approved. The office is on the 2nd floor. Hours are 8 am to 3 pm Monday to Friday. On the weekends, immigration

To Highway 1 &
Trailer Parks

Calle Rangel

Calle Topete

Calle Abasolo

To Airport

Calle Belisario Domínguez

Calle Francisco Madero

Calle Revolución

Calle Aquiles Serdán

Calle Guillermo Prieto

Calle Ignacio Ramírez

Calle Ignacio Altamirano

Calle Valentín Gómez Farías

Calle Héroes de la Independencia

Calle Josefa Ortiz de Domínguez

Calle Lic. Verdad

Calle Conde de Revillagigedo

Calle Gral Félix Ortega

Camino A Las Garzas

Calle Isabel La Católica

Calle Meliton Albanez

Calle México

Calle Durango

Calle Chiapas

Calle Yucatán

To Cabo San
Lucas 221 km

Calle Mijares

Calle Isabel La Católica

Calle Meliton Albanez

Calle México

Calle Durango

Calle Chiapas

Calle Yucatán

Calle Padre Kino

School

Govern-
ment
Buildings

Calle Cuauhtémoc

Calle Sonora

Calle 5 de Febrero

Calle Navarro

Calle Encinas

Calle Legaspy

Calle Márquez de León

Calle Pineda

Calle Juárez

Calle Allende

Calle Rosales

Calle Bravo

Calle Jalisco

Calle Oaxaca

Calle Nayarit

Calle Puebla

Calle Sinaloa

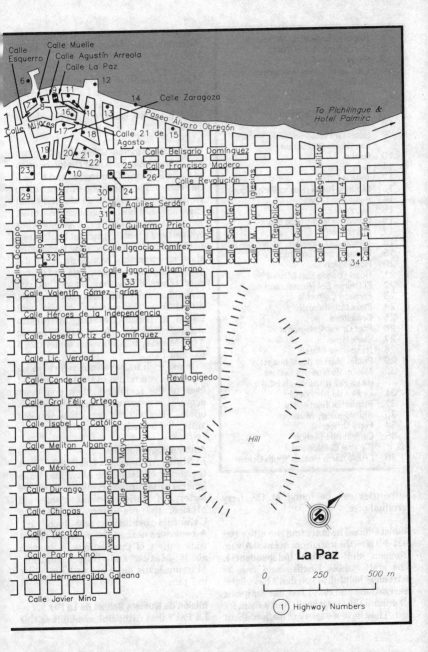

Calle Esquerro
Calle Muelle
Calle Agustín Arreola
Calle La Paz
Calle Zaragoza
Paseo Álvaro Obregón
To Pichilingue & Hotel Palmirc
Calle Mijares
Calle 21 de Agosto
Calle Belisario Domínguez
Calle Francisco Madero
Calle Revolución
Calle Aquiles Serdán
Calle Guillermo Prieto
Calle Ignacio Ramírez
Calle Ignacio Altamirano
Calle Valentín Gómez Farías
Calle Héroes de la Independencia
Calle Josefa Ortiz de Domínguez
Calle Lic. Verdad
Calle Conde de
Revillagigedo
Calle Gral Félix Ortega
Calle Isabel La Católica
Calle Meliton Albanez
Calle México
Calle Durango
Calle Chiapas
Calle Yucatán
Calle Padre Kino
Calle Hermenegildo Galeana
Calle Javier Mina
Calle Ocampo
Calle Degollado
16 de Septiembre
Calle Reforma
Calle Victoria
Calle Salvatierra
Calle M. Torre Iglesias
Calle República
Calle Guerrero
Calle Heroico Colegio Militar
Calle Héroes Del 47
Calle Ejido
Calle Morelos
Avenida Independencia
Avenida 5 de Mayo
Avenida Constitución
Calle Hidalgo
Hill

La Paz

0   250   500 m

(1) Highway Numbers

1	Registro Federal de Vehículos
2	Restaurant/Bar El Cheff
3	Hotel de los Arcos
4	Las Casas de las Artesanías de Baja California Sur
5	Aero California
6	Wharf
7	Post Office/Telegrams
8	Immigration Office
9	Hotel La Perla/Hertz/ Las Brisas Restaurant
10	Banks
11	Dive Shop
12	Tourist Office
13	Medrita Travel (Bus to Pichilingue)
14	Restaurant Kiwi
15	Aeroméxico
16	Dorian's Department Store
17	Chinatown
18	Palacio de Gobierno
19	Hostería del Convento
20	Hotel Palencia
21	Hotel Posada San Miguel
22	El Quinto Sol (Restaurant)
23	Pensión California
24	Plaza Constitución
25	Bookstore
26	Post Office/Telegrams
27	Clark Hotel
28	Hospedaje Mareli
29	Public Market (local buses)
30	Misión de Nuestra Señora de La Paz (mission church)
31	La Flor de Michoacán
32	Bismark II Restaurant
33	Anthropology Museum
34	Ferry Office
35	Central Bus Station (Central Camionera)
36	CREA Youth Hostel/Youth Centre

authorities can be found at the ferry terminal pier.

Tourist Office The state tourism office (tel 2-11-99) is on the waterfront at Paseo Álvaro Obregón and Avenida Independencia. The staff speaks English and can be extremely helpful. If you don't have hotel reservations and don't feel like traipsing all around the city, they'll find a room for you. They have a variety of leaflets about

Baja. Hours are 9 am to 7 pm daily except Saturday, when hours are 9 am to 1 pm. Holiday hours are the same.

Money There are several banks and casas de cambio in downtown La Paz. Most are on or around Calle 16 de Septiembre. Bank hours are 8 am to 1 pm Monday to Friday.

Vehicle Registration Office The Registro Federal de Vehículos is near the intersection of Calle Belisario Domínguez and Calle 5 de Febrero. They issue you a free permit to transport your vehicle on the ferry and drive on the Mexican mainland. You must have this permit before the ferry officials will sell you a ticket; it cannot be obtained in Cabo San Lucas. To obtain it you must show an ownership certificate or a valid vehicle registration certificate and tourist card (Form FM1) that shows that you brought a vehicle into Mexico. Form FM1 differs from the standard tourist card issued to people travelling in Mexico without vehicles. Hours are 8 am to 3 pm Monday to Friday and sometimes 4 to 7 pm.

If you wish to leave your vehicle in La Paz while you return to the USA or head over to the mainland, then you must acquire the proper authorisation from this office. They will tell you where you can 'officially' leave it.

Anthropology Museum
El Museo Antropología (tel 2-01-62) is at the corner of Calle 5 de Mayo and Calle Ignacio Altamirano. Exhibits show the history of various ethnic groups in Mexico, the pre-history of the Baja California peninsula and local art. A bookstore next to the museum sells a wide variety of publications in Spanish about Mexico and Baja California. Museum hours are 9 am to 1 pm and 4 to 7 pm.

Misión de Nuestra Señora de La Paz
La Paz's first cathedral was built at this

site on Plaza Constitución (Constitution Square) in 1720 by Jesuit missionaries Jaime Bravo and Juan de Ugarte. The present church was built on the foundation of the mission only this century.

Beaches

There are several fairly good but somewhat short beaches north and west of La Paz. To the west are the bay beaches of El Comitán and Las Hamacas. If you do not have your own vehicle, you must hire a taxi to get to these beaches. The beaches to the north are on the Pichilingue Peninsula.

From south to north, the first set of beaches are Palmira, Coromuel and Caimancito. Playa de Palmira has a hotel, restaurant and bar. The latter two beaches have a restaurant and bar, toilets and plenty of shade huts or palapas. Playa Tesoro is the next beach to the north; it also has a restaurant and shade. Playa de Pichilingue 100 metres north of the ferry terminal has a restaurant and bar, toilets and shade. Camping is definitely possible on this beach. This is the last stop for the 'Medrita' bus from town. The bus leaves from the Medrita Travel Agency on Paseo Álvaro Obregón near Calle 5 de Mayo.

Farther north are the exceptional beaches of Balandra, Tecolote and Coyote. You must have your own sturdy vehicle to drive the approximately eight km of dirt roads and tracks to these beaches. Playa Balandra is beautiful but not good for camping because of flies and mosquitoes. Playa del Tecolote (Owl Beach) is spectacularly located across from Espíritu Santo Island. It is ideal for camping, but there are no facilities (including drinking water). Playa del Coyote, a short distance east, is more isolated than Playa del Tecolote.

Diving

Diving and snorkelling in the Bay of La Paz are fantastic. Equipment rentals and day trips can be arranged from dive shops in La Paz. There are dive shops at Independencia 107-B and Paseo Álvaro Obregón 1680. Both are run by Fernando and Francisco Aguilar. An all-day snorkelling trip which includes equipment, lunch and soft drinks costs US$30. An all-day scuba diving trip, which includes two tanks, weight belts, backpacks, lunch and soft drinks, costs US$55. They claim that they can provide anything you need.

Places to Stay – bottom end

The *Hotel Posada San Miguel* at Calle Belisario Domínguez 15140 is a pleasant colonial-style place with lots of blue-and-white Spanish tiles and black wrought-iron set around a courtyard. Rooms are dark but clean. Singles are US$3.50, doubles US$4, triples US$5, quads US$5.80. All rooms have bathrooms, but there is hot water only from 6 to 11 am and 5 to 11 pm.

The *Pensión California* (tel 2-28-96) at Calle Degollado 209 between Calle Madero and Calle Revolución is a long-time favourite among budget travellers and has lots of character. Each room is basic, with an overhead fan, poor fluorescent lighting, old wooden vent-like windows and a shower. The courtyard is a jungle maze of tropical plants and trees. Singles or doubles are US$4, triples US$5, quads US$6.

The *Hostería del Convento* (tel 2-35-08) at Calle Madero 85 is a budget hotel on par with the Pensión California; in fact it's owned by the same people. Singles are US$3.50, doubles US$4, triples US$5.

Camping There are several trailer parks in and around La Paz where you can camp for US$5 to US$10 per vehicle or tent. You can also camp for US$1 or sometimes free at the beaches on the Pichilingue Peninsula.

If you are coming from the north, the first park you'll see is *El Centenario Trailer Park* in the small community of El Centenario. It is 15 km north of La Paz on the Bay of La Paz. The park is also known as the *Oasis Los Aripez Trailer Park*. All spaces face the bay and have full hook-ups. Facilities include toilets, hot showers, a restaurant, a bar and a laundry room. They charge US$8 per night for two people.

One of the next parks on Highway 1 is *El Cardón Trailer Park* four km from town. It is not near the beach, but in a nicely wooded area. There are full hook-ups and facilities including a laundry room, small grocery store, hot showers, toilets and restaurant. They charge US$5 per night for a vehicle or tent.

La Paz Trailer Park is a deluxe park 1½ km south of downtown La Paz. Their luxury camping facilities include very clean bathrooms and showers, a great restaurant, a jacuzzi, a grocery store and a swimming pool. Not surprisingly, rates are US$10 for a vehicle and US$6 for a tent. If you feel like camping in comfort, this is the place to do it.

Places to Stay – middle

The *Hotel La Perla* (tel 2-07-77) is one of the best deals in La Paz. It is in the centre of town at Paseo Álvaro Obregón 1570 and Calle La Paz across from a short stretch of bayside beach. There are three classes of rooms with rates ranging from US$6 to US$15 per night; all have air-conditioning and showers. The hotel has a restaurant, bar and nightclub.

Hospedaje Mareli (tel 2-10-17) is a small guest house at Calle Aquiles Serdán 283 between Calle Bravo and Calle Ocampo with clean, pleasant, air-conditioned rooms. It is not far from the centre of town, only about a 10-minute walk from Plaza Constitución. A double room costs US$8.50.

Places to Stay – top end

The *Hotel de los Arcos* (tel 2-27-44) at Paseo Álvaro Obregón 498 is one of the best hotels in town. All rooms have air-conditioning, telephones, colour TVs and showers. This is essentially a tourist-class hotel and a pleasant place to stay if you want to pay the price. Rates are US$36 single, US$38 double and US$40 triple.

Reservations can be made in the USA by calling (800) 421-3772; in California call (800) 352-2579 or (714) 827-3933. The address of their US agent is Baja Hotel Reservations, 4332 Katella Avenue, Los Alamitos, California 90720.

Places to Eat

Try the *Bismark II Restaurant* for excellent seafood at US$3 to US$4 for a full meal. This place is popular with local Mexican families.

Las Brisas Restaurant is on Paseo Álvaro Obregón near the Hertz Rent-a-Car office.

Restaurant/Bar El Cheff is on Paseo Álvaro Obregón one block south of the Hotel de los Arcos. Part of the restaurant is nicely situated on a veranda overlooking the bay. They serve big, filling dishes of Mexican food and various types of seafood for US$3 to US$4 per meal.

Restaurant Kiwi serves delicious seafood including lobster, shrimp and oysters. It is on the bay side of Paseo Álvaro Obregón between Constitución and 5 de Mayo – a romantic though touristy place to watch the sunset. Prices average US$5.

Restaurant/Bar El Cheff is on Paseo Álvaro Obregón one block west of the is the place to come for a cheap, delectable steak.

Getting There & Away

Air There are daily flights on Aeroméxico and Mexicana between La Paz and

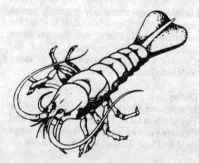

Culiacán, Durango, Guadalajara, Guaymas, Los Angeles, Mazatlán, Mexico City, Puerto Vallarta, Tijuana and Tucson.

Aerocalifornia operates daily flights between La Paz, Tijuana and Los Mochis. The flight to Los Mochis departs daily at 8 am, arriving at 8.30 am. The fare is US$30. In the USA their representative has an office at the Tijuana Baja Information Center (tel (619) 299-8518, toll free (800) 522-1516). Their address is 7860 Mission Center Court, Suite 202, San Diego, California 92108. Their office in La Paz is at the airport.

The Aeroméxico office (tel 2-00-91, 2-00-93, 2-16-36, 2-76-36) is on Paseo Álvaro Obregón between Calles Hidalgo and Morelos; the Mexicana Airlines office is at Paseo Álvaro Obregón 340.

The only way to get to and from the La Paz airport is by taxi. The fare is US$3 to US$4.

Bus Two inter-city bus companies operate from La Paz: Autotransportes Aguila y Tres Estrellas de Oro and Autotransportes de La Paz. The buses of Aguila y Tres Estrellas leave from the Central Camionera (central bus station) that is at Calle 5 de Febrero and Calle Valentín Gómez Farías. The buses of Autotransportes de La Paz leave from in front of the public market at Calle Guillermo Prieto and Calle Degollado.

Following is some fare and schedule information:

Tres Estrellas buses northbound:
Loreto, US$4.75, 9 am, 12 noon, 5.30 pm
Santa Rosalía, US$7.25, 9 am, 12 noon
San Ignacio, US$8, 10 am and 1, 4, 6, 8 and 10 pm
Guerrero Negro, US$10, departures as for San Ignacio
Ensenada, US$18.25, departures as for San Ignacio
Tijuana, US$20, departures as for San Ignacio
Mexicali, US$22, departures as for San Ignacio

Tres Estrellas buses southbound:
San José del Cabo, US$2.75, 7, 9, 9.30 and 11 am, 1, 2, 3, 5, 6 and 7 pm
Cabo San Lucas, US$3.05, departures as for San José
Todos Santos, US$1.80, 9 am, 2 pm and 6 pm

Following is fare and schedule information for Autotransportes La Paz. These buses take the new highway through Todos Santos on the western side of the Baja cape area:

Autotransportes La Paz buses southbound:
Todos Santos, US$1.80, 8.30 am, 1.30 pm and 4.30 pm
Cabo San Lucas, US$3, departures as for Todos Santos
San José del Cabo, US$3.50, departures as for Todos Santos

Ferry La Paz is a major terminus for ferries to the mainland. The ferry office (tel 2-01-09) or Oficina de Transbordadores is at Calle Ignacio Ramírez and Calle Ejido, 13 blocks east and five blocks south of the state tourism office. Reservations should be made as far in advance as possible. Supposedly you can do this three weeks in advance by calling (706) 822-01-09 (from the USA). If they tell you that cabin tickets are sold out, don't believe them. Many people make reservations for cabins and then do not confirm them in time. Tickets must be confirmed by 2 pm one day prior to departure. At 3 pm the cabins which were not confirmed are sold on a first-come, first-served basis. Sometimes this degenerates into a shoving match to see who stays at the beginning of the line. Hold your ground.

Tickets should be purchased a day in advance before 2 pm either at this office or at the ferry terminal on the Pichilingue peninsula 22½ km from downtown La Paz. Your tourist card and/or vehicle permit must be valid, otherwise you will not be sold the tickets.

The city office is open daily from 7.30 am to 1 pm and 2 to 6 pm. To get there from downtown La Paz take the 'Panteón' bus from the market at Calles Degollado and Revolución; catch it on Calle Revolución. To get to the ferry terminal catch the 'Medrita' bus from in front of Medrita Travel at Paseo Álvaro Obregón and Calle 5 de Mayo. A taxi to the ferry office costs US$1.50.

Following is rate and schedule information for the ferries to and from La Paz. For an explanation of the various classes, see the 'Getting There' chapter. Fares are estimates only:

class	Mazatlán	Topolobampo (Los Mochis)
salon	US$0.55	US$0.55
turista	US$1.10	US$1.10
cabina	US$2.35	US$2.35
especial	US$4.65	US$4.65

To either destination, vehicles up to five metres cost US$3.75, five to 6½ metres US$4.25, with trailer up to nine metres US$7.35, with trailer up to 17 metres US$11.25. Motorcycles are US$0.55.

The ferry departs for Mazatlán every day at 5 pm and arrives at 9 am the following day. Departures for Topolobampo (near Los Mochis, the terminus for the Copper Canyon train trip) are every Thursday and Sunday at 8 pm, arriving at 4 am the next day. Westbound ferries leave Topolobampo every Tuesday and Friday at 10 am and arrive in La Paz at 6 pm.

On Friday there is usually a ferry from La Paz to Puerto Vallarta, which leaves at noon and arrives at 10 am the next day. Check on this because the schedule has been changing over the last few years. At one point this was supposed to be a temporary service.

Getting Around

Walking, local buses and taxis are the principal means of getting around. Most of the local buses begin their journeys in front of the public market at Degollado and Guillermo Prieto.

The bus to the Pichilingue ferry terminal and beaches is called the 'Medrita' bus. It departs from in front of the Medrita Travel Agency at Paseo Álvaro Obregón and 5 de Mayo.

TODOS SANTOS

Until recently the small town of Todos Santos was rarely visited by outsiders because it was not connected to La Paz and Cabo San Lucas by paved road. When the road was finished in 1985 many people began to visit, the effects of which are gradually being noticed. Fortunately, the town has not yet been transformed into a tourist centre, although it is likely that the beauty and isolation of nearby beaches will attract increasing numbers of visitors.

There are only two hotels in town, but that is certain to change. The *Hotel La Misión* is a favourite among budget travellers. It is just off the main road; you'll see the signs as you enter town. They charge US$5 for a basic but clean double room.

Some of the most beautiful beaches you'll ever see are only 1½ km from Todos Santos. To get to them walk through the fields behind Hotel La Misión. You may have an entire beach all to yourself.

EL TRIUNFO

If you decide to follow the eastern route down the cape, then El Triunfo will be the first town you pass. In the latter half of the 19th century, it was one of the most important towns in Southern Baja California. When gold and silver were discovered in the area the town's population swelled to more than 10,000. The mines were closed in 1926. Today El Triunfo is a quiet place with only a smokestack and old mill left from its mining days.

SAN ANTONIO

In 1748 silver was discovered eight km south of present-day San Antonio by a retired Spanish soldier. By 1756 silver had been discovered farther north and the town of San Antonio was founded. The mines produced plenty of silver until about the middle of the 19th century.

The town is in a picturesque location on the side of a canyon. It is a small farming centre with nothing of great interest.

LOS BARRILES

After going south from La Paz through the Baja Cape mountains of Sierra de la Laguna, you return to the coast at the small town of Los Barriles. Over the last decade a few attempts were made to transform this wind-blown fishing and farming town into a minor resort. The great fishing attracted visitors only from May to October. The rest of the year the town was deserted because there were few attractions.

However, in 1981 a pair of wind-surfing fanatics named Jay Valentine and Dusen Mills discovered that the spectacular winds of Los Barriles and the Bay of Palms were perfect for wind-surfing; they had searched all over the world for a winter locale like this. They established The Baja High Wind Center to organise group trips and competitions in Los Barriles.

From the launching site in front of the Rancho Buena Vista Hotel the shoreline runs south and then east out to the Sea of Cortés. Theoretically it is possible because of the curved shoreline and side-shore wind, to sail 32¼ km out to sea and still be close to the beach. The shoreline acts as a long leeward safety net. If you venture too far, the tide will eventually take you back to the shore. A few words of warning: because of high wind conditions, this area is suitable only for experienced wind-surfers.

The Baja High Wind Center is based in the San Francisco area. Each winter the Center is located at the Rancho Buena Vista Hotel in Los Barriles. Courses are held weekly from November to April with world-class instructors and prototypes of the latest wind-surfing equipment direct from the manufacturers. Seventy boards are available for course participants.

Each participant is videotaped while wind-surfing and then evaluated later by the instructors. In January the Center sponsors the Baja International Board Wind Surf Championships. The Center's address is: PO Box 1374, Sausalito, California 94966, USA (tel (415) 332-0110, toll free in California (800) 323-1991, toll free in the rest of the USA (800) 222-5697).

Accommodation and lesson packages include seven nights and eight days in deluxe 1st-class rooms at the Rancho Buena Vista Hotel, unlimited use of the equipment, three meals per day, airport transport to and from La Paz and instruction. Prices range from US$610 to US$655 for a single, US$610 to US$784 for a double. Group rates are available.

If you are not participating in the Baja High Wind Center's programme, it's not recommended that you stay at the *Rancho Buena Vista Hotel*. Their room rates seemed high for what you get.

The most inexpensive option for staying at Los Barriles is camping for free on the beaches, but you probably won't be allowed access to nearby facilities. The 'official' parks are just north of the Rancho Buena Vista Hotel.

The *Playa de Oro* park is recommended by many campers. It is on a low plateau overlooking the ocean. The spaces and facilities are surrounded by palm trees. Facilities include hot showers, a laundry room, clean toilets and full hook-ups. They charge US$6 per night.

Martin Verdugo Trailer Park charges US$4.50 per night for a small vehicle and US$6 for a larger one. Tent camping costs US$4.50 per night. Vehicles and tents are crammed close together. Facilities include hot showers, electricity, full hook-ups and a laundry room. The park is close to the beach, though you can't see it. Paperbacks can be bought or borrowed from the park office.

La Capilla Trailer Park is 3¼ km south of town right on the beach. It is run by Jorge Geraldo and his family. They charge US$6 per day or US$150 per month. Facilities include full hook-ups and brand-new bathrooms with hot showers. Jorge gladly arranges fishing trips from the beach.

A last note – Los Barriles is one of the few places in Baja California where you can actually drink the water, because it comes from a mountain spring.

The Tropic of Cancer This is marked by a big concrete sphere placed precisely on the 23.5° North Latitude parallel just south of Santiago on Highway 1. The Tropic of Cancer also passes through Hawaii, Taiwan, the middle of India, Saudi Arabia and the Sahara Desert.

SAN JOSÉ DEL CABO

Population: 10,000

San José del Cabo, a quaint place of small streets, Spanish-style buildings and a tree-shaded plaza, is quickly being transformed into a major tourist resort. Most of downtown sits on a hill 1½ km from the Sea of Cortés, 32¼ km north-east of Cabo San Lucas and 181 km south of La Paz. The city's altitude is four metres. The maximum temperature is 42°C; minimum is 19°C.

Orientation

The town is divided into two distinct halves: resort hotel complexes and downtown San José. The row of resort hotels lining a beautiful wide stretch of beach west of San José was built in only the last 10 years by Fonatur, Mexico's tourist development agency responsible for the mega-resort complexes of Cancún and Ixtapa on mainland Mexico. Fonatur is also building a massive resort complex on a bluff overlooking the beach.

The resort half of San José is connected to the actual town by Boulevard Antonio Mijares. The last two or three blocks of Boulevard Mijares have been transformed into a mini-gringo-land of restaurants and souvenir shops. The boulevard ends at the tree-shaded Plaza Mijares, a pleasant

place to have an ice cream and do some serious people-watching.

Calles Zaragoza and Doblado are two other principal streets. Both intersect Mijares and lead up to Highway 1. If you are walking towards town from the beach, turn left on either of these streets to go through the Spanish-style heart of San José – small red-tiled buildings, the colonial-style church and the plaza. The town's few relatively inexpensive hotels and restaurants are on or near these streets.

Information

Money There are two banks on Calle Zaragoza (see map) two and three blocks from the plaza.

Post The post office is part of the Palacio de Gobierno building on Plaza Mijares.

Telephone Calls The public telephone office is on Calle Doblado next to the bus

1	Pemex Gasoline Station
2	Hotel Pagamar
3	Bus Station
4	Public Telephone Office
5	Tortilla Factory
6	Banks
7	La Fogata (Restaurant)
8	Restaurant Diana
9	Hotel Ceci
10	Restaurant Fisher
11	Post Office/City Hall
12	Mexicana
13	Marco's Pizza
14	Aeroméxico
15	Budget Rent A Car/ Swensen's Ice Cream
16	Hotel Colli
17	Restaurant Français L'Ecuyer de Roy
18	Liliana's (taco stand)
19	Municipal Market (Mercado Municipal)
20	Hotel Calinda Aquamarina (Comfort Inn)
21	Castel Cabo
22	El Presidente Hotel

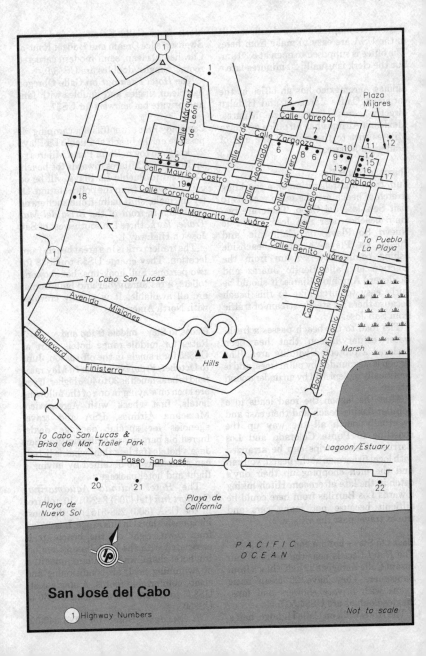

San José del Cabo

① Highway Numbers

Not to scale

PACIFIC OCEAN

station (see map). Direct and collect calls to the USA are easy to make from here. The office is supposed to open at 8.30 am, but the clerk is usually 20 minutes late.

Airlines Aeroméxico has an office at the corner of Calles Zaragoza and Hidalgo directly across from Plaza Mijares. Mexicana Airlines has an office on Plaza Mijares just to the right of the end of Boulevard Mijares.

Things to See & Do

Fun, frolic and relaxation on a sparkling stretch of beach are the main reasons to visit San José del Cabo. There are two main beaches near San José: Playa de Nuevo Sol/Playa de California and Pueblo La Playa, a small beachside fishing community 2½ km from the junction of Calle Benito Juárez and Boulevard Antonio Mijares. It should be fairly easy to hitch-hike to this beach because there's a steady stream of traffic from San José.

The road to the beach passes a fresh-water estuary/lagoon that has been declared a protected wildlife area. The lagoon is surrounded by palm trees, and is continually replenished by an underground stream.

After the lagoon the road leads to a popular fishing beach and then east and eventually north all the way up the coastline to Punta Colorado and Los Barriles. Fishing trips can be arranged with local fishermen at the beach; you can find the men chopping up their day's catch in the late afternoon. Hitch-hiking towards Los Barriles from here could be difficult because not many cars and trucks travel past the village.

Places to Stay - bottom end

The *Hotel Ceci* is near the heart of San José at Calle Zaragoza 22 half a block from Bancomer. They have 20 clean basic rooms with private showers and fans. Singles/doubles are US$4.50/5.50.

The *Hotel Colli* on Calle Hidalgo, half a

block from Calle Zaragoza and above Swensen's Ice Cream and Budget Rent-a-Car, has 12 clean, semi-modern carpeted rooms. Singles/doubles are US$8/9.

The *Hotel Pagamar* on Calle Obregón has clean singles and doubles with fans and private hot showers for US$7.

Camping Free 'unofficial' camping is possible on the beach at Pueblo La Playa 2½ km from town. From Plaza Mijares go up Boulevard Mijares towards the beach. The road to Pueblo La Playa will be on your left across from the police station. Or try the make-shift palm-frond shelters on the beach in front of the *Brisa del Mar Trailer Park*, three km south-west of San José on Highway 1.

The trailer park is in a great beach-front location. They charge US$5 to US$8 for two persons. Full hook-ups, hot showers, toilets, a restaurant/bar and laundromat are all available. It is usually crowded with North Americans.

Places to Stay - middle & top end

Rates for middle-range hotels start at US$35 for a single in the off-season, June to October. From November to May rates tend to be as much as 30 to 40% higher. If you are keen on staying in one of the following hotels, first check with Aeroméxico, Mexicana Airlines, PSA and travel agencies for special package deals. Incredible bargains and discounts on San José's hotels (far less than what is listed) can sometimes be obtained by buying a flight and hotel package.

The *Hotel Calinda Aquamarina-Comfort Inn* (tel (706) 842-01-10, toll free in the USA (800) 228-5151) is the most inexpensive hotel in this range. It is 2½ km from town, right on the beach. It is associated with the USA-based Comfort Inn hotel chain, with standard amenities of swimming pool, air-conditioning and clean, comfortable rooms. A single costs US$35 to US$45 and a double US$40 to US$50.

El Presidente Hotel (tel (706) 842-02-

11, toll free in the USA (800) 472-2427) is on the beach near the lagoon. Rates are high: US$58 to US$85 for a single and US$61.50 to US$88 for a double. This is one of the hotels built by Fonatur. Check into special travel packages if you want to stay here.

The *Castel Cabo* (tel (706) 842-01-55, toll free in California (800) 336-5454) is also on the beach. They have slightly lower rates than El Presidente Hotel.

Places to Eat

La Fogata is a restaurant across from Bancomer on Calle Zaragoza that caters primarily to Americans. They serve typical Mexican fare and seafood and are considered expensive by local standards (US$5 to US$6 for a full meal).

The *Restaurant Diana* is a predominantly local hang-out across from La Fogata and next to Bancomer. They will cook just about anything you request if they can obtain the ingredients. The waiters have been known to search the town for cows' tongues and frogs' legs to fulfil a dinner order.

Liliana's serves the best tacos in San José. It is a little blue stand run by Liliana and her sister at the crest of a hill on Highway 1. If you are headed for Cabo San Lucas, look for the stand on the left after Calle Doblado; it's well marked by a large sign. Be prepared to stuff yourself on delicious meat, chicken or fish tacos – three for less than US$1.

Back in town, the *Restaurant Fisher* on the corner of Hidalgo and Zaragoza serves filling meals of seafood and typical Mexican food for US$2 to US$3.

Restaurant Français L'Ecuyer de Roy on Calle Hidalgo is a French restaurant serving delicious home-made pâtés and various fish filet dishes as well as a chocolate mousse that will satiate the sweetest sweet tooth. Prices are not cheap for Mexico, but reasonable by American standards (US$4 to US$10).

The *Mercado Municipal* (Municipal Market) is a great place to get cheap eats, but your stomach should already be used to local cuisine. One section of the market is restaurant stalls and the other is for staples. Try the juice stall for freshly squeezed juices and licuados.

Getting There & Away

Air Pacific Southwest Airlines (PSA) has flights to and from most major cities in the western USA on Wednesday, Saturday and Sunday. They offer various fare deals. For example, if you book a round-trip flight from Los Angeles two weeks in advance, leave on Wednesday and return on Saturday, the flight will cost US$250. If you leave on Sunday, the flight costs US$270.

Aeroméxico and Mexicana have almost daily flights between Los Cabos and destinations throughout the USA and Mexico. The standard round-trip fare between Los Angeles and Los Cabos is US$280. A round-trip excursion fare is US$230 while a special round-trip fare can be as low as US$201.

Bus Tres Estrellas de Oro is the principal bus company serving San José del Cabo. The station is downtown on Calle Doblado (see map).

Departure times for the half-hour trip from San José del Cabo to Cabo San Lucas are 7 and 10 am, and 12.30, 2.30, 3, 4, 6, 8 and 10 pm. The fare is US$0.50.

Departure times for the two-hour trip from San José del Cabo to La Paz are 6.30, 7, 7.30, 9.30 and 11.30 am, and 1.30, 3, 4.30 and 6.30 pm. The fare is US$3.

Departure times for the trip from La Paz to San José are 7, 9.30 and 11 am, and 1, 2, 3, 5 and 7 pm.

Getting Around

Airport Transport The Los Cabos International Airport is 11 km north of San José del Cabo. Bright yellow taxis and minibuses operated by the official government-run company Aeroterrestre take passengers between the airport and Los Cabos (Cabo San Lucas and San José del Cabo). The fare averages US$6, but was subject to change soon.

Local Transport The town is small enough to walk just about everywhere. If you want to get out of town, take the bus or rent a car. Budget Rent-a-Car charges US$24 per day and 11c per km including insurance. They have a weekly rate of US$175 plus US$52 for insurance.

CABO SAN LUCAS

Cabo San Lucas was originally founded as an outpost to protect Spanish shipping lanes. Eventually, the garrison settlement became a sleepy little village whose inhabitants primarily depended on fishing and fish-canning for their livelihood. Today fishing is still popular in Cabo San Lucas, but for very different reasons. After WW II private American pilots landed in Cabo and returned to the USA with tales of big fish and magnificent beaches.

More people began to arrive from North America. Hotels and restaurants with names like the 'Palmilla', 'Gigglin' Marlin' and 'Sushi Bar' appeared. An 'international' airport was built near San José del Cabo. Cruise ships included Cabo in their itineraries. A ferry began service to and from Puerto Vallarta on the mainland. An important result for the local economy were the hordes of North American tourists and elderly people looking for a place to retire who converged upon the area. Most of this has happened in the last 15 years. Despite what some long-time expatriate residents call transmogrification (great change often with humourous or grotesque effect), Cabo is still basically a sleepy little town.

As soon as you walk more than a block or two inland away from the harbour and streets of curio shops, restaurants and hotels, you will begin to see a different Cabo San Lucas. This 'other' Cabo is where the local people live. Streets are unpaved or so pocked with potholes that they may

as well be unpaved. Donkeys and pigs wander in and out of yards. Some houses are compact pre-fabricated structures built by the government, but many are shanty-town shacks and huts. Even so, living standards are still better here than in many other parts of Baja and the rest of Mexico. Unemployment is not a problem as it is in most of Mexico.

The city's altitude is four metres. Maximum temperature is 42°C, minimum 6°C.

Orientation

Cabo San Lucas is at the southernmost tip of the Baja peninsula, 1704 km from Tijuana and 221 km from La Paz. Highways 1 and 19 are the only paved routes from La Paz to Cabo San Lucas. Highway 19, completed in 1984, goes through Todos Santos.

Information

Tourist Office There is a Fonatur office next to the ferry landing. The staff can provide maps of Los Cabos, but not much else in the way of information.

1	Faro Viejo Trailer Park & Restaurant
2	Restaurant Chan
3	Hotel Casablanca
4	Bus Station
5	Jugos y Preparados de California
6	Candido's
7	Golondrina
8	Hotel Mar de Cortez
9	Taquería Miramar
10	Café Petisa
11	Gigglin' Marlin
12	El Rey Sol Restaurant
13	Club Cascadas de Baja
14	Hotel Marina
15	Galleon Restaurant
16	Hotel Hacienda
17	Ferry Terminal
18	Hotel Finisterra
19	Tourist Office (Fonatur)
20	Government Crafts Centre/Docks
21	Hotel Solmar
22	Lover's Beach/Land's End

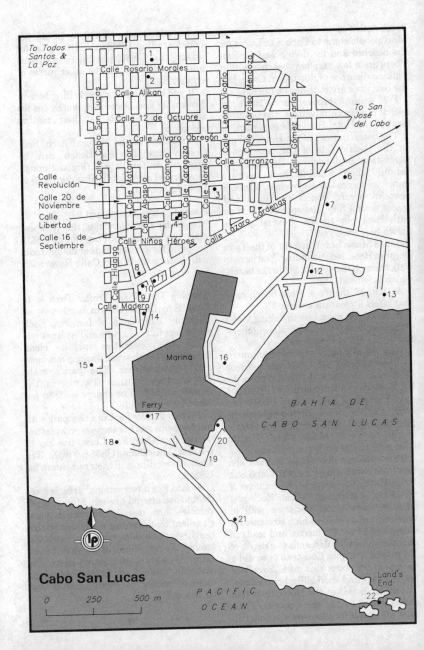

To Todos Santos & La Paz

To San José del Cabo

Calle Rosario Morales
Calle Alikan
Calle 12 de Octubre
Calle Alvaro Obregón
Calle Carranza
Calle Revolución
Calle 20 de Noviembre
Calle Libertad
Calle 16 de Septiembre
Calle Niños Héroes
Calle Lázaro Cárdenas
Calle Madero

Calle Cabo San Lucas
Calle Matamoros
Calle Ocampo
Calle Zaragoza
Calle Morelos
Calle Leona Vicario
Calle Narciso Mendoza
Calle Gómez Farías
Calle Abasolo
Calle Hidalgo

Marina

Ferry

BAHÍA DE CABO SAN LUCAS

Land's End

Cabo San Lucas

0   250   500 m

PACIFIC OCEAN

Beach Activities

Most people come to Cabo San Lucas for the beaches and for diving and fishing. There are a few excellent beaches within walking distance of downtown Cabo, but the best ones are outside the town.

For sun-worshippers and those in search of very calm waters, the beach in front of the Hotel Hacienda is perfect.

The beach in front of the Hotel Solmar on the Pacific side of the cape has a reputation as dangerous. Be extremely careful when walking here because immense waves suddenly emerge from a peaceful ocean, pound the sand and recede with a fury that sucks all in their path back out to sea. Several people drown here each year.

Santa María beach in front of the Twin Dolphin Hotel is outstanding. You have to walk through the hotel to get to the beach, which is federal land.

At Km 12 there's a great beach cove that offers a pleasant escape.

Some of the most breath-taking views of the beach are from the Whale-watchers' Bar at the Hotel Finisterra.

Baja Sports rents various equipment such as bicycles for US$2 per hour or US$10 per day; snorkel, fins and mask for US$8 per day; a surfboard for US$10 per day. Horseback-riding costs US$10 per hour, and a total diving-equipment package costs US$25 per day. The shop is at the corner of Madero and Vicente Guerrero. Hours are 9 am to 9 pm.

There are two dive shops in the Cabo San Lucas area. One is next to Cabo San Lucas Hotel. According to the manager of this shop, starting at Pelican Rock just offshore there is an undersea wall of vegetation and sea life which stretches for a depth of 18 to 27½ metres and leads to another wall which descends to a depth of 274 metres. Jacques Cousteau once did a documentary about this area. Excellent beach diving and snorkelling are possible. The other shop is at the Hotel Hacienda and is owned by the same people. Their rates are US$16 for a four-person boat trip to Lover's Beach, US$10 to US$15 per hour for sailing, US$8 to US$10 per day for an air tank, US$10 per day for a wetsuit and various rates for the other pieces of equipment.

If you are diving or snorkelling here in November and December, watch out for the sea lions; this is their mating season.

Boat trips to the Natural Arch, Seal Colony and Lover's Beach can be arranged on the Yate Trinidad through most travel agencies in town for US$5 to US$10 per hour.

Places to Stay – bottom end

The *Hotel Casablanca* is the cheapest place to stay in town. They charge US$10 per night for a clean single or double room with bathroom. It's on Calle Revolución just off Calle Morelos.

Camping *Faro Viejo Trailer Park* is in Cabo San Lucas 1½ km north-west of Highway 1 on Calle Matamoros. Each space has full hook-ups and at least one shade tree. Facilities include clean bathrooms, hot showers, washing machines and restaurant/bar. The park's main disadvantage is that it's not in the downtown area. The charge is US$6 per night for two people.

El Arco Trailer Park is a new park with full hook-ups and hot showers on a plateau overlooking Cabo San Lucas five km to the east. They charge US$5 per night. Try a full lobster dinner in their restaurant for US$10.

At Km 9 is a recreational vehicle park established around a beach. More than 50 vehicles are usually stationed here. Excellent tent camping is possible on this beach west of a shipwreck. You can roam around the rusted hull of the ship, but be extremely wary of sharp, rusty parts. The camping charge of US$5 per night includes access to clean showers and bathrooms.

Places to Stay - middle

Hotel Mar de Cortez is a colonial-style building in the centre of town. Each room has air-conditioning and a private bathroom. There is a swimming pool and an outdoor bar/restaurant. A single costs US$25 to US$37, a double US$29 to US$44 and a triple US$42.50 to US$47.50. Their USA representative's address is PO Box 1827, Monterey, California 93942 (tel (408) 375-4755).

The *Hotel Marina* has overpriced, motel-style air-conditioned rooms arranged around a small swimming pool. Rates are US$24 single, US$26 double, US$28 triple; suites are US$70 per night. A restaurant and bar are attached to the hotel. Live music accompanies the rowdy drinking of yachties just off their boats.

Places to Stay - top end

Hotel Finisterra is a luxury hotel perched on a bluff overlooking the town on one side and the ocean on the other. Singles are US$60 per night, doubles US$69 and triples US$79. Service charges and taxes are added on. Reservations can be made in the USA by calling (800) 352-2579 (California only) or (800) 421-3772 (nationwide). The address of the USA representative is 4332 Katella Avenue, Los Alamitos, California 90720.

The *Hotel Hacienda* is a resplendent five-star luxury hotel designed to resemble an old Spanish hacienda with tropical gardens and fountains. The hotel is a convenient base for water sports. A variety of rooms are available – townhouses, deluxe suites, beach cabañas and garden patio rooms. However, there is nothing for less than US$45 per night for a single unless you come with some sort of package tour.

Hotel Solmar is on the Pacific side of Cabo San Lucas. It is a secluded resort with rooms which all face the ocean. Singles are US$55, doubles US$65 and triples US$77.

Club Cascadas de Baja claims to be similar to Club Méditerranée. The cutesy representatives in front of stores and at street corners stand behind podiums advertising 'free tourist maps', which are indeed free, but you have to listen to the sales pitch.

Places to Eat

The restaurants of Cabo San Lucas cater primarily to vacationing tourists. Consequently, prices tend to be higher than in more isolated Baja towns. However, a few places offer fairly good meals at relatively low prices.

Try *El Caracol Restaurant* for a Mexican-style breakfast which includes a Spanish omelette, tortillas, frijoles, coffee and orange juice for US$2 to US$3.

Restaurant Chan serves a full meal of soggy chow mein for US$4. It is across from the Faro Viejo trailer park (see map). Eat here only if you cannot live without Chinese food.

Café Petisa is on the 2nd floor of the building across from the Hotel Mar de Cortez. They serve cappuccino and espresso. In the evenings the atmosphere is friendly and Bohemian, with singing and guitar-playing. Hours are 8 am to 9 pm.

Faro Viejo Trailer Park Restaurant, hidden within the confines of the trailer park, has one of the best restaurants in Cabo San Lucas. It is often crowded with Americans. They have an outstanding reputation for barbecued ribs. A full dinner that includes several dishes costs US$6 to US$12 and is more than enough for one person.

Candido's is a European-style restaurant which typically serves a meal of seven or eight courses. Classical background music, excellent service and an incredible filet mignon make this a big but worthwhile splurge.

The *Galleon Restaurant* is the rotunda-shaped building across from the ferry terminal. Try the hearts of fillet, one of their specialities prepared right at your table. Breakfast is pleasant on the veranda overlooking the bay. Prices range from US$3 up for a meal.

El Rey Sol Restaurant serves fantastic Mexican food for breakfast, lunch or dinner. The breakfast is great (US$4). Try the *machaca* and eggs (resembles a beef omelette). If you want fish prepared a special way, bring it in.

Gigglin' Marlin is a popular watering-hole for local gringos and anyone out for a good drunken time. Read the fine print on the sign in front which promises two drinks for the price of one; the drink selection is very limited. The food has not been recommended. Some say that their appetisers are better than their meals; try the quesadillas and potato skins. Aside from eating, drinking and watching big-screen TVs with music-video satellite broadcasts from the USA, patrons enjoy being hoisted up and hung like marlins from chains around their ankles. Great fun!

Estrella's is a good all-around place serving burgers and hot fudge sundaes.

Taquería Miramar around the corner from the Mar de Cortez Hotel serves some of the best tacos in Baja. Four tacos cost US$1.50. They also serve Mexican-style *shwarma* sandwiches.

Unbelievably, there is a *Sushi Bar* in Cabo San Lucas on the corner of Calle Zaragoza and Calle Niño Héroes. Japanese-style sushi costs US$3 to US$5. Try their seafood cocktails. Locals were not optimistic about the survival of this place.

Things to Buy

One of the local specialities is hand-crafted black coral jewellery. The Southern Baja California government sponsors a centre where the jewellery is made and sold. It is conveniently located at the dock where cruise-ship passengers disembark for brief shopping sprees. Most of the passengers never get past the centre and into town where merchants who depend on tourist dollars for survival say they are hurting.

Getting There & Away

Air The closest airport is north of San José del Cabo. See that section for information.

Bus The bus to La Paz leaves at 6.30, 7, 9 and 11 am, and at 3 and 6 pm. The fare is US$4.50. The bus to Tijuana goes via La Paz and departs at 4 and 6 pm. The fare is US$22. Confirm your tickets at least half an hour before departure.

The bus to San José del Cabo leaves at 7, 9 and 11 am, and at 1, 2, 4, 4.15 and 6 pm. The fare is US$0.50.

The bus station is at the corner of Calle Zaragoza and Calle 16 de Septiembre.

Ferry Every Wednesday and Sunday there is a ferry to Puerto Vallarta. In November and December the ferry leaves at 11 am and arrives the next morning at 7.30 am. From January to October the ferry leaves at 4 pm and arrives at 1 pm. The return trips from Puerto Vallarta are on Tuesday and Saturday. Reservations should be made by calling the ferry office (tel (706) 843-00-79) in Cabo San Lucas at least two to three weeks in advance – that is, if you would like better than a salon seat. Salon seats are unreserved seats which recline just slightly and not really enough to doze. They are located in unventilated rooms packed with families of puking kids and smoking men. If you get stuck with a salon seat and the weather is good, take your sleeping bag or blanket on to the deck. If you manage to get a cabin, then consider yourself lucky because they are one of the best travel deals in the world. The best cabins are in the *especial* class – suites with a bedroom, living-room and bathroom that cost US$4 per person.

Obtaining better than a salon seat can be challenging and incredibly frustrating. Do not believe the ferry officials when they say that salon seats are the only ones available. Reservations cannot be made for the majority of cabins because most are reserved until 3 pm the day before departure for VIPs who rarely appear. That means that after 3 pm you can usually change your salon ticket to a cabin ticket, though there is no guarantee that you will be able to. You will not be the only person trying to upgrade your ticket; expect complete chaos at the ticket window. Some people pay others to stand in line for them, but this is not recommended. Get there early and plant yourself at the window.

Fares are US$0.70 for a salon seat, US$1.50 for turista class (roomette with a bunk) and US$3 for cabina class (double room with bathroom).

Rates for vehicles are US$5 for up to five metres, US$5.50 for 6½ metres, US$10 for a vehicle and trailer up to nine metres, US$7 for motor-homes.

Confirm and reconfirm reservations and departure times. The former occasionally disappear from official records and the latter tend to change.

Getting Around

Airport Transport Taxis or minibuses will take you to the airport. The front desk of any of the major hotels in town will help you arrange transport. Fares to the airport are officially set by the government so you will not have to haggle with the driver about the fare.

Taxi Taxis for getting around town are plentiful; catch them in front of any hotel. Fares for destinations within Cabo San Lucas average US$4.

Glossary

Atlante – pre-Hispanic sculptured column.

Barrio – district, neighbourhood.

Billete – bank note, unlike in Spain where it's a ticket.

Boojum – strange *cirio* tree found only in Baja California. Named after the 'Boojum' in *Alice in Wonderland*.

Caballeros – literally 'horsemen', but corresponds to 'gentlemen' in English; look for it on toilet doors.

Cacique – Aztec chief; also used to describe provincial warlord or strongman of newly independent Mexico.

Callejón – alley or small, narrow or very short street.

Cardón – world's largest cactus, found on the Baja peninsula. It can grow up to 17 metres high.

Casa de cambio – place where currency is exchanged. In Mexico it offers exchange rates comparable to or better than banks and is much faster to use.

Caste War – bloody Mayan uprising in the south of Mexico during the chaos following the US annexation of California.

Caudillo – a kind of national *cacique*.

Cazuela – clay cooking-pot, usually sold in a nested set.

Cenote – large well used for water storage in Mayan regions, sometimes with a ceremonial purpose as well.

Chac – Mayan god of rain.

Chac-mool – pre-Hispanic sacrificial stone sculpture.

Charro – cowboy.

Chilango – citizen of Mexico City.

Chinampas – floating gardens of the Aztecs at the time of the Spanish invasion, versions of which still exist in Xochimilco near Mexico City.

Chingar – literally 'to rape' but in practice a word with a wide range of colloquial meanings similar to the use of 'to screw' in English. If you've been 'screwed' then you might ruefully admit that *me chingaron*.

Chulten – Mayan brick reservoir found at the Puuc Hill sites south of Mérida.

Churrigueresque – Spanish late baroque style found in many Mexican churches.

Cigarro – cigarette.

Coatlicue – goddess of death.

Colectivo – taxi or minibus which picks up and drops off passengers along its route.

Completo – full up, a sign you may see on hotel desks in crowded cities.

Conasupo – government-owned store that sells many everyday basics at subsidised prices.

Conquistador – early Spanish explorer-conqueror.

Coyote – guide who helps illegal immigrants slip across the border into the USA.

Criollo – Mexican-born Spaniard considered inferior by the Spanish.

Cristeros – religious fanatics who caused much havoc during the general unrest of the Revolution.

Curandero – Indian medicine man.

Damas – ladies, the sign on the toilet doors.

De lujo – deluxe, often used with some licence.

Descompuesto – broken, out of order.

DF – Distrito Federal; the initials often follow the name 'Mexico City'.

Diligencia – stagecoach-like horse-drawn vehicle.

Ejido – communally owned Indian land; frequently taken over by landowners but returned under a Lázaro Cárdenas-inspired programme.

Embarazada – literally 'embarrassed' but usually means pregnant.

Embute – regular bribe paid by politicians to newspaper journalists.

Encomienda – early Hispanic practice of putting Indians under the guardianship of landowners, almost akin to medieval serfdom.

Estación ferrocarril – railway station.

Excusado – toilet.

Fajo – tequila cup.

Ferrocarril – railway.

Fotonovela – comic-book-like paperbacks which have an enormous following in Mexico.

Frontera – border between political entities; more often the border between the USA and Mexico.

Gachupines – derogatory term for the peninsulares during the Spanish period.

Gringo – European or North American visitor to Latin America.

Gringo trail – trail followed down through Latin America by gringo visitors.

Grito – the cry for independence by parish priest Miguel Hidalgo y Costilla in 1810 which sparked the struggle for independence from Spain. His *Grito* is still repeated by political leaders on 15 & 16 September each year.

Guayabera – also *guayabarra*, thin fabric man's shirt with pockets and appliquéd designs up the front, over the shoulders and down the back.

Guarache – also *huarache*, woven leather sandal, often with car-tyre tread as the sole.

Güero – white person. *Una güera* is a blonde woman.

Hacienda – estate.

Hay – 'there is', 'there are'. You're equally likely to hear *no hay*, 'there isn't' or 'there aren't'.

Henequen – cactus fibre used to make rope, grown particularly around Mérida in the Yucatán.

Hombres – men.

Huevos – eggs. Also colloquial expression for testicles.

Huipil – woven white dress from the Mayan regions with intricate, colourful embroidery.

IVA – the *impuesto al valor agregado* or 'ee-vah' is a sales tax which can range as high as 15% and is added to many items.

Jaguar – principal symbol of the Olmec civilisation.

Jarocho – citizen of Veracruz.

Jefe – boss or leader, especially political.

Kukulcán – Mayan name for the plumed serpent Quetzalcóatl.

La Noche Triste – the 'Sad Night' when Cortés was besieged by the Aztecs and retreated from Tenochtitlán with massive losses.

Larga distancia – long-distance telephone.

Latifundio – large land-holding; these sprang up after Mexico's independence from Spain.

Latifundista – powerful landowner who usurped communally owned land to form the latifundio in independent Mexico.

Licenciado – university graduate, a status claimed by many who don't actually possess a degree.

Lista de correos – poste restante or general delivery; literally 'mail list' because names of people for whom letters are waiting are supposedly posted on a daily list.

Lleno – full, as with hotels and gas tanks.

Machismo – maleness, masculine virility. An important concept in Mexico.

Maguey – sap from this cactus-like plant is used to make mezcal and tequila.

Mañana – tomorrow. The mañana syndrome is blamed for many of Mexico's problems.

Maquiladora – assembly-plant operations in Mexican border towns and cities that are usually owned, at least in part, by foreigners and are allowed to import raw materials duty-free under a customs bond on the condition that the products manufactured are re-exported to the US.

Mariachi – small ensemble of street musicians; strolling mariachi bands often perform in restaurants.

Mestizo – people of mixed blood (Spanish and Indian); the word now more commonly means 'Mexican'.

Mezcal – alcoholic drink produced from maguey cactus.

Moctezuma's revenge – Mexican version of 'Delhi-belly' or travellers' diarrhoea.

El Monstruo – 'the monster', Mexico City.

Mordida – 'little bite', or small bribe that's usually paid to keep the wheels of bureaucracy turning. Giving a *mordida* to a traffic policeman may ensure that you won't have a bigger traffic fine to pay.

Mudéjar – Moorish architectural style.

Mujeres – women, another possibility on the toilet door.

Música – music, especially ranchero or country & western.

Obrajes – small factories during the early Hispanic period.

Palapa – thatched roof.

Parada – bus stop, usually for city buses.

Paseo – walkway or pedestrian way. Also the habit of circling the plaza in the evening (men and women in opposite directions).

Pastry war – a struggle with France over compensation for French citizens due to riots in Mexico City. The conflict took its name from a baker's claims.

Pemex – government-owned oil-company monopoly.

Peninsulares – Spaniards sent by the government in Spain to run Mexico during Spanish rule. They were posted to Mexico, unlike the criollos who were Spaniards born in Mexico.

Peyote – hallucinogenic mezcal cactus.

Plan of Ayala – Zapata's denouncement of Madero's policies regarding land reform; this was a major factor in the Revolution.

Plazuela – small plaza.

Porfiriato – Porfirio Díaz's reign as president-dictator of Mexico for 30 years until the 1910 Revolution.

Portales – arcades.

PRI – Institutional Party of the Revolution.

Propino, propina – a tip, though not the same as a *mordida*, which is closer to a bribe.

Pulque – fermented maguey cactus juice. The traditional, mildly intoxicating drink is also nutritious.

Puro – cigar.

Quetzalcóatl – plumed serpent god of pre-Hispanic Mexico.

Rebozo – long wool or linen scarf covering the head or shoulders.

Rejas – wrought-iron window guards.

Retablo – ornate gilded, carved decorations of wood in churches.

Rurales – federal police force used to suppress opposition during the Porfiriato.

Sacbe – ceremonial avenues between great Mayan cities.

Sanatorio – hospital, particularly a small private one.

Sanitario – literally 'sanitary'; usually means toilet.

Sarape – traditional woollen blanket.

Simpático – sympathetic, amiable, friendly or likeable; the word also has wider meaning.

Supermercado – supermarket. Can range from a small corner store to a large, Western-style supermarket.

Taller – shop or workshop. A *taller mecánico* is a mechanic's shop, usually for cars. A *taller de llantos* is a tyre-repair shop.

Telenovela – TV soap opera.

Templo – church; anything from a wayside chapel to a cathedral.

Tequila – vodka-like liquor produced, like pulque and mezcal, from the maguey cactus, though tequila can only be produced from the *agave tequilana* species.

Tezcatlipoca – god of evil.

Tierra y Libertad – 'Land and Liberty', the rallying call of Emiliano Zapata which still has much importance in Mexico today.

Típico – typical or characteristic of a region; particularly used to describe food.

Topes – speed-break ridges found on the road in many Mexican highway towns. Keep an eye out for the sign if you're driving.

Tostón – obsolete 50-centavo coin. In Yucatán, Campeche and Chiapas it can refer to thinly sliced bananas dipped in batter and deep-fried.

Voladores – Totonac Indian ritual in which men whirl around a tall pole, suspended by their ankles.

Viajero – traveller.

Yácata – stone ceremonial structure with an eternally burning flame, constructed by the Tarascan civilisation.

Zócalo – town's main plaza or square. Literally means 'pedestal' or 'base', which derives from the pedestal begun in the Plaza de la Constitución in Mexico City.

Index

934 Index

MAPS

MAPS

Dear traveller

Prices go up, good places go bad, bad places go bankrupt...and every guidebook is inevitably outdated in places. Fortunately, many travellers write to us about their experiences, telling us when things have changed. If we reprint a book between editions, we try to include as much of this information as possible in a Stop Press section. Most of this information has not been verified by our own writers.

We really enjoy hearing from people out on the road, and apart from guaranteeing that others will benefit from your good and bad experiences, we're prepared to bribe you with the offer of a free book for sending us substantial useful information.

Thank you to everyone who has written and, to those who haven't, I hope you do find this book useful – and that you let us know when it isn't.

Tony Wheeler

President Salinas, who took a strong stand against corruption and promised to get the Mexican economy on a road to recovery in 1988, seems to be succeeding. Corruption is declining while the economy is strengthening. Inflation is slowing down as indicated by a 21% increase in the first nine months compared to 28.6% in 1989.

Mexico City is an ecological and demographic disaster area. The air and noise pollution is so bad that residents are advised not to open their house and car windows. Many people suffer from respiratory diseases, and birds are dying. People who can afford them use air purifiers in their homes. Garbage dumps are open pits in which the garbage from the city is disposed, and unpleasant odours engulf the surrounding areas.

The following section was compiled using the letters sent to us by the following travellers: Australian Embassy in Mexico, Ingemar Carlsson (Sw), Mike Coop (NZ), Peter Dowling, D J Dyke (Aus), Joseph Halpin (USA), Stephen Hopkins, Stephen Hysking, Raul Lopez, Liesbeth van Ommeren (Nl), Freddy Rabenau (D), Conrad Richter (C), Tony Smyth, Henk Tukker (Nl), Jill Yesko (USA) & Werner Zwick (D).

Visa & Permits

Currently you will be issued with no more than a 30 day permit when you enter Mexico at the airport in Mexico City. The officials claim that it is possible to extend the visa in any of the state capitals of the republic. If you decide to extend the visa in Mexico City, don't go to the address published on your visa, as this is now incorrect. The new address is: Servicios Migratorios, Albañiles No. 19, Esquina Eduardo Molina, Colonia Penitenciaria.

Money & Costs

Hotel and food prices have skyrocketed because the Mexican economy is strengthening, the US dollar is weakening, and the peso is being artificially supported. Most hotel and food prices are around 50 to 100% higher. However, bus fares have remained fairly stable. The current official exchange rate is MEX$2961.8 to US$1.

As of 1 June 1990, entrance fees to all archaeological sites, museums and monuments were increased by 800%. Sites are graded from A, being the most important, to D, being of minor importance. The new price scale is as follows: Grade A sites cost MEX$10,000, Grade B Sites are MEX$8000, Grade C sites are MEX$5000 and Grade D sites are MEX$2000. The Grade A sites include those at Teotihuacán, Tula, Cholula, Monte Albán, Palenque and Chichén Itzá. The entrance fee to the Museum of Anthropology in Mexico City has also gone up to MEX$10,000.

There's a Casa de Cambio Lacatún (tel 8-25-87) in San Cristóbal De Las Casas, on Real de Guadalupe 12-A, less than half a block east of the main plaza which has no queues like the banks and staff there will not ignore you. A traveller reported that they changed their money in ten minutes with a 2.5% commission at competitive exchange rates, and a minimum exchange of US$50. Opening hours are from 8.30 am to 2 pm and 5 to 8 pm Monday to Saturday, and 9 am to 1 pm on Sunday.

Dangers & Annoyances

We heard from a traveller who was imprisoned for two days for not having their passport with them. They were caught at an internal customs/immigration checkpoint a couple of hours out of Palenque between Acayucan and Minatitlán whilst travelling on a bus from Palenque to Mexico City. This internal border is between the main part of Mexico and Yucatán/Chiapas region. The border runs north-south along the narrowest part of the Isthmus of Tehuantepec. There's another customs/immigration checkpoint just east of Juchitán in the southern part of the Isthmus. While it is not common for travellers to be arrested it can happen, so it is advisable to have your passport with you at all times.

A traveller strongly advises never to take a night bus from Taxco, Guerrero as these buses are a constant target of night robbers.

Information

It's hard to find information in Western Europe on Mexico. The *Staatliches Mexikanisches Verkehrsamt* at Wiesenhüttenplatz 26, 6000 Frankfurt am Main, Germany, can provide some information.

The tourist information office in Guadalajara has moved to Morelos 102, Plasa Japatia, Palacio de Gobierno, Calle Corona.

Getting There

The airport departure tax is US$10 o MEX$28,000. Only cash is accepted.

Getting Around

It took two and a half days and many phone calls for a traveller to get their luggage back after their bags were lost on a flight from Mexico City to Oaxaca with Aeroméxico. Apparently it is possible to claim US$100 compensation for inconvenience if receipts for replacement goods bought are provided. This of course rules out buying any items from the markets. The airlines won't volunteer this information, but if you insist and have receipts the money will be refunded. On a flight through Mexico City or any other flight that involves a change of airports within Mexico, it's best to only ticket your bag to the first airport, go through customs with it and then check it in again for the next stage of the flight.

Travellers should be very careful when arriving during the night at the Northern Bus Terminal in Mexico City, as the taxi drivers try to extort unnecessary tips from the tired gringos as they disembark.

It's difficult to leave Zacatecas if heading towards Mexico City. The buses fill up early, and a traveller reported that while they were there no reservations were accepted, and Mexicans had priority on seats.

Some travellers have encountered difficulties while travelling on trains including double booked seats, no sleepers, no dining car, and very expensive fares. Buses are recommended as they are considerably cheaper and more efficient. One of the best bus companies is ADO. They run modern luxurious buses all over Mexico at low fares.

First class bus companies like ADO generally provide labels for baggage stored in the compartment of the bus. This is quite safe and definitely more comfortable than having the luggage with you on long distances. During breaks you just get off the bus with your hand luggage without having to worry about your main luggage. This is also better when the bus is held up by bandits, as they generally take only what the passengers have on them, leaving the storage compartment under the bus untouched. On second class buses it is better to keep all luggage with you, or if this is not possible, keep an eye out on what is happening near the bus at every stop.

Mexico City

The American Express office at Hamburgo 75 has moved to a new address on Paseo Reforma 234.

The British Embassy, while remaining at the same address, has changed its opening hours. It is now open from 8.30 am to 3.30 pm and the new telephone number is 207 2089.

The new address for the Australian Embassy is (Tel 395 9988 - Fax 395 7870), Jaime Balmes no 11, Plaza Polanco, Torre B, 10th floor, Colonia Los Morales, Mexico 11510 DF.

Travellers Tips & Comments

Customs at the airport in Mexico City was a curious affair. A group of inspectors sit about not moving until the uninitiated travellers finally open up and ask what must be done to be cleared. The answer is quick and surprisingly simple.

You have to push the green button which lights the green light marked PASE. Pushing the green button apparently means 'I have nothing to declare' and you're on your way!

Howard Scotland III – USA

At the Temple of the Warriors in Chichén Itzá, I saw many tourists sitting on the Chac Mool. I told a few of them to get off, but there were too many there. The top of it was worn shiny by so many bums sitting on it. The two magnificent serpents just behind the Chac Mool still contain the original red colour inside the mouths, but I saw people sitting on them wearing their shoes and one man had organised his daughter to lie inside the mouth of the serpent at the same time! The colour won't last long at this rate.

Tony Smyth

Playa del Carmen is now an unmitigated tourist trap with every Mexican seemingly out for tourist bucks. It's a good place to meet young Americans and Europeans if that's what you want, but we thought it utterly lacking in charm. On our first day on the beach, a Mexican man grabbed the bag of an unsuspecting sun bather. My wife tried to head him off, whereupon he pulled out a pistol and waved it at her.

Daniel Lieberfeld – USA

Lonely Planet Guidebooks

Lonely Planet guidebooks cover every accessible part of Asia as well as Australia, the Pacific, South America, Africa, the Middle East and parts of North America and Europe. There are four series: *travel survival kits*, covering a single country for a range of budgets; *shoestring guides* with compact information for low-budget travel in a major region; *walking guides*; and *phrasebooks*.

Australia & the Pacific
Australia
Bushwalking in Australia
Islands of Australia's Great Barrier Reef
Fiji
Micronesia
New Caledonia
New Zealand
Tramping in New Zealand
Papua New Guinea
Papua New Guinea phrasebook
Rarotonga & the Cook Islands
Samoa
Solomon Islands
Tahiti & French Polynesia
Tonga

South-East Asia
Bali & Lombok
Burma
Burmese phrasebook
Indonesia
Indonesia phrasebook
Malaysia, Singapore & Brunei
Philippines
Pilipino phrasebook
South-East Asia on a shoestring
Thailand
Thai phrasebook
Vietnam, Laos & Cambodia

North-East Asia
China
Chinese phrasebook
Hong Kong, Macau & Canton
Japan
Japanese phrasebook
Korea
Korean phrasebook
North-East Asia on a shoestring
Taiwan
Tibet
Tibet phrasebook

West Asia
Trekking in Turkey
Turkey
Turkish phrasebook
West Asia on a shoestring

Indian Ocean
Madagascar & Comoros
Maldives & Islands of the East Indian Ocean
Mauritius, Réunion & Seychelles

Mail Order

Lonely Planet guidebooks are distributed worldwide and are sold by good bookshops everywhere. They are also available by mail order from Lonely Planet, so if you have difficulty finding a title please write to us. US and Canadian residents should write to Embarcadero West, 112 Linden St, Oakland CA 94607, USA and residents of other countries to PO Box 617, Hawthorn, Victoria 3122, Australia.

Europe
Eastern Europe on a shoestring
Iceland, Greenland & the Faroe Islands
Trekking in Spain

Indian Subcontinent
Bangladesh
India
Hindi/Urdu phrasebook
Trekking in the Indian Himalaya
Karakoram Highway
Kashmir, Ladakh & Zanskar
Nepal
Trekking in the Nepal Himalaya
Nepal phrasebook
Pakistan
Sri Lanka
Sri Lanka phrasebook

Africa
Africa on a shoestring
Central Africa
East Africa
Kenya
Swahili phrasebook
Morocco, Algeria & Tunisia
Moroccan Arabic phrasebook
West Africa

North America
Alaska
Canada
Hawaii

Mexico
Baja California
Mexico

South America
Argentina
Bolivia
Brazil
Brazilian phrasebook
Chile & Easter Island
Colombia
Ecuador & the Galápagos Islands
Latin American Spanish phrasebook
Peru
Quechua phrasebook
South America on a shoestring

Middle East
Egypt & the Sudan
Egyptian Arabic phrasebook
Israel
Jordan & Syria
Yemen

The Lonely Planet Story

Lonely Planet published its first book in 1973 in response to the numerous 'How did you do it?' questions Maureen and Tony Wheeler were asked after driving, bussing, hitching, sailing and railing their way from England to Australia.

Written at a kitchen table and hand collated, trimmed and stapled, *Across Asia on the Cheap* became an instant local bestseller, inspiring thoughts of another book.

Eighteen months in South-East Asia resulted in their second guide, *South-East Asia on a shoestring*, which they put together in a backstreet Chinese hotel in Singapore in 1975. The 'yellow bible' as it quickly became known to backpackers around the world, soon became *the* guide to the region. It has sold well over ½ million copies and is now in its 6th edition, still retaining its familiar yellow cover.

Today there are over 80 Lonely Planet titles – books that have that same adventurous approach to travel as those early guides; books that 'assume you know how to get your luggage off the carousel' as one reviewer put it.

Although Lonely Planet initially specialised in guides to Asia, they now cover most regions of the world, including the Pacific, South America, Africa, the Middle East and Eastern Europe. The list of *walking guides* and *phrasebooks* (for 'unusual' languages such as Quechua, Swahili, Nepalese and Egyptian Arabic) is also growing rapidly.

The emphasis continues to be on travel for independent travellers. Tony and Maureen still travel for several months of each year and play an active part in the writing, updating and quality control of Lonely Planet's guides.

They have been joined by over 50 authors, 40 staff – mainly editors, cartographers, & designers – at our office in Melbourne, Australia, and another 10 at our US office in Oakland, California. Travellers themselves also make a valuable contribution to the guides through the feedback we receive in thousands of letters each year.

The people at Lonely Planet strongly believe that travellers can make a positive contribution to the countries they visit, both through their appreciation of the countries' culture, wildlife and natural features, and through the money they spend. In addition, the company makes a direct contribution to the countries and regions it covers. Since 1986 a percentage of the income from each book has been donated to ventures such as famine relief in Africa; aid projects in India; agricultural projects in Central America; Greenpeace's efforts to halt French nuclear testing in the Pacific and Amnesty International. In 1990 $60,000 was donated to these causes.

Lonely Planet's basic travel philosophy is summed up in Tony Wheeler's comment, 'Don't worry about whether your trip will work out. Just go!'